THE GREAT
CONTEMPORARY
ISSUES

FOOD AND POPULATION: THE WORLD IN CRISIS

OTHER BOOKS IN THE SERIES

DRUGS
Introduction by J. Anthony Lukas

THE MASS MEDIA AND POLITICS
Introduction by Walter Cronkite

CHINA
O. Edmund Clubb, *Advisory Editor*

LABOR AND MANAGEMENT
Richard B. Morris, *Advisory Editor*

WOMEN: THEIR CHANGING ROLES
Elizabeth Janeway, *Advisory Editor*

BLACK AFRICA
Hollis R. Lynch, *Advisory Editor*

EDUCATION, U.S.A.
James Cass, *Advisory Editor*

VALUES AMERICANS LIVE BY
Garry Wills, *Advisory Editor*

CRIME AND JUSTICE
Ramsey Clark, *Advisory Editor*

JAPAN
Edwin O. Reischauer, *Advisory Editor*

1975 Publications

THE PRESIDENCY
George E. Reedy, *Advisory Editor*

POPULAR CULTURE
David Manning White, *Advisory Editor*

U.S. AND WORLD ECONOMY
Leonard Silk, *Advisory Editor*

1976 Publication

SCIENCE IN THE TWENTIETH CENTURY
Walter Sullivan, *Advisory Editor*

THE GREAT CONTEMPORARY ISSUES

FOOD AND POPULATION: THE WORLD IN CRISIS

The New York Times

ARNO PRESS

NEW YORK/1975

SENATOR GEORGE MC GOVERN

Advisory Editor

Library of Congress Cataloging in Publication Data
Main entry under title—

Food and population.

(The Great contemporary issues)

Articles from the New York times.

1. Food supply—Addresses, essays, lectures. 2. Population—Addresses, essays, lectures. 3. Birth control—Addresses, essays, lectures. 4. Surplus agricultural commodities, American—Addresses, essays, lectures. I. McGovern, George Stanley, 1922 – II. New York times. III. Series.

HD9000.5.F593 338.1'9 75-23476

ISBN 0-405-06663-5

Manufactured in the United States of America by Arno Press, Inc.

The editors express special thanks to The Associated Press, United Press International, and Reuters for permission to include in this series of books a number of dispatches originally distributed by those news services.

A HUDSON GROUP BOOK

Produced by Morningside Associates. Edited by Gene Brown.

Contents

Publisher's Note

It would take even an accomplished speed-reader, moving at full throttle, some three and a half solid hours a day to work his way through all the news The New York Times prints. The sad irony, of course, is that even such indefatigable devotion to life's carnival would scarcely assure a decent understanding of what it was really all about. For even the most dutiful reader might easily overlook an occasional long-range trend of importance, or perhaps some of the fragile, elusive relationships between events that sometimes turn out to be more significant than the events themselves.

This is why "The Great Contemporary Issues" was created—to help make sense out of some of the major forces and counterforces at large in today's world. The philosophical conviction behind the series is a simple one: that the past not only can illuminate the present but must. ("Continuity with the past," declared Oliver Wendell Holmes, "is a necessity, not a duty.") Each book in the series, therefore has as its subject some central issue of our time that needs to be viewed in the context of its antecedents if it is to be fully understood. By showing, through a substantial selection of contemporary accounts from The New York Times, the evolution of a subject and its significance, each book in the series offers a perspective that is available in no other way. For while most books on contemporary affairs specialize, for excellent reasons, in predigested facts and neatly drawn conclusions, the books in this series allow the reader to draw his own conclusions on the basis of the facts as they appeared at virtually the moment of their occurrence. This is not to argue that there is no place for events recollected in tranquility; it is simply to say that when fresh, raw truths are allowed to speak for themselves, some quite distinct values often emerge.

For this reason, most of the articles in "The Great Contemporary Issues" are reprinted in their entirety, even in those cases where portions are not central to a given book's theme. Editing has been done only rarely, and in all such cases it is clearly indicated. (Such an excision occasionally occurs, for example, in the case of a Presidential State of the Union Message, where only brief portions are germane to a particular volume, and in the case of some names, where for legal reasons or reasons of taste it is preferable not to republish specific identifications.) Similarly, typographical errors, where they occur, have been allowed to stand as originally printed.

"The Great Contemporary Issues" inevitably encompasses a substantial amount of history. In order to explore their subjects fully, some of the books go back a century or more. Yet their fundamental theme is not the past but the present. In this series the past is of significance insofar as it suggests how we got where we are today. These books, therefore, do not always treat a subject in a purely chronological way. Rather, their material is arranged to point up trends and interrelationships that the editors believe are more illuminating than a chronological listing would be.

"The Great Contemporary Issues" series will ultimately constitute an encyclopedic library of today's major issues. Long before editorial work on the first volume had even begun, some fifty specific titles had already been either scheduled for definite publication or listed as candidates. Since then, events have prompted the inclusion of a number of additional titles, and the editors are, moreover, alert not only for new issues as they emerge but also for issues whose development may call for the publication of sequel volumes. We will, of course, also welcome readers' suggestions for future topics.

Introduction

We have seen those eyes, the stark, anxious eyes, the eyes which plead without words, the eyes of the hungry children, for whom the early years will be the last years. Americans saw them in the Depression and in World War II; I saw them in South America and Asia as Food for Peace Director during the Kennedy Administration; we can still see them in the United States.

Despite all our food and agricultural foreign aid and domestic food programs, despite all men have written and spoken about hunger (as the articles in this book so eloquently show), millions continue to be malnourished; thousands are condemned to die each day. The United Nations Food and Agricultural Organization estimates that 400 million people on this planet are hungry or starving, twice the population of our entire nation.

The needs seem so limitless, the means of food production so limited, that the apocalyptic prediction of Thomas Malthus, cited by most with disdain only a few years ago, now appears to many to be nearly proven. "The power of population," Malthus wrote in 1798, "is indefinitely greater than the power in the earth to produce subsistence for man . . . I see no way by which man can escape from the weight of this law which pervades all animated nature."

In the present food and population crisis, pessimists among us have focused on the concept of triage. The idea of "sorting" was first applied in World War I as a method of allocating scarce medical supplies and personnel so that only the wounded who could most benefit from treatment received it. In applying it to the problem of hunger, it has been assumed that our agricultural resources are insufficient to feed all of us. This is simply not the case—not, that is, if we have the will and desire to utilize those resources. Those who see triage as a realistic choice under the present circumstances also make the mistake of assuming that it is our option whether or not to make the effort to produce enough food to feed the world. If for no other reason, the choice is not ours to make because we do not hold all the cards.

For the last two centuries, an indispensable condition of industrialization has been access to raw materials, without which the machines would have nothing to process, the factories would close, farm products would be unsold, the consumer economy would enter a permanent Great Depression. Essential raw materials were once secured through colonization; when World War II ended that era, they were obtained through trade and investment policies. Some prosperous countries, especially the United States, have been less dependent on foreign sources of supply. Now American economic independence has been eroded, and the fruits of any "Project Independence" seem distant and difficult to attain. Simultaneously, we contend with a new consciousness in the Third World, which has perceived and asserted the power of its natural resources. The Arab oil embargo was an historic event; for the first time, Third World nations made their natural resources a weapon of world political bargaining.

The embargo failed to end or erode the American commitment to Israel, but it succeeded in that purpose with much of Western Europe. In addition, it has been followed by higher prices, which the consuming nations have paid even as they have protested them. The oil embargo had a meaning beyond the particular circumstances of the Middle East crisis: it demonstrated to other producing nations that raw materials are a powerful leverage, both for direct economic gain and larger political purposes.

Consequently, the American economy is shifting from single-minded emphasis on consumption to an inescapable concern for conservation. Today families are buying smaller cars, with fewer frills, and keeping them longer. One imperative of economic policy thus becomes the expansion of employment in the production of "essentials" in order to prevent higher rates of unemployment due to the declining production of "extras."

The most serious potential shortage, and the most inevitable reliance on others, will occur in the area of non-renewable resources such as oil and minerals. Until the 1940's, the United States was a net exporter of raw materials; by the year 2000, our economy will import 80 per cent of all its ferrous metals other than iron and 70 per cent of all its non-ferrous metals.

One sadly predictable reaction to the oil embargo has been the proposal to invade and occupy oil producing countries—a proposal which conceivably could be extended to future resource shortage situations. The result, of course, could be more Vietnams; it surely would be the hostility of the Third World and a crippling withdrawal of other primary products from the American market. In the end, the United States would face a Hobson's choice between an unsupportable empire and an unsupportable economy.

Another course of action that has been suggested is a production and stockpiling policy of scarcity which forces a higher return for American food exports. Rising prices can improve the nation's balance of payments and offset the increased price of petroleum imports, but "food for crude" has a devastating impact in the developing world and on the entire world economy. The import cost of cereals to the poorer nations more than tripled from $3 billion in 1971 to $10 billion in 1974. Grain scarcity generates worldwide inflationary pressures and sentences millions more to hunger or starvation. It is not only an inhuman policy, but it is likely to be ineffective. For the American capacity to produce food requires intensive inputs of oil and mineral derivatives, and sufficient quantities are not within domestic reach or secure foreign markets.

The second report to the Club of Rome, *Mankind at the Turning Point*, concludes that while efforts to obtain raw materials at deflated prices may bring short term benefits they will prove disastrous for the consuming nations in the long run. The computer model of the Club of Rome study concludes:

> . . . the conflict between the two sides in the dilemma over finite resources is more apparent than real. In the long run, when all important factors are accounted for and the long-range benefits considered, cooperation is the only sensible and the most beneficial path for all participants. Attempts by one side to take significant advantage over the other backfire; they reduce the benefits to all . . .

Complete independence is impossible. Our circumstance is interdependence. Our policy must be a "Project Interdependence."

In this context the ethically decent choice is also the economically sensible course. It is to expand trading opportunities for the poorer nations. It is to pay a fair price for raw materials, not to enforce an artifically cheap price, even if that is feasible. This is the only policy which can yield the most important and lasting return—a stable world economic order, the preservation of peace, the prospect of continuing human progress.

As the world's great food exporter, the United States must contribute to this process by greater food production. The escalating price of food has been a cause of economic crisis over the last three years and the major barrier to adequate nutrition for much of mankind. Current American food policy is predicated on maximum commercial sales; production is planned—or more accurately, unplanned—to result in insufficient supply and inflated prices. There are no significant stockpiles; supply is whatever happens to come out of the ground. The survival of millions and the standard of life everywhere are subject to unpredictable and capricious shifts of climate.

Instead of obsessive pursuit of profit, the United States must make and keep a commitment to produce enough food not merely to meet commercial demand, but to provide reserves which can stabilize prices and prevent starvation. Such reserves would be insurance against both bad crop years and unexpected cutoffs or shortfalls of fuel and fertilizer.

This guaranteed supply requires insurance of farmers incomes. Today the American agricultural economy makes bumper crops, which should be a blessing in a hungry world, a burden for those who farm the land. It is a disincentive system, under which farmers are penalized for their abundance because its effect may be a decline in the commodity market. This nation must provide an incentive for maximum production through a new program which offers realisitic income support instead of inadequate price supports. Only in this way can the United States both reserve grain and preserve the viability of its agriculture, especially the family farm.

Expanded production can sustain major expansion of foreign food assistance. The developing world ultimately must become self-sufficient in food production if it is to survive. But Third World nations must be able to feed their people in the short term in order to become capable of growing their own food in the long term. An impoverished society with a hungry population cannot plan or implement a decade of agricultural development. More food aid to the Third World now is a precondition of enough food production by the Third World in the future. The United States provided more than four fifths of all food aid between 1965 and 1972. But the primary purpose was the disposal of surplus. As this surplus was depleted and commercial demand expanded, food assistance was reduced. As drought struck and food shipments slowed, developing countries did not even have promises to eat. And for the United States food aid was no longer a promise to keep.

Food assistance must be more than surplus disposal. It must be planned to serve its most important purpose—that the recipients will have proper nutrition, on a regular basis, with an incentive for shaping over time the means of their own sustenance. Our policy, therefore, also must face honestly another problem in many recipient nations. Too often our aid has been overlaid on systems of such manifest economic injustice that it has been ineffective or even counterproductive. If we truly seek to end hunger and to stabilize the world economy, then as we feed individuals, we must encourage their governments to undertake vital reforms. This is a difficult and delicate process. We cannot expect to dominate these nations; their fierce sense of independence will not yield even in the face of a vast dependence on our food. But we need not accept the waste of our aid or of the chance it offers for them to aid themselves. Farmers in the developing world can grow food if they have the incentive. The incentive will come with sensible international trade relationships and progressive economic policies in Third World nations.

New approaches will be expensive to the United States and other industrial nations; they are inexpensive in comparison with the certain alternative of economic warfare and the probable alternative of armed conflict. Yet we still seem reluctant to pay the price of change. World War II left us the world's strongest military power, and we became used to thinking of ourselves as all-powerful. But in Vietnam especially and in the world generally, we have discovered recently the limits of American arms and influence. The continued assertion of omnipotence will be refuted by events and rewarded by the hostility of other countries.

Rather, we must redefine our national purposes to fit new realities. Some directions that redefinition should take were provided by the Reverend J. Bryan Hehir of the United States Catholic Conference, testifying in December 1974, before the Senate Select Committee on Nutrition and Human Needs, of which I am chairman:

> To define the personal and policy choices we face in the food crisis in terms of charity is to distort the empirical problem, to dilute the moral decision we confront and to distract us from the key policy questions.
>
> Humanitarian charity depicts our moral responsibility in terms of an option or voluntary program. To say we are called in charity to feed the hungry is to say we are being asked to be exceedingly generous. The language of charity reduces our moral responsibility to this level of going far beyond what we have an obligation to do.
>
> To pose the food problem as an issue of justice is to sharpen the moral dilemma we face as a nation. Charity is concerned with the needs of others and our freedom to choose to help them. Social justice is concerned with the rights of others and our responsibility to meet these rights.
>
> The global food crisis is about the right to eat; to say others have a right to eat is to pose our problem in terms of an obligation we have rather than an option we face.

A government with unrestrained power abroad has a way, even if it is wrong, to scorn the rights of others. An omnipotent nation can choose to confront or co-operate with its neighbors, to take or to share. But when a nation's power is limited, its only option is its obligation of conscience to attend to the will and needs of others. Morality then becomes practicality.

Thus triage is not practical, but chimerical. It would be hard not merely on others, but on ourselves. Triage is not a necessary solution, but the spiritual and material suicide of the West. The Club of Rome report states the imperative of international social justice:

> A more equitable long-term allocation of global world resources would require that the industrialized regions put a stop to further overdevelopment by accepting limits on per capita use of finite resources. If development aid is to lend a truly helping hand to the hungry billions who must find a way out of poverty, more than investment capital is needed. Unless this lesson is learned in time, there will be a thousand desperadoes terrorizing those who are now "rich," and eventually nuclear blackmail and terror will paralyze further orderly development . . .
>
> Ten or twenty years from now it will probably be too late, and then even a hundred Kissingers, constantly criss-crossing the globe on peace missions, could not prevent the world from falling into the abyss of a nuclear holocaust.

Seldom in history has choice been so stark, yet so obvious. Here selfishness and selflessness are the same. The national interest requires what the eyes of the hungry children implore—a policy which recognizes that earth is a single lifeboat, that we are sailors on the same crew, and that we will all sink or be saved together. The Scripture says: "Whatever you do unto these, the least of my brethren, you do unto Me." Now whatever we do unto them, we do also to ourselves.

George McGovern

CHAPTER 1

The World in Crisis

Hunger in Bengal.

Courtesy The New York Times.

MYRDAL SEES END OF FARM SURPLUS

Says U.S. Must Produce to Bar Death of Millions

By DONALD JANSON
Special to The New York Times

CHICAGO, March 15—Gunnar Myrdal forecast today an end within a decade to the farm-surplus problem that has plagued the United States since World War II.

The Swedish economist told the National Farmers Union that the time was fast approaching when this nation must shift gears and produce all the food its advanced agricultural technology permits.

Otherwise, he said, the burgeoning populations of underdeveloped countries faced starvation of "hundreds of millions of people."

Repercussions that could be expected, he added, include political totalitarianism ushered in by violence.

In another address, Vice President Humphrey said that the mounting world need for food was a "great challenge" to American agriculture.

Rises in Poor Nations

He noted that the world's population was growing at a rate of 2 per cent a year. The biggest increases, he said, are coming in nations least able to feed their people.

Mr. Myrdal and Mr. Humphrey addressed opening-day sessions of the 63d annual convention of the farmers' union at the Sherman House here. The union represents some 225,000 farm families, many of them small producers.

Mr. Myrdal is on his way home after completing studies of the food problem in South Asia.

Even "under the best auspices," he said, "birth control will spread only slowly" in the underdeveloped countries.

His studies indicate, he said, that the United Nations has underestimated in calculating that total world food supplies must be doubled by 1980 and trebled by 2000.

A world food-aid program to prevent starvation and calamity must be "internationalized" to be most effective, he said.

He suggested a major expansion of the pioneering World Food Program administered by the Food and Agricultural Organization of the United Nations.

"All that the American farmers can produce will be needed," he said, "as also what Canada, New Zealand and other similar countries can produce."

The cost should be shared, he said, by all nations able to contribute.

Headache For Taxpayers

An indication of the extent of the farm surplus headache for United States taxpayers for a generation is seen in figures for the last fiscal year alone.

In the year ended last July the Department of Agriculture spent $3.2 billion to buy crop surpluses. In addition, it gave away or sold for local foreign currencies commodities it had bought earlier for $2.1 billion

Mr. Myrdal has accurately pointed up major crises in the past. In the United States he is best known for his intensive study of the Negro problem a quarter of a century ago. In "An American Dilemma," he forecast the revolution under way today.

He is now "very hopeful," he said at a news conference, of a lasting solution to the racial question. He praised President Kennedy and President Johnson for "running very fast to keep far enough ahead of the movement" to maintain order.

March 16, 1965

U.S. Storage Bins Coming Down As the Surplus of Crops Dwindles

By WILLIAM M. BLAIR
Special to The New York Times

WASHINGTON, Jan. 1—Government storage bins are coming down.

The round bins and quonset huts that were the symbol of surplus grain are being sold Farmers are picking up the bins for storage on farms, and the huts for machine shops and farm-implement sheds. Nonfarmers are buying them too.

In 1957, the Government owned 238,439 structures in 24 states. These had a combined capacity of nearly one billion bushels of wheat, corn, oats, barley, soybeans and other grains.

On Dec. 1, the number was down to 154,000 structures in 15 states and a capacity of 636 million bushels, a reduction of one-third in storage capacity since the peak year of 1957.

Nearly all of the storage structures sold, representing more than 300 million bushels of capacity, were moved through public sales for farm or commercial use in the period between July 1, 1963, and Dec. 1, 1966.

Cost Was $234-Million

The storage facilities cost the Government about $234-million, or about 24 cents a bushel, at the height of the surplus production period. No figures are available yet on the amount recovered by the Government in the sale of the bins and other storage facilities, although the amount is small in relation to cost.

Many of the storage structures are in poor condition and have been depreciated by the Government.

Small bins have sold at auction for about $120. Larger bins have sold for as high as $235 on bids. The quonset huts have gone for as much as $500.

One example of the reduction in Government storage is De Witt County, Ill. That county had a storage capacity of more than 3.4 million bushels, but at present the Government storage is down to 490,000 bushels.

Most of the storage facilities are in the Middle West. The bins are of steel or aluminum construction and are situated on leased land that the Government is turning back to individual farmers or county governments.

The Commodity Credit Corporation, the Government's farm price support and storage agency, now has opened up its storage sales policy to enable public and nonprofit organizations to buy bins for non-agricultural use.

Officials said that they expected these groups to be primarily interested in the so-called flat storage structures, such as quonset huts, rather than the round bins. These structures have capacities of 25,000 to 55,000 bushels of grain. Buyers must arrange for moving the structures and installing them on their own property.

Previously the nonfarmers acquiring the surplus bins had been agricultural supply concerns such as seed and feed dealers and fertilizer suppliers.

The decline in farm stocks has put the Commodity Credit Corporation in its best financial position since 1953. This institution had only $4.5-billion of its assets invested in farm products as of Nov. 1. This compares with $6.3-billion a year ago and a record of $8.5-billion in February and November of 1959.

The Nov. 1 figure is the lowest since the $4.4-billion of October, 1953. Officials said that year-end figures probably would show less than $4-billion invested in farm stocks.

Wheat Holdings Down

The continued depletion of farm stocks is shown in the agency's figures as of Nov. 1, the latest available. At that time, it owned, for example, only about 273 million bushels of wheat worth $535-million. This compared with 610 million bushels worth more than $1.2-billion a year earlier.

This situation was brought about by the combination of idling land and filling foreign demand, mainly relief shipments.

The Government increased the national wheat acreage allotment for the new year by 30 per cent. A survey of farmers' intentions for the new year indicates that they will use more than 26 per cent of the increased acreage. This would make a potential record crop in 1967, which would enable the United States to fulfill domestic and foreign demand and start to rebuild reserves.

Reserves as of next June 30 are estimated at 375 million to 425 million bushels. The new crop could push the reserves to 450 or more million bushels, still shy of what many officials believe is the desirable level of about 600 million bushels or a year's domestic supply.

January 2, 1967

U.S. to Let Russians Buy 136-Million in Feed Grain

Terms Deal 'First Step' in Expansion of Trade — Maritime Unions Waive Demand for Use of American Ships

By WILLIAM M. BLAIR
Special to The New York Times

WASHINGTON, Nov. 5 — The Nixon Administration announced arrangements today for the commercial sale of nearly $136-million worth of corn and other livestock feed grains to the Soviet Union.

Nixon Administration officials termed the planned sale by two United States grain companies "the first step in the expansion of trade with the Soviet Union," and said that the impetus had been generated for more sales in the future. But they declined to speculate on whether such sales would extend to China in the near future. President Nixon will visit China after the first of the year.

According to Administration officials, the key to the sale was a waiver of American maritime unions' long-time demand that at least 50 per cent of grain shipments to the Soviet Union be carried in American ships.

The officials attributed the maritime unions' action to the Administration's efforts to revitalize American merchant shipping, which include a 10-year program of subsidies to enable domestic shipping to compete with foreign-flag ships.

The sale was expected to have a significant political effect in the big mid-Western corn states. Farmers have complained of depressed prices caused by increasing stocks of grain, including wheat.

There has been a record corn crop this year, and The Administration recently announced a program to combat the price slump — it was also designed to offset political unrest — by paying farmers $600-million more in subsidies to take more acres out of production next year.

The pending sale to the Soviet Union is the first since President Kennedy authorized a $100-million wheat sale to Russia in 1964, a move that stirred controversy.

The new sale will be made by the Continental Grain Company and Cargill, Inc. Spokesmen for the companies declined, for competitive reasons, to disclose how much of the total sale each company would handle. The sale covers 80 million bushels of corn, 28 million bushels of barley and 21 million bushels of oats.

Officials said that the shipments could start immediately, mainly from Great Lakes ports.

The grain deal was described as an indication of an improved climate of relations with the Russians, who were reported to want more trade with the United States to help overcome consumer problems, including the need for high-protein foods.

The Russians are expected to use the grains particularly for greater pork and poultry production. The $136-million worth of grain exceeds by $18-million the total of $118-million representing all commodities exported to the Soviet Union last year.

Richard V. Allen, President Nixon's Deputy Assistant for International Economic Affairs, and Andrew E. Gibson, Assistant Secretary of Commerce for Maritime Affairs, said at a news conference that the grain sale arose from a series of developments that started last June.

Union Officials Summoned

In June, Mr. Nixon lifted some of the barriers for trade with the Soviet Union and China. These included removal of special licensing requirements for shipments and the 50 per cent requirement for American shipping.

Mr. Allen related that last week Continental Grain and Cargill told the White House that they had received offers from the Soviet Union for the feed grains. Earlier this week, at Mr. Nixon's direction, union officials were summoned to the White House and, according to officials, were convinced that the Administration intended to make American shipping competitive in world trade.

This, officials said, was in the spirit of the Merchant Marine Act of 1970, proposed by Mr. Nixon. The act provides for a subsidy program for construction of 300 merchant-marine vessels and for operating subsidies to offset lower foreign operating expenses.

At the first White House meeting were Paul Hall, president of the Seafarers International Union, and Jesse M. Calhoon, president of the National Marine Engineers Beneficial Union. Yesterday, at another meeting, those present were Joseph Curran, president of the National Maritime Union; Thomas W. Gleason, president of the International Longshoremen's Association; Thomas F. O'Callahan, president of the International Organization of Master, Mates and Pilots, and William R. Steinberg, president of the American Radio Association.

Question Sidestepped

In the news conference, Mr. Allen, Mr. Gibson and J. Phil Campbell, Under Secretary of Agriculture, referred to Mr. Nixon's "deep personal involvement" in the grain sale but sidestepped the question whether he had talked directly to the maritime-union leaders.

The unions reversed their position on shipping because they were convinced that in the long run more contracts and jobs would be gained by permitting competitive bidding for shipments to the Soviet Union and China.

In answer to questions, Mr. Gibson said that the grain sale "will not be used to put pressure on unions in their negotiations with management" to end current dock strikes on the East Coast and Gulf of Mexico. The Great Lakes are not affected by the strikes. Mr. Gibson and other officials said that the unions had not asked for anything in return for permitting the grain to be loaded on foreign vessels.

On Capitol Hill, Senator Jack Miller, Republican of Iowa, said after a briefing by Administration officials on the sale that the Russians would probably transport the grain in their own ships although this had not definitely been decided.

According to the Agriculture Department, the corn will come from the free market and the barley and oats will come from Government supplies.

November 6, 1971

SOVIET PURCHASE OF GRAIN FROM U.S. MAY TOTAL BILLION

Estimate by the Agriculture Department Points to New One-Year Trade Peak

BAD HARVEST REPORTED

Brezhnev and Aides Meet on Farm Issues—Attempts to Spur Output Indicated

By BERNARD GWERTZMAN
Special to The New York Times

WASHINGTON, Aug. 9—The Agriculture Department estimated today that the Soviet Union would purchase a billion dollars worth of farm products from the United States over the next 12 months. This would raise Soviet-American trade to unprecedented heights.

The forecast was compiled by leading department officials on the basis of recent talks with private commercial dealers negotiating with the Russians and of reports from Moscow indicating a bad Soviet harvest this fall.

The spring harvest was called a "disaster" by many officials and it was reported from Moscow today that Leonid I. Brezhnev, the Soviet Communist party leader, had held a new high-level meeting on farm issues, evidently in an effort to spur the harvest.

$500-Million in Wheat

The Agriculture Department's projection of a billion dollars in sales goes far beyond the $200-million in grains that Moscow agreed to purchase as part of a $750-million, three-year deal announced July 8.

Department officials said that about $500-million of the billion-dollar sales would probably be in wheat. This indicates that Moscow is anticipating shortfalls in its chief crop, vital to the bread supply that is a staple of the Soviet diet.

The rest of the total will probably be in corn, sorghum, rye, barley, oats and soybeans, the Agriculture Department estimated.

Department officials said that an American company, Cook Grains of Memphis, had just about completed arrangements for the first sale of soybeans to the Russians—one million tons, valued at about $100-million.

These products are used in producing animal feed. Soybeans in particular are valued for their high protein content, useful for the growth of cattle. Under the current Soviet five-year economic plan, Moscow is committed to a 25 per cent increase in protein consumption, to be achieved principally through an increase in the amount of meat and dairy products in the Soviet diet.

The large sales to the Soviet Union will cause a severe imbalance in trade between the two countries. Last year, the United States exported about $125-million worth of goods to the Soviet Union and imported about half that amount. The disproportion will grow with the extensive agricultural purchases as well as with a step-up in Soviet purchases of American industrial equipment for a truck factory on the Kama River.

Gold Sales Possible

Because of this anticipated trade imbalance, Moscow will have to find ways of paying for its purchases. Under the original $750-million three-year deal, the Administration, through the Commodity Credit Corporation, had agreed to extend a maximum of $500-million in credit.

Agriculture Department officials said that the additional purchases would be paid for "privately," meaning, in most cases, by cash.

Some officials here believe that the Russians may have to sell gold on the world market to cover the heavy agricultural purchases.

It is believed that under the terms of the deals, some of the farm products will be delivered by third-country ships and the rest by Soviet and American ships.

The Russians, aware of the trade imbalance, have been seeking to persuade the United States to participate in joint efforts to exploit the untapped oil, gas and metal resources of Siberia.

This was a major topic discussed by Commerce Secretary Peter G. Peterson and Mr. Brezhnev when they met two weeks ago in the Soviet Union.

Mr. Peterson was there as head of the American delegation to the first session of the newly created Soviet-American commercial commission.

So far, American companies have expressed an interest in such joint ventures, but the Government has been wary of a drain on Government credits that would be needed for such large undertakings.

The Soviet Union would probably be able to sell its products more successfully in the United States if a trade agreement is signed and it receives regular tariff treatment. But such an accord has been help up pending resolution of the lend-lease negotiations to settle the Soviet Union's World War II debts.

The Soviet Union and other Communist countries, except Poland and Yugoslavia, are barred from receiving what is known as "most favored nation" treatment. This means that goods from those countries are taxed at a higher rate than those from the rest of the world—the most favored nations. The Russians have been pressing to receive most-favored-nation treatment.

August 10, 1972

Effect of Big Grain Purchases Worries World Aid Agencies

By KATHLEEN TELTSCH
Special to The New York Times

UNITED NATIONS, N.Y., Nov. 14—The impact of Soviet and Chinese purchases of American wheat is being eyed anxiously by relief organizations worried about higher prices, bottlenecks in shipping and the possibility of dwindling reserves in 1975.

The United Nations assistance program for Palestinian Arab refugees could run into similar difficulties, a spokesman said, because of the higher prices for wheat. The United Nations Relief and Works Agency, which has operated this program in the Middle East, last year received 105,000 tons of flour from the United States.

Wheat Production Watched

These relief agencies, and also private aid operations, have been following with rising concern the indications that 1972 world wheat production will be well below last year's record, mainly because of the Soviet crop failures. The Soviet decline prompted the $1-billion grain deal with the United States this summer, boosting prices from $1.63 a bushel to $2.25.

Because of the large purchases, it is expected that American reserve stocks will drop to their lowest level in several years, but an official of the Department of Agriculture predicted that supplies would not fall so low as in 1967, when big shipments were made to India after two disastrous crop failures there.

Barring a repetition of such events and disappointing crop yields in the main producing countries, adequate grain will be on hand. "The problem is not of shortage; the pinch will be in the price," the official said.

The aid agency known as CARE—Cooperative for American Relief Eveywhere — and other private agencies said that the most pressing worry concerned shipping relief goods.

CARE, which operates free-lunch programs in 14 countries, including India, Turkey and Colombia, has been assured that it will continue to get wheat and other food supplies through next June 30 under Public Law 480, the so-called Food for Peace act, which provides for the sale and distribution of United States surplus foods to other nations.

However, since Soviet and Chinese purchases all may be moving out of the United States at the same time, CARE officials are worried about bottlenecks in railway freight yards and higher shipping costs. "Here's where we see our problem—not in the commodities," Fred Devine, deputy executive director, said.

Roman Catholic Relief Services, which also depends on supplies donated under Public Law 480 for its assistance in 52 countries, also was seeking assurances from Washington. The agency has been told that "it can more or less count on it" through June 30, according to Anthony Foddai, director of program and supplies.

Under the same law, 20 to 25 countries purchase American food under liberal terms, among them Indonesia, Pakistan, Korea and Israel.

The agreement with Israel was signed in October after the Soviet sales. An official of the Agriculture Department pointed this out to show that there had been no change so far in policy.

On the other hand, there have been reports from Washington that the Department of Agriculture intended to propose a cut of 50 per cent or more in the funds appropriated under Public Law 480, which amounted to $1-billion for the current year.

Both the programs for donated foods and for sale to governments on liberal terms would be affected by the cutbacks.

Herbert J. Waters, who was assistant administrator for the Agency for International Development until 1967, has written to the Secretary of Agriculture, Earl L. Butz, saying such a cut would be a "tragic mistake" leading to a storm of disapproval in Congress and among private agencies.

November 15, 1972

Days of 'Cheap Food' May Be Over

Soviet Demand and Farming Costs Alter Trend

By MORTON I. SOSLAND

As food prices continue to soar, Washington officials have been offering relief in the form of promises that prices will decline sharply in the last half of 1973. Such an outcome seems to be predicated on recent changes in Government crop programs.

However, such predictions arise from an oversimplification of what has happened in world commodity markets in the last six months.

The assumption of both the Cost of Living Council and the Department of Agriculture is that record high crop prices — not only in the United States but in practically all other countries — have been caused by demand outpacing supply.

The assumption is that by increasing supply, prices for wheat, corn, soybeans, beef and poultry (the list is endless and not necessarily limited to things grown on farms) will fall back to levels that prevailed early last summer.

While it would be unwise to posit that present price levels will be sustained over a long period of time, it is equally foolish, as well as self-deceptive, to hold out hope that recent upward price moves are only an aberration on a long-term trend that assures the availability of "cheap food" ad infinitum.

A case can be made that cheap food in that context is a thing of the past, that the world is moving through a true watershed in food production and demand and that this is an economic development of historic importance all too little appreciated and most dangerous to neglect for any length of time.

In this discussion cheap food is defined as meaning that food costs represent a smaller share of annual family spending than would be the case if true supply and demand forces were allowed to function in a commercial farming situation.

Within that definition, cheap food has prevailed in the United States since the nineteen-thirties. It has been the cornerstone of Britain's economy since the middle of the 19th century and provided a key foundation for Japanese economic growth since World War II.

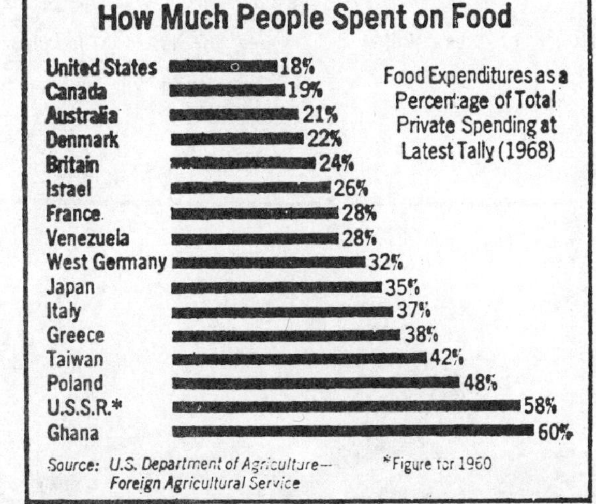

To a great extent, United States farm programs that began in the nineteen-thirties have been more of a cheap food subsidy to American consumers than their more widely criticized and publicized role as a subsidy to American farmers. Until the price advances that began this last summer, American families on the average spent only about 16 per cent of net disposable income on food, the lowest share of any country.

This was made possible by a farm program that subsidized growers through direct income supplements and payments for withholding land from production that might not, in the long run, have been planted anyway.

American consumers have not been the sole beneficiaries of these policies. Japan and Britain, traditionally the largest food importers, have relied on cheap American food for many years.

The fact that such availability is coming to a swift end has been perceived first by the British. The chairman of a leading British food company declared recently that "the era of cheap food is over." And one of that country's labor leaders said a few days later, "We no longer have the divine right to be cheaply fed."

These dramatic declarations go considerably beyond the impact on British food prices of membership in the European Economic Community. They reflect an appreciation in Britain that fundamental changes have occurred in the world supply-demand situation for food.

Even though this impact may first be recognized in Britain and Japan, where reliance on food imports causes supersensitivity to basic changes, it will be only a matter of time before food prices in the United States will call forth similar realizations.

Two fundamental forces are at work of a dimension that is yet very difficult to measure.

On the demand side is the apparent decision by leaders of the Communist bloc to raise the "standard of eating" of their peoples. That commitment has been an important part of five-year plans for decades.

This year the intent has been made crystal clear by huge purchases by the Soviet Union in world grain markets in order to do everything possible to prevent shortages of bread and to sustain rapidly increasing livestock and poultry numbers. In stark contrast with past poor crop years, the Soviet leaders made a very conscious decision to maintain food supplies at tremendous costs.

Now that the Soviet Union has learned how easy it is to buy on the American market and even to fool the capitalists in the bargain, it would be the height of folly not to expect continued takings.

Upgrading of the diet in the Communist-bloc nations poses the need for massive additional quantities of grains that will have reverberations into every American supermarket.

A pronounced multiplier effect comes into operation when consumption patterns shift from grain-based diets to diets of meat and poultry. Each unit of beef production requires eight units of feed. In the case of pork it is a 4-to-1 ratio and for chickens it is 2½ pounds of feed to make one pound of poultry.

If the Soviet Union succeeds in meeting its 1980 goal of raising livestock and poultry consumption by 25 per cent (which would still leave that country's consumers with 40 per cent less meat than the average American), the Soviet Union and Eastern Europe will require annually at least 75 million more tons of grains than presently utilized.

Industry experts say the Soviet Union can be expected to supply half of that increased need by expanding domestic production. The remainder will have to come from the United States and other suppliers, creating quite a strain in view of the fact that American feed grain exports this year are expected to be 33.2 million tons.

The great uncertainties of Soviet demand are nearly overshadowed by the mystery of potential buying by China. Just consider that one more pound of chicken a year for every Chinese requires slightly more than 900,000 tons of feed grains.

Introducing the Soviet Union and China as potential buyers of unknown dimension on the world food market comes at a time when political and budgetary realities in the United States are dictating a major shift away from old methods of agricultural support.

On the supply side, President Nixon has called for a gradual phasing out of income supplements, the keystone of farm programs for some years. He and his advisers would have the marketplace, not the Government in Washington, tell the farmer how much wheat, corn and soybeans should be planted and how many cattle or broilers should be raised.

He recognizes that farming has become an industry and that the concept of living on a farm as a way of life is past.

But the President has not stated that encouragement of crop and livestock production at a total large enough to satisfy expanding American and usual world needs—much less the explosive potential of buying by the Soviet Union and China — will require continued high prices in the absence of income supplements. Otherwise, the market will not function as a signal to farmers.

Land suitable for crop production in the United States is limited. Witness the fact that farmers last fall, in response to the highest prices in a quarter of a century, seeded only 1 per cent more acres to winter wheat.

Inputs such as fertilizer, insecticides, herbicides and better seeds are, in a very real economic sense, substitutes for land.

In the past, relatively few American farmers have considered land as a cost. Accelerating commercialization of farming will change that attitude. If we are approaching the limits of cropland, then prices very near present high levels will be required to stimulate the inputs that substitute for land.

Much about the present situation heralds expanded corporate participation in farming — perhaps not by national companies but by area and regional business entities. Before such companies will commit the capital inputs required, they will have to look to market returns substantially above the cheap food of the past.

As an economic benchmark of this magnitude is reached, it is important that the national leaders who are making important policy and legislative decisions become aware of these new realities.

For example, farm programs must be structured to allow for the establishment of reserves that will make this country's ability to supply unprecedented business more than an accident, as was the case this year.

The end of the era of cheap food is the price American consumers will pay for an adequate domestic supply and for establishing the United States as a reliable source of food for hundreds of millions of people around the world, including new and important customers in the Soviet Union and China.

Mr. Sosland is editor of Milling & Baking News, Kansas City.

March 11, 1973

Sovfoto

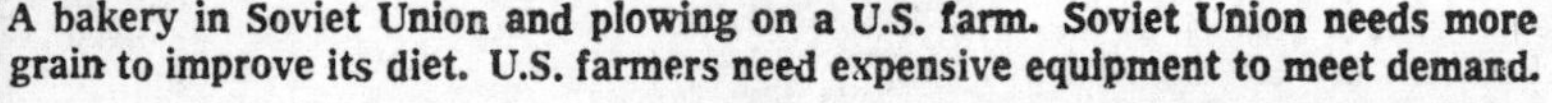

A bakery in Soviet Union and plowing on a U.S. farm. Soviet Union needs more grain to improve its diet. U.S. farmers need expensive equipment to meet demand.

Too Many to Feed

By James P. Brown

Six years ago in a book prophetically entitled "Famine 1975," William and Paul Paddock warned that world population growth was outstripping food production and that an international food crisis was probable by the middle of the decade.

The widespread skepticism that greeted that dire prediction was reinforced in subsequent years by the encouraging results of the so-called Green Revolution, as farmers in many lands adopted new "miracle seeds" developed at about the time the Paddocks were writing their book. Optimism rose steadily as the new seeds sharply increased acreage yields in such perennially hungry countries as India, where grain production leaped from 72 million metric tons in the disastrous 1965-66 crop year to 108 million tons two years ago, giving India for the first time since independence an actual surplus. By early last year there was even talk of a "rice glut" in Asia.

Then that old bugaboo of farmers everywhere through history — bad weather — struck savagely. A drought of unprecedented severity sharply reduced crops last year over wide areas of the globe from Australia to the Soviet Union, through Asia, across Africa and into Central America. Food shortages have already produced civil unrest in India, a mass migration of hungry nomads in six African nations along a 2,000-mile strip south of the Sahara and declarations of emergency in Costa Rica and Honduras.

The struggling new nation of Bangladesh, which was kept afloat by generous foreign food aid last year, is appealing for even more grain this year—but it may not be forthcoming because of the heavy demand for limited supplies, especially the recent large purchases from normally surplus nations by the Soviet Union and China. The Food and Agricultural Organization has reported that the world's reserves of grain have dropped so low that some areas may face starvation if the coming harvest is poor.

It appears that the Paddock brothers' prophecy for 1975 could begin to become a reality as early as 1974.

The problem of food shortages does not arise primarily from failure of the Green Revolution, although it is evident that much more can and must be done to extend the benefits of the new food technology. The basic problem, as the Paddocks foresaw, is that population growth has kept pace with, if not exceeded, increases in food production in those areas of the world where the Malthusian food-population squeeze has always been most acute.

The experience of India is illustrative. Contrary to widespread opinion, the Indians have made quite spectacular strides in agricultural production over the last two and one-half decades—with significant assistance incidentally, from public and private United States agencies. Even before introduction of the new seeds, total Indian food grain output had climbed from 50.8 million tons in the 1950-51 crop year to 82 million tons in the mid-sixties, just before that disastrous drought of 1965-66. This year, even with the drought, India expects to harvest 100 million tons, or nearly twice her 1950-51 production.

The trouble is that during the same period India's population has risen, not quite proportionately, but still from around 350 million in 1950 to more than 570 million today, or by about two-thirds. Some Indians, the relatively few who have profited from post-independence development in agriculture and industry, are undoubtedly better fed than ever. The overwhelming majority, however, remain close to the starvation line and highly vulnerable to the vagaries of the monsoons which are the lifeblood of Indian agriculture.

It is not that India has been indifferent to her population problem. The Indian Government was one of the first among developing nations to launch a serious official family planning effort. Small-family propaganda, the pill, the loop, sterilization—the whole arsenal of birth-control weapons has been promoted with zeal by Indian family planners for years. But nothing seems to have worked, Prime Minister Indira Gandhi conceded in an interview early this year, except for a few scattered successes around large cities.

Similar frustration has been experienced in neighboring Pakistan, which in 1965 launched the most ambitious family planning program then existent in any developing country. In 1969, a United Nations survey team gave the Pakistani program high marks for good organization and imaginative promotion. But today population officials in Pakistan and in Bangladesh, formerly East Pakistan, agree that the program has been almost a complete failure.

The disappointing results of intensive family planning efforts so far in such large developing countries as India and Pakistan, and the rapidly diminishing capacity of the world to help feed their exploding populations, point to a deepening crisis that can be alleviated only through greatly intensified international effort to solve the population problem. The developing food-population crisis adds grim urgency to United Nations plans for a World Population Conference next year in Bucharest.

James P. Brown is a member of the editorial board of The Times.

May 30, 1973

Wheat for an Anxious World

Hunger Threatens Despite Big Crops

By H. J. MAIDENBERG

"The period from now until the end of September is the critical one, during which we shall continue to live in an atmosphere of troubled uncertainty, assuming that uncertainty is not brutally cut short by a sudden disaster."

These were not the words of a hairshirted political campaigner or of someone planning a costly vacation.

Rather, they were spoken the other day by Addeke H. Boerma, Director General of the United Nations Food and Agricultural Organization. Mr. Boerma was talking about the world wheat crop.

His words were the latest reminder that the world today is experiencing the greatest shortage of foodstuffs and other basic commodities ever seen in a relatively peaceful period.

Ironically, the specter of hunger looms at a time when the world's production of wheat is about to set another record, at a time when people are, on balance, living better than at any time in history and at a time when international trade is being unfettered from political restrictions.

For the vast majority of Amercans, worried about fitting into a bathing suit that has mysteriously shrunk since last summer, talk about food shortages has always had a foreign ring. The only rationing that Americans have ever experienced is "price rationing," or the ability to pay for food.

But all that is history. For the first time since World War II, the Government has no surpluses of wheat or other foodstuffs, either to give away to foreign friends or to put a lid on domestic prices.

And, for the first time ever, Americans may have to share what they have with the rest of the world or fight to keep it from them (by peaceful or other means) because starving people are being told they need not go hungry, either here or abroad.

What has caused this dramatic state of affairs? Aren't the American farmers, 2 per cent of the nation's population, able to feed the other 98 per cent by wringing annual miracles from the soil? And aren't the foreigners learning to produce better and larger crops?

In the case of wheat, the answers are simple for agricultural experts such as the F.A.O.'s Mr. Boerma, commodities brokers, exporters and others worried about the weather this summer.

American farmers have increasingly produced more wheat over the years, although their numbers have shrunk. Aided by science, they averaged a record 36.6 bushels an acre last year and produced a record total of 1.6 billion bushels.

Farmers in the Soviet Union produced 2.3 billion bushels of wheat last year, despite adverse weather that cut production by 25 per cent.

Over-all, world wheat production increased from 6 billion bushels to 11 billion bushels (of 60 pounds each) between 1950 and 1972. And it is expected to rise 5 or 10 per cent this year, according to the Federal Reserve Bank of Kansas City, the heart of this country's wheat industry.

That 80 per cent increase in wheat production between 1950 and 1972 compared with a 52 per cent rise in the world's population during the same period. Of the 5-billion - bushel increase in wheat output during the period, China, the Soviet Union and Eastern Europe accounted for 2.2 billion bushels, with the United States and the rest of the world making up the rest.

Why, then, should there be any concern about a shortage of wheat or other basic foodstuffs?

The answer the experts give is that, despite widespread poverty suffered by most of the world's 3.8 billion people, they are living better than ever before, even if the improvement is almost imperceptible to many foreigners. And every 24 hours there are 200,000 more mouths to feed.

The obvious improvement in living standards of the Chinese and Russians alone means that more than a billion people, for the first time, have become consumers rather than window shoppers.

The 500 million people of the Indian subcontinent are demanding to be fed, and fewer of them each year are resigned to starvation. Paying the wheat bill for the hundreds of millions of Pakistanis, Indians and Bengalis is a major problem for them and Washington. Again, there are no American surpluses left to give away.

Elsewhere in the world people, swarming from rural to urban areas, are no longer able to raise their own food.

Brazil, for example, was an economic basket case nine years ago, with 65 per cent of her 100 million people living in rural areas scratching for their own sustenance. Now only 35 per cent of Brazil's population live outside cities and towns.

Moreover, the industrialization of Brazil has given that country the capital to expand wheat output at home and pay for what she must import.

The Japanese economic miracle has put an additional 100 million customers at the door of wheat producers.

As this global demand for wheat began building some 20 years ago, it was largely ignored because United States surpluses were ample to the point of irritation. American taxpayers complained of the cost of subsidies. Farmers complained that the subsidies were too little to assure them a profit and too much to shut the farm down.

Politicians framed farm programs to suit their immediate needs, and the nation's agricultural industry seemed to stumble along without any purpose.

Then came last year's massive Soviet grain purchases at "bargain prices." Of the 30 million tons bought by Moscow, 18 million came from this country.

The purchases included 11 million tons of wheat—one-fourth America's annual output and about equal to Canada's total production in an average year.

China came into the market for smaller quantities of grain, and other countries began buying to assure themselves of supplies.

With political trade barriers falling, a purchase of wheat in one country is equivalent to a purchase in another. For example, if the Chinese buy Australian or Canadian wheat, as they do regularly, other buyers have to shift to this country and that will be the pattern in the future. In short, the buyers are all reaching for the same table.

That is one reason why the price of American wheat is now more than twice the $1.40 a bushel it was a year ago. Another reason is that, while science can come up with better seed and fertilizers, nature has the final word. And the word this spring was rain, which delayed planting. If the word turns to drought this summer it will spell the disaster Mr. Boerma was talking about.

The farmers of the world know that the Soviet Union and China can be expected to have more poor crop years in the future.

Most Soviet wheat-growing areas are at the latitude of Canada and subject to the same vicissitudes of nature. Drought will probably continue to plague China.

And each time nature frowns on the farmers of the world, there will be more mouths to feed.

June 24, 1973

An Age of Scarcity

Abundance is a modern idea. For millennia, men had to live with the hard, grinding knowledge that resources of land, water and minerals are scarce and that poverty is the lot of most. That is still true in many parts of Asia, Africa and Latin America.

In the past century, however, the idea of abundance has taken hold. People who exploited the seemingly limitless land and resources of North America and Australia naturally took the yeasty notion that for the first time in human history, widely shared prosperity was possible. Western Europe began to believe in this exciting vista, not because its own resources had suddenly expanded but because modern science and technology seemed to have shattered old constraints.

Today, thousands of persons are starving to death in sub-Saharan Africa. The upheaval in oil prices and the temporary reductions in oil supplies have exposed the vulnerability of even the most advanced and powerful nations. Inflation has always been endemic in underdeveloped countries and—concealed behind a facade of totalitarian controls—in Communist countries. But today, in every free, wealthy, industrialized nation, inflation subverts the economy.

With regard to each of these critical problems—famine, energy, inflation—the facts and portents are plain to read. Men have not transcended the limits imposed by the finite resources of a small planet. It is not neo-Malthusian doctrine but mere common sense that impels men everywhere to come to terms with a new age of scarcity.

Each of the critical problems has an American as well as a worldwide dimension. America is the breadbasket of the world, but this country's farmers cannot help feed the world and also produce the surpluses that once kept food prices low here at home. Yet the United States has no food policy, either for building a reserve for further domestic needs or for feeding the hungry overseas on a consistent basis.

* * *

Americans are 6 per cent of the world's population but consume 35 per cent of the world's energy. In moral terms, Americans have no right to pre-empt so large a share of the world's resources; in practical terms, the economic costs and strategic risks are too great. Nor is this country's energy consumption static.

It increases by about 5 per cent a year. If that rate persists, the likelihood is that despite coal gasification, oil shale development, nuclear energy, and long-range efforts such as solar energy, the United States will be importing one-half of its oil by 1980.

Yet the United States has no policy for limiting economic growth and reducing the regular increase in the demand for energy. There are, for example, no national plans to require the recycling of all industrial and household wastes or to establish energy-conserving standards for the heating and lighting of commercial buildings or to require commuters to abandon their energy-wasting private automobiles in favor of trains and buses. Instead, Congress and the Administration haggle over a "stand-by energy bill" that is based on the myopic premise that Americans can evade the imperatives of scarcity.

Rapidly rising prices for food, for oil, for raw materials are the economic signs that people everywhere are bidding ever higher for scarce resources. This country's industrialized trading partners in Western Europe and Japan cannot get their inflation under control until the United States, the most powerful economic force in the free world, gets a grip on its own economic problems.

* * *

Yet this country has no inflation policy. On Friday, the House Banking Committee killed the Administration's request for stand-by wage and price controls. Democrats plausibly complained that Mr. Nixon and his economic advisers had managed the control program in such a feckless and inconsequent manner as to destroy the program's credibility.

A policy to cope with inflation would have to go beyond the slapdash imposition of wage and price controls. It would have to be comprehensive, embracing world food needs, the conservation of energy, and the cooperative international sharing of scarce resources. Self-sufficiency and economic isolationism are as delusive goals today as military and political isolationism proved to be at the outbreak of World War II.

To cope responsibly and effectively with an age of scarcity is going to require some sacrifice and some new forms of self-discipline in the ways in which Americans and other free people work and spend and live. Neither Congress nor the Administration has distinguished itself in providing leadership in developing a conservationist ethic, a new style of cooperation to cope with the exigent problems of famine, energy and inflation. Important and necessary as government leadership is, however, ordinary citizens have to show themselves responsive to changed conditions and make decisions in their private spheres of activity that reflect their recognition of those conditions.

As it has been throughout human history, scarcity is a challenge to men's capacity to act together in civilized ways.

April 7, 1974

Experts Ask Action to Avoid Millions of Deaths in Food Crisis

By BOYCE RENSBERGER

From drought-besieged Africa to the jittery Chicago grain market, from worried Government offices in Washington to the partly-filled granaries of teeming India, the long-predicted world food crisis is beginning to take shape as one of the greatest peacetime problems the world has had to face in modern times.

With growing frequency, a variety of leading individual experts and relevant organizations are coming forth to warn that a major global food shortage is developing.

A Different Situation

While there have always been famines and warnings of famine, food experts generally agree that the situation now is substantially different for these reasons:

¶World population is expanding by larger numbers each year, especially in the poor countries that are most susceptible of famine. Last year, the population increased by 76 million, the largest increase ever. The number of mouths to feed throughout the world has almost doubled since the end of World War II.

¶While agricultural production has generally kept pace, it has done so by increasing reliance on new, high-technology forms of farming that are now threatened by shortages of fertilizer and energy and soaring prices of raw materials.

¶The grain reserves that once made it possible to send emergency food to stricken areas are now largely depleted. The huge American farm "surpluses" that were such an item of controversy in the nineteen-sixties have long since been given away or sold and eaten. The world stockpile of grain that, in 1961, was equivalent to 95 days of world consumption has fallen to less than a 26-day supply now.

As the Arab oil embargo hastened the beginning of the energy crisis, so a major global shortage of fertilizer, precipitated by the oil squeeze, is cutting into this year's agricultural productivity in several populous countries.

The lack of fertilizer and rain and the untimely arrival of rains in some areas, are, in the view of many international food authorities, bringing the world to a food crisis sooner than had been expected a year or two ago.

The fertilizer shortage has already stunted the latest wheat crop in India an will lkely reduce the succeeding crops so severely that by this autumn India could be experiencing a famine of sizeable proportions. Unless massive international aid is forthcoming, Norman Borlaug, the Nobel Prize-winning developer of high-yielding wheat, has forecast, from 10 million to 50 million persons could starve to death in India in the next 12 months.

His forecast is based on the calculated number of people the wheat shortfall would have fed plus a factor for the shortfalls expected in crops not yet harvested but lacking fertilizer and rain.

In other parts of Asia and in Latin America where supply has long barely met and sometimes failed to meet demand, people are beginning to experience unusually severe food shortages. The food that is available has become so costly that the meagerest of meals for millions of poor families take from 80 to 100 per cent of their incomes.

Experts Not Optimistic

And in Africa the long drought continues. International relief agencies forecast that the effects in coming months could be more severe than ever because the people have been weakened by previous years of deprivation.

Before this year is out, many food experts fear, the soaring curve of food consumption will have overtaken the gentler slope of food production for the vast majority of the world's people, bringing more of mankind to hunger than ever before.

Many food and international relief experts say privately that they are not optimistic about how fast the rich countries will respond to a large famine. "It may take 50 or 100 million deaths before people are moved to find some kind of effective, long-term solution," one foundation official said.

A number of experts believe that the crisis may try the humanitarian potential of the American people—who control the world's largest source of food—as never before. Increasing social and political pressures within affected countries and growing stresses on "business as usual" international trading practices may test to the limit the ability of world leaders to cooperate.

Addeke Boerma, director general of the United Nations' Food and Agriculture Organization, said that the international community must soon come to terms with "the stark realities facing the people of this planet."

"Remember," Mr. Boerma said, "that, for one thing, prolonged deprivation leads people to desperation. Desperation often leads them to violence. And violence, as we all know, thrives on enlarged prospects of breaking down restraints including those of national frontiers."

Norman Borlaug often warns of the same thing when he says, "You can't build peace on empty stomaches."

The growing food shortage began to become critical in 1972, when a lack of rain in many countries led to poor crops. World grain production fell 4 per cent, a significant drop because the demand for food grows by 2 per cent each year. Drought in the Soviet Union caused that country to buy in 1973 one-fourth of the United States wheat crop.

"This small change was enough to cause violent responses in prices and shifting of foreign exchange expenditure and human suffering," said Lowell Hardin, head of agricultural programs for the Ford Foundation, a major supporter of agricultural research.

Poor weather this year, coupled with the fertilizer shortage, is expected to limit crop yields sharply again. The effects will, of course, be felt most severely in countries where the nutrition levels are already inadequate.

Although areas of malnutrition exists in virtually all underdeveloped countries, by far the greatest food problems now exist among the 700 million people of India, Pakistan and Bangladesh. Other large problem areas are in the drought-stricken regions of Africa, in northeastern Brazil, among the Andean Indians, and in the poorer parts of Mexico and Central America.

The Overseas Development Council, a private "think tank" that studies the world food situation, estimates that one billion people suffer serious hunger at least part of the year. The F.A.O. estimates that 400 million people are malnourished but adds that "a less conservative definition [of malnutrition] might double the figure."

According to the World Health Organization, ten million children under the age of 5 are now chronically and severely malnourished, and 90 million more are moderately affected. While undernourished children may remain alive for a while, they are extremely vulnerable to minor infectious diseases.

"Where death certificates are issued for preschool infants in the poor countries, death is generally attributed to measles, pneumonia, dysentery or some other disease when, in fact, these children were probably victims of malnutrition," said Lester Brown, senior fellow of the Overseas Development Council.

W.H.O. figures show that of all the deaths in the poor countries, more than half occur among children under five, and that the vast majority of these deaths, perhaps as many as 75 per cent, are due to malnutrition complicated by infection.

While most people recognize that protein deficiency is

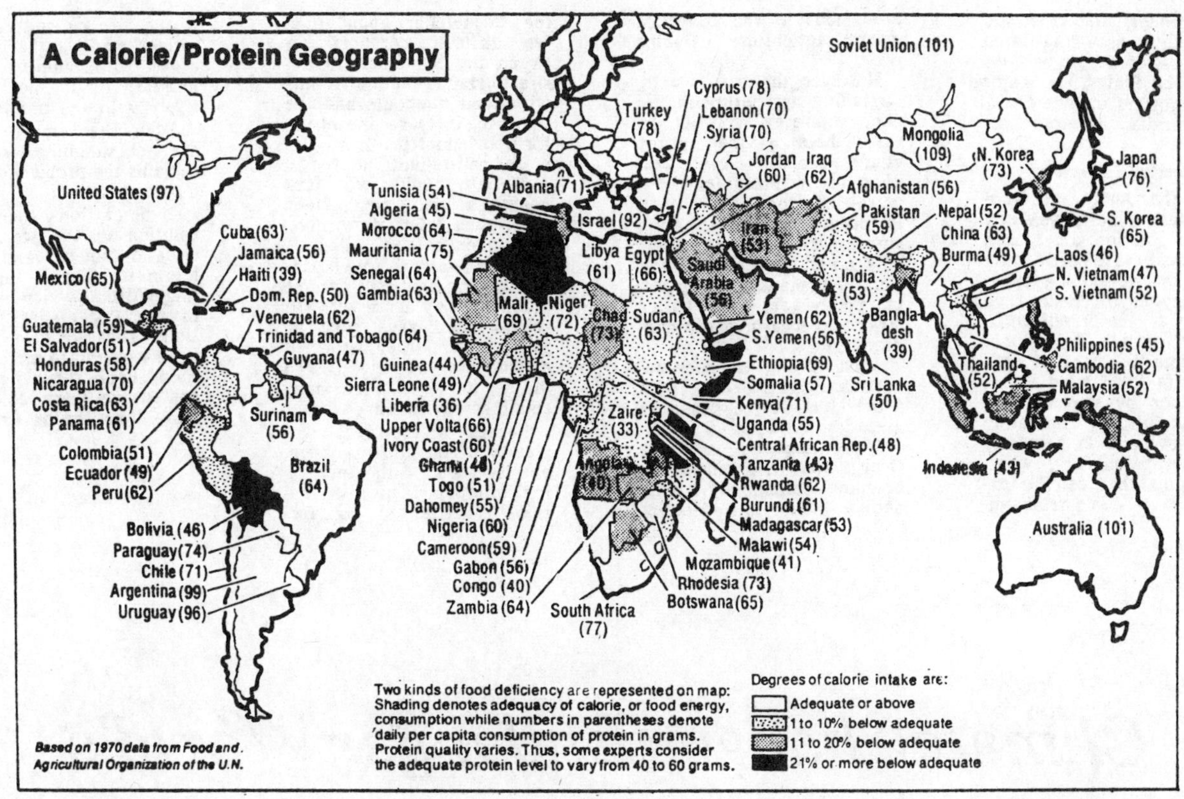

A Calorie/Protein Geography

Two kinds of food deficiency are represented on map: Shading denotes adequacy of calorie, or food energy, consumption while numbers in parentheses denote daily per capita consumption of protein in grams. Protein quality varies. Thus, some experts consider the adequate protein level to vary from 40 to 60 grams.

Degrees of calorie intake are:
- Adequate or above
- 1 to 10% below adequate
- 11 to 20% below adequate
- 21% or more below adequate

Based on 1970 data from Food and Agricultural Organization of the U.N.

The New York Times/July 26, 1974

a major problem, few appreciate that many people also suffer from a lack of starchy foods, which supply calories for energy.

Below the Minimum

"Average calorie intake in countries containing close to two-thirds of the world's people is below the nutritional minimum required for normal growth and activity," Dr. Brown said.

Even in countries where protein and calorie intake may be adequate, there can still be malnutrition due to deficiencies in one or more trace nutrients. W.H.O. authorities estimate that 700 million people now suffer iron deficiency anemia severely enough to impair their ability to work.

Every year hundreds of thousands of children, especially in Southeast Asia, go blind due to a lack of the leafy green or yellow vegetables that supply vitamin A.

Perhaps the most widely publicized recent hope for improving world food production is the controversial "Green Revolution," the use of new seed varieties that respond to irrigation and fertilizer with vastly increased crop yields.

Although the new, high-yielding strains involve mainly only two kinds of crops, wheat and rice, the potential benefits are significant because each of these grains supplies one-fifth of the world's food, more than any other source, plant or animal.

In Asia, where the situation is most critical, cereal grains, meaning wheat and rice almost exclusively, supply 74 per cent of the calories consumed. In North America, cereal grains supply only 24 per cent of the caloric intake. The difference is that North Americans and, increasingly Europeans and Japanese, consume large quantities of meat, milk and vegetables.

However, because much of the meat and dairy products consumed in the United States require grain for their production, the average American diet requires about five times as much grain to be grown as does the average Indian diet.

The "Green Revolution" has been criticized as giving all the advantages to large-scale high-technology farmers who then squeeze out their smaller competitors. Because most of the world's farmers have been too poor to buy irrigating equipment and fertilizer and too isolated to get the needed technical advice, they have not taken advantage of the new farming methods as readily as have wealthier farmers.

New Credit Sought

For these and other reasons, Green Revolution farming has not been practiced on one-half the arable land in any developing country, and in most of those countries it has been used on less than one-tenth the farmland.

Thus, agricultural researchers like Mr. Borlaug note, the full gains to be made through the Green Revolution have yet to be realized. Efforts are now under way through many angencies to develop credit mechanisms for small farmers to enable them to invest in higher yields and to improve the teaching of new farming methods to small farmers.

In small countries where this has been done, such as Taiwan, where the average farm size is 2½ acres, it has been found that small farms outproduce the huge "agri-business" farms of the United States. American farms yield an average of 3,050 pounds of grain per acre per year, Taiwanese farmers get 3,320 pounds.

While a long-term solution of the world food crisis depends on fundamental changes in the policies and practices of most small countries, the short-term solutions, many authorities feel, depend more on United States policy.

From the mid-nineteen-fifties to the nineteen-seventies, while the United States Government was buying surplus grain to keep market prices up, much of the developing world relied on this excess production to prevent famine. Through a change in Department of Argriculture policy, American grain reserves have now been largely eliminated.

To an extent greater than many people realized, it was American surpluses that stood as the world's buffer between enough to eat and famine. Now there is considerable controversy over whether the United States should reestablish large grain reserves or, as an alternative, contribute to a proposed world granary that famine-stricken nations could draw upon.

The debate includes concern over the impact of an American reserve on domestic prices, with the perennial conflict between farmers who want to sell for high prices and consumers who want to buy for low.

Although many food experts see a world grain reserve as essential in dealing with sporadic famines, most agree that, for the long range, even the vast productivity of American farms cannot forever make up the world's food deficits. Population is growing too large.

While every country produces all or most of the food it consumes only a handful produce much more than enough for domestic needs, thus providing large quantities for export. Besides the United States, the major food exporters include Canada, Australia and Argentina.

Realistic Solution

For the long-term solutions, few experts see any realistic solution other than to intensify the agriculture within the developing countries, trying to make each country as nearly self sufficient as possible. The agronomists note that because agriculture in the United States and other developed countries is already operating near the limits of presently available technology, whatever gains that can be expected must come from improvement in the countries where agriculture remains poor.

However, the experts note, upgrading agriculture in the poor countries will not be easy, because that effort would depend on ample supplies of fertilizer (and the petroleum from which much fertilizer is made), irrigation equipment and know-how, new credit mechanisms and continuing plant-breeding programs to adapt the better strains to local climatic conditions.

Much of this effort is becoming increasingly costly in a world of scarce resources and tight markets.

Many experts, such as George Harrar, a pioneer in breeding better food plants and a former president of the Rockefeller Foundation, see difficult conflicts between the humanitarian desire to rescue famine victims with food handouts and the need to increase incentives for poor countries to become more self-reliant in food.

"Why should we feed countries that won't feed themselves," Dr. Harrar often challenges.

While no one advocates abandoning innocent famine victims, many agree with Dr. Harrar that ways must be found to end the history of dependence on the United States for food that many small countries have had.

Because of the great complexity of the food problem, and because of the increasing interdependence of nations in matters of food, fertilizer, energy and raw materials, many authorities see a need to develop new world institutions to deal effectively with the problems.

Even then, most experts are not sanguine, for there remains the problem of population growth.

"I don't think there's any solution to the world food situation unless we get population stabilized," said Sterling Wortman, vice president of the Rockefeller Foundation. "Those of us who have been working to increase the food supply have never assumed we were doing any more than buying time."

July 26, 1974

Climate Changes Endanger World's Food Output

By HAROLD M. SCHMECK Jr.

Bad weather this summer and the threat of more of it to come hang ominously over every estimate of the world food situation.

It is a threat the world may have to face more often in the years ahead. Many weather scientists expect greater variability in the earth's weather and, consequently, greater risk of local disasters in places where conditions of recent years have become accepted as the norm.

Some experts believe that mankind is on the threshold of a new pattern of adverse global climate for which it is ill-prepared.

A recent meeting of climate experts in Bonn, West Germany, produced the unanimous conclusion that the change in global weather patterns poses a severe threat to agriculture that could lead to major crop failures and mass starvation.

Others disagree, but are still concerned over the impact of weather on man's ability to feed the ever-increasing number of human beings.

Whether or not this year's events are harbingers of a major global trend, some of those events are, of themselves, causing concern.

The monsoon rains have been late and scant over agriculturally important regions of India, while Bangladesh has been having floods.

Parts of Europe and the Soviet Union have had problems at both ends of the weather spectrum this year—too hot and dry at some times and places, too wet and cold at others.

There have been similar problems in North America. An American weather expert recently received reports that ice was lingering abnormally on the coasts of Newfoundland and that new evidence showed that the Gulf Stream was fluctuating toward a more southerly course.

In the United States, the world's most important food producer, a severe drought that began last fall in the Southwest has spread northward and eastward, and may have potentially serious effects in the Corn Belt. There have also been reports that spring wheat in the United States has been badly hurt by hot, dry weather.

Earlier this year, there had been hopes of bumper crops in North America and elsewhere. But the weather's adverse impact has trimmed back some of these hopes.

The situation is not all bad, by any means. Canada's prospects are said to be reasonably good, depending on what happens during the next few weeks. Aside from some floods, Australia has had no serious problems, according to experts in the United States. The Soviet Union has predicted a high grain yield, largely on the basis of a good winter wheat crop. But spring wheat, accounting for about 35 per cent of that nation's total wheat crop, may be suffering from persistent high temperatures and strong winds.

It appears that what is happening now and what will happen in the next few weeks in many areas of the world may be crucial for food production this year.

The Department of Agriculture's mid-July world grain outlook called the situation somewhat less favorable than it was a month earlier.

"The June 14 production estimate was 1,000.5 million metric tons," said the department's estimate, "but as of mid-July, the total output is estimated at only 983.8 million metric tons."

Soviet Estimate Rises

"The most important changes in crop prospects over the past month have been in the U.S.A. and the U.S.S.R.," said the report on wheat and feed grains. "The latest U. S. crop estimate is approximately 22 million tons below mid-June, whereas the U.S.S.R. estimate has been revised upward by about 11 million tons."

All of the signs, both good and bad, are being watched closely by specialists in weather and its effects on agriculture.

In the whole complex equation of food, resources and population, the element that is least controllable and probably least predictable is weather. Yet, weather can spell the difference between abundance and disaster almost anywhere.

This year, experts in weather, climate and agriculture have given much thought to the prospects for the coming years and decades.

The Rockefeller Foundation sponsored a conference on essentially this subject. A unit of the National Academy of Sciences is preparing a major report on climate change. The Environmental Data Service of the National Oceanic and Atmospheric Administration is organizing a special group of experts to keep close watch on global weather as it relates to food production. And a workshop sponsored by the International Federation of Institutes for Advanced Study prepared a

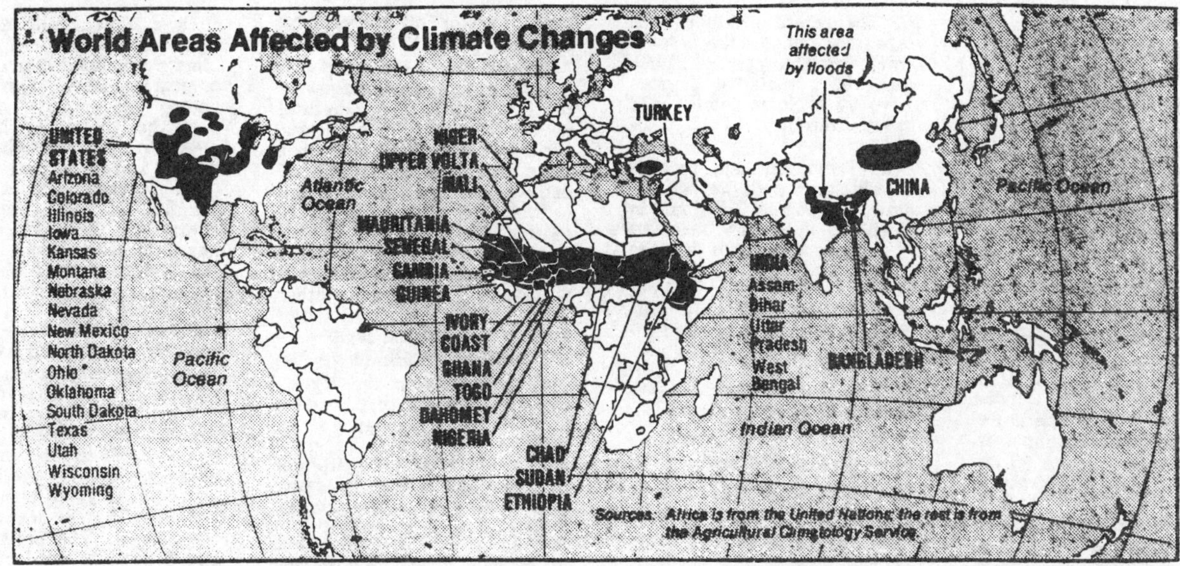

Severe weather changes, ranging from floods to drought, have struck many of the world's major agricultural areas so far this year. Climate experts say that even greater variability of weather can be expected in years to come, bringing changes to arable areas that have adjusted to past patterns, thus threatening future output.

detailed report on the impact of climate change on the quality and character of human life.

The summary statement of that report is one of the grimmest forecasts to be made in recent years. Dr. Walter Orr Roberts, one of the nation's foremost experts on climate, believes there is a growing consensus in his field that agrees with the workshop's assessment.

New Pattern Emerging

"The studies of many scholars of climatic change attest that a new climatic pattern is now emerging," the workshop's summary said. "There is a growing consensus that the change will persist for several decades and that the current food-production systems of man cannot easily adjust. It is also expected that the climate will become more variable than in recent decades."

"We believe that this climatic change poses a threat to the people of the world," the summary continued. "The direction of climate change indicates major crop failures almost certainly within the decade. This, coinciding with a period of almost nonexistent grain reserves, can be ignored only at the risk of great suffering and mass starvation."

Dr. Roberts, who is program chairman of the federation, said that scientists of several nations participated in the workshop. Its conclusions were unanimous.

Although all scientists do not put the matter in such stark terms and many doubt that a clear change in climate is demonstrable, there is widespread agreement on one point: The weather patterns that have prevailed in recent decades are anything but normal when viewed against the history of the past several centuries.

The mean temperature of the northern hemisphere increased steadily from the early nineteen-hundreds through the early nineteen-forties. Since then, it has been on its way downward toward the colder circumstances of the last century. The drop since the nineteen-forties has only been about half a degree, but some scientists believe this is enough to trigger changes that could have important effects on the world's weather and agriculture.

In recent publications, Dr. Reid Bryson of the University of Wisconsin, one of the chief proponents of the view that climate change is overtaking mankind, has cited India as an example of the possible hazards.

Early in this century, severe droughts seemed to hit northern and northwestern India roughly once every three or four years. In more recent decades, the monsoon rains moved northward and the frequency of droughts declined to about once or twice in 20 years. Dr. Bryson and other scientists now believe that the trend is back toward the less favorable conditions of the early nineteen-hundreds.

Meanwhile, the Indian population has greatly increased and demands on the nation's agriculture have risen accordingly.

Apart from that kind of long-range consideration, the situation in India this year is being watched with particular attention because, in the view of several experts, it is potentially serious.

The heavy monsoon rains vital to India's agriculture seem to be at least a month late, according to the latest world summary of the weekly weather and crop bulletin, published by the Departments of Commerce and Agriculture.

7th Year of Draught

Dr. Richard Felch, one of the weather experts involved in producing the bulletin, said the latest data available to them showed that three-fourths of the total grain-producing area of India was below normal in rainfall this year. Rainfall was normal at this time last year throughout most of the sub-continent.

The sub-Saharan region of Africa, another area of the world ultimately dependent on monsoon rains, is now in its seventh year of drought.

The region is currently experiencing a brief reprieve as the result of a somewhat wetter rainy season than has been the pattern in recent years. Some observers say the rains may even allow modest crops of sorghum and millet to be harvested.

Even so, most experts view the current rains as only a temporary fluctuation. Dr. Bryson and others believe that the sub-Sahara will continue to suffer the effects of a change in weather patterns that is likely to persist. This, like most other aspects of current climate, is subject to considerable debate among specialists.

One important reason that all of the world's weather signs are being watched closely this year is that the world does not have the margin of safety in food grains that it had a few decades ago.

One specialist said that the world's total grain reserves were equal to the approximate difference between a good crop year and a bad one. Thus, it would take only one bad crop year to draw the safety margin in world food down close to the vanishing point.

That is why experts are keeping a close watch on such diverse phenomena as the tary monsoon rains over India, hot weather in the Soviet Union east of the Urals, and the moisture in the soil of sun-baked Iowa. Now, perhaps more than ever before in man's history, they all tie together.

Indeed, some scientists believe efforts to build up world food reserves ought to be a major international concern.

Although there is no prospect of a food shortage in North America, specialists are keeping a watchful eye on the Southwest, the Plains States and the Corn Belt because the United States is so important to the world's total food supply.

Lyle M. Denny, who helps Dr. Felch to produce the weekly weather and crop bulletin, said a drought began last fall in West Texas and adjoining areas of the Southwest and has since spread northward and eastward. He said ranchers have had to haul water to their cattle in New Mexico, Arizona and Utah.

Problems in Iowa

Dr. Louis M. Thompson, associate dean of agriculture at Iowa State University in Ames, said hot, dry weather had reduced Iowa's potential corn and soybean crops by at least 10 per cent. A sophisticated statistical study of temperature, soil moisture and their effects on crops has led Dr. Thompson to a rough rule of thumb relating temperature to crop yield.

According to this rule of thumb, he said in a recent interview, the corn crop will be reduced one bushel an acre for every cumulative 10 degrees that the temperature rises above 90. For example, if the temperature rises to 95 on a given day, he would record that as a five. If it rises to 100 the next day, he would add 10.

By the end of the third week in July, Dr. Thompson said, the cumulative total reached 114 degrees above 90. For both corn and soybeans, this would mean a reduction in yield of about 10 per cent, according to his calculations. But Dr. Thompson sees more potential significance to the number than the effect on this year's crop.

The record of 114 has not been approached since the drought year of 1954, when the total through July 21 was 96. The record has not been surpassed since the "dust bowl" drought year of 1936, when the cumulative degrees above 90 in Iowa totaled 236 through the first 21 days of July.

Dr. Thompson said records to 1800 show that the agriculturally important region in which he lives has been hit by a severe drought in a cycle that occurs roughly every two decades. The most recent cycles came in the mid-nineteen-thirties and the mid-fifties, according to his figures. And he notes with little complacency that the next drought would be "due" in the mid-seventies.

Dr. Thompson and those scientists who agree with him think the timing of the current harsh weather in the West may be more than coincidence.

But there is sharp disagreement among experts on this point. Some see no evidence of any cyclical 20-year pattern, and no logical or scientific basis for it.

Specialists in the Department of Agriculture, for example, are among those who disagree with Dr. Thompson. They believe that weather is a random variable, obeying no regular cyclic pattern over the years except, of course, the seasons.

Richard C. McArdle, an economist and climatologist in the Department of Agriculture, doubts the reality of a 20-year cycle and does not think that there will be a global run of bad weather this year or in the near future. The more likely pattern for any year, he believes, is one in which some areas of the world have good weather for crops while other areas do not. This year's pattern is like that, he says.

Benefits of Technology

He and others in the department also argue that modern agricultural technology and irrigation are capable of mitigating the effects of drought in the United States. This, too, is an area of disagreement among experts. Some doubt that American agriculture, proficient as it is, can be "drought resistant" in any major sense.

Regardless of their views on the existence of a 20-year cycle and the drought resistance of modern agriculture, many scientists are agreed on one important point: The United States has had a run of remarkably good weather during the last 15 years. And many think it foolhardy to expect that good fortune to continue indefinitely.

Dr. J. Murray Mitchell of the National Oceanic and Atmospheric Administration's Environmental Data Service is among the experts who believe that the world should be alert to the probability of change in weather patterns.

Dr. Mitchell, who is one of the nation's leading experts on climate change, says scientists have learned a great deal in the last five years about the fluctuations that have disturbed the earth's climate in the past. He also says there is no doubt that the earth is now at the peak of a very warm period. Change is to be expected.

The point made by many experts is this: World population has soared in the last few decades. World agriculture, adapting to the present norm, has only barely managed to stay ahead. The pressures of population and food need are so great now that the system has lost much of its flexibility. In such a situation, any change from the present "normal" weather could bring serious trouble.

"The normal period is normal only by definition," Dr. Bryson said in a recent article. "There appears to be nothing like it in the past 1,000 years."

August 8, 1974

Computer 'Model' of World Sought to Cope With Food Shortage

By WALTER SULLIVAN

Few, if any, problems confronting modern man are more complex than that of assuring an adequate food supply to the peoples of the world in the decades to come.

With near-famine conditions in some parts of the world pushing the problem to the forefront, specialists in the analysis of interacting global issues have begun to apply their expertise and their computers in search of possible solutions.

Success, they emphasize, will depend on identifying those key factors that will control the outcome and, not unexpectedly, they have found that curbing population growth is by far the most vital element.

One projection, in fact, suggests that, if this is not done soon and with special vigor where food supplies are already short, mass starvation by the end of this century is inevitable.

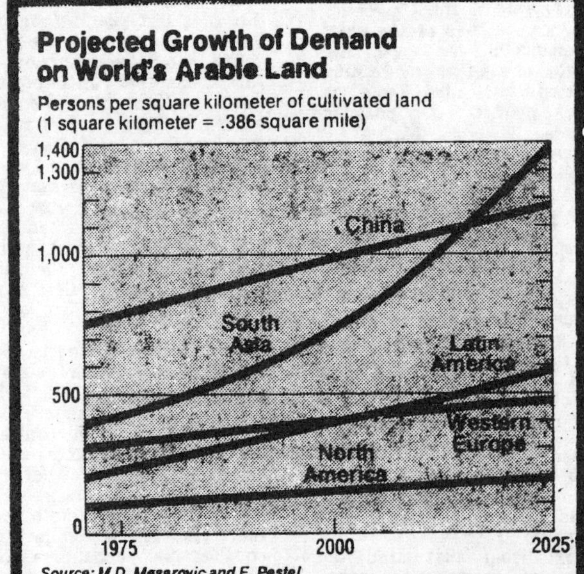

This has emerged from an international effort at computer analysis of all factors believed to bear on food production and population growth over the next half century. The analysis indicates that, unless births in South Asia are brought down to the death rate level within a few decades, half a billion children will die between 1980 and 2025.

Trends Are Projected

The analytical method consists of developing a computer "model" that can project trends by simulating the interactions of all factors believed to determine the direction of such trends.

Those persons responsible for the model that projects

mass starvation, unless population is drastically curbed, emphasize that their motive is to identify measures most likely to avoid such a catastrophe, rather than to make "doomsday" predictions.

They are mindful that in the past such projections have been criticized on a variety of grounds—notably that the models did not take into account the "common sense" reactions of humanity to situations that obviously call for changes.

Other long - term projections indicate that total world food production will remain adequate, at least for a decade or two, assuming that the problem of getting food from surplus-producing countries, like the United States, to hungry lands can be solved. On this score, however, there is not much optimism.

It is expected that the countries most in need of food to avert famine will be the least able to pay for it. Some projections set the needs so high that they could be met only if the industrialized countries slaughter much of their livestock to release feed grain for human consumption, assume a considerably greater tax burden and voluntarily lower their living standards.

One proposal for averting famine is setting aside bumper crops to cover the needs of lean years. Such a proposal for "ever-normal" granaries is to be discussed at the United Nations World Food Conference in Rome this November.

It is likely, however, that such granaries would be in surplus - producing countries, leaving unresolved the question of who would pay for the relief shipments.

Some projections envision such widespread famine that a form of "national triage" will be necessary. Triage is a term of French origin (rhyming with camouflage) that refers to a procedure for sorting battle casualties.

Normally, the purpose of triage is to minimize deaths by focusing medical attention on those who can only be saved by immediate attention. It denies such attention to those fated to die, regardless of efforts to save them.

"National triage" would direct limited available relief resources to those countries best able to use them effectively.

The possible need for such measures was predicted as early as 1967 by William and Paul Paddock in their book (widely discounted at the time) entitled, "Famine-1975!" One of the Paddock brothers is an Iowa agronomist and the other a retired Foreign Service officer.

National triage is treated at length in a study nearing completion at the Massachusettes Institute of Technology. It deals with "The Ethics of Humanitarian Food Relief" and is being drafted by Dale Runge of the System Dynamics Group led by Prof. Jay W. Forrester.

Its conclusion, in essence, is that food relief—if it promotes further population growth in the relieved area and denies food to those elsewhere committed to population control—can be "unethical."

As the world food situation has approached a crisis state, there has been a proliferation of efforts to look at it from a "systems" point of view—that is, to look at it in terms of all the interacting factors. It is argued by some experts that so many factors interact to determine the food supply in any one region that only a computer "model" of those factors can make even remotely reliable projections.

Thus, in a telephone interview last week, Dr. Howard Raiffa, head of the International Institute of Applied Systems Analysis near Vienna, said that, if abundant energy were available, there would be no major food problems.

Energy can be used to produce fertilizer. It drives tractors, harvesters and other farm euipment. It turns the pumps used for irrigation in many hungry lands—notably South Asia. It moves food from surplus to needy regions. And it can be used to desalinate water and make the deserts bloom.

But the world's energy supply is limited by a complex of factors including fossil fuel reserves, economic and environmental considerations, and constraints on the development of nuclear power or more exotic energy sources.

As growing world population has placed an ever heavier burden on food-producing lands, adequate food production has become increasingly energy dependent. The outlook for future food supplies has therefore become inextricably entwined with the energy picture, which itself is a classic "systems" problem.

Systems Analysis

The International Institute of Applied Systems Analysis, which set itself up last year in a palace outside Vienna, was founded on joint American - Soviet initiative. Its assignment is to apply the techniques of operations research — originally developed for strategic and big-business decision-making —to such problems as the world's energy supply.

Before taking over as its director, Dr. Raiffa was professor of managerial economics at Harvard University.

The institute decided, initially, to avoid taking on problems that involved the whole "world system," concentrating instead on what seemed more manageable issues, such as water resources and energy. The problem of food supply, linked as it is to delicate problems of population control and economics, seemed too touchy for an institute with equal representation from the Soviet bloc and the West.

But in recent months the increasing severity of the food crisis has dissolved such inhibitions. This fall a meeting will be held at the institute to assess what can be done in its 1975 program bearing on the food situation. Furthermore the institute recently devoted one week to

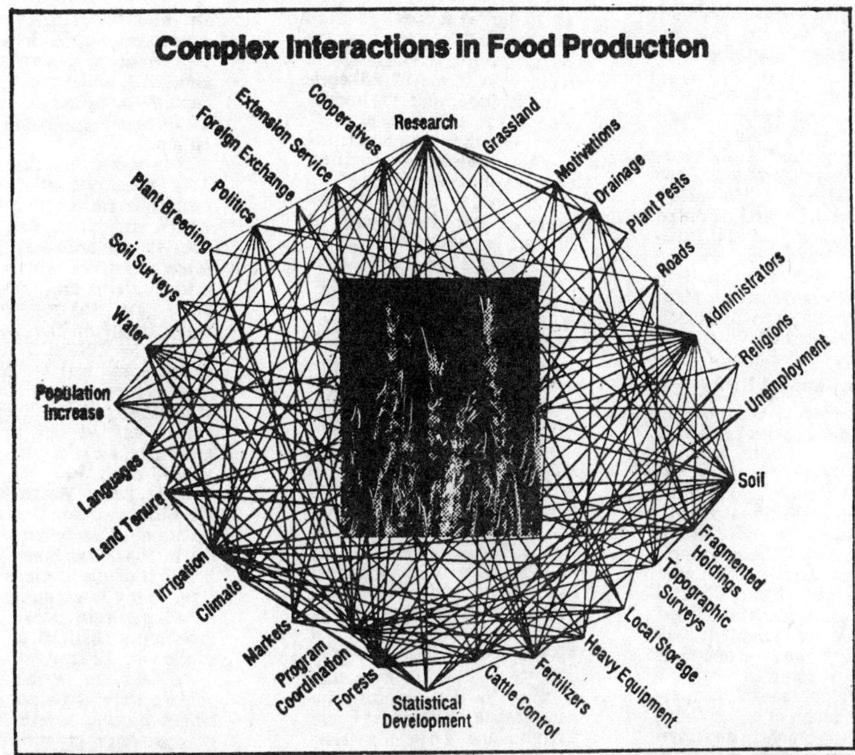

Ford Foundation experts who studied India's food production problems found there were no two or three easy steps to allay the crisis. This diagram shows less than half of key interrelationships found by scientists to be major factors in solving food shortages.

assessing the world modeling effort that has led to some of the most alarming predictions.

The world effort, known as the Mesarovic-Pestel Model, was devised by Mihajlo Mesarovic, director of the Systems Research Center at Case Western Reserve University in Cleveland, and Eduard Pestel, director of the Institute of Mechanics at the Technical University of Hanover in West Germany. Maurice Guernier, French specialist in problems of tropical agronomy, collaborated.

The Club of Rome

They present a summary of their findings, with particular relevance to South Asia, in the July-August issue of the UNESCO Courier, journal of the United Nations Educational, Scientific and Cultural Organization. Their efforts have been carried out under the auspices of the Club of Rome, an international organization of scientists, industrialists and economists formed in Rome in 1968.

The "club" seeks to apply modern techniques of business management and systems analysis to the more threatening global problems. It promoted the study, carried out at M.I.T. by Dennis L. Meadows of Dr. Forrester's group, that resulted in the 1972 report entitled "The Limits to Growth."

The latter was criticized in some quarters as a simplistic analysis of world trends, based on generalizations with little meaning for the real world.

According to Dr. Meadows, now at Dartmouth College, a detailed explanation of the computer model that led to the report will be published under the title "Dynamics of Growth in a Finite World."

Bid to Meet Criticism

The Mesarovic-Pestel Model is an attempt to meet some of the criticisms leveled at the Limits to Growth study. The data relating to food, fertilizer, energy, population and other factors on which it is based are stored in computers in Cleveland, Hannover and Grenoble in France. These can be interrogated by telephone from anywhere in the world.

Two years of work by a large team of specialists went into the study, according to the Courier account. Financial support was provided by the Volkswagen Foundation, which has long aided Club of Rome efforts.

Because issues affecting the "world problem complex" tend to be regional, the analysis has been done in terms of 10 large regions. In each of them, 87 age groups are considered. The local diet is defined in terms of 26 varieties of food, and the model also takes into account effects on the population of protein deficiencies arising from various shortages.

The model makes it possible to test the effects of various attempts to avert mass starvation. One such "scenario" envisions a population policy in South Asia that 50 years after its iniatiation in 1975, would reduce the birth rate to match the death rate.

Because older people would survive while the younger ones were reproducing, population would continue to grow for several more decades. The only way to feed the resulting population of South Asia, according to the analysis, would be to import more grain than the most optimistic predictions for the entire production of all northern countries.

Since this is unlikely, according to the report, "the catastrophe would start some time in the early nineteen-eighties and would reach its peak around the year 2000, when deaths related to food deficit would more than double."

After that, the report says, the population would be so cut back that deaths from starvation would begin to decline. However, the cumulative total, by 2025, would come to some 500 million The report continues:

"Starvation would not be limited to isolated small areas from which people could escape, but would extend its stranglehold over vast regions inhabited by hundreds of millions. The population would be trapped and there would be no fertile areas to go to as the recent events in semi-arid Africa have so tragically shown.

"There is no historical precedent for this kind of slow, inexorable destruction of the population of entire regions which at their peak were inhabited by several billion people."

In a more optimistic scenario, by the same group, a reduction of births to a one-for-one level is envisioned in 25 to 30 years, rather than in 50. The excess population would then be considerably less, and wide starvation might be averted through reasonable imports.

Imports and Investments

However, for South Asia to be capable of such imports, the region must develop export industries. To that end, Dr. Mesarovic said in a recent interview, the industrialized nations, between now and 2020, will have to make capital investments in the area totaling about $300-billion.

It is significant that South Asia was chosen for this prognosis, rather than Africa, where population density is not so severe and where some residents suspect demands from the north for population control are racially inspired. The same issue of the UNESCO Courier carries an article entitled "False Prophets of Doom," attacking the "numbers game" carried out by men and machines in more advanced countries.

Its author is Maaza Bekele, an Ethiopian educator, who points out that whereas Africa, in 1650, was home for 20 per cent of the world population, today it accounts for 9 or 10 per cent occupying a little more than 20 per cent of the world's land.

Africans, he writes, must achieve their "true potential" before putting severe brakes on population growth. Indeed it is widely believed that no form of voluntary control can be achieved until a society has become sufficiently stable and affluent to offer security to its citizens in old age. Until that comes, producing capable offspring is the only hope of such people for security.

The Land Problem

One problem, however, as noted by the Paddocks, is that the United States and Canada account for 22.7 per cent of all cultivated land in the world. Yet, for example, South America, with a comparable population, has only 6.5 per cent. Other analysts point out that, while more South American land could be brought under the plow, earlier hopes for cultivation of the Amazon Basin no longer seem very promising in that much of the land is unsuitable for cultivation.

There are a variety of dissenters from the school that believes in elaborate computer modeling and analysis of world problems. There is the "garbage in—garbage out" school that believes most of the data put into the analysis are so unreliable that the results have little meaning.

Some would prefer a much simpler computer analysis, using only what seem determining factors. Others avoid computers entirely, relying on intuition (based on long experience) or blackboard calculations.

Thus, five years ago the United States Department of Agriculture developed a relatively simple computer program to predict American harvests as well as demands by the less-developed countries for American grain.

Its long-term predictions were thrown off by such unforseen developments as the huge Soviet and Chinese grain purchases of recent years, fertilizer shortages resulting from fuel limitations, and droughts like that which has struck Africa.

American Crop Land

According to Dr. Quentin M. West, director of the Agriculture Department's Economic Research Service, 25 million acres of unused American crop land were put back into production in 1973 and by 1985 27 million more acres should have been added to this figure. As a result, in the next 15 years corn crops could grow 25 per cent and soybean yields, 20 per cent.

"Our projections," he told a meeting last April, "suggest that the United States could meet nearly all the world's increased import demand for coarse grains," through 1985. However, he said, poorer nations may continue to depend on food donations that will not always be forthcoming.

"In this connection, we see no easy solution to the agonizing problem of localized famine in this otherwise increasingly prosperous world."

Lester R. Brown of the Overseas Development Council, who has long specialized in such prognoses, makes far less optimistic predictions. In a book entitled, "By Bread Alone," to be published by Praeger this fall, he and his colleague Erik P. Eckholm predict that starvation may strike "millions, perhaps tens of millions."

Reordering Priorities

A fundamental change in the world situation, they say, calls for a reordering of American priorities. With countries like the Soviet Union periodically dependent on the efficiency of American farmers, as well as on imports of American technology, they write, such nations are unlikely to attack the United States.

"It is becoming more and more difficult," they say, "to justify the current scale of U.S. global military expenditures." Profligate consumption of energy by the industrialized countries, they add, "may be a greater threat to future global security than many commonly recognized dangers."

Their study was done,

essentially, without recourse to computers. Next door to the Washington headquarters of their Overseas Development Council the Brookings Institution has also began studies of world food prospects for the remainder of this century. A computer model with limited inputs is being used.

Early results of these studies have led to no predictions of severe global food shortages before the year 2000, although local crises may occur like that associated with the drought and southward march of the Sahara.

It is in the year 2000, on the other hand, that according to the Mesarovic-Pestel Model, population loss by famine would hit its peak in South Asia if population growth is not checked relatively soon.

Among other efforts to project future food needs is a computer program of the Food and Agricultural Organization of the United Nations in Rome. It was initiated in the nineteen-sixties as an "Indicative World Plan," directed primarily at crop yields and movements of foodstuffs between nations.

According to specialists here its published findings have run into difficulties when they clashed with national findings that sought to paper over unfavorable statistics. A more sophisticated model is said to be in preparation for the Rome meeting.

August 10, 1974

Rising World Fertilizer Scarcity Threatens Famine for Millions

By VICTOR K. McELHENY

A worldwide shortage of fertilizer, gripping rich and poor nations alike, is intensifying a danger that millions may die of starvation in poor countries in the coming year.

With inventories of food and the fertilizer needed to grow it at the lowest levels since World War II, many experts are concerned with what they see as a global maldistribution of scarce fertilizer.

They have begun searching for potential emergency supplies to reverse sharp declines in food crops caused by shortages in the three main fertilizers—nitrogen, phosphate and potash—in nations like India and Bangladesh.

One possible source is the fertilizer used on American lawns, flower gardens, golf greens and cemeteries. This comes to nearly three million tons a year and would be easier to tap, politically as well as economically, than fertilizer used by American farmers.

Twice as Large Yields

A Senate resolution calling on President Ford to ask Americans to reduce such ornamental uses of fertilizer, freeing it for crops in nations where food is shortest, has gained the backing of 38 Senators. It is an idea that is supported by many food experts as part of a broad program to encourage food self-sufficiency in poor nations.

In this view, scarce fertilizer should be directed to the countries where it will grow the most food. Fertilizer will produce yields at least twice as large on the nutrient-starved soils of Asia, Africa and Latin America as on the already generously fertilized cropland of the United States.

Yet, with food shortages pushing farm prices and farm income to record levels, farmers in developed nations are scrambling for every extra pound of fertilizer they can get to plant more acres and grow more food—some of it for sale to poor nations. The United States and Japan have imposed "quasi-embargoes" on fertilizer exports.

Prices of fertilizer and such fertilizer raw materials as petroleum have doubled and tripled in the last two years. There have been two main reasons—the energy crisis and an exhaustion of reserves because demand outran construction of new fertilizer-manufacturing capacity.

Just a few years ago, spurred by the adoption of the high-yield grain types in the widely heralded "green revolution" in many poor countries, the fertilizer industry built so much capacity that it was threatened with bankruptcy. Construction halted. Then scarcity came again much sooner than expected.

Now, mines and factories are being built and opened all over the world—including eight nitrogen fertilizer "complexes" in China—but not enough of them are expected to go into operation in time to alleviate the present emergency.

For lack of sufficient fertilizer, the green revolution is stalled all over the developing world. With nearly all of the world's land suitable for agriculture already exploited, with a world population of nearly four billion growing at better than 2 per cent a year, experts estimate that generous supplies of fertilizer are essential to avert chronic famines.

Dependence on Fertilizer

They estimate that one billion people, one fourth of the world's population, already depend for their food on the extra food yields from fertilizer. Virtually all the more than two billion extra mouths to feed in the next quarter century will depend on fertilizer.

In the current emergency, close observers are disturbed when a nation like India, for lack of a pound of fertilizer costing 15 cents, fails to grow 10 pounds of wheat that she must try to buy on the world market for at least $1. Such demand from food-short nations is one of the pressures driving American food prices up.

Food experts are convinced that generous supplies of fertilizer are a key to growing the food needed for the world's nearly four billion people, and for the population of more than six billion expected in the year 2000.

Their concern about unequal distribution and worldwide shortages of fertilizer focuses on India, which has been hit with about half of the estimated 2 million-ton "shortfall" of fertilizer in food-short developing nations around the world.

The nearly three million tons of nitrogen, phosphate and potash that Americans use on lawns and rose gardens and for other ornamental purposes each year roughly equals the entire amount that Indian farmers applied—until the sudden shortage of the last year—to a cropland area only slightly smaller than the 360 million acres of United States farmland. American farmers use at least seven times as much fertilizer per acre as Indian farmers do.

Cut by 10 Million Tons

In the last year, because the Indian supply of the main plant nutrients fell from three million tons to two, food grain yields have been cut, despite relatively favorable weather, by some 10 million tons. This amount, which is a year's supply for 50 million people, would cost $2-billion to buy on the world market.

According to such observers as James Grant and Lester Brown of the Overseas Development Council, the best place to use scarce fertilizer supplies is the developing countries, where levels of nitrogen, phosphate and potash in the soil are so low that the extra yield from a pound of fertilizer would be at least 10 pounds of grain. Only two to five pounds could be expected from already richly fertilized American or European fields.

Prof. Raymond Ewell of the State University of New York at Buffalo has estimated that an increase in the world grain yield of 100 million tons—above the present world total of 1.2-billion tons—would require 24 million tons of fertilizer if grown on the fields of rich nations like the United States. The same increase would require only 10 million tons of fertilizer if placed on the fields of the developing nations, such as Bangladesh, where food shortages are greatest.

The problems of fertilizer allocation now affect all parts of what many observers see as a single global food community. In testimony before the House Foreign Affairs Committee in July, Mr. Grant said: "It is no longer possible to insulate U.S. food prices from the outside world. Food prices in the United States are now determined by world price levels."

Mr. Grant said that a $1-billion increase in food and fertilizer aid by the United States would still "be less than half of the more than $2-billion we will receive in 1974 from the developing countries as a result of our higher food prices."

Concern about maldistribution and shortages of fertilizer has triggered these official actions:

¶A proposal from the Government of Sri Lanka for establishing a world fertilizer "pool" through which rich nations would share fertilizer supplies with poor ones.

¶Creation by the United Nations Food and Agriculture Organization of a special fertilizer commission, which held its first meeting in July.

¶Introduction of House Resolution 1155 and Senate Resolution 329 in the Congress, with sponsorship by more than 100 members, urging enlarged food and fertilizer aid by the United States and reduction of "non-critical, non-food-producing uses of fertilizer."

¶Pledges by Secretary of State Kissinger, in a speech to the United Nations April 15, of American technical assistance to help improve the operation of fertilizer factories, to help make more effective use of fertilizers, and help build new fertilizer plants in areas like the Persian Gulf where raw materials for nitrogen fertilizers are plentiful.

Such moves are arousing anger among American farmers, who oppose fertilizer exports that would cut into their own supplies. Their complaints led last fall to action by the Cost of Living Council, now defunct, in which decontrol of United States fertilizer prices was allowed in return for a promise by the fertilizer industry to reserve an extra 1.5 million tons of fertilizer for domestic sale.

This action was termed a "quasi-embargo" by Mr. Grant in testimony before the House Foreign Affairs Committee in July. At the moment, farmers fear that fertilizer manufacturers might step up exports, since world fertilizer prices are 50 per cent above American levels. A Senate staff aide called the issue "politically red hot."

Wide-Ranging Impact

Ripples from the fertilizer problem have spread all over the developing world, where leaders suddenly realized last fall—when oil exporting nations set their prices sky high—that both industrial and agricultural development prospects were in pawn to the oil-exporting nations.

Developing nations stepped up their plans for self-sufficiency in fertilizer raw materials and products. The most significant moves came in Southeast Asia, where Indonesia, rich in natural gas and petroleum, dedicated one large fertilizer plant at Palembang on Sumatra and promptly signed a contract for one twice as big.

To save up to a year in its drive for self-sufficiency, Indonesia ordered a ship-borne fertilizer plant from Europe. It will be sailed to a point offshore from Samarinda in Kalimantan, as the Indonesians call Borneo.

Some of the ammonia to be produced at this plant will be shipped to the Philippines, where it will be made into ammonium phosphate or ammonium sulphate fertilizer. The sulphuric acid byproduct from the Philippine copper industry can be used to make the ammonium sulphate, or to process imported phosphate rock to put into the ammonium phosphate.

Similar arrangements could make Southeast Asia self-sufficient in fertilizer manufacture within a few years, according to experts from the National Fertilizer Development Center in Muscle Shoals, Ala., who have visited the area.

Several Plants Planned

Discovery of important natural gas reserves 100 miles north of Dacca, the capital of Bangladesh, has led to plans for several nitrogen fertilizer plants, according to observers interviewed at the Muscle Shoals center, which is operated by the Tennessee Valley Authority. The fertilizer plants would not only supply the needs of Bangladesh but also a portion of those of neighboring India.

The fertilizer shortage in India, which has little of its own petroleum or natural gas, has led to the signing of World Bank-sponsored contracts for two nitrogen fertilizer plants meant to tap India's large deposits of lignite, or brown coal.

Such efforts point toward more generous supplies of fertilizer a few years from now—so generous, indeed, that the world might seek to "stockpile" surplus fertilizer factories as part of a world fertilizer "bank" and thus avoid the boom-and-bust sequence being experienced now.

A suggestion for this was made in the June issue of War on Hunger magazine, published by the Agency for International Development, by Dr. Donald McCune, head of the international group at the T.V.A. fertilizer development center.

"It appears that adequate capacity is being built to meet long-range needs," Dr. McCune wrote. "In fact, caution may be needed to prevent the pendulum from swinging so far that production may greatly exceed demand."

Fertilizer experts stress that the food needs of a world population growing at 2 per cent a year have long since outrun natural supplies of fertilizer.

Among these are inert nitrogen gas in the atmosphere converted into nitrates by the heat of lightning bolts, at the estimated rate of eight pounds per acre per year. This falls in rain, and helps replenish a little of the nitrogen taken from the soil by food plants.

Another natural source is nitrogen extracted from the air by micro-organisms living in nodules in the roots of such plants as soybeans and alfalfa, or in the soil, or in the water of rice paddies.

Also outrun by man's voracious need for extra food are such recycled materials as bones for phosphate, wood ash for potash, manure and slaughterhouse waste for nitrogen—or mined nitrate. The functions of these fertilizers were first understood scientifically in the eighteen-forties.

Although the raw materials of nitrogen, phosphate and potash fertilizers are plentiful in nature, each requires elaborate, massive technology to convert it to substances that plants can use.

Huge centrifugal compressors convert nitrogen from its "aloof" form in the atmosphere, as the fertilizer expert Dr. A. V. Slack calls it, into ammonia, where the nitrogen is combined with hydrogen "donated" by natural gas, an oil byproduct called naphtha, or coal. The plants then use nitrogen compounds as part of every one of the amino acid building blocks of all their proteins, including the enzyme catalysts that carry out thousands of different operations in the cell.

Phosphate rock is mined in Morocco, or scraped from the earth by electric-powered draglines in Florida, separated from other substances and finally treated with sulphuric acid. In the plants, phosphorus atoms linked together in so-called adenosine molecules provide most of the energy for the operations of living cells.

Sulphur a Key to Phosphate

Sulphur, because of its use in sulphuric acid, is a key to phosphate fertilizer supply. As it happens, sulphur itself forms "bridges" within many proteins, holding them to the exact shape that is essential to the proteins' functions.

Almost all the potash originally named from the source farmers once used, comes today from potassium chloride mined in ancient, dried out, salty lake beds. The potassium, according to Dr. Slack in his book, "Defense Against Famine," helps promote the assembly of proteins from amino acids, and the forming of carbohydrates.

The scale of the nitrogen fertilizer industry, which now accounts for half the fertilizer of the world, jumped dramatically in the nineteen-sixties with the invention of the centrifugal-compressor ammonia plant by the M. W. Kellogg Company, a division of Pullman, Inc., in Houston, Tex. Today's typical ammonia plant, producing 1,000 tons a day, is three times larger than the typical older plant.

The invention meant that if underdeveloped countries wanted to manufacture their own low-cost fertilizer to raise the productivity of their most primeval industry, agriculture, they would have to leap into an enormously complex technology, operating at a vast scale with the help of huge supplies of energy.

If the plants operated below capacity because of bad management or a shortage of spare parts or interrupted electricity supplies, their economies suffered. With the exception of a factor or two in Indonesia, fertilizer plants in developing nations typically operate at 60 per cent of capacity.

Rich resources of natural gas for nitrogen fertilizer are being lost every year in oil-producing nations because markets have not been developed for them. In Venezuela, Nigeria, North Africa and the Persian Gulf region, a total of 4.5 trillion cubic feet of natural gas is burnt, "flared off" into the atmosphere and lost forever each year.

The amount is 10 times what is used in the United States annually to make nitrogen fertilizer. It is enough to make twice the present annual consumption of nitrogen fertilizer.

The existence of such resources, including thousands of years' supply of potash for the entire world in the mines of Saskatchewan, and new discoveries of phosphate rock in Australia and even India, increase confidence that a balance between demand and supply can be established by the end of the decade.

Recent reviews of the world fertilizer outlook by the Economic Research Service of the Department of Agriculture and by the National Fertilizer Development Center indicate that world consumption of plant nutrients, which was 78 million tons in 1973, would rise at least 30 per cent, to 113 million tons in 1980.

While fertilizer experts study how to meet future demands, agricultural researchers are giving new attention to how hundreds of millions of small farmers in developing nations could economize on fertilizer and still achieve larger food yields than they and their

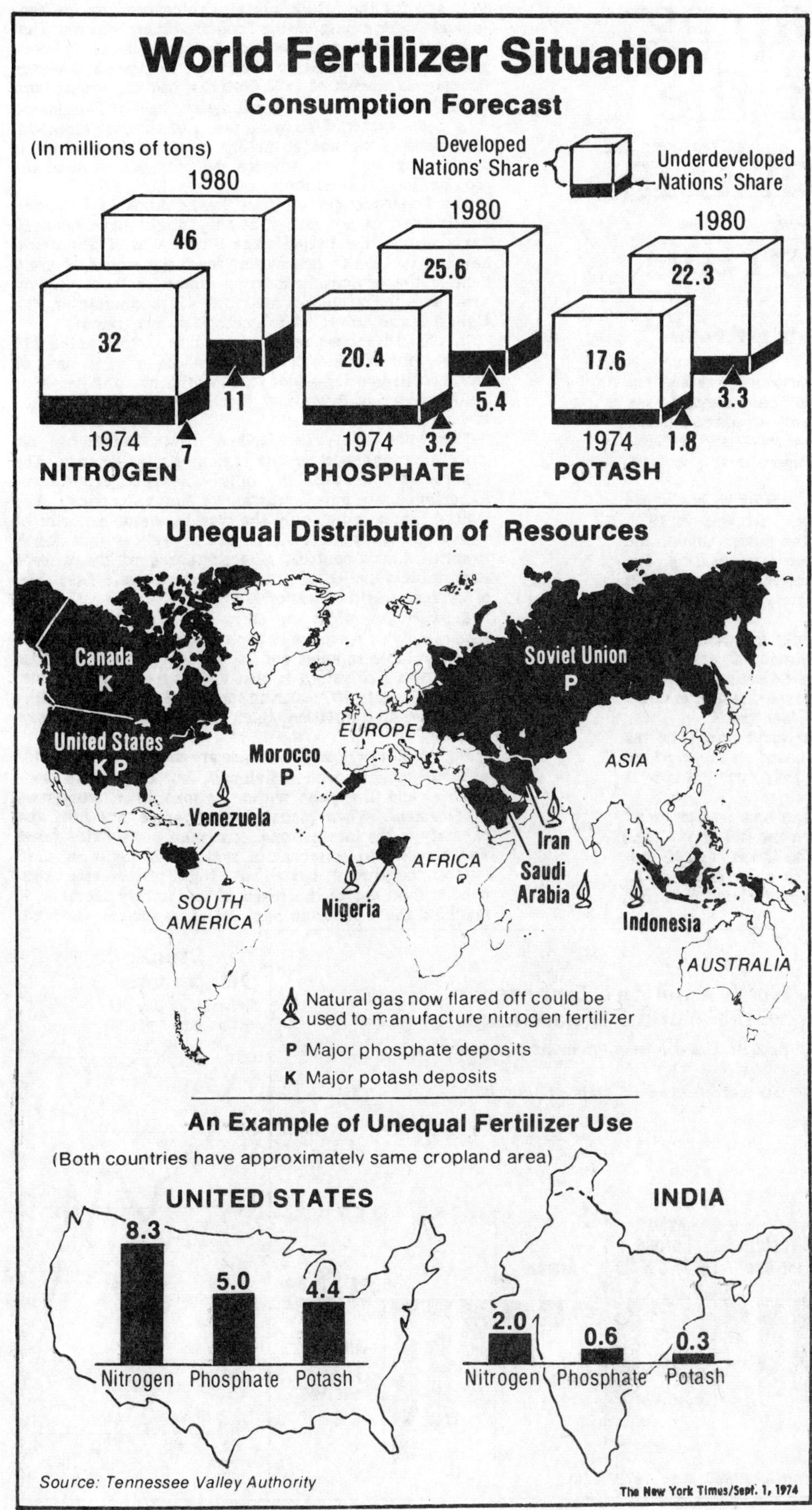

families are accustomed to do now.

Laboratories such as the International Rice Research Institute are studying simple ways to apply fertilizers at just the times plants need them.

The National Fertilizer Development Center at Muscle Shoals is pushing development of a sulphur-coated form of the urea fertilizers, which are fast becoming the most-applied type in Asia, as a kind of "timed-release" nitrogen fertilizer for rice paddies that are alternately flooded and dried.

By releasing the nitrogen more slowly to the rice plants, the sulphur-coated urea, which can be applied in one dose at the start of the growing season on intermittently flooded paddies, yields have been increased in trials from Peru to the Philippines.

Nutritious soybeans, whose rich protein now is fed largely to animals, are receiving new emphasis. Soybean plants supply much of their own nitrogen needs, thanks to the work of bacteria living in nodules in their roots.

At the Asian Vegetable Research and Development Center in Taiwan, genetic work has begun to extend the range of the soybean plant from the temperate zones in the United States and China, where it grows best now. This would cut fertilizer needs and aid multiple-cropping plans to enrich diets in rice-growing areas.

At North Carolina State University, plant breeders have been reporting some success in developing hybrid soybean plants, which would allow farmers to increase soybean yields per acre. Up to now, the only way to grow more soybeans has been to plant more acres of soybeans.

One hope, which many scientists had reserved for the distant future, has acquired new sharpness in the last year. This is the idea of genetically "tailoring" bacteria living in the soil or plant roots to do a better job of "fixing" nitrogen from the air.

Scientists in California discovered a new technique of using bacterial "plasmids," small rings of genetic material alongside the main rings of genes, to transfer properties from one strain of bacteria to another.

It is thought that this technique might be used to transfer the genes for the nitrogen-fixing protein called nitrogenase into many soil microorganisms now lacking it. The result might be a significant new way to meet the desperate need of the world's farmers for new supplies of nitrogen for their food crops.

September 1, 1974

Grim Reaping: This Year the Whole World Is Short of Grain

By LESTER R. BROWN and ERIK P. ECKHOLM

WASHINGTON—Despite the vagaries of weather and crop disease, world grain production rises almost every year. But not this year. Most recent estimates indicate the world's 1974 harvest will be nearly 2 per cent less than in 1973, and with 70 million more people to feed, the drop is serious.

Once before in the past dozen years or so has world grain output declined significantly. That was in 1972, largely due to a poor harvest in the Soviet Union, and the world food market was thrown into disarray. But there is an important difference between 1974 and 1972; then the world had substantial grain reserves, today it does not.

This year's decline reflects sharply decreased output in the world's two principal food-producing areas, Asia and North America. In addition, the Soviet grain harvest though still the second largest in Soviet history, is down from its exceptionally high level of last year.

A drop in the Asian harvest is not surprising. This was predictable as early as last spring, based on the shortage of fertilizer for the 1974 crop. The only question now is how much it will drop.

A preview of the 1974 grain crop in Asia was provided by the Indian wheat crop planted in the fall of 1973 and harvested in the spring of 1974. The target was 30 million tons, but the harvest turned out to be closer to 23 million tons. The reasons: shortages of fuel and fertilizer, and poor weather.

Food prospects on the Indian subcontinent, both this year and for the future, are also threatened by the ecological undermining of the food-producing system. That imbalance starts with overpopulation; it leads to overgrazing and deforestation, then more frequent and severe flooding. In August of 1973, Pakistan had the worst floods in its history. In recent weeks nearly half of Bangladesh was under water, destroying much of the rice crop. Unfortunately, but not surprisingly, the deforestation is accelerating. In North America the principal cause of the crop decline has been drought.

The consequences of these lower crops in Asia and North America are not what they might have been 10 years ago. In the period since World War II, the world has had two major reserves of food: the stocks of grain held in the principal exporting countries from year to year and the cropland held out of production in the United States under government farm programs.

In 1961 these two reserves combined represented 222 million tons of grain, or a "cushion" equal to 95 days of world consumption—food the world could have if it really needed it. Right now, these reserves have declined to just 26 days.

The vulnerability is further demonstrated by the world's dependence on one region, North America. The exports of Australia, the only other net exporter of importance, are only a fraction of North America's. The United States is not only the world's major exporter of wheat and feedgrains, but of rice as well. In fact, North America today controls a larger share of the world's exportable supplies of grain than the Middle East does of current world oil exports.

Between late 1972 and early 1974, world food prices rose rapidly in response to the growing excess of demand over available supplies and the decline of food reserves. Wheat and rice prices tripled and soybean prices more than doubled. In 1974 soaring food prices are contributing to the two-digit inflation which now affects almost every nation.

High food prices and shortages are an inconvenience for affluent societies and individuals, but they place poor nations and the poor within nations in a dangerous predicament. When global food reserves are low, the capacity of the international community to provide relief and respond to emergencies such as droughts or crop failures is greatly diminished. High prices help keep needed food out of the reach of the sizable segment of mankind that spends 80 per cent of its income for food.

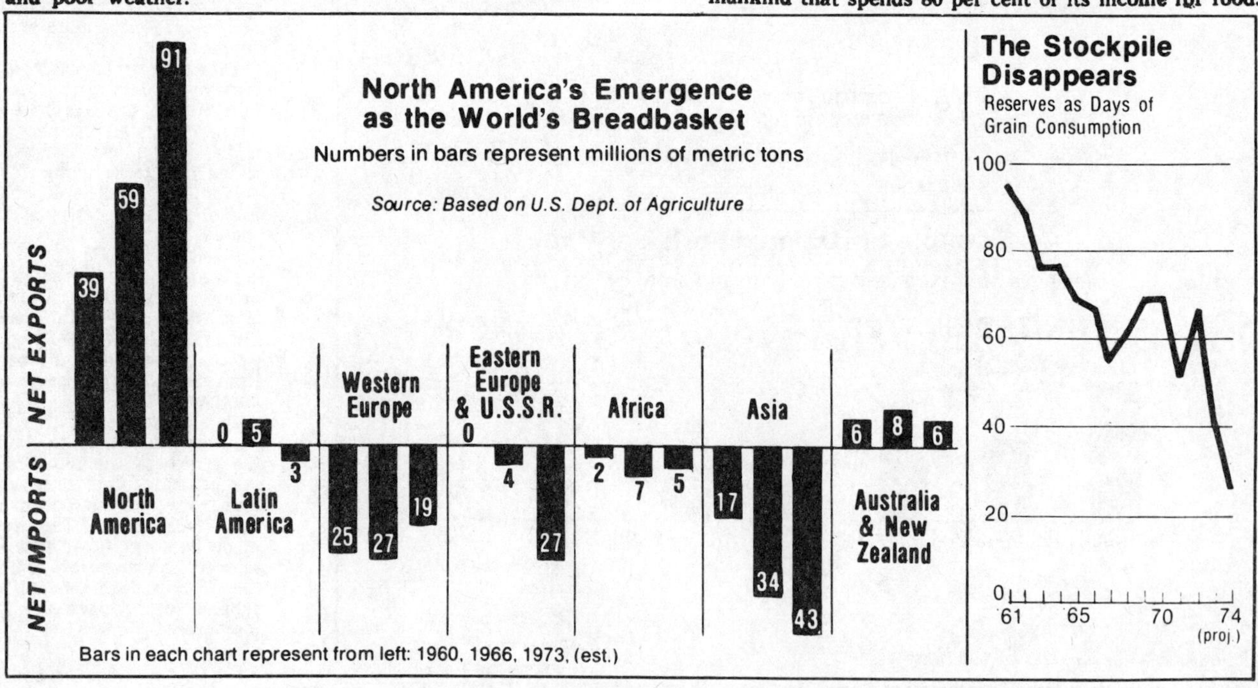

Pressure on world food supplies is leading to the emergence of a global politics of food scarcity. This produces such actions as the Soviet use of secrecy to corner the world wheat market two summer ago, or restrictions on exports of basic foodstuffs by suppliers. Thailand has limited the export of rice; Brazil has restricted the exports of soybeans and beef; the United States imposed a soybean export in the summer of 1973.

The current precarious food outlook is not entirely accidental. As a matter of political philosophy, the Nixon Administration consciously planned the liquidation of government food stocks, but the result has been to leave consumers dependent on the marketplace and the uncertainties of weather.

The resulting situation, according to those who have discussed the situation with him, has left Secretary of State Kissinger deeply troubled by the potential consequences for United States foreign policy. Instability and insecurity in a starving world could make a mockery of efforts to bring peace to the world.

While reserves of food worldwide and idle cropland in the United States have been diminishing, another kind of "reserve" is generally overlooked: the expanding herds of livestock in the northern tier of industrial countries. Those herds consume huge amounts of grain.

If those in the affluent countries, especially in North America, were asked to do the food equivalent of turning thermostats down 6 degrees, large quantities of grain could be freed for emergency relief in threatened countries. The "sacrifice" might involve abstaining from meat consumption one day a week, or reducing consumption of livestock products by 10 per cent.

The result could be the availability of large quantities of grain for shipment to famine-threatened Asia and sub-Sahara Africa.

Lester R. Brown and Erik P. Eckholm are fellows at the Overseas Development Council and authors of the forthcoming book, "By Bread Alone."

September 15, 1974

Malnutrition Is Up Sharply Among World's Children

By HAROLD M. SCHMECK Jr.

Special to The New York Times

WASHINGTON, Oct. 5—In parts of rural Bangladesh, during relatively good times, villagers hope to eat one meal a day. This year, during the aftermath of the summer floods, many of them were eating only once every other day, sometimes only once in every three.

An authority on world malnutrition, Dr. Nevin S. Scrimshaw, cited these grim figures recently to put in human terms the impact of hunger in 1974.

The consequence of prolonged hunger is malnutrition. It is widespread in the underdeveloped world. It appears to be getting worse. It hits children hardest, killing many and stunting the growth of many others both mentally and physically so that they are likely to be handicapped for life.

Since early this year, nutritionists say, there have been sharp increases in serious malnutrition among young children in many regions, notably Barbados, Guatemala, Bangladesh, Thailand and India.

There are no good global figures on malnutrition and never have been, but some experts estimate that a billion or more people suffer from it during at least part of the year. That means that almost a third of the human race are suffering today from hunger and its consequences.

Malnutrition and its ultimate form—starvation—are the real causes of world concern over the teetering balance between food supplies and population across the globe.

Real progress against malnutrition has been made during the last two decades. But some specialists, including Dr. Scrimshaw, head of the Department of Nutrition and Food Science at Massachusetts Institute of Technology, say there has been a sharp turn for the worse in recent months.

Among the underlying causes are bad weather, inflation in energy and food costs and the inexorable growth of world population. Rising petroleum prices have sent the costs of fertilizer and transportation up, too, blunting the promise of the "green revolution."

Hazards of Weather

Floods, droughts and other anomalies of weather have hurt crops in some of the world's main food-producing regions and in other places where shortage can be least tolerated.

Nations that appear to be particularly hard-hit include India, Pakistan, Bangladesh, the sub-Saharan countries of Africa, Indonesia and parts of several Latin-American countries.

It has been estimated that roughly 15 million children a year die before the age of 5 of the combined effects of infection and malnutrition. This annual toll represents a quarter of all the deaths in the world.

Some experts believe virtually all of the children born to poor parents in the underdeveloped nations have some degree of malnutrition at one time or another. For millions the malnutrition is severe.

The human tragedy of this is clear to anyone who has ever seen the staring, apathetic eyes, match-stick limbs and swollen belly of a seriously malnourished child. The whole social and economic cost is harder to grasp, but no less tragic.

In adults, malnutrition can ruin health and productivity; in a child it can all but foreclose the future. The world malnutrition covers many possible deficits, sometimes simply too little food of any kind, sometimes the lack of certain crucial nutrients. The results can vary too—anemia and apathy, or deformed bones, or stunting of growth in both mind and body. When prolonged and drastic enough, malnutrition becomes starvation—a word that needs no definition.

In regions where malnutrition is common, Dr. Scrimshaw observed during a recent interview, laborers often have to be given tasks that take only two or three hours a day. Men and women can't work longer on the calories their meager diet provides. This lack of productivity trends to be self-perpetuating. The person who can work only a few hours a day can't earn enough to buy the food that would make a longer work day possible. Even when the malnutrition reflects primarily deprivation of certain specific nutrients rather than overall lack of food, the loss of productivity can be drastic.

Effects on Efficiency

A field study in Indonesia last year, sponsored by the World Bank, showed a strong correlation between iron-deficiency anemia and reduced take-home pay among rubber tappers. The study, by scientists at M.I.T., showed a 38 per cent rise in income when the rubber workers were fed extra iron to correct the anemia.

Malnutrition is bad enough by itself, but it almost never occurs alone. The malnourished person is more likely than a well-nourished American children. In places such as Africa, where malnutrition is a common childhood experience, measles is a killer.

Furthermore, repeated bouts of infection can intensify and aggravate malnutrition. When a malnourished infant develops diarrhea—often a combined effect of too many germs and too little food—the mother responds by withholding solid food. When the only alternative is a thin gruel of little nutritive value the malnutrition inevitably gets worse.

In many poverty-stricken regions of the world, infant diarrhea and respiratory infections in the young are among the leading over-all causes of death. Many experts agree that this toll is as high as it is primainly because of malnutrition.

While malnutrition can be disastrous at any age, health workers concerned with the problem are most alarmed about the effects on children and pregnant women. The alarm is over those who survive as much as over those who die.

The combined assault of poverty and its social deprivations along with the lack of good nutrition, both before and after birth, can leave a young child permanently handicapped virtually from the start of life. For at least 20 years, evidence has been accumulating that infants thus deprived may grow up with permanent mental as well as physical handicaps.

'Increasing Threat' Foreseen

"The world is producing literally hundreds of thousands of children who will be at risk of poor mental development later on," said Dr. Myron Winick, who has done pioneering studies on the effects of malnutrition on the developing mind and brain.

"These are the very countries that are underdeveloped and can least afford to have many of their 20-year-olds retarded 20 years from now," he said. Dr. Winick is director of the Institute of Human Nutrition of Columbia University's College of Physicians and Surgeons.

The same worry has been expressed recently by many experts, including Dr. Scrimshaw of M.I.T.

"We will see an increasing threat to the population on which the developing countries will depend to bring them into the modern age," he said.

That is a factor of utmost concern to health scientists: Today's malnutrition may already be shackling tomorrow's generation of adults.

Part of the evidence for this lies in the way the human brain develops. There are two relatively distinct key periods in its growth. The first of these is a rapid multiplication of nerve cells coming during the second trimester of pregnancy—months three-through-six.

The second key phase extends through the first two years of a child's life. During this phase, according to Dr. Merrill S. Read, of the National Institute of Child Health and Human Development, comes major growth of the brain's non-nerve cells and of the intricate multiple connections between cells.

This latter phase is particularly important to human mental performance. Dr. Read said in a survey report on the effects of malnutrition on learning.

It had once been thought that the human fetus was almost entirely protected against malnutrition while still in the womb and that the infant could recover satisfactorily from even severe temporary lack of nourishment. Today, both of these views seem overly optimistic. A malnourished mother may not be able to give the fetus the optimum nutrition that it needs. The infant lacking proper food during early critical stages may never recover completely.

There are at least three ways in which early malnutrition can permanently stigmitize its victims, Drs. Read, Winick and others agree. Evidence from humans and animals shows that malnutrition at key times early in growth may affect the development of the brain so as to impair learning ability. The second and third factors appear to be as much social and behavioral as physical. The seriously malnourished baby tends to be apathetic, less demanding of attention from its mother—and therefore getting less. The result is likely to be further malnutrition and withdrawal into a bleak empty world of its own. It's a situation that tends to perpetuate itself among the survivors with later changes in personality and behavior that may interfere with learning and almost everything else.

Experiments with nonhuman primates have shown that severe malnutrition in the young results in emotional problems and difficulty in adapting to change later on.

From long studies of deprived children in Latin America and Cambridge, Mass., Dr. Ernesto Pollitt of M.I.T. has concluded that the victims of early malnutrition inhabit a world virtually separate from the more fortunate, and that food alone would hardly suffice to bridge the gap.

Yet, for millions, enough food seems to be getting more and more out of reach.

A Summary of Conditions

In oversimplified summary, this is the picture several specialists have drawn recently:

In poor areas of the world, inflation in both human numbers and the cost of everything is driving rural people off the land and into appalling city slums. Work is scarce and government dole of food offers the only hope of survival. In this natural breeding ground for malnutrition, infants are further compromised because their mothers can't both breastfeed and look for work.

In city after city in countries where hunger is already a problem there seems to be a trend away from breast feeding. Nutritionists are concerned because they see evidence that it is reflected in serious malnutrition at the age when the baby is most likely to suffer irreparable damage. The reason is that the infants often get their substitute food under unsanitary conditions and the formula food itself is often watered down to save the family money.

"It's too dilute to do any good," one doctor said, "but it still looks white."

Some nutritionists say a major aggravation of the problem is the tendency of some poor mothers to abandon breast feeding in emulation of more prosperous women—but without the resources or knowledge to provide their babies with adequate substitute nutrition.

The result, all too commonly, is a grave type of malnutrition called marasmus. It results from a prolonged deficit in total food—too few calories, too little protein, too little of everything else that is important in food.

Dr. Winick said marasmus in the very young is particularly dangerous because it hits during a stage of development when the risk of permanent brain damage is probably greatest. Dr. Joe Wray, a pediatrician who has worked in community health projects in many parts of the world as a field staff officer of the Rockefeller Foundation, says he has been appalled by the extent of urban malnutrition.

His most recent assignment was several years in Thailand. There he said, breast feeding was still the custom in rural families. Malnutrition was neither common nor often severe.

Over Half Malnourished

Dr. Wray said that when he left Bangkok earlier this year, the drift away from breast feeding was so strong that most women were no longer doing it after the first six months. In the urban slums of that city, he said, well over half of the babies were malnourished and as many as 15 per cent suffered from marasmus. He suspects that the same thing would be found in many of the other big cities of Asia.

Dr. F. James Levinson, director of M.I.T.'s International Nutrition Planning program, called the lack of breast feeding among the poor "a dreadful syndrome" that is having effects all over the world.

In the midst of all the evidence of malnutrition in various regions of the world, there are a few notable exceptions.

Dr. Georgio Solimano, head of the nutrition programs under the Allende regime in Chile, said his country had made significant progress against infant malnutrition by intensive programs of giving milk supplements to poor women and children, together with a large-scale public health education program.

Dr. Solimano, who is now at M.I.T., said the program began before the Allende regime but was accentuated during his presidency. Infant and maternal death rates have declined in Chile in recent years, he said, partly under the impact of the long-term policy.

China Visitors Impressed

Others familiar with the situation in Chile said the present regime was continuing to follow a strong nutrition policy under the direction of Dr. Fernando Monckenberg, an internationally known scientist.

Several nutritionists and experts in child health have been surprised and much impressed by the lack of visible malnutrition in mainland China. Evidence of severe and widespread malnutrition would not be easy to hide from the visitors' expert eyes. Many who have been to China believe she has indeed managed to provide adequate food for her 800 million people. Visitors to North Vietnam in recent years have reported much the same thing.

Decades ago, China and Indochina had the reputation of being the traditional home of periodic famines. Today, in much of the rest of Southeast Asia, malnutrition is widespread, some experts say.

As Lester R. Brown of the Overseas Development Council notes in a new book, "By Bread Alone," to be published this fall by Praeger, neither malnutrition nor famine is anything new to the human race. Millions died of famine in the Soviet Union during the early nineteen-thirties; millions died in Ireland during the potato famine of more than a century ago.

In 1943 floods destroyed the rice crop in West Bengal, India, causing a famine in which some two to four million died.

There have been smaller famines since World War II in various parts of the world and one case in which a large-scale threatened famine was avoided in India because of food aid shipments made largely on American initiative.

Mr. Brown, who has devoted much time and energy to warning of world food problems, said India might have experienced one of the worst famines in history in the mid sixties had it not been for the nearly 10 million tons of food aid shipped in during two successive years.

India's Need Is Vast

Observers say it appears that India may need several million tons of food aid this year, possibly as much as their annual needs for aid during the episode of the mid sixties. But this year, one American nutritionist, said, we don't have the surpluses to send them.

Some of the great famines of history have devastated whole countries or regions, threatening almost everyone when food supplies ran out. In his new book, Mr. Brown worries about subtly different famines that may confront today's world. The modern version, influenced by population pressure and rising prices, could affect primarily the poor, leaving the affluent, even in poor nations, largely untouched.

"The modern version of famine does not usually confront the world with dramatic photographs such as those of the morning ritual of collecting bodies in Calcutta during the Bengal famine of 1943," he said, "but it is no less real in the human toll it takes. Reports in 1974 of rising rates of nutrition-related deaths in several poor countries underscore the need for closer attention to this ominous trend." In a recent conversation. Dr. Wray of the Rockefeller Foundation also underscored the ominous look of things today, particularly in the urban slums of major Asian cities.

October 6, 1974

Curb on U.S. Waste Urged To Help World's Hungry

By BOYCE RENSBERGER

As the daily ration of rice becomes steadily smaller in several poor countries, some Americans are beginning to look at their dinner plates of steak and potatoes not with pleasure but with a trace of guilt.

They are among a small but growing number of people who are coming to realize that the dietary habits that are commonplace in the United States are among the most wasteful of the world's agricultural resources.

As a result, a growing number of voices are urging that individual Americans help to stretch the food resources of a hungry world by modifying their traditional diets to favor less wasteful sources of protein.

If there were cutbacks on grain-fed meat, the food experts contend, it would be possible to divert the grain saved to famine-relief efforts. The move would be similar to turning down the thermostat and reducing speed limits to conserve energy for other uses.

Because most Americans eat the way they do, consuming two to four times as much meat as the body can use and excreting the excess protein, agricultural experts say that a sizable share of this country's land, fertilizer and farming skills has been committed to growing food for animals and not directly for man.

Cattle, swine and poultry consume several times as much protein in grain as they yield in meat, dairy products and eggs.

Dr. Lester Brown of the Overseas Development Council estimates that if Americans were to reduce their meat consumption by only 10 per cent for one year, it would free for human consumption at least 12 million tons of grain. This amount, enough to feed 60 million grain-eaters for a year, would be more than enough to prevent the famine now developing in India and Bangladesh.

Humanitarian reasons aside, the American Heart Association is emphasizing personal health in its current recommendation that Americans cut their meat consumption by one-third. Mindful of the contribution of animal fats to deterioration of the arteries, medical doctors say this reduction would go a long way toward preventing heart disease.

Even a few citizens groups, with names like Freedom From Hunger, Bread for the World, and the Hunger Action Coalition, will attempt to persuade Americans to substitute vegetable protein for animal in their diets.

Some authorities say that such campaigns may be unnecessary because rising meat prices have already begun to reduce consumption. The trends are expected to continue.

While most authorities concede that the traditional American reliance on meat, particularly beef, is perhaps the single largest inefficiency in world dietary patterns, it is, of course, not the only one.

Nutrients Removed

In many Asian countries, for example, people prefer a highly polished rice. That the process of polishing removes much of the protein- and vitamin-rich layers of the grain seems to prompt little change in preferences.

In much of South America, where the corn has been yellow for centuries, people spurned a new variety of corn that had protein of as high a quality as milk or meat. The new variety was white and people said it was "sick."

Plant breeders seeking to develop improved varieties of many crops frequently encounter such seemingly arbitrary local preferences for various characteristics in staple foods. In addition to breeding higher yielding or disease-resistant potatoes, for example, plant scientists must remember that if they are to help Venezuela, the potato must have a white skin but that if the neighboring Colombians are to adopt it, the skin must be red.

Traditional taboos also deny available nutrients to some peoples. Among a few tribes in Tanzania, for instance, women are forbidden to drink milk. In parts of Thailand pregnant and nursing mothers may not eat a variety of fruits and other foods. Some Jews and many Moslems observe proscriptions of pork.

Efficient Food Use

On balance, however, the underdeveloped countries are thought to be making remarkably efficient use of the foods they have, even to consuming plants, animals and organs of animals that many Americans would consider repellant.

Despite the wide variety of unusual sources of food some people draw upon, the vast majority in virtually every country, rich or poor, rely upon a narrow range of foods as staples. They are chiefly wheat, rice and corn.

All of man's food comes initially from plants. The great dietary difference distinguishing affluent societies from those in poverty is the number and kind of "middlemen" between the plant harvest and the dinnertable.

In India the plants are almost entirely consumed directly in a largely vegetarian diet. In the United States only a small fraction of the edible plant products are consumed directly by people. A large fraction—mostly corn—is consumed by animals which, in turn, feed man with meat, dairy products and eggs.

Because animals consume so much more food than they return, diets that rely heavily on meat claim a larger share of primary plant nutrients than do diets that are more vegetarian.

Statistics from the Food and Agriculture Organization of the United Nations and the United States Department of Agriculture show that the average Inture consumes about 400 pounds of grain each year, of which about 85 per cent is eaten directly in such things as chapati, an unleavened bread, and gruel.

The average American consumes, directly and indirectly, nearly a ton of grain a year, of which only about 7 per cent is eaten directly in the form of bread, breakfast cereals, baked goods and the like. The other 93 per cent is fed to cattle, swine and poultry for meat, milk and eggs.

Thus the average American consumes about five times as much of the earth's primary food as does the average Indian. In Western Europe, for comparison, per capita grain consumption is about half that of the United States.

Growing awareness of these disproportions is raising questions about the capacity of human societies to work out systems for the equitable distribution of food. The complex food production and distribution systems that operate within and among most countries have largely come into being without plan or control.

Food is generally treated not as a basic human right but as a commodity to be sold to the highest bidder. As a result, the demands of the wealthy can claim disproportionate shares of a finite resource.

"Morally," Willy Brandt told the United Nations General Assembly a year ago, "it makes no difference whether a man is killed in war or is condemned to starve to death by the indifference of others."

In the view of some experts, the demand for food is increasing so rapidly that any growth in production of primary foods, meaning mostly grain and beans, that can reasonably be expected will be too little to meet the need.

"Efforts to insure an adequate diet for all mankind can no longer concentrate almost wholly on expanding the supply of food," Dr. Brown warns in "By Bread Alone," a book to be published next month. "Almost equally important is the need to curb the growth in per capita consumption among the more affluent people in the world, those who are already overeating."

Erroneous Belief

As it affects the world food supply, "overeating" means eating meat, particularly beef. Although man is biologically an omnivore and not a carnivore, many Americans believe — contrary to the findings of nutritionists—that a healthy diet must include large quantities of red meat. Beef is regarded as one of the good things that money can buy and one of the most familiar indicators of the affluence a family feels is the frequency with which steak is served. This affinity for beef is of relatively recent origin.

For the first 50 years of this century, figures from the Department of Agriculture show, beef and pork were consumed in approximately equal and unchanging quantities. From the turn of the century until about 1950, for example, consumption of beef in the United States fluctuated little from about 60 pounds per person year after year. But from 1950 to 1972 beef eating soared in popularity, nearly doubling to an annual per capita rate of 116 pounds. In 1973 it declined slightly to 109 pounds, the first decline since the early nineteen-fifties, largely because of rising prices.

Pork consumption has changed little over the same period, hovering at about 65 pounds per person annually. Poultry-eating patterns remained stable at 16 pounds a year per person until about 1940 when it began rising to reach about 50 pounds in the nineteen-seventies. Adding lamb and other minor sources of meat, the average American directly consumes about 250 pounds of meat each year.

It is not fully clear why the sudden boom in beef occurred, but it is generally ascribed to the popular view that large quantities of meat are nutritionally desirable. With the rapid growth of personal income in the United States over the last 25 years, many Americans appear to have chosen more beef as a way of seeming to improve their standard of living.

Few realized that in 1950 most people in the United States were already consuming as much meat as their bodies could use.

Similar patterns have developed in many other countries where affluence has been spreading. The famous Soviet grain deal of 1972 was a direct result of the Soviet government's desire to sustain increasing levels of meat consumption. Normally, in a bad crop year, cattle would have been slaughtered to conserve grain for human consumption and six or eight years would have to pass before the herds could be built up again. This time the Russians chose to continue feeding the cattle, necessitating massive grain purchases.

Despite the belief that large quantities of meat are nutritionally desirable, meat-heavy diets have not made Americans significantly healthier than, for example, West Germans, who eat about 200 pounds of meat per year, or the British, who consume 170 pounds annually, or the Swedes, who eat about 110 pounds, or the Japanese, who eat about 50 pounds per year.

In the view of many medical authorities the rise in beef consumption may, indeed, be linked with the rise in heart disease. Similar increases in heart disease are being noted in other countries adopting the American beef-heavy diet, and some experts now consider too much meat-eating to be a form of malnutrition.

The beef boom has led to a dramatic increase in the demand for grain. Because Americans want more beef and more "marbled" beef than can be raised on grazing land, livestock producers have increasingly resorted to "feed lots," where young steers that started out on grass are penned together outside slaughter houses and fattened on grain.

Once a steer is in the feedlot, it consumes about 10 pounds of grain for every pound of meat added to its weight. When it is ready for slaughter, having gained some weight on grass and some on grain, each average pound of meat will have required four to five pounds of grain.

Growth in Per Capita Meat Consumption in Some Industrial Countries*

	1960 Meat Consumption	1972 Meat Consumption	Increase
	(Pounds per year)		(Per cent)
United States	208	254	**22**
Australia	234	235	**0**
France	168	212	**26**
Canada	167	211	**26**
United Kingdom	158	171	**8**
West Germany	144	192	**33**
Sweden	109	112	**3**
Soviet Union	80	104	**30**
Italy	70	136	**94**
Yugoslavia	62	75	**21**
Spain	51	96	**88**
Japan	14	51	**264**

*Includes beef, veal, pork, mutton, lamb, goat, horse, poultry, edible offals, other.

Sources: Organization for Economic Cooperation and Development. Soviet Union data from U.S. Department of Agriculture.

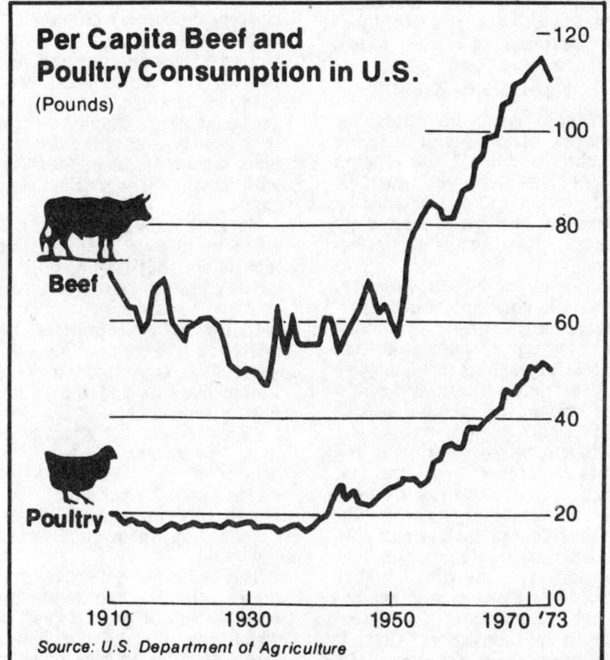

Source: U.S. Department of Agriculture

Among the principal meat animals used in the United States, cattle are the least efficient converters of grain into meat. While it takes 10 pounds of grain to add a pound of beef, it takes only four to make a pound of pork. Still more efficient are chickens, which produce a pound of meat on only two pounds of grain.

These differences in grain-to-meat efficiency have prompted some food conservation groups to try to persuade Americans to switch from beef to pork or chicken in their meals.

They note, for example, that if Americans substituted a pound of chicken for a pound of beef (the protein contents are similar), it would reduce the animal consumption of grain by eight pounds. That extra grain could be used to grow an additional four pounds of chicken or it could be used for direct human consumption. In that case, it could feed one adult for a week.

If the American demand for beef were reduced to a level that could be met by grass-fed cattle, it could, hypothetically, release more than enough grain to feed all of India's nearly 600 million people.

The same switch from beef to chicken would also substantially reduce the intake of fat and cholesterol, a fact that the American Heart Association emphasize in its public education efforts.

Still less wasteful of basic food resources, food experts say, is a largely vegetarian diet that substitutes protein from grains, beans and other plant sources for animal protein.

While there has, in the past, been some controversy among nutritionists over whether a strictly vegetarian diet provides good nutrition, it is now generally agreed that with proper selection of foods, it does. Earlier this year the National Academy of Sciences concluded that "a vegetarian can be well-nourished if he eats a variety of plant foods and gives attention to critical nutrients."

Virtually all nutrition experts condemn as inadequate some vegetarian diets, such as the unvaried "macrobiotic" regimen adopted by some people for religious reasons. Serious, near fatal, cases of malnutrition have been discovered among some followers of macrobiotic diets.

Nutritionists say the most important factor to consider in substituting vegetable protein for animal protein is the balance of amino acids, the building blocks of all protein molecules. In digestion proteins are broken down into their component amino acids. There are 18 principal amino acids, of which eight cannot be manufactured within the adult human body and must be included in the diet. A ninth amino acid is essential in the diet of infants. Once the bloodstream has transported the amino acids to human tissues, each cell constructs new proteins by linking the various amino acids in precise combinations. If one of the requisite amino acids is not available at the time, the others that are present cannot be used and are either excreted or broken down.

Amino Acid Sources

Unlike animal proteins in meat, dairy products and eggs, most vegetable proteins are deficient in one or two essential amino acids. Consumption of a single vegetable source alone results in the waste of much of its protein content. But if two or more vegetable sources are properly combined, each can compensate for the deficiencies of the other. Theombinations must be made within the meal.

Two groups of protein-rich vegetable foods that nutritionists have found to compensate well for each other's deficiencies are legumes and nuts on the one hand and cereal grains of the other. The combinations cludes beans, peas, lentils, nuts and peanuts. The second includes wheat, oats, corn, rice and rye in whole-grain products.

Combinations recommended by nutritionists include beans with corn, beans with rice and peanuts with wheat. The most familiar form of the latter, is of cours, a peanut butter sandwich.

Jeanut butter is generally regarded as one of the richest sources of vegetable protein. It is also, according to the Agriculture Department's Research Service, the cheapest source of protein in the American grocery store. The quantity necessary to yield 20 grams of protein, the requirement of an adult for each meal, could be bought for 15 cents as of August, 1974.

By comparison, the most expensive source of the same quantity of protein were veal cutlets and porterhouse steak at 74 cents for 20 grams worth in protein. The least expensive meat on a pennies-for-protein basis was whole chicken at 20 cents for the same quantity of protein. Among the most expensive meat sources was bologna at 54 cents.

Vitamin Deficiencies

One of the drawbacks of a strictly vegetarian diet, nutritionists warn, is that it can easily be deficient in vitamin B[12] vitamin D and calcium, nutrients that are available in significant quantities only in animal products. Milk commonly fortified with vitamin and mineral supplement in pill form, would fill al these deficiencies, nutritionists point out.

Even in the efforts to persuade Americans to cut back on beef and substitute pant protein for animal—sometimes called simplification of diet or "lowering one's self on the food chain"—were successful, there is no guarantee that the grain or fertilizer saved would be diverted to feed starving people or to build a reserve for future famine relief.

While it is obvious that a decline in domestic consumption would initially eave a larger share of grain available for export, the exact amounts could not be determined until the trend had become stable. Increased supplies might, for example, depress prices so much that farmers would grow less. Or the rie in world demand might well be more than enough to absorb the increase.

It is generally held that extending the benefits of an American food conservation program for poor countries would require some form of Government regulation compatible with guidelines on the international food trade that may be worked out at next month's World Food Conference.

October 25, 1974

World Fish Supply Too Depleted to Fill Needs of the Hungry

By HAROLD M. SCHMECK Jr.
Special to The New York Times

WASHINGTON, Oct. 25—New England haddock has been a staple of American fish markets since Colonial days. Today the fish are so scarce that stocks are endangered and commercial fishermen are forbidden to seek them anywhere off the East Coast.

There used to be a large-scale sardine fishery off California. Today California sardines are commercially extinct. There are a few left, but so few that it is not worth putting to sea after them.

Herring have virtually disappeared from the North Sea and the Atlantic coast of Europe. Fishermen learned all their migration points and systematically fished them out.

Such is the reality behind the popular conception of the teeming seas as a source of limitless food for the world's hungry humans.

In various ways mankind is already putting unprecedented strain on the resources of the seas and showing these resources to be finite. The impetus has come from expanding population, the world's increasing need for food and, in the case of some nations, from affluence.

The lure of large-scale supplies of food from the sea has led to the development of big ocean-going fishing fleets capable of going anywhere on the high seas and virtually fishing out any stock of fish at any depth. The Soviet Union and Japan have been notable for the development of such fleets. Only in its tuna fleet does the United States compare with them, some experts say.

The sharp decline of haddock off New England and the Atlantic coast of Canada is widely attributed to intensive fishing by a Soviet fleet in the late nineteen-sixties. It is expected to take years for the stocks to regenerate. Meanwhile, by international agreement, commercial fishermen are forbidden to take haddock except for small numbers caught incidentally in the quest for other species.

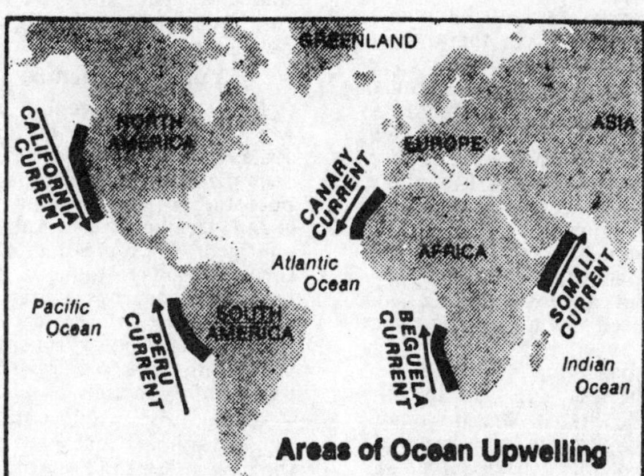

The New York Times/Oct. 26, 1974

Along current paths shown above, prevailing winds and the earth's rotation cause surface water to move away from coast and be replaced by nutrient-rich water rising from the ocean depths. The upwellings make these waters especially fertile areas for concentrations of fish, but not so fertile that they cannot be depleted.

Intense Fishing Efforts

The California sardines seem to have been depleted because of intense American commercial fishing efforts from the midnineteen-thirties through the early nineteen-sixties and some bad climate years during that time. There has been no sign yet of any subsequent return. The herring off Europe disappeared more gradually after the assault of fishing fleets of several nations over a span of more than a century.

These are only examples of what over-fishing can do—coupled probably with unknown and unpredictable natural assaults on fish populations.

Specialists say most of the best-known food species of fish and shellfish are already being harvested close to the practical maximum. Some have been pushed beyond that, according to experts on the world's fisheries.

If there are to be substantial increases in the next several years, this apparently must come from wider use of squid, skate, croaker, hake and some other species seldom featured on American menus.

Fisheries experts have singled out some striking examples of fisheries that should be made more productive by taking species that are either ignored at present or even thrown back.

One such case, according to Donald R. Whitaker, of the National Marine Fisheries Service here, is the so-called "by-catch" of shrimp fishing in the Gulf of

Mexico. The by-catch means the fish taken incidentally in nets set for something else.

Much Thrown Away

For every pound of shrimp taken in the gulf, Mr. Whitaker said, a shrimp boat is likely to haul in five to 10 pounds of other kinds of fish, primarily croaker, a source of edible even tasty, food. Thus, he said, in a catch of 200 million pounds of shrimp as much as two billion pounds of fish may be thrown away.

In fact, shrimp-fishing boats aren't equipped to handle the by-catch and would probably have no American market for it if it could.

Nevertheless, some specialists believe it could be developed into a valuable source of food if the necessary effort were made.

The fisheries service has, itself, been criticized for not doing more to popularize some under-used fish species that are plentiful in American waters and for not doing more to help American fishermen make the most of their opportunites.

For example, Mike Weiner, president of a cooperative called the Florida Fishermen's Marketing Association, says the king mackerel is plentiful, but little used in waters off our southeast coast mainly because no effort has been made to promote it.

He also charges that the fish marketing system in this country is antiquated and corrupt and, for years, has exploited American fishermen and fish-eating consumers alike.

Yet another example of seafood wastage is that of the tanner crab, plentiful in the seas off Alaska.

A fisheries expert of the National Oceanic and Atmospheric Administration said the Japanese catch more than 100 million of these edible crabs each year in the course of fishing for pollack but have to throw many of them back because the permissible catch is limited by international agreement.

Several specialists say there appears to be large quantities of squid available for the catching if more people could be persuaded to eat them.

There are other expliotable seas, but the total foreseeable gains from using them are modest. Mankind takes some 70 million metric tons of fish and shellfish from the sea each year.

Many experts say this might be boosted, with current technology, as high as 100 million. Some put the possibilities a little higher, but there is widespread agreement that the seas offer no easy answer to world hunger and that seafood is by no means inexhaustible.

One recent estimate was that no more than about 12 per cent of the annual protein eaten by humans comes from the sea. Some experts put the total at about half that.

"We have a finite resource which we have only recently discovered is finite," said David H. Wallace, associate administrator of N.O.A.A. during a recent interview. "It's kind of frightening."

Optimism Now Doubted

Five years ago, a national commission on marine resources estimated that the total harvest of food from the sea might be raised as high as 500 million metric tons or higher.

In 1969, when the report was completed, the huge anchovy fishery off the coast of Peru was growing dramatically year by year. Its potential seemed all but inexhaustible—and was treated that way.

Not until the mid-nineteen-fifties did commercial fishermen in Peru begin serious efforts to exploit the Peruvian anchovy. By 1958 the anchovy harvest had growth to more than one million metric tons a year and, by 1962 to over seven million — making Peru the world's foremost fishing nation. Most of the catch was used for fish meal.

"Large financial investments were made in the harvesting of this seemingly endless resource until 1970 when the landings were 12.3 million tons," said an analysis published a few months ago by the National Marine Fisheries Service. The catch of that one species off one stretch of the South American coast yielded more than a fifth of the world's total harvest of fish from the sea.

But in 1971 it became tragically clear that this resource was not endless. A combination of over-fishing and a shift in the Peru current, also known as the Humboldt, cut the anchovy population drastically.

By April of 1973, the Peruvian fishery was in deep trouble. At mid-year anchovy fishing was prohibited to preserve the species. By then only 1.8 million tons had been caught despite all the efforts of a huge fishing fleet. Much of the industry was near bankruptcy.

Some anchovy fishing was permitted again this year, but only on a tightly restrictive quota basis.

Fisheries experts in the United States aren't unanimously agreed on the main cause of this debacle. Some say it was primarily over-fishing. Some change in ocean conditions. Most agree it was a combination of these two factors.

In either case there is a lesson in the experience for a world growing desperate for increased sources of food: Even the vast abundance of the sea can be pushed too far.

The Pacific waters off Peru are usually an almost ideal incubator for anchovies because of something called ocean upwelling. This is caused by complex interaction between prevailing winds, currents and the effects of earth's rotation. Under this influence warm surface waters are blown away from a coast and replaced by an upwelling of cold nutrient-rich waters from the bottom.

The ocean's one-celled plants called phytoplankton thrive on these nutrients when they become available in sunlit waters near the surface.

Upwelling nourishes a complex and abundant food chain, but one that can be subject to perturbation. Changes in the prevailing winds can displace the coastal currents and either disperse the upwelling or shift it to places where its nutrients will be wasted. The offshore crop of phytoplankton fails. Much of the local food chain withers.

In terms of mankind's needs this can be important because there are only a few places on earth where major ocean upwelling occurs dependably. A publication of the National Science Foundation this year estimated that coastal upwelling, occurring in only about one-tenth of 1 per cent of the area of our planet's oceans, yields a good deal more than half of the world's total fish catch.

The principal regions thus favored are waters off the coast of California, off Peru, northwestern and southwestern Africa, along the path of current from East Africa past the southern tip of Arabia. There are also important areas of upwelling in the Antarctic and at midocean spots along the equator, according to the National Science Foundation.

Untapped Potential

Most of the upwelling areas are already being thoroughly fished today. One that still seems to have great untapped potential is the fertile region of ocean around the Antarctic continent. For more than a century, ships have gone to these icy and dangerous waters for whales—and in recent years have brought most species of these huge sea mammals into danger of extinction.

While some whales are the biggest animals that ever lived, the new interest in the Antarctic waters focuses on animals that are among the smallest. These are little shrimp-like creatures called krill. Dr. William F. Royce, associate director for resource research of the National Marine Fisheries Service estimates it might be possible to harvest 50 to 100 million tons of krill a year from the Antarctic—if anyone knew how to use them effectively.

The Soviet Union has been trying to develop a home market for krill, according to other experts at the fisheries service, offering pure frozen krill for salads, making a paste from it for use with butter and cheese. It is still too early to tell how popular these products will be.

In any case, krill are widely believed to be the ocean's main untapped food resource.

Most of man's effort to gather food from the sea is essentially hunting—whether this be gathering clams by hand or capturing whole schools of ocean fish with huge power-driven purse seines.

In recent years there has also been increasing interest in sea food production of a kind more akin to agriculture on land. The general name for it is aquaculture. It has been practiced in various times and places for thousands of years. These efforts to produce fish and shellfish under controlled conditions give the world some four-to-five million tons of seafood a year, and the U.N.'s Food and Agriculture Organization has estimated that the total might be increased several fold.

Oysters are produced in large quantity under these semi-domesticated conditions in Japan, the United States and elsewhere. Milkfish are raised for food in brackish ponds and enclosures in many parts of Southeast Asia. Large quantities of mussels are raised in Spain and Portugal. The United States is the world's biggest producer of hatchery-bred trout.

Culture of Other Species

Culture of many other species is under study for early commercial developments here and elsewhere — including shrimp, salmon, scallops and abalone.

For the United States particularly shrimp cultivation could be a major asset, according to Dr. Albert K. Sparks, a National Marine Fisheries Service expert in this field. He noted that the United States catches more shrimp than any other nation—but also eats more and, in fact, has been importing shrimp for more than a decade.

Nevertheless, shrimp growing and most of the other newly developed forms of aquaculture still have a substantial way to go in research and development before they can make much impact on total food supply. In this country particularly such efforts seem more likely to develop further supplies of essentially high cost foods than low cost, mass-produced items that might make a difference to the most drastically food-poor regions of the world.

In fisheries in general, the position of the United States is a tangle of paradoxes. While many American fisheries remain static or are actually in decline, the United States is the world's largest importer of food from the sea. Americans eat only a moderate amount of sea food directly — about 12½ pounds for each person every year, but agriculture uses huge quantity of fish products for animal feed and for many industrial uses.

A draft outline of a national fisheries plan now being circulated among Government and other specialists, notes that American total consumption of fish products increased from about three billion to seven billion more during the next decade.

Roland Finch, a national marine fisheries officer who has played a major role in developing the draft plan, said most of the increase during the last quarter of a century has been provided by imports.

It seems clear that the nations of the world are becoming more and more interested in the seas as a major source of food and other needs. As the pressure increases on those resources, food from the sea may increasingly become a source of dispute as well as nourishment for mankind.

Philip M. Roedel of N.O.A.A. said there is recent evidence that nations with extensive coastlines, but no present capacity for commercial fishing, may be interested in leasing off-shore fishing rights to one or another of the major fishing nations.

This potential trend together with recent tragic experiences in the over-fishing of some important food sources, suggests a new era. In this, food from the sea may be more diligently sought than ever before—but also more carefully exploited so that these major resources are kept alive and forever renewable.

October 26, 1974

Experts Back Pest Control To Multiply World's Food

By JANE E. BRODY

Each year an estimated half of the world's critically short food supply is consumed or destroyed by insects, molds, rodents, birds and other pests that attack foodstuffs in fields, during shipment and in storage.

Experts believe that control of even part of these losses may be the fastest and least costly way of substantially increasing the food available to the world's millions of hungry and malnourished people, who survive primarily on grains.

If the field pests and pathogens that attack the world's principal cereal grains—wheat, rice, corn, sorghums and millets—were more adequately controlled, these experts estimate that an additional 200 million tons of grain would be available to feed one billion people each year.

More effective control of storage pests in large and small granaries throughout the world could mean an immediate 25 per cent increase in edible grains without any change in agricultural productivity.

At the World Food Conference, which opens in Rome on Nov. 5, the United States is expected to emphasize the need for research and investment directed toward "reducing the enormous losses between the farmer's field and the consumer's table," according to Ambassador Edwin Martin, who is coordinating American participation in the United Nations-sponsored conference.

In some cases, solutions to pest problems, such as keeping rodents out of grain stores, are already in hand and need only to be applied, particularly in those poor countries where most of the world's grain eaters live. But other pest defenses require considerable research to develop simple, economical and ecologically sound control measures with worldwide applicability.

The problem of food losses to pests is by no means limited to the developing countries where traditional agricultural practices, haphazard shipping and primitive storage methods often prevail. In the United States, according to the best estimates of the Department of Agriculture, a third of the nation's potential harvest is sacrificed to insects, disease and weeds despite control measures.

Dr. Elvin C. Stakman, plant pathologist at the University of Minnesota, has calculated that American farmers plant "the equivalent of 75 million acres of crop land to feed weeds, insects and plant pathogens instead of human beings."

Up to 10 per cent of crops may be left in the field after harvest and another 5 to 10 per cent are consumed or destroyed by insects, molds and rodents during storage. An estimated total, then, of between 40 and 60 per cent of the potential American crop is unavailable for human consumption.

Losses of 70%

In the less developed countries, the problem is similar but often of much greater magnitude. In India, for example, losses of 70 per cent of foods placed in storage are reported to be not uncommon.

A half dozen rats consume the amount of grain that could sustain a man, not to mention what the animals may stash away as "reserves." A consultant for the Food and Agriculture Organization in Pakistan dug out a rodent burrow in a rice field and uncovered a 10-pound grain reserve. The consultant, E. W. Bentley, said that local farmers commonly allow poor people to raid these burrows after the rice is harvested, with perhaps 20 per cent of what the rats store being reclaimed for human food.

Insects and micro-organisms that feed on stored grain not only reduce the amount of grain available but also reduce its nutritional quality, since these pests preferentially attack the protein-containing portions of the grain.

On a worldwide percentage basis, losses in the fields of developing countries are not much greater than those in the United States. But sporadic raids by rodents and other animals, epidemics of diseases and invasions of insects can, and frequently do, devastate an area's food supply.

Toll of Rice Disease

An epidemic of a rice blight disease in India led to the starvation of a million people in the 1940's. During the last major locust plague in Africa, in one month of 1959 in Ethiopia alone the insects devoured a year's supply of grain for one million people, the F.A.O. reports.

An annual African pest almost as voracious as a horde of locusts is the quelea bird, a small weaver that has virtually no natural enemies and "holds the power of life and death over innumerable small farmers," the F.A.O. says in a report on food losses. The killing of hundreds of millions of these sparrow-sized birds made hardly a dent in their destruction of food grains.

All told, the organization estimated that "35 million Africans could be fed for a year from the [native] grain finding its way to the wrong consumers — rats, locusts, quelea birds, beetles, moths and weevils and countless micro-organisms."

In some areas, pest problems have totally prevented the production of important food sources. Peanuts, for example, could be a valuable dietary item and export crop for many islands in the South Pacific, but plots have been so badly damaged by rats that attempts to grow the highly nutritious peanut have been all but abandoned.

In Africa, 4.25 million square miles of good grazing land is unavailable for cattle production because it is dominated by the tsetse fly, which spreads epidemics of sleeping sickness among domestic animals.

Other sources of "waste" that deprive people of potential foodstuffs include poor use of land, lack of erosion control, shipping delays and mishaps and losses during milling and processing.

The quickest gains in reducing food losses can be made by contolling storage wastes, according to various experts.

"Once the grain is produced, we ought to be able to keep it," remarked Dr. David Pimentel, entomologist at the New York State College of Agriculture and Life Sciences at Cornell University.

Noting that "conservatively $2-billion worth of grain is lost each year in storage and transit," scientists from 27 nations who attended a meeting on stored products entomology in Savannah, Ga., earlier this month sent a resolution to the United Nations pleading for "the patronage and assistance of national and international leaders to accelerate the utilization of available methods and skills" in controlling storage pests. The scientists expressed their belief that "comprehensive adoption of our technology could make a major contribution to mitigation of worldwide food shortages."

In many countries, only a small percentage of the grain is scientifically stored in large warehouses by government or other agencies. Most is kept by individual farmers or small villages under less than ideal conditions. In India, for example, agricultural experts estimate that 90 per cent of the country's food grain is stored in substandard facilities.

For small farmers in poor countries who store their families' grain supply in burlap sacks or simply heaped in a corner, such simple methods as keeping it in sealed clay pots, burying it in the ground or hanging it in trees can go a long way to reduce storage losses, according to Dr. Robert Davis, a storage pests expert with the Department of Agriculture in Savannah.

A Freedom From Hunger program in Africa promoted the use of corn cribs elevated from the ground with shields on the legs so that rats would be unable to climb up.

Other methods aimed at preventing storage losses that were discussed at the Savannah meeting include the following:

¶ Hermetic storage of grains in Africa in large, airtight rubber bins. The stored grain and insects already present in it respire, and when all the oxygen is used up, the insects die.

¶ Pumping cool, dry air into storage bins at night and during the cooler months. This chills the grain, depresses the activity of insects, which are cold-blooded, and prevents the build-up of infestations.

¶ Storage in plastic bags underwater or in mines to keep grain at a relatively constant low temperature. This method is being used in some Pacific countries, including Japan.

¶ Partly replacing the air in storage bins with inert gases so that less oxygen is available to support insect life.

¶ More effective drying of grain before storage and sealing leaks in the roofs of storage bins can help to suppress mold growth, which can render grain poisonous as well as distasteful.

Chemical fumigants and insecticide sprays as pretreatments to prevent insect infestation of grain stores are already widely used in developed countries, but their cost and the technology involved in their application is prohibitive in many areas of the world. Therefore, Dr. Burkholder and others are trying to develop simple, low-cost techniques to control the world's most serious storage pests.

His approach includes the use of traps baited with a chemical that attracts the insect, such as a sex attractant. Once in the trap, the insect may be killed by an insecticide or exposed to a disease that it would then spread to its co-invaders.

In India, where treatment of stored grain with DDT is widespread (although illegal), the amount of DDT regularly found in the bodies of the people is the highest in the world. Prof. O. S. Bindra of Punjab Agricultural University has been promoting the use of malathion instead, since this chemical is not stored in the body, is readily broken down in the environment and is relatively nontoxic to mammals.

Since weeds compete with food crops for soil nutrients, sunshine and water, the control of unwanted plant growth, either by hand weeding where labor is cheap or by use of herbicides, can substantially increase yields. Experiments in five Asian countries showed that hand weeding of rice paddies increased yields by an average of 45 per cent.

Partly controlling the rice stem borer in the Philippines by spraying with insecticide produced minimum yield increases of about half a ton an acre.

Much research is being devoted to the development of crop varieties that are resistant to attack by various insects and diseases, obviating the need for any pesticides. The rice institute in the Philippines has released rice varieties that are resistant to five major pests. Such breeding work is a continual process, since sooner or later the pest organism evolves a way of overcoming the plant's resistance, but the use of resistant varieties makes pest control simple and economical for the farmer.

Along the tsetse fly belt in Africa, the Agency for International Development is conducting a major study to reduce the population of these live-stock-attacking insects by releasing large numbers of sterilized male flies. Since the female mates only once, mating with a sterile male will prevent her from reproducing.

Experts say that long-lasting solutions to the problem of food losses to pests will require intensive study of the natural behavior of each pest and the development of effective methods of intervention.

Then, as with most other approaches to increasing the world's food supply, the problem remains of "getting the new pest control methods out into the countryside," as Ambassador Martin put it.

October 28, 1974

Latin America's Role of Food Exporter Is Threatened

By JONATHAN KANDELL
Special to The New York Times

LIMA, Peru, Oct. 24—Under the crush of a rapidly increasing urban population and a strong government bias in favor of industrial growth, Latin America is threatened with losing its status as a net exporter of food in coming years.

The region has always suffered from widespread problems of malnutrition. According to studies by the Food and Agriculture Organization of the United Nations, as many as half of the 280 million Latin Americans live on moderately to seriously deficient diets.

But the area has traditionally maintained a favorable trade balance in agriculture on the basis of strong exports from key countries—beef and grains from Argentina, fish products from Peru and Chile, sugar from Cuba.

The concern of food experts is that Latin America—with its vast, but unrealized potential for strong agricultural surpluses—will become instead an increasingly heavy buyer of costlier and scarcer food supplies on the world market.

Crisis 'No Longer Regional'

"It is no longer possible to consider the food crisis in regional terms," said an official of the Food and Agriculture Organization "Even if Latin America manages to maintain its deficient food standards in the coming decades, it may be doing so by placing even more afflicted Asian and African countries in deeper crisis."

With one of the highest birth rates in the world, the region almost tripled its population from 1930 to 1970.

Even more dramatic was the migration to the cities. Urban population accounted for less than 40 per cent of the area's inhabitants in 1950. The proportion rose to 56 per cent in 1970. By 1990, two out of every three Latin Americans will be living in urban areas.

Along with this shift to urban living, there has been a deterioration in the strength of the agricultural sector in the regional economy. In general the prices farmers pay for goods and services have increased far more rapidly than the prices of farm products.

Prices Depressed

Faced with volatile and more politically demanding urban constituencies, governments have tended to depress agricultural prices artificially in inflationary times.

Often such measures backfire, leaving governments with even more difficult options. In Bolivia, for example, strict food-price controls led to a booming contraband trade that sent thousands of tons of agricultural products into neighboring countries.

To counter the growing food shortages, Bolivia's President, Hugo Banzer Suárez, increased the prices of basic necessities by almost 100 per cent last January. Ensuing protest strikes by miners and professional employes, and a peasant revolt in the Cochabamba Valley almost toppled the regime.

In Argentina—the most important agricultural exporter in Latin America—farmers have long complained that they are subsidizing both the urban population and the country's efforts to industrialize.

Food prices in Argentina—even for beef—remain among the lowest in the world, and heavy taxes on farmers have prevented them from benefiting fully from rising food prices on the world market.

There are no significant food shortages in Argentina, but there is a heavy contraband trade across the country's borders that the Finance Ministry estimated earlier this year to be running at more than $500-million annually. More important, the inadequate farm income has discouraged farmers from investing more heavily to increase production.

As a result of such factors, Argentina—which some experts assert could double or triple her agrarian production—has failed to increase food exports notably for decades. The country achieved its highest wheat exports in 1929.

At times, government attempts to ameliorate the plight of agriculture have caused serious disruptions in farm production.

In Chile, for example, a badly managed agrarian-reform program under the Government of President Salvador Allende Gossens resulted in the formation of overcrowded, inefficient agrarian cooperatives and numerous illegal land takeovers that created widespread insecurity among private farmers. Agrarian production fell 30 per cent from 1970 to 1973, and food imports cost more than $600-million—four times the previous annual record.

The right-wing military junta now in power in Chile sought to stimulate agrarian production by allowing food production to rise according to demand. But the resulting inflationary spiral has created the threat of widespread malnutrition among the poor urban majority.

In Mexico, increased government credit to food producers has not increased agricultural output. Food production continues to fall further behind the demand for food, which is rising at about 5 per cent a year compared with a 3.6 per cent increase in the population growth rate.

A long drought through the last two winters followed by rare frosts and serious flooding brought by two hurricanes this summer are largely responsible for reduced agricultural production. But peasant unrest and insecure land tenure have also discouraged many farmers from investing.

As a result, Mexico is importing large quantities of basic grains. Beans, another staple food, were hit badly by recent frosts and about 10 per cent of the 1-million-ton consumption will be met by imports. There have been sharp increases in food prices, in the case of beans and cooking oils over 75 per cent in the last 12 months.

The Central American republics have also suffered the effects of droughts and hurricanes. Honduras will be forced to import large quantities of corn, wheat and oil seeds.

Crops in Guatemala, El Salvador and Nicaragua were also damaged by heavy rains, and the eruption of three volcanoes in Northwest Guatemala has covered farmland with sulphurous ash.

Even with normal harvests, malnutrition affects the rural populations of Central America. With a food shortage and the consequent increase in prices, intensified malnutrition is inevitable.

The Latin American agricultural picture has been further clouded by adverse developments abroad, including world inflation, the energy crisis, shortages of fertilizer, and increasing protectionism.

Although Venezuela is in good shape because of her oil revenues, other nations have felt pressures. Argentina has seen her beef exports to the Common Market countries drop from 270,000 tons in 1973 to 65,000 tons this year after European Governments met their farmers' demands.

The situation has been far more critical in Uruguay, which imports all her oil. In an attempt to increase export income, the government banned domestic beef consumption, only to see its efforts thwarted when the Common Market restricted meat imports.

Haiti offers the classic example of a population permanently undernourished.

Although the Haitian economy has begun to improve, 85 per cent of the rural population are worse off because inflation has placed many foods out of their reach.

October 30, 1974

FOOD CONFERENCE, IN LAST DAY, FORMS NEW U.N. AGENCY

130-Nation Parley Approves Organization to Supervise Anti-Hunger Programs

A COMPROMISE ACCORD

Talks in Rome Also Set Up Agricultural-Aid Projects for Poorer Countries

By WILLIAM ROBBINS

Special to The New York Times

ROME, Nov. 16—A new United Nations agency to supervise programs to give the world, and particularly the less-developed nations, more and better food, was approved by the World Food Conference here today.

The new organization, to be called the World Food Council, will have a secretariat in Rome, associated with the Food and Agriculture Organization, but will report to the United Nations in New York.

Though it requires endorsement of the parent organizations, that action is expected to be a formality, considering the worldwide representation at the conference here.

A Key Accomplishment

The new structure represents a key accomplishment of the conference, whose plans it is to help carry out. It was the result of an intricate compromise between underdeveloped and developed nations that was reached in the final session of this 11-day meeting of 130 nations.

Edwin M. Martin, deputy chairman of the American delegation, said that the United States was pleased with the results of the conference.

"This conference was not called to get food to people tomorrow but to lay out a plan of action to prevent the crisis that we have now from recurring," Mr. Martin said.

His apparent allusion was to President Ford's refusal to commit the United States to a million-ton increase in emergency food aid. However, Mr. Martin acknowledged publicly what others have said privately, that "we will probably be giving that much" in additional food aid, but added, "It would not be useful to announce a figure."

As the delegates gathered here Nov. 5, many hoped that pledges of immediate aid for some 460 million people imperiled by hunger would be made while they worked on long-term food-supply problems.

Those hopes for immediate pledges during the conference faded, but before the delegates closed their sessions today they gave the projected council a number of new programs to supervise and coordinate, with details and machinery to be worked out later. The major plans were the following:

¶An agricultural development fund, originally proposed by several Arab nations, including major oil producers, but later sponsored by many other nations.

¶A fertilizer-aid program, with help for increased supplies for developing nations as well as for new and improved plants.

¶A pesticide-aid program, with research into residual effects and other environmental questions.

¶An irrigation, drainage and flood-control program to aid developing countries.

¶Expansion of agricultural research and training and methods of disseminating findings among growers.

¶A nutrition-aid program, including special feeding for malnourished children and studies on fortification of staple foods with vitamins.

¶Recognition of women's role in agriculture and food, their right to equality and the special nutritional needs of mothers.

¶A call for "achievement of a desirable balance between population and the food supply."

Earlier in the session, the conference completed work on a 10-million-ton-a-year food aid program for developing nations, an internationally coordinated system of national grain reserves, and an early-warning system of data-sharing to help alert the world to any climatic or other threats to food supplies or sudden surges in demand.

In another action, the developed nations effectively resisted demands of the underdeveloped nations for trade preferences, saying that the conference was not a forum for trade negotiations. Instead the conference adopted a resolution that requests improved treatment of exports from the poorer countries.

The compromise reached today on a World Food Council ended a deadlock between developed and underdeveloped countries over what sort of follow-up mechanism should be created to supervise and coordinate food-aid and development programs.

The United States and other developed countries had wanted a coordinating body to be created and controlled by the United Nations Economic and Social Council. The underdeveloped countries had wanted establishment and control by the United Nations General Assembly of whatever body was created.

A Matter of Influence

The major powers have more influence on the Economic and Social Council, where representation is on a regional basis, than in the General Assembly, where each nation has one vote and the developed countries are outnumbered.

Had the meeting ended in a deadlock, the developed countries would have automatically won their point, because the conference must report to the Economic and Social Council. Apparently, however, no one wanted that kind of result.

A strong influence on the outcome, according to some delegates, was the Soviet Union's support for those who wanted the Economic and Social Council to be the umbrella organization.

The solution gave recognition to the positions of both sides. Under the agreement, the new World Food Council will be established by the General Assembly as a United Nations body reporting to the Assembly through the Economic and Social Council.

Members of the group will be officials of ministerial or other high level who will meet from time to time, but the everyday work will be done by the staff of the secretariat in Rome.

The secretariat's staff and budget will be drawn from the Food and Agriculture Organization, but it will be independent of that agency.

A Coordinating Group

The new World Food Council will be responsible for coordinating the work of all United Nations agencies now dealing with food.

Mr. Martin emphasized, however, that the new body would not have the power to order action but would have a coordinating role and the responsibility for reporting to the United Nations on needed actions.

The conference also recommended creation of two subsidiary units & a world food security council and a food aid committee, which would take over responsibility for the present World Food Program and coordinate both bilateral and multilateral aid operations.

In one of its final actions tonight, the conference adopted a carefully worded declaration that a committee had spent the entire time of the conference in drafting.

It calls on all governments to "accept the removal of the scourge of hunger and malnutrition as the objective of the international community as a whole," asks "all governments able" to "substantially increase their agricultural aid" and urges all to "reduce to a minimum the waste of food and of agricultural resources."

November 17, 1974

ISSUE AND DEBATE

Can Eating Less Meat Here Relieve Starvation in the World?

By BOYCE RENSBERGER

As the significance of the world food crisis becomes more apparent to well-fed Americans, the call for people to cut down on consumption of meat, especially grain-fed beef, is increasingly being voiced by citizens' groups, religious and humanitarian organizations and some food and nutrition experts.

Their argument is that if meat consumption were to decline enough, the agricultural resources now devoted to feeding cattle, pigs and chickens could be diverted to rescue famine victims and to build grain reserves against almost inevitable future food shortages.

Several advocates also suggest that such actions would be in the enlightened self interest of the affluent countries because they would help fight inflation. Rising food prices, they note, are now leading the over-all inflation rate. In a world competing for the same food resources, any effort to expand the supply in one place would tend to hold down prices everywhere.

On the other hand there are a number of agricultural economists, meat industry representatives, and experts on the food problems of poor countries whose views range from less enthusiasm to opposition.

They contend that such a voluntary campaign would be unlikely to overcome a well-developed American preference for grain-fed beef and that, even if it did, the action would not be likely to result in food for starving people, especially in the near future.

The skeptics contend that such an outcome would require the Federal Government to buy the diverted grain specifically for famine relief. Otherwise the grain would simply go to the highest commercial bidder. If the Government must take that step anyway, the argument goes, it might as well enter the grain market now and buy what is needed.

Price of Milk Affected

In addition, some economists see that too hasty a retreat from beef would not only wreck one segment of the agricultural economy but also sharply drive up the prices of other foods. For example, the price of milk would be higher if dairy farmers could not sell their calves to the beef producers.

Only a few years ago, when the American cornucopia was still full, such a debate would have seemed unthinkable. Now that the more or less unplanned drift of American tastes and farming priorities have been called into question, experts on all sides are finding they have little hard data from which to predict the results of sudden shifts in consumption and production trends.

While the debate on this issue is sharpest on the question of whether much extra grain could be diverted to humanitarian purposes in the short run, there is somewhat more agreement that a long-term change in American dietary patterns could indeed result in the availability of larger quantities of grain for export.

In fact, some of those who doubt that charitable motives will cut the beef demand significantly note that the high price of beef is already lowering the demand. Per capita beef consumption dropped last year, for the first time in nearly 20 years, from a peak in 1972. There are indications the decline is continuing through 1974.

Because cattlemen now benefit little from the high retail price of beef and must pay high prices for corn, grain feeding is becoming uneconomical and the industry is already shifting toward more use of grass and other forage crops.

Thus there seems to be agreement that whether or not the steak given up today results in more food for people starving now, it could be the beginning of a trend that over the next few years would increase the United States ability to help prevent or relieve future famines.

Many of those urging a cutback in meat eating say that even if it didn't release enough grain to meet the present crisis, there are likely to be similar crises recurring with increasing frequency in the next few years. If a trend in reduced meat eating can be begun now, they contend, American corn farmers will soon shift to growing desirable food grains such as wheat, thus increasing the quantity available for export or for donation to a world food reserve for future emergencies.

Background

Twenty five years ago the average American ate about 60 pounds of beef a year, about equivalent to the rate of pork consumption. Poultry consumption stood at about 25 pounds a year per person. Americans were not, on the average, malnourished then.

These days Americans eat about the same amount of pork, but the annual consumption of poultry has doubled to about 50 pounds per capita and beef eating soared to 116 pounds before declining slightly to 110.

Nutritionists agree that the swollen meat consumption is not necessary or even desirable for health. Many heart specialists believe the increased eating of meat, particularly the more expensive grades with more fat, sometimes called marbling, has contributed to the rise in disability and death due to heart disease.

The extraordinary surge in beef eating is generally attributed to the then rising affluence of the middle class and to the development of a taste for soft, juicy beef. The juiciness comes largely from melted fat.

A large share of the increased beef production demanded by this change in preference has come not from pasture and grazing lands which yield a leaner, often tougher beef but from the use of feedlots where young steers that are started on grass are virtually force-fed on fattening grains.

Because meat production consumes several times as much food in grain as is returned in meat, the growth in meat eating has used up grain at a disproportionately high rate. The American meat-heavy diet uses up five times as much grain each year as does the Indian grain-heavy diet.

In the nineteen-forties only about one-third of the beef cattle slaughtered had received any special feed but by the nineteen-seventies about 82 per cent of the beef cattle were coming from feedlots. The animals that are still grass fed are largely ground into hamburger, a fact that those urging the sacrifice of "one hamburger a week" have apparently overlooked. Skipping a hamburger will save little or no grain. It is the highest grades of beef that monopolize the grain.

Lately, due to increasing costs of feed grain, the beef industry has been returning to more reliance on grass. The National Livestock and Meat Board, an industry group, estimates that in coming months as much as 30 per cent of beef will be grass fed, up from about 18 per cent in recent years.

Skeptical Views

While few outside the meat industry itself flatly oppose a reduction in meat consumption, many of the most knowledgeable experts on world agriculture are skeptical that it will do much good, particularly in the short run. They also worry about the impact on American meat producers, already hard hit by costs rising faster than sales.

The first point usually raised by the skeptics is that too few people would cut back far enough to make an identifiable and useful difference.

Even if there were large reductions, the grain that would be diverted would be mostly corn of types that are not widely attractive to human beings. Although corn is a staple in parts of Latin America and Africa, it is not as widely eaten in India and Bangladesh, two of the countries where food shortages are most acute.

It is sometimes argued by skeptics that, if the demand for grain declined within the United States, the price would fall and farmers would be inclined to reduce production or even go out of business.

"In the short run it is not a feasible or consequential idea," said Dr. Kenneth Farrell, deputy administrator of the Department of Agriculture's Economic Research Service. "In the long run, however, the argument is not without merit."

Dr. Farrell said the first result would be a drop in the price of corn, the main feed grain, discouraging corn production. He said farmers would tend to switch to growing wheat and rice. One requirement for a meat cutback to have effect in famine areas, Dr. Farrell stressed, would be for the Government to announce its intention to buy a specified quantity of grain. Assured of a demand and a good price, he said, farmers would continue to produce.

Dr. Sterling Wortman, vice president of the Rockefeller Foundation which supports much agricultural research in poor countries, contends that if averting famine soon is the goal, a meat cutback is at best an indirect solution.

He notes that the Federal Government would probably have to buy the diverted grain for famine-stricken countries or at least earmark quantities available for purchase by those countries.

"There are much more direct and forceful ways to get the grain," Dr. Wortman said. "If the American people really want to send food aid, they should urge the Government to buy the grain as the first step."

Another point Dr. Wortman raises is that it is the very lack of ready American food aid in the present crisis that is now motivating poor countries to develop their own food-producing potential.

"For the first time in history we've got people seriously interested in getting food production up in the underdeveloped countries," Dr. Wortman said.

It is generally agreed, even among those who urge meat cutbacks, that the most important solution to the food crisis in the long run is to upgrade farming in the poor countries.

Lowell Hardin, who heads agricultural research programs for the Ford Foundation, notes that whether or not the grain diverted from steers reaches starving people depends on an intricate web of agricultural, economic, and other factors. Not the least of which is the political implication of inflicting further hardship on the already beleaguered meat producers. There are about 150,000 commercial feedlots in the United States, each buying its calves from many sources including dairies and many thousands of small farmers.

Dr. Hardin suggested that the only way the needed Government action might be politically acceptable would be if it included some measure to ease the economic impact on the beef industry.

Food Conservationists' Views

The most prominent food experts supporting the campaign to reduce meat consumption have been Lester Brown, an economist with the private Overseas Development Council, and Jean Mayer, a professor of nutrition at Harvard Medical School.

Dr. Brown has calculated that if the total American consumption were reduced by only 10 per cent, it would save about 12 million tons of grain, an amount greater than India's food deficit this year. This would be the equivalent of returning to the meat consumption level of ten years ago.

Beyond the economic and health arguments of the food conservationists is the assertion by some that a moral issue is at stake.

"In a world of scarcity," Dr. Brown wrote in his latest book, "By Bread Alone," "if some of us consume more, others of necessity must consume less. The moral issue is raised by the fact that those who are consuming less are not so much the overweight affluent but the already undernourished poor."

A number of religious organizations have urged their followers to observe regular meatless days, a move recalling President Truman's call in 1947 for Americans to go without meat on Tuesdays to conserve food for famine relief.

Most of those calling for reduced meat consumption concede that Government action would be needed, at least in the short run, to assure that the diverted grain gets to hungry countries. Until that happens, many groups are suggesting that Americans send the money saved to private famine relief programs, which would acquire the grain and donate it.

No Choice for the Hungry

Although corn is not the preferred grain in the most critical countries, the conservationists say genuinely starving people would be unlikely to turn it down.

Supporters of food conservation argue that in many of the regions where corn is grown, the land is good for other crops for which the demand is strong, such as wheat and soybeans.

Dr. Folke Dovring, an agricultural economist at the University of Illinois, has found that many Midwestern farmers could easily switch from corn to a combination of wheat and soybeans and achieve the same or better income.

Because an acre's production of corn sells for more than an acre's worth of wheat, Dr. Dovring said it would be necessary for farmers to plant a second crop on the same land in the same growing season. He said farmers in southern Illinois have found it economically feasible to sow soybeans in the unplowed stubble of a harvested wheat field and reap a crop before the first frost.

One advantage of this alternative is that it requires much less fertilizer. Corn is one of the most fertilizer-demanding of plants. Wheat requires less and soybeans need no nitrogen fertilizer. The release of scarce fertilizer could ease shortages in the poor countries.

"I think it is quite realistic to free agricultural resources this way," Dr. Dovring said.

While there are too few data upon which to project the precise immediate effects of a meat cutback, there is little doubt among agricultural experts that if food production fails to move much ahead of present increases in demand, the wasteful character of dietary habits in affluent countries could become difficult to defend.

November 28, 1974

On Argentina's Fertile Pampas, The Bitter Harvest of Neglect

By JONATHAN KANDELL

Special to The New York Times

BUENOS AIRES, Jan. 22—As soon as the plane ascends from the sprawling capital on the Río de la Plata, the pampa comes into view, stretching in a semicircle for hundreds of flat, green, treeless and fertile miles.

The pampa, an agricultural zone matched only perhaps by the American Midwest, remains the source of Argentina's wealth. It sets the country apart from the rest of Latin America, elevates its people to the brink of a European standard of living and makes the nation potentially one of the most affluent in the world.

But year after year that potential is only barely tapped. Argentina, which 30 years ago was the second largest wheat exporter and accounted for half of the world's exports of beef and as much as 80 per cent of corn, has ceased to be a food producer of international importance.

"Of all the great exporters, only our country has failed to take advantage of its great natural conditions and has remained behind," noted Horacio Fernández Harper, the president of the Center of Cereal Exporters, in an interview with a Buenos Aires newspaper.

Four Surge Ahead

Since the thirties, the world trade in grain has risen from 40 million tons a year to 150 million tons. The United States, Canada, Australia and France have surged ahead as producers and exporters, but Argentina now accounts for only 8 per cent of the total.

"In its best years, our country contributes only 12 million to 12.5 million tons to the international grain market," said Mr. Fernández. "If during the last 30 years we had increased our production and pursued an aggressive trade policy abroad, we could have been exporting 45 million tons or more a year."

For Argentina, the lag represents an annual loss of billions of dollars in foreign exchange earnings. For the world, it is a missed opportunity to alleviate the food crisis somewhat.

World production of cereals, which reached 1.2 billion tons in 1972, should have increased by 25 million tons a year to cover the growing demand, according to G. N. Vogel, president of the Canadian Wheat Board, who visited Buenos Aires last week.

He noted that the wheat reserves of exporting countries fell from 49 million tons in 1972 to 29 million tons in 1973, and declared, "An especially poor harvest in any important zone in 1975 would be truly critical."

Within days the Argentine Government announced that only 4.8 million tons of wheat would be harvested this year—the poorest crop in a decade. Argentina will probably have to import wheat again to meet commitments made with Latin-American and European buyers; after overselling the last harvest, the Government was forced to buy 500,000 tons of wheat abroad.

Bad weather or unforeseen trade barriers have sometimes been behind the disappointing performance. The poor wheat harvest was partly a result of a drought in the three richest provinces, and trade barriers in the European Common Market caused Argentina's beef exports last year to fall to less than half the 556,000 tons of 1973.

But most experts agree that the country's agriculture has been undermined for decades by a Government policy of depressing farm prices in favor of urban dwellers, new industry and public spending.

The policy began three decades ago when the late Juan Domingo Perón first came to power. Faced with a growing population shift to the cities, he imposed price controls on basic food products.

The governments that came after the fall of General Perón in 1955 largely maintained economic programs aimed at underwriting the welfare of the cities at the expense of agricultural expansion.

Today, with 85 per cent of Agentines living in urban areas, the political pressures are greater than ever to keep food prices down.

Government officials proudly point out that food prices in Argentina are the fourth lowest in the world behind those in Colombia, India and the Philippines. The average Argentine eats 240 pounds of beef a year—twice as much as an American. Restaurants are packed every day and often do not accept reservations.

The Government, which is the only authorized buyer of grains and which also controls the price of meat, offers farmers only a fraction of the world market prices for their produce.

Until two weeks ago, cattlemen were getting only 21 cents a pound for steers delivered for slaughter; farmers are receiving only about one-half the prices quoted in international commodity centers for wheat and corn.

Still the Money-Maker

"We have reached the point where the Government is absorbing 50 per cent of the international price of corn," noted La Nación, the leading newspaper, in a recent editorial, "And at the same time, in a demonstration of incoherence, our representative at the World Food Conference in Rome declared that the cause of the food deficit that is scourging mankind is the inadequate resources allocated to agriculture."

Despite heavy taxes and price controls, agricultural products last year accounted for about 70 per cent of the estimated $3.8-billion in exports. With a favorable trade balance of more than $600-million, there was little pressure on the Government to change its agricultural policy.

Farmers have been able to withstand lean years partly because their production costs have been low compared with those of other countries. There are few feed lots—areas where cattle are fattened for market—and steers graze in open pastures. The pampas, with top soil often six to 12 feet deep, produce crops with a minimum of fertilizers.

For many farmers, particularly along the borders with Brazil, contraband is important. The Government estimated that last year $500-million in food products was smuggled into neighboring countries.

But the Government policies have taken a heavy toll of agricultural productivity. A recent study noted that yields per acre in the United States were 7.4 per cent higher than in Argentina in the 1937-1948 period, but now are 67 per cent higher because of the much larger investment in modern techniques and fertilizers.

Faced with low beef prices at home and trade barriers abroad, cattlemen are again depleting their herds, mainly by sending large numbers of animals to slaughter.

Only two weeks ago, the most important agricultural association in the provinces of Buenos Aires and La Pampa, the richest agrarian zones, urged all farmers "to get ready to meet the situation of economic and financial crisis that is approaching for all farm activities by not buying machinery, tools, implements, or anything else that is not essential to keep your concerns in production."

January 23, 1975

FOOD SUPPLIES UP AS HARD-HIT LANDS FIND SOME RELIEF

Large Part of Grain Needs Being Met by Imports, Particularly in India

By WILLIAM ROBBINS
Special to The New York Times

WASHINGTON, Feb. 1—The world food picture has improved sharply in the last two months, most notably for India. This changed picture has emerged from interviews with Government officials and other experts here and from data from United States and United Nations sources.

While the food gap in the deficit nations will still amount to millions of tons between now and June 30 and untold numbers of lives continue to be threatened by malnutrition, several countries that faced the most serious problems when the World Food Conference met in Rome in November have succeeded in contracting large parts of needed supplies.

Many of the arrangements are still in the form of commitments yet to be shipped, but agriculture officials say the food is moving smoothly. India, for example, is reported to be receiving all the grain her ports can handle, and her officials are optimistic about the spring harvest.

Gap Greatly Narrowed

The remaining food gap worldwide is at least three million tons, an unofficial tabulation of data from governmental and United Nations sources indicates. This compares with a generally accepted estimate of 7.5 million tons at the end of November.

Experts emphasize that much of the improvement has come from costly purchases on commercial markets, entailing deferment of developmental needs with possibly serious consequences. They also emphasize that additional needs will continue beyond June 30, the end of the current crop year.

"As just one example," said James T. Grant, president of the nonprofit Overseas Development Council, a research organization, "the money India must spend now for food cannot be used to improve fertilizer production, and that can be even more costly in terms of future hunger."

Meanwhile, the availability of American food for export to the needy nations has improved, though financing remains a problem.

"We have more wheat available now, and it's moving smoothly," Richard E. Bell, a Deputy Assistant Secretary of Agriculture, whose responsibility is foreign trade, said in an interview. The Texas winter wheat crop, which will become available in May, looks good, he added.

"We've got plenty of rice, and we're anxious to move it so it won't be taking up space for the next crop," he said. The 1975 harvest begins in August.

Record Stock of Rice

The Agriculture Department has reported record stocks of rice on hand and 19 per cent more wheat on hand than a year ago, with consumption down in recent months.

A problem in moving the rice and other grain is a result of delays in Ford Administration approval of food-aid goals for the rest of the 1975 fiscal year, other agriculture aides say. When it comes it is expected to provide substantial increases over last year.

The improved grain supply is reflected in an internal memorandum provided to agriculture officials with reference to the November estimate.

"As of Dec. 16, 1974, the United States alone was in a position to supply all of the wheat required, two million tons of corn and 1.5 million tons of rice, provided the financing can be found," it said.

The deficit figure consisted of 5.2 million tons of wheat, 1.4 million tons of coarse grain such as corn and 900,000 tons of rice.

Softening World Demand

The easing of the situation is largely a result of economic decline and softening world demand, the experts say, with the biggest factor the reduced use of livestock feed lots in the United States.

India and Bangladesh are classed by the United Nations Food and Agriculture Organization as having the most serious shortages, but if United States estimates are accurate, each has obtained all but about 500,000 tons of the deficit.

The F.A.O. lists 10 other countries as suffering from lesser shortages, while one, Sri Lanka formerly Ceylon, is listed as being in danger of a shortage.

The designations are in a restricted report circulated to member governments under an early-warning system adopted at the food conference. At that time Sri Lanka was included with India, Bangladesh, Pakistan and Tanzania as the countries regarded as suffering the most serious shortages.

India was viewed as having the greatest total need although she had already begun to make substantial purchases in commercial markets. Her original need for imports to offset a disastrous drought was estimated by United States officials at 7.5 million tons. She now has commitments for about seven million tons, largely through purchases on commercial markets, Mr. Bell said.

New U.S. Aid in Works

In addition, India is negotiating with the United States for a new commitment—in the form of sales on credit at low interest rates—that originally involved 300,000 tons of wheat but has been raised to 500,000 tons, United States and Indian sources said. An Indian diplomat added that only technical details remained to be resolved in the arrangement, about which there had been some confusion as a result of Indian denials.

One problem is that India has used up two-thirds of her currency reserves to buy food and fertilizer, with purchases totaling over $1-billion. She will need new shipments in July, Government officials said, toward which she is reported to have contracted for 200,000 tons from the next United States wheat crop.

India's Cruch Is Over

"It looks like India's crunch is about over for now," a United States official said. "But each year she needs two million tons more food just to meet the increase in population."

Bangladesh estimates that her need this year is 2.2 million tons, 500,000 tons more than the United States estimate. The F.A.O. has reported that as of Dec. 20 Bangladesh had commitments for 1.45 million tons —150,000 of it from the United States, according to Mr. Bell.

The United States puts Pakistan's deficit figure at 1.2 million tons. About a million of that has been supplied. Mr. Bell said, 800.000 tons of it in commercial purchases and 200,000 in aid, with 100,000 tons from the United States.

United States officials estimate Tanzania's deficit at 360,000 to 450.000 tons. About 250,000 tons has been committed, Mr. Bell said.

Sri Lanka has commitments for 750,000 tons of a total need of a million tons, the agriculture official said. That includes 100,000 tons in aid from Australia and the European Common Market, with more to be provided eventually by the United States, Mr. Bell said.

Looking beyond June 30, another official said Sri Lanka would need sizable imports—230,000 tons of wheat and 200,000 tons of rice after commercial purchases, barter deals and aid.

In all other countries Mr. Bell put the remaining deficit at about 1.9 million tons, including 400.000 tons for the sub-Sahara section of Africa, which has been swept by drought and famine in recent years but where conditions have improved.

The countries listed by the F.A.O. as suffering from lesser shortages are the following:

BURMA—The amount is uncertain. Flood damage has left rice supplies that may prove inadequate.

BURUNDI — Principal crops are said to have been reduced by 50 to 70 per cent by heavy summer rains: the supply situation is listed as critical.

ETHIOPIA—Pockets of shortages are said to remain, but with harvest prospects for main cereals reasonably good, other areas are likely to have surpluses.

GAMBIA—The government is seeking 3,000 tons of aid to meet shortages feared later in the season.

HONDURAS—The deficit is estimated at 55,000 tons because of hurricane damage, but expanded crop areas may reduce it.

MALI—The shortage is estimated at 150,000 tons.

NIGERIA—Grain is available to meet demand, but aid is needed.

RWANDA — Crop losses in floods have totaled 200,000 tons, but about 17,000 tons of aid and some cash have been supplied. Two million people are said to be affected by shortages.

SOMALIA — Some 100,000 people are said to be affected by shortage because of drought.

SOUTH YEMEN — Shortages of uncertain dimensions are said to persist partly because of droughts.

The human toll has not been determined. Officials say there has been some starvation in India and that at least 25 per cent of the population of Sri Lanka is below the F.A.O.'s minimum nutrition standards. An American study in a rural area of Bangladesh found 54 per cent of the children checked to be suffering from severe malnutrition; 12 per cent were not expected to survive.

February 2, 1975

Hard Economics the Key to World Livestock Supply

By SETH S. KING

Special to The New York Times

CHICAGO, Feb. 7—American farmers who have been fattening cattle, hogs and poultry with corn and soybeans are now cutting back on their feeding operations more sharply than in any period since the nineteen-fifties.

These deliberate reductions in the production of feed grains —and thus of livestock, America's prime source of protein—are not moral responses to appeals for Americans to eat less meat and free the unused grains for the world's hungry.

Nor is this country, the world's largest producer and consumer of animal protein, nearing the point where it cannot raise any more animals.

The reason, rather, is purely economic. After last summer's drought, the world's supply of feed grains is now at the lowes point since World War II. The costs of feeding livestock anc poultry have soared above the prices these animals bring in the market.

To dilute their losses, American farmers are reducing their feeding operations. By reducing supply, they hope to force meat prices higher. Meanwhile, they are waiting for a bumper grain crop next fall to push feed costs down and bring them a profit.

There are now 133-million head of beef cattle on American ranges, the largest number in this century. In Australia the

The New York Times/Gary Gulsinger

Cattle being fattened in Colorado. The use of grains for this purpose is lessening.

Average Per-Capita Meat Consumption in Various Countries

(in kilograms—2.2 pounds)

Continent and country	Average 1965-69	1969	1970	1971	1972	1973*
NORTH AMERICA						
Canada	69	72	73	74	74	71
Costa Rica	14	13	14	15	14	15
Dominican Republic	8	8	9	10	10	10
El Salvador	11	9	9	9	8	9
Guatemala	10	10	10	10	10	9
Honduras	9	8	8	10	9	8
Mexico	17	17	18	18	18	19
Nicaragua	20	22	21	23	22	22
Panama	25	26	27	29	28	29
United States	80	83	84	87	86	80
SOUTH AMERICA						
Argentina	97	107	96	82	78	81
Brazil	25	27	26	24	25	30
Chile	26	26	26	25	24	21
Colombia	22	23	23	25	22	19
Paraguay	40	39	41	32	29	21
Peru	15	16	15	15	12	11
Uruguay	97	78	89	93	71	66
Venezuela	24	26	23	24	23	23
WESTERN EUROPE						
European Community						
Belgium-Luxembourg	57	60	64	63	68	70
Denmark	58	56	61	56	58	63
France	62	63	63	64	64	63
West Germany	58	60	63	66	66	53
Ireland	57	55	59	61	61	55
Italy	32	37	41	42	42	46
Netherlands	46	46	47	50	48	46
Britain	63	62	63	66	63	59
Average	53	55	57	59	59	58
Austria	57	59	60	61	62	63
Finland	38	40	43	44	46	50
Greece	32	35	38	41	39	45
Norway	38	39	37	39	39	39
Portugal	20	23	23	25	27	28
Spain	26	28	31	29	31	35
Sweden	45	46	48	47	45	46
Switzerland	55	58	60	61	60	62
EASTERN EUROPE						
Bulgaria	37	35	34	36	40	39
Czechoslovakia	49	50	53	58	60	60
Hungary	40	39	42	41	46	45
Poland	40	41	41	44	46	49
Yugoslavia	30	29	30	36	32	33
SOVIET UNION	36	37	38	40	41	40
AFRICA						
South Africa	34	35	37	37	34	33
ASIA						
Taiwan	21	22	24	25	24	28
Iran	9	10	9	9	9	9
Israel	19	20	20	20	11	8
Japan	8	9	12	12	15	16
Philippines	13	14	12	12	12	11
Turkey	14	14	15	15	12	13
OCEANIA						
Australia	94	93	94	99	96	90
New Zealand	102	88	93	81	96	89

*Preliminary

World Meat Production

Includes beef and veal, pork, lamb, mutton, goatmeat and horsemeat; excludes rabbit, poultry meat and miscellaneous.

Thousands of metric tons
One metric ton=2,200 lbs.

	1964-68 average	1972	1973*	Per cent change 1973 from 1964-68	Per cent change 1973 from 1972
North America	17,488.4	19,799.7	18,806.5	+8	-5
South America	6,448.6	7,119.6	7,491.9	+16	+5
Western Europe	14,272.8	16,251.5	16,379.4	+11	-1
Eastern Europe	4,289.2	5,048.2	5,185.5	+21	+3
Total Europe	18,562.0	21,299.7	21,564.9	+16	+1
Soviet Union	7,956.4	10,012.7	9,952.0	+25	-1
Africa and Asia	3,311.6	4,294.1	4,458.8	+35	+4
Oceania	2,547.4	3,424.5	3,323.6	+30	-3
Total world	**56,314.4**	**65,950.4**	**65,597.7**	**+16**	**-1**

*Preliminary Note: Totals may not add due to rounding

beef herds are at record levels. The European Common Market countries have a beef surplus that they are having difficulty selling.

When it is once again more profitable to raise and fatten hogs, poultry and feed-lot cattle in this country, the food forecasters are confident that all meat supplies will increase again.

The more optimistic of these experts believe that for the rest of this century, if weather patterns are normal, supplies of animal protein in the affluent nations can be increased faster than the population is growing.

If the underdeveloped countries can somehow find the money to acquire feed grains and create transportation systems for distributing meat, these forecasters also believe, enough can be produced to increase the animal protein in these countries and improve the diets of their people.

Like most forecasts involving the global food situation, these are predicated on "ifs" that could turn out much less favorably than is expected by the optimists. In the view of some experts, it would be foolish to assume that weather will be consistently normal and that supplies of fertilizer and fuel will always be adequate.

Recent suggestions of climatic shifts and the volatility of international politics, for example, could drastically reduce the supplies of rainwater, fertilizer and oil.

Another assumption that some food experts would hesitate to make is that the poor countries will be able to find financing for their expensive import needs.

If the assumptions by the optimists should prove wrong, the supplies, not only of animal protein but of all food resources, could be seriously jeopardized.

Affluence and Religion

The rest of the world, like the United States, derives its animal protein from the same sources: beef, poultry and eggs, pork, and dairy products. The numbers of these animals and the amount of meat eaten vary in direct proportion to affluence and religious beliefs rather than to human populations.

Most of the world's meat and dairy supplies are now concentrated in North America, the Soviet Union, Western Europe, and parts of South America. Last year North America and Western Europe produced more red meat—beef, pork and mutton—than all the rest of the world. Australia and New Zealand, with their tiny populations. produced almost as much as Asia, with its millions, and Africa combined.

The world's champion red meat consumers are the Australians and New Zealanders, who eat nearly 198 pounds per person each year. The Americans and Argentinians are close behind at 177 pounds each. In 1973 the Western Europeans consumed 128 pounds each, while the Russians ate only 88 pounds per citizen.

But in most of Asia and Africa, red meat consumption was only a fraction of the leaders'. The affluent Japanese, despite a national effort to increase meat consumption, ate only 35 pounds each and the Filipinos consumed only 24.

Hogs and poultry can be raised almost anywhere in the world in a minimun of space. Thousands of chickens, confined from birth to slaughter in tiny pens, can be raised each year in an area no larger than a supermarket parking lot. Hundreds of hogs can be handled at one time on a few acres. And in most modern dairy operations the cows are kept in small feed yards and milked in sheds no larger than a small house.

But beef cattle and sheep need rangeland or pasture on which to graze, and the number of animals an acre will sustain varies with the amount and quality of the forage on it.

Thus the world's capacity for raising hogs and poultry is limited, in theory, only by the amount of feed grains that can be grown for them. Hogs and poultry compete with humans for cereal grains in the sense that humans can, and to varying degrees do, eat the same wheat, corn, soybeans, and sorghum grains.

Virtually all of the American wheat crop is now used for human foods. But more than 90 per cent of the American corn and sorghum crops and virtually all of the soybean meal, after the edible oil is removed, are fed to livestock.

The United States exports two-thirds of its wheat crop, almost half of its soybeans, and about 20 per cent of its corn. Foreign buyers of American corn and soybean meal use virtually all of it for livestock feeding, mostly for hogs and poultry.

But cattle and sheep are ruminants. Their digestive systems convert forage, which humans cannot eat, directly to meat protein.

The soybean meal and feed grains now fed sheep and beef and dairy cattle put extra fat on them, making their meat tender and juicy or increasing their daily yield.

A beef steer or heifer fed only on forage can attain a choice grade weight, with its meat almost as flavorful as a grain-fed animal's, if the forage is abundant. But it takes nearly twice as long to fatten an animal on forage as it does on grain.

Fattening beef cattle on grains is a relatively new practice in the United States and still relatively rare in other countries. Since 1952 the percentage of American beef cattle fed on grain rose from 45 to 78 per cent, though it is declining slightly now as more grass-fed animals are going directly to the packing houses.

The burgeoning of grain-fed beef has been caused by economics and eating taste. From the end of World War II until 1973, the Russians and Japanese began buying tons of American grain in a deliberate effort to increase their own livestock production. This country had towering surpluses of feed grains. Stuffing them into livestock was the only profitable way to use them.

At the same time, take-home pay of Americans rose and so did their preference for beef and their ability to buy it.

In the last decade beef production in the United States has jumped 36 per cent. Broiler production has increased 58 per cent. But pork production increased only 10 per cent and there has been an actual drop of 23 per cent in lamb and mutton slaughter. Americans preferred more beef and poultry and more money could be made raising them.

Key Is Rising Grain Output

The world's population is growing by more than 2 per cent, or about 75-million persons, each year. Among the questions pondered constantly by the farm and food experts is whether the production of livestock and poultry can keep pace with this human growth and whether the current high animal protein diets of the more affluent countries can be continued into the next century without more of the poor starving.

Although most of these experts agree that much more grain can be grown in the United States and some other parts of the world in the next decade if the weather is normal, there is no consensus on how much.

They agree that if grain production can be increased sharply, then poultry, pork, and dairy production can be increased as well in most of the world. But the chances of the underfed sharing in these increases will depend more than anything else on their achieving the means to pay for it.

Dr. Leroy Quance, program leader of the Agriculture Department's Economic Research Service, foresees the possibility that, given average weather and continuing supplies of fertilizer and fuel, the world's capacity for growing cereal grains could increase faster than consumption in the next decade.

His study envisages the opportunity, if the money is available, of adding about 30-million acres of cropland to the roughly 350-million now being cultivated in the United States.

Assuming that the 1 to 1.5 per cent annual yield increases of the 1 ast 20 years will continue — an assumption questioned by some private forecasters — American farmers could produce by 1984 a corn crop of 9.1-billion bushels. This would compare to the 6-billion bushel crop expected in 1974 had the weather been normal. The Quance projection also foresees American soybean crops by 1985 increasing nearly 40 per cent, and a jump of 42 per cent in grain sorghums.

With these sharp increases in feed grains, the study also predicts a 33 per cent rise in American beef supplies, and a 13 per cent increase in pork production by 1985. Broiler production could rise 36 per cent and the egg supply could be increased by 2 per cent. The projections point to an increase of only 2 per cent in dairy supplies and a huge decline of 65 per cent in sheep production, based on project demand and not capacity.

The National Academy of Sciences, in a lengthy analysis of agricultural efficiency published in mid-January, was more conservative. The academy agreed that increases in per-acre corn yields would probably continue in the coming decade. It also foresaw a continuing improvement in broiler feeding efficiency.

But the academy warned that progress in increasing efficiency in feeding livestock was not as likely as some experts believe.

"Advances in animal production have not kept pace with those for crops," the academy declared. "It seems clear that nothing as dramatic as the increase in corn yields, nor even as the increase in broiler meat production per unit of feed, has occurred with beef, pork and lamb."

The greatest potential for a quantum leap in red meat supplies, some food experts believe, is on the grazing lands. With better management of herds and the use of now idle grassland, they believe that additional thousands of cattle and sheep could be raised with little new demand on the grain supply.

Today there are a record 133-million beef cattle and calves in the United States. Range experts with the American National Cattlemen's Association believe Western ranges, as they are now used, are at near capacity for beef cattle without being overgrazed.

But there are thousands of acres of grassland in the Southeastern and Eastern states that are now idle because there has been little economic incentive to graze cattle or sheep on them.

In the last decade alone, the number of beef cattle in the Southeast has increased by nearly 700,000. Part of the land they graze on was once in cotton and tobacco. Most of these animals now go into fattening pens. But they could be marketed at grassfed weights if Americans again accept leaner beef.

Citing Agriculture Department studies published earlier last year, the Council for Agricultural Sciences and Technology notes that 63 per cent of America's total land area is classified as grazing land. Currently, these grazing areas, most of them in the West, produce about 213-million animal-unit-months of grazing for domestic livestock. This means they have the forage required to keep a mature, calf-producing cow for a month. The study estimates that if more fully developed and intensively managed, this country's total forage lands could reach 1.7-billion animal-unit-months.

While this might sound wildly optimistic to the more cautious, the council cites other recent studies showing that in many parts of the West and Southwest, ranges would actually yield greater amounts of usable forage if sheep and cattle were allowed to graze together. This offers the possibility of increasing the red meat supply by including sheep with the cattle.

Substitutes for Grain

Australia, the largest exporter of beef, could, if the economic incentives developed, increase its cattle herds from the current 30-million head to at least 50-million with the forage the country now has.

The American Forage and Grassland Council cites an assessment made this summer by W. F. Wedin, H. J. Hodgson, and N.L. Jacobsen, plant and livestock specialists, in which they foresee increased grain production barely keeping even with increasing demand for livestock if these animals get the same amount of grain as they do now.

"But the fact remains that there are tremendous acreages in the United States and in the world where the only chance for having high quality protein food available is through conversion [of forage] by ruminant livestock [cattle and sheep]", the assessment states.

Dr. Paul Putnam, assistant director of the Agriculture Department's Beltsville, Md., research center, points to the availability of many livestock and poultry feeds that can now be substituted for grain.

These have not been fully utilized, Dr. Putnam said, because there have always been cheaper feed grains available.

These substitutes include sugar beet tops, citrus pulp, "tankage" matter left from slaughtered animals, grain mash left from distilling alcohol, apple pomace, whey left from making butter and cheese, high nitrate animal wastes, and even cellulose fibers from wood pulp, newsprint, and sawdust.

The Wedin-Hodgson-Jacobson study notes that in the United States enough rough forage is left largely unused on 75-million acres of corn and sorghum stalks, after the grain is harvested, to maintain between 12-million and 30-million additional head of beef cows annually.

Looking toward the future, Dr. James Smith, chairman of the Animal Physiology and Genetics Institute at Beltsville, said recently:

"If economic incentives are great enough, we believe the world's farmers have the capacity to breed and feed livestock and poultry in numbers great enough to keep pace with the population increase and provide a better diet for the hungry—certainly during the rest of this century."

February 8, 1975

Somali Nomads Dying as Drought Depletes Herds

By R. W. APPLE Jr.
Special to The New York Times

MOGADISCIO, Somalia, Sept. 2—Even in the best of times, the nomads who inhabit the wilderness of sand, rock and thornbush at the tip of the horn of Africa must struggle for their lives and livelihood.

"They live," says a man who knows this bleak country well, "from rain cloud to rain cloud."

But these are not the best of times. The drought that has hit many countries along the southern edge of the Sahara has been particularly punishing in northeast Somalia, where it has not rained for more than two years.

U. S. Aid Expected

Premier Mohammed Ibrahim Egal of Somalia grew so alarmed by the situation that he held a news conference last week to describe the plight of the nomadic herdsmen and their livestock. He appealed for help from friendly countries and international organizations to avert mass starvation.

The United States is expected to provide an emergency grant.

Premier Egal estimated in an interview that it might take as much as a million dollars to sustain the drought-stricken area, even if the rains come on schedule late next month. If the dry spell continues, the need will be far greater.

In nine years of independence, Somalia, with a population of about 2.6 million, has received about $400-million in aid from Eastern and Western countries and the United Nations — more per capita than any country during a similar period. But Somalia cannot hope to finance a major relief operation from her resources.

"We agreed at a Council of Ministers meeting to devote 2 per cent of the budget to the disaster," the Premier said. "But that is theoretical. There's no money in the treasury."

The New York Times Sept. 6, 1969

The afflicted region, which includes all of Mijirtein and some adjacent areas as well, is poor even by the standards of Somalia. It has no secondary schools, no qualified doctors, no paved roads and sporadic airline service. About 250,000 people live in the region.

Wells Are Dry

Dressed in loose-fitting robes, usually gray, the nomads wander barefoot across the semidesert, herding their sheep and goats and cows and camels with long crooks. Their diet consists of camel milk and meat, and it produces tall, lean, and durable men.

The failure of the rains has dried up three of every four water holes and wells in the area. Herds have been depleted, according to Government spokesmen, thereby eliminating not only the nomads' source of food but also their only source of cash with which to purchase supplemental food.

In Somalia, life revolves around the camel, and the deaths of animals threaten human life. Bride prices and reparations for clan murders are paid in camels—usually 50 for a woman and 100 for a man. The Somalis even profess to see a camel in the heavens—the Southern Cross forms the animal's neck.

A Government official who recently toured the northeast said that he was almost made ill by the stench of dead animals as he drove along the bush roads.

Another recent visitor, an Italian doctor, said the penniless nomads were wandering into the tiny towns that serve as governmental centers in search of sustenance. When they found none, he said, many walked or crawled back into the bush to die.

Because Government records are incomplete, it is impossible to estimate the number of deaths so far. But the Government believes that starvation and disease brought on by malnutrition have caused a "substantial" loss of life.

The only remedy is to import grain and other foods from Aden, across the mouth of the Red Sea, and elsewhere. Water must be trucked from the few remaining water holes to places where the nomads are camped—a task that will require a fleet of 100 vehicles.

September 6, 1969

Drought in Kenya Results in Famine

By CHARLES MOHR
Special to The New York Times

BARAGOI, Kenya—The skeletons of cattle littered the roadside near this remote village and a cloud of vultures swarmed restlessly over the remains of a starved zebra.

A church bell tolled mournfully as a strong, hot wind swung it relentlessly against the clapper.

A hundred naked children, bellies swollen and legs thin as sticks, gathered on the packed dirt of a schoolyard to receive famine relief from a soup kitchen.

For 10 months almost no rain has fallen here and, like much of Kenya, this area of the northern frontier is gripped in a terrible, intense drought. It has brought famine and economic ruin to tens of thousands of nomadic, pastoral tribesmen.

After nine good years in East Africa, the so-called short rains failed last October and November. Grass burned into an unnutritious stubble or was grazed to the roots by starving cattle. Small wells and ponds dried up.

150,000 Are Being Fed

About 150,000 people are being fed by the Government and voluntary relief agencies, and many more have been reduced to poverty by the loss of their herds. Red Cross officials estimate that in the north and northeast 75 per cent or more of the cattle have died, leaving the people with few resources for the future.

The long rains, which usually begin in March and extend to May, have made only a fitful, unsatisfying start—a quarter of an inch here, a third of an inch there. Most has fallen in the wetter, richer central highlands around Mount Kenya and almost none in the dry north and northeast.

If the long rains fail, the effect on people, livestock and Kenya's famous wildlife may be devastating. There is a widespread feeling of what Isak Dinesen described in her book, "Out of Africa," as a "being in disgrace with the great powers." Recalling a drought long ago, she said that "it was as if all force and gracefulness had withdrawn from the world" and that "it was not bad weather or good weather, but a negation of all weather."

In an act of uncharacteristic desperation, one old Samburu tribesman at Maralal tried recently to give the small remnant of his cattle to a Government officer since they were doomed to die anyway. Ordinarily, the Samburu, like their southern cousins the Masai, hesitate even to sell cattle, which they cherish as a visible form of wealth.

Overgazing Hurts Land

The traditional reluctance to

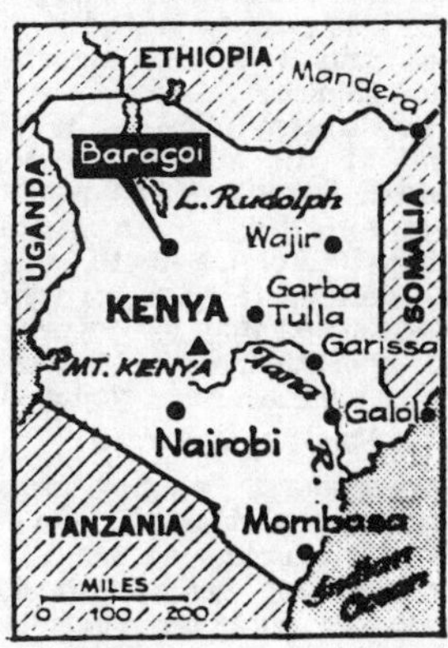

The New York Times April 7, 1971

live in a monetary, market economy has contributed to the impact of the drought, for overgrazing had left the land lean.

"The situation is very bad," said John Mullei, secretary general of the Kenya Red Cross. "In many areas most of the cattle have already died. Thus even if the rains now come, it will be necessary to provide relief for several months."

"The condition of the people is piteous," said an African teacher south of Lake Rudolph. "People ordinarily find water by digging in the sand beds of empty rivers, but now they go down 15 feet and still cannot reach water. Even the elephants have trouble digging for water."

An official in the region of Isiolo reported to the Red Cross that 5,000 cattle a week were dying.

The worst areas are the Samburu and Turkana districts near Lake Rudolph and the section stretching from Garba Tulla and Wajir to Mandera, in the Northeast.

An outbreak of cholera on the Tana River near Garissa and Galole has caused about 30 deaths. The drought may have contributed to the disease since such water supplies as exist are filthy because people and cattle share them.

Richer Regions Affected

The effects of the drought have begun to spread to better watered, populated areas, including even the fertile doughnut of land around Mount Kenya.

Poor grazing for dairy cattle has caused a mild shortage of butter in Nairobi. The Kenya Meat Commission has warned of possible shortages.

The Wakama tribal area in east-central Keyna has begun to suffer as supplies of feed and water for stock herds have run short. One Wakamba estimated that 30,000 people in the district needed urgent assistance.

The Government is using soldiers and others to move food into the affected areas and is reported to be considering a "destocking" program to buy emaciated cattle from nomads, slaughter them and feed them to the owners.

In some areas such a program may be too late. The Rev. Raymond Borello, an Italian priest who runs the Roman Catholic mission in Baragoi, said: "There is now no water at all here. The Government brings water in three tanker trucks but it is salty. The hyenas now don't even eat all the dead cattle. They have had more than they can eat."

April 7, 1971

Ethiopia Says Famine Was Covered Up

Special to The New York Times

DESSYE, Ethiopia, Nov. 11 — The Ethiopian Government says that for months it was kept in ignorance of the gravity of drought and famine in a remote northern province, and it has ordered an inquiry into the disaster.

Not only will the reported cover-up of the facts be investigated, but also the circumstances in which at least 17 students were killed at Dessye, the capital of Wallo Province, in May.

According to the United Nations 50,000 to 100,000 people died in the famine and drought.

Official sources in Addis Ababa, said that the students were shot by the police in a demonstration following the refusal of the acting governor general, Sololeman Abraham, to meet with them to discuss the famine. According to the official sources at least six were killed immediately, others were put to death later and an unknown number were wounded.

Shooting Criticized

Government sources said they believed that the shooting was unnecessary and that the governor general should have met with the students.

Mr. Abraham has been suspended and, according to sources in Addis Ababa, he has already appeared before investigators.

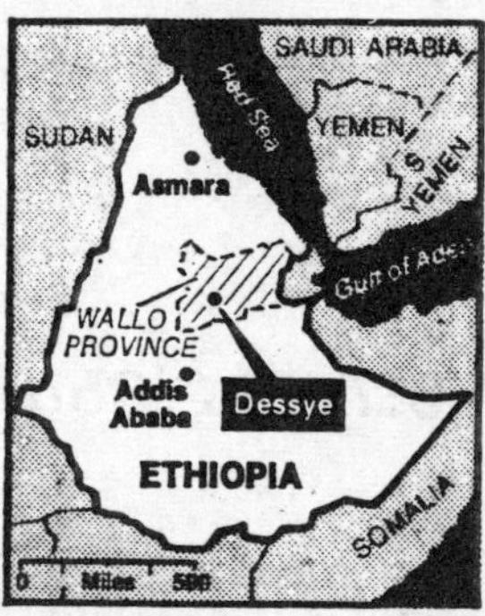

The New York Times/Nov. 18, 1973

Details about the inquiry have not been disclosed but it is said to be primarily concerned with ascertaining why the famine was kept secret from Emperor Haile Selassie. When the Emperor visited Wallo Province a year ago no mention was made of the drought.

It was not until this March, when the head of a subdistrict traveled to Addis Ababa because he felt his reports were being ignored by the provincial administration, that the central government realized the magnitude of the catstrophe.

Request for Help

Seven days after the Government says it became aware of the facts, the Council of Ministers met. On March 26, with the Emperor presiding, the Crown Council met in emergency session and set up a relief committee with nine subcommittees to deal with specific areas such as transport and coordination of relief aid. Appeals went out immediately to international donors. As of last week, however, none of the 35,000 tons of grain committed seven months ago by the United States, China, European countries and the World Food Program had arrived.

In fact in June, the Ethiopians requested that one of two American grain ships heading for Yemen with relief supplies be diverted. In response an American official in Addis Ababa observed in a letter that Ethiopia would have to show justification before extra supplies could be committed.

The suspended governor general is reported to have said at the inquiry that he had been too busy with administrative matters in Dessye. Officials there charge that during his three-year tenure he never left the provincial capital for the rural areas.

Dessye is in the heart of the famine area. Almost all the people of Wallo Province are cut off from any form of transportation or communication. It was not until starvation conditions reached the main road between Asmara and Addis Ababa that the tragedy became apparent.

Among the reasons given for the disaster are a reported breakdown of administration in Wallo Province and later the attempt by the central government to deal with the problem behind the scenes, without the international publicity that might have brought about the rapid delivery of relief supplies from major donors.

November 18, 1973

DROUGHT

Nature and well-meaning men have combined to produce a catastrophe imperiling many millions

By Martin Walker

BOUTILIMIT, Mauritania. "We are living in a catastrophe," said Dr. Moustapha Siddatt. "Last year, the babies started to die in May when the measles came. This year, they started to die in March, with the flu. We are all that much weaker this year."

Above us on a hill brooded the curiously squat shape of an old French fort. It had once been three stories high, but now the two lower floors were filled with drifting sand. This part of the dry season was always windy, but years of drought had killed off what little vegetation held down the sand. The sandstorms had never been so bad.

Boutilimit—a garbled phrase of the Legionnaires' that means "the end of the line"—was home last year to 4,000 people. This year, there are 12,000, and more arrive every day from the desert that has finally proven too much for them. They arrive without their animals. Mauritania had some 11 million head of cattle last year, and a million people. This year, says the Minister of Health, there are perhaps two million cattle left. Even the camels have died. In Boutilimit, they saved five camels to haul up the water from the wells. The water level has fallen so far—it is now more than 200 feet deep—that the men are too weak to haul up the buckets.

It was 140 degrees Fahrenheit in Boutilimit, and it had taken us a day to drive the 160 miles from the Mauritanian capital of Nouakchott in a four-wheel-drive Land-Rover. Much of the time was spent digging the truck free from drifting sand, and it had become horribly clear to us why no food trucks had reached this place since the week before Christmas, why the food ration for the 12,000 people had been cut to less than 200 grams per person per day, why the French doctor who came here went back to the capital and told the Ministry of Health: "There is nothing to be done. These people are lost."

Dr. Siddatt led me through the crowded tents that made up his hospital. One hundred and thirty-four families had trekked in from the desert in the last week. Their tents surrounded the little mud building where the dwindling supplies of drugs were kept, sprawled across what had been the main street, and crept up the hill to the old fort. "Here is where we keep those with TB. There are the typhoid patients. They all have anemia, and

Martin Walker is a columnist for The Guardian. He recently spent five weeks traveling in the drought-affected areas of Africa.

In Africa, the drought is such a vast calamity that our statistical machinery is unable to measure it meaningfully.

soon they will all have jaundice. There is not very much I can do. I write to doctors who were at medical school with me in France, asking for their free samples. But what they really need is protein —meat and milk from the animals that died last year."

The flu came to Boutilimit in March and killed more than 400. Nobody had the time or the strength to keep exact figures. Now chicken pox was racing through the tents. We stopped at one tent, where three children had died recently of chicken pox. The other four children were still sick. Dr. Siddatt thought that two would live.

We walked through the tents, looking at feet that had swollen, like footballs, from protein deficiency, at eyelids chalk-white from anemia, at limbs so like sticks that the knee joints looked gross and deformed. Something seemed to be missing, and it suddenly occurred to me that there were no children following us. In most villages in Africa, a white man strolling around bears a long train of giggling, thumb-sucking children. But here, not one child had the strength to play or to follow or even to wave away the flies that crawled on his sores.

The drought that afflicts Boutilimit stretches across the African continent, all the way to Mecca. As well as Mauritania, its dry hand has touched the adjoining countries of Mali, Niger, Chad, the Central African Republic, the Sudan and Ethiopia. It has crept down to Kenya and it has killed the animals in the game park outside Nairobi. It has divided huge Lake Chad into four ponds. (The fishing village of Bol once stood on the lake's shore but now is stranded 18 miles from water.) Right across the waist of Africa, the belt of drought stretches 4,000 miles long and 1,000 miles wide. And beyond the Indian Ocean, in a similar latitude, the drought continues through India's Maharashtra province, into China's Yangtze Valley and right on around the world into Central America.

It is such a vast calamity that our statistical machinery is unable to measure it meaningfully. In the African drought belt, observers think there are about 50 million people, of whom one-third have been severely affected. Bill Price, the British Overseas Development Minister who has just returned from West Africa, reckons that five million now face starvation. Kurt Waldheim, the Secretary General of the United Nations, says that up to 10 million may face starvation across Africa. Nobody really knows for sure.

It is perhaps easier to comprehend in geographic terms: As a result of the ongoing drought, the Sahara Desert has been creeping south, reclaiming huge sections of the marginal land between the desert and the great River Niger, an area known as the Sahel, from the Arabic word meaning shore. The Sahel supports the herds—cattle, camels and the ubiquitous goats—of such desert-dwelling nomads as the Fulani and the Tuareg in the dry season, as well as thousands and thousands of tiny villages and hamlets that exist on subsistence crops of millet and sorghum. Last year, the desert advanced about 60 miles, leaving behind village after village where only sand blows through abandoned huts, where the desert has already covered the stubble of millet.

Thus, in addition to causing widespread physical suffering and death, the drought has incalculable social consequences. The scarcity of food and other resources has aggravated existing tensions in the underdeveloped societies of the Sahel—in recent months, the Governments of Niger and Ethiopia have fallen, and in both countries the drought has contributed to unrest.

The ancient nomadic and peasant cultures of the Sahel were already under considerable pressure as the national boundaries of new African nations cut across their traditional paths of migration and as modern cash economies disrupted their normal way of making a living. The drought has proved a final blow in many places, and some observers of the Sahel have come to believe that the traditional cultures are no longer viable. Meanwhile, Sahel governments must cope with the problem of feeding and caring for settlements of refugees that begin to look more and more permanent.

Rain still falls in the Sahel—enough each summer, in fact, to wash out fragile roads necessary to transport food stores—but in recent years these rains have been sharply diminished. In normal times, 200 millimeters of rain would fall on Boutilimit between July and September, but last year only 41.6 millimeters fell. That was typical —it was a lucky Sahel zone that received even half its normal rainfall last year, and any area that received that much was immediately deluged with refugees. Rosso, on the Senegal River, gets 350 millimeters in a normal year. Last year, 164.5 millimeters fell, and the town exploded from 8,000 to 35,000 people in eight weeks.

It is becoming increasingly clear, furthermore, that this drought is no temporary meteorological aberration, but a basic shift in weather patterns that is causing a progressive reduction in Sahel rainfall. For centuries, weather in the Sahel had been governed by the shifting of a body of cold polar air. In spring and early summer, it would begin to recede to the north. As it did so, temperate air masses would follow, and so, in turn, would moist air belts that carry monsoon rains. Then in October, the polar air would begin moving south again, bringing the dry season to the Sahel. Now, however, an increasing number of climatologists believe the polar air mass is not

First there were health and other aid programs; then came the drought; the combination has dealt a devastating blow to the fragile ecology of the Sahel.

To fight starvation, a Sahel woman scrapes spilled cattle feed from the ground.

receding so much with summer, and so the temperate air, and the monsoon bearing moist air, cannot move so far north. No one knows for sure why this has happened, although some scientists believe it has to do with the recently observed fact that the temperature of the earth has dropped gradually over the past few decades. This has resulted in an expansion of polar air masses, in a way that keeps monsoon rains below a line that corresponds closely to areas now experiencing drought.

If the theory of the polar air mass is valid, however, the implications are dire for the Sahel, for there is little man can do to deal with it. Thus, the British meteorologist Derek Winstanley argues that massive reforestation projects in the Sahel will have little effect on the southward march of the Sahara. For the rain will still not fall.

The effects of the drought are compounded by an ironic factor: Well-meaning aid projects over the last decade or so have resulted in an overpopulation of men and livestock that makes the current reduced ability of the land to support them far more disastrous in terms of lives than it might have been before. In the Sahel, the good years began shortly after 1961. There were six years of unusually high rainfall, which improved the thin and scraggly desert pasture. Then came the aid projects — U.S.A.I.D. built more than 1,400 wells where people seemed to need them most, which meant where there were most people and most cattle. In a desert society, which exists in a subtle ecological balance, one of the key restraints upon the size of herds has been the amount of water the tribe can haul up for its cattle by hand. The new power wells were soon surrounded by too many cattle for the available pasture. And with the vaccination programs, fewer cattle died prematurely. The human population explosion, fueled by the beginnings of health care, needed the extra cattle, and the frail ecology of the Sahel began to crumble. Even in 1968, a relatively mild drought led to the desertification of vast areas, as the herdsmen cut down trees so their cattle could eat the foliage, as the hungry and numerous goats ate the very roots in the ground. Nineteen-sixty-nine was an almost normal year for rains, and the crisis was avoided, but the diminished rains of 1970, '71 and '72 condemned the bulk of the Sahel herds to death in 1973, and brought the Sahara into thousands of square miles of hitherto fertile land. The sheer scale of the human population increase terrifies local aid officials. Achim Kratz, the director of the European Development Fund mission in Niger, last year produced an authoritative report that concluded that even with good rains for the next 10 years, the food-population ratio will be worse in 1982 than in disastrous 1973.

There are a handful of towns scattered through the Sahel, most of them, like Agadez and Timbuktu, centuries old—the only reminder of the great and prosperous civilizations that flourished here six centuries ago when the desert was fertile. When the nomads and the peasants, their traditional way of life shattered by the drought, decide to flee, they move to these towns and to the modern cities on the Niger. There they live in pathetic and disease-riddled shantytowns. Fewer and fewer people remain on the land to plant next year's harvest, to tend what cattle are left. Food production has thus declined and can be expected to continue at reduced levels, but the uprooted nomads and peasants gathered in the towns must still be fed. And though the crisis that has left them starving is awesome in magnitude, organized attempts to help them have shown an appalling lack of urgency and competence.

The major food donors and local officials have agreed that about seven million people in the Sahel will need emergency food aid this year, and an investigating committee of donors decided after a factfinding tour last September that some 650,000 tons of food would be required. The food itself was not a problem —in fact, almost 600,000 tons were pledged by various donors (in particular, the U.S. and the European Economic Community) by January of this year. But the food is useless unless it can be shipped to northern areas where the hungry people are.

Roads are few in the Sahel. When they exist, they are simple dirt tracks that are covered by drifting sand in the dry season and washed away by the rains. On the average, a Land-Rover can cover 100 miles a day. The normal life of a truck, in these conditions, with few servicing

The drought, stretching across the continent, has brought hunger and social disruption to the Sahel region on the edge of the Sahara Desert. Left, drought refugees at a camp near Niamey, Niger.

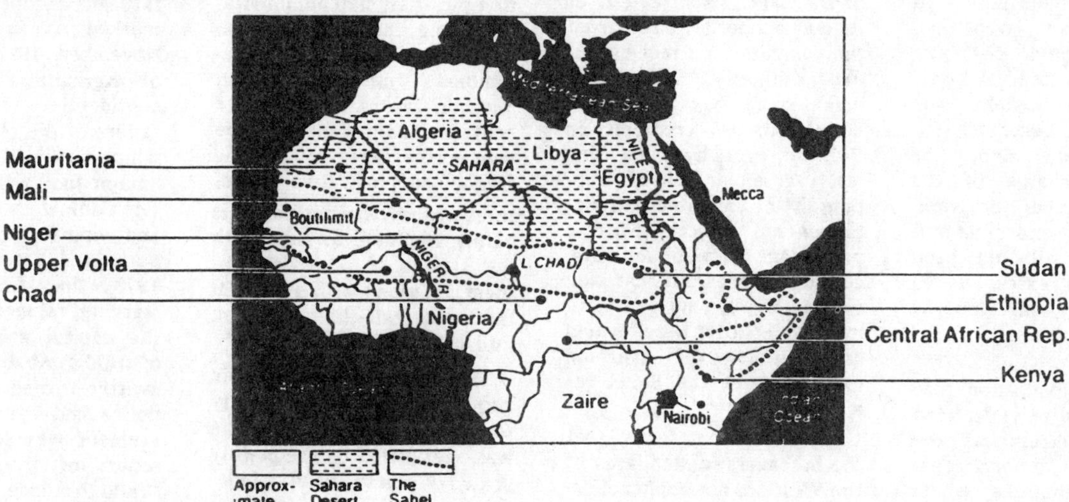

facilities, is about 1,000 hours. There are also four old and frail railroads that go from the ports on the coast up to the southern part of the marginal zone. The capacity of these road and rail links is about 100,000 tons of food per month, and so if the required 600,000 tons of food is to be moved into place by the time the rains come in July, the shipments shoulc have begun in January.

That should have been possible. Last year, when an emergency program was hastily patched together to deliver 400,000 tons, so little time was left to deliver before the rains came that aircraft were being used from May. But the airlift was so cumbersome and expensive that local aid officials hoped to avoid it this year. They worked out a plan for transporting food by land and forwarded it to Brussels, Rome and Washington last October. That left more than three months for the bureaucratic work and for the shipments to be arranged.

But on Jan. 31, the Food and Agricultural Organization's Sahel Relief Office (OSRO) issued report No 8. Clause 6 reads: "The timely shipment of donated commodities is of considerable importance. OSRO has prepared tentative shipping schedules for each country by month and by port, taking into account port and internal transport capacities. These schedules will be discussed at a meeting of major donors called by the E.E.C. in Brussels on 12 February 1974."

In other words, by the time that meeting began, six vital weeks of delivery time had been wasted. And it was not until mid-March that the Council of Ministers in Brussels gave the full and final agreement for the deliveries. Only in April did the food begin to arrive in any real quantity. In Niger, for example, a steady supply of 23,000 tons a month was needed. Anything less meant transport capacity wasted. Anything more meant transport capacity swamped and food stockpiled on the wharfs at the mercy of rats and weather. But the monthly arrivals at the ports for Niger look like this:

February	10,438
March	7,662
April	49,102
May	20,232
June	11,017

(All figures are in tons.)

It takes five weeks to get the food from the ports to the distribution points, so anything delivered after June will be blocked by the rains, which close the roads. The transport plan was never put into effect.

So another airlift will have to be undertaken this year, a fact that amounts to an indictment of the international aid community. President Hamani Diori of Niger pointed out to me shortly before he was ousted in a military coup that "the international community spent over $40-million on transporting food to Niger last year. Most of that money went on the airlift. For that kind of money we could have irrigated 11,000 hectares of land near the Niger River, which would have produced 110,000 tons of food. That is not far from our total needs — the economics of airlifts simply does not make sense."

Moreover, aircraft need fuel. The Belgian Air Force Hercules planes were using 19 tons of aviation fuel to deliver one ton of medical supplies to northern Chad last year. The U.S. Air Force used a ton of fuel for every ton of grain it flew from the railhead at Bamako to the refugee camps at Gao. That aviation fuel has to compete with food for limited rail space on the long slog from the ports.

The delay in approving food shipments was not the only administrative mistake. The multidonor mission that visited the Sahel last September to ascertain the total food needs agreed with the Mauritanian Government that Mauritania needed 100,000 tons in 1974, in addition to the 40,000 tons already in the pipeline for the country. Once back in the F.A.O. office in Rome, that 100,000 ton requirement was cut to 60,000 tons, to the horror of the Mauritanians.

To quote from a confidential World Food Program report dated Dec. 8, 1973, the reduced F.A.O. estimates were "based on either a misinterpretation of the recommendation made by the members who visited Mauritania or on a misunderstanding of the situation by the latter. It had been agreed between the mission and the Government that 100,000 tons of cereal would be required in 1974 in addition to the 40,000 tons in the pipeline at the beginning of October, 1973."

In other words, somebody had put a minus sign where there should have been a plus sign. The immediate result was that the Mauritanian Government cut the food ration to below 300 grams per head per day—a level of slow starvation.

The confidential report goes on: "In a report of the proceedings of the multidonor mission in Rome it is claimed that the Mauritanian Government indicated that it could only handle the distribution of 58,000 tons of food aid or relief supplies. This is absolutely inaccurate. No such statement was ever made, nor is it contained in any report originating in Mauritania." In fact, the report went on, Mauritania could distribute about 120,000 tons a year. Although this mistake was uncovered last December, Dr. Abdallahi Ould Bah, the minister in charge of the Mauritanian relief program, told me at the end of March that he had still not been promised the extra 40,000 tons. Belatedly, this food is now on its way.

The organization that should have detected this error was the Sahel nations' own emergency committee, which was established more than a year ago. Based in the Upper Volta capital of Ouagadougou, it was meant to coordinate food deliveries and provide the link between the bulk deliveries of the donor nations and the local transport of the individual nations. In fact, it has done little, largely because the various nations of the Sahel, each jealous of its own authority, have given the committee no real executive authority. Its major action so far has been to undermine its own credibility in Western eyes by presenting last year an unrealistic shipping list of unrelated and ambitious aid projects, with a price tag of $1-billion. According to one American soil expert, the committee's estimate of fertilizer needs would have poisoned every river and every acre of the Sahel for a decade.

We should not forget that the bureaucratic standards of the West are not applicable in the Sahel. These nations are among the poorest in the world. Insofar as the figures mean anything, Upper Volta has an annual G.N.P. per capita of about $60. Niger's is about $80. Independence 14 years ago found these countries with but a tiny band of educated leaders. Niger had but one high school. Education facilities, civil administrations and the accouterments of statehood had to be assembled from scratch. In "normal" years, about 40 per cent of Tuareg children die before the age of 5. The fragile administrative structures of the Sahel nations were barely adequate to cope with the strains of underdevelopment, let alone with a drought that made half the population into refugees.

This fundamental economic and administrative incapacity to handle a crisis of this scale was aggravated by the prickly pride of these newly independent nations. It is never easy for a government to announce to the world that it is incapable of saving its own citizens, and this kind of confession can be politically dangerous in countries where traditional tribal hostilities and jealousies are in an uneasy state of truce. Nowhere was this official reluctance to face up to the problems as marked as in Ethiopia. In November, 1972, its Ministry of Agriculture circulated a confidential report on the failure of the rains and crops, which would necessitate "major food imports" in 1973. The Cabinet chose to suppress and virtually ignore this report. And then in February, 1973 the first batch of starving refugees approached the capital and the tourists of Addis Ababa. They were swiftly turned away by the police and the alarmed Government was soothed by the report of the Governor of Wallo Province that there was "a problem of drought," but all was under control.

This official complacency meant that the local U.N. aid agencies, whose charter forbids them to work in anything but close association with the host Government, were not

In Ethiopia, a German Red Cross helicopter brings help. "Food is useless unless it can be shipped to where the hungry people are."

able to mobilize any effective relief. A stormy meeting took place in Addis Ababa on Aug. 14 last year, when an ex-Peace Corps UNICEF official presented a report saying that 60,000 people had already died in Wallo Province and the area was devastated. The Minister of Health suppressed this report, and said that such events could not occur in the great Empire of Ethiopia. But a copy of this report found its way to Britain, and journalists and TV crews went to Ethiopia and reported the crisis to an alarmed world. Then the Government, with incompetence and corruption, began to handle its "problem of drought." Terrified that adverse news would ruin the tourist trade, the Government refused to admit that Wallo Province was raging with cholera. The Government insisted that the ailment be called "gastro-enteritis C." But the Government was only too happy to accept doses of free cholera vaccine — and then to sell them for the equivalent of two American dollars a shot. The people who had to pay were the desperate, starving, impoverished victims of Wallo.

These were the events that led to the student and military outrage which erupted early this year and led Emperor Haile Selassie to dismiss the Government of Premier Aklilou Wold and install the avowedly reformist regime of Endalkachew Makonnen. That old and discredited Government is gone, but the inflation and the national trauma that drought has brought have injected a basic instability into a system that has preserved Ethiopia in feudal stasis for centuries. For the drought's effects are all the more vicious in the context of that archaic system. Drought or no drought, the church, owning one-third of all the land, has demanded its rents from the impoverished peasants. And so has the aristocracy. The peasant farmers of Ethiopia have paid about 90 per cent of their crops in rents and taxes. Corrupt officials have abused their power to enrich themselves at the expense of drought victims.

The results have often been violent. In April, I drove deep into southern Ethiopia, towards the Kenyan border, where the drought of last year had left the inhabitants desperate. Encouraged by the political unrest in the capital, peasants who had been docile for generations exploded into a sudden rural revolt. All down the fertile Rift Valley the sky was trailed by the smoke from the burning farms. In the town of Arba Minch, we had barely crossed the only bridge before the local people tried to blow it up. Fifteen people were shot dead in the town that day, three by the nervous police, and the rest by landlords defending their farms against angry mobs of peasants. The provincial Governor had fled back to Addis Ababa, leaving his home in flames behind him. He was no great loss—he had persistently refused to distribute any of the aid food until every last bushel of his own harvest had been sold at three times the normal price. The local priest fled with him. The Governor had been donating $500 a month to the church, and the priest had threatened the townsfolk with mass excommunication if they attacked the Governor. They attacked anyway. The local Mayor was in hiding from a lynch mob.

In Ethiopia, whether the Emperor lives or dies, whether the rains come or not, life will never be the same again. The new Government has already begun to draw up more radical programs of land reform, because its first timid proposals were howled down by an outraged National Assembly. The peasants have shaken off the apathy of centuries. The Emperor has been forced to name an heir. The armed forces have come of political age.

Besides contributing to political unrest, the drought has cut savagely into Government revenues. In Mali, almost 20 per cent of the tax revenues came from poll taxes on cattle. And in Niger, the relatively mild drought of 1968 cost $20-million in lost agricultural production and $14-million in lost livestock—this in a country with a budget of $65-million. The oil crisis served to twist the economic knife inside the wound. The third world as a whole faces an oil bill that is $11-billion higher than last year, and yet total financial aid to the third world is only $8.5-billion. Even in relatively wealthy Senegal, this year's higher oil bill is costing over $70-million, which is slightly more than a quarter of the national budget. And one cannot relieve a famine without gasoline. In Senegal, the Government even has to take water in trucks to the people who live along the shores of the mighty Senegal River, because its flow is now so weak that the water is salt 80 miles from the sea. It has not passed unnoticed in the Sahel Governments that their fellow Moslems control the oil and have some say in the final gasoline prices, but the desperate Sahel governments are still paying the full commercial cost.

The prostration of the Sahel countries by the drought has undermined their economic negotiating position, particularly since the oil price rise has emphasized oil-rich Nigeria's role as Africa's new superstate. Diplomats and aid officials are already suggesting that the Sahel's future lies in much closer economic and political links with the stronger nations that surround them. Traditionally, these nations have been firmly tied to the apron strings of France, the original colonial power. But at the end of March, France agreed to withdraw her last troops from Senegal, and to hand over the key naval base of Dakar. The death of President Pompidou has simply accelerated an established trend of diminishing French influence. The oil-rich neighbors, Libya, Algeria and Nigeria, are increasingly concerned about who governs the nations in their rear. And the trans-Sahara road, from Algeria down through Niger to Nigeria, is arguably the single most strategic road in Africa. Although the social problems and dislocation of the drought were the underlying reasons for the recent coup against Niger's President Diori, its immediate cause was the defense treaty he had just signed with Libya, a move that upset the delicate new balance in the area and alarmed the neighboring Nigerians. Power politics has come to the Sahel, and the impact of the drought has left the Sahel nations with pitifully few cards to play.

If these countries are to stand on their own at all, they will need to solve the basic problems of underdevelopment that the drought has masked. They will need an agricultural revolution, producing cash crops with adequate roads to move the harvest to the markets. And yet, any change in the economic structure of the Sahel will need the agreement and cooperation of the markets for their cattle and manpower in the south. In addition, the Sahel nations argue that they need guaranteed prices for their primary produce from Europe, which will give their farmers incentives to increase production for export. But after the Arabs' use of the oil weapon and the explosion of commodity prices in general, Europe is wary of guaranteed price structures; the third world countries seem quite capable of getting better prices for themselves.

More profoundly, any attempt to modernize agriculture in these countries will require massive adjustments in attitude on the part of the people. Mauritania, a nation that is perhaps 90 per cent nomad, has already decided that the desert has become too much for the old way of life to continue. The Minister of Health, in charge of drought relief, openly suggests that the future of his country lies in having the vast majority of the population settle down to a static, peasant life in the fertile strips along the coast and along the Senegal. "There will be oases inland, and no doubt many of the older people will return to the desert if they can. But if this drought has given us the opportunity to modernize our society, we must not ignore it," he argues. In Niger, the only country which had a Minister for Nomads (who was himself a Tuareg), the future is seen to lie in irrigated farming along the banks of the Niger, with non-nomadic stock-raising in the marginal zones. Man has endorsed the verdict of nature.

> Experts talk of 're-education,' but when a peasant loses faith in his land, and when a nomad loses his trust in the fertility of the desert, the effect is a kind of psychological castration.

A massive re-education project will be needed to turn the nomads into settled farmers, and to take the peasant refugees from the shantytowns and out to new, irrigated areas near the fertile river. In Mauritania, this is beginning to happen; a network of local radio stations to focus on agricultural education is being established. But there is little sign of such prescience elsewhere. This drought, and its social effects, has come as a traumatic psychological shock to the people of the Sahel. When a peasant loses faith in his land, and when a nomad loses his trust in the fertility of the desert, the effect is a kind of psychological castration.

Aid officials, too, are despondent, having seen the drought's brutal negation of a decade of development. In northern Senegal, the rice plantations and sugar-cane groves, all developed in the last 10 years, are dead, poisoned by the salt water that has crept up the river from the sea. In Mauritania, the famous gum trees of Mededra, whose gum arabic was a key source of foreign exchange, are dead. Small market-gardening projects, stock improvement programs—so many are now wasted by drought. The panic of the last two years and the overriding need to keep people alive have left little time for the planning of long-term reconstruction. The World Bank is looking at a $70-million dam project on the Senegal, but there are fears that the reduced water flow may make such a dam superfluous.

Meanwhile, to the frustration of those who hope for rural development, many of the refugees are digging in to become a permanent feature of urban life. In Nouakchott, for example, whose population swelled from 40,000 to 120,000 last year, walls of mud brick are beginning to appear around the tents in the shantytowns.

Inevitably, the old ways will pass, and the passage may not be very smooth. What few nomads the desert will support will have to give up their goats, the basis of their old way of life, for goats eat the bark from the trees, the roots from the ground and, in terms of erosion, are the advance guard of the Sahara. The Governments of Mauritania, Mali and Niger have already — with reluctance — decided to follow the example of Tunisia and declare war on the goat. The few remaining herdsmen will also have to learn to sell their beloved cattle for slaughter when they are 5 years old, rather than cherish them until they die, for reasons of custom and prestige, as they still do. The herds will be rebuilt, up to a point, but they will never be allowed to overpopulate again. This can and will be attacked as cultural rape, but the Sahel governments have little choice but to try and absorb the nomads into the developing economy.

And so there is a deeper sadness about the drought, beyond the immediate despair and suffering. The archaic feudal system of Ethiopia can pass unmourned, perhaps, but the nomad way of life in the Sahara, the style of the Tuareg, has probably contributed something utterly intangible but rather valuable to the human experience. It was a strikingly effective way of using limited resources to the best effect, and more than that, it generated an ethic of freedom and eternal challenge against the most hostile environment in the world. In that sense, it was always in some indefinable manner inspiring, and in a particular way the human race may never see again. ■

June 9, 1974

7 DROUGHT LANDS GET FOOD SUPPLY

Million Tons of Grain Sent to Africa, but Distribution Remains a Problem

By THOMAS A. JOHNSON
Special to The New York Times

LAGOS, Nigeria, July 14—United Nations appeals for food for seven drought-stricken nations at the southern edge of the Sahara are being met, relief officials here report.

The officials say that more than a million tons of food, or slightly more than had been asked for at the beginning of this year, is being transported to aid the 25 million people of Chad, Gambia, Mali, Mauritania, Niger, Senegal and Upper Volta. The food shipments are mostly of sorghum and corn.

While the total food available is thought to be adequate, officials are reluctant to declare that the emergency in the region has ended. African and international relief workers are not relaxing their efforts in this second consecutive summer of large-scale aid, for they face complex logistical problems.

"There is the problem of getting food from ports to capital cities, then to village distribution points and then to even smaller distribution centers," K. A. P. Stevenson, director of the United Nations office for relief operations in the area, said.

"For the smaller distribution centers, we must have four-wheel-drive vehicles, and if the rains come for five or six days straight, even our four-wheel-drive vehicles are useless for a time."

Summer Rains Begin

The summer rains have started in some parts of the region, where it takes about 90 days to produce harvests of sorghum, millet and peanuts.

Farmers planted seeds for the three crops in the vast fields of yellow sands on the morning after the first rains. The surviving herds of sheep, goats, camels and horses are being moved northward from the savannah regions as new grass sprouts.

International relief workers say that the grain needs of the region total about 3.5 million tons a year. Before the six years of drought that began in 1969, the region produced about 2.5 million tons of grain and imported about one million tons annually.

The successive years of drought greatly reduced annual harvests and exhausted food reserves and seed supplies. Domestic animals died for lack of pasture. An unknown number of people—often estimated in the hundreds of thousands—died of starvation or of diseases resulting from their weakened condition.

Complaints Were Few

Inhabitants of the area, conditioned by the customary hard times between the first rains and the harvest, did not generally complain to officials. And local governments generally did not appeal for aid until destitute farmers and herdsmen congregated by the thousands in desert slums around cities and villages in quest of food. The affected nations began asking for international aid in late 1972 and in 1973.

Last spring the Food and Agriculture Organization of the United Nations warned that some six million people might die if huge quantities of food were not brought into the area.

Most grain for the region arrives at Atlantic coastal ports such as Nouakchott, Mauritania, and Douala, Cameroon, and is then sent inland by rail, road or air.

Trucks Across Sahara

The United States Agency for International Development, which has contributed more than a third of the emergency grain shipments, has rented a fleet of trucks in Algiers to move 5,000 tons of grain from there through the Sahara for more than 1,000 miles to Gao, Mali. Although the trip will take three weeks, its cost will be less than a quarter that of an airlift, Mr. Page said.

Major pledges of grain for November, 1973, to October, 1974, were made by the United States, 216.769 tons; the European Common Market, 110,000 tons; France, 74,000 tons; West Germany, 35,000 tons; World Food Program, 33,957 tons; Belgium, 13,400 tons; Denmark, 13,000 tons; Britain, 10,000 tons; the Soviet Union, 10,000 tons; North Korea, 8,000 tons; Hungary, 5,000 tons, and Sweden, 3,500 tons. The League of Red Cross Societies is giving 484 tons. Officials expect another 100,000 tons not yet in the pipeline plus at least 37,000 tons of highly nutritious foods.

Among the numerous international relief efforts are the 10 medical camps operated by the Red Cross affiliate in Niger. Highly nutritious foods are also distributed there.

An American airlift that was highly praised last year by the Government of Mali has returned this summer under the same commander, Col. Solomon Harp of the Air Force.

In the American airlift, three C-130 cargo planes make four flights daily from Bamako, Mali, to desert regions of Gao and Timbuktu. Another airlift is of two Soviet cargo planes flying two missions daily from Ndjamena, the capital of Chad, to desert cities such as Mao, Largeau and Abéché.

July 15, 1974

Rains Bring Relief to Sub-Saharan Region

Niger Town Looking to Improved Crop After Drought

By HENRY KAMM

Special to The New York Times

DAKORO, Niger, Sept. 15—Fields of millet, taller than a man and heavy with ripening grain, surround the large camp of nomad herdsmen and their families who were driven to this southern region of Niger by last year's drought and famine.

Here at last, and along a 500-mile drive eastward from Niamey, the national capital, it looks as though the drought is over. The rains have been plentiful and timely since the beginning of the wet season in late June.

Heavy monsoon clouds still hang over the greening landscape, indicating that more rain may fall before harvesting can begin in earnest later this month. The villagers who live in the south as well as the nomads who fled as the Sahara advanced southward in the drought are cheerful.

But, even with a good harvest, Niger will not be able to feed herself this year. The untold damage of the drought, which began slowly six years ago before becoming a disaster along a broad belt between the desert and the lush tropical coastal lands, will be difficult to repair.

Experts of the many nations, and international groups that have contributed to the relief effort know that much work remains to be done and continuing help is needed.

Rains Bring Problems

Paradoxically, the rains that are bringing so much hope are also bringing problems. Flooding has washed out roads on which food supplies must be carried.

The countries of The Sahel—the Arabic name meaning "fringe" that describes the sub-Sahara region — are some of the world's poorest. The scarceness of all-weather roads is one of the indices of their poverty.

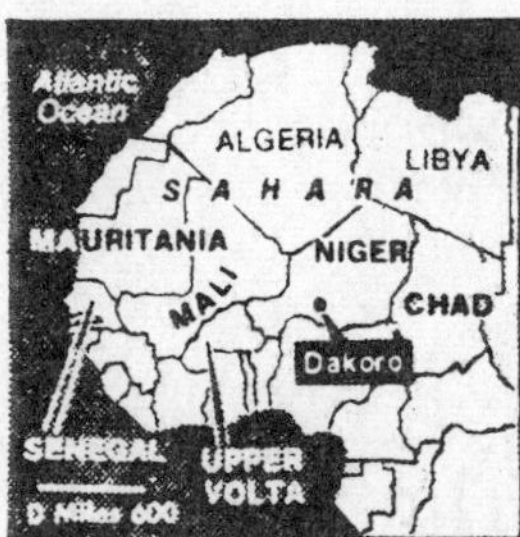

The New York Times/Sept. 22, 1974

Despite plentiful rains that have brought an apparent end to the drought in the sub-Sahara region (shown in white), many refugees remain in camp at Dakoro, Niger.

The 75-mile dirt road leading here from the principal east-west highway —also only partly surfaced —has been able to bear a steady flow of relief food northward to Dakoro. Earlier this year, the road was one of the tragic scenes for many of the moving photographs of starving children and dead cattle.

Two thousand to 3,000 persons remain in the camp at the edge of this way station, which lacks only the Foreign Legion fort to be a perfect setting for a remake of "Beau Geste."

"We need only two more weeks of rain," said Tahirou Moussa, the tall and elderly, robe-clad subprefect, in a conversation in the cool, co-

Associated Press

Camel caravan financed by the United Nations carries food to remote areas of Niger

lonial-style house that belonged to his French predecessor before independence in 1960. "The nomads will leave here then, when the millet is ready."

Nomads Lost Herds

Asked how the Tuareg and Fulani tribesmen, traditional cattle, camel and goat herders, would fare on their own after having lost so many animals, Mr. Moussa shrugged and replied in French.

"That will be a little difficult. But what can we do? It happened, and that's that."

The millet fields that surround the camp do not belong to the refugees but to the villagers. The Government's eagerness to see the nomads head northward once more stems in large measure from traditional suspicion between the sedentary and the nomad.

The herdsmen seem as eager to leave as the villagers are to be rid of them. The scarceness of men in the camp is believed to indicate that some have stayed with at least part of their herds and found grazing land across the border in Nigeria and others have more recently gone to join the herders to help them drive the livestock northward.

The town of Maradi, on the main highway, after having been swollen to double its size of 40,000 with nomads, is now almost empty of outsiders. The refugees, mainly Tuaregs, were rounded up and trucked northward last May. Many left the certainty of regular feeding with reluctance.

Feeding the nomads on their northward trek will remain a relief operation until they can reconstitute viable herds. There remains also the results of the famine on many of those who survived it.

A Fulani woman, walking about with her suckling baby, squeezed her thin breast and shook her head, to indicate she had not enough milk. The baby squalled. No signs of extreme hunger were evident, but many women offered their traditional necklaces, bracelets and earrings for sale to raise money for food.

Tuaregs and Fulanis, people of limited commercial ambitions, put their wealth into herds and into jewelry for their women.

Malnutrition is a serious problem also among the villagers. Although their plight has been less dramatic than that of the herdsmen, because they did not have to trek southward to find relief, they have also been hard hit by the drought and have lived largely on the dole.

"Right now they are picking head by head the millet that is ripe," said Dr. Burt Long, an American who runs the hospital of the Sudan Interior Mission near the village of Galmi.

"And I'm afraid they're picking some before it's ripe."

Dr. Long, who has been at Galmi for 24 years, said the famine had greatly reduced the life expectancy of a people who even in years considered good suffer from malnutrition.

"They have no reserves," Dr. Long said.

"If this year's crop breaks the famine," the doctor continued, "we will see for five years to come a much higher rate of deaths and then five more years of more deaths than is normal.

September 22, 1974

After the Drought, a Shaken Niger Faces Long Uphill Struggle

By HENRY KAMM
Special to The New York Times

NIAMEY, Niger—An extensive international relief effort has substantially ended the famine in Niger, one of the countries most tragically afflicted by last year's catastrophic drought that spanned the African continent immediately below the Sahara.

This year's rainy season, now drawing to an end, gives hope for a good harvest. But for years to come, even with continuing good harvests, Niger will need help in feeding her population of about 4.2 million and in overcoming the long-term effects of the drought.

Many people are presumed to have died of starvation or of illnesses fatal only because of the hunger-weakened state of the victims. Mortality was highest among young children, who will also suffer most from the long-term effects of malnutrition. But in a region where even the number of the living is a far-from-precise statistic, it is impossible to know how many died.

Both President Seyni Kountche and the Public Health Minister, Moussa Sala, said in interviews that they could not estimate the number of dead. They said that the international rescue effort averted the worst. Certainly the gloomiest predictions of last year, forecasting mortal danger to millions in the sub-Sahara region, proved excessive.

But even fewer might have died or suffered grievously if relief had arrived faster and more nations had helped.

Food Behind Schedule

Although a study mission prepared an accurate blueprint of Niger's needs last October, it was March before the flow of food began in earnest.

Taking into account port and road transport facilities an optimum goal of 25,000 tons a month, beginning in January, was set for the arrival of food supplies. But by mid-March, no more than 10,000 tons had reached Niger.

The optimum flow, which would have adequately stocked forward distribution centers before the summer rains made much of the country inaccessible, became instead an unmanageable flood of 50,000 to 60,000 tons a month through Nigerian and Dahomeyan ports in April, May and June.

The United States provided more than half of the nearly 200,000 tons of food, mainly sorghum, that pulled Niger through. The European Economic Community, as well as West Germany, France Belgium and Canada, and the United Nations World Food Program, were the other major contributors.

Others capable of helping have been more reticent.

The assistance from Arab countries to this Moslem nation was "infinitesimal," President Kountche said.

Kuwait and Algeria each sent about 1,000 tons of wheat and Iraq 850 tons of dates. President Kountche, a devout supporter of Moslem unity, said that since he seized power in a military coup April 15, Libya and Algeria had provided some help.

Saudi Arabian Report

In a recent news conference, the head of the Saudi Arabian diplomatic mission here, Hassain al-Rachach, said that his country had contributed about $2-million. But international development experts here put the cost to Niger so far of increased fuel prices close to $9-million, or about one-fifth of the total national budget.

The Soviet Union has donated 2,412 tons of rice and five trucks. China has provided no help, unless 400 tons of rice given in the name of Prince Norodom Sihanouk, nominal head of insurgent forces in Cambodia, was of Chinese origin.

Aid missions here are at a loss to explain the three-month delay in the start of food deliveries. At the United States Embassy and at the European Economic Community and United Nations offices, distraught officials offer to show stacks of telegrams that they dispatched in the critical months importuning governments and international organizations to act.

"We felt a heavy responsibility," said Alexander H. Rotival, representative of the United Nations development program and a coordinator of the aid effort. "The people had eaten their reserves and were down to their stoic ability to resist death without food."

Bureaucracy Blamed

The slowness of bureaucracy is the reason most often advanced. The United States Ambassador, L. Douglas Heck, said he believed the decision in Washington to make the American effort as much as possible part of the international program made a slow start inevitable.

Drawing a lesson from this performance, the United States has already set aside 100,000 tons of food grains for the sub-Sahara area for the coming year. A quarter of that is destined for the stockpiles of this country.

The pressures on the White House resulting from the Mideast war and Watergate may have been responsible for the Cost-of-Living Council's one-month delay, from December to January, in approving the 400,000-ton grain program for the drought area.

The results of the delay are still being felt here in the inordinate difficulties of distributing the food to the remote regions of this thinly populated, landlocked country, which is larger than Texas and California combined.

Camel caravans have taken over where even four-wheel-drive vehicles fail. Three convoys of Algerian trucks are crossing the Sahara from Algiers, carrying 1,500 tons of American sorghum to the northern regions of Niger not reachable from the south. The United States and the United Nations Food and Agriculture Organization are sharing the transport costs.

In the most hopeful of estimates, it will take at least three years of continuously good growing seasons for Niger to regain what President Kountche called her "food equilibrium."

In those years, Niger will need donations of grain to replenish the two to three years' reserve that her farmers normally stock for food and seed. That reserve has been wiped out. She will also need grain to feed the nomads until their herds of cattle, camels, sheep and goats—about half of which are thought to have been lost to the drought—have been renewed to a viable minimum.

If the weather and the donor nations remain favorable, there is optimism here that Niger will return to where she was when the weather cycle turned to increasing drought seven years ago. She is a country where in the best of circumstances all but a few people live on the margin of subsistence and look forward to a life span of no more than 40 years.

October 3, 1974

Chad's Hungriest See Little of Food Given by World

By HENRY KAMM

Special to The New York Times

NDJAMENA, Chad, Oct. 6—At a cost of more than $1-million, the United States is airlifting 2,000 tons of sorghum to Chad. Half is being flown to a remote desert region that has suffered only marginally from the great African drought and has little immediate need of relief.

The grain is being flown to Chad from Maiduguri, Nigeria, 154 miles from here, where thousands of tons of sorghum have been arriving since last March and thousands more are on their way.

Great as her food needs are, Chad has failed to absorb and distribute to the hungry most of the supplies furnished by the world communtiy.

Of about 4,000 tons of American sorghum remaining in Maiduguri, an inspector has found 1,000 to be rotten and 700 infested with bugs.

Many Share Dilemma

The expensive airlift to a region of marginal need and the backlog in Maiduguri with more grain on the way illustrate the dilemma of the American relief effort to Chad. It is shared by the many other donors—governments, international organizations and private groups: The need is great, assistance has been made available but donors are powerless against Government handling of transport and distribution.

Ten days of conversations here with representatives of most of the principal donors—the United States, France, The United Nations and various affiliates, the Common Market's European Development Fund and private groups—as well as two field trips disclosed remarkable unanimity in assessments of the problem.

The Government of Ngarta Tombalbaye is believed to be mismanaging the relief effort.

The principal reasons cited are incompetence, apathy and participation in or toleration of profiteering on the part of persons close to the national leadership.

'Here to Help'

It is part of the dilemma of those attempting to help the people of Chad that if they criticize the Government's performance they incur a high risk of being barred from further assistance to those stricken by drought and famine. Consequently, all persons interviewed insisted on anonymity.

"We are here to help the people of Chad, Government or no Government," an international official said.

One price exacted by President Tombalbaye for allowing his four million people to receive assistance is that all decisions are made by his Government; whatever goods and services are put at Chad's disposal, the Government decides how to use them.

The American airlift to the Sahara is an example. Last June, with the rainy season at hand, which makes most of Chad's roads unusable, the Government urged the donors to provide air delivery. The United States, mindful perhaps of the large stocks lying useless in Nigeria and with a desire to give no offense to groups at home, agreed reluctantly and at the same time said it would carry its sorghum where Chad wanted it.

Interview With Prefect

The American Embassy was surprised when Public Works Minister Abdoulaye Ndjoumouna, in charge of all drought relief, ordered 1,300 of the 2,000 tons to be delivered to northern locations. It was aware that the 70,000 nomads of the Uaharan region there live in permanent drought and have for centuries coped without outside assistance. The embassy persuaded the minister to reduce the allocation to half the 2,000 tons and proceeded with the airlift.

The Prefect, or Governor of the region, said in an interview in his oasis capital, Faya-Largeau, that the people had had less food during the drought period because less arrived from the south but had survived without too much hardship. Now, he said, caravans are again arriving with millet from the first harvest of the new crop.

The American planes, a vastly more expensive form of transport, are arriving at the same time. About 700 tons have arrived so far, 15 tons at a time carried over distances of about 1,000 miles each round trip.

The Prefect, Bakary Diallo, said all but 50 tons would be stocked until April or May, when the nomads will be running out of the proceeds of this year's date crop and before next year's can be marketed. Throughout rural Africa the period before the new harvest is one when people have a difficult time making ends meet, but it is not considered an emergency.

Mr. Diallo appeared to see no paradox in carrying grain by emergency airlift only to put it in storage for seven months. The American Embassy does but feels powerless.

Aid and development officials here can only guess at the reasons motivating this surprising allocation.

One line of speculation is that Mr. Tombalbaye is sending American grain to the north because he wants to appease the nomads, who are openly disaffected and who have often rebelled against all governments trying to dominate them. Another reason offered is that grain sent so far away can be disposed of without anyone's knowing its ultimate use. A third speculation is that the grain can be used to feed Government troops sent north to keep the nomads in check.

There is no need to guess, however, at the reason for the constant backlog of relief food, which made airlifts necessary last year as well and has caused great hardship to many of the two million Chadians estimated to have been affected by the drought. The reason is the Government failure to break the monopoly of the Chadian trucking industry in this landlocked country without railroads.

Throughout the relief operations beginning last year, the donors have carried on a running fight with the Cooperative of Chadian Transporters, the truck monopoly.

"We have the monopoly and we fix the tariffs," boasted Cameron Agar, a Syrian-born Lebanese of French citizenship who founded the monopoly 20 years ago. The truck owners used it to enforce the highest ton-per-mile rate in the world and to keep the cheaper, faster and larger Nigerian trucks from carrying grain here while Chadians starved.

Mr. Agar said he gave "temporary authorization" for Nigerian truckers to come as far as this capital last May. In an interview, Public Works Minister Ndjoumouna said the Government had ordered the lifting of the monopoly.

An international official said that the Government "could not impose its will on the truckers," and one of his colleagues called the truckers "a mafia." But a leading figure in the trucking industry said that most members of the Government had an interest in truck ownership through close relatives, including President Tombalbaye's wife.

Mr. Ndjoumouna opened the interview with an unsolicited declaration that Mr. Tombalbaye owned no trucks and added that no Government members did.

It is difficult to know what happens to the goods after they leave warehouses for distribution points.

"It is difficult to verify anything in this country," an international official said.

But like many of his colleagues he believes that much grain remains in warehouses at distribution centers without going to those who need it.

Despite a rainy season that was mostly good, Chad's food problem remains vast. Some areas can look forward to mediocre harvests at best. In others, little was sowed because the population was on the move looking for food. In the densely populated region around Mongoan in the center, grasshoppers are destroying much of what should be a good harvest.

About 30,000 tons of relief food remain destined for Chad out of 1974 pledges. Representatives of the donors here want very much to be hopeful that it can be got to those who need it.

October 10, 1974

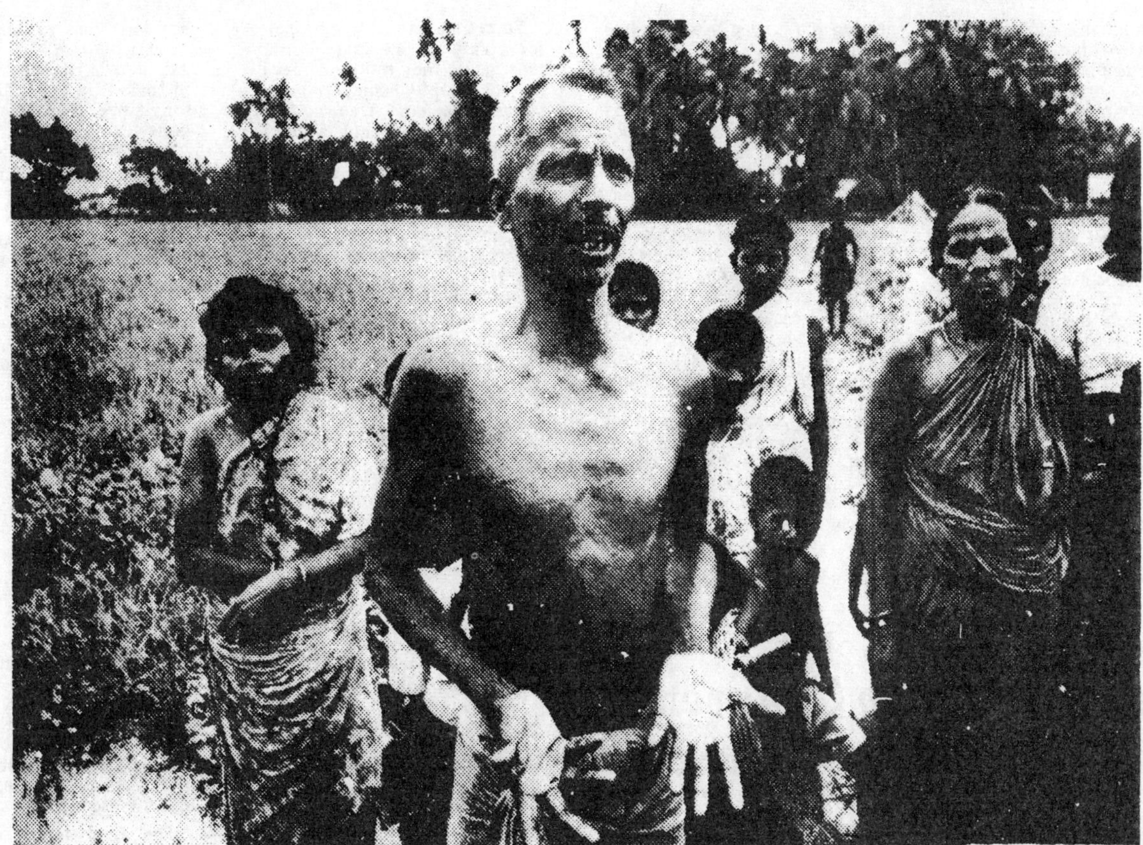

The New York Times/Baldev

Marudai, a 55-year-old farmer, stands before land lying idle during disputes between the landlords and farmers

Land Disputes Thwarting Green Revolution in India

Ownership, Pay and Politics Involved in Rice-Area Fight

By KASTURI RANGAN
Special to The New York Times

PACHAMPETTAI, India—This tiny South Indian village on the banks of Cauveri River is typical of the lush rice-growing countryside, where efforts to bring in the Green Revolution have been hamstrung.

Use of new hybrid seeds, fertilizers, pesticides and modern farm implements have transformed wheat fields in the north, but here the rice-growing has been curbed by endless disputes over wages, ownership, ceilings on holdings and, most of all, politics.

"Green Revolution?" asked a Communist leader, M. Kalyanasundaram, who lives at Tiruchirappalli, 15 miles west of here, and whose pro-Moscow Communist party is organizing peasants against landlords. "Oh, yes. It's coming. But there has to be a Red revolution first."

Rich Land Lies Fallow

Pachampettai has a population of 1,000 and 800 acres of rice and banana fields. A third of the cultivable land, where three rice crops a year used to be harvested, has been lying fallow for 18 months because of a dispute between the landlords and their tenants.

"We've been cultivating the land for generations," said Marudal, a 55-year-old tenant farmer. "Suddenly our landlord has decided to evict us. We are not allowed to work on his land and we are not allowing him, either."

Marudai has a family of nine, his wife, two sons, two daughters-in-law and three children. After giving a third of the crop to the landlord, who lives in the nearby town of Srirangam, there was just enough rice left to support the family.

Twenty other tenant farmers in this village have been similarly evicted. All the land will remain uncultivated until the issue is decided in the courts, where thousands of similar cases are pending and where decisions are not made before two years at the least. Peasants, forced off the land, must work as casual labor, part of their earnings going to lawyers to fight their cases.

'Tears of Blood Flow'

"Tears of blood flow from our eyes when we see our fields lying parched and untended," said Veeramma, the wife of Marudai. "And we walk 10 miles a day crossing two rivers in search of work."

Adding to the distress, and the fury, of the peasants, most of the court cases are going against them. The law usually protects the tenant farmer, making eviction almost impossible. But there are many loopholes and the landlords, who can afford the best lawyers, manage to win most cases. Most landlords, before deciding to evict the tenant, persuade him to sign a statement declaring himself only a paid laborer.

Srirangam Thathachariar, Marudai's landlord, who owns 65 acres in Pachampettai and 200 in other villages of the district, denied that he was doing anything illegal.

"I go strictly according to law," he said. "These people were never my tenants. They were all laborers on my land. I have documents to prove it."

Landlord Demands Share

He also said he would not have evicted them if they had been regular in paying him his share of the crops.

"I give them my land to cultivate," he said. "I have dug wells for them. I was going to buy a tractor for their use. But they started behaving as if they owned the land. They appropriated all the produce as their wages."

Mr. Thathachariar, an 82-

year-old Brahman patriarch, is so conservative that he refused to be photographed because he said "photos shorten one's life." He has nominally distributed most of his land among near relatives, to conform with the Land Ceiling Act, which limits a family to 15 acres.

Mr. Thathachariar blames "the Government and the Communists."

"My workers are innocent," he said. "I've known them since they were born. They are my children. It's just that they are lead astray by Communists. They will come back to me finally."

When landlords win eviction cases they often force their way onto the land, paying outside labor three times the local price for sowing and harvesting. The operations are usually carried out under heavy police escort.

Communists Interested

The peasants who lose and those who fear they will lose turn to political parties. The Communists are only too willing to take up their cases.

Many Pachampettai villagers have joined the pro-Moscow Communist party. In other villages of this region, the rival Marxist Communists have organized casual laborers to agitate for higher wages, bringing them in conflict with both the landowners and the tenant farmers.

In this three-way conflict many landowners, most of them small holders living in cities, are anxious to sell away the land, which brings a higher price without a tenant.

Sometimes tenants are paid for giving up the land, but in most cases they refuse to leave.

"They are told they are going to get the land free if they hold on to it," said a landowner at Mannargudi. "Many have stopped paying their annual rent. That's why we are anxious to sell away the land and invest the money in a less bothersome business, like selling saris."

Other landlords have diverted fields to cotton or cashew nuts to escape the Land Ceiling Act. The act permits the holding of four to five times as much land for these crops.

In the last two years the area under rice has shrunk by 5 per cent in Tamil Nadu state and the trend is continuing.

The trend is also reflected in other rice-growing states—Kerala, Mysore, Maharashtra, Andhra, Orissa and West Bengal. India's rice production has increased by only three million tons since 1965—from 39 millions tons to 42 million tons.

In contrast, wheat production has doubled in the period, from 12 million tons to 24 million tons.

But rice is the largest crop in India and is the staple diet of most Indians.

"Hereafter all the increases in food production should come from the rice areas," said an official at the Agricultural Ministry in New Delhi. "But we are not sure which way the wind is blowing there."

October 12, 1971

Starving Afghan Children Await Death Along Roads

By JAMES P. STERBA

Special to The New York Times

CHAKHCHARAN, Afghanistan, June 9—The boy's spindly body sank slowly to the dusty gravel road. He lowered his head to the pebbles, resting his sunken cheek on his hand. His dry, cracked lips did not close. He tried to cover his feet, but the torn, dirt-encrusted rags he wore were not long enough. He placed an empty tin can, his only possession, near his stomach. And then he started to cry.

Fifty feet away, near a mud building, another small boy lay motionless in the midmorning sun. In a ditch 20 yards away was a tiny, rag-covered body, and beside it still another boy, perhaps 6 years old, sat on his haunches and stared blankly at the road, his eyes not following two bearded men as they coaxed their sagebrush - laden mules toward the bazaar.

The reality is clear: Afghanistan has been suffering from the worst food shortages in memory.

The final days of life for the sick and starving children in this small, dust-swept provincial capital in the barren hills of central Afghanistan are spent pleading for a nugget of mutton fat from the town butcher, drinking water from a puddle, dodging the flailing sticks of the newly arrived sellers of wheat, flour, onions and tomatoes, picking a precious few spilled grains of rice out of the dirt, and trying to swallow roots and the toxic grass that swells their faces and puffs their eyelids nearly shut.

The final nights are spent stumbling from mud house to mud house, knocking on locked doors and gates moaning for food and warmth, and huddling in corners of abandoned buildings to escape the cold wind.

The final hours are spent alone.

No one knows how many children, abandoned by parents who had no food for them, have died or are dying in Chakhcharan, in the surrounding hills of Ghor Province or in the other towns and hills in central and western Afghanistan. Fewer are dying now. Roads are opening and food is beginning to trickle in.

After two rainless years followed by a severe winter, the symbols of the past few months have been the sounds of once-

Photographs for The New York Times by JAMES P. STERBA

A PARCHED AND BARREN LAND: A small boy and a young burro walk beside old man riding a burro near Chakhcharan, Afghanistan

strong and proud men weeping and the sights of veiled women grazing like animals on field grass and of children lying like tiny rag heaps beside roads.

It is a quiet tragedy in an isolated part of the country—a crisis probably compounded by the facts that undeveloped Afghanistan minds her own business, although not very well at times, and that the suffering has been dwarfed by the misery on the neighboring Indian subcontinent.

Some Help From Abroad

The United States, several European countries, the Soviet Union and a few others, responding to reluctant pleas from the Government for emergency aid late last fall, sent wheat and advice. Except for the work of a few diplomats and Government officials, and the impassioned appeals of a hundful of American and West German volunteers living in the worst-hit areas, the response have been modest, low-keyed and slow-moving.

There has been little of the urgency and attention that accompany similar catastropries in other countries that have been linked to a cause, a war, political villainy or a contest between world powers.

Aid-granting countries like the United States demand precise estimates for donations that are not politically inspired.

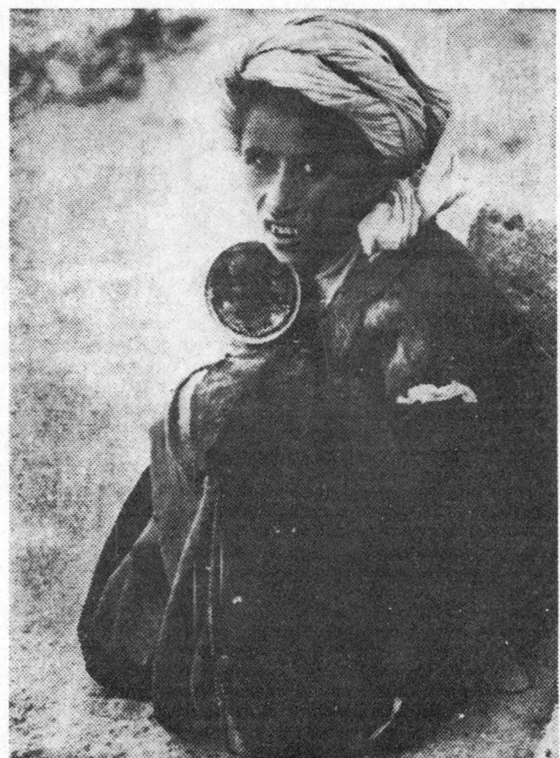

Staring blankly, a boy with beggar's cup sits by road

Leaders of many small nations in Asia have noted in the past year that as great-power competition for influence lessens and as the United States turns more inward to its domestic problems, donors have become more demanding of facts and figures.

Those are impossible requirements for a country like Afghanistan, where one can travel hundreds of miles overland without crossing a road and where the Government does not know whether it has 9 million or 17 million citizens.

When a child died in James Mathewson's arms six weeks ago, the 22-year-old Peace Corps volunteer from Kansas City, Kans., was marked for life. But in the view of officials who know he is young and impresssionable, his pleas for fast help did not have the force of a pile of statistics showing how many people and animals have died, how many are hungry, how much food is left, how much wheat was planted this year and how much will be harvested—statistics that are virtually impossible to get.

Warnings of famine were sounded as early as 1970 by Richard Saunders, a consultant on agricultural economics who has worked in Afghanistan for seven years. But his projections were disputed and largely ignored because of squabbles in the central Gov-

The New York Times

STARVING AND IGNORED, a boy lies in the dust of Chakhcharan, central Afghanistan, an area plagued by famine ernment and among foreign advisers.

Mr. Saunders worked with a consultant team of Robert Nathan Associates, a United States concern that advised the Ministry of Planning under a grant from the Agency for International Development. He projected a wheat shortage of 409,000 metric tons in 1970 and 606,000 in 1971, the actual shortages were about 60,000 tons less.

American officials working with the Ministry of Agriculture projected little or no shortage in 1970 and less than half the actual shortage in 1971.

The two ministries and their advisers have never gotten along because of differences in approach to development and because the ministers have never been close.

The six-year-old central Government in Kabul, set up as an "experiment in democracy" by King Mohammed Zahir Shan, has always been more concerned with conditions in the relatively prosperous Kabul Kandahar region in the east than with the isloated western provinces, traditionally a source of wheat for the east. As the famine drew near, the central region was relatively well off since imported food always comes to it first.

Furthermore, student and labor unrest in the central region attracted much more Government attention than the early reports of hunger in the west, where communications are difficult, roads are impassable in winter and many officials are exiled for poor performance.

"I doubt that Afghanistan has ever had this bad a situation," said Abdul Wakil, Minister Without Portfolio in the central Government. "People are dying of hunger. We have reports of this in localized areas."

There are no estimates of how many people have starved to death, but the number suffering from hunger ranges up to half a million. Roughly 20 per cent of the population live in the five central and northwestern provinces most seriously hit.

Two weeks ago a survey team of United States aid officials visited four of these provinces—Herat, Badghis, Faryab and Ghor. In the Badghis town of Qalainau, where a nurse guessed that 20 people had died per day over the winter months, some 200 hungry people surrounded the survey team's car, banging it with their fists and asking for food. Policemen had to chase them away.

The team found Herat City flooded with refugees. There was no medicine for the many sick, and an epidemic is feared as spring temperatures rise.

'Hungry People Everywhere'

A Peace Corps volunteer reported that in Herat "you can see hungry people everywhere." Of neighboring Qalainau he wrote:

"Walking in the bazaars you are followed by hundreds of small kids, men and women asking for food. And more than that, you can see some men and children lay down in the streets—either they are hungry or sick. You can see some people are sick from eating different kinds of grass. Their faces, hands and legs are swollen and finally some are bleeding from the face."

Mr. Wakil, who holds a doctorate in agriculture from the University of London, estimates that half the livestock in the country has been slaughtered. This includes 15 million to 16 million head of sheep that produce a vital export commodity —karakul skins used for making Persian lamb coats in Europe and America. For debt-ridden Afghanistan, it means years of hardship.

Seed wheat that farmers would have planted was eaten. Many bullocks used for plowing were slaughtered for food along with sheep and goats because there was no fodder. The weak bullocks remaining had to be rested for two or three days instead of the normal one after a day's plowing, so some wheat was not planted on time.

Many farmers abandoned their homes to seek food in the district towns, and when little food was found there, they left their children to beg and headed for the cities. There were reports that some families sold children as slave labor so the remaining members of the family could buy food.

No Food to Buy

In some isolated sections money became irrelevant because there was no food to buy.

By late fall some of the wheat previously purchased on easy credit under the United States Food for Peace program arrived, but some was held up by the Indian-Pakistani war. High officials toured Europe to get what commitments, but shipment through the Soviet Union by train, truck and barge was slow. The United States Ambassador, Robert G. Neumann, who is credited with spurring some urgency into Kabul officials, made a special trip home to arrange a grant of 100,000 tons of wheat, but it has only begun to arrive.

When relief did arrive it was almost impossible to get it to the stricken areas. Bridges were washed out. Mountain passes were clogged with snow. Trucks were scarce. And Government officials had no experience in dealing with such a problem.

In Chakhcharan, it appears, not much was done by provincial officials to deal with hunger until a new Governor, Abdul Razaq Lala, was appointed six weeks ago. Some 160 tons of wheat were sent between March 21 and May 22, but 58 tons are missing from the new German-built storehouse. The Governor has arrested the storehouse keeper.

When the Governor arrived he found thousands of hungry people from the surrounding hills clustered in town and around the dirt airstrip but little effort by local officials to provide food. He expanded the two town bakeries to 12, including one in the town jail, to bake nan—a flat wheat bread that was sold at low cost to people with money and given free to people without money. Yet many children still do not get any.

Before the Governor arrived a local doctor estimated that 2,500 people had died of starvation in the vicinity of the town.

The problems have eased drastically in the past few weeks. Roads have opened, allowing in Government wheat and private food truckers from Kabul and Kandahar. Many families with money but no food purchased supplies and moved back to their farms.

But children continue to die or be ignored and men and women go hungry as local officials hinder relief projects.

There is a hospital here, but no one from it ventures out to treat the sick. In a country where only one person in 10 is literate and is aware of such things as modern medicine, few people know enough to go in for treatment. Those who do know enough also know that while examinations are free, medicine costs. And if the choice is between food and medicine, most people choose food.

Today it would not have mattered anyway. No one was at the hospital because it was Friday, the Moslem sabbath.

The acting director of provincial development walked down the main road of town yesterday with visitors, and

A boy, one of many abandoned by their parents, lies in ditch. He showed no sign of life.

The New York Times/June 16, 1972

when he saw this reporter photographing a small boy who had collapsed on the road, he picked up the boy and shouted to a stranger to take him and buy him a piece of nan.

The stranger carried the sobbing boy off the road, placed him under a bush and left him as the acting director of provincial development walked on. Today the police chief, who would not give his name, called the reporter in for questioning.

When the Governor arrived yesterday from Kabul, where he had attended meetings, Timothy F. McCormack, 23 years old, of Kansas City, Mo., the second Peace Corp volunteer in Ghor Province, told him that a Food for Work road project had stopped because local officials would not provide a truck to haul gravel from the river that runs through town.

Food for work projects, in which men are paid in relief wheat, were started throughout the country last fall as a way of circumventing Government objections to straight welfare programs and to American community-development projects.

Trucks There But Unused

Trucks are in short supply. The army, which is more or less under the direct control of the King, has plenty, but was reluctant to use them to haul relief wheat. After weeks of coaxing, the army finally agreed to rent 20 trucks at $7 a day each.

Four army trucks that had brought wheat to Chakhcharan had been sitting unused for days, as were four trucks belonging to the Public Works Department.

The Governor immediately ordered the foreman of the road gang to get a truck. Then, as the Governor attended to business elsewhere, the provincial development director told the foreman that the army trucks could not be used, allegedly because of new orders from Kabul. The public works director said his trucks could not be used because he had no authority to pay for gasoline.

When the Governor heard of the delay, four local officials and Mr. McCormack had to accompany the truck driver to the Government gasoline pump, where a 15-minute debate took place over who would eventually pay for the gasoline and where the local reporter for the Government news agency had to sign a statement saying he had witnessed the gasoline being pumped.

Shortly thereafter road work began, probably for the benefit of visitors.

A new grader and roller sat unused beside the airstrip; they are restricted to clearing snow from the runway in winter and, according to the aviation authority, could not be used for upgrading a road to bring wheat that might help the people survive next winter.

June 16, 1972

Afghans Striving to Aid Famine Areas

By HENRY KAMM

Special to The New York Times

KABUL, Afghanistan, Nov. 13 —Countless Afghans are still dying of hunger and many more will perish in the months to come. But under strong American guidance, Afghanistan is carrying out a major effort of bringing food to the hungry, and many lives are being saved.

Three years of drought in the central and northern part of this mountainous country have brought famine — and deaths that will never be counted.

No one knows how many people live in Afghanistan—estimates range from 9 million to 17 million — and no estimate even exists of those who have starved to death.

What killed the people stricken by the drought, in the view of Afghan and foreign observers, was not only lack of food in their regions but also governmental indifference, and greed and official corruption.

Operation Help, an Afghan project that would not exist without the United States, is sending large quantities of food into the stricken areas while guarding, with apparent success, against misappropriation and lack of energy in its distribution.

Credits Opinion in U.S.

The Health Minister, Mohammed Ibrahim Majid-Seraj, chairman of the operation's coordinating committee, said that public opinion in the United States, which he said was mobilized mainly by two articles in The New York Times last June, "pushed the Government to help those people."

The consensus of informed sources, Afghan and American, is that publicity in the United States strengthened Ambassador Robert G. Neuman's hand in drawing the attention of King Mohammed Zahir Shah to the suffering of many of his subjects. Mr. Neumann is in his sixth year here and dean of the diplomatic corps. His relations with the King are excellent.

Mr. Neumann, who went to the United States from Austria as a refugee from the Nazis, is known to feel that his role in helping to save these lives would have been enough to make worthwhile his leaving the academic life to accept the ambassadorship.

Assured of maximal American assistance, the King last September took the unusual steps of entrusting the program of saving the hungry to a group outside the apathetic and venal bureaucracy and of giving the group extraordinary powers.

In essence, Operation Help is run by Dr. Majid-Seraj and a group of youngish, modern-minded officials relying on the logistical support of the army.

U.S. Expert Credited

Although the United States is eager to understate its role and present Operation Help is a strictly Afghan project, Dr. Majid-Seraj and his associates give full credit to an American expert for the conception and management of the enterprise.

He is Abe S. Ashcanase, a tall, middle-aged management expert of the Agency for International Development.

After enumerating American contributions of wheat, cooking oil and medicine, Dr. Majid-Seraj said:

"But the biggest contribution is that we have Mr. Ashcanase as adviser and responsible for the management of the operation."

Another senior Afghan official said, "This program is the child of Ashcanase, the whole conception and the safeguards. Ashcanase is the kingpin."

Mr. Ashcanase, a veteran of American aid programs since the immediate postwar days, shrugs this off and insists that he is merely a consultant.

The safeguards that he included in Operation Help are mainly constant supervision of all distribution processes through frequent field trips by all the top officials. Such field trips are as new for Afghan officials as another Ashcanase innovation: a daily public financial statement of all disbursements.

Peace Corps Volunteers

The Afghan officials and Mr. Ashcanase put strong reliance also on the observations of 20 Peace Corps volunteers who are active in the field. The volunteers were among the first to bring reports of the famine to Kabul and urge action.

Operation Help is taking food into three disaster areas: the northwestern triangle between the Soviet and Iranian borders, the central area and the northeastern province of Badakhshan.

Distribution in the first two areas began last month and will be completed late this month. Between 55,000 and 60,000 of an expected total of 85,000 to 90,000 people have received a six-month supply of wheat, as well as such oil, clothing and medicines as are available.

The Badakhshan operation, where 60,000 people are to be fed, is just getting under way and racing against the first snows.

Distributing about 10 tons of wheat is a major achievement in regions where there are few passable roads and where most of the loads have to be carried by pack animals for long distances. Many friends advised Mr. Ashcanase not to take on the job for it was bound to fail.

Many Afghans Surprised

Many Afghan officials still seem surprised by the measure of their success.

In August, one recalled, Deputy Premier Abdul Samad Hamed, Dr. Majid-Seraj and the provincial governor were stoned by a hungry crowd in the town of Chaghcharan; the emaciated bodies of children had been stacked in front of the schoolhouse where the officials were meeting. Now, the official said, officials are cheered when they go there.

No one pretends that Operation Help will save all of the people in the areas this winter. Many are inaccessible, particularly in Badakhshah, and it is doubted that wheat alone will save people who have lived on dried mulberries and grass for a long time.

Ambassador Neumann hopes that the program has taught Afghans that they can do something to help themselves. But a high Government official active in the program said that unless the Government "gets out of its coma," Operation Help is only "prolonging the death agony of these people."

November 19, 1972

With Economy in Ruins, Bangladesh Faces Food Crisis

By SYDNEY H. SCHANBERG

Special to The New York Times

DACCA, Bangladesh, March 29—As a column of horsecarts carrying bagged rice plods along a dirt track on the edge of Faridpur, ragged children scramble in the dust for a few kernels that have escaped from a hole in a bag.

In Khulna 20 big United Nations relief trucks sit idle outside a Government office — either for lack of anything to carry or because the Government cannot pay for drivers and maintenance crews.

Disturbances—some observers have called them small riots—have broken out in several areas where shortages of rice and wheat have driven prices far beyond the reach of any but the well-to-do.

Many factories, shops and businesses have not reopened since the December war and unemployment has rocketed. Beggars are multiplying at an unusual rate as the rural poor pour into the cities in the futile hope of finding work or at least a subsistence dole of food.

A Flattened Economy

In short, the food situation and the economic picture in general are bleak and worsening in the new Bengali nation of Bangladesh, formerly East Pakistan, which won independence from Pakistan after an eight-month guerrilla struggle and a two-week Indian-Pakistani war that destroyed hundreds of thousands of homes, damaged most roads and bridges and left the economy flattened.

Just about everything is wrecked, and trying to repair the wreckage is like trying to plug a sieve.

By Western standards the situation seems desperate and to some newcomers hopeless. Even by Bengali standards it is a serious crisis. Long-time Western relief workers—always reluctant to predict famine or other cataclysms in a land where the resilient Bengalis have survived chronic floods, epidemics, tidal waves and, lately, widespread slaughter and a civil war—are nevertheless describing the situation as dangerous.

"Even the most inventive and most resilient destitute people," Toni Hagen, the Swiss who heads the United Nations relief operation, wrote in a recent report, "have no chance to survive if they are not given a minimum standby to start with."

The United Nations relief effort, the largest ever attempted, has not really gotten off the ground.

Money Just One Problem

One big reason is lack of money, but there are others: appalling bureaucratic delays in both the Government and the United Nations Headquarters in New York; corruption; the failure of the United Nations, the Government and the myriad foreign private relief agencies to coordinate their programs. Confusion and infighting are rife.

"The Prime Minister has asked how long this mess is going to continue," a Government official told a meeting of relief agencies earlier this month, referring to Sheik Mujibur Rahman.

With things gone sour, at least so far, everyone is blaming everyone else—and there is some truth in all the charges.

The private agencies, most of which have meager funds and can undertake only small projects, say the United Nations is inefficient and incompetent. United Nations officials, hamstrung by their slow-moving bureaucracy in New York, say the private agencies have a "short-timer" relief mentality — just dumping charity goods here and moving on to the next disaster without addressing themselves to the real problem, which is rehabilitating the economy and the people.

And the Bangladesh Government, itself debilitated by confusion and delay, accuses them all on occasion of acting like sovereign fiefdoms and not consulting on their activities.

Government Gets the Blame

The Government says further that the wide publicity surrounding the private agencies has "led people to believe that if adequate relief was not

Jason Laure/Rapho Guillumette

Food being given to residents of Dacca, capital of Bangladesh. The food situation in the new nation is bleak.

reaching them, this must somehow be the fault of the Government."

So far the Government has conveyed no sense of urgency or crisis to the people. There are no signs of mobilization for what may be a famine emergency—no efforts to commandeer river boats and vehicles, no campaign in the interior to organize the convoys of bullock carts and coolie crews that will be the only means of moving the food in remote areas when the rains come.

"Any foreigner who visits Dacca," a disgusted Bengali official commented, "would not have the faintest notion that we are in the middle of what amounts to a wartime emergency. The hotels are full, the girls are dancing, the movie houses are thriving, people are politicking and the Government has imposed no special taxes or issued any special orders."

Observers who are not quite so pessimistic point out that the Government is really less than three months old—dating from Sheik Mujib's return Jan. 10 after more than nine months in West Pakistani prisons—and that it is too soon to make any definitive judgments.

The conventional wisdom about the food situation—in Washington, for example—is that the problem is not so much getting supplies to Bangladesh as it is distributing them to the interior. Experts here agree with this, but at the same time they note that for the moment there is virtually no food in the ports to distribute.

Big Food Gap Foreseen

With the food gap for this year estimated at two million tons or more, less than 100,000 tons of food grains have been brought in through the United Nations program so far, and the next substantial shipment —66,000 tons — is not due until the last half of May.

"The dangerous time is the next six weeks, before the food begins to arrive," a food expert here said. "Stocks are very low and the rice price is getting dangerously high. In many cases it has doubled. People can't afford it. There could be trouble, maybe riots, and this could have political implications."

Of the $350-million pledged to the United Nations operation so far—the appeal for this year is for about $600-million — the United States has offered about $100-million, but almost none of this, which includes nearly $60-million in food, has arrived.

Many Bengalis and some foreigners contend that the relief situation would not be half so bad if the United States—the only country, they feel, with the resources to make a real dent —had moved in sooner. They feel that President Nixon allowed his foreign policy to get in the way of a humanitarian relief effort. The Nixon Administration adopted an anti-India, pro-Pakistan policy during the Bangladesh struggle, and it has still not recognized the new nation of about 75 million.

India Holds the Key

The Russians, though their relief commitment is much smaller, have moved in quickly to take advantage of the political vacuum. They got a salvage contract to clear mines and sunken hulks from the Chalna and Chittagong ports which some observers think will give them a naval foothold here. The United Nations had first option on the contract, but when headquarters dragged its feet for over two months, the Bangladesh Government got fed up.

Whatever the results of either Western or Soviet aid, the key to the relief crisis for the next few months and perhaps longer will be India, which has the largest stake in keeping Bangladesh not only afloat but reasonably stable.

Enjoying a food surplus for the first time as a result of the "green revolution" in wheat, the Indians have promised to pump at least 500,000 tons of grain into Bangladesh by the end of June.

Yet relief officials here concede that even if all the food promised by India and the United Nations arrives on schedule, there will still be pockets of severe shortage and some people will die—if not of outright starvation then of such diseases as cholera and pneumonia as a consequence of hunger.

Mr. Hagen, the United Nations relief official, whose bluntness about the situation has brought him an admonition from New York to stop talking with the press, wrote in a widely circulated report last month:

"The situation in Bangladesh is desperate. Practically no food grains are in the pipeline. Entirely insufficient measures have been taken so far to restore the transport system. Blankets won't do. Baby food won't do. Midwifery kits won't do. Charity won't do. Cash is required for employment and reconstruction. Plain cash."

March 30, 1972

ASIA THREATENED BY RICE SHORTAGE

Indonesia Is Hard Hit as Rains Reduce Crop

By JAMES P. STERBA
Special to The New York Times

JAKARTA, Indonesia, Dec. 5—Less than a year after agricultural experts predicted that Asia would soon face a rice glut caused by increased production, the weather has caused the opposite to happen: the continent is facing a serious rice shortage.

It rained too much during the period in the Philippines and South Korea, and not enough in Indonesia, Malaysia, Cambodia, Thailand and Burma. As a result, rice yields are far below normal and prices are soaring, threatening new inflationary trends that could seriously upset fragile economic stability in some countries.

Indonesia is already hard hit. Rice prices have doubled since the last major harvest in June, and the next big crop will not begin to be harvested until next spring.

No one knows how much rice is left for the critical months to come, but there have already been reports of hoarding and in a few isolated regions of farmers' eating some of their seed for the next crop.

In addition, provincial and district officers in central Java—Indonesia's big rice bowl—have asked the Government to begin delivering rice to the region from central stocks.

A Comparison with U.S.

The severity of the situation can be illustrated by a comparison with the United States, where the average family spends less than 20 per cent of its income on food. The average Indonesian family spends about 60 per cent of its income on food, half of which is rice.

Protests directed at the Government have begun in Indonesia. High-school students, charging both Government inefficiency and corruption and hoarding by ethnic Chinese rice merchants, demonstrated in Jakarta last week. Several were arrested.

Indonesia weathered a rice shortage in 1968, but this year's is more severe. Rice prices then did not double until February. This year, they have already doubled, and there are four more months until harvest.

As do most Asian countries, Indonesia grows most of the rice she needs and imports the rest from countries such as Burma, Thailand and the United States.

In recent years, Indonesia grew about 94 per cent of what she needed, and bought the remaining 6 per cent. This year, she may have to buy double that amount.

A harvest of 13.4 million tons was predicted. But because of the drought, production may have been less than 12 million tons.

Thus Indonesia needs to buy more than a million tons of rice. Her problem is that few countries have enough to sell, and those who do have drastically raised their prices.

The United States, the world's leading rice exporter, has little excess available because of heavy rice aid commitments to many Asian countries, including South Korea, the Philippines, South Vietnam, Cambodia, and Bangladesh. These countries buy American rice on long-term easy credit under the Food for Peace program.

Supply From Japan Expected

The United States is already committed to sell 319,500 tons of rice to Indonesia this year, but Indonesia clearly needs much more. Japan, with a huge rice surplus, is expected to supply about half that much on similar credit. The rest will have to be paid for in cash wherever it can be bought.

Both Burma and Thailand, normally rice exporters, were also hit by drought and are thus reluctant to sell rice they might need later themselves. Prices of medium-grade rice in Thailand have jumped from $89, to nearly $140 per ton, and for the first time in years, countries wanting to buy rice have had to plead with the Thai Government to sell it.

Indonesia's rice shortage would have been worse if she had not converted about 20 per cent her rice-growing land to raise high-yielding "miracle" varieties in recent years.

In good years, these varieties provided yields double or triple the yields of regular rice strains. But they are also the most delicate, and in years of floods or drought, yields plummet.

December 6, 1972

Worst Drought in Decade Perils India's Food Supply

By BERNARD WEINRAUB
Special to The New York Times

NEW DELHI, Feb. 19—India, struck by the worst drought in a decade, is facing severe food shortages and rising prices, and criticism of the Government is growing.

Although the food shortage has raised the specter of famine in such states as Maharashtra, Rajasthan, Mysore, Gujerat, Andhra Pradesh and pockets of Orissa, Government officials deny that there is widespread starvation.

At this point, however, Prime Minister Indira Gandhi's Government, as well as critics, Western economists and food experts agree that the monsoon season, which starts in June, will be the most crucial in years and that a scarcity of rain could stir famine across the country.

"The drought now is serious, it is there," said T. P. Singh of the Agriculture Ministry. "We can only hope that the monsoon will be good."

One Western farm expert said simply: "India can just about squeak through now and we're holding our breath for the monsoon. If there's a bad one—like the past few years—then we'll have famine, a bad one."

The balance between food and population—a fundamental one in India—is especially perilous in view of the drought. Farmers have swarmed into crowded cities like Bombay, set up makeshift tents and turned to begging. Hundreds of thousands of farmers have been placed on Government relief projects—widening roads, excavating canals, breaking stones—at salaries as low as 30 cents a day.

Reports of Starvation

There have been reports of families in remote villages living on one meal every two days, and of half-starved farmers eating lana, a shrub normally consumed by camels. There is a shortage of fodder, and hundreds of head of cattle are perishing daily. Drinking water is rationed in drought-stricken areas, forcing families to spend hours on line waiting to fill their buckets from Government tankers and bullock-carts.

The drought has also been a harsh blow to India's pride. Just two years ago India seemed on the verge of self-sufficiency, a profound yearning since independence in 1947. Now, facing a crisis, India is importing grain. Last month the Government announced the purchase of at least two million tons of food grains, mostly from the United States.

The gravity of the food crisis is underlined by the statistics. In 1970-1971, the bouyant Government said that Indian farmers produced 107.8 million tons of grain, at least three million tons more than had been expected. This made it possible for the Government to fulfill its promise to halt imports from the United States, giving a profound lift to a nation embarrassed about its perennial role as a supplicant.

With the population swelling at a rate of 13 million a year—almost twice the size of New York City's population—the nation faced a bitter setback last year when only about 104 million tons of grain were harvested. In the current farm year—1972-1973—the yield is expected to hover around 100 million tons, a crisis figure.

What makes the drought even more depressing is the fact that India's 9.5-million-ton buffer grain stock, carefully saved as a cushion against shortages, has dropped by at least six million tons. "It is now a perilous situation," said one Western economist who has worked closely with the Indian Government.

Although prominent Government officials. including Annasaheb P. Shinde, the Agriculture Minister, insist that the food situation is "manageable," a rising chorus of voices is grumbling about the Government's handling of the drought.

Protests as Parliament Opens

These voices were heard when Parliament opened today amid protest and sharp opposition. Five major parties boycotted the opening, protesting the Government's handling of the drought situation. The parties also protested what one group called the "all-around failure of Government policy" in easing unemployment, food shortages, price rises and the problems of the stricken state of Andhra Pradesh, where troops have clashed violently with demonstrators seeking to split up the state.

It was the first time since independence in 1947 that five major opposition groups—ranging politically from left to right—had boycotted the President's traditional opening address to the two houses of Parliament.

The only major opposition party that did not join the boycott was the Communist party of India, one of three Communist factions and the only one that has generally supported Mrs. Gandhi.

Food for Bangladesh

The Government asserts that the war against Pakistan depleted India's food stocks by two million tons — India sent one million tons to Bangladesh after the nation, which was formerly East Pakistan, became independent and distributed a million tons of food to the 10 million refugees who streamed into India during the war.

The Government also says that emergency programs — irrigation projects, the dispatch of seeds and fertilizers to villages, work relief operations — have effectively averted widespread hunger. "The challenge has been met bravely," Mr. Shinde said recently.

Critics of the Government's food policies make numerous charges. Perhaps the most damaging allegation commonly heard is that the Government did not respond to the drought quickly enough because officials feared panic buying and further inflation.

Inaction Charged

"They knew as far back as August and September that they were in trouble, but they did very little," said one agricultural expert. "Partly it's misguided pride. They refused to admit, especially vis-à-vis the United States, that they couldn't raise enough grain for themselves."

One Western agricultural expert said: "If they hadn't made this terrific pose of independence, and reacted in August instead of last month, they could have received larger imports on far better terms than now." In fact, some economists say that the recent decision to buy wheat—with prices at the highest level in a decade mostly because of Soviet wheat purchases in the United States — meant that India was buying two million tons of food grain for $200-million, a price that would have purchased nearly three million tons last August.

There have been other charges: sufficient fertilizer and electricity to power irrigation wells was unavailable to farmers; over-all development in India has lagged, with some states spending as much on relief projects in the last two years as on irrigation projects over the last 20; corruption is rife at the village level, especially in the distribution of welfare funds, and the bureaucracy is top-heavy at all levels, creating confusion and uncertainty.

Pattern Called Familiar

As it was put in the moderate and influential journal Economic and Political Weekly, published in Bombay: "The Government, mostly existing in New Delhi, has little clue to what is happening around the country—to the distribution of fertilizers, the allocation of high-yielding seeds, the provision of irrigation water, the state of power supply, and so on. The pattern by now is wearily familiar; the complaisant officials tell the junior ministers what they want to hear, the junior ministers tell the senior ministers what they want to hear and so on till the chain ends with the Prime Minister."

The magazine added: "It is a twilight world of imperfect knowledge and uncertain estimation."

February 20, 1973

Sri Lanka's Universities Closed by Food Shortages

Special to The New York Times

COLOMBO, Sri Lanka, Oct. 6 —All five of Sri Lanka's university campuses have closed because of an acute shortage of food.

The food crisis in Sri Lanka, formerly Ceylon, has not been eased by a Government measure halving the free ration of rice and raising the price of bread and flour, two other basic items in short supply.

A shortage of foreign exchange with which to buy food abroad and the worldwide increase in the price of grain have brought about this situation.

The free rice allotment which 11 million of Sri Lanka's 13 million people depend on is now one pound a week.

October 7, 1973

Australian Wheat Rise For Export Questioned

By IAN STEWART

Special to The New York Times

SYDNEY, Australia, — Throughout Asia, countries in need of grain have been increasingly looking to the vast continent of Australia as a possible source of supply. But they are likely to be disappointed.

Australia has the potential for a significant increase in wheat production. But the Australian Wheat Board, a statutory authority created to market wheat within Australia and abroad, believes prevailing factors weigh against any major expansion of farming areas allocated for the growing of wheat.

"I don't see any increase in wheat production in Australia that is going to have a significant impact on the total world situation," said John P. Cass, chairman of the Wheat Board, in an interview at the board's headquarters in Melbourne.

He added that there had been "a lot of disencouragements" from the wheat growers' point of view.

No Positive Action

In his report on the 1972-73 season, Mr. Cass spoke of the urgent need for increased production so that Australia could play its part "in meeting the present world demand for wheat and at the same time give the industry the opportunity to reap the benefits of the high prices presently prevailing."

But in the interview he said that the board could not take any positive steps to increase production.

Mr. Cass said that some increase in wheat production could be expected as a reaction to declining demand abroad for Australian meat and wool. However, he forecast that the increase would be moderate because farmers who increased the area of land sown to wheat at the expense of other crops would be keeping in mind the long-term possibility that the favorable situation for food grain could change.

Wheat production has fluctuated over the past few years following a fairly steady increase throughout the nineteen-sixties. In the 1960-61 season, the area sown to wheat was 13.3 million acres and by the 1968-69 season it had doubled to 26.6 million acres. Production rose in the same period from about 272 million bushels to 544 million bushels.

Pinch on Trade

The Australian growth coincided, however, with expanding output elsewhere, which resulted in a decline in the world wheat trade and a rise in stocks.

One of the factors tending to discourage farmers from growing more wheat, despite the increasing world demand, is the existing payment arrangement. On delivery of his crop, a farmer is given what is called a "first advance," now pegged at $1.80 a bushel, or less than half the current export price of about $4.80.

Subsequent payments are made as revenue accrues to the Australian Wheat Board for sales at home and abroad. A farmer may have to wait from two to four years before he is fully compensated for his crop.

Mr. Cass has called for a "substantially higher first advance" and recommended that payments to farmers be completed within 15 months. But this would require agreement by the central bank, which provides the board's financing.

Delivery quotas were imposed and by the 1970-71 season, the area in wheat production had fallen to 16 million acres and production had declined to about 250 million bushels.

Some expansion in the area sown to wheat occurred in the 1971-72 and 1972-73 seasons but severe drought condtions resulted in a production figure of only 235 million bushels in the latter years.

In the 1973-74 season, production topped 409 million bushels but output is not expected to register any significant increase in the 1974-75 season and may even down slightly. The area sown to wheat during the last season was about 22 million acres. It is expected to be about the same or a little less for the next season.

The quotas, meanwhile, have been raised, with a total of 54 million bushels now permissible. At the discretion of the Minister for Primary Industry, Senator Kenneth Wriedt, production could be expanded by another 73 million bushels.

Revaluations of the Australian dollar—by 7 per cent in December, 1972, and another 11 per cent in February, 1973—considerably reduced the number of local dollars that Australia's wheatgrowers got for their exports, another factor discouraging expansion over the past two years.

Mr. Cass said growers would have been "in real trouble" if not for the world shortage of wheat and resultant escalation of prices.

The wheat board has received an increasing number of inquiries for supplies this year, and Mr. Cass said the country could not supply all the quantities requested this year and would have insufficient wheat next year "to meet all of th sales opportunities that could be presented to us."

India, China and the Soviet Union are among the countries expected to be in the market.

Mr. Cass added: "We know that Japan will be seeking bigger quantities or at least a quantity equal to what it took. They would have taken more this year but we didn't have the grades they wanted."

Export Availability

If Australian production in 1973-74 is around the 400 million bushel mark, domestic requirements and the amount withheld by farmers can be expected to account for about 140 million bushels. This will leave about 260 million bushels for export.

An indication of the strength of the demand earlier this year was the interest being expressed by various countries in long-term wheat supply arrangements with Australia. The Wheat Board, which has long-term agreements with China, Egypt and Zambia, was approached by East Germany, India, Bangladesh, North Korea and others for supplies spread over periods of up to five years.

Although Australia is happy with its existing long-term agreements, which include an agreement to supply China with 40 million bushels in 1974 and 55 million to 66 million bushels in each of the following two years, all the new requests were turned down.

While long-term agreements set a basis for production and guarantee market, Mr. Cass said, the board feels production is not sufficiently reliable to warrant any new commitments of this nature "without jeopardizing sales to other regular markets."

Mr. Cass said this attitude was based on the assumption that the area sown to wheat in Australia was unlikely to expand much beyond 24 million acres in the present uncertain climate and that yields might vary anywhere between 12 and 22 bushels an acre.

August 8, 1974

INDIA LOSES 10% OF STORED GRAINS

Rodents and Insects Among Causes of Waste

NEW DELHI, Dec. 8 (UPI)—In food-short India, where the Government has had to go shopping in the United States and the Soviet Union, millions of tons of food a year are lost to pests, poor storage and bad transportation—enough to feed 50 million people for one year.

India so far this year has bought nearly three million tons of food from the United States and accepted a $2-million "food loan" from the Soviet Union.

The Industrial Development Minister, Chidambaram Subramaniam, said recently: "India is losing a minimum of 10 per cent of grains during storage, and by insects, rodents, fungi and fire each year. This works out to a minimum of about 10 million tons—a little more than the amount by which we fall short of our needs."

Big Money Loss

"In other words," Mr. Subramaniam said, "some people go hungry, or precious foreign exchange is used, not because we have not produced enough, but because we have not taken adequate care of the output."

An official of the Food Corporation of India, which looks after the procurement and distribution of food in the country, said "this 10 per cent loss is not very high in comparison to world standards. But, for a country like India, this food wasted can easily feed 50 million people annually." He said that in terms of hard cash it meant a loss of $1-billion a year.

India's annual food production has varied from 94 million to 108.4 million tons in the last five years. Some 96 million tons are expected this year. This works out to about 1.1 pound daily for each of India's 560 million people.

Nearly 70 per cent of the grain produced in India is kept by the farmers for personal consumption and for next year's sowing. The rest enters organized trade channels for marketing, either private or governmental.

Poor Storage Techniques

Though India has made important strides in food production, she still is using antiquated techniques; it is common to see farmers cutting their crops with sickles and drying them on the roads.

An agricultural scientist said that storage in rural areas was so old-fashioned that nearly 25 per cent of certain grains was lost because of high humidity and temperature, which are conducive to rapid multiplication of insects and rodents.

He said that the actual loss was greater since insects consumed the most nutritious portion of the grains and contaminated the rest. Molds that grow on badly stored grains also become active under high moisture and temperature conditions and produce poisonous toxins, he said.

Then there are the rats. A recent study by the National Institute of Communicable Diseases said the number of rats in the country was nearly 10 billion. "These rodents eat away 26 million tons each year," the study said.

December 9, 1973

Food an Obsession in Misery-Ridden Calcutta

By **BERNARD WEINRAUB**
Special to The New York Times

CALCUTTA, India — This is a hungry city. It is a place where thousands "survive" each day on a slice of bread or a bowl of rice, a potato or a scrap of garbage.

It is a metropolitan area of nine million people where the line between life and death seems precariously thin. Long a stricken city, it is now beset by tens of thousands of impoverished peasants who have surged in over the last few months because of hunger and drought in surrounding West Bengal and such neighboring eastern states as Bihar and Orissa.

Rice and wheat, the dietary essentials, are in short supply. Fish, chicken, vegetables and the spices that are an important part of Indian fare are out of the grasp of millions. Prices have climbed inexorably, and the lives of middle-class clerks, shopkeepers, teachers and businessmen are tormented. Food — its cost and availability, its preparation and consump-

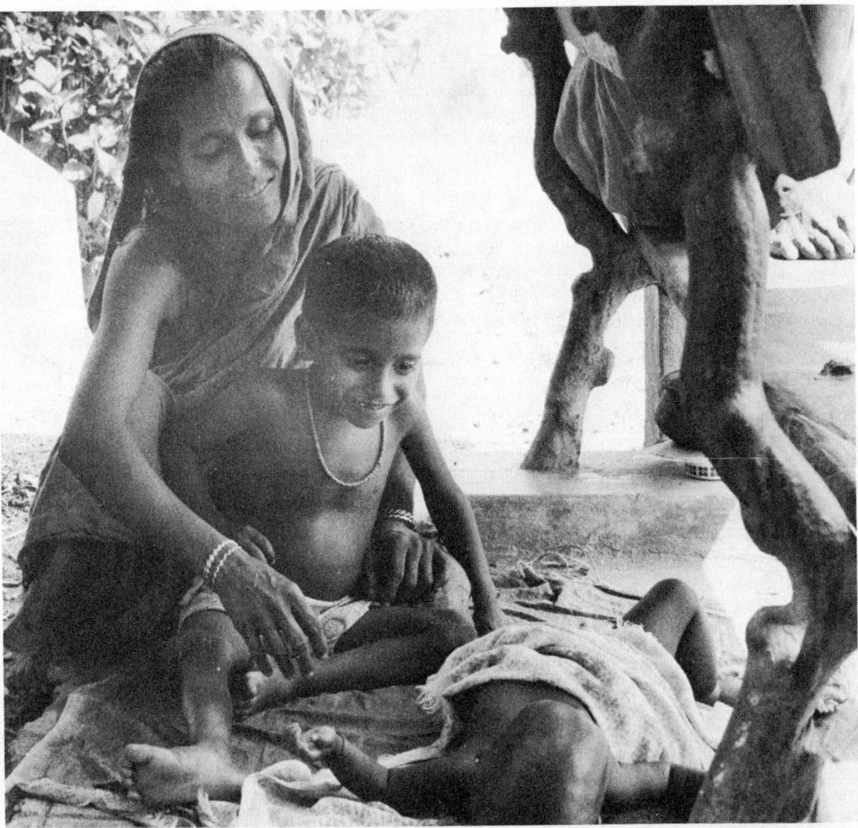

Noorjehan, who fled with her four children from a village where they could get nothing to eat, tends her ailing daughter on a street in Calcutta. They sleep on the pavement.

nine years in a Calcutta bustee, a mud hut that rents for $3 a month.

In a single room 9 or 10 people cook, eat, argue, study, make love and sleep.

There are only eight ration cards for the family. It is too complicated to get cards for the younger children, Mrs. Haque said, because the clerks are nasty and the lines are too long.

The weekly ration lasts four days. There is a rice dish in the morning, mixed with a boiled vegetable, and a wheat chapati, a thin bread, at night. Mrs. Haque spends her days preparing dhal, a lentil sauce, cooking the chapati and rice, and shopping.

On the fifth day of the week the family cuts back. Last year Mrs. Haque could afford spices, bananas, biscuits, some carrots and sweets. This year prices have doubled. "We suffer through the fifth and sixth days," she said in Bengali. "We take one meal. I take the last portion, and nothing is left over now."

"There's so little we can afford, and we go without food, except for the baby," Mrs. Haque said. "Sometimes the children cry. Sometimes I cry. It is not enough. It is never enough. We are all half-starved." ●

Photographs for The New York Times by BERNARD WEINRAUB

tion, its quality and taste — is an obsession.

Government officials and relief workers voice alarm. "We may just tide over this crisis," a senior state official said. A relief worker commented: "There's not much starvation in Calcutta, but there's so much hunger now. For a person to starve in Calcutta, he would have to be in social isolation— either a crazy person or an old and sick person who literally can't cry out for help. People are not starving, but they're at the bottom."

If Calcutta always seems on the precipice—it has long served as a metaphor for urban disaster—the food problem this year is especially dangerous. Like a vacuum, Calcutta sucks in thousands of tons of rice and wheat a week from state and national stocks. This year the production is dismal, reserves have dwindled and the food bins here threaten to go bare.

●

Akhtari Haque, a lithe, long-fingered woman, speaks with fatigue through dry lips, her eyes half-closed. She has eight children, ranging in age from 2 to 22. Her husband earns $35 a month as a tailor. The family has lived for

Children on a cloth spread beside the gutter. In the city, 200,000 people are homeless.

Calcutta exists on a ration system that seems vulnerably simple. Although statistics are slippery, this, roughly, is the food situation:

There are 9.3 million ration-card holders in West Bengal, 8.5 million of them in the Greater Calcutta area. One day a week people line up at the 2,400 ration shops in the state to get their weekly allotments.

The rations for the city have gone steadily down. In 1972 an adult Calcuttan received nearly eight pounds of food grain weekly—then considered a reasonably adequate diet since it meant the daily consumption of at least a pound of wheat or rice (children receive half rations).

In 1973 the weekly ration was cut to between 4.6 and 4.8 pounds; this year it is 4.4 pounds, and even this seems precarious. Late in July the vital rice ration was cut by 25 per cent, but the wheat ration was increased to keep the weekly total from falling below 4.4 pounds.

The wheat ration is in the form of a coarse flour known as atta, which is pounded and baked into bread or used in stews and gruels.

Until the rice cutback wheat cost about 8 cents a pound and rice was about 10 cents. On the open market the prices were more than triple.

Calcutta receives its food from the Central Pool, the Government's supplies. Because the national procurement and distribution system is in even more disarray than ever, Calcutta officials are doubtful that they can keep the city fed.

Dr. Gopal Das Nag, the Acting Food Minister of West Bengal, said in an interview that the state was receiving a monthly supply of 50,000 tons of rice and 80,000 tons of wheat from the Government. However, other officials place the figures at 40,000 tons each.

Furthermore, some sources say that Government shipments have occasionally been even more deficient. In June only 18,000 tons of rice arrived, they say, and the flow was dismal last month.

The problem in Calcutta is intensified by the hundreds of thousands without ration cards: the 200,000 who live on the streets, where the gutter serves as a bathroom; the thousands in bustees; the floating populace of the destitute, beggars, homeless children, families. Desperate and terrified, they are all in the shadow of starvation.

●

Noorjehan, a frail, wide-eyed woman in her thirties, lives on the pavement on Chowringhee, the main avenue in the downtown center. She has four small children with her; her husband is dying of tuberculosis in a coastal village.

She came here six months ago because there was no food in the village. She begs with one or two of her half-naked children, who range in age from 5 months to 5 years. The other children beg on their own and pick through refuse cans. When it rains the family sleeps beneath a park bench. She says the children are always screaming for food.

Each morning, Mrs. Noorjehan gets a bagful of chick-peas from a Roman Catholic charity. The children line up at night outside restaurants whose proprietors dole out leftovers.

"People do not have much to give any more," Mrs. Noorjehan said in Bengali. "No one has money. There are too many children beggars now. No one wants to give them anything."

The mother is illiterate and the children have no hope of going to school. Mrs. Noorjehan is trying to breast-feed her infant, which has dysentery. Her daughter is frightened of the city and has stopped talking. Her sons run wild.

"I am too ashamed to go back to the village," she said, adding: "There is no food there, nothing. Everyone is in trouble."

●

Although officials insist that no one has died of starvation in Calcutta recently, there are dozens—perhaps hundreds—of deaths weekly from dehydration, dysentery, cholera and tuberculosis.

At Mother Teresa's home for dying destitute people, an associate, Sister Agnes, said: "The people are suffering so much. We see it. It's hard, it's very difficult, it's getting worse. The prices have gone up. People are hungrier."

"By nutritional standards some of these people should be dead," a foreign relief worker said. "You see some children eating grass, rats, the green scum off tanks."

A survey has found that 98 per cent of the children under age 4 are undernourished and that the avearge Calcuttan suffers from acute vitamin deficiency.

"Everyone's hungry now," said Maj. Dudley Gardiner, a former British Army officer who runs the Salvation Army social-service center, which feeds 5,800 people a day. "Infant mortality is very high, but if they survive the first 12 months in all of this filth, they get robust. They seem to thrive."

"Even my supply is down and I begin to worry about the shipments coming in," he added.

CARE, the Salvation Army, Mother Teresa and other charities maintain daily feeding programs. The state provides three slices of bread for 40,000 children daily.

"These children will get the bread, squirrel it in their shirt and run home," a relief worker said. "Everybody is so close to the borderline."

The most searing scenes are visible. A child watches another eat an ice-cream stick. When the ice cream is finished and the wooden stick tossed in the gutter, the watcher picks it up and sucks it. On the Howrah Bridge a woman squats in the center of the crowded road and picks up grains of rice that have fallen from trucks.

●

Mrs. Dorothy Henderson, whose grandfather was English, and her friend, Mani, also an Anglo-Indian, go to the Salvation Army every day at 12:30 P.M. for their only meal of the day—a curry of vegetables, flour, tomato sauce, apples and soya bean soup. They eat in silence and then lift their bowls and lick the remaining drops of gravy.

It is only in the last two months that the two women have gone to the Salvation Army. "I take tea in the morning," Mrs. Henderson said, "and this is what I have during the day."

"I've got nothing and no one," she went on, with a shrug. "I have some relatives in Sheffield, but I haven't heard from them in years. It's only in the last year, with the prices and all, that I couldn't make out. I'm a 60-year-old woman. I can't work. I'm scared, a bit."

Her friend said: "I had two ration cards and both were stolen. The last time, a man just grabbed it at the fruit stand and ran. I went back for another ration card and the clerk called me a parasite."

Shaking her head, Mrs. Mani continued:

"My husband died 18 years ago. I wanted to leave Calcutta but I couldn't. And now look at the prices. How can you live?

"The vegetable men used to be so nice to me. They used to call me Mem-sahib. They used to give me a nice little concession, an extra fruit here and there. The older men were kind, but these young boys are rough."

"Can you imagine?" she said abruptly, referring to the official clerk. "That man called me a parasite." Her face was wet with tears. "The nerve! the nerve! A parasite!"

Mrs. Henderson leaned toward her and said: "Hush up! Stop!" Mrs. Mani smiled and nodded.

●

As the center of eastern India Calcutta was founded on a malarial swamp 285 years ago by British merchants seeking to expand trade with the heartland. The port, growing chaotically out of three marshy villages, became the headquarters of the British East India Company, which dominated trade.

Appropriately, Calcutta's diety—and its namesake—is Kali, the Hindu goddess of death, who represents, according to one commentary, "the supreme night, which swallows all that exists."

After independence from Britain and the partition of the subcontinent in 1947, the already-jammed metropolitan area was swollen by 1.5 million refugees from what had become East Pakistan, now Bangladesh. Since then the foul-smelling city's erosion and decay—its inability to cope even minimally with sanitation, water supply, transport and housing—have been exploited by politicians and journalists, overwhelmed social scientists and aid agencies and embarrassed the Indian Government.

As for the current food crisis, West Bengal—a state of 60 million that is one of the sickest in India—has received less than a third of its goal of 500,000 tons of rice. That is what the state government sought to purchase, at a fixed price, to feed the Calcutta area and hard-hit rural districts.

Affluent farmers and traders have failed to heed the state's demands, mostly because hoarding and smuggling are extraordinarily profitable. Moreover, the state has failed to take tough measures against them since they are politically powerful contributors to the governing Congress party.

"The situation would not have been as desperate as it actually is had not the Government's procurement drive been such a dismal failure," said The Hindustan Standard, a Calcutta newspaper. "Two factors were responsible. First, administrative incompetence abetted by corruption; secondly, lack of political will. And the latter perhaps is the more important factor."

Enmeshed with the political constraints are subtle but powerful changes in West Bengal, particularly landlessness, which is increasing sharply. One estimate says that landless agricultural laborers, who were 15 per cent of the work force in 1961, were 26 per cent in 1971.

•

Banchu, who drives a ricksha, came to Calcutta from Barauni, a village in Bihar, about two years ago. He had three children, one of whom died in the village.

Mr. Banchu earns about 3.5 rupees a day, or nearly 50 cents. He sleeps in his ricksha, bathes outdoors and spends most of his money on food — chattu, coarse grain rolled into a pastry ball mixed with chillies and onion. He tries to send his wife a dollar a month.

Echoing others, Mr. Banchu said that no one in Calcutta had money, and his earnings had fallen. Even the rich are walking to work, and Mr. Banchu said that his friends who wash cars or watch them in parking places outside hotels and restaurants were in trouble.

Prices are frightening, he said. A dhoti, a loose cotton wraparound that cost 21 cents last year costs 40 cents now. Roasted corn cost a cent and a half last year and 4 cents now. How can a man live? asked Mr. Banchu.

Another ricksha driver, Sarjad Mohammed, a tough, aggressive man who is a bachelor, said he had raised his prices. Six months ago he charged 12 cents for a 600-yard ride—from one end of Wellesley Street to the other; now he demands 16 cents. "I manage to stay alive," he said with a grin.

•

To officials the hopes for keeping Calcutta fed rest on increased rice production in West Bengal and, in the long run, on lifting the darkness and misery in such neighboring states and Bihar and Orissa. As long as they remain at the mercy of the primitive plow and the bullock, and in the grip of large landowners, the peasants will stream into Calcutta.

"We still wait for the rain god in India," said Shyamal Ganguly, an agricultural specialist and journalist. "After 27 years of freedom we still have so little.

"We could do miracles in eastern India if we had the water, the insecticides, the fertilizer. It's not the lack of imagination and skill at the bottom—we have hard-working farmers, some of the best in the world. It's the lack of imagination and skill at the top."

•

Outside the Grand Hotel on Chowringhee: "Hey, mister, shine your shoes, please? Very hungry. No food today. Hungry baby. Please, mister! Shine your shoes, O.K. Tomorrow; you promise, tomorrow, tomorrow. I see you tomorrow. You promise, tomorrow. Tomorrow. . . ."

September 5, 1974

United Press International

Indian women marching on Government House in Bombay on Wednesday to protest against the high cost of living

New Delhi Is Blamed for the Worsening Food Crisis

By BERNARD WEINRAUB
Special to The New York Times

NEW DELHI, Sept. 11—Prime Minister Indira Gandhi and her advisers have come under increasingly bitter criticism as a result of the intensifying food crisis in India.

Economists, agricultural specialists, politicians and journalists maintain that the Government has bungled the situation by failing to develop coherent policies, concentrating on heavy industry and relying on food imports.

As a result of the policies, the critics say, the production of wheat and rice, the basis of the diet of the 580 million people, has faltered. At the same time, they say, insufficient attention has been paid to increasing the output of the fertilizer vital to improved yields.

According to the critics, the Government, by failing to focus on the crucial role of agriculture, has distorted the priorities of a nation in which 80 per cent of the people live on farms. They say it must accept a sizable share of the blame for the food problems.

The Government attributes lagging output to the absence of imported fertilizer, insecticides and seed. Moreover, it maintains that hoarding among farmers and grain dealers is helping to increase prices.

Dr. B. S. Minhas, a prominent economist and former adviser to Mrs. Gandhi, has said that the Government has steadily decreased outlays for agricultural development in the last three years. "The neglect of agriculture is unpardonable," he added.

Another critic has said: "Our ideology dictated, while common sense deplored, that we invest in basic heavy industries instead of agriculture and production of consumer goods."

Too Little Fertilizer

Fertilizer plants, of which there are too few, are running at less than 60 per cent of capacity, which experts attribute to mismanagement and power shortages. The procurement of food by the Government, which distributes wheat flour and rice in urban ration shops, and import planning have gone "haywire," another critic said. Hoarding and accelerating inflation, plus the soaring cost of oil, have deepened the problems.

"The present crisis is indeed a crisis of frustrated expectations, of patience wearing thin, where millions have waited for years for a better deal and better food," Dr. D. K. Rangnekar, editor of The Economic Times, wrote recently.

"In our country, where so many areas are as often parched as not and where crop failures are an unfortunate feature of a long history, people justifiably expect national policy to build on experience, anticipate a setback and insure efficient management of the food economy. Unfortunately, food management has been less than efficient."

Mrs. Gandhi, who has summoned the Chief Ministers of India's states to New Delhi next week to discuss food problems, is touring the country to exhort farmers and officials to step up production. In one state, Maharashtra, she told officials publicly that she was disappointed in the level of production there in recent years.

What one expert has termed the bankruptcy of policy is reflected in food production. In the 1970-71 agricultural year, ending in June, the crop was 108 million tons; in the 1973-74 year the total fell to 103 million tons while the population increased by 36 million.

Officials are especially apprehensive now because reserves have dwindled to about two million tons, the rationing system in the cities is under severe stress and drought has struck the north. Hunger—perhaps even starvation—is on the increase. Imports are deemed vital, with officials saying privately that 4 million to 11 million tons are needed in the next six to eight months.

A parliamentary committee's report said that over the last five years the Government had treated the production of fertilizer in "a leisurely manner" and had not paid "as much attention to the use of fertilizers for agricultural production as it deserves."

Although the Government has now undertaken an ambitious fertilizer program, the failure in recent years to sanction projects quickly, to issue licenses to private concerns and to provide the needed foreign exchange has severely increased the shortage. Since a ton of chemical nutrients yields 9 to 10 tons of food grain, even a slight change in production has an impact on supply.

Last year India used 2.7 million tons of fertilizer. Of this she produced 1.4 million tons, importing the rest. The initial production goal of four million tons was not met because of power shortages, the inability to get raw materials abroad and mismanagement.

This year, according to reliable estimates, production will probably remain the same, but imports are uncertain, and some sources say that India will be fortunate if consumption reaches the same level as last year. Others say it may be three million tons—even that a melancholy figure since farmers could consume double or even triple that amount.

'Obvious Needs' Ignored

Dr. Minhas, a member of the Planning Commission who resigned in anger last year to protest Government policy, said that the yearly outlay for agriculture had declined to $850-million in the current agricultural year from $1.03-billion last year and $1.1-billion the year before. With inflation running at 30 per cent a year, the real outlay is even less.

Prem Shankar Jha, another economist, has written in The Times of India:

"The main needs of any poor country are obvious—food, clothing, shelter, health and gainful employment. This may be precisely the reason **why they are so often ignored. One only has to turn the pages of the successive plan documents to notice the stepmotherly treatment which the planners have given to these basic goals.**

"The share of agriculture in successive plans has dwindled from 31.4 per cent in the first plan (1951-56) to 20.7 per cent in the fourth (1969-74). It has been slashed further in the annual plan for 1974-75."

Furthermore, economists point out, the per-capita availability of such basic necessities as cereals and legumes, edible oils and cloth has declined in the last 10 years.

In the view of most experts the so-called green revolution is faltering because the muscle behind it has weakened. The shift from traditional methods in the nineteen-sixties through the use of high-yield seeds, irrigation, improved equipment, chemical fertilizer and insecticides resulted in a production breakthrough and led India to proclaim that she was self-sufficient.

Nonetheless, per-acre wheat yields have declined in the Punjab, the most productive state, because the high-yield seeds have been prone to disease, and fertilizer, irrigation and insecticids have been inadequate. Moreover, policy decisions and administration have proved tradition-bound and, according to the critics, incapable of dealing with technological needs.

September 13, 1974

Sri Lanka, Short of Food, Faces an Economic Crisis

By BERNARD WEINRAUB
Special to The New York Times

COLOMBO, Sri Lanka, May 6 — At dawn hundreds of people wait in bread lines. Elderly men and women pick through garbage. Thieves harvest vegetables and rice in the countryside.

Although the earth is bountiful in Sri Lanka, which was formerly Ceylon, the nation of 13 million has a critical food shortage. Moreover, it is going broke, jolted by inflation, torn by internal dissension and plainly alarmed about the future.

Prime Minister Sirimavo Bandaranaike, a tough politician and a Socialist, said recently that the economic crisis had "almost squeezed the breath out of us—we are literally fighting to survive."

Mrs. Bandaranaike, who is the target of bitter attack, repeatedly pronounces a single, stark slogan for her nation: "Produce or perish."

People Are Well Fed

What makes the crisis at once melancholy and bizarre is that the Ceylonese, because of Government largesse, have been among the best fed, best educated and healthiest people in South Asia. Their fertile tropical Indian Ocean island, the size of West Virginia, is covered with dense vegetation.

Perhaps the fundamental reason for Sri Lanka's plight is that the cost of food imports has spiraled while export earnings have remained stationary. A blend of Government mismanagement of farmland, meager incentives to growers, the take-over of private estates under land reform and the residue of colonial tradition—the British ignored food production to spur tea and rubber exports—has left a lush nation virtually begging for rice and wheat.

At one stage last month, some sources say, Sri Lanka had only two weeks' rice supply in stock. An emergency shipment of 40,000 tons from China averted an immediate crisis. Other nations selling food here are Australia, Pakistan, the Soviet Union, Canada, the United States and even India, which has serious food problems of her own.

A diplomat remarked that Sri Lanko was living a ship-to-mouth existence." An economist said: "The country is now operating on a week-to-week basis. We check how much comes in and how much goes out. We don't think beyond the week. We can't."

$2-Billion in Debt

The nation is about 2-billion in debt to other nations and is increasingly unable to get loans because of its poor credit position. This year it will spend about two-thirds of its foreign-exchange earnings, or about $300-million, just on imports of rice and wheat, whose cost has tripled in the last two years.

In the meantime the key exports — tea, rubber and coconut, which account for 80 per cent of the foreign-exchange earnings — have failed to generate enough to meet the food bills. The reasons for this include fertilizer shortages, bureaucratic restrictions and low investment in new equipment, plus export prices, especially of tea, which have not followed those of grain.

"It's a spectacular non-achievement," an economist said. "They're importing 50 per cent more than they're exporting. They're broke, and because they're forced to spend so much money on food, they have very little left for petroleum, fertilizer and manufactured products to keep the economy going."

Compounding the crisis, according to critics of the Government, is an ideological addiction to take-overs, coupled with a tradition of far-reaching social-welfare measures, which are extravagant and perhaps crippling.

Big Rise in Population

Even Ceylonese concede that the decades-old system of free medical care, free education and free food dole each week to every nontaxpayer — the vast majority — has proved economically unfeasible, especially with a population that has doubled in 25 years. In addition the Government subsidizes and underwrites wheat, sugar and flour at unrealtistic low prices.

It would be political suicide to end the handouts, and Mrs. Bandaranaike's coalition United Front was swept to power in 1973 on the promise of supplying more free rice than ever.

Now the Government has cut the ration of rice, flour and sugar to about three pounds a week, compared with as much as 10 pounds a week in the nineteen-fifties. The rice ration is about a pound and a half a week, compared with four pounds last spring.

An indication of the topsy-turvy quality of politics is that the Opposition leader, J. R. Jayewardene of the United National party, said that he would make the food ration eight pounds a week if he came to power.

Because of the free education in a nation where half the population is under 30—and because the floundering economy is still based on agriculture — about 700,000 educated people are without jobs. This is a main source of unrest.

In 1971 this group staged an insurrection against the Government that was quietly but harshly crushed by security forces. The number of insurgents rounded up and killed runs in the thousands.

Mrs. Bandaranaike, whose husband, S.W.R.D. Bandaranaike, was assassinated in 1959 when he was Prime Minister, heads an anticapitalist coalition of three parties — her own Sri Lanka Freedom party, which emphasizes "democratic socialism," the pro-Moscow Communist party and the Troskyite Lanka Sama Samaja party.

Private investment is under severe constraints and the Government has spurred a measure that allows the nationalization of any company—a move that has virtually dried up foreign investment.

A ceiling on disposable income of $330 a month after taxes as well as limitation of landholdings to 50 acres has further curtailed investment and production.

"The only salvation lies in making the country self-sufficient," the Prime Minister told a May Day crowd. "We are facing a crisis such as the country has never yet faced in its history."

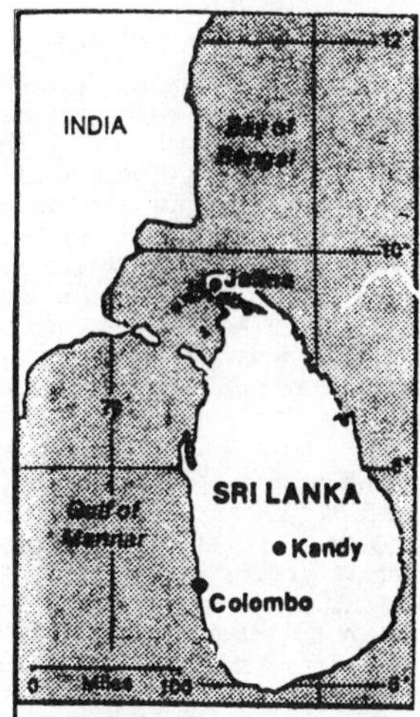

The New York Times/May 13, 1974

May 13, 1974

Disputes Add to Bangladesh Food Crisis

By BERNARD WEINRAUB
Special to The New York Times

DACCA, Bangladesh, June 10—**Bangladesh, torn by economic crisis, is facing a food shortage complicated by sharp conflict among claims and growing uncertainty about the scope of the scarcities.**

At the heart of the tangled problem is an unresolved question: Will Bangladesh receive enough food in 1973 from overseas donors to avert widespread hunger, possibly famine?

United Nations officials say that the 2.4 million tons of imported food expected by the end of the year will tide the country over; Bangladesh officials now insist that a half-million tons more of food is needed because of recent monsoons and floods that destroyed crops.

Intertwined with this are a set of economic variables that have begun to disturb local relief officials. Essentially, economists now say that the numbers, the estimates and the predictions issued publicly by both the Government of Bangladesh and the United Nations are based on fragmentary data that are subject to wide discrepancies.

'All We Can Do Is Guess'

"We operate on agreed fictions here, and this is the problem," said an official. "We know there's a human need but to define it, to quantify it, is impossible. All we can do is guess."

Examples of this abound. In his United Nations food report that is the cornerstone for aid to Bangladesh, Dr. Robert F. Chandler, who headed the international research institute that developed high-yield "miracle rice" in the Philippines in the nineteen-sixties, uses a population estimate of 75 million for this country.

The report sets a figure of 11.5 million tons of food as Bangladesh's requirement this year, based on the 75 million people eating 15 ounces per capita each day. To meet that requirement, the United Nations says that Bangladesh needs about 2.4 million tons of imported food.

Officials say that the population has been variously estimated at 72 million to 77 million and that a "working figure" of 75 million has been adopted. The 15 ounces of foodgrain, meaning rice or wheat, represents about 1,500 calories, a sustenance level but not a minimum level.

Flood Damage Debated

The Food and Civil Supplies Minister, 71-year-old Phani Busan Majumdar, said in an interview that recent rains and floods had "seriously damaged" crops and that 300,000 to 500,000 tons of food were needed badly. Relief officials, however, say that aerial surveys indicate that the recent heavy rains resulted in "slight and certainly not widespread damage."

Officials outside the United Nations maintain that it has deliberately sought to avoid controversy with the Bangladesh Government, which has repeatedly stressed the need for more food. "The U.N. keeps quiet and the Bangladesh Government makes all these dire statements about famine," said an agricultural expert who has been here for several years. "Do they need more food now beyond the U.N.'s estimate?" he asked. "I seriously doubt it."

The problem is compounded because the Government, which is now setting its food needs for 1974, has settled tentatively on a population figure of 76.2 million and has raised the minimum daily food requirement per person to 15.5 ounces. "It will project a huge consumption requirement, and you then panic because of the gap between what's needed and what's produced," a Western economist said. "And yet, no one knows what the population is and how much food is absolutely necessary."

The Food Minister, Mr. Majumdar, defended the increase in the minimum food calculation, saying: "Five years ago it was 18 ounces per capita and we had to cut it back. Our people have suffered enough now. Why shouldn't we raise our food figure?"

What makes the problem murkier is that the food imports are actually distributed to a relatively small and ever-changing number of Bengalis—at most, 20 per cent of the population, and generally in urban areas. How much food the rest of the nation eats a day or a week or a month is uncertain. "The question is," said a Western economist, "how much food do you really need and how do you have to buy in the face of all the other needs in the country?"

'Very Erratic' Deliveries

About five million people, most of them in cities, receive rations on a "statutory" basis each week. In addition, 6 million to 10 million are on a "modified" ration system, mostly from July to November when food supplies are low here. About 80 per cent of the population is dependent upon agriculture and receives little, if any, food aid.

The delivery of rations is, in the words of one relief official, "very erratic"; the amount distributed changes weekly; corruption and theft are rife; on any week or month no relief official is certain how much food goes where.

Since the three-week war in December, 1971, which resulted in the birth of Bangladesh in what had been East Pakistan, the United Nations has undertaken a relief effort here of about $1.3-billion. Now the United Nations' emergency mission, under a French diplomat, Francis Lacoste, is being phased out. Officials say that funds for the operation are allocated only until the end of the year.

The nation's economy is in dismal condition. Food prices have risen as much as 100 per cent in a year and a half. Nationalization of industry, coupled with labor unrest and "managerial ineptitude," a phrase heard often, have brought a critical drop in production.

The production of jute, the main industry, is at 40 per cent of capacity. Exports are expected to total $375-million this year when planners were hoping for $500-million. Accumulated orders are so backed up at the docks at Chittagong that ships arrive and depart unladen.

Other Imports Cut

A Bengali economist, optimistic three months ago, said: "We've been very unhappy with the performance of the economy—its managerial incompetence, its labor indiscipline, its general disorder. What makes the labor problems here somehow inexplicable is that the pro-Government unions and youth groups have rampaged through industrial plants, causing chaos in the hunt for 'corrupt and Pakistan-minded' officials."

The Government is spending at least $140-million on purchases of food, forcing itself to cut importation of such items as fertilizer, water pumps and raw materials, which Bangladesh also needs.

"It's a consumption-oriented Government that feels under terrific pressure to deliver as much food as it got during the Pakistani period," said an economist. "These are Opposition politicians, now in power, who are very much obsessed with shortage issues. In a country as poor as this, it is a question of priority, and their priority is not to tighten belts, but to say 'we'll give you as much as we possibly can.'"

June 12, 1973

Subsiding Floods Leave Dacca Desperate for Aid

By KASTURI RANGAN
Special to The New York Times

DACCA, Bangladesh, Aug. 14—Flood-devastated Bangladesh is desperately seeking help to pull through a developing calamity of epidemics and famine.

"Without assistance from friendly countries," said Abdul Momen, Minister for Relief and Rehabilitation, "anything might happen."

What has frightened the Government of this new nation, which was formerly part of Pakistan, is not so much the floods as their aftermath. The mighty Himalayan rivers, the Ganges, the Meghna and the Brahmaputra, which flow through Bangladesh and into the Bay of Bengal, rose simultaneously in recent weeks, flooding two-thirds of the country. Some 80 per cent of the summer crop was destroyed along with the seedlings planted for the main winter crop.

Officials estimate that at least 40 per cent of the annual food output of 12 million tons was lost in the floods, which are finally subsiding after nearly a month. The country already imports two million tons of grain a year to help feed its 75 million people.

To provide relief to about three million people who have been uprooted by the floods and are now living in Government relief centers, 700,000 tons of grain are needed.

Mr. Momen said that in response to appeals, half a dozen countries had given "token" aid. Only 4,000 tons of grain have been promised, mostly by the

Associated Press

A boy guiding his mother to safety aboard a makeshift raft as floods inundated their village near Mymensing, in Bangladesh. Country has been severely stricken by flooding.

United Nations world food program. The rest of the aid is medicine, milk powder and cloth.

However Mr. Momen said that he was pleased at reports quoting a State Department spokesman as having said that the United States would be "very active" in helping Bangladesh recover from the floods.

[In Washington the State Department has announced a $4-million grant to Bangladesh for building materials to restore homes damaged by floods. The grant will also provide for the local purchase of seeds to replant crops. The State Department said that in addition, 59,000 long tons of wheat would be sent to Bangladesh. Family-size tents and blankets were being airlifted.]

In Dacca, the capital of Bangladesh, 107 relief camps serve as homes for 10,000 people uprooted by floods in the surrounding area.

The waters of the swollen Dhaleswari, a branch of the Jamuna River that skirts Dacca on the west, have reached the busy Motijheel commercial center in the eastern part of the capital. In Narayanganj, a bustling town 10 miles south of Dacca, the waters poured into most of the houses. Schools are crammed with people who have lost their homes.

Although medicine and shelter are available, flood supplies are inadequate.

"We get some wheat flour and milk powder," said Abdul Rauf, a 35-year-old casual laborer who has taken refuge here with his wife and five children. Mr. Rauf, who lived in the Narayanganj slums, now stays here without a job. His home is under 10 feet of water. He gets enough flour for one meal a day and he has cooking problems because of the lack of fuel.

The floods themselves were neither unprecedented nor unmanageable. Twenty years ago a similar flood crisis was handled by the Pakistani Government without much foreign help. Then the economy was relatively sound and the area had not gone through the disasters that have befallen Bangladesh. In 1970, three million people were killed by cyclones. And 1971 was the year of Pakistani military repression and war that led to independence. This was followed by a year of drought, and now the floods.

Already the Government, led by Sheik Mujibur Rahman, seems at the brink of economic disaster.

Faced by a severe food deficit, the country is threatened by a famine that can only be averted if it receives vast help from abroad. The immediate threats, however, are epidemics of cholera and typhoid. Most of the country's 2,000 relief camps do not have pure drinking water. As a result the two diseases have spread. According to official figures, 100 people die every day in the camps. The flood death toll has reached 1,400.

Several reasons are given for the sluggish response to appeals for foreign help. Many governments are said to have tired of frequent distress calls from Bangladesh. Some say that relief goods are misappropriated by corrupt officials and intermediaries and that the Bangladesh Government is exaggerating the situation to get more foreign aid.

Foreign observers feel that there may be substance in these allegations but it is a fact that Bangladesh is "so down and out" that she cannot fend for herself in any abnormal situation.

August 18, 1974

The Rome Food Conference Is Forgotten

Bangladesh, The Hungriest Of Them All

By BERNARD WEINRAUB

DACCA—The scenes are numbing. A woman howling with a dead infant in her arms. Naked, emaciated children sitting on pavements with tin begging cups. Old men lying on burlap bags outside markets, staring vacantly and open-mouthed at strangers.

In this nation of 75 million, probably the most underfed and overcrowded nation in the world, mass hunger and starvation is no longer a threat. It is here. It is visible, on the choking streets of Dacca. The foreigners who take taxi cabs or rickshaws struggle to read newspapers to avoid gazing.

Anywhere from 15,000 to 100,000 persons have died in recent months of starvation or malnutrition that weakened their resistance to disease. Thousands of hungry farmers have sold their land and bullocks to buy rice. There are beggars everywhere. "We are a sick nation," said a Bengali economist. "We are a nation that must beg to stay alive."

Government officials say that Bangladesh needs at least 2.3 million tons of food imports, about 20 per cent of her total requirements. So far she has obtained about 1.3 million tons, 400,000 bought commercially and the rest long-term assistance from the United States, Canada, Australia and Europe.

Even despite this aid, no nation has yet reached a point where the Malthusian nightmare seems so imminent. If the population is outstripping food supplies, if hundreds of thousands, possibly millions, are on the knife edge of starvation, if international handouts are unable to cope with the needs, it is taking place in Bangladesh.

Born in tragedy four years ago and staggering from cyclones to civil war to drought and then floods, Bangladesh, a nation about the size of Wisconsin, is a virtual metaphor for the world food shortage. Government and relief officials barely mention the Rome Food Conference that was specifically designed to assist nations such as Bangladesh but ended inconclusively.

At the moment, with the winter harvest, the immediate threat of starvation has eased. But officials are fearful of the upcoming lean months, February and March, before the spring harvest. Some Bengali officials say privately that the situation then could prove worse than the 1974 famine.

So desperate has the situation become that yesterday Prime Minister Sheikh Mujibur Rahman declared a national state of emergency. "The Government had no option but to proclaim an emergency under the compelling circumstances of repeated acts of violence, sabotage and destruction," the announcement said.

Several elements have contributed to the grave situation. Nearly half the nation was flooded last summer. The government estimated the crop loss at more than one million tons; foreign experts put the loss at 300,000 tons.

Compounding the loss was inept distribution of food and large-scale smuggling of rice into neighboring India. Again, the figures vary broadly: From 100,000 tons to as much as a million tons. "The smuggling is serious," said one foreign aid official. "Even if one per cent of your crop is smuggled out, with your population increasing by three per cent, you have a serious problem."

Specific estimates of Bangladesh's food needs are fuzzy. Relief officials say that Bangladesh has damaged her own case in the past few years, "crying wolf" about starvation. "People are cynical about Bangladesh and about all the nepotism and corruption," said one European. "The aid is still coming in. No one's stopping. But a time is going to come soon when these donor countries will have had it. You hear people talking now. They're just tired of this place."

Three years ago, the United Nations estimated that Bangladesh would need $1.5-million of foreign assistance to recover from the nine months of Pakistani army terror and three weeks of war that wrecked factories, bridges, crops, homes and railways. The war resulted in the birth of Bangladesh, the former eastern wing of Pakistan.

By next summer, nearly $3-billion will be committed to Bangladesh. But far from recovering, Bangladesh remains overwhelmed by corruption in the handling of foreign aid, a tottering bureaucracy, surging prices—the cost of rice has climbed 300 per cent since independence—natural disasters and the 3 per cent population growth. Seven babies are born here every minute, the population is growing by two million a year and will double in two decades.

Even in normal times, Bangladesh must import about ten per cent of her food needs. With the recent disasters, she must now raise that to 20 per cent.

The largest aid donors have been the United States, which has sent more than $520-million in bilateral aid, as well as India, the United Nations and the World Bank. Only in the last year, and after the repeated pleas of Sheikh Mujib, have Iraq, Saudi Arabia, Kuwait and the United Arab Emirates started assisting Bangladesh, probably the poorest Moslem nation in the world. Aid from the oil producers is now about $100-million.

Bernard Weinraub is The New York Times correspondent in the Indian subcontinent.

December 29, 1974

Java Is Lush, but Not Rich Enough to Feed All Its 80 Million People

Photographs for The New York Times · JOSEPH LELYVELD

Workers harvesting rice in Sawahrejo, Indonesia. Rice and fruits seem plentiful, but crops do not match Indonesia's population density, which in the county where Sawahrejo is situated is 2,200 a square mile.

By JOSEPH LELYVELD
Special to The New York Times

SAWAHREJO, Indonesia— The name of this hamlet in Central Java means "prosperous rice fields," and a glance at the lush landscape is enough to reach the conclusion that the word hunger ought never be uttered here.

The irrigated paddies are vivid variations on the theme of green as the grain ripens in the sun; ducks cruise the irrigation canals, evoking far-fetched comparisons to swans in an English village stream; fruit trees grow everywhere, offering a seemingly endless supply of plantain, mango and papaya, in addition to more exotic fruits with names like belimbing, jambu and nangka, whose textures and tastes are simply beyond the imagination of denizens of the Temperate Zone.

If the word hunger is rarely uttered, that is only because the Javanese—a people of elaborate politeness and reserve—regard it as unseemly to speak bluntly about their most urgent needs. In fact it soon becomes obvious that most of Sawahrejo lives on the edge of hunger.

For the fecundity of Java extends to its people, and although it has been said for decades that the saturation point had surely been reached, the population has continued to rise. Now there are about 80 million living in an area only slightly larger than the state of New York. In rural Pemalang County, where the hamlet is situated, the density is about 2,200 a square mile. If the United States had that density, its population would exceed that of the world.

In Sawahrejo 420 households—about 2,000 people in all—live on 673 acres, a little more than a square mile. The hamlet, which is divided into two clusters of houses by an irrigation canal, is neither especially well off nor especially poor by the standards of the area.

The village office and the school are set on the banks of the canal, which is crossed by a narrow bamboo bridge. Beyond the bridge is a broad path, the hamlet's main thoroughfare, which is lined on both sides by the stucco houses of the prosperous farmers and the rattan huts of those whose buildings are so small that they can be nothing more than spectators of whatever prosperity the hamlet experiences.

The first impression is of tranquility and order. Every hut on the path has a fence of some sort and all but the poorest have a gatepost with a small lantern on it.

Even when the sun is directly overhead, the path is shaded by the myriad fruit trees. And at night the kerosene flames in the lanterns glimmer beguilingly.

If Sawahrejo had several hundred fewer residents or several hundred more acres, the first impression would remain the strongest. But, finally, it is statistics that describe the place most vividly. Of the households 284 farm less than an acre; 78 are classed as landless.

Consider the case of Kayin—Indonesians typically have one name—whose holding, like that of 184 other peasants in the hamlet, is a mere fifth of an acre. It is really a patch of garden rather than a farm, and because it is so small Mr. Kayin is able to lalavish loving attention on every seedling, checking daily for weeds, insects and rats that might threaten his tiny harvest.

By careful cultivation he can reap nearly 500 pounds of rice in a good season—barely enough to sustain himself, his wife and their two surviving children. (Three other children died; in Java, a quarter of all deaths are of children under a year) How barely the land sustains them can be seen in Mr. Kayin as he trudges barefoot through the fields. At about 45—he is unsure of his exact age—he is gaunt rather than wiry, not middle-aged but old.

Mr. Kayin sells only enough rice to buy seeds for the next season and small doses of fertilizer. For his present crop, nine pounds of fertilizer, costing less than $1 even at a black-market price, was all he thought he could afford.

Not because he resists change but because he is a realist, he takes it for granted that he will never penetrate the cash economy sufficiently to be able to afford the high-yield seeds, insecticide and quantities of fertilizer that have dramatically increased the output and incomes of larger landholders in recent years. All he can hope for is opportunities to work as a day laborer in their fields at the going rate of 50 rupiahs — about 12 cents—a day, plus meals.

Such work, which he appears to find no more than 120 days in the year, provides his family with its only cash income, nearly all of which goes for cassava, the starchy root that he and other poor Javanese eat as a supplement or alternative to rice (any desirable fruit is sold). There is not much nutrition in cassava but there is bulk; when there is nothing else it staves off hunger.

Mr. Kayin does not describe himself as desperate. On the contrary, he says that he is better off than he used to be, thanks to repairs this year to an irrigation canal that flows near his field. Built in the period of Dutch colonial rule, it had silted up and fallen into disuse, leaving plots like his subject to the weather. Now, although his lack of means firmly limits his ability to increase his output, his crops are at least safe.

The condition of Wartam, a landless father of two, is much worse. For him nearly everything depends on his ability to find work, but the very pressure of population makes that a matter of chance. Even at the height of the harvest there is not enough field labor to go around.

The actual facts of Mr. Wartam's situation emerge only indirectly. Asked whether he finds work every day or whether his family has enough rice, he avoids a negative answer; a man should be able to work every day and feed his family, and Mr. Wartam does not want it to be thought that he does less than a man should.

When he works he earns 50 rupiahs. He needs 300 to buy what he deems to be an adequate amount of rice for his family. He masks the discrepancy by saying that he goes to market to buy rice whenever he is "feeling good."

That means, it develops, when he has worked for several days consecutively. "Did you work today?" he is asked.

"No, not today."

"Yesterday?"

"Not yesterday."

"This week?"

"No."

A Feudal Arrangement

Like most of Sawahrejo's landless Mr. Wartam lives on state land on the banks of an irrigation canal, the best available property in the hamlet. Irrigation officials allow the landless to grow cassava, bananas and rice in minuscule patches there. It is a personal, extralegal, basically feudal arrangement between the landless and the officials, who periodically turn up to ask for a share of whatever rice is grown or, in lieu of that, an informal cash tithe.

Mr. Wartam does not have enough land to cultivate rice, so he feeds his family on a root called perut, which is so much less appealing even than cassava that it is never on the local market, Still, it is all Mr. Wartam has available, and he offers a plate to a foreigner who has come to call. What taste the root has is vaguely turnipy, but it is mostly cellulose and barely digestible; the sensation is that of eating paper.

"Every day there are a couple of families that have nothing to eat," says Damhuri, another landless laborer, who spends most of the year as a sidewalk hawker of food in Jakarta, 200 miles to the west. When there is nothing, the landless say, they borrow from friends. But according to the landed that is not quite the whole story; not infrequently, they allege, they discover that their cassava

People of Sawahrejo posing outside a home. There are 420 households on a little more than a square mile.

plants have been uprooted or their fruit trees stripped.

Drift to the Cities

Chasmin, a neighbor of Mr. Wartam's on the canal bank, does not wait for a job to turn up. When there is no prospect of work—the usual situation — he hikes four miles to a forest and picks leaves until he has enough to form two tightly packed bundles of about 20 pounds each. The next day he hauls these six miles to the nearest market, where he sells them for 150 rupiahs, about 35 cents, to traders who use the broad, sturdy leaves for packaging.

The pressure of population can be inferred from such makeshift efforts or from the fact that women in the hamlet account for about 60 per cent of its adult population. Those men who cannot scratch out a living tend to drift off to the towns, usually Jakarta, which has been proclaimed a closed city but is actually growing faster than any other in Asia.

The pressure of numbers is not simply inferred. It is palpable, and the hamlet is aware of it as something extraordinary, especially at harvest time, when 300 to 500 people may show up to cut the rice on a mere two acres.

Observing the Old Ways

By Javanese tradition the harvest is an occasion for sharing: Anyone can take part. The work, done by hand with a blade called an ani-ani, is usually assigned to women and children, who are rewarded with a fraction of whatever they cut, an eighth or a 12th.

These days the numbers looking for work are so great that it is commonplace for people to be turned away. Kambali, a relatively prosperous farmer with a holding of three and a half acres, says that if too many harvesters show up he sometimes has to delay for a day for fear of loss through careless handling, trampling or even pilferage.

What is involved is the delicate social mechanism, the balance wheel, of the Javanese village, which has made it possible for it to absorb an ever-increasing population. Now that mechanism is being strained, not just by rising population but by the sudden injection of an element of dynamism into the economy through the new agricultural technology that is available to the minority whose holdings are large enough to be viable.

The old sense of obligation has not died. On a recent Friday an announcement was made at the village mosque inviting worshipers to the home of a landowner who was holding a traditional ceremony called slametan, in memory of his father, who died 1,000 days before.

One of the Three Biggest

After the ceremony the landowner distributed 500 boxes in the village, each crammed with bananas, rice, dried fish and chicken. In his own mind this was a necessary part of the memorial to his father; for most of the recipients it was the first good meal in days.

There are slametans before the harvest and on other important occasions such as births and marriages. But such ceremonies are no longer enough, if they ever were, to bridge the gulf that separates the prosperous farmers from the small holders and the landless.

Supadi, a retired police officer, has five irrigated acres and five and a half that are rain-fed, enough to make him one of the three biggest landowners in the hamlet. In a three-month season, he says, he needs to hire labor only on five days—one day for transplanting, three for weeding and one for the harvest.

Some prosperous farmers invest their new profits in a pilgrimage to Mecca, which costs about $1,500. Mr. Supadi's money has gone into the hamlet's most imposing house, a comfortable whitewashed structure with a bricked-in terrace where he has planted an orange tree. But he does not feel entirely secure there.

"In the coming 20 years," he said, "the situation will get worse and worse. If the landless and the poor have nothing to eat, they will become robbers, they will become hoodlums."

The 185 smallest holders in the hamlet own only 5 per cent of its land. More than half is owned by the prosperous farmers who use the new techniques and seeds, which have improved their yields by as much as 50 per cent.

There is little doubt, then, that Sawahrejo grows enough food to feed itself, but self-sufficiency is an abstraction as far as the hamlet is concerned. Only a minority of farmers have a surplus, and those who do naturally send it to market. If the rest are self-sufficient, that is only because they lack the means to be anything else.

From the perspective of the hamlet it is apparent that increasing production has no necessary bearing on the actual food consumption of the rural poor whose foothold in the local economy seems increasingly tenuous. For those who cannot count on eating rice, per capita rice consumption is a meaningless statistic.

Insofar as the local government responds to their predicament at all, it is with slogans about modernization. It offers neither work nor rations.

In Sawahrejo local government is personified in the paternalistic figure of the village headman, an army veteran named Amin Sojitno, who was installed by the military authorities in 1965. The previous headman, now said to have been a Communist, was killed in the bloody reprisals that swept Java and Bali in the wake of an attempted Communist coup d'état.

Mr. Sojitno and his wife—she is the hamlet's kindergarten teacher and family-planning officer—have worked hard to be accepted in Sawahrejo and, by all accounts, they have succeeded. But their status is essentially that of gentry. The headman rides a Honda scooter, smokes imported Dunhill cigarettes and buys the latest cassette recordings in town. On his right hand he cultivates a thumbnail more than an inch long, evidence of what is only obvious—that field labor is outside his experience.

Self-Sufficiency Distant

On Java as a whole, rice production is expanding faster than population, and it is even arguable that per capita rice consumption is higher than it has been at any time in this century, but self-sufficiency remains a vague and ever-receding goal. Last year, with the best rice harvests on record, Indonesia had to import 1.6 million tons, more than any other country in the region.

Village government has changed little in Java in the last two centuries. Essentially the headman's function is to maintain order and assist in the collection of taxes. In return he is given exclusive rights to a large amount of land instead of a salary for as long as he holds his position.

Other local officials are compensated in the same way; even the man who sweeps the village office is given an acre and a half. By definition then, it is government by the landed.

Sometimes it is alleged that this basically feudalistic system impedes development. But Mr. Sojitno is at pains to be sure that the latest methods and seeds are used on the 35 acres—three times as much as he could legally own outright—that have been set aside for him. Crops on that much land could bring in as much as $8,000 in a year, which is breathtaking by the standards of rural Java.

Mr. Sojitno, not oblivious to the plight of the small holders and the landless, hopes that eventually there will be small-scale industry in the county to employ them. In the meantime he advocates family planning.

Birth-control pills and the intrauterine device, commonly known as the loop, were first introduced in Sawahrejo two years ago. According to records kept by Mrs. Sojitno, 52 women accepted the loop and 45 women started on the pill. But the pill-takers gave up within a few months, complaining of headaches, and no loops have been accepted for a year.

It is not so much resistance to birth control as skepticism over the methods and a certain fatalism about the results. By Asian standards the rate of population increase in Central Java is relatively low—1.7 per cent a year—and with the high density the advantages of a small family are widely recognized. But high infant mortality undercuts the very notion of family planning.

'It Doesn't Matter'

The question was raised in one of the small colonies of the landless on the banks of the canal. Not a single man or woman there, it was said, had used modern contraceptives. Several times they were asked why. The answer was given by a 15-year-old named Lukimah, who had just had her first child. "It doesn't matter," she said. Asked what she meant she merely repeated herself.

In the final analysis each small holding is an overcrowded lifeboat. A young farmer named Kasmari was asked how many people had to be sustained on the slightly more than an acre and a half that his father had farmed; he recited 22 names.

Half the holding had been deeded to two elder brothers; seven siblings had equal claims on the rest. This season they contrived to rent an additional two-fifths of an acre by selling their last water buffalo. Next season there will be no buffalo to sell.

August 28, 1974

Chinese Farm Gains Impress Visitors

By BOYCE RENSBERGER

China appears to have raised agricultural production and evened the distribution of food so successfully that she seems well protected against the food shortages now afflicting the underdeveloped world, according to 10 leading American farm researchers who recently visited China.

"We were tremendously impressed everywhere we went with the high quality of Chinese farming," said Dr. Sterling Wortman, the group's leader, in an interview.

"I came away feeling I'm going to worry less about whether China is able to feed her people or not," said Dr. Wortman, a plant breeder who oversees agricultural research grants for the Rockefeller Foundation.

With nearly one-quarter of the world's people and a history of widespread poverty, malnutrition and episodic famines, China has long been a major concern of those working to improve the world food supply. Until recently the country's isolation had restricted available information about Chinese agriculture.

The 10 scientists, experts in nearly all major crops and other aspects of farming, found on a four-week tour that although China's isolation had kept her from achieving some of the scientific advances that have helped improve yields elsewhere, major strides have been made by combining traditional farming methods and domestic scientific advances.

For example, to supply growing quantities of fertilizer needed to increase yields, the Chinese have augmented the traditional use of compost, manure and human excrement with inorganic fertilizer produced by some 800 "backyard factories" that turn coal and water into nitrogen fertilizer.

Each such factory produces a few thousand tons of fertilizer a year. Together, they supplied half of China's consumption of inorganic fertilizer in 1973. The balance was derived from fertilizers produced domestically on an industrial scale or imported. In addition, China has planned or is constructing eight fertilizer factories capable of producing a thousand tons a day.

The American scientists said the backyard fertilizer plants, which produce ammonium bicarbonate, a chemical not generally used as a fertilizer outside China, appeared to be using a simple technology that might well be adapted to other areas of the world.

Dr. Norman E. Borlaug, a world authority on wheat and a member of the group, visited one of the small fertilizer plants and is preparing a report.

Dr. Wortman said he and his colleagues, who toured most of the major farming regions, by train and private vehicle, found a wide variety of other innovations and techniques that might also be adapted for use in poorer countries.

The group, organized by the American-based Committee on Scholarly Communication with the People's Republic of China, stopped in Peking, Shanghai, Nanking, Sian, and Canton and visited farms and research centers in the surrounding provinces and in Kirin Province, north of Korea.

Dry Area Not Seen

Although the group had high praise for the quality of the crops, they noted they had not visited drier western and northern regions, where agriculture might still be poor.

One of the biggest surprises to Dr. Nyle C. Brady, director of the International Rice Research Institute in the Philippines and a member of the group, was that the rice being grown was almost entirely of a new, high-yielding dwarf variety similar to the "miracle rice" developed at Dr. Brady's institute. The Chinese varieties, it turned out, had been developed before the Philippine center was established.

Members of the group also noted that special cropping systems—such as growing several crops simultaneously or in close succession on a piece of land—were widely used.

Farmers would, for example plant rows of wheat, wait for it to sprout and then plant two rows of corn between the wheat rows. Before the corn was high enough to shade the wheat, the grain would be ripe and harvested. Two months later the corn would be ready.

Chinese farmers told the scientists that this particular system yielded 40 per cent more food than would the same acreage if the two crops were planted separately.

This system is obviously impossible with American-style mechanization. But China, lacking the machinery, does have the labor for hand harvesting.

One of the American group's major conclusions was that innovations such as intercropping and backyard fertilizer production are found throughout China. One of the major problems of upgrading farming in many poor countries has been the difficulty in persuading farmers to adopt new methods.

Aided by Organization

"They have been tremendously successful in getting all available knowledge into use at the farm level," Dr. Wortman said. He added that agriculture seemed to be organized in a way that facilitated the spread of new techniques.

The basic farming unit in China is the "production team," a group of 30 to 40 households that till large individual plots of land. Each family also has its own smaller plot, mostly for its own vegetables.

From 20 to 40 production teams are organized as a "production brigade." Ten to 20 such brigades constitute a commune. A commune may include 25,000 to 30,000 people.

Income Linked to Crops

Management decisions are made at commune level, though brigade and team leaders share in responsibility. Each commune specializes in one crop, which is sold to the government. But communes also devote a portion of land to a variety of other crops in an attempt to be as self-sufficient as possible.

A family's income is determined by the success of the crop raised by its production team. The scientists said they felt that this maximized the incentive for hard work. The method contrasts with that of other collectivized-farming countries where the farmer's income depends little, if at all, on the result of his work.

In China, the government buys the team's major crop at stable prices, the scientists were told. Accountants for each production team then subtract costs from income, take out a further 6 to 7 per cent in tax for the government, and apportion the remaining money equitably among the member households.

Whether this system makes China truly self-sufficient in food has been a matter of some disagreement. Figures published by the United States Department of Agriculture show that last year China imported about six million metric tons of wheat and corn but exported 1.3 million metric tons of rice. A metric ton is 2,200 pounds.

Ton for ton, rice costs more than wheat and China has for several years sold rice and used the money to buy larger quantities of wheat. Considering that the per-capita grain consumption in China is about 400 pounds a year, the country can be said to have exported enough rice to feed about seven million people and imported enough wheat to feed 33 million.

Whether this means that 26 million people — the net difference — would have gone hungry without imports is unclear. The purchases may represent an attempt to provide more than the bare minimum of food.

The American scientists found it difficult to get exact figures on Chinese crop tonnages or per-capita production. "Whenever we asked," Dr. Wortman recalled, "they would say production is up 'twofold' or 'threefold.'"

In any event, without highly detailed information, it could be misleading to infer the adequacy of nutrition in China from crop-production statistics.

For one thing, the scientists found, each family is urged to be as self-reliant as it can. Each farm family raises most of its own vegetables and usually keeps a few chickens and pigs for eggs and meat.

'They Recycle Everything'

The pigs live mostly on vegetable material that is not used in many other countries—leaves and stalks of vegetables, corn stalks, table scraps and cottonseed hulls. In turn, the pig provides manure that is spread on the fields.

"They recycle everything in China," Dr. Wortman said.

He told of one commune that specialized in carp and silk. Dirt dug out to make ponds for the fish was heaped for the planting of mulberry trees on which silkworms live. The carp, considered an underwater pig, is fed much the same way. Droppings from the silkworm, rich in digested mulberry leaf, are also fed to the carp.

Periodically the rich bottom sediments from the ponds are scraped out and spread under the mulberry trees as fertilizer. The ponds are set among the trees to share the moisture.

Seed Exchange Made

One of the chief goals of the visiting scientists was to begin an exchange of seeds so that plant breeders outside China might be able to cross Chinese varieties with their own to improve plants. Chinese scientists might have new seed types to work with in the same way. A wide variety of seeds were exchanged and plans were made for further exchanges.

One of the more significant exchanges involved soybeans, a crop rich in protein that it has so far defied plant breeders' efforts to develop a higher yielding type. Because China is the home of the soybean and many wild varieties grow there, Dr. Richard L. Bernard, a soybean expert with the United States Department of Agriculture, rambled along hillsides and fences collecting wild soybeans. He brought back the only new soybean varieties that American breeders have had in many years.

Training in Disarray

The group found China still needed more fertilizer. Dr. Wortman said that while no obviously deficient fields were seen, he and his colleagues did believe that yields could be improved with more fertilizer.

They said a more serious problem for the long run, however, was the disarray of agricultural research and training programs.

China's efforts to sharply modify the nature of some educational and research institutions for political reasons have meant few new scientists have been trained in recent years, the group found. Dr. Wortman said the highly trained scientists and scholars were nearly all over the age of 60.

Unless schools and research centers could enjoy some stability, Dr. Wortman said, his group feared that further agricultural progress over the next few decades could be seriously retarded.

Dr. Wortman said that a detailed report on the group's observations in China has been written and is being prepared for publication.

Other scientists in the group were Dr. Glenn W. Burton of the University of Georgia, an expert on forage grasses and millet; Dr. John L. Creech, director of the United States National Arboretum and formerly head of the United States Plant Introduction Service; Dr. Jack R. Harlan of the University of Illinois, an authority on the origins of agriculture and cultivated plants; Dr. Arthur Kelman of the University of Wisconsin, an expert on the diseases of small grains; Dr. Henry M. Munger of Cornell, a specialist in vegetables, and Dr. George F. Sprague of the University of Illinois, an authority on corn and sorghum.

Burma and Thailand Seen as Possible Rice Suppliers to Neighbors

By JOSEPH LELYVELD
Special to The New York Times

BANGKOK, Thailand — When the world food crisis is discussed, the talk usually focuses on the rich nations' surpluses and the poor nations' deficits. Little is said about poor nations that have surpluses or about the possibility that those surpluses might be used to meet the threat of famine in neighboring countries.

The possibility exists in Thailand and, to a lesser extent, in Burma, which have usually had surpluses and which have barely begun to explore the green revolution in rice through the high-yield varieties.

Before World War II the Thai and Burmese surpluses, taken together, were on the order of five million tons a year. As recently as 1962 the two countries were able to export more than three million tons. In the coming year Thailand is expected to export about a million tons, but Burma's exports, aside from undetermined quantities that smugglers slip to Bangladesh and Malaysia, will be negligible or nonexistent.

Even if the old level of exports could be restored, there would be no mechanism for regional distribution beyond the open market. It remains an easier proposition to ship food from the United States, Australia and Canada to deficient areas of Southeast Asia than from Bangkok, geographically next door.

Foreign advisers have been unanimous until recently in urging Thai planners to concentrate on diversification of export crops. The argument, advanced by representatives of the International Bank for Reconstruction and Development and others, was based on a rosily optimistic assessment of the green revolution. Progress in other countries in the region, it was said, would rapidly undermine prospects for rice as a marketable commodity.

Thailand's current five-year plan, adopted three years ago, did not list rice production as a priority. Since then, because of growing shortages, the price of rice has more than quadrupled on world markets. Given the higher prices and concern over the impoverished lot of most paddy farmers in Thailand, there is renewed interest in stepping up output.

In the last decade Thailand has steadily increased rice yields and acreage, with production rising fast enough to outpace a dangerously high population growth rate by a slight margin. The population, expanding by more than 3 per cent annually, is 41 million.

The Burmese agricultural failure, unparalleled in Asia, makes a startling contrast. Essentially yields, acreage and production have been stagnant for 35 years. In 1939, when there were 14 million Burmese, the output of paddy, or unmilled rice, was 7.4 million tons. This year, with the population at about 30 million, it will be no higher than eight million.

Despite that contrast the problems that would have to be overcome to increase production rapidly in the two countries are strikingly similar.

First is a lack of any strong sense of urgency. An effort to expand exports just does not arouse the same response as an effort to avert mass starvation at home—a danger neither country has had to face, though Burma's economy is chaotic and there are severe shortages.

Then there are problems of administration. In both Burma and Thailand the price the farmer receives has traditionally been kept low, so he has never had much incentive to take investment risks or to toil over a second crop.

A third problem, and the one on which there is probably the greatest prospect for headway, is the lack of high-yield varieties suitable to the deep-water culitvation that prevails in both countries. Indeed, in the view of plant breeders, removal of the obstacles that have kept Thailand and Burma from having a green revolution of their own would go a long way to removing obstacles to it elsewhere in the region.

Too Much Water

Only about 5 per cent of Thai and Burmese rice acreage is planted with high-yield varieties. The basic problem is water—not the lack of it, as in sub-Sahaha Africa or parts of India, but a superabundance in the monsoon season that invariably floods the paddy fields. It is this season that produces the main harvests.

The traditional varieties usually withstand the floods. Some Thai "floating rice" is able to grow, as much as six inches a day, to survive in water as deep as 15 feet. But the dwarf high-yield varieties developed at the International Rice Research Institute in the Philippines cannot be grown in deep water.

Deep-water conditions also prevail in the Mekong Delta of South Vietnam, in Bangladesh and in heavily populated areas of eastern India. It has been estimated that deep-water cultivation is used on 50 million acres in Asia.

"The new varieties are dry-season varieties," commented Dr. Ben R. Jackson, a Rockefeller Foundation plant breeder who came to Thailand eight years ago from Oklahoma State University to work on rice. "They assume good water control. But this is not the way Asia is situated today or likely to be situated for a long, long time."

Dr. Jackson and his Thai colleagues started by breeding high-yield varieties that, halfway in height between traditional varieties and the new dwarf types, were able to survive in fairly deep water but not the deepest. These "semi-dwarf" types are in limited use in Thailand. Now the breeders are seeking a variety that retains the growth capacity of the "floating rice."

Recognizing that the problems of deep-water cultivation have been slighted, the International Rice Research Institute announced recently that it was extending its activities to Thailand. Under an agreement with the Thai Department of Agriculture it will station research personnel at the station where Dr. Jackson has been working and underwrite part of an expanded program.

Deep-water conditions prevail in most of the fertile Irrawaddy River Delta in Burma, but there has yet to be contact between Thai and Burmese breeders. The Burmese authorities have even refused to contribute to the rice institute's seed bank.

Going it alone, the Burmese breeders have modified dwarf types from the Philippines, but their new variety is being grown on an even smaller area now than it was several years ago.

Plainly, a comeback for Burma as a major exporter would require more than new varieties. Thirty to 40 per cent of Burmese farmers, it has been estimated, are planting by broadcasting the seed—that is, tossing it into plowed furrows instead of going through the back-breaking labor of transplanting. The result of broadcasting is smaller yields.

In an effort to reverse the trend the autocratic Government of President Ne Win has raised the price it pays farmers in three successive seasons, but with little effect so far. Last season it sought 2.6 million tons for distribution to urban consumers and for export, but it got 1.5 million.

This season it raised the price again and, simultaneously, forbade private trade in a desperate effort to gain full control. But the black-market price is twice the official rate, so the effort seems doomed.

Unlocking the vast potential of the verdant fields of Thailand and Burma could undoubtedly buy Asia time against famine, but the two countries are in no position to give away their rice, which is high in quality and relatively high in price. In any case, there has never been a serious look at the possibility that Asian surpluses could be used to meet Asian deficits.

January 6, 1975

REDBOW
SUNRISE
FOOD
EXCHANGE
LEVITTOWN
FOR
SACRAMENTO
FOR INDIA
Connell
Rice
CONNELL RICE & SUGAR CO.
HOUSTON, TEXAS
REDBOW
GREEN SPLIT PEAS
REDBOW
BABY LIMA BEANS
GLASS
GREAT CARE
JUNIOR FOODS
Surf
24 LARGE
STARLAC
LOG CABIN
SOUP

CHAPTER 2
Food

Collecting food for India—Levittown, Long Island, 1951.

Courtesy The New York Times.

'The Most Distressful Country'

From "The Great Hunger."

Famine funeral, as drawn for the Illustrated London News, Jan. 30, 1847.

THE GREAT HUNGER. By Cecil Woodham-Smith. Illustrated. 510 pp. New York and Evanston: Harper and Row. $6.95.

By D. W. BROGAN

THE great disaster, described and explained in this somber and moving book, had, of course, its chief effect in Ireland, fully confirming her title to being "the most distressful country." Ireland has never been the same since the Famine. In the famine years at least one and a half million Irish died, another million emigrated. The population, which had been almost nine million in 1845, had dropped to 6,552,385 in 1851. It was the greatest and, in many ways, the most inexcusable catastrophe in Western Europe since the Thirty Years War. In Mrs. Woodham-Smith, the Famine has found not perhaps its Brecht but its Tacitus.

To this account of the greatest disaster in the sad history of her country, Mrs. Woodham-Smith brings controlled passion, deep learning and a sense of justice that make her book a historical landmark. She is not a neutral academic historian ready to believe in the inevitability of whatever has happened. She was born a Fitzgerald and does not forget it. She thinks that in addition to the ruthless forces of nature, like the potato blight that no one knew then how to counter, there was a great deal of stupidity, conceit, callousness and racial and religious prejudice displayed by the complacent rulers of "John Bull's Other Island." It *was* John Bull's island but he had little concern for its well-being but a great deal for its solvency—seen in British terms.

In Irish popular mythology, the Famine is the great disaster. But Mrs. Woodham-Smith has shown that popular mythology is far more nearly right than the official complacent history of the English Establishment. Thus Brendan Behan has recently repeated the legend that Queen Victoria gave £5 to her starving subjects. She did, in fact, give £2,000—a lot less than a week's income. Mrs. Woodham-Smith shows that the absentee landlords often behaved better than the local bankrupt gentry. A "half-mounted gentleman" couldn't afford to be generous, and while men, women and children were dying in conditions to be equalled only in modern times in Hitler's camps, taxes and rents were ruthlessly collected. It is true, as modern Irish historians have shown, that even if all the food produced in Ireland had been kept there, there would still have been starvation. Even so, the sight of food exported under armed guard to pay the rent due to scum like Lord Clanricarde still turns the stomach.

Memory of the Famine is still the bitterest memory of the descendants of the Irish Diaspora in Boston, Sydney, Liverpool, Glasgow. (I hasten to add that I have good reason to fear that my family did well out of the Famine.) Any British politician who talks peevishly of the attitude of Irish-Americans should read this book and the Irish-American politician might well say to the descendants and representatives of Lord John Russell and Lord Palmerston, "Vous l'avez voulu."

In the folk memory of the Famine there is, of course, a lot of mere legend. Ireland was, in the traditional story, if not a paradise, a happy country. It was the country of the "wild sports of the West," of "the days of the Kerry dancing," of rough pleasures and rough plenty. This is to paint a golden age that never was. There were minor famines. Food for the vast majority of the population was potatoes and nothing else. The cabins would have been thought disgraceful on a bad plantation "down the River." Visitors to Ireland saw a poverty that was almost unbelievable and intolerable in the days of the great Victorian boom when England was leading the world in industry and in the free supply of censorious advice. Tocqueville was horrified not only by the poverty but by the bitter virulence of religious bigotry. Ireland was, indeed, a house divided even before the Famine struck and forced the peasants to fight for their lives and the landlords for their rents. The landlords won if only because the British government attached more importance to rent than to life.

SOME of the most brutal exhortations to severity in the nineteenth century came from highly educated and formally Christian English officials. Mrs. Woodham-Smith cites documents that would have done credit to a *Sturmbannführer*. There were, of course, no gas ovens. Typhus was nearly as effective.

How did this triumph of insensitivity occur? There was in a great many British official's minds a contempt for the Irish and a hatred for their religion that blinded them to reality. (Typhus killed Protestants, too, as well as the heroic Quakers and doctors.) Ireland was overpopulated. Its social structure was highly defective for it was the result of a series of conquests and confiscations. Often

Mr. Brogan, the British historian and political scientist, is fellow of Peterhouse in the University of Cambridge.

there was no genuine human or humane relationship between the landlord and "his" tenants. The middlemen, often Catholics, were no better. In 1846, Ireland was already sick. If government in Russia was "tyranny tempered by assasination," Irish landlordism was absolute property tempered by assasination, if not of the landlord, then of his agents. "If you think you can intimidate me by shooting my bailiff you are very much mistaken," as one of the worst of landlords was later to write from his London club. But little or nothing was known of Ireland in official circles or rather what was known was ignored.

The horrible history of how the Famine was turned from a disaster to a catastrophe is a fine example of the maxim which tells us "with how little wisdom the world is governed." The British official most concerned was Sir Charles Trevelyan, Macaulay's brother-in-law, later reformer of the British Civil Service and founder of a dynasty of distinguished scholars and public servants. He was a man of courage, of dogmatic views, of real though narrow abilities. But he was a doctrinaire. He was probably influenced by Malthusian doctrines. The Irish married young and bred too many children. (They learned their lesson as the sad state of modern Ireland shows.) To feed them free was to break the sacred laws of political economy. That the alternative was to let them die was never faced. To their credit, English officials broke the rules and fed when they could, but usually they couldn't.

THERE is a curious parallel between Herbert Hoover and Sir Charles Trevelyan. Mr. Hoover was, of course, a far better administrator and would have handled the Famine much better than Trevelyan did. But both men were blinded by doctrine to the realities of the collapse of an economy. In a way Trevelyan was right. Dead men, women and children don't perpetuate the habit of asking for a handout.

The most important result of the Famine was not the bleeding of Ireland white. (Alas, the modern Irish are not jolly, improvident, carefree peasants!) It was the great "lemming flight" of the survivors all over the English-speaking world. The survivors poured into Boston, Montreal, New York; they created the Irish ghettos. They remembered.

With a fine sense of irony, Mrs. Woodham-Smith ends her story with the visit of Queen Victoria to her distressful island. There were grumblings and protests, but the Queen was given a gold reception. The Dubliners on the social make were as servile as was desirable, although the results of the Famine were visible on every hand. It makes a note of bitter comedy and justifies John Mitchel's denunciation of Dublin as a "city of bellowing dastards." I don't think there is any reason to recommend this book to John Fitzgerald Kennedy, but it can be warmly commended to Her Majesty's Ambassador.

April 14, 1963

THE CAUSES OF FAMINE IN INDIA.

It is commonly supposed that famines in India are due to the failure of the crops, and that the crops are cut off by the sudden droughts which sweep over the entire country; but when in Southern India alone six millions have perished by starvation in one year's famine, the causes must lie deeper beneath the surface. A people must be poverty-stricken beforehand to be thus absolutely cut down by want of food. The social condition of the native population is at fault somewhere, and Miss FLORENCE NIGHTINGALE, in the August *Nineteenth Century*, reveals the difficulty, with her usual penetration and sympathy. The land in India is not specially subject to famine; the cultivators of the soil are industrious; the native races compare favorably with other races in capacity to take care of themselves. The difficulty lies elsewhere, and it is summed up by Miss NIGHTINGALE in her accusation of the English nation, in one sentence: "We do not care for the people of India." By this she means that the British Government has put such burdens upon the people that they are crushed down by them. For instance, salt in India, which costs 12 shillings 6 pence a ton, has a tax of £7 a ton. This restricts the preservation of food, and absolutely forbids native manufactures. No man can live there without nine pounds of salt a year, and the cry for salt is only equaled by the cry for bread in ancient Rome. Then, in the famine districts, there is great suffering from the scarcity of water. Plenty of water there means irrigation, cheap canal communications, improved methods of agriculture, and forest plantations. Where the water supply is adequate, or has been made so by Government aid, there has been no famine. Then, again, the native man has no voice, no education, no method by which his grievances or sufferings may reach the public ear. The Government has been so hard upon him at its points of contact with his life that he shuns it even if it comes to him bearing relief from the middlemen, who oppress him the most. There is little to show in the British rule of India that the Government has had any higher idea than that of great returns for small outlays from that distant section of the Empire. It is to be said, as an offset to this rapacity, that the voluntary subscriptions for famine relief in England and the colonies during the famine year have been £800,000; but for all this, the wheels of the Government still cut just as deeply into the lives of the Indian peasantry as they did before. It is only a relief, not a cure, for the difficulty which besets the Indian population.

Miss NIGHTINGALE sets forth the greatest difficulty in India in words which must make every Englishman's heart burn with indignation. Her facts seem scarcely credible at the present day, and yet, being drawn from public documents, or amply authenticated by her personal experience, we have no alternative but to accept them. They show a state of society in India whose only parallel in recent times was to be found in American slavery, and whose only result is to make English rule in India a disgrace to civilization. The difficulty arises from a class of men who have established themselves all over the country as money-lenders to the ryots or cultivators. They lend the ryot money on his forthcoming crop, or to buy oxen or seed, charging him anywhere from 50 to 100 per cent. interest. This he cannot pay when his crops are gathered, or, if he does pay it, he has nothing left for his family, and must again borrow money on his next crop. In many cases the interest amounts to more than the principal. Where this is so, the Hindoo law protects the debtor, but the money-lender, aware of this, obtains a new bond from the debtor, who knows nothing of legal obligations, and can neither read nor write, and compels him to pay interest anew on the previous principal and interest, now reckoned as altogether principal. By this means the poor debtor is compelled to sell his land, or rather the money-lender, whom the law maintains in his extortions, brings an action against him for debt, and has his property sold. No one bids against the money-lender, and thus the laborer's property comes into the usuror's grasp for a song. If the debtor has nothing to pay, the money-lender has authority to sell the man himself, his land, and everything he possesses, even to the honor of his wife and daughter. It was the saying of a native, "The English law makes the sale of our land as easy as the sale of a bullock or a turban." The changing of the ownership of the land in this way is going on all over India, and so far the Government has not been able to check it. It is by this concentration of the land ownership in the hands of men whose only purpose is to rob the natives, and whom the English law, unfortunately, protects, that the rural population, which means almost the entire people, are placed in a position which exposes them to many of the horrors of slavery, and reduces them to such poverty that upon any light change in the success of the crops famine sweeps them away in vast numbers. The trouble with India is that the native does not count for a man, and has no rights which he can maintain without the risk of his life. Miss NIGHTINGALE cites several instances in which natives, reduced to beggary by their money-lenders, and maddened beyond control by a sense of their wrongs, took the laws into their own hands, and murdered the men in open day who had effected their ruin. The English law promptly put the murderers to death, and there the matter ended; but the cases are few and far between in which the natives are able to obtain justice as against the men who live by plundering them. Miss NIGHTINGALE's words of condemnation are severe, but they will hardly be thought to exceed the facts which support them. She says: "Here is shipwreck, utter, disastrous, of some, not hundreds, but millions of souls; it is a shipwreck which is repeated every year. No hand is stretched out to save. It is a shipwreck which will be repeated, more disastrous, more complete, if that be possible, *every year*. It is not a famine, or storm-wave induced by the elements, which comes once in a period. It is the utter demoralization of two races—the race that borrows and the race that lends." It is evident that, unless the money-lenders, who in most cases are not natives, are speedily arrested in their endeavors to grasp the land, a very large part of the people will be reduced to chattel slavery. It has been the proud boast of Englishmen that their flag floated in every clime over the homes of the free, but it is plainly evident that if England does not soon take the condition of the native Indian population in hand, and correct the abuses which now exist, civilization at large will hold that nation guilty of neglecting a great responsibility. Miss NIGHTINGALE has seen with her own eyes many of the evils which she describes, and the picture which she paints is awful and thrilling. The sufferings of the people at their best season come from their extreme poverty, and neither education nor religion are to be thought of when the great problem is how to get enough to eat. There is nothing in the present administration of Indian affairs to prevent the return of the late famine, with its unimaginable horrors, if the crops fall short in the districts which have not been irrigated, or in which the money-lenders have prosecuted their nefarious business. Miss NIGHTINGALE's paper is not a pleasant subject for discussion by the English press, but nothing can help its making a profound impression wherever it is read.

August 25, 1878

THE FARMER'S GOLDEN YEAR.

From The Chicago Inter Ocean.

Western farmers are likely to be swamped with money next Winter. Reports from all the great agricultural States of the Middle West indicate that the crops now being harvested and those that are approaching the harvest season will excel those of any former year. This is true in Illinois and Wisconsin, throughout Iowa, Missouri, Minnesota, the Dakotas, and Nebraska. From everywhere come reports of phenomenal crops. The farmers are crying for help for the harvest fields and are offering wages that would have seemed impossible a few years ago.

Last year Nebraska produced 150,000,000 bushels of corn, and it was called a great crop. This season's yield is estimated at 320,000,000 bushels, or more than double the yield of 1898. The Kansas crop last year was 130,000,000 bushels. Crop experts compute the yield this year in Kansas at 340,000,000 bushels. These figures are given by State officials. Full allowance, they say, has been made for damage by grasshoppers, hot winds, and other adverse conditions. The same story is told by other corn-growing States.

The wheat crop of the Northwest simply dazes the farmers, and they are trembling lest they will not be able to harvest it. They are making frantic appeals for harvest hands at wages running from $2.50 to $6 a day, and employment agents are overrun with applications for men to go out into the fields and gather the crops. In the meantime the women and children have been impressed into service and have dropped housework to help in the harvest field. The corn crop of the great "corn belt," extending from Illinois through Missouri, Kansas, and Nebraska, now gives promise that the coming season's proceeds will pay off the last mortgage and put an organ, a Bible, and a plush album in every home in the district.

The effect of this tremendous crop can scarcely be realized by the people of the cities or the farmers of the East. The big crops of last year, together with the high prices, very nearly cleared off all mortgages on Western farms. The prospects for the present year are that the farmers will clean up the last vestige of debt and provide themselves with all necessary machinery, furnish their homes with comfort, if not with luxury, and have money in the banks for future use.

The cornfields of Iowa, Nebraska, and Missouri are almost beyond the belief of anybody who has not looked them over. The corn stands high above the heads of the tallest man, and, barring some unlooked-for and appalling disaster, the yield will be almost unprecedented. One good result of the years of the poor crops is that the farmers have developed along lines allied with the raising of the crops. Time was when corn was worth so little that the farmers used it for fuel. But the farmers of the West and Northwest have found a way to use their corn without selling it to the elevator man at whatever the latter chooses to give. In nearly every one of the Western States the growers of corn have become breeders of cattle and hogs. If they cannot get a decent price for their corn they keep it and feed it to the live stock and sell the stock at a figure that gives them a good profit for the corn and the work of converting it into meat.

Throughout Minnesota and the Dakotas the wheat crop as it stands to-day presents a picture to gladden the hearts of the farmers and of all other people as well. It is one of the greatest crops ever grown on the Western prairies. Of course, there will be local mishaps, such as the hailstorm in Cass and Traill Counties, in North Dakota, where the crops on some 200,000 acres of land were destroyed. But while these accidents are deplorable to the district and the people interested, they affect only in a small way the general conditions.

This tremendous crop in the West means as much to the merchant as to the farmer. With debts paid and money in the bank, the farmer become a good customer. And when the merchant is selling freely for cash the jobber and the manufacturer are kept busy supplying him, and the manufacturer then reaches out for more men to whom he can offer permanent work—and so it goes down the entire line. And, to go a step further, the increased number of laborers in the factories call for more food supplies, and thus the prosperity again helps the farmer.

August 20, 1899

POLITICAL NOTES

It is supposed that the horrors of the Chinese famine, which are almost solely the result of imperfect means of internal communication, will lead the Mandarins to reconsider their bigoted opposition to the introduction of railroads within the Empire. That is hardly probable. A complacent fatalism, which has been the growth of many more centuries than the Anglo-Saxon race has known of civilization, is not likely to be overthrown even by the lessons of a famine which directly affects fifteen millions of people. Not that the Chinese officials have been at all negligent in their efforts to cope with this stupendous calamity. On the contrary, they have shown an amount of energy and promptitude which has won the hearty admiration of all observers. But to sanction the employment of the works of the Devil by way of neutralizing a visitation of Providence would be regarded in China merely as a way of inviting worse disasters. The Celestial Empire has shown itself ready to utilize Western adaptations of inventions which had reached their rudimentary stages in China; it has never, willingly, tolerated mechanical appliances which were so far removed from Chinese conception as to be intelligible only on the assumption that they were the work of the powers of darkness.

May 21, 1878

INDIA'S PECULIAR CLAIM.

The committee having in charge the collection of a fund for the relief of the famine-stricken people of India plan that to-day there shall be made in each of some twelve thousand of the churches in the United States an appeal for that purpose. Certainly nothing could be more appropriate as a subject for Sabbath appeal. Not in our time has there before been so vast an affliction visited on any people, or one demanding more instant relief, so far as any relief now remains possible. The testimony of the missionaries who were at the council recently held in this city is still fresh in the minds of the public, and must powerfully reinforce the efforts of the committee.

There is, however, a peculiar claim on the American people in the case of the suffering millions of India. We are actually profiting by the calamity that has befallen them. A considerable portion of the exports of India is in cotton and in wheat, which come into direct competition with our own exports, and though the supply from the Indian sources is small compared with that contributed by the United States, a failure of it has its effect. That is a fact on which our people may well reflect in the present appalling situation in India. We are as a Nation generous in charity when we realize the need, and in this case the need is tremendously urgent. Our contribution to its relief is in a sense only the payment of a debt. It should be prompt and liberal.

May 20, 1900

SHOULD AMERICA HELP INDIA ?

To the Editor of The New York Times:

I have noticed with interest the appeals being made through the press for contributions toward the relief of India's famine-stricken myriads. So far as I know, the Rev. Charles M. Sheldon started the movement in the first issue of his experimental Christian daily in Topeka. His plea was based on a broad Christian altruism which would relieve suffering wherever found without asking any questions.

This sort of charity may perhaps be as unwise between American and Hindu as between millionaire and pauper in New York City. In your last Sunday's editorial on "India's Peculiar Claim" you appealed to American charity for India on a much more definite and tangible ground. You brought up the question of international responsibility and urged that the spirit of charity, which sometimes softens the relations between individual competitors when one has gone to the wall, should hold in international relations.

I do not wish in any way to raise my voice against the practice of the Golden Rule among the nations. But the Golden Rule may be foolishly interpreted to mean that I should do for my neighbor just what an urgent distress might make me want him to do for me; whereas it seems to me that the Golden Rule enjoins upon us to treat our neighbors as we think they ought to be treated, as we think we ourselves ought to be treated under like circumstances. What I am trying to get at is the question as to how far do the circumstances of the present case justify a general appeal to the American people to save the Hindus from starvation?

I have seen nowhere in this discussion any reference to the question of overpopulation. Is it not true that India could not support her present population in a degree of comfort consistent with western ideals, even if she could be made to change her spots and become like the countries of Europe and America?

If this is the case, does not the Western world assume an impossible responsibility in trying to civilize and keep alive India's millions? Perhaps England may be said to have assumed this responsibility for good or ill.

If England made a mistake, surely we ought not to be called in to bolster up a policy that is ruinous to the world. We are responsible for the relief of India or we are not. If we are, let's be quick and united to the full extent of that responsibility. If we are not, let's turn away from the terrible spectacle and not stultify our consciences and our intellects by spooning out our little dole of relief.

I do not see that there can be any effective plea based on the sacredness and worth of human life in this case, for human life is not sacred when it is fathered by vice and misery, and it is not worthy when there is absolutely too much of it.

In India human life seems to be "dirt cheap," and we cannot raise the price by a fiat of philanthropy. Is India to be counted in the circle of nations which are seeking a common level of civilization and co-operative helpfulness? If so the level must be a lower one than could be attained by Western nations.

Is it not clear that we cannot assume responsibility for the relief of such an immense nation without having some control over the increase of its numbers? Is not starvation in India plainly the penalty for overpopulation and improvidence?

DELOS F. WILCOX.

Elk Rapids, Mich., May 23, 1900.

May 27, 1900

WHEAT PRICES SOAR TO A NEW RECORD

Riotous Scene on Chicago Exchange as Crop Is Quoted at $1.41¾ a Bushel.

MAY HAVE TO TURN TO CORN

Question of Feeding Two Continents on Our Supply Becomes Vital—Some Would Bar Export.

Special to The New York Times.

CHICAGO, Jan. 8.—May wheat soared today to the unprecedented price of $1.41⅝ a bushel, amid riotous scenes on the Board of Trade, and after a day of tension on the part of traders closed at $1.40⅞. The warring nations are making so great a demand on this country for wheat that conservative operators predicted that the crop would sell for $1.50 a bushel. A few large grain brokerage houses even go further by stating that a standard price of $1.75 will be ultimately reached.

The opening of the Dardanelles, releasing the many millions of bushels of Russian wheat, which cannot now be shipped, will be the first signal for a break in American prices, it was promised. Argentina made her first shipments this week, exporting only 40,000 bushels, compared with 288,000 bushels last year at this time.

Julius Barnes, a New York and Duluth exporter, was on the Chicago Exchange today and reported France and Italy still coming after wheat regardless of prices. An immense trade in wheat futures forced the price up in the Chicago pit. Eleventh-hour investors bought heavily and there were many important sales made on the bulges.

Export sales of wheat from the United States today were reported as 1,600,000 bushels, in addition to 750,000 bushels of corn and 500,000 bushels of oats. The business was limited by the offerings, as exporters feared to make sales until they felt sure of getting the grain in the country. Farmers were offered $1.25 a bushel for wheat in many sections, but were not disposed to sell.

The remarkably strong cash wheat situation impressed the trade more than any other feature, particularly the strength displayed by Kansas interior markets, where the wheat surplus is supposed to be stored.

Leaders from outside points on Exchange today were predicting that if wheat goes much higher there will be a general turning to corn in place of wheat bread, both in this country and in Europe.

Resolutions calling upon Congress to place an embargo upon the export of wheat and flour will be introduced at the next meeting of the Chicago Retail Grocers' and Butchers' Association. S. Westerfeld, Chairman of the Trades Relations Committee of the National Association, plans to inaugurate a new fight against the high cost of flour on more aggressive lines than the war of agitation, which brought down the "high cost of living" late last Summer.

One well-known expert put the breadstuff situation this way: "It is not so much a question of price for wheat as a question of supply. Will there be enough to feed two continents? If wheat goes to $2, it will mean eating of corn as never before."

Flour was sold to grocers and bakers at from $7 to $7.10 a barrel today, and the market of elevated prices was declared to be "firmer" than last August and September, when the first series of high marks was reached.

The Chicago Police Department has tackled the bread problem. The police have undertaken to bake their own bread. Hereafter, it was announced today, the Bridewell will bake all the bread for prisoners both there and at the police stations.

WASHINGTON, Jan. 8.—Department of Justice officials expressed interest tonight in reports that the price of a loaf of bread was about to jump from five to six cents in New York, Chicago and possibly other large cities. No complaints have reached the department, however, and no immediate action is contemplated.

It is realized at the department that with wheat far above normal figures, bakers undoubtedly have been forced to face the prospect of higher flour. Officials are interested, however, in learning whether there is any conspiracy among bakers over the country to effect a raise in price of their commodity. Concerted action that involved bakers in different States would allow prosecution under the anti-trust act.

Several years ago the department began an investigation to see if there was any ground for believing that there was a bakers' trust. At that time it was understood that at least forty cities were involved in the operations of the reported combination. No action ever was taken as a result of the investigations then.

January 9, 1915

ONE YEAR OF HOOVER'S CONTROL: FOOD ENOUGH FOR ALL ALLIES

Taking a Chance on His Faith in Nation's Loyalty, the Administrator Has Succeeded in Using Volunteer Spirit to Assure Supplies for Democracy's Hosts

Below is the record of a careful inquiry to determine just what has been accomplished in one year of Food Control by the United States Government.

The vital result is that the Allies in Europe are assured of enough food to keep them going until the next harvest, while this country is equally sure of adequate supplies. But the American Nation must continue the same economics and sacrifices which it has undertaken successfully in the first year of war.

ALONG the allied battlefront and throughout the allied nations American food is now being distributed in greater quantities than ever before. But for the food this battlefront and these nations would not have the strength to stand up and fight. Fifty per cent of the food for the Allies must now be sent from North America.

In an office at Washington, as plain with its beaver board wall covering as that of the Superintendent of some third-class mining camp, there sits from 8:30 a.m. to 7:30 p.m. dialy the man who is chiefly responsible for this flow of food to the Allies. He has, in a true sense, become Food Administrator for the Allies as well as Food Administrator of the United States, though Herbert Hoover would be the first to disclaim that distinction; but in support of it might be cited the fact that with him the needs of the Allies come first, as due them for what they have borne and are bearing; next come the food needs of the United States. Both must be satisfied.

How have they been satisfied? What has been accomplished? Every American has contributed to the results, though what these are has been subordinated to the campaign for food saving. It is a fitting time to ask the question, for it is just a year since Mr. Hoover took charge of food conservation, though the law creating him Food Administrator was not passed until later.

Take wheat: Owing to the shortage of last's crop we had scarcely 20,000,000 bushels above our normal consumption and seed requirements. Practically all this had been shipped by Christmas. Then, in January, came the British Food Commissioner's urgent call for 75,000,000 bushels before the new crop, if the Allies were to have food enough to carry on the war. In response to that call, the American people saved 50,000,000 bushels out of their normal consumption; it was shipped to Europe, and the war goes on!

For the last four weeks wheat consumption in this country has been 40 per cent below normal. Whole communities have "sworn off" from wheat, for the pressure of the Allies' needs is now at its highest. In the list are many churches and lodges; at the top is an entire State, Texas. From July 1, 1917, to March 31, 1918, America has exported to her allies 80,000,000 bushels of wheat and flour, or 124 per cent of the amount available for export on July 1, while a year ago, during the same period, we exported to the Allies only 51 per cent of the amount available for export.

There is another side, in what has been accomplished in wheat price stabilization. In the face of the wheat shortage this is what has been brought about: In May of last year the difference between what the farmer got for his wheat and the wholesale price of flour was equivalent to $5.68 a barrel; in early May of this year the difference amounted to 64 cents. In May, 1917, the wholesale price of flour at Minneapolis was $16.75; it was predicted that it would go to $20 a barrel and higher; in early May of this year the price of flour was $9.80 a barrel, a decrease of 41 per cent.

Exports of rye and rye flour from the beginning of the fiscal year, July 1, 1917, through March, 1918, were 32 per cent larger than last year; of barley 55 per cent larger, of oats and oatmeal 34 cents larger.

Before we entered the war we were exporting to the Allies 50,000,000 pounds of pork a month. There was even at that time the menace of a hog shortage. When we entered the war the high prices offered by the Allies had increased our exports of port to 125,000,000 pounds a month. A severe cut in our reserve supplies was the result. In 1917, a month before the conservation program went into effect, the export of pork had fallen to 70,000,000 pounds a month. In March of

Map and Diagram © Nat. Geographic Magazine. Washington, D. C., 1918.

The Boundary Lines of European Nations, as Drawn by the Gaunt Hand of Hunger.

this year the amount of pork exported to the Allies amounted to 308,000,000 pounds, more than six times the normal and 50 per cent greater than any previous month in the last seven years. There is in addition 1,100,000,000 pounds of pork and pork products in storage. This is what "porkless days" have done.

Our average monthly production of hog products is 750,000,000 pounds.

Before the war our average monthly exports of beef to the countries of the Allies were less than 1,000,000 pounds. During the last two years we have averaged about 22,000,000 pounds a month. In January the Allies called on us for 70,000,000 pounds a month for the next three months. In March we shipped 86,000,000 pounds of beef and beef products to the Allies. This was 20 per cent larger than any previous month in seven years and more than twice as great as the highest amount exported in any month in the four years before 1915. Our cattle have not increased since the war, and these increased drafts to the Allies have been provided by reducing our own consumption. It is a result of meatless days.

The production of beef in the United States is about 650,000,000 pounds a month.

Our annual saving on sugar is expected to foot up 400,000 tons. A year ago the wholesale price of refined sugar was 8.33 cents a pound; in April, 1918, with sugar much more scarce, it was 7.3 cents a pound, a decrease of 12 per cent. In the same period the margin between the price of raw and refined sugar was reduced from 2.12 cents a pound to 1.3 cents. A reduction of one cent a pound means a saving to the people of the United States of $16,000,000, measured by annual consumption. As to general price changes since the Food Administration has been in charge, the index number of producers' prices for March, 1918, shows an increase of 27 per cent over August, 1917, while the index number of consumers' prices decreased 13 per cent. Wheat is the only commodity the price of which the Food Administration has authority to fix. For other commodities the prices may be reached indirectly only through regulation of profits. By far the greater part of the reductions have been through volunteer agreements—about 90 per cent, it is estimated.

That, briefly, shows what has been done in food conservation. How has it been done?

Mr. Hoover can't tell; neither can any of his aides, for there is something to be accounted for that does not get into records. A European Food Administrator could give full explanation, out of records, for he has a stringent system, through food cards, which reaches every consumer. It is an explanation that concerns discipline, but what discipline has reached the millions here who have observed the wheatless days and the meatless days?

One of Mr. Hoover's aides in trying to explain fell back on a story.

"A man came up from my State," he said, "to attend a conference that concerned one of the most important food industries in our State. This man is a prominent official at home and a citizen of much influence. He was aroused over proposed interference in the industry by the Food Administration. 'We won't stand for it,' he said. 'It isn't fair. We are willing to be reasonable; we don't ask to make what we are entitled to, but this proposal is too raw. If Hoover insists on it, we'll go after him as he never has been gone after before.'

"'Better wait and see what he says,' I suggested.

"After the conference the State official came to me. 'How much longer can Germany hold out on their food supply?' he asked. I told him Germany was practically self supporting before the war, and had since seized some of the richest farm lands in Europe. 'But, he broke in, 'It doesn't matter. We'll get them in the end. Of course, we have to make every sacifice; think of what the Allies are doing over there. All that's worth living for is at stake! We're in to the limit. Hoover can take the whole industry if he wants it, do with it as he pleases. We've got to win. At a time like this who would think of profit?

"That man did not seem to know that a change had been wrought in him, that something bigger than he had ever known before had got hold of him; for the first time he realized what we are standing for. And you see he wasn't forced to do anything!"

Other volunteers in other sections had experiences as remarkable.

The third step was the preparation and distribution of written propaganda for food conservation. The volunteers believe wholly in their work; they consider it a rare privilege to be a member of Mr. Hoover's organization. Whatever they prepare, therefore, has the impulse, the emotional drive, of deep conviction. They are well posted on the restrictions which the Food Administration has through the license control of wholesalers, but their purpose is to arouse the volunteer spirit in the consumer and to set it eagerly to work. So that even in preparing a new placard they strive to evoke the ideal of democracy and of service without compulsion.

One of them, a college professor, pointed to a recent utterance of Mr. Hoover on "The Motive of Service":

"Aside from the prime necessity of protecting our independence and our institutions, there is but one possible benefit from the war, and that is the stimulation of self-sacrifice in the people, the lifting of its ideals, and the diversion from its peace-time inclinations toward the purely material things in life, to a strengthening of the higher purposes. I do not say that such compensations are full compensations for the war, but they are at least ameliorations of the terrible currents which are threatening our existence. Therefore we felt if there could be brought home to the sense of every American household the necessity of this personal and individual sacrifice we would have spread the opportunity for service beyond those who sacrifice in giving their sons to immolation on the national altar."

Voluntary—that is the word nearest to an explanation of what has been accomplished. More than 100 of the Washington staff give their services, paying their own expenses, and many of them are not men of large wealth, but persons who have resigned their positions to come to Washington for work with the Food Administration; in the national organization there are more than 4,000 who work for nothing and pay their own expenses. Others, it is added, merely accept what it cost to live in Washington. They have forgotten about the connection of money with work.

These volunteers, deriving their inspiration from Mr. Hoover, who in the beginning made the stipulation that he receive no pay for his services, carry this spirit to Omaha and Memphis and other towns. Producers' organizations receive them with frowns, and, in the end, tingling somehow with a new feeling about the war, wonder what has struck them. This is a sample, related by a Hoover aide in Washington:

"One of our men went out to confer with a hog producers' association in the Middle West. They were up in arms and had protested against any interference with the price. They wanted more money instead of less; the time had come for a clean-up, and they demanded the right to make the clean-up. That issue, soon after our representative began to state the situation as it actually was, dropped out of sight, and the really important issue came to the fore. The meeting ended with a resolution in which the members of the hog association pledged themselves not to kill another hog for family use or eat another piece of port until the Food Administration asked them to."

Mr. Hoover took a chance on his faith in the American people. That is the uncertain quantity he undertook to deal with, on a hazard that a mere Prussian materialist would have regarded as inexcusably reckless; the response of the American people to the appeal for voluntary conservation is the one part of the food saving that cannot be explained; it is too deep for that; they did not have to—something utterly unintelligible to the Prussian materialist, but it is sufficient to say that Mr. Hoover's faith was justified. It is assured that the Allies' needs will be provided for until the next harvest, and there is food enough for the American people.

A rationing system in the United States would face many more difficulties than it does in Europe. Fifty per cent of the people of the United States are either producers or live in close contact with the producer, and effective restraint on their consumption by rationing would be a problem no European food administrator has had to face; in Germany, however, this very phase of the problem has presented the worst difficulties. In addition, owing to the great variety in habits of consumption among the industrial population, another difficulty would be raised in employing a rationing system. In some parts of the South workers consume no more than two pounds of wheat a week, using other and less needed substitutes for the nutrient qualities of that cereal, while in some parts of the North the worker uses eight pounds of wheat a week. In this commodity a rationing system would force more wheat on the Southern worker than he wants and would cut the supply of the Northern worker below what he needs.

A third consideration is that a rationing system would impose a great cost on the Government.

In Mr. Hoover's opinion only some unexpected emergency, such as a disastrous slump in the sugarcane crop prospect, would make the installation of a card system necessary. If it were required that normal consumption be reduced 75 per cent, it could be handled only by means of food tickets. The same situation might be brought about in wheat if the crop were suddenly struck by smut. The rationing system weighs heavily both on the people and on the administrator of it, and in this country the possibility of its introduction can be made more remote by increased simplicity of living and the elimination of all waste. Mr. Hoover thinks that the comparative short term of office of European Food Commissioners is due largely to the friction that is caused by the enforcement of the rationing system.

The crop prospects are full of encouragement, but the same self-denial will be necessary by the American people even if there are bumper yields. A surplus is needed to face the future without apprehension. Food saving also increases the shipping space for the Allies and our own troops; the more food that is conserved in this country the more ships can be withdrawn from the longer routes, as to South America. It takes a ship twice as long to go from an allied port to Argentina as it does to come to this country or to Canada; in addition, the danger of loss from submarine is greater. Just recently, on account of the greater demand for ships by the United States and the Allies, it has been necessary to make withdrawals from the long route to Argentina. Later, emphasizing how food and ships and winning the war are becoming more and more closely interrelated, 50,000 tons of shipping have been withdrawn from the sugar trade between Cuba and the United States. These ships were transferred to the service of the Allies, whose needs are pressing. It may be necessary to reduce our present consumption of sugar by 15 per cent.

Mr. Hoover's sway over the staff of the Food Administration might lead one to expect what is called a "tremendous personality." On the contrary, you hardly know he is in the room until you get right up to his desk, and he is shaking hands, with a trace of a smile. He does not emphasize what he says with clenched fist, as a master of men is expected to do. As he talks, you do not think of Hoover at all, but wholly of the food needs of the Allies and ourselves; you apprehend those needs as never before, and Hoover seems to have forgotten himself. That is probably the secret if it — he has forgotten himself, and he makes others forget themselves, first the circle of his associates, and through them the greater circle of the nation—thus achieving the necessary food conservation by self-denial instead of by compulsion.

REASONS FOR FEEDING OUR BEATEN FOES

Not Merely Humane, But Expedient--- Our Food Administration Spreading Over the Whole World

For a year or even longer, it may be necessary to keep in Europe the 2,000,000 soldiers we now have in France, for the purpose of maintaining order in those parts of Europe where, under the strain of readjustment and reconstruction, riots and uprisings threaten. This will be a shock to the vast number of people in this country who have had most closely associated in their minds with the coming of peace the picture of the beginning of the return of our men to America, although there has been within the last few days more than one intimation of the gravity of the situation under the surface in Europe which may make such action necessary or, indeed, might require the increase of our forces there.

This danger is directly connected with the food shortage in Europe, and upon the handling of that problem in the months immediately following the cessation of hostilities depends not only the length of the stay of our men in Europe but whether, in the transition from war to a new regime of constructive peace, there may not be a period of wide-spread disorder, with our soldiers facing wild armed mobs in various countries in Europe. There is no doubt that secret promoters of revolt, urging the doctrines of anarchy, are at work in many places, and that with the relaxation of the military discipline and control of war time they look to privation and want to set the flames of insurrection going.

The clearest intimation of this menace comes from the man who is best posted on the food situation in Europe, Herbert Hoover, Federal Food Administrator, in these words from a published letter to Frederic Coudert, with regard to our aims and responsibilities in Europe:

> Our object in the overthrow of all autocracies in Europe and the establishment of government by the people is but part of our great burden, for beyond this, when these immediate objects are attained, we still have before us the greatest problem that our Government has ever faced if we are to prevent Europe's immolation in a conflagration of anarchy such as Russia is plunged in today.

As to the extent of this burden and the increased responsibility that will fall upon the people of the United States in food saving: This country is now contributing food to the support of 120,000,000 within the territory of the allied nations. To these will be added, according to an estimate obtained at the Federal Food Administration at Washington, not less than 138,000,000 people who will be chiefly dependent on the United States for food to save them from starvation, when all the barriers which cut us off from the hungry millions of Europe are removed. Close to 200,000,000 people in Europe, according to the latest information from Europe, are in dire need of food. Behind the German lines whole nations have been cut off from help. Large sections of the population in many of the European neutrals are on the verge of starvation.

It was estimated by the Food Administration, before the prospect of an early peace appeared, that in an ensuing year of war the number of deaths from starvation would equal those caused in battle. With the signing of an armistice it is considered that this situation will be aggravated instead of lessened. The machinery of war which parceled out the food available with a fair hand will be weakened, and even the small filter of supply to large classes cut down or stopped. Before the armistice negotiations were concluded there were numerous signs that systems hitherto efficient were beginning to fail in their service to the civilian part of the population. Cognizance of this situation and the menace that it contained no doubt led the Supreme War Council at Versailles to adopt the resolution announcing its desire to cooperate with Austria, Bulgaria, and Turkey, and now Germany, in furnishing the necessities of life to the suffering peoples of those nations.

President Wilson, in his address before the houses of Congress on Monday, laid great emphasis on this phase of the peace settlement. He said:

> The humane temper and intention of the victorious Governments have already been manifested in a very practical way. Their representatives in the Supreme War Council at Versailles have by unanimous resolution assured the peoples of the Central Empires that everything that is possible in the circumstances will be done to supply them with food and relieve the distressing want that is in so many places threatening their very lives; and steps are to be taken immediately to organize these efforts at relief in the same systematic manner that they were organized in the case of Belgium. By the use of the idle tonnage of the Central Empires it ought presently to be possible to lift the fear of utter misery from their oppressed populations and set their minds and energies free for the great and hazardous tasks of political reconstruction which now face them on every hand. Hunger does not breed reform; it breeds madness and all the ugly distempers that make an ordered life impossible.

Here it is recognized that the call to the people to save food to prevent Austrians, Bulgarians, Turks, and, most of all, Germans, from starving, is the most difficult problem of the whole food conservation campaign. Such is the feeling of horror among people of the United States over German atrocities that the humanitarian appeal has lost its force and is replaced in many minds by the wish that the Germans, in retribution for wrongs they have done, suffer in full the pangs and effects of hunger. For countries such as Serbia and Rumania sympathetic response, of course, is assured, and also of nearby neutral nations that have been drained of food by the heavy hand of Germany.

For enemy countries, or those until recently so, there will be two appeals for food saving of far greater popular force than any humanitarian ground that could now be presented. One of these is that a supply of food and the consequent assurance of order will promise the earlier return of our troops to this country, including relief from putting down insurrection while there. The other is that, in order that the Germans and other nations which have been at war with us may be able to pay back the great debts of reparation which will be imposed on them, they must be provided, for economic reasons, with maintenance until their own production places them on a footing to go ahead with this. But the problem of food conservation will be one, and those who deny themselves will not know what fraction of their saving will go to Germany. Certain it is that the needy countries of the Allies and of neutrals will be supplied first.

Our food obligations it is certain will be enormously increased, with the ending of hostilities, even if the immediate needs of recent enemies were left out of consideration. The letting down of the barriers that the war erected will permit us to reach with food the people of Poland, Rumania, Serbia, European Russia, Armenia, and others who now lack an adequate supply of food. Some of these have partial food resources and some are near the verge of starvation: their total number has been estimated at 180,000,000.

Food, it has been said, will win the war. Food, it now turns out, is the one necessary bridge that will carry Europe over from the state of war to an orderly productive peace. Back of the lines, during the war, thousands have starved, but attention was fixed on the battle line where the great issues were at stake and starvation was looked on as a secondary effect. Now, it is seen, with the prospect of an end of the fighting, that no real peace can be assured until this vast food problem is on its way toward solution. A vast machinery of distribution under the direction of the Allies and the United States, with arms to penetrate into many parts of Europe, is seen to be urgently necessary. At stake is not only the saving of millions from starvation but also the protection of large sections of Europe from the disaster that overtook Russia. Therefore the need for food conservation and the elimination of all waste by the American people was never considered to be so great by the Food Administration as it is today.

In the three years prior to the war our average annual exports to the Allies averaged 5,533,000 tons of food. Last year, under the stimulus of a well-directed food conservation and food-production campaign, we succeeded in sending to the Allies 11,820,000 tons of food. The minimum pledged for this year is an increase of close to 6,000,000 tons. That was based on a continuance of the war. With peace, and the added responsibility to head off starvation in large areas of Europe that could not be reached before, it is estimated that this country will have to add another 6,000,000 tons, if not more, raising the requirement from this country to close to 18,000,000 tons. This takes into consideration such relief as available shipping facilities can provide from South America and Australia.

Owing to the attention which the large increase in the wheat crop received, there is an opinion in the public mind that the food resources of the 1918 crop are much larger than those of 1917. But after the wheat harvest adverse weather conditions out down production in other crops. The October report of the Department of Agriculture shows the production condition of the 1918 crop to be, as compared with the 1917 crop:

INCREASE.	Bushels.	DECREASE.	Bushels.
Wheat	268,000,000	Corn	442,000,000
Barley	27,000,000	Oats	52,000,000
Rice	5,000,000	Potatoes	32,000,000
Rye	17,000,000	Sweet potatoes	2,000,000
Buckwheat	2,000,000		
Beans	3,000,000		
Total	322,000,000	Total	548,000,000

On the whole, however, the actual food resources are about the same as last year, due to two main facts: the nutritive value of corn is much higher in this year's crop than last year's and a portion of last year's crop, in the form of a greater number of hogs to which 1917 corn was fed, remains on the farm. The food situation as respects the United States then is, according to the present prospect, an increased demand of between 5,000,000 and 6,000,000 tons from resources that are no larger than those of last year.

As to the scope of the demands on the United States information on which the following reports are based was obtained from the Federal Food Administration at Washington; they concern some of the peoples who, in greater or less degree, will look to the United States as soon as they can be reached by transportation. It is stated:

Poland—A state approaching famine exists throughout the country. Through the "Centralen," established by the Central Powers, a large proportion of the foodstuffs of the country, naturally productive, passed into Germany and Austria. There was a bread famine in many Polish towns as far back as last March. Bread that was offered was mixed with sawdust in many instances and was absolutely inedible. Cattle requisitioned by the military authorities in Galicia left the towns with barely 20 per cent. of their normal supply. On July 1 a meatless period of six months was proposed for the civilian population, from which creches, hospitals, and charitable kitchens were to be exempt. For some time fats have been unobtainable. Although in normal times Poland produces great quantities of sugar beets sugar is very scarce. According to September reports, however, this year's sugar beet crop in Poland promises a favorable result, but before the war 23 per cent. of the agricultural land of Poland was customarily sown in sugar beets.

The Baltic lands: Famine exists in parts of Finland. One of the worst famine-stricken places is in the vicinity of Helsingfors. Since the middle of September Kuopic has been without bread, except for a small amount of wheat later furnished by Germany. Many deaths have occurred from actual starvation at Viborg: from Aug. 1 to Sept. 15 there was no bread at Viborg. Both Suojarvi and Karelen are in the throes of famine. Corn was harvested in many places before it was ripe to prevent deaths from starvation. In numerous places in the Baltic lands bark and lichen have been mixed with the scanty supply of flour in order to make a larger loaf. Finland is almost entirely dependent on imports, in normal times, for wheat, rye, and barley, and the grave situation in the Baltic lands, said to be as serious as anywhere else in Europe, is aggravated by the fact that in ordinary times agriculture is only a secondary industry there. The paper and timber industries stand first, and the people found it more advantageous to import quantities of their food. In Courland less than 30 per cent of the soil is cultivated. Throughout the Baltic lands only 24 people are fed to the kilometer, (three-fourths of an acre,) whereas in Germany 232 people are fed from the products of the same amount of land. In order to preserve present available amounts of fresh and salted meats and fish, butter and sugar, the daily ration throughout the Baltic lands has been cut down to 740 calories a day. On account of the meagre bread ration in Finland the entire food intake is only one-third of what it ought to be. Grain imports have been reduced in Finland to 474,320,000 pounds less than average imports in pre-war times. This has made necessary in Finland a bread ration of 2.8 ounces a day. Consequently the 1,900,000 in Finland dependent on these rations are brought to the border of famine.

Holland—The worst-felt shortages are fats, breadstuffs, meat, feeding stuff, coffee, tea, and chocolate. All foods are strictly rationed. Riots on account of the lack of bread have occurred within the last year at The Hague, Amsterdam, and other large cities. Both horse meat and dog meat have been resorted to, in the hope of relieving the acute meat situation. In order not to deplete the herds in Holland, now amounting to 1,795,195 head, a meatless period has been contemplated for some time. Butter production has fallen off from 135,000,000 pounds in 1916 to 67,500,000 pounds, due in marked degree to underfeeding of the cattle. Poultry production has dropped 60 per cent, potatoes 50, and eggs are practically unobtainable. The fat ration is less than one ounce a day, inclusive of all uses. Only by the extremest care in saving and by strenuous effort to stimulate home production has Holland been able to maintain the present ration of four ounces of meat a day, seven ounces of bread a day, eight ounces of potatoes a week, and one-half pound of sugar a week. Holland will renew her demands for American food, it is certain.

PROGRESS ALREADY MADE BY UNITED STATES IN FEEDING THE WORLD

The following table shows the increase over normal in exports of foodstuffs by the United States since it became the food reservoir for the world on account of the war:

TOTAL EXPORTS.

	3-Year Pre-war Average.	1916-17 Fiscal Year.	1917-18 Fiscal Year.	July, 1917, to Sept. 30, 1917.	July, 1918, to Sept. 30, 1918.
Beef Products, pounds.......	186,375,372	405,427,417	565,462,445	93,952,477	171,983,147
Pork products, pounds.......	996,230,627	1,496,302,713	1,691 437,435	106,256,750	540,946 324
Dairy products, pounds	26,037,790	351,958,336	590,798,274	130,071,165	161,245,029
Vegetable oils, pounds.......	332,430,537	206,708,490	151,029,893	27,719,553	26,026,701
Grains, bushels..............	183,777,331	395,140,238	*349 123,235	66,383,084	121,668,823
Sugar, pounds...............	621,745,507	3,084,390,281	2,149,787,050	1,108,559,519	1,065,398,247

*Wheat harvest 1917-18 was 200,217,333 bushels below the average of the three previous years.

potatoes a week, and one-half pound of sugar a week. Holland will renew her demands for American food, it is certain.

Denmark—The outlook in Denmark, according to a Danish newspaper, is the worst since 1881. Dairying is a great industry there. The number of milk cows have been reduced from 1,147,000 last year to 950,000 on Sept. 1. Within the next six months a drop by another 100,000 is expected. The hay crop this year was less than one-third of the average, and a large slaughtering is therefore regarded as inevitable. With the reduction of cows and limited feeding the output of butter has gone down until now it is necessary to reserve 40 per cent. of the production for home consumption. Before the war there were 2,500,000 hogs in Denmark, which has a world reputation for ham and bacon; the number that remains is 433,000; Denmark's sugar output is reduced by 60,000,000 pounds, to 296,000,000 pounds, but she still has enough of a surplus to make exports to Norway and Sweden. A large potato crop is expected this year from 200,000 acres. On the other side of the ledger the herring fisheries were a complete failure this year, causing a loss of millions of dollars. On the whole, Denmark is probably the least hard pressed for food of any of the surrounding countries from which Germany has drained supplies. Conditions in Iceland are much worse than in Denmark proper, the island being almost wholly dependent on fishing.

Norway—There is a serious shortage of both potatoes and fodder. The potato scarcity falls heavily on the country as a whole, as potatoes are served there with every meal, and in large quantities. Causes for the shortage are given as: Increased consumption due to low bread rations, the necessity of saving 50,000 tons for seed purposes, and that potatoes have been used to take the place of fodder. Scarcity of fodder has compelled farmers to slaughter a larger proportion of live stock than usual. Butter is practically unobtainable in the open market. In its place margarine made largely of whale fat, has been introduced. To control this supply the Government has taken over the whole of the whale catch. Number of whales caught this year are reported to be 593. A whale yields about thirty barrels of fat. Bread, flour, sugar, coffee, beans, sago, oats, rice, potatoes, and tea are all under a rationing system. Tea is so scarce that the Government has fixed the retail price at $2.20 a pound. The Norway Statistical Bureau gave the increase in the cost of living from prewar times to the beginning of the year as 139 per cent., and since that time there has been a steady rise. The Storthing has granted a $27,000,000 subsidy to take care of those upon whom the increased cost of living falls most heavily. It is known as the "hard times" subsidy. Live stock in Norway has not suffered such a falling off as in some other countries. The reductions according to a statement made by the Norwegian Food Commissioner, are: Cattle, 4 per cent.; hogs, 20 per cent.; sheep, 13 per cent. Poultry stocks have gained.

Sweden—Among the middle and laboring classes there is considerable suffering, but no actual starvation. The prevailing opinion is that the laboring and middle classes have not enough of anything; most of their incomes goes for the two items of food and rent. A card rationing system is in use, and it is certain that for manual workers the rations are too low. The rations are estimated at about two-thirds of the normal food intake. Of single items cut down in the rationing bread allowance is reduced to one-half, sugar to one-third, and butter to one-fifth. As a reflection of the system in use there is a new regulation requiring that the bread allowance of those whose income exceeds $1,620 a year is to be reduced. Maximum prices have been established for many articles, but in order to obtain a supply sufficient to keep up strength, the people are forced to trade outside of the regular channels of distribution. Here are some private trades prices: Tea, per pound, $9.45; coffee, $4.85; white flour, 45 cents; butter, $1.20 to $1.50; enough cocoa for six cups, $1.66. Before the war the price of beef was 11 cents a pound; now it is up to a few points above $1. Considerable apprehension is felt as to the effect on the people of this under-nourishment. Fats and sugar in this northern country are particularly necessary, and these are now quite unobtainable in the necessary quantities. To sum up, there is a very real and great food shortage in Sweden.

Serbia and Armenia — So far as information is available a state of famine exists in these countries very much like that in Poland; that is, starvation is taking a heavy toll.

As to the Ukraine, no two authorities seem to agree on the Ukrainian situation, but they do agree that it will not present serious difficulties. The present crop is fair, and although the amount is not ascertained, it is reasonably certain that there will be a surplus of wheat, rye, and corn.

In Germany famine is in sight. A crop shortage, with which Germany entered the year, has been aggravated by the breaking down of the food system in some of its important parts. Since the tide turned definitely against Germany the successive shocks of defeat have had a steadily weakening effect on the once firmly administered distribution of food.

In Austria the menace of famine is reported to be as bad, and in some parts of Turkey the conditions are worse.

In all the hunger-ridden countries of Europe the lack of food, competent observers realize, carries explosive elements which, unless relieved with all possible promptness, may spread wreck and ruin over large areas. There are two assurances, considered to be controlling, that the problem will be met. One, the efficiency of distribution of food achieved by the United States and the Allies in their own territories during the high stress of the war; an extension of this vast machinery of distribution will transport food into the great famine-stricken areas where aid is most urgently needed. The other assurance is that the American people, upon whom in new self-denial the greater part of the burden falls, will meet the responsibility as they have met every one in this war, even rising above just aversion when brought face to face with the fact that some part of the food they save will go into enemy countries whose barbarous conduct in the war was enough to set them outside of humane consideration.

November 17, 1918

SPEEDING CHINA RELIEF

American Fund Must Grow Fast if Tens of Thousands Are to Be Saved From Famine

TRAVELERS just home from China, recent witnesses of the ravages of perhaps the greatest famine in all history, say that the selection of those chosen for rescue is about the most trying duty thrust upon relief workers. Literally, the power of life and death is frequently in the hands of the foreigners, mostly Americans, who are trying to make the most of every cent contributed to the Famine Fund.

At some relief centre the famine victims are lined up to be passed upon by a man in charge of a certain district. There is not enough to feed them all, and the American has to decide which ones will be saved and which must be left to die. Of course, he always tries to get more food in and carry aid to the last man; but sometimes this is impossible, and the cruel choice must be made.

The problem is to make the available supplies do the most possible good. A man who has a fair chance of recovery, who can plant seed for next season's crop and then cultivate the fields, has to be preferred over a victim whose life could probably not be saved, and who, if it were saved, would be unfit to help others.

Not long ago the Governor of the State of New York told a friend that of all his duties none weighed upon him so heavily as the exercise of the pardoning power. The realization that his decision meant the saving or the taking away of a human life, he said, almost overcame him at times. But the periodic ordeal of the Governor is no harder than that faced by the merciful-hearted Red Cross or International Relief Committee workers now in China. At least the Governor does not have to witness the victim's dread of death. The relief workers in China, on the contrary, see a starving Chinese with his hand outstretched for bread and have to say to him in effect:

"No, you must be left to die—the man next to you in line looks more worth saving."

$4,055,000 Sent by Cable.

Up to the present time the amount of money which has been cabled to China for famine relief is put at $4,055,000 by the American Committee for the China Famine Fund, of which Thomas W. Lamont is Chairman. The committee has forwarded $2,255,000, the churches have sent $800,000, and the American Red Cross has appropriated $1,000,000 out of its treasury.

This is but a small fraction of what the Hoover Committee raised for the starving children of Europe, though the sufferers from hunger in China far outnumber those in Europe. Contributions are still coming in, so that the China fund is mounting steadily, but it is still insufficient to meet the demands upon it, and the committee is striving to stimulate still greater generosity.

The planting of the next crop is of vital importance. The loss of one crop means severe hunger for multitudes, and North China has already lost two. A third season without a harvest will add millions to the toll of death. That is why the men in charge of distributing the foods are trying to save those men and women who are most able to work.

Americans of every calling have been brought into the service of relief. Missionaries and Red Cross folk are assisted by employes of business houses who have volunteered their help and in many instances have obtained furloughs from their regular duties in order to assist in the distribution of food. It is the missionaries upon whom the main responsibility must fall. They are not neophytes who have to be taught to fight in the midst of battle. They have lived among the Chinese for years, and even their ordinary year-to-year routine partakes of the nature of relief. It is these men and women, by their very nature and occupation Good Samaritans, who have to be as hard-hearted as executioners in condemning the least fit of the sufferers to die.

Missionaries' Valiant Work.

Practical business men, engineers and merchants, who hitherto have had at best a sort of good-natured tolerance for missionaries as a collection of well-meaning visionaries, are bearing witness to their practical ability in emergencies like this one. Charles Davis Jameson, an engineer who was for years in the service of the Chinese Government and made important examinations and surveys for the Red Cross in preparation for flood control operations, was an active participant in relieving the sufferers from a famine in another part of China. He says of the missionaries:

"It was necessary, in our undertaking, that food centres and famine camps should be in charge of non-Chinese who would have charge of the money and food and the payment of the workers. There was no money to pay wages for such men. But China's revolution inadvertently supplied them. The unrest in Western China became so acute that the Protestant missionaries were ordered to the coast and there was thus set free for famine work a magnificent body of young, vigorous and enthusiastic men who worked for their bare expenses.

"They were a revelation to me. I had known them as missionaries, preaching the fear of God and the beginning of wisdom, in season and out of season. Now they were hard-headed, efficient organizers and leaders of men in manual construction work. Among them were engineers, surveyors, machinists and accountants. It seemed that for any special work the perfect man appeared."

Children Sold or Slain.

"There is snow on the ground, and there are no leaves on the trees or even leaves left for fuel," is one of the latest messages received by the Famine Fund Committee. It comes from a missionary at Au Ping, China, who adds: "The doomed throng my doors every day and have to be sent away with kind words, but no food."

The Y. M. C. A. man in charge of the relief work at Paotingfafu writes:

"In our one district alone we will need 50,000 tons of grain before June if wholesale starvation is to be prevented. Our district is only one of a dozen such, and not the worst one in the famine area."

Authentic accounts of the killing or sale of children to save them from the sufferings of starvation continue to come in. Wells are found poisoned by the bodies of babies thrown into them by crazed parents. Whole families lie dead by the roadside. China has had many famines in its history, but none on record approaches this one in the havoc wrought. It is estimated that 10,000 victims succumb each day.

There has come to the Famine Fund Committee from an engineer what is perhaps as succinct and clear an explanation of the extent of the famine, geographically, as has yet been given. He says:

"The areas affected are the Province of Shensi, the Province of Shansi, that portion of Chihli from the coast on the east to the mountains on the west and from Peking on the north to the southern boundary of the province; Shantung from the northwest border to the mountains, east to the mouth of the Yellow River and south to the southern boundary of the province, and that portion of the Province of Honan north to the Yellow River.

"There is along the coast a stretch some twenty miles in width that is not suitable for cultivation at any time and has an inappreciable population.

"The acute areas in Shensi are said to be of less extent than in the other provinces. In Shansi the famine area is extensive, and the number of deaths may run into the millions. There is no water transportation in or into the province. There is one narrow-gauge railway only, which connects the centre of Shansi with the coastal plain. Owing to the urgent call for help in the acute areas easier of access, in Chihli and Shantung, only the most heroic measures, in money and personal effort, can save Shansi from a terrible disaster.

"The rich tillable land in Shansi runs north and south along the central and western part of the province upon a plateau some 3,000 feet above the sea. This plateau is fenced in on the north, south and east by rugged mountains rising thousands of feet higher. There is only one cart road from the east and only one narrow-gauge railway.

"Because of their greater accessibility, more is known of conditions in Chihli and Shantung than in Shensi and Shansi. Shantung is the most densely populated part of China—545 persons to the square mile. This is the second year they have had no food and no money. They have sold their belongings for a few cents, and land is being sold at a quarter of its value."

Relief Through Schools.

Schools constitute one of the mediums for relieving the famine sufferers. Attendance cards are kept, and parents presenting the cards receive a certain allowance of money with which to buy food. This method is of special value in keeping homes together and preventing the sale of children, in that it provides parents with a powerful motive to keep their children close by. It is reported as giving splendid results in certain sections.

To prevent overcrowding in large cities, the relief organizations are making every effort to distribute grain in the country districts. There is not much coal, but enough wood fuel to make grain relief feasible. The recipients of grain have the opportunity of mixing other ingredients, and thus the supplies go further than if distributed through soup kitchens.

The American Committee for the China Famine Fund, conducting its fieldwork through the existing agencies in China, and through newly organized committees, has its most pressing task here at home—the collection of money. Speeding up is the program; for speed means, definitely, saved lives. Funds are cabled across the Pacific, as fast as received, by two banking corporations that transmit them without cost.

China life-saving stamps, to be placed on the backs of letters, are being sold in ever-increasing volume. More than 5,500,000 of these stamps have been ordered by local committees and individual purchasers in forty-four States. They sell at 3 cents each. Oregon is leading in the stamp sale thus far. Churches are redoubling their effort to raise funds from their congregations. Rotary clubs have begun to take part in the campaign. The United States Chamber of Commerce, representing local chambers throughout the country, is co-operating. Vernon Munroe, Treasurer, Bible House, New York, receives contributions to the fund.

March 13, 1921

NO U. S. GOVERNMENT AID FOR CHINA YET.

Special to The New York Times.

WASHINGTON, March 10.—No action has been taken by the United States Government in the direction of transporting grain from the United States to China for distribution to the starving millions in the five northern provinces of that country. Failure of the Government to act in the matter is the result of the neglect of Congress to appropriate funds, or enact the necessary legislation to enable the United States Shipping Board to utilize vessels which are idle, or operating on a half cargo basis, in the transportation of surplus grain from this country to ports nearest the Chinese famine districts.

The Senate, late in February, passed a resolution offered by Senator William S. Kenyon of Iowa, proposing to appropriate $500,000 for the relief of the famine-stricken people of China. This appropriation was to be used for the transportation in vessels of either or both the navy or the Shipping Board, which use was thereby proposed to be authorized by Congress, of corn in bulk and other food products from the United States to China. American farmers were prepared to furnish corn to the extent of 5,000,000 bushels. The All-American Committee for Famine Relief in China, at Peking, on Feb. 22 announced its acceptance of such a tentative offer, stipulating that the grain, to accomplish its purpose, should arrive in China by the middle of May.

The Senate had been informed that American Farm Bureau and the Chinese Relief Committee stood ready to co-operate in the effort to get this grain to the points where it would serve the most humanitarian purposes in China. Railroad officials of the United States were willing to provide the necessary transportation of the corn to the seaboard. The railroad brotherhoods had agreed to handle the grain, and in every way facilitate its movement. Naval vessels could not be used without authority from Congress, and this was likewise true of Shipping Board steamers. The Senate not only granted such authority, but voted an appropriation of $500,000.

The Kenyon resolution struck a snag in the House of Representatives. It was referred to the Appropriations Committee, which met on Feb. 28 and heard testimony from General W. D. Connor, Chief of the Transportation Service of the Army; Lieutenant Commander C. J. Moore of the Office of Naval Operations; Lieutenant A. B. Canhan and R. D. Vining of the Bureau of Supplies and Accounts of the Navy, as well as Captain Paul Foley, Director of Operations of the Navy. The Kenyon resolution failed in the House. Chairman Good of the Appropriations Committee wrote a letter, however, to Captain Foley of the Shipping Board indicating that if the board's vessels were used for sending American grain to China, there would be no criticism of the matter in Congress. But the board itself was not provided with an appropriation by the Congress which adjourned sine die on March 4 and was left in an anomalous state.

Admiral W. S. Benson, Chairman of the board, submitted to the members of the board, before it was virtually legislated out of office, the question whether the board's ships could be utilized. Admiral Benson and members of the board agreed that vessels could not be used for Chinese relief purposes without special legislation by Congress.

When members of the House committee wanted to know whether it would require as many as ten vessels to haul 10,000,000 bushels of corn to China, Captain Foley responded that it would require forty-four vessels to do it in one trip for each vessel. He said it would cost $5,009,840 to transport this much grain to China, including the cost of unloading the vessels. The statement was also made that it would "demoralize the commercial trade in the Pacific if we brought back any commercial cargo."

Testimony by Lieutenant Commander Moore was that the $500,000 which the Senate voted would transport about 1,000,000 bushels of corn only. It was developed that the Shipping Board had tied up at present in Pacific ports twenty-nine vessels of 7,000 to 9,000 tons, all idle in the Pacific. These vessels carry skeleton crews and would have to be manned with naval reserve if put into service. There are forty-four other Shipping Board vessels operating in the Pacific which carry only half cargo on their outward voyages. It was thought that these vessels might be utilized, but the Shipping Board, in the face of the Treasury decision, has decided it has no authority of law to use them for hauling corn at lower than regular rates.

The new Administration has taken no steps to bring about the use of any of the Shipping Board vessels. As a matter of fact, pending the decision of President Harding as to the future status and personnel of the board, its establishment in Washington is largely an empty shell, operating without appropriations, with its Chairman holding only as a custodian of its affairs and properties, but making no decisions that involve policy.

The executive branch of the Wilson Administration took an active interest in the Chinese famine situation. Mr. Wilson on Dec. 9 issued a statement in which he appealed to the humanitarian sentiments and generosity of the American people in behalf of the famine-stricken people in China and at the same time named the nation-wide relief committee, the Chairman of which is Thomas W. Lamont. While the attitude of the Harding Administration toward Chinese relief has not been officially announced, there is no indication that the State Department, under its new management, will have any but the most sympathetic attitude toward the famine sufferers.

March 13, 1921

Our Aid to Russia: A Forgotten Chapter

In 1921-22, millions of Russians were saved from starvation by swift American action.

By GEORGE F. KENNAN

THE exchange that took place recently between Soviet First Deputy Premier Kozlov and Secretary of State Herter over the question of who paid for the American relief action during the Russian famine of 1921-22 suggests that few people now recall the detailed circumstances of this episode into which so much American interest and effort were poured at the time. Since this is one of those points at which the Soviet historical image is beginning to diverge rapidly from that of historians in this country, it might be worth while today to review the facts of this episode.

During World War I, up to 1917, the area under cultivation in Russia declined by about 25 per cent. For this, the Bolsheviki were in no way responsible. But after their assumption of power, this decline continued unchecked until 1921, so that by that year the area sown to crops can scarcely have been much more than half of the prewar figure. There is solid evidence to show that while the civil war played a part in this further decline of agricultural production after the revolution, the major cause of it lay in the reckless and ill-advised policies of the Soviet Government itself, and particularly in its failure to provide adequate incentives for the individual peasant.

In 1921 Russia was struck by a first-class drought in certain of the main grain-growing regions, notably the Trans-Volga district and the southern Ukraine. In the prevailing conditions, the effects of this drought were serious in the extreme. The total crop in the year 1921 fell short by some seven million tons of the minimum amount required for feeding the country. Had there been normal reserves and distribution facilities, famine might still have been prevented. But, in addition to the lack of reserves, Russia was at that time in a general state of economic ruin.

AGAINST this background, the effects of the drought were appalling. By midsummer an estimated fifteen million persons were threatened with sheer, stark starvation; and there was absolutely no prospect that this disaster could be appreciably mitigated by action undertaken within Russia itself.

At some time in the late spring or early summer of 1921, the Soviet Government became at least partially aware of the dimensions of the catastrophe and also of its own inability to remedy it. How seriously the Soviet leaders viewed the situation we do not know. This was a bad time for them. They had just been severely rocked by the Kronstadt mutiny. They had already been sufficiently sobered by the general economic breakdown to inaugurate the New Economic Policy in March. The famine now came as a new blow.

Walter Duranty, the well-known correspondent of The New York Times, wrote that the Soviet leaders were aware "that the whole machinery of state * * * was liable to be wrecked on the rocks of the food shortage." Others took a less serious view of the political dangers which the famine presented for the regime. However that may be, the extremity in which the leaders found themselves must really have been great.

THE appeal for help was not made in the name of the Soviet Government. It was made by Maxim Gorki, the writer, who, while close to the Communists, was known and respected as a literary figure far beyond Russia's borders. Gorki issued his appeal on July 11, 1921. Hinting that he himself did not believe in humanitarian impulses, he pointed out that the Russian famine nevertheless presented "a splendid opportunity" for those who did so believe to apply their convictions. He invoked the images of Tolstoy, Dostoevski, Mendeleev, Pavlov, Mussorgski and Glinka as bonds likely to appeal to cultured European and American people. He ended with the bald injunction: "Give bread and medicine." Two or three weeks later, Lenin, in his own name, issued a similar appeal to the international proletariat for aid to the Russian comrades.

Gorki's appeal aroused the immediate interest of Herbert Hoover and those who had previously been associated with him in the work of famine relief. Mr. Hoover, though by now Secretary of Commerce in the new Republican Administration, was still head of the American Relief Administration, usually known as the A. R. A. The A. R. A., following completion of its famous wartime program in Belgium, had administered post-hostilities relief, mostly for children, in some twenty-three countries.

THE idea of work in Russia by the A. R. A. had come up at the time of the Paris Peace Conference, but had been vitiated by the fact that the offer to Russia was coupled with conditions which were wholly unacceptable to the Soviet Government. The matter had come up in the following year, 1920, during the Russian-Polish war, when the advance of the Red Army into Poland had interrupted the work of the A. R. A. feeding stations in that country. The retreat of the Red Army from Poland had been followed by talks between A. R. A. officials and the Soviet authorities in Moscow about possible A. R. A. work in Russia. But these had broken down because the Soviet Government insisted on complete control of actual supplies brought in, and refused to guarantee the protection of any A. R. A. personnel in Russia unless the United States Government would enter into official relations with the Soviet Government.

Following the breakdown of these talks, Communist-controlled organizations had kept up a drumfire of criticism of Hoover for failure to send food to Russia on Soviet terms. Now, with the evidences of the Russian famine, and the news of Gorki's appeal, it seemed to Hoover that there might be a real chance of agreement.

The State Department, on being consulted, made only one condition. This was that the Soviet Government release a number of Americans, whom it was holding in its prisons as hostages in order to bring pressure to bear toward the resumption of official relations. These were men who had fallen foul of the Soviet authorities in one way or another between 1919 and 1921.

ON July 22, 1921, Hoover replied to Gorki's appeal, explaining that the prisoners would first have to be released before any American aid could

---

GEORGE F. KENNAN, a former Ambassador to Russia, is the author of a history entitled "Soviet-American Relations, 1917-1920."

be extended, and then listing the technical conditions on which the A. R. A. would consider extending aid. These were, in fact, exactly the same conditions on which the A. R. A. had been distributing food in a number of other countries. This offer was promptly accepted by Maxim Litvinov as a basis for negotiations; and a batch of six American prisoners was released across the Estonian border the next day as a starter. About 100 were finally released.

Two days later at Riga there began negotiations which ended with the signing, on Aug. 20, of a curious sort of treaty between the A. R. A. and the Soviet Government. This agreement defined the conditions under which the A. R. A. might act within Russia to bring aid to famine sufferers, particularly children.

The A. R. A. operation in Russia lasted roughly a year and a half. About one-fifth of the total dollar costs, running to some sixty-two million dollars, were covered by the Soviet Government itself which released some twelve million dollars from its gold reserve for this purpose. Of the remainder, about one-half was put up by the American Government. The rest came from private donations in the United States. In addition, the Soviet Government expended an estimated fourteen million dollars on behalf of the program in local currency.

THE American staff of the A. R. A. in Russia numbered something less than two hundred Americans. Within a few weeks after inauguration of the program, i.e., by February, 1922, as a result largely of exertions by these Americans that were little short of heroic, some 1,200,000 Russian children were being fed. By August, the figure had grown to a peak of 4,173,000 children, plus over six million adult sufferers whose condition was too urgent to be ignored—a total of over ten million people.

There were at one time 18,000 feeding stations in operation. In all, some 788,000 tons of food were imported and distributed by the A. R. A. alone. Medical relief was brought to many millions to control the raging typhus which accompanied the famine. The program lasted, so far as the adults were concerned, until the relatively favorable harvest of 1922 had been gathered. Long before the A. R. A. program was finished, the Soviet Government had resumed export of its own grain.

The A. R. A. was not alone in this work. Valuable independent contributions were made by other American and European organizations, including the Quakers, but these were on a far smaller scale. The Soviet Government, too, stimulated—one senses—by the A. R. A.'s example and competition, greatly increased and improved its own efforts to meet the situation.

It has been soberly and authoritatively estimated that, as a result of the A. R. A.'s efforts alone, approximately eleven million lives were saved, of which at least a third were those of children and young people.

The Soviet Government plainly wished to see the A. R. A. succeed in bringing famine relief to certain of the stricken districts (for some reason, the southern Ukraine does not seem to have been included in this benevolent intention) and in many basic respects it supported the A. R. A.'s operations. But the memories of the recent civil war were still fresh, and the Soviet leaders made it a principle, then as later, to put the preservation of Soviet power ahead of every other consideration. Their view of world capitalism, furthermore, left no room for the possibility that Americans might be sincere in the humanitarian sentiments on which they based their readiness to extend this aid, and made it necessary to search for ulterior motives on the American side.

FOR these reasons, the dominant consideration underlying Soviet treatment of the A. R. A. and its doings—a consideration overshadowing any interest in its success as a famine-relief agency—appears to have been an absurdly overdrawn concern lest the operation should become a focal point for opposition to the Soviet regime. To this end, efforts were put in hand (a) to intimidate the A. R. A.'s local employes to a point where they would, while nominally serving A. R. A., take their orders actually from Communist commissars sent out for the purpose and (b) by this and other means to bring distribution of the food under direct Soviet control. The A. R. A. had no choice but to resist these efforts, and it was generally successful in doing so.

By the same token, official liaison with the A. R. A. was entrusted to the organization whose main function was to see that it did not become the seat of conspiracy: the secret police. The A. R. A. was obliged, throughout the major period of its existence, to deal with the organs of the central government through the agency of a senior official of the dreaded "Cheka" (special secret police). He was A. V. Eiduk, a man known during the civil war for his merciless severity to the enemies, or supposed enemies, of the revolution. From the A. R. A.'s standpoint Eiduk had the advantage that, whenever he could be persuaded to issue an order on A. R. A.'s behalf, he had the means to make it respected. But he was suspicious and hostile, and obviously took more seriously the duties of surveillance and penetration of the A. R. A. operation than he did the task of assisting the Americans with their work.

MEMENTO—A scroll presented in 1923 to Herbert Hoover, A. R. A. chairman, says Russians will never "forget the aid rendered to them."

THE head of the mission, Col. William Haskell, was repeatedly obliged, in his dealings with Eiduk, to come to the verge of closing up the entire program (at one time he even had to stop all shipments from the United States for a considerable period) in order to protect the integrity of the operation.

The treatment of the A. R. A. in Soviet public statements was varied and contradictory. Lenin, for his part, seems to have kept scrupulously aloof from the American relief undertaking and to have avoided committing himself in its favor or disfavor. Other Soviet leaders did not hesitate, even while the program was in progress, to impugn the A. R. A.'s motives and to encourage hostility to it and suspicion of it among the population.

At the farewell dinner for the senior A. R. A. staff in 1923, Leonid Kamanev, one of the senior Soviet figures of the time, spoke warmly of the A. R. A.'s work, and presented Colonel Haskell with a Resolution of the Soviet of People's Commissars professing most profound gratitude and declaring that the Soviet people would never forget the help given by the American people. Yet historians note that at about this same time Kamenev's wife (Trotsky's sister) was saying in speeches that foreign relief was just a subterfuge for the penetration of Russia and for getting rid of undesirable food surpluses.

RECENT Soviet historical works do indeed mention the famine, but they ignore Gorki's appeal; they portray the A. R. A. as having taken the initiative in proposing American assistance; they show the Soviet Government as having graciously accepted the proposal while rejecting the A. R. A.'s efforts to encroach on Soviet sovereignty. They slide quickly over the question of what the A. R. A. really did in the way of famine relief (one recent book says cryptically that the A. R. A. "gave a certain help to the starving") and they go on to tell at length of what the Soviet Government itself did, and of the assistance given by the foreign proletariat. The latter assistance, measured against the A. R. A.'s, was in a ratio of about one to fifty.

The best that may be said in retrospect is that, despite all the friction and difficulty, both sides got, basically, what they most wanted. The A. R. A. did not become a source of conspiracy; the Soviet Government was not overthrown. Several million children, who would otherwise have died, were kept alive.

July 19, 1959

HUNGRY INDIA LEARNING AMERICAN FARM METHODS

Princeton Man Demonstrates Use of Machinery to People Near Starvation, But Finds Many Difficulties—Sacred Cows and Caste System Cause Great Loss

By ELSIE WEIL.

THE new Viceroy of India, Lord Irwin, has recognized that the future of India depends on its agricultural development. In his reply to the address of welcome of the Bombay Chamber of Commerce he said he was heartily in accord with the appointment of a Royal Commission of Agriculture for India, recommended by Lord Reading, the retiring Viceroy. Lord Irwin, who was formerly Minister of Agriculture in England, indicated that his chief interest would be a coordination between the people and the Government to harness modern science to the development of agriculture in India.

Dr. Sam Higginbottom, recently home from India, where he has been successful in introducing up-to-date American methods of farming, paints a grim picture of the poverty there. Dr. Higginbottom confirms Gandhi's statement that 100,000,000 people in India are in a state of chronic starvation. And this in a country where 80 per cent. of the population is engaged in agriculture—a country that grows more rice and sugar cane than any country in the world, leads all in the production of tea, oil seeds, sorghums and millets, and is second only to America in cotton raising.

Under proper conditions of cultivation India could become a most prosperous country, asserts Dr. Higginbottom, superintendent of the Allahabad Agricultural Institute, who has recently received the degree of Doctor of Philanthropy from Princeton—his alma mater—the first American to be thus honored.

"There are three primary causes for poverty in India," he said. "First, the belief in the transmigration of souls, in which the destruction of animal life is regarded as murder; second, caste, and third, the low place given to woman."

$2,250,000,000 Loss Yearly.

Dr. Higginbottom can discourse impressively on the theme of cow-worship.

"There are 65 horned cattle to every 100 acres of land and 61 to each 100 of population," he said. "The result is a severe economic pressure on the soil of India. Over 90 per cent. of the cattle are an economic loss to the country. The cow does not pay her board bill in milk and calves. Roughly estimated, the loss per year is $2,250,000,000.

"Free-lance cattle, unattached to any home, are permitted to wander through the country and eat as they can. Naturally, if the rains fail, the cattle suffer and many die because of lack of fodder. Few farmers keep more than one cow for their own use. It is the custom to give bull calves to the temples, where they are stamped with the sacred brand and turned loose to wander through fields and villages to subsist as they can. The obvious remedy—to send surplus cattle to the slaughter-house as in Europe and America—would horrify the Hindus.

SAM HIGGINBOTTOM

"Hindus regard the killing of a cow as the most hideous crime that can be perpetrated. The cow, in a country that believes in transmigration, is worshipped as a god and stands as a symbol of the whole animal world striving for higher life. A Hindu child is taught at its mother's knee to venerate the cow above all living things. The Hindu regards the cow as we regard God or Christ. You might as well expect a Christian to express approval of the Crucifixion as a Hindu to sanction the slaughter of a cow.

Can't Be Sold for Beef.

"Everything connected with the cow is sacred. All orthodox Hindus who come to Western countries, all Hindu boys in American or English universities, must go through a ritual of purification before they return to their high-caste homes. The purification ceremony requires that they partake of the products of the cow.

"In India a man who wishes to be regarded as a benefactor does not, as a rule, erect a university, a library, a hospital or a home for convalescent children. He establishes a Gowshala, a home for indigent, aged and decrepit cows. The welfare of the cow is far more important to a Hindu than the welfare of the child. And yet in a country that venerates the cow, the cattle are stunted and dwarfed. The best dairy animal in India gives 5,000 to 7,000 pounds of milk a year in contrast to the best American breed, yielding 20,000 to 30,000 pounds. Under present conditions the cow is eating India out of house and home.

"In India the Western way of utilizing surplus cattle cannot be applied. A constructive program must take into account the sensibilities of the Hindu and manipulate them for progress. The Brahman boy should be trained to appreciate the economic value of the cow. All cattle collected in the Gowshalas should be studied. The deformed should be allowed to die and only the best animals should be used for breeding. The best breeds of other countries should be introduced. On our farm we have obtained excellent results from American Jersey bulls. Cows bred from one of our American Jersey sires and an Indian mother gives 6,000 to 9,000 pounds of milk a year, while the mother gives only 2,000.

Non-Injury to Animals Expensive.

"The doctrine of ahimsa, or non-injury to any living thing, keeps alive not only cattle, but all other animals. As a consequence, the animals suffer as well as the human beings. Monkeys are sacred. Unmolested and unharmed, they raid gardens and orchards so often that farmers, in a country where fruit can be cheaply and abundantly grown, are discouraged from planting fruit trees. It has been estimated that rats alone cost India $70,000,000 annually in the grain they consume. In the Punjab, the Government started a campaign to eliminate rats. They distributed traps to the farmers, but the high-caste Hindus ordered the release of the rats as soon as they were caught."

With high youthful hopes of doing evangelistic work among the outcasts of the United Provinces, Dr. Higginbottom went to India for the North India Presbyterian Mission. Because of the scarcity of missionary teachers he was assigned to Allahabad Christian College, there to teach economics. He did not teach his students by books alone. He took them on tours of factories, machine shops and brick kilns, and to neighboring villages to study the life of the native farmers. In studying village life he was appalled at the frightful poverty. He saw that his mission in India was to show the natives how to grow bigger and better crops.

He went to Government officials and to missionary bodies. "The crying need in India is more food, more education," he said. "India must have agricultural schools and colleges."

He got little encouragement. In those days all roads led to a polite education of the Oxford or Cambridge type, fitting Indians for Government service. And for every vacancy in the Government 100 disappointed Indian A. B.'s were turned away from the position. But high-caste Indians were as enamored of "white collar" education as the Britons and the missionaries who sponsored it. Any innovation that suggested manual labor was unpopular.

Dr. Higginbottom's earnestness finally won the mission authorities to his point of view. They sent him back to Ohio State University to study advanced methods of **agriculture. He was graduated in 1911 and returned to India. With $30,000 collected from friends, 275 acres on the Jumna** River, near **Allahabad, were** purchased, stocked and equipped.

His work has more than justified itself. The Allahabad Agricultural Institute is a model farm that radiates its usefulness throughout the United Provinces. His trained young men are now carrying the message of better tools, better cattle and better farming to all of India.

"The caste system is an overwhelming burden," said Dr. Higginbottom. "The low-caste people are kept down and live in enforced and wretched idleness half their time. If a man belongs to the washerman caste, in a community where 40 per cent. of his neighbors have clothing that costs less than a dollar a year, there will be little to wash. If his sons cannot get laundry work to do the neighbors shrug their shoulders: 'It's too bad.' But nothing can be done about it. In any other part of the world the son of a washerman could drive a team or hoe a field. Not in India. The son of a washerman is a washerman to the end of his days.

"I employed a sweeper whose duties were of the lightest description. He complained that he could not support his wife and six children on $2 a month. I suggested that he help the gardener and I would gladly pay him. A few minutes later the gardener gave me notice. He could not work with a sweeper. He would be shunned by the members of his own caste. That settled it. Had I employed the sweeper the whole tribe of gardeners would have boycotted me. There are seven classes of sweepers alone. One can feed and wash a dog, another cannot. A second cannot wash a cat's saucer. A third can feed chickens, but a fourth cannot. And so on through a complicated list of sweeper commandments.

Illiteracy of Women.

"The sixty million outcasts have just as rigid rules of caste as those higher up. Among leather workers some will eat the beef of an animal that has died of old age or disease, but not one that has been butchered. No orthodox Hindu of caste would touch beef. It is even regarded as a criminal offense to beat a man with a shoe, because an orthodox man touched by leather, which is the product of a dead animal, becomes defiled. Lower than the leather worker and the washerman in the social scale is the dom, who buries the dead. Beneath all of these is the scavenger who handles the offal.

"All this has a direct bearing on agriculture. To grow bigger and better crops in India we must have manure to enrich the soil. Cow dung is almost entirely consumed for purification rites and fuel. Any other kind is defiling to Hindu caste ideas. India's soil responds gratefully to bone fertilization, but this is on the taboo list because the majority of Indian farmers will not handle the bones of dead animals.

"It is not only caste that keeps the people down but also the low status of woman. Only 2 per cent. of the women of India are literate. The 98 per cent. pass on to their children the superstitions of their own ignorance.

"The poverty of the Indian farmer drags him down and makes him accept his situation as hopeless. Because he lacks capital to start with he builds houses and roads of mud, which because of the constant need for repair, are in the long run an expensive luxury. I can speak out of my own experience. I had to spend $2,000 in ten years to maintain a bamboo and grass thatch shed 200 feet long and 30 feet wide over my silos, and even with constant and diligent repair I could not keep out rain, snakes and ants. Another shed with iron pillars and tiles required an original outlay of $2,600, but at the end of ten years it was as good as new, while the bamboo and grass shed was not worth a penny.

Need American Tractors.

"The actual cultivator of the land, the farmer, who determines the sowing and ca: dispose of his own produce, makes about three dollars a month. The farm laborer does not average more than two or two-fifty. The farmer is so heavily in debt to **the money lender that his crop is usually mortgaged before it is harvested. A wedding feast impoverishes him for life. The money lender takes the crop from the threshing floor and doles out to the farmer from week to week just enough grain to keep body and soul together.**

"In the villages in Central India with which I am most familiar the interest on loans varies from 36 to 100 per cent. And once in the clutches of the money lender the farmer never gets free, for the lender either will not give receipts for payments made or takes advantage of the farmer's illiteracy to frame up preposterous terms that can never be met.

"Two and a half to four acres represent the average holdings in the Ganges Valley and in the congested districts of the Punjab, but because of the fragmentation of holdings this land is not all in one piece. Such division of the ancestral land among the heirs would not be so bad if the whole amount of the property was divided into equal portions among, say for example, four sons. Bu each field has to be broken up into four equal portions. The holdings are often so small that they resemble checkerboards. Many fields are so narrow that it is impossible to turn the plow. In America one man with his tractors and up-to-date farm machinery can look after twenty-four acres. In India one man can handle only one acre.

"There is no reason why India cannot become one of the prosperous countries of the world instead of remaining one of the most backward," Dr. Higginbottom says. "India now records the lowest yield per acre of cultivated land of any country. What India needs is better tools and implements. The limiting factor is not money, but men trained to use them. American plows and tractors could be purchased through the rural cooperative societies.

"The most important thing for India at present is to have enough to eat. Christ Himself always ministered to the people according to their particular needs. I firmly believe that good religion and good economics are two sides of the same coin."

June 13, 1926

2,000,000 STARVING IN CHINESE FAMINE

With 2,000,000 Believed Dead Already, Situation Is Called the Worst in History.

INVESTIGATOR SEES NO HOPE

American Tells of Villages Near By Wiped Out and Mercury at 32 Below Zero, Coldest Recorded.

Special Cable to THE NEW YORK TIMES.

PEKING, Jan. 13.—One-third of the 6,000,000 population of the Provinces of Shensi and Shansi have perished of starvation in the last twelve months and 2,000,000 more are doomed to certain death before June, according to a grim report brought here today by foreign investigators.

The intensely cold Winter is aggravating conditions. On behalf of the Chinese International Relief Commission, it is stated, a breakdown in local cart transport has made its practically impossible to get stores into the distressed areas from the outside. The animals which drew the carts have been eaten and the carts smashed for firewood.

Kansu Province, which last year was the scene of a wholesale massacre by Moslem bandits, now is unapproachable except by walking. More than 6,000,000 persons, it is stated, are destitute in this region owing to the failure of crops last season, to which has been added the miseries attendant on civil war and brigandage.

Starvation, according to the report, is rampant over an area of 5,000 square miles. The people are eating elm leaves, chaff and any rubbish obtainable, and desperate parents are ready to give their children away to anybody who will feed them.

Investigator Describes Scenes.

PEKING, Jan. 13 (AP).—The China International Famine Relief is confronting the most hopeless situation it has ever faced in famine-ridden China in the Northern province of Shensi, where thousands of persons are dying daily from famine and exposure.

Grover Clark, a former Peking newspaper editor, returning from a six-weeks inspection trip in the Wei River district, declared today that there is no hope for saving the famine sufferers.

He says thousands were frozen to death in the recent cold wave, when with the thermometer at 32 below Shensi province suffered the coldest weather recorded in its history. The people, accustomed to a minimum temperature of fifteen above for more than forty years, were caught unprepared.

Mr. Clark reported "the most disheartening scenes I have ever witnessed in all my years in the Orient and in all my travels in the interior.

"Thousands begged for a piece of bread, for coppers, for anything I could give them.

Local Authorities Helpless.

"I consulted the various local authorities, but no remedy was suggested because of transportation difficulties and dangers from bandits, the bandits being the stronger peasants who have taken to robbeery for food.

"Even if the China Famine Relief had plenty of grain to pour into the **area we could not reach it for months. The local authorities are helpless and in many instances are themselves on the verge of starvation."**

Mr. Clark said entire villages had been wiped out by cold and starvation. Only five or ten persons remained alive in village after village that he visited. All the woodwork in houses had been burned as a last resource for heat.

He said that he saw thousands upon thousands of persons slowly starving and without the strength to commit suicide. Men and women begged him to take their children with him.

Mr. Clark considers the Shensi area one of the worst examples of famine conditions that have ever existed in China.

This section of the country has repeatedly suffered from droughts since the Spring of 1927, and the drought extends to Southwestern Shensi, where conditions are nearly as bad as along the Wei River.

The China International Famine Relief is making every effort to send millet to the Wei River in large quantities, but the only quantities it has been able to get into the district scarcely suffice for 2,000 children and 100 old women, who have been assembled at Siam-fu and are being kept alive with rations of a pound of millet a day each.

Mr. Clark reports that 300,000 of General Feng Yu-hsiang's soldiers are reduced to the same rations of a pound of millet a day.

January 14, 1930

ANOTHER FAMINE IN CHINA.

The latest reports from the Chinese famine districts are the more appalling because there is no likelihood that effective help can be given by outsiders. Now, as before, the difficulty lies primarily in the lack of transportation facilities. Except along the few railroad lines and the canals, the mass of the Chinese people can be reached only on foot or by slow-moving carts or wheelbarrows. There are few highways in China suitable for transportation on a large scale. The difficulty of distribution of food throughout most of the famine districts is almost insurmountable.

There is one encouraging new factor in the situation. From Nanking comes the report that a set of "Hooverizing" orders have been promulgated whereby it is hoped to save food for the use of the famine sufferers. While it is true that spreading the knowledge of such an order is a hard task, and that carrying it into practical effect is even harder — since they have never known that sort of self-denial in the interest of the community in China—it is an indication that the Nationalist Government realizes the basic truth in the statement of the American Red Cross investigators last Summer to the effect that the most effective relief can come only from within—by Chinese working in the interests of their own people, rather than by foreigners using their own funds.

To Americans and Europeans the thought that they are powerless to alleviate the suffering of China's starving millions is most depressing. Nor is it made any the less awful by realizing that for at least forty centuries China has been swept by periodic famines which have carried away millions of people within a few months, and that throughout this period a large proportion—today probably more than half—of the population of China has lived on what to us of the West would be a starvation diet.

Those who have studied the problem on the spot agree that the only permanent relief must come from a change in present conditions. This is why some of the charitable organizations have in the past devoted their money to the building of roads and the damming of rivers. In this way they hope at the same time to prevent some of the causes of famine—of which floods in certain sections are the most important—and to make it possible to send supplies quickly and readily into the smitten districts. This work is, however, rightly that of the Chinese Government. So also is the actual organization of lasting relief measures. There is plenty of money in China to be devoted to such purposes. In the past it has rarely been forthcoming in adequate amounts.

January 18, 1930

100,000 Reported Driven From Sahara by Famine

Wireless to THE NEW YORK TIMES.

LISBON, Portugal, May 30 (by mail to London).—Reports from Tangier, International Zone, Morocco, say 100,000 natives are on the verge of starvation in the zone bordering on the southern frontier of French Morocco.

Long caravans of camels bearing natives with all their worldly possessions are said to be trekking northward. A third consecutive year of drought in the northwestern part of the Sahara Desert, it is said, has driven them to the north coast of Africa, 300 to 400 miles away.

French Morocco authorities have been sending hundreds of truckloads of rice to the famine-stricken population, and water is distributed by the quart for drinking purposes only.

On the Moroccan coast beggars have increased by the hundreds in the last few months. The French Government has sent high colonial officials to investigate and supervise relief.

June 8, 1937

U. S. FOOD PURCHASE FOR RUSSIA REVEALED

First Lend-Lease Items Is 17,500,000 Pounds of Sugar

WASHINGTON, Jan. 17 (AP)—The United States has started accumulating food for shipment to Russia under the lease-lend program.

Although it has been made known officially that this country would help supply food to its allies, the first indications that purchases were being made for Russia came today in reports by the Department of Agriculture on lease-lend buying operations.

In announcing that the government had delivered $300,000,000 worth of food and other farm products to the British Government for lease-lend shipment, the department added that "war in the Pacific has not changed our basic program for agricultural commodity lease-lend operations."

"We are continuing heavy purchases to make available the vital supply of food for England and Russia," the department's summary read. "We are also buying food and feed supplies to meet the needs of our territories under separate Congressional authority."

The first item bought for Russia was 17,500,000 pounds of sugar. Larger imports of this vital food are needed by the Russians because of German occupation of sugar-beet producing areas of the Ukraine. Wheat and flour and other cereal products are among other items expected to be made available to the Russians.

The department made known that agricultural commodities turned over to Great Britain between the time the lease-lend program was started last April and Dec. 1 amounted to more than 2,650,000,000 pounds, the total including canned and dried fruits and vegetables, cereal products, cotton and tobacco.

January 18, 1942

WEEKLY FOOD RATIONS HERE AND ABROAD

	MEAT	BUTTER & FAT	COFFEE OR TEA	SUGAR
U.S.A.	32 oz.	16 oz.	COFFEE 3⅕ oz.	8 oz.
BRITAIN	16 oz.	8 oz. ONLY 2 OZ. OF BUTTER	TEA 2 oz. COFFEE NOT RATIONED	8 oz.
U.S.S.R	18 oz.	7 oz.	TEA COFFEE NOT RATIONED	15 oz.
GERMANY	12½ oz.	7¼ oz.	SUBSTITUTE ONLY 3½ oz.	8 oz.

March 28, 1943

FAMINE GRIPS BENGAL

British Threaten to Intervene Unless Prompt Relief Is Given

British authorities in New Delhi, India, have threatened to intervene in the domestic affairs of Bengal unless the the local Indian Government is able to alleviate the famine raging there, the British Broadcasting Corporation said in a broadcast recorded yesterday by the National Broadcasting Company in New York.

Charging that the famine was due to "profiteering and bad distribution," the broadcast said that "in October, the British authorities will call a food conference, which will draw up plans for compulsory rationing in every Indian town with a population over 100,000."

"Advices from Calcutta," it added, "indicate that the food shortage in Bengal has now reached the proportions of a famine. * * * Men are reported dying in the streets of Calcutta, and there is not a single village in the province in which the inhabitants are getting two meals a day. In one town the average death rate from malnutrition is 20 to 25 persons a day."

September 19, 1943

INDIA ARMY CALLED TO HELP IN FAMINE

Wavell Takes Relief Steps as 8,000 Die in Calcutta Within Sixty Days

TROOPS TO HANDLE FOOD

Commons Plans Debate—A Cyclone and Loss of Burma Caused Shortages

CALCUTTA, India, Oct. 28 (U.P.)—Field Marshal Viscount Wavell, Viceroy of India, has called on the Indian Army in an emergency move to help the Bengal Government deal with the situation created by a famine in which thousands of persons have died, it was announced today.

The Viceroy's secretary said that Lord Wavell, after a three-day inspection tour of the starvation areas, where hundreds of persons were dying in the streets, and after a day-long conference with authorities, announced that the following relief program would be put into effect immediately:

1. The Bengal Government would take prompt action to send Calcutta's growing destitute population to rest camps in the suburban areas where they would be given adequate food and medical attention, after which they would be returned to their villages.

2. Since the movements of food and grain from Calcutta to the rural areas was a major problem, Gen. Sir Claude J. E. Auchinleck, commander of the Indian Army, agreed to make available to the Government an officer who was expert in supply movements to improve the distribution of food.

3. Lord Wavell will ask General Auchinleck to make the resources of his army available for the movement of food, providing shelters, the establishment of relief stores, distribution of food locally and medical relief.

Lord Wavell hurried to Calcutta shortly after his arrival in New Delhi from England to assume his duties as Viceroy, spurred by the increasingly desperate food shortage which led to appalling scenes in the larger cities. A total of 2,154 persons died in Calcutta alone in the week of Oct. 10 to 16, as compared with a "normal" death rate of 600 weekly, according to official reports.

October 29, 1943

GRAIN HOARDING IMPERILS BENGAL

Famine Threat Acute Because of Inability to Break Grip of Black Market

By GEORGE E. JONES
By Wireless to THE NEW YORK TIMES.

CALCUTTA, India, July 14—Some tremendous undercurrent seems to be driving Bengal Province and its swarming sixty millions into a probable famine this year.

This writer has returned to Bengal after a tour through drought-stricken Southern India where there is a genuine crisis. In Bengal one sees a crisis, also, but it is generated by greed on the part of the Indian grain dealers and by lack of a vigorous Provincial Government policy.

It now appears that Bengal's rice crop has suffered more damage than was estimated last February when the Province was not even listed among the critical food areas of India. The Government says today that Bengal, normally a deficit province which has to import some rice from the outside, has suffered a 7 per cent deficit this year.

This figure is open to dispute. Anti-Government sources assert that 10 or 15 per cent is more nearly accurate.

In any event, Bengal's actual shortage cannot be compared with that of Madras Province or Mysore State in the south. They have suffered far more actual crop damage, yet maintain a relatively efficient rationing and procurement program.

In those areas a peasant can buy his ration at a rate of slightly less than $3.50 per maund [eighty-two pounds] of rice. In Bengal, the villager must turn chiefly to the black market where he may pay at the rate of more than $7.50.

The entire situation brings memories of the 1943 famine. Once again the bulk of the rice stocks has fallen into the hands of dealers who speculate happily on the possibilities of further price increases. Most responsible persons not connected with the Provincial Government agree that there will be a famine starting perhaps in September — although some are hopeful that the famine will be localized and will not attain the proportions of the 1943 disaster in which a million persons died of starvation and allied causes.

It is well to note that while there is no starvation on a large scale as yet, the Government of Bengal has ceased to list starvation deaths separately in its weekly tabulation of mortalities. They are now classified with deaths "from unknown causes." Until a few weeks ago deaths of two or three destitutes a week from starvation were reported regularly as a matter of routine.

About that time prices on the "free market"—a local euphemism for black market—began to shoot upward from a variety of causes. Among these were newspaper publicity of the crop shortage, which aroused the fears of the excitable Bengali, and measures to halt grain smugglers, to name only two contributing factors.

Prices advanced from eighteen rupees a maund of rice on the black market to nearly thirty-five rupees. They have since subsided, but increasing numbers of villages are now unable to afford the black market prices. It is probable that not more than half of the population is on either the formal or informal rationing.

The black market, therefore, knows its strength and flourishes accordingly. Honest officials dare not prosecute it too vigorously lest they cut off the villagers' main source of supply. Dishonest officials and police who seek to supplement their miserable salaries with bribes and illegal activities look the other way for quite different reasons.

A British Army officer, in hard-hit Dacca district, told this writer in a weary tone of voice that he had discovered forty-two ways in which money passed illegally from one hand to another in circumventing the Government's rationing and procurement machinery.

For 30 cents for each maund involved, police ignore the smuggling boats plowing up the Ganges River. Forged ration cards are selling freely for approximately 45 cents.

It is incorrect to assume that the Provincial Government has done nothing about this. Unfortunately, however, it has done too little.

Fearing panic on the part of the excitable Bengalis, it has not pushed rationing, nor has it procured more than a tenth of this year's crop for use in Government channels. Most of that crop is being accumulated by the grain dealers, while some remains in the hands of the individual farmer.

At this stage the Government now hesitates to move too strongly against the Indian grain dealers who have — quite literally — the power to feed or starve Bengal's millions.

July 15, 1946

EUROPE IN DIRE NEED OF U.S. FOOD

It Goes to Liberated Lands —Germans Will Have to Depend on Themselves

By LANSING WARREN

WASHINGTON, May 12—With victory the Allies in Europe will inherit what may develop at once into perhaps the most stupendous feeding problem in history.

Europe is liberated, but with administrations, local and national, disrupted, and with her transport and production disorganized by war. The problem thereby becomes infinitely complicated and the need for action on a huge scale absolutely imperattive.

Director General Herbert H. Lehman of UNRRA has made an urgent appeal to Governments of the United Nations to provide the tools with which to meet this tremendous emergency, and ex-President Herbert Hoover, Director of Relief in Europe and Food Administrator in the last war, has suggested that the Army move the supplies if UNRRA does not receive the facilities.

"It is 11:59 on Europe's starvation clock," he is reported to have told the audience in Carnegie Hall.

It is not only a question of finding supplies from already depleted Allied stores but involves a most complicated problem of distribution that will take relief with the greatest possible speed to widely separated centers which have been most gravely affected and a careful supervision to insure that the food is delivered to the persons the most in need.

Problem Multiplied

Already the roads leading out of Germany are congested with throngs of footsore and famished prisoners of war and displaced persons who have been released from camps and are trying without means of conveyance or provisions to reach their homes in the four corners of the Continent. Others too weak to walk are waiting for help in the places where they have been confined. Millions of these wanderers are being taken into new refuge centers to be cared for until they can be assisted on the way. And civil populations of the Reich and even in the liberated lands are crying out for food. Added to this the troops engaged in action and the work of occupation must be constantly supplied.

Some areas are worse stricken than others. In Rotterdam, Amsterdam and other cities of Holland rations have sunk to 450 calories a day, when 2,000 calories are held to be the normal minimum. Large numbers of people are in imminent danger of starvation. Some have been living on soup made from tulip bulbs from which the poisonous centers have been cut. Now that these bulbs are sprouting the poison is carried through the bulbs and they have become inedible. Efforts are being made to drop emergency supplies from airplanes to these districts but more systematic measures must start now that the Allied armies have free access to these impoverished towns.

Land Ravaged

Desperate conditions prevail elsewhere. Recent revelations of conditions found in German camps for prisoners and internees have shown what is expected in all parts of the Reich. Wide areas of fertile country are ravaged and cannot produce this year. The Nazis plundered food-producing areas and drove off livestock. Lands have been flooded, houses destroyed and roads and railways wrecked.

Europe's needs and the Allied possibilities for meeting them, have formed the subject of intensive studies.

According to estimates Europe will need 375,000,000 bushels of wheat and flour. It will need additional fodder for livestock. It will need 800,000 long tons of fats and oils.

"FOOD IS AMMUNITION"

The Baltimore Sun

The strain on our production will be the greater since it has been estimated that the United Nations are faced in 1945 with larger food requirements but with supplies in many categories less than in 1944. The Allied shortages exist in just those products which the European will need most—such staples as meat, sugar, rice and fats and oils.

May 13, 1945

Truman Call for Food to Europe

By The Associated Press.

WASHINGTON, Feb. 6—Following is the text of President Truman's statement on the world food crisis:

For the world as a whole, a food crisis has developed which may prove to be the worst in modern times. More people face starvation and even actual death for want of food today than in any war year and perhaps more than in all the war years combined.

The United States and other countries have moved food into war-torn countries in record amounts, but there has been a constantly widening gap between essential minimum needs and available supplies.

Although this country enjoyed a near-record production of food and a record crop of wheat, the wheat crops of Europe and North Africa and the rice crops of the Far East have proved to be much shorter than anticipated; in fact some areas have experienced the shortest crops in fifty years because of extreme droughts and the disruption of war.

We in this country have been consuming about 3,300 calories per person per day. In contrast, more than 125 million people in Europe will have to subsist on less than 2,000 calories a day; 28 million will get less than 1,500 calories a day and, in some parts of Europe, large groups will receive as little as 1,000 calories.

Under these circumstances it is apparent that only through superhuman efforts can mass starvation be prevented. In recognition of this situation Great Britain only yesterday announced cuts in rations of fats and a return to the dark wartime loaf of bread.

"Share of the Burden"

I am sure that the American people are in favor of carrying their share of the burden.

Accordingly, I have instructed the appropriate agencies of the Government to put into effect a number of emergency measures designed to help meet critically urgent needs to the greatest possible extent in the shortest possible time.

The cooperation of every man, woman and child, the food trades and industries, the transportation industry, and others will be needed to make these measures effective. I know the conscience of the American people will not permit them to withhold or stint their cooperation while their fellow-men in other lands suffer and die.

The measures to be taken are as follows:

1. The appropriate agencies of this Government will immediately inaugurate a vigorous campaign to secure the full cooperation of all consumers in conserving food, particularly bread. Additional emphasis will be placed upon the cooperation of bakers and retailers in reducing waste of bread in distribution channels.

2. The use of wheat in the direct production of alcohol and beer will be discontinued; the use of other grains for the production of beverage alcohol will be limited, beginning March 1, to five days' consumption a month; and the use of other grains for the production of beer will be limited to an aggregate quantity equal to that used for this purpose in 1940, which was 30 per cent less than the quantity used in 1945. This will save for food about 20 million bushels of grain by June 30, 1946.

Flour Controls Planned

3. The wheat flour extraction rate (the quantity of flour produced from each bushel of wheat) will be raised to 80 per cent for the duration of the emergency. Also, steps will be taken to limit the distribution of flour to amounts essential for current civilian distribution. This will save about 25 million bushels of wheat during the first half of 1946.

4. The Department of Agriculture will control millers' inventories of wheat and bakers' and distributors' inventories of flour. The inventory controls will be designed to maintain the wheat and flour being held for civilian use at the minimum necessary for distribution purposes.

5. Specific preference will be given to the rail movement of wheat, corn, meat, and other essential foods in order promptly to export maximum quantities to the destinations where most needed.

6. The Department of Agriculture will exercise direct control over exports of wheat and flour to facilitate movement to destinations of greatest need.

7. Necessary steps will be taken to export during this calendar

year 375,000 tons of fats and oils, 1.6 billion pounds of meat, of which one billion pounds is to be made available during the first half of 1946, and to increase the exports of dairy products, particularly cheese and evaporated milk.

8. The War and Navy Departments already have aided materially the movement of Philippine copra (the raw material from which cocoanut oil is produced) by releasing 200 LCM and J boats for the inter-island trade in the Philippines. These departments and the War Shipping Administration will take immediate steps to make available the additional ships needed for this purpose.

Release of Ships Planned

The Secretaries of War and Navy will release for the movement of food to Europe all refrigerated ships not essential to the maintenance of the flow of food to the armed forces.

9. The Department of Agriculture will develop additional ways in which grain now being used in the feeding of livestock and poultry could be conserved for use as human food.

These steps may include means to obtain the rapid marketing of heavy hogs, preferably all those over 225 pounds, and of beef cattle with a moderate rather than a high degree of finish; to encourage the culling of poultry flocks; to prevent excessive chick production; and to encourage more economical feeding of dairy cattle. Regulations to limit wheat inventories of feed manufacturers and to restrict the use of wheat in feed will be prepared.

We are requesting the cooperation of retailers and other distributors in informally rationing commodities that will be in scarce supply for the months immediately ahead. Actual reductions in the volume of distribution may be suggested, with the obligations placed on the industry involved to handle distribution equitably.

I believe that with the wholehearted cooperation of food manufacturers, wholesalers, and retailers the job can be done.

The measures which I have directed will no doubt cause some inconvenience to many of us. Millers and bakers, for example, will have to adapt their operations to produce and to use flour of a higher extraction rate, while consumers may not be able to get exactly the kind of bread that many prefer.

Many Products Affected

We will not have as large a selection of meats, cheese, evaporated milk, ice cream, margarine, and salad dressing as we may like. However, these inconveniences will be a small price to pay for saving lives, mitigating suffering in liberated countries, and helping to establish a firmer foundation for peace.

In attempting to alleviate the shortages abroad, this country will adhere to the policy of giving preference to the liberated peoples and to those who have fought beside us, but we shall also do our utmost to prevent starvation among our former enemies.

I am confident that every citizen will cooperate whole-heartedly in the complete and immediate mobilization of this country's tremendous resources to win this world-wide war against mass starvation.

February 7, 1946

New 'Famine' Board Asks U.S. Cut Wheat Use by 25%

By FELIX BELAIR Jr.
Special to THE NEW YORK TIMES.

WASHINGTON, March 1—An appeal to all Americans to deny themselves a substantial part of their daily bread "so that millions may survive who are otherwise doomed to death by starvation," was voiced today by a newly formed Famine Emergency Committee under the honorary chairmanship of former President Herbert Hoover following its first meeting with President Truman.

Warning of "death by starvation of untold millions in other lands" unless all citizens cut down on calories, the committee asked a 25 per cent reduction in the national consumption of wheat and wheat products, and all possible savings of food, oils and fats.

The group, which was addressed informally by the President and his Cabinet committee at the outset, was unanimously of the opinion that "our people, knowing the facts, will want to stop all wastage of foods and to deny themselves a substantial proportion of their daily consumption of certain foods."

"Americans of good will can do more and do it faster than any system of Government rationing orders," the committee said. "Speed is vital."

Next Four Months "Vital"

In a press conference following the meeting, Mr. Hoover explained the need of concentrating all possible aid to the deficit countries in the next four months before their harvests. He added:

"The fate of civilization depends on whether the American people are willing to make a sacrifice for the next four months, if they are willing to save the world from chaos."

The new Government-sponsored organization was set up during their first White House meeting by the twelve civic leaders called by the President to meet with Federal officials to implement his announced "war on mass starvation."

The group accepted an invitation of Secretary Anderson to constitute themselves a continuing committee to aid him in formulating a detailed program through which the public, by voluntary cooperation, could meet the crisis. Chester C. Davis, president of the Federal Reserve Bank of St. Louis, was named chairman of an organizing

CONFERRING ON THE PROBLEM OF FEEDING OVERSEAS NEEDY

President Truman and Herbert Hoover, former Chief Executive, at the White House yesterday
The New York Times

committee to give it broader representation.

Secretary Anderson explained that the present nucleus would be expanded to a Famine Emergency Committee of seventy-five members which would work through hotels, restaurants and industry groups and with the Department of Agriculture in formulating specific conservation measures.

While the group was perfecting its organizing plans in the East Wing of the Executive Mansion, John W. Snyder, Director of the Office of War Mobilization and Reconversion, was conferring throughout the afternoon across the hall with transportation experts in an effort to crack the bottleneck of box-car shortages to expedite grain shipments from the West.

Truman Expresses His Hopes

In opening the meeting today, President Truman expressed his appreciation to the individual members for attending and added his belief that "with your advice and help we will be able to work this program out, so that the people who are now on the verge of starvation may live through the next year."

"It is the most important meeting, I think, we have held in the White House since I have been the President," said Mr. Truman.

Mr. Hoover, who sat on the President's right, said:

"The inevitable aftermath of war is famine, and with famine civilization itself is jeopardized."

He added that "the last reservoir from which starvation can be halted is in the United States."

"There is thrust upon us one of the greatest obligations of these troubled years," said the former President. "It is my belief that the American people will respond again, as they did after the last war. And we cannot fail."

Secretary Anderson stressed the need for personal sacrifice here if starvation were to be prevented abroad and said: "We have to strain ourselves a little more to make that possible."

Secretary Wallace, the other member of the Cabinet committee, said that once the people knew the true facts of the situation, they "will take such action during the next six months that they will not be ashamed of themselves a year hence."

The need for a greater measure of authority in the hands of the Secretary of Agriculture to organize conservation measures throughout the country was stressed by Mr. Hoover during his press conference, and dealt with also in a telegram which he sent to Secretary Anderson in accepting the invitation to today's meeting. Mr. Hoover made the telegram public today.

To illustrate the need, the former President said that "due to incorrect price differentials," farmers already had fed 100,000,000 to 150,000,000 bushels of feed grains including wheat to cattle, and added that "it is going to be necessary to disturb price levels to some extent" to end the practice.

Calls for Food Administrator

"We never have had a food administrator in the United States and the emergency is such that we should have one," said the former food director of the first World War.

The ex-President remarked that with American occupation troops in many countries, this country would have "100 troubles" if the food situation were not handled. He said the situation was one of "holding together Western civilization against chaos."

"We are asking a four-months' sacrifice by the American people," he repeated.

He explained the four-month term by the statement that the next harvest would not come in before the end of that period.

Mr. Hoover, who recalled that after the last war he dealt with famine in eighteen countries, stated that in the present emergency it was necessary to provide "simply wheat and fats," thus leaving the American people free so far as other commodities are concerned.

"That's not much to ask from Americans," he commented.

The world supply of wheat, he said, was only 15,000,000 to 16,000,000 tons, whereas the need was for 20,000,000 tons, and that was "a very close shave."

Would Bar Wheat as Feed

"We have got to cut out the use of wheat for feed to animals," he stated. "We can't feed wheat to animals and expect the sufferers to starve."

The present situation was made "more acute," he went on, by the failure of the rice crop in Asia, and crop failure in Argentina.

Germany, Austria and Japan would have to be included in the relief, said the former President.

"We have got to face the facts," he remarked. "I have never regarded starvation as a matter of race or creed. Starving people are entitled to solicitude. Even if we did not do this from a humanitarian motive, we would have to do it on the basis of protection of our troops abroad."

However, he said, the amounts of foods needed for enemy countries would be "comparatively small." The great requirement was in the other regions.

Mr. Hoover would not discuss how far he pressed his idea of a central food administrator upon President Truman. He and his hearers all laughed when he added:

"I make it a practice to never say what I say to a President."

The actual number of persons to be fed, Mr. Hoover said, was not larger than after the last war. But he pointed out that, at that time, our part of the war lasted only two years and surpluses had been piled up. Now, he said, there had been a four-year war and surpluses were not available.

Needy Set at a Half Billion

Mr. Hoover estimated that 300,000,000 in Europe would require aid and another 100,000,000 might be added in Japan, China and Russia. The over-all figure might be 500,000,000, he said.

India he considered a problem, but said that country would have to be aided from the Pacific zones.

"It has been said that creation of this committee would lead to hoarding," said Mr. Hoover. "I do not believe that, because the matter will be a moral appeal to the American people, and I think they will respond."

Americans, said Mr. Hoover, now consumed about 3,400 calories of food daily, whereas more than half the Europeans were living on 1,500 or less, all against a minimum health requirement of about 2,000.

The ex-President hoped the American farmer would now be as cooperative as in the last war, when "he emptied his granary to the last grain."

In his telegram to Mr. Anderson, Mr. Hoover said that he did not believe the proposed general committee organization, though helpful, could cover the whole emergency.

"I recommended to the President last May that all control of food, scattered over different Government agencies, should be lodged in you as Food Administrator, because that office is inseparable from the Secretaryship of Agriculture," Mr. Hoover wrote.

"I am advised that was not done. It should be done now."

Wide Authority Proposed

The complete authority Mr. Anderson should have, Mr. Hoover stated, should apply to the elimination of waste and unnecessary consumption, hoarding, substitution of foods, and control of exports and imports.

After constituting State agriculture directors as State food administrators and county agents as county administrators, Mr. Hoover proposed that each of the food trade associations, such as those of hotels, restaurants, bakers, packers, millers, etc., be asked to appoint emergency famine committees under some respected leaders to work out ways and means of avoiding waste and unnecessary use of food and bringing about adherence of the trade members to the voluntary program.

Mr. Hoover further urged "a simple program for housewives which will eliminate waste, save unnecessary consumption and make use of substitutes."

He said this should be a voluntary program like the others and that State and county food administrators should organize the women in their localities and see that food trades were fully organized as well.

March 2, 1946

U. S. Met Famine-Aid Goal, Truman, Anderson Declare

Year's Shipments Exceeded Commitments, President Says, Hailing Producers and Public—Future Help Called Vital

By BESS FURMAN

Special to The New York Times.

WASHINGTON, July 12—President Truman today made public, with a commendatory statement, the United States' record in shipping food overseas for relief in the famine year ending June 30 as given to him in a special report by Secretary of Agriculture Clinton P. Anderson.

A total United States export of 16,500,000 long tons of food was reported, of which 10,336,000 tons were bread grains. Shipments were nearly double what was planned when the crop year opened, and exceeded actual commitments as of the year's end by 17,000,000 bushels.

This country sent foreign Governments more than 40 per cent of its wheat; more than 35 per cent of its rice; more than 20 per cent of its cheese; more than 10 per cent of its fats and oils, and about 6 per cent of its meat.

President Truman pronounced this a record of accomplishment in which the American people could take pride, and said that it had been made possible only by cooperation and determined effort on the part of every one—the public, food producers and handlers, transportation companies, organizations and Government agencies.

He emphasized the need for continued cooperation and sharing with the rest of the world to relieve the hunger still existing, and said that the importance of this effort to relieve human suffering and establishing world peace could not be overestimated.

Secretary Anderson also stressed in his report the continuing urgen-

BASIC IN THE FOOD PROBLEM—THE WORLD'S NEED FOR WHEAT AND THE AVAILABLE SUPPLIES

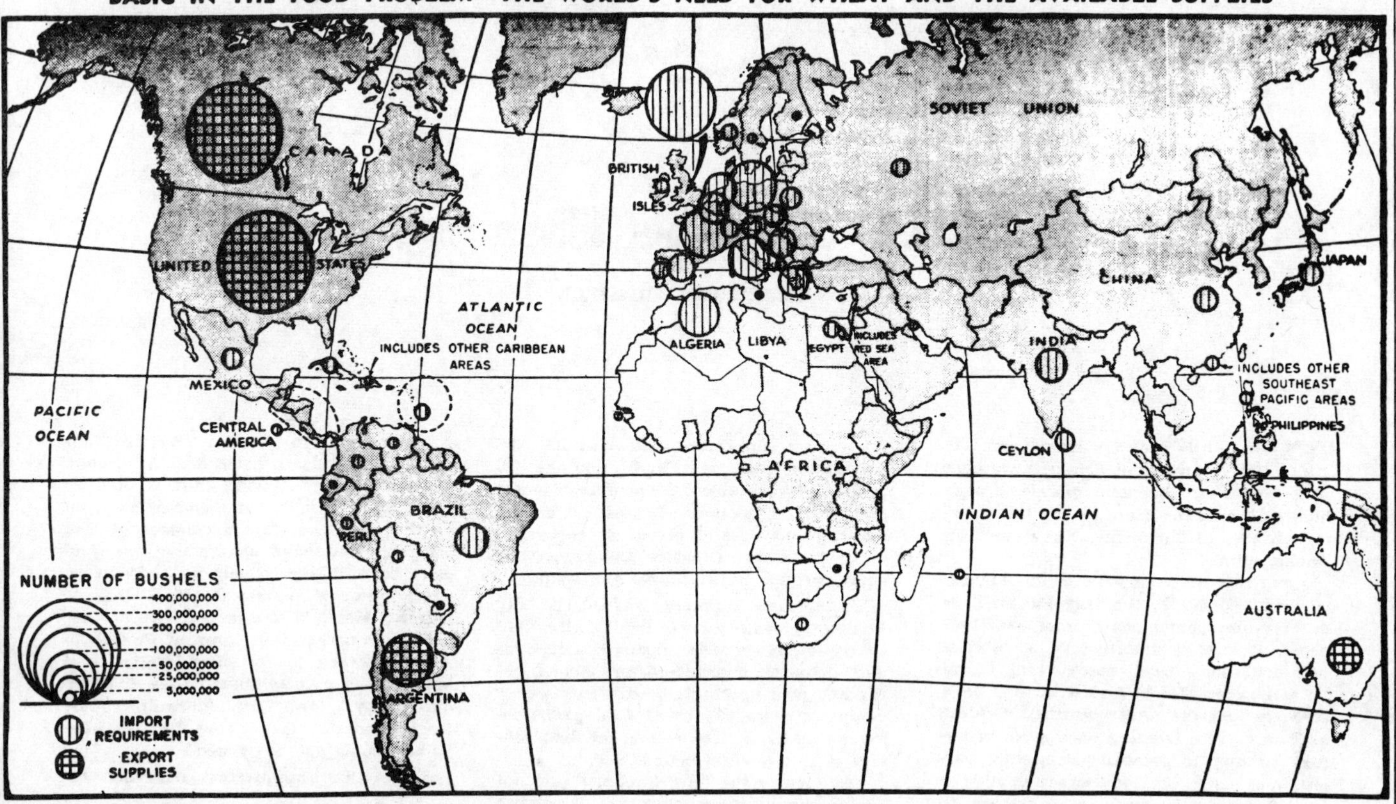

This map, based on a chart issued by the Foreign Agricultural Relations Office of the Department of Agriculture, shows the latest available compilations. Import requirements are constantly changing.

March 3, 1946

cy of relief needs, although he said the worst immediate dangers of famine had been forestalled. When this year's harvests were completed for the Northern Hemisphere, he stated, a good deal more would be known about the situation. In the meantime he urged continuance of relief shipments and a readiness to meet at least a minimum of future needs.

He told of the planned export of up to 250,000,000 bushels of wheat in the 1946-47 crop year, from which this year's excess shipments would not be subtracted. He said that tentative plans were also being made for the shipment of other commodities.

Bread-Grain Commitment Met

The Anderson report on the nation-wide campaign to ship grain into the famine countries gave these final results: The bread-grain commitment of 400,000,000 bushels for the year was met by June 30. Wheat and flour exports, plus the corn and corn products shipped after May 1 from stocks acquired under the corn-bonus plan, reached a total of 401,000,000 bushels.

Bread grains shipped from Jan. 1 through June 30 totaled 5,556,000 tons, with enough in the ports to bring the total for the half-year above the 6,000,000-ton goal. The grains in ports will have cleared by the middle of July, a few days hence.

During June the export was record-breaking, a total of about 1,500,000 tons. Rice, oats, rye, and barley were also shipped, bringing the total of all grains exported for the year to 11,747,000 long tons.

On meats, the report was that about 614,000 long tons were shipped, as compared with 714,000 the year previous, the lesser amount being ascribed to work stoppages and supply shortages.

Most Meat Sent to Europe

Countries supplied by the United Nations Relief and Rehabilitation Administration received 288,000 tons, or nearly half the total. Of the 614,000 tons total, 588,000 tons went to European countries, including the UNRRA countries; the rest to the Far East, Latin-American countries, and others.

The total of fats and oils was 356,000 long tons exported, of which 268,000 went to Europe. Shipment to the UNRRA countries in Europe totaled 73,000 tons, other large recipients being the United Kingdom, France and French North Africa. The 1945-46 shipment totaled more than the export goal for fats and oils set for the 1946 calendar year, which was 347,000 tons.

Export shipments of dairy products totaled about 764,000 long tons, about 28 per cent of the total distribution of these products. Of this amount, 669,000 tons went to Europe, UNRRA receiving 316,000 tons, and other shipments going to the United Kingdom, France, French North Africa and Belgium, with small amounts to the Far East.

July 13, 1946

CARE for the Hungry

By GERTRUDE SAMUELS

TWO words recently introduced into the languages of Europe have done more to quicken morale among hungry thousands than all the fine flowing phrases of diplomacy. They are "Big Package."

America's most eagerly sought ambassador of good-will, the "Big Package" is a forty-nine-pound, waterproof, weatherproof, practically indestructible cardboard box containing that most urgent of all human needs—food. And it is food on a scale to lure the undernourished children of Europe into trusting once more in human nature; to persuade struggling parents and elders that democracy is alive in the hearts of fellow-men across the sea; to give, finally, comparatively well-off Americans the opportunity to share their bounty—personally—with the less fortunate of the world.

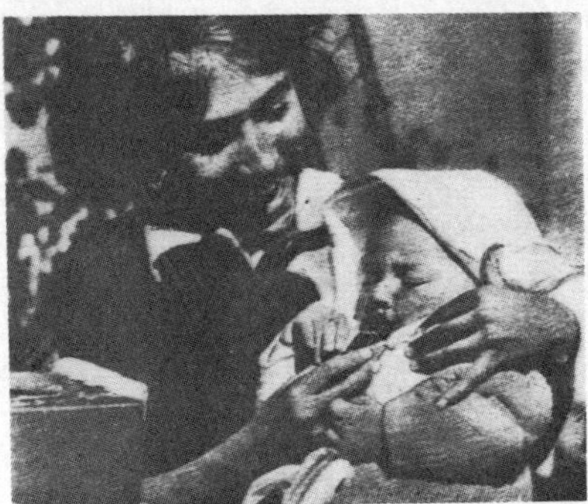

Food arrives—and the young rejoice.

Three million "Big Packages" have been stored in Government warehouses in the United States since last April. Some 300,000 have already been bought by individual Americans at a cost of $15 apiece. The goal is a sale of 500,000 a month.

THE "Big Package" is Army surplus. Originally earmarked to feed ten American combat soldiers for one day in preparation for the invasion of Japan, it contains food enough for thirty well-planned meals, or some 40,000 calories (compared with a European's average daily diet of below 1,500 calories). It includes 9.8 pounds of solid meat, stews and hashes; 6.5 pounds of cereal and biscuits; 3.6 pounds of fruit jam and pudding; 2.3 pounds of vegetables; 3.9 pounds of sugar and candy; 1.1 pounds of cocoa, coffee and beverage powders; .8 pound of evaporated milk; .5 pound of butter and cigarettes, chewing gum, paper towels and soap.

To experienced senders of food, the "Big Package" with a net food content of twenty-eight pounds, insured, duty-free and delivery guaranteed or money refunded, is a spectacle of dizzying riches compared with the usual food packages, averaging $7 to $10, with a net food content of five to eight pounds.

The idea of the "Big Package" did not evolve simply from charity. It sprang also out of self-interest—that by sending food gifts to those overseas, the bond between peoples, and so the chances of peace, would be strengthened. Thus last April the organization CARE (Cooperative for American Remittances to Europe, Inc.), a non-profit agency with headquarters at 50 Broad Street in New York, was born, sponsored by the President's War Relief Control Board and twenty-five public and private agencies. President Truman, buying 100 "Big Packages," said: "I commend it to the people of the United States."

Distribution is unique, speedy and wholly traceable. CARE has a "revolving residue" of some 500,000 packages in warehouses of the areas it serves—Austria, Belgium, Czechoslovakia, Finland, France, the American and British zones of Germány, Greece, Italy, the Netherlands, Norway and Poland. The packages are ration-free (not deductible from regular rations) and safe from pilfering—the recipient Governments guarantee delivery.

HOW do the recipients feel toward their American benefactors? Lincoln Clark, assistant executive director of CARE, just back after three months in Europe checking on distribution arrangements, says, "The big reaction is something we've been taking for granted, but they can hardly believe, especially the Poles. 'My God,' they cry, 'this thing works! The food packages are actually getting to the people they're addressed to.' "

Letters pouring in to CARE and to the senders tell their own story:

From the Netherlands: "We are four * * * Pim, 12; Han, 9; Herman, 5; Ronald, 2½ years old. You don't know us, and we don't know you, but our father has told us that you and we are children of One Father. You have understood this, and have been willing to help us." From M. Szatkowska of Warsaw to Mrs. B. T. of Durant, Miss: "I was a prisoner in that terrible concentration camp at Oswiecim. And so every bit of consideration and kindness as well as humaneness gives us untold joy." And from Marseille: "The most wonderful part is that it's all sealed up and could not be opened."

At CARE's headquarters, men and women from all walks of life spoke quietly with this reporter while they filled out remittance blanks. One couple was sending four packages to "relatives, three in the British zone and one in the American zone in Germany." A woman was purchasing "one every two months for my new foster family in Paris." Another was sending one to her "first cousin in Vienna."

A grandmother signs package receipt.

"It is very sad there now," she said. "First we sent packages from Denmark, then from private sources here. But it took months and they could starve before they got there. Many never got there. I am very happy that I can do this."

She turned back to her task. In the bare little room with its makeshift-office atmosphere and deliberately spelled-out posters—"C.A.R.E."—democracy without fanfare was finding some fulfillment. Tom Paine's famous words seemed to stand out clearly: "The world is my country, all mankind are my brethren."

CUTS BUYING IN '47 FOR OVERSEAS AREA

The Department of Agriculture Will Confine Purchases to Wheat on Cash Basis

Special to THE NEW YORK TIMES.

WASHINGTON, Nov. 1—The Department of Agriculture said today that except for wheat it will not purchase farm products for other countries after the end of this year.

On most of the important commodities the Department of Agriculture has ceased acting as purchasing agent. It is still doing some buying, however. The list of commodities which it will procure for foreign governments being wheat, fats and oils, canned salmon, canned pilchard, rice, dried eggs, cheese, evaporated milk and dried milk.

The department said that it will continue to procure for the United Nations Relief and Rehabilitation Administration until about March 31, when UNRRA's buying operations are expected to be over, and until Dec. 31 it will make purchases for cash buying countries to meet previous commitments.

During the war and famine periods when this country was acting as purchasing agent for foreign governments, a total of $667,000,000 was deposited with the Commodity Credit Corporation, for purchases of the American farmers' products, the Department said.

Countries for which the purchases were made were the United Kingdom, France, The Netherlands, the Netherlands East Indies and Burma.

N. E. Dodd, Acting Secretary of Agriculture, made clear that the Department reserved the right to buy for export "when it is in the best interest of American farmers and consumers."

Dropping of wartime set-asides and of price controls in this country ended Government buying programs which often had been extended to include the purchases of other countries. Next year these governments will buy in the open market as before the war.

November 2, 1946

Billion Bushel U. S. Surplus Will Ease World Grain Need

By WILL LISSNER

The United States has an expected carry-over this year of more than 1,000,000,000 bushels of the major exportable grain crops, wheat and corn, assuring the world of an adequate "cushion" against basic food shortage next year, it became known yesterday.

From United States crops alone, the indicated carry-over of these grains computed from requirements and commitments is nearly equal to world export requirements on a pre-war basis, adjusted for population and other changes.

This prospect is of great political significance, since it reassures Europeans against a return of the specter of famine that has haunted the Continent since the war produced a world food shortage.

With bumper crops indicated for other surplus grain producing areas, the United States prospect assures Europeans of an adequate minimum diet even if adverse weather conditions halt the recovery of European agriculture next year.

The improved food situation already having resulted in eliminating rationing in several European countries, this prospect may be expected to spur recovery in European agriculture, warranting expansion in meat and dairy production, and in European industry as well, through its promise of better diets for workers.

Warn Against Relaxation

The carry-over indicated from the United States Department of Agriculture's Aug. 1 crop report, released last Tuesday, was computed from data on our requirements and commitments by Dr. Julius Hirsch and Mrs. Edith Hirsch, economists for industry interests.

In making public their private estimates, Dr. and Mrs. Hirsch emphasized that the happy prospect that a great improvement was taking place in the whole world food supply situation did not warrant relaxation by farmers of their production efforts this year or next.

If properly handled, they said, our surplus will be a blessing for humanity; but on the other hand, it is one that may be needed. As the Bureau of Agriculture Economics noted the other day:

"Despite the marked recovery in production of European bread grains this year, several considerations point to a continued need for substantial imports by the traditionally deficit areas. These include increased population, extremely low reserves of grain in many areas, the need to increase bread rations from the low level of the past year, and low quality bread resulting from high extraction rates."

The indicated carryover is computed as follows:

MAJOR EXPORTABLE GRAINS

WHEAT

(In million bushels)

Carryover, July 1, 1947		195
Crop, 1948		1,284
Total supply		1,479
Human consumption	500	
Feeding (maximum)	150	
Seed and industrial usage	90	
Export goal (minimum)	350	1,090
		389

CORN

(In million bushels)

Carryover, Oct. 1, 1948		125
Crop, 1948		3,506
Total supply		3,631
Feeding	2,500	
Other farm & indus'l usage	278	
Seed	12	
Exports	175	2,965
		666
Total indicated carryover—		
Wheat		389
Corn		666
		1,055

Cite Prewar Average

The world export of wheat before the war averaged between 630,000,000 and 640,000,000 bushels a year, the Dr. and Mrs. Hirsch estimate. This figure must be revised upward not only to take care of population and other changes, they point out, but to make up for the deficits in rice production in Japan and India. From 1950 on, world exports of 750,000,000 bushels may be needed to cover the deficits of Japan and India and possible needs of China.

The world export of corn may be taken as 400,000,000 bushels. This figure need not be revised upward, since it can be used only in a limited way for human consumption abroad and expansion of the demand abroad for animal feeding is inhibited by the slow recovery of animal numbers and by the shortage of dollars, encouraging the use of substitute grains.

Taking 750,000,000 bushels as the probable upper limit of world export requirements of wheat next year and 400,000,000 bushels as the requirement of corn, Dr. and Mrs. Hirsch estimate world export requirements of the major exportable grains next year as 1,150,000,000 bushels. Thus the indicated carryover for both grains from the 1948 United States crops would be within 95,000,000 bushels of world requirements.

Before the war world wheat exports of the important exporting nations for the years 1934-38 averaged as follows, in millions of bushels:

United States	49
Australia	102
Argentina	123
Canada	177
Danubian countries	50
U.S.S.R.	25
Poland	4
India	10
French N. Africa	18

Food Controversy Cited

The estimates cast some light on the controversy over revision of our export goals between Dennis A. Fitzgerald, director of the food division of the Economic Cooperation Administration, officials of the Department of Agriculture and of the Food and Agriculture Organization, on one side, and Secretary of Commerce Charles Sawyer on the other.

Mr. Fitzgerald has proposed that the United States step up its shipments of wheat and coarse grain over earlier ECA goals. Mr. Sawyer said that the prospects for improved crops in Europe should permit a substantially reduced level of wheat exports from the United States this year. The former wheat export goal was 300,000,000 to 350,000,000 bushels, but this was increased to 450,000,000 bushels when it was clear that crops would be big.

With a billion-bushel United States grain reserve in prospect, the carryover is likely to strain storage facilities in this country, Dr. and Mrs. Hirsch pointed out.

If exports are maintained, they believe, part of the grain may be stored in Europe, which would constitute part of the indicated United States reserve. It would be unwise, however, they warned, to force wheat on nations that would rather use their dollars for industrial machinery, fertilizers, raw materials and other production goods to spur their recoveries.

From the point of view of world needs, the indicated carryover in the United States is not yet an embarrassing surplus but actually a reserve, Dr. and Mrs. Hirsch declared. However, it does bring nearer the time when agricultural policy in the United States will have to deal with crop surpluses, they said.

"For the future, especially the years from 1951 on, it might be important to decrease somewhat our wheat production," they said. "This of course, will only be possible if the price supports and other political measures are adjusted to bring about willing collaboration from the farming community.

"The great long-term aim may be to find broader uses in industry for the main products of our farmers."

August 15, 1948

TRUMAN WILL URGE GRAIN GIFT TO INDIA

Plans 2,000,000-Ton Request to Congress to Avert Famine —No Strings Attached

By W. H. LAWRENCE
Special to THE NEW YORK TIMES.

WASHINGTON, Feb. 1—President Truman is expected to recommend to Congress shortly that the United States give 2,000,000 tons of grain to India to avert a major famine affecting millions of people. There will be no political conditions attached to the relief measure as it is submitted by the Chief Executive to the legislative branch.

Coming within a week after India's representatives had fought the United States bitterly in the United Nations debate over branding Communist China an aggressor in Korea, the relief proposal, which will cost the people of this country approximately $180,000,000, is calculated to demonstrate throughout the world, but especially in Asia, the humanitarian nature of American foreign policy.

The action of the President also is counted upon to dramatize the contrast between the foreign policies of the United States and the Soviet Union which milks even its satellites of products for shipment to Russia. The Administration already has made much of the fact that the Soviet Union took grain from the northern provinces of China at a time of serious famine in that country.

However, it is believed that the issue will stir heated Congressional debate against giving aid to countries that do not follow the lead of the United States in resisting the expansion of international communism led by the Soviet Union.

Administration strategists, who informally with members of the House Foreign Affairs and Senate Foreign Relations Committees, expect eventual approval of the recommendation. They believe that the American people as a whole will react favorably to any proposal to prevent widespread death by starvation, and would not sit idly by while people were dying because the United States refused to ship them grain from its ample reserves. The Government will urge Congress to act speedily so that the first grain shipments can be at sea before April.

Vast Shipping Problem

The project is a tremendous one, involving approximately 75,000,000 bushels of the current United States wheat reserves of approximately 375,000,000 bushels. It presents transport difficulties in getting the grain from storage elevators to ports of loading.

This amount of grain represents 220 shiploads on a voyage that takes approximately three months to complete on a round-trip basis. Shipping experts have indicated a need for fifteen cargo vessels to be brought out of the "mothball" fleet and added to the shipping now available between this country and Indian ports

India officially had asked the United States to grant her long-term credits for the purchase of the 2,000,000 tons of grain needed to prevent widespread starvation. The Indian statistics indicated a shortage of approximately 5,500,000 tons of food grain this year as a result of a series of natural disasters, including an earthquake in Assam, followed by floods, and a series of droughts in other parts of the country.

The Indian Government made it clear that it had resources available for the purchase this year of about 4,000,000 tons from the United States, Canada, Australia and other suppliers. With approximately 120,000,000 of India's 330,000,000 people already receiving food grains on a rationed basis, the Government found it necessary Jan. 19 to cut the ration from twelve to nine ounces a day.

While India requested a loan, Administration experts have decided that it would be better to make the grain transaction an outright grant.

The Administration's position is that India faces a national disaster resulting from natural calamities and that it is in the interests of the United States, with ample reserves of grain, to see to it that people do not starve.

In the weeks the grain issue has been under consideration by the State Department and other agencies, the Administration ruled out the possibilities that India might receive a credit from the Export-Import Bank or the International Bank for Reconstruction and Development. These agencies, it was noted, do not make loans for consumable items such as wheat and rice that do not offer any prospect of return on investment.

The United States Government considered also the financial position of the Indian Government which has sterling balances that, computed in dollars, amount to approximately $1,500,000,000. About half of this sum is regarded as an essential reserve of the Indian Government, and the other half is earmarked for a program of internal development in India designed to make less likely recurrences of the grave food shortage this year.

The Administration will argue before Congress that it would not be in the best interests of the United States to demand payment from these funds, which, to become transferable, also would create a heavy drain on the British Commonwealth's dollar "pool," thus defeating some of the economic recovery measures that the United States already has sponsored under the Economic Cooperation Administration.

Different Situation Now

The Administration will contend also that the current situation, with the indisputable threat of famine before October, is far different than conditions were about eighteen months ago when the United States turned down an "informal" Indian request for a long-term credit to obtain 1,000,000 tons of grain in this country.

Administration witnesses before Congressional committees will attest to the gravity of India's food outlook this year, confirmed by first-hand reports of governmental representatives on the spot.

But the continuing rivalry between India and Pakistan, created by partition and fanned by religious and territorial disputes, also probably will creep into Congressional discussion on the food grant proposal.

The Pakistani charge that the Indian famine is partly the fault of the Nehru Government arises from the assertion that the Indian Government has diverted a large acreage of food-producing land to the production of cotton and jute.

Pakistan asserts that she can supply all the cotton that India needs and produce enough jute for the whole world but that her neighbor seeks self-sufficiency in these two products "in order to strangle Pakistan's economy even at the cost of starving herself."

India's reply to the charge that she had cut down food production to increase cotton and jute output is that the acreage devoted to food crops actually increased in the period from 1949 to 1950. The rice acreage went up 2 per cent to a total of 71,660,000 acres, while wheat acreage increased 6.1 per cent to 23,627,000 acres.

India, has, however, been engaged in a vast land-reclamation program — amounting to about 500,000 acres in the last few years—and much of the new land has been devoted to cotton and jute. Cotton acreage now totals 11,498,000 acres, a gain of 5.7 per cent in the last year, and the total amount of land devoted to jute growing now is 1,158,000 acres, a gain of 39 per cent in a year.

The Indians added, however, that jute was now their No. 1 export.

Wheat Accumulation Cited

As a result of its price support activities, the Federal Government in the last few years has accumulated a few hundred million bushels of wheat. Since only about 75,000,000 bushels are involved in the gift to India, the Government would not have to enter the market to obtain the necessary wheat.

For the present season, shipments of wheat abroad have been lagging. Clearances since July 1 are estimated in the trade at 122,000,000 bushels, or about 60,000,000 below the similar period last season. With the proposed shipments to India included, shipments abroad for this season may still be below those of last season.

INDIAN LEADERS ENJOY A CHUCKLE IN BOMBAY

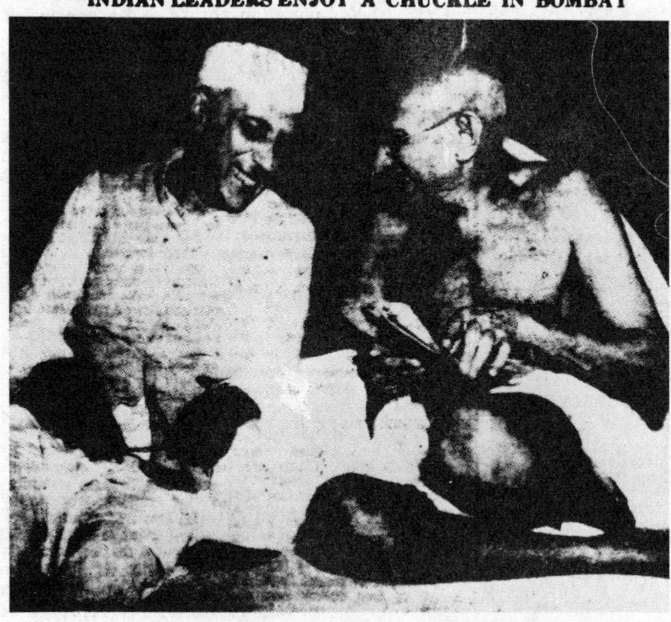

Associated Press

Pandit Nehru (left) and Mohandas K. Gandhi during an intermission on the opening day of the All-India Congress committee meeting.

February 2, 1951

INDIAN AMBASSADOR SIGNING CONTRACT FOR GRAIN

Mme. Vijaya Lakshmi Pandit arranging for long-term credit with the Export-Import Bank. President Truman, who had just signed the Indian aid bill, is holding the agreement flat for the envoy.
Associated Press Wirephoto

Special to THE NEW YORK TIMES.

WASHINGTON, June 15 — President Truman signed the long-delayed Indian aid bill today, authorizing a loan of $190,000,000 to provide approximately 2,000,000 tons of food grains to India.

Madame Vijaya Lakshmi Pandit, the Indian Ambassador, witnessed the signing in the White House Executive Office and immediately signed, on behalf of her Government, a long-term credit arrangement with the Export-Import Bank so that the grain could start to move at once. The loan agreement provides that the Indian Government will make its first semi-annual payment of $1,125,000 on June 30, 1957, and its final payment of $4,942,033.56 on June 30, 1986.

In signing the bill, Mr. Truman noted that the loan supplemented already large supplies of grain being shipped to India from this country at the rate of 250,000 tons a month and for which that country was paying cash. He said the United States would provide about two-thirds of all the food India received from abroad to avert famine.

Madame Pandit replied that the American loan would give the Indian people "more than mere physical sustenance and will be instrumental in strengthening a friendship which has always existed between them and the peoples of this great country."

The President also noted voluntary American efforts to aid India and declared they should be continued and expanded. "This kind of help to stricken humanity is a tradition of the American people — whether to the sufferers of the great Russian famine and the victims of the Japanese earthquake in the early Twenties or to the starving in Rumania in the late Forties," he said.

Sirdar J. J. Singh, president of the India League of America, characterized the aid measure yesterday as indicative of "a new era of friendship and goodwill between the peoples of India and the United States" and a means of "abridging the gulf that has, unfortunately, come to exist" between the two nations."

June 16, 1951

INDIAN LARDER FULL, 20 MILLION HUNGER

Peasants in 4 States, Jobless From Crop Failures, Cannot Buy Food That Is Available

By ROBERT TRUMBULL
Special to THE NEW YORK TIMES.

NEW DELHI, India, Aug. 9—About 20,000,000 Indian peasants are suffering acute distress because of crop failures in Madras, Bengal, Uttar Pradesh and Rajasthan States, according to reports reaching here.

Paradoxically, Government warehouses are so filled with grain that the United States and Canada have been asked to postpone shipments of 750,000 tons of wheat until next year and the central Food Ministry hopes to reduce next year's total grain imports by 25 per cent or more.

The explanation for this contradictory situation, according to Government analysts, is a lack of purchasing power on the part of the population. This, in turn, is caused by droughts and monsoon failures, which have cut down the scope for hired labor in the fields of the larger landowners. Thus peasants who are unable to support themselves and their dependents on the products of their own small holdings are being denied the work on which they normally have depended for income to buy the additional food that is available.

Free Food Distributed

India's current problem apparently is not a food shortage or famine, therefore, but widespread unemployment. To meet the situation the state Governments have sanctioned a total expenditure equivalent to more than $5,000,000 for various works projects in recent months, in addition to remission of land taxes and rents, plus the provision of loans and grants by the central Government amounting to about $6,000,000.

Food has been shipped to scarcity areas to be distributed free or to be added to the ration available at controlled prices. However, unless the Government undertakes the impossible task of indefinitely paying for the feeding of up to 30,000,000 peasants, substantial immediate relief must await an improvement in crop conditions.

The weather being extremely uncertain in India, it appears that, without a perpetual dole, permanent alleviation of the food situation in many districts depends on the success of long-term agricultural development projects, some of which now are under way with United States Point Four technical aid.

India's own five-year plan for irrigation dams and many other projects represents the largest physical field of attack upon the perennial problem. The United States' contribution of nearly $100,000,000, including the amount expected under this year's foreign aid allocation—not mentioning last year's $190,000,000 wheat loan—is dovetailed into the five-year plan but still represents only a fraction of the more than $1,000,000,000 in economic assistance that India needs from abroad, by her own calculations, if development is to proceed on the present optimistic schedule.

Land Reform Critical Issue

Even more basic in the problem of unemployment may be the progress of land reform. Under present conditions most peasants hold so little land—if any at all—that they must depend to a large extent on earnings as hired labor. Government surveys have shown that in the best of times these landless or almost landless farmers are unemployed one-third of the year or more, and are likely to go hungry during these long periods of idleness.

Unfortunately, land reform has not yet gone very far and even when it is effected the peasant's obligation to continue to pay rent to the Government for a period of years, plus his lethargy in adopting better farming methods, leave discernible benefits still some years away.

On the bright side of the picture it can be said that every effort to improve conditions in rural areas—which include nearly 90 per cent of the Indian population—is being made by the Government within the limits of its finances and the conservative character of the average farm-dweller.

August 10, 1952

LAND REFORM PROBLEM IS WORLD-WIDE IN SCOPE

Developments in Egypt and Iran Point Up Critical Importance of the Issue

By A. M. ROSENTHAL

Special to THE NEW YORK TIMES.

UNITED NATIONS, N. Y., Aug. 23—Recent developments in Egypt and Iran have highlighted the issue of land reform. In Egypt the Government has taken steps to give peasants a larger share of the land, while in Iran it has moved to give them a larger share of the harvest.

There have been years of debate on the world's farm-land problems, pounds of reports and batches of charts and analyses of impressive complexity. But at the center of all the reports and talk are a few quite simple facts:

In many parts of the world, Asia especially, farms are simply too small to provide the farmer and his family with enough to eat, to say nothing of producing for his countrymen. In other areas—South America, especially—huge and often uneconomical estates spraddle the land, leaving most farmers as insecure, hungry tenants.

In some countries, in the Balkans especially, a farmer's holding is divided into scattered plots—fragmentation, the specialists call it—that make for waste of time and effort. And in too many countries farmers suffer from other production-destroying problems—perpetual tenancy, credit hard to come by and at exorbitant interest rates, rents up to 70 per cent of the crop, insecure land tenure, lack of tools and know-how.

For years now the United Nations has recognized the land reform problem as one of the world's most important jobs. Poor land distribution means less food for a growing world population, and a U. N. report prepared in cooperation with the Food and Agriculture Organization sums it up this way:

"To a very large extent, the problem of the underdeveloped countries of the world is the problem of the poverty of their farm populations."

There is no one easy cure; it is not simply a matter of making little farms out of big ones. The F. A. O. and the U. N. long have preached that land reform is most effective when it is an integrated, over-all attack on the problems of the farmer. Different areas of the world have different problems. Region by region, the problem of the agrarian structure—the way the land is owned, distributed, financed and taxed—shapes up this way:

ASIA

The outstanding features of the agrarian structure are large numbers of holdings too small for economic production, fragmentation, high rents, and a heavy debt-burden on the cultivator. Asia suffers from the old problem of density of population — too many people on the land. In Japan, Korea, Indonesia, Indo-China, Ceylon, China and India there is less than one acre per head of total population.

SOUTH AMERICA

Many holdings, according to the F. A. O. and the U. N., are "uneconomically large." In Latin America as a whole 1.5 per cent of individual holdings add up to 50 per cent of all agricultural land. In Argentina, 85 per cent of the privately held agricultural land is in estates larger than 1,250 acres, while 80 per cent of the farm population own no land. Concentration of ownership in huge estates reduces a large part of the rural population to the status of laborers. In some countries, estates are worked by unpaid labor in return for tiny subsistence holdings. The land economy prevents full utilization of land resources and depresses the peasant's living standards.

WESTERN EUROPE

Fragmentation and extremely small holdings are major problems. One report says that a farm of twelve acres in Yugoslavia may be divided into thirty separate plots.

MIDDLE EAST

Chief problems are insecurity of land tenure, high rents, indebtedness. Land shortage, the F. A. O. and U. N. report, does not affect the region as a whole except in Egypt. But the peasant's insecurity is a major problem. In some Middle Eastern countries, the peasant does not even cultivate the same plot of land from year to year. Favored tenants get the most fertile plots. The result is that the peasant tries to exploit his bit of land for the year without thinking of the soil's future fertility.

CARIBBEAN

This is one of the most densely populated areas of the world, where the plantation system has given rise to great hostility. But as far as sugar cane is concerned, the yield per acre would be less if the plantations were divided, and that would mean more economic trouble. The yield of sugar per acre is from 50 to 100 per cent greater on plantations than on small farms, according to one estimate.

For many countries, therefore, the agrarian structure prevents a rise in the standard of living of small farmers and farm workers, hampers economic development by preventing the expansion of food production, brings on agricultural stagnation.

What's being done about it? The United Nations and the F. A. O., spurred by the underdeveloped countries and encouraged by the United States, are providing land-reform experts, conducting seminars, making studies and reports.

But the U. N. and the F. A. O. have recognized that the key to the problem remains in the hands of the national governments. In many countries—outside the Middle East, where only Turkey has put important land reform measures into operation, according to an F. A. O. and U. N. report last year—some remedial steps already have been started.

Politically, the problem of land reform is enormous. The promise of more land remains one of communism's most effective weapons, and the West knows it. A couple of years ago Charles F. Brannan, Secretary of Agriculture, said something that pretty well capsules the feeling of the U. N.'s own specialists in land reform:

"A little bit of land, a little bit of opportunity can do for world peace something that great armies cannot possibly accomplish. It is something that happens inside a person. It is something that cannot be shot or chained."

August 24, 1952

Food Production at Pre-World War II Level But Underdeveloped Areas Still Go Hungry

Special to THE NEW YORK TIMES.

ROME, Sept. 11 — Food production in the world as a whole regained its pre-World War II level for the first time in the agricultural year 1952-53, the United Nations Food and Agriculture Organization announced today. This is the central fact of the agency's annual report, which will be released on Sunday.

Though the world level of production is now equal to what it was before the war, this is by no means true of all areas, the report will point out. Thus, in the Far East, excluding China, per capita production is 15 to 20 per cent below the insufficient prewar level. Latin America is about 5 per cent short of its prewar level. Europe as a whole is about at the prewar level, which has been exceeded by about 20 per cent in North America. The result is that whereas the number of hungry people has increased in some parts of the world, surpluses have piled up in others to a point where sharp reductions are in prospect for wheat and maize.

As a result, the Food and Agriculture Organization is now laying emphasis on producing more food in areas where it is most needed, especially in the less-developed regions where production lagged far behind the population. Formerly, the United Nations agency had recommended a general increase of food production.

The new policy was dictated by the fact that any other program would result in an accumulation in some areas that could not alleviate the shortages in others.

The organization report estimated that 70 per cent of the people in the world do not eat enough to maintain their health and strength. This creates a problem of such magnitude that it cannot be solved by moving foodstuffs from surplus to deficit areas because there are not ships enough to carry the food required nor money enough to pay for it.

As compared to the pre-war period, food exports from underdeveloped areas have fallen by two-thirds and the Far East, formerly a large food exporter, has become a large importer. It is for this reason that Europe has become more dependent on North American exports than before the war.

As far as prices of farm products is concerned, the United Nations agency's report foresees the trend continuing downward in most countries. The downward trend, it adds, is so far reflected to a limited extent in general wholesale prices and only slightly in the cost of living.

September 12, 1953

Common Disease

Protein Malnutrition Found in Many Lands by the F. A. O.

A publication of the Food and Agriculture Organization of the United Nations lists about fifty names for protein malnutrition. In South Africa the name is "infantile pellagra," in Jamaica "fatty liver disease," in India "nutrition dystrophy." In some parts of Africa nearly every child suffers from it at some time in his life. The mortality rate may run as high as 50 per cent. Yet the treatment is simple. The very name "protein malnutrition" indicates that a cure can be effected by a diet of animal milk.

Though the disease needs more study, the basic facts are simple. Infants and young people need a diet rich in protein for growth. Mother's milk provides enough protein, so long as there is mother's milk. As the child grows, the diet must be supplemented from outside sources. This is easy in a country like the United States, where cow's milk and other forms of protein are obtainable everywhere. But protein is scarce in many parts of the world where the staple foods are starches, such as manioc, corn or banana.

At various international conferences it has been emphasized that if animal milk is not obtainable soy milk will do. Soy milk has been prepared for years by a factory in Hong Kong and distributed in hermetically sealed bottles. In other parts of Asia experiments are being made with soy and peanut preparations.

The F. A. O. also approves of fish as a corrective of the diet in protein malnutrition. Its Nutrition Committee for South and East Asia has recommended the inclusion in the diet of fish so small that they can be eaten whole. Fish flour also has possibilities. The new kind is free from the objectionable smell and flavor of the old.

May 23, 1954

Food: Bountiful 1955

With Incomes at an All-Time High, U. S. Enjoyed a Year of Good Eating

By JUNE OWEN

WITH incomes at an all-time high in 1955, Americans have eaten well. They have consumed more meat this year than ever before, an estimated 161 pounds a person. Egg consumption has been at a record high. Though poultry cost more than in 1954, more has been enjoyed than at any time in our history. This has indeed been a year of chicken in every pot.

With plenty to spend on food, the American housewife has been able to take advantage of quick-to-use products that have appeared in groceries in increased numbers and varieties this year. The housewife who taps typewriter keys by day could get home at 6 o'clock, grab individually packed frozen dinners from her refrigerator, "cook" them in the oven and have them on the table in jig time.

Frozen dinners costs more than meals from scratch, but in servantless 1955, when many demands were being made on housewives, their convenience proved worth their price. And this year there have been even more packaged cake mixes from which to choose; innovations have included chocolate angel food, pound cake and caramel cake. In some cases, an aluminum foil baking pan of exactly the right proportions for the loaf has been included in the mix package.

But not all the emphasis in 1955 has been on the expedient. One food authority, who regularly talks with home cooks across the country, is convinced Americans have traveled farther on their way to becoming gourmets this last year.

New Tastes Developed

"Going to Europe has had a lot to do with it," she said. "About a million Americans went abroad this year. They savored all kinds of interesting dishes while away, and came home with new tastes they wanted to satisfy at home on their range."

In St. Louis as well as Boston, our authority said, women have been able to buy Neopolitan pizza during 1955. A few years ago they had never heard of it. To be sure, she said, they may have purchased a frozen pizza, not always good, but at least they were progressing toward more varied dishes

Along the same lines came a bulletin from Borden's that Americans ate more natural, less processed, cheese during 1955. The buying trend, because of developing palates for foreign foods, has been in the direction of blue, Swiss, Parmesan and Romano cheeses

Another strong trend in cooking in 1955 has been the vogue for preparing meals al fresco. It has been estimated that about $30,000,000 was spent on outdoor cooking equipment during 1955.

And this was one bill to which husbands did not object, for more often than not it was the man of the family who presided at the fresh-air grill. He did more, also of the family food shopping this year than ever before, according to reports from retailers throughout the country.

Despite higher incomes in 1955, most Americans could not afford to invest in the newest and most exciting of home cooking appliances—the electronic range. Ranges that operate electronically have been used in commercial establishments and by the armed forces for several years. And last fall the Tappan Stove Company introduced the first model for home cooks, a truly remarkable device that roasts meat in a matter of minutes. The price—$1,200.

December 28, 1955

RICE IS THE GRIST OF INDIA POLITICS

Ruling Party Tries to Keep Prices Down While Reds Sound Famine Tocsin

By A. M. ROSENTHAL

Special to The New York Times

CALCUTTA, Nov. 6 — The wife of a Calcutta bank clerk counted out a few rupees today, handed them to a man squatting in an open-front stall and walked away with a bag of rice.

That is the most basic business transaction in Calcutta—and one of the most important political factors in the life of this city.

There is one thing that every politician in town knows: The price of the sack of rice can mean more to the way people vote, can send more people protesting into their dingy streets than any high-powered international controversy.

It is difficult for anyone who comes from a supermarket society to realize just how much rice means. More than 75 per cent of the diet of a Bengali is rice. Rice shortages mean famine and high rice prices mean hunger.

That is why the Congress party, a majority party—but in this leftist city always with its back to the wall—knows it must keep rice prices down to keep the peace and keep political power.

That is why the Communists, a well-organized party with good leadership, hits hard these days at two themes: Prices are too high and a rice famine is coming.

Hard Hit by Drought

Bengalis produce a lot of rice, about 11,300,000 tons. But the elemental economic fact of this state is that it eats more than it produces, about 200,000 tons more.

Calcutta depends on the states of Bihar and Orissa for the difference. And every Bengali knows that those states have been hit hard by drought, as has West Bengal. Next year there will be no relying on Bihar and Orissa for rice, and the housewife and the politician know it.

The number of rupees the wife of a bank clerk pays for her sack of rice, of course, depends on the amount of rice in the market. It also depends on what action the Government takes to prevent hoarding.

The Government of West Bengal has made it plain to commercial rice hoarders that it will move against them. Government agents recently requisitioned about 16,000,000 pounds of rice from mills.

Price Hard to Budget

The Government also fights its greatest threat—panic—by assuring the people that the Central Government will move in supplies in case of emergency and by keeping an eye on thousands of fair-price shops.

Rice costs a Bengali housewife about $5.25 a maund, which is about eighty-two pounds. That is a considerable amount of money for a housewife who budgets, if she is quite lucky, on about $6 to $8 a week.

B. C. Roy, Chief Minister of West Bengal, has urged the people to eat less rice. He is a physician and he says they can get along on fifteen ounces a day.

That is not likely to be a popular political slogan. Bengalis can eat two pounds of rice a day without feeling at all stuffed. That means that rice is the main budget item for every family and the dollar-a-maund rise of the last year is much more grim than any amount of talk about foreign exchange or sterling reserves.

November 10, 1957

FOOD PRODUCTION OF WORLD UP 3%

Increase Gives No Relief to the Underfed Populations, F.A.O. Reports in Rome

By ARNALDO CORTESI

Special to The New York Times.

ROME, Sept. 3—World agricultural production rose by 3 per cent in 1955-56, the United Nations Food and Agriculture Organization reported today.

However, this increase over 1954-55 will bring little or no relief to areas where hundreds of millions of the world's underfed live because the main increases were registered in North America and Oceania, both already plagued by surpluses.

A production report was distributed to members of the twenty-four-nation F. A. O. Council, which opened a two-week session at its headquarters here today. Next week a plenary conference of the seventy-two nations belonging to the F. A. O. will meet in a special session. On the agenda is the election of F. A. O.'s fourth director general to replace Dr. Philip V. Cardon of the United States, who resigned last March for reasons of health.

In addition to North America and Oceania, said the F. A. O. report, the Far East showed substantial gains in food production. In some regions there was little change and in others production declined.

Output Lags in Some Areas

In 1955-56 food production per capita in Latin America, Oceania and the Far East was still 5 per cent less than before World War II.

Total additions to stocks by the end of 1955-56 were likely to be fairly small, the F. A. O. report said. There were large increases of grain and cotton stocks, mostly in North America, but stocks of some other commodities were somewhat reduced.

In view of the further small increase of production expected next year there is no immediate prospect that stocks of the main commodities will be substantially reduced. Nevertheless, the report added, measures to curtail output in the United States should begin to take effect next season.

World trade in agricultural products increased by about 5 per cent in 1955-56, reaching its highest post-war level. However, there was a contingent fall of prices with the result that the value of world trade in agricultural products increased by only 1 per cent.

It is believed that the decline of agricultural prices is coming to a halt in the last quarter of the present year, the report said. Despite this year's substantial increase, world trade in agricultural products is only about 5 per cent above the 1934-1938 level while world trade as a whole has increased by 70 per cent.

A feature of the report was the large imports of grains and sugar by the Soviet Union and Western Europe. However, their imports of livestock were reduced from the high levels of the previous two years.

East-West trade now appears to account for 3 to 4 per cent of world trade in agricultural products.

Prices continued move against the farmer in most countries. The cost of farm requisites increased and farm incomes decreased almost everywhere. The fall in farm prices was not accompanied by any general or appreciable fall of retail food prices, apparently because of a new increase in marketing margins.

The accumulation of surplus stocks and falling farm prices caused a change in several countries' agricultural policies. The most important was in the United States, which seeks to curtail production by the soil bank. Changes elsewhere were less radical.

After stating that the present economic situation seems likely continue, at least during the early part of 1956-57, the report concluded:

"The main problems facing the world's agriculture remain broadly the same. The basic dilemma of most governments is how to reconcile their dual responsibilities to maintain the economic position of farmers and at the same time provide consumers with adequate food supplies at low prices.

"The deteriorating position of the farm population continues to cause anxiety. In spite of the added urgency caused by surplus stocks only a beginning has been made so far toward reducing production and marketing costs to bring more and better food within reach of the poorer consumer."

Special to The New York Times.

NEW DELHI, India, Sept. 3—United Nations representatives will hold an election in Rome this month that may not get much publicity but will mean considerable to the Indian Government.

Indian official sources made it clear today that they were campaigning actively to get a top-ranking Indian civil servant elected director general of the Food and Agriculture Organization.

September 4, 1956

RED LAND REFORM IN CHINA TRACED

Agrarian Revolution Pushed by Peiping Government to Assure Food Supply

This article comes from Dr. Sripati Chandrasekhar, prominent Indian social scientist, who recently returned from extensive travel in Communist China.

It is natural that in any underdeveloped country the problem of agriculture and food supply should assume paramount importance. This is particularly true in China, where famine has stalked the land from time immemorial.

During the last 100 years, what with a series of wars with Western nations, Japanese aggression after 1931, a thirty-year civil war and World War II, there has been a constant state of political unrest, economic dislocation and recurring famine. China has not known peace for even two consecutive years during the last century.

About twenty-five years ago, when China, in the throes of widespread famine, appealed to the International Red Cross, the Red Cross declined help on the ground that it was designed to meet national emergencies but that famine in China was not an emergency but a chronic state of affairs.

No One Starves Now

The situation between 1946 and 1949 was so desperate that the price of a measure of rice, because of rocketing inflation, soared and kept changing from hour to hour.

What have the Communists done to solve the food problem?

While there was some shortage of food and famine three years ago, the problem has been solved today from the quantitative point of view. No one starves in China now. Though the common man does not have meat or fruit, everybody gets at least a bowl of rice and some cabbage.

This is saying a great deal when you remember that China's population today is about 650,000,000.

Any satisfactory solution of the food problem in Asian countries implies revolutionary changes in land ownership and methods of cultivation. The Chinese Communists have effected, by and large successfully, such drastic changes. Their agrarian reforms have passed through four distinct changes between 1949 and 1958.

Four Changes Listed

The first stage witnessed the public trials of landlords. And when the long-suffering peasantry knew that the new regime meant business, they accused the landlords of all the crimes known to man—from harsh treatment, withholding grain from a starving peasant's family, raping the peasant's daughter or taking his women as concubines, down to brutal murder.

It is possible that some landlords were guilty, of these crimes, but there were no lawyers to defend them. Most landlords pleaded guilty for the simple reason that they knew their end was near no matter what their defense. It is estimated that about 2,000,000 landlords were executed.

The second stage involved the distribution of land to landless peasants. The average peasant received a few mou of land. (A mou equals about a sixth of an acre.)

Within two years the third stage was launched. It was said that private ownership of land was neither socialism nor communism, that it was both a serious economic barrier to greater production, so desperately needed, and a theoretical obstacle to Socialist reconstruction. Thus collectivization was ushered in.

The peasants were made to see the need for collective ownership, for intensive cultivation, use of abundant fertilizers and mechanization were impossible on tiny plots.

From a modest beginning of 300 cooperatives in 1952 the number rose to 14,000 in 1953 and to 600,000 in 1954. By the spring of 1956, China had 1,300,000 cooperatives. This meant that only a small number of the 500,000,000 peasants were outside the cooperatives.

But China was not yet out of the woods from the point of view of food supply.

Therefore the fourth and present stage—the people's communes, which were causing such heart-searching when I was in China.

February 19, 1959

Associated Press

MECHANIZATION IN COMMUNIST CHINA: Workers use harvesting machine in a rice paddy. Increased use of such equipment has been stressed in raising production.

Red China Accepting Food

Special to The New York Times.

HONG KONG, July 16—The Macao general post office announced today that food parcels, including American relief milk powder, were being accepted by the Chinese Communists. Acute food shortages, aggravated by floods in Kwangtung and other southern mainland provinces, were said to be the reason for the lifting of the previous ban on food shipments.

July 17, 1959

Freedom From Hunger Is the Goal of World-wide 5-Year Campaign

Irrigated fields on former jungle land in Ceylon will supply rice, basic food of the inhabitants. The United Nations Food and Agriculture Organization has launched campaign to raise food output and improve its distribution.

World Drive Opens To Erase Hunger

By ARNALDO CORTESI
Special to The New York Times.

ROME, July 1—A world-wide, five-year "Freedom From Hunger" campaign was launched by the United Nations Food and Agriculture Organization at its Rome headquarters today.

Binay Ranjan Sen, Director General of the organization, described as "historic" the decision by the agency to undertake a campaign for the "eradication of hunger in its manifest and hidden forms."

Many countries are expected to publicize the campaign through public announcements and messages over radio and television stations. Cooperation has been promised by many religious leaders, heads of state and prominent statesmen. Messages were read at today's ceremonies from Pope John XXIII, President Eisenhower and de Gaulle and Prime Minister Macmillan.

President Eisenhower's message said:

"The world is confronted by two great problems in nunger—the needs of the present and of the future. And the last is greater than the first. We must try to raise the level of nutrition for many millions who now subsist on an inadequate diet and we must find new sources of food for the rapidly expanding family of man."

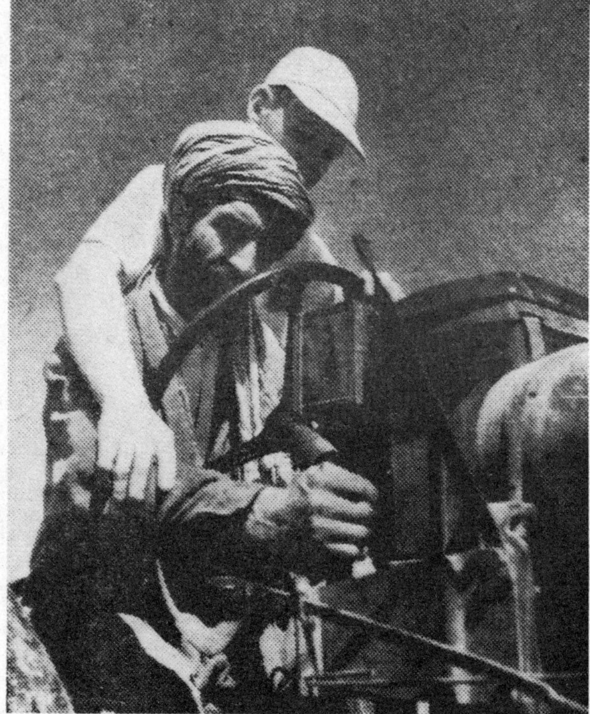

Food and Agriculture Organization

F. A. O. specialist teaches Afghan how to operate tractor

Committees to Be Set Up

National campaign committees will be established in all F. A. O. member countries. First, an intensive study will be conducted of the problem of hunger in the world. The research will seek to throw light on aspects of the problem that are not yet fully understood.

This part of the campaign will culminate in a World Food Congress to be held in 1963 in Rome. The congress will coincide with the twentieth anniversary of the Hot Springs, W. Va., conference that led to the founding of the Food and Agriculture Organization.

The World Food Congress will provide a forum for discussing "action programs" to be undertaken in the concluding years of the campaign.

Half of World Ill-Fed

In launching the campaign, Mr. Sen said:

"More than half of the world's population today does not have enough food or the right kind of food. Many go hungry. Others suffer malnutrition, which leads to ill-health and impaired capacity for work. They live mostly in the less developed countries of Asia, Africa and Latin America.

"They are caught in a vicious circle of stagnation, apathy and poverty. At the same time, population is increasing at a faster rate than ever before, particularly in those same regions which are deficient in food supply.

"However, the central problem, as we see it, is not overpopulation but underproduction. There are vast resources still to be exploited. But unless food production can be stepped up sharply and within a short time, we shall be faced with chronic malnutrition for increasing millions of people, and possibly with disastrous famines. Such developments are bound to affect the peace and well-being of the world as a whole."

Mr. Sen said he was confident that the food problem could be solved.

"Hunger is neither inevitable nor irremediable," he said. "It is within our power to bring this old affliction under control."

Work Already Under Way

Special to The New York Times.

UNITED NATIONS, N. Y., July 1—The implementation of the five-year program to stimulate world food production and to improve distribution in underdeveloped countries already is under way.

Prior to the start of the campaign, a Food and Agriculture Organization spokesman said, the Roman Catholic bishops of West Germany raised $8,000,000 in a one-day drive for funds for campaign projects. A check for $100,000 to help cover the expenses of the campaign has been sent to Rome, he added.

The Netherlands Government has forwarded $20,000 as an initial contribution and has set a goal of $1,000,000 to be spent for research and improvements of production of barley and wheat. To raise the money, reproductions of the bread ration cards used in the Netherlands in World War II will be sold to the public.

A few weeks ago representatives of the fertilizer industry met in Rome and suggested a contribution of $1,000,000 to be paid in two $500,000 installments.

The F. A. O. is seeking similar support from other industrial groups with an interest in increasing food production.

Seed Year Scheduled

The activities of the campaign will be integrated with those of the World Seed Year to be held in 1961. The objective is to convince farmers that the use of scientifically developed seed is one of the most effective ways of insuring bigger and better crops.

Some national committees have already been established and are drafting programs to be adopted in their countries.

The committees are seeking the cooperation of nongovernmental organizations and industrial and professional associations.

Donations of money, equipment and supplies are being sought from these sources as well as from governments. Help is expected in the form of trucks, mechanized farm tools and hand tools, in shipping space and in railway transport, in supplies of seeds and other materials and in advice from experts.

July 2, 1960

Canada to Sell China 362 Million in Grain

By RAYMOND DANIELL

Special to The New York Times.

OTTAWA, May 2—The Canadian Government announced today that it had negotiated an agreement with Communist China for one of the biggest grain sales in Canada's history.

The agreement, between the Canadian Wheat Board and the China Resources Company, was negotiated by Alvin Hamilton, Minister of Agriculture, in two days of conferences in Hong Kong. It covers the period from June 1 of this year to December, 1963. Payment will be in sterling.

In the two-and-a-half-year period, Canada has agreed to supply 6,000,000 tons of wheat, barley and flour, with a total value of about $362,000,000. About 1,000,000 tons of this will be barley. The sale amounts to 186,700,000 bushels of wheat and 46,700,000 bushels of barley.

Earlier this year Canada sold Communist China 28,000,000 bushels of wheat and 12,000,000 bushels of barley, valued at $60,000,000. Total sales in the three-year period thus are expected to come to approximately $422,000,000, with 214,700,000 bushels of wheat and 58,700,000 bushels of barley shipped to China.

The new agreement is in keeping with Canada's policy of selling to any market available. The Canadian Government does not recognize the Peiping regime diplomatically.

Widespread famine conditions have been reported in Communist China in recent months as a result of draught, storm damage and floods in agricultural areas.

The terms of payment for contracts negotiated under the new Canadian-Chinese agreement are 25 per cent cash and the balance in 270 days. The Government, which is making extensive effort to reduce Canada's huge surplus of grain by sales to new markets, will guarantee necessary credit up to a maximum of $50,000,000.

In announcing the transaction to the House of Commons, Mr. Hamilton said that "a sale of this order will spread substantial benefit through the Canadian economy.

"Not only will it provide a welcome increase in western farm incomes, but this in turn will release new purchasing power for the goods and services required by farmers from the business community at large," he said. "Additionally, the sale will generate increased employment for the country and terminal elevator workers and others engaged in the domestic handling and export movement of grain and flour.

"It is apparent," Mr. Hamilton declared, "that new grain sales of this magnitude will add significantly to Canada's total earnings from exports. Business activity in general will therefore be stimulated to a marked extent by the conclusion of this new sales contract with China."

Lester B. Pearson, leader of the Opposition, expressed concern over the effect of the sale on relations with the United States, suggesting that Washington might become less willing to consult with Ottawa on agricultural sales.

"We sell wheat to our friends for cash," he said, "yet we sell to a country we do not recognize on credit."

May 3, 1961

So. African Grain for Peiping

DURBAN, South Africa, Aug. 10 (AP)—South Africa has contracted to sell corn and other grain to Communist China, officials said today. The first cargoes, totalling 25,000 tons, will load here next week for Peiping.

August 11, 1962

ASIA FOOD OUTPUT REPORTED GAINING

It Is a Step Ahead of Rise in Population, F.A.O. Says

Special to The New York Times.

KUALA LUMPUR, Malaya, Sept. 15 — Asia is increasing food production 1 per cent faster than its rise in population, Binay Ranjan Sen of India, Director General of the United Nations Food and Agriculture Organization, said today.

He addressed the organization's sixth regional conference for Asia and the Far East, which opened here this morning.

Mr. Sen said there had been an improvement in terms of calories in the diets of millions of Asians, but that the quality of Asian food was "grossly inadequate and malnutrition remains widespread."

Mr. Sen emphasized that efforts to achieve adequate food levels for the 910,000,000 people of Asia—excluding Communist China—must be stepped up vigorously.

Twenty-two governments were represented at the conference, which was opened by the Prime Minister of Malaya, Tunku Abdul Rahman. The Prime Minister directed the conference's attention to commodity price problems. Stable prices, he said, are necessary to insure planned and steady economic development.

Mr. Sen said that although the volume of Asia's agricultural exports increased 7 per cent in the last decade, export earnings actually fell.

Measured against the imports of manufactured goods, he said the larger exports of last year would buy 10 per cent less than in 1959. He said this situation was likely to continue.

Mr. Sen said Asian agricultural production must be in-

REPORTS FOOD GAIN: Binay Ranjan Sen, head of United Nations Food and Agriculture Organization.

creased at an annual rate of 4 to 4.5 per cent. He noted that this figure was higher than the present level of expansion in some countries, but below what other countries were achieving. He said such an increase was "undoubtedly within the capacity of all."

All agricultural planning should be guided by this target figure, Mr. Sen declared. The figure takes into account Asia's population growth.

The F. A. O. chief predicted that by the year 2000 there would be two and a half times as many people in Asia as there are today. This would make Asia's population equal to the present world population.

A conference working paper on planning said that national self-sufficiency programs for rice growing should not be carried to extremes. It said that under conditions of a growing demand marginal costs would rise sharply. This would cause a serious misallocation of resources to the detriment of general economic growth, the paper said.

The same subcommittee pointed out that wheat was available to Asia at relatively low prices on special terms not involving foreign exchange. This situation may continue for some years, the subcommittee said. If there is a marked fall in rice prices, the paper said, the diversion to wheat may be halted.

Another working paper reported that while food production had been growing steadily, it did not reach the per capita prewar level until 1960-61 and now appears to have fallen off somewhat.

September 16, 1962

Sales of Snack Foods Up Sharply; More Gains Seen

By ALEXANDER R. HAMMER

Sales of the snack foods industry, a potpourri based on people's diverse appetites, are expanding at a rapid pace.

Industry-wide figures are hard to come by since there are many component parts such as potato chips, pretzels, crackers, biscuits, popcorn, nuts, relishes, pickles, meats and fish.

However, a breakdown of some of the most important segments clearly pinpoints the advance. Sales of crackers, biscuits and cookies in this country have risen from $924 million in 1960 to $993 million in 1962.

Potato chips volume soared from $519 million in 1960 to $581 million in 1962. In 1961, nut sales amounted to $438 million. By 1962 they had risen to $467 million. Trade sources report that sales rose again last year and are expected to grow further this year.

Popcorn is another illustration of how the snack food business has grown. Its sales rose from 295 million pounds in 1961 to 360 million pounds last year. About 65 per cent of the popcorn sold is eaten in the home and the rest in theaters, bars, etc.

The growing popularity of snack items is mainly a result of changes in the social and eating habits of Americans. These include increased home entertainment, including television and parties, and the growth of self-service supermarkets.

Another important factor is that snack foods such as potato chips and corn chips, in addition to providing for between-meal consumption, have now become standard parts of many luncheon menus as well as a basic ingredient in casseroles, meatloaves, salads and fish sticks.

Similar changes in social and eating habits are starting to show up abroad. Recent marketing studies conducted in Europe disclosed a bright outlook for the industry.

For instance, the Potato Chip Institute International, worldwide organization of potato chip manufacturers founded in 1937, now represents more than 400 concerns in this country and more than 60 in 30 overseas countries.

Among the leading companies in the snack foods industry are the Borden Company, Frito-Lay, Inc., General Foods Corporation, Jay Company of Chicago, National Biscuit Company, Pet Milk Company, Standard Brands Company, Sunshine Biscuit Company, United Biscuit Company and Wise Potato Chip Company of Berwick, Pa.

A recent survey of 2,440 chain supermarkets throughout the country showed that specialties accounted for about 1 per cent of total store sales with a gross margin of 25 to 30 per cent.

Numerous supermarkets have increased sales by tying snacks in with other items. For example, some store managers have linked potato chips with sour cream, pretzels and corn chips with prepared dips and beer. One helps sell the other.

An example of how the snack food industry has grown is Frito-Lay, Inc., a concern that has done more than its share to make corn chips and potato chips popular.

Net sales of Frito-Lay jumped in the year ended Aug. 31, 1963, to $165,226,031 from $146,632,364 in the preceding year. In 1960 the company had sales of $123,737,185.

Net income of Frito-Lay in fiscal 1963 rose to $6,644,493, or $1.56 a share, from $5,405,164, or $1.29 a share, in fiscal 1962. Two years before, the company cleared $4,077,142, or 99 cents a shre.

The common shares of Frito-Lay were admitted recently to trading on the New York Stock Exchange. The shares formerly were traded in the over-the-counter market.

April 12, 1964

Many Who Are Starving Reject New Foods, Nutritionists Find

WASHINGTON, Dec. 9 (UPI—People cannot be forced to eat strange new foods, not even to save their lives, a Brazilian expert said today at an international conference on the prevention of malnutrition in children.

Oswaldo Ballarin, president of a food company at São Paulo, said that even the hungry were choosy about what they ate, often preferring familiar bad foods to unfamiliar good ones.

Mr. Ballarin told the conference that "any new type of food must be tested for acceptance." Even hungry children will reject nutritionally good food if they don't like the taste, he said.

Food Tastes Are Local

Fish flour is accepted in Africa, he asserted, but is rejected by the inhabitants of northeastern Brazil. Children used to certain flour or corn can't stand the flavor of soybeans.

Some authorities have tried to make new foods palatable by adding an aroma that would cover up an unfamiliar taste. But, Mr. Ballarin said, this doesn't always succeed.

By education and demonstration, however, nutritionists have been able to induce large numbers in India and Latin America to accept cheap substitutes for meat, eggs and milk.

It was brought out that local traditions sometimes keep a malnourished people from eating good foods virtually laid at its doorsteps by nature.

This, it was said by Prof. Ritchie Calder of the University of Edinburgh, has led to an oddity in food economics. According to Professor Calder, when a seafood fancier in New York orders a dish of shellfish, or a Parisian gourmet eats a plate of froglegs, it is helping an Indian who wouldn't think of eating either food.

Shellfish, prawns and rock lobsters abound on the coast of the Indian state of Kerala. Frogs swarm by the millions in the backwaters of this coast. Since Indians won't eat them, these culinary items can be exported.

With the money thus earned, Indian fishermen can buy the power boats they need to "catch more abundantly" the kind of fish that they and their compatriots are willing to eat.

December 10, 1964

INDIANS INCENSED OVER GRAIN ISSUE

Regime Scored on Failure of Raids as Prices Rise

By JACQUES NEVARD

Special to The New York Times

NEW DELHI, Aug. 1—The Government was strongly criticized today as Delhi food prices began to rise again after an announcement by the police that raids on traders suspected of illegally hoarding grain would be stopped.

Officials said an investigation of grain stocks and records seized in three days of highly publicized raids had shown some "technical" accounting irregularities but no evidence of hoarding. No arrests were made.

Suspicions of "whitewash," or covering up, were voiced. It was recalled that three days ago officials were pointing to seized grain stocks as evidence that traders were holding back food to force prices higher.

Many Indian leaders believe that the country's acute food shortage results largely from artificial scarcities through profiteering.

Some Opposition politicians were quoted as having said that the raids were "ill planned and ill executed and gave ample opportunities for hoarders to go scot free."

A leader of Jan Sangh, a right-wing Hindu party, said that several days before the raids began there was a "hectic movement of trucks" carrying grain out of the Delhi market area. He implied that dealers had received advance warning.

A Socialist leader said it was surprising that the police could not bring a single case of hoarding against the dealers.

"After all, what was the provocation for the administration to launch the raids?" he asked. "I believe they acted on some definite information."

Dealers to Take Action

A Communist party spokesman asserted: "It was nothing but a hoax. The failure of the administration will only encourage the hoarders."

One leader of the ruling Congress party was as critical as the Opposition. "The raids began with a bang and ended with a whimper," he said.

The Grain Dealers Association said it was planning "suitable action" against Delhi officials for "unnecessarily harassing" members and damaging their reputations.

The Times of India reported that the prices of grain, edible oils, sugar and pulses had "recorded an unprecendented rise during the past year." Pulses, or edible seeds such as peas and beans, make up the bulk of protein in the diet of most Indians.

The paper found that the prices of the inexpensive varieties of grain eaten by poor people were 100 per cent higher than a year ago

In the key port of Bombay, the Government went into the stevedoring business in a move aimed at speeding the flow of imported grain to distribution points. The Government will now hire dock workers directly instead of relying on commercial labor contractors.

To increase the productivity of port workers, the Government will pay incentive bonuses.

Under the increased program of United States assistance, the equivalent of two fully laden 10,000-ton ships will leave American ports each day from now through next February.

The Government announced new maximum wholesale and retail prices for coarse rice in the south Indian states of Andhra, Madras, Kerala and Mysore. Price ceilings will gradually be extended throughout India.

August 2, 1964

U.S. and India Sign $398 Million Food Agreement

By THOMAS F. BRADY

Special to The New York Times

NEW DELHI, Sept. 30—The United States signed an agreement here today to provide India with $398 million worth of food grains and edible oil under the Food for Peace program.

The agreement covers pledges already made to India to help meet the current food crisis, which has forced up the price of wheat by more than 30 per cent since May.

The agreement, covering the fiscal year ending next June 30, was signed by Joseph N. Greene Jr., United States minister-counselor, and P. Govindan Nair, Secretary of the Finance Ministry.

The United States promised to provide four million tons of wheat, 300,000 tons of rice and 75,000 tons of soybean oil.

Wheat deliveries will actually amount to 6.7 million tons because 2.7 million tons remain from a previous agreement. Talks are already in progress for a similar Food for Peace agreement for the year beginning next July 1.

Food Aid Totals $2.7 Billion

The agreement brings to more than $2.7 billion the value of surplus food provided to India since 1956 under Public Law 480. India has paid 13.7 billion rupees for this commodity aid, but the rupees have remained blocked in India.

Under Public Law 480 a country receiving surplus United States food pays in its own currency, which then can be spent by the United States only in that country.

Total blocked funds generated here by all forms of United States aid will now reach more than 17 billion rupees.

In addition to large outright grants to the Indian Government and local expenditures by the United States Embassy, more than 12 billion rupees of this amount is on loan or earmarked for loans to Indian development projects or is drawing interest here as bank deposits.

American rupee holdings or credits are consequently equal to about half the money in circulation in India.

Under a secondary accord also signed today, "the bulk" of the 1.9 billion rupees to be generated by the new agreement will be lent to the Indian Government for 40 years at three-quarters of 1 per cent interest.

In the current food crisis, United States wheat is arriving in India at a rate of about 20,000 tons a day. Mr. Greene said that today's agreement reflected American confidence that India would solve her food production problem on a long-term basis, and that the American aid was designed to provide the time needed to achieve that goal.

Another United States project was inaugurated today when King Mahendra of Nepal and President Sarvepalli Radhakrishnan of India exchanged messages over a new telecommunication service linking Katmandu, the Nepalese capital, with New Delhi and Calcutta and thence with the rest of the world.

Greetings from President Johnson were relayed from here to King Mahendra over the new circuit.

October 1, 1964

INDIA WILL RATION GRAIN IN CITIES

Sets a 12-Ounce Daily Limit to Counter Shortages

By J. ANTHONY LUKAS

Special to The New York Times

NEW DELHI, Aug. 6—India decided today to impose food rationing on her city dwellers.

In a major move to meet the country's chronic food shortage, the Government will limit men, women and children in urban areas to 12 ounces of wheat or rice a day.

Twelve ounces of wheat will make six chappatis, the large slabs of unleavened bread that are the staple of the North Indian diet.

In South India, where rice is the staple, 12 ounces covered with boiled vegetables, curd or curry will provide about two meals.

The national average consumption of food grains is now about 14.4 ounces a day, according to Government statistics.

The rationing system, which is expected to begin in about two weeks, will put city dwellers under more controls than at any time since World War II, when nationwide rationing was in effect.

Initially, the new rationing will affect only the eight cities with more than a million residents and certain highly industrialized areas.

However, it will eventually be extended to 114 other cities with more than 100,000 inhabitants. This will bring a total of 40 million persons, or one-twelfth of the country's population, under the rationing system.

The decision, announced today by Food Minister Chidambara Subramanium, is a triumph for the policies of Mr. Subramanium and Prime Minister Lal Bahadur Shastri.

The two men recommended a similar system last year. It was rejected by most of the country's 16 states.

Today's decision does not reflect any worsening in India's food situation. In fact, the situation is appreciably better this year than last, when serious shortages caused near-famine conditions in many parts of the county.

Harvest 10 Per Cent Better

Although the food-grain harvest this year has been 10 per cent better than last year's and the best on record, the Government wants to establish a food distribution system that will work in good years as well as bad.

Despite large-scale irrigation projects, the country's agricultural production is still heavily dependent on the weather. A two-week delay in the arrival of the southwest monsoon caused some crop damage even this year.

At present, rationing is in force only in Calcutta and in the cities and towns of the State of Kerala. It was also used temporarily last year in the City of Madras.

However, the 16 state Chief Ministers, at a meeting here today, decided to adopt the system as a national policy.

Prime Minister Shastri presided at the meeting. The five-hour closed-door session, held in the Government auditorium, was also attended by Mr. Subramanium, Gulzarilal Nanda, the Home Minister; T. T. Krishnamachari, the Finance Minister; Bali Ram Bhagat, Minister of Planning, and other Government officials.

The decision must now be ratified by the full Cabinet. However, this is considered a formality.

8 Cities Are Listed

The first stage of rationing will apply to the following eight cities, all with more than a million inhabitants—Bombay, Calcutta, New Delhi, Madras, Bangalore, Hyderabad, Ahmadabad and Kanpur.

The next stage will embrace cities with populations over 300,000. The third stage, which the Government hopes to complete within two years, will extend the system to cities with more than 100,000 people.

On the basis of the experience during the first two years, the Government will then decide whether to extend the system to cities with more than 50,000 inhabitants.

The ministers decided today that the ration for manual laborers would be increased by 10 per cent.

By restricting consumption by all but manual laborers to 12 ounces, or 2.4 ounces under the national average, the Government hopes to do the following:

¶Limit consumption in surplus areas and thereby provide more grains for deficit areas.

¶Cut down on the import of grains, particularly of rice, which must be paid for in scarce foreign exchange.

India imports 6 million tons of wheat a year under the United States agricultural surplus program. However, such imports are paid for in rupees.

Two million tons of rice are imported every year, chiefly from Thailand and Cambodia, and are paid for in foreign exchange.

August 7, 1965

Food: Not Enough Where It's Needed

By KATHLEEN McLAUGHLIN

Special to The New York Times

UNITED NATIONS, N. Y. —Pope Paul VI touched a sensitive nerve in the United Nations when he told the General Assembly last October: "You must strive to multiply bread for the tables of mankind."

The Pontiff was aware that the world organization had been working steadily for 20 years at this task through the first specialized agency to be set up under its auspices—the Food and Agriculture Organization. The Vatican maintains a permanent observer at F.A.O. headquarters in Rome, holds reserve membership in the unit and is in constant touch with developments.

•

But the stalemate that has arisen in the struggle to expand food production may have inspired the Pope's emphasis on the problem, which is currently furrowing the brows of officials inside and outside the United Nations.

For, despite notable gains registered in the last two decades in total output of food, population growth has been steadily drawing abreast of production volume. And the pace is mounting.

Unless the ratio can be reversed through some type of crash program, the "number

The world food problem was underlined last October when Pope Paul VI exhorted the United Nations to "multiply bread for the tables of mankind." Statistics show food output lagging in precisely those regions that have the highest birth rate. Some nations, like India, are seeking two solutions — more food and a slower population rise, through family planning.

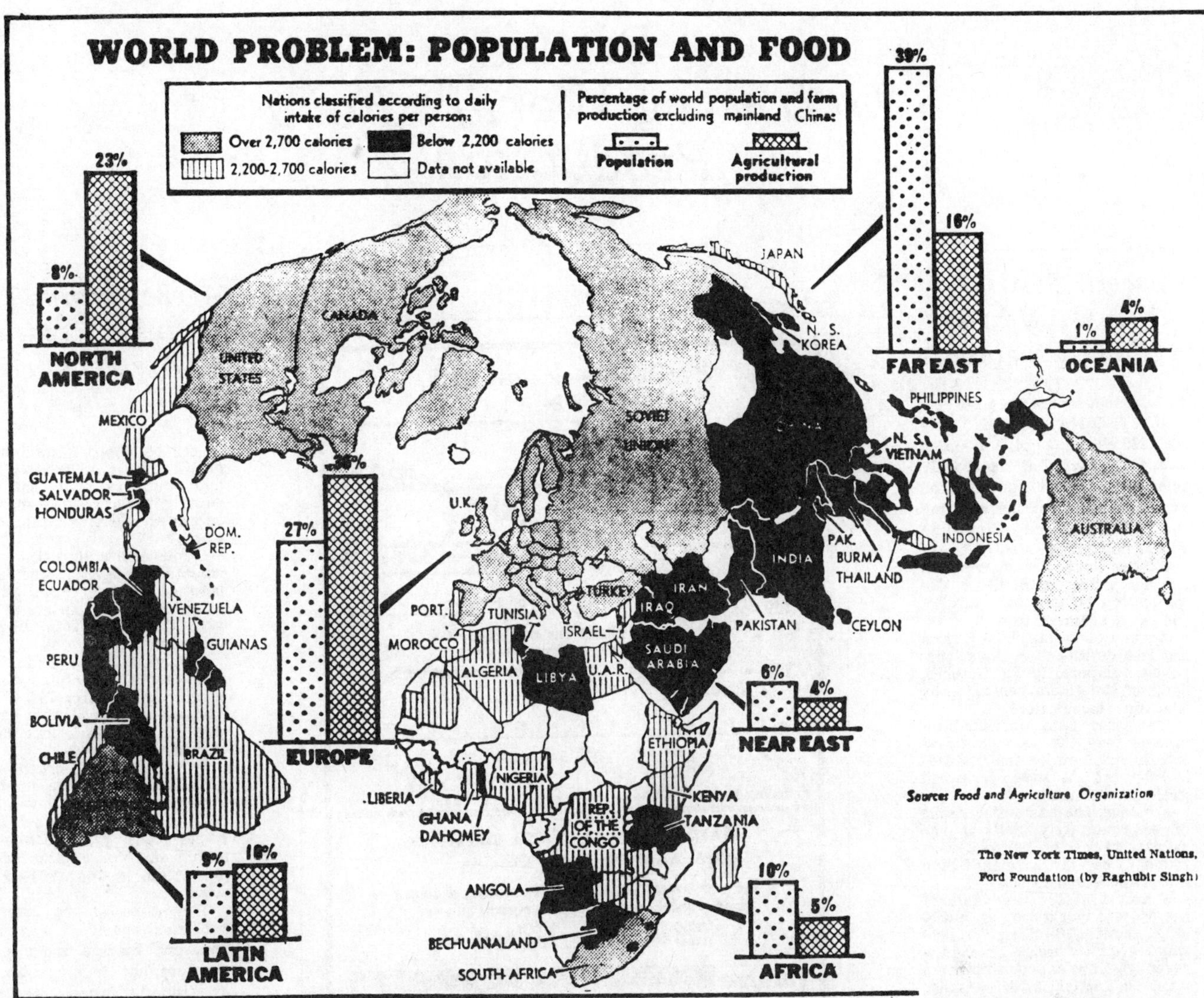

of guests at the banquet of life," to which Pope Paul referred in his comment on birth control, threatens to reduce still further the per-capita share of bread in the years ahead.

The background of the existing situation is summed up by the F.A.O. in a recent publication, "The State of Food and Agriculture 1965," a 273-page review of developments covering the second postwar decade.

At the threshold of the third such decade, the fact that emerges is that output of food has been lagging precisely in those regions of the world that have the highest rates of population growth. It has expanded most quickly in those areas that need it least—the more prosperous nations with the more moderate increases in population.

The next few years are expected to reflect the quickening tempo of population increases, as infant-mortality rates are reduced and life expectancy is extended.

Over the last several years Latin America has lead the world regions in this sphere, with annual growth rates at 2.6 per cent in the 1958-63 period and an average of 2.9 per cent from 1960 through 1963. In the Caribbean area exclusively, it was up from 1.9 per cent in the earlier span to 3.2 per cent in the later period.

•

Demographic experts are closely watching the statistics from Africa, where comparisons are difficult because of the sparsity of data before World War II. Signs are emerging there that the pace is already faster than had been suspected, and that Africa may before long rival the southern part of the Western Hemisphere in population growth.

The F.A.O. review reports that in the harvest season of 1965 output of food crops in the more advanced countries rose 14 per cent above the 1953-57 average. In the poorer, emerging lands output gained by only 1 per cent.

Exclusive of mainland China, F.A.O. analysts comment, the 1958-59 season brought good harvests practically everywhere. The rise in world production reached 6 per cent—by far the largest gain of the decade.

The situation has stagnated since then. Lagging per-capita output in many of the poorer lands has had to be bolstered by increasing imports or decreasing exports of food, the economists note. Thus in Latin America less grain and meat have been shipped abroad in the last few years than before World War II. Imports of wheat in Brazil between 1956 and 1962 rose from 63 per cent of the total food supply to 76 per cent; in India, imports climbed from 12 to 24 per cent.

An F.A.O. balance sheet covering production, imports, exports, supplies and population in 53 countries from which figures are obtainable show a decrease of 4 per cent in the per-capita availability of food for Africa and a decline of 1 per cent for North America.

In the latter case the significance is negligible, since it stemmed from government policies in countries with an immense potential for reversing the trend.

On the contrary, the African record reflects the most disappointing performance of any world region in the farming sector. It underlines the anxiety about rates of population growth now under discussion by top officials throughout the world.

Star performers among food crops in order of importance in average annual gains between 1954 and 1965 are listed in the review as soybeans, cocoa, peanuts, barley, corn, coffee, apples, bananas, sugar, vegetable oils, meat, tea, rice eggs, citrus fruits, wheat, milk and olive oil.

January 24, 1966

Births Outracing World's Food Production

Concern Growing in F.A.O. Despite Some Progress

Special to The New York Times

UNITED NATIONS, N. Y. — As 1966 ebbed, concern mounted about the fact that the world's relatively static output of food was lagging increasingly behind the needs of an expanding global population.

At the Rome headquarters of the Food and Agriculture Organization revised estimates of the year's harvest, still dribbling in slowly—especially from the less developed regions—dispelled temporarily in October, some of the gloom generated by the June calculations.

The later data projected increases over the preceding season for most major commodities inclusive of a recovery for world grain production.

For rice, the basic diet staple of approximately half of the human race, the outlook was found to be "much better" than in the 1965-1966 season.

F.A.O. assesses the value of the present world crop at "probably about $20-billion." It estimates the foreign exchange revenues from export shipments —for countries with supplies of the commodity available—at about $900-million. The 1966 rice volume is now expected to equal the record yield of about 7.5 million tons in 1965.

October figures also brightened the forecast for world output of all grains. Wheat yields, in particular, appeared headed for new highs in Canada and the Soviet Union. The United States yield for 1966 was expected to be only 2 per cent less than that of 1965, instead of the 7 per cent retreat predicted earlier.

Confirming these trends in part, the Soviet Union announced in December that its grain harvest would total 171 million metric tons (of 2,204 pounds each), exceeding the previous record of 152 million tons in 1964.

In contrast, the drought-ridden season of 1963 had cut Soviet production to 107.3 million tons, necessitating imports costing hundreds of millions of dollars.

Communist China recently publicized official claims of "the biggest grain crop in history," while omitting vital statistics.

The F.A.O. has learned unofficially that bad weather in China

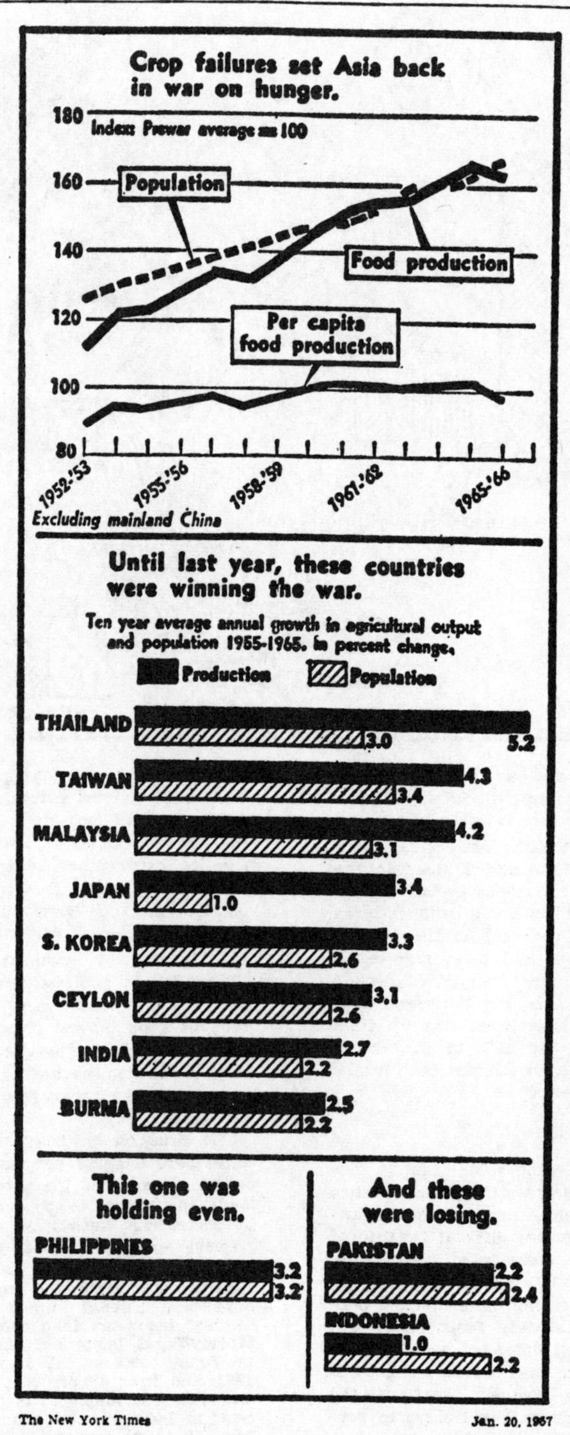

The New York Times Jan. 20, 1967

Agency Warns That Signs of Recovery Are Tentative

destroyed about 3 million tons of the rice crop in the South and Southwest, but that yields on irrigated areas elsewhere had improved despite unfavorable weather.

While continuing to import wheat, the agency said, mainland China has materially increased its rice exports in 1966, with the year's total likely to reach one million tons.

To forestall any undue optimism about the enhanced short-term food situation, F.A.O. statisticians cautioned that it was still too early to assess the extent of the recovery.

It is already certain, they commented, that the final figures for the year in low-income regions will be well below the 7 per cent gain required to match the per capita level of production in the 1964-65 season.

The scope of the long-term problems involved was made apparent by the most recent demographic reports compiled at United Nations headquarters. They showed that the world population was growing at the net rate of 180,000 persons every 24 hours, or the equivalent of a city of moderate size.

Annual birth rates in the poorer countries, least able to feed their inhabitants adequately, have reached 40 for each 1,000 persons, against 20 per 1,000 in the industrialized nations.

Average life expectancy has been extended in many areas as mortality rates, especially among infants, have been reduced, leaving more mouths to be fed.

On the other hand, the stirrings among governments that had been slow to recognize the importance of stimulating agriculture as well as industry within their borders, picked up momentum last year. Requests for technical aid on food production projects have continued to rise.

In 1966 Tunisia joined those governments that have included some version of population stabilization among their official plans for national development.

January 20, 1967

JOHNSON SPEEDING TWO MILLION TONS OF GRAIN TO INDIA

Asks Congress for More and Urges Other Countries to Meet 'Inescapable' Duty

By FELIX BELAIR Jr.
Special to The New York Times

WASHINGTON, Feb. 2—President Johnson advised Congress today that he was making an immediate consignment of two million tons of food grains to India. He asked for Congressional approval to send three million tons more, "provided it is appropriately matched by other countries."

In a special message sent to the Senate and House of Representatives, the President laid down the proposition that food aid to India or any other country without enough to eat was "an inescapable duty of the world community." Rich and poor nations alike must join in the effort, he said, giving food if they have it, or capital, equipment and fertilizer.

"The first obligation of the community of man is to provide food for all its members," the President said. "This obligation overrides political differences and differences in social systems. The United States is prepared to do its share."

Shortage Is Estimated

The Indian "food package" outlined by the President was predicated on a shortage of about 10 million tons this year. With 1.6 million tons of United States wheat and other grains already in the pipeline, his proposal would mean a 6.6-million-ton contribution from this country.

The President estimated the cost of filling India's 10-million-ton food deficit at $725-million. He valued at "nearly $150-million" the two million tons he was allocating immediately and asked that $190-million of Commodity Credit Corporation funds be used to finance the three million tons additional.

There was no explanation for this apparent discrepancy in costs.

Agreement in Consortium

The President also recommended an allocation of $25-million in food commodities for distribution by CARE and other American volunteer agencies in an emergency program in Bihar and Uttar Pradesh, states in India where drought has persisted.

Under the President's proposal, food aid would be treated as part of assistance provided through the 10-member India aid consortium headed by the International Bank for Reconstruction and Development, the World Bank. He said there was "substantial agreement" among the consortium members on these major points of the United States proposal:

¶Meeting food needs of India during this emergency should be accepted as an international responsibility in which each nation should share.

¶Emergency food and food-related aid should be coordinated through the World Bank consortium.

¶This aid should not diminish the flow of resources for other development programs. It should be in addition to the targets for each country suggested by the World Bank.

Although he could have made the immediate and future allocation of grain to India without asking Congressional approval, the President said he was requesting authority by joint resolution because the nature and scope of the issues made it "important that we act together."

The President noted at one point that the Soviet Union had contributed 200,000 tons of grain as part of an impressive effort to help India. Canada and Australia also have provided substantial amounts, and India had used her own foreign exchange to buy 200,000 tons.

Administration officials estimated that two million tons would take care of India's food needs approximately through June. They said this United States grain would be sold for Indian rupees. But a gradual shift to credit sales for dollars for at least a part of the three million additional tons will be considered during the consortium's discussions in March.

Special emphasis was put on two related factors in the President's message. One was fertilizer. The other was the necessity for effective voluntary population control in all countries lacking enough food to feed their people.

"We know that land can be made to produce much more food — enough food for the world's population, if reasonable population policies are pursued," the President said. "Without some type of voluntary population program, however, the nations of the world—no matter how generous—will not be able to keep up with the food problem."

India's avoidance of famine last year "ranks among the proudest chapters in the history of international cooperation," the President said. She imported nearly 11 million tons of grain and used several million more from her own food reserves.

This year, unless the country's own production can be supplemented with the 10 million tons she is estimated to need "more than 70 million people will experience near-starvation," the President added.

Of last year's efforts, the President said that Canada had been especially generous, as had Australia, which is not a member of the consortium. Simiarly, he said, the private contributions of the Dutch and Italian people had been especially heartwarming.

"But the bleak facts require a substained international effort on a great scale," the President said. "Today I propose that all nations make the new Indian emergency the occasion to start a continuing worldwide campaign against hunger."

Move Welcomed in New Delhi

NEW DELHI, Feb. 2 (Reuters)—Indian officials tonight welcomed President Johnson's announcement that the United States was allocating two million tons of food grain to India immediately.

A Government spokesman said: "We certainly appreciate this as a first step. It will help keep the pipeline full and prevent an interruption of supplies."

Food Ministry circles estimate the new allocation would keep the pipeline full until May, tiding over the lean months of spring and preventing a breakdown of supplies to scarcity areas.

February 3, 1967

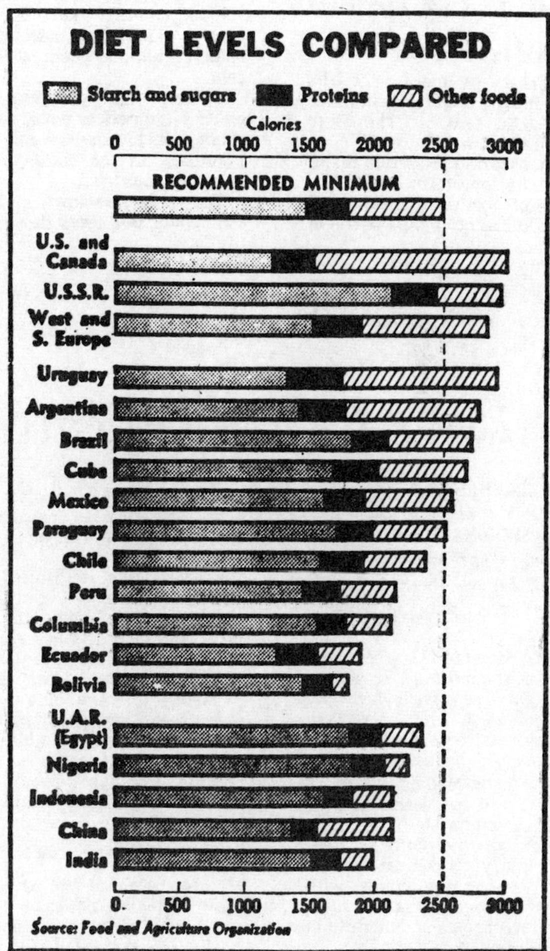

The New York Times Jan. 22, 1968

January 22, 1968

Poorer Countries Lag Further in Food Production

By C. GERALD FRASER
Special to The New York Times

UNITED NATIONS, N.Y., Oct. 9—Three major studies by the Food and Agriculture Organization indicate that developing nations — even with foreign aid, expert help and modern technology — cannot grow enough food to meet their needs.

Developing nations with agricultural products to sell abroad are also reported to have a hard time competing in the world market because of the import-export policies of the technologically advanced nation. These policies are said to be restrictive and protective and to reflect maladjustments in the developed countries' own farm sectors.

The three reports just published are the "FAO Commodity Review and Outlook 1971-1972," "Agricultural Adjustment in Developed Countries" and "The State of Food and Agriculture 1971."

World Increase Maintained

Addeke H. Boerma of the Netherlands, director general of the F.A.O., said in "The State of Food and Agriculture":

"That world production maintained its long-term annual increase of about 3 per cent was due to substantial expansions in the developed countries, where incomes are relatively high and nutrition generally adequate.

"In the developing countries, according to preliminary information so far available, the rise in production was between 1 and 2 per cent, which is much less than in recent years."

The commodity review reported that agricultural exports of the developing countries declined about 3 per cent. Keen competition and the larger exports by developed countries in most commodities caused the decline.

Wide Gap in Value

The products of the developing countries are not selling that well, nor bringing in that much money when they do sell.

In food and feed products, for example, developed countries increased the value of their exports 11 per cent over the previous year. But developing nations gained only 1 per cent.

In beverages and tobacco, developed countries gained 8 per cent in export value, while developing nations declined 9 per cent.

Commodities showing declines were coffee, wool, cocoa, rubber, oilcakes and meals—all important in the trade of developing countries.

The trade slowdown in 1971, the report said, was due to "a significant recovery of agricultural output in Western Europe, the largest importing region."

"The State of Food and Agriculture 1971" said that expertise, technical assistance and foreign aid have not succeeded in helping developing nations meet agricultural production goals.

While 60 to 80 per cent of the increase in agricultural output in developed nations can be attributed to technology, the review said, "a direct transfer of their experience and knowledge to developing countries has not generally proved a success."

Foreign aid is also spotty. "The year 1971," the review noted, "was particularly critical for foreign assistance programs and raised doubts over future levels of aid, chiefly as a result of developments in the main donor country, the United States."

In the United States, the review said, "international financial problems and world political developments stimulated domestic opposition to aid legislation."

Market Difficulties

In the third report, "Agricultural Adjustment in Developed Countries," Mr. Boerma said:

"The difficulties encountered in trying to expand the agricultural exports of developing countries are to be found rooted in the market adjustment difficulties experienced at the national level in developed countries, which in turn are associated with the maladjustments in the farm sector.

"Agricultural structures and policies in developed countries must be and will be modified. It is important that these modifications should facilitate rather than handicap the development of agriculture in other, less developed regions of the world."

Mr. Boerma said that in the developed countries—the United States and Western Europe, for example—resources and manpower "have not moved out of agriculture quickly enough." This results in too many small farms that are unable to exploit modern production factors and that bring only low incomes to their owners.

The F.A.O. is a United Nations intergovernmental agency with headquarters in Rome. Membership is voluntary and not all United Nations members are in the organization.

Summing up his feelings on agriculture, Mr. Boerma said, "All in all, 1971 was not a very encouraging year."

October 10, 1972

Poor Lands Do Little on Protein Deficiency

By KATHLEEN TELTSCH
Special to The New York Times

UNITED NATIONS, N. Y., April 18—The musical sensation in Zambia these days is a catchy lyric sung in Nyanja dialect:

"On Monday, I feed my baby a spoonful of powdered milk. On Tuesday, I feed my baby some peanuts to make him grow strong. On Wednesday, mashed beans."

The "baby-feeding song" is part of an energetically pursued campaign by the Government of the Central African country to combat malnutrition among the young with more and better-quality food. Few low-income countries in Africa, Asia or Latin America have utilized such methods to combat this pressing problem.

Two-thirds of the 800 million children on the three continents are affected by malnutrition, according to experts in the United Nations and elsewhere.

Six years ago, the United Nations warned of an "impending protein crisis." Today, the experts say, the crisis has arrived and protein malnutrition is increasing alarmingly, particularly among the rural and urban poor. The situation is rendered more acute by crop failures in India and in African countries because of droughts, but the extent of the problem is still uncertain.

Not So Dramatic as Famine

Malnutrition is not so dramatic as famine nor does it demand such urgent attention as smallpox, says Alan Berg, a World Bank official who has worked on nutrition problems in the poorer countries and who habitually takes along a recording of the Zambian feeding song.

Science recognizes that not enough food and a deficiency of protein in the diet of the young result in protein-calorie malnutrition that can cause physical and mental impairment. But Mr. Berg maintains that governments still do not appreciate the importance of proper diet in their economic planning.

Proteins are complex substances made up of a combination of amino acids essential for health and growth. They are available to the prosperous in protein-rich foods such as meat, fish, eggs and dairy products. However, the poor, unable to afford high-priced foods, must depend for protein on cereals and vegetables, which have some but not all the essential amino acids.

It is for this reason that the international community has been seeking to improve the qualities of plants by breeding—to enrich them with the missing amino acids—and to develop new sources of protein.

Concerned officials maintain that it will take concerted action by governments, both the prosperous and the poor, to solve the protein problem, and so far the response has been discouraging.

Apathy Laid to Governments

Philippe de Seynes, an Under Secretary General of the United Nations, who heads its Department of Economic and Social Affairs, complains of the apathy of government leaders, saying: "The world does not have the will power or enthusiasm to eradicate protein malnutrition." He notes that only Denmark and Norway reacted favorably to a proposal for the establishment

A child in Bangladesh holds a ball of food derived from corn, soya and milk, used by the United Nations Children's Fund to combat protein malnutrition.

of an international "protein fund" comparable to those already functioning to deal with problems of environment, population control and drug abuse.

In Washington, Dr. Martin Foreman of the Agency for International Development says that many low-income countries now recognize the existence of the protein problem but that their leaders have not been galvanized into action. A.I.D. has provided $800-million to supply protein foods and promote protein research for the benefit of needy countries.

"The technology we can solve," says Dr. Foreman, who heads A.I.D.'s office of nutrition. "The important thing is to get governments to give enough of a damn to put a meaningful nutrition program into their national plans and budgets"

The development of high-yield strains of wheat and rice, probably one of the most beneficial agricultural achievements of this century, has also had a negative impact.

The spread of the Green Revolution could double cereal production in the next 25 years, says Dr. Lewis M. Roberts of the Rockefeller Foundation, which helped pioneer the "miracle" seeds. He believes they hold out the best hope for coping with the total food problem and with part of the protein shortage.

However, enthusiasm for the new varieties has led to a shift toward these corps at the expense of legumes—the high-protein peas, beans and lentils frequently called the "meat of the poor." Legumes have two to three times the protein content of cereals.

In a new study, "The Nutrition Factor," to be published by the Brookings Institution, Mr. Berg stresses what he calls the "silent loss" of a major protein resource—the dramatic drop in breast feeding in low-income countries. Governments seem reluctant to try to reverse this disturbing trend, he says, "but an effective public effort would be of greater significance than any other means for improving infant nutrition."

Probably the most encouraging development, Mr. Berg maintains, is the increase in government interest in malnutrition. "Nutrition is not being seen as just vitamin pills and sliced peaches," he said.

Many exports concede that overoptimism concerning prospects for solving the protein problem arose from the possibility that private industry, with its technological skills, could attack the protein problem and devise new foodstuffs that magically would be attractive, cheap enough for the poor to afford and still profitable for the companies involved.

More than 100 such ventures were initiated, with A.I.D. alone sponsoring 14 feasibility projects, each at a cost of $60,000. Though some are continuing, most of the undertakings failed.

Many were unsuccessful because of the inability to turn out a product at a price the masses could afford. Others were dropped after marketplace fiascoes. For example, a high-protein cereal was rejected in Peru because of its "wet dog" odor and taste, while a protein-fortified beverage in Indonesia failed as a weaning drink for babies although it became popular as a party drink with the élite.

Funds and Influence Lacking

Some experts say that the United Nations has succeeded in alerting governments to the protein problem but has failed to provide leadership or impetus for action.

The Protein Advisory Group set up in 1955 and financed by the World Health Organization, the Food and Agriculture Organization, the United Nations Children's Fund and the World Bank, has remained the main body promoting research and acting as a clearing house. Although Dr. Nevin Scrimshaw of the Massachusetts Institute of Technology, a leader in the field, is chairman of the 14-member expert group, participants concede that it lacks the money and influence to make much of an impact.

Despite general discouragement, experts see some favorable developments.

The Protein Advisory Group has singled out as a major new protein source the recent progress in developing the single-cell-protein known as SCP, the generic term for protein flour derived from yeast, bacteria and fungi. It can be grown on oil or papermill wastes or even sewage. France and Britain have made considerable progress in developing SCP for animal fodder, which contributes to increased animal protein.

The "hottest thing" in agriculture these days, says Dr. Max Milner, a leading food technologist, is the work being done at six international agricultural research centers, financed mainly by the Ford and Rockefeller Foundations and the United States Government together with the World Bank, the United Nations Development Fund, Canada, Britain and some others; $15-million was contributed to the six centers last year.

April 19, 1973

The Hunger Belt

	Average Daily Caloric Intake Per Person*	1974 Projected Overall Deficit (In millions of dollars)
Bangladesh	1840	375
Central African Republic	2200	19
Chad	2110	16
Dahomey	2260	9
Southern Yemen	2070	45
El Salvador	1930	48
Ethiopia	2160	**
Ghana	2320	23
Guinea	2020	21
Guyana	2390	16
Haiti	1730	8
Honduras	2140	33
India	**	820
Ivory Coast	2430	57
Kenya	2360	84
Cambodia	2430	**
Laos	2110	**
Lesotho	**	**
Madagascar	2530	32
Mali	2060	42
Mauritania	1940	17
Niger	2080	30
Pakistan	2160	155
Senegal	2370	69
Sierra Leone	2280	31
Somalia	1830	27
Sri Lanka	2170	69
Sudan	2160	46
United Republic of Cameroon	2410	25
United Republic of Tanzania	2260	120
Upper Volta	1710	10
Yemen	2040	11

** not available

*In the United States the average daily caloric intake is 3,000. The recommended minimum daily caloric intake is 2,300. In some countries above, regional disparities and wastage may mean that substantial portions of the population are far below the figure shown.

Source: F.A.O. and the U.N.

October 20, 1974

ROOSEVELT URGES FOOD PARLEY WAIVE TARIFFS FOR HEALTH

Asks World Agriculture Rise to Meet Nutritional Needs Without Trade Barriers

PART OF FOUR FREEDOMS

Chairman Tells Delegates of 45 Nations Treaties Won't Be Made at Hot Springs

THE UNITED NATIONS FOOD CONFERENCE OPENS IN VIRGINIA

The first meeting of the chairmen of the forty-five delegations attending the sessions at Hot Springs. Judge Marvin Jones, who was elected president, is in the right foreground. Associated Press Wirephoto

By RUSSELL B. PORTER
Special to THE NEW YORK TIMES.

HOT SPRINGS, Va., May 18—The United Nations conference on food and agriculture, attended by representatives of forty-five nations, opened tonight with a message of welcome from President Roosevelt.

Reporters were allowed to pass through the military police lines into the Homestead for the plenary session. Newsreel and still cameras clicked as Judge Marvin Jones, chairman of the United States delegation and permanent president of the conference, ordered the message read to the delegates, advisers, technical experts and staffs from all parts of the non-Axis world.

Mr. Roosevelt, declaring that the purpose of the meeting was to further the policies of the Atlantic Charter, the declaration of the United Nations, and the Rio de Janeiro conference of the twenty-one American republics with respect to the post-war consumption, production and distribution of food and other agricultural products, announced that this was to be the first of a series of international conferences extending United Nations collaboration from war to peacetime problems.

Urges Food Production Rise

He urged that world food production be increased to meet "the essential nutritional needs of the world population" and that no barriers of international trade, transportation or internal distribution be allowed to prevent any nation or group from "obtaining the food necessary for health." Only in this way, he declared, could mankind be made free from want and from fear so that the Four Freedoms might become universal and "peace, prosperity and security" assured for the world.

President Roosevelt expressed regret that he could not attend this "historic occasion" in person because of "urgent matters in the prosecution of the war," but said he hoped to meet the delegates "later."

Judge Jones of the Court of Claims, a Texan who was formerly chairman of the House Agricultural Committee and is now assistant to James F. Byrnes, Economic Stabilization Director, delivered an address of welcome in which he "dedicated" the conference to the philosophy of "a new day for humanity" through the achievements of the objectives as stated by the President.

Explaining that the conference was concerned with the long-range "rebuilding" of world agriculture, Mr. Jones said that it would not deal with the problems of immediate post-war relief for the liberated countries, which were in the province of former Governor Lehman's Office of Foreign Relief and Rehabilitation.

To Make No Treaties There

He also made it plain that the conference would merely explore and assemble facts and make recommendations to the participating governments and that the delegates had no power to negotiate treaties or make binding agreements.

Judge Jones urged the delegates to use their influence to bring about a "neighborly attitude" among the nations of the world, so that economic rivalries might not lead to war in the future, as they had in the past.

He said that apparent surpluses of food products were not actually surpluses, but rather "results of accumulations caused by defects in the systems of distribution and the inability of the masses to purchase the food they need." Such conditions, he went on, had caused "starvation in the midst of great plenty," and brought about a cycle of low prices to producers and subsequent scarcity.

He hoped the conference would help to increase food production, promote the flow of farm products into world markets and distribute surplus products. Any temporary devices which might be necessary to deal with immediate "gluts, geographic surpluses and adjustments of production," he added, should be geared to the long-range program. Conservation of natural resources, the rebuilding of those which had been depleted and efficient methods of cultivation, he said, were among the subjects on which valuable information could be exchanged among the participating nations.

Referring to the coming hundred years as "the people's century," Judge Jones called for action to prevent hunger and famine after the war and said that "a better distribution of products of farm and field will materially aid in whatever provision is hereafter fashioned for maintaining the peace of the world."

Kuo Hails Leadership Step

Dr. P. W. Kuo, chairman of the Chinese delegation, responding on behalf of all visiting delegations, called the conference an event of "great historic significance," and said the mere fact that it was being held now meant that "we are all convinced that no matter how long the war may still last, final victory will surely be ours, and we believe the moment has come for us to give common consideration to problems which will confront us all after the war."

He said a great responsibility rested upon the delegates and "the attention of the entire world is being focused upon us." A satisfactory solution of the problems of food, clothing and shelter today called for international cooperation, Dr. Kuo declared. The willingness of the United States to take the lead in calling the conference, he said, was a significant indication that she was prepared for world leadership.

An adequate supply of proper food and other essentials of life for every one, besides an expanding world trade, he continued, would go far toward preventing another world war and "ushering in a new era in human history."

Dr. Kuo voiced the gratitude of the delegates to President Roosevelt for calling the conference into being, and to Secretary of State Hull for making the arrangements. He also expressed himself in favor of drawing up tentative plans for setting up machinery to continue and carry forward the work of the conference.

English Adopted as Language

English was adopted as the official language of the conference at a meeting this morning of the executive committee, composed of the chairmen of the forty-five delegations.

Herve Alphand, chairman of the French delegation, made the reservation that this was not to be considered as a precedent for abandoning the use of French as the official language at other international conferences. He emphasized the traditional use of his language at such events and for recording international agreements. The delegations from Belgium, Luxembourg, Greece and Haiti associated themselves with this reservation.

Judge Jones, who had been designated by President Roosevelt as temporary president of the conference, was nominated for permanent president by the executive committee and was elected to that post at tonight's plenary session. The committee approved a motion made by G. S. H. Barton, chairman of the Canadian delegation, that the conference adjourn not later than June 3.

One of the articles in the conference regulations adopted by the executive committee permits a majority vote of the delegations to order the holding of public sessions in addition to the opening and closing plenary sessions already provided for.

Parley Setting One of Plenty

The delegates assembled for their first meeting in an atmosphere of tranquillity and abundance far different from wartime life in parts of Europe, Africa and Asia from which many have come. This has been a fashionable watering place for a century and a half and Thomas Jefferson, who came here for the baths, wrote about it.

The first inn on the site was put up by an officer who commanded Fort Dinwiddie, the stone ruins of which are preserved a few miles from here, within a few years of the time George Washington visited the fort soon after Braddock's disastrous expedition against the French and Indians.

Set in a beautifully landscaped park with fountains, gardens and shady paths, and surrounded by a 17,000-acre estate with golf links, tennis courts, trout streams, swimming pools, bath houses, riding trails and hiking routes through woods and forests, the Homestead stands like a huge castle on the crest of a hill overlooking the pleasant green valley where the thermal springs are situated.

Without any uniform architectural design, the hotel consists of several ivy-clad colonial brick wings, red with white trimmings, from three to five stories in height, and a ten-story tower which has a suggestion of the Independence Hall tradition. It is surrounded by wide piazzas and its entrance is an old-fashioned porte cochere with white columns.

Reporters Chat With Delegates

The press was admitted to the hotel this afternoon for the official reception given by the United States delegation in honor of the visitors, and was permitted to mingle and talk with individual delegates. Because of the war, this was one of the few social events planned for the conference. Many of the delegates from abroad had to travel light on crowded ships or planes, and did not bring formal attire. Therefore business suits predominated instead of the striped trousers and cutaways normal to such receptions in peacetime. A few military and naval uniforms were matched by as many sports suits.

The reception was held from 4 to 6 o'clock. The guests congregated in the Great Hall, the 175-by-45-foot colonial lobby, with two rows of white columns supporting a high ceiling, and a row of French windows looking out on the Spring blossoms and green shrubbery of peaceful Warm Springs Valley and the magnificent views of the Virginia Alleghenies.

In the adjacent Silver Room the receiving line was formed by Judge Jones and the other United States delegates — Paul H. Appleby, Under-Secretary of Agriculture; W. L. Clayton, Assistant Secretary of Commerce; Thomas Parran, surgeon general of the United States Public Health Service; Murray D. Lincoln, executive secretary of the Ohio Farm Bureau Federation, and Miss Josephine Schain, member of the commission to organize the study of peace.

Mingling of Many Races

Thence the guests moved into the ballroom, where a stringed orchestra played and many of the world's races mingled, and the principal languages were spoken—except German, Japanese and Italian.

Beginning at 9 o'clock tonight, the plenary session, at which the conference was officially and publicly opened, was held in the Empire Room, a large, brightly lighted auditorium, with thick carpetings, light green walls, large wall mirrors in the French manner all along one side, and on the opposite side windows overlooking the park. Flags of all the participating nations were hung in the room.

The reporters and still photographers were at press tables directly in front of the speaker's stand. Across the room was a platform for the movie men. Space was provided also for the radio men.

May 19, 1943

Official Summary of the Food Conference of 44 Nations

By The Associated Press.

HOT SPRINGS, Va., June 3—Following is the text of a summary of the results of the United Nations Food Conference as prepared by the parley's secretary general:

The conference met to consider the goal of freedom from want in relation to food and agriculture. In its resolutions and its reports, the conference has recognized that freedom from want means a secure, adequate and suitable supply of food for every man.

All men on earth are consumers of food. More than two-thirds of them are also producers of it. These two aspects of gaining subsistence from the soil cannot be separated. Men cannot eat more and healthier foods unless these foods can be obtained from the land or the sea in sufficient quantities. If more and better food is to be available for all people, producers must know what they are called upon to do. They must equally be assured that their labors will earn them an adequate livelihood.

The work of the conference emphasized the fundamental interdependence of the consumer and the producer. It recognized that the food policy and the agricultural policy of the nations must be considered together: It recommended that a permanent body should be established to deal with the varied problems of food and agriculture not in isolation but together.

The work of the Conference also showed that the types of food most generally required to improve people's diets and health are in many cases those produced by methods of farming best calculated to maintain the productivity of the soil and to increase and make more stable the returns to agricultural producers. In short, better nutrition means better farming.

The conference declared that the goal of freedom from want can be reached. It did not, however, seek to conceal the fact that it will be first necessary to win freedom from hunger. In the immediate future, the first duty of the United Nations will be to win complete victory in arms; as their armies liberate territories from tyranny their goal will be to bring food for the starving. The need to reach freedom from hunger before seeking freedom from want was understood and resolutions were adopted on this subject. These covered both the planning of agricultural production and the adoption of measures to prevent violent fluctuations in prices resulting from the shortages of the transition period.

Many delegates informed the conference about the state of health in their respective countries. It was made clear that there was a close connection between many prevalent diseases and deficiency in diets. The important part played by malnutrition in maintaining child mortality rates at a high level was also established.

It was apparent that in all countries there are large sections of the population who do not get adequate and suitable food for health; in many countries the majority of the people are in this situation.

The conference has not attempted to lay down ideal standards of nutrition for all peoples. It has recognized that, while the ultimate objectives must be a world in which all people are fed in full accordance with the requirements of good health, it will be necessary as a practical measure to concentrate on intermediate goals which can be progressively raised as conditions improve. These intermediate goals must differ from region to region according to climate, taste, social habits and other circumstances. These goals are therefore primarily a matter for individual governments to determine.

One of the most important recommendations of the conference is that the governments represented should declare to their own people and to one another their intention to secure more and better food for the people. Various measures which might be taken for this purpose were discussed. These included education, special provision for particular classes of the population, and the improvement of the quality of food available.

The conference recognized that a great increase would be needed in the production of food if progress was to be made toward freedom from want. Section II discussed how this increase could be brought about. It was recognized, however, that to a varying extent in different countries and at different times there would be insufficient food of kinds required for health. It might therefore be necessary to take measures to see that special groups of the population, such as young children and pregnant women, who most needed these foods, obtained at least their minimum requirements, even if this meant reducing the supplies for the rest of the population below what they would otherwise consume.

In Section II, the conference considered how agricultural production could be increased and adapted to yield the supplies most needed by consumers. It began its work with the assumption, which was confirmed by the conclusions of Section I, that more production was needed if the people of the world were to have sufficient food for adequate nutrition and that both new and existing production would have to be adjusted to secure more of those "protective" foods which are most necessary for good health.

Before discussing methods by which these changes could be brought about, the section examined the short-term position immediately after the liberation of occupied territories. It was generally agreed that this period will be one of shortage, the exact incidence and extent of these shortages being governed by the circumstances in which various territories are liberated from the enemy. During this period the first call will be to reach freedom from hunger in areas devastated by the war.

Until these lands themselves are able to produce a harvest, the most urgent demand will be for cereals and other foods which maintain human energy and satisfy hunger.

The conference agreed that while shortages lasted there should be coordinated action by governments both to secure increased production and to prevent speculative and violent fluctuations in prices.

The conditions of shortage existing at the end of hostilities will be exceptional and it should not be too long before the production of the basic energy foods is sufficiently restored to provide for freedom from hunger. When that state is reached it will be necessary to increase wherever possible the emphasis on production of foods containing first-class protein and other protective qualities necessary to good health, according to the standards considered by Section I of the conference.

There is danger that the heavy demand for energy foods which will arise from the immediate period of shortage may lead, as the shortages are overcome, to overproduction of these foods unless governments act with foresight in guiding producers to alter their production programs in accordance with the long-term requirements. The actual programs must be drawn up to suit the particular circumstances of each country, but the conference agreed upon broad general principles which should serve as a guide in making these programs in all countries.

These principles cover not only the adjustment of production to fit the long-term requirements of a better diet but also improvements in the general efficiency of production. The conference also recommended certain particular measures of more general application for carrying them out.

In addition, the conference recommended measures for new agricultural development. It was the opinion of the conference that some parts of the world which at present are unproductive could be brought into agricultural production if the appropriate measures were applied. At the same time, it was recognized that, in some areas of rich potentialities, development is impeded by overcrowding of farmers on the land. While something can be done to increase the productivity of these areas by improving methods of farming, by drainage and similar measures, it was recognized that in some cases the development of industry to provide employment for agricultural populations or emigration to other areas were the only measures likely to offer any significant contribution to a solution of the problem.

The conference recognized that it is useless to produce food unless men and nations have means to acquire it for consumption. Freedom from want cannot be achieved unless there is a balanced and world-wide expansion of economic activity.

The deliberations of the conference in Section III, which was set up to investigate the improvement of distribution, clearly showed that consumers would not be in a position to buy the food they needed, and producers of food could not be assured of adequate returns, unless progress was made through national and international action to raise the general level of employment in all countries. Moreover, as discussions in Section I emphasized, poverty is the first cause of malnutrition and hunger.

The work of Section III established the close interdependence between the level of employment in all countries, the character and extent of industrial development, the management of currencies, the direction of national and international investment, and the policy adopted by the nations toward foreign trade.

The conference was not invited to conduct a detailed investigation into policies which should be adopted by the governments of the world in order to promote an expansion of economic activity; but it declared that freedom from want of food could not be fully achieved without such an expansion and urgently recommended to the governments and authorities represented to take action individually, and in concert, in order to secure this objective.

Having drawn attention to the fundamental importance, in the approach to freedom from want of food, of policies to expand and quicken economic activity, the conference discussed the place and functions which might be given, within the framework of such policies, to international arrangements for the control of basic staple foodstuffs entering international trade. There was agreement that the objects of any such arrangements must be to eliminate excessive short-term movements in the prices of food and agricultural commodities, to mitigate general inflationary or deflationary movements and to facilitate adjustments in production which may be necessary to prevent economic dislocation.

The conference agreed that any such arrangements should include the effective representation of consumers as well as producers. It was not possible for the conference, in the time available, to discuss future international commodity arrangements in detail. Discussion in Section III was directed to general questions of principle affecting the operation of such arrangements as might later be made. The two questions to which most attention was paid were—

(A) The place which buffer stocks should occupy in these arrangements, and

(B) How far it would be necessary to achieve the desired objectives to include within the general arrangements agreements for the regulation of production.

The conference agreed that further international discussion of these questions ought to take place with a view to the formulation of broad principles to govern the formulation and operation of future commodity arrangements.

There was general agreement that, whatever the nature of the arrangements eventually made for individual commodities, machinery would be needed for coordinating their operations in the light of the broad principles to be agreed upon.

It became clear at a comparatively early stage of the conference that there was general agreement that the nations represented at the conference should establish a permanent organization in the field of food and agriculture. It was also generally agreed that this organization should act as a center of information and advice on both agricultural and nutrition questions and that it should maintain a service of international statistics.

The conference did not, however, attempt to lay down in detail what the scope and functions of such an organization should be or its relationship to other national or international bodies. It was agreed that these questions would have to be worked out in detail between representatives of the participating governments. Accordingly, the conference recommended the establishment in Washington of an interim commission, one of the functions of which would be to draw up for submission to governments and authorities represented a detailed plan for the permanent organization.

The United Nations conference on food and agriculture has shown that the governments and authorities represented are agreed upon the necessity of their taking action individually and in concert to achieve freedom from want of food. The reports and recommendations of the conference indicate further agreement on the methods to be followed. The conference has accordingly recommended that the governments and authorities represented should recognize their obligation to their own people and to one another to raise the levels of nutrition and the standards of living of their citizens, to improve the efficiency of agricultural production and to cooperate one with another for the achievement of these ends. The conference resolved that the interim commission to be established in Washington should prepare such a declaration or agreements in this sense for the consideration of governments and authorities represented.

WORLD FOOD PACT DRAFTED BY BOARD

Interim Commission of United Nations Maps Agreement on Standards of Living

TO GO TO GOVERNMENTS

Organization Following Parley at Hot Springs Preparing for Permanent Set-Up

Special to THE NEW YORK TIMES.

WASHINGTON, Sept. 9—The United Nations' Interim Commission on Food and Agriculture has proposed a draft agreement regarding the obligations of governments to one another and to their respective peoples to raise levels of nutrition and standards of living, and is now consulting the various governments informally concerning it.

In making this announcement today, L. B. Pearson of Canada, chairman of the commission, said that after the governments' views were received the agreement would be put in final form for formal submission to the governments with a view of receiving their official approval.

The commission was formed on July 15, after the Food Conference at Hot Springs, Va., and has been sitting here since. Details of the draft agreement were not revealed but Mr. Pearson said the agreement followed the lines of Resolution Two of the Hot Springs Conference. While it was more detailed than that resolution, he indicated that it was, nevertheless, somewhat general in form.

Living Standard the Issue

Resolution Two binds the governments accepting the work of the Hot Springs Conference to collaborate by effective measures in raising the standards of living of their own peoples and of all peoples after the war.

At present a committee in the Interim Commission is working on a draft proposal covering functions and powers of a permanent organization to carry out the ideas of the Hot Springs Conference. Mr. Pearson expressed the hope that its report would be completed and placed in the hands of the various Governments by the end of this year for adoption. In this event the permanent organization would presumably be set up some time next year.

The Interim Commission, in carrying out its duties, has set up an executive committee and three main working committees. Of the main committees, the first has concentrated on the draft agreement now under consideration; the second is studying the structure of the projected Permanent Commission, and the third is considering what activities the Interim Commission should undertake pending the establishment of the Permanent Commission.

Panels of Experts Set Up

The first committee is under the chairmanship of Eurico Penteado of Brazil, the second of Sir Girja S. Bajpai of India and the third of H. P. L. Steenberghe of the Netherlands.

In addition, two panels of experts have been set up, one of economists and the other of scientists in the field of agriculture and nutrition.

The chairman of the economic panel is Dr. Howard Tolley of the United States, chief of the Bureau of Agricultural Economics. The chairman of the scientific panel is James A. Scott Watson of the United Kingdom, Professor of Rural Economy at Oxford.

The panels will report on the extent to which the permanent organization can assist in the promotion of scientific and economic research and the collection and dissemination of information.

September 10, 1943

30 COUNTRIES SIGN FOOD BODY CHARTER

Constitution Adopted to Start World Organization—First Plenary Session Held

By WALTER H. WAGGONER
Special to THE NEW YORK TIMES.

QUEBEC, Oct. 16—Representatives of thirty countries signed today the constitution of the Food and Agriculture Organization of the United Nations, pledging their Governments' cooperation in this new international body.

The heads of delegations from thirty of the forty-five eligible nations thus officially started a conference that has as its objective the ending of world-wide hunger through "separate and collective action" by their Governments.

Twenty signatures would have given the FAO and the conference official status.

The purposes of the FAO, toward which this conference is the first step, are listed in the preamble of the constitution as follows:

Raising levels of nutrition and standards of living of the peoples under their respective jurisdictions.

Securing improvements in the efficiency of the production and distribution of all food and agricultural products.

Bettering the condition of rural populations.

And thus contributing toward an exjanding world economy.

Members of the FAO, it is stated, will report to one another "on the measures taken and the progress achieved" toward these goals.

The nations that, by their action today, agreed to these objectives and promised to work toward them were:

Australia	Iraq
Belgium	Liberia
Canada	Luxembourg
China	Mexico
Czechoslovakia	Netherlands
Denmark	New Zealand
Dominican Republic	Nicaragua
	Norway
Egypt	Panama
France	Peru
Greece	Philippines
Guatemala	Union of South Africa
Haiti	
Honduras	United Kingdom
Iceland	United States
India	Venezuela

Although the Soviet Union did not sign the constitution, its chief delegate, Vasili A. Sergeyeff, Deputy Commissar for Foreign Trade, has arrived with the intention of joining the FAO. L. B. Pearson, Canadian Ambassador to the United States and chairman of the Interim Commission on Food and Agriculture, now out of existence, assured a news conference that Mr. Sergeyeff was merely awaiting the arrival of his credentials from Moscow. These papers, demanded by the secretary for the conference, state that the Soviet delegate is authorized to sign the constitution on behalf of the Soviet Union.

Other nations that have delegations here but which did not sign the constitution are Yugoslavia, Iran, Poland, Ecuador and Uruguay. Their reasons for not signing are believed to be similar to those that delayed the endorsement by the U.S.S.R., it was said.

Brazil Stands Aloof

Brazil has not joined the conference on the grounds, it is reported, that she has an extensive agriculture improvement program of her own under way. Other nations are said to have been delayed by travel difficulties.

An Argentine delegation is present, but only to observe.

In a brief welcoming address to the combined delegations in the ballroom of the Chateau Frontenac, the Hon. Ernest Bertrand, Postmaster General of Canada, observed that Quebec had twice been the meeting place of statesmen of the United Nations for deciding "questions of war."

"This time," he declared, "representatives of the United Nations are meeting not on questions of war tactics but on everlasting questions of peace and charity.

"Charity between nations is possible under the constitution of the Food and Agricultural Organization of the United Nations and undoubtedly will do more for lasting peace than armies, airplanes and even atomic bombs.

"If we have found this truth under the guidance and inspiration of the late President Roosevelt, after twenty centuries of Christianity, mankind cannot boast of having been too alert; but, however slow we have been, there is hope for the future, and freedom from want might well be achieved, thereby laying grounds for lasting peace."

Tanguay Prigeant, French Minister of Agriculture, said that he had been authorized to convey the unreserved support of the French Government, but he added that action was required on the social, political and economic fronts in addition to the effort at improving the world food situation.

Indian Emphasizes Task

Sir Girja Shankar Bajpai, Agent General for India in the United States and leader of the Indian delegation, asserted that "No task to which the United Nations have turned their hand is more important than the one taken up here."

Among the delegates there is an undertone of disagreement about the proper function of the FAO. It has been described by one official as an "international expert consultant." As such, it would be able to recommend action on any aspect of food and agricultural production.

Another body of opinion is expressing the view that the organization should be able to advise on economic matters such as commodity agreements and world price stabilization for agricultural products moving in international trade.

This issue may be resolved soon. At the insistence of several leading delegations, including Secretary of Agriculture Clinton P. Anderson, who heads the United States group, the schedule for meetings and other matter on the agenda have been speeded up. The first plenary session originally planned for tomorrow afternoon, was moved ahead to tonight.

October 17, 1945

Banishing Drudgery from the Farm

Automatic Sprays Have Replaced the Patient Pest Slayers of Other Days, and Hay Is Loaded by Machinery—Tilling, Planting, and Reaping with the Inventor's Aid

By C. E. CAPEN.

WHEN a Chinese comes to America his slant eyes soon take in the reason for his country's backwardness and the reason for our prosperity is plain to him. Machinery! That word spells "plenty" to us, but the Celestial hardly knows the meaning of the word. China is an agricultural nation, but the farmers there make the seed beds and harvest the crops in much the same way as their ancestors did 3,000 years ago. We, too, started in a humble way with our main reliance on a good strong back and plenty of elbow grease. But we soon quit that.

The farmer may sing the praises of the seedsman and extoll the virtues of the experiment station, but if he goes carefully over the long list of blessings that have come to him in the last fifty years he must give the inventor a place near the top. He has done as much as anybody to keep us from living in China. There is hardly a farm operation from the breaking of the ground to the storing or marketing of the crop that has not been revolutionized by new implements or vast improvements on the old ones. A bushel of wheat, which once required more than an hour of man's labor in its production, takes today only about ten minutes of his time. Where would the hungry Belgians be now had the old methods been in use in America during the last four years?

Before land can produce good crops it is often necesssary to carry away an excess of water and let in the air. The old way was to dig a ditch and call the job finished. Then some one with a better head threw stones loosely into the bottom of the trench and put the dirt back. Then came the wooden box to take away the water. Now we have tile made in all sizes and of all sorts of material and machines turn them out at a rapid rate at low cost. The tiler who used to make the ditches with a long-nosed spade is losing his job to the big ditching machine that walks over the soggy field with its web feet and leaves a ditch of just the right depth at either end. The amount of backache this machine has saved would be enough to fill Atlas with envy.

The general style of the plow has remained much the same for centuries. To be sure there has been a great improvement in the design of mold boards and in the materials used. But in recent years we have learned to group several plows and concentrate a lot of power, engine or horse, under the direction of one man. In the last year a new hitch has been devised which enables a farmer to drive four, six, eight, or ten horses in tandem pairs with little difficulty. Weights keep the line of draft at right angles to the shoulders and the pull being all in a straight line ahead, there is no waste of power in side draft. The secretary of the Percheron Society of America, the largest pure-bred horse recording association in the country, says he can take such an outfit and plow more land in a month than any tractor ever built to pull three bottoms. It would be interesting if a challenger were to come forth on his iron horse or steel mule.

And after the plowman comes the planter. The sower used to go out to the field with a bag slung over one shoulder and used the other arm to scatter the seed over the ground. He still does it with some seeds, grass seed, for instance, but more often he has a little whirligig arrangement attached to the sack for throwing the little pellets far and wide or he pushes a long slim box on a skinny wheelbarrow up and down the field. But like as not across the fence you will find some young fellow steering a tractor that is hauling a combination grain drill and seeder. The disks cut into the soil and deposit the seed of wheat, barley, rye or oats, and from a separate compartment comes a sprinkling of grass, clover or alfalfa seed that does not require deep covering of earth.

While the crops are growing there is usually an army of pests that must be destroyed or held at bay. They range from the ultra-microscopic bacteria to the visible army worm and others as shameles. In the old days one of the numerous jobs for small boys on the farm was killing bugs. Any middle-aged man (and some younger) who has spent his youth on the farm will remember how he trudged along those endless rows knocking the gaudy Colorado potato beetle into a tin pan or an old paint pail. That job is about lost to the country boy, and he probably is shedding no tears over it. The spraying machine, which covers severals rows at once, now deposits a poison mist on potatoes, cantaloupes, cucumbers, and any other crops likely to be benefited by that treatment.

Of all the more modern farm machines the grain harvester has probably had more influence on the welfare of bread-eating millions than any other. The gap between the old cradle and this complex implement is as wide as that between the simple sundial and a fine watch. Now the harvester is pulled by a gas or kerosene tractor which can be guided from the seat of the former just as a team of horses would be driven. An engine may become overheated more easily in the hot weather of harvest, but the driver never fears to keep it working because of sunstroke.

Horses and mules are still far from extinction on American farms—we have about 25,000,000 of them—but if they ever disappear before the advance of the motor-driven machine we will still have to make hay for the cattle and sheep. Haying is a big, bulky job, and requires a lot of perspiring effort, but the inventor has made the work easier at many points. The picturesque haying scene with the strong-backed pitchers throwing the big bunch of fragrant feed to the top of the high load has disappeared on the larger farms. The mechanical loaders, with various improvements to make it operate well in thin or light hay and in the wind, makes it possible for one man and a boy to do the job that formerly took three men, and the load is on the wagon in a jiffy.

These are only a few of the big things that the inventor has done for the farmer, but these alone have done enough to change farming from drudgery to a business that should appeal to anybody who doesn't mind getting up early in the morning and cranking the machinery.

August 10, 1919

SYNTHETIC FERTILIZER GAINING, HE ASSERTS

Dr. Landis Says That Chemicals Are Replacing Waste Products in the Industry.

Chemical products are replacing waste products in the manufacture of fertilizer, Dr. W. S. Landis, vice president of the American Cyanamid Company, said last night in a lecture on "The New Fertilizer" at Cooper Union. The meeting was under the auspices of the People's Institute and the American Institute. Dr. Landis outlined the history of fertilizers from prehistoric times to the present.

"The fertilizer industry," he said, "has come to depend more and more upon chemical products for its raw materials. The natural nitrate of soda and the by-product sulphate of ammonia, to which have been added of more recent years various synthetic nitrogen chemical products such as cyanamid, nitrate of lime, urea, and ammonium phosphates, now form the bulk of our nitrogenous ingredient. There is little chance to return to the waste organics, and with better education of our farmers the little still used will further decrease."

He declared that nitrogen as obtained by electrical fixation of the atmosphere did not provide a complete fertilizer but lacked certain ingredients, and went on to say that "the future fertilizers will be much more concentrated in the common plant foods than even past history would lead one to suppose. The elder organics of animal or vegetable origin will disappear to still greater extent and will be replaced by newer synthetic salts mostly of inorganic nature."

March 13, 1929

PEDIGREED CORN BRED BY SCIENCE

Mendel's Principles of Heredity Have Been Applied to Produce a Sturdier and More Uniform Type for the Farmer

CORN, one of the most valuable plants in the New World, has been set on the road to greater glory—more bushels to the acre, more protein and carbohydrates to the bushel, more vitamins locked away in each kernel. Our oldest crop has been transfigured by men in the laboratory. Breeding for pedigree, they have given it new strength and quality. Maize, like Hereford bulls, now has ancestry, released and utilized according to the principles of the Austrian monk, Johann Mendel, and of Thomas Hunt Morgan, formerly of Columbia University, now at the California Institute of Technology.

Sturdy, rich-yielding corn that was only a hope of farmers before 1900 today waves its tassels high in the air, the fulfillment of science. Row after row, it grows as uniform as a mural decoration and every stalk bears a good ear. Over New England, the wide Middle West and the South, on soil baked hot in late August, is maturing such grain as the American Indians, who nurtured maize up through the centuries, would have thought impossible.

One of the men most responsible is Dr. Donald F. Jones of the Connecticut Agricultural Experiment Station in New Haven, where some of the first experiments had been made in 1906. He writes of a trial of one of his own varieties of sweet corn that it "yielded six tons an acre, in comparison with three and one-half tons from Evergreen corn," a standard variety. His work with sweet corn is to be the principal exhibit of the annual field day on Aug. 28 at the Station Farm at Mount Carmel. For nine years Connecticut farmers have been raising Double-Crossed Burr-Leaming corn, a variety produced by Dr. Jones, and getting on the average one-sixth more grain than they obtain from the type of the next highest yield. On field day they will see how such corn was evolved, how other varieties are now in the process.

Science of Genetics Applied.

Wandering among many exhibits, the visitors will puzzle over some like this: Two rows of puny, spindling corn, unattractive and freakish. Corn possesses both male and female functions, and for generation upon generation those plants have been bred to themselves in strange, artificial matings brought about by the use of ordinary paper bags to guard the flowers. As plants, they show the degeneracy that may come with inbreeding. But within themselves they treasure enormous capabilities. In between those two rows visitors will behold tall, vigorous corn, glossy green and beautiful. It is the child of the two inbred strains, the result of crossing the dwarfish plants.

This performance was first observed twenty years ago, almost simultaneously, by Edward Murray East at the Connecticut Experiment Station and by George Harrison Shull at the Carnegie Institution Station for Experimental Evolution at Cold Spring Harbor, L. I. That was soon after Mendel's principles of heredity were dug up from obscurity and handed around the world to found the science of genetics. Dr East went to Harvard in 1910 and there largely gave up corn breeding. **After eight years Dr. Shull turned to the breeding of primroses and to lecturing as Professor of Botany at Princeton University.**

No farmer yet had profited from the enormous yields and superior quality of crossed corn when Dr. Jones in 1915 came to the experiment station in New Haven.

Planting corn that first Summer on the Connecticut Station's farm under Sleeping Giant Mountain, Dr. Jones determined that he would produce, if possible, some of the wonderful crossed corn of pure science for farmers to raise to fatten their cattle and hogs. Still in an academic stage, at no other place was it pursued to get seed for general use. Dr. Jones laid out plot after plot, planted and carefully tended them. Seed he selected from the best corn that William L. Slate, director, was growing in a survey of all kinds which were raised in Connecticut. Also he used such old reliable varieties as Illinois Leaming and Burr's White Dent. Summer after Summer they came up, self-fertilized at Dr. Jones's hands. No freshness and vigor appeared in them, only purity.

When July came on and silks threatened to show, Dr. Jones went down each row of his experimental maize and clapped a paper bag over each ear-shoot on selected plants. No pollen, save that ordained, was to get on those silks and father the unborn ears. Two or three days later he walked along and pinned a bag over the tassels that blossomed above the silks. Another day he took that fine yellow pollen collected in the bag and dusted it over the silks, which were finally crowned with a large bag to prevent the contamination of any foreign pollen.

Thus he breeds pure corn. He is separating corn from its germinal mixture and producing it true. He is ordering an original variety into its several strains. They may be weak, they may be small and they may be largely unproductive, but they are pure and by and by they come to be uniform. Generation after generation, "like will produce like." If crossed, they will every time show the same bouncing growth in each plant.

When Dr. Jones began cultivating his corn at New Haven, crossing was held to be the important thing about crossed corn. He saw that inbreeding was the great factor. Corn could be grown on pedigree. Its ancestors could be known and its descendants predicted. On that belief he selected corn by family, not by appearance, as the old method was, and he proceeded to the accomplishment of the Double-Crossed Burr-Leaming field corn and the Redgreen sweet corn, which is grown for canning. Another variety, Canada-Leaming, has been on trial the last two years, and next Spring it will be offered for sale. It yields 20 to 30 per cent higher than the best corn now grown in New England and New York, for which it is intended.

In about two years Dr. Jones expects to have a new sweet corn for market gardeners, to whom the remarkable uniformity of the single cross is particularly desirable. Most of his experiments are with sweet corn, because of its value to Connecticut.

August 25, 1929

HAILS MODERN FARMING AS REDUCER OF COSTS

Kansas Wheat Grower Points to Machine Operation as Time-Saver.

Special Correspondence, THE NEW YORK TIMES.

TOPEKA, Oct. 28.—Evidence of how modern machinery and mass production under scientific methods are reducing the cost of food raising has been compiled by John S. Bird of Hays, head of one of the large Kansas wheat farming corporations.

Under the old hand-cradling methods, Mr. Bird declares it used to take three and a half hours to produce a bushel of wheat; now, under the most modern methods, the same result is accomplished in about three minutes. Here is the way Mr. Bird puts it:

"A good man with a cradle in the cradle days could cut three acres a day.

"With the self-rake a man and three or four horses could cut fifteen acres.

"With the self-binder and four or five horses one man could cut from thirty to thirty-five acres.

"With a tractor and the combine two men can cut and thresh fifty acres in about ten hours—an operation that but yesterday required twenty-three men and the same number of hours."

Putting it another way, Mr. Bird, who believes mass production alone can restore prosperity to the wheat-producing sections, says:

"In the earliest days of American agriculture, with the only implements then at hand, a man could cultivate approximately ten acres of land in a whole year.

"With the machinery of yesterday the average farmer cultivated eighty to 120 acres.

"Today, with modern power machinery, one man cultivates a thousand acres or more, and every year sees additional capacity for work accomplishment added to this. Each worker thus equipped with power machinery cultivates an acre in approximately one and one-half hours. If he produces an average of twenty-five bushels of barley, corn and wheat the time required per bushel is between three and four minutes. It used to be more than three hours."

Attention also is called to the fact that the big farming corporations have installed automatic time-clocks on their machinery which measure the actual operating time, and thus make it impossible for modern farm hands to "go to sleep in the shade" when the bosses are not looking.

November 2, 1930

SCIENTISTS UPSET FARM-CURB PLAN

They Seek to Double Output as Government Struggles With Crop Surpluses

ROTATION IS WORKED OUT

Cattle Feeding Experiment Is Now Topic of Discussion at Kansas State College

By JOHN M. COLLINS

Special to THE NEW YORK TIMES.

MANHATTAN, Kan., May 14.—As government agencies struggle with the problem of farm surpluses, scientists in the field of agricultural research continue studies which seek to make the proverbial "two blades of grass grow where one grew before."

In recent years the various agricultural experiment stations on the high plains have developed and publicized the fact that letting fields lie idle one out of every two or three years, meanwhile fallowing them to conserve moisture, will increase the subsequent yield of wheat more than 50 per cent in years of normal rainfall. Under the acreage reduction program of the Agricultural Adjustment Administration this practice has spread widely in the last two years.

In recent years in Kansas, Oklahoma and Texas the drought-resistant sorghums have been the most dependable grain crop, but they have been difficult to harvest and thresh for grain. So the scientists deliberately bred a heavy-headed, dwarf, upright variety of milo which can be cut and harvested with wheat combined harvester threshers.

Then there is the introduction into Missouri and Eastern Kansas in recent years of lespedeza, "the poor man's clover," a legume crop which will grow and stand abuse on poor soils, where it is impossible to produce other legumes without expensive soil treatment. Lespedeza can be grazed, cut for hay or for seed. It flourishes in the middle Summer period when blue grass is dormant.

Works Out Rotation System

As lespedeza reseeds itself annually, the Missouri experiment station has worked out a short rotation of lespedeza with small grains, such as barley, wheat or oats, which makes possible two crops a year on the same field. The small grains are planted on the same land with the lespedeza. After the small grains have been grazed off in the late Spring, or cut for grain or hay, the lespedeza is up high enough to be pastured. In the Fall the lespedeza land is disked and drilled again to a small grain. Enough lespedeza seed will scatter during the operation to reseed itself.

At the Missouri station there are fields of this combination four years old which have not been plowed since the inception of the rotation, the expensive plowing job being eliminated. One such field last year produced forty-five bushels of barley an acre. After the grain was taken off, beef cattle pastured on the lespedeza gained 280 pounds an acre from July 8 to Sept. 25, while blue grass in the same period produced only ninety-eight pounds of beef an acre.

Lespedeza is growing on about 4,000,000 acres in Missouri, a larger area than that planted to corn in the State.

Along with these developments have gone the constant effort to improve varieties, and here the plant breeder's alc emy again has come into play. Atlas Sorgo is a new forage crop which is being widely accepted. It is a cross between the sweet, heavy yielding stalks of cane, and the sour, heavy grain yielding grain sorghums. It produces from twelve to twenty-five tons an acre of a sweet stalked forage containing a heavy grain yield, for use as dry fodder or for silage. It combines the palatability of the cane with the grain production of the kaffirs.

Interest in Hybrid Corn

Most interesting present topic of conversation is hybrid corn, a development in which Secretary Wallace himself was a pioneer. Hybrid corn is the result of several years of inbreeding of selected older varieties, the plant breeder seeking to concentrate such desirable characteristics as heavier yields, low hung ears, strong stalks and drought resistance. Yields of commercial corn from adapted hybrids are said to average 20 per cent more than the usual open pollinated varieties.

Indicating the growing interest in hybrid corn, it has peen estimated there is sufficient hybrid seed available this Spring to plant one-fourth the normal corn acreage of the entire country.

Which brings up the latest scientific achievement in this area, the discovery that the "sorghum belt" of Nebraska, Kansas, Oklahoma and Texas has in its drought resistant sorghums practically as good a cattle fattening ration as the Corn Belt has in the older feed grain, providing care is exercised in getting the cattle on feed and the feeding period is continued long enough.

This point was made at the twenty-seventh annual Cattle Feeders Day at Kansas State College here by A. D. Weber of the college staff. Several hundred livestock men from all parts of the State attended the event.

Professor Weber gave preliminary figures in a comparison now under way of No. 2 ground white kaffir, consisting mostly of hegari grain, with No. 2 ground shelled corn in fattening steer calves. In addition to the grain, which is being self-fed, each lot of calves is receiving atlas sorgo silage, full fed; one and one-half pounds of cottonseed meal a head daily, and one-tenth pound of powdered limestone.

The calves were started on feed with a pound of the grain daily and the grain ration was increased at the rate of a pound a day for seven days, the calves later being put on self-feeders. The calves went on feed on Nov. 22 and the test will end about June 15. Ground sorghum grain was used because tests at other stations definitely have shown grinding increases the value of threshed sorghum grain approximately 40 per cent and grain sorghum heads about 60 per cent.

While the corn-fed calves have eaten more grain, made larger gains and are somewhat fatter than the sorghum-fed lot at this time, Professor Weber termed the performance of the steers on the ground sorghum grain as satisfactory.

May 15, 1939

The Farm Revolution Picks Up Speed

The new group of machines promise bumper crops—and economic and social troubles, too.

By VERNON VINE

DOWN South in the cotton country, out West where they raise sugar beets, and in the dairy lands of the North, farmers are talking machinery.

The news about machinery is exciting. It is a dramatic new chapter in the story of agriculture's mechanical revolution that began when John Deere invented the moldboard plow and Cyrus McCormick perfected the reaper. A new group of machines, just coming into use, or being readied for market, will produce not only bigger farm crops, but a bumper crop of social and economic consequences as well.

Among the most impressive of these machines are the mechanical cotton picker, forage harvesters for the hay fields, sugar beet, peanut and potato harvesters and corn pickers.

Flame cultivators are important factors in the mechanization of both cotton and sugar beets. So are machines which thin both crops. Barn cleaners, manure loaders and silo unloaders offer farmers relief from some of their most odious and backbreaking chores.

There are even such exotic machines as tree shakers, which knock nuts off trees, and vacuum cleaners which pick the nuts off the ground (and which will harvest cranberries, or clean out chicken houses as well). There are adaptations of the Army's fog generators, which may make economically practical the use of new, more effective but higher-priced insecticides.

PROBABLY the most significant of these new machines, because of its social and economic implications, is the mechanical cotton picker. This factory-built field hand costs about $5,000, and cuts the cost of growing cotton by $25 a bale when the wage for hand-picking is $1.50 per 100 pounds (considerably less than current wages).

Although the cotton picker was first announced a decade ago, its acceptance was delayed by a number of factors. It was high priced. It gathered leaves as well as cotton, and green bolls as well as ripe ones. Important as these objections were, however, they were not the paramount drawback.

Cotton economy requires that the crop be mechanized in its entirety. So long as cotton growers remain dependent upon hand labor for such jobs as chopping (thinning) and weeding, they might as well keep their share-cropper system, and plow and plant with mule power, and pick by hand also.

But now machines have been devised to chop cotton. Flame weeders have outmoded the hoe. Chemical defoliants, sprayed from airplanes, cause the leaves to drop in the late summer, so the sun can get to the bottom-most bolls, causing them to ripen and open uniformly with the bolls at the top of the plant. Thus, the yield per acre that can be harvested mechanically is increased, and most of the problem of trashy cotton is solved.

Mechanization also has come apace to the hayfield. If your interest in farming is esthetic, rather than economic, you will resent what this means to the rural scene. The haycock is gone, and the hay rack is rapidly going. On some farms, equipped with driers capable of handling freshly cut hay, forage harvesters cut the hay, chop it, and blow it into trailing wagons. The chopped hay is hauled to dehydrators, unloaded mechanically, and the grass is converted into bone-dry feed, all leaves, vitamins and proteins intact.

ON other farms, the hay will be mowed as usual (although power-driven mowers do a better job than old friction-drive models). After a few hours curing, it will be picked up by balers pulled behind tractors, the balers automatically depositing the bales in a wagon behind. Or the hay may be picked up by a field chopper and blown into a wagon. At the barn, curing will be completed in a mow fitted with a huge electric fan, blowing air through a series of ducts.

Sugar beet growers in the West confidently expect that within five years machines will reduce their labor requirements by 50 per cent. The first problem their engineers went to work on was what to do with the beet seed. It grows in the form of a ball, containing several seed germs. The engineers learned how to split the seed so only one plant would grow where several grew before. They devised a planter which evenly spaces these segments, so that much of the thinning job has been eliminated.

Next came mechanical "blockers," which do for beets what mechanical choppers do for the cotton crop. Weeding now can be done with "sizz-weeders," to give agricultural flame throwers their accepted name. And now, to complete the mechanization of the crop, comes the mechanical harvester. Beets have to be plowed out of the ground. (It is backbreaking to pull up a beet that has not had the soil loosened around it.) It has to have its leafy top sliced off. It has to be pitched onto a wagon or truck. The new harvester does all of these operations at once.

SIMILAR machines have been devised for the potato harvest. They dig potatoes, pick them up, shake the loose dirt off, and deposit them in bags. Peanut harvesters, which reduce by seven-eighths the labor required to harvest an acre of peanuts, also have been developed. Peanut shellers, that can do in an hour what a man can do by hand in 300 hours, have been perfected.

Corn pickers are not so new as many other machines, but more of them are coming into use each season, and new models are bigger and more efficient. Some of the current pickers harvest as many as four rows at a time; some are self-propelled, and some have a built-in stalk-shredder which provides automatic control of the corn borer. One casualty of the corn picker is one of the nation's largest sporting events—the national corn husking championship, which used to draw crowds larger than the Army-Navy game.

The self-propelled principle applied to grain combines (no tractor is needed to pull them) has resulted in strange-looking machines which proved important factors in getting the bumper wheat crops into the bin in the last two labor-short harvests.

ON the dairy farm, barn gutters now can be cleaned mechanically by an arrangement of electric motor, chain, sprockets, and angle irons which deposit the contents of the gutter into a manure spreader without a hand ever being put to a shovel. Tractor-mounted manure forks take the load off the cattle-feeder's back when the time comes for him to clean out his feed lot.

Mechanical chicken pickers —a blur of rapidly revolving rubber "fingers"—strip the feathers from broilers, capons and turkeys in a matter of seconds. New tillage tools, especially designed for the smaller farm, in one operation plow, disk and harrow, while propelling themselves.

Electricity, in an estimated 200 farm uses, already serves 2,500,000 farms, and may come to as many more within the next five years. The final touch, however, has been supplied by a Wisconsin manufacturer, who has designed a glass-lined silo, complete with power unloading device.

There can be no mistaking the intention of farmers to mechanize as rapidly as they can. (Because of labor disputes, the outlook for machinery production is poorer this year than last.) They have the money. They also are thoroughly fed up with their labor problem—high wages, inexperience, unreliability, and in many cases no help of any kind at any price. They know that economics favors more machinery. A recent survey indicated machinery costs are up only 14 per cent from prewar; labor costs, 180 per cent.

The effect of this expansion of farm mechanization is bound to be far-reaching. The result, in the case of cotton, may be nearly as significant as the invention of the cotton gin. The price of the cotton picker puts it far beyond the reach of small growers. They are not going to buy pickers. Instead, they eventually will go out of the cotton business, and some out of farming.

THE cotton picker also spells the end of the sharecropper and his mule. And as the mule gives way to the tractor, millions of acres that have grown corn to feed him may now be seeded down to pasture and hay to feed still more cows.

As in the other mechanized areas of the nation, the coming of the tractor in the South means fewer farms and larger ones; fewer towns, and larger ones; fewer schools, and larger ones; fewer farm families, and smaller ones. The rural South faces the prospect and problem of catching up with the twentieth century fifty years after it began.

The effects of mechanization on the economics of cotton seem fairly predictable. Shortly before he resigned as Secretary of Agriculture, Claude Wickard proposed a five-year plan for subsidizing the mechanization of cotton production on land best suited to it, and the subsidizing of other types of farming on land now in cotton but not well adapted to mechanical production methods. At the end of the five-year period, Mr. Wickard predicted, the combination of mechanization and the concentration of the crop on the best-suited land not only would enable cotton growers to get along without subsidies but also would make it possible for them to compete on the world markets with foreign cotton, and on the domestic market with synthetic fibers.

Mr. Wickard's plan apparently was buried when he became Rural Electrification Administrator. His successor, Clinton P. Anderson, gloomily recognizes the arrival of mechanization by predicting that it will probably depress prices, although he believes it will benefit agriculture in the long run.

UNLESS the Wickard plan, or a similar one, is adopted, the adjustment period is bound to be painful. Small farmers, manfully but vainly trying to pit their mules and hands against tractors and machines, will cry out for subsidies and more subsidies, each one benefiting the mechanized producer more than the mule-power operator, and thus only further widening the gap between them.

The impact of machinery on the sugar-beet crop will be less severe because it will involve fewer persons, and because the West's agriculture is more diversified than is that of the Cotton Belt. One result will be less use of transient labor in the sugar-beet producing States. This may disrupt a large share of the West's migratory labor economy, which functions as smoothly as it does because it is based on a succession of crops which provide the workers with a "circuit" of seasonal jobs through the coastal and mountain States.

The political ramifications of beet mechanization are interesting to contemplate. The domestic sugar industry has long urged a policy of continental self-sufficiency for sugar, but they have had to combat an opposition which made the most of the industry's high labor requirements and consequent high-cost operation. If the new machines give the beet-sugar lobbyists effective answers to these criticisms, they may also give our statesmen new headaches as they wrestle with the future of our commercial relations with Cuba and the Philippines.

WHAT the results of new machinery in other branches of farming will be is not quite so apparent, because only some, and not all, phases of production are affected. This much, however, is clear: These new machines mean less drudgery for farmers and their families; better incomes; more leisure, and more widespread enjoyment of modern amenities.

For the nation as a whole it brings closer the day when we must face up to some fundamental problems. As farmers increase their productive capacity through mechanization it becomes more necessary than ever that we develop a system of distribution so the output of our farms and ranches can be consumed at prices fair both to producers and purchasers. Unless the solution to this problem can be found within the framework of a free economy, we face the choice between more Government control and agricultural regimentation than we ever have had, or chaotic surpluses.

No less significant is the effect of farm mechanization on our population pattern. For years metropolitan areas have not produced enough children to maintain their populations. Our cities have grown because our farms and small towns have exported to them their "surplus" young people. Dwindling numbers of farmers, plus the depressing effect of mechanization on the farm birth rate, mean that rural America will fall increasingly short of meeting our metropolitan deficits.

This flame cultivator kills weeds, does not damage crops.

MEANWHILE, farmers are not worrying about such abstruse problems. For the rest of the world the air age, or the electronic age, or the atomic age, may just be dawning. But on the farm front this is the beginning of the era of the mechanical cotton picker and the automatic barn cleaner. It is the electrical epoch, the self-propelled century. It may conceivably be the time in which the farmer's day can be cut to twelve hours.

The dawn of this new day already is coming up like thunder—the thunder of the exhausts of myriad new and potentially terrifying machines. It will be a bright, streamlined day. There will be few of the nostalgic reminders of the kind of farming dear to the sentimentalists of the old school.

But the modernists, who find beauty in stark functionalism, have before them a rich experience reporting and depicting an agriculture in which the horse is iron and the old familiar odors have been supplanted by the sweet fumes of a Diesel engine.

June 30, 1946

Our 'Lazy Acres' Can Yield Far More Food

Unconventional techniques, proved on American farms, points the way to much bigger harvests.

By JAY RICHTER

WASHINGTON.

THERE is new hope among men who know the land that within the lifetime of most of us we can dispel the ubiquitous ghost of Thomas Robert Malthus, the gloomy English clergyman-economist who envisaged a world in constant misery and want because it could not produce enough food to match the rate of population growth.

Although this dim Malthusian outlook still might be valid if we fail to solve formidable problems of distribution, the production of enough food for all peoples is now possible through widespread application of modern technology. This country's recent production record provides a measure of what can be accomplished elsewhere, since our vast land area includes a wide range of soils exposed to a variety of weather and other growing conditions.

In the seventy years prior to 1940, our acre-yield of major crops increased little, if any. Since 1940, crop production per acre has increased by approximately 30 per cent. Reduction in the rate of soil loss, and reinvigoration of deteriorated soils, are two of three major reasons why the production stalemate has been broken. The third is the fact that more producers have adopted improved technology, a trend hastened by wartime and post-war production imperatives and good farm prices.

These gains may look small ten years from now. Food production in the next decade can be increased by 50 per cent, or five times our expected population growth of about 10 per cent, in the view of many conservative agricultural scientists. Their rosy outlook is prompted in large measure by a revolutionary new approach to crop production research which is resulting in truly amazing increases in yields. The scientists sum it up in the phrase "the proper integration of all production factors." That means, as one of them explained, "working cooperatively with individual farmers under ordinary farm conditions" and trying several new techniques at varying rates and in different combinations.

JAY RICHTER is the Associate Director of Agricultural Services, a Washington farm news bureau. He has written extensively on farm subjects.

Chemicals at work—A Virginia farmer displays corn from untreated land (left) and corn treated with nitrate of soda.

CONRAD H. PARKER, a chunky, middle-aged man who cultivates about 70 acres in Johnston County near Princeton, N. C., is a typical example of the new approach. Four years ago this harvest, he brought in a corn crop which was the biggest surprise of his hard-working life. One of his twenty-five acres planted to corn had outyielded the others by at least three to one.

He could see the difference with the sure vision of a man who had planted, fertilized, and cultivated a dozen corn crops, then prayed them to an indifferent maturity out of a reluctant soil which yielded twenty to twenty-five bushels per acre when Providence was generous. Seventy-five bushels, harvested from an acre surrounded by land producing less than twenty-five bushels, added up to quite an occasion.

What nitrogen will do—Figures show pounds of nitrogen used per acre in a series of tests; ears of corn show relative amounts yielded.

Parker's surprise was freighted with considerable chagrin because of the indifferent reception he had given young Bert Krantz before planting time the previous spring. The tall, lanky soil research scientist from Raleigh had persuaded Parker, against his judgment, to apply to his seventy-five bushel acre production practices which did violence to techniques evolved over 150 years by the best farmers in the area.

"I thought Dr. Krantz was nuts," Parker admits today, "but I stuck my toe in the pond. In 1946 I went in swimming and tried his way on all my corn land. I've stayed in the pond ever since. In 1946 and 1947 we got ninety to one hundred bushels to the acre over the whole farm. Last year we didn't get much more than fifty bushels. It was the driest year in our community that I can remember, but since I've learned how to grow corn I feel ashamed to admit a fifty-bushel yield."

PARKER was not the only North Carolinian to do a double-take in his corn fields during the harvest of 1945, and then plow under the hallowed traditions of his fathers, come planting time 1946. Some 350 other farmers in the state, sold what most of them thought to be a "bill of goods" by Federal-state agricultural experts, discovered they were in possession of a gold mine whose resources are renewable. Ten thousand of the state's farmers, since converted, are now producing corn at more than triple the pre-1945 rate.

The news was too good to keep. By 1948 more than 50,000 farmers throughout the seven-state area of Alabama, Georgia, Mississippi, North Carolina, South Carolina, Tennessee, and Virginia had worked into the act. Their yield has been quadruple that of average yields throughout the area for the ten years, 1935-44. Last year, they outyielded neighbors using the old techniques at the rate of two and one-half bushels to one. Their per-acre harvest of sixty-five bushels even topped the average in corn-conscious Iowa by four bushels.

"The last quarter of 1949 will see more meat on the market (at lower prices) than the same months of 1948," observes the United States Department of Agriculture. "Hog growers were sure of an abundance of corn, and an increase of about 15 per cent in the spring pig crop is the principal item in the prospect for more meat. There will also be more good-quality, corn-fed beef this season. Increases in chickens and turkeys will also build up the meat supply."

WHEN he visited Parker, Krantz was bringing with him considerably more than his own specialized knowledge of soil types, fertilizer, and plant spacing. He was also offering the plant breeder's knowledge of new varieties; the agricultural engineer's knowledge of new equipment and fertilizer placement; and the agronomist's knowledge of weed control and other cultural practices.

Adoption of the integrated production technique for specific crops rules out the traditional approach to agricultural research known as the "single factor" concept. This theory holds that only one new production practice should be tried at a time, preferably in a hothouse atmosphere where other factors can be held rigidly constant. That notion now belongs with the man-powered plow, and inevitably will be abandoned even by the agricultural experts still in the thrall of their own specialties.

A DIRECT comparison brought the lesson home to researchers at the State Experiment station in Raleigh. Single-factor experiments were carried out in plots adjoining one where the combined approach was used. In the first plot, a hybrid corn variety boosted yields fourteen bushels an acre above the twenty-seven-bushel average; in the second, extra heavy doses of nitrogen brought a similar increase; in the third, where the number of plants per acre was increased, yields fell almost twelve bushels below the average.

Totaling the two increases and subtracting the decrease gave the scientists a theoretical gain of about sixteen bushels. That is the result they expected in the fourth plot, where all three practices were tried in combination. Actually, the increase was fifty bushels above the twenty-seven bushel average. In a similar trial, yields bounded from a twenty-bushel average to an incredible 120 bushels. In Mississippi improved corn production techniques, when tried separately, added up to a theoretical gain of forty bushels per acre. When the practices were combined the increase was sixty-one bushels. Two conclusions were abundantly clear:

(1) A single crop practice may increase yields, but production can be pyramided when several practices are used together in the right combination; and,

(2) A single practice, although it reduces yields in a solo run, may actually bring substantial increases when combined with others.

FURTHER trials in North Carolina have produced results with oats, wheat, and soybeans similar to those achieved with corn. The techniques and combinations vary; the principle remains the same. Larger crops foreshadow an expanded livestock production, currently the major objective of agricultural policy makers.

Parker now has more than one hundred hogs in an area where a crop of porkers is a phenomenon, and frequently a thin one at that. He is selling swine breeding stock to his neighbors, and also milking a half-dozen cows. His explanation is simple and the connotations vast: "I have to do something with all this feed."

Improvement and increase of forage production in the Southern tests indicate that production of dairy products could be doubled throughout what is as yet a region tragically deficient in milk to meet the needs of its population. By use of the new approach in management of pastures, beef production has been increased as much as 150 per cent. Such results have been achieved against the advice of leading farm economists who, only a few years back, were telling the South to forget about expanding its livestock numbers. Feed crops, the economists said, could not be produced economically.

THE new production records are not being made on "brag acres", planted and harvested at high cost for purposes of show. North Carolina's corn production champion last year, F. L. Albritton, manager of the Parott farm near La Grange, harvested more than 148 bushels to the acre. His net profit per acre was $91.68 using the new method. Average gross return in the state, where two-thirds of the farmers still employ traditional practices, was $40.31 per acre.

Most important and dramatic results of the new production approach are being achieved in the South with corn. There is a certain poetic justice in such a state of affairs, since corn is our most important crop and the South is a symbol of the economic folly of a one-crop agriculture dependent upon either cotton or tobacco.

A LEADING advocate of the combined approach to crop production, and perhaps its most vocal spokesman—Dr. Robert M. Salter, Chief of the Agriculture Department's Bureau of Plant Industry, Soils and Agricultural Engineering—recently passed the word along to a corn belt audience in Chicago:

"Unless Midwestern farmers adopt more effective measures for protecting their God-given heritage of productive soil, it is not inconceivable that future generations will look south when they speak of the great American corn belt."

Salter was perhaps exaggerating for emphasis. Actually, the new approach is catching on outside the South. In nine tests with soybeans in various states, yields were increased threefold. Last year's corn champion in Iowa, Carroll Brown of Rose Hill, produced an astronomical 224 bushels to the acre. In Washington State, researchers found that heavier irrigation alone reduced potato yields by twenty-four bushels per acre, but that more water, in combination with nitrogen, brought yields up to 522 bushels per acre compared with a normal 392. In Utah, thirteen tons were added to normal sixteen-ton yields of sugar beets.

In a corn experiment on irrigated land in Oregon, extra water brought a four-bushel gain; a normal water supply, with nitrogen side dressing, added forty-one bushels. When the two practices were combined, however, the normal yield of fifty-two bushels was increased by eighty bushels per acre.

IN most other nations, a widespread application of the modern technology on land already being cultivated could increase world food production by 25 per cent within five years at a conservative estimate. Total world food supplies are still tragically short of needs, but we are making some progress toward closing the gap. American hybrid corn varieties, planted in Italy's Po Valley, are increasing yields by approximately 40 per cent. Eventually, this project may become an important factor in expanding livestock production throughout the whole of Europe.

There is an unprecedented rate of exchange among the nations of technical agricultural experts. American officials report that foreign nations are drawing heavily upon the unique ability of United States farm experts to put their knowledge to work on the land. Materials for insect and disease control, seeds, and planting stocks of proved superiority are important items in world commerce.

Increasing food production in underdeveloped areas is a formidable task depending upon solution of complex social, economic, and political problems, but we can start at once to do some things: expand fertilizer manufacture; start a few more irrigation projects in the most promising areas; and prepare the way for hydroelectric projects, especially in the tropics where potentialities for power are promising.

NORTH of the temperate region in northern Eurasia and northern North America, there are at least 300 million acres which could be developed for successful dairying and vegetable production. Of far greater importance are great areas in East Africa, South America, Central America, South eastern Asia, and the Pacific islands. Altogether, it would be possible to increase by approximately 40 per cent the 3-billion-acre land area now under cultivation throughout the world, according to estimates of the U. N.'s Food and Agriculture Organization.

Application of modern technology on new lands, plus production increases in sight on land now under cultivation, would provide more than enough food for the estimated world population in 1960. It comes to this: man himself now may choose whether he is to have an adequate diet.

October 9, 1949

Blueprint for Hungry Nations

A Mexican-American agricultural project demonstrates the means of multiplying the food output of low-yield granaries.

By GEORGE W. GRAY

AN event not reported in any newspaper, but a picturesque reflection of a movement that seems likely to have far-reaching consequences, occurred not long ago in the Mexican village of Juchitepec. The villagers gathered to welcome (with an arch of flowers) and to honor (with a feast of native dishes) a group of young American agricultural scientists. Working as one with Mexican *tecnicos*, they had, in five years of research, developed improved varieties of corn and wheat especially adapted to Mexican conditions.

Juchitepec has celebrated many fiestas in its history, but never one like this—a fiesta honoring *Norteamericanos*. But then, never before had the village granaries been so filled with precious maize. Never before had its children been so well fed. This year there was corn enough, not only for the tortillas, but for feeding the chickens and a few pigs. This year there would be meat as well as bread.

Juchitepec is only a tiny part of Mexico, and Mexico is only a small segment of the globe, but the agricultural research project which this gay fiesta celebrated may well prove to be historic. Years hence, economists may look back on it as the beginning of a new kind of attack on the problem of supplying the world with food.

The project had its origin in a conference between the Mexican Secretary of Agriculture and officers of The Rockefeller Foundation. It had been suggested that scientific research be undertaken on a cooperative basis to see if it could increase the productivity of Mexico's food crops. The foundation agreed to provide a staff of agricultural scientists and to help build, equip and operate the necessary laboratories. The Mexican Government, on its part, agreed to set aside land and facilities for the experiments and to assign young Mexican men and women to serve as research assistants and associates, thus creating a group of native scientists who, it is expected, will eventually take over direction of the work.

THE joint effort has been in operation since 1943 and truly remarkable results have been achieved. The most dramatic is the development of improved strains of corn, wheat, and beans, some of which are producing from 20 to 100 per cent larger yields than the old native varieties. Today, in numerous experimental plots scattered over Mexico, two ears of corn are ripening where only one ear grew before.

When the idea was broached in 1941, it was evident that a survey of Mexico's agricultural resources would be necessary. The Rockefeller Foundation had long been engaged in public health work there, but it had had no experience in agricultural research. Accordingly it called upon three distinguished experts—Drs. Richard Bradfield of Cornell University, Paul C. Mangelsdorf of Harvard, and E. C. Stakman of

GEORGE W. GRAY is on the Rockefeller Foundation staff and often writes about science. His books include "The Advancing Front of Science."

the University of Minnesota—to serve as a survey commission. The three Americans spent two months in Mexico, traveling some 5,000 miles by automobile, airplane, and in the saddle. They visited sixteen of the thirty-three Mexican states; observed the characteristic soils, climates, crops, and other conditions; pored over the statistics of crop yields; inspected the current methods of farm cultivation—and came back to write a memorable report.

The report pointed out that despite the fame of its oil wells and the fabulous stories of its gold and silver mines, Mexico was predominantly agricultural. More than three-fourths of the population had its hands in the soil. And yet, much of Mexican agriculture was operating at a miserably low level. More than half the farm land was planted to corn, but Mexico still had to import corn to meet its own necessities. The average farmer's yield was less than ten bushels per acre, compared with an average of twenty-five at that time for the United States. International statistics showed that in wheat production per acre Mexico ranked fifty-ninth among the countries of the world. In beans and other food crops production was similarly meager. "While Mexico is not blessed with a great surplus of productive land," concluded the commission, "there seems to be every reason to believe that her land resources are adequate, if well-managed, to supply all the needs of her people at a standard of living much higher than at present and at the same time provide a surplus of several tropical crops for export."

The New—Wheat farms like this are becoming more numerous as a result of using new hybrids and techniques.

Iowa-sized corn—but grown in Mexico.

WHAT to do, then, to help Mexico pull herself out of the agricultural doldrums? Drs. Bradfield, Mangelsdorf and Stakman agreed that it called for something different from the foundation's normal procedure of making grants to support research in existing institutions. They felt that the situation required a group of experienced agricultural specialists in full-time Mexican residence "to cooperate with and advise the Mexican Department of Agriculture in its various activities, including experimentation and research, regulatory work, resident teaching at its various levels and adult education."

The Mexican Department of Agriculture welcomed this venture with keen enthusiasm and Director Warren Weaver of the Natural Sciences division of the foundation began to look for a scientist to head it up. He found his man in J. George Harrar, plant pathologist at Washington State College and head of the Department of Plant Pathology at the near-by Washington Agricultural Experiment Station. Dr. Harrar had formerly taught at the University of Puerto Rico, and spoke and wrote Spanish fluently. He was designated director of the *Oficina de Estudios Especiales* which the Mexican Department of Agriculture set up to embody the new project, and was assigned office space in its ancient, fortress-like building in Mexico City. For several months in 1943 Dr. Harrar, as sole scientific member of the *Oficina*, perspired his way over thousands of miles of rugged terrain, from the lush tropics of Vera Cruz to the arid plateaus and mountainous peaks of the north. Frequently he was accompanied by Mexican colleagues from other bureaus of the department. On these travels he began to collect seeds for later appraisal.

ABOUT twenty-five miles east of Mexico City, at the old hacienda of Chapingo, is the Mexican National College of Agriculture. The faculty extended a warm welcome to the new research bureau and sixty acres of college lands were placed at Dr. Harrar's disposal. The plantings made there were the beginnings of studies which brought hybridization to its present high stage of achievement. But between those early experiments and the attainment of the improved disease-resistant, high-yielding crops which thousands of Mexican farmers are growing today, lies a whole epoch of pioneering research in which many devoted workers shared.

Corn was tackled first. This Indian maize has been cultivated here for thousands of years. It is the Mexican staff of life. From it is made the tortilla, the ancient pancake of the Aztecs, the universal dish of Indian and *mestizo*. It is both food and utensil, for rolled into a scoop as "Montezuma's spoon" it serves to convey soup chile and other foods to the mouth. Tortillas are eaten at breakfast, lunch, dinner and supper, and someone has estimated that the well-fed Mexican laborer consumes an average of forty a day.

More than 1,500 varieties of corn were collected by Dr. Harrar and his associates from Mexican fields. They were found in a wide range of climates. Some grew in isolated, protected valleys, others clung to dry hillsides; a few were found in the rarefied air of mountain steeps. The more numerous were stocks gathered from the great central plateau known as the Valley of Mexico and from the luxurious tropics. Brought to the *Oficina's* headquarters, the ears were shelled, the seeds packaged and labeled according to the places of origin. Then specimens of each variety were planted in experimental plots in different regions to see how they would fare. Farmers all over Mexico voluntarily gave the use of a few acres for these plantings. Today there are 300 sites at which such tests are under way.

The tests showed that only sixteen of the 1,500 varieties were definitely superior. They differed in time required to mature, in size and shape of grain, in adaptation to different altitudes and latitudes. Some gave a good yield in one region and were poor in another, but each had qualities which recommended it. The sixteen varieties were then sown for seed increase, and, following extensive yield tests, six were offered to Mexican farmers for planting. One of these chosen varieties, tested for three years in the Valley of Mexico, yielded 25 per cent more crop than the best hitherto grown in that area.

But the plant breeders are not satisfied with merely seeking out the best native species. They know that by controlled crossing of two or more varieties it is possible to produce hybrids which are better yielders than any strains found in nature. And so, while the more promising of the natural varieties are being released, to give farmers the benefit of their increased yields, the bureau's geneticists have been crossing natural stocks.

IN the fields of Chapingo—where 250 acres of the college grounds are now occupied by these plantings—one sees row after row of hybridization experiments. As soon as the ear begins to form on a stalk it is covered with a paper bag. Similar bags are tied over the tassels to catch and hold their pollen. After a few days have passed the tassel bags are removed and the pollen they contain is applied to the ear shoots of the plants selected for cross-fertilization. By these means, crosses have been made between the sixteen superior native varieties and their progeny, and between these and other varieties, some imported from other lands. In this way several excellent hybrids have been developed, some with yields 50 to 100 per cent better than the best of the native varieties.

But hybrid corn, the kind which has revolutionized the agriculture of our own Corn Belt, requires slow and costly procedures. In order to obtain seed quickly in the quantities required and at reasonable cost, the *Oficina* resorted to the corn-breeders' short-cut known as "synthetic varieties." In this technique a number of the better strains of two varieties are planted in the open field in alternate rows. Then all the rows of one variety are detasseled and left to be pollinated by the other variety through the action of the wind. Some of the resulting ears may be better than others.

BUT in the course of two or three years of successive breeding these variations will level off and the corn will reach equilibrium. The synthetic does not give as high a yield as a double-cross hybrid —it may give only a 20 per cent increase—but improving one of the sixteen already superior native varieties by a factor of 20 per cent is something worth doing.

Through five years of corn-breeding experiments eight acceptable synthetic varieties have been obtained. Last year, enough seed was produced to plant about 500,000 acres. From the seed saved from last year's crop, some 750,000 to 1,000,000 acres were planted in 1949, or nearly one-tenth of Mexico's entire corn acreage. At this rate of acceleration, with the distribution of seed wisely controlled by the Government, and with the continuing cooperation of the farmers, it should not be long before the improved varieties completely supplant the inferior native stocks.

DISTRIBUTION of seed is administered by a Federal agency, the National Corn Commission, which was appointed by President Alemán in 1947. This Corn Commission of three members has custody of all seed produced under the corn program. Seed of the improved varieties is given to farmers in exchange for their old seed. There is a follow-up system to instruct them in improved methods of cultivation, pest-riddance, irrigation techniques, and other measures of scientific agriculture. Last year the commission staged a contest to see which farmer could show the greatest increase in yield per acre. The prize, a Ford tractor awarded by President Alemán, was won by Pedro Barto of the village of Texcoco. On his small farm, Señor Barto planted the Rockefeller-Mexican variety known as Rocamex V-7, and harvested 125 bushels per acre. His best previous crop had yielded forty-five bushels an acre.

WHEAT was the second crop tackled by the researchers. The problem was to find or develop varieties which would resist the rust and other fungus diseases. Rust flourishes in a moist atmosphere. The two principal wheat-growing areas are Sonora, the northwestern state which borders on Arizona and fronts on the Gulf of California, and the great inland plateau known as the *Bajío* which embraces several states north of Mexico City. Sonora is the richer, but it has a long coastline, and when winter fogs blow in to blanket the fields with weeks of humidity, growing wheat becomes an easy prey to rust. This happens about one year in four.

Today, thanks to the scientific labors of the *Oficina*, Mexico has eight varieties of wheat which are highly resistant to rust. In 1948, for the first time, Mexican farmers saw high-yielding, high-quality wheat growing normally during the rainy season. Last winter, there was a heavy rust epidemic in Southern Sonora, with losses so complete that farmers burned their crops to rid the fields of the useless, infected stalks. But those who had ventured to try the new Rocamex rust-resistant varieties were mostly immune to such disaster. One enterprising farmer in Sonora obtained from forty-five to fifty bushels per acre from the new seed, whereas in favorable years his yield from the native variety averaged only twenty-five to thirty.

A WHEAT COMMITTEE appointed by Secretary Nazario S. Ortiz Garza of the Department of Agriculture is in charge of a program for the increase and distribution of seed of the new wheat varieties. From the 1,000 acres which were sown in the summer of 1948, enough seed was obtained to plant 15,000 acres last winter.

What has been done in wheat and corn is an index to what is being attempted in other crops. And the plant breeders or geneticists are only part of the team. In addition, there are plant pathologists, entomologists, soil chemists, microbiologists, and ecologists, each of whom is contributing his bit toward increasing the yield of Mexico's food crops. In the final analysis, yield depends on how well the plant is able to withstand untoward conditions. The program of the *Oficina* is, therefore, concerned with fortifying the plant's natural resistance to diseases, to insect depredations and to drought; and its studies are also directed at increasing the fertility of the soil, saving areas from erosion and improving the methods of cultivation.

HEADQUARTERS of the *Oficina* remain in the Department of Agriculture building in Mexico City, but its principal laboratory facilities are on the grounds of the National College of Agriculture at Chapingo. Here a convenient and commodious building has been erected with Rockefeller and Government funds. It is set in the midst of the fields where the new varieties are in process of development and it is only a step from the test tube and the microscope slide within to the waving rows of hybrid grains without.

The staff consists of eleven American scientists, fifty-six Mexican associates, and five Mexican technicians, in addition to administrative workers. Usually, there are a few visiting scientists and students. At present, the visitors number two from the United States and twelve from Central and South America.

The program aims to do more than improve the stock of plants on which Mexico depends for its food crops. A more fundamental objective is to improve the stock of agricultural scientists, so that the work begun in this cooperative project may be carried on as a permanent Mexican program. The Rockefeller Foundation is providing fellowships to enable promising Mexican students to pursue advanced courses in the United States.

Four such students are now studying on fellowships in this country—at Mississippi State College of Agriculture, Ohio State University, the University of Minnesota, and the University of California. Eighteen earlier appointees have completed their fellowships and returned to posts in Mexico, three of them to become faculty members of the National College of Agriculture.

An important practical question is the cost of such a project. To date, the Rockefeller Foundation has put $1,301,825 into it, including $321,555 for the current year. The figures for the Mexican Government are not known to the writer, but in 1949, in addition to providing many hundreds of acres of land for the experiments and paying the salaries of Mexican scientists and others whom it assigned to duty there, the Mexican Department of Agriculture invested 430,000 pesos in the *Oficina*. In relation to the results accomplished, the money expenditures, both Mexican and American, have been trifling. Compared to the cost of direct subsidy, the expense has been infinitesimal.

PERHAPS the deepest significance of the Mexican agricultural program lies not in what it has accomplished in Mexico, but in what it may augur for other agriculturally undeveloped areas of the world. The United States has succeeded, perhaps more than any other nation, in applying science to the improvement of its agriculture. Instead of giving away to hungry countries the surpluses resulting from our own efficient agriculture, as Henry Morgenthau proposed in a recent article in THE NEW YORK TIMES Magazine—a procedure which is only palliative at best, and which in fact means giving away part of our soil fertility—would it not be more sensible to export our agricultural "know-how," and thereby help our neighbors to help themselves? The Rockefeller-Mexico agricultural program has demonstrated that a mere handful of well-trained scientists, freed of the strangling restrictions of governmental red tape, can, in an amazingly short time, catalyze the agricultural economy of a nation.

January 1, 1950

LAND FERTILIZERS WIDELY EXPLORED

Rise in Synthetic Output Cited in F. A. O. World Output—Gains Are Significant

By KATHLEEN McLAUGHLIN

Special to THE NEW YORK TIMES.

UNITED NATIONS, N. Y., Feb. 21—Lands that lay unnourished for centuries are now yielding harvests because of enrichment of their soil strata, according to a world report by the Food and Agriculture Organization. This development is credited to a growing understanding of the role that commercial fertilizers can play in food production.

The annual F. A. O. review covers a three-year period and shows significant developments in many countries. Designed primarily for technicians in the field, it includes many sections of interest as well to the average farmer or gardener.

From this factual presentation, for instance, the layman is able to see the increasing construction of synthetic fertilizer plants and the acceleration of the hunt for additional raw materials. Experts confirm that Asian and other farmers are eagerly exploring the potentialities of proper soil-feeding to stimulate larger and finer crops.

The survey, made partly from official Government sources and partly from unofficial estimates for 1954, includes several major points.

Proposals are under consideration to erect nitrogen plants in certain Near Eastern oilfields, using natural gas or refinery waste gases as sources of energy and sulphur. Ample supplies of such valuable materials can be obtained at virtually no cost, the survey notes, and it should be possible to supply nitrogen fertilizers at lower prices than at present to the expanding markets of the East.

New sources of high-grade phosphate rock have been discovered, augmenting deposits in the Negev in Israel. Two large deposits are reported unofficially in Jordan. One near Amman, the capital, has assured reserves of 16,000,000 tons, which may run to a maximum of 100,000 tons. The other is near Hasa.

In Brazil, the Araxo apatite deposits, estimated at 100,000,000 to 300,000,000 tons, are said to be of good quality although below those of the United States deposits.

Europe's exportable surplus of nitrogen fertilizers is said to have increased to more than double that of South America's (mainly Chile). Previously these sources each had contributed about 200,000 metric tons annually to fill the needs of other continents.

The reclamation of vast tracts of formerly inaccessible areas in Australia and New Zealand through utilization of aircraft to spread superphosphate is noted in the report. This type of "aerial farming" employs half the civilian aircraft in New Zealand and is responsible for tremendous acreage gains for grazing.

"It is even suggested that aircraft could load up fertilizers at the works and fly direct to the land to be treated, eliminating bagging and the transport by rail or road with much expensive handling," the survey observes.

In many parts of the world, particularly in Asia, the use of commercial fertilizers has been concentrated mainly on nitrogen types, although phosphatic and other varieties are also required for balanced crops.

With the growing trend toward construction of domestic production plants, increased supplies of sulphur are expected to improve the phosphatic fertilizer situation, which is characterized in the study as "still perhaps the most crucial factor" for general expansion in this field.

Countries that have programs to build fertilizer plants include Canada, Finland, Iceland, the Netherlands, Turkey, Israel, Italy, Yugoslavia, India and Mexico.

February 28, 1954

SHARP RISE SHOWN IN FARM RESEARCH

Special to The New York Times.

WASHINGTON, Nov. 11—The National Science Foundation, a Federal agency, said today that expenditures for research by its agriculture experiment stations had increased more than tenfold since 1920. In the 1953-54 fiscal year such outlays were $74,000,000, it reported.

The figure was based on a survey of its research stations in the United States, Alaska, Puerto Rico and Hawaii. Nearly all the stations are administered by land grant colleges and universities.

The largest expenditures, the survey showed, were for applied research in the fields of animal production, field crop products, horticulture crop production and soil and plant nutrition.

State governments are the primary source of support for the stations. The states provided $44,900,000 in the 1953-54 fiscal year and the Federal Government $13,500,000.

* * * * *

November 12, 1957

NITROGEN BRINGS VAST CROP GAINS

Increased Use of Fertilizers Produces Record Yields—Corn a Prime Example

By WILLIAM M. BLAIR

Special to The New York Times.

ST. PAUL, Minn., March 7—An underground explosion is rumbling across the Farm Belt. It is setting off a chain reaction in farm production.

Some people call it a "nitrogen binge." Some term it a "fertilizer fantasy." Whatever its name, it is a significant part of the technological revolution that is changing the face of agriculture, bringing about an upheaval in the economic, sociological and cultural structure of the rural areas.

Take Leslie C. Boler of Martin County, Minn. Seven years ago he was growing forty-five bushels of corn an acre. Today his yield is 100 bushels an acre.

Seven years ago he was rotating crops in traditional fashion to get natural nitrogen back into the soil for corn. Today, he grows corn year after year on 570 of his 600 acres and puts the nitrogen back as he plants with time-saving machinery. His goal is 150 bushels an acre.

Yield Doubles in 5 Years

Five years ago Emil Eickhoff and his son, Donald, were getting about seventy-two bushels an acre from their good farm land in Fillmore County, in southeastern Minnesota.

In 1953, they entered the "X-tra yield corn test" of the University of Minnesota's Institute of Agriculture. They won with a test yield of 126.1 bushels an acre. They won again this year with a yield of 155.1 bushels an acre.

These farmers, along with thousands of others, poured on the fertilizer. There is disagreement in the farm country on precisely what turned the production trick, but nitrogen is given a major share of the credit.

Some ascribe the startling yields to a combination of better farming methods: sound management, more efficient use of farm machinery, better hybrid seeds and fertilizers. Others contend that the production increases of the last three years are due entirely to the "nitrogen binge."

This monoculture of corn is spreading with the inflow of nitrogen and a host of farm practices unheard of a few years ago. These new farming methods, singly and in combination, are causing the increase in yields on shrinking acres for products ranging from corn to tung nuts.

Another example is minimum tillage. This is simply less and less tillage than a few years ago. It means less time for the farmer in the field. It means more capital expenditures through new methods, and increasing quality while increasing quantity.

Two pounds of nitrogen equals one bushel of corn. One hundred pounds of nitrogen, at 10 cents a pound, make for an outlay of $10 to get fifty more bushels. Even with corn at $1 a bushel, the extra $50 helps to offset rising farm costs.

Leslie Boler's continuous corn operation is not unique in the farm areas today. But it is startling. A few years ago agriculture colleges and experimental stations preached the merits of crop rotation to keep the land fertile and productive. Some still do. But many now approve it only for the better soils on which erosion can be held to a minimum.

New Theory Taught

Tests at Iowa State College, for example, show that soil structure has no bearing on yields, so long as organic matter is returned to the soil through corn stalks and new tillage measures maintain adequate aeration and porousness. This is a sharp reversal of the teachings of twenty years ago.

Mr. Boler said his soil structure was better because of the abundance of organic matter returned by the corn. Water now is soaking into the soil instead of running off, and there is less loose soil for the winds to blow away.

Minnesota farmers alone used 15 per cent more fertilizer last year than in 1956. Nitrogen use has climbed 600 per cent in the state since 1950. Potash use has risen 250 per cent.

Over-all, the straight materials, such as nitrogen, have gained 21 per cent in a year and mixed commercial fertilizers only 13 per cent, although mixed fertilizers continue to account for the bulk of the total tonnage used throughout the Farm Belt.

More Fertilizer Needed

Farm authorities say that even with present gains the fertilizer applied still is short of the amount needed to replace the plant nutrients removed from the soil in harvested crops and animal products.

But a swing through the Farm Belt uncovers the "explosive" situation. It promises even greater production to meet the needs of the future, but at the moment poses serious surplus problems and leaner farm pocketbooks. Nevertheless, farmers are fighting to gain volume to offset rising costs and lower prices, a human trait often overlooked by the politicians.

Among those who believe in nitrogen is Roswell Garst, the Coon Rapid, Iowa, business man and farmer who penetrated the Iron Curtain to sell his hybrid seed corn to Rumania.

Mr. Garst noted that at the end of World War II, the Government had about a dozen plants capable of producing about 100,000 tons of actual nitrogen a year. It is the main component of TNT, the big material of war bombs.

The 'Binge' Begins

"At the end of the war, this nitrogen was used mainly in fertilizers," Mr. Garst said. "It was the first time that nitrogen was available in sufficient quantity and at a cheap enough price to be widely used. Farmers and experiment stations soon found out that it was perfectly explosive to crops. In fact, as explosive to crops as it was to bombs."

Prof. William C. Martin, head of the Department of Soils at the University of Minnesota's College of Agriculture, said the production situation had been aptly named a "nitrogen binge."

The increasing use of fertilizer, he said, has been "influenced by the farmer's increasing awareness that fertilizer is one of the best weapons against the cost-price squeeze."

Commercial fertilizers are cleaner, easier to handle and can be applied faster than the farmer's long-time friend, manure. There are still no accurate figures on the difference between the cost of artificial nitrogen and nitrogen fixed through clover in crop rotation.

Vast Potential Seen

Agronomists differ. Some say the cost ranges from 50 cents to $1 a pound for fixing nitrogen through a legume crop. This compares with 10 cents a pound for artificially produced nitrogen, a comparison that does not escape the farmer faced with rising fixed costs and varying prices.

Professor Martin and others who watch the changing farm scene foresee an untapped potential in nitrogen used in balance with other fertilizers.

These balanced fertilizers are well known to suburban dwellers. Estimates on the nonfarm use of fertilizers run to about 2,500,000 tons, or at least 10 per cent of the total national consumption of more than 20,000,000 tons a year.

The story of nitrogen, the colorless, tasteless, odorless element that makes up about four-fifths of the atmosphere, is not confined to the Midwest.

In two decades, cotton acreage has fallen from about 40,000,000 acres to 16,000,000. Yet cotton producers raise as much cotton as they did two decades ago.

Fertilizers have been slow in reaching the Western and Southwestern Wheat Belt. There, the emphasis had been on improved varieties and efficient farming. Now, the 1958 winter wheat crop promises to set yield records. Nitrogen was pumped into the wheat land as the seed was planted.

Added to the World War II nitrogen plants were plants built with fast tax write-offs during the Korean war. Nitrogen capacity rose far beyond the country's needs. As a result, the price of nitrogen has dropped from about 16 cents a pound in 1950 to about 10 cents now.

Farmers gobbled it up after the Korean war. Consumption now is estimated at more than 3,000,000 tons annually and is steadily pressing against a plant capacity of about 4,000,000 tons.

The demand has brought added capacity. Fifteen big Midwestern farm cooperatives recently contracted to take the entire output of a new $16,000,000 plant at Pine Bend, Minn.

Like a good many other farmers, Les Boler on his 570-acres in southern Minnesota faced the problem of keeping his costs low and getting a maximum net return per acre without a loss of soil fertility and soil structure.

Soil samples showed him what he needed. Significantly, soil sampling is growing rapidly with the use of commercial fertilizers.

Cuts His Volume

He began by broadcasting bulk loads of phosphorus and potash. He used 115 pounds of each material an acre at the start. Now that the land-fertility level is higher than when he started he has cut back to sixty pounds of each an acre.

He applied 120 pounds of nitrogen to each acre. He uses it either in gaseous or granular form.

In the first four years of building his land to the present 100-bushel-an-acre yield, his fertilizer costs averaged $30 an acre. His costs now have dropped to between $15 and $20 an acre, and he has been able to hold a high fertility level.

In the fall, he plows under the corn stalks with an application of nitrogen. Thus, he holds fertility, maintains the soil structure and cuts his costs and labor.

He pumps the nitrogen into the field at planting time. He plants with a six-row planter. Attached to this planter are a box or tank for the fertilizer and others carrying an insecticide and weedicide.

The wire worms and cut worms that the farmer formerly killed by rotation practices now are doomed by a chemical. The chemical compounds also get at the weeds before they sprout and eliminate two crop-season cultivations of the fields, another labor- and time-saver.

In the cotton and wheat country there are even bigger behemoths of the farm. In the Pacific Northwest, and elsewhere, giant fertilizer tanks atop planting machinery are a familiar sight.

Tank and cargo trucks carry the "explosive" materials to the field side. The farmer hitches up his horses, fifty or more fed on gasoline or Diesel oil. Six hours of labor produces a bushel of corn. Twenty-five years ago it took the farmer twenty-five hours.

March 8, 1958

RICE YIELD STIRS FARM SCIENTISTS

Research Grants Seek Way to Increase Harvest of Major World Food

A basic scientific puzzle is how to increase the harvest of one of man's oldest and most popular foods—rice.

Rice fills the major food requirements for about half the world's population, yet there is less scientific knowledge about this cereal than any other major crop.

The problem is particularly acute in India, which produces only about 750 pounds an acre. A Chinese rice acre produces about 1,550 pounds; an Egyptian, 2,060; an Italian, 3,100.

The Rockefeller Foundation reported yesterday that it had appropriated $537,000 in the last six years in direct grants in support of rice research, fellowships and travel grants.

Foundation officers in 1950 began exploratory visits to Brazil, India, Burma, Indonesia, Thailand, the Philippine Islands and Japan.

Dr. J. George Harrar, director of the foundation's agriculture division, said the greatest single need in agricultural development in the Orient was for trained personnel who could carry on a successful agriculture program.

The programs, Dr. Harrar emphasized, are designed to supplement "indigenous projects" being developed by local governments concerned with rice yield and very large population increases.

Grants here and abroad were directed toward rice improvement through studies in soil science, genetics, cytology, microbiology, plant pathology and biochemistry.

The grants included two totaling $195,000, to Louisiana State University for a training center for American and foreign agricultural scientists specializing in research on rice and for a study of the genetic and cytogenetic relationships in rice.

Other grants followed. One of $30,000 was made to Texas A. & M. College for training foreign students specializing in rice improvement and management.

Japanese organizations got $213,000 for the study of the origin of rice and rice genetics, problems of fertility and the control of rice diseases. Smaller grants were made for studies in Ceylon, the Philippine Islands and Indonesia.

Dr. Harrar said one of the problems in the study of rice was the enormous number of varieties — at least 7,000. He said 4,000 of these were in India. A rice that does very well in one country may not do well in another; some respond very favorably to fertilizer, others do not, he said.

Researchers look toward a hybridized species with a good growth, disease resistance and fine yield. But, he said, that goal is a long-range one. Additional problems in India, he said, are outmoded farming methods, local traditions, lack of a profit motive in raising a crop and insufficient land for rice growers to think broadly about their agricultural economy.

March 9, 1958

Artificial Breeding Of Livestock Rises

By WILLIAM M. BLAIR

Special to The New York Times

NEW PRAGUE, Minn., March 12—One of the greatest scientific developments in agriculture is changing the face of a whole sector of American farming.

Artificial insemination of livestock has achieved a "scientific revolution" in the dairy industry and among purebred cattle. Now it is spreading to the country's vast commercial beef cattle herds and covering all of the livestock business with a promise of more and better quality meat products.

Artificial breeding is comparatively new among modern farming methods. It dates to ancient times but has been developed here as part of the big technological and scientific breakthrough in farming during World War II. And in the last eight years it has helped to bring a 20 per cent increase in milk production from 22 per cent fewer cows.

Experiment stations and agriculture laboratories in colleges and universities, farm cooperatives and private groups across the land are working to improve and extend hog production through artificial insemination. It is being used with chickens and now has spread to turkeys. The latest big development is in beef cattle.

Programs Began in 1938

Last year about 6,500,000 dairy cows, or one-third of the 20,500,000 cows milked in the United States, were bred artificially under organized programs by individual farmers.

Twenty years ago it was a 100-cow business in the experimental stage. Today there are fifty-seven farmer cooperatives and fourteen private businesses. Their total annual income last year was more than $36,000,000.

The effects of the new science can be seen in milk statistics. The 20,500,000 cows milked last year were the smallest number on record, but their output reached another peak. They produced 126,400,000,000 pounds (about 588,000,000 quarts) of milk. This production was 907,000,000 pounds more than the previous record of 1956 despite a 2 per cent drop in the number of cows between the two years.

But white milk output increased and caused trouble in some areas—mainly because of marketing problems—it is the one phase of agriculture that failed to keep pace with an expanding population. Milk production provided only 738 pounds of milk per person last year against 746 pounds in 1956.

This situation has been accepted as a challenge by dairy producers and particularly by the artificial breeders in farm groups who are now engaged in long-range programs to get a better cow, a better product for consumers, and more income for farmers.

The ancient Egyptians knew of artificial breeding. The Russians moved the science forward with work on sheep. The Danes and English, with limited land and other resources, advanced it rapidly.

The first organized cattle group in this country was the New Jersey Artificial Breeders Cooperative in Annandale. It began in May, 1938, followed in June by a cooperative in Hughesville, Mo. A year earlier, D. L. C. Cole of the University of Minnesota was doing research achieved successful field results on sheep and dairy cattle and at the School of Agriculture, Grand Rapids, Minn.

Colleges Get Inquiries

Today, inquiries on the possibilities in commercial beef herds are coming to Midwestern colleges and universities from ranchers in Nebraska, Colorado, Kansas and Western states.

Some cattle producers figure they can increase calf production from the current 70 to 75 per cent to at least 85 per cent, improve quality and cut disease. They also see a reduction in big bull herds on the range and problems of management.

Such a move would mean more cows bred per sire and the elimination of shipping bulls long distances, such as friends of President Eisenhower have done to help him build his purebred Aberdeen Angus herd on his Gettysburg, Pa. farm.

By cutting costs, some cattle producers hope to help beat the cost-price squeeze on agriculture and profit as dairy producers have in their programs. Dr. Harry Herman of the National Artificial Breeders Association in Columbia, Mo., estimated that dairy producers "find enough extra milk to pay for the extra service three times."

He said he had some doubts about extending the service to beef cattle until he recently visited Washington State College. He said he had found livestock producers there "enthusiastic" because they wanted a better calf crop and could cut disease spread by bulls in herds.

Not Enough Good Bulls

A farmhand on horseback will ride through the herd two hours each morning and evening on the lookout for cows ready to be bred. These will be penned for artificial breeding.

Dr. Greg Raps, manager of the Iowa Co-Op, pointed out that through this method some 10,000 to 20,000 cows could be bred. Otherwise, there would be a need for about thirty bulls and "there simply are not enough good bulls to go around."

This is the type of operation that has an appeal to the Western rancher. He can cut down his bull herd and get a higher rate of conception and thus a higher and better calf crop.

It will enable ranchers to band together, as dairy producers have done, to have a bull stud in a central location. The bull semen can be transported in extended, frozen or dried state.

Large purebred beef cattle breeders have been using the technique for years. But it is coming fast in the commercial herds of beef cattle. About 600,000 commercial beef cows were artificially inseminated with good results last year.

The Iowa co-op is about to begin service with frozen semen on a 316-head Angus beef herd in southwestern Iowa.

Here in this small community south of Minneapolis and St. Paul is one of the country's largest breeding cooperatives. The Minnesota Valley Breeders Association is embarking on a progeny-testing program that may provide the answers to much higher quality dairy cattle and more milk to meet the needs of a growing population.

It is believed to be the first program of its type in this country.

Studies in Heredity

Wallace Miller, association manager, is gathering a herd of more than 300 cows in a controlled program with the advice of Dr. Edward Graham, a young researcher from the University of Minnesota. These cows will be serviced by forty bulls owned by the association to provide studies on hereditary characteristics aimed at getting better sires and better milk cows—and fatter pocketbooks for its members.

Today the association heads a list of some sixteen breeding groups in the state. Thirty-five per cent of the dairy cows in Minnesota are bred by artificial insemination. The association owns a set of modern buildings and 500 acres of farmland, from which it gets most of its feed.

When the association started, the dairy herd improvement figures showed average state production of 320 pounds of butter fat per cow a year. Today the average is 370 pounds and rising. Meanwhile, the association has provided the inheritance for 1,200,000 offspring.

Dr. Graham explained they were looking for many things to improve milk production. These included the rate of milking; the letdown of milk by cows; better udder conformation, temperatures, and to some extent the feed utilization. Some cows are slow milkers; some do not let down all of their milk, some put their feed back on their bodies and "some in the milk pail."

Dr. Graham said:

"By breeding some of the new daughters back to the sire we may reveal some abnormalities which will give us a chance to get better bulls and dams. Perhaps we can change by inheritance the milking rate and other factors now barring greater output."

Mr. Miller and Dr. Graham went to Denmark, where 80 per cent of dairy cows are artificially inseminated, to study the progeny programs there. They adapted the two systems for association use. Departing from the Danish system, which borrows cows from farmers, the association will have its own herd on its own farm.

A Chance Remark

The association, which last year bred more than 279,000 cows from its bull stud, was started with the chance remark that Martin Beckman, a Jordan, Minn., farmer, made to Mr. Miller, then Scott County agriculture agent.

Bull rings, formed by a group of farmers who either took a bull to their cows or brought a cow to the bull, then were a standard operation. "Bull rings are a slow method of improving dairy cattle," Mr. Beckman said to Mr. Miller in 1940. "I have read about artificial insemination. When that program gets started I will be interested."

Mr. Miller investigated. A unit of Scott and Lesueur Counties, with 1,400 cows, was formed. Resources were limited and crude. Even the three bulls acquired then were trained and hitched to wagons to haul supplies. Assets now are $324,000 and members received $106,000 in dividend payments last year.

It has attracted widespread attention, although similar lines of inquiry are in progress in Iowa in cooperation with herds owned by state institutions and elsewhere in the cattle country.

"We believe that through a progeny-testing program such as we're setting up we can get some answers that have eluded us on the physiology of the cow," Mr. Miller said.

He said that present methods of analyzing sires were inadequate. "Now we'll be able to service twenty cows to each bull under optimum controlled conditions, even to feed. The daughters of these bulls and dams will be grown out and bred and when they come in milk we'll have a chance to check for the things we're looking for."

Mr. Miller also hopes they may be able to find out what bulls will produce offspring that give more milk solids, not fat.

"Butterfat or butter," he said, is on the wane. "There are too many good substitutes." Last year Americans consumed more substitutes — including margarines from cottonseed, soybean and other oils—than butter.

Buffers Dilute Semen

The association's operation is typical of the cooperatives in the field. Semen is collected under extremely sanitary conditions four times a week. It is immediately diluted with buffers. The association uses an egg yolk citrate.

At first the dilution was three or four parts of buffer to one part of semen. Some breeders now use thirty to forty parts of buffer to one part of semen.

The extended semen is put in vials and packed in special insulated cardboard boxes around a can of frozen water that keeps the temperature at about 38 degrees Fahrenheit. These packages are rushed to inseminators employed by the association.

The association recently developed a new package, using as an insulator a core of styrene, a new type of plastic several ounces lighter than the fiber material used previously. This has provided better insulation and lower shipping costs.

On hand also is a quantity of frozen semen for use in special selected matings. It came from bulls who died in a fire that swept the association's cattle barns a year ago. Som[e] [f]orty bulls were lost in the fi[re].

Largest in Ithaca

The largest livestock breeders cooperative is at Ithaca, N. Y. It is the New York Artificial Breeders Association, which works closely with Cornell University's College of Agriculture. The next in line is Badger Breeders of Shawano, Wis. The No. 1 private organization is the American Breeders Service of Chicago, which serviced 1,000,000 cows last year in forty-three states, Cuba and South America. The Curtis Candy Company of Chicago has the second largest private service.

The private companies sell semen wholesale to farm cooperatives and other groups in addition to having their own distribution systems. The cooperatives do about 75 per cent of the business in the country, with the rest shared by the private concerns.

Frozen semen, which is coming into wider use, is used more extensively in the East than in the Midwest. The Iowa Breeders Co-Op recently installed the automatic freezing equipment, said to be the first west of the Mississippi.

The average rate per cow is about $6. Inseminators employed by the cooperatives usually get a fee of $2 to $3 each insemination.

March 16, 1958

Livestock Grow Fat On Chemical Feeds

By WILLIAM M. BLAIR
Special to The New York Times.

MANHATTAN, Kan., March 28—Four white-faced calves from the New Mexico range loll placidly in a small room of the new sandstone and glass animal husbandry building at Kansas State College.

They are there in isolated splendor because nutrition scientists want to know more about what makes their stomachs tick, how they utilize certain feeds and such things as "nitrogen balance" and "digestible energy."

These Herefords are a part of a new era in agriculture science and a symbol of the impact of science down on the farm.

This impact is most startling in livestock, which now get such wonders as antibiotics, sex hormones and tranquilizers in a measure calculated to startle the father who has to pay the doctor's bill for little Johnny's shots.

Farmers' acceptance of these "tools" has come in a far shorter time than similar revolutionary ideas in crop production.

For example, only four years ago Iowa State College came up with a synthetic chemical compound with estrogenic properties.

This synthetic female sex hormone was greeted by hot debate in the Farm Belt. Fears were expressed that it would adversely affect the humans who ate the meat from steers given the hormone.

But diethylstilbestrol, or stilbestrol for short, is now so widely accepted that some estimates say it is used on at least three-quarters of the cattle coming to market each year.

Many New Techniques

Today new debates are sputtering over a host of new scientific "tools" and techniques for livestock. Within the last month, Iowa State has come up with another feed additive that promises even faster, cheaper gains on cattle, plus an increase in the quality of meat.

The feed additive is a material now used for human patients afflicted with oversecretion from the thyroid gland, or hyperthrodism. Hyperthyroid individuals tend to be thin.

Dr. Wise Burroughs, livestock nutritionist, said that laboratory studies showed that the thyroid-blocking material "seemed likely to help cattle produce the interior fat or 'marbling' which makes for tenderness and flavor in meat."

At the same time, he said, it "might not add to the outside fat often cut off in the meat market or kitchen."

Tests Encouraging

This new additive still is in the experimental stage. Further tests will be made before it will be released with the approval of the Food and Drug Administration.

But, the first feedlot tests have shown that it increased daily weight gains in cattle by as much as 21 per cent and improved the consumer taste appeal of beef.

The additive slows down the metabolism, the burning-up of energy in the body. It goes hand in hand with a new feeding concept, that of high-energy, low-protein diets for more and better beef.

Dr. Burroughs said that before the introduction of stilbestrol five tons of grain had been needed to produce 1,050 pounds of gain on a steer. With the advent of stilbestrol in 1953, five tons of grain produced 1,150 pounds of beef. Now, he said, with stilbestrol and the new thyroid-blocking additive added to the feed ration, five tons of grain will turn out 1,250 pounds of beef.

Stilbestrol is implanted in a steer's ear with a spring-type "gun" especially designed for the operation. The tiny implants of ten milligrams are absorbed into the blood stream. The amount is rigorously controlled by the Food and Drug Administration.

The success of the synthetic compound and four years of tests are expected to bring an increase in the allowable implant up to twenty milligrams.

Researchers have been experimenting with even larger amounts.

Dr. Rufus F. Cox, head of the Kansas State Animal Husbandry Department, viewed the long leaps in science as "a steady collection of a lot of little facts" in all phases of livestock, starting with breeding and moving through feeding, management of herbs and marketing.

At Purdue University, yearling steers that received seventy-five milligrams of the "wonder drug" each day, gained sixty-seven more pounds of beef a head than steers that got no antibiotic. Feed conversion was increased 10 per cent.

Cattle at Kansas State also are getting ammoniated blackstrap molasses. This is simply more nitrogen. The increase of a milk cow's intake of nitrogen has produced more milk. Some scientists believe that synthetic nitrogen will prove as "explosive" within livestock as it has in crop production.

In one college feedlot, a bunch of steers received low-level doses of a tranquilizer to determine whether it would make them less active and thus produce more beef, in combination with other new feeding ideas. One day this week they were as active as their non-tranquilized companions.

Because stilbestrol has failed to do much in gains for heifers, Dr. Drake Richardson, nutrion researcher at Kansas State has begun trying testosterone, the male sex hormone, on heifers. His initial experiments show that the heifers gained one-quarter pound more a day than heifers without the hormone.

At Kansas State also, a series of running tests on feeding seventy milligrams of an antibiotic, Aureomycin, show increased gains on steer calves wintered on the pastures of the college farm before they are fattened for market. The antibiotic is mixed with soybean meal.

Pellet Feed Tested

The University of Illinois' College of Agriculture Experiment Station at Dixon Springs also has compiled results of experiments making a timothy-alfalfa hay mixture into pellets for feed. This change doubled daily-gain rates on beef cattle.

By using baled hay, the traditional roughage for livestock, **the test cattle gained 0.63 pounds per day. In pellet form the gain was 1.73 pounds per day.**

Dr. Richardson at Kansas State said pelleting of all kinds of feed, either singly or in combination, held a "bright promise." He hopes to find out why this is so, in his digestive studies on the Herefords.

Perhaps, he said, it is because the pellet exposes a larger surface to enzymes in the stomach than does rolled, cracked or ground corn and other feed grains. Thus, the digestive system utilizes more of the feed, and not so much moves through the animal rapidly to be lost as waste.

Farm colleges and county agents across the Midwest already are getting calls from farmers on the pelleting of all kinds of feed. Some feed firms have developed pelleting machines but the machines and the process still are relatively expensive.

However, the results from pellets indicate that as more machines are built, the price will come down, and farmers will be able to buy them individually or to form cooperative ventures.

Pelleting also is part of the new technique of stepping up the calories and cutting the amount of protein feed, a sharp reversal of standard practices.

The pay-off for such scientific endeavors come in dollars and cents. Experiments by Iowa State and other institutions, show, for example, that there is a return of $7 more a head on steers fed more calories and less protein while on stilbestrol.

March 30, 1958

Sorghum Story: Obscurity to Surplus in Six Years

Grain Popular After Long U. S. History as 'Small Crop'

By RICHARD RUTTER

Grain sorghum, the bushy-headed youngster that in six short years has come from near-obscurity to become the nation's fourth largest grain crop, has developed some of the problems that go along with bigness.

With its new eminence as a leading farm product, sorghum has attracted not only the flattering attention of farmers, grain merchants, feed companies and seed producers, but the keen interest of the Federal Government as well in the form of controls. Meanwhile, a surplus problem has developed.

Sometimes called "dry-land corn," grain sorghum can survive with far less moisture than either corn or wheat. It is particularly suited for growing in the low-rain fall areas of Texas, Oklahoma, Nebraska and Kansas. When a drought occurs that would wipe out less hardy grains, this rugged crop's growth is halted only temporarily. Sorghum resumes growing when moisture is again available and ultimately produces a normal or near-normal crop.

This year, according to the latest crop forecast by the Department of Agriculture, farmers will grow 480,100,000 bushels of grain sorghum. That is an amount exceeded only by the "big three" of agriculture: corn,

A field of grain sorghum in Nebraska is inspected by executives of Cargill, Inc. The inset shows buckshot-size kernels of the grain, which has become a leading farm crop.

3,548,813,000 bushels; wheat, 1,210,000,000, and oats, 993,000,000. In each case the 1961 figure is less than that in 1960, reflecting the effects of the 1961 feed-grain law and other Government acreage-cutting measures.

Surplus Grows

Despite the cutback in this year's crop, the burgeoning production of sorghum has propelled it proportionately into second place behind wheat as a surplus crop.

Its phenomenal popularity has made the grain a major factor in a variety of marketing and manufacturing enterprises. Cargill, Inc., of Minneapolis, a leading grain handling and processing concern, describes the present situation:

"Sorghum is a major item for purchase in the Southwest, for merchandising to a constantly expanding market in this country, and for foreign export to Europe and Asia through Gulf port facilities. It is interchangeable in our Nutrena-Feeds division with corn in most feed formulas and is the main formula at our plants in Texas, Kansas and Nebraska. In our hybrid seed department, processing sorghum is a major operation at Aurora, Neb."

The 1961 law, which reduced sorghum production, represents the first year-to-year decline in harvested acreage since the crop began its meteoric climb in 1955. The legislation guarantees growers high support prices and compensatory payments in exchange for acreage reductions. The end-result has been a 26 per cent drop in the number of acres planted.

How Program Works

The sorghum support program works this way:

Farmers agreeing to reduce acreage by 20 per cent are guaranteed a support price of $1.08 a bushel (usually quoted at $1.93 a hundredweight) for grain produced plus payment in kind (grain from the Government's stocks). Or they can take cash at 50 per cent of the value of the retired land's average yield. Farmers cutting acreage by 40 per cent receive the base amount plus 60 per cent in kind of a cash payment on the additional land's average harvest value.

Those growers who do not choose to participate in the price support program must sell their grain on the open market. Prices there at present are considerably below the guaranteed price.

Meanwhile, hitches have developed in the support program, creating a complicated pattern of action and counteraction that has left most farmers confused and many angry. Among the sorghum snags are these:

¶A practice among farmers to sign up for the full 40 per cent acreage cut-back program and then to retire only 20 per cent of their land. Watching the weather and the commodity markets, growers tend to wait until the last possible moment — fifteen days after their land is measured for compliance — before deciding whether to plow under the second 20 per cent and thereby receive the full government payment or to harvest that acreage and either put it under Government loan or sell the yield on the open market. Actual acreage could be measurably less than forecast.

¶Uncertainty over prices that acts against the Department of Agriculture's program to step up the conversion of surplus grain into edible meat. It is likely, according to some observers of the farm scene, that livestock and poultry producers, leery over grain price fluctuations, will turn to Government-guaranteed cash grain farming as a less risky proposition. The result would be to increase, rather than to reduce, government grain stocks.

Game of Pool?

Where will it end?

"End? We don't even know where we'll be tomorrow," one close follower of the grain market says. "This is the Department of Agriculture's pool game. All we can do is to play along until some logical pattern begins to appear."

f.salvia

Uncertain and fast changing as the future appears, the development of grain sorghum is long and clearly defined. In one variety or another it has been grown around the world from earliest history. Africa is considered the most probable place of origin.

Ancient varieties are millet, still grown in India and southern Europe, guinea corn grown in the West Indies, and kafir and hegari grown in West Africa and the Middle East.

All of these, as well as varieties of sweet sorghum used as a forage for livestock, have been traditional "small crops" on American farms for generations, but until six years ago were of only minor consequence to the total farm economy.

The change came in 1955 when hybrid sorghums were first introduced. The need for such hybrids had long been recognized, but researchers were stumped by a characteristic of the plant itself.

In corn, where the pollen-shedding "male" tassels and the kernel-producing "female" silks are separate, it is relatively easy to control pollination and to make a successful cross of one variety with another. But in bushy-headed sorghum, the pollen shedding organs are contained in the same envelope as the female parts, making pollination control appear to be impossible.

The breakthrough came with the discovery of a male-sterile variety, a genetic "freak," which produced no pollen. This sterile plant, unable to fertilize itself, was crossbred with other sorghum strains and the elusive hybrid was created.

New Seed in Demand

Farmers, remembering the bonanza brought by hybrids to corn production, bought every available bushel of the new sorghum seed in 1955 and in each succeeding year until 1958. Only then, according to industry leaders, were commercial seed companies completely able to supply their customers' wants.

Enthusiasm for the new varieties has been justified, for most recent reports show hybrids consistently out-yielding standard varieties by 15 to 25 per cent, with some varieties recording a 40 per cent bonus yield.

Today, in the great western plains, 90 per cent of all irrigated sorghum acreage and 50 per cent of dry-land acreage is being planted in hybrids. The hybrids have already taken over more than half the sorghum acreage of the more humid eastern great plains.

The present average yield to the acre is 41.3 bushels, almost twice the ten-year average of 22.6 bushels. This year, though total plantings were down 26.2 per cent from the 1960 level, they were 80.5 per cent higher than the average for the last ten years.

November 12, 1961

World Fishery Production Doubled From 1950 to 1961

WASHINGTON, June 8 (UPI)—The Interior Department's Bureau of Commercial Fisheries reports that world fishery production after 1950 more than doubled to reach a total of 41,200,000 metric tons in 1961.

The bureau estimated that this production would continue and might further double within the next several decades.

The bureau said fisheries have a significant role in feeding the expanding populations of many regions of the world and contributing to the battle against protein deficiency. This is a malady that affects an estimated two-thirds of the world's peoples, the bureau said.

June 9, 1963

Fish Flour to Feed Hungry Perfected

By FELIX BELAIR Jr.
Special to The New York Times

WASHINGTON, Dec. 23—Federal scientists have made a major breakthrough in the universal search for a solution to the world food crisis.

The answer, already perfected by experts of the Interior Department's Bureau of Commercial Fisheries, is a new process for producing a clinically pure fish concentrate with a rated protein content of 80 per cent. Eventually the concentrate could end "protein starvation" for about two-thirds of the human race.

Feasibility studies indicate that if only the unharvested fish in United States coastal waters were translated into the concentrate it would provide the normal protein requirements for one billion persons for 300 days at a base production cost of half a cent a person a day.

The product is almost odorless and tasteless and has the appearance of a light-gray flour. Intended as a food supplement or additive, it mixes readily with baked goods, noodles or beef gravy mix without any trace of fish taste. It has been used in "milk shakes" and formulated baby foods with the same results.

The new fish flour has been certified as "pure and wholesome" by the National Academy of Sciences and National Research Foundation, which carried out extensive investigations covering bacterial and toxic aspects as well as cost engineering studies.

The two private research organizations were called in by Secretary of the Interior Stewart L. Udall to work with the Bureau of Commercial Fisheries after the Food and Drug Administration had banned a similar but less refined concentrate from interstate commerce in 1962 on the ground that it was "polluted and filthy" within the meaning of the Food, Drug and Cosmetics Act.

The agency based this decision on the use of whole fish in the process then under review, including the head, tail fins and viscera.

Since then, however, a small group of Federal scientists working quietly in laboratories and in a pilot processing plant in nearby Maryland have developed an isopropanol extraction process that completely eliminates from the whole fish any bacterial or other toxicity in the finished product.

Spotlessly clean, the pilot installation has been operated as a food processing plant and is producing 100 pounds of the fish protein concentrate daily.

Pending a formal acceptance of the product by the Food and Drug Administration a tight lid of secrecy has been clamped on the project. Another reason for official reticence about the breakthrough is the personal interest taken in the development by President Johnson, who is expected to announce it during the Christmas holidays.

Food and drug officials, however, have indicated that they will interpose no objection to the domestic marketing of the product.

The agency let it be known as part of its original decision that it would have no objection to marketing of the product in food deficit areas overseas. But elsewhere in the Government officials promptly dismissed any such course of action on grounds that it risked a Communist propaganda attack charging the United States with palming off on others a product it considered unfit for human consumption at home.

By bringing out the product as a food supplement the Food and Drug Administration retains control over its commercial manufacture.

Under the new extraction process the whole fish is first ground in much the same way as beef is reduced to hamburger. This pulp is then put through a moving bath of cold isopropyl alcohol, which eliminates most of the water and fatty content. It is then put through two more stages using hot isopropyl alcohol in kettles that stir the contents.

This final treatment eliminates all remaining fatty substances and most of the water. After being spray dried, what remains is an off-white, flour-like substance of 80 per cent protein content. The other 20 per cent consists of beneficial minerals including calcium, phosphate and somewhat less moisture than is chemically present in wheat flour.

Mental Effects Seen

Government officials consider development of the new fish concentrate to be dramatically significant in terms of the mathematics of increasing populations, declining food production and malnutrition in the underdeveloped countries of Asia, Africa and Latin America.

Studies by the United Nations Food and Agriculture Organization and World Health Organization have pinpointed protein hunger as the most pressing human problem of the century. Over 80 per cent of the world's population does not receive sufficient daily protein, while some 60 per cent of the world population verges on actual protein stravation.

A recent task force report to President Johnson brought out that about 50 per cent of infants and pre-school-age children in underdeveloped countries suffered from protein malnutrition. There is evidence that the condition retards mental and physical development of between 10 and 25 per cent.

The report to Mr. Johnson said that overcoming the vitamin and protein deficiencies of young children in most underdeveloped countries would do more to reduce disease and eventually raise productivity than any other health measure that could be taken.

The vital function of protein in human development is easily understood in terms of the nutritional process. Water and minerals aside, food consists of proteins, fats and carbohydrates. If the diet is low on fats and carbohydrates there is no great problem since the body can manufacture both from proteins. It cannot manufacture proteins from fats and carbohydrates.

Animal proteins contain more of the essential amino-acids needed for human growth than do plant proteins. Milk, eggs and meat are the best source of animal proteins. But milk and eggs are scarce in the tropical areas that include most of the underdeveloped nations.

Moreover, high prices make meat beyond the reach of those who need it most. And livestock production is considered uneconomical in such areas since meat animals consume three times the protein sources that they return in the form of food.

Least Exploited Source

All of this supports the belief that the greatest and least exploited source of animal protein in terms of quantity, quality and economy is the oceans. The annual harvest of fish from the United States coastal water is about five million pounds. Federal experts believe this could easily be increased to 12 million pounds.

One Academy of Sciences study looking to worldwide potential supply and demand for the concentrate puts the total harvest of fish at about 50 million tons annually. It cites expert estimates of the potential limit at about 400 million tons and says that 250 million tons of fish, sufficient for 50 million tons of the new concentrate, can be obtained with present methodology.

Cost projections were made for the new process based on various plant production capacities. For a plant producing 10 tons of concentrate daily, a selling price of 18 cents a pound, including profit, was indicated. For a 100 ton plant, the selling price would be about 13 cents a pound.

The Academy of Sciences study made a number of evaluations based on a price of about 18 cents a pound of fish concentrate having 80 per cent protein content. The academy said this was the more "realistic" price for the product under commercial production. Average price markups in underdeveloped countries where the product would be used were added to the base cost with the following results:

On the assumption that a three-year-old child received all his daily protein from the fish concentrate, an intake of slightly less than half an ounce would be required, according to Food and Agricultural Organization calculations. The base price of this would be ½ cent. This figure was multiplied by six to cover costs of subdividing, distributing, retailing and peddling to give a cost of 3 cents.

On another assumption—that of an 8-year-old child getting 1,700 calories a day from white rice—he would have to eat slightly more than a pound of rice to attain this intake. This would provide him with about 1.2 ounces of protein against a requirement of about 1.7 ounces. The cost of the fish concentrate that the 8-year-old would need in addition to his rice intake would be about 4 cents, including typical markups.

December 24, 1965

Aquiculture Is More Than A Dream

By LAWRENCE GALTON

MAN, for centuries a random hunter of the sea, is developing ways to farm it. Confronted by the increasingly acute food shortage on land and visualizing much richer harvests than conventional agriculture can produce, pioneers in the new science of aquiculture, or mariculture, have plans to raise fish, shellfish and even plants by plowing the sea, warming areas by atomic energy, fertilizing and weeding the ocean, fencing off underwater farms electronically. Only a few years ago such ideas seemed mere "raptures of the deep" but today they are taken seriously.

The President's Science Advisory Committee last year published a re-

LAWRENCE GALTON specializes in articles on science and technology.

port calling for technological studies to expand the yield of food from the sea. The National Academy of Sciences, issuing its own study, also underscored the need for scientific sea farming. And Congress passed the Marine Resources and Engineering Development Act, establishing a Cabinet-level Council on Marine Resources, headed by Vice President Humphrey. Racing a deadline for 1968 Federal budget allocations, the council recently turned over an interim report to the President in time for him to ask Congress to finance several high-priority projects.

Leading the list was a program to produce fish protein concentrate—a low cost, odorless substance made from whole fish that can be used as a plentiful substitute for flour. Two pilot production plants will be built in the United States and three more in foreign countries to be selected. Also receiving high priority was the concept of "sea-grant colleges," patterned after the land-grant colleges of the last century which did so much to develop agricultural technology. With new Federal financial aid, sea-grant colleges would train sorely needed oceanographers, create regional marine development centers and forge a partnership between scientists and fishermen to apply the fruits of research, much as agricultural experts helped farmers boost the nation's food output.

Summarizing the urgency of increasing worldwide food production, Earl Butz, dean of the School of Agriculture at Purdue University, recently noted that it took mankind hundreds of centuries to develop the capacity to sustain some 3.5 billion people, many only meagerly. Now we need to develop the capacity to feed almost double that number "in the short term of one-third of a century . . . at a time when nearly all the virgin lands of the world have been brought into production and when we face increasing inroads on arable land by urban sprawl."

While the world food supply has been increasing by 1 per cent a year, world population has been rising 1.8 per cent. The result has been a steady decrease in average individual caloric intake. If present trends continue, by the year 2000 the average number of calories available for a world population of about 7.4 billion will be 1,340 a day—below the absolute starvation level, which is pinpointed by nutritionists at 1,350 calories.

Quite apart from the obvious need for higher gross food production is the particular need for protein and protein components in the diet, those essential basic constituents of body tissue and body fluid. (Protein deficiency, according to various studies, may also permanently damage the learning ability of infants and children.) Yet many authorities agree with Dr. William M. Chapman, research director of the Van Camp Sea Food Company, that "the world ocean is producing more fish and animal protein than a human population of 3.5 billion persons can use and it appears to be capable of producing somewhat more than 30 billion would need."

The trouble is, man is not exploiting the resources of the sea, or else he is exploiting them destructively. The annual worldwide fish catch is now 50 million tons, more than double the 1953 catch of 23 million tons, but still a tiny fraction of the possible haul. At the same time, the hunt for fish has been concentrated in areas known to be lucrative, which has led to the depletion of valued stocks.

Sea farming would eliminate such waste and recklessness. The concept, embracing all waters where tides ebb and flow, shares the goal of land agriculture: to control the growth of organisms in order to increase productivity beyond the level possible in harvesting a wild crop.

IN their effort to farm the sea, many marine scientists believe that the best start might lie in inshore waters and the intensive cultivation there of three common forms of aquatic life: algae, mollusks and crustaceans.

Marine algae are plants that range from single-celled forms visible only under a microscope to gigantic growths 100 feet long. For centuries in the Orient, kelp, sea lettuce and seaweed—all algae—have been used in making soups and condiments. The plants are cultivated in shallow estuaries on bamboo poles sunk in muddy bottoms or on ropes strung in bays or inlets. On the California coast, where kelp production is big business, some 160,000 tons are harvested annually. Kelp beds are leased to harvesters for extended periods, providing the incentive to farm and husband the crop.

Such algae cultivation is only a

SEA RANCH—Beneath Japan's Okachi Bay, salmon and trout are raised in net cages and fed from the surface (right). Oysters also grow in the bay, on ropes hung from rafts (below).

beginning, however. "The bulk of the earth's vegetation grows under water," points out Athelstan Spilhaus, dean of the University of Minnesota's Institute of Technology and the man credited with originating the proposal for sea-grant colleges. "Some estimates place ocean vegetation at 4,000 tons per square mile. Ocean plants could be cultivated in much the same way our wild grasses were cultivated to give us wheat, barley and other grains."

Microscopic algae would be nutritious as a human food, or food for cattle and chickens, since the plants often consist of more than 50 per cent protein after they are dried. In the opinion of Jean A. Gross of the Illinois Institute of Technology, "algae could be developed for direct consumption by man and become as normal for human use as potatoes or rice."

Although the taste of algae may not tempt the American palate, the Japanese use one type, Chlorella, whose flavor is similar to lima beans, as an additive to noodles, rice crackers, soups and even jelly beans. Green-colored vanilla ice cream, containing algae powder, is considered a delicacy by many Japanese. In the New World the Aztec inhabitants of Tenochtitlán (now Mexico City) ate large amounts of a blue-green algae with a flavor like cheese which the Spaniards learned to find palatable.

Algae can be grown in large open basins excavated by bulldozers to about a 3-foot depth or in long tubes of transparent plastic that allows sunlight to penetrate. Fertilizers can be injected into the tubes, as well as chemicals, to prevent contamination by undesirable organisms. The Government's Bureau of Commercial Fisheries laboratory at Milford, Conn., has pioneered in mass-producing algae and studying their use. One promising possibility: food for shellfish, but since 10,000 species of algae are known to exist in sea water, the possibilities are almost endless. The need, says Victor L. Loosanoff of the Bureau of Commercial Fisheries, is to develop hybrid strains of the best species, "as it is done in agriculture and cattle breeding."

COMPARED with algae cultivation, the farming of mollusks such as mussels and oysters is well-developed. In the Dutch Waddenzee, for example, the mussel catch rose from 37 million pounds in 1950 to 154 million pounds in 1961—and the system of intensive scientific farming that produced the increase utilized only 30 square miles of the 540-square-mile area.

Each Waddenzee mussel farmer has a plot that ranges from 12 to 25 acres of sea bottom. Mussel seed is transported from "banks" to the plots in autumn or spring when the seed is an inch long, then tended until it is 2½ inches long and ready for market. Natural predators such as starfish are controlled by dredging up both mussels

CALL IT AQUICULTURE, mariculture or sea farming, the scientific cultivation of fish, shellfish and underwater plants could yield a rich harvest, vastly increasing the world's food supply. Below, scientists of an Interior Department research station in Oxford, Md., check oysters planted in a tributary of Chesapeake Bay. Right, from top, checking sperm used in fertilizing female oysters; inspecting algae oyster food; examining oysters injected with a virus.

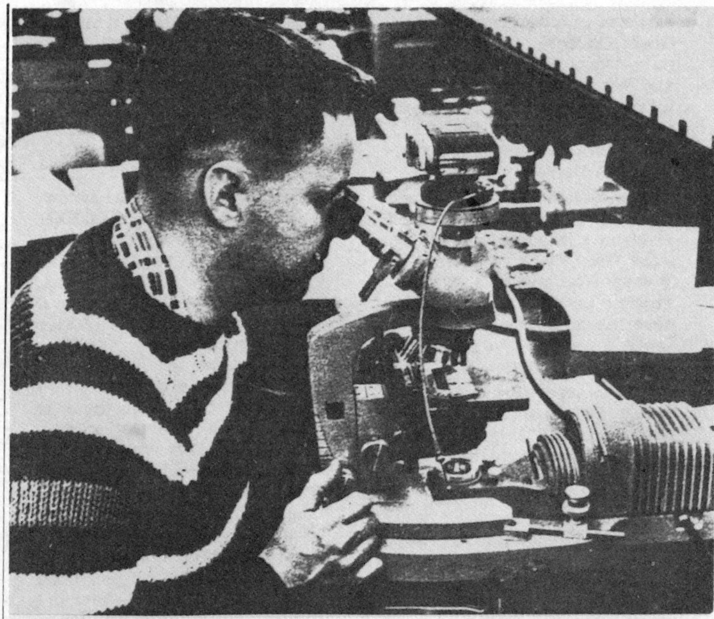

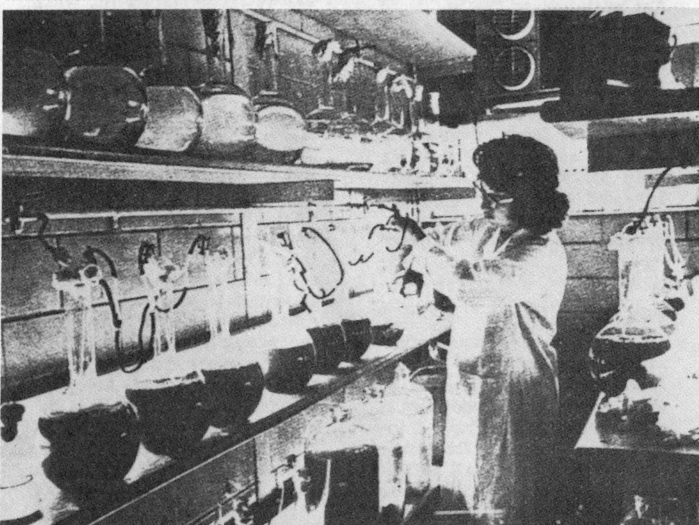

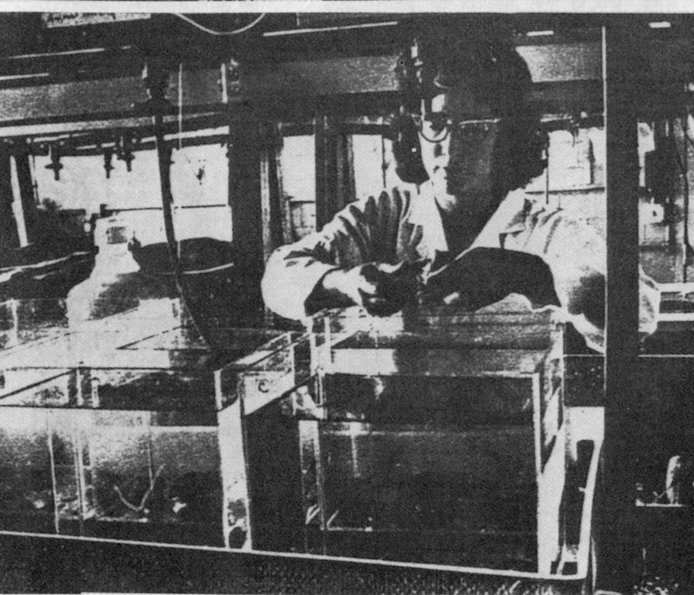

New York Times photographs by GEORGE TAMES

and starfish. The starfish soon die, out of the water, but the mussels are unaffected and can be put back safely to grow.

OYSTERS, anyone? The Japanese are getting 32,000 pounds an acre, using a "raft" technique in which long ropes, strung with full-size oysters or scallop shells to which the young oysters cling, are suspended in the water. Loss from predators is reduced, growth rates are increased and harvesting is simplified. The result is a 50-fold increase over ancient methods of oyster production, which produced, at best, 600 pounds an acre.

In this country, biologists in the Government's Milford laboratory and elsewhere have achieved a series of notable successes during the last 20 years. One of the most impressive advances has been their ability to grow laboratory-ripe ready-to-spawn mollusks the year round. The natural spawning season for oysters, clams and most other bivalve mollusks that dwell in Long Island Sound, for example, is during two and a half summer months. Bivalves brought to the Milford lab in midwinter are subjected to gradually increased temperatures and are ready to spawn in three weeks. With ripe spawners available throughout the year, small oysters and clams hatched in winter can be planted outdoors as soon as the water is warm enough for them to grow; the period of extra growth during the first season can shorten the time needed to reach marketable size by as much as a full year. And to suit the taste of different bivalve larvae, scientists have also mass-produced special algae food which can be stored by means of a new freeze-drying process and used by hatchery operators whenever the need arises.

A popular crustacean delicacy—shrimp—may become more easily and cheaply available as the result of new forms of cultivation. Robert Lunz, of Bears Bluff Laboratories in South Carolina, has demonstrated the feasibility of creating shrimp farms in marsh ponds. The ponds can be built for as little as $35, and considering the cost of a modern, ocean-going shrimp trawler the incentive for further research into shrimp ponds is powerful indeed.

The U.S. Public Health Service has identified 10 million acres as suitable for shellfish farming. Even at a production rate of 600 pounds an acre, the output of 6 billion pounds would be equal to our entire fish catch at present. Within the next 25 years, some marine scientists believe, shellfish farms could be commonplace in the U.S. "Atomic reactors for electric power and desalination plants," says David H. Wallace, director of marine fisheries of New York State, "will supply a cheap source of warmed brackish water for these aquaponds, [even] in northern areas, on a 12-month basis."

Pointing toward another aspect of marine research, Wallace predicts that genetic studies leading to selective breeding for fast-growing and maturing stock will stimulate industrialization of shellfish cultures. "Oysters, ready for market in 12 months or less, should be the attainable goal when trained technicians control the systems," Wallace says.

SUCH genetic juggling is by no means a distant dream. Nor are such experiments restricted to creatures that live in shallow inshore waters.

Almost 20 years ago, Lauren Donaldson of the University of Washington culled the best female Chinook salmon he could find in Soos Creek, near Tacoma. Then he removed their eggs, fertilized them with sperm from choice male Chinooks, and let the eggs mature in laboratory trays. Once hatched in local ponds, the fingerlings were marked (by snipping off a small fin) and dumped into a nearby lake to start their migration through Puget Sound to Alaska. In hopeful expectation of the Chinooks' return, Donaldson dug a ditch from the lake to the ponds, which was promptly labeled "Donaldson's Folly." Four years later, right on schedule, the salmon returned—big, healthy and in large numbers. They were called "Donaldson's Dandies."

Since then, Donaldson has reduced the age at which they reproduce from four years to two years. Moreover, 30 times as many Donaldson Dandies survive the rigors of migration as do ordinary Chinook. Donaldson is now experimenting with another species. By crossing a select breed of rainbow trout with steelhead trout, he is growing fish that are virtually full grown in less than a year.

In addition to selective breeding, more prolific breeding also seems feasible. Two biologists at the Max Planck Horticultural Institute in Hamburg, Reinhold von Sengbusch and Christophe Meske, are experimenting with hormones on special fast-growing carp. Carp normally breed once a year, in the spring. With hormone injections, they are expected to spawn every five months, regardless of the season.

Some mariculturists are confident that within 25 years fish will be raised in offshore pens, tended by divers living for months at a time in undersea houses. Japan—unquestionably the world leader in salt water farming—is already moving in that direction. In 1965 the Government established a sea farm in Okachi Bay, some 200 miles northeast of Tokyo, at a depth of approximately 65 feet. About 4,400 salmon and trout are raised in nylon net cages, fed enriched food pellets and chopped raw sardine through a "chimney" net leading to the surface and inspected once a month by diver-keepers.

The farm has been remarkably successful, in large measure because the deeper water is less polluted than shallower water and circulates more freely. (A shallow farm stocked with salmon and trout, built to compare results with farming at greater depths, had a disastrous mortality rate.) Encouraged by the experiment, the Japanese are preparing to move into depths of 100 feet and more as diving equipment and techniques improve.

Farming at even greater depths may well become possible before long. Says Dr. Milner B. Schaefer, director of the University of California's Institute of Marine Resources: "Already, Yves Cousteau's aquanauts in the Mediterranean and our aquanauts from Sea Lab II, off California, have been able to live and work in depths of 300 feet. It is almost certain that this limit will soon be extended to 1,000 feet. With pressure protection for deeper habitations, men will certainly be able to operate, within the next decade, anywhere on the bottom of the ocean and through the overlying waters."

The new horizons will open vast opportunities. "Once people can work and live at 1,000 feet," predicts Athelstan Spilhaus, "the whole of the continental shelf, an area of 10 million square miles—larger than North America—will be opened up as a new continent for our use. Oil drilling, mining, salvage and even fish farming can be done by people down there and not, as now, on the end of the string from a wobbly surface."

THE ocean is a huge sump, a repository for all the nutrient chemicals that have washed off the land from the beginning of time. But chemicals are generally useful for plant production only when they lie within about 300 feet of the surface, where sunlight is adequate for photosynthesis. And as plants grow and are eaten by animals which die or are eaten by other animals, the chemicals continually drift downward.

But nutrient-rich deep waters can be raised toward the surface. Natural winds that plow the ocean already help bring them up. Some scientists suggest that the same results could be achieved artificially by installing a nuclear reactor at the ocean bottom to heat up deeper water layers so they would rise to the top. Economical? Perhaps not, if heating water were the only purpose of a reactor. "But," argues Dean Spilhaus, "the waste heat from nuclear reactors used for other purposes may well be used in this way." Among the cost-spreading other purposes would be oil drilling and mineral mining on the sea floor.

The answer to the problem of fertilizing stretches of ocean lies in what are known as trace elements, or micronutrients—chemicals such as iodine, zinc, boron and cobalt which are found in minute quantities in plant and animal tissue but which are essential to life processes. Parts of the sea, as well as areas of land, may lack the necessary micronutrients, but to correct the deficiency may be easier than many people think. As Harvard's Roger Revelle, one of the nation's most distinguished oceanographers, points out:

"In Australia, for example, there is a deficiency of cobalt, a basic substance of one of the vitamin B compounds. By simply flying over sheep ranges in an airplane and spraying a thin layer of cobalt-containing material, sheep production can be greatly increased. Apparently exactly the same kind of deficiency occurs in the sea. Substances present in very, very small amounts — a few parts per billion — exercise a controlling effect on the productivity of the sea. But it may be possible, by spreading a few thousand tons of micronutrients off the coasts of the world, for us to greatly increase the harvest of the sea."

Mariculturists also visualize two other analogues to land farming: weeding and fencing.

"By using what the marine scientists know about the food chain," Spilhaus told a recent National Conference on Sea-Grant Colleges, "we can eliminate some of the unnecessary and less useful species; that is, intervene in a way that might be called 'weeding the sea.'" Even simpler would be dragging with nets.

Proposals for fences include barriers of air bubbles and electronic impulses. Recently, Paul M. Fye, president of Woods Hole (Mass.) Oceanographic Institution, told of discovering a natural underwater fence during a dive in a tiny research submarine.

"As we went across the coral sandy reef close to New Providence Island," Fye said, "we crossed what might be considered a barren desert in the ocean—no plants, no fish, almost nothing of any kind. Suddenly, we came into an area with a great profusion of fish, the likes of which I hadn't imagined existing in the ocean. Yet just across the width of the submarine — a six-foot sphere—looking out the other window, there wasn't a single fish.

"For two hours I observed an invisible fence in the ocean as sharp as you could possibly draw it. Why was it there? How did nature create such a fence? Is it one we could reproduce for our own convenience?"

THOUGH this and other mysteries suggest that marine research is still in its infancy, enthusiasts are already making plans for the future. Suppose, for example, fishermen decided to farm a 10,000-square-mile section of the sea off Cape Cod. The area could be fenced by means of perforated air hoses on the ocean floor that would send streams of bubbles to the surface, preventing the cultivated fish from wandering. (If necessary, chemicals could be introduced into the bubble curtain to make it more effective.) With the fish fenced in, their growth could be stimulated by raising nutrient-rich water from lower levels and by adding fertilizing trace elements from the top. By periodic dragging with nets, the area could be weeded and trash fish removed so that the cultivated fish would get all the nutrients.

"One of the most fascinating future possibilities," says Frank Hester of the Bureau of Commercial Fisheries, "is the use of marine animals as 'sheepdogs' to tend fish and run errands." As if to underscore the possibility, Navy scientists recently reported that dolphins have been trained to attach wires to torpedoes and missiles lying on the ocean floor to simplify recovery operations; the dolphins are so domesticated that even though they are swimming freely in the open sea they swim back to their base when their job is done.

Encouraged by some recent successes in training fish, Hester also suggested that killer whales might be trained to herd schools of blue whales, whose massive bodies of red meat grow bigger and faster than any Black Angus. A blue whale doubles its birth weight in a week; it grows from two tons to 20 tons in six months --about 200 pounds a day. And if the killer whales prove to be poor herdsmen, Gifford Pinchot, a Johns Hopkins biology professor, offers another plan. He proposes raising mammoth blue whales in lagoons on a diet of enriched plankton (algae and other organisms) for harvesting when the creatures reach their adult weight of 130 tons.

CONSUMERS, of course, may not care for blue whale steak—or seaweed vinaigrette or algae soufflé. Tastes in food are difficult to change, and it may take a while until they reach the status of sought-after delicacies. Yet, educated to the high protein content, even relatively well-fed people may be induced to include more products from the sea in their diet. After all, smoked shark fillets have become a British delicacy. In Russia, whale meat is now blended in beef and pork sausages. Japanese tuna hot dogs taste like the original but cost much less.

The technical and scientific obstacles to large-scale sea farming are more to the point, perhaps. And not the least set of problems will stem from the attempt to change man's natural environment. No one can closely predict the effect on land temperatures of a nuclear reactor that heats part of an ocean, for example, but it might be that a warm-water fish farm in the Bering Sea, say, would change the prevailing weather pattern in the area near Seattle.

Nevertheless, man's instinct for inventive exploration, sharpened by the prospects of a worsening food shortage for a rising world population, promises to make sea farming not only necessary and feasible but inevitable. ■

SHORT-PLANT RICE MAY DOUBLE CROP

IR8 Type Makes Philippines Self-Sufficient in Cereal

By HOWARD TAUBMAN

Special to The New York Times

LOS BANOS, Philippines — May 26—The half of the world that depends on rice as its staple food can put an end to its chronic shortages if it will turn to the short, sturdy plant type known as IR8, or the improvements now being studied at the International Rice Research Institute.

This dazzling prospect was outlined here with the typical understatement of a Maine man by Robert F. Chandler, who has been the head of the research institute since its establishment in 1959 on the rolling, wooded campus of the University of the Philippines College of Agriculture.

Mr. Chandler has a strong distaste for the kind of ballyhoo that has accompanied IR8 since 1966 when it was made available to farmers in the Philippines and other rice-growing countries. However, he does not deny that IR8 and its successors, now being studied at I.R.R.I., could make a vast difference in the world's food problems.

"It would be possible to double the world's rice crop," said Mr. Chandler, "if all the rice-growing areas turned to the short plant type, and farmed it properly. Doubling the crop would satisfy present rice demands."

Impact on Nation

Mr. Chandler warned that the solution would only be a holding operation. "We would still have to do something about this increase or make further advances in rice culture," he said.

IR8, which has been dubbed "the miracle rice" in the Philippines and other countries where it has produced impressive results, has made a tremendous difference to this nation.

In less than two years, according to Mr. Chandler, the Philippines has become self-sufficient in rice after years of shortages. He was careful, however, to give the Government a large share of the credit.

"President Ferdinand E. Marcos and his Government," he said, have conducted an intensive educational campaign and followed it up with constant supervision and advice in the villages and on the farms."

The first versions of IR8 were developed at I.R.R.I. in 1965. The scientists were not willing to pronounce it ready for distribution until the next year.

Despite the results obtained by IR8, the rice has become a subject of controversy in the Philippines. Probably because the first local newspaper reports were too ecstatic, there was a reaction.

May 27, 1968

Developers of High-Yield Grains Report a Victory Over Drought and Disease

By JUAN de ONIS

Special to The New York Times

MEXICO CITY, Sept. 15 — The developers of the high-yield cereals that are increasing food production dramatically in hungry countries reported today a major victory for their seeds over drought and disease.

The International Maize and Wheat Improvement Center here, which has developed and propagated the new wheat and corn varieties, said in its annual review of its worldwide program that Mexican dwarf wheat varieties had produced record harvests in India and Pakistan despite unfavorable rainfall that would previously have meant crop failure.

"The 1969 harvest should convince all skeptics that the green revolution has deep, strong roots," the report said. It predicted that India's 500-million people would be self-sufficient in wheat in two years.

New Varieties Popular

As a result of the spreading use of the "miracle" wheat, corn and rice, food production specialists here said that crucial decades had been gained in the race to keep food output apace with population growth in developing countries.

The success of the high-yield wheat varieties has contributed, the report said, to farmers' rapid adoption of new seed varieties and improved technology for production of corn and rice.

"The new yield level of wheat, rice and maize in several food-deficit countries combined with greatly increased efficiency in multiple cropping systems has drastically changed the outlook for world food production for the next two or three decades," the report said. It added:

"It is now clear that these developments can provide a brief period for bringing population growth into balance with the rapidly expanding demand for more jobs, schools, housing, medical and recreational facilities, as well as that indispensable item — food."

Demand Is Stimulated

The report estimated this year's wheat production in India at 19.5 million metric tons, while it said that Pakistan had achieved a slight surplus in wheat — after years of requiring United States wheat to avoid famine — with a production of eight million tons.

These outputs compare with 1965 crops of 12.5 million tons in India and 4.6 million tons in Pakistan.

"The production increases have stimulated the demand for fertilizer, pesticides, farm machinery, sewing machines and transistor radios," the report said. "There is growing demand for better housing, more and better schools, more warehouses, more trucks, better roads and more electricity."

For many years development experts have identified the weakness of productivity and farm income in developing countries as the key obstacles to industrial growth. These countries hold two-thirds of the world's population.

The center, which is supported by the Rockefeller and Ford Foundations as well as the Mexican Government, said that wheat production in Mexico and Turkey was also at record levels because of wider sowing of the high-yield varieties.

These have been developed during 25 years of research by the Rockefeller Foundation here. The seeds began to be commercially available in quantity in the 1967 crop year.

The Ford Foundation has entered the program recently. It has emphasized the irrigation and fertilization methods required to realize the production potential of the new varieties.

Showing good resistance to rust, root rot and other diseases harmful to production, the seeds are being sown increasingly in North Africa — particularly in Tunisia — and in Afghanistan, Iran, Kenya and other developing countries. The center has opened an office in Lebanon to help Middle Eastern countries.

The report said that 20 million acres were sown in the new wheat varieties this year. The center also reported major strides in its program to increase both production and the nutritional quality of corn, particularly in the Andean and tropical countries where corn is a more basic food than wheat.

A major objective has been to incorporate high-protein strains into local corn. Consumption of such improved corn can double the protein intake in countries where protein deficiency among the poor is a major health problem.

The center, under the direction of Dr. Edwin Wellhausen, trains specialists in agricultural research and production technology from all over the world.

September 16, 1969

High-Protein Food, Created in Laboratories, Is Starting to Enter the Consumer's Diet

By SANDRA BLAKESLEE

In the dank basement of a laboratory on Long Island the other day, a research scientist crouched before a glass cauldron filled with a yellowish, translucent liquid that bubbled furiously beneath a bright light.

"Grow, my darlings, grow," he murmured. "Are you warm enough? Want some more ammonia?"

He craned his neck up and around to face a visitor and said with a sigh, "They're very finicky; if you don't give them everything they want — the right minerals, the right temperature — they'll up and die on you."

Hours later the liquid in the vat had changed—into a deeper, creamier yellow, richly opaque. "Aha," the scientist exclaimed, "they're growing!" He then skimmed off a cupful of the liquid, held it at arm's length, grinned and pronounced, "Food!"

The laboratory-produced food is called Single Cell Protein, and it is one of the newest in a line of "man-made" protein foods that are derived from the chemistry set rather than the pig, pond or peapatch in response to alarming signs of a growing world food shortage.

A New Kind of Food

SCP is a totally new kind of food—a tasteless, odorless mass of edible micro-organisms that are treated, dried and fed to animals. Toxic effects have been minimal, depending on the nature of the process used. In a few short years, SCP may become human food.

Some other new high-protein foods or food components that are engineered in the laboratory, however, are already filtering into the American consumer's daily diet. They include spun soybean fiber and synthetic amino acids.

And still some other foods are just around the corner—alfalfa extract, fish protein concentrate, cultured algae and a group of "superplants" that may one day pack the nutritive wallop of "steak on the stalk."

Spun soybean fibers doctored to taste like real meats are being test-marketed in several Northeastern states, often without the consumer's knowledge. Dozens of hospitals, prisons, public restaurants, schools and industrial cafeterias are using such "meat analogues" in their everyday recipes.

Called 'Mock Meat'

Skeptics are fond of calling the new food products "imitation meat," "fake food," "food of the loom," "mock meat" and so on. They are disturbed by the fact that up to 50 per cent of the ingredients in the final product are chemically derived food additives. Manufacturers prefer to call the new foods "vegetable proteins" because they are derived from a natural food source. In any case many soymeats are almost impossible to tell from the real thing, especially when prepared in highly seasoned dishes.

But at least one ersatz "meat" is being sold, successfully so, on its own merits. It is a General Mills product called "BacOs." It looks like bacon bits but is actually spun soybean. The company estimates that more than six million jars of BacOs were purchased last year at an average retail price of 69 cents. United Airlines serves BacOs in its salads.

Most soybean "meats" today are being sold to food processors, who use the products to extend real meats in their convenience preparations. The law requires that such processors list "vegetable protein" as an ingredient on their package labels.

Food processors are attracted to these ersatz meats for several reasons. They are slightly cheaper than real meats, ready cooked and frozen, will not shrink in preparation and require less prep-preparation. In 10 years imitation meats are expected to be a \$2-billion industry.

The New York Times (by Neal Boenzi)

Research worker developing high protein food components

Scientists, population experts and international leaders are interested in new sources of protein because conventional food supplies are already dwindling the world over. There is not enough meat, cereal and fish being harvested for everyone now on the planet. It is estimated that 10,000 people die each day of malnutrition, which is simply the lack of adequate protein in their diets. Meantime, the experts say, the population is exploding with the ferocity of an unchecked nuclear reaction.

More Protein Is Target

For this reason many scientists have become modern-day foragers, armed with microscopes and technology rather than guns and plows. They are looking not only for ways to grow more food on available land, but also for ways to improve the quality of the existing food supply. The quarry is more protein, not just more food.

This is because not just any protein will do. The problem of adequate protein nutrition is analogous to a very complex jigsaw puzzle. The key to the puzzle is in the structure of protein itself.

There are about 20 amino acids, a class of organic compound, that combine in various ways to produce protein in the human body. The body is able to synthesize most of these amino acids except for eight (nine in children) which are called "essential amino acids." These essential amino acids must be gotten into the body through foods eaten.

Many foods provide enough calories for energy and even some nonessential amino acids. But it is the essential amino acids that are important and in short supply around the world.

One of the most exotic of the new foods is the Single Cell Protein being produced in the Long Island laboratory.

Shortcut in Food Chain

The main advantage of SCP is that it provides a shortcut in the food chain. Cattle must graze on tons of grass and feeds to produce a few pounds of protein. Single cell organisms, however, are able to convert one pound of "waste" material (such as crude oil, methane gas, bagasse, old newspapers and so on) into one pound of cells, or about one-half pound of pure protein. The organisms can also be grown in the factory, in a kind of farm that is not dependent on weather or pesticides.

Paradoxically, man through the ages has sought to control, often to kill, many single cell organisms (yeasts, bacteria and fungi) that brought disease and discomfort. Now the reverse is becoming true. Not all microscopic organisms are bad; some are and always have been truly beneficial to man. [Blue cheese and yogurt owe their zesty tastes to micro-organism.] Now many scientists are working to cultivate more of these friendly "bugs."

The "bugs" are legion. Millions upon millions of them live in the air, soil and water of the earth. They are such basic units of life that scientists are really not sure if they should be labeled plants or animals. In any case, they possess inside their cell walls all the vital components of life—especially proteins that the scientists aim to extract.

Many micro-organisms thrive on materials that man has traditionally thrown away—on garbage of all sorts. The tiny organisms use hydrogen, carbon and cellulose components of waste material for their own food. They convert into protein what man could not possibly eat himself.

One excellent source of hydrocarbon (food for the friendly "bugs") comes from the petroleum industry. Today 26 major oil companies are engaged in SCP research, trying to find an economical way to grow the "bugs" on petroleum products.

Means of Cultivation

There are many different ways to cultivate SCP and each oil company has tended to strike off on its own, cloaking its projects in secrecy with hopes of eventually patenting the process they find most economical.

SCP is now being grown experimentally on methane gas, paraffin and crude oil. So far yeasts and bacteria have shown most promise.

Generally the techniques used include setting up a culture medium in which water and the hydrocarbon substrate are mixed. The micro-organism is introduced into the bath. Since the "bugs" are finicky, temperature must be strictly controlled. If it gets too cold or too hot they simply refuse to multiply.

The organisms also demand to be fed extras—nitrogen, potassium, phosphorus, magnesium and sulphur. These minerals can be manipulated in various concentrations to alter the protein content of the individual cells. The best mixture of minerals will produce the best quality protein.

Once in the bath the micro-organisms begin to divide, some as quickly as every two minutes, some as slowly as every two days. Different organisms divide at different rates.

As they multiply, batches of the organisms are skimmed off, put through a centrifuge, dried and fed to animals.

Work on the System

While SCP in human diets may be 10 years off, another unusual source of protein is here today.

The source is the lowly soybean, a bitter nugget that humans find hard to digest. Soybeans are an excellent source of protein, from 40 to 60 per cent in each bean, and they have traditionally been fed to animals after valuable oil has been squeezed out. The left-over mash can also be used to manufacture pressgate, glue or other industrial products.

Several major food manufacturers have now found ways to engineer soybean mash into food "analogues," that is, into entirely new foods analogous to traditional foods.

Such soy products are able to imitate, with varying degrees of success, such things as ground beef, diced chicken, scallops, bacon and turkey. One manufacturer now sells an "imitation" turkey loaf that comes with a plastic wishbone.

Soy meal is also being widely used, in an unprocessed form, as an ingredient in various high-protein "formulas," such as gruels, for use in developing countries. Such mixtures are meant as dietary supplements. They include Incaparina, Pro-Nutro, Fortifez, Multi-Purpose Food and L'Aubina.

'Junk Fish' Concentrate

Synthetic amino acids, which are just being chemically synthesized in the laboratory at viable costs, can be added to traditional foods to increase nutritive value.

Fish Protein Concentrate, another new source of protein, is derived from ground-up, whole fish that would not normally be eaten. "Junk fish" such as hake can be turned into a safe, tasteless, odorless powder high in protein, which in turn can be added to familiar foods.

The process by which soy meal is fashioned into familiar foods involves some cribbing from the textile industry. The mash is actually spun, like cotton fibers, into stringy soy fibers that are further treated to taste, look and feel like real foods.

Forage plants such as alfalfa, water hyacinths and elephant grass are a good source of protein, but one that man may not use directly because of hard-to-digest cellulose encapsulating the protein. Scientists have found ways, however, to squeeze the "protein juice" from the plants. Bitter tastes and green color can be removed, leaving another nutritious powder for addition to familiar foods.

Finally, new "superplants" may be developed with all the protein value of a T-bone steak inside their kernels. Lysine, one of the eight essential amino acids, has already been bred into a variety of corn, called opaque-2 after a lysine-carrying gene.

March 1, 1970

U.S. Agronomist Gets Nobel Peace Prize

By BERNARD WEINRAUB
Special to The New York Times

OSLO, Norway, Oct. 21—An Iowa-born crop expert who has sought to ease the world's hunger with research into improved strains of wheat and rice was awarded the Nobel Peace Prize for 1970 today.

Dr. Norman E. Borlaug, who heads a team of scientists from 17 nations experimenting in Mexico with high-yield grains, was given the prize, valued at $78,000, for his "great contribution" in spurring food production, especially in Mexico, India and Pakistan.

He is director of the International Maize and Wheat Improvement Center of Mexico, a research organization operated by the Rockefeller Foundation in cooperation with the Mexican Government.

"Dr. Borlaug, as the prime mover in the 'green revolution,' has made it possible for the developing countries to break away from hunger and poverty," said the chairman of the five-member prize committee, Mrs. Aase Lionaes, who is president of one of the segments of the unicameral Norwegian Parliament.

"Dr. Borlaug, through his improvement of wheat and rice plants, has created a technological breakthrough which makes it possible to abolish hunger in the developing countries in the course of a few years," she said.

Dr. Borlaug, 56 years old, the son of Norwegian immigrants and a resident of Mexico City, said during a visit to Norway in August: "The world's population problem is a monster which, unless tamed, will one day wipe us from the earth's surface."

The most recent award of the Nobel Peace Prize to an American was made to Dr. Martin Luther King Jr. in 1964. Other recent American peace laureates were Dr. Linus C. Pauling in 1962, Gen. George C. Marshall in 1953 and Dr. Ralph J. Bunche in 1950. Last year's winner was the International Labor Organization.

The 1970 laureate—one of 38 nominees—was born in Cresco, Iowa, and educated at the University of Minnesota. Since 1944 he has worked on plant pathology and agricultural projects, mostly in Mexico, to increase food production in countries where hunger remains a searing problem.

The award was announced in a third-floor board room of the green stone Norwegian Nobel Institute, which is across the street from the United States Embassy.

Mrs. Lionaes, seated before television cameras and reading in Norwegian and later in English, said:

"The Nobel Committee of the

Norwegian Parliament has decided to award the Nobel Peace Prize in 1970 to Dr. Norman E. Borlaug for his great contribution toward creating a new world situation with regard to nutrition."

Helps on Population Also

After taking note of his efforts to improve wheat and rice strains, she said:

"By his work he has also contributed to the solution of another main problem of today, namely the population explosion.

"The kinds of grain which are the result of Dr. Borlaug's work speed economic growth in general in the developing countries. In short, we do not any longer have to be pessimistic about the economic future of the developing countries."

"If the economists and politicians of the world today can make a similar contribution toward a peaceful balanced development in the third world as Dr. Borlaug has made in the field of nutrition, we can all be more optimistic with regard to a peaceful world," she added.

The five committee members then left, declining, as in past years, to discuss the other nominations for the 70-year-old prize and the committee's private meetings over the last few months.

The other committee members—nominated for a period of six years by the Norwegian Parliament—are Bernt Ingvaldsen, President of Parliament; Helge Refsum, a High Court judge; John Sanness, a University of Oslo professor and director of the Norwegian Institute of International Affairs, and Sjur Lindebraekke, director of Bergens Privatbank, the largest in Bergen.

The judges will award the prize in Oslo on Dec. 10, the anniversary of the death of Alfred Nobel, who endowed the prizes.

United Press International

Dr. Borlaug in Mexico yesterday with wheat he developed

The award came as something of a surprise. In recent weeks two prominent names have been mentioned, publicly and privately: the most Rev. Helder Câmara, Roman Catholic Archbishop of Olinda and Recife, Brazil, who has spoken out against alleged torture and repression of dissidents and has been a center of controversy in the Brazilian Government, and Danilo Dolci, who has spent more than 20 years crusading against poverty, injustice and the Mafia in Italy.

Candidates ofr the peace prize—as for all prizes—must be proposed before Feb. 1. Recommendations for the peade prize may be made by a wide range of individuals, including former laureates, members of parliaments and governments, officials of the International Arbitration Court at The Hague, and university professors of political science, law, history and philosophy.

Prize to Aid Research

Special to The New York Times

MEXICO CITY, Oct. 21—Dr. Borlaug said here today he would use the $78,000 prize to further his research in richer strains of wheat to alleviate world hunger and "perhaps win another Nobel Prize."

Dr. Borlaug was informed of his Nobel Peace Prize award late this morning by his wife while he was working on an experimental farm some 40 miles west of here at Atizapán de Metepec. He refused to return to Mexico City for a news conference until he had finished his day's work in checking a new type of "triple-dwarf" wheat.

Dr. Borlaug said that the Nobel Prize should have been awarded not just to him but to all members of his team of Mexican experts with whom he has been working since 1944.

He predicted a gloomy fate for mankind if the present rate of population increase continued.

"We have only delayed the world food crisis for another 30 years," Dr. Borlaug said. "If the world population continues to increase at the same rate, we will destroy the species."

October 22, 1970

Corn

Double Threat To a Staple

Corn, the most extensively harvested crop in the United States and the food staple for most of Latin America, is being threatened on two fronts, according to reports issued in recent weeks:

- The plant breeders responsible for the extraordinary productivity of hybrid corn have produced varieties so uniform and universally planted that the crop is highly vulnerable to new blights, such as the one that struck the United States in 1970.
- The wild corn-like weed that is believed to cross-breed with corn, periodically reinjecting vitality into the plant, is threatened with extinction.

The threat to corn is but a dramatic example of a hazard that faces most of the world's basic food crops. Despite many millenia of agriculture, those basic foods are still few in number: rice, wheat and corn, with sorghum and potatoes of lesser importance.

The genetic uniformity of such crops has been a triumph of plant breeding, satisfying farmers who want high-yield crops suited to machine cultivation, machine harvesting and machine processing. Now, according to a report to the National Research Council of the National Academy of Sciences, plant science must produce varieties that not only meet such demands but also retain enough genetic diversity to survive a fungus or other blight to which one or two strains are vulnerable.

In warning of the perils of crop

uniformity, the report, entitled "Genetic Vulnerability of Major Crops," cites ominous precedents.

In the 1840's the Irish grew a single variety of potato called the Lumper. Since potatoes are typically grown by cutting up and planting the previous year's potatoes (rather than from seed), cross-fertilization is eliminated and crops tend to become regionally uniform. A fungus to which Lumper potatoes were highly vulnerable appeared in Ireland in the 1840's and a catastrophic famine followed.

In 1942 a fungus to which the rice grown in Bengal was vulnerable struck a crop already weakened by a typhoon. Tens of thousands of persons died in the resulting famine.

In 1870 Ceylon grew most of the world's coffee and it was the favorite beverage along Piccadilly and the Strand in London. But the coffee was vulnerable to a rust and in 1885 not a single bag was exported. As a result, said the report, "the British became a nation of tea-drinkers."

The latest such calamity, and the one responsible for the new report, was the corn blight that hit Florida early in 1970 and moved north with the spring season. About half the crop was destroyed in the South and 15 per cent was lost nationally. The blight was caused by a fungus whose spores, in heavily infected fields, "boiled blackly" above the harvesting machines, according to the report.

The alarm was sounded for the wild weed—a cousin of corn—by Dr. H. Garrison Wilkes of the University of Massachusetts in the Sept. 22 issue of Science. The cousin, which some believe was the ancestor of corn, is teosinte. It is native to Mexico, where the cultivation of corn is thought to have originated, and its cross-breeding with corn, over thousands of years, is thought to have helped sustain the vigor of that food crop.

Teosinte grows within Mexican corn fields and around their edges but, Dr. Wilkes said, current farming practices are wiping it out. It appears to be only half as extensive as it was in 1900 and, he reported, "in the last 10 years I have watched the rate of extinction accelerate." He added: "We can ill afford the loss of such genetic wealth in this day of exploding population."

The origins of corn remain controversial. It is said to be the only food crop whose cultivation began so long ago and which was so drastically changed that its origins are obscure.

In a lecture at the Connecticut Agricultural Experiment station in New Haven last month Dr. George Beadle, Nobel Laureate and former president of the University of Chicago, pointed out that when Columbus first sighted America, the Indians had already developed 200 or 300 types of corn—essentially all that exist today. "Theirs," he said, "was the most remarkable achievement in plant breeding in all of man's existence."

He said that the Indians bred the wild ancestor of corn into a plant that was—and is—completely dependent for survival on human hands.

A corn plant has the ability, to fertilize itself. The tassel at the top produces male pollen that fertilizes the female flowers that become ears. In the early days, to achieve the cross-breeding of different strains, self-fertilization had to be prevented. Thousands of boys were hired to pull the tassels from one corn strain so that it would only be fertilized by pollen from a neighboring strain.

Then a type of corn was found in Texas whose tassels are sterile, obviating the need for tassel-pulling. This characteristic is carried in the cellular material, or cytoplasm, of the corn and in 1970 virtually every corn farmer in the United States grew corn containing this "Texas cytoplasm." The blight, to which this corn was highly vulnerable, was a disaster for many farmers.

The corn strains planted this year were selected for resistance to such a blight, but if the world's food crops become too uniform, with no variations or wild forms in reserve, at some future time a resistant strain might no longer be available.

—WALTER SULLIVAN

October 8, 1972

Research Finds Rich Sorghums To Bolster Diet of World's Poor

By HAROLD M. SCHMECK Jr.

Special to The New York Times

WASHINGTON, Sept. 28—A scientific discovery that promises a powerful new weapon against starvation and malnutrition among millions of people in the poorest nations of the world was announced today by the State Department and Purdue University.

Agricultural scientists at Purdue, supported by the Agency for International Development, reported discovering two naturally occurring strains of sorghum that are nutritionally far superior to the varieties of that cereal on which more than 300 million people throughout the world subsist. The scientists said the nutritionally valuable trait should be easy to transfer to other types of sorghum.

Although used little for food in this country, sorghum is the fourth most important cereal crop in the world. Only wheat, rice and corn are more widely used.

Because sorghum can be grown on land that is too dry and, often, too infertile for other cereals, it has become the subsistence crop of the most impoverished communities. Unfortunately, it provides a low quality of protein, having little of the essential amino acid lysine—a building block of protein found in more generous amounts in meat and dairy products.

The scientists at Purdue, analyzing 9,000 kinds of sorghum from all over the world, found two strains from Ethiopia that were far richer in protein and lysine than any commonly used types. The trait for lysine richness proved to be governed by a single gene, the scientists said at a news conference today, thus making the trait relatively easy to transfer to other varieties.

"When we recall that sorghum is the principal subsistence cereal for more than 300 million people — indeed the poorest people in the world's poorest countries — improving its protein quality will amount to a gift of life, especially for children," said Dr. John A. Hannah, administrator of the Agency for International Development.

In many parts of Africa, he said, almost every child under five years or age suffers from protein malnutrition; in Latin America more than half of childhood deaths are related to malnutrition, and in India an estimated 80 per cent of preschool children are retarded in growth by malnutrition.

AID, which has supported the research at Purdue under a $1.7-million contract, estimated that it would be three to five years before improved sorghum varieties became available for human consumption. How long it will be before the new sorghums would make any impact on agriculture and nutrition in the protein-poor regions of the world, however, remained problematical.

First, agriculturally useful strains have to be developed. Next, farmers have to be persuaded to use them. Lysine-rich corn was introduced nearly a decade ago but is still much less widely used than its proponents would wish.

Dr. John D. Axtell, a member of the Purdue scientific team, said today that the two Ethiopian strains were presumably grown as crops in some parts of that African country. He said investigators would visit Ethiopia this year to find out where this sorghum was grown, how widely it was used and how useful it was nutritionally to the people who consumed it.

Dr. Axtell said that an Indian graduate student at Purdue, Rameshwar Singh, who was credited with a principal role in finding the two valuable strains, had returned to India and was presumably working already to transfer the strains' important trait to locally grown sorghum.

Tests in Puerto Rico suggest that the two Ethiopian strains give a good crop yield, but the scientists as yet have no solid data comparing them with other sorghum.

Another key discovery in the research at Purdue helps to explain why some widely used types of sorghum are so poor nutritionally. Dr. D. L. Oswalt explained that dark colored varieties of sorghum were widely grown in some of the countries that depended on this cereal because birds did not seem to like them. Crops of other, light colored varieties, are sometimes destroyed by birds before they can be harvested, he said.

Dr. Oswalt's studies have shown, however, that the dark varieties have large amounts of pigment-containing chemicals called tannins that somehow reduce the nutritional effectiveness of the cereal even if it is enriched with lysine. Research is in progress to make lysine-rich varieties of sorghum "bird resistant" without lowering their nutritional value, or to remove the tannins through the milling process after harvesting.

In the most direct studies of the nutritional value of the two Ethiopian strains of sorghum, weaning rats were fed them for 28 days as the principal part of their diet. The rats fed one of the two strains gained three times as much weight as rats fed ordinary sorghum. The weight gain was twice that of rats eating ordinary sorghum when the other strain was used.

The scientists present at the news conference today said the research on sorghum was a multi-disciplinary effort involving scientists from several institutions and that the work had been in progress for at least seven years.

September 29, 1973

New Corn Type Exceeds Beef in Quality of Protein

By BOYCE RENSBERGER
Special to The New York Times

EL BATAN, Mexico—Scientists at the International Corn and Wheat Improvement Center here have developed a new variety of corn that surpasses beef in protein quality and, pound for pound, contains twice as much protein as milk.

Despite the advantages, however, farmers are not growing it. Ignorant of the principles of nutrition and beyond the reach of present education efforts, they are unable to perceive any advantage in the new corn over traditional varieties that look and grow the same.

In experiments in Colombia, where large numbers of poor people depend on ordinary corn as their chief food source—as do millions throughout Latin America and Africa—feeding of the new variety have dramatically reversed cases of near fatal protein deficiency.

'Dramatic Demonstrations'

The subjects in the experiments were children dying because of too great a reliance on ordinary corn, which lacks two essential amino acids, without which the human body cannot take up much of the protein in ordinary corn.

The researchers who developed the new corn are now faced with the difficulty of persuading farmers to raise it. Because its yields in weight are no greater than ordinary corn it brings no more at the market because farmers are paid for the quantity and not the quality of what they sell.

"We've had all these dramatic demonstrations of what this means to sick children and could mean to people in general," said Dr. Ernest W. Sprague, director of the center's corn research, "but the average small farmer doesn't know about this."

At present the new variety, known as opaque-2 corn, is being grown only in relatively small areas in the United States, Brazil and Colombia. Virtually all the production goes to make animal feed.

The story of opaque-2 corn began in 1963 when scientists at Purdue University in Indiana discovered that a mutant of the corn plant that produced opaque rather than translucent kernels also had unusually high levels of the two amino acids in which ordinary corn was deficient.

The protein that human beings must consume to live is broken down through digestion to 18 component amino acids. For the amino acids to be reassembled in the body into various types of protein, certain quantities of all the amino acids must be available in the proper balance. If some amino acids are missing, many of the others cannot be used and are excreted.

Ordinary corn is so deficient in the two amino acids lysine and tryptophone that nearly half the protein available in corn is unusable by the body. Opaque-2 corn, it was found, had enough lysine and tryptophane that 90 per cent of the protein could be used by the body, thus nearly doubling the effective protein content.

After the Purdue discovery, Dr. Sprague and his staff at CIMMYT (the acronym from the center's name in Spanish: Centro Internacional de Mejoramiento de Maiz y Trigo) began work to turn what was essentially a laboratory find into an agriculturally useful crop.

Despite its high nutritive value, opaque-2 corn suffered from having a soft, white, floury kernel instead of the hard yellow kernel that corn growers know. Farmers did not like it because the less dense kernel weighed less than normal, reducing an acre's yield 10 per cent by weight. The softer kernel was also more vulnerable to rot and insects. Furthermore it did not grind well into the meal or grits from which most corn dishes are cooked.

"With disadvantages like that," Dr. Sprague said, "there was just no way we were going to feed people with it. For the last few years we've been engaged in a breeding program to combine the opaque-2 gene with the other desirable characteristics."

By crossing opaque-2 corn with others, CIMMYT corn breeders have now produced a number of high-protein varieties that are yellow, harder kerneled and give yields comparable with ordinary corn. They have also incorporated the desirable characteristics into corn varieties adapted to a range of climatic zones.

Dr. Sprague said that not all the modifications were fully reliable however. On kernel color, for example, the goal has been to make opaque-2 corn that is the traditional yellow. Experimental varieties are now sufficiently developed that better than 90 per cent of the ears from a field will be yellow.

"That's not good enough. The farmer will look at the white ears and consider them sick," Dr. Sprague said. "He'd rather plant his old corn that always comes up yellow."

Some Special Problems

And there remain some special problems. In the Andes, for example, people are familiar with a type of corn that has kernels two or three times the size known in most of the world. Samples of that corn have been obtained and CIMMYT breeders are trying to make crosses with opaque-2 corn to produce a fat-kerneled but super-nutritious corn.

Another problem is that small plots of opaque-2 corn planted near ordinary corn may not yield grain of as high a protein quality because the pollen from the ordinary plants can drift over and fertilize the richer-protein variety. Without the opaque-2 gene in the pollen, the resultant kernels will not be of high protein quality. Whatever seed the farmer saves to plant the next season will be of poorer quality.

Dr. Sprague said the only way around this problem seemed to be the development of local programs to encourage widespread adoption of the new corn, reducing the extent to which it will be planted near ordinary corn.

September 4, 1974

Green Revolution Passes Over Asia Without Expected Upheaval

By VICTOR K. McELHENY
Special to The New York Times

LOS BANOS, Philippines, Sept. 20—Studies in half a dozen Asian countries show that the introduction of revolutionary high-yielding rice varieties is not making the rich richer and the poor poorer, as many social scientists had predicted it would.

The predictions had been that high-yield wheat and rice would favor mechanization of farms, drive labor off the land, concentrate land holdings and generally heighten social and economic inequities in the countryside.

However, studies summarized this month at the International Rice Research Institute here show that the green revolution, which has spread the new varieties through much of Asia since 1966, has exerted little pressure toward enlarging or mechanizing farms.

The survey, conducted in 1971-72 by 30 social scientists from research centers and universities in Pakistan, India, Thailand, Malaysia, Indonesia and the Philippines, covered 2,400 farms in more than 30 villages in those countries.

No Dramatic Change

According to Randolph Barker and Teresa Anden of the institute's department of agricultural economics, the survey found that the size of farms and the form of tenure had "not changed dramatically since the introduction of the modern varieties."

Furthermore, although more machinery, fertilizers and pesticides were used as output and income grew, over half the farms adopting the new technology used more hired labor from within the village, 40 per cent used more family labor and 30 per cent hired extra labor from outside the village.

"The villages where labor-saving technology had been most widely adopted since the introduction of modern varieties also reported the largest number of farmers with increased employment of family and hired labor," the summary asserted. "Thus, any savings in labor appear to have been more than offset by labor requirements due to the new technology."

A Rapid Spread

Recent estimates are that the new varieties of rice are planted on 40 million to 50 million acres in Asian nations outside China—about 20 per cent of the region's rice land. New wheat varieties have spread even further, to an estimated 30 per cent of the region's wheat acreage.

Whether this adoption of the new varieties in less than a decade constitutes success is vigorously disputed. The agricultural technologists who developed the new varieties stress that the rapid spread of the new grain types shows that Asian farmers are eager to adopt higher-yielding grains.

Many other observers say that adoption or proper cultivation of the new varieties has been hindered by ancient social inequalities, which are proving difficult to overcome. They say that glowing predictions in the late nineteen-sixties of rapid movement in Asia toward self-sufficiency in food or even oversupply have proven false.

Such developers of the new varieties as Dr. Robert Chandler, the founding director of the International Rice Research Institute, stick to their opinion that the potential exists to double rice yields in Asia.

Clouding the forecasts is a sharp rise in the price of fertilizer, along with severe shortages in Asia. There are some reports of farmers reverting to traditional varieties for lack of fertilizer.

Good Yields Expected

Interviewed at the Asian Vegetable Research and Development Center in Tainan, Taiwan, which he now heads, Dr. Chandler questioned whether the fertilizer shortage would cut rice yields as drastically as some now fear. He noted that rice varieties more resistant to insects and diseases than earlier modern types, now being planted widely, should give good yields even with low levels of fertilizer.

The surveys summarized at Los Banos were performed before the fertilizer shortage and focused on a point separate from the total spread of the new varieties. The social scientists went to villages where the green revolution would be most likely to take hold and where any social damage would be most likely to be visible. The results of their multination survey differed from reports of increased social disparities made earlier in specific locations, such as the wheat-growing region of the Punjab in India.

Dr. Robert Herdt of the agricultural economics department said the survey was being followed by a much more detailed inquiry into the factors that prevent farmers from getting high yields from the improved varieties. The deterrents include deficient irrigation and shortages of fertilizer and pesticides and of agricultural credit.

The new varieties, short-strawed types that perform best with high levels of fertilizer and generous irrigation, were largely developed from strains bred at the International Rice Research Institute.

The new varieties are said to have added more than 20 million tons annually to the food supply of South and Southeast Asia, which is the yearly rice intake of 100 million people.

Rice yields have been increased from 1,200 pounds an acre to perhaps 2,500 pounds, though this is still less than half of what is regularly achieved at agricultural experiment stations.

Because the study was looking for effects of the green revolution, it focused on villages that were ready for change. They tended to be more prosperous than average and to have become accustomed to fertilizers and pesticides and, in some cases, machinery.

Dr. Herdt said in an interview: "These are not typical of the situation in Asia at all. These are very advanced villages." Because of this, he noted, the villages could be expected to show the effects of the green revolution early and indicate any social hazards.

The survey was performed at a time when many of the farmers were shifting from a first generation of scientifically tailored rice strains toward even more advanced varieties with wide resistance to insects and diseases.

Varieties with even wider ranges of resistance, with even stiffer straw—the straw keeps the plant erect—and built-in adaptation to special conditions, such as the deep water of Bangladesh and Thailand and the cold of Korea, are emerging from the institute.

The farmers surveyed planted the first-generation modern types during the dry season, when insects and disease reduce yields less than during the rainy season. They told interviewers that insect and disease problems were the chief drawbacks of the types then available.

The survey found new rice varieties being planted on farms whose size varied from less than two acres in Indonesia to nearly 20 acres in Thailand and Pakistan. The new types found favor in villages where farm sizes were disparate, where cultivators were diverse and where either machines, or animals provided most of the motive power for plowing. The reliability and completeness of the irrigation systems varied greatly, and the new varieties were often planted with little or no fertilizer.

September 23, 1974

Search for Protein Crucial In Struggle Against Hunger

By JANE E. BRODY

Scientists are juggling plant genes, squeezing juice out of leaves and growing microorganisms on manure in a wide-ranging assault on one of the most fundamental problems of the world's food shortage—how to get more protein for more people.

The push for protein is a major part of the worldwide effort to fight the growing specter of hunger aggravated in recent years by unbridled population growth in already food-poor countries, crop failures caused by droughts and floods, fertilizer shortages and the energy crunch.

As a result, malnutrition is now epidemic in many countries. Experts estimate that nearly a third of the world's people are suffering from hunger and its consequences and that the diets of half the world's children lack adequate protein, the nutrient most essential to proper physical and mental development.

While carbohydrates and fats are most important as energy sources, protein is the core substance of the body's vital organs, including the brain. If a child's diet lacks sufficient protein during critical growth periods, body and mind may be permanently stunted. In adults, protein deficits prevent the proper rebuilding of body tissues.

Protein deficiency also increases susceptibility to infections which, combined with the stress of malnutrition, is the main cause of death among young children in developing countries.

Thus, in laboratories and farm fields throughout the world, scientists from government, industry and the universities are seeking to improve the protein quantity and quality of conventional foods as well as to develop novel sources of protein nutrition.

The approaches, besides extracting protein from leaves, using protein-rich wastes and breeding crops with more and better protein, include fortifying traditional foods and developing new foods from under-utilized proteins.

The United States, the world's major breadbasket, is the leading center for this research and the main source of funds for projects abroad. But the effort is worldwide, with considerable work under way in such industrialized countries as Japan, Scandinavia and England and at internationally supported research centers in Mexico, the Philippines, India, Nigeria and other developing areas.

Proteins (from the Greek for first or primary) are constructed out of about 20 different chemical building blocks called amino acids, all of which contain nitrogen. The human body is able to manufacture 12 of these amino acids from various sources of dietary nitrogen —proteins or parts of proteins that the body digests into molecules called amino groups.

But the remaining eight building blocks, called essential amino acids, cannot be

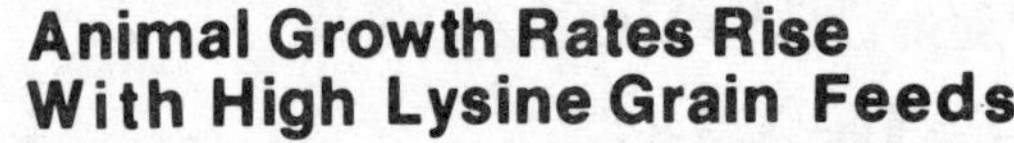

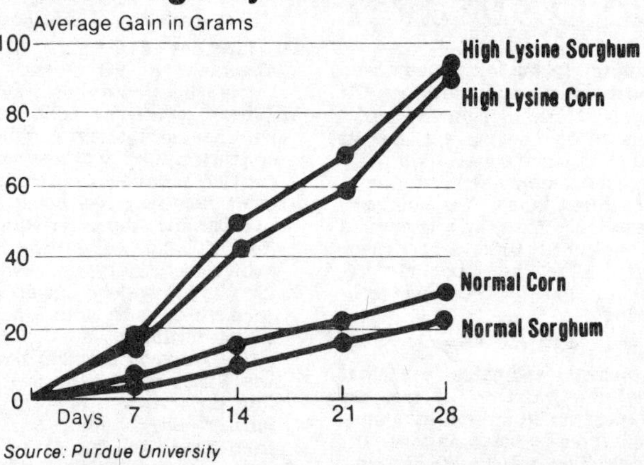

made by human beings and must be supplied as such in the diet. In addition, in order for the body to make the proteins it needs, all the essential amino acids must be consumed in balanced amounts at approximately the same time.

Most Balanced Proteins

The most balanced proteins (that is, those that supply all eight essential amino acids in adequate amounts) come from animals—meat, fish and dairy products—but they provide less than a third of the world's protein.

Plants, which supply about 80 per cent of the protein for people in developing countries, are normally deficient in one or another essential amino acid. In order to obtain usable protein from vegetarian sources then, two different kinds of plant proteins that make up for each other's deficiencies—say, cereals and beans—must be eaten in the same meal.

Most of the current research has centered on plant proteins, which have the potential of adequately nourishing more people at less cost than meat proteins.

For a steer in this country to produce one pound of beef requires the average consumption over its lifetime of four to five pounds of grain. The pound of beef could provide protein for two persons a day, but the grain the animal consumed to produce that meat could theoretically feed four.

Despite all the research, science has not yet had significant impact on the world's protein deficiency. The complexities of the problems are such that new protein foods can take years, even decades, to move from the laboratory bench to the mouths of the hungry. Such factors as tastes, habits, incentives and price as well as the lack of technical and agricultural resources and adequate number of trained personnel all make for delay.

Nonetheless, the scientists are hopeful. Their efforts are founded on the premise that if the earth's resources were optimally used, it should be possible to provide adequate nutrition for the present world population and the more than six billion people who are expected to inhabit the earth in the year 2000.

A survey of scientific results to date has revealed a wide range of promising prospects — some that are now ready for application, others that need minor further development and many that will require years more research.

Plant breeders, who by increasing productivity of crops have thus far kept the world from mass starvation, are now re-engineering some of the most fundamental characteristics of plants to improve their protein yield and quality. Breeding for better protein is one of the key efforts in the current protein thrust and one that is most likely to pay off in the near future.

Plant breeding is the painstaking, prolonged and somewhat unpredictable task of attempting to change the genes of one kind of plant by crossing it with close relatives that contain the desired genetic characteristics.

Perhaps the best known success of plant breeding toward boosting the world's protein supply is the development of the so-called miracle seed of the Green Revolution. These were semidwarf varieties of wheat (an achievement for which Dr. Norman Borlaug received the Nobel Peace Prize in 1970) and rice that, when properly culti-

Above: dented kernels of high lysine corn. Below, tropical type natives like.

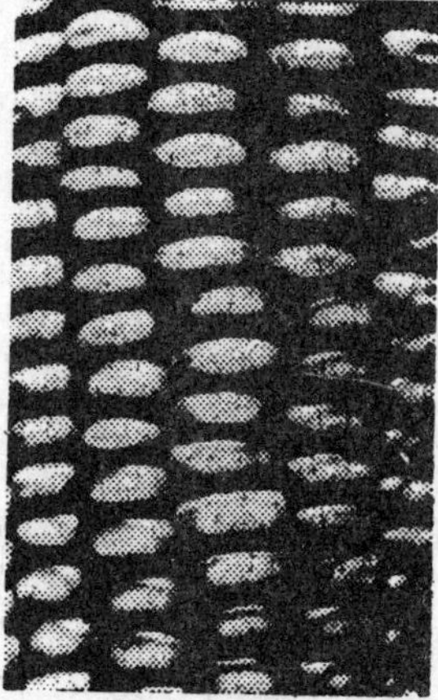

vated with adequate fertilizer and water, can double the yield of grain per acre.

But the grain of the Green Revolution is still deficient in certain essential amino acids, and the emphasis of most of the current breeding work is on improving the amino acid balance of cereal crops.

Studied Protein in Corn

Twenty-eight years ago, when American grain elevators were bursting at the seams with excess grain, Dr. Edwin T. Mertz of Purdue University received a state grant "to figure out some way to use up all this surplus food in a nonfood manner." Since Dr. Mertz was a protein chemist, he began by studying the protein in corn.

Seventeen years later, this low-key effort led to an unexpected success—the discovery, with the plant geneticist Oliver E. Nelson (now at the University of Wisconson), that certain varieties of corn contained twice as much of the amino acids lysine and tryptophan as are found in ordinary corn varieties.

Since these are the two deficient, or limiting, amino

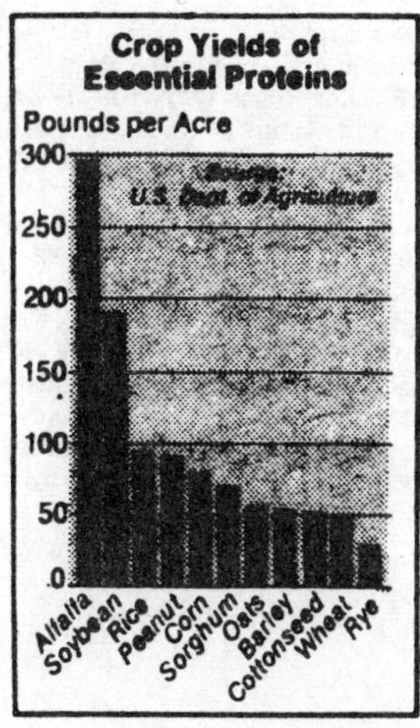

The New York Times/Oct. 11, 1974

acids in corn, the discovery held the prospect of greatly improving the nutritive value of this grain, the principal staple in many countries of Latin America and Black Africa. Indeed, when young rats were raised on high-lysine corn, they grew nearly as well as rats raised on milk protein.

Piglets fed the new variety grew three and a half times faster than piglets fed ordinary corn. In fact, in Colombia a high-lysine corn diet was able to cure children of the severe protein deficiency disease, kwashiorkor, which they had developed from living on a diet of ordinary corn.

But the discovery of high-lysine corn was only the beginning. An incredible amount of work lay ahead to breed the high-lysine gene into otherwise successful native varieties without adversely affecting the desirable characteristics of those varieties.

The high-lysine gene changed the corn kernel from hard to soft, which affected milling characteristics. In addition, explained Dr. Loval (Pete) Bauman, who heads the breeding work at Purdue, the softer kernels were more susceptible to ear-rot and, because the kernels weighed less, the yield per acre was lower.

Yields Almost Normal

Ten years of "backcrossing" have virtually solved the ear-rot problem and yields are now up to 90 per cent of normal. Dr. Bauman said. In backcrossing, the original high-lysine corn was crossed with standard high-quality varieties. The resulting new high-lysine hybrid was then repeatedly crossed with the original standard variety to breed out unwanted genetic characteristics while preserving the high level of lysine.

In each area where corn is grown, the breeding work must be repeated with local varieties in order to preserve the disease resistance and other agronomic characteristics necessary in those regions. High lysine corn is now being tested in many countries around the world, and American farmers grew some 200,000 acres of it last year for animal feed.

Purdue scientists have calculated that by eating only high-lysine corn plus a vitamin-mineral supplement, an adult could eat adequately on 10 cents a day.

As Dr. Mertz put it, the discovery of high-lysine corn "upset the apple cart of plant genetics," which had previously assumed that plant protein could not be changed by breeding. This inspired a search for better quality protein in other cereals.

Thus far, the search has paid off for barley, used mainly as animal feed in this country but an important food grain for about 200 million of the world's disadvantaged people in Eastern and Northern Europe, the Mediterranean and Near East, India and the Andean countries of South America. A high-protein, high-lysine barley strain from Ethiopia was found in screening 1,000 varieties in the World Barley Collection in Beltsville, Md.

Similar success has been achieved for sorghum, the world's fourth most important grain (after wheat, rice and corn), on which some 300 million of the very poorest people in the developing countries of Africa, East Asia and India depend.

High-Lysine Sorghum

Sorghum grows in towering stands, with heavy heads of edible seeds—produced atop tall, thick stalks.

High-lysine sorghum was discovered last year at Purdue by Drs. John D. Axtell, Dallas L. Oswalt and Rameshwar Singh. In six years of analyzing the protein of some 10,000 varieties of sorghum from all over the world under a grant from the Agency for International Development, the Purdue scientists found two varieties from Ethiopia that contain nearly a third more protein and twice as much lysine as other sorghum strains.

Tenant farmers of Ethiopia like to roast the nutty-flavored seeds of these two strains and eat them like nuts, Dr. Axtell discovered on a recent visit there. But only small amounts of these strains are grown because landlords, who get a share of what the farmer sells but not of what he eats, discourage their cultivation.

The varieties have been maintained largely because the tenant farmers plant them hidden in the middle of stands of other sorghum varieties so that landlords would be less likely to notice them, Dr. Axtell said.

Dr. Axtell, an enthusiastic but realistic scientist, estimates that a decade of work lies ahead to breed the high protein quality into native sorghums. Work is already under way toward this end in India, Lebanon and Mexico.

Once the scientists have completed their work, the task remains to convince farmers to grow the new varieties. "It's extremely difficult to get farmers to grow something you tell them is nutritionally superior when they've never even heard of nutrition," Dr. Axtell noted. "In Brazil, with high-lysine corn, they're telling farmers to feed it to their hogs. Once the farmers see how well the hogs thrive, it's easy to convince them that the corn is good for their children, too."

Protein in Oats Studied

A push is also on now to increase the protein content of oats, which have an exceptionally good balance of amino acids and already contain more protein than most cereals, said Dr. Vernon Youngs, a chemist who heads the Agriculture Department's National Oat Quality Laboratory at the University of Wisconsin. Last year, his laboratory analyzed the protein in 28,000 oat samples sent in by breeders throughout the country.

Until now, oat breeding emphasized larger kernels—which gives farmers bigger yields—but larger kernels meant a lower percentage of protein, Dr. Youngs said.

As a result of the new emphasis on protein, two new oat varieties containing about 22 per cent protein have already been released. Their protein content compares to the 17 per cent average of the World Oat Collection and rivals that of meat, which ranges from 20 to 30 per cent.

"Right now, even though oats are such a good food, only 5 to 10 per cent of the U. S. production goes into human foods," Dr. Youngs remarked. "We'd like to change this. We're feeding our animals better than our people."

Another cereal grain that has attracted much research interest is triticale (pronounced trit-i-kaley), a man-made hybrid of wheat and rye that surpasses wheat—the world's main cereal—in both total protein and lysine content. Its main drawback is that its hybrid genes are somewhat unstable, making it an unreliable producer of quality seed, according to Dr. Kenneth Lebsock, an Agriculture Department scientist who is overseeing Government-sponsored work on triticale in India.

Wheat itself appears to be resistant to much change in its protein quantity or quality. Thus far, 15,000 lines in the World Wheat Collection, also housed in Beltsville, have been analyzed but nothing yet has come near the improvement in high-lysine corn.

However, steady progress has been made in developing hybrid wheat, which holds the promise of considerable increases in yield per acre. Scientists at Cargill Wheat Research Farms in Fort Collins, Colo., have just harvested their first crop of hybrid wheat, the seeds of which derived from two high-quality inbred lines.

Hybrid Vigor Concept

Theoretically, according to the concept of hybrid vigor, the hybrid seed should produce a crop better than either of its parents. The achievement depends on the development of one line in which the male part of the plant is sterile, preventing self-pollination, and a second line containing fertility-restoring genes so that fertile seeds will result from a cross with the male-sterile plant

Beans, which Americans look upon as a source of carbohydrate but which much of the world uses for protein, have also begun to attract the interest of plant breeders. Although higher in total protein content than the cereal grains and adequately endowed with lysine, most beans are deficient in other essential amino acids, mainly methionine and cysteine.

At the University of Ife in Nigeria, Dr. Frederick Bliss, a University of Wisconsin plant breeder, helped develop a high-protein (30 per cent) cowpea (also known as black-eyed or southern pea), an important protein source in many tropical and subtropical areas. According to what he calls his "skyscraper" philosophy, he is now trying to improve the productivity of the African pea, in part by changing it from a viney plant that grows along the ground to an upright one.

Dr. M. Wayne Adams at Michigan State University estimates that by changing the architecture of the field bean from a short bushy plant with lots of branches to a taller, nonbranching type that can produce the same number of pods in less space, the protein yield per acre could be increased by a third.

This season, Dr. Adams, who works under a grant from the Rockefeller Foundation, will examine "one by one" some 22,000 plants—the results of crosses he made last year—to select for those that grow tall and narrow.

Cross-pollinating bean plants is in itself an arduous, backbreaking task that requires the dissection and emasculation of flower buds one-sixteenth of an inch wide. Theodore Hymowitz, a plant geneticist at the University of Illinois, has enlisted bees to do the pollination for him. A table of soybean plants in a greenhouse is covered with a screened cage that is home for a hive of bees, whose diet of nectar and pollen from soybean flowers is supplemented with synthetic pollen. The result is thousands of hybrid seeds all year round, Dr. Hymowitz said.

Soybean Seed From China

He is seeking, among other things, to breed out some of the plant sugars that humans have difficulty digesting, resulting in the classic "gassiness" of beans. In the search for better soybeans, Dr. Hymowitz had been disturbed that no breeding material was available from the Chinese mainland, where the soybean originated. Last week, however, American scientists returned from China with many native soybean seeds, including some wild soybeans, to test in American breeding programs.

Soybeans, with an average of 40 per cent protein (nearly twice that of most meats), contain more and better protein than any other edible plant. But like all beans, its yields are low compared to cereal crops such as corn and wheat, a fact that Richard Cooper, an Agriculture Department researcher in Urbana, Ill., is trying to change by developing a more efficient, semidwarf soybean plant.

As he explained it, when a lot of fertilizer is used to increase the yield of ordinary soybeans, they get so tall that they fall over, or "lodge," which diminishes yield. Using the approach that produced the greatly increased yields of miracle rice and wheat, Mr. Cooper has bred a 22-inch plant that produces as many beans per acre as the 44-inch plant. This year he has planted the short variety closer together to see if yields will increase.

Other scientists at the Regional Soybean Laboratory are trying to create soybeans that will bloom regardless of how long the day or night is, a characteristic that would allow the soybean to spread into the food-short tropics. One such "day-neutral" variety is now being tested in Puerto Rico.

Rather than wait for desired genetic variants to occur naturally and, following their discovery, breed them into native crops, some scientists are attempting to induce genetic change in existing crops with radiation or chemicals. This approach, which has already succeeded in producing a high-lysine barley and a high-yielding semidwarf rice, can potentially save the plant breeder much time and effort.

October 11, 1974

Soybean Has Become the Focus of Drive to Give More Protein to the World's Hungry

By JANE E. BRODY

One of the geatest hopes in the drive to provide more and better protein for the peoples of the world is the soybean, a bitter-tasting legume that has been used by Asians for centuries as a major protein source.

It has only been in the last two decades that Western food technologists have sought to adapt this most nutritious of vegetable proteins to a wider range of tastes and dietary habits.

Scientists believe that the soybean can do much to resolve the pervasive problem of protein malnutrition, now rampant in developing countries. A protein-deficient diet can increase susceptibility to disease, permanently stunt the brains and bodies of young children and prevent the proper rebuilding of body tissues in adults.

Creating new, protein-rich foods from the old soybean is part of a multi-faceted effort to increase world supplies of this most essential major nutrient. In addition to breeding crops that contain more and better protein, research is also being directed toward fortifying foods with protein supplements, extracting protein from leaves and utilizing protein-rich wastes.

Much of the current popularity of the soybean, which recently surpassed wheat as a cash crop in this country, is due to its oil, a key factor in the fast-growing magarine and vegetable oil industry. Now, however, increasing interest is focusing on the protein-rich residue left in the bean after the oil is extracted.

Americans are already familiar with at least two products of the worldwide soybean research effort — bacon-flavored bits and hamburger extender (also known as "textured vegetable protein.") Americans also consume breakfast foods, biscuits, breads, sausages and other foods that contain soybean meal.

Aimed at U.S. Market

While such products are currently designed primarily for the American market, the technology involved in their preparation could be readily applied to the creation of highly nutritious foods for protein-starved peoples with vastly different dietary habits and tastes. The price of soybeans is now at a new-record level, but they are still a much less costly protein source than meat.

Scientists anticipate that Americans will be among the hardest to please with novel sources of protein. General Mills, Inc., is currently test-marketing two soy protein meat analogues called "Country Cuts"—frozen, ready-to-eat cubes with the flavor and texture of chicken or ham.

Despite the ready availability of the "real thing" in this country, General Mills expects the convenience, economy (a savings of 25 to 40 per cent over the meats they imitate) and lack of waste to attract considerable consumer interest.

In producing meat-like fibers from the "defatted" soybean flour with which General Mills starts, first the carbohydrates are removed and the remaining hone-like solution of pure protein is pumped through a "spinnerette"—a showerhead-like device with microscopic holes. As the protein emerges from the holes, it hits an acid bath that precipitates the protein as individual fibrils, which are neutralized and washed.

The resulting tasteless, odorless, off-white fibers are then mixed with flavorings, coloring, fat, water and egg albumin, which acts as a binder. A cooking process coagulates the mass into slabs three-eighths of an inch thick.

The "chewiness" can be varied by increasing or decreasing the stretch on the fibrils as they go through the spinnerette.

At the University of Illinois, food scientists have taken a different approach — using the whole soybean, oil and all. They have come up with a wide range of products, from cereal flakes to "milk" and "yogurt," and nearly all of them have been rated as very acceptable by taste panels. They have developed a simple, inexpensive processing method that skirts the soybean's limitations while taking full advantage of its virtues.

"Since most people who are deficient in protein also need more calories, using the whole bean—oil and all—makes better nutritional sense," said Dr. Marvin Steinberg, who directs the Illinois research.

If calories for energy are in short supply in the diet, the body—which normally uses sugar, starchy foods and fats for energy—burns protein for energy instead, leading to a "wasting" of consumed protein needed for building body tissues.

Previously, processors avoided the whole soybean because the oil imparts a characteristic "beany" or "painty" flavor that is difficult to mask and unacceptable to consumers outside the Orient. Dr. Steinberg found he could get rid of this flavor right at the start by heating the beans to inactivate the enzyme that causes it.

But the heat makes the soy protein insoluble, a limitation that Dr. Steinberg circumvents by "homogenizing" it with a miniature dairy homogenizer. His process also removes most of the gas-causing sugars, and he ends up with a high-protein material that has 90 per cent the nutritional value of milk protein.

As Dr. Steinberg and Drs. Lun-Shin Wei and Alvin Nelson downed a mid-morning snack of soy "milk," a visitor sampled some of their soy products. Soy flakes, mixed one-to-one with flakes of corn rice or banana, tasted like what they were mixed with and did not get pasty when liquid was added.

A variety of canned goods in which soybeans were substituted for traditional navy beans—three-bean salad, pork and beans, for example—were indistinguishable from their traditional counterparts.

Homogenized soy beverages —3.6 per cent protein (the same as milk) and 1.8 per cent fat (half that in milk)—were refreshing and good-tasting. The milk-flavored drink had a slight cereal-like flavor, the cream-flavored one tasted like melted soft ice cream and the chocolate drink was indistinguishable from chocolate milk.

The Illinois team has also turned the drinks into flavored yogurt, an ice cream-like desert and a custard. Other prototype soy products they have developed include a whole soy bean diet margarine, soybean butter and a soy-rice snack.

Flavored Yogurt Desert

Soybean beverages are already popular in several countries, where they compete successfully with bottled sodas. As Dr. Steinberg pointed out, the beauty of soy protein products is that their form and flavor can be tailored to the tastes of peoples with vastly different dietary habits.

Other oilseeds besides soybeans also lend themselves to the development of food analogues. Considerable research is now under way on cottonseed protein which, in addition to flour, can also be texturized to make a meat extender or other meat analogues. At Texas A & M University, Drs. Karl F. Mattil and Carl M. Cater are also working on converting peanuts, coconuts, sunflower seeds and sesame seeds into low-cost, high-protein foods.

A variety of areas in soybean research follows:

FORTIFYING FOODS

Rather than improve the quantity and quality of protein in natural foods, some scientists have focused on adding substances that would boost nutritional value.

One approach, already widely used in mills and bakeries around the world and in certain nutritional programs in develoipng countries, is the use of combinations of flours or cereals, such as corn, soy and wheat, which compensate for each other's amino acid deficiencies. The formula for these composites can be adapted to the dietary customs of the region in which it is to be used. Thus, cassava, coconut, sorghum or other foods can be included.

Several of these fortified cereals have been used successfully to correct protein malnutrition in children.

Another, related approach is simply to add the missing amino acids to the food in question. Thus, artificial rice grains containing the two amino acids in which rice is deficient, lysine and threonine, can be added at the mill to ordinary rice. Lysine produced by the chemical industry can be added to cereal grains, and methionine added to beans to produce a more balanced protein.

The protein content of foods can also be improved by adding a balanced protein concentrate, such as fish flour prepared from species that are not ordinarily used for food. The National Marine Fisheries Service developed a process of producing an odorless, tasteless, off-white flour containing 90 per cent fish protein. This concentrate can be added to processed foods or baked into bread, cookies and crackers.

A Swedish company, Astra, which already produces fish flour for human consumption, is now studying ways to make fish protein concentrate into a form that could be fashioned like soybeans into meat analogues.

PROTEIN FROM LEAVES

Green leaves from grasses, plants and trees are the largest source of protein on earth. Although leaves from such crops as grass, alfalfa and corn supply of most of the protein for livestock, they have been used only in very limited amounts in human diets. Anyone who has tasted a leaf, aside from conventional leafy vegetables, can readily tell why they are not popular foods: They lack palatability and they contain large amounts of fibers and other indigestible materials.

But science has found a way around such drawbacks. Rather than use the whole leaf, protein-containing juice is squeezed out and processed into protein concentrates. What remains behind still contains enough protein to make excellent animal foods.

Interest in leaf protein dates back to World War II when Britain, fearing that its food supply would be cut off by the Germans, enlisted N. W. Pirie, a biochemist, to figure out how to get edible protein out of leaves. Although never used to feed the British, the substances he developed led among other things to the use of leaf protein to treat malnourished children in India.

Most leaf protein workers have concentrated on alfalfa, although the same process is applicable to any kind of leaf, including pea vines, carrot tops, potato plants and other leaves that are currently just waste. In terms of protein quality and protein yield per acre, alfalfa surpasses all other crops, including the revered soybean.

In experiments at Michigan State University by Dr. J. Robert Brunner, about 25 per cent of the plant's protein is "creamed off" by squeezing the fresh-cut alfalfa. The green juice is spun in a centrifuge to remove the chlorophyll-containing chloroplasts and the resulting amber-colored liquid is treated with acid or heat to precipitate a whitish protein concentrate. The final almost tasteless powder (it has just a hint of hay) can be spun into meat analogues or used as flour or a food fortifier, Dr. Brunner said.

At the University of Wisconsin, a 15-member team has developed pilot equipment for processing leaf protein. Part of their goal is to design a machine with the cost of a hay bailer for use on smaller farms. Among the advantages of extracting alfalfa, they say, is that it reduces losses encountered in drying hay in the field, the juiceless alfalfa makes high-quality silage, and the left-over juice can be used for fertilizer.

George O. Kohler, a scientist with the Agriculture Department, operates a pilot leaf protein processing plant at the Western Regional Research Laboratory in Berkeley, Calif., where farmers harvest seven crops of alfalfa a year. A further advantage of this approach, he said, is that it saves fuel used in plants that dehydrate the crop.

Dr. Kohler said commercial interest in his process is keen. "We receive a steady stream of visitors from food companies, as well as from alfalfa dehydrating firms, but we're not yet ready to hand out large quantities of our white protein for testing by processors."

PROTEIN FROM WASTES

With the current emphasis on pollution and recycling wastes, it is not surprising to find that the searchers for protein have turned to currently discarded materials as potential sources of food for both man and animals.

Whey, the whitish liquid left after milk is processed into cheese, is one such product that is nutritionally too good to throw away. Yet, less than a third of the 22 billion pounds of liquid whey produced annually in the United States goes into human or animal foods. (Ricotta cheese, for example, is made by coagulating the protein in whey.)

If the whey that is now discarded each year were dried and treated, it would yield at least 170 million pounds of protein, one billion pounds of the milk sugar, lactose, plus water-soluble vitamins.

Whey can be added to fruit drinks (Dr. Steinberg at the University of Illinois mixes it with his soy milk). In addition, coagulated whey protein makes an acceptable ground meat extender and whey protein can be whipped into foam suitable for cake frosting.

At Michigan State, Dr. C. A. Reddy, veterinarian and microbiologist, is fermenting whey and mixing it with ammonia to produce a syrupy, high-quality feed for ruminant animals. The resulting feed, which he calls "bactolac," contains 50 per cent protein (as good as soybean meal in protein quality) "and it is made from stuff that does not compete with the human food chain, as does the soybean," the Indian scientist pointed out.

"It is also a completely recycled process—the cow produces the whey and the whey is fed back to the cow to make more whey-containing milk," Dr. Reddy added.

With his whey feed process about to be used commercially by a new plant in Okemos, Mich., Dr. Reddy is now working on another waste-recycled feed from manure. He said that if only a third of the three to five billion tons of cattle manure produced annually in the United States were used to make feed, it would exceed in protein value all the soybean protein produced in this country each year.

Dr. Rerry is studying a process whereby the mircoorganisms already in the manure convert it without air into organic acids. When ammonia is added, the acids form ammonia salts which the cattle can use to make protein.

Waste products are also being studied as a substrate on which to grow protein-rich microorganisms—bacteria, and other fungi—that might be used to feed people as well as animals. A Louisiana State University team is harvesting bacteria with 60 per cent high-quality protein that were grown on cellulose wastes, such as paper and plant fibers. Bechtel International of San Francisco is building a $10-million demonstration plant that will use the Louisiana process to make protein supplements for animal feeds.

Much work has already been done demonstrating the feasibility of growing edible microorganisms on petroleum.

As human food, microorganisms (often referred to as "single-cell protein") have a disadvantage of resulting in too much uric acid, which can cause gall stones and kidney stones. But the Louisiana team believes ways will be found to get around this limitation so that someday these organisms may be converted into analogues of steak.

The Japanese, among others, are culturing single-celled algae which, after the protein is separated out and coagulated, can yield a high-protein powder that can be added to flour or other foods or used as an animal feed supplement.

These various approaches represent the major efforts in the current worldwide thrust for protein. Other avenues being explored include breeding crops that can be irrigated with salt water, increasing the drought tolerance of plants so that they can be grown in desert areas and using soil bacteria to fertilize crops that currently require large inputs of chemical fertilizers, which are costly and in short supply.

Some of these ideas are currently little more than that—an idea on which a great deal of research must still be done. For others, such as fish protein concentrate and various soy foods, the technology has been nearly completely worked out on a pilot scale and could theoretically be incorporated soon into the diets of protein-starved people.

But the obstacles to such incorporation are substantial. They include such political and economic questions as who should sponsor the effort and is there money in it for private industry. Moreover, needed technology and personnel are usually not available in the developing countries and the new foods often do not suit individual tastes and dietary customs.

General Mills says, for example, that the main stumbling block to introducing soybean "meats" in this country is getting people to try them for the first time. It would be even harder to feed them to undernourished people in developing countries who are unaccustomed to any kind of meat in their daily diet.

Since there can be no one solution for all the protein-malnourished peoples of the world, the search for adequate protein resources continues to go in many different directions at once. In recent years, growing numbers of American scientists, industries and organizations have joined this search, and some of the results of their labors are expected to find a substantial place on the American table before the decade is out.

But the primary goal of this effort is to provide ample quantities of well-balanced protein for the growing numbers of people in developing countries whose diets are protein-deprived. There is little doubt among both scientific and political experts that the achievement of this goal is essential, not only to the well-being of these people, but to the future health of the world as a whole.

October 12, 1974

Big-Scale Agriculture

Trend On Farms Is Toward More Acreage

By LEN RICHARDSON

FRANKFORT, Ill.—"Our policy has been to say yes to everything," declares Wayne Heberer, who farms 1,800 acres near Belleville, Ill. "That means taking on expansion by buying or leasing farms as soon as they become available." Starting with 183 acres just 10 years ago, he is typical of the captains of a new big-scale agriculture.

Ten years ago, when Mr. Heberer started business, there were only 350,000 farms that produced $20,000 or more gross sales from farm products a year. By 1965 that number had jumped to nearly 450,000 Now, the United States Census estimates the number at nearly 600,000.

How could such growth occur? During the same 10-year period over a million farms disappeared—merged into new and larger farms.

What's more, the new managers of America's farm land handle more acres with less labor. Twenty years ago farmers were spending 15 billion hours of labor on farm work each year. Last year they used only 6.5 billion hours while producing 29 per cent more than farmers did in 1950.

Big farms are efficient. Last year each farmer produced enough to feed 47 other persons, while 20 years ago he supported only 15. Productive differences are even more dramatic by farm and income size. The 223,000 farms that grossed over $40,000 last year fed 563 people per farm while the 1,184,000 small farms (average 202 acres) fed only a family of four.

How can a farmer produce more with less labor? Big farmers are using giant, four-wheel drive tractors, many of which average more than 200 horsepower. These industrial monsters come complete with air-conditioned cabs and stereos. Tractor horsepower per farm worker rose from nine in 1950 to 46 in 1970, and will probably reach 60 or more by 1975.

This added comfort seems small compared with what it means in lower cost and labor. An Iowa State University study shows that small farms averaging 160 acres had costs per crop acre of $85 per acre. Larger farms, with over 600 acres per farm, averaged only $56 per acre.

Mr. Heberer emphasizes this point. "My most important management decision was made three years ago when we decided to buy equipment big enough to get the job done," he says.

A farmer plowing at four and one-half miles an hour, for example, can cover 36 to 40 acres a day with eight 14-inch plow bottoms—twice as many acres as he can plow in the same day with four 14-inch plows.

"In the future I see more double-cropping [in the same year] where soybeans are planted right after wheat. We tried planting wheat stubble to eliminate all cultivation," Mr. Heberer says.

This trend, commonly called no-plow tillage, also reduces costs. Norman Rask, Ohio State University economist, estimates that no-plow tillage may reduce labor requirements 70 to 80 per cent during the spring rush. It would also cut machinery cost as much as 75 per cent, he adds.

Mr. Heberer's experience with big farming matches that of Dave Shumway who, at 33, farms 4,500 acres near Queen Creek, Ariz. Ten years ago Mr. Shumway started his operation with a down payment on 320 acres.

One of the biggest problems, according to Mr. Shumway, is the ability to generate enough liquid capital to keep an operation going. He was nearly wiped out by severe hailstorms on his cotton on 1964. He says:

"You've got to keep expanding at a fast enough clip to generate capital. I've watched homebuilders in this area use the same technique."

The 4,500-acre Shumway operation is based mainly on the idea of leasing land and selling on a contract. Leasing worked best for Mr. Shumway because he was in need of liquid assets. Principal payments were not tied up in the buying of farm land.

"I put all of my cash into the stock market and mutual funds. I think I have had as great a return or greater than if I had invested mainly in farmland." During the recent downturn in the stock market, however, Mr. Shumway found land a bargain and bought 1,800 acres.

Mr. Shumway points to another advantage of his stock and land holdings. "While I have an elaborate record system, including computer printouts, you learn pretty fast that records don't talk. You have to explain the entire operation every time you want to borrow money.

"Today all I have to do is take my portfolio of stocks and land holdings to any lender and I get cash without explanation. Another thing, when you always have cash at hand and when you can move in with both cash and volume, you usually get 60 per cent of the deal."

The trend to bigger farming is not without its problems. As this year's gigantic harvest demonstrates, farmers must learn to manage markets or bury them-

The Big Farmer.

Big farms with new, big equipment are more efficient than small. There are about 600,000 farms with sales of over $20,000.

Mr. Richardson is feature editor of Big Farmer magazine.

selves in what they produce. This is leading to a new style of farm management.

No one is in a better posittion to recognize this new management trend than Ernest Fuchs, who with his partner, John M. Ashley Jr., farms 6,000 acres near Centreville, Md.

Until recently, Mr. Fuchs managed this and similar operations for H.L. Hunt, the Texas millionaire. When Mr. Hunt decided to get out of the food business, Mr. Fuchs and his partners purchased the entire operation.

"We have to think in terms of keeping processing plants running. When we can, we are lowering the overhead and fixed costs on every case of product," Mr. Fuchs says.

"Too often, farmers are more concerned with meeting their production-yield goals than helping to manage supplies in terms of time, quantity and quality."

Mr. Fuchs has built his reputation by being a dependable source for quality products. He does it by meeting deadlines for both quality and quantity. "That eight-row planter equipped with a 300-gallon liquid fertilizer tank is one way we save time and cut costs," Mr. Fuchs explains. The liquid polyphosphate fertilizer makes it possible to spoon-feed micronutrients on a prescription basis. "We replaced three tractors and three drivers with this unit," he adds.

Farms and farmers like these carry more clout than all of the "politics" involved in the current agricultural power struggle. The struggle is now embodied in the Sisk bill, which would give farmers the right to bargain. The struggle, however, is much broader and boils down to these points:

¶Integration of production into giant food supply companies resulting in a corporate agriculture.

¶A public utility agriculture regulated by Federal marketing orders.

¶Fewer and larger farms that are meshed into a commodity system where a fair price fits the market objectives of the total industry.

It is in this last direction that agriculture is moving and the reason the Sisk bill is getting at least qualified support. The bill, introduced by Representative B.F. Sisk, Democrat of California, would set up a three-man board to certify qualified bargaining groups, establish bargaining conditions and broaden marketing orders to include all farm commodities except canned or frozen products.

This differs from other bills that would establish prices and terms of sales between farmers and handlers. These proposals would also replace voluntary associations of producers with a Presidentially appointed board to select handler committees. This direction, favored by the Farmers Union, would move agriculture in the direction of a public utility.

Significantly, the Department of Agriculture believes the Sisk bill should apply mainly to vegetable and other specialty crops. Production of these crops are now concentrated on large farms, mainly in the West.

The reasons are clear. All crops are moving in the direction of vegetable production. Large farms producing a crop become an industry. As Mr. Fuchs points out, "once an industry is formed, middlemen are eliminated and farmers and processors can share in greater marketing efficiency."

November 14, 1971

Rise of Corporate Farming A Worry to Rural America

By B. DRUMMOND AYRES Jr.

Special to The New York Times

KANSAS CITY, Mo., Dec. 3—Few things are growing faster down on the farm these days than corporate influence.

All across the United States, from the wide-open prairie surrounding this cattle and grain center to Maine's fertile potato fields and California's irrigated grapefruit groves, big business is diversifying and moving in on what once was strictly a family enterprise, a way of life.

International Telephone and Telegraph now produces not only transistors but also Smithfield hams.

Greyhound now runs not only buses but also turkey processing plants.

John Hancock now sells not only insurance but also soy beans.

Corporate farming or conglomerate farming or agribusiness—by any name it strikes deep fear in rural hearts, such deep fear that the new Secretary of Agriculture, Dr. Earl Butz, was almost rejected by the Senate after he had espoused the advantages of agricultural giantism and had disclosed membership on the boards of such super farm firms as Ralston Purina and Stokely-Van Camp.

Senator Gaylord Nelson called Dr. Butz's views "brazen" and has begun to investigate corporate influence in agriculture with an eye toward limiting legislation. The Wisconsin Democrat says: "Corporate farming threatens an ultimate shift in power in rural America, a shift in control of the production of food and fiber away from the independent farmers, a shift of control of small town economies away from their citizens."

The Agribusiness Accountability Project, a non-profit study group with headquarters in Washington, has been looking into corporate farming for more than a year and reports:

"Corporations generally have become the dominant force in rural America. Their concentration of agricultural markets and their power over rural people is increasing every day. Control of American agriculture has moved from the fields to the board rooms of New York, Kansas City, Los Angeles and other centers of big business."

Farmers themselves speak even more directly about the problem. Summing up the position of one of the largest farmer associations, the National Farmers Organization, Roger Blobaum of Creston, Iowa, said:

"A corporate takeover of the food industry would be a national disaster."

Corporations everywhere deny any takeover is threatened.

"We're not trying to run anybody out of business," says George Kyd, a spokesman for Ralston Purina.

A Misleading Picture

At first glance, corporations do not seem to loom large on the agricultural scene. Of the 2.7 million farms left in the United States, only about 1 per cent are carried on the Agricultural Department's books as incorporated or owned by corporations. And most of the incorporators still insist they are "family farmers."

But that picture is misleading.

Corporate farms are big farms. Many consist of thousands of acres of the best land obtainable. Their owners often have backlogs of development capital and, if diversified, obtain numerous tax advantages.

On the other hand, the average American farm, the unincorporated farm, consists of only about 400 acres, some of them nonproductive. The man who owns this relatively small plot probably has no big capital backlog, often is deep in debt, and seldom receives any special tax breaks.

Eventually, he may have to sell out, flee to the already jammed city, surrender to those who have the capital to compete in a business where $6,000 deals have replaced $60 mules.

This surrender, in one form or another, takes place 2,000 times a week all across America. That is the average number of farm sales weekly, according to the Agriculture Department. Often, a well-heeled corporation comes in to fill the void, or maybe a wealthy city doctor looking for a tax deal or maybe a neighboring farmer who has somehow found the means to expand and is on the brink of incorporation.

Actually, not all farming corporations own land. Some only lease and thus do not farm statistics.

Other farming corporations neither own nor lease land. They simply contract for crops, an operating method that now accounts for about a fifth of the country's total agricultural output.

A few corporations use a combination of operating methods.

For instance, the Tenneco Oil Corporation owns and farms about 35,000 acres of Southern California's best crop land. It leases 100,000 acres more. And it contracts for the crops of dozens of other farms in the area.

The overall effect is to make Tenneco one of the dominant agricultural forces in one of the biggest farming areas of a state that provides more than a third of all vegetables eaten in the United States.

Tenneco has no monopoly on the vegetable market. But in some other agriculture sectors, corporations have achieved dominance or near dominance.

Three companies — Purex, United Brands and Bud Antle—produce a large share of the lettuce eaten in America, a situation that has led to a rare agricultural antitrust investigation by the Federal Trade Commission. Many Government officials contend that a corporation cannot grow lettuce any cheaper than a family farmer, a point farm economists have frequently made, not only about lettuce but also about most other crops.

Another sector of agriculture dominated by corporate America is the broiler industry. There, 20 or so corporations are in control, producing everything from chicks to feed to packaged drumsticks. Among these companies are Pillsbury, Perdue and Ralston Purina, with which Secretary Butz was associated.

Change After World War II

Until shortly after World War II, many broilers were raised in the barnyards of family farms. Small flocks of chickens, though always underfoot, supplied added income, cash for birthday presents or a winter weekend in the city.

Today, there is virtually no market for barnyard chickens. Instead, the family farmer is usually growing broilers under contract for one of the big agrigiants.

In a shed built with a loan from a corporation, he feeds mash produced by the corporation to chicks hatched in the corporation's incubators. When the birds are mature, the corporation takes them away, slaughters them in its own processing plant, packages them prettily, then ships them off to a supermarket—perhaps its own.

The farmer is paid $50 or so for every 1,000 chicken raised. But in any year, if times are hard or management particularly tough, the corporation may cut the growing fee in half.

Should the farmer refuse to sign a new contract, fine—so long as he pays off his loan on the corporation-financed chicken house.

Only last week, chicken farmers on the Delmarva Peninsula—comprising parts of Delaware, Maryland and Virginia—threatened court action when some broiler corporations proposed cutting growing fees in half.

And two years ago, in northern Alabama, growers became so incensed about reduced growing payments that they refused to sign new contracts and began to picket the offices of broiler companies. The companies refused to negotiate, however, and eventually the strikers gave in and returned to work.

Commenting on the strike's failure, one grower, Crawford Smith of Cullman, said:

"Us folks in the chicken business are the only slaves left in this country."

George Kyd of Ralston Purina counters:

"Chicken is cheaper to eat today than it was after World War II, and besides, a lot of farmers have been given work."

'The Lesson Is There'

To which Harrison Wellford, one of Ralph Nader's agriculture "raiders," replies:

"Poultry peonage. One economist cranked in every applicable factor and concluded that most chicken farmers make minus 36 cents an hour. The broiler industry is the most corporatized in American agriculture and the lesson is there."

Foes of corporate farming refer to the broiler industry as being "vertically integrated"—that is, the corporations control almost everything from field to table. Few other segments of agriculture are so thoroughly integrated. But the trend is in that direction.

Tenneco recently told stockholders:

"Tenneco's goal in agriculture is integration from seedling to supermarket."

In fact, the corporation has almost achieved its goal. Not only does it own land, but it also makes tractors, tractor fuel and pesticides. Furthermore, it packages farm products and sells them in little groceries attached to its service stations.

In the potato industry, some companies have achieved full integration. This became evident several years ago when Idaho farmers tried to get more money for their potatoes by withholding them from processors for several months.

The processors refused to give in. Instead, they dipped into storage houses filled with spuds they had quietly grown themselves or had quietly obtained through growing contracts.

Eventually, the growers surrendered. Their potatoes were beginning to rot.

In the hog and cattle industries, vertical integration remains limited. But corporate influence is being felt.

For instance, some concerns like Ralston Purina now rent gilts and boars to farmers, sell the farmers grain to feed the resulting pigs, then offer to market the pigs once they reach maturity.

In the cattle business, a few petroleum corporations have set up huge feed lots in the Southwest, some with 50,000 head or more. As a result, oil companies are steadily becoming an influential force in cattle feeding, encroaching on the family farmer, the man trying to pick up a little extra income by raising a dozen steers out in the barnyard where the chickens used to scratch.

Big food chains often buy directly from feed lots or set up their own feeding operations. Thus, they reduce the need for stockyards, the one place where the family farmer can always be sure of getting the best price for his cattle because the bidding there is always competitive.

Victor Ray, an official of the National Farmers Union, a large farmers association, contends that several years ago Denver supermarkets whipsawed steer prices down from 29 cents a pound to 21 cents a pound simply by repeatedly shifting purchases from feed lot to stockyards and back to feed lots. Mr. Ray says:

"When the chains weren't buying at the yards, prices naturally would drop. Of course, the chains denied any connection. But interestingly enough, all the while that wholesale meat prices were going down, retail meat prices stayed the same. I figure the people of Denver paid at least $4-million more for food during that period than they should have."

Here in Kansas City, there is a company that specializes in investing the excess capital of wealthy corporations or individuals into cattle and other agriculture operations. Called Oppenheimer Industries, it takes on no client with a net worth of less than $500,000 or an income tax bracket of less than 50 per cent.

Its specialty is "cowboy arithmetic," tax savings for the rich through depreciation, favorable capital gains levies and other legal loopholes. One of its clients is Gov. Ronald Reagan of California, who paid no state taxes in 1970.

The president of Oppenheimer Industries, H. L. Oppenheimer, argues that the money he steers away from the United States Treasury and into farming actually helps keep the family farmer in business and does not contribute significantly to the corporate invasion of rural America.

Federal tax records indicate that at least three out of every four people with annual incomes of $100,000 or more are involved in farming in some way, most of them reporting agricultural losses that can be written off against taxes on nonfarm income.

If Federal tax laws seem to help the city corporation that farms on the side more than the family farmer who farms full-time, they are not the only ways in which Federal programs tend to work against the little man.

The biggest farms receive the biggest subsidies and also the most Government-supplied irrigation water.

Recently, Congress placed some limits on subsidies. And the courts are beginning to crack down on the big water users. But the gap between the rich and the poor still widened.

Even so, the fight over the Butz appointment crested hope among some family farmers. Roger Blobaum of the National Farmers Organization says:

"We lost the battle against Earl Butz but the struggle sure swung attention toward the farm issue. I've never seen Washington so upset over an agricultural thing. Maybe Earl Butz will turn out to be the best thing that ever happened to us."

No Keeping Them Down on the Farm

By GEORGE L. BAKER

Having waited in vain for a golden harvest, many corporate giants are sadly coming to the conclusion that the farming business is not for them.

Scores of companies rushed into farming, mostly in the West, during the late nineteen-sixties. They were mesmerized by the profit potential, the long-range prospect of food shortages, tax advantages and the notion that a 10,000-acre farm would be 10 times more efficient than a 1,000-acre farm.

It seemed like such a good plan at the time, but these corporate latecomers might have saved themselves considerable grief had they looked at the experience of the Di Giorgio Corporation.

Twenty years ago, Di Giorgio derived 100 per cent of its revenues from agriculture and related enterprises. Last year only 2 per cent of this company's $459.8-million in revenues came from farming—a stunning about-face.

In 1959, Di Giorgio set as its goal an annual growth rate of 10-15 per cent, according to its chairman, Robert Di Giorgio.

"If you want regularity of earnings over a period of five to 10 years, it's hard to do that in farming," he declared. "When you're in farming, you are subject to things beyond your control—weather, oversupplies, undersupplies and market conditions."

Di Giorgio phased out just as the rush began. This turned out to be wise strategy since the projected cornucopia of profits never came.

After taking their financial lumps, such companies as the S. S. Pierce Company, CBK Agronomics, Inc., the Gates Rubber Company, Multiponics, Inc., and Gulf & Western Industries, Inc., later got out entirely. Others, such as the Purex Corporation, Ltd., and Telleco, Inc., are now retreating.

Not all diversified corporations, however, have pulled up stakes and gone back to the city. Some of them remain involved in farming in an indirect way (mostly through limited partnership syndicates).

Yet there is a lesson to be learned from the failure of corporate farming ventures: It seems that the usual corporate standards of productivity, pricing, quality, control and lower-level management cannot be transferred to a $130-billion industry where so many imponderables predominate.

One of the most startling failures has been that of Purex, the Lakewood, Calif., producer of home-use products. As part of its diversification program, the company went into the business of lettuce and fresh produce, hoping to capitalize on its marketing skills.

Today Purex is retrenching as fast as it can. Now it is growing only 11,500 acres of grain and cotton, campared with 40,000 acres in California and Arizona two years ago.

Roger R. Robbins, executive vice president of Purex, attributed the poor performance of its Fresh Pict subsidiary to a "horrible labor situation" stemming from a contract it signed with Cesar Chavez's United Farm Workers of America in 1970. (Other people in the farming industry say that Purex's problems were more deeply rooted and that a proposed Federal Trade Commission complaint alleging monopolization of the lettuce industry also was a factor.)

"When we started we had all kinds of charts showing price averages," said Mr. Robbins. "But I think the thing we didn't anticipate was inflation. We looked at the averages and it looked good to us. We ended up not being able to harvest a lot of crops and this increased our costs a lot more. Production costs went up, prices went down and we were caught in a cost-price squeeze."

Mr. Robbins said he had originally expected Fresh Pict to be able to return at least 25 per cent on stockholders' equity, but in one year alone it sustained a loss of almost $800.000.

Eric Thor, agricultural economist at the University of California and former administrator of the Agriculture Department's Farmer Cooperative Service, says that diversified corporations simply are not good farmers.

"There's an old saying of who wants to sit up with the corporate sow at night," he said. "There is plenty of data to show that large (absentee) corporations have higher production costs and get lower yields than do farms where the operator is a part-owner.

"The real risk in a hired manager is that he can't make decisions very well. He's more concerned about his job than about production of crops. He knows that if he makes a bad decision he might get fired, so he waits for someone higher up to approve it. Sometimes it's too late to save a crop."

Gates Rubber, a privately held corporation in Denver, found out about management problems. It invested several million dollars (the company won't say how much) in 10,000 acres of sugar beets and wheat in eastern Colorado and waited for the profits to roll in.

They never did. Gates lost money three years in a row. In 1971 it unloaded its land, expensive irrigation system and equipment.

Robert Schramm, vice president of the Superior Farming Company, a subsidiary of the Superior Oil Company, Houston, thinks there can be a place for corporations in agriculture if management understands the cyclical and uncertain nature of farming.

Superior, which farms 35,000 acres in California, has some of the most sophisticated and expensive equipment in the state. But its venture has not turned a profit in five years and probably won't for the next 15.

Even when a company attempts to stabilize prices, however, trouble can arise. United Brands, Inc., known for its Chiquita bananas, paid $17-million for seven West Coast lettuce firms and set a goal for 25 per cent of the national lettuce market.

With so big a market share, the company figured it could afford a heavy advertising program of brand identification, thus helping to stabilize prices, which can swing from $1 to $7 a carton.

But now United Brands is fighting an F.T.C. order to liquidate its fresh produce subsidiary, Inter-Harvest, Inc., which had a deficit of $8,287,000 in 1970.

The illusion of corporate efficiency was shattered. United Brands told the F.T.C. "at the farm level (the company's) size does not bring with it any significant cost benefits." It added, "farming has severe built-in limitations on size in terms of diseconomies of scale."

S. S. Pierce, based in Boston, also knows about diseconomies of scale. This distributor of quality food products attempted to apply its corporate management techniques to California's strawberries, a fruit normally grown with great care on sites of 25 to 50 acres.

Pierce planted more than 2,000 acres and tried to grow strawberries in blocks as big as 500 acres, a perilous undertaking for even an experienced farmer. It quickly ran into financial problems. Pierce had a loss of $4.5-million on sales of $10-million.

Even Tenneco, the Houston based multinational company with sales last year of $3.27-billion, has pulled back from its vow of handling food from "seedling to market place."

A former executive of Tenneco said it had de-emphasized farming because of "all the heat," including disputes with Mr. Chavez's union, criticism from social reform groups and an investigation of its grape-growing activities by the F.T.C.

Economist Thor believes the trend toward corporate farming has abated.

"The outlook is brighter now than it was four or five years ago in terms of local autonomy and control," he said. "Back then it looked as if the big companies were going to take over California agriculture."

FARMERS AGAIN FACING A SURPLUS OF WHEAT

By W. M. KIPLINGER.

WASHINGTON.

THIS year we have in the United States what is called a "wheat situation," which means an abundant crop on top of two previous abundant crops, with a world surplus and consequent low prices. Since wheat is the principal staple food of the world with which we deal, it might seem that plenty of wheat at a low price were a boon. Perhaps it is to the world, but not to the United States. We normally grow between 800,000,000 and 850,000,000 bushels a year; we eat 650,000,000, and we export 200,000,000—these figures being rough and changing from year to year. The 200,000,000 bushels of exports form the crux of the situation.

The fact is that the world is overstocked with wheat—it has not more than the world can eat, but more than it ordinarily is prepared to pay for. Supply is an actual thing, measured in bushels of wheat in the storehouses and coming along now from the ripening wheat fields. Demand is a flexible thing, depending ultimately on the cash available for flour and bread in hundreds of millions of homes. It is a case of bushels against coins, with more bushels offered than coins. Thus coins go further, buy more bread, cut the price of wheat.

In the sense of actual consumption, there is no such thing as oversupply. People will eat all the grain made into flour, made into bread. There is merely a temporary lack of adjustment between the amount of wheat available and the amount which can conveniently be consumed. There may be hunger among peoples of many lands, but if they have not the money to pay they are beyond the economic pale. This may be a hard-hearted doctrine, but it is the rule by which the game is played.

A Part of the World Situation.

To get the picture, start with the United States, but bear in mind that the wheat situation here is an integral part of the world situation. Let us say that we grow 850,000,000 bushels, which ordinarily sell well above $1 a bushel, but which just now are promising to bring considerably less than $1 on the farms. The 850,000,000 bushels may be considered this year's crop, although actually the size of the crop is not yet estimated. It may be larger, for Winter was kind to wheat sown last Fall, causing abandonment of less than half the usual acreage. It may be smaller, for there are still three months for sun and rain to make or break the crop, harvesting of which has just started in the "early" Southwest, to continue progressively northward until early Fall.

On top of the 850,000,000 bushels we have the carry-over from last year, which was 423,000,000 on April 1. The total is then 1,273,000,000 bushels, or more than half of what the United States consumes yearly. The stock on hand the two previous years was just above 300,000,000. Thus, record-size old stocks, plus higher acreage this year, plus good weather and good yields, give us unwelcome abundance.

The reason for our big "unsold stocks" is primarily the bounty of previous years, but there is one incidental reason of particular interest. Canadian wheat last Fall was frost-bitten, and there was high glee among American wheat producers, for this seemed to indicate higher prices for our wheat. But it turned out that the Canadian frosted wheat was still suitable for flour, and when sold at heavy discounts it was eagerly bought abroad, thus undercutting our wheat and leaving us with more stocks than we had planned.

* * * * *

The first world exporter, therefore, is Canada. Second is the United States, third Argentina and fourth Australia. There is no comparable fifth. Just now it is Canada and the United States which, more than any others, are making possible a bargain sale of wheat. The United States bears the brunt even more than Canada, because the largest "unsold stocks" are here.

The big world customer is Europe, as a whole, with Great Britain first, followed by Germany, Italy and France. Europe is the centre toward which wheat flows in thousands of ship bottoms from the four principal producing countries.

True, Europe grows one-third of the world's wheat, but not enough for her millions of mouths. Even the bountiful yellow wheat fields along the blue Danube—in Austria, Hungary, Rumania, Czechoslovakia, Yugoslavia and Bulgaria—cannot fill the needs of Europe. Russia is an unknown factor, out of the picture for the present. India, normally an exporter, contributes nothing to the world this year.

The whole world's production of wheat has been 3,800,000,000 bushels a year, and this is (roughly) what it may be this year. On hand April 1 were 837,000,000 bushels. These are dry figures for the layman, but they give a sort of distance and perspective scale to the picture.

It is natural to wonder where wheat is leading us, both in the immediate and in the distant future. Considering this year only, it is obvious that wheat is plentiful and cheap and will so continue. But these are relative terms, and the Fall is still a long way off, with influences of weather in between. Weather in Kansas and North Dakota, weather in Alberta and Saskatchewan, weather along the Danube—weather of the world holds the dollars of American farmers and may scatter or withhold them.

Wheat Areas Expanding.

Looking further into the future, one sees unlimited acres of land which can and will be tilled and set to wheat. Canada, Argentina and Australia are expanding their wheat areas more rapidly than any other countries, and all are capable of indefinite extension. All have the idle and cheap lands, all have the opportunity to buy tractors and thrashing combines, which cut, thrash, clean and sack the yellow grain as the machines are pulled through the fields. All have labor, cheaper than that of the United States, although with the new combines, and with power tractors, less and less man-labor is required.

One sees Russia. The revolution there sent Russian into eclipse as a world wheat exporter and set the wheat statisticians to devising new scales of production. It was as if Pennsylvania were dropped out of the coal story. Russia may come back ultimately and help fill the wheat bin.

Political leaders of most European nations are urging their farmers to grow wheat. This is part of the nationalistic program for economic self-sufficiency, but, on the whole, European acreages are not increasing rapidly as compared with those of Canada, the United States, Argentina and Australia.

World wheat acreage is increasing from year to year, so that the average yearly additional production is about 75,000,000 bushels. This probably exceeds the normal growth of demand, but not much, and "demand" is easily stretched into "consumption" by lower prices. It is easy to say, but difficult to prove, that world production of wheat is increasing more rapidly than world requirements. It is easier to prove that the big four wheat-growing nations can and will increase their acreage and production, thanks to lands and machines.

This particular piece of the world called the United States, the greatest grain grower, the second greatest wheat exporter, must determine for itself what its future policy shall be.

* * * * *

The total gross value of farm production in 1926 was nearly $13,000,000,000, of which wheat represented $1,000,000,000.

Of the 6,300,000 farms less than 2,000,000 grow wheat, and most of these are not dependent on it. It is apparent that American agriculture runs on many legs, of which wheat is only one of the foremost.

There are two classes of remedies for the wheat situation in the United States so far as the problems of the producers are concerned, and both may be applied under the system set up by the new agricultural act.

One is to limit production and acreage to our domestic requirements. The other is to let wheat culture go the limits and "control" the surplus, so that the domestic price shall not be determined by the world price, as at present, but shall go higher on a domestic preferential basis, like the prices of our tariff-protected industrial commodities. A corollary of the second plan, more moderate in effect, is to market wheat more systematically so as to eliminate some price fluctuations without going so far as to raise price levels artificially.

Limitation of the Crop.

Limitation of acreage for wheat is in the back of the minds of those who have espoused the new agricultural law. The Federal Farm Board, which is set up by that law, has as one of its functions the task of studying the effect of limiting production in wheat and other commodities and of passing advice on this subject down the line to the farmers through the medium of crop advisory councils to be attached to the board. Limitation of acreage means substitution, however, for lands do not lie idle. The question will be: What shall be substituted for wheat? Dairy cows come first to mind, because they have crowded out wheat in Minnesota and other regions. Per capita consumption of wheat is decreasing in the United States and consumption of milk, cream, ice cream, butter and cheese is increasing. Yet the process of substitution is slow.

Prices themselves will probably cause farmers in the East and the Ohio valley regions to diminish their acres planted to wheat, while the big producers of the Western plains States will be able to grow wheat at a lower price and still profitably.

Control of the exportable surplus will be attempted by the Federal Farm Board and its subsidiary agencies, the stabilization corporations and cooperative associations. There are two kinds of "control." Under the more rigid plan it is proposed that a wheat stabilization corporation shall buy up the surplus, say 200,000,000 bushels, and proceed to sell it abroad at the world price. This would raise prices in the United States to something like the level of the wheat tariff. At the same time it would involve the marketing corporation in a loss, represented by the difference between the domestic cost and the foreign selling price, or some part of this. The loss might be carried by the government under the new law, and indeed this is about the only way of carrying it, inasmuch as losses in stabilization operations may not be passed back to the cooperative marketing associations which are members or owners of the stabilization corporation. It is doubtful whether such a method will be used.

A more probable course will be this: The Farm Board, after its organization, will use part of the $150,000,000 immediately available for the purchase, storage and "orderly release" of a substantial part of this year's grain crop. This is likely to raise the price to some extent, but by little more than natural forces would do otherwise. It will not depress the world price and will not injure the wheat growers of other countries. It will tend to stabilize but not to raise wheat prices materially from year to year.

June 23, 1929

PRESIDENT SIGNS FARM BILL, MAKING INFLATION THE LAW

But He Is Silent at the White House Ceremony on Use of Broad Currency Powers.

ASKS FORECLOSURE DELAY

Mortgage Creditors Are Urged to Grant Time to Make Measure Effective.

WALLACE ACTS AT ONCE

Wagner Bill, Setting Up $500,000,000 for Unemployment Relief, Is Also Signed by Roosevelt.

FARM RELIEF-INFLATION MEASURE BECOMES LAW.

Associated Press Photo.

The President signing the bill. Others in the group, left to right, include Representatives Doxey, Mississippi; Fulmer, South Carolina; George Peek, Illinois, who will administer the farm enterprise; Jones, Texas; Louis J. Taber, head of the National Grange; Senator Smith, South Carolina; Henry Morgenthau Jr., farm credit director, and Secretary Wallace, of Agriculture.

Special to THE NEW YORK TIMES.

WASHINGTON, May 12.—Affixing his signature to the farm relief-inflation act today, President Roosevelt not only made effective one of the greatest phases of his legislative program, but became empowered with the widest range of authority over the economic affairs of the nation ever granted to a President in peace time.

In the one measure are included threefold powers authorizing unprecedented control over agricultural production and marketing, refinancing for billions of dollars of agricultural debts and a complete adjustment of the currency system of the United States.

No suggestion by Mr. Roosevelt elicited greater vocal opposition in Congress, but none was adopted with less opposition on the roll-calls. Three important roll-calls on the bill in the Senate revealed an average of only twenty-three opposition votes.

The inflation section is considered generally as the broadest factor in the act, involving as it does authority to increase Federal Reserve credit by $3,000,000,000, to issue an equal amount of new currency and to reduce the gold content of the dollar by as much as 50 per cent.

No Statement on Inflation.

There is no indication as to how much, if any, of this sweeping authorization will be utilized by Mr. Roosevelt, except that in a recent radio speech he reaffirmed his promise to maintain a sound money system.

In public statements today the President and Secretary Wallace, who will have direct authority under the farm-relief sections of the act, mentioned the agricultural potentialities.

Following the signing of the bill in his office at the White House, where the President was surrounded by a group of men who participated in framing the relief program, he issued a statement requesting holders of farm mortgages to withhold foreclosure proceedings until the bill becomes operative. This, he remarked, "is in line both with public duty and private interest."

Pointing out that applications for loans cannot be acted upon instantly, as time for examination, appraisal and "perfection of records" will be necessary, the President said:

"I urge upon mortgage creditors, therefore, until full opportunity has been given to make effective the provisions of the mortgage refinancing sections of the farm relief act, that they abstain from bringing foreclosure proceedings and making any effort to dispossess farmers who are in debt to them. I invite their cooperation with the officers of the land banks, the agents of the Farm Loan Commissioner and their farmer debtors to effect agreements which make foreclosures unnecessary."

Wallace Present at Signing.

Those present at the signing of the bill were Secretary Wallace, Assistant Secretary Tugwell, Senator Smith of South Carolina, Henry Morgenthau Jr., farm board chairman; Professor M. L. Wilson, author of the allotment plan; Edward A. O'Neal of the Farm Bureau Federation, Louis Taber, head of the National Grange; Mordecai Ezekiel, Jerome Frank, who figured in the shaping of the farm section; Representatives Doxey of Mississippi, Clarke of New York, Jones of Texas and Fulmer of South Carolina, W. W. Meyers and George N. Peek of Moline, Ill.

While no announcement was made today, it is understood that Mr. Peek, long a student of farm problems, whose advice was sought throughout the preparation of the bill, will be named as administrator of the act.

In a radio speech over the National Broadcasting Company's system this evening, Mr. Morgenthau explained the aid provided in the bill for farm debtors.

The measure started its journey through Congress solely as a farm-relief bill, authorizing optional methods for control of crop production and marketing, but for legislative convenience the farm-mortgage and inflation sections were added as amendments by the Senate.

1909-1914 Price Level the Goal.

Under the terms of the farm-relief section proper, methods are established for the control of basic commodities until such commodities in most cases shall have reached a parity with the average prices for the years 1909-1914. Incidentally, it is conceded here that should the sharp rises recently registered by commodity prices continue at the present rate, such parity will have been achieved before the bill can be put into operation.

As finally enacted, the relief bill defines wheat, corn, cotton, oats, hogs, tobacco, rice and milk and milk products as "basic commodities."

In supervising these commodities, the Secretary of Agriculture is authorized either to set quotas for production and sale or to lease land for withdrawal from production in order to reduce the marketable quantities to the level of domestic demand. The cost of this program is to be borne by processing taxes levied upon manufacturers of products made from the commodities.

Since enactment of the bill, Congress has passed a concurrent resolution authorizing the extension of control by the Secretary to the marketing and processing of all farm products should this be necessary to control competition of other products with the so-called "basic commodities."

May 13, 1933

21 NATIONS IN WHEAT PACT, CURB OUTPUT AND EXPORTS

ACCORD AFFECTS TARIFFS

Duties to Be Cut After Price Holds at 63.02 Gold Cents 4 Months.

15% CUT IN ACREAGE SET.

Chief Exporters Are Limited to 560,000,000 Bushels in Total of Shipments.

10 NATIONS FAIL TO SIGN

But Are Expected to Come In Soon—Compact Is Hailed by Washington Officials.

By FERDINAND KUHN Jr.
Special Cable to THE NEW YORK TIMES.

LONDON, Aug. 25.—After four months of patient effort an agreement was signed by twenty-one countries tonight to restrict the production of wheat, lift its price in the international markets and improve the living conditions of hundreds of millions of farmers and their families throughout the world.

If the agreement works out as planned it will mean the disappearance of the colossal surplus of more than 450,000,000 bushels in the United States and Canada, much of which has overhung the world wheat market for years.

At the same time it is intended to reopen the blocked channels of international trade and restore some of the conditions that prevailed before the 1929 collapse.

The agreement embodies the first pledge made since the world depression began that all the great wheat consuming nations of Europe will reduce their tariffs and other nationalistic restrictions on foreign grain.

They have promised not to increase their acreage in the next two years and agreed to revise tariffs as soon as the price of wheat shall have been maintained for four months at an average of 63.02 cents, gold, a bushel (91.33 cents at the closing value of the dollar here yesterday).

At present the world price is about 55 cents gold. This means it must rise by about 15 per cent before the tariffs can begin to come down.

Many Loopholes Left.

There were many loopholes in the importers' pledge, among them a provision that all changes are "dependent upon the domestic conditions in each country," and therefore must be approved, in many instances, by national Legislatures.

Nevertheless, the great exporting nations regarded the agreement as good enough to enable them to go ahead with the reductions they had agreed upon provisionally a month ago.

The four greatest exporters—the United States, Canada, Argentina and Australia—now agree definitely to restrict their exports in the next two years, basing their action for 1934-35 on a 15 per cent cut in production.

Their total exports during the year 1933-34 will be limited to 560,000,000 bushels, to be allocated by mutual agreement.

At the same time the Danubian countries, which are exporters on a smaller scale—Bulgaria, Hungary, Rumania and Yugoslavia—agree to limit their combined exports next year to 50,000,000 bushels.

The single recalcitrant nation among the exporters was Russia.

Russians Are Non-Committal.

Her delegates signed the agreement, but refused to accept the cut in acreage and even refused to say how much they would be willing to limit their exports. The figure will be worked out later in further negotiations with the big overseas exporting nations, but it will be ratified, so the Russian delegate warned tonight, "only if it satisfies Russia's essential requirements."

Until Russia comes into the scheme, therefore, the whole agreement may be jeopardized by a sudden flood of Russian exports. It is not believed, however, that the Russians want to upset the plan, and in any case their export surplus this year is reported to be small.

The nations signing the compact were Germany, Austria, Belgium, Bulgaria, France, the United Kingdom, Greece, Hungary, the Irish Free State, Italy, Poland, Rumania, Spain, Czechoslovakia, Sweden, Switzerland, the Soviet Union, the United States, Canada, Australia and Yugoslavia.

Ten of the thirty-one countries represented at the conference failed to sign the agreement. One was Argentina, whose delegate could not be present at tonight's meeting, but will sign tomorrow.

The others who did not sign were Denmark, Estonia, Finland, Holland, Lithuania, Latvia, Portugal, Turkey and India, but all are expected to come in when their governments have had more time to consider the document.

Most of these countries are of small account in the world wheat situation and were represented here by subordinate officials who were not empowered to make decisions.

The leading delegates were elated by the agreement, despite its obvious shortcomings. Frederick E. Murphy, chief American representative, was wreathed in smiles when he emerged from the closing session at 10:30 o'clock tonight.

"This is bound to clean up the enormous carryover in North America that has depressed the price of wheat for years," he said. "It is going to bring the price of wheat back to normal."

Prime Minister R. B. Bennett of Canada, who presided at the conference, told the delegates the agreement would "do much to overcome the universal depression from which every country is suffering."

While leading grain merchants of London professed to be indifferent, they were really more impressed by the agreement than they would admit publicly. The wheat trade in Liverpool regarded the agreement as "bullish," and its effect was felt even before the actual signature, for the price of wheat rose 1⅜d a quintal in the afternoon.

The expectation here is that the agreement will be reflected in an immediate rise in all the grain markets of the world tomorrow.

Price Question Was Vital.

As was foreshadowed yesterday, it was the decision on the vexed question of average price that led to the final agreement. The difference between the importers and exporters had been narrowed to 8 cents a bushel yesterday, but this led to a flood of reservations, which almost wrecked the conference.

By this morning, the two groups had compromised. The French delegate announced that his government was ready to accept twelve gold francs a quintal, or 63.6 gold cents a bushel, as the prerequisite to tariff reductions.

Italy still hesitated, but Prime Minister Bennett, who was presiding, announced that the exporters had accepted this figure. Germany and Switzerland quickly followed with their assent, and the conference was on the way to success.

In the end the importers accepted the entire draft agreement as suggested to them by the exporters earlier this week, but added a safeguarding article. This was the "loophole" stating that the sanction of national Legislatures must often be obtained before tariff reductions could become operative.

To show their good faith, however, the importers added the pledge that they would not "take advantage of the voluntary reduction of exports on the part of the exporting countries by developing their domestic policies in such a way as to frustrate the efforts the exporting nations are making in the common interest to restore the price of wheat to a remunerative level."

An advisory committee has been formed to supervise the working out of the agreement. It will not be permanent, but will watch the way the agreement is being applied, especially in the matter of average price.

It was announced tonight that the committee would hold its first meeting in London on Sept. 18.

The London Times, in commenting on the agreement tonight, says every country will gain more from it than it has sacrificed.

"The greatest gain in prospect is, of course, revival of international trade in general—not merely of wheat trade—which can hardly fail to follow if wheat-growing becomes once more a profitable occupation," it declares.

The Times expresses especial satisfaction at the pledges made by importing countries.

"These undertakings, despite their vague and indefinite character," says The Times, "are to be welcomed as the first real indications on the part of countries which have hitherto pursued a policy of extreme agrarian protection that they are prepared to consider some modification of that policy in the general interest, provided that the interests of their own producers are properly safeguarded."

Asserting that the wheat agreement is "only the first instalment" in the program of recovery that the World Economic Conference was intended to frame, The Times suggests that it should be followed by similar agreements in other fields.

"The world price of wheat can be raised and restrictions imposed by the principal consuming countries in self-defense upon the importation of wheat can be removed," The Times concludes. "The consequent improvement in the purchasing power of agricultural countries should make it easier to deal with the fundamental problem of indebtedness and with other financial and monetary difficulties which appeared insuperable at the World Conference."

August 26, 1933

CROPS CURB IDEA IS NOW WORLD-WIDE

Movement Is Broadening as Nations Seek Further Power of Control.

FRANCE HAS NEW METHOD

Will Rule Varieties of Wheat to Be Planted—Australia to Pay $20,000,000 Bounty.

WASHINGTON, Dec. 25 (AP).—A movement among governments throughout the world toward closer control of agriculture seems to be broadening, as the situation is presented by the Bureau of Agricultural Economics. The bureau keeps watch upon international developments.

Almost everywhere, according to Loyd Steere, a foreign observer for the bureau, back from a tour abroad, nations are maintaining broad powers and in several instances arming, or preparing to arm, themselves with further authority.

The United States, regarded as one of the most Democratic of countries, opened the way with its adjustment programs toward an essentially new policy of government regulation of agriculture, or intervention into its difficulties. Mr. Steere says, and other nations have not been slow in following.

The prospect, he believes, is for a further march in the direction of control during the coming year, a march that may vary in detail and in method, as peoples and governments vary in habit and philosophy, but an effort, nevertheless, toward substantially the same goal.

Selecting wheat as a great world crop and illustrative of general trends, Mr. Steere gives this sketch of the present status of that crop and what, in his opinion, may be expected to develop in the movement.

FRANCE—Preparing to abandon minimum prices fixed by law, under which restriction of production was not included, this country will soon initiate a scheme of control over the planting of certain types of wheat, never before attempted there; it hopes to keep production in hand and to effect what amounts to a price guarantee satisfactory to the French farmer. Prices, after the institution of that system of production regulation, will be allowed free play.

GERMANY—Already in "almost complete control" of grain marketing and grain imports, Germany is expected to bring about indirectly a reduction in wheat acreage by encouraging the planting of other crops, although no specific drive at cutting wheat is likely. A minimum price law probably will be maintained.

CANADA—Is empowered to set up marketing quotas under certain circumstances, but is more likely to encourage retirement of some wheat acreage, although not by direct action. The country might have no great objection to a system of subsidy and production control. Mr. Steere believes, but probably would not find it economically feasible.

AUSTRALIA—Preparing to pay a price bounty of about $20,000,000 to wheat growers. Has full authority to control exports, and might consider the possibility of direct action toward regulating production, although that step is not regarded as planned now.

ARGENTINA—Reinstituting a minimum price law, under which the Government takes the loss if the price is not as high as the bounty it pays. Low prices over a considerable period might lead this country to act directly toward control.

ENGLAND—Here, too, subsidies will continue on set quantities of production.

RUSSIA—No great change in technique expected here, control already being virtually all-inclusive.

THE UNITED STATES—Going forward with the acreage restriction and benefit program. Probably leads the way in the number of crops under government regulation, save, of course, for Russia.

December 26, 1934

SUPREME COURT FINDS AAA UNCONSTITUTIONAL; 6 TO 3 VERDICT DOOMS OTHER NEW DEAL LAWS; ROOSEVELT STUDIES UPSET; MORE TAXES NEEDED

FARM ACT IS SWEPT AWAY

States' Rights 'Invaded' and Compliance Bought, Roberts Declares.

STONE LEADS HOT DISSENT

With Brandeis and Cardozo He Ridicules a 'Tortured' View of Constitution.

CONFUSION IS WIDESPREAD

Effect on Payments in Doubt—Republicans Are Jubilant, Seeing Campaign Aid.

By ARTHUR KROCK.

Special to THE NEW YORK TIMES.

WASHINGTON, Jan. 6.—The Supreme Court by a two-thirds majority vote today demolished the Agricultural Adjustment Act (the AAA) as completely as last year it destroyed the NRA. These two were the major legislative devices of the New Deal for orderly recovery in industry and agriculture, and for economic parity between them.

The AAA, like the NRA before it, was held by the court majority to be an invasion of the rights of the States to regulate their local activities. It specifically banned the use of processing taxes to regulate crop production. The minority of three, in a bitter attack on the reasoning of their brethren, termed the decision a "tortured construction of the Constitution."

The decision definitely forecast the later invalidation of the cotton, potato, tobacco and other crop control laws, appeared definitely to doom the TVA, railroad pensions and Guffey coal-mining regulation acts, and seemed to offer to the New Deal only the device of a constitutional amendment to legalize all its recovery methods unless a State-aid plan can be used in the case of AAA.

Longer Congress Session Likely.

It foreshadowed a longer session of Congress, if the President and his aides decide to try to find a way around the stone-wall decision; cut down expected government revenues by at least half a billion; jeopardized the legality of $1,126,000,000 already distributed, and $979,000,000 already collected, in the processing taxes under AAA; and threw back the whole farm-relief issue into the lap of partisan politics, with a Presidential campaign at hand. Its finality struck the Department of Agriculture with bewilderment, brought silence to the White House and a general order that all the government agencies should be silent also.

But, while the NRA decision in the Schechter case was unanimous, today's evoked from Justice Stone, speaking also for Justices Brandeis and Cardozo, words burning enough to light fires of dissatisfaction in the vast areas where AAA enjoys great popularity. The objects of his legal attack, and sometimes scorn, were the Chief Justice of the United States, Justices Van Devanter, Sutherland, Butler, McReynolds and Roberts, who read the opinion of the majority.

Justice Stone, in brief, denied the view of his six colleagues that Congress, which they admitted had the right to levy processing taxes, had not the right to use them as they have been used.

The fate of the AAA came before the court with more dignity than did the NRA, which perished in a chicken-coop in Brooklyn. Receivers of the Hoosac Mills in 1933 declined to permit the company to pay the government's claim for processing taxes. A district court in Massachusetts ordered the moneys paid. The Circuit Court of Appeals reversed this ruling, and today the Supreme Court majority upheld the secondary Federal tribunal.

Budget Estimates Involved.

Since the lower court spoke, the AAA had been amended in an effort to cure defects arising out of loosely delegated power by Congress to the Secretary of Agriculture. But in a curt last sentence Justice Roberts swept away this Congressional effort, saying that, since there was no original power to impose the contested tax, Congress could not confirm what an executive officer had done in levying or disposing of it.

The effects of the court majority's ruling are both political and economic. More than half a billion dollars in expected government revenue must be subtracted from its hope chest, upsetting the budgetary plans outlined to Congress by the President at the very moment the court was speaking. Unless by act of Congress the courts are closed to those processors whose taxes to the amount of $1,126,180,089 have already been distributed to producers by the government, they will have an excellent chance to recover them.

So sweeping was the finding of the six justices who composed the majority that plans to substitute another legislative device for the AAA must be revised, and the task is desperately difficult. It is made so by the firm repetition of the dictum that agriculture, like mining and manufacture, is a local affair and can only be regulated by the States themselves, unless the Constitution is amended.

McNary Proposes Substitute.

The original Agricultural Adjustment Act was to terminate when the President declared the emergency to be at an end. But the purpose of the amendments of 1935 was to set up a permanent farm adjustment program and the President said that specifically in his budget message today. Senator McNary, the minority leader in his branch of Congress, moved to substitute a plan resembling the twice-vetoed McNary-Haugen act, with an equalization fee instead of bounties for crop control. The Democrats preferred to con the majority decision and the minority opinion before coming to any conclusions. Republicans hailed the majority decision with delight, for the AAA has been a political handicap to them.

Senator Frazier, a Republican, demanded a statute forbidding the Supreme Court to invalidate acts of Congress, with impeachment for the Justices if they attempted it thereafter.

There was a conference at the White House among the President, the Attorney General, the Secretary of Agriculture, Congressional chairmen and others. The President was presumed to have been ready for an adverse decision because his agriculturally minded colleagues were on hand at noon when the court began reading.

But whether he was prepared for a decision so broad that few New Deal acts before the court now seem to have any chance of being upheld, so conclusive as to seem to compel a choice on his part between surrendering the whole concept of the New Deal or proposing a constitutional amendment—that is not known. No comment was forthcoming, and the President's secretaries said none would be.

Divergence of Attitude Sharp.

The two extracts that follow from the majority decision and minority opinion will give some idea of the division in the court on what room there is in the Constitution for the New Deal:

Justice Roberts: Until recently no suggestion of the existence of any such power in the Federal Government has been advanced. The expressions of the framers of the Constitution, the decisions of this court interpreting that instrument, and the writings of great commentators will be searched in vain for any suggestion that there exists in the clause under discussion [the taxation clause], or elsewhere in the Constitution, the authority whereby every provision and every fair implication from that instrument may be subverted, the independence of the individual States obliterated, and the United States converted into a central government exercising uncontrolled police power in every State of the Union, superseding all local control or regulation of the affairs or concerns of the States.

Justice Stone: Courts are not the only agency of government that must be assumed to have the capacity to govern. Congress and the courts both unhappily may falter or be mistaken in the performance of their constitutional duty. But interpretation of our great charter of government which proceeds on any assumption that the responsibility for the preservation of our institutions is the exclusive concern of any one of the three branches of government, or that it alone can save them from destruction, is far more likely, in the long run, "to obliterate the constituent members" of "an indestructible union of indestructible States" than the frank recognition that language, even of a Constitution, may mean what it says: that the power to tax and spend includes the power to relieve a nation-wide maladjustment by conditional gifts of money.

Spectators Crowd Court Room.

The administration had hoped that Justice Stone's reasoning would be that of a majority, and, were the court differently manned, it might well be. But today's majority decision makes it evident that, as now constituted, the court has turned its thumbs down on the Stone-Brandeis-Cardozo school of flexible interpretation of the rights of Congress.

While today's decision stopped the flow of processing taxes into the Treasury, and exposed to suits for collection the taxes already collected and distributed, it did not specifically determine the status of over 200 millions in these levies now held impounded by the courts. These may be released to processors as a result of a decision in the injunction case of the Louisiana Rice Millers, now before the court.

The finding of the AAA was the second to come from the bench after the court assembled in a chamber jammed with spectators shortly after noon today. Justice Roberts began by analyzing the original AAA Act, section by section, and then he stated how the Hoosac Mills case came before the court. Here follows the substance of his decision:

The government argues, based on Massachusetts vs. Mellon, that a taxpayer has no right to question the use made of money he pays in as taxes. But this case transcends that situation. These taxpayers are resisting the levy as a step in an unauthorized plan. The government asks that the court separate the AAA into two acts and consider them separately—one, a levy on processors; the other, an appropriation of public moneys. This is a "novel suggestion"; at any rate, the legislation does not permit the requested separation.

The act can be sustained only if the court ignores its avowed purpose and operation. That sole purpose is to restore the purchasing power of agricultural production to an earlier parity. In this purpose the tax plays an indispensable part; it is the "heart of the law," as Administrator Davis said. It is effective only when the Secretary of Agriculture determines to reduce or produce a farm commodity, and ceases when payment to the producer ceases. The whole levy is for crop control, none is for general government use, and [in the 1933 act] ends with the proclaimed end of the depression.

There is a marked difference between an "exaction" and a "tax." This one is an exaction. The tax never signified the right to expropriate from one group for the benefit of another. But, that aside, this tax is a mere incident of agricultural regulation. Therefore the thing to determine is whether that regulation is within the powers granted to Congress by the Constitution. If it is, as in the Head Money cases, even if the tax is an exaction, it stands.

Agriculture a Local Activity.

The government relies on Article I, Section 8, of the Constitution, which contains the taxation and general welfare clauses. That is the controlling question in the case and the court approaches it with a sense of its grave responsibility to render judgment according to the principles set down to guide the three coordinate branches of the government. The court assumes no power to control or overrule the representatives of the people in Congress. But on the court is imposed the duty to decide when legislation does and does not conform to the national charter. It has no enforcement powers. It can only speak.

We live under a dual form of government, Federal and State. The Federal Union is a government solely of delegated powers. The States have all others. Agriculture, as the court has often said about mining and manufacture, is a purely local activity. Therefore, the powers of Article I, Section 8, do not apply. Justice Story pointed out that the general welfare clause could be construed to cover unlimited Federal powers. In this case the government has asked the court to say that Congress at all times decides what is the general welfare.

That phrase would not have been used were it not meant as a limitation on taxing and spending. Madison thought it confined the powers to tax and spend to the enumerated legislative field of Congress. Hamilton and Story said it was a separate power, and they were right. Monroe agreed with Hamilton.

Even though the court majority agrees with Hamilton, it is not called on in this case to decide the point. The AAA is unconstitutional for another reason: It invades the rights reserved to the States. The regulation of agricultural production is beyond the enumerated powers of Congress—the tax is "a means to an unconstitutional end." (Here followed numerous citations, including Marshall in McCulloch v. Maryland, also used by Justice Stone to buttress his contrary position.)

Buying of Compliance Not Valid.

Can Congress purchase compliance and thus attain constitutionally the regulation of local affairs directly denied to it? The court thinks not. The government says the plan is voluntary, but it isn't, since the price of noncompliance is the loss of benefits to the producer. The payments are arranged on that basis, and this involves the power to destroy. Nonconformists get less for their crops than conformists. In the Bankhead Act Congress proceeded logically with the AAA method to "use the taxing power in a more directly minatory fashion to compel submission." That is coercion by economic pressure in a progressive form.

But even when the reduction is voluntary, it cannot be constitutionally achieved by Congress. It is still a scheme to purchase with Federal funds the submission to Federal regulation of a subject reserved to the States. Congress can neither purchase nor compel that submission. The plea of an emergency is no defense, for on that plea Congress could usurp State powers at any time.

If the AAA should be permitted to stand, all industry could be regulated. A producer could be taxed to pay a processor. By offering premiums to employers conforming to wage and hour regulations, Congress could invalidate the dictum of the Supreme Court in the Schechter case. Sugar refiners, shoe manufacturers could be paid with taxes levied on producers if Congress thought they were not getting enough for their manufactures. The Federal Government could by such devices redistribute the country's population. These possibilities are cited, not to stamp them as unworthy objectives, but to illustrate the scope of the AAA method—the use of taxing power to achieve prohibited aims. States' rights would end.

Stone Points to Ballot Box.

The retort of Justice Stone for himself and his two colleagues was in substance as follows:

Courts are concerned only with the validity of acts of Congress, not with their wisdom. The only check on the Supreme Court is its "own sense of self-restraint." The ballot box, not the court, is the proper appeal from unwise laws.

Congress's power to levy processing taxes is undisputed. Only their use is disapproved by the majority. Certainly the effect of farm economy on national economy brings its relief within the terms of the general welfare, and the majority says nothing to the contrary. Also, in the 1935 amendments, Congress cured the original act of loosely delegated powers and the fixing of the taxes by executive fiat.

The majority invalidates the act as a step in regulating agricultural production, and therefore an invasion of State power. It holds that the Federal Government has no right to invade the States' domain by purchasing the performance of acts it has no power to compel. But the taxpayers made no claim of coercion. The majority went outside the record to argue this. The act has no such consequences. "Threat of loss, not hope of gain, is the essence of economic coercion." Many farmers did not participate in the reduction plans. The appearance of the Bankhead Act proves how widespread was this nonconformance since its 50 per cent tax is an effort to force conformity. The majority's argument as to coercion is "groundless speculation."

The power of Congress to spend is inseparable from persuasion to action it has no right to control. Grants to State colleges for the teaching of agricultural science—the Morrill act—prove this. It is a furtherance of national purpose through distribution of public moneys. The majority has reversed the "time-honored principle" that granted power includes all incidents thereto, and McCulloch vs. Maryland is cited to prove the venerability of that principle.

Implications of Ruling Cited.

Incidents of granted power by Congress are many. There is the power through Congress of the I. C. C. over intrastate railroad rates, the effects of tariffs on farm and industrial prices. The court has often upheld these incidents of other powers, but it contends that the incidents of the powers to tax and spend are different. The limitations it has set on these are incapable of sensible application. The power of the purse presupposes freedom of selection in spending. It is "a contradiction in terms" to hold that Congress can spend for the general welfare but cannot impose conditions to attain that general welfare through the spending.

The effects of the majority reasoning would be, for example, that the government may distribute free seeds but not condition their use; that it may give money to the unemployed, but neither require them to work nor to support their families; that it may give money to areas stricken by calamity but not enforce sanitary or other regulations in the spending. This the majority calls "purchased regulation, infringing State powers."

The government henceforth cannot supervise the vocational education it pays for. It cannot require farmers receiving money to fight the boll-weevil, not to plant in infected areas. It cannot enforce standards in the rural schools it supports. Must the RFC close down now because it imposes conditions on local loans? Such are the consequences of the working of "minds accustomed to believe it is the business of courts to sit in judgment on the wisdom of legislative action."

"A tortured construction of the Constitution is not to be justified" by imagining what would be done by a Legislature "lost to all sense of public responsibility."

Both justices uttered their sharply differing views calmly and clearly, and the AAA, the most popular measure of the New Deal, the President's political armor in the Republican farm areas and in the cotton States of the South, was dead as a doornail.

January 7, 1936

BILL FOR NEW AAA PASSES CONGRESS; WIDE POWER VOTED

Measure Orders Wallace to Restore Pre-War Ratio of Farm and City Incomes.

BORAH ATTACKS CLAUSE

He Says It Gives Secretary Control Over the Earnings of All Workers.

Special to THE NEW YORK TIMES.

WASHINGTON, .Feb. 27.—With scarcely a dissenting voice and with little argument, the Senate and House completed action on the administration's $500,000,000 Soil Conservation Bill today. President Roosevelt's signature is said to be assured before the end of the week.

No record vote was asked to bring adoption of the conference report which resolved differences between the Senate and House versions of the new farm-relief program. In the House Speaker Byrns had to pound repeatedly for order to remind members they were about to pass this most important legislation.

As adopted, the bill remained in substantially the form in which it was first passed by the House.

It gives broad discretionary authority to the Secretary of Agriculture to. restore the pre-war relationship between farm and city incomes for those farmers complying with prescribed soil conservation and erosion-control methods.

When brought up in the Senate following its adoption in the House, Senator Borah took the floor to express doubt as to the workability of the direction that the pre-war farm-city income ratio be restored. He had stated previously that the provision would give Secretary Wallace virtual control over the incomes of all workers.

Payments to Farmers Provided.

Under the bill, until January, 1938, Federal payments made directly to cooperating farmers would be in order as rewards for their voluntary contributions toward conservation of soil resources. After two years, Federal payments would be made only to States having adopted authorizing legislation and a conservation plan acceptable to the Secretary of Agriculture.

The measure goes considerably further than the invalidated provisions of the AAA, in the direction of soil conservation, adjustment of agricultural output and the restoration of farm income on a prosperity basis.

During the temporary two-year period, payments could be made for:

"Preservation and improvement of soil fertility.

"Promotion of economic use and conservation of land.

"Diminution of exploitation and wasteful and unscientific use of national soil resources.

"Protection of rivers and harbors against the results of soil erosion in aid of maintaining the navigability of waters and watercourses and in aid of flood control."

In seeing that these purposes are carried out the Secretary is directed to base payments to farmers, among other things, on their treatment or use of their land for soil conservation, restoration and erosion control; changes in historic land uses; shifts from intensive to extensive cultivation below the normal proportion of these two methods, or any of these used in combination.

Food Supply to Be Maintained.

Although the Secretary is directed by the new statute to restore the ratio of farm and city income which existed between 1909 and 1914 at as rapid a rate as practicable, this requirement is conditioned on the maintenance of a volume of food supplies for the nation not less than the average for 1920-29 with certain moderating factors considered.

Subject to the practical limitation that no more than $500,000,000 be spent on the program in a single year, the Secretary receives carte blanche to do whatever he considers necessary to achieve the purposes of the measure within the field of soil conservation and erosion control.

Widely differing conservation and erosion-preventing methods are likely to be prescribed for the separate areas of the country. These are to be determined by State conservation committees working through county and local committees composed just about as they were under the old AAA.

State land grant colleges and the Federal Agricultural Extension Service are to be called upon in carrying out the new program.

Thus it would appear that, even after the initiation of the State-aid plan in 1938, the Federal Government will be in complete control of the disbursement of benefit payments and the conditions necessary to be met before farmers are eligible to receive them.

Dairy Interests Held Unprotected.

While the measure was being debated, Senator McNary said for the record that it failed to give protection to dairy farmers against surplus production resulting from lands converted to grasses from cash crop cultivation, but he made no effort to block passage.

Senator Nye added a novel touch to the debate on various farm relief problems when he introduced a proposal for a constitutional amendment giving Congress the power to regulate "the sale and marketing of all agricultural products."

Mr. Nye contended that there had been "so many inconsistencies in Supreme Court decisions regarding agriculture's place in interstate commerce, that it becomes apparent that if the government is to be empowered to help agriculture, it can only be by constitutional amendment giving Congress the clearly defined power to deal with that industry."

As soon as the new measure is signed by President Roosevelt Secretary Wallace is expected to call regional meetings of farm experts with a view to working out details of the new system.

AAA Officials Puzzled.

At the Agricultural Adjustment Administration, the agency to be intrusted with carrying out the most far-reaching farm relief measure ever enacted in this country, officials had only a vague idea as how it was to be placed in operation.

Only one thing was certain in the minds of those charged with the responsibility of carrying out the conservation program—about 30,000,000 acres of land, normally planted to cash crops, would have to be shifted to grasses and legumes if the program was to be successful and cash rewards of about $500,000,000 probably would be disbursed.

Meanwhile, Chairman Smith of the Senate Committee on Agriculture announced that he intended on Monday to try to overturn President Roosevelt's veto of the $50,000,000 feed and seed loan legislation. Although administration supporters were confident the veto would be sustained, Senator Smith claimed sufficient strength to override it.

Preparing the ground for a test of such a move in the House, Representative Bankhead, majority leader, said he understood that the President was prepared to approve a measure appropriating as much as $30,000,000 for feed and seed loans.

February 28, 1936

WALLACE URGES "BALANCED ABUNDANCE"

In the "Ever-Normal Granary" the Secretary Sees the Salvation of the Farm and the City

The "ever-normal granary" plan will be one of the important issues before the special session of Congress opening this week. In the following article the proposal is explained and the agricultural future of the country discussed.

By HENRY A. WALLACE
Secretary of Agriculture

IN the Summer of 1934 hot winds and drought swept the Corn Belt and there was a smaller corn yield per acre than ever before in the recorded history of the United States. Again in 1936 the same thing happened and the yield of corn per acre was less than in any other year with the one exception of 1934. Not one person in a hundred on the Atlantic seaboard can imagine the wreckage caused by drought. But one needs no imagination to understand high meat prices. The newspaper articles on the New York kosher meat strike might well have carried the headline "The Droughts of 1934 and 1936 Finally Visit New York City."

Meat prices and livestock production are determined more by the size of the corn crop than by any other single thing. But the corn crop unfortunately is very subject to drought. The corn supply affects not only the price of beef and pork but also, to a lesser extent, that of butter and eggs. It can accurately be said, therefore, that the variability of the weather in the Corn Belt is one of the leading sources of national disequilibrium.

It is rather surprising that in the past we have ordinarily carried over from one year to the next only about 7 per cent of the corn crop as compared with 15 per cent of the wheat and 30 per cent of the cotton crop. The carry-over of corn on the farms of the United States from one year to the next is ordinarily only about 170 million bushels. This means that when a drought like that of 1936 comes along, which reduces the yield by nearly a billion bushels, the shortage is so appalling as to affect in one way or another every person in the United States.

IN view of the droughts of recent years it is essential that the nation should have a corn carry-over from one year to the next several times as large as it has been having. In normal years it should have a carry-over of at least 350 million bushels instead of only 170 million. The welfare of the entire nation demands this. Such supplies would insure New York consumers against meat shortage like that experienced this Fall.

But while the larger carry-over seems to be vital from a consumer's point of view, there are many corn farmers who feel strongly that their prices and incomes ought to be protected against the price-depressing effect which it would be certain to have in the absence of adequate protective measures. Some of them remember that back on Oct. 1, 1932, there was a carry-over of 250 million bushels, which was only 90 million bushels in excess of the normal carry-over, and that corn prices in the Western Corn Belt went down to 10 cents a bushel in November of that year. In South Dakota certain elevators actually offered as low as 2 cents a bushel for corn.

The big supplies of corn and other farm products in 1932 were accompanied by grief to farmers which they are not likely to forget soon. Moreover, their grief was communicated at once to the farm machinery and automobile factories and then on to the steel mills and finally in a thousand different ways to the people in New York City. Corn was so superabundant in the Fall of 1932 as to be almost worthless. But the abundance brought waste, not plenty, to the people in the cities. Thousands of bushels of corn were burned because corn was a cheaper source of heat than coal.

Consumers are right in asking that they be protected from the aftereffects of droughts like those of 1934 and 1936. They don't want to pay so much for meat as they did this Fall. But farmers are equally right in asking that they be protected in the situation which results when corn supplies are too large. The problem is how to help both farmers and consumers by making it practical to have on hand a normal carry-over of corn from the preceding crop of from 300 to 500 million bushels.

SO far as corn and meat are concerned, this is what the ever-normal granary legislation is all about. We want to bring greater stability to the supplies of corn from year to year so that the meat supplies also will have greater stability from year to year. We want to make it impossible for either a 1932 superabundance or a 1936 drought to do us such great harm.

It is therefore proposed in years of abundance that the Federal Government should lend enough money on corn at low rates of interest to make it possible to carry over corn from the good years into the bad years. It is further proposed that the loans be handled in such a manner that in the good years there will be enough corn available to feed sufficient livestock to take care of the needs of the consumers of the United States at a reasonable price, but not enough to cause the corn price to slump to a point destructive to the purchasing power of the corn farmer.

Ever since the Civil War we have had again and again a situation when hog prices one year would be twice as high as they were three or four years later. When the prices were high the consumer was hurt, and when the prices were low the farmer was hurt. What both farmers and consumers want is a more uniform price and a more uniform supply from year to year. The ever-normal granary legislation is designed to iron out the peaks and fill up the valleys.

THE suggestion has been made in New York City that the ever-normal granary would not be practical until the country has ever-normal weather, ever-normal bugs and ever-normal plant-disease pests. In reply I would say that it is because weather, bugs and pests are so abnormal that the nation should build an ever-normal granary to equalize between the good years and the bad.

Farmers have already had experience with this kind of thing. In the Fall of 1933 the Federal Government lent 45 cents a bushel on 270 million bushels of corn. This corn was stored under government seal on the farmer's own farm. That is the cheapest place to store it. That is the place where as a rule it will finally be needed. We can say quite definitely because of our knowledge and experience that the cheapest and most practical way to operate the ever-normal granary for corn and meat is by means of government corn loans and corn storage on the farm.

The most difficult administrative problem is presented by the need for controlling the surplus when the granary overflows. We need in this country now only about 2,370,000,000 bushels of corn annually to feed our horses and mules, our chickens and dairy cows, and to produce a supply of pork and of fat beef about 30 per cent greater than has been consumed in 1937. With the present income of the United States and present productivity of city factories, corn crops of 2,370,000,000 bushels will most nearly bring the interests of both farmers and consumers into harmony. But suppose we should have two corn crops of 2,800,000,000 bushels and the granary was overflowing. Obviously the government loans would be imperiled and we would be in danger of repeating the Farm Board fiasco. To guard against this the farmers must use government power to control the overflow.

The most practical way of controlling the overflow is by means of marketing quotas and storage quotas. These would be used only in the Corn Belt extending from Eastern Nebraska to Western Ohio and from Southern Minnesota to Northern Missouri. Marketing and storage quotas would not be used in this area unless the Corn Belt farmers by two-thirds vote approved them. The essence of marketing and storage quotas is to require farmers who have overplanted their land to corn or who have had an unusually large yield per acre to seal up a certain percentage of their corn under government loan. The objective would be to bring the total amount of corn thus sealed to a point which would leave available for market about 2,370,000,000 bushels.

Non-cooperators in the soil conservation program who have overplanted their land to corn and who have a small percentage of their land in soil-building crops would be given the right to borrow money on their sealed-up corn but at a somewhat lower rate than the cooperators. It is obvious that these men who have been overplanting corn or destroying the nation's precious heritage of soil fertility should not have the privilege of borrowing from the government at a rate per bushel which might later result in the government's having to take over their corn at a loss to itself. The non-cooperators should be treated fairly but they should not be allowed to unload on the government.

If, during the years ahead, there should be three or four years of good crops in succession, the plan I have described would result—in case of affirmative votes by two-thirds of the farmers—in the government's requiring the sealing under loan of larger and larger percentages of the crops. After the second year of good weather many farmers would find it necessary to build more cribs. Even the non-cooperators would then begin to cut down their corn acreage. However, they would know that the corn sealed under government loan on their farms could come out from under seal whenever the total national supply was cut to a manageable point. A year or two of bad weather would bring the sealed corn out onto the market.

IN the system I have described it is obvious that a lot depends on the amount lent by the government per bushel. If too much is lent, the result will be an eventual Farm Board disaster, no matter how tightly the overflow from the granary might be controlled. A high loan would make every farmer eager to produce to the limit and therefore most farmers would object strenuously to any action hampering their corn planting or corn marketing. The combination of high loans and drastic controls to back up such loans would inevitably lead to an explosion which would blow up the whole system unless the vast majority of Corn Belt farmers fully understood and were agreed as to the desirability of the system.

In saying this I am speaking about the undesirability from the standpoint of the farmers themselves of high loans and high-powered, drastic control of marketing and production. It is much safer from the farmer's point of view to have more reasonable loans which can better be defended to the consumer and which will not cause so many farmers to want to expand their production beyond the true needs of the market.

At the present time corn would have to be selling for 87 cents a bushel in order for a farmer to buy as much with a bushel from the cities as he bought before the war. It can hardly be said, therefore, that 45 cents a bushel is an excessive loan so long as cities are charging farmers such high prices.

Under many

Times Wide World

Wheat ready for export—A dock in Oregon.

conditions a higher loan than 45 cents would be justified in order to set up an ever-normal granary in such a manner as to minimize the likelihood of $1.20 corn in years of drought. Every year the conditions are different and there must be examined all the surrounding factors, such as the size of the new crop, size of the carry-over, number of head of livestock and the way in which the corn loan will best stabilize the livestock cycle.

The point I am making is that considerable freedom should be left to the Administration in determining loans. As in other business enterprise, the program should be carried out over a period of years so as to make it possible to improve the ever-normal granary model, as we improve our automobile models from year to year.

It is essential that the loan policy should in the long run bring the maximum of security and stability to both farmers and consumers. It must be high enough to encourage the carrying over of abundant corn supplies from the good crop years to the poor crop years. If it does this there will never again be quite such a meat shortage as we experienced this Fall—unless, of course, we should have year after year of bad weather. On the other hand, the loan must not be so high as to pile up surpluses impossible to control with any ordinary means. Corn farmers would not want the loan policy to cause the government losses running into the hundreds of millions of dollars. There is a sensible middle view which can and should be embodied into legislation.

I WILL not take the space here to discuss the details of the proposed ever-normal granary legislation as applied to cotton and wheat. The principles are much the same, except that it is essential to make sure that the loans do not interfere with exports. This is especially true with cotton.

Because our high tariffs have destroyed the ability of many foreign countries to pay a decent price for our extra cotton and wheat, it is proposed to pay both cotton and wheat growers a special adjustment payment to compensate them for the market lost to them by our tariff policy. The money for this would come from a tariff-equalizing tax.

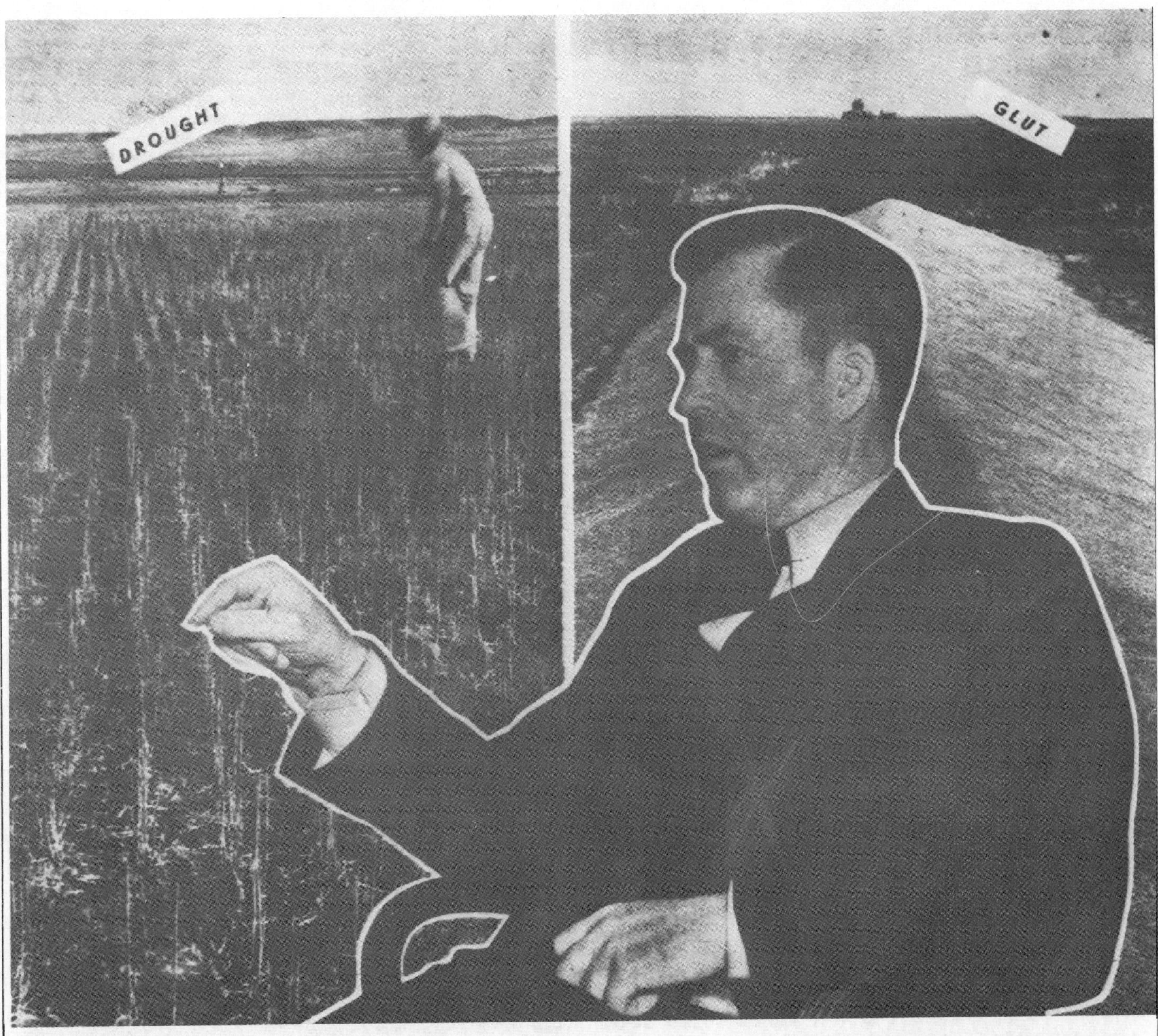

Ewing Galloway and Underwood & Underwood

"We want to make it impossible," says Secretary Wallace, "for either a 1932 superabundance or a 1936 drought to do us such great harm."

But in no event is there any likelihood that the market price of wheat and cotton, plus the tariff-equalizing tax, would be sufficient to give the farmers as a five-year average a total equal to the share they had in the average consumer's income before the war. With all the benefits of loans, soil-conservation payments and adjustment payments, it is impossible to give cotton and wheat farmers an income which will return them on the average more than 3 per cent on their investment and more than $300 to $400 a year for their labor and capital above out-of-pocket costs. Wheat may average a little more than this and cotton somewhat less. The Dakota wheat farmer and Alabama cotton farmer both have an income which, with all government payments added in, is pitiably low, and their standard of living in many cases is below that of the tenantry and peasantry of Western Europe.

Some people say farm land values are too high, not realizing that, if we take 1921 to 1925 as a base, farm land today is less than one-half as high as industrial stocks after the October, 1937, crash. No, farm land has had the water squeezed out until it is cheaper than before the World War, whereas industrial stocks are still several times as high as they were before the war. But on the bone-dry values for farm land the return is low, and the labor return is much lower on both an hourly and a yearly basis than labor in the cities.

Before the war, even after counting in the value of the house rent and the value of the home-raised food, the average farm family received only $1 as compared with $2 for the average city family. In the decade of the Twenties the farm family received only 90 cents as compared with the city family's $2.

A few city people will say: "What do we care about the farmer? What if he is hard up? His loss is our gain."

But most city people now understand the interdependence of farm and city. City workmen know that low farm income constantly threatens their jobs. Low farm income means that farm children will come to town willing to work for low wages. City business men know that low farm income means small sales in the farm territory.

The problem obviously is to find that happy middle course which will give the farmers enough income to keep them in proper balance with labor and business. Since 1920 farmers in nearly every year have received less than the amount necessary to bring about such proper balance. Our tariffs, our changed relationships to the outside world, certain practices of our corporations and some of our labor policies have all contributed to the farmer's disadvantage.

The farmer does not want to attack tariffs, corporations or labor unions. Rather he wants such bargaining power as other groups have, and he wants all groups to exercise their separate grants of power jointly under the common limitation that they all serve the general welfare. He believes the Soil Conservation Act and the new farm legislation now being proposed are the means by which he may serve both himself, the consumer and the general welfare. He believes he can achieve balanced abundance for both the consumer and himself if the soil is sensibly handled, if the farm income is fairly maintained and if highly variable weather is offset by a workable ever-normal granary policy.

Acting under a joint resolution adopted by both houses of Congress and signed by the President on Aug. 24, the first order of business when Congress reconvenes tomorrow will be ever-normal granary legislation. All the farmer organizations are agreed as to the fundamental principles of such legislation, though there is difference of opinion as to details. They all believe the farmer should get a fair share in the national income and that the consumer should be protected against scarcity. They all believe in commodity loans and in storing up crops in the good years which can be of service in the bad years. When there is this much agreement in principle it is certain that the details can eventually be adjusted.

I am convinced ever-normal granary legislation will be enacted into law and that it will be looked on by future generations of farmers and consumers as vital to their mutual welfare.

November 14, 1937

ROOSEVELT CROP CONTROL VOTED BY SENATE, 56 TO 31; 'JUST PRICES' ARE SOUGHT

SENT TO PRESIDENT

Bill Vests in Wallace Wide Powers to Rule Farm Production

FINAL DEBATE IS BITTER

'Regimentation' Is Charged—Cotton, Wheat, Corn, Rice and Tobacco Covered

Special to THE NEW YORK TIMES.

WASHINGTON, Feb. 14.—The Senate adopted and sent to the White House today the crop control bill asked by President Roosevelt as one of the four major pieces of legislation needed to complete his New Deal program.

The vote was 56 to 31, with two Republicans and one independent joining fifty-three Democrats in support of the measure and ten Republicans, eighteen Democrats, two Farmer-Laborites and one Progressive opposing it.

The bill was rewritten by a conference committee from the two rival measures passed at last Fall's special session. It applies to cotton, wheat, corn, rice and tobacco and gives the Secretary of Agriculture broad scope for administering a program designed to control production and thereby obtain for the farmer what is considered by the Secretary a just price for his products.

Despite the overwhelming vote of approval in both houses, opponents heaped upon the measure charges that it meant "regimentation" of the farmer, that it was unconstitutional in that it invaded State and individual rights.

Party Leaders in Debate

The closing debate saw the majority and minority leaders locking horns, Senator Barkley, Democrat, defending the measure from an attack by Senator McNary, Republican, author of farm bills of the past.

Leading the attack of a coalition group, Mr. McNary declared that there was nothing in the bill but a "policy of scarcity" at a time when "we find more and more agricultural imports coming into this country." He asserted that the bill called for "coercion" of farmers and recalled that President Roosevelt, in his 1936 speech at Wichita, Kan., advocated "voluntary" control of production by farmers.

Mr. Barkley, with only a minute or two at his disposal under the agreement by which a vote was to be taken at 3:30 o'clock, shouted that both major political parties had advocated production control in their platforms, and that this measure represented the best effort of Congress to give the farmers legislation for which they had been asking.

He said that the measure "undoubtedly is not perfect," but promised that amendments to the act would be offered as experience dictated them.

Regimentation Charged

Senator Johnson of California declared that the measure was the beginning of regimentation of all industry, and assailed the power it bestowed on the Secretary of Agriculture. This was more power, he added, than had ever been given to any one man.

"You penalize the Creator Himself," he shouted.

Senator McAdoo questioned the constitutionality of the measure, asserting that he could not reconcile it with his views on the power of Congress to legislate.

"I don't think it is constitutional to go out on a man's farm and measure off portions that he may use and portions that he cannot use," he said.

As the result of acreage restriction under the AAA and soil conservation programs, he asserted, at least 250,000 persons migrated into California.

Senator Shipstead, pointing to charts held by several Senate pages, declared that the measure did not go far enough to bring farm income into proper relationship with national income.

Comparing the "spirit" of the bill with Nazi regimentation in Germany, Senator Burke argued that the Federal Government had no right to enforce the compulsory features of the bill.

Senator Borah said he disapproved of the doctrine of scarcity "still in the bill," but admitted that the program was somewhat improved over those in the measures originally passed by the two houses.

He added that he would speak tomorrow on supplementary legislation he believed necessary. After the vote he declared that one need was legislation to control food trusts and prevent undue price increases. He cited the bill sponsored by himself and Senator O'Mahoney to license concerns doing an interstate business.

Senator Pope, co-author of the original Senate Farm Bill and one of the conferees, defended the measure as one which would give agricultural interests control of their acreage and production and said he was preparing legislation to raise additional wheat and cotton benefit payments through processing taxes. This legislation would call for 15 cents a bushel tax on wheat and 2 cents a pound on cotton, he said. Many legislators favor an excise tax.

Court Changes Aid Plan

Constitutional prospects for the measure passed today are favored by changes in the Supreme Court more than by introduction into it of legislative safeguards not contained in the first AAA, which the court rejected. To the three justices who voted for the AAA have been added two justices presumed to believe in the principles of the new measure.

These are Justice Reed, who argued the constitutionality of crop control before the court in the Hoosac Mills case, and Justice Black, who voted for the original crop-control plan and headed a group of Senators who sought to force action on the new adjustment plan in the last regular session of Congress.

Passage of the complicated measure did not end the fight against it by the National Grange, which was the chief farm organization opposing it before Senate and House committees. In an analysis of the measure by Francis J. Clair, economist, the Grange said today:

"It is conservatively estimated that if this bill should go into effect and become a law there will be established within the realm of this overlordship of American agriculture more than 100,000 'local committees,' together with 3,070 'county committees,' 48 'State committees' and, assuming that only one farmer in each so-called 'commercial producing area' should request the review of his allotment in the production of any one of the crops subject to control in the act, the further establishment of an additional indeterminate number of 'review committees, or a total of possibly more than 300,000 persons, installed on the Federal payroll, in order to place and to weld this yoke of absolute regimentation upon the neck of the American farmer."

February 15, 1938

MARKETS FOR FARMERS NOW A MAJOR CONCERN

Federal Authorities Are Grappling With Problems of Agriculture in The War Years and After

By LUTHER HUSTON

WASHINGTON, Feb. 22—The first World War started American farmers on a prosperity spree that ruined many of them. The present war has created problems of its own that are now the deep concern of the very highest officials in Washington.

The extent to which agriculture figures in the consideration of wartime problems is manifested by the facts that Claude R. Wickard, Secretary of Agriculture, sits often in what might be called the President's "War Council" and that a major segment of the plans being devised to cushion the adverse effect of war's dislocations upon our national economy embraces the welfare of the farmer.

It is not feared today that the demands of European markets will cause inflation of the American agricultural structure, as in the World War when farmers went deep into debt to acquire land at high prices to raise crops which were sold at boom price levels. On the contrary; one of the outstanding problems faced by American agriculture is what to do with the things it produces that Europe no longer buys and may not ever buy again.

The plain fact is that agriculture in this country has suffered almost complete loss of its export markets. Continental Europe now buys nothing from us. Great Britain, our best customer, is using her money and credit to buy munitions instead of food.

Estimates of Loss

Department of Agriculture officials are chary about estimating the dollar value of the loss of export trade since the war began. One unofficial estimate is $800,000,000. That may be high, but $500,000,000 would be conservative.

An indication of the volume extent of the loss is supplied by these figures:

Exports of wheat in 1938-39 amounted to 107,000,000 bushels. In 1939-40 the figure was 45,000,000 bushels. This year the best estimate is that our wheat exports will not exceed 20,000,000 bushels.

Last year we exported 6,000,000 bales of cotton: the top estimate for this year is 1,500,000.

Tobacco growers have lost export markets for 250,000,000 pounds; hog producers have lost markets for 75,000,000 pounds of pork and 140,000,000 pounds of lard; fruit growers will not sell abroad this year 10,000,000 bushels of apples and 3,000,000 boxes of oranges that were normal export quotas before the war.

ON THE FARM FRONT

Times Wide World

Claude R. Wickard, Secretary of Agriculture, is tackling the farm problem from many angles.

One plan now under discussion, in connection with efforts to coordinate agriculture's part in the defense program, would help offset this loss of markets by requiring Great Britain to increase her purchase of farm products as part compensation for the aid to be given her under the lease-lend bill. This would be a temporary aid to the farmer, but could not be regarded as a long-time solution of the export problem.

Counting Europe Out

Peace, it is supposed, will bring about a partial restoration of export markets, but official opinion is agreed that long-range planning for American agriculture must discount European markets as a major outlet for its surplus products in the future.

"It would be in error if we say that World War No. 2 is the sole cause for our almost complete loss of exports and that as soon as war ends we shall have what we think of as 'normal' export," Secretary Wickard says. "World war number two climaxed a trend in our export trade that had been going on for four decades. Likewise it brought into sharp relief the situation that American farm products face in the world export markets today."

Surpluses in basic commodities are the chief, but not the only, problem in an agricultural situation that Secretary Wickard describes as "extremely complex" and as having "social implications that are simply tremendous."

Price parity for farm commodities, which has been a major objective of the New Deal farm program, is still unattained. The prices of all five basic farm commodities—cotton, wheat, corn, tobacco and rice—are still lower in relation to what the farmer has to buy than they were in established base periods: 1919-29 for tobacco and 1909-14 for the others.

The seriousness of the surplus production situation is matched by the surplus population problem. If the ever-normal granary is bursting at the seams, so too is the human granary represented by the more than 32,000,000 people that live on farms.

There are seven or eight million people in agriculture who are not needed to supply existing markets for farm products. The curtailment of export markets will add more. Too many farmers are competing for a share in an agricultural income that is not big enough to go around. Close to one-fourth of the people on farms are being supported on a bare subsistence level under conditions that exhaust the re-

FACTS ABOUT THE FARM PROBLEM

	CASH FARM INCOME FROM CROPS AND LIVESTOCK	GOVERNMENT PAYMENTS
1930	$ 8,883,000,000	NONE
1931	$ 6,283,000,000	NONE
1932	$ 4,682,000,000	NONE
1933	$ 5,278,000,000	$131,000,000
1934	$ 6,273,000,000	$447,000,000
1935	$ 6,969,000,000	$573,000,000
1936	$ 8,212,000,000	$287,000,000
1937	$ 8,744,000,000	$367,000,000
1938	$ 7,590,000,000	$482,000,000
1939	$ 7,733,000,000	$807,000,000
1940 (estimated)	$ 8,354,000,000	$766,000,000

FARM POPULATION
1930 – 30,169,000
1940 – 32,245,000

Each disc equals one billion dollars

sources of the soil and debase human standards of living.

Problems Listed

The major problems facing farmers now and for the coming years have been summarized as follows:

Adjustment of farm production to find alternative opportunities for farmers who have been producing for export markets.

Working out of methods and conditions under which the United States may be able to regain some foreign markets after the war is over.

Improvement of the marketing and the expansion of domestic use of farm products.

Preparation for readjustments which will be required at the end of the war and at the end of our own defense effort.

Continuation without interruption of the conservation of soil, timber, water and grass—the basic elements of agricultural and national wealth.

Despite the loss of export markets, cash income of farmers from sale of crops and livestock is going up. The Department of Agriculture estimates the total cash farm income for 1940 at $8,354,000,000, as compared with $7,733,000,000 in 1939. The prediction is that 1941 will see a further increase.

This will be due, it is said, to increased purchasing power of consumers brought about by expansion of industry under the defense program.

Nutrition Campaign

The nation-wide nutrition campaign soon to be undertaken to build up the health of American citizens is another element agriculture is counting upon to bring about a substantial increase in per capita consumption of farm products, needed for farm prosperity.

Secretary Wickard believes that agriculture would be aided and "cut-throat competition" for world markets avoided by international agreements among the producing nations. L. A. Wheeler, director of the Office of Foreign Agricultural Relations, thinks that an extension to other countries on the American Continent of the method of surplus commodities distribution represented in this country by the food stamp plan would be beneficial. He also sees merit in a plan that has been suggested for an adequately financed hemispheric cartel to buy up surpluses as they appear and control their marketing.

If the United States financed the development in other American republics of facilities for growing commodities now imported from Europe or Asia, such as rubber, abaca, tea and camphor, cinchona bark, etc., there would be created in those countries, some believe, industrial activity which would make them a better market for things grown on farms in this country.

Some of the Plans

Plans being discussed for improving farm conditions by purely domestic measures involve, as one major possibility, the imposition of quota limitations on marketings of the 1941 corn and wheat crops, and a referendum of growers on a quota for wheat will be held on May 31. Other elements in the plans under discussion include a "two-price" program on domestic consumption and exports; higher loan rates on crops, whose result would be to place virtually all surpluses under government ownership, and the so-called "income certificate plan," highly favored by some farm leaders. This last would be in effect a processing tax designed to make self-financing a large part of the farm program now financed by government payments.

It is the consensus in official quarters that most of the plans being discussed to alleviate the ills of the farmer, prevent wartime conditions from pushing back his social and economic horizons, could be carried out under existing legislation. It is not expected, therefore, that much new legislation purely domestic in its application will be proposed at this session of Congress.

Whether President Roosevelt will ask Congress for legislation to carry out farm policies linked directly with the war and the national defense program is not known. His recent conferences with Secretary Wickard have given rise to the belief that some such move may be in the making.

February 23, 1941

POST-WAR WHEAT ASSURED

Canada, Argentina, Australia and U. S. Discuss Problems

Special to THE NEW YORK TIMES.

WASHINGTON, Aug. 9—The post-war world will be assured of an ever-normal granary of wheat, free wheat for countries in danger of famine, and wheat in plenty for all nations at prices reasonable to consumers and producers, according to plans being made at a series of conferences being held here by representatives of the United States, Great Britain, Argentina, Canada and Australia.

Wheat problems have been under discussion since July 10 by representatives of the governments concerned, according to the Department of State, and a provisional agreement has been reached which has been submitted to authorities in Washington, London, Buenos Aires, Ottawa and Canberra. Replies are expected by Aug. 18, when the meetings here will be renewed.

The problems of furnishing post-war relief to countries which suffered invasion and devastation have been considered, as have methods for avoiding cut-throat competition and of controlling production so that present wheat stocks may not continue to rise. Wheat-growing countries have on hand in granaries supplies which under normal conditions of trade would supply export demands for at least two years

August 10, 1941

CAN SUBSIDIZE SALE OF PRODUCE ABROAD

Commodity Credit Corporation Shown to Be So Empowered by Surplus Disposal Act

By JOHN H. CRIDER

Special to THE NEW YORK TIMES.

WASHINGTON, Oct. 5 — The surplus war property disposal bill which President Roosevelt signed on Tuesday contains a provision permitting the Commodity Credit Corporation to subsidize the export "of any farm commodity or product," and some officials regard this as a significant new step in the Administration's foreign economic policy.

While from time to time during the present Administration there have been provisions for subsidizing exports of some agricultural commodities, notably cotton and wheat, this is the first time that a Government agency has, in effect, received carte blanche to sell "any" farm product abroad at give-away prices, if necessary.

"The Commodity Credit Corporation," the act says, "may dispose of or cause to be disposed of for cash or its equivalent in goods or for adequately secured credit, for export, and at competitive world prices, any farm commodity or product thereof without regard to restrictions with respect to the disposal of commodities imposed upon it by law."

Insertion of the provision in the bill by the Congressional farm group was generally interpreted as an attempt to face the fact that Administration price-support policies for farm commodities, for which the same Congressional group was responsible, virtually foreclosed the possibility of exporting surpluses except at prices considerably less than those which the Government maintains domestically.

"Dumping" Is Made Possible

Some officials of the Department of Agriculture admitted that the provision in the new law would make possible the "dumping" of surplus agricultural commodities abroad, a fact which in their opinions makes it imperative that the United States proceed soon to negotiate commodity agreements with other large producing countries to prevent competitive "dumping" of surpluses after the present abnormal demand has subsided.

The objections of some other Government agencies to the Agriculture Department's commitment to the use of international commodity agreements to solve the problem of world surpluses has been the principal pitfall holding up the interdepartmental executive committee on economic policy in drafting its final report to the President on cartel and commodity policies.

The attitude of officials at the Agriculture Department is that whether the Administration's policy of maintaining artificial supports under domestic farm prices is right or wrong, the department must carry out the Congressional mandate.

Thus, they contend, if it is national policy to maintain domestic farm prices so high that commidities cannot be sold in the international market without subsidies, then it is essential that chaotic competitive marketing conditions be avoided by drawing up agreements with other producers not to resort to practices which might work hardship on all countries in the end.

In some quarters the new export subsidy policy was viewed as in conflict with the aspiration expressed in Article 7 of the master lend-lease agreements to work for "the elimination of all forms of discriminatory treatment in international commerce."

A Practice Not Commended

The practice of "dumping" commodities overseas, for which Japan and Germany became notable during the Thirties, is generally regarded as one of the most undesirable forms of economic nationalism and discriminatory trade practice.

The surplus property disposal bill's provision authorizing the CCC to sell abroad surplus agricultural commodities and products "at competitive world prices," means that the Government absorbs the differences between what it paid for the products and what it can sell them for in the foreign market.

Prior to this, since some time in 1941, the law prohibited the sale of such commodities at below-parity prices, but under earlier legislation it was possible for the Government to sell some products abroad on a subsidy basis, using 30 per cent of annual customs receipts, which were made available for farm subsidies for either domestic or foreign sale, to pay the bill.

October 6, 1944

42 NATIONS ADOPT WHEAT AGREEMENT

Export and Import Quotas Set for 456,283,386 Bushels for Each of Four Years

By BESS FURMAN

Special to The New York Times.

WASHINGTON, March 23 — Forty-two countries today unanimously adopted the international wheat agreement, described as a "trading instrument" to make possible "planned production and organized marketing of wheat throughout the world."

At a final plenary session full of felicitations among the delegates on a difficult task well done, many leaders expressed the hope that the treaty would prove a trail-blazer for multilateral pacts on other main commodities in world trade.

Five exporting and thirty-seven importing countries voted for a trade pact allocating 456,283,389 bushels of wheat a year, for each of four years beginning with the crop year 1949. The ceiling price set was $1.80 a bushel with the floor starting at $1.50 a bushel and receding by 10-cent intervals to $1.20 for the crop year 1952.

The wheat conference spokesmen today deplored the fact that two great exporting nations, Soviet Russia and Argentina, were not among the negotiators. These two countries were represented by observers all through the long negotiations, including today. The door was left open for their possible entrance into the pact later.

Russia withdrew from the negotiations as they neared their conclusion because she could not obtain an export quota of 75,000,000 bushels. The quantities to be exported proved to be the thorniest problem, and the final figure was settled only today.

Thirty countries signed the wheat agreement in ceremonies that followed today's plenary sessions. All five exporting countries signed. The importing countries that were first-day signers were Austria, Belgium, Ceylon, China, Colombia, Cuba, Denmark, Dominican Republic, Egypt, El Salvador, Greece, Guatemala, India, Ireland, Israel, Italy, Lebanon, Liberia, Netherlands, Nicaragua, Philippines, Portugal, Saudi Arabia, Union of South Africa and the United Kingdom.

The Arabic countries were applauded as they signed, for there had been some doubt as to whether they would join Israel in a multilateral agreement, as they had opposed her admission.

The rest of the countries have until April 15 to sign, and until July 1, which starts the 1949 crop year, to ratify.

The exporting countries agreed to furnish the following quantities:

	Bushels.
Canada	203,069,635
United States	168,069,635
Australia	80,000,000
France	3,306,934
Uruguay	1,837,185

The importing countries agreed to take the following quantities, in bushels:

Austria	11,023,113
Belgium	20,209,040
Bolivia	2,755,778
Brazil	13,227,736
Ceylon	2,939,497
China	7,348,742
Colombia	734,874
Cuba	7,422,229
Denmark	1,616,723
Dominican Republic	734,874
Ecuador	1,102,311
Egypt	6,981,305
El Salvador	404,181
Greece	15,726,308
Guatemala	367,437
India	38,286,946
Ireland	10,104,520
Israel	3,674,371
Italy	40,418,081
Lebanon	2,388,341
Liberia	36,744
Mexico	6,246,431
Netherlands	25,720,597
New Zealand	4,592,964
Nicaragua	293,950
Norway	7,716,179
Panama	624,643
Paraguay	2,204,623
Peru	7,348,742
Philippines	7,201,767
Portugal	4,409,245
Saudi Arabia	1,837,125
Sweden	2,755,778
Switzerland	6,430,149
Union of South Africa	11,023,113
United Kingdom	177,067,938
Venezuela	3,306,934

U. S. Ratification Predicted

The text provides that as of July 1, the signators must include 70 per cent of the guaranteed purchases and 80 per cent of the guaranteed sales.

"The next three months is not a long period to allow for acceptance, but it is all the time there is," said Charles Wilson, Canada's representative and spokesman for the exporting nations.

Secretary of Agriculture Charles F. Brannan, the conference chairman, said that the State Department would determine how and when the treaty would go to Capitol Hill. Last year, a similar agreement was regarded as a treaty and was sent only to the Senate, where it was considered by the Foreign Relations Committee. It then failed of ratification, and became a campaign issue. Secretary Brannan today expressed a "firm belief" that the current Congress would ratify it.

He said it would have the following advantages for the United States:

1. It will stabilize our foreign market for wheat. Added to supplies to Germany and Japan, the agreement assures export of well over 300,000,000 bushels a year over the four-year period, precluding such a débâcle as followed the first World War.
2. It will make it less difficult to support wheat prices at home, thus making more firm the domestic program.
3. It will set a pattern of international cooperation in solving agricultural problems.

The conference today set up a preparatory committee to function until the International Wheat Council set up by the agreement, to consist of a representative from each of the signatory countries, takes over. It is provided that the first meeting of the wheat council will be held in the United States early in July.

March 24, 1949

SUBSIDIES REPLACE PARITY TO FARMER IN FULL-FOOD PLAN

Long-Range Brannan Program Involves a New Support Idea Based on Purchasing Power

MILK GRANT IS ASKED NOW

Quick Help Also Urged to Spur Pork Production — Truman Classes Project as Sound

By BESS FURMAN

Special to The New York Times.

WASHINGTON, April 7—Plentiful food for consumers and assured incomes for farmers were announced as the aim of the new long-range farm program, presented by Secretary of Agriculture Charles F. Brannan today at a joint meeting of House and Senate Agriculture Committees.

Asked to comment on the program at his news conference today, President Truman said that it spoke for itself, that he knew what was in it and that it was all right.

The thirty-five page plan would involve, in place of "percentage of parity" price supports of recent years, a new "minimum standard of purchasing power" price-support formula. This would be based on a recent ten-year average for the staple, storable crops. These constitute about 25 per cent of United States production.

The program would provide production payments, that is, subsidies, to absorb the gap between what it costs a farmer to produce a product and what the consumer can afford to pay, on the perishable crops. These constitute about 75 per cent of United States crops, including most of the "protective foods" which assure high nutritional levels in American living.

Government buying programs would continue as a price-support device, and Secretary Brannan made clear that he would like to see perishable surpluses channeled into a larger school-luncheon system.

But he said that for the present he had definitely discarded a "food-stamp" or "food-allotment" program of food aid to the neediest as "administratively expensive and of only indirect aid to agriculture."

Equal funds put into production payments, he said, "would give the farmer more aid, and would benefit all consumers of the commodity involved."

Secretary Brannan recommended a start right now with a milk subsidy, such as was paid farmers during the war when consumer prices were held down by OPA, to bring milk at around 15 cents a quart back to the urban table. He also recommended production payments to pork growers this season, for an immediate build-up of meat stocks which had been low since the failure of the 1947 corn crop.

Under questioning, Secretary Brannan said that the Government would soon have to start a whole-milk price support program anyhow, since support of butter and skim milk had failed to stabilize the market. The most important thing, he said, would be to see that fluid milk went into the market-place to users. He indicated that milk consumption was rapidly going down because consumers were being priced out of the market.

Wants Criticism Relieved

"It (subsidy) will relieve us of the criticism that the Government is using billions of American dollars to maintain at high levels the prices of things that consumers need," he said. He added that this criticism would have to be met if taxpayers were to be expected to keep on putting up their dollars.

Secretary Brannan told the two committees that no new principles were involved in his new, long-range farm plan. However, several committee members indicated some astonishment at its scope, and Senator Clinton P. Anderson, Democrat, of New Mexico, former Secretary of Agriculture, said he wanted time to study it before asking questions.

Chairman Harold D. Cooley of the House committee said the Secretary had spoken in a "bold and brilliant fashion." Chairman Elmer Thomas of the Senate committee said that he had "set forth the philosophy of agriculture in relation to other industry." Both chairmen asked him to draft the plan into legislation.

One of the four big farm groups spoke up immediately. President James G. Patton of the National Farmers Union issued a statement terming the agricultural income and parity proposals "a milestone in the history of American agriculture."

Secretary Brannan told the two committees that he believed his plan would cost the United States Treasury no more than the present price-support program but said that he had as yet no actual cost estimates.

Emphasis on Conservation

Under the new plan, all payments to farmers would be predicated on strict compliance with conservation practices, and with acreage-allotment and marketing-quota plans.

Perhaps the most unusual feature of the plan is a "unit-system" of production limits beyond which big commercial growers, estimated at 2 per cent of present United States producers and now growing about 25 per cent of the crops, would get no Federal aid. This was said to be in the interest of preserving the family farm and rural community life.

Units suggested were ten bushels of corn, almost eight of wheat, fifty pounds of cotton—their equivalent in other products. Not more than 1,800 units per farm would be eligible for support, with, however, the possibility of some special consideration for strict adherence to acreage-control and marketing-quota programs.

Discarded under the new plan would be both the rigid 90 per cent of parity price support of the Hope part of the current Hope-Aiken act and the flexible 60 to 90 per cent of parity of the long-range Aiken part of the act to take effect Jan. 1, 1950.

New Criteria Are Proposed

The aim of the old parity formula was to make the farmer's bushel of wheat or hundredweight of hogs buy as much in goods and services as it bought in a base period regarded as a region of "normalcy," 1909 to 1914. The Aiken bill recognized this period as far removed from the present day, and provided a more modern base period.

Secretary Brannan, however, said that income, and not price, was what actually counted, and that the time had come to use income criteria, instead of price, in figuring farm supports. A recent ten-year period was selected as base—at first 1939 through 1948 and then moving forward annually to the first ten of the preceding twelve years.

He presented the committee with a formula which he termed as more simple than any yet written into law for figuring farm prices. Under the new principle, the main commodities are figured out in comparison with current parity prices.

As of now, the wheat support price would be lower, that of hogs, beef and lambs higher, indicating the shift to livestock production and away from grain surpluses desired by the Administration.

The Secretary said the two-year lag in the forward-moving base period would give Congress, the department and farmers time to make better production plans.

Secretary Brannan recommended first support for commodities of first priority: corn, cotton, wheat, tobacco, whole milk, eggs, farm chickens and the meat animals—hogs, beef cattle and lambs.

He recommended that all other commodities be supported in line with first priority commodities, taking into account available funds and authorities and the ability of producers to keep supplies in line with demand.

He cited potato supports, still a costly program, though acreage has been curtailed and prices supported at only 60 per cent of parity, as an outstanding example of how the Government could save money under the new system. One committee member said he would like to hear the Secretary "spell that out" at a later date.

The Secretary said that his plan would contribute to continued full employment and high participating power, and to the brisk international trade envisaged by the International Wheat Agreement.

He called price supports "the farmer's equivalent of the laboring man's minimum wage, social security and collective bargaining." He said authority should be available to support any commodity at whatever level was required to increase supplies or meet national emergencies.

April 8, 1949

FARM BUREAU VOTE HITS BRANNAN PLAN

Group Sees Nationalization of Agriculture in Program—Opinion Unanimous

By WILLIAM M. BLAIR

Special to The New York Times.

CHICAGO, Dec. 15—The American Farm Bureau Federation charged today that the ultimate effect of the Brannan Plan "would be nationalization of agriculture and the distribution system" for farm products.

The first official stand of the country's largest farmer organization was contained in a three-page resolution adopted at the final session of the four-day annual meeting. There was no debate. The standing vote was unanimous.

In a lengthy series of resolutions dealing with related agricultural and governmental activities, the federation went further and struck at Federal activities that have been described as tending toward a "welfare state."

Voting delegates backed up their resolutions by electing Allan Blair Kline of Vinton, Iowa, to a second term as president. He has been one of the bitterest foes of the Brannan Plan. They also re-named Romeo E. Short of Brinkley, Ark., chairman of the resolutions committee, as vice president.

The anti-Brannan Plan resolution was the climax of three days of castigation of the program advanced by Secretary of Agriculture Charles F. Brannan, who was not invited to the meeting.

The delegates reaffirmed faith in a system of flexible price supports for farm products under a parity concept and laid down seven reasons for opposition to the Brannan Plan as follows:

1. Government payments to farmers are not a desirable substitute for price supports or a satisfactory means of bringing income into agriculture.
2. The cost of the program would be staggering.
3. There is no good reason why the Government should pay part of the grocery bill of every citizen.
4. Per-unit goals of the plan (including direct payments to farmers) are so high as to make for certainty of rigid controls over all phases of agricultural activity.
5. A unit limitation on the amount of farm production eligible for price support would place a ceiling on opportunity in agriculture.
6. The plan discards the fair-exchange concept of parity, which has been the basis of farm programs since 1933 and would substitute an untried concept in the post-war adjustment period.
7. The bipartisan approach to development of farm policy has been jeopardized by the unusual procedure employed in the creation of this plan and its presentation to the public.

Opposite Result Seen

"A plan which promises high per-unit returns (including payments) to farmers and cheap food to consumers with little cost to anyone, actually would result in low farm prices and high food costs when the resulting inefficiencies and the inevitable tax costs are included," it stated.

"The great bulk of the American people are able to buy agricultural products at prices which will reflect fair market prices to farmers. The nutritional needs of low-income families can be met most effectively by continuing those efforts through which remarkable progress has been made in raising income levels in America."

It is a well-known economic fact, the resolution said, that "the demand for most agricultural products is such that an increase of a given percentage in supply makes a greater than proportionate decrease in price."

"Farmers do not intend," it added, "to get themselves into the position of having their entire net income, and probably a part of their actual production costs as well, dependent upon the precarious possibility of annual appropriations from the Federal Treasury. Here is the basis for real regimentation."

The Brannan plan would employ a combination of supports and direct payments to farmers. Farm products would be permitted to seek their own price levels in the market. To achieve a "fair return" to farmers, the Government would pay the difference between what he received in the market and stated price props. It also provides for certain farm unit production goals and control measures, which Secretary Brannan has said are available to him in present legislation.

Compromise Endorsed

Under the existing price support system the Government bolsters prices through buying with loans and purchase agreements.

The federation endorsed the 1949 compromise farm legislation for a "fair trial," but with reservations.

It also differed with inclusion of hired farm labor in calculation of the parity formula, continuation of the 90 per cent of parity price supports on so-called basic commodities through 1950, and an amendment permitting basic commodities to use the higher of the old or modernized parity formula.

December 16, 1949

U. S. SURPLUS FOODS OFFERED 62 LANDS

Agricultural Department Would Sell Millions of Pounds at Nominal Prices

WASHINGTON, Aug. 4 (UP)—The United States offered some of its surplus food to other friendly nations today under a cut-price arrangement.

The Agriculture Department said the food was offered at "nominal" prices to sixty-two other nations which are members of the United Nations Food and Agriculture Organization.

It did not disclose the price nor the amount of food being offered, but it was reported to run into millions of pounds."

The food offered included butter, cheese, Mexican canned meat, dried milk and eggs, beans and peas. They are among the surplus foods the Government has accumulated under the farm price support program.

The offer to the foreign governments was the latest of several moves the department has made in recent months to dispose of huge stocks of perishable foods before they spoil.

The department has been giving away food for domestic relief feeding and for relief feeding of foreigners by private, American-sponsored relief agencies. The food also has been offered at cut rates to commercial exporters.

The only string attached to the new offer was that the foreign governments use the food as a supplement, and not a substitute, for the food supplies they normally buy in regular trade channels.

The governments that buy the food will have to use their own dollars. They will not be allowed to use foreign aid funds that the United States Government provides to many of them.

August 5, 1950

KOREAN WAR HELPS TO HALT SURPLUSES

But F. A. O. Experts Caution World to Act to Curb Prices and Assure Distribution

Special to THE NEW YORK TIMES.

LAKE SUCCESS, Oct. 19—United Nations members received a report today saying that the Korean conflict—with its heavy demands for foodstuffs and supplies—had incidentally brightened economic conditions in most countries.

This improvement in the global economic picture was reported by experts of the Food and Agriculture Organization in their annual survey of the "world's outlook." Their findings were summed up in the wry judgment of Norris E. Dodd, director general of the United Nations' agency, that the bitter fighting in Asia and the expansion of armaments production apparently had been more beneficial to the international food situation than all the peaceful efforts under taken in the last four years.

"This is not a flattering commentary on international statesmanship," Mr. Dodd said, "but by all means let us take full advantage of this by-product of a troubled situation, and hope that in the future we can do better in developing methods that will work in an atmosphere of international good-will."

As a result of the Korean crisis, the F. A. O. experts predicted, the demands on producing and importing countries would be so strong in the next two years that all threat of unmarketable surpluses would fade. They cautioned however, that prices would go so high on some products that governments might have to clamp down on speculators and hoarders to assure fair distribution for consumers.

In the agricultural field, the price of wool and rubber already has risen "dangerously," the report said.

Sees Trade Stimulated

Before the war in Korea, the experts said, currency difficulties "loomed as a great barrier" to world-wide distribution of supplies, particularly in the instances of soft-currency nations such as those in Western Europe.

As an outcome of mobilization for war and the stepped-up defense program of the United States, it was said that "world trade in food and other agricultural products should be stimulated."

"For the next two years at least," the report predicted, "the amount of dollars available to the rest of the world should continue to increase." By the middle of next year, it added, United States military spending should reach $30,000,000,000 and the gross national income should approach an annual rate of $300,000,000,000. As a consequence, the demand for imports into the United States of raw materials and manufactured goods, as well as foodstuffs, should rise "appreciably," the experts said.

Many countries, the F. A. O. report stated, will be unable to cope with the increased United States demand for products since many of the commodities take time to produce and output cannot be raised rapidly.

Within the next few months other products besides wool and rubber will be affected by the increased demand, the report said.

One approach, the experts asserted, would be to place items in short supply under some form of international control. Aside from products already in "extreme scarcity," the report posed the question of what arrangements should be made to prevent the exhaustion of cereals, livestock products, cotton, tobacco and other commodities. While these commodities were not necessarily in short supply national stockpiles could be drained rapidly, the specialists cautioned.

The report asked that consideration be given to what action the agency should take in the United Nations' efforts to forestall civil disturbance and war. It suggested that the F. A. O., with the approval of members of the United Nations, might make preliminary studies of land reforms, a basic problem in Asia.

October 20, 1950

PROBLEMS LOOMING ON CROP SURPLUSES

With Export Demand Abating, New Markets Are Needed For Record Output

By J. H. CARMICAL

The incoming Republican Administration may have to deal with a difficult surplus problem in some farm products. To satisfy the heavy demand abroad in recent years, the American farmer has stepped up production to record levels. Now, with the foreign demand abating, the farmers must depend more and more upon local markets. The result is that farm product surpluses are building up rapidly.

With food scarce in many areas following the end of World War II, the export movement of United States farm products increased rapidly and the dollar value reached record levels. Through the various foreign aid programs the dollar exchange shortage was overcome. Prices moved up sharply, which stimulated production, and in 1952 the combined output of domestic crops and livestock, according to the Department of Agriculture, was the largest in history despite droughts in several important producing areas.

Mechanizing Pushed

From profits on their steadily increasing production, the United States farmers in the post-war years speeded their mechanization efforts and today are prepared to produce at a still higher rate. With the United States Government pledged to support prices of the basic crops at 90 per cent of parity through 1954 the incentive to produce still exists, despite the decline recently in prices of some products to around the support level. No production controls have been established on the basic crops for this year, and the chances are that if weather conditions are not too adverse, heavy yields again may be expected.

It is true that the winter wheat crop has gotten off to a poor start because of drought conditions over a part of the belt. However, this condition has been alleviated materially recently. With the acreage sown to winter wheat this year approximately the same as a year earlier, there is a fair chance that a normal yield may be made if adequate moisture is received in the next two or three months.

The first report of the Department of Agriculture is that the yield from the present winter wheat crop will be 611,141,000 bushels or around 400,000,000 bushels below the yield from the 1952 winter crop. The spring crop has averaged around 285,000,000 bushels in recent years, so the total yield on the present preliminary estimate from this year's wheat harvest is tentatively placed at 896,000,000 bushels. This would compare with 1,292,000,000 bushels from both the winter and spring crops in 1952.

Reflecting last year's near-record crop and a decline in the export movement, the carryover of wheat on June 30 is expected to be around 560,000,000 bushels. This would be only 82,000,000 bushels below the record carryover on June 30, 1942. The domestic consumption of the cereal in a crop year, which is from July 1 to June 30, at present averages about 700,000,000 bushels.

With a record supply of wheat in Canada seeking an export outlet and both Australia and Argentina now harvesting good crops, the United States growers face stiff competition for exports. Since the importing countries have increased their supplies, the international movement of wheat this season may be substantially below that of recent years.

Because of the rapid expansion in wheat production in most countries the importance of United States production in the world wheat market was at a low level just prior to World War II. Although this country was the "granary for the world" prior to World War I and the years immediately following, shipments of wheat from the United States to world market dropped rapidly in the Nineteen Twenties and the Thirties. To some in the trade, a similar situation now seems to be developing.

At the Commonwealth Economic Conference held in London in the first two weeks of December, a communiqué was issued listing a number of plans for increasing the output of food in several areas. It stated that these projects are to be given priority.

In Australia, it stated that food production is to be increased 20 per cent over the 1947-52 level by 1957, with wheat acreage to be expanded from 10,500,000 acres to 13,650,000. Exports of oats are to be doubled and sugar exports increased from 168,000 tons to 718,000. By 1954, New Zealand is scheduled to have an extra 20,000 tons of meat, 6,000 tons of butter and 4,000 to 5,000 tons of chese for export.

In Ceylon, the communiqué noted, a great expansion of food output, particularly rise, is planned to reduce imports. Large irrigation schemes were reported under way there.

India has a five-year development plan, which is now before the Indian Parliament. This plan the communiqué stated, involves an expenditure of £690,000,000 to be on irrigation, power and agricultural projects aimed at increasing food production.

Although more or less self-supporting in food, Pakistan reported that it has initiated several massive irrigation schemes to bring a very large additional acreage under production.

Other Areas Plan Increases

Other areas outside the British Commonwealth also are increasing production of foodstuffs to conserve exchange and to become self-sustaining so far as possible. Russia and the satellite nations, some of which in the past have bought agricultural products here, are not expected to be important customers of the United States soon.

With the United Kingdom, the largest purchaser of foodstuffs in the international market, expected to depend more and more on the Commonwealth members and the sterling area for its food supplies, the outlet for surplus farm products may be expected to shrink still further. Since exports of farm products have been a factor in keeping the nation's economy at a high level, the loss of these foreign markets may have an influence on industrial activity even though farm product prices may be held in the domestic market around current levels for the next two years through Federal price support activities.

January 4, 1953

SURPLUSES IN A HUNGRY WORLD

The Food and Agriculture Organization of the United Nations, meeting in Rome tomorrow, will face among other problems that of chronic hunger in vast areas of the world and that of an agricultural surplus in the United States. It has been estimated that the United States Government's purchase of such surpluses will amount to six billion dollars by the end of the present year. At the same time there are literally hundreds of millions of people in India, Pakistan and doubtless on the Communist-dominated mainland of China, and elsewhere, who do not, from birth to death, get enough food to sustain them in good health and full vigor. These undernourished millions may not die of starvation, but they fall victim to diseases to which the underfed are particularly subject.

The Netherlands Government announced on Friday that it would propose a special world conference to discuss the United States farm surplus problem. There is no reason why we should not welcome such a meeting, assuming that the subject cannot be fully threshed out at F. A. O.'s Rome conference. We ought to be able to take advice as well as to give it, and there are experts in other countries who might throw light on what is really a distressing and ironic problem.

Actually, of course, the question is financial. We have been accustomed in recent years to raise food for export, and we could go on doing it if the arrangements for paying the farmer could be made. We cannot, of course, set up as a permanent Lady Bountiful, collecting taxes to buy food for free distribution abroad. But certainly this problem cannot be beyond the possibility of solution. And in the long run, of course, the food supply for the peoples of the underdeveloped countries in the world can be increased by improved methods under the too much neglected program of technical assistance and Point Four aid.

November 22, 1953

SURPLUS DISPOSAL IS VOTED BY HOUSE

Billion-Dollar Bill Bars Curb on Trade—Restrictions Decried by President

By WILLIAM M. BLAIR

Special to The New York Times.

WASHINGTON, June 16—The House of Representatives passed the Administration's $1,300,000,000 farm surplus disposal bill today without any curbs on East-West trade.

Passage came on voice vote as President Eisenhower made clear at his press conference that he opposed any restrictions that would bar trading in nonstrategic materials with Iron Curtain countries. He viewed any such restrictions as tending to drive satellites closer to the Soviet Union.

What was needed, he said, were centrifugal forces to draw Soviet-bound countries away from the Red center.

The House accepted, however, an amendment that would forbid shipment of farm surpluses to any country before the President had determined that the commodities would not enable a country to trade in farm products with Iron Curtain nations.

Sponsors of the bill regarded the amendment as not limiting trade and requiring only simple certification by the President of surplus shipments. It was offered by Representative Martin Dies, Democrat of Texas, who yesterday unsuccessfully tried to block all trade in farm products with any country that dealt with Russia or her satellites.

The amendment was approved by a standing vote of 64 to 45.

The House also accepted fourteen other amendments, mostly clarifying language. One was a major blow to the State Department. By a voice vote on the motion of Representative Thomas G. Abernethy, Democrat of Mississippi, the House killed an "anti-dumping" provision. It would have required the President to take "reasonable precautions to safeguard" the usual marketing of friendly countries and assure that sales for foreign currencies would not disrupt world prices.

Representative Clifford R. Hope, chairman of the House Agriculture Committee, which approved the bill, did not oppose the Abernethy amendment but told the House he would try to work out alternative language in a Senate-House conference. This was needed, the Kansas Republican said, to state clearly that Congress opposed dumping and wished to prevent any international price war.

State Department Assailed

Mr. Abernethy, also a member of the House Agriculture Committee, said the original language would give the State Department a "veto" over agricultural trading. He and other opponents contended the provision had been written by the State Department. They accused the State Department of being more interested in protecting markets of foreign countries than in helping American farmers to dispose of their surpluses.

The bill will go to the conference committee because the Senate passed a similar measure last year. The Senate measure, however, provided a $500,000,000 disposal program and the House bill was expected to be substituted with some Senate suggestions.

The House measure gives authority to the President to dispose of up to $1,000,000,000 in farm surpluses in exchange for foreign currencies, goods and services. The monies acquired could be spent abroad for strategic materials, for foreign economic and military aid programs, such as bases abroad, for expanding world markets for American farm products, and for loans to promote multilateral trade and economic development.

Relief Authority Provided

The bill also provides authority for the President to use $300,000,000 worth of surpluses for output gifts in famine and other relief assistance. It provides for liberal disposal by the President of surpluses to meet disaster or distress from economic conditions at home.

Also on the farm front, the President indicated to his news conference that he might favor a readjustment of dairy price supports because he was for gradualism in everything the Government did on farm matters. He said, however, that an action of the House Agriculture Committee on dairy supports had not been brought to his attention.

The committee voted to increase by five points the price supports that Ezra Taft Benson, Secretary of Agriculture, cut sharply April 1 to try to stem the flood of butter, cheese and dried milk the Government is compelled to purchase under price support operations.

On April 1 Secretary Benson cut dairy price supports fifteen points on the parity scale—from 90 per cent of parity to 75 per cent.

Parity is a standard intended to give farmers a fair return for their products in relation to the prices of things they must buy.

June 17, 1954

CONGRESS PASSES FARM COMPROMISE

House, Senate Vote Flexible Supports in Major Victory for the Administration

By CHARLES E. EGAN

Special to The New York Times.

WASHINGTON, Wednesday, Aug. 18—The Senate completed Congressional action on the compromise farm bill early today, giving President Eisenhower a major victory.

The Senate approved the conference bill, 44 to 28. The House had passed it, 208 to 47.

The action of the two houses approved the compromise bill worked out by a joint conference committee. The measure, which will make effective the Administration's flexible support principle, now goes to President Eisenhower for his signature.

In both the Senate and the House, segments of the shattered farm bloc made futile efforts to reject the compromise.

The flexible supports, ranging from 82.5 to 90 per cent of parity, would replace the 90 per cent rigid price supports that five basic crops—wheat, corn, cotton, rice and peanuts—have enjoyed since the end of World War II. President Eisenhower and Secretary of Agriculture Ezra Taft Benson sought a flexible range of 75 to 90 per cent of parity, which is a Government-calculated formula designed to give farmers a fair price in relation to the costs of things they must buy.

At his news conference yesterday President Eisenhower said he was convinced that the majority of farmers backed his flexible support program.

The President added that if it was apparent that the farm measure needed to be changed he would propose such changes to the next session of Congress.

Although the farm bill rode through to an easy victory in the House yesterday, it was bitterly attacked from both sides of the aisle before the final vote was taken. Most of the denunciation from members of the farm bloc was concentrated upon the dairy price support feature of the bill.

Critics expressed dissatisfaction over the fact that House conferees had consented to drop a House-approved provision calling for dairy price supports of 80 per cent of parity in place of the 75 per cent that the Agriculture Department had put into effect April 1. The support level had been 90 per cent of parity before that date.

The Senate had rejected all attempts to increase the dairy support price.

Spokesmen for the Administration say flexible supports will help achieve a better balance in agricultural production and cut surpluses. The new flexible system would become effective Jan. 1.

Representative Franklin D. Roosevelt Jr., Democrat of Manhattan, joined the farm bloc in opposition to the Administration bill. Asserting that next to Wisconsin, New York State was the largest producer of dairy products in the country, Mr. Roosevelt sought to push a motion to recommit the bill to conference with instructions to insist upon an 80 per cent dairy support.

Before Mr. Roosevelt could present his motion, Representative Pat Sutton, Democrat of Tennessee, acting for the conference group representing the House, forestalled the move. He offered a motion to recommit the measure ,but omitted any reference to the dairy price support feature.

The motion was defeated, as Mr. Sutton had hoped. The motion to approve the bill followed.

In the debate that preceded House adoption of the bill, Representative Harold D. Cooley, Democrat of North Carolina and ranking minority member of the House Agriculture Committee, said that the Administration had wona "hollow victory." He said that if the Administration was the "victor" in today's action, the farmers were the vanquished.

Says Consumers Won't Save

Representative H. R. Gross, Republican of Iowa, protested that Congress was "selling the farmers down the river" and said that the lower prices to farmers "won't save consumers a nickel."

The bill as it emerged from the conference committee called for:

¶Flexible supports ranging from 82.5 to 90 per cent of parity, beginning next year, for cotton, wheat, corn, peanuts and rice.

¶A $2,500,000,000 "set-aside" of surplus crops for a national stockpile and for domestic and foreign relief. These stocks will be eliminated from price-support calculations, thus in some cases tending to give various products a slightly higher support than if the stocks were included. The President had suggested the "set-aside" to ease any abrupt downward economic shock in the farm economy.

¶A new direct payment program to encourage the production of wool as a security measure. Wool producers, beginning next year, will get direct Treasury payments for the difference between a support price not to exceed 110 per cent of parity and what growers receive in the open market. The program is aimed at raising domestic wool production to 300,000,000 pounds from the present level of 229,000,000 pounds annually.

¶A modernized parity formula that will become effective in 1956 on the five basic crops. The new formula will generally reduce support levels.

The bill provides, however, that such reductions would be limited to five points a year until the formula became fully effective.

August 18, 1954

U. S. JOINS SURPLUS UNIT

New U. N. Agency Will Try to Solve Crop Problem

Special to The New York Times.

UNITED NATIONS, N.Y., June 22—The United States, now struggling with its domestic wheat surplus, has joined other states in setting up a new international body to seek means of disposing of farm surpluses.

The new agency will function under the aegis of the United Nations Food and Agriculture Organization as a subsidiary body of F. A. O.'s Committee on Commodity Problems. Its first meeting, according to word received here today from F. A. O. headquarters in Rome, will be held in Washington some time next month.

Establishment of the new subcommittee at this time, F. A. O. officials observed, reflected the concern of governments in the mounting difficulties encountered in absorbing excess agricultural stocks in wheat, some oils, dairy products and cotton.

June 23, 1954

CANADA WRESTLES WORST WHEAT JAM

Big Crop Seeks Storage but Farms and Elevators Hold Vast Carryover

NO CASH AID TO GROWERS

Income Is Limited to $400 Each on Grain Actually Delivered to Elevators

Special to The New York Times.

WINNIPEG, Sask., Sept. 24—Canada is faced with what is probably the worst grain surplus in its history. Grain handling and marketing facilities from country elevators to lake and seaboard terminals are jammed with the carryover from the 1954 crop and the first deliveries of the 1955 crop.

The Canadian Wheat Board, the Federal Government's grain marketing agency, is confronted with the job of disposing of nearly 1,000,000,000 bushels of wheat. The 1955 wheat crop alone is estimated at 500,000,000 bushels.

The carryover of wheat on July 31, end of the official 1954-55 crop year, was 481,383,000 bushels—the third largest wheat carryover on record in spite of the near failure of the 1954 prairie wheat crop.

Nearly 100,000,000 bushels of this carryover was in granaries and makeshift bins on farms—about 90 per cent of it on farms in Western Canada. This was 95,000,000 bushels less than the carryover on farms in 1954 but was still the third largest farm carryover on record.

Export Lead Lost to U. S.

Canada's wheat exports have declined for three consecutive years. In the 1954-55 crop year Canada took second place to the United States, as the world's leading wheat exporter.

Preliminary figures released this month by the Board of Grain Commissioners show Canada exported 251,800,000 bushels of wheat and the grain equivalent of wheat flour during the 1954-55 crop year. The United States moved ahead with shipments totaling 275,000,000 bushels. Canada's 30-year wheat exports from 1923 to 1953 averaged 255,400,000 bushels.

Now in addition to the carryover from 1954 and preceding years, the 500,000,000-bushel 1955 wheat crop is ready for delivery. But in spite of the fact that nearly nine-tenths of the prairie wheat crop has been harvested, only about 25,000,000 bushels have actually been delivered to elevators. Congested grain-handling facilities offer wheat growers little hope of being able to step up deliveries in the immediate future.

Last year farmers were permitted to deliver eight bushels of wheat per seeded acre to elevators. Farmers in some areas of central Saskatchewan are still waiting for elevator space to market their 1954 eight-bushel quotas.

$400 Per Farmer

No farmer in Western Canada

is permitted to deliver more than his initial quota of 1955 grain. The initial quota has been set at 100 units. In practice this works out to 300 bushels of wheat, or 500 bushels of barley or rye, or 800 bushels of oats.

The initial quota is not related either to the number of seeded acres or the amount of grain stored on the farm. Regardless of the size of the farm, each farmer is permitted to deliver only 100 units. This quota would put less than $400 in the hands of the producer if deliveries took the form of No. 1 Northern wheat.

The large amount of grain stored on farms is reflected in farmers' cash position. In Canada there are no advance payments on farm-stored grain, nor is there a program of Government assistance for farm storage. Grain growers receive no return until their produce is delivered to elevators.

Information from the Wheat Board, the Board of Grain Commissioners and other sources indicates that deterioration of the stored grain is not yet an acute problem, although there have been some cases of loss of grade through heating of out-of-condition grain.

More Wheat on Less Acres

The bumper half-billion bushel wheat crop this year was not due to an increase in wheat acreage. Farmers seeded fewer acres to wheat in 1955 than they had for many years. The Dominion Bureau of Statistics reports that this year wheat acreage dropped to the twelve-year low of 21,504,000 acres compared with 24,266,800 acres in 1954. The ten-year average, 1944 to 1953, was 24,953,900 acres.

In spite of this sharp drop in acreage, Canadian farmers have harvested a bumper crop of high grade wheat. The delays caused by excessive rain and flooding in some areas last spring were overcome by ideal growing weather over most of the Prairies. Warm dry weather in August and September speeded harvesting operations.

The brighest spot in the Canadian grain picture is the good quality of the new crop. Preliminary estimates by the Board of Grain Commissioners place the average protein content of samples delivered so far at 13.4 per cent, 0.8 per cent above the 1954 average.

Wheat is Higher Graded

The wheat delivered to date is grading better than the 1954 crop. Much of the new wheat is being graded No. 1 and No. 2, in contrast to the large quantities of No. 3 or lower in the weather and rust-battered 1954 crop. At least 80 per cent of the 1955 wheat crop is now farm-binned in dry condition.

The Saskatchewan Department of Agriculture announced last Tuesday that with 90 per cent of the wheat in that province threshed, it is indicated that 95 per cent of the crop will grade Nos. 1, 2 or 3.

Grain dealers say there would be a ready market for considerable quantities of this high grade bread wheat and Durum wheat if it could be moved through plugged grain pipelines from Prairie farms to the Great Lakes before the close of navigation, about ten weeks away.

Low Grades at Lakehead

At present there are about 46,000,000 bushels of wheat in store at the Head of the Lakes. Nearly half this wheat grades lower than No. 4, the lowest recognized milling grade. Only 4,000,000 bushels of high grade wheat is stored in this easy marketing position.

The problem is to move supplies of the new high grade wheat through the plugged elevator system to positions where it will be readily available to buyers.

So far the problem has not been solved. Deliveries of all grains to date have been less than half delivery totals for the corresponding period in 1954. Deliveries of wheat have totaled only about 25,000,000 bushels.

George H. McIvor, head of the Wheat Board, has declined to discuss prospects of wheat sales, but informed observers believe exports will total no more than 250,000,000 bushels. This would leave a carryover of about 600,000,000 bushels at the end of the 1955-56 crop year.

Grain Handlers Laid Off

Normally in September Canadian railroads and grain dealers hire extra men to help transport and store the new crop. This September some grain handlers were laid off at Lakehead terminals.

Farm organizations in the West are demanding that something be done to move the grain surpluses, but they leave little doubt that they want sales increased without lowering prices. These farm groups insist that lower wheat prices would not lead to significant increases in sales.

In recent weeks, however, the Wheat Board has shown some disposition to lower prices. The price of No. 1 Northern wheat was lowered 1 cent to $1.75 basis in store at Fort William. Decreases of 1 or 2 cents a bushel have been announced in all other grades of bread wheats.

Limit to Price Cuts

But there is a limit to price cuts the Board may make. The Federal Government sets the initial price, in reality a floor price, that the Board must pay farmers for wheat delivered to the elevator system. This year the initial price has been set at $1.40 a bushel.

In practice, the Board is squeezed between the initial price it must pay to farmers for wheat and the price it can get for the wheat in domestic and world markets. The board is expected to pay the cost of storing and handling the vast quantities of grain that come into its possession, to pay its own costs of administration and to show a profit on its operations to be paid out to farmers as a final settlement for the grain they have delivered.

Any drastic action to move Canada's grain surpluses and to get cash into farmers' pockets must originate with the Canadian Government.

Government spokesmen in the past, particularly C. D. Howe, Minister of Trade and Commerce, have repeatedly declared that there would be no fire-sale price cutting of Canadian surplus grain and no attempt to compete with giveaway programs of other countries.

Concern Over U. S. Policy

But there is increasing concern on the part of Government officials and farmers over what Secretary of Agriculture Ezra T. Benson declared in Regina, Saskatchewan, in August was to be a policy of "aggressive but fair" United States efforts to dispose of agricultural surpluses in world markets.

They regard the United States policy of disposing of surplus wheat for unconvertible local currency as little more than giveaway deals that are seriously disturbing international wheat marketing. They believe these giveaway sales are cutting directly into Canada's established markets in such countries as Japan, West Germany, Italy and Brazil.

This question will almost certainly be brought forward for discussion when Canadian and United States cabinet ministers meet in Ottawa on Sept. 26 as the joint committee on trade and economic affairs.

September 25, 1955

WORLD'S MARKETS FACING RICE GLUT

Burma Turns to Iron Curtain Outlets for Barter Deals—U. S. Has Own Overload

By JAMES J. NAGLE

Rice producing countries are finding it difficult to locate foreign markets for this daily food staple of more than half the world's population.

Burma, for instance, is making barter deals with Iron Curtain countries to rid itself of its surplus rice output. The deals were made after an unsuccessful attempt by the Burmese to dispose of the rice here in exchange for a technical assistance program. (Burma and Thailand are the two biggest rice exporting countries of Asia.)

The United States, however, has its own surplus rice problem. This government on Sept. 30 held 718,731 tons of rough rice, valued at $165,462,098. This despite the fact that the country produces less than 2 per cent of the world total.

The chief reason for the lack of foreign markets for the popular cereal is a profound change in the output of rice in recent years.

Production Doubled

For example, non-Asiatic countries have doubled their production since World War II, although 90 per cent of the world supply still is grown in Asia. In this country alone, rice production has increased from 890,000 tons in 1935 to 2,955,000 tons in 1954.

For eight years after World War II rice was scarce and a marked increase in price occurred. This resulted in a shift in consumption to cheaper and more abundant substitute cereals. In the Far East the shift was made only because of this scarcity and not because of any change in diet preference.

On the basis of import unit values between rice and other cereals imported into Asia between 1937 and 1953, the average prices for imported rice rose twice as much as those paid for other cereal imports, according to the Commodity Research Bureau.

Simultaneously, the relative share of rice in all Asian cereal imports fell sharply. In 1937, rice made up 88 per cent of the total cereal imports, compared with 31 per cent in 1953, when rice was scarce and prices relatively high. In 1953 Japan had one of its poorest rice crops in decades and India began building up heavy stocks.

Another disturbing factor is the heavy exporting of rice by Red China while Chinese go hungry

This year production has been going up everywhere except in North America. The 1955-56 world crop is expected to reach 135,000,000 tons, compared with 130,650,000 tons in the 1954-55 period, a rise of 3%. These figures exclude Communist China, North Korea and Soviet Russia. Burma alone is expected to produce 7,400,000 tons of rice in the 1955-56 season compared with 7,250,000 tons in the 1954-55 period.

Estimates for This Year

Other principal producing countries for which estimates of this year's output are available include:

India, 42,500,000 tons, the same as last year; Japan, 15,000,000 tons compared with 12,500,000; Pakistan, 14,250,000 against 14,150,000; Thailand 8,500,000 against 6,450,000; Philippines, 3,600,000 against 2,250,000; Taiwan, 2,450,000 against 2,250,000, and the U. S. 2,500,000 against 2,850,000 tons. No figures are available for such major producers as Brazil, China, Indochina, Soviet Russia, Indonesia and Korea, North and South.

Rice is one of the world's oldest foods. It originated with wild species indigenous to Africa, India and Indochina. Most of it is grown on submerged lands but some, known as "upland rice" is found on higher ground. It is most prevalent on coastal plains, tidal deltas and river basins in tropical, semi-tropical and temperate regions where fresh water is available to submerge the land.

In this country, the principal producing states are Texas, with an output of 805,000 tons in 1954; Louisiana with 750,000 tons, Arkansas with 735,000 tons; California, 545,000 tons, and Mississippi, 110,000 tons.

Seeded By Plane

In America, seeding is done by airplane and harvesting is carried out by machines after the water is drained off. The yield per acre, however, is not nearly as large as in most Asiatic countries, where practically all functions are carried out by hand and every plant is carefully nurtured.

Rice grown and sold here is polished much more than that grown in Asia, with the result that it is usually much whiter in appearance. Asiatics contend that too much polishing robs the rice of its nutritive value and those who try to exist on such rice alone often wind up with beri-beri, a vitamin deficiency disease.

Two basic types of rice are grown here — long grain and short grain. Known by the trade name "Carolina," the long variety is gaining in popularity with producers because of its higher yield per acre and with processors because it is fairly firm. General Food's Minute Rice is of this type. It is made in a large plant at Houston, Tex. After being cleaned, precooked and rinsed of the pasty starch film, it is dehydrated and dried by a special patented process.

Short grains, some carrying the trade name River Brand, are softer and recommended for puddings, croquettes and other dishes where a starchy consistency is desirable.

December 4, 1955

Surplus Export Plan Deemed Inadequate

By CHARLES E. EGAN

WASHINGTON, May 24—A staff report just submitted to President Eisenhower has found the prospect of solving farm overproduction by exporting surpluses to be unpromising.

The results of an eighteen-month study on the problem were recently handed to Clarence Francis, former head of the General Foods Corporation, who is a special adviser to the President on farm surplus matters. Mr. Francis passed the report to the President and Ezra Taft Benson, Secretary of Agriculture. He recommended an overhauling of Government policy to meet the problem.

A foreword says the report has been submitted "for consideration" and does not necessarily "reflect the views of the Administration." Even in the unlikely circumstance that current rates of agricultural surplus exports could be raised by 50 per cent, the study finds, it would take nine years or more to dispose of existing surpluses of feed grains and cheese, six years for surplus wheat, five years for cotton, four years for rice and tobacco and eighteen months for soybean stocks.

"Since foreign disposal does not appear to offer outlets adequate for the disposition of current surpluses in the next few years," the report says, "the situation strongly suggests that domestic production, price support and sales policies be carefully reviewed."

"It would appear that current output of supported commodities should be brought within the bounds of prospective dispositions; that all opportunities for decreasing production and marketing costs, as well as for increasing domestic utilization, be thoroughly explored; that legislative provisions that prohibit domestic sales except at levels materially above current prices should be reexamined; and that rigid domestic support prices for some commodities that cause the United States to be a residual supplier to world markets should be adjusted."

The report notes that obligations of the Commodity Credit Corporation resulting from price-support programs totaled $7,200,000,000. Of this amount, it says, $5,000,000,000 represented inventory and the remainder other price-support obligations, such as loans and purchase agreements made or underwritten to support prices and not redeemed by farmers.

In the 1954-55 fiscal year, it goes on, more than 40 per cent of the $3,100,000,000 worth of agricultural commodities shipped abroad was aided by one or more governmental programs to facilitate exports. The special aids included subsidies, barter deals, foreign currency sales, donations and special shipments for relief.

The question whether surplus exports to Soviet-bloc countries should be permitted has been raised in several quarters, the report notes. Sales or barter to Eastern European countries are now prohibited.

The report concedes that a potential market for additional surplus commodities seems possible through legislative modifications to permit the President to exploit at his discretion such opportunities as may be deemed appropriate.

Soviet-bloc purchases of United States products have included few agricultural commodities, the report finds. The Communist countries have chosed to use their dollar earnings for other purposes that they consider important it says.

"It is significant, however," it adds, "that recently large purchases of wheat have been made from Canada by Poland and Hungary, and of butter from Canada by Czechoslovakia, and that Hungary has asked to buy wheat from both Canada and the United States."

Although little is known about the prospective market for American exports to Communist China, the report finds evidence that the food situation there has become precarious following the 1954 drought.

The United States still maintains a full embargo on trade with Red China. But even if it did not, that country would provide only a limited market for surplus agricultural commodities except cotton.

The best opportunities for increasing exports without risking a substantial displacement of United States exports for dollars are in low-income, low-consumption areas, the report declares.

May 25, 1956

NEW FARM BILL IS SIGNED; PRESIDENT HAILS SOIL BANK, DEPLORES LAG IN PAYMENT

VOICES CRITICISMS

But Sees Gain Despite Objections to Many Parts of Measure

By EDWIN L. DALE Jr.
Special to The New York Times.

WASHINGTON, May 28 — President Eisenhower signed the farm bill today, praising its soil bank feature as "a concept rich with promise for improving our agricultural situation."

But the President declared:

"The delay in the bill's enactment * * * makes it virtually impossible to put the soil bank properly into effect in 1956, and I am disappointed that advance payments to farmers are not provided for."

The President sharply criticized several of the bill's sections, but said "its advantages outweigh its harmful provisions."

He had vetoed the first bill to reach him, mostly because it contained provisions restoring rigid price supports at 90 per cent of parity on five major crops.

Ezra Taft Benson, Secretary of Agriculture, said in a statement that he was "glad the President signed the bill." Mr. Benson had urged the veto of the earlier bill.

The key provision of the second bill, as of the first, is the soil bank—one of the first major innovations in Government agricultural programs since World War II. It provides $1,250,000,000 to pay farmers for taking crop land out of production and placing the land into soil-building cover crops or trees.

It is designed to cut surpluses and improve the land without impairing the farmers' income.

The President was critical of the new bill's cotton provisions as they related to foreign trade.

These provisions require the disposal of about 5,000,000 bales of the Government-held surplus at a price of at most 25 or 26 cents a pound. This is far below the original Government acquisition cost of 32 cents a pound and upward, and is also below the price at which cotton moves in world trade.

The President said the bill "requires the Government to follow an inflexible program of cotton export sales with little regard to costs and without adequate regard to the far-reaching economic consequences at home and abroad." He added that "in order to avoid seriously disruptive effects, this section of the bill will have to be administered with extreme caution."

The President also objected to these provisions of the bill:

¶Import restrictions on long-staple cotton.

¶Authority for the President to negotiate agreements limiting imports of farm commodities. General Eisenhower termed this "an undesirable complication in the field of foreign trade."

¶Provisions freezing acreage allotments for rice and cotton for 1957 and 1958 at this year's level. By preventing any further reduction in acreage, the provisions "run counter to the adjustment principle which underlies our basic agricultural legislation," the President said.

Sees Problems on Rice

He also noted that "the effective operation of a two-price plan for rice [as provided in the bill on a discretionary basis] is faced with several serious problems, which must be carefully evaluated before a decision is made as to whether to institute such a plan."

The President had no criticism of the section of the bill that caused the most controversy in Congress—price supports for the feed grains, oats, rye, barley and grain sorghums. The bill for the first time puts these supports on a quasi-mandatory basis.

However, it raises support levels for this year only slightly above the Administration's intentions, from 70 to 76 per cent of parity, a formula designed to give the farmer a fair price for what he sells in relation to the cost of what he buys. And it contains no provisions for acreage controls on the grains, which the President had made plain that he opposed strongly.

Today's action by the President ended for this session of Congress perhaps the hottest political issue of this political year. The battle has raged since Congress met. But it was difficult to say which party had gained an advantage.

Both because of provisions in the new bill on feed grains and administrative actions by the President when he vetoed the first bill, Government price supports are higher on most major crops. Meanwhile, mainly for seasonal reasons, the prices of hogs and cattle, which are not supported, also have risen.

The bill directs the Secretary of Agriculture to use the soil bank this year as much as possible. Mr. Benson said today that his department was "moving immediately to put the soil bank program into effect."

Aside from the criticized portions, the bill contains a long list of relatively noncontroversial provisions. These are the main ones:

¶Addition of $500,000,000 to present funds authorized for removing perishable farm items from the market to prevent price declines. This is the authority used in recent months to bolster the price of pork.

¶Authority for payment of ocean shipping costs on surplus food donated to church and charitable agencies for distribution abroad.

¶Authority for the Agriculture Department to pay the costs of processing farm crops it holds into edible form for donation to the needy in the United States.

¶A series of provisions requiring Mr. Benson to produce within ninety days plans and recommendations for a "food stamp" program, additional surplus disposal and strategic food stockpiles.

Associated Press Wirephoto

BILL BECOMES LAW: President Eisenhower signs substitute farm measure for the bill he vetoed last month.

May 29, 1956

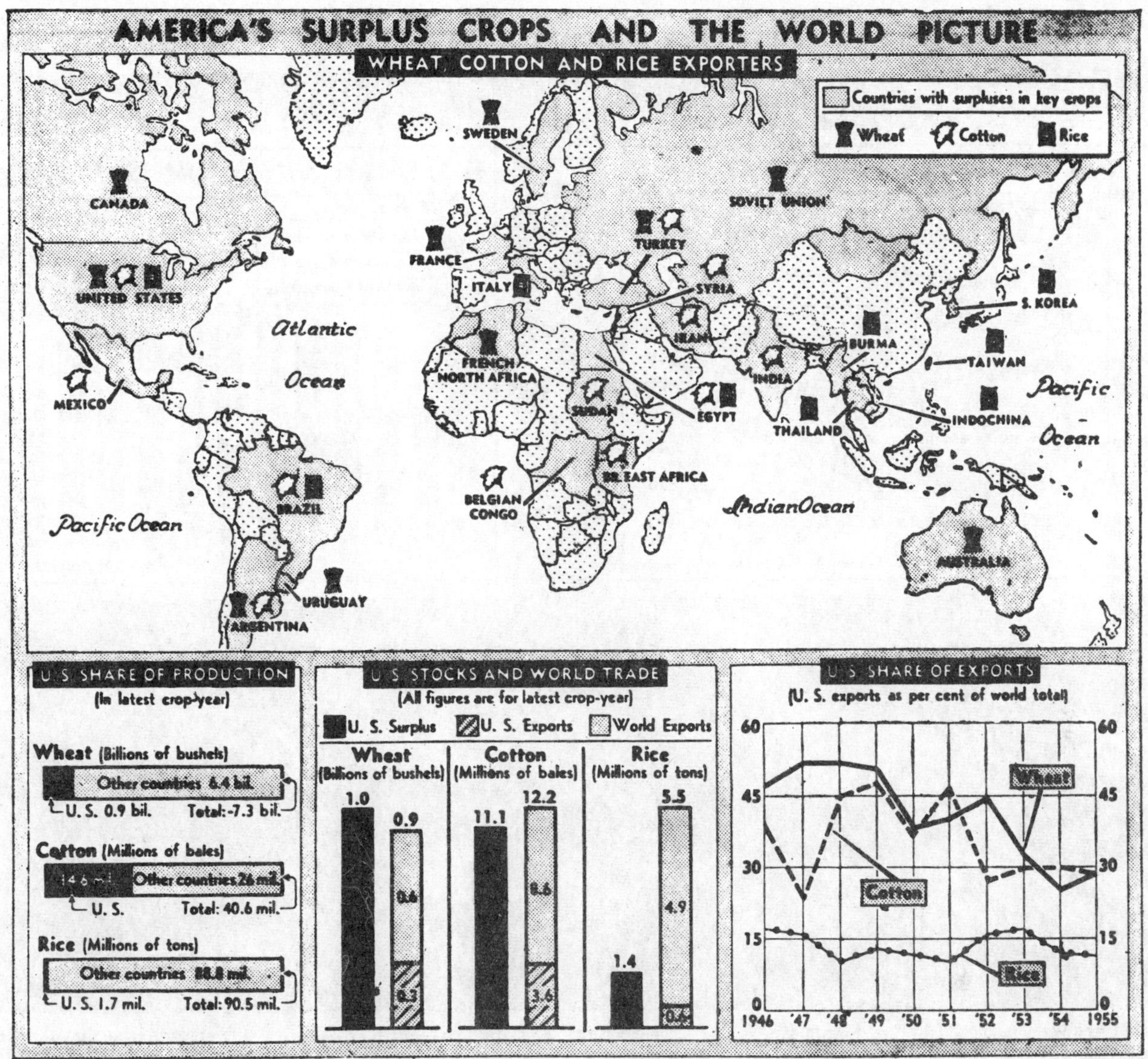

Corn, another heavy U. S. surplus, does not figure in world trade and is not included in overseas disposal plans.

January 29, 1956

BENSON RULES OUT FOOD GLUT ABROAD

Promises World Organization U. S. Will Avoid Disrupting International Markets

By PAUL HOFMANN

Special to The New York Times.

ROME, Nov. 7—The United States promised today that it would not dump its agricultural surpluses on foreign markets.

Addressing the seventy-four-nation plenary conference of the United Nations Food and Agriculture Organization here, Ezra Taft Benson stressed that the United States, in its efforts to get rid of excess stocks, aimed to "avoid depressing prices and generally disrupting world markets."

Misgivings over the methods adopted by "some governments" to sell, barter or give away agricultural surpluses were voiced during the first week of the organization's meeting by delegates from Canada, Australia, New Zealand and other countries. None mentioned the United States by name.

Douglas Harkness, Minister of Agriculture of Canada, said his Government was watching "with concern the mounting of stocks of wheat that have been accumulating in exporting countries, particularly in North America, and the measures employed in surplus disposal."

Canadian Asks Selectivity

He said Canada certainly would not oppose "such generous action" as donating food to underdeveloped countries, but advocated "greater selectivity to insure that such programs did not interfere with commercial marketing."

In his speech the Secretary of Agriculture seemed to realize that United States agricultural exports were worrying some nations. He set forth these three principles that he said were guiding the agricultural export operations of the United States.

"1. We will compete fairly on the world market.

"2. We will be competitive in quality.

"3. We will participate in mutually profitable international trade that gives our customers abroad continuous opportunity to earn the foreign exchange they need to buy our products."

Mr. Benson reported on the soil-bank plan and other United States devices to reduce excessive crops. Under the soil-bank plan, farmers are paid Federal subsidies to keep out of production acreage that would produce surplus crops.

Mr. Benson strongly emphasized that the United States wanted to see agricultural commodities used for the purpose for which they were grown—"to be consumed by people who need them."

The Secretary said the United States would tighten programs to barter surpluses for other commdities to avoid interfering with normal trade. The sale of United States agricultural products for local currencies is being done "with much checking, deliberating and negotiating on every transaction" to avoid possible injury to third countries, Mr. Benson declared. He invited observations on individual arrangements and expressed the willingness of the United States to "talk frankly" about any complaints.

Mr. Benson arrived in Rome from Greece. It was his eighth stopover on an eleven-nation tour primarily devoted to observing the results of the United States agricultural export program. He is due to leave for Spain tomorrow.

November 8, 1957

Ever-Mounting Surplus of Wheat and Feed Grains Remains Administrative Nightma

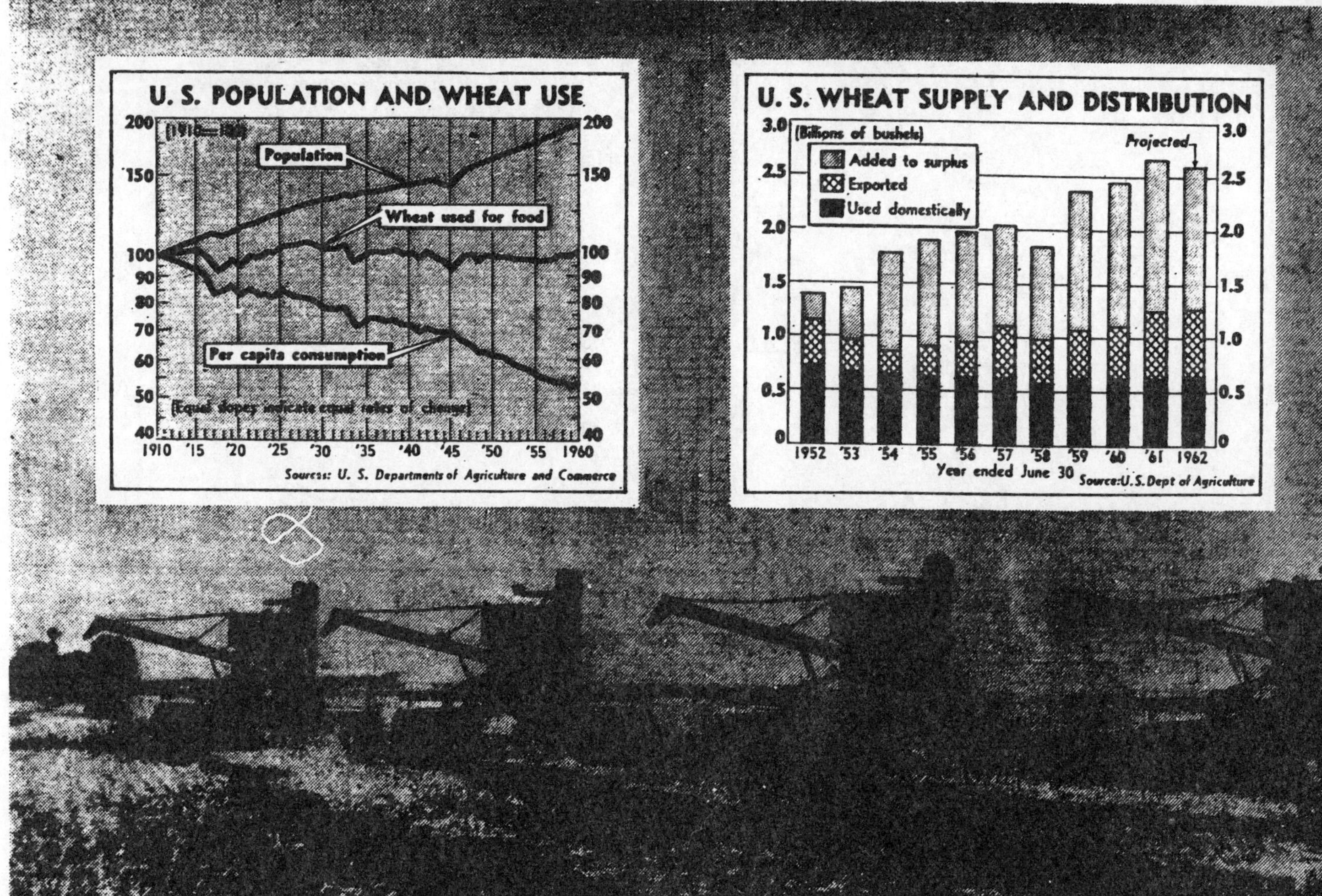

New legislation has been proposed by the Administration to reduce output of farm products increasingly in oversupply, such as wheat, here bei harvested in Kansas. Charts reveal how wheat surplus has been mounting over the years, in contrast to consumption of product at home and abro

June 10, 1962

CROP CURB SCORED AT FOOD CONGRESS

Laos Princess Asks Parley to Condemn Practice

WASHINGTON, June 6 (AP) —Local problems and traditions plus flagrant mistakes by well-intentioned people often make it difficult to provide food for the hungary people of the world, Princess Aline, wife of Premier Souvanna Phouma of Laos said today.

The wife of the neutralist Premier of Laos, without mentioning crop production controls by name, told the World Food Congress also:

"Since we have come together here to make the world aware of this suffering from hunger, you will understand me if I ask you to condemn those who throw fish back into the sea because they will not bring a good price and those who destroy their crops because the vegetables will not sell."

Finds Shortages Less Acute

The princess said, however, that because of technical aid given to underdeveloped nations "shortages and even famines are no longer as terrible as they used to be."

But she said "flagrant mistakes must be avoided in this humanitarian zeal." Princess Souvanna Phouma cited the case of a special issue of the World Health Organization publication showing a young Negro eating flour distributed in Dahomey in 1962.

"This picture is poignant because the expression on the face of the child is particularly tragic," she said. "But it is especially distressing to see that, in this emergency case, a product that was not ready for immediate consumption was distributed to this starving child.

"Among the foodstuffs of prime necessity distributed was cheese, which the rural people used for soap; they were very much surprised when it failed to produce suds."

Princess Aline said that in the backward countries "where food has retained its original form or appearance, it would be charitable to substitute dried meat for frozen meat and salted fish for the canned fish."

Udall Cites Fish Protein

The Congress, attended by some 1,200 delegates from more than 100 countries, is meeting here through June 18. It is sponsored by the United Nations Food and Agriculture Organization.

Secretary of the Interior Stewart L. Udall told the session his department was pressing the use of low-cost fish protein concentrate "into large-scale production." This produce, he said, "holds great promise for the benefit of mankind" and is easily added to cereals or other basic foodstuffs.

"By utilizing the unharvested fish of United States waters alone," Mr. Udall said, "It can provide supplemental animal protein for one billion people for 300 days at the cost of less than one-half cent per person per day."

June 7, 1963

Canadian Wheat Pricing Provokes U.S. Criticism

By WILLIAM M. BLAIR
Special to The New York Times

WASHINGTON, Oct. 8—United States officials have in effect charged Canada with seeking to fix the world price of wheat and with damaging this country's efforts to market wheat abroad. The latest flare-up in Canadian-United States relations arose from Canada's agreement, announced yesterday, to sell 800,000 tons of wheat to Japan at the same price paid by the Soviet Union in Moscow's $500 million wheat deal with Canada.

[Ottawa concluded another wheat agreement Tuesday. The Canadian Government announced it would sell 300,000 metric tons to Bulgaria over a three-year period.]

It was learned that officials of the Department of Agriculture engaged in a heated discussion here yesterday with representatives of the Canadian Wheat Board. The Americans argued that the price offered Japan by Canada could hold world wheat prices at a fixed level for the next eight months.

See Disruption of Trade

The Canadian-Japanese agreement calls for the delivery of 100,000 tons a month for eight months. The Americans contended this was forward, or advance, pricing that would disrupt normal commercial transactions.

The new Canadian sale came at a time of a rising wheat market. Wheat prices have climbed nearly 5 cents a bushel above the price paid by the Russians, who are also seeking United States wheat. President Kennedy is expected to announce tomorrow his approval of the sale to the Soviet Union of American wheat with an estimated value of $250 million.

The White House announced late today that President Kennedy was delaying his news conference tomorrow by two hours. There was speculation that he would hold a briefing on the wheat sale for Congressional leaders before the news conference, which is now scheduled for 6 P.M., Eastern daylight time.

Market's Worth Noted

Of great importance, in the American view, is the potential of the Japanese market. The United States has made considerable efforts to cultivate the commercial Japanese market in recent years, in the form of subsidies and other special considerations. Private wheat interests have likewise promoted the Japanese market.

The Canadian-Japanese agreement is Government-to-Government trading, which enables the countries to fix a price for deliveries over a period of time. American commercial transactions are carried out on a flexible futures market. Thus, the price of wheat for future delivery might vary from the current price.

The Canadian sale to Japan, at the same price paid by the Russians, was reported to be a total of nearly $52 million at an average price of about $1.74 a bushel. This compares with the current world price of nearly $1.79 a bushel.

The Japanese purchase accounts for nearly 75 per cent of Canada's normal dollar wheat trade with Japan. The United States also expects to sell in other markets that the Canadians will not be able to supply because of Ottawa's sales to the Soviet Union and Soviet-bloc countries. One large market, to which some American wheat has already moved, is Western Europe, where crop conditions have been poor this year.

The United States exported nearly 37 million bushels of wheat to Japan this year, a gain of 10 per cent since 1959-60. Canada's exports to Japan have been slightly higher.

Humphrey Predicts U.S. Deal

Senator Hubert H. Humphrey Democrat of Minnesota, predicted today that the United States would sell about 5 million tons of wheat to the Soviet Union and three of its allies—Bulgaria, Czechoslovakia and Hungary. This would mean a sale of more than $300 million, $250 million from the Soviet and $60 million from the three satellites.

"I think a decision is close at hand," Mr. Humphrey, the Senate Democratic whip, said after a weekly meeting of Congressional leaders with President Kennedy at the White House. He said the Administration had **been "able to ascertain that there is broad support for a one-shot wheat sale for cash or gold."**

PREDICTS WHEAT SALE: Sen. Hubert H. Humphrey, Democrat of Minnesota, who commented on proposal for a Soviet-bloc transaction.

After the White House meeting, Senator Mike Mansfield of the wheat state of Montana, said he did not know when President Kennedy would make a decision on a Russian sale. He said the problem was both "economic and political."

The "economic" side is the benefit that would accrue to United States farmers through a reduction of surplus wheat stocks and a long-run strengthening of markets. Some Administration officials have calculated that sales to the Soviet and to Western Europe this year could reduce the present surplus of 1.1 billion bushels to about 700 million bushels. This level would be in sight of the reserve of 600 to 650 million bushels that is considered adequate to meet emergency needs.

The "political" side is mainly Republican opposition to a sale and the possibility of a Republican advantage in next year's Presidential election.

Senator Thomas J. Dodd, Democrat of Connecticut, introduced today a resolution calling for the establishment of a select Senate committee to study "the proposed wheat deal" with the Russians. It would also express the "sense of the Senate that no grain deal should be concluded with the Soviets until the results of this study are available for the guidance of the Administration."

Co-sponsors of the resolution included Republican Senators John Sherman Cooper of Kentucky, Peter H. Dominick of Colorado and Karl E. Mundt of South Dakota and Democratic Senator William Proxmire of Wisconsin.

The master of the National Grange, Herschel D. Newsome, said today he had told the Administration he believed his organization "would not necessarily oppose the sale of wheat to the Soviets at this time."

The Grange and the American Farm Bureau Federation have opposed foodstuff sales to the Russians in the past. The National Farmers Union, the third major general farm organization, has favored such sales.

Any sale to the Soviet Union would be at the world price, which at present ranges about **55 cents below the domestic price of about $2.40 a bushel. The Government makes up the difference in an export subsidy.**

KENNEDY AUTHORIZES WHEAT SALE TO RUSSIANS TOTALING $250,000,000

AID TO PEACE SEEN

President Also Calls Deal Beneficial to U.S. Economy

By WILLIAM M. BLAIR
Special to The New York Times

WASHINGTON, Oct. 9—President Kennedy approved today the sale of $250 million worth of wheat to the Soviet Union.

The wheat—150 million bushels—will be sold through private commercial channels at the world price for cash or short-term credit. It will be for use only in the Soviet Union and Eastern Europe. This ruled out wheat to Cuba and Communist China.

The President's action opened the way for sales to other Soviet-bloc countries. Czechoslovakia, Bulgaria and Hungary have asked for wheat. Their request covers about $60 million. This would make the total sale $310 million.

[Wheat futures advanced smartly Wednesday on the expectation that the President would approve the sale of the grain to the Soviet Union. Prices rose 2 to 3 cents a bushel on the Chicago Board of Trade.]

Seeking Other Products

At the same time, the President told his news conference that the Soviet Union and satellite countries were interested in American surplus livestock feed grains and other farm products.

In what amounted to a summation of his views on the wheat deal, Mr. Kennedy said:

"This particular decision with respect to sales to the Soviet Union, which is not inconsistent with many smaller transactions over a long period of time, does not represent a new Soviet-American trade policy. That must await the settlement of many matters.

"But it does represent one more hopeful sign that a more peaceful world is both possible and beneficial to us all."

The President said the Soviet was being treated "like any other customer in the world market." The proposed sale, he said, demonstrates the "willingness" of this country to help countries with short supplies of foodstuffs and to relieve world tensions.

Sees Payments Deficit Cut

The wheat sale will benefit other sectors of the United States economy besides farmers, he said. These include shippers and the whole agricultural complex of traders and food processors. It also would reduce the United States balance-of-payments deficit.

The balance of payments represents the money coming into and going out of the country. The payments for the grain would increase the money coming into the country and thus cut the United States deficit by the amount of the payments.

The world price that the Russians will pay is expected to be about $1.79 a bushel. The domestic price includes also a Federal subsidy of about 55 cents a bushel, which would make it $2.34.

Part of the subsidy is used to pay the farmer the difference between the world price and the support price guaranteed him by the Government, now $2 a bushel. The rest of the subsidy goes toward handling, transportation and related costs in getting the wheat to the ships. This latter part of the subsidy benefits the farmer also, because it pays for charges that otherwise would be deducted from the price he received for his wheat.

Mr. Kennedy struck at critics' contentions that subsidized wheat should not be sold to the Soviet. He said the wheat could be sold only at the world price and that the export subsidy paid by the United States was not a subsidy to a foreign purchaser but an aid to American producers.

Mr. Kennedy emphasized that "the Russian people will know they are receiving American wheat," a question raised by opponents of the sale.

"We have our means of informing the Russian people," he said. He mentioned the Voice of America, whose radio broadcasts he said were now getting through to the Soviet Union. Besides, he added, "there is no reason for the Russians to keep it quiet."

After "careful consideration" of international and domestic political elements involved in such a sale, he said, it would be "foolish to halt sales of our wheat when other countries can sell." To tell private traders they could not sell, he said, would "accomplish nothing."

Some persons will disagree with his decison, he said in anticipation of political repercussons. Whte House sources believe the wheat sale will be politically costly to the President, despite its general economic advantages. They think the President will be heavily criticized by conservatives for "trading with the enemy."

Mr. Kennedy said any legal barriers to a sale had been cleared. His advice came from his brother, Attorney General Robert F. Kennedy. Opponents of the deal have contended that Federal law bars the extension of credit to Communist countries by either private or Government corporations.

Calls Johnson Act No Bar

The President expressly denied that the Johnson Act closed the door on sales to the Russians. This act prohibits loans to any foreign government in default to the United States, as the Soviet Union is on loans made to Russian governments that preceded the Soviets.

In this case, however, no loans are involved. Mr. Kennedy pointed out that grain traders would have to make their own credit arrangements with private banks and "take the risk."

As set down by the Presi-

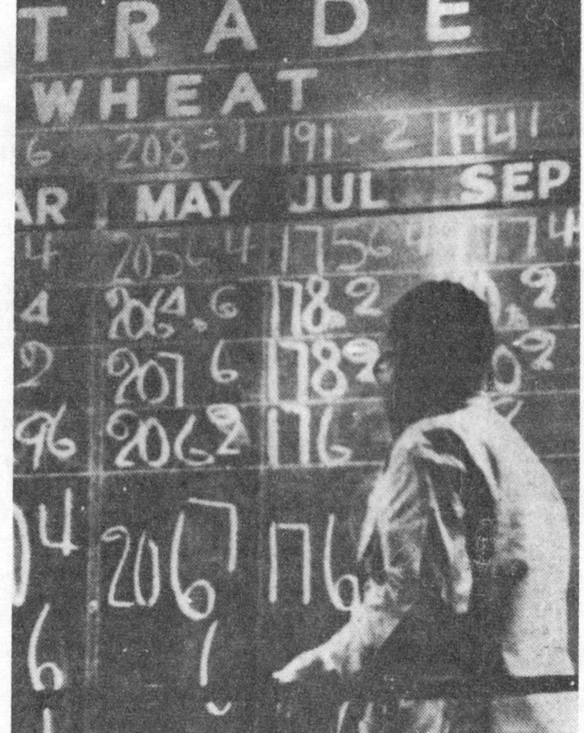

United Press International Telephoto

WHEAT MARKET ON THE RISE: Marker posts changes in futures prices on board at the Chicago Board of Trade.

dent, the wheat will be transported to the Soviet Union in American ships, supplemented as may be required by foreign shipping.

The Department of Commerce will grant the necessary export licenses. The department also will be charged with preventing "any single American dealer from receiving an excessive share" of the sale. This was an indication that the traders might form a pool to divide the wheat, as was contemplated by the private United States traders who initiated talks with the Russians in Ottawa last month.

It was believed that the sale would be the second-largest in history. It follows the biggest, the $500 million deal made by the Canadians with the Russians on Sept. 16. The Canadian sale was on a government-to-government basis, through a trade agreement, over 18 months.

Big Cash Payment Seen

Mr. Kennedy said he expected the Russians to make a large cash payment, presumably in gold, to avoid a high interest rate. They did this, he said, in Canada, and the United States interest rates are higher than those in Canada.

The immediate impact of the sale will come in reduction of the great surplus stocks of wheat piled up in storage through the Federal price-support program. Agricultural officials expected that the sale to the Soviet plus other expected sales would shrink the surplus stocks from a billion bushels down to about 750 million bushels. The lower level would be near a normal for an emergency reserve and would strengthen market prices in the year ahead.

The Government will use surplus wheat stocks, now in storage in public and private facilities throughout the country, to replace grain used by the private traders in the sale. It is expected that most of the wheat will come from 1962 and 1963 wheat now on hand.

President Kennedy said the reduction of wheat stocks, the country's No. 1 surplus headache, would mean a saving to taxpayers of at least $200 million in storage, handling and other costs, thus reducing the agriculture budget. This budget is now about $6 billion a year.

There is little likelihood, however, that consumers would either benefit or be hurt directly, by higher wheat prices. Most of the cost of a one-pound loaf of bread goes to millers, bakers, wholesalers and other off-the-farm handlers.

Announcement of the sale came soon after the Senate Foreign Relations Committee had agreed to a review of United States trade policy, with an eye on expansion of sale of foodstuffs and other nonstrategic materials to the Soviet Union.

After the Canadian sale to the Russians and the negotiations of the group of private United States traders with the Russians in Ottawa, many of Mr. Kennedy's advisers had urged him to go into a review of restrictions that blocked expansion of trade. The Russians' interest in United State wheat to fill out their needs, caused by a near-disastrous crop year, opened the way for executive action and a push in Congress.

Before announcing the sale to the Soviet, Mr. Kennedy had conferred several times with the National Security Council and with Congressional leaders, to discuss security implications as well as the effect on the Western nations and the general easing of world tensions.

President Kennedy did not state specifically that the Russian sale was for $250 million, but this is the known amount of wheat the Soviets have sought so far. This is some 4 million metric tons, or about 150 million bushels. There are 60 pounds in a bushel. A metric ton is 2,205 pounds.

October 10, 1963

National Affairs: New Policy on the Farm

By EDWIN L. DALE Jr.

Special to The New York Times

WASHINGTON, Aug. 21—Although few people but farmers appear to realize it, the United States has been undergoing a major change in the way the Government subsidizes agriculture. The change took a giant further step this week as the House passed a complicated omnibus farm bill that was difficult even for the members to understand.

The first thing to be said about the farm program is that much of agriculture is not subsidized at all. There are no Government price support programs or other subsidies for any kind of meat, nor for eggs, fruits and vegetables.

But, starting back in the days of the Great Depression, there has been major and costly Government intervention for what came to be called the "basic" commodities—wheat, feed grains (such as corn), rice, cotton, tobacco and peanuts. Dairy products were added later.

The method called price support, was basically the same for all of these crops. The Government set a "fair" floor price for each crop and if a farmer could not get that price in the market, the Government would pay him for his crop and take that part of the supply off the market This was eventually accompanied by acreage controls, but still the Government-held surpluses--and costs — piled up.

This system lasted until 1962 when the change began. It has three main features:

First, crops are treated somewhat differently, instead of having the same program for all.

Second, farmers hava a choice of alternatives—grow as much as they want with no Government price support or other help, or retire some of their acreage from the crop in question and benefit from the Government program.

Third, as a general principle, floor prices are lowered, sometimes sharply, and the Government uses the equivalent of a straight cash subsidy to make up the difference between the new floor and a "fair" price. One key result is to reduce the market price, both for home users and, equally important, for export.

Although results have been slow in coming, it now appears that the new method stands a good chance of accomplishing all the major objectives of the farm program--maintaining or improving farm income, reducing surpluses and reducing costs to the taxpayer.

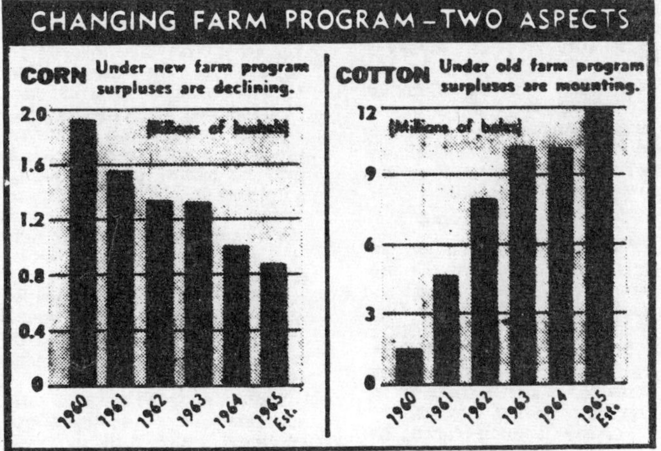

It has been applied so far principally to the feed grains. Stocks of corn in the hands of the Government have been reduced from a peak of 1.9 billion bushels in 1960 to an estimated 870 million this year. Domestic and export demand has taken the entire annual crop, reduced by voluntary acreage retirement, and more.

The price of corn to users of feed, and for export, has dropped from around $1.50 a bushel in the mid nineteen-fifties to around $1.10 now. And the income of farmers who grow feed grains has been maintained or even increased.

Some of the principles of this program here began last year for wheat, and this year for the first time, assuming the farm bill clears the Senate, the new system will be applied to the chief current problem crop, cotton. If it is, one of the main advantages will be to permit United States cotton, with a much lower floor and hence market price, to compete again in the world market.

The farmers are not losing from the change. Net income per farm rose to a record $4,320, at an annual rate, in the second quarter of this year. The taxpayers are still paying enormous sums for the farm program—nearly $5 billion in the fiscal year just ended, but the Administration is convinced that the new system, where it has been applied, is already costing less than the old.

August 22, 1965

World's Food Glut Strains Trade Relations

Breakdown Feared for International Grain Pricing

By BRENDAN JONES

Increasing world production of major food crops—a bright potential for feeding larger populations — is currently building up costly surpluses and straining international trade relations.

The rise in production has been spurred by a combination of developments: a drive by more countries for self-sufficiency, increasing use of subsidies, dramatic technological advances and, in recent years, favorable weather conditions.

Last year, the world had record and near-record yields on a wide range of key food crops—wheat, barley, soybeans, rice, sorghum, millet, sugar and citrus.

Much of the production gain, however, was in the developed countries, where it exceeded domestic demand and created both export surpluses and restrictions on competing farm imports.

A river barge taking on grain at a Cargill elevator in St. Louis for shipment to export elevators on the Gulf of Mexico. Big crops have contributed to growing surpluses.

Grain Accord Threatened

An exceptionally high yield of wheat—a record 305 million metric tons — has recently caused sharp competitive price cutting by the major exporting countries.

The price cutting, the result of a huge worldwide surplus, has threatened a breakdown of the International Grains Arrangement under which minimum prices are supposed to be maintained.

A pre-Easter meeting in Washington of the major wheat exporting countries — the United States, Canada, Australia, the European Common Market (chiefly France) and Argentina—failed to resolve the pricing issue.

Proposals for lowering the minimums, which are considered too high in relation to the prevailing glut, were made, but no agreement was reached.

According to grain-trade sources, the I. G. A. pricing schedules apparently will be ignored for the present, although the agreement technically remain in effect.

At the start of this year, the main exporting countries had supplies of wheat available for export and carry-over stocks —in effect, surpluses—totaling 3.2 billion bushels.

This is more than twice the amount of wheat exported in world trade in a single year. With the forecast of a further 9 per cent increase in world wheat production this year, surplus stocks are expected to grow.

The wheat problem, however, is only one facet of mounting world problems in the management of farm production and crop distribution.

Agricultural policies of the European Common Market currently are causing serious concern for the United States and other farm-produce exporters.

In an effort to increase efficiency and output of its farms, the Common Market has adopted a program of subsidies and restrictive levies on imports.

Presently under consideration is a stiff levy on soybeans. United States exports of this commodity to the Common Market—$500-million a year—are expected to be cut sharply by the tax. Common Market officials are to meet later this month on the question.

Proposal Protested

Meanwhile, Washington officials have protested the proposed levy. There have also been threats, mainly in Congress, that the United States will retaliate, either with special subsidies on soybean exports, or with restrictions on Common Market exports.

For the Common Market, the effort at increased farm production has proved costly. A major problem has been a huge butter surplus, presently rising at a rate of 300,000 tons a year.

While steps have been taken to reduce the dairy subsidy that has produced the glut, the cost of butter price support has risen to $1-billion a year.

Total farm subsidies under the Common Market program are now $2.4-billion a year, five times the amount in 1960. The Common Market also has been faced with a serious problem of finding storage facilities, not only for butter, but for wheat, barley and rye.

Problem Arises

According to reports by the United States Department of Agriculture, the Organization for Economic Cooperation and Development and other organizations, world food problems are on the way to becoming a problem mainly of distributing surpluses to the less fortunate countries.

Technological advances, chiefly in high-yielding varieties of wheat, rice, corn and grain sorghum, have, theoretically, made it possible for most countries to increase food production faster than their population growth.

India and Pakistan, outstandingly, have achieved exceptional gains with the new wheat varieties.

Yields on the new crop strains are two to five times greater than with conventional varieties. Some wheat strains also are drought resistant.

Meat Over Grain

Their successful use, however, requires expert cultivation, fertilizer and, in some areas, irrigation, all of which require substantial investment.

In the developed countries, surplus food production exceeds demand, particularly as higher incomes increase preferences for meat instead of grains.

For the developing countries, the basic problem is a shortage of foreign exchange either to buy surpluses or to finance new agricultural expansion.

This is a problem which, according to the economic and agricultural experts, has still to be worked out. But it is emphasized also that the predictions of a few years ago that rising populations would bring widespread famine are no longer valid. Even in developing countries, according to authoritative reports, food grain production, as the result of increased emphasis on agriculture, is now growing as fast as their 2½ per cent annual birth rate.

April 14, 1969

Rice Boom in Asia Raises Doubts

By PHILIP SHABECOFF
Special to The New York Times

LOS BANOS, the Philippines —The new strains of rice, wheat and corn that are producing the so-called green revolution in Asia, holding out a promise of plenty for underfed millions, are beginning to stir objections.

Some of the traditional rice-exporting countries such as Thailand and Burma—and even a few voices in the United States, which is also an exporter—have been complaining that the new strains will produce a glut.

Dr. Robert F. Chandler, a 63-year-old Yankee from Maine who is head of the research institute here that developed the high-yield "miracle rice," commented: "Only three years ago people were screaming, 'How are we going to feed the teeming millions of Asia?' Now some of those same people are yelling about overproduction and lost export markets."

The miracle rice was developed at the neat, quiet experimental farm, set among coconut palms and framed by blue mountains, that is run here by the International Rice Research Institute.

The new miracle strains, which have brought about a tremendous rise in South Asian agricultural productivity, raises a variety of problems that have led experts such as Clifton R. Wharton Jr., president of Michigan State University, to ask if the green revolution was a "cornucopia or Pandora's Box."

The New York Times (by Philip Shabecoff)

Dr. Robert F. Chandler, director of the International Rice Research Institute, in one of the institute's rice fields at Los Baños, the Philippines, where "miracle strain" was developed.

Marketing Often Disrupted

Dr. Chandler estimates that this year there will be at least 15 million acres of paddy field planted with the strains developed in his fields. Four years ago it grew only at the institute, which was established by the Ford and Rockefeller Foundations in 1960 in association with the Manila Government and the University of the Philippines.

Certainly the skyrocketing rice yields have caused new problems in many Asian countries without adequate storage, drying and transportation facilities. Age-old marketing systems have been disrupted.

Some critics have charged that the new seeds will only serve to make the rich richer and the poor poorer in Asia. Because of the high monetary investment and management skills needed to cultivate the new rice, the critics say, it is largely the landlords with already large resources who can afford the outlays that bring such high rewards.

The poor farmer, this argument runs, falls further behind because he cannot afford to increase his own production, while generally higher world productivity means he gets a lower price for the amount of rice he does grow.

Dr. Chandler, a former president of the University of New Hampshire, who saw his first growing rice plant when he was 40 years old, reacts vigorously when these criticisms are brought up.

Problems Accompany Change

"Sure there are problems—there must be when a new technology is introduced," he said. "But how can it be wrong to increase the amount of food for people who eat and to increase the incomes of farmers?"

"Don't forget, it is true that half the world still goes to bed hungry every night. Next year there will be 15 million more Indians, a million more Burmese, a million more Thais, a million more Filipinos to feed."

He acknowledged that the new strains of rice and other food staples might create a food surplus during the next decade but said: "We should be planning for 1980, 1990 and beyond instead of worrying about a temporary recession in rice prices in 1971."

"The long-term future still looks awfully grim despite the technological increases in food production," he asserted. The recent advances, he said, are just a stopgap arrangement to stave off hunger.

"It will take more than high yield rice plants to stop disaster," he went on. "We must curb our populations. After all, the amount of land, water and air available for food is constant, but people are not."

It was in the planting season of 1966 that the institute's first high-yield strain — IR-8 — was made available to farmers in the Philippines and several other countries.

The results were so immediately dramatic that even conservative peasants saw the value of changing over. **Rice yields began doubling and tripling. Two crops were possible where only one had been reaped in the past.**

Despite high expenditures on fertilizers, insecticides and herbicides required by the new rice and despite a declining trend in world rice prices, farmers who have planted the miracle strains have also doubled their incomes in many cases.

April 6, 1970

SURPLUS OF GRAIN REPORTED IN INDIA

Breakthrough May Lead to Export of 8 Million Tons

By KASTURI RANGAN
Special to The New York Times

NEW DELHI, April 29—India has made a breakthrough in food output this year, becoming a surplus nation in wheat and rice.

Officials have started looking for export markets for a grain surplus of eight million tons that they expect to have in hand at year's end.

Observers, caution, however, that the talk of surplus may be misleading. The bulk of Indians live in unimaginable poverty and the per-capita food consumption is at least 25 per cent below health requirements. Starvation and malnutrition are major problems that the Government has been unable to surmount.

The average consumption of grains is about 12 ounces a day, four ounces less than the required minimum. So India is simultaneously trying to industrialize the nation to help increase the purchasing power of the average Indian.

5-Million Ton Gain

Preliminary estimates show that this year's grain is exceeding by five million tons last year's record level of 108 million tons. The major gain is in wheat, with the output expected to reach an unprecedented level of 26-million tons.

Annasaheb Shinde, India's Minister of State for Food, said in an interview that at this rate India would "outstrip the United States in seven to eight years." American wheat output is some 40 million tons a year.

India has already stopped importing American wheat under the Food-for-Peace program. Since 1956, India has imported more than 50 million tons to meet a chronic food shortage in a country whose population has soared to 550 million.

This year, India was able to achieve relative self-sufficiency. As a result, according to Food Ministry officials, she will not renew her importing agreement with the United States, which runs out in June.

Exports in Asia Likely

Iqbal Singh, chairman of the Government-owned Food Corporation of India, said that in six months India would be exporting wheat to west Asian nations, where the demand is heavy.

India has already started her own Food-for-Peace program, with 700,000 tons of grain provided to Bangladesh, which has a severe food shortage.

Officials believe India never again will have to depend on foreign countries for food. Indian agricultural research and crop planning has been set up so that even if there is a drought in one area the surplus in another can fill the gap.

In West Bengal, a state with a chronic rice deficit, farmers have experimented successfully with the raising of wheat during the summer season when their rice paddies normally are left fallow. The state no longer depends on monsoon rains but on the vast reservoir of underground water from the Ganges River.

'West Bengal Miracle'

Now officials are extending what they call the "West Bengal Miracle" to other states. Punjab, a rich wheat-producing area, is now also growing rice by using underground water.

The Government is also successfuly promoting hybrid seeds in wheat and rice. What has come to be known as the "green revolution" has almost doubled food output in 10 years. This "revolution" is largely attributed to the hybrid seed and related developments.

M. S. Swaminathan, an agricultural expert, said that the green revolution really consisted of four different revolutions —in seeds, in fertilizer, in pesticides and in crop-planning. "We have discovered that rice and wheat can be produced throughout the year regardless of seasons," he said.

April 30, 1972

PRESIDENT SIGNS FARM BILL ENDING PRICE SUBSIDIES

Growers to Be Paid in Cash if Income for Products Falls Below 'Target'

FULL PRODUCTION SEEN

Nixon Says Revised Plan to Support Main Crops Will Help Inflation Battle

Special to The New York Times

WASHINGTON, Aug. 10—President Nixon signed today legislation establishing a four-year farm program with a new method of subsidizing the main crops.

Under the new approach for wheat, feed grains and cotton, the Government will make no effort to keep prices up by the various means used in the past. Instead, prices will be set wholly by market forces of supply and demand, and the Government will pay farmers in cash if prices for their products fall below the "target" prices established in the law.

These target prices are well above the prices that were customary in most past years but are far below the record prices now prevailing in the commodity markets. If market prices remain high, the new program will mean virtually no cost to the Government and the taxpayer.

Although Mr. Nixon did not recommend the new approach, he called the bill a "constructive" compromise and said, "It will encourage full production and dampen inflationary pressures without risking a market disaster for America's farm families as they respond to new demands."

Capacity Output Seen

He said that the law "should help in our battle against inflation by encouraging American farmers to produce at full capacity."

In his statement, issued here although the President signed the bill at nearby Camp David, Mr. Nixon sharply criticized one provision of the many-sided bill. This involved the continued availability of food stamps to the aged, blind and disabled, who were scheduled to lose food stamps Jan 1 because they will get extra Social Security payments.

The President said he was willing to continue this program but objected that the administrative method provided in the bill "is highly undesirable and must be corrected."

Secretary of Agriculture Earl L. Butz said the bill represented "a historic turning point in the philosophy of our farm programs." He said the philosophy was now "geared to expanding output" after years of a philosophy of "curtailment and shrinking of our agricultural plant."

Dr. Butz previously announced that there would be no restrictions in 1974 on the acreage that farmers could plant. He told reporters today that he expected "expanded demand at home and abroad a long way down the road," probably meaning that farmers would receive prices above the new target prices.

Dr. Butz reaffirmed his strong opposition to export controls on farm products, despite the report by his department yesterday estimating that the harvest of several important crops would be somewhat less than was predicted a month ago and despite continued sharp price increases in the commodity markets.

He said that the reduction in the estimated corn crops would be partly offset by an "unhead-

Associated Press

Agriculture Secretary Earl L. Butz comments on farm bill signed by President Nixon

lined" increase in the estimated crop of grain sorghums. He also stressed that in seven out of the last 10 years the corn crop was larger than the August estimate.

In another development connected with the farm bill, Senator George McGovern, Democrat of South Dakota, urged Dr. Butz to act "within the next several hours" to end the price freeze on beef, using a provision of the new law.

This provision, first introduced by Senator McGovern, requires the President to "adjust" price controls in cases where the Secretary of Agriculture certifies a shortage of the product in question. In a telegram to Dr. Butz sent from Sioux Falls, S. D., Senator McGovern said, "Certainly the beef shortage experienced throughout this nation, including the White House itself, in recent days is a classic example of a shortage caused by price controls."

Dr. Butz, speaking to reporters before he saw the McGovern telegram, said he would not move to end the beef price freeze. He confirmed that he did not like it but said he was a "team player" and that the President's decision would prevail.

If he sent the President a finding that the President did not like, Dr. Butz said with a smile, "the President could always get another Secretary of Agriculture."

In his statement on the farm bill, Mr. Nixon, in the case of several provisions that he did not propose or even opposed, sought to create a sense of compromise with Congress.

For example, in a section of the message dealing with loans under the new Rural Development Act—where the bill required a larger Federal Government role than Mr. Nixon wanted—his statement said, "I respect the wishes of the Congress on this point and will adhere to this legal prescription."

But he said, "I plan to administer these programs in a way which will give the fullest possible consideration to state rural development goals and the local priorities expressed in those goals."

August 11, 1973

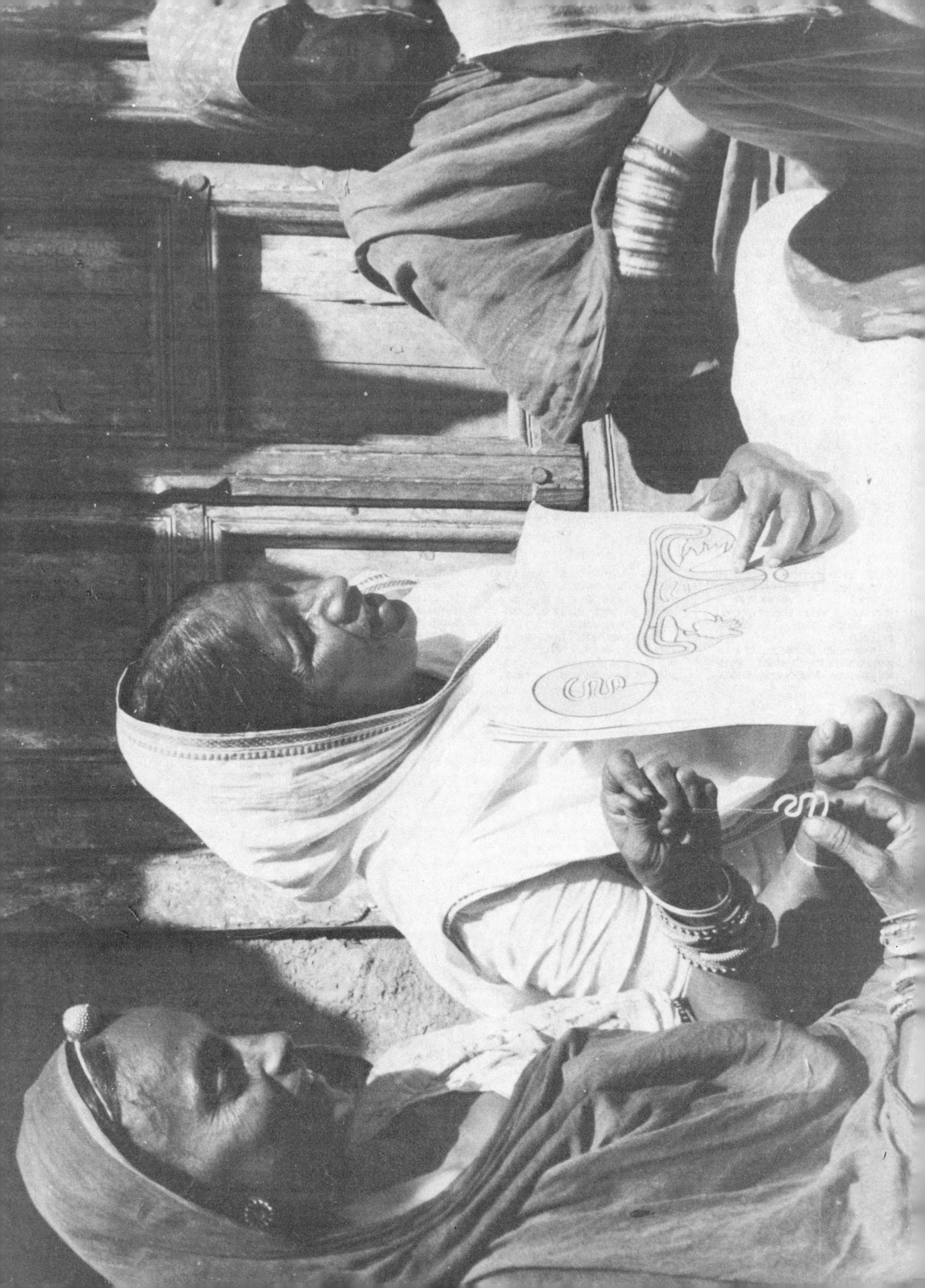

CHAPTER 3
Population

"The loop," a birth control device, is explained to village women in Rajasthan, India.

Roland Michaud. Courtesy UNICEF Photo.

WORLD OVERCROWDING

Saturation Point for Earth's Population Soon Will Be in Sight, With the Safety Limit for United States Estimated at 200,000,000 People—How the Nations Grow

By RAYMOND PEARL.

Head of the Department of Biometry and Vital Statistics, Johns Hopkins University.

"THEY breed like flies!"

Most cynical persons who make this remark about the inhabitants of the congested quarters of our great cities, or about any sort of people whatever, do not realize that that is an accurate statement of scientific fact. I have lately had occasion to demonstrate this experimentally and statistically. The methods and results of this particular adventure into the unknown may well serve to orient the mind on the great problem of population growth.

Population is a problem only because this giddy globe on which we live is strictly limited in size. It does not and cannot grow or increase in size, to any indefinite degree, in the way that every living thing can and does increase in numbers by reproduction. The earth constitutes a universe of strictly limited size. Man's efforts to increase its usable size by building sky-scrapers and the like are plainly of an extreme insignificance in proportion to the whole. But there is no way to grow potatoes or fatten beeves on the successive floors of a flat building, desirable as such a form of agriculture might be from some points of view.

What happens when a living organism capable of indefinite multiplication of its numbers by reproduction finds itself confined to a universe strictly limited in size? This question was put in an experimental way to a small family of fruit-flies of the genus Drosophila, a form now much used in many sorts of experimental inquiries. These minute flies live mainly on yeast which grows upon decaying fruit and other vegetable material. For experimental purposes the yeast is sown upon a semi-solid medium of banana pulp and agar-agar. To these flies in the laboratory a pint milk bottle represents their universe. They cannot get out. The universe is limited strictly in size by the walls of the bottle, which cannot grow nor multiply.

So then an experiment like this was performed: A pair of flies, one male and one female, corresponding to Adam and Eve if you like, were put with a few of their children (say 10 or 12) of different ages into a pint milk bottle, on the bottom of which was a layer of banana-agar, corresponding to the tillable soil of the earth, properly sown with yeast for food. Then the bottle was closed with a cotton stopper which would admit air, but would not permit the flies to pass out. Then this young and conveniently sized universe was put into an incubator and kept at a uniform temperature of 25 degrees Centigrade.

Living went on within it in a manner in many fundamental respects like that of human beings. The original parents had some more children, finally grew old and died. Their children grew up and had offspring of their own, and so on. Every three days a census was taken of the population which had accrued up to that time. The results were those shown in Figure 1.

Men Much Like Flies.

We see at once that the increase of the fly population in its limited universe followed no haphazard course, but proceeded along a smooth and regular curve. The growth of population was at first slow, then at an ever more rapid rate. At the middle portion of the whole curve the rate of growth per unit of time was most rapid. From that point on the population, although it kept growing in numbers, decreased in rate. Finally the universe became densely crowded with flies, supporting the greatest possible number that the agricultural potentialities, in the way of yeast crop in this particular pint universe, could sustain. The population had reached the saturation point.

Now, what of the growth of human populations? Theoretically and a priori there are so many complex factors involved in the growth of human populations that it would seem hopeless to expect that any simple mathematical expression could possibly describe its course. But in science he is lost who lets his inquisitive bent be hampered or curtailed by a priori logic. The Pauline injunction to "try all things" is, or should be, his guiding motto. In accordance with this principle we have examined with much care the known population history, as derived from census figures, of some twenty-odd of the leading countries of the world, all indeed that had enough reasonably accurate census data to make any analysis possible.

The results are indeed astounding. It appears that the population growth of every country we have tried has in its past history followed a course which is described with the greatest accuracy and completeness either by the same mathematical equation which served for the experimental Drosophila populations, or by a superimposed combination of two or more of these curves (Ireland, Germany and Japan). Space is lacking here to present the detailed proof that this is so. I can only present three typical examples, the United States, France, and England and Wales.

The United States, in respect to its present cultural epoch or cycle, is a relatively new country in which the population only just recently (in 1914) passed its point of most rapid growth per unit of time. On the other hand France is an old country, and the known population data for it lie toward the upper end of the curve, describing its population growth in this cultural epoch.

It is evident enough from mere inspection of these curves, which could be extended to many other countries, that it is in the highest degree probable, having regard to the complete evidence, that human populations in limited areas grow in essentially the same manner as experimental populations in closed universes. In other words, population growth in respect of its rate appears to be a fundamental biological phenomenon in which insects and men are on much the same footing.

Having ascertained the mathematical law in accordance with which this phenomenon operates, we are in a better position to predict future populations than we have ever been before, and shall get an accurate result just so long as the same kind of forces, social, economic, and the like, as have operated in the past, continue in effect. Of course, if wholly new factors come into operation, the curves will have to be revised to take account of them.

Knowing the law according to which past growth of population has taken place, in order to predict we have merely to extend the curve to future time. Doing this for the United States, for example, we find that the saturation point probably will be represented by about 200,000,000 of people in continental United States. Professor East has lately examined the question from the standpoint of our future agricultural potentialities and comes to the conclusion that this figure is about what could be expected from that angle.

From a social standpoint the first result of our experimental and statistical study is that all human populations are proceeding at a lawful and predictable rate toward a point of complete saturation, where within any defined area of the earth's surface there will be living the maximum number of people that can be supported.

Projecting our thought for a moment to that time, at most a few centuries ahead, we perceive that the important question will then be: What kind of people are they to be who will then inherit the earth? Here enters the human and social phase of the problem. Man, in theory at least, now has it completely in his power to determine what kind of people will make up the earth's population when saturation is a fact.

In proceeding to the analysis of this phase of our problem let us first examine what man has, in the past, done about the problem of population, either consciously or unconsciously. In general, attempts have been made in two fundamentally different ways to meet the problem of population pressure, by acquisition of new territory through conquest or more or less peaceful penetration; secondly, limitation of reproduction, by operative interference through segregation and "birth control."

The first method of meeting the population problem is a very ancient one. At one time or another every people has gone out looking for new territory into which its people, crowded at home, might expand. Virtually always some one already is living in the desired territory and has to be got rid of. The methods used to accomplish this end have varied somewhat, but not greatly, with the progress of history. On the whole, the surest method of getting undisturbed possession of another's territory, internationally speaking, has been to kill him. Advancing civilization has decreed that the moral tone of the excuse or justification put forward for the killing should be progressively higher, but this thoughtful provision has inured solely to the benefit of the killer and not at all to that of the killed. It is by this direct and logical procedure that the peoples now inhabiting Europe and America have come into possession of their lands. The latest attempt to put this plan into operation is still so fresh in the mind as to need no expanded presentation.

The slightest thoughtful consideration of the matter shows that this method of solving the population problem leads finally to no solution at all. It works at the best only so long as there are parts of the earth so sparsely inhabited as to be easy of conquest, and at the same time inherently capable of supporting a considerable population. Eventually there will be no such places, and mankind upon the whole earth will find himself in precisely the same situation as the Dosophilae in the pint bottle. There will, perhaps, even then be some attempted readjustments, some strong peoples will endeavor to kill off others whom they judge weaker, but in time even this sort of activity must come to an end, because it will be found to work out that the survivors of different nationalities, if separate nations then exist, will be so evenly matched that war will be still more like the famed battle of the Kilkenny cats than it is now. All this, of course, is only another way of saying what must be obvious, that the solution by acquisition of territroy is not applicable to the world problem of population, but at best only to that of nations.

Turning now to the other attempted solutions, we must recognize at the start that there are a number of ways of limiting the inherent reproductive capacities of mankind. First of all is the so-called "sterilization" method. By one or another form of surgical operation it is easily possible to render men incapable of begetting offspring without in any other way affecting their sexual life. With considerably greater surgical difficulty the same thing can be accomplished for women. Therefore, in theory, the program is simple. Let some wise person or persons decide what kind of people ought not to reproduce, for the best good of the body social, and then turn the surgeon loose upon them. Two difficulties beset the practical implementation of this so simple scheme. In the first place, who is to separate the honorable sheep from the goats? And by what and whose standard is he to work?

High Cost of Unfit.

Where laws to this end have been passed their operation has been confined, in the main, to criminals, the feebleminded and insane. The ardent eugenist argues that surely no one can logically object to the sterilization of these classes. Which is, of course, true. But the legal difficulties are great against any sterilization program sufficiently large to be socially effective. For it has been shown that, from well known and established principles of heredity, if a sterilization program is to be socially effective within any reasonable period of time, say one or two centuries, it would be necessary to sterilize a good many apparently normal persons whose germ plasm is defective. To get legislative power to do this would be even more difficult than if one contemplated sterilizing only the patently defective. But without such power the program could not possibly show socially significant results. The difficulty is that not all feeble-minded or insane or criminals, or what you please, have parents falling in the same defective categories.

Precisely the same arguments apply in principle regarding segregation as apply to sterilization. Indeed, sterilization is to be regarded socially as an ambulant form of segregation. And the obviously insuperable obstacle to segregation as a means of limiting reproduction on any large scale is economic. It costs too much. It has been estimated, though the writer cannot vouch for the accuracy of the statistical computations, that already this country spends $500,000,000 more to keep unfit persons alive than it does on such constructive social forces as schools and churches.

This brings us to a consideration of so-called "birth control" methods of limiting reproduction. This means in direct language the use of measures which either prevent or make conception extremely unlikely. In general, measures of this sort are in widespread use by the more intelligent elements of the population in most countries standing high in the scale of civilization. Except in a few countries, notably Holland, the use of these measures in the less intelligent social strata is distinctly infrequent. The propagandists of the birth control movement urge that all classes of people should be freely taught the use of these methods, with the expectation that one or both of two important social consequences would follow. In the first place, the birth rate of the socially less desirable classes would fall to a plane of at least equality with that of the socially more desirable classes, thus effecting a direct contribution to the problem of population by reducing the birth rate generally; or it might be hoped that the more socially desirable classes would increase their birth rate with the lowering of the rate of the socially less desirable, so that the result would be a generally better quality of population.

It is impossible to say with any scientific accuracy just what would be the social consequences of any entirely unrestricted birth-control propaganda. The plan, however, obviously faces certain practical difficulties. It inevitably weakens in a military sense any country that unreservedly practices it, because it leads to a higher average age of the population. Consequently, from the point of view of statesmanship, any country before adopting birth control as a national policy would want rather a definite assurance that wars of conquest would not occur.

That birth control will become more and more widespread as the pressure of world population increases seems to be certain, because it so obviously is in accord with individual self-interest, both economic and social. It seems to me personally that after making due allowance for the increased powers of control over nature, which may reasonably be expected from the future development of science, the most hopeful outlook for a working method of so organizing society that a maximum of comfort and happiness will be associated with a maximum saturation of the earth is to be looked for in a combination of the idea of birth control, directed along eugenic lines, with those ideas of co-operation which in themselves are eugenic, so brilliantly expounded by Dr. William Patten in his recent book, "The Grand Strategy of Evolution."

But at the best the outlook does not arouse any furious optimism in the minds of the thoughtful. Our children's children will have to face a standard of living much below that which we enjoy.

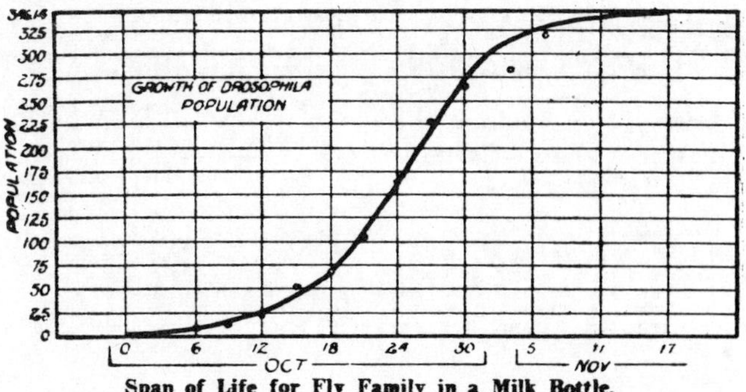

Span of Life for Fly Family in a Milk Bottle.

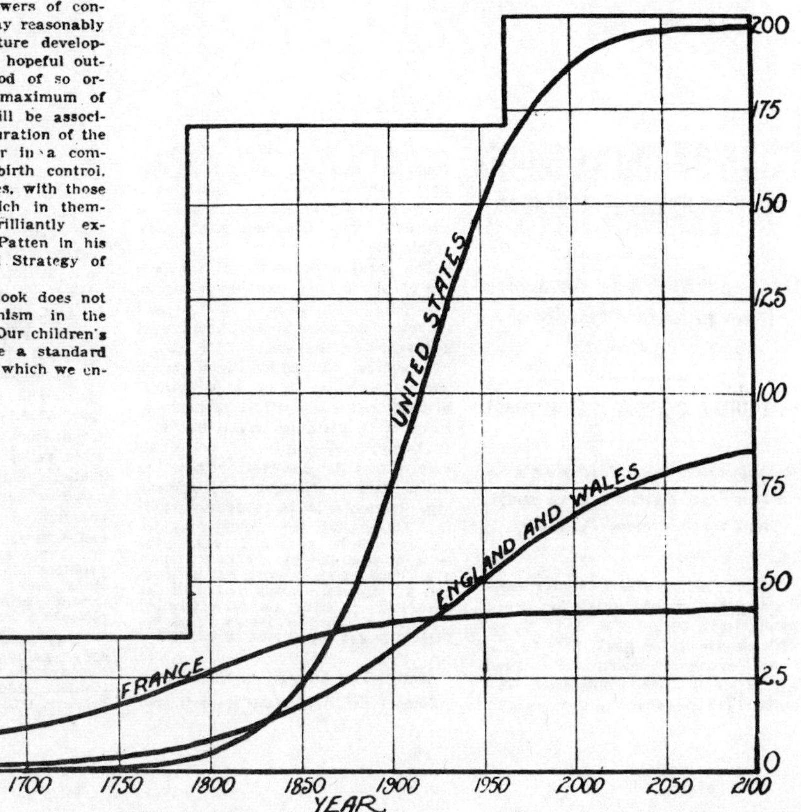

Growth of Population in Three Typical Countries.

October 8, 1922

SEES FAMINE PERIL IN PROLONGING LIFE

Dr. D. B. Myer Says Progress in Disease Prevention Also May Lead to Wars.

CITES POPULATION RISE

Tells Medical College Association Total of 1,920,000,000 May Be Reality Here in 240 Years.

That a real danger to the welfare of society may lie in the progress which medical science is making in eliminating disease and prolonging life was suggested last night by Dr. Burton D. Myers, president of the Association of Medical Colleges, at a dinner of the association in the Pennsylvania Hotel. The 200 medical educators representing the institutions composing the association opened a three-day business session yesterday morning at the Medical Centre.

Dr. Myers declared the possible menace of medical progress lay in the resulting increase of population, which might breed famine or war. The population of the world at the present rate doubles every sixty years and the population of the United States has been shown by the Census Bureau to have doubled every thirty-three years, he declared.

Foresees 1,920,000,000 Here.

Using the world rate of increase to figure his totals, Dr. Myers said:

"Assuming our present population to be 120,000,000, then in three successive sixty years we would have 240,000,000, 480,000,000, 960,000,000 and in 240 years 1,920,000,000, a figure materially in excess of the present population of the earth. That is, in about one-half the time that has elapsed since Columbus discovered America the warning, 'standing room only,' might be a reality."

Dr. Myers pointed to an eighteen-fold increase of English-speaking whites since 1800, the growth of the population of India by 50,000,000 in forty years and the doubling of the population in Porto Rico in thirty-seven years as examples of expansion. In the last sixteen years in this country the death rate was so reduced that there were two births to one death, he added.

"We may abolish war, throttle pestilence and for a time we may muzzle famine, but if the present rate of population increase maintains long enough it seems an inescapable conclusion that famine will again be a world-wide menace," he said.

Although Dr. Myers said that the solution of the problem "seems evident," he urged a correlated scientific study to consider trends and work out a remedy if necessary. As a minor point of attack on the problem he suggested sterilization legislation for mental defectives.

Dr. William Darrach, dean of the Columbia University College of Physicians and Surgeons, presided. President Nicholas Murray Butler of Columbia, who was to have been a speaker, was unable to attend.

November 8, 1929

INDIA'S POPULATION JUMPS 30,000,000

Freedom From Pestilence and Famine a Factor—Madras Has 22% Gain.

Special Cable to THE NEW YORK TIMES.

NEW DELHI, March 8.--India's population has increased 30,000,000 during the last decade, it is estimated from the preliminary census returns thus far received. The census of 1921 put the figure at 318,000,000, but figures now available show that during the last ten years there has been an increase in population exceeding all estimates.

Freedom from pestilence and famine, the lessons the natives have learned in sanitation, generous medical facilities and more enlightened living generally have contributed to the increase in population which appears certain throughout India.

Burma's population has risen at least 10 per cent and probably 12 per cent. Bikanir State takes the lead, however, with an increase of 41.7 per cent, largely due to the completion of a large irrigation project and the consequent immigration. This immigration, however, while it explains the increase in Bikanir, has not left a gap elsewhere.

Population increases of 35 per cent in the Ahmednagar district of Dekkan and 32 per cent in the adjoining Poona district may perhaps be similarly ascribed to new irrigation works, but here again the immigration leaves no gap elsewhere. It merely shows such general pressure of population that the people immediately flow into the areas providing support for fresh inhabitants.

In Madras Province, where there is an active birth control society, the population has increased 22 per cent. The census of 1921 showed an increase in population in Madras since 1911 of slightly more than 1 per cent. The fact that it was not larger was ascribed to the influenza epidemic of 1918, which accounted for 6,000,000 deaths.

The census of 1921 gave Madras third place among the provinces of British India, with a population in excess of 42,000,000. The increase indicated by the year's tabulation would place the figure above 51,600,000.

March 9, 1931

CURB ON CHINA SEEN IN OVERPOPULATION

Dr. Condliffe Finds Resources Inadequate for Pressure of Racial Growth.

POSSIBLE CURES DISCUSSED

Economist in New Book Points to Modernized Agriculture as Only Hope for Distressed Peasantry.

China's root problem is a tremendous pressure of population upon available resources, Dr. J. B. Condliffe asserts in his book, "China Today: Economic," recently published by the World Peace Foundation. The author was for several years research secretary of the Institute of Pacific Relations and was called from that post to the Secretariat of the League of Nations to undertake the task of preparing the League's world economic survey.

The pitiless pressure of numbers too great for the available resources to support nullifies the sacrifices and labors of the most patient and frugal peasantry in the world. Dr. Condliffe writes. "Since land is so scarce and valuable in China, it is natural to find that every effort is made to force it to yield its maximum productivity," he points out. "Whatever effort is possible within the limits of size, technique and auxiliary organization must be made incessantly. Even then the industrious ingenuity of the peasant-farmer must be supplemented by the most rigorous economy of a sort hardly conceivable in other lands, and still the standard of living remains pitiably low so that there is always a 'famine factor' in the death rate of China."

Emigration Viewed as Remedy.

Some relief, Dr. Condliffe believes, will be gained by redistributing the population so as to utilize to better advantage land hitherto neglected, "but the extent of this possible relief is often overestimated. Redistribution of an agricultural population is a difficult and slow process, and meantime any improvement caused by emigration from crowded areas is quickly swallowed up by the further increase of population.

"Some relief may come in time also from more equitable organization of land tenures," continues Dr. Condliffe, "but here again the possible relief should not be overestimated. China's peasantry already owns a considerable proportion of the land it cultivates. While there are abuses in the tenurial system and rents are high, the root of the problem lies in the small-scale operations and poverty of the tenant-farmer rather than in his undue exploitation by the landlord."

There seems to be a consensus not only among the foreign experts working in China but also among Chinese students who have received modern training in the agricultural sciences that improvements in the traditional methods of Chinese agriculture offer the best and most immediate means for the amelioration of China's poverty, Dr. Condliffe points out.

Would Arrest Population Cycle.

"The problem is to arrest the population cycle, to provide a surplus of production over immediately pressing needs so as to give a breathing space in which the process of education and social reform may work to reverse the cycle and raise living standards."

Dr. Condliffe expresses the opinion that the cultural tradition and unity of the Chinese people is so deep and strong that the development of national consciousness is only a matter of time. "The size and diversity of the country, the strength of local groupings and attachments, and indeed the whole social genius of the people make it almost inevitable that there shall be a large element of decentralization and federalism in any effective government of China as a whole."

August 19, 1932

POPULATION DROP SHOWN IN JAPAN

Demography Experts Here Are Told Modernizing Economy Was the Apparent Cause

Changes in population trends as a result of the war were discussed yesterday by leaders in the field of demography at the fall meeting of the Population Association of America, held in the Hotel New Yorker.

Frank Lorimer, Professor of Population Studies at the American University, Washington, welcomed visiting scientists from abroad.

Before the war the interest of both governmental agencies and private institutions in matters of demography was centered on national or local problems, Mr. Lorimer said.

"The exigencies of the war and prospect of post-war problems," he continued, "directed the attention of many American demographers to research on conditions in other countries. The imaginations of all men have been stimulated by world problems which suddenly seem directly related to our personal security and interests."

Dr. Irene B. Taeuber of the Office of Population Research traced "the pattern of fertility decline in Japan" for the period extending from 1920 to 1943, from which she drew the hypothesis that "decline in fertility is a necessary reaction to the condition of living in a modernizing economy, whether the culture be Western or Eastern."

"However, this is still conjectural," she said, "for the Japanese constitute only a small fraction of Asia's billion people and, in many ways, they are an atypical fraction."

"Hence, one demographic history of Japan cannot predict the rate of the demographic transition that may occur in mainland Asia, just as the demographic history of European peoples did not predict the speed of that transition in Japan."

Discussing future population growth in the Netherlands, Dr. Johannes B. D. Derksen of the Central Bureau of Statistics at The Hague, observed that "the rapid rise in the birth rate during the war and especially after the liberation of the country caused a much more rapid natural increase in the population than was envisaged before, and has also rendered it much more difficult to estimate the future trend of the birth rate."

Other factors that have influenced the increase of population, according to Dr. Derksen, include the repatriation of larage numbers of Dutch from the Dutch East Indies, Germany, Belgium, France, Switzerland and other countries.

Noting the existence of a serious housing shortage due to these increases, he predicted that "even under optimistic assumptions with respect to the possible expansion of building activity, it may take from ten to fifteen years before pre-war conditions are restored."

David V. Glass, a member of the Population Investigation Committee of Great Britain, explained the tabulation program, set up by the Royal Commission in March, 1944, to study current population trends in that country.

October 26, 1946

Food and World Population

Necessity Pointed Out for Long-Range Planning to Assure Resources

TO THE EDITOR OF THE NEW YORK TIMES:

In Sir John Orr's latest press conference at Geneva he calls attention again to the fact that world population is growing more rapidly than the world's food supply. As reported in THE TIMES of May 19, I gather that his immediate appeal is for action to relieve shortages in areas where food supply is too low for minimum nutritional needs.

Obviously, our first attempts to improve the food-population ratio must deal with the food-supply side of the problem. But serious long-range efforts must also be made to determine how rate of population increase will affect the feasibility of providing an adequate diet for all the peoples of the world. The possibilities for increasing food supplies are more limited than are the propensities to multiply the race.

Perhaps no other single issue is more significant in our present attempts to bring the benefits of modern science and technology to a larger portion of the world's people than is this continuing historic race between population and food.

A century and a half of controversy over the merits of the Malthusian idea have resulted largely in academic quibbling over minor points of application. The basic thought advanced by Malthus and by others before and since remains to confront us today: namely, that population increases have tended to outstrip increases in food production, in long-term historical experience. Although the extensive colonization and exploitation of new lands in the nineteenth century has obscured this fact somewhat, it is once again becoming increasingly evident that the problem must be faced and solved as a prerequisite or condition to any well-ordered form of a future world political organization.

Adequate Living Standard

A "social policy" with respect to food resources seems scarcely enough. The distribution of food and other material benefits of modern civilization occupy many of our energies, and problems arising therefrom underlie the social and political revolution which is now going on in many parts of the modern world. However, before such problems can be satisfactorily solved, it may be necessary to consider whether the total to be divided will provide an adequate living standard for all.

The present food supply of the world is not adequate to the needs of the present population—that is, in the sense of supplying a diet which enables men to make the most efficient use of their capabilities. Even in the United States it may well be argued that this statement holds true, in spite of our large food wastage and soil exploitation. How, then, can the world's people hope figuratively to "lift themselves by their bootstraps" to a higher economic plane when this terrible pressure of numbers of people on the food supply destroys their greatest asset—that of human ambition and human energies?

From the standpoint of food supply alone, the future outlook need not appear to be a gloomy one. On the contrary, there is every reason to believe that continued technical advances in such things as land reclamation, irrigation and farm management practices, plus the startling achievements of the chemists, agronomists, and plant and animal breeders, will make possible considerable increase in food supplies in future years. It is only when we consider that population pressure may nullify the benefits which could otherwise be expected from such nutritional gains that the outlook becomes less optimistic.

Study Suggested

Therefore, it seems reasonable to urge that some authoritative educational agency conduct extensive study to determine how world population may best be kept in proportion with a food supply which is the maximum for any given level of agricultural technology. Undoubtedly, educational work must be conducted on a large scale in preference to governmental restrictions.

People do not alter the social mores of centuries by edict alone. The immediate problem may well be whether such educational processes will be effective or possible before a world government has been achieved, or if we must raise the level of living for the world's people before political unification can be accomplished. The intense nationalistic feelings which were brought to bloom during the nineteenth century stand as a tremendous obstacle, in either case.

In other words, which must come first: economic improvement or settled political organization? The most likely answer is that both must go forward together. For that reason, the problem of the food-population ratio must be considered now.

ROBERT N. HAMPTON.

Ithaca, N. Y., May 29, 1948.

June 8, 1948

WILL THERE BE FOOD ENOUGH?

A Census Bureau report which gives the country an estimated population of 143,414,000 focuses attention on the old problem of food supply. This country has no reason to worry, but mankind has. World population has never increased at anything like the present rate. So far as the statistical evidence goes there were 445 million people on earth 300 years ago, and the density was eight to the mile; today there are 2,251 million, and the density is forty to the mile. The billions who are now on earth and who will come must live on the land, periodically visited by such disasters as premature frosts, droughts, storms, earthquakes, floods that wash away soil. Not all the land is good enough for human habitation or good enough for agriculture or mining. The late Dr. Raymond Pearl went into these matters thoroughly and painted a black picture of an increasing human horde which would rapidly exhaust the chemical elements that sustain life. If the rate of increase that prevailed from 1936 to 1946 (a little less than 1 per cent) is maintained there will be over 21,000 million people by 2240. Even if we cut this estimate in half, as the more cautious demographers do, the world will have to cast about for means to feed itself.

Can science help us in the extremity that must ultimately be faced? During the war we learned how to cultivate edible yeasts. Starches and sugars have been synthesized in the laboratory, a success which, though enormously expensive, warrants the belief that the factory may yet supplement the farm in the production of food. Virtually nothing has been done to harvest the vast amount of plankton in the sea. The synthetic chemist is still baffled by the structure of protein, for which reason his attempts to synthesize it in one of its many forms have failed. Yet there is nothing absurd in the idea that the synthetic equivalent of beefsteak, a glass of milk or white of egg may some day be produced at a cost low enough to be of practical importance. Even pessimistic Dr. Pearl did not think humanity would some day have to follow the lemmings and drown its excess numbers in the sea in order to solve the problem of food and overcrowding. Science is the algebraic "X" with which statisticians cannot reckon because its frontier is boundless and its discoveries are unpredictable.

August 15, 1948

World Population Increasing 1% Annually, Mounting by 544,000,000 in Last 3 Decades

Special to THE NEW YORK TIMES.

UNITED NATIONS, N. Y., March 27—According to the latest population estimates, the total of people in the world has increased during the last three decades from 1,834,000,000 to 2,378,000,000, United Nations population experts reported today.

That is, the world's population has increased by 544,000,000 between 1920 and 1949, or about a generation. During the period, the estimated population of the world increased by slightly less than 1 per cent a year, although the increases, obviously, varied a great deal from year to year.

If this rate of growth were to be maintained over a long period of time, the experts said, it would mean the present world population would be doubled in less than a hundred years. Because for several regions of the world population information is poor, it is likely that present estimates understate the world's population.

Latin America appears to be the fastest growing part of the world. In this region, relatively high birth rates and the reduction of mortality by improved environmental conditions have combined to produce a rather high rate of increase, about 2 per cent a year. In other parts of the world, high birth rates in combination with high death rates, or low birth rates in combination with low death rates, have resulted in somewhat lower growth rates, between 0.8 and 1.5 per cent a year.

The density of the world population has increased steadily in recent decades from fourteen persons a square kilometer (or 247 acres) in 1920 to eighteen in 1949.

The world's estimated population in mid-year 1949 was distributed as follows: Africa, 198,000,000; the Americas, 321,000,000; Asia, 1,254,000,000; Europe, 593,000,000 and Oceania, 12,000,000.

The density of the world's population varies greatly among its regions. In Africa it is estimated at seven persons a square kilometer, in Oceania one person a square kilometer. In Africa, however, large parts of the Continent consist of desert area unsuitable for human habitation. This is also true of some parts of Oceania, such as Australia.

In the United States and Canada and in Latin America the density is eight persons a square kilometer. For Asia, as a whole, the figure is forty-seven, but this is not a typical figure. In the Near East it is twelve; in South Central Asia, 100; in Japan, 223 and in the remaining Far East, forty-one.

In Europe, as a whole, excluding the Asiatic part of the Soviet Union, the density is twenty-two persons a square kilometer. Within the region, however, there is also great variation: seventy-eight in Northwest-Central Europe; eighty-eight in Southern Europe, and twelve in Eastern Europe.

March 28, 1951

Lower Death Rates

Ceylon Epidemic Control Saves Lives—and Upsets Balance

Dr. Robert C. Cook, acting director of the Population Reference Bureau, cites in its bulletin Ceylon's experience to show how easily and cheaply modern epidemic control measures can lower death rates. The decline in the death rate is a blessing, but it also upsets the balance between birth and deaths and often precipitates economic and political crises.

Cook states that in Ceylon a malaria-control campaign cut the death rate from twenty to fourteen in only one year. This low death rate has been maintained since 1946. The annual cost has been about 12-15 cents per person.

Because Ceylon's birth rate per thousand population remains high (40.3), the annual rate of growth is nearly 3 per cent. Should that rate persist, the population of Ceylon will double in no more than twenty-five years; the population density will be 600 per square mile.

The average world rate of increase is today about 1 per cent a year—the highest in history. Cook likens the rate of increase to compound interest. An increase rate of 1 per cent will double the population of the earth in about seventy years. In terms of people, this 1 per cent means that the net gain each year amounts to about 25,000,000 people, or 68,000 additional mouths to feed each twenty-four hours. Should the rate for the entire world increase to that of Ceylon—almost 3 per cent—the world's 2.4 billion people would become 4.8 billion before 1980 and over 9 billion shortly after the year 2000.

Over half of the people of the earth have a very low level of living in terms of food, clothing and housing. To achieve any improvement, economic production must increase more rapidly than the population. At present population is winning the race.

October 19, 1952

Infant Mortality Declines

GENEVA, Aug. 2 (UP)—The infant mortality rate, which rose sharply during World War II, is dropping now throughout the world, the United Nations World Health Organization said today. The agency published a survey of forty-four countries covering infant mortality from 1950 to 1952. Before the war 3 to 24 per cent of live-born children in the countries surveyed died before they were 1 year old. In 1952 this figure dropped to from 2 to 16 per cent. The survey showed that in the United States during this period infant mortality dropped 50 per cent.

August 3, 1953

SCIENCE IN REVIEW

Rome Conference on Population Trends Raises Serious Questions Concerning Food Supply

By ROBERT K. PLUMB

Five hundred delegates from seventy nations meeting in Rome last week and this are pondering a problem that many believe to be the key to the future history of the world. The problem: world population trends.

The conference is sponsored by the International Union for the Scientific Study of Population, the International Labor Organization, the Food and Agriculture Organization, the World Health Organization, the United Nations Educational, Scientific and Cultural Organization and the International Bank for Reconstruction and Development.

The conference was formally opened by Guillaume-Georges Picot, Assistant Secretary General of the United Nations for economic affairs, and official representative of the Secretary General. Liebmann Hersch of the International Union for the Scientific Study of Population at Geneva was elected chairman.

Four previous population conferences, Mr. Hersch recalled, were concerned chiefly with falling birth rates in the highly developed Western countries. The concern today, he said, is in Asia: particularly acute is the problem posed by the rapidly increasing birth rates in economically underdeveloped countries. In many of these areas (India is the prime example) the spread of Western medical and hygienic practices has caused life expectancy to rise. Birth rates remain high. Population increases.

There are many opinions but not many hard facts about population problems. Inevitably discussions center on food supply and the availability of materials for clothing and shelter.

Gloomy Malthus

A hundred and fifty years ago Thomas Robert Malthus, an English economist, published his pamphlet "An Essay on the Principles of Population as it Affects the Future Improvement of Society." The treatise contended that the tendency of population was to outrun the means of subsistence. This view became widely known in the first half of the nineteenth century. It led Carlyle to dub economics "the dismal science."

Later it became the fashion to disparage the Malthusian idea. In his early discussion, Malthus had underestimated the importance of industrialization on agricultural output. The development of modern means of transportation and communication altered the food supply picture.

After the World War of 1914 to 1918, however, the specter of over-population returned and, indeed, Malthus' views gained new supporters.

The population of the world has increased from 500,000,000 to 2,500,000,000 in the last 300 years. The United Nations Department of Social Affairs has published a study that forecasts an additional world population increase by 1980 of 1,500,000,000.

Last spring in the House of Lords, the subject of "World Population and Resources" was introduced as the most important problem facing the world. The Secretary General of the United Nations, Dag Hammarskjold, has cautioned that "the world is skating on thin economic ice." The problem has often been put this way: "An extra hundred thousand persons turn out for dinner every day."

And Many Starve

This picture is not at all relieved when one considers that as much as two-thirds of the present 2,500,000,000 world population is starving or close to starving. What will happen when population increases?

Improvement of agricultural methods can increase the availability of foodstuffs. This is coming about. Two weeks ago, the Food and Agriculture Organization reported that for the second growing season in succession, food production outstripped population increase. This is not to say that starvation was relieved: there are surplus areas and shortage areas.

But present improvement in farming methods is actually getting more food from the available supply of cultivable land. Improvements in fertilizers, the addition of nitrogen to growing soils, crop selection and the **rise of high-yielding seed strains fitted to particular areas has been important.**

Animal husbandry has provided another basis for improvement. Emphasis has been on encouraging the raising of animals that provide a good return in animal protein for the amount of cereal feed expended.

A third area of improvement being pushed now is the extension of farming into new areas. Good growing bottom land is already nearly 100 per cent cultivated. But in the Far West of the United States "dry land" wheat farming has moved up the slopes and valleys of previously unfarmed mountains.

'Rice' Out of Wheat

And in other directions efforts are made to improve the food-supply situation. We have an excess of wheat. But Asians demand rice. Our wheat can be parboiled in an ancient method and then prepared and eaten like rice. By altering traditional customs through education some improvement in food-supply utilization can be achieved.

In addition to better use of crops and animals on a limited amount of cultivable land area in the world, many believe that fish should be a more important item in world diet. Vast areas of the oceans support quantities of vitamin-rich and protein-rich fish that can be harvested by conventional fishing methods. Fresh-water lakes are not exploited. Wide use of the current improvements in farming and animal raising, and the exploitation of new food sources by available means, is now increasing the world's food supply, authorities say. But the same authorities generally agree that methods now known cannot begin to provide for the expected vast increase in population, particularly when it is realized that it is necessary first to make up the food deficit by adequately feeding those now malnourished or starving.

It is the future, which is probably as difficult to envisage now as it was in the time of Malthus, which occupies the thoughts of many population authorities today. Some hints of what technology may accomplish in food production are now at hand. Algae can be farmed in fresh and salt water ponds and tanks, harvested and processed chemically into a palatable food. Yeast-foods can be grown from molds.

The current issue of "Population Bulletin," publication of the Population Reference Bureau, Inc., Washington, is devoted to excerpts from the recent Viking Press book "The Challenge of Man's Future," by Harrison Brown, California Institute of Technology chemist. Dr. Brown states:

"Indeed, if food habits were to change sufficiently so that the people of the world were content to derive their main nourishment from the products of algae farms and yeast factories, a world population of 50 billion persons could eventually be supported comfortably from the point of view of nutritional requirements."

Food From Power

Dr. Brown asserts that this goal probably cannot be achieved. But it does give a measure of what might be accomplished. Other factors suggest that some vast multiplication of food may be possible. Scientists studying the nuclear fusion reaction under Sir John Cockcroft of Britain reported last week at the British Association for the Advancement of Science that the possibility of "power without limit" was being considered. Power can produce food, by-passing agriculture, if necessary.

The Rome population conference is considering these possibilities in the long view and it is also considering the elements now in use that might provide for an increase in food in the near future.

And foremost among the subjects studied is conception control. Although many of the conception control techniques are not acceptable to large religious groups, there remain areas, in India and Japan, for instance, where ignorance is the only barrier to achieving a lower birth rate. Representatives of the International Planned Parenthood Federation are presenting this aspect of the population problem in Rome.

September 5, 1954

Life Expectancy in India Raised From 27 to 32, Minister Says

By KATHLEEN McLAUGHLIN
Special to The New York Times.

UNITED NATIONS, N. Y., Oct. 29—In the last five years life expectancy in India has been raised from an average of 27 years to 32.

That fact pleases, but does not elate, the woman who directs the vast public health job, Rajkumari (Princess) Amrit Kaur, India's Minister of Health, who is on a trip to the United States, Canada and Puerto Rico.

The Princess, a slender, graying woman in a saffron-colored sari, told correspondents here yesterday that she was too much aware of the scope of tasks still ahead to feel any complacence about results thus far.

She cited progress in the anti-malaria campaign, unexcelled anywhere, as "one of the triumphs of international cooperation." Top credit for aid to the Indian Government in this respect, she said, belonged to the United Nations Children's Fund,

Rajkumari Amrit Kaur

which allocated $667,000 to supply 700 tons of D. D. T. to spray swamps and homes, and gave $850,000 worth of equipment for a D. D. T. plant at Delhi. Next, she ranked the United States Foreign Operations Administration's gifts of D. D. T. for the same purpose.

Tuberculosis Problem

At the present pace, she foresees the disappearance of malaria as an Indian national problem within the next seven years. There remains tuberculosis for which 40,000,000 children and mothers have been tested and 13,000,000 given vaccinations, she reported. For these activities, the Children's Fund has donated $1,529,700 to date.

Princess Amrit said the infant mortality rate declined since 1949, from 158 per 1,000 a year to 124 per 1,000, and maternal mortality 10 per cent as a result of the maternal and child-care programs in which the World Health Organization participated extensively.

Training facilities for Indian doctors and nurses have been enlarged gradually, Princess Amrit added.

Recent floods have caused great damage to health, as well as crops and property, she said, but the food situation now is less critical than it was, although the average intake of 1,750 calories still is nearly 400 below that of Asia generally. Again she credited the United Nations Children's Fund with aid in a crucial situation, mentioning its gifts of $3,000,000 toward emergency relief.

Born in a palace of Lucknow, the Princess abandoned a life of luxury to serve her people. She is the daughter of Raja Sir Harnam Singh of Kapurthala, was educated in England and became a championship tennis player in her native country.

She spent the years 1942 to 1945 in a prison cell for her activities in the independence movement. As a welfare worker, she became a disciple of Mohandas K. Gandhi and served for sixteen years as his secretary.

Her appointment as Minister of Health dates from 1947, when India won separate status as a nation.

October 30, 1954

POPULATION RISE: WHAT IT IMPLIES

Vast Opportunity for Growth Here and Abroad Will Also Bring Problems

By RICHARD RUTTER

One of the biggest stories of 1959 wasn't even a new one.

For many years a population "explosion" has been in the making in this country and throughout the world. But last year attention was focused on the problem as never before.

Economists, Government officials, various commentators all pointed out the political, social and economic implications.

The cold statistics are startling enough. In the next ten years—by 1970—the world's population is expected to soar from 2,900,000,000 to 3,500,000,000. By the year 2000, there are likely to be about 6,300,000,000 humans on the globe.

Accelerating Trend

The rate of population growth in the United States will not be so rapid, but it'll still be quite explosive. Right now there are about 179,000,000 Americans. The projection for 1970 is from 204,000,000 to 217,000,000. And in 2000? At least 360,000,000.

This trend has been accelerating almost ever since World War II. Only recently, however, has its bearing on the nation's economic growth been apparent. In the Nineteen Fifties about 25,000,000 were added to the population; there were more than 4,300,000 births in 1959 alone. In the coming decade an increase of 30,000,000 more will will undoubtedly occur.

What does the population "explosion" portend for the national economy? Overseas, it should mean a tremendous opportunity for investment, especially in under-developed areas.

Even now, private American enterprise has invested at least $28,000,000,000 abroad. That investment is growing at the rate of $3,000,000,000 a year. It will undoubtedly rise further in the coming decade.

More and more American companies are starting their own manufacturing or sales operations overseas. In some instances, they are buying into established foreign companies or forming joint-venture projects.

The foreign market looms as an ever more important source of new business and new profits. For instance, the six nations of Europe's Common Market have 165,000,000 potential consumers.

A Dramatic Impetus

Back home, the impetus to the economy from the sheer addition of numbers may prove even more dramatic. It should be noted, incidentally, that the population forecasts may be on the conservative side. They invariably have been so in the past.

Back in the early Ninteen Thirties a research committee appointed by President Hoover surveyed the population outlook and decided that "the United States might have a stationary population before the end of the twentieth century * * * with the total population close to 145,000,000."

How far off this finding was from actuality needs little emphasis. In recent years, there has been a trend to earlier marriages and earlier births. Meanwhile, the death rate continues to drop thanks to major new medical advances—some of the most important of which may lie just ahead.

A new rise in the birth rate is seen in the mid-Sixties and the succeeding years as the post-war baby crop reaches marriage age. Women are now marrying at an average age of 20 and men at 22.5.

There seems little doubt that —barring a major international war—the growth in population will largely dictate the course of the economy. Already, the economists and other observers are referring to forthcoming decade as, variously, "The Soaring Sixties," "The Golden Sixties," "The Fabulous Sixties." Glowing forecasts are being made by the sheaf-full.

Problems Lie Ahead

It's true also that the population spurt will bring problems as well as opportunities for growth. It will require an enormous upsurge in productive capacity and output to meet consumer demand.

Traffic problems, already near the nightmare stage in some metropolitan areas, will become even more nightmarish. Sufficient and decent housing must be provided unless the cancer of slums is to spread unchecked. Educational facilities will be strained.

But as of now, at least, the consensus is that the problems will be solved—with far-sighted planning as the key—and that the Sixties will be genuinely an era of spectacular growth and prosperity.

January 11, 1960

World's Population Well Past 3 Billion

By KATHLEEN TELTSCH

Special to The New York Times.

UNITED NATIONS, N. Y., Sept. 1—The world population has raced well past the 3,000,000,000 mark and is rushing ahead at an annual rate of increase of 1.8 per cent.

Two new United Nations studies found that the highest growth rate was in the regions of Central America and Southwest Asia. The lowest rate was reported in Northern and Western Europe.

United Nations statisticians also noted the fact that in all parts of the world married men and women lived longer than unmarried people.

No single satisfactory explanation for this phenomenon has yet been found, experts here said. They offered the suggestion that "married people have a reciprocal concern about each partner's wellbeing and a sense of responsibility about preserving one's own health."

The studies made here also showed that girl babies born in Sweden could expect a long life span—slightly more than seventy-five years. In twenty-five countries the average girl baby can be expected to live for more than seventy years. By contrast, only five countries give boy babies the same chance.

United Nations statisticians base their findings on data collected for the 1961 demographic yearbook and for a quarterly report of population and vital statistics, both made public here today.

The world total of at least 3,000,000,000 was reached by the middle of last year, the statisticians said. The estimated rate of increase, averaging 55,000,000 yearly, would place the population total by the middle of this year at 3,115,000,000.

Among other findings, they reported that West Berlin and Hungary had the world's highest suicide rate.

Austrians appeared to be more accident prone than any other people. They also hold the world record for deaths from motor vehicle accidents—27.5 for each 100,000 inhabitants. The rate in the United States was 20.6 for each 100,000.

Heart and Cancer Deaths

In the world's more economically advanced countries with high levels of living, half or more of all deaths were found to have been caused by heart disease or cancer. These two causes accounted for more than half of all fatalities in the United States, Canada and Britain in 1960.

Iceland had the most favorable record on infant mortality, a low of 13.3 deaths for each 1,000 babies born. The United States was in twenty-ninth place with a record of 25.2 deaths reported in 1961 for each 1,000 babies born.

A more favorable record was achieved by the Netherlands, which reported a low of 15.4, Sweden with 15.5 and by Norway, Australia and Finland.

In most countries and particularly the more prosperous states, accidents account for more deaths than tuberculosis and, with few exceptions, take more lives than childbirth. Accidents were the leading cause

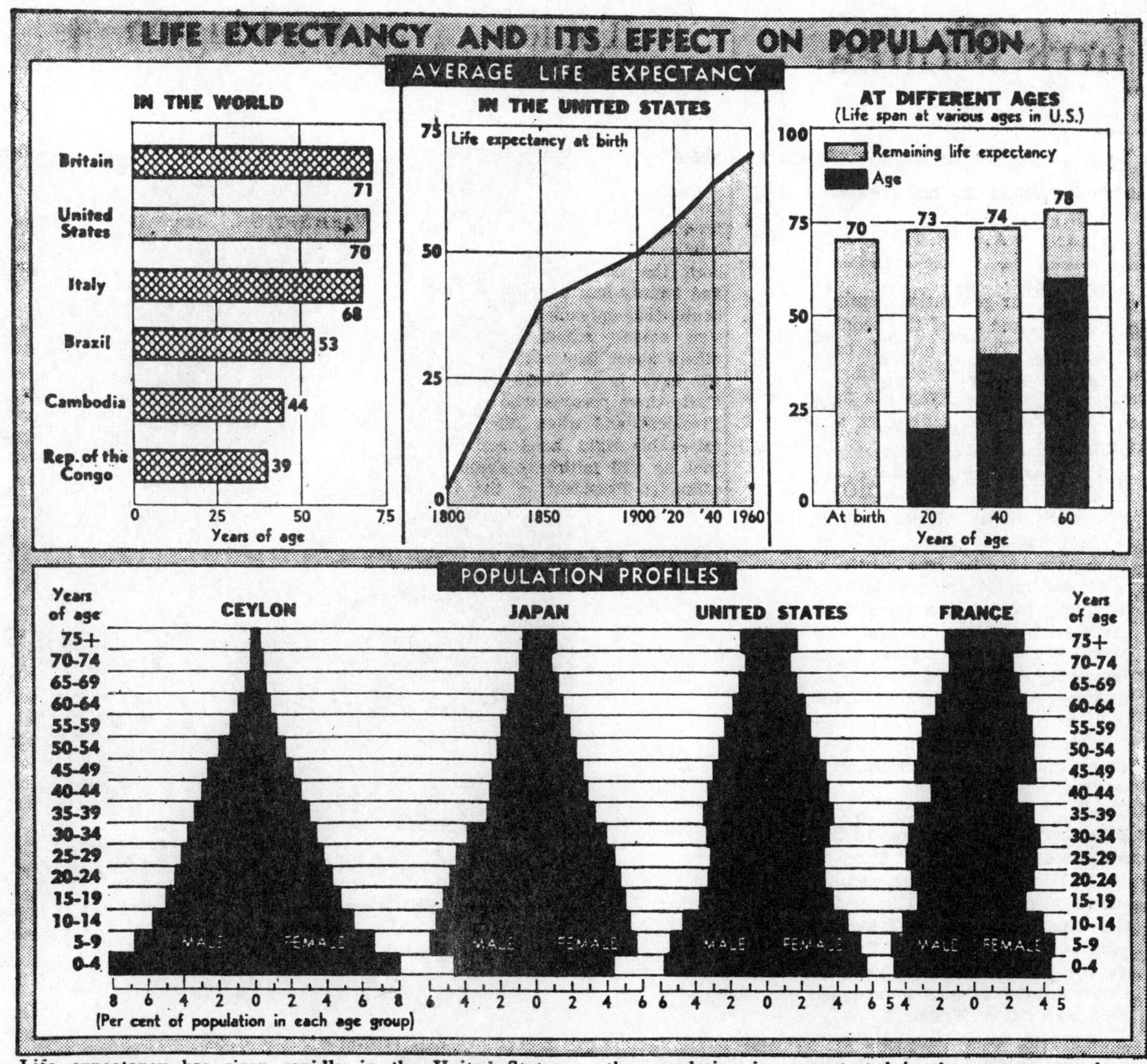

Life expectancy has risen rapidly in the United States and is much higher in the Western nations than in the underveloped areas, as the charts at top show. Lower charts, adapted from Population Bulletin, show different age patterns in underdeveloped and Western societies. In underdeveloped Ceylon, where birth and death rates are high, the population is concentrated in the younger age brackets. In Japan, a society in transition, the birth rate is falling. In the U. S. and France, with lower birth and death rates, population is spread more evenly through the lifespan. In the case of France, the population 'gap' at ages 15-19 and 40-44 is due to the effects of two world wars.

January 15, 1961

of deaths in forty out of forty-seven countries and the leading cause of death among young males in the 15 to 24 age group. The rate for girls and women was considerably lower.

Women not only live longer in most countries but also have a lower death rate than men and boys, the United Nations data said. The male death rate was reported 36 per cent higher than the female in the United States.

Statisticians here pointed out that the differential might be laid to various environmental and biological factors: one of these could be the greater stresses of living confronting men. However, it was also suggested that the more favorable showing of women could be laid to a greater capacity to withstand physical and emotional stress.

In all parts of the world, married men and women have lower death rates than the single, the widowed or the divorced population, according to the data collected. A slight tendency for divorced persons to have a lower death rate than the widowed also was reported.

Statisticians posed the possibility that the lives of some divorced persons might be regarded as lengthened because they had escaped an unsatisfactory marriage or the lives of widowed persons shortened by grief.

Evidence of the continued population explosion was strongest in Central America, where an annual rate of 2.7 per cent was reported, and in Southwest Asia, where a rate of 2.6 was given. By contrast, Northern and Western Europe increased by only 0.7 per cent.

Japanese efforts to curp.population by birth control programs appears to have had an appreciable effect in recent years. The annual birth rate of 23.5 for each 100,000 in 1952 has been reduced to 16.9 in 1961.

The population figures for Communist China were based on the Peiping Government's estimate of the 1958 population as between 670,000,000 and 680,000,000.

September 2, 1962

Malthus—Again

Searing population figures call to mind the forebodings of an English clergyman.

By ELIOT FREMONT-SMITH

MALTHUS—"There is only so much standing room."

THE word "Malthusian" has been taking on fresh significance of late. In New York, United Nations demographers have announced that the world's population passed the three-billion mark in the middle of last year and is now rushing ahead at an average annual rate of increase of 1.8 per cent—as much as 2.7 per cent in Central America and some parts of Asia—a figure not far from the Malthusian projection of the population's doubling every twenty-five years. And China, whose population is fast approaching 700,000,000, has given signs of relaunching the intensive birth-control program it abandoned five years ago with the "Great Leap Forward." In doing so, it has opened itself to charges of what the Communists call the "Malthusian heresy."

"Malthusian" refers of course to the English economic philosopher Thomas Malthus, and to the theory of population growth he published in 1798 under the title: "An Essay on the Principle of Population, as it Affects the Future Improvement of Society, With Remarks on the Speculations of Mr. Godwin, M. Condorcet, and Other Writers."

"The power of population," Malthus wrote, "is indefinitely greater than the power in the earth to produce subsistence for men. * * * Population is always and everywhere, in some measure, pressing against the available food supply."

More specifically, Malthus' essay held that population, unchecked, increases geometrically while the earth's food resources can increase only arithmetically: "In two centuries and a quarter, assuming a doubling every twenty-five years, [the population] would be to the means of subsistence as 512 to 10: in three centuries as 4,096 to 13 * * *."

Although the theory was not entirely new—Plato, Aristotle and Hume had previously addressed themselves to demographic problems, and Benjamin Franklin had first suggested the twenty-five-year doubling period—it was Malthus who brought the matter to public attention. Clearly, if one accepted his figures and assumptions, catastrophe was at hand.

Many did not, and for more than half a century—until Darwin engaged the theologians—"The Principle of Population" was the subject of heated debate. In the past decade, "Malthusian" has once again come into common usage.

Thomas Robert Malthus was born in 1766 in the town of Dorking, Surrey, where his father owned a small estate. He attended Cambridge University and, despite a pronounced shyness, owing to a cleft palate and resulting speech impediment, took holy orders. In 1798, the same year he published his essay, he was appointed to a curacy. In 1804 he married and the following year was appointed to the East India College at Haileybury as professor of political economy, a post he held until his death in December, 1834.

For two centuries the study of social philosophy had gyrated around the issue of man's "innate" moral quality. Jean-Jacques Rousseau was the principal spokesman for the positive or optimistic view (optimistic because, if man was good, Utopia was possible), and among Rousseau's English followers was his close friend and executor, Daniel Malthus.

IT can be argued that it was partly in revolt against his father that son Thomas aligned himself with the opposite view—that man was fundamentally evil and, left to his own devices (that is, without authoritarian guidance), would soon degenerate into a morass of "misery and vice." Yet "misery and vice" were also important factors in Malthus' theory of population control.

"The Principle of Population" was explicitly prompted by the writings of Rousseau's disciples, the Marquis de Condorcet and William Godwin. An extreme rationalist, Godwin had claimed, in his "Enquiry Concerning Political Justice" of 1793, that mind would triumph over matter in the coming perfect society to such a degree that death itself would be conquered. Further, "there will be neither disease, anguish, melancholy, nor resentment. Every man will seek, with ineffable ardor, the good of all."

To Malthus, this was not only ineffable poppycock, but dangerous as well, for disease, anguish and the rest, which Malthus lumped under "misery and vice"—"all unwholesome occupations, severe labor and exposure to the seasons, extreme poverty, bad nursing of children, excesses of all kinds, the whole train of common diseases and epidemics, wars, plague and famine," plus celibacy, nonprocreative promiscuity and "vicious practices" (by which he meant birth control)—these were the essential checks against overpopulation.

In 1796, Prime Minister William Pitt proposed to formalize this practice and, further (reading a lesson from the Napoleonic wars, which suggested population as an index of a country's might), actually to promote population growth by establishing relief rates in accordance with the number of children in any given family.

IN Malthus' view, the proposed bill would not only negate the necessary checks of "misery and vice," but compound disaster. Direct relief, he reasoned, would kill incentive to work—to produce more food—for man is naturally "inert, sluggish, and averse from labor, unless compelled by necessity."

Thus, while population leaped, food supplies would actually decline; the poor would increase in suffering as they increased in number. (Despite his harsh theories, Malthus was not without humanitarian feeling. "The parish prosecution of men whose families are likely to become chargeable, and of poor women who are near lying-in," he added, "is a most disgraceful and disgusting tyranny.")

Largely because of "The Principle of Population," Pitt finally withdrew the proposed law, but Malthus became the center of a storm of criticism. Not only did Godwin attack him, but such luminaries as Coleridge as well, charging him with hypocrisy and worse. William Hazlitt accused him of having a "warm constitution and amorous complexion" and a tale sped the rounds that the "parson" had fathered no fewer than eleven daughters (which added nine fictional daughters to fact and curiously ignored Malthus' son).

Both Dickens and Disraeli later satirized Malthus in their novels, and Karl Marx denounced Malthusian theory as a vicious capitalistic plot to limit the proletariat and stifle revolution—a judgment that has caused considerable handwringing in the Communist world.

© Punch.

MALTHUS assumed that the bottom of the social pyramid was always at the bare minimum of subsistence; thus in effect, the fate of the poorer classes determined the size of the total population. Disaster came either (1) when the food supply suddenly increased (through new agricultural resources, or following a great plague), so that life for the poor became more comfortable, people married earlier, had more children and died later—thereby quickly increasing the population which, multiplying geometrically, soon outran the food supply—or (2) when one or another of the natural checks was legislated out of existence. This second possibility Malthus saw as an immediate danger arising from the Government's new poor-law bill.

For some time the old English workhouse had become increasingly limited to the old and infirm, poor relief being made in the form of direct payments whenever wages fell below a set minimum.

IN 1804, Malthus published a greatly expanded and revised edition of "The Principle of Population." It contained an implicit but crucial shift of emphasis, from "natural" forces to social forces—specifically, acknowledgment of the aspirations of the poor to middle-class status and to liberty.

Because this shift compromised some of his previous conclusions—and also because a man is more likely to be remembered for his extreme first assertions than for his gentler second thoughts—Malthus is known today for the essay of 1798, not the revision of 1804.

Since Malthus' time, the population of Great Britain has multiplied itself five times over, the population of America thirty-five times. The total number of people in the world, estimated at 907 million in 1800, has more than tripled—and half the additional number has arrived in only the last three decades.

The current Malthusian "crisis" was postponed during most of the nineteenth century because of technological progress (inadequately foreseen by Malthus) in agriculture and the processing and distribution of food.

But with the social and medical revolution of recent years, which has so mitigated "misery and vice"—especially infant mortality—in the underdeveloped areas, demographers, economists, politicians and social scientists on both sides of the Iron and Bamboo Curtains have been training worried attention to the potentially disastrous population spiral.

A variety of methods for increasing the food supply have been suggested, and it now appears technologically feasible to feed many times the earth's present estimated 3.1 billion inhabitants. Eventually, however, the Malthusian explosion will have to be contained; there is only so much standing room. Unless, of course, we colonize other planets, or as one writer recently suggested in a flash of inspiration, we find a way to reduce the size of the human animal.

September 23, 1962

Americas Surpass Europe In Population for First Time

WASHINGTON, Oct. 6 (UPI)—The world population stood at an estimated total of 3,180,000,000 in mid-1963, the Population Reference Bureau reported today.

For the first time, the population of the Americas exceeded that of Europe excluding the Soviet Union, it said. The figures were 441 million and 437 million, respectively.

Asia has the largest share of the world's people—1.8 billion, or 56 per cent.

China leads the nations with 731 million people, the bureau said.

October 7, 1963

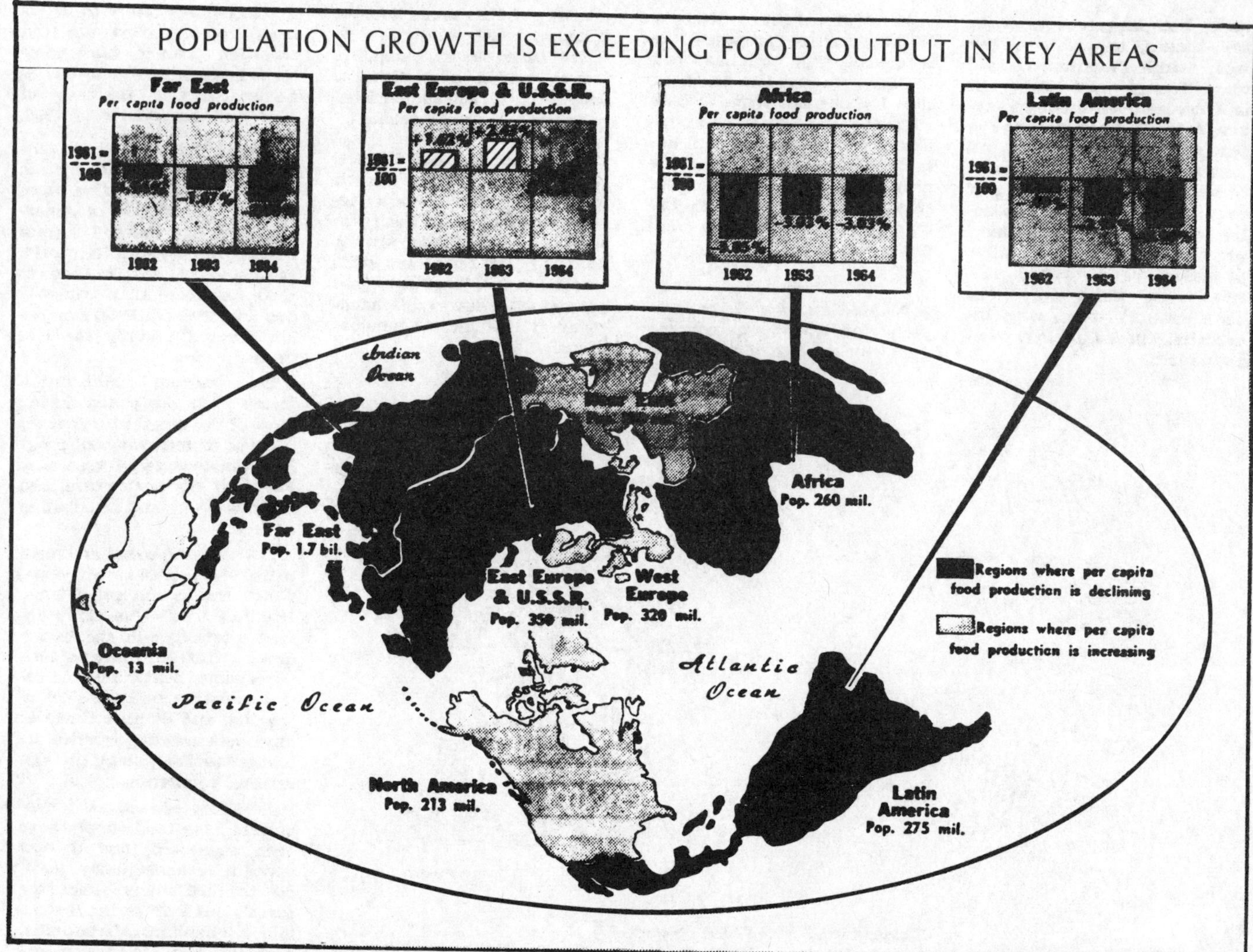

The world's food problems—already serious in some under-developed areas—are getting worse, and it is believed that shortages may persist through the rest of this century. This gloomy prospect was outlined recently by Lester R. Brown, a staff economist of the U.S. Department of Agriculture, at a symposium on population problems. The symposium was held at Cornell University Medical College in New York City. World food production, Mr. Brown noted, is rising—but population is rising even faster. Thus there is a continuing decline in per capita food production in important regions, including the Far East, with about half the world's population. Map shows regions where per capita food output rose or fell between 1961 and 1964; charts show the recent trends in the four major regions where per capita food output is going down. Reliable statistics on China's food output are unavailable, but it is generally agreed that she is suffering a downward trend in per capita food output comparable to the trend for the Far East as a whole.

May 30, 1965

Educator Sees Distribution As Key to World Survival

PHILADELPHIA, Nov. 11 (AP)—A Harvard University professor of economics believes that the key problem in world survival will be the distribution of the world's wealth, not population control.

Dr. Simon Kuznets said technological and economic resources were adequate to support the number of people who are expected to inhabit the earth in the year 2000.

Speaking today at a session of the autumn meeting of the American Philosophical Society here, Dr. Kuznets said,

"The population problem is reduced by, not resolved by, a p oulation policy. It will be resolved by changes in economic and social institutions."

November 12, 1966

POPULATION HUGE IN EAST PAKISTAN

Political Issues Compound Problem of Growth Rate

By SYDNEY H. SCHANBERG
Special to The New York Times

RAWALPINDI, Pakistan, April 1—"East Pakistan is a special crisis on a crisis subcontinent. It's got 72 million people jammed into a space just a little bit larger than Arkansas, which has only two million. That's twice the density of Japan and Holland."

That is how one family-planning expert here in the Pakistani capital recently described the seriousness of the country's population problem—a problem compounded by political issues created by the overthrow of President Mohammad Ayub Khan a year ago.

The problem is critical in

both wings of this geographically divided Moslem nation of 132 million people, but in East Pakistan—separated from West Pakistan by 1,000 miles of unfriendly Indian territory—the dimensions are overwhelming.

East Pakistan has 12 million more people then West Pakistan's 60 million. It is only one-fifth the size of the western part, has a much lower per-capita income, has a food deficit and has received far fewer development funds from the central Government.

Growth Rate 3 Per Cent

All the experts agree that East Pakistan's population growth rate ideally ought to be zero, or even a minus figure, but they agree that this is an impossibility.

The growth rate now is 3 per cent in both wings, and even if it can be cut to the 2 per cent level considered "successful" by the United Nations, the population will double by the year 2000.

The Pakistani's are aiming at a growth rate somewhat around 1 per cent by 1985, but even if that is achieved, which is uncertain at best, it would be too high for East Pakistan.

Much of the pessimism about the future of the family-plan-stigma it received—and which which it still has not completely shaken off—during the nationwide uprising against President Ayub. Throughout his 10-year reign, the President—who had eight childen—made family planning one of his special concerns. As a result it was attacked along with everything else identified with him.

"We are suffering because Ayub was closely identified with it," said one Government family-planning official. "There is not a total Government commitment."

Yahya Avoids Stand

Both Pakistani and foreign family-planning experts say that President Agha Mohammad Yahya Khan, the head of the martial law Government that replaced the Ayub regime, is personally committed to the program but chooses not to push it publicly because of its political sensitivity.

"Yahya says publicity has to be low-key," said a Pakistani official, "even though family planning is the most crucial thing to Pakistan."

The President never mentions the subject in his speeches, not only because of its identification with the Ayub decade, but also apparently to avoid arousing the conservative Moslem political parties that believe the Koran opposes any form of birth control.

Further, there are some Government ministers from West Pakistan who, it is thought, would like to see the program work only in East Pakistan so that the western wing can gain population superiority.

There is much bad blood between the two parts of the country, with the Bengalis of East Pakistan charging that the Punjabis of West Pakistan, who dominate the Government, have exploited the eastern section.

Though the population growth rate is the same in both sections, there is evidence that the less tradition-minded East Pakistanis have been more receptive to at least some of the family planning techniques.

Many Vasectomies Performed

For example, the Government chose intra-uterine devices as its principal method, but its popularity declined while the use of surgical sterilization of men—given a minor role in the program — suddenly increased in East Pakistan.

No one knows why this happened in a male-oriented Moslem culture that usually places a premium on virility, but several possible explanations have been offered — such as the money inducement (about $4 in a low-income area), the East Pakistani's sensitivity to the pressure of their greater population density and the fact that women have more influence in the family in East Pakistan than in the western section.

Whatever the reason, about one million vasectomies have been performed so far, almost all of them in the east, and the experts now regard this as the most desirable and effective of the methods now in use.

Pakistan's fourth five-year plan, which begins on July 1, has earmarked $129-million for family planning. This is 70 per cent more than was spent during the five years of the third plan, but is still less than 5 per cent of what Pakistan spends of defense.

"This is not a tremendous amount," said one family-planning official. "It can only be called reasonable."

April 12, 1970

Population:

The Panic As You Approach Zero

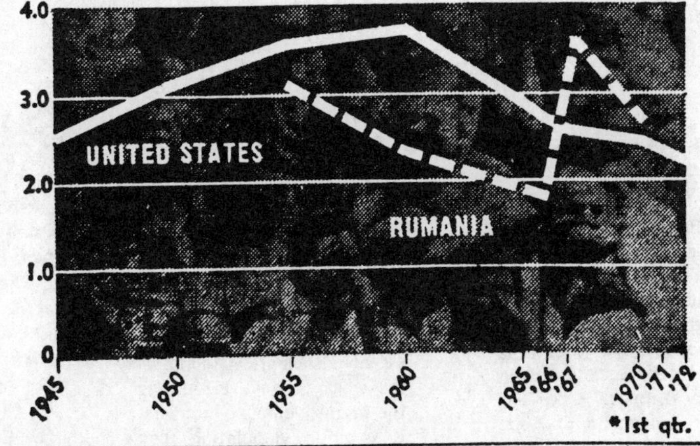

Z.P.G.—The Magic Number is 2.11

That's zero population growth. The United States is getting there; Rumania was there for five years when state planners decided the future dictated not Z.P.G. but population explosion.

WASHINGTON — Zero population growth has long been an earnest, if Utopian goal, of many Americans concerned about the quantity of national resources and the quality of national life.

But in the closing days of May came two strong signs that for the first time in history the nation may actually have reached the threshold of the "Z.P.G." Utopia. And with that possibility came the realization that even this form of Eden may harbor its own kind of serpent.

The signs of change:

• National birth statistics for the first quarter of 1972 showed that births had dropped sharply, even from the already declining 1971 rate. The drop is so great, in fact, that the total fertility rate—a sophisticated demographic measurement—is now virtually at the "replacement level." This is the milestone level which, maintained over decades, would bring a population of stable size.

• The authoritative National Fertility Study indicated an even more lasting decline than the short-term quarterly birth figures. In just five years, the study reported, American women have markedly reduced their estimates of the number of children they intend to have in the future. The most pronounced decline was among Catholic women, despite their tradition of large families. The findings so impressed the study's authors that they abandoned their otherwise technical prose to conclude: "American couples have changed their reproductive behavior radically . . . stabilization of population size is within reach."

All this was good news indeed to the growing and varied core of citizens concerned about population. They range from professors to publicists and their contributions range from technical research to distributing bumper strips that read "Trouble Parking? Support Planned Parenthood!"

They are the first to recognize that reaching the threshold to Z.P.G. is not the same as no growth. For the population to stabilize firmly, very low fertility rates would have to persist for perhaps 70 years. No authority believes that is even imaginable.

The demographic "magic number" —the replacement level—is 2.11. That is the number of children women must bear, on the average, to replace themselves, their husbands, single people and young girls who die before they reach child-bearing age. Yes, experts acknowledge, the current rate may be under 2.14, the lowest in history. But, for perspective, they caution, one need only examine the abrupt fluctuations in recent American rates: 1937—2.23 children; 1947—3.27; 1957—3.77; 1967—2.57.

At the same time no one is ready to dismiss the present low-fertility trend as a fragile fad. It is just as strong as the social forces that explain it and these appear entrenched: the accelerating use of contraception, abortion, and sterilization; more single people and later marriage; swelling interest in women's liberation and more working wives; increasing concern for over-crowding and pressure on the environment.

These forces are not likely soon to diminish. And thus it becomes realistic to anticipate at least several years in which the fertility rate grazes—and even drops below—the stabilization level. If that happens, Americans may conclude with fervor that 2.11 is no magic number at all and that the Z.P.G. Utopia is flawed.

That is exactly what has happened elsewhere. Country after country has awakened with shock to the fact that its fertility rate has fallen below the replacement level. Sometimes, governments have reacted so sharply that they have destroyed not merely the serpent, but the potential Eden as well.

Generally, low fertility excites three principal fears. One is economic stagnation. Most authorities dismiss that fear out of hand. If a family has fewer mouths to feed, it has more to spend for sailboats, or second homes.

A stronger fear is that as the number of people in each age group starts to equalize, the population would grow older. Now, half the population is under 28. In a stationary population, the median age will be 38. It would not take long for impatient young people to recall such somber dicta as the French writer's view that a stationary population is "a population of old people ruminating over old ideas in old houses."

The third fear is psychological and it is the strongest. When, in the Depression, European countries dropped below the replacement level, Cabinet Ministers and bartenders alike loudly bewailed the declines as signs of decadence and the end of grandeur. Patriotism — chauvinism — demanded remedial steps.

In 1969, a Japanese Government study—noting that the fertility rate had dropped below the replacement level for nine out of 11 years—urged a small increase in fertility. According to a study by Princeton demographer Michael S. Teitelbaum, the mass media reacted passionately, forseeing "imminent national decline" and clamoring for a return to high fertility. And the Government has since entertained a program of financial allowances for children.

The most striking modern example comes from Rumania. In late 1966, after the fertility rate had fallen below replacement for five straight years, the reaction come like a thunder clap. State Decree No. 770 drastically limited abortions, restricted divorce, banned importation of contraceptives and increased taxes on the single and childless.

In exactly nine months, the results were evident. In September of 1967, there were *three times* the number of births as in the preceding December. The immediate effect was severe. Newspapers reported three pregnant women to one hospital bed. The long-range effect—on schools, jobs, housing—will come later.

If, as appears likely, the American fertility rate should now hover around or below the replacement level, such experiences offer a clear lesson—the name of the serpent is panic.

—JACK ROSENTHAL

June 4, 1972

Mankind Warned of Perils in Growth

By ROBERT REINHOLD
Special to The New York Times

CAMBRIDGE, Mass., Feb. 26—A major computer study of world trends has concluded, as many have feared, that mankind probably faces an uncontrollable and disastrous collapse of its society within 100 years unless it moves speedily to establish a "global equilibrium" in which growth of population and industrial output are halted.

Such is the urgency of the situation, the study's sponsors say, that the slowing of growth constitutes the "primary task facing humanity" and will demand international cooperation "on a scale and scope without precedent." They concede such a task will require "a Copernican revolution of the mind."

The study, which is being sharply challenged by other experts, was an attempt to peer into the future by building a mathematical model of the world system, examining the highly complex interrelations among population, food supply, natural resources, pollution and industrial production.

The conclusions are rekindling an intellectual debate over a question that is at least as old as the early economists, Thomas Malthus and John Stuart Mill:

Will human population ultimately grow so large that the earth's finite resources will be totally consumed and, if so, how near is the day of doom?

The study was conducted at the Massachusetts Institute of Technology under the auspices of the Club of Rome. In the findings, to be published next month by the Potomac Associates under the title "The Limits to Growth," the M.I.T. group argues that the limits are very near—unless the "will" is generated to begin a "controlled, orderly transition from growth to global equilibrium."

The study would seem to bolster some of the intuitive warnings of environmentalists. In Britain last month,

Prof. Dennis L. Meadows directed the M.I.T. study.

Two Projections in 'Limits to Growth' Study

I. What Happens Without Regulation

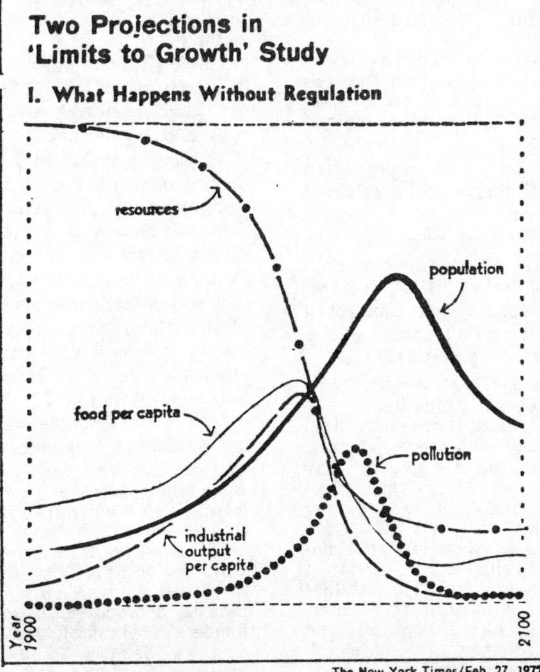

M.I.T. group used a computer global model to project trends in five key growth factors to year 2100. This computer "run" shows rapidly diminishing resources eventually slowing growth, assuming no major change in physical, economic, or social relationships. The time lags in decline of population and pollution are attributed to natural delays in the system. Rise in population is finally halted by an increase in death rate.

II. What Happens in One Pattern of Regulation

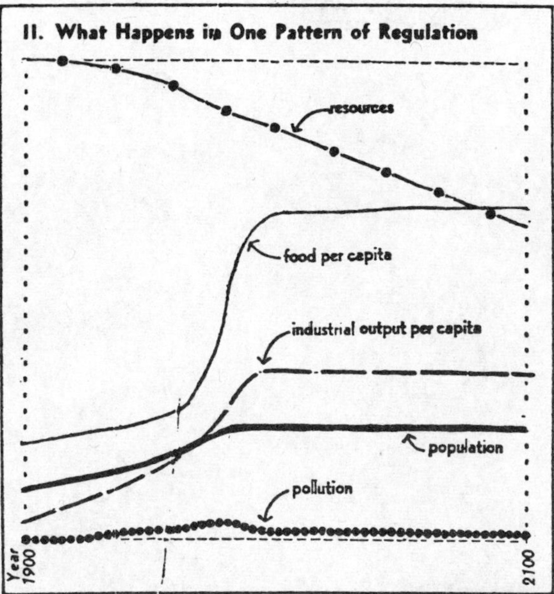

This computer "run" projects relatively stable future on assumption that "technology policies" are combined with other growth-regulating mechanisms. Study says policies would include resources recycling, pollution control devices, increased lifetimes of all forms of capital, methods to restore eroded and infertile soil.

for example, a group of 33 leading scientists issued a "blueprint for survival," calling on the nation to halve its population and heavily tax the use of raw materials and power.

But others, particularly economists, are skeptical.

"It's just utter nonsense," remarked one leading economist, who asked that he not be identified. He added that he felt there was little evidence that the M.I.T. computer model represented reality or that it was based on scientific data that could be tested.

Another economist, Simon S. Kuznets of Harvard, a Nobel Prize-winning authority on the economic growth of nations, said he had not examined the M.I.T. work first hand, but he expressed doubt about the wisdom of stopping growth.

"It's a simplistic kind of conclusion—you have problems, and you solve them by stopping all sources of change," he said.

Others, like Henry C. Wallich of Yale, say a no-growth economy is hard to imagine, much less achieve, and might serve to lock poor cultures into their poverty.

Malthus Again and Again

"I get some solace from the fact that these scares have happened many times before — this is Malthus again," he said.

Malthus, the 19th-century British economist, theorized somewhat prematurely that population growing at exponential rates that could be graphically represented as a rising curve would soon outstrip available food supply. He did not foresee the Industrial Revolution.

Don't Have Alternative

Prof. Dennis L. Meadows, a management specialist who directed the M.I.T. study—which is the first phase of the Club of Rome's "Project on the Predicament of Mankind" — conceded that the model was "imperfect," but said that it was based on much "real world" data and was better than any previous similar attempt.

The report contends that the world "cannot wait for perfect models and total understanding." To this Dr. Meadows added in an interview: "Our view is that we don't have any alternative — it's not as though we can choose to keep growing or not. We are certainly going to stop growing. The question is, do we do it in a way that is most consistent with our goals or do we just let nature take its course."

Letting nature take its course, the M.I.T. group says, will probably mean a precipitous drop in population before the year 2100, presumably through disease and starvation. The computer indicates that the following would happen:

¶ With growing population, industrial capacity rises, along with its demand for oil, metals and other resources.

¶ As wells and mines are exhausted, prices go up, leaving less money for reinvestment in future growth.

¶ Finally, when investment falls below depreciation of manufacturing facilities, the industrial base collapses, along with services and agriculture.

¶ Later population plunges from lack of food and medical services.

All this grows out of an adaptation of a sophisticated method of coming to grips with complexity called "systems analysis." In it, a complex system is broken into components and the relationships between them reduced to mathematical equations to give an approximation, or model, of reality.

Then a computer is used to manipulate the elements to simulate how the system will change with time. It can show how a given policy change might affect all other factors.

If human behaviour is considered a system, then birth and death rates, food output, industrial production, pollution and use of natural resources are all part of a great interlocking web in which a change in any one factor will have some impact on the others.

Interrelations Studied

For example, industrial output influences food production, which in turn affects human mortality. This ultimately controls population level, which returns to affect industrial output, completing what is known as an "automatic feedback loop."

Drawing on the work of Prof. Jay W. Forrester of M.I.T., who has pioneered in computer simulation, the M.I.T. team built dozens of loops that they believe describe the interractions in the world system.

They then attempted to assign equations to each of the 100 or so "causal links" between the variables in the loops, taking into account such things as psychological factors in fertility and the biological effects of pollutants.

Critics say this is perhaps the weakest part of the study because the equations are based in large part on opinion rather than proved fact, unavailable in most cases. Dr. Meadows counters that the numbers are good because the model fits the actual trends from 1900 to 1970.

The model was used to test the impact of various alternative future policies designed to ward off the world collapse envisioned if no action is taken.

For example, it is often argued that continuing technological advances, such as nuclear power, will keep pushing back the limits of economic and population growth.

To test this argument, the M.I.T. team assumed that resources were doubled and that recycling reduced demand for them to one-fourth. The computer run found little benefit in this since pollution became overwhelming and caused collapse.

Assumptions Tested

Adding pollution control to the assumptions was no better; food production dropped. Even assuming "unlimited" resources, pollution control, better agricultural productivity and effective birth control, the world system eventually grinds to a halt with rise in pollution, falling food output and falling population.

"Our attempts to use even the most optimistic estimates of the benefits of technology," the report said, "did not in any case postpone the collapse beyond the year 2100."

Skeptics argue that there is no way to imagine what kind of spectacular new technologies are over the horizon.

"If we were building and making cars the way we did 30 years ago we would have run out of steel before now I imagine, but you get substitution of materials," said Robert M. Solow, an M.I.T. economist not connected with the Club of Rome project. "It is true we'll run out of oil eventually, but it's premature to say therefore we will run out of energy," he added.

At any rate, the M.I.T group went on to test the impact of other approaches, such as stabilizing population and industrial capacity.

Zero population growth alone did very little, since industrial output continued to grow, it was found. If both population and industrial growth are stabilized by 1985, then world stability is achieved for a time, but sooner or later resource shortages develop, the study said.

System Suggested

Ultimately, by testing different variations, the team came up with a system that they believe capable of satisfying the basic material requirements of mankind yet sustainable without sudden collapse. They said such a world would require the following:

¶Stabilization of population and industrial capacity.

¶Sharp reduction in pollution and in resource consumption per unit of industrial output.

¶Introduction of efficient technological methods — recycling of resources, pollution control, restoration of eroded land and prolonged use of capital.

¶Shift in emphasis away from factory-produced goods toward food and nonmaterial services, such as education and health.

The report is vague about how all this is to be achieved in a world in which leaders often disagree even over the shape of a conference table.

Even so, critics are not sanguine about what kind of a world it would be. Dr. Meadows agrees it would not be a Utopia, but nevertheless does not foresee stagnation.

"A society released from struggling with the many problems caused by growth may have more energy and ingenuity available for solving other problems," he says, citing such pursuits as education, arts, music and religion.

Many economists doubt that a no-growth world is possible. Given human motivations and diversity, they say, there will always be instability.

"The only way to make it stable is to assume that people will become very routine-minded, with no independent thought and very little freedom, each generation doing exactly what the last did," says Dr. Wallich. "I can't say I'm enamored with that vision."

"Can you expect billions of Asians and Africans to live forever at roughly their standard of living while we go on forever at ours?" asked Dr. Solow.

Dr. Wallich terms no-growth "an upper income baby," adding "they've got enough money, and now they want a world fit for them to travel in and look at the poor."

The M.I.T. team agrees there is no assurance that "humanity's moral resources would be sufficient to solve the problem of income distribution." But, they contend "there is even less assurance that such social problems will be solved in present state of growth, which is straining both the moral and physical resources of the world's people."

The report ends hopefully, stating that man has what is physically needed to create a lasting society.

"The two missing ingredients are a realistic long-term goal that can guide mankind to the equalibrium society and the human will to achieve that goal," it observes.

Collaborating with Dr. Meadows in writing "The Limits to Growth," were his wife, Donella, a biophysicist; Jorgen Randers, a physicist, and William W. Behrens 3d an engineer. They were part of a 17-member international team working with more than $200,000 in grants from the Volkswagen Foundation in Germany.

The major conclusions of the study have been circulating among experts for a few months. The full details are to appear in next month's publication and in future technical documents. This Thursday, a symposium on the study will be held at the Smithsonian Institution in Washington.

February 27, 1972

BIRTH CONTROL STIRS INDIA

Lectures by Mrs. Sanger Inaugurate a Debate Upon Family Limitation

By F. M. DE MELLO.

BOMBAY.

MRS. MARGARET SANGER, American advocate of birth control, is now in India, lecturing on family limitation. She has spoken in Bombay, Calcutta and Delhi, and the newspapers have opened their columns to a debate on birth control, a subject heretofore neglected because it was not regarded as important to the welfare of the Indian people.

The census of 1931 first opened the eyes of the public to the increase in population, accompanied by high birth and death rates. In ten years 34,000,000 people had been added to the country's population, despite the recurrence of plague, cholera and smallpox, the prevalence of malaria, typhoid fever and hookworm and periodic visitations of famine.

In Madras a Neo-Malthusian League has been formed to direct public opinion toward birth control. This league has as two of its patrons the Maharajah of Pittapur and the Maharajah of Jeypore and it includes among its vice presidents such public men as Sir C. P. Ramaswamy Aiyar, formerly a member of the Viceroy's Executive Council and now legal adviser to the Travancore Durbar, and two judges of the Madras High Court, Justice Sir Vepa Ramesan and Justice M. Venkatasubba Row. No women are associated with the movement because of the shyness of the sex in India and their disinclination for a contentious public life.

Government Remains Aloof.

Though propaganda is not forbidden, the government so far has taken little interest in the establishing of birth-control clinics. One Indian State, Mysore, has established clinics in all the public hospitals, and this led to a movement in the neighboring province of Madras, culminating in a demand for public clinics. The Madras Government called on the surgeon general for a report on the subject, but there was a great deal of opposition, especially from the Catholics, and nothing was done.

Though India has no Margaret Sangers, the women's organizations have not been slow to take up the study of the subject. The All-India Women's Conference in 1932 and 1933 and again in January 1935 passed resolutions favoring birth control and advocating the opening of public clinics. The women are now agitating for equal rights, and are centering their attacks upon polygamy, purdah, child marriage and the denial of education and political rights to women. When these positions have been won more attention doubtless will be given to propaganda for birth control.

Masses Are Uninformed.

Among the masses, however, profound ignorance prevails. There is a powerful religious sentiment which causes people to regard their lives as unimportant items in the great fabric of past and future, justified only by the advance they make toward spiritual perfection. It is the general belief that children are God's gift to man. Women are prepared to bear as many as God will give them.

Among the poorer classes sons are regarded as potential sources of economic support, and there is an eager desire for more and more sons. Among the propertied classes, however, the birth of a son with a claim to a share in the father's property is not always an occasion for rejoicing. Thus among the Punjab landowners, family limitation already is practiced to some extent.

As Moslems increase rapidly by the practice of polygamy, Hindus are not anxious to diminish their rate of increase. In a country where there is keen competition for power between religious groups, any movement calculated to reduce voting strength is looked at with suspicion.

Support for propaganda, however, is obtained from many economists and humanitarians. Against the numerical advantage which the politicians are keen upon securing, the economists suggest that quality rather than quantity of population matters.

Considerations such as these are making an impression upon municipalities, social service leagues and similar bodies which Mrs. Sanger has addressed in India. It will take some time for them to act, but it seems probable that family limitation will be publicly encouraged sooner or later.

Nesmith.

An Indian Child Mother and Her Baby.

January 26, 1936

SOVIET ENACTS LAW TO INCREASE BIRTHS

Abortions Are Banned, Divorces Taxed and Aid Is Ordered for Big Families.

MOSCOW, June 27 (AP).—A big family project which taxes divorces and grants State aid to families with numerous children became law tonight on approval by the Soviet Central Executive Committee.

As finally signed by President Mikhail Kalinin, the law contained only slight modifications from its previous draft, which had caused some criticism. The law retains the main clauses prohibiting operations for the prevention of childbirth, establishing graduated taxes of from 50 to 300 rubles for divorces and providing for government financial help to families with more than six children.

Abortion operations will be permitted only when the health of the prospective mother is bad or where there is serious hereditary disease. Doctors performing illegal operations will be punished by imprisonment. Men who induce women to undergo such operations will be liable to two years in prison. The women will be publicly rebuked.

The amounts fixed for support of children in case of divorce was changed to one-quarter of the parents' income in the case of one child, one-third the income in the case of two children and one-half the income in the case of three or more children.

June 28, 1936

BIRTH CONTROL FOR EGYPT

Grand Mufti Approves Moslem's Increasing Practice

Wireless to THE NEW YORK TIMES.

CAIRO, Egypt, Feb. 2.—Replying to inquiries from many Moslems, Sheikh Abd el-Magid Salim, Grand Mufti of Egypt, issued today a statement generally approving birth control by married Moslems. He said birth control was not contrary to the sacred law of Islam provided it was necessary and not harmful to the health. Abortions were condemned in the strongest terms.

Birth control has been steadily gaining in Egypt in recent years and is now reaching the peasants who wish to avoid the huge families of the past.

February 3, 1937

WORLD BIRTH CONTROL GOAL OF 4-NATION UNIT

CHELTENHAM, England, Aug. 27 (AP)—A four-nation committee was formed today to promote birth control on an international scale.

The action was taken at the final session of the International Congress on Population and World Resources in Relation to the Family, which has expressed concern over whether the globe can continue to feed its expanding millions.

Frank Lorimer, Professor of Sociology at American University, Washington, said the move would "make this Congress a historic occasion."

The committee will "promote research and education for the furthering of human welfare through planed parenthood and progressive sex education."

It will consist at the start of representatives of national birth-control organizations in the United States, Great Britain, Holland and Sweden. Its secretariat will be set up in London.

Mrs. Margaret Sanger, American birth-control advocate, termed the action "one of the most important steps to be taken at this crucial period in our world of insecurity."

Mrs. Moya Woodside, representing the Institute for Research and Social Science at the University of North Carolina, called it "an important step toward ending the menace of a growing world population with falling world food production."

August 28, 1948

INDIA TRIES BIRTH CONTROL

Will Create Family Planning Clinics With U. N. Help

Special to THE NEW YORK TIMES.

NEW DELHI, India, Dec. 24—In cooperation with the United Nations World Health Organization, India will establish a number of "family planning clinics" in various parts of the country, the Government announced today.

The clinics will teach the rhythm system of birth control advocated by Dr. Abraham Stone of New York, family planning consultant for the United Nations agency, who recently finished a six weeks' tour of India, studying excess population problems. This method utilizes infertile or "safe" periods.

Following Dr. Stone's suggestions, the Indian Health Ministry will set up "pilot" projects at various centers, with couples volunteering to demonstrate the efficacy of the system through tests.

December 25, 1951

POPE STRENGTHENS PROCREATION VIEW

Asks Midwives and Doctors to Bar Abortion, Sterilization, Artificial Insemination

SET OF NORMS SWEEPING

Special to THE NEW YORK TIMES.

ROME, Oct. 29—Alarmed by the spread of birth control and also by licentiousness in modern society, Pope Pius XII urged midwives and doctors today to oppose abortion, artificial insemination, sterilization and any other practice that would violate the fundamental Roman Catholic principles of the sacrament of marriage: procreation and the education of children.

The papal directives were contained in a speech delivered to members of the Catholic Union of Obstetricians, which has been holding a congress here. They formed probably the most comprehensive set of norms on the subject ever issued by the Church because they took into account new developments in the biological field and dealt frankly and clearly with the Catholic conception of the duties and rights of husbands and wives.

The Pope made it clear that he was restating the attitude of the church on marriage because of some confusion in interpretation existing today even among Catholic authorities, and he issued the following guidance for all Catholics:

Abortion—Doctors and midwives must refuse to cooperate in any action that may destroy both born and unborn life. To save the life of a mother is a noble aim, but "direct killing of a child as a means to that end is illicit," even if sanctioned by "public authorities." The Catholic Church holds that "every human being, even a child in the mother's womb, receives the right to life directly from God, not from his parents nor from any human society or authority."

Therefore no human authority, regardless of what the reasons may be, has "valid juridical title" to measures that would eliminate an innocent human life because "man has been created for God" only and "man is also a child even if unborn" and has the same rights as a mother. Therefore the life of a child is "intangible."

Sterilization Called Illicit

Sterilization—Any attempt on the part of the husband or wife "during the connubial act or during its natural development"—that may prevent procreation is immoral. "Direct sterilization, namely that practice that aims to make procreation impossible, is a grave violation of moral law and therefore illicit." Even public authority — Government officials — has "no right" to permit it.

Rhythm of conception—Instruction on the part of midwives and doctors as to the biological and technical aspects of periods of natural sterility of woman is permitted. However, even in this case the "moral norms to which application of that theory is subordinated must be made known and upheld."

In other words, if application means that husband and wives may enjoy their matrimonial right even on days of natural sterility, no objection exists "inasmuch as they do not prevent or vitiate consummation of the natural act and its subsequent natural consequences."

But if the "connubial act" is performed only on those days, then the behavior of the couple "must be examined more closely." There may be cases in which either of the two participants in marriage at the time of wedding had the intention of denying the other participant the right of the connubial act except on those days. In these cases the marriage is not considered valid because the right deriving from the matrimonial contract is a "permanent, uninterrupted and not an intermittent right" of both participants.

On the other hand, if both participants "without serious motive" deliberately avoid the duty they have of procreating while "fully satisfying their sensuality," they sin against the very essence of marital life.

Exclusion of motherhood—If there are serious reasons to avoid motherhood, the Church recognizes only one natural way to attain that purpose — abstinence — because "God compels a husband and wife to observe abstinence if the consummation of their union cannot be attained according to the norms of nature."

Artificial insemination—Cohabitation of a married couple must not be "reduced to a purely organic function for the transmission of germs" because in that case marriage would be nothing more than a "simple biological laboratory." The Church regards the connubial act as a "personal action; simultaneous immediate cooperation on the part of a married couple * * * it is much more than the fusion of two germs, which can be achieved even artificially, that it, without the natural act of a married couple."

Therefore, when a natural act between a husband and wife is "permanently impossible from the beginning," then the marriage is imperfect. In such a case the Church points out that abandonment of the goal of procreation, "especially if due to the most noble motives, is not mutilation of personal and spiritual values."

Sexual excess, depravity and hedonism—It is quite normal that a married couple should enjoy themselves physically and spiritually. However, they must use moderation and not abandon themselves recklessly to sexual pleasure. Moreover, the pleasure must be the result of natural action. No other means must be used "to make pleasure more intense through preparation and actual accomplishment of connubial union."

October 30, 1951

SOVIET IRKS INDIA BY A DIG AT WEST

Charge That Birth Control Is Another 'Warmongers' Plot' Is Resented

By ROBERT TRUMBULL

Special to THE NEW YORK TIMES.

NEW DELHI, India, Jan. 28—Soviet propaganda in India, which is particularly active at this time, came a rare cropper this week.

Prof. G. F. Alexandrov, leader of the Russian delegation to the Indian Science Congress, tried to persuade this overpopulated country that birth control was another plot of the "Western warmongers." He asserted in a speech at Delhi University that "the population theory of the West sought to justify wars."

Russian scientists, according to Prof. Alexandrov, believe that the world can support 9,000,000,000 to 11,000,000,000 inhabitants instead of the present 2,400,000,000 with present-day technological progress and scientific advance.

India, with a population of 357,000,000 growing at the rate of nearly 5,000,000 a year, has adopted birth control as a national policy. The 1951 census report predicting a population of 520,000,000 by 1981 pointed out that the saturation point on the basis of the country's natural resources and foreseeable production capacity would be reached in about 1969 when the population should be about 450,000,000. After that the prospect is famine, according to Census Commissioner R. A. Gopalaswami's analysis.

This morning's New Delhi Hindustan Times, a conservative orthodox publication that usually supports the Government, retorted sharply to Professor Alexandrov that "it is unfair to import East-West differences into a discussion on population."

"Apart from the question of the food shortage, which only two years ago was 3,500,000 tons, there is the problem of finding employment for the added population and keeping up the standard of living, let alone the possibility of raising it," the paper commented. The Hindustan Times is edited by Devadas Gandhi, son of the late Indian leader who disapproved of contraceptives but advocated population control by abstinence.

Remarking that "conditions in India and elsewhere make it imperative that there should be a planned drive for checking an abnormal increase in the population" and that "the public should be educated on the subject," the paper declared that Professor Alexandrov's charge against the West "can hardly be taken seriously."

This time a Soviet representative apparently overstepped himself by bringing propaganda into conflict with what most Indians regard as hard fact. Such immediate repudiation has seldom been encountered here.

January 29, 1954

POPULATION LIMIT PROPOSED IN CHINA

Communist Deputy Favors Disseminating Knowledge of Birth Control Means

By HENRY R. LIEBERMAN

Special to The New York Times.

HONG KONG, Nov. 9—When the British Labor party mission visited Red China in August its members were told that mainland China's huge population—already the world's largest at 582,603,000 for 1953—was increasing at the rate of 12,000,000 a year.

Clement R. Attlee, head of the mission, said later he had been disturbed to find the Chinese Communist leaders considered the population increase a boon. He expressed the view the Peiping Government was facing a "terrible" overpopulation program.

Notwithstanding the official line, however, at least some quarters in Peiping seem not to regard an unchecked population as an unmixed blessing.

In a little-noticed speech at the September meeting of the National People's Congress Shao Li-tze, one of the Deputies, declared:

"It is a good thing to have a large population, but in an environment beset with difficulties it appears that there should be a limit set."

Mr. Shao is a former Nationalist official who went over to the Communists in 1949. Although the Communists reject what they call the "bankrupt Malthusian theories" [that the population tends to multiply faster than the means of subsistence can be made to do], his observations on overpopulation were published by the Peiping People's Daily, official party organ, Sept. 18.

So far as is known here this was the first public acknowledgement by anyone associated with the Peiping regime that China's population might be too big.

Up to now the Communists have held that China's "Socialist" economic growth can keep ahead of the population increase. The standard arguments appear to have been that China has considerable undeveloped natural resources including "a vast amount of virgin land" and that inasmuch as "labor produces value" the more "labor" the better.

Associated Press

URGES LIMIT: Shao Li-tze, Chinese Communist official, who displayed concern over rising mainland population.

In his speech to the People's Congress Mr. Shao raised the population problem after a discussion of China's "backwardness." He said the Government would have to cope with many difficulties until this "backwardness" had been "eliminated."

Pointing out China is still subject to recurring "natural calamities of a localized nature" every year, Mr. Shao stressed the need for intensified flood control work. Then he brought up the matter of "difficulties" caused by "too large a population."

He restricted himself to "difficulties" associated with "culture and education." One of the difficulties, he said, involved the Government's inability to provide educational facilities for "all our children of school age."

Mr. Shao called for a campaign to spread "medical theories" and provide "practical guidance" on birth control, but added the "question of abortion" could be left undisturbed.

November 10, 1954

SOVIET LEGALIZES ABORTIONS AGAIN

Move After Twenty Years Viewed as Part of General Easing of Restrictions

Special to The New York Times.

MOSCOW, Nov. 30—The Soviet Union has legalized abortion for the first time in almost twenty years.

The step, announced today in the Government newspaper Izvestia, was interpreted as part of a general easing of restrictions on Soviet citizens. It was also linked with a net annual population increase of 3,000,000 persons that has more than offset the wartime depopulation.

The edict, passed last Wednesday by the presidium of the Supreme Soviet, says it is "possible to dispense at the present time with the prohibition of abortion carried out according to law."

Henceforth the state will rely on education and propaganda to encourage motherhood and prevent unnecessary abortions, the edict says.

It asserts that "unceasing awareness and the rising cultural level of women" in every walk of life have made it possible to abrogate Article 1 of the decree of June 27, 1936, prohibiting abortions.

Under the Soviet criminal code, physicians were subject to one to two years' imprisonment if they carried out illegal abortions. An operation was authorized only when birth would be dangerous for the life or health of the mother or when it would make possible the inheritance of a serious illness.

Relaxation in the official attitude toward abortion began Aug. 5, 1954, with the issuance of a decree abolishing criminal responsibility for women who consented to abortions.

Provisions of the criminal code prescribing up to three years' imprisonment for unqualified persons who perform abortions, or physicians who perform the operation in unsanitary conditions, are maintained, today's edict declares. A penalty of two years in jail is still in effect for anyone who obliges a woman to have an abortion.

One clear aim of the new edict is to minimize the considerable number of abortions now carried out in the Soviet Union by quacks or other persons without access to medical institutions.

Abortion in the Soviet Union has had a checkered history. Between the Bolshevik Revolution and 1936 it was freely practiced, especially in major cities. With the onset of a more conservative trend, the legal ban was rigidly enforced.

By the end of 1955 the Government's drive to step up the birth rate through bachelor's taxes, family allotments and other devices appears to have met with signal success. Indeed, the population increase is far outstripping the Government's ability to provide more housing, schools and other facilities.

December 1, 1955

RED CHINA AIMS AT CUT IN BIRTHS

Economic Troubles Linked to Excess Population by Party Newspaper

PEIPING, March 5 (Reuters)—The Chinese Communist party newspaper, People's Daily, said in an editorial on birth control today that economic development, however fast, could not yet catch up with China's rapid rate of population increase.

The editorial was the first carried on birth control by the party newspaper, and it was the first time that the current economic campaign had been linked officially with population problems.

The paper said that China's population of more than 600,000,000 was increasing at a yearly rate of 2.2 per cent (more than 13,000,000 a year, or roughly twenty-five a minute).

These 600,000,000, the newspaper said, are doing wonderful things under the leadership of the Communist party, and density of population is not in itself a bad thing. It added, however, that it would take several decades to bring the country from its backward position and many difficulties remained, especially for those with many children.

The editorial said that in August, 1953, the State Council instructed the health department to give instruction in birth control to the public.

No forcible orders should be given on birth control, the paper said. It suggested that Chinese should change their custom of early marriage and that propaganda should be directed toward encouraging youths not to marry until they were 25.

Contraceptives should be sold at cheap prices and all methods of birth control should be investigated and those that are safe should be widely practiced, the newspaper said.

Intensive propaganda has been going on throughout the country recently on birth control; contraceptives are now on display in drug stores, and next Friday a birth-control exhibition will open in Peiping.

Soviet Seeks More Population

The Communist Chinese effort to limit population growth appears to be sharply at variance with the Soviet effort to encourage maximum population increase. Several yeas ago Nikita S. Khrushchev, First Secretary of the Soviet Communist party, declared that the Soviet Union needed 300,000,000 or more people rather than 200,000,00C.

Population growth is encouraged in the Soviet Union by prizes given to mothers of many children, by tax benefits that increase with the number of children, and the like.

March 6, 1957

India Offers Sterilization To Lower Her Birth Rate

Special to The New York Times.

NEW DELHI, India, Feb. 15—The Indian Government has decided to provide surgical facilities in the state-owned hospitals as a means of controlling population growth, Health Minister D. P. Karmarkar said today.

He told a meeting of the Indian Family Planning Board that the ruling Congress party unanimously approved a resolution some weeks ago supporting the idea of evolving drastic measures to curb the rise in population.

The Health Minister said the Government then decided to provide facilities in all hospitals to carry out operations for all who desire to restrict the size of their families. He said at first these facilities would be available only for sterilization of males.

Controversy on Program

For some months there has been a controversy throughout the country on the merits of encouraging sterilization of men and women and induced abortions. The central Government had remained silent on the issue, but the state governments of Madras and Kerala had promoted the sterilization of men.

Yesterday Prime Minister Jawaharlal Nehru told the sixth International Conference on Planned Parenthood meeting here that, although the Government had adopted family planning as an official policy, the results of the last eight years had not been encouraging.

India, the most populous country in the world after China, has an estimated population of 406,000,000 and it has been rising at an annual rate of nearly 7,000,000.

Addressing today's plenary session of the international conference, Dr. Homi J. Bhabha, secretary of India's Atomic Energy Commission, proposed the development of a substance that could be mixed with the daily diet to reduce the conception rate by almost 30 per cent.

He said the problem was so vast in India that no tangible results could be attained by propaganda and door-to-door canvassing or even by large-scale free distribution of contraceptives.

Huxley Sounds Warning

NEW DELHI, Feb. 15 (Reuters) — The world's population will reach 5,500,000,000 by the year 2000 unless efficient birth control counters the death control brought by medical science, Sir Julian Huxley, British biologist, said today.

The present world population is estimated at nearly 3,000,000,000.

Sir Julian, addressing the family planning conference here, called for international research to develop a cheap and satisfactory oral contraceptive.

Already, he said, two-thirds of the world's population is undernourished and deforestation and erosion have reduced the possibilities for increased agricultural production.

Prof. Juitsu Kitaoka of Tokyo's Kokugakuin University reported that Japan had halved her birth rate in ten years. He said magazines in Japan published regular and detailed information on contraception.

Chinese Program Lags

The world's most populous country, Communist China, also has been beset with the problems of limiting a rapid population growth. The state planners counted on the population's reaching 660,000,000 in 1958, a rise of 13,000,000, or a little more than 2 per cent.

In 1957 it was announced that abortion and sterilization would be legalized. In 1953 the State Council instructed the Health Ministry to give instructions on birth control to the public. The Government has disseminated birth control propaganda extensively, contraceptives are on display in drug stores and a birth control exhibit has been held in Peiping.

However, in the opinion of observers, the Chinese birth control program has met with only moderate success, partly because of vacillation on the part of the Government. This was believed to stem from concern over popular resistance to restricting births.

February 16, 1959

POPE'S ENCYCLICAL URGES RICH NATIONS TO AID POOR

HAILS LABOR GAINS

Welfare State Given His Backing—Birth Control Assailed

Special to The New York Times.

ROME, July 14—Pope John XXIII appealed in an encyclical today for aid to under-developed areas without the creation of a "new form of colonialism" or the spread of the materialistic "poison."

The Pontiff also warned against the element of fear in today's changing world. Obviously alluding to past and possibly future East-West talks he said that leaders of nations were unable to understand one another because they were being inspired by radically opposed philosophies.

"Each fears that the other harbors plans of conquest," he said.

The Pope declared that necessary trust among men and states required respect for a moral order founded on God. He denounced as futile all attempts at creating a godless civilization.

Nuclear Threat Seen

As for nuclear warfare, the Pope warned that "the gigantic forces placed at the disposal of technology" could be used for both constructive and destructive purposes. He said this "makes evident the pressing importance of spiritual values."

A search for social justice and a condemnation of materialism were the underlying themes of the long-awaited Papal letter to the Roman Catholic hierarchy and laity throughout the world.

The encyclical, entitled "Mater et Magistra" ("Mother and Teacher"), marked the seventieth anniversary of a similar encyclical on social and labor matters issued in 1891 by Pope Leo XIII under the title "Rerum Novarum" ("Of New Things").

Main Points Listed

The other points in the document of more than 20,000 words were:

¶A stern restatement of the Roman Catholic condemnation of birth control.

¶A plea to allow workers to have a greater voice in industry at all levels.

¶Strong statements upholding private property and private initiative as safeguards against political tyranny.

¶The acceptance of the advantages of socialization and state welfare programs provided that "negative aspects" are removed.

¶A detailed discussion of the world agricultural crisis.

Discussing assistance to emerging nations, Pope John said, "Probably the most difficult problem of the modern world concerns the relationship between political communities that are economically advanced and those in the process of development."

"The solidarity which binds all men and makes them members of the same family," he asserted, "imposes upon political communities enjoying abundance of material goods not to remain indifferent to those political communities whose citizens suffer from poverty, misery and hunger and who lack even the elementary rights of the human person."

The Pontiff hailed foreign aid programs adopted by wealthy nations and by international bodies and private foundations. He urged stepped up efforts in this direction.

Social progress in developing countries should proceed at the same pace as economic advance, the encyclical said. It warned against foreign aid with political strings attached.

The Pope said such strings could be cleverly disguised colonialism no less blameworthy than that from which many peoples have recently escaped. He warned that they could constitute a menace to world peace.

In calling for a greater role for workers, the Pope welcomed profit-sharing plans and part ownership of businesses by the workers. The encyclical did not deal with strikes.

Pope John departed from social and economic themes at one point to stress that "among different peoples the conviction of the urgent necessity of mutual understanding and cooperation is becoming ever more widespread."

He appeared to sound a warning note about summit talks, explaining that the lack of reciprocal trust between statesmen was caused "by different or radically opposed concepts of life." Thus, he added, such terms as "justice" may take on different and opposite meanings, depending on who uses them.

Spiritual Elements Stressed

While acknowledging that progress and the betterment of living conditions "are certainly positive elements in a civilization," the Pope warned against fostering material well-being as the "unique reason of life."

He warned also that the instilling of disregard for spiritual things in under-developed countries was a dangerous gift to "people in whom ancient tradition has quite often preserved a living and operating consciousness of some of the most important human values." To undermine this consciousness "is essentially immoral," the Pope asserted.

In his renewed condemnation of birth control, Pope John referred to "the all-wise laws of God: laws inviolable and immutable that are to be recognized and observed."

He added that it was "not permissible to use means and follow methods that can be licit for the transmission of plant or animal life."

Overpopulation Can Be Problem

The Pope conceded "that in certain areas and in the political communities of developing economies really serious problems and difficulties" connected with overpopulation might arise. But even in such circumstances birth control is forbidden, the Pope made clear.

He suggested that nature had inexhaustable resources, which human genius could harness and distribute evenly.

In view of the world population explosion, the Pontiff advocated "cooperation on a world scale that permits and favors an ordered and fruitful interchange of useful knowledge of capital and manpower."

Considering the role of states in economic matters, the Pope warned that state participation must not be "exercised so as to reduce ever more the sphere of freedom of the personal initiative of individual citizens."

He said that in societies suppressing private initiative there existed politically political tyranny, economic stagnation and a lack of consumer goods. This was an allusion to the Communist states.

The Pope insisted that the right of private ownership, including the ownership of productive facilities, had "a permanent validity." He said history and experience had shown "that in those political regimes which do not recognize the right of private ownership of goods * * * the fundamental manifestations of freedom are suppressed."

The Pope mentioned national education and health plans and remarked that human beings had the "almost irrepressible" tendency to join together for the attainment of objectives that were beyond the capacity and means of the individual.

While underlining the advantages of socialization, the Pontiff warned that it might restrict individual liberty. However, he denied that growing socialization necessarily reduced men to automatons.

Low Wages Deplored

Pope John deplored the low wages that forced masses of workers to live in subhuman conditions in contrast to the luxury of a few. The Pontiff stated that workers should receive wages that enabled them to live "a truly human life" and support their families.

A large part ot the encyclical was devoted to agriculture, which was termed a "depressed sector." The Pope called for the stabilization and integration of farm income and he declared cooperatives and family-size agricultural enterprises to be the most desirable forms of rural life.

Pope John noted that "there are not a few countries where gross disproportion between land and population exists." However, the encyclical failed to elaborate on needs for land reform.

In the social field the Pope noted the development of social insurance systems, the spread of labor movements, increased social mobility and related developments.

The encyclical cited as new international factors the "end of the colonial regimes and the attainment of political independence of the peoples of Asia and Africa" and a growing feeling of global interdependence.

Critically evaluating present day civilization, the Pope contrasted the "limitless horizons opened up by scientific research" with the danger of atomic destruction and what he described as a sense of increasing dissatisfaction spreading in the most affluent nations.

He condemned a contemporary "hedonistic conception and tendency which would reduce life to the search after pleasure and the full satisfaction of all the passions."

The Roman Catholic Church today "is confronted with the immense task of giving a human and Christian note to modern civilization," the Pontiff said in conclusion.

July 15, 1961

USE OF ABORTIONS IN JAPAN IS NOTED

1.5 Million Are Performed Yearly, Scientist Says

By WALTER SULLIVAN

As a consequence of the legalization of abortion in Japan, about half of all pregnancies in that country are terminated artificially, a sociologist reported here yesterday.

In this way, he said, the Japanese have been able to check the population growth—a critical problem in most countries.

The speaker was Philip M. Hauser, professor of sociology at the University of Chicago. He took part in a symposium at the Albert Einstein College of Medicine.

He estimated the annual abortions in that country at 1,500,000. For the United States, he used a figure of 1,000,000 a year. Because most abortions are illegal in this country, reliable figures are unavailable. The estimates of other specialists range from the hundreds of thousands to more than a million.

Professor Hauser spoke at a symposium on Man and Environment organized in connection with commencement at the college. The college, a component of Yeshiva University, is at Eastchester Road and Morris Park Avenue in the Bronx.

The sociologist pictured overpopulation as a serious and growing environmental problem of mankind.

'Death Control'

In underdeveloped areas, he said, the idea of controlling family size has not penetrated the minds of most people. They are beginning to enjoy the benefits of "death control," without the balancing effects of birth control, he said.

The result, if the trend continues, he predicted, will be "mass frustration, political instability and threats to world peace."

While there is no culture in the world where abortion is not resorted to, he said, there is deeply felt antagonism to it in some areas. In India, for example, the Hindus consider it a form of murder.

On the other hand, he said, there is no religious or ethical segment of the world population for whom some form of birth control is not acceptable. To his predominantly medical audience he said the medical profession has been "something less than progressive" in its attitude toward the population problem.

The moderator of the program, Dr. Robert S. Morison, discussed ethical problems that have arisen as a result of man's ability to alter the environment. Dr. Morison is Director of Medical and Natural Sciences at the Rockefeller Foundation.

If someone clubs a baby to death, he said, it is unanimously regarded as a terrible crime. Yet he added, far more deaths result from "statistical" negligence.

He quoted from a 1948 book by C. H. Waddington that said: "The whole community of England and Wales kills 8,000 babies a year by failing to bring its infant mortality rate down to the level reached by Oslo as early as 1931."

To do so, the author said, was "perfectly feasible," yet, he added, "few people seem to think this a crime."

The difficulty in such cases, Dr. Morison said, is that "each one of us contributes a tiny bit to a situation which ultimately becomes such as to jeopardize the welfare or the actual life of a number of other people."

Bentley Glass, Professor of Biology at The Johns Hopkins University, spoke on the effects of radiation. Gordon M. Fair, Professor of Engineering and Sanitary Engineering at Harvard, discussed water pollution.

The other speakers were Dr. Nevin Scrimshaw, Professor of Nutrition, Food Science and Technology at the Massachusetts Institute of Technology; John R. Pierce of the Bell Telephone Laboratories in Murray Hill, N. J., and Theodosius Dobzhansky, Professor at the Rockefeller Institute and an authority on population genetics.

May 28, 1963

DUBLIN CLINIC AIDS FAMILY PLANNING

Now Facility Is Established by a Catholic Hospital

Special to The New York Times

DUBLIN, Oct. 5—Parents in Roman Catholic Ireland for the first time this year are able to go to a Catholic hospital in Dublin and get advice and instruction on the spacing of births, or family planning as this is known in Britain.

The help is available at a new clinic of the National Maternity Hospital.

Under Irish law the import and sale of contraceptives is illegal, and books and magazines advocating the use of contraceptives are banned by the Censorship of Publications Board.

But Catholics in Ireland, as in the neighboring United Kingdom of Britain and Northern Ireland, have had to face up to the problem of limiting their families to the number of children they can reasonably support and educate within their economic resources.

This problem is being discussed openly in the lay and Catholic press of England, but the subject is still taboo in Irish newspapers, where family limitation and spacing of children is ignored.

The first hospital in Ireland to show its awareness of the need for providing some guidance in these matters was the Rotunda Hospital, which established a Marriage Guidance and Infertility Clinic in 1948, under the direction of one of its consultants.

Founded in 1745, the Rotunda was one of the earliest maternity hospitals in Europe and through a succession of many brilliant masters won world renown in the field of obstetrics and gynecology. Its medical staff is undenominational, and patients of all religions are admitted.

Clinic Gives Advice

The Rotunda's clinic does not, the present master, Dr. Alan Browne, said, give any instruction in the use of contraceptives, but it does give advice to those who desire some degree of family limitation "within the prevailing ethical code of the patient." But the help is limited to cases referred to it by the hospital's gynecology department.

With Catholics the only method of family planning permissable, apart from mutually agreed total continence, is the use of the rhythm, or "safe period" during which marital relations can take place without the risk of pregnancy.

Many Catholic, as well as non-Catholic couples availed themselves of this marriage guidance at the Rotunda as the only hospital at which it was available until April of this year.

Now the Catholic authorities, clerical and medical, realizing that they must take some positive action, have opened the first marriage guidance clinic at the National Maternity Hospital, Holles Street, Dublin, the largest Catholic teaching maternity hospital in Ireland.

October 6, 1963

Birth Curb Review Urged on Vatican

By ROBERT C. DOTY
Special to The New York Times

ROME, Oct. 19—An international group of Catholic laymen of 12 learned professions has petitioned Pope Paul VI and the Ecumenical Council to make a "far-reaching reappraisal" of the Roman Catholic Church's teachings on birth control.

The 182 signatories of the memorandum, from 12 countries in Europe and the Americas, respectfully left determination of the issues to the church. But they argued that the present absolute ban on any chemical or mechanical means for contraception was based on a view of "natural law" that failed to take sufficient account of modern developments in physical and psychological sciences. It was man's very interference with "natural law" in such matters as elimination of decimating plagues and in matters affecting the biological balance, the memorandum said, that had produced the overpopulation problems that made the birth control problem urgent.

The memorandum suggested also that this implied refusal by the church to consider the problem realistically had made Catholic doctors and scientists "painfully aware" of a conflict between their professional and religious convictions in dealings with those who consult them.

The memorandum said that priests also had been "forced to make a most unfortunate distinction between a formal directive [the absolute ban on artificial contraceptive means] and its practical application."

"Man's intervention in nature can raise delicate problems," the memorandum said, "but he has a norm for their solution in the over-all good of the individual and mankind. It is not a question of denying the absolute sovereignty of God, but of recognizing man's part in the creative process for which God has endowed him with intelligence and will."

It was this sense of the basic responsibility of man that was the central theme of the document distributed to the more than 2,000 prelates of the church attending the Ecumenical Council on the eve of the discussion of the important draft on "The Church in the Modern World."

This draft contains sections indicating that the church is considering the birth control problem, but has reached no affirmative conclusions.

The document reaching the bishops gave no hint of its source of inspiration, except that certain locutions in the English version indicated strongly that it was drafted in French. But there was no indication of who had inspired the signers to sign the memorandum.

Among the signers from the United States was Dr. John Rock, Harvard professor emeritus of gynecology and author of the controversial book "The Time Has Come," which urges that something be done about the population explosion.

There were physicians, psychologists, psychiatrists, jurists, philosophers, gynecologists, editors, authors, sociologists, publishers, legislators, educators and lawyers listed as signatories.

They came from Australia, Austria, Belgium, Bolivia, Britain, Canada, the Congo, France, West Germany, Italy, the Netherlands and the United States.

A random sampling of those who signed included Richard J. Blackwell, associate professor of philosophy at St. Louis University; J. B. Bouckairt, professor of physiology at Louvain University in Belgium; Joseph J. Caulfield, editor-in-chief of the Helicon Press, Baltimore; David L. McManus, identified as a publisher, of Baltimore; Roberto Melchior, an officer of a Catholic social organization of La Paz, Bolivia; Joseph Sullivan, associate professor of psychiatry at Cornell University; Joseph T. English, chief psychologist of the United States Peace Corps; Philip J. Scharper, editor-president of the Religious Education Association of the United States and Canada.

The draft on "the Church in the Modern World," scheduled for debate by the Council beginning tomorrow, recognizes the "conflict" between "the intimate drive of conjugal love" and the "sense of responsibility" of parents for refraining from producing more children than they can care for adequately.

The schema urges scientists, married laymen and the theologians to collaborate on a problem. And it urges Catholic married couples "not to be discouraged" if the church fails immediately to resolve problems brought on by human sexuality.

In general, the Roman Catholic Church has held for many centuries that any manifestation of conjugal sexuality that sought to frustrate conception was sinful.

The earliest Biblical authority for this is the story of Onan in Genesis who, forced by tribal custom to marry his dead brother's wife, "spilled his seed upon the ground."

Some modern Biblical interpreters say the Old Testament reproval is rooted in early Hebraic social customs having nothing to do with the morality or immorality of contraception.

In the New Testament, the Apostle Paul urged continence as the most holy way of life—"It is good for a man not to touch a woman"—but conceded that, if this were impossible for an individual, "it is better to marry than to burn."

October 20, 1964

Japan's Birth Rate—The Trend Turns

By EMERSON CHAPIN

TOKYO

WITH slightly more than 96,000,000 people compressed into an area the size of California, Japan is the fifth most densely populated nation. But since only one-sixth of the land area is arable, Japan must be rated, with the possible exception of South Korea, the most crowded country in the world.

Yet, paradoxically, Japan's booming industries are beginning to experience a labor shortage. The number of young people entering the productive age group will begin to decline sharply next year. An industrial and economic structure always hitherto geared to an excess of people faces the need for major readjustments to make maximum use of available workers. A sociological revolution is under way.

What is happening in Japan is that for the first time an Asian nation has succeeded in limiting population growth and making its birth rate one of the lowest in the world. The Japanese rate of 17.2 per thousand is roughly comparable to the Western European average (18), somewhat less than the rate of the United States (21.6) or the Soviet Union (22.4) and a great deal less than those estimated for other Asian nations—mainland China (34), South Korea (40.6), India (40.9), Thailand (42), Indonesia (43), Burma and the Philippines (50).

AFTER the close of the Second World War, when much of the country lay in ruins and 6,000,000 Japanese servicemen and civilians were brought back home to add to the burdens of a faltering economy, the nation's future was bleak and the population problem seemed overwhelming. A birth rate already high rose to a peak of 33 to 34 per thousand during the "baby boom" of 1947-49. In the five years after the war, the population increased by 11,000,000 from the 72,200,000 of 1945.

EMERSON CHAPIN is a reporter in the Tokyo bureau of The Times.

But in 1948, the Diet (parliament) adopted legislation known as the Eugenic Protection Law which, with subsequent amendments, provided the basis for ultimate success in curbing the trend. It was drawn up by a Diet committee in which medical men were influential and its ostensible purpose was only to safeguard maternal and child health and promote family welfare. But its most significant provisions had direct impact on the nation's birth rate.

One section of the law authorizes induced abortion when a woman's health "may be affected seriously by continuation of pregnancy or by delivery, from the physical or economic viewpoint." It requires only the decision of a single approved gynecologist to determine when termination of pregnancy is justified by "economic hardship." Another clause permits termination for women who have conceived "through violence or threat or while prevented through incapacity from resisting or refusing."

These requirements have been interpreted liberally, with the result that Japan has the reputation of being one of the easiest countries in the world in which to have an abortion. Legal abortions rose to a total of 1,170,000 in 1955 and continued above the 1,000,000 mark until 1962. In addition, officials of the Health and Welfare Ministries estimate that unreported abortions have run between 500,000 and 1,000,000 annually.

Thus, in recent years there has been one abortion for each live birth. Fees for abortions are generally no more than $10, and critics assert that it is easier for a woman to avoid an unwanted child in this way than to have her tonsils removed. One result of the practice has been the virtual elimination of illegitimate births.

IT has been estimated that 60 per cent of abortions followed the failure of contraceptive measures. The rate is now dropping as couples gain more reliable knowledge of birth-control methods—and to disseminate such knowledge was another major aim of the Eugenic Protection Law.

CHANCE TO LEARN—Better education for fewer children is a major goal of birth control in Japan.

The law provided for establishment of "eugenic protection consultation offices" in the governments of each of Japan's 46 prefectural districts to conduct marriage counseling and to "popularize and give guidance in adequate methods of contraception." Consultation offices were set up in about 800 health centers already in existence throughout the country.

Local governments conducted special courses for midwives and nurses under auspices of the Health and Welfare Ministry. Not only methods but also incentives for family planning were stressed. About 50,000 nurses and midwives now have been trained to give birth-control guidance — a number that some experts say is still far from sufficient. They say funds should be made available to triple the number, permitting one instructor or counselor for every 500 families.

In addition to its own efforts the Government welfare program encourages nongovernmental birth-control organizations, among them the Foundation-Institute for Research in Population Problems. This group, established in 1953, concluded that family-planning programs could be carried on most effectively through local agencies. Its "new life movement," conducted through family-guidance centers in almost 400 business and industrial concerns, is said to reach 3,200,000 households.

SUCH methods of operation are particularly successful in the still-paternalistic Japanese business structure, in which companies often provide low-cost housing, shopping facilities and a host of welfare benefits to employes who devote all their working life to a single employer.

At the Tokyo Steel Company plant at Kawasaki, near Tokyo, a pilot project was set up among families of the 20,000 workers. Housewives were given the opportunity to receive family-planning guidance as an alternative to such other instruction courses as cookery or household economics. A leader met with groups of about 10 women and explained not only birth control techniques but ways in which family life would be improved if there were fewer children.

Initially the labor union charged that the program was a plot by management to reduce the outlay for family allowances—wage supplements paid to workers according to the number of their children. But the women accepted the courses eagerly and as word spread, enrollment in family-planning instruction rose to almost 100 per cent. The birth rate among company families dropped markedly, the rate of pregnancies and abortions declined and the number of those practicing contraception rose quickly by more than 25 per cent.

IN appraising the results, the institute noted that the families were able to eat and live better and provide more educational opportunities for their offspring and that, in addition, as an interesting by-product, the factory's industrial safety record improved. This was attributed to the workers' getting more rest in their smaller households and being subjected to less family tension.

Since the eu. enic program began, surveys have discovered that there has been not only an increasing acceptance of the idea of family limitation but a shift in the reasons given for it. In the immediate postwar years simple economic factors were dominant. Now, in a more prosperous and competitive society in which education is the key to advancement, 43 per cent of mothers say that their chief purpose is to provide better education for a smaller number of children. Twenty-nine per cent mentioned safeguarding of the mother's health and 9 per cent the desire for a more pleasant life, while only 12 percent mentioned financial strain.

The result of the eugenic program has been that Japan's birth rate has been cut in half. But because medical advances have caused the death rate to drop just as dramatically, the population will continue to increase for at least three more decades, reaching a projected peak of 113,293,000 in 1995. Twenty years later, according to forecasts, it will have dropped back to 107,500,000. As early as next year, however, one significant effect of the eugenic program's first successes will be felt—a sharp decline in the supply of new, teen-age workers, born since 1949. This will have wide implications for the future of Japan's booming economy, now expanding at a rate unequaled among industrial nations.

Dr. Minoru Tachi, head of the Health and Welfare Ministry's Institute of Population Problems, believes that the low birth rate, and the increase in the number of older persons will force several desirable changes — in particular, modernization of the numerous small and medium-size industries that have unduly relied on young, unskilled and low-paid labor. Already wage scales in such industries are being pushed up in the competition for workers, and companies will have to streamline their operations or fail, he says.

A REPORT presented by the Population Council, an advisory body to the Health and Welfare Ministry, urged last year that the Government deal decisively in its future economic planning with the effects of the shortage of young labor and the changing economic and social structure. In addition to the modernizing of small enterprises, it urged development of rural areas and full use of older workers.

One change that seems inevitable is a delay in the retirement age of Japanese workers, most of whom now must terminate their employment at 55. With the life expectancy of Japanese males now up to almost 70, a number of leading companies have started to offer workers the choice of continuing in employment to the ages of 60 or 65. As the need for skilled workers grows, training and retraining programs for older workers and increased effort to induce older women into employment are to be expected.

THIS outlook represents a complete transformation in the nature of Japan's population problem. United States Ambassador Edwin O. Reischauer, one of the West's foremost experts on Japan, observed recently that "there is no doubt now of the country's ability to provide for the growth in population. . . ." He said that the population problem had been shifted from the economic field to the psychological — from the economic problem of providing for so many people to the psychological one of achieving satisfactory living conditions in such crowded circumstances.

"This is the one country in the non-Western world to have shown that the population problem—under certain conditions — can be solved," Dr. Reischauer declared.

It is these "certain conditions" — the high degree of literacy, economic advancement, urbanization and industrialization — that limit the applicability of Japan's example to other, less-developed nations of the vastly overpopulated Asian region. Experts here believe it may require several generations before the Japanese experience can be emulated elsewhere in the Orient.

Nevertheless, wherever population experts hold international meetings, delegates gather around the Japanese representatives, eager to learn of Japan's accomplishment. For other crowded, impoverished and underdeveloped nations, where at last the population problem is beginning to be recognized as the most pressing and serious of all problems, the Japanese example holds much long-range promise.

October 25, 1964

3 PRELATES URGE VATICAN REVIEW OF BIRTH CONTROL

Plea of Leading Churchmen Is Called Turning Point in Church's History

COUNCIL APPLAUDS CALL

But the Basic Instruction on Marriage Is Not Expected to Change for Years

By ROBERT C. DOTY
Special to The New York Times

ROME, Oct. 29—Three of the most influential Roman Catholic prelates called today for an urgent and searching re-examination of the church's teachings on marriage and birth control.

Convergent views on this vital issue expressed at the Ecumenical Council by Paul Émile Cardinal Léger of Montreal, Leo Jozef Cardinal Suenens of Mechlin-Brussels and his Beatitude Maximos IV Saigh, Melchite Patriarch of Antioch, won prolonged loud applause from the more than 2,000 prelates attending today's session.

All three emphasized the need for study of the theological meaning of marriage, enlarging this to give new recognition to the importance of conjugal love as a true end of marriage—"good in itself," in Cardinal Léger's term.

All indicated that from this study of principles would flow naturally the applications in terms of birth control through the combined studies of theologians and scientists.

Debate to Be Pressed

The sanction of three such senior churchmen for restudy of the church's total ban on any artificial means of birth control was described by theologians as a "turning point" and "watershed" in church history.

They indicated that, from today, uninhibited theological speculation and debate on the issue replaced the uncertainty and nervousness that had prevented serious Catholic students of the problem from speaking their minds on it.

But it was clear, also, that any basic change in the church's teaching was still years away. Until there is an agreed finding by commissions of lay and clerical experts appointed by Pope Paul VI and a similar body to be sponsored by the bishops in the Council, the Catholic faithful are still under obligation to observe the norms of marital conduct currently in effect in the church.

Violation of Rule Charged

These authorize Catholic couples to limit fecundity only by timing sexual relations to the sterile period of the female menstrual cycle.

But the most outspoken of the three prelates, the Eastern Patriarch, said bluntly today that this rule was not observed in "the immense majority" of Catholic homes. There is, the Patriarch Maximos said, a "gap" between the "official doctrine of the church" and the "contrary practices" of this majority.

"The authority of the church is put in question on a vast scale," he said. "The faithful find themselves forced to live in rupture with the law of the church, far from the sacraments, in constant anguish, because of the inability to find the viable solution between two contradictory imperatives: conscience and normal conjugal life."

This appeared to be a recognition of the fact that the normal sexual drives of most Catholic spouses far exceed their will or ability to accept the responsibility for rearing the children that would result

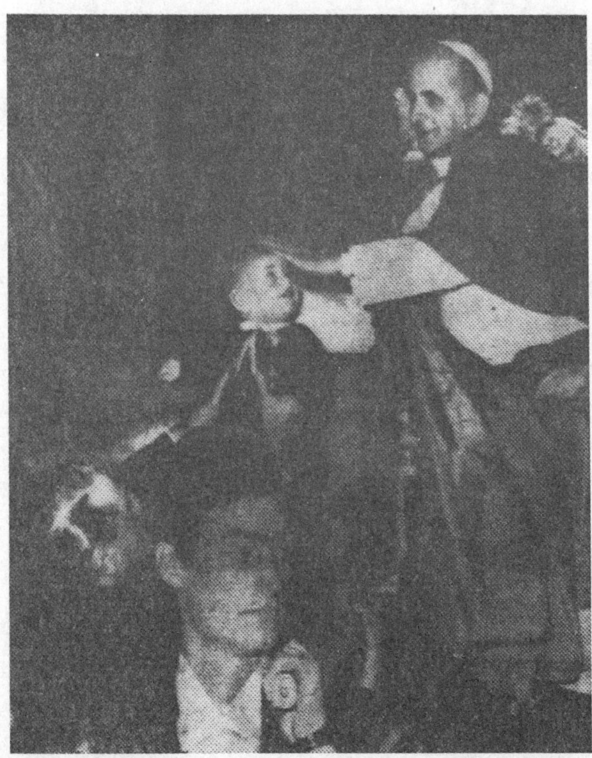

Associated Press Cablephoto

FOND GREETING FOR A SMALL BOY: Pope Paul VI touches the head of a boy held aloft by his father as the Pontiff's chair is borne through St. Peter's Basilica.

from observance of current Catholic teachings on contraception.

He suggested implicitly that many Catholic husbands and wives refrain from communion, the central sacrament of receiving consecrated bread and wine representing the body and blood of Christ, because they are unwilling to do so in a state of unconfessed sin resulting from nonobservance of the church's birth-control strictures.

Turning to social aspects of the question, the Patriarch asserted that unregulated human fecundity condemned "hundreds of millions of human beings to unworthy and hopeless misery." The church, he said, must say "if God really wants this depressing and antinatural dead end."

'Outdated Conceptions'

He suggested that "certain official positions" resulted from "outdated conceptions and perhaps also from a psychosis of bachelors foreign to this area of life," a reference to Catholic priestly celibacy.

Cardinal Suenens, one of the four moderators or presiding officers of the Council and a leader of its progressive wing, rejected any suggestion that the church change essential traditional doctrine.

"But," he said, "it behooves us to know whether we fully open our hearts to the Holy Spirit for an understanding of divine truth." He added:

"Venerable fathers, we do not have the right to remain silent. Let us not be afraid to study this thing. What is at stake is the salvation of our souls and families, if not of the world itself."

Help of Church Awaited

He said the "best among the faithful and not the depraved" were waiting for help from the church so that they could be "true at the same time to the church and to their married life."

Cardinal Suenens warned that the church must not again find itself at cross purposes with science. One "Galileo case," he said, was "certainly enough for the church."

He was referring to the condemnation by the Church during the Renaissance of the Italian astronomer Galileo Galilei, who was forced to recant formally his assertion that the earth moved around the sun.

"Nevertheless it does move," the astronomer is reported to have muttered under his breath after his formal denial of his thesis.

The Belgian prelate appeared to demand a greater role for the bishops of the Council in formulating any new church doctrine on marriage and birth control.

It was recalled to the Council late last week that Pope Paul had appointed a commission to study all aspects of the birth-control question, including such technical aspects as the practicability and morality of various pills halting or regulating female ovulation, and had reserved for himself a decision on the question.

Cardinal Suenens said the papal and Council commissions, and their lay scientific and theological experts drawn from the widest possible fields, should work together.

The members of the papal commission and its meeting place have not been identified. Cardinal Suenens indicated that they should be and that the deliberations of the commission be made a matter for public information.

Another 'Turning Point'

This idea, if accepted, would represent another "turning point" for the church, in the opinion of one of the clerical experts of the American bishops' press panel set up to clarify the issues of the Council.

Cardinal Léger, too, spoke of the "daily difficulties" of the Catholic faithful in seeking solutions for marital problems compatible with their faith and of the "doubts and uncertainties" that assailed Catholic confessors in dealing with these problems.

He stressed the idea that marriage was the total union of two human beings, dedicated to mutual help, and not merely a device for procreation.

A continuing fundamental aim of marriage must be a generous but prudent fecundity, the Canadian Cardinal said, but this must be viewed in the light of the total married state and not in terms of "every individual act"—presumably, every conjugal act.

Against these progressive views, Ernesto Cardinal Ruffini, Archbishop of Palermo, Sicily, the most consistently conservative voice in the Council, entered a demurrer. The schema on "The Church in the Modern World," which the three other prelates found too timid in its approach to marriage problems, is dangerous, in Cardinal Ruffini's view, because it appears to leave too much to the discretion of individuals.

The rulings, not infallibly proclaimed but still authoritative, of Pope Pius XI and Pope Pius XII, affirming the ban on any chemical or mechanical means of birth control, should be the basis of the Council's action on marriage problems, he said.

October 30, 1964

INDIA TRYING LOOP TO REDUCE BIRTHS

Seeks to Popularize Plastic Contraceptive Device

By JACQUES NEVARD

Special to The New York Times

NEW DELHI, May 9—India is turning to a small bit of plastic that costs about 2 cents in a new effort to come to grips with her biggest problem — more Indians.

The Government is opening a nationwide drive to popularize birth control by means of an intra - uterine contraceptive known as a Lippes loop. The loop has been extensively tested in India and found "safe, effective and most acceptable."

India is trying to stem a birth rate so high that, by the end of this year, there will be 14 million more Indians to be fed, housed and clothed by an impoverished nation than there were when the year began. That is not the total number of babies that will be born—it is the excess of the newborn over all those who will die in a country where disease, hunger and ignorance hold average life expectancy to about 40 years, about half of what it is in the United States.

In tests conducted over recent months by the Indian Council of Medical Research, 3,300 women wore Lippes loops. The S-shaped bit of polyethylene, named for the doctor who developed it, cut the pregnancy rate nearly to zero.

The vast majority of Indian women were without loops, however, and their pregnancy rate remained well above 4 per cent. Every day India's population went up 40,000. That kind of growth means that India's current estimated population of 475 million cannot be considered a base for planning but is really more like a bottomless pit.

Although other methods of birth control are becoming more widespread, family planning experts believe that the intra-uterine device may represent a breakthrough.

To get the program started, the Population Council, an American organization supported by the Ford Foundation, is sending 600,000 Lippes loops to India as a gift. Meanwhile, arrangements are being made to manufacture the device in India. Within the next few months two plants are expected to go into production, one of them designed to turn out 2 million loops annually.

The main effort will be to make the device popular in rural areas where ignorance and illiteracy have hampered previous efforts to bring the birth rate down. The great virtue of the loop, according to doctors who have worked in India, is that once it is installed there is nothing for the woman wearing it to remember.

A problem with the loop, however, is that 10 per cent of the Indian women tested found they were unable to continue wearing it. Some simply expelled the device; others experienced bleeding or other adverse reactions that necessitated removal.

If the program is to be successful, the probable key will be local family planning centers that give advice and service on birth control. Ten years ago there were 150 throughout India. Now there are 11,000, of which 9,000 are in rural areas.

Largely as a result of these centers, rural prejudices against birth control practices are slowly disappearing. The most dramatic proof of this is that, over the last 10 years, there have been more than 100,000 sterilization operations in India.

Hopkins Tests New Device

Special to The New York Times

BALTIMORE, May 9—Johns Hopkins Hospital has been successfully testing an intrauterine contraceptive for the last year.

Known as the Incon, it is a small plastic ring, about the size of a quarter, that is placed in the uterus. It has proved cheap, effective and relatively free of side effects.

"Preliminary data are very encouraging," said Dr. Hugh J. Davis, the developer, who is an assistant professor of gynecology and obstetrics at Hopkins. He reported that only one of 400 women fitted with the Incon had become pregnant.

Equally important, Dr. Davis said, is that the device has caused less than 1 per cent bleeding among the women tested. Only 5 per cent of the rings have been expelled, and half of these were successfully replaced, he added.

May 10, 1965

W.H.O. Authorized To Give Members Birth-Control Data

Special to The New York Times

GENEVA, May 21 — The World Health Organization was authorized for the first time today by its assembly of member nations to include birth control in its official program.

The authorization was given in a resolution that was unanimously approved at the close of the United Nations health agency's 18th annual assembly.

A carefully worded compromise was reached with the predominantly Roman Catholic countries. It provides for the development of a program "in the fields of reference services, studies on medical aspects of sterility and fertility control methods, and health aspects of population dynamics."

Authorization was given to supply "technical advice on the health aspects of human reproduction" to member states at their request. However, it was stipulated that this was not to "involve operational activities."

More than 10 years ago the health organization acceded to a request from India that it make available a consultant on birth control. This move provoked such criticism from the Roman Catholic countries among the agency's members that no further action was taken in the field of birth control.

The approval of a guarded approach to family planning reflects the more liberal attitude that the Roman Catholic Church has been showing while reviewing its policy on the question.

May 22, 1965

Peking Urges Birth Curbs; Big Families Are Penalized

By SEYMOUR TOPPING

Special to The New York Times

HONG KONG, April 26—Communist China, using economic and ideological pressures, is compelling its people to practice birth control. According to reports received here, provincial officials are penalizing parents who have more than three children.

Government food and clothing allowances usually granted at the birth of a child are being withheld in the case of a fourth child. In some areas allowances are withheld for the third child.

Officials are encouraging abortion, sterilization and the use of contraceptives. Government and party organizations are appealing to patriotism to convince women to delay marriage until the age of 25. Men are being urged to wait until they are 30.

Birth-Rate Figures

The Peking leadership is apparently convinced that the rapid population expansion must be slowed if the country is to attain its ambitious industrialization goals. About 40 per cent of the country's yearly expenditure of hard foreign exchange abroad goes for importing wheat instead of machines, and the gap between the population's grain needs and grain production is widening.

The birth rate is believed to be more than 2 per cent annually in a population estimated at 725 to 750 million. At least every fifth person in the world is Chinese.

Peking has avoided publicizing the birth-control campaign abroad, possibly to spare the leadership embarrassment. In 1957, the regime repudiated birth control, asserting that a bigger population would aid the economy rather than hinder it.

Sometime in 1963 the state quietly sanctioned birth control again, and measures have been introduced since then to enforce family planning.

Peking has not disclosed any statistics to indicate what success the birth-control program has had. Private reports suggest that progress has been made in urban centers.

In Shanghai, the great coastal metropolis, birth-control propaganda is common. Lectures are given in factories and offices and by neighborhood organizations. Contraceptives are sold cheaply at cigarette kiosks and in shops. The Government is still experimenting with a contraceptive pill, but it is not made generally available.

Women who delay marriage for the sake of their careers are warmly praised in party propaganda. Marriage and child-rearing among students are severely criticized. In many Government institutions maternity leave is not granted after the third child.

In Canton, to the south, factory clinics issue certificates entitling the holder to free abortion. Men are urged to accept sterilization.

In the countryside, where traditional attitudes persist and children are regarded as a form of insurance against poverty in old age, the birth-control program is lagging, and the Government is giving special attention to persuading the peasantry to accept family planning.

Thousands of touring health teams were sent into the countryside last year. Their purpose ostensibly was to improve medical facilities and sanitation in villages, but they also preached birth control.

According to reports from some areas, peasants' incomes have been restricted to keep families small. Peasants are also being compelled to pay back to village production teams loans that often were drawn to meet the needs of large families.

April 27, 1966

W.H.O. REBUFFS U.S. ON BIRTH CONTROL

U.N. Unit Declines to Take Leading Role in Campaign

Special to The New York Times

GENEVA, May 18 — The World Health Organization refused today to assume international leadership in developing family planning as an answer to the population explosion.

The United Nations agency's program committee adopted by a vote of 64 to 19, with 13 abstentions, a resolution confirming that W.H.O.'s role was to "advise members, upon request, in the development of activities in family planning."

This vote indirectly killed a United States-endorsed proposal that would have given the agency a much more positive role.

Dr. Marcolino G. Candau, the agency's director general, came out strongly for the lesser role embodied in the resolution that was adopted.

Once a Threat to Agency

The birth-control issue once threatened to disrupt the 18-year-old agency because the predominantly Roman Catholic member states opposed its even being raised.

It was not until last year that the assembly approved for the first time some action in the field. It authorized the supplying of "technical advice on the health aspects of human reproduction" to member states on request. It was carefully stipulated, however, that this was not to "involve operational activities."

When urging more positive action, Dr. Malcolm Merrill of the United States expressed Washington's hope that the agency would provide "leadership in the health aspects" of family planning.

The United States delegate, health service director of the Agency for International Development, said that a "vigorous W.H.O. and country program" in family planning would help to promote the activities of national health services in other fields.

Candau in Callenge

This was challenged by Dr. Candau, a Brazilian. He said that the attention being given family planning was already resulting in some countries in the diversion of funds from program to control malaria, cholera and other diseases.

Dr. Candau also said it was necessary to have adequate public health services organized before population control campaigns were undertaken.

France took the lead in urging the adoption of the resolution that was approved. She was a co-sponsor with Argentina, Austria, Belgium, Brazil and Mexico.

India, Pakistan and Britain were among the 18 countries that joined the United States in sponsoring the proposal that lost.

May 19, 1966

JAKARTA BACKING A CURB ON BIRTHS

New Leadership Reverses Policy of Sukarno

By ALFRED FRIENDLY Jr.
Special to The New York Times

JAKARTA, Indonesia — Former President Sukarno often used his considerable capacity for scorn against advocates of birth control and family planning. Touring villages in Java, he would proudly single out, as community exemplars, mothers who had borne a dozen or more children.

Birth control, he was fond of saying, "conduces to moral laxity." Moreover, he said to one American visitor years ago, Indonesia, which now has a population estimated at 110 million and an annual population growth rate close to 3 per cent, "could feed 250 million."

Prof. Sarwono Prawirohardjo, chairman of Indonesia's Family Planning Association, said recently that in such a climate of official opposition "there were not many people who dared to joint our movement." Even before Mr. Sukarno's removal from power here in March, however, the new Indonesian leaders had discarded this policy.

Officials Endorse Policy

The Minister of Health has agreed in principle that family planning should become an official project. The Governor of Jakarta has given his enthusiastic support to plans for an effort in the city. And Indonesia has announced that it will seek membership in the International Planned Parenthood Federation, to whose meetings it had previously sent only observers.

According to the professor, who is also a member of a special team of civilian economic advisers on the private staff of Indonesia's Acting President, General Suharto, the change in policy has come not a moment too soon.

In a recent speech here, he warned that without any restraints Java's population, now estimated at 70 million on an island only slightly larger in area than New York State, could reach one billion in less than a hundred years.

Already the crowded, fertile plains of Central Java have the highest rural population density in the world, calculated at 1,158 people to a square mile. By the middle of the next century, he said, it could average close to 30 people an acre, or 19,200 a square mile.

Under the circumstances, Professor Sarwono (like many Indonesians, he uses only his first name) somewhat surprisingly advocates a slow, cautious approach to family planning. He is elated by statements of Government support and surprised by the speed with which religious groups, particularly Moslems, whose nominal adherents represent 90 per cent of the people, dropped their objections to birth control.

An advocate of intrauterine devices as the contraceptive method requiring the least "strong and sustained motivation," he believes that nondoctors should be trained to perform the insertions, but adds that with any program "you have to go very carefully, because if you fail, there will be a setback of many, many years."

Already, he concedes, there is strong interest in birth control from the better-educated segments of the population. The 15 clinics sponsored by his association in Indonesia "cannot give enough services to meet the great demand of this group."

In fact, Dr. E. Looho, a Dutch-educated chemist whose Jakarta company is manufacturing and selling some 20,000 packets of birth control pills monthly at $1.50 a packet, says sales of his product are constantly rising.

Interest in family planning among the relatively well-to-do is not enough, said a recent editorial in the official Indonesian Armed Forces weekly newspaper. To insure economic prosperity and closer knit families, the authoritative publication of the nation's military rulers added, "It is more important to bring the idea and the practice of family planning to the general public, to the rural areas, where 85 per cent of our people live."

April 10, 1967

British Abortion Reform Bill Wins Approval in Commons

By W. GRANGER BLAIR
Special to The New York Times

LONDON, July 14—A controversial bill to reform Britain's abortion laws was approved this morning after an exhausting all-night session in the House of Commons.

At 11:45 A.M., after 13 hours and 13 minutes of debate, weary Members of Parliament voted 167 to 83 to approve the reform measure in its third and final reading in the Commons.

The measure will now go to the House of Lords, where it has already passed two readings successfully.

But even before the current legislation, the House of Lords had twice initiated similar reform measures, only to have them blocked in the Commons.

Thus, in the view of most observers, there is little chance that this time the measure will fail to win final passage, although the Lords may seek some minor modifications in the bill.

The reform bill would legalize abortions—and permit them to be done free under the National Health Service program—if two registered physicians found that "continuance of pregnancy would involve risk to the life or of injury to the physical or mental health of the pregnant woman or the future well-being of herself and/or the child or her other children."

Furthermore the bill provides that "in determining whether or not there is such risk of injury to health or well-being, account may be taken of the patient's total environment, actual or reasonably foreseeable."

These provisions without question will put the burden of responsibility on the doctors. The prospect that such a burden will pose questions of conscience for the medical profession was reflected in a key amendment introduced during committee discussion of the bill last spring and incorporated in the final measure.

This amendment held that "no doctor, nurse, hospital employe nor any other person shall be under any duty, nor shall they in any circumstances be required, to participate in any operation authorized by this Act to which they have conscientious objection, provided that in any civil or criminal action the burden of proof of conscientious objection shall rest on the person claiming it."

Deletion Rejected

During the debate an attempt by Mrs. Jill Knight, a Conservative opponent of the measure, to eliminate the "burden of proof" provision was defeated.

The new measure will replace the existing statute, dating from 1861, which makes abortion a crime under all circumstances. In practice, however, the court have permitted abortions when there was medical testimony that the mother's physical or mental health was endangered by pregnancy.

Perhaps no other recent measure involving social reform has caused so much controversy as the abortion bill, which was sponsored and largely piloted through the Commons by David Steel, a 29-year-old Liberal party Member from Scotland. The Government, which unofficially favored the measure, permitted a free vote in which party discipline was not enforced.

Mr. Steel, who was congratulated by opponent and supporter alike for the skill and moderation he had shown in the long months of committee discussion and floor debate, told the House shortly before the vote that the main case for the bill rested on the ground that "the scourge of criminal abortion would be substantially removed from our land."

Illegal Abortion Rate High

The number of "backstreet" illegal abortions performed annually in Britain has been unofficially estimated at 20,000 to 200,000. The Home Office, whose secretary, Roy Jenkins, supported the private member's bill, has placed the figure in the region of 100,000. In any case, it is widely agreed that the measure will substantially reduce the number of abortions performed by unqualified practitioners.

The controversy that surrounded the abortion measure rested on theological, moral and sociological grounds. Not only were churchmen divided but also doctors and sociologists. In such an atmosphere it was not surprising that a year passed between the bill's approval in principle on its second Commons reading and the decisive vote this morning.

Not all the opponents of the measure went down to defeat gracefully.

Hugh Fraser, a Roman Catholic, Conservative party member, remarked that it was "a rather sad commentary—but accurate—that after a thousand days of this [Labor] Government there should have been no extension of freedom except to the bugger and the abortionist." This comment brought cries of "disgraceful" from the benches.

Mr. Fraser was alluding to the passage 10 days ago of the Homosexual Conduct Act, under which all criminal penalties for homosexual acts committed in private by consenting adults were repealed.

July 15, 1967

Population

For the Latins the Birth Rate Spells Disaster

By PAUL L. MONTGOMERY

CARACAS — The women of Latin America, from the wretched hillside slums of Lima to the dusty Bolivian lowlands, call it "la sonda"—the probe. Doctors call it "el carnicero"—"the butcher."

It is a pointed metal implement about a foot long, crude and unclean. Sometimes it is a knitting needle. Sometimes it is made from a broken length of car aerial.

La sonda is used by the women, most of them married and with children, to rupture the placenta protecting their unborn, unwanted babies. This causes convulsions and eventual expulsion from the uterus of the destroyed fetus. The jagged instrument is used several million times a year in Latin America, and in many cases produces massive hemorrhages, tenacious infections and painful deaths.

Cause of Death

According to some studies, la sonda is the leading cause of death among Latin American women between the ages of 15 and 45. It is certain that it has been a prime reason for turning the attention of the teeming region toward population control.

Perhaps the most significant manifestation of the sudden interest in family planning has been the first inter-American conference on population policies, which was held here last week.

The government-level conference, which would have been unheard of even two years ago, brought together representatives of the United States and 16 Latin American governments — all the members of the Organization of American States except Mexico, Uruguay, Paraguay and Haiti—to discuss with demographers and economists the problems of population in relation to economic and social development.

In the background of the conference was the birth rate in Latin America, the fastest growing region in the world (see map). The average annual population growth of 2.7 per cent—encompassing rates ranging from 1.4 per cent in Uruguay to 4.3 per cent in Costa Rica — will swell the area's population from the present 250 million to 365 million in 1980, and 650 million by the end of the century.

Large parts of Latin America are not equipped to care for their present populations, and these are precisely the areas where the birth rate is highest. Some economists say the nations have a simple choice: Control population growth now, or have the population growth controlled automatically in the future by starvation and economic ruin.

The conference discussed many aspects of population—statistics, training of demographers, the effect of growth on educational and health facilities, the adequacy of food production, unemployment, migration from rural to urban areas. Its principal recommendation was that future population rates and movements be taken into account in development planning—something that is not presently done.

The Next Step

Birth control was barely mentioned. But in the opinion of most of the experts, it was implicit in all the discussions. In this view, the sponsors of the conference, especially the O.A.S.,

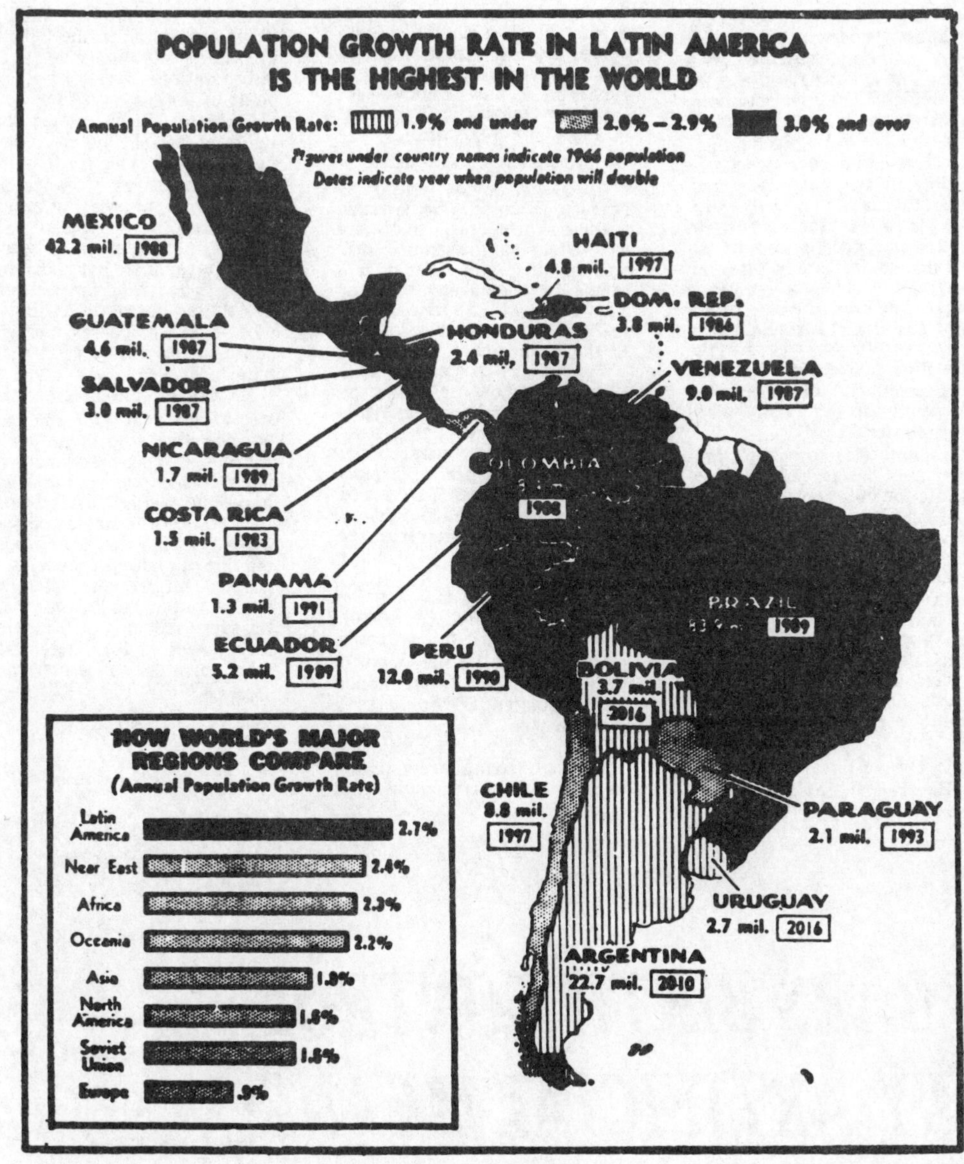

want to consolidate public discussion before they go onto the next logical step of promoting national family limitation plans.

In fact, family planning programs have already been established by Chile, Columbia, Peru, Honduras and Costa Rica. These programs include clinics that give advice and dispense contraceptives.

It seems clear from the studies presented at the conference that Roman Catholic opposition to chemical and mechanical methods of contraception has had its main effect on the political level. Public officials are still wary of repercussions from advocacy of family limitation, but the people appear to have chosen it already.

Use of contraceptives is increasing among Latin Roman Catholic women. It is estimated that 1.5 million Latin Americans of the middle and upper classes now use the pill. The majority of Catholics surveyed in a number of studies replied that they would use contraceptives if they were available.

The Latin American hierarchy, which used to thunder pronouncements at every mention of birth control, has been largely quiescent lately. It is assumed that the bishops, like some governments, are waiting for the new statement from Rome on family limitation. The statement, which could include liberalization of current doctrine, is expected around the end of the year.

September 17, 1967

Birth Rate Decline in 2 Nations Is Attributed to Contraceptives

By RONALD MAIORANA

A group that has been active in promoting international population control programs reported yesterday that "for the first time in history" the use of a contraceptive device for women in family planning programs had succeeded in lowering birth rates—in Taiwan and South Korea.

At the same time, an article in the current issue of Science, the weekly journal of the American Association for the Advancement of Science, said that it was a questionable and "ostrich-like approach" to equate planning programs in the two countries and elsewhere to declining birth rates.

The article, written by Prof. Kingsley Davis, director of international population and urban research at the University of California at Berkeley, did not address itself to the report issued by the Population Council, a nonprofit foundation. Titled "Population Policy: Will Current Programs Succeed?," the article is a general discussion of current family programs.

Proffers 'Fresh Hope'

The report by the Population Council said that its findings in Taiwan and South Korea offer "fresh hope to many nations in the less developed world, where mounting population growth consumes all or most of per capita gains" in economic growth.

"The first family planning successes in the newly developing world are a testimonial to the intrauterine device," said Frank W. Notestein, president of the council and author of the report.

The success of the program in Taiwan and South Korea was based on the female population's acceptance of the Lippes loop, a plastic contraceptive device. The loop, which was developed by Dr. Jack Lippes, a Buffalo obstetrician and gynecologist, has a double-S shape designed to fit the contours of the uterine cavity.

A study by the council, according to Mr. Notestein, showed that the use of the device accounted for an annual decline in the birth rate in Taiwan, at the end of 1966, of 3 to 5 for 1,000 population and 3.77 to 5.3 for each 1,000 in South Korea. The birth rate in Taiwan at the end of 1966 was about 31 for each 1,000. A similar figure was not available for South Korea because, the report said, accurate statistics have not been maintained.

Midway through a five-year program started in 1964, 261,000 Taiwanese women have accepted the contraceptive; it is hoped that 600,000 women will be using it by the end of the program. At the same point in a similar program in South Korea, where the goal is to reach one million women, 737,000 have accepted the loop.

Mr. Notestein said that the birth rate in Taiwan had been declining before the family planning program got under way, primarily because of a rising age for marriage and increased contraceptive practices, but that the planning program lent impetus to the decline.

"There is no question that a decline in the birth rate took place," he said. "The only question is about the extent to which that decline can be attributed to the family planning program. Since that program began, however, the rate of decline has accelerated and, moreover, within the island the reduction of the birth rate has been positively correlated with the depth of the family planning service."

In South Korea, he said, contraception has served as a substitute for abortion.

"It is not possible to suppose, however, that the contraceptive program has not brought a substantial decline in birth rates," he said.

The success of the program in Taiwan was said to have been aided by a rise in prosperity and literacy and in South Korea "because recent political events have broken the cake of custom in that somewhat secular population."

The report said also that "strong family planning programs" in Hong Kong and Singapore had been "important factors" in reducing birth rates. However, it said "much less" could be claimed for their effect in India and Pakistan.

Sees Semantic Confusion

Professor Davis, writing in Science, disputed whether such planning programs had any real effect on the ground that nations undergoing rapid economic development, such as Taiwan and South Korea, usually experienced a decline in the birth rate.

"Taiwan is acclaimed as a show piece because it has responded favorably to a highly organized program for distributing up-to-date contraceptives and has also had a rapidly dropping birth rate," he wrote. "Some observers have carelessly attributed the decline in the birth rate" to family planning programs.

Professor Davis said that the issue was confused by semantics because the terms family planning and fertility control suggested that reproduction was regulated according to a rational plan.

"And so it is," he continued, "but only from the standpoint of the individual couple, not from that of the community. What is rational in the light of a couple's situation may be totally irrational from the standpoint of society's welfare."

Professor Davis argued that the need for society's regulation of individual behavior in other areas—explosives, dangerous drugs and natural resources—was readily recognized.

"But in the sphere of reproduction, complete individual initiative is generally favored even by those liberal intellectuals who in other spheres most favor economic and social planning," he said.

He suggested that the "next step" would be to eliminate policies that encourage childbearing. He proposed such avenues as postponing marriages, imposing a child tax, stopping the taxing of single persons more than married ones, aborting illegitimate pregnancies at government expense, charging a substantial fee for marriage licenses, reducing paid maternity leaves and paying people who volunteer to be sterilized.

November 13, 1967

POPE BARS BIRTH CONTROL BY ANY ARTIFICIAL MEANS; TAKES NOTE OF OPPOSITION

TONE FORTHRIGHT

Encyclical Binding on Catholics but Is Not Immutable Dogma

By ROBERT C. DOTY
Special to The New York Times

ROME, July 29—Five years of uncertainty over how the Roman Catholic Church would view modern methods of birth control ended today with the official presentation of a papal encyclical letter that upheld the prohibition on all artificial means of contraception.

The 7,500-word declaration by Pope Paul VI, "Humanae Vitae" ("Of Human Life"), reaffirmed that Roman Catholics might limit the size of their families only by the rhythm method—confining sexual intercourse to a woman's infertile period—or by abstinence.

This, it was conceded both by the Pontiff and Msgr. Ferdinando Lambruschini, the Lateran University moral theologian who presented the text at a news conference, "will perhaps not be easily received by all."

'Great Act of Courage'

But, the monsignor said, "in its human aspect the pontifical decision, which concedes nothing to popularity, is a great act of courage and perfect serenity."

In the opinion of other Roman churchmen, the Pope's decision, overruling the recommendations for liberalization by a majority of his own study commission of clerics and laymen and running counter to widespread pressure for change inside and outside the church, may produce a serious crisis of authority.

Monsignor Lambruschini said that the encyclical—a papal letter sent to all bishops of the church—was not an infallible pronouncement, that is, an immutable part of the central dogma of the church. But he insisted that it was an "authentic pronouncement" binding "the consciences of all Christians, hierarchy and faithful alike." The Pope offered his

United Press International

SPEAKS FOR PONTIFF: Msgr. Ferdinando Lambruschini reading the Papal encyclical in the Vatican.

teaching to "all men of good-will," but specifically demanded obedience only from Roman Catholics.

Pills Are Outlawed

By affirming only the rhythm method, the Pontiff outlawed, without specific mention, the use of birth control pills, intra-uterine loops, diaphragms or condoms.

In the case of women whose physicians had prescribed "therapeutic plans" to cure "diseases of the organism" the Pope ruled that it was not illicit to apply such means even if they impeded procreation, "provided such impediment is not, for whatever motive, directly willed."

The Pontiff dismissed demographers' warnings of an imminent world population explosion, holding that more effective action by governments to increase the development of resources was the proper answer, not "utterly materialistic measures"—birth control—that he said were incompatible with human dignity and natural law.

Other sections of the encyclical repeated well established church prohibitions of abortion and sterilization, "temporary or permanent," and restated the Pontiff's right to interpret natural law authentically with the aid of the Holy Spirit.

It reaffirmed the principle of "responsible parenthood"—the need to take into account the ability to provide for the well-being of offspring. But the encyclical said that this could be done only by "the deliberate and generous decision to raise a numerous family" or by deciding for "grave motives" to avoid procreation "for the time being" by the use of periodic abstinence from intercourse.

The heart of the Pope's declaration was his reaffirmation of the doctrine proclaimed 38 years ago by Pope Pius XI "that each and every marriage act [of sexual intercourse] must remain open to the transmission of life."

This was a rejection of the interpretation of the principle of totality advanced specifically by the majority of the Pope's own study commission of clerics and laymen in June, 1966, and, implicitly, by Ecumenical Council Vatican II.

Takes Issue With Council

This holds that the morality of married sexuality rests not on the significance or motive of any given sexual act but on the total approach of the couple to their obligations to God, to each other and to the creation of a family. Within this context, it would be possible for Roman Catholic couples to exercise responsible parenthood—another aim approved by council, the commission and the Pope — spacing children properly by contraception.

But the Pope overrode the commission because, he wrote, "certain criteria of solutions had emerged which departed from the moral teaching on marriage proposed with constant firmness by the teaching authority of the church."

The Pope accepted the general principle affirmed by the council putting the uniting quality of conjugal love and its procreative function on an even plane as ends of marriage. But he denied the contention, implicit in some council discussions and explicit in the commission report, that husbands and wives could give physical expression to their love for each other in ways that eliminated the possibility of procreation.

The Pontiff also discussed fears of human population explosion. The threat should be met, he said, by "social and economic progress" compatible with human dignity rather than by adoption of "utterly materialistic" measures to limit births.

He attributed the existence of the problem to the lack of wisdom of governments, an insufficient sense of social justice and "indolence" in making sacrifices necessary to raise living standards.

Any relaxation of the ban on contraception, he warned, would would have the effect of encouraging marital infidelity, premarital promiscuity by the young and "dangerous" actions in the field of birth limitation by governments.

"Who," he asked, "will stop rulers from favoring, from even imposing upon their peoples, if they were to consider it necessary, the method of contraception which they judge to be most efficacious."

An Issue of Authority

In the opinion of some churchmen here, the encyclical raises a serious issue of authority. They noted that it demands of scores of Roman Catholic theologians and half a dozen bishops and cardinals a capitulation to views that are diametrically opposed to those they have publicly expressed in the past.

It runs counter to the practice of leaving the issue of contraception to the consciences of individual Roman Catholics, which is already widely sanctioned by prelates in the Netherlands and parts of Germany and Mexico, and is applied, sanctioned or not, by millions of Roman Catholic laymen.

"It can be foreseen," the Pope wrote, "that this teaching will perhaps not be easily received by all: too numerous are those voices—amplified by the modern means of propaganda—which are contrary to the voice of the church."

But, he went on, the church is merely the costodian and interpreter of moral law, not its arbiter and author, and can do nothing but maintain humble firmness in its exposition.

Three elements of the encyclical and the manner of its announcement seemed to some informed observers to increase the problems of dialogue for Christian unity with Protestant and Anglican communities.

It complicates the resolution of the problem of marriages between Roman Catholics and other Christians because, as one student of the problem observed, "it is not so much an issue of who marries them at what altar as it is of how they live together for 50 years."

A second aspect likely to offend Protestant and Anglican sensibilities was the total reliance of the Pope on church tradition rather than scriptural revelation in his ruling. Non-Roman Christians hold, generally, that the most promising basis for restored Christian unity is supplied by revelation rather than by the interpretations and additions of successive Popes and theologians, and they note that the Bible is nowhere categorical on the subject of contraception.

Meeting this objection raised at his crowded news conference, Monsignor Lambruschini asserted that none of the faithful disputed the church's right to interpret authentically "the natural moral law even if not based implicitly or explicitly on revelation."

Finally, Monsignor Lambruschini chose the moment of the meeting of the world Anglican community in the Lambeth conference in London to criticize specifically an Anglican document taking a view of sexual problems differing from that of the Pope.

This was the 1966 report of the British Council of Churches, "Sex and Morality," which terms immoral, the Vatican spokesman said, only those sexual acts that trample on personal values such as liberty of choice and autonomy of the individual. This failed to recognize the primary evil of violations of chastity, he said.

Nowhere in the encyclical, it was noted, is there any trace of the cautious "on-the-other-hand" language that has marked many of the Pontiff's pronouncements. Such language in the past has permitted Roman Catholics to interpret encyclicals broadly enough to accommodate many divergent points of view.

"This was putting it on the line on a gut issue," said one observer, "and it poses a real problem of discipline and authority."

The five years that have elapsed since the late Pope John XXIII first raised the contraception question by appointing the study commission have divided the Roman Catholic world into three groups, this observer said. One minority has decided that past teaching is erroneous and has discarded it irrevocably. Another, he said, has anticipated the Pope's ruling and embraced the ban as immutable.

The majority in between, he continued, has remained in a state of doubt, most of them resolving the doubt conditionally in favor of the use of contraceptives.

"The crunch is going to come in the reaction of the members of this group," he said. "They are presented with a severe problem of conscience. Will they accept the ruling or drop out?"

A similar problem faces those prelates who have already loosened disciplinary bonds by telling priest confessors that they need not deny the sacraments to parishioners who had employed contraceptives. Among them are Julius Cardinal Doepfner, Archbishop of Munich, Bishop Bernhard Stein of Trier, Bishop Sergio Mendez Arceo of Cuernavaca, Mexico, and the late Bishop Willem Bekkers of the Netherlands. Bishop Bekkers's precedent of leaving the birth control issue to the individual conscience has been widely followed elsewhere in the Netherlands.

July 30, 1968

Studies Indicate Link Between Use of Contraceptives and Economic Progress

Religion Appears as a Lesser Factor in Most Areas

By JANE E. BRODY

Various studies have indicated that, in Roman Catholic countries, as in non-Catholic countries, the birth rate and the practice (or absence) of birth control are more closely related to the state of economic development than to religion.

In an as yet unpublished study, a major family-planning organization found that even the most devout Catholics in Western countries have and want smaller families than nominal Catholics and Protestants in less developed countries.

In the more advanced countries, Catholic women are somewhat less likely to practice birth control than are non-Catholics. But within several Catholic populations surveyed—including American Catholics—more than half the married women admit to having used some method of contraception other than the rhythm method.

In the developing countries, the use of contraceptive methods has been found to be limited by knowledge and availability rather than by religious beliefs.

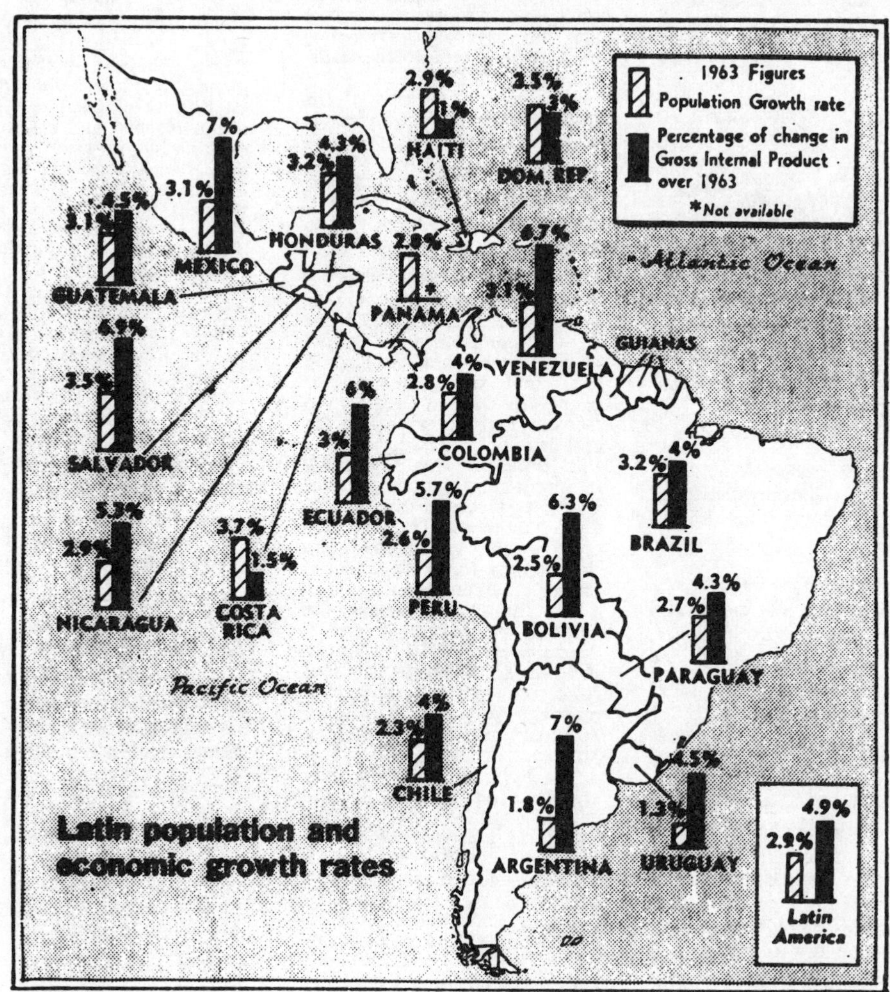

The New York Times — July 30, 1968

Surveys Are Cited

Surveys conducted by the United Nations Latin-American Demographic Center and Cornell University in six Latin-American cities have shown, in fact that devout Catholic women have, on the average, a slightly smaller number of children than women who are only nominally Catholic. Although the exact reasons for this are not known, the studies did find a wide acceptance of birth control among Catholic women.

In these surveys, levels of income and education were found to be far better predictions of family size than degree of religiosity—the higher the economic and educational level, the smaller the family.

In Panama City, for example, women who attended mass once a week or more had an average of 2.41 children whereas those who never went to church had an average of 3.15 children. In Rio de Janeiro, the comparable figures were 1.88 children for the more devout women and 2.5 children for the less devout.

In Santiago, the number of children ranged from 5.9 to 2.4, depending on economic levels, and from 4.4 to 2.1, depending on the level of education.

In Latin America, where virtually the entire population is Roman Catholic, there is scarcely a country without an affiliate of Planned Parenthood. The international family planning organization will spend $2.5-million—more than a third of its worldwide budget—for family-planning aid to Latin America this year.

In addition to the numerous voluntary and private family-planning clinics that have sprung up in the last few years, 18 Latin-American Governments provide some degree of support for family planning, and in 12 countries this support is extensive.

Family planning programs in Latin America, as in other parts of the world, rely heavily on artificial methods of birth control such as the intrauterine device and oral contraceptives. Despite the strict prohibition on such methods by Catholic

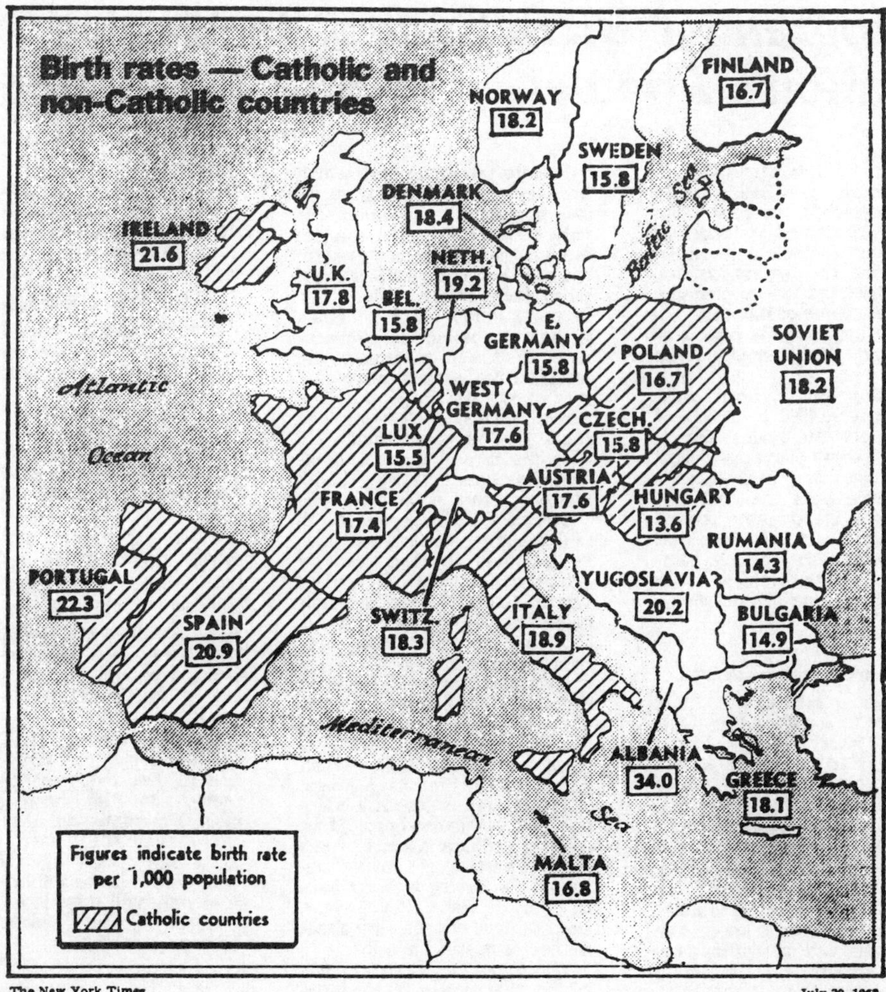

The New York Times July 30, 1968

doctrine, these programs have not met with vocal religious opposition.

Public family-planning programs in Latin America have expanded with what some observers describe as the "tacit cooperation" of the Catholic leadership.

These programs were developed largely to curb the steadily rising abortion rate and the damage to the health of—and sometimes the death of—potential mothers. They are intended to ease the strain that population growth has placed on economic development.

The birth rate in most Latin-American countries has been stable at around 45 per 1,000 population in recent years. But the introduction of modern medicine and technology has brought about a tremendous drop in the death rate, particularly among infants and children.

As a result, the rate of growth of the population—especially that part of the population dependent on others for food, clothing and education—has risen sharply.

This population growth has made serious inroads on, and at times has overridden, the increase in the gross national product and thus has stifled the countries' economic development.

Abortion has long been one of the most popular methods of birth control in Latin America, despite the position of the Catholic Church that it is a form of murder. Uruguay has one of the lowest birth rates in Latin America because of an abortion rate estimated at three for every live birth.

Resistance to the introduction of birth control generally has been along nonreligious lines. In Puerto Rico, for instance, researchers found that one of the strongest impediments to birth control was a complex of superstitious beliefs about failing health.

In one poll of 30 Catholics, 18 were aware that the church was opposed to birth control, bu. 15 of them disagreed with the church. The 12 who did not know the church position said it would make no difference to them if the church opposed birth control.

The extent to which European Catholics practice birth control is not well-established in all countries. But, in general, birth rates in the Catholic countries of Europe are nearly the same as those in non-Catholic countries.

In France, the decline in the birth rate, which began falling nearly 200 years ago and is now at 17.4 per 1,000, was caused by "the prevention of births within marriage by contraceptive means," according to Alfred Sauvy, former director of the French National Institute for Demographic Studies.

Poland, an overwhelmingly Catholic country, is considered the abortion center of Europe. It also has a state-approved family planning organization known as the Association of Consenting Motherhood, which provides the full gamut of birth control advice and devices.

In Spain, where 99.5 per cent of the population is Catholic, birth control is a matter of growing interest to middle-class families. The sale of oral contraceptives rose 78.8 per cent there last year.

A recent study of birth control practices in the United States revealed that nonconformity of Catholic wives to the church's position on contraception has increased steadily since 1955.

The study, conducted by Drs. Raymond Potvin of Catholic University, Charles Westoff of Princeton University and Norman Ryder of the University of Wisconsin, found the increase in nonconformity to be "widespread and not limited to any Catholic age or socio-economic category, nor to women who are less faithful in participating at mass or receiving communion."

Catholic women with more education and with husbands in white-collar occupations were found to heed the church's prohibition most, and women who married younger the least. Catholic wives with Irish and French mothers were more likely to conform to church doctrine than wives with mothers of Italian and Latin-American or Spanish background.

Over all, 78 per cent of American Catholic wives surveyed said they had used some form of contraception, and two-thirds of these said they had used a method other than the rhythm method, which is approved by the church.

July 30, 1968

Pakistan's Program of Birth Control Is Making Progress but Nation's Population Is Still Increasing

Special to The New York Times

LAHORE, Pakistan, Nov. 25 — Last February the family-planning clinics here in the capital of West Pakistan were able to perform only 45 sterilization operations. Now it is an ordinary thing for them to perform 45 in a day.

The sharp rise in operations has upset the calculations of the Government's closely administered Family Planning Division. It seems likely that more than 50,000 such operations will have been performed when the administrative year ends next June, a total that will far surpass not only the goal set for the year but the following year's as well.

Pakistan's family planners had been wary of pushing a sterilization program. No form of birth control, they reasoned, could be more offensive to Moslem traditionalists, and a bad reaction to a campaign on behalf of sterilization might defeat their whole program.

They had reason to be wary. Unlike India, where there is little active opposition to family planning, conservative religious elements here believe that there should be a ban on contraception and that Moslems should be encouraged to increase their numbers.

"Every child is born with one stomach and two hands to fill that stomach," observes Mian Tufail Mohammed, a leader of the powerful Moslem revivalist movement, the Jamaat-i-Islami, which lists the family-planning program as one of its main reasons for opposing the regime of President Mohammad Ayub Khan.

All this month, with West Pakistan engulfed in a tide of student protests against the regime, family-planning signboards and clinics in town after town have been the first targets when the students started throwing rocks. Before that there was a whispering campaign that the clinics were sadistically sterilizing young boys.

Numbers Continue to Rise

Yet the graphs in the clinics continue to show a steep climb, though West Pakistan has a long way to go before it will match East Pakistan, where 250,000 sterilizations were performed in the administrative year that ended in June.

Male sterilization operations, known as vasectomies, are simple. In less than 10 minutes the duct that carries sperm can be cut and tied off without impairing in any way the ability to have sexual relations.

Female sterilization, which involves more complex surgical procedures, accounts for only a tiny fraction of the operations performed in Pakistan.

Until the middle of last year, when there was a sudden rise in the number of vasectomies in East Pakistan, the Government had been promoting the intrauterine contraceptive device known as the loop as the surest means of slowing the rapid gain in population.

In the three years that Pakistan has been stressing family planning, the population has shot up from 115 million to 125 million. The Government asserts that it has already achieved a 10 per cent reduction in the birth rate, but concedes that this is only a guess based on incomplete and unreliable statistics.

It is particularly difficult to estimate what has been accomplished with the loop, a curlecue of plastic or other synthetic material that, when placed in the uterine passage, prevents conception in a manner not yet determined. More than a million women have been reported as having accepted the device in West Pakistan alone, but after a year, surveys have shown, only about 50 per cent still have it.

There has also been the suspicion that heavy and continuous pressure to meet "targets," combined with the payment of monetary incentives for doing so, has produced a certain amount of overreporting.

The Ultimate Question

The ultimate question is not how many vasectomies are performed or how many loops are accepted but how many children Pakistani parents actually want. A survey has shown that a married Pakistani woman who lives to the age of 49 will have had, on average, 8.8 live births.

Given present mortality rates, she would have to have five children to be sure that one son would still be alive when her husband reaches 65. The Government says two children are enough, but not everyone in the Government is persuaded.

Fakhar Zahman, who heads the family-planning program in Lahore, has two daughters already. But he believes, as most Pakistanis do, that it is "very important to have a son." In a few years he and his wife plan to have a third child. And what will they do if that is a girl? "I don't know," he answers ruefully.

December 2, 1968

China's Changing Society Seems to Cut Birth Rate

By TILLMAN DURDIN

Special to The New York Times

SHANGHAI, April 20—Mrs. Hu Fang-tsu was emphatic about it. "Children are a lot of trouble," she said. "Nobody wants very many of them any more." The leader of a production team in the Machiao commune in the countryside 18 miles west of Shanghai, the 35-year-old Mrs. Hu has one child, and she and her husband have no plans to add another.

Other couples in her team feel as the Hus do, she said, and their reasoning is incisive and practical.

Both husband and wife work in the fields or at other jobs on the collective farm. Two very young children can be left at nurseries during the day while the parents are at work but they need home care and feeding and this is a burden

And as children grow up in the society of the Machiao commune, there is progressively less and less interdependence between them and their parents. The children are taken into the activities of schools and youth programs and by the age of 16 are on their own in the communes as self-supporting workers.

By the time they are teenagers, the children have little need of their parents and the parents have little material need of their children, for the elderly in China today rely not on their offspring for support in their old age but on the organization to which they are attached.

Petite and attractive despite her garb of padded trousers and jacket of faded blue, Mrs. Hu gave her views on children and birth control in the clean, plain but neatly furnished upstairs bed-living room of her two-room home in an apartment building near the fields in which she works.

"The old idea that parents should have lots of children to honor and support them is finished," she said. "Most parents in this production team have one or two children. The largest family has only four."

Mrs. Hu's team forms a collective that is roughly the equivalent of the traditional Chinese village with its surrounding fields. Out of 248 persons in the team, 80 are married women, and Mrs. Hu said 20 had had sterility operations while others were taking birth-control pills or using contraceptive devices so they would have no more children.

At the commune hospital nearby, the doctor in charge said he not only was operating on women to make them sterile but was performing vasectomies on men at the rate of three a week.

Steady Decline Indicated

The evidence provided at the Machiao commune, where a group of foreign newsmen visited today as part of a four-day stay at Shanghai, and at other institutions in the Shanghai area where the correspondents have asked questions about birth control, points to the probability that a steady decline is taking place in the birth and population growth rates in China.

The vice chairman of the commune, Wu Chiu-ling, with whom the newsmen talked, had no comparative figures from earlier years. But he said the present birth rate in the commune, which consists of 196 collective farms and 35,000 people, was 15 to 17 per 1,000. He had no figures on the death rate, so a population growth rate for the commune could not be calculated.

Factories and other establishments the newsmen have visited also reported declining birth rates. The so-called extended Chinese family of former times seems to have virtually disappeared, replaced by just a man and wife with one, two or three children.

Officials queried here have no information on national population growth or the effectiveness of birth control on a nationwide basis, and the lack of statistics in the Machiao commune would indicate that social organizations throughout the country are not recording very good population growth information for forwarding to a central authority.

Thus it seems doubtful that Peking has at present any very

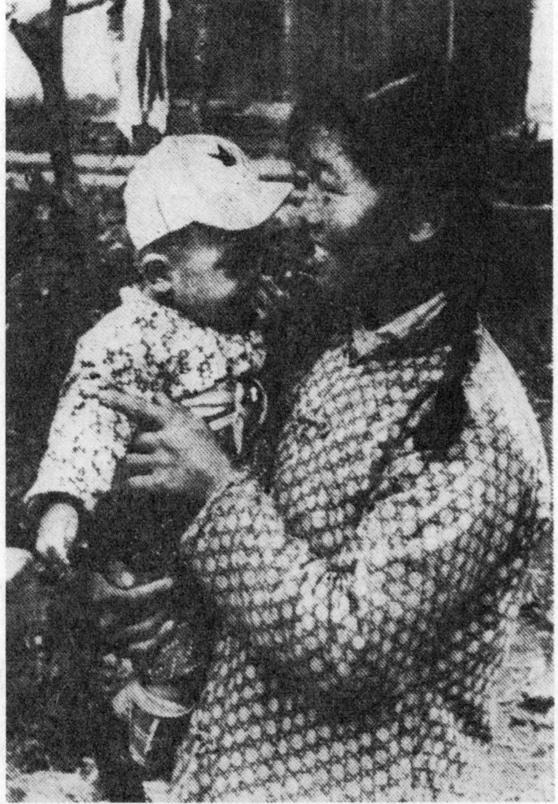

Norm an Webster/© The Globe and Mail, Toronto

The present life style in China does not encourage large families, as did the old. Here, a young woman holds her baby, but children spend much time away from parents.

exact data on the rate of population increase. It is clear, however, that the central Government is encouraging birth control without making an intensive publicized campaign out of it.

Late Marriage Favored

The encouragement consists, for one thing, of constant pressure on the young not to marry before the age of approximately 28 for men and 26 for women. Additionally, birth-control pills and other contraceptive means are made available free. Vasectomies for men and sterilization for women can be had at nominal cost in hospitals.

China's population is usually estimated today at around 800 million. Peking itself has used a peak figure of 750 million.

The growth rate has for years been estimated at about 2 per cent annually, but it is possibly below this figure now.

Growth in China's enormous population has been one of the basic problems of the Communist Government. The increase has steadily curtailed the effects of economic expansion in improving the livelihood of the people.

Now it appears, as much because of factors stemming from the new way of life in China as because of the use of artificial contraception, that the birth rate and population growth rate are dropping appreciably.

April 21, 1971

FOR ITALIAN POOR, BIRTH-CURB HELP

Family-Planning Consultant Now Works Legally

Special to The New York Times

ROME, May 29—For more than a decade Maria Luisa de Marchi has technically been a lawbreaker as the lone birth-control consultant in Italy.

On March 17 it became legal for her to hand out contraceptive pills to women who were afraid of having another child, and to offer advice on planned parenthood.

A landmark decision by the Constitutional High Court that day struck down a 1926 law from the Mussolini era that had made dissemination of birth-control information a punishable offense in Roman Catholic Italy.

The ruling by Italy's highest tribunal that the ban has violated the basic right of free speech ended a 20-year crusade by Mrs. de Marchi's husband, Luigi de Marchi, a writer and advocate of social reforms. He had fought his legal battle as secretary of a birth-control movement called the Italian Association for Demographic Education.

The association has long been operating Italy's first and only birth-control clinic, with Mrs. de Marchi its principal field worker.

Visits Shantytowns

Mrs. de Marchi, who has a son and a daughter, regularly visits the tenements and teeming shantytowns that ring Rome, giving advice on how to avoid unwanted births.

One neighborhood where she is well known is Pietralata, on the eastern outskirts.

"I suppose this must be my first year of married life without a pregnancy," said Maria, one of Mrs. de Marchi's charges there. Maria lives in a shack with her husband, a house-painter, and 10 children. She told a visitor that she had had as many abortions as children.

Maria's neighbor, Bianca, who has seven children, admitted a little ruefully, "I think I've had 14 abortions." Both women have been using birth-control pills for some months. Containers of contraceptive pills may now bear labels telling what they are; before the Constitutional High Court's ruling they had to be camouflaged as remedies against female ailments.

Mrs. de Marchi said that in 12 years of social work she had met only one woman who was reluctant to use contraceptive methods because of religious scruples.

After Pope Paul VI condemned all artificial birth-control techniques in his encyclical "Humanae Vitae"—"Of Human Life"—in 1968, Mrs. de Marchi wrote a book, "In Human Life," in defense of planned parenthood.

Her husband's legal victory, she thinks, has opened great possibilities. "Doctors may now be encouraged to give contraceptive advice, hospitals may fit devices, and medical students will be taught birth-control techniques," she said.

Planned-parenthood information, Mrs. de Marchi hopes, will also reduce the danger of "kitchen-table abortions." Her long experience has convinced her that there has been at least one abortion for each living child in Italy. The next aim of the de Marchi crusade is to legalize abortion in Italy.

May 30, 1971

Moslems Back Birth Control

RABAT, Morocco, Dec. 31 (Reuters) — The first Islamic conference on family planning has ruled that birth control is permissible in Moslem law but that sterilization and abortion are prohibited, according to a statement issued here today. The five-day conference was organized by the International Planned Parenthood Federation.

January 1, 1972

Population Growth Said to Slow In Countries of the Soviet Bloc

As a result of a marked fall in the birth rate since the middle nineteen-fifties, population growth in the Soviet Union and other countries of the Warsaw Pact has slowed, according to a report by the Economic Committee of the North Atlantic Treaty Organization.

As a result, the population gap between the Eastern and Western alliances is expected to widen in favor of NATO. The population of the Warsaw Pact countries in 1970 was 345.9 million and that of the 15 Atlantic Alliance countries 553.8 million. For 1980 the figures forecast by demographic experts are 377 million and 596.1 million respectively.

United States, British, West German, and French demographers submitted reports to the Economic Committee recently. Danish and Belgian experts also attended the meetings, which examined population trends in the Soviet Union, Poland, Rumania, East Germany, Bulgaria, Czechoslovakia and Hungary.

The experts found that abortion has been the chief cause of the decline in the birth rate in the Warsaw Pact countries in the last 15 years. Since the liberalization of abortion laws in the middle nineteen-fifties the number of legal abortions has grown strikingly.

60% Abortions In Hungary

They estimated that 60 per cent of all pregnancies are aborted in Hungary and that this figure probably applies also to the Soviet Union. Other estimates were 44 per cent of pregnancies aborted in Bulgaria, 36 per cent in Czechoslovakia and 23 per cent in Poland.

Authorities in these countries, alarmed by the decline in births, have attempted to raise the rate. The abortion law was tightened in Rumania and the birth rate rose from 12 per thousand in December 1966 to 40 in September 1967.

Since then, however, the rate has declined steadily because, it is believed, of use of contraceptives and illegal abortions. In the first quarter of 1971 the birth rate was 20 per thousand.

Decline in 1980's Seen

Despite the general decline in the birth rate, the experts foresee no shortage of military manpower over the next decade in the Warsaw Pact in comparison with NATO.

United States projections submitted to the committee showed about 2,250,000 men reaching the military age of 18 years in the Soviet Union each year at present. This figure, it is believed, will rise to about 2,500,000 in the early nineteen-eighties, when it will begin to decline slightly.

In the other countries of Eastern Europe, the number of men reaching military age each year—about 1,000,000 at present — is seen as beginning to diminish by the middle of this decade.

"Neither the Soviet Union nor the East European countries are likely to resort to reductions in armed forces because of lack of manpower," the report stated.

One main point that emerged from the experts' papers was that future industrial growth in the Warsaw Pact countries will depend almost exclusively on higher productivity. In the past such growth depended largely on a rapid expansion of the labor force through the recruiting of the young, the transfer and migration of young peasants to industrial areas and increased participation of women.

Peasant Force Depleted

Although an appreciable number of young people will be reaching working age in the future, the experts concluded that the reserve work force of peasants and women is almost exhausted.

Within the Warsaw Pact the Soviet population makes up 70 per cent of the total, and, if current trends continue, this share is expected to rise in the future.

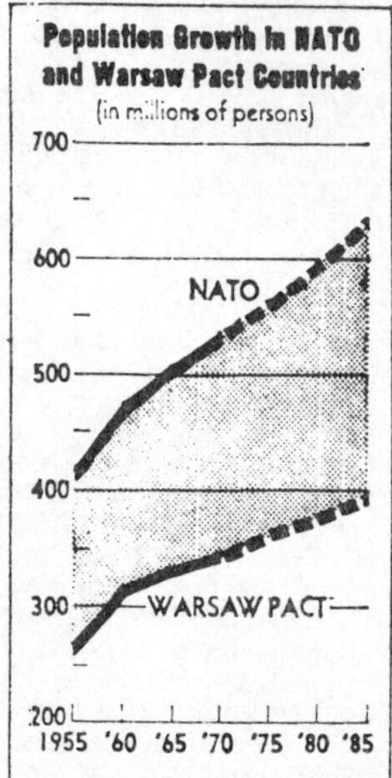

The New York Times/March 5, 1972

Inside the Soviet Union, the non-European peoples of Central Asia, the Caucasus and Siberia, although a minority of about 20 per cent of the total population of 242.8 million in 1970, are increasing much faster than the Europeans: the "Great Russians," the Byelorussians, the Ukrainians and the Baltic peoples.

March 5, 1972

COSTA RICA LEADS BIRTH CURB TREND

Decline in Rate Began Even Before Drive Was Started

By RICHARD SEVERO
Special to The New York Times

SAN JOSE, Costa Rica, June 21—Costa Rica, which had one of the world's highest birth rates during the nineteen-fifties, has become something of a trend setter in population control.

Although there is no question that population growth and birth rates have declined, there is a question as to why. The drop began well before the programs that were designed to bring it about.

"The decline started in 1960," said Tin Myaing Thein, a Columbia University research associate who is studying the reasons for the drop in Costa Rica. "But it wasn't until 1962 that the first doctor started introducing birth-control methods and the Ministry of Health didn't become active in family planning until 1967.

Situation Watched Closely

The Costa Rican phenomenon is being watched closely by demographers because it contrasts so vividly with the situation in much of Latin America. Family planning concepts are not taken for granted in Latin America and the subject is enormously controversial.

Politicians regard the words "birth control" as a liability because, they say, their constituents consider it a Government attempt to tell couples what they may do in their own homes.

In Mexico, for example, where the Government appears ready to undertake some of the programs Costa Rica's leaders adopted five years ago, there remains a great deal of uneasiness about where it will all lead. And, unlike in Costa Rica, population growth figures in Mexico show no sign of declining on their own.

Latin Americans sometimes say that opposition to family planning has to do with their ideas of individualism and "machismo," the need for the male to prove his virility. But there are those who say this factor has been overemphasized.

Dr. Arturo Cabezas López, who started preaching the virtues of family planning in Costa Rica a decade ago, has more recently found that men here are quite willing to consider vasectomy as a means to control family size. Some 800 vasectomies have been performed here and Dr. Cabezas has told associates that he regards machismo as a sociological myth, at least in Costa Rica.

Dr. Jack Reynolds, who is Tin Myaing Thein's husband and is associated with Columbia's International Institute for the Study of Human Reproduction, has found that Costa Rican women were turning to voluntary sterilization well before the country's family-planning program started. He said that factors not related to the program played a significant part in the decline in population growth. But neither the doctor nor his wife were sure just what motivated the Costa Ricans to take steps that are still regarded as drastic in many Latin-American nations.

Little Church Opposition

Although Costa Rica is a Roman Catholic country, no major problem has been created by the church's long-standing opposition to artificial means of preventing conception. The hierarchy has not made an issue of it and many young priests have stressed parental responsibility among their parishioners, leaving the means by which birth control is achieved to the individual. Only in some rural areas among a few older priests is there a real stand against artificial controls.

The population of Costa Rica is now estimated at 1.8 million to 2 million. The census department estimated the population growth rate at 2.6 per cent for 1970. Some sources have called the estimate conservative. But some demographers say that even a rate of 2.6 per cent is too high for the country.

Although Costa Ricans seem to have accepted the idea of limiting family size to what they can afford, they tend to be optimistic as to what the number will be.

June 27, 1972

Declaration to Waldheim Urges Nations to Promote Birth Control

By ERIC PACE

Special to The New York Times

UNITED NATIONS, N. Y., April 25—A declaration stressing the urgency of world food and population problems was presented to Secretary General Waldheim today. The document speaks of the "responsibility of governments to provide their peoples" with birth control information and equipment.

C. P. Snow, the British writer and scientist, made the presentation here on behalf of more than 1,000 persons from 94 countries who signed or declared their support for the document, called the Declaration on Food and Population.

The declaration's supporters include John A. Scali, the United States delegate; Senator Jacob K. Javits, Representative Jonathan B. Bingham and Representative Bella S. Abzug of New York; former Attorney General Elliot L. Richardson, the anthropologist Margaret Mead and the writer Bernard Malamud.

Others supporting the declaration are Giovanni Agnelli, the Italian industrialist; Gunnar Myrdal, the Swedish economist and Lon Nol, the Cambodian President. The list also includes several Nobel Prize-winners.

"The precarious state of world food production made critical by predicted expectations of continued population growth calls for concerted action by the world community," the declaration says. It warns that "in this new and threatening situation, a bad monsoon in Asia (which could occur in any year), or a drought in North America (like those in the nineteen-thirties and nineteen-fifties), could mean severe malnutrition for hundreds of millions and death for many millions."

The declaration is addressed "to governments, organizations and men and women everywhere" and it notes that the United Nations is now providing leadership on solving both population and food problems. In August the United Nations will convene the World Population Conference in Bucharest. In November it will convene the World Food Conference in Rome.

In accepting the declaration during a ceremony in a Security Council antechamber, the Secretary General did not specifically endorse its recommendation concerning birth control. But he said, "the unprecedented growth of the world's population is compounding man's difficulties in feeding himself.

"The time at our disposal is very short," he continued. "You point out that the world's food production has barely kept pace with population increases. Our goal is not mere survival, but a life of dignity and peace with hope for each new generation to improve the condition of life."

After the ceremony, a scientist on the staff of the United Nations Food and Agriculture Organization, John A. Howard, said a variety of techniques for gathering data at long distance were proving helpful to nations in appraising their resources more efficiently.

April 26, 1974

French Assembly Allows Wide Contraceptive Sales

By FLORA LEWIS

Special to The New York Times

PARIS, June 28—The French Assembly gave overwhelming endorsement today to a law not only authorizing general distribution of contraceptives but also providing that the cost be borne by the social security system.

There was only one vote against the bill, which was sponsored by the Government. It was a dramatic reversal of attitudes in a country that had one of the world's most restrictive set of laws on contraception and abortion.

Passage of the law by near unanimity came as such a surprise that it was the day's biggest news in the major Paris newspapers. It was hailed by many commentators as a sign that the new Government of President Valéry Giscard d'Estaing is going to be much more liberal than anyone expected.

Many reasons were given for what seemed a sudden, drastic shift in social judgments. The one most widely advanced was that a highly vocal, militant campaign for liberalized abortion in the last two years had turned the traditionalists completely around, so that they were now prepared to accept free birth control as the lesser evil.

Special Severity

The special severity of previous French law in this area dates mainly to 1920. It probably had more to do with the slaughter of young men in World War I and fear of a steady population decline than it did with religious dictates.

Roman Catholic France has always listened to the church and republican France has always resisted its demands. And by and large, with a narrow band of exceptions, the two have pretty much represented the same Frenchmen according to pressures of the moment.

The new law replaces one passed with difficulty in 1967, permitting the distribution of contraceptives only on medical orders and requiring personal prescriptions with a time limit.

Medical experts have charged that even that modest legalization of birth control was systematically sabotaged by the authorities. Estimates of the number of French women currently using the contraceptive pill vary from 6 to 10 per cent, compared with 46 per cent in Britain.

The new law also wipes out the requirement that girls under 18 have written permission from their parents, as well as from a doctor, to obtain contraception. Proponents of the measure argued that it was exactly among the very young girls that the lack of birth control produced the greatest number of social tragedies and illegal abortions.

Health Minister Simone Veil, who presented the Government's bill to the Assembly, promised a vigorous public information campaign to spread word that birth control was now a matter of "common right," freely available to all without question. The social security system will also establish clinics to provide free medical examinations and counseling.

Despite the thesis that traditionalists acepted birth control in an effort to head off legal abortion, the victory of those who argued that family planning is a human right was expected to lead to renewed efforts to change the abortion law.

Current Law

The current law permits therapeutic abortions only when the life of the mother is found to be in danger by two doctors in addition to the mother's own doctor. Between 1966 and 1970, 132 legal abortions were performed in the Paris area.

Nobody knows the exact number of illegal abortions performed in France each year, but estimates run from 300,000 to 800,000, with a population of 10 million women of childbearing age. Mortality rates are high: 1 to 3 per cent of the women involved.

The courts have enforced the law with unpredictability, sometimes imposing heavy fines and long prison sentences on the women as well as the abortionists.

Famous Case

For decades, the subject was taboo. But a case in the fall of 1972 suddenly drew wide public attention and became a focal point for advocates of reform. A 16-year-old girl who refused to bear her child was tried along with her mother for violating the law. After much public debate, the judge acquitted her.

Last year, a somewhat reluctant Government introduced a bill to liberalize the abortion law, but abandoned it without formal debate when it ran into quiet opposition from what the politicians evidently considered the powers that be on moral and social issues.

That retreat, considered pusillanimous by reformers, became an issue that was frequently brought up against the Gaullists during last May's presidential election campaign, although Mr. Giscard d'Estaing himself did not take a stand on the issue.

June 29, 1974

130 NATIONS BEGIN POPULATION TALKS

Outlook for Decisive Action at Bucharest to Control Growth Seems Dim

By GLADWIN HILL
Special to The New York Times

BUCHAREST, Aug. 19—The likelihood of any decisive international action soon to defuse what many experts have called the global "population bomb" seemed dim today as the United Nations World Population Conference opened here.

There was an impressive turnout of delegations from 130 nations for the first worldwide parley on population at the governmental level.

But a succession of illustrious keynote speakers at opening ceremonies—Secretary General Waldheim, President Nicolae Ceausescu of Rumania, and Dr. Antonio Carrillo Flores, the secretary general of the conference—all stressed the theme of absolute national sovereignty in formulating population policies, regardless of global impact.

Waldheim's View

Referring to the conference's proposed international "Plan of Action," Mr. Waldheim said, "There should be no question that the plan emphatically recognizes the prerogatives of national sovereignty."

President Ceausescu said that every country "has the sovereign right to promote that demographic policy and measures that it considers most suitable, consonant with its national interests, without any outside interference."

And Dr. Carrillo Flores declared that while nations comprising a majority of mankind had recognized the need to try to reduce their rates of demographic growth, "it is also understandable that several nations in Europe, Arica and Latin America, where the objectives are different, look at the problem in a different way."

The world's population is increasing at an annual rate of 2 per cent—or more than 70 million people a year. At that rate the present population of four billion will double in 35 years, producing what many experts see as potentially catastrophic stresses on supplies of food and other key resources under present patterns of production and distribution.

An Historic Parley

Despite th inherent limitations on the conference's actions, Dr. Carrillo Flores said, it was historic in that governments for the first time "are beginning to deal with questions such as population growth, distribution of people between rural and urban centers, and even in a limited way with the age structure of populations."

"The task of the international comunity," he added, "is to promote research, the knowledge and interpretation of the demographic realities, its trends and prospects, and to provide cooperation to all peoples who might need that cooperation."

More than 3,000 people attended the opening session in the main auditorium of Rumania's legislative Palace of the Republic.

President Ford, in a message read by the head of the United States delegation, Caspar W. Weinberger, Secretary of Health, Education and Welfare, said that the global population problem would "remain one of our primary concerns for the remainder of this century."

"The policies and programs you recommend could affect the peoples of all our nations. I pledge that the United States will work unceasingly with you in seeking solutions that are both sound and right."

Rumania's Foreign Minister, Gheorghe Macovescu, was elected presiding officer of the 10-day conference.

Tomorrow, while the full session marks time with speeches, three committees open to participation by all nations will begin discussing special aspects of the population problem and a fourth will begin debate on the draft of the Plan of Action. It outlines broad policies nations may choose for managing population problems.

That confrontations between the developing and affluent nations, particularly the United States, are in prospect was was suggested by the candid observation of Mr. Waldheim, an Austrian.

"Eminent voices have been raised against patterns of consumption prevalent in the industrial world. While this may not be a major focus of the discussions it should remind us of our immense obligation to satisfy certain basic and universal needs—for food, shelter, education, and health care."

August 20, 1974

Marx vs. Malthus: Ideas Stir Rancor at Population Meeting

By GLADWIN HILL
Special to The New York Times

BUCHAREST, Aug. 25—The United Nations World Population Conference, at midpoint, is shaping up as a struggle between the doctrinal ghosts of Malthus—who stated that population, increasing geometrically, would inevitably outstrip the growth of food supplies—and Marx—who contended that the population characteristics of a society were determined by its political and economic structure.

The consensus of the affluent industrialized Western nations at this first global conference on population is that overpopulation—centered in the underdeveloped "third world" of Asia, Africa, and Latin America, which contains a majority of the world's nearly four billion people—threatens to overstrain world resources, particularly food.

The Communist bloc, along with a number of the poorer nations at the conference, counters that overpopulation is an effect, not a cause, of underdevelopment and that additional population is needed in many areas for development.

Coping With 'Population Bomb'

The view of the advanced nations is that the global "population bomb" can best be defused by fertility reduction through means ranging from "family planning" to tax incentives, along with international economic assistance.

The opposing view is that a widescale redistribution of the world's wealth and resources, including decreased consumption in the affluent countries, automatically would bring populations into satisfactory equilibrium.

These diverse lines of thought were pursued so adamantly at this gathering of some 1,100 representatives from 135 nations that it appeared the conference's projected product—a "world plan of action"—would inevitably end up as an ambiguous document that would give less support to the limiting of population than it would to economic innovations beyond the scope of the conference.

While nearly 100 spokesmen from various nations occupied the conference's plenary sessions, the most specific item in the statement is the proposal that the world's nations, acting individually, try to bring the present global population growth rate of 2 per cent—which currently means an increase of over 70 million people in a year—down to 1.7 per cent by 1985.

An indication of what the tone of the final document may be came at the outset when the panel agreed to remove from its preamble the barest allusion to the existence of any population problems.

U.S. a Target of Criticism

In the debates, the United States—whose views favoring a major reduction in population growth were presented by Caspar W. Weinberger, Secretary of Health, Education and Welfare—was a major target in assaults on the rich nations by the far more numerous poor ones.

But China criticized the Soviet Union as well as the United States, accusing the "superpowers" of "ruthless imperialism and colonialism."

"The superpowers' false alarm of a 'population explosion,'" said Huang Shu-tse, China's Deputy Minister of Health, "reminds us of the notorious Malthus, who more than 170 years ago driveled about the impossibility of production's ever catching up with population. Today, the world population has more than trebled that of Malthus's time, but there has been a much greater increase in the material wealth of society."

Maurice Strong, executive director of the United Nations Environmental Program, the coordinating agency that grew out of the 1972 World Environment Conference, told the conference:

"A simplistic and illusory notion all too common to the more developed world is that population growth in the less developed countries is the greatest threat to the global environment.

"The fact is that the main risks of environmental damage on a global scale and the greatest pressures on natural resources come from the population growth and economic activities of the rich countries and the exploding appetites of their inhabitants.

"A citizen of an advanced industrialized nation consumes in six months the energy and raw materials that have to last the citizen of a developing country his entire lifetime."

August 26, 1974

POPULATION TALKS REVISE PROPOSALS

Poor Nations, in Bucharest, Succeed in Subordinating Population Curbs

By GLADWIN HILL
Special to The New York Times

BUCHAREST, Aug. 28—After dealing with 340 proposed amendments, delegates to the World Population Conference tonight were completing a "plan of action," a set of suggested guidelines for nations in formulating population policies.

The document that was emerging was markedly different from the draft plan that had been presented as the 135-nation conference sponsored by the United Nations opened here Aug. 19.

Its original theme was that excessive population threatened worldwide development and resources and that population limitation should be a major component of development policies.

In the revised text, population limitation is pointedly subordinated to economic and social development itself, which is regarded as the prime means of solving population problems.

Richer Nations Outnumbered

The change in the declaration's tone was attributable largely to the fact that the underdeveloped nations—many of which are indifferent to population limitation and which were less active in the original drafting process — outnumber the industrialized nations by more than two to one both in the United Nations and in the conference here.

Noting that most of the amendment proposals had come from underdeveloped countries, Ali Oubouzar of Algeria, who presided over the principal debates, said at a news conference today:

"The underdeveloped countries want to restore the paramountcy of development over the matter of negatively influencing fertility rates."

In many of their parliamentary moves here the underdeveloped countries have been supported by the Soviet-led Communist bloc. They also have received a degree of tacit support from some of the advanced nations, such as Sweden, that attach great importance to economic development and have seen their own birth rates decline as their economies grew.

The basic recommendation of the draft declaration is that nations strive to reduce the present 2 per cent annual increase in world population to 1.7 per cent by 1985, with the reduction to be effected entirely among the underdeveloped nations, which have about two-thirds of the world's nearly four billion people.

The United States proposed a more ambitious objective—a systematic effort to attain "a replacement level of fertility, an average of two children per family, by the year 2000." But the trend of the conference has been away from such a recommendation.

Mr. Oubouzar has been chairman of the conference's important "working group," which is open to all participating nations and which has been revising the action plan. Most of the panel's decisions presumably will stand since it will take a two-thirds vote in the two final full sessions to make any substantive changes.

The conference's conclusions must be ratified by the United Nations General Assembly, which voted in 1970 to hold the population conference. Even then any recommendations will not be binding on any nation but would stand as criteria for international actions.

August 29, 1974

Assembly in France Backs Abortion Bill After Bitter Debate

Special to The New York Times

PARIS, Nov. 29—In a historic precedent for a Roman Catholic country, the French National Assembly has voted by a surprisingly wide margin to legalize abortion during the first 10 weeks of pregnancy.

Barring unforeseen circumstances, the measure will become law by early next year after completion of the formal legislative process.

In essence the bill will allow any permanent resident "distressed" by a pregnancy to have an abortion during the first 10 weeks. The operation must be carried out by a doctor in an established hospital or clinic. Girls under 18 must obtain their parents' permission.

The cost will not be borne by the social-security system, as the Socialists and Communists had wanted, but the Government plans to fix a ceiling on charges to make sure that poorer women are not excluded.

The Government of President Valéry Giscard d'Estaing, which proposed the profoundly controversial reform, could not have won without the overwhelming support of his Communist and Socialist opponents in Parliament. Only 99 of the 291 deputies belonging to the President's party and its political allies favored the measure, which overturns an antiabortion law adopted in 1920. The vote was 284 to 189 with 17 not voting.

Minister's Role Held Vital

Government leaders and Assembly members said the legislation would never have gone through without the gentle firmness of the Minister of Health, Simone Veil, the mother of three and the bill's floor manager, who has never sat in Parliament. They added that no other Cabinet minister could have been successful in Parliament, which let a much more restrictive proposal die in committee a year ago when Georges Pompidou was President.

The measure goes to the Senate, the much weaker upper house, which will debate it in December. If it votes to block the legislation, the Assembly can override.

The debate, which lasted three days and nights and grew increasingly bitter, was finally concluded by the roll-call at 3:40 A.M. The Gaullists voted nearly two to one against; only one Communist and one Socialist deputy voted no. Three-quarters of Mr. Giscard d'Estaing's Independent Republican party deserted him; like the President its members are mainly upper-middle class, conservative and Roman Catholic.

The 1920 law makes abortion a crime unless the mother's life is in danger and carries heavy fines and prison sentences for anyone who performs or aids in an abortion and for the woman who undergoes it. Mr. Giscard d'Estaing termed it hypocritical, chaotic and archaic.

Opponents of the new legislation flung at Mrs. Veil, a career civil servant, such phrases as "trading in death" and "murder."

Her initial speech Tuesday seemed timid and apologetic, but as the debate waxed fiercer, she grew more resolute and convincing though she was sometimes staggering from fatigue.

"This law takes account of reality," she said. "The facts are that 300,000 Frenchwomen who are neither ignorant nor immoral have abortions in France every year."

The actual figure is believed to be several times higher since the statistic she cited involves those who seek hospital treatment for aftereffects.

'Never a Victory'

Asked whether the vote should be regarded as a victory for women, Mrs. Veil responded: "Abortion is never a victory. I would rather say this is progress."

Much of the extraordinarily long debate, which fascinated France, was televised live. At one point an opponent of reform played over the loudspeaker system what he said was the heartbeat of a nine-week-old fetus.

On Monday the Vatican issued a strong antiabortion statement that was approved by Pope Paul VI five months ago but was released only on the eve of the Assembly debate. Yesterday the Grand Rabbi of France, Jacob Kaplan, issued a declaration noting that abortion is a crime under Judaic law.

The French Federation of Protestants has approved the bill on humanistic but not theological grounds.

November 30, 1974

TOP GERMAN COURT REJECTS ABORTION

Bonn's 1974 Law Allowing Termination in the First 3 Months Is Struck Down

By PAUL KEMEZIS

Special to The New York Times

BONN, Feb. 25—The West German Constitutional Court in Karlsruhe, in a highly controversial decision, today struck down as unconstitutional a law allowing abortions on request during the first three months of pregnancy.

The court's 6 to 2 decision said the measure legalizing abortions, which was approved by the West German Parliament last June but never became effective, violated the Constitution's guarantee of the right to life for everyone.

The court, whose authority is similar to that of the United States Supreme Court, did however rule that abortions could be performed in the first three months of pregnancy in cases of rape, of danger to the mother's health, when there was a prospect that the child might be born deformed and when the birth could cause "grave hardship."

The court president, Ernst Benda, read the decision at the tense, heavily guarded Karlsruhe court building as about 1,000 pro-abortion demonstrators staged a protest march in the city center. Other demonstrations against the decision, involving thousands of protesters, were held later today in many German cities including Munich and Hamburg.

The decision is a major setback for the Government of Chancellor Helmut Schmidt, a coalition of Social Democrats and Free Democrats. The Government is now expected to propose a new law that will probably interpret in the widest possible legal terms the "grave hardship" principle of the court's ruling.

Nevertheless, the decision means that West Germany will not join the growing number of West European countries, which now includes Britain, France, the Netherlands, Austria, Denmark, Sweden and Finland, where all abortions performed in a certain period, usually the first three months of pregnancy, are either legal or are not subject to prosecution.

Instead it will remain among those countries, such as Italy and Belgium, where any abortion must meet sharply defined criteria.

In Bonn today Justice Minister Hans-Jochen Vogel said that the Government would accept the decision as reflecting the law but still considered its arguments for the three-month unconditional abortion period "sound and conclusive."

Leaders of the opposition Christian Democratic Union said they were now ready to work with the Government to find a solution to the abortion problem along constitutional lines, but the leader of the West German Roman Catholic Church, Julius Cardinal Döpfner of Munich, welcomed the ruling as a "limitation to the growing trend of watering down basic social values."

It is estimated that hundreds of thousands of West German women get illegal abortions in this country each year or go abroad for them and there have long been calls for reform of the 104-year-old abortion law, which prescribes a five-year jail sentence for infractions. As opposition to any change, especially from the Roman Catholic Church, has stiffened in recent years, bitter debates and incidents have developed.

The Social Democrat-Free Democratic Government made the issue a central element in its social reform program in 1972. Last June it pushed the liberalizing law through the lower house of Parliament by a vote of 260 to 218, overriding a veto by the upper house, which is controlled by the conservative, church-linked Christian Democratic Union.

The Christian Democrats immediately appealed the law to the Constitutional Court, which issued an injunction on June 24, 1974 suspending the legislation while it deliberated.

The court's conservative majority ruled today that the Constitution gave top priority to the preservation of life and required that this principle be given the widest possible interpretation in the laws. Thus, according to the court, the state has a duty to protect the human being from the beginning of its existence, which, the ruling said, means the 14th day after conception.

The decision took note of more liberal laws in other countries, but said that the "bitter experience" of the Nazi period in Germany provided historical grounds for determining that protection of human life should receive absolute priority. This order of values, the court said, can be overridden only in the special instances that were cited.

February 26, 1975

Associated Press

Ernst Benda, president of West German Constitutional Court in Karlsruhe, announcing its decision on abortion. The court ruled, 6-2, against a law allowing abortions upon request in the first three months of pregnancy.

TOPICS OF THE TIMES.

Going Back to Rock Bottom.

"Recently," remarks Colonel ROOSEVELT, "in certain circles, some popularity has been achieved by a song entitled, 'I Didn't Raise My Boy to Be a Soldier'—a song which ought always to be sung with a companion piece entitled 'I Didn't Raise My Girl to Be a Mother.'" That is an observation which will give great joy to the unregenerate and great annoyance to the vaguely benevolent people who are teaching the world to rise to great heights by lifting itself up by its boot-straps. It is frankly old-fashioned and, from their standpoint, barbaric. It revives, with unpleasantly startling vigor, the old primitive conception; the object of life is to live and to increase, the woman has the greater part of that duty, which is the fostering of the new life until it is strong enough to stand alone, and the man stands outside the cave with his club and keeps the enemy off. When he is not doing that he is getting meat to aid the woman in her work, and if he cannot get the meat because some other man wants it he fights the other man. A horribly low conception to our milk-and-honey twentieth century—or rather the twentieth century that existed before the murder at Serajevo shook it loose from its moorings—and yet it is debatable whether all our intricate civilization, if analyzed down to the ground, has not that basis.

Some of those who are singing that uplifting song will not quarrel with the Colonel's statement. Not all the people who do not want other people to raise their boys to be soldiers are also opposed to having other people raise their girls to be mothers; but most of the people who are advocating what they call birth control as a propaganda are also pacifists. It would not be far short of the truth to say that all of them are. The New-Thoughtists are pacifists, the philosophical anarchists are pacifists, the advocates of all the buttery theories so popular just now are pacifists. The people who are advocating—and advocating as a social theory—any such thing as free love, race suicide, or "the right of every man to live his own life"—are singing "I Didn't Raise My Girl to Be a Mother," even if they do not sing it in words; and you will find the same crowd in every audience that enthusiastically applauds the singing of "I Didn't Raise My Boy to Be a Soldier." For soldierhood and motherhood both represent the same primitive thing that this chocolate-fed generation is so nervously anxious to forget.

July 21, 1915

Dismisses Birth Control Case

WASHINGTON, Nov. 17 — The Supreme Court today dismissed, without an opinion, for lack of jurisdiction, the appeal of Margaret Sanger on the constitutionality of the New York State Birth Control act. Miss Sanger was sentenced to thirty days' imprisonment for conducting a "birth control clinic" in Brooklyn.

November 18, 1919

APOSTLE OF BIRTH CONTROL SEES CAUSE GAINING HERE

Hearing in Albany on Bill to Legalize Practice a Milestone in Long Fight of Margaret Sanger—Even China Awakening to Need of Selective Methods, She Says.

BY MARGARET SANGER.
President American Birth Control League.

After ten years of incessant agitation and activity the much-discussed question of birth control has invaded the legialative halls of Albany. A bill intended to amend existing laws so that New York physicians may be authorized to disseminate contraceptive advice has been introduced. There will be a hearing on the matter in the Assembly Chamber on April 10. If enacted, we hope for the beginning of a new era of social welfare and racial hygiene. But whatever the outcome, this bill means that birth control is no longer looked upon, even in the judicial and legislative field, as a topic "obscene and indecent," worthy only of ribald jest and suggestive leer.

No other great problem affecting the welfare of nation and race has been more misinterpreted and misunderstood, even by Americans who consider themselves well informed. Advocates of this doctrine do not beg for mere assent or approval. They ask for investigation and understanding, as the initial step toward support and adherence to their doctrines.

Much of the opposition to birth control has had its source among clergymen and other professional moralists. This ecclesiastic opposition is amazing in view of the fact that the "onlie true begetter" of the whole birth control movement, Robert Malthus, was himself a clergyman of the Church of England. He advocated "prudential checks" on the grounds of austere morality. Our clerical opponents also ignore the fact that many of the most noted champions of birth control today are clergymen. The most noteworthy example is that of the distinguished Dean of St. Paul's, London, William Ralph Inge.

There is a confusion in the public mind concerning the origin of the present movement, which must be distinguished from the so-called Neo-Malthusian movement of Great Britain and the Continent. The Neo-Malthusian League was the direct outcome of the celebrated trial in London in 1877 of Charles Bradlaugh and Mrs. Annie Besant, who had frankly admitted distributing among the English poor thousands upon thousands of copies of the pamphlet of a Boston physician, Dr. Knowlton, entitled "Fruits of Philosophy," originally published in this country in 1833. The Neo-Malthusian League, sponsored by those valiant pioneers, Charles and George Drysdale and Dr. Alice Vickery, soon spread to all countries of the continent, and its doctrines were put into practice in Holland, where fifty-three birth control clinics, approved by the Dutch Government, have been conducted with great success for forty years.

The birth control movement, which has now absorbed the earlier Neo-Malthusian movement, originated right here in New York just a decade ago. While the Neo-Malthusians based their propaganda on the broad general basis of Matlthus's theory of population, the expression "birth control" was devised in my little paper of advance feminism, The Woman Rebel, as one of the fundamental rights of the emancipation of working women. The response to this idea of birth control was so immediate and so overwhelming that a league was formed — the first birth control league in the world.

WHY SHE TOOK UP TASK.

With all the flame-like ardor of pioneers we did not at first realize the full scope of this fundamental discovery. At that time I knew nothing of Malthus, nothing of the courageous and desperate battle waged by the Drysdales in England, Rutgers in Holland, of G. Hardy and Paul Robin in France, for this century-old doctrine. I was merely thinking of the poor mothers of congested districts of the East Side who had so poignantly begged me for relief, in order that the children they had already brought into the world might have a chance to grow into strong and stalwart Americans. It was almost impossible to believe that the dissemination of knowledge easily available to the intelligent and thoughtful parents of the well-to-do classes was actually a criminal act, proscribed not only by State laws but by Federal as well.

My paper was suppressed. I was arrested and indicted by the Federal authorities. But owing to the vigorous protests of the public and an appeal sent by a number of distinguished English writers and thinkers, the case against me was finally abandoned. Meanwhile "birth control" became the slogan of the idea and not only spread through the American press from coast to coast, but immediately gained currency in Great Britain. Succinctly and with telling brevity and precision "birth control" summed up our whole philosophy. Birth control is not contraception indiscriminately and thoughtlessly practiced. It means the release and cultivation of the better racial elements in our society, and the gradual suppression, elimination and eventual extirpation of defective stocks — those human weeds which threaten the blooming of the finest flowers of American civilization.

In our efforts to effect the repeal of the existing laws which declare the use of contraceptive methods indecent and obscene, birth control advocates have been forced to battle every inch of the way. To get the matter before the Legislature of New York my path has led completely around the earth. Our effort has been to enlist the support of the best minds of every country, an object we have achieved even beyond our fondest expectations.

The backbone of the birth control movement has been from the time Malthus first published his epoch-making "Principles of Population" essentially Anglo-Saxon. John Stuart Mill, Francis Place, Matthew Arnold, Thomas Huxley and our own Thomas Jefferson, James Madison, Ralph Waldo Emerson and Robert G. Ingersoll spoke openly in favor of control of the population. Today such thinkers and writers as H.G. Wells, Harold Cox (editor of The Edinburgh Review), Arnold Bennett, Dean Inge, William Archer, Havelock Ellis, Gilbert Murry, Bertram Russell, John Maynard Keynes (editor of The Nation), and Lord Dawson, one of the King's physicians, and innumerable others in Great Britain speak openly and valiantly for birth control.

It is not without significance that since the inauguration of our agitation in 1913 there has been an immense recrudescence of interest in the persistent problem of population; and a number of new efforts, notably that of A.M. Carr-Saunders, to reinterpret the thesis so brilliantly advanced by that obscure clergyman, Malthus.

Most gratifying to the battle-scarred propagandist for birth control has been the awakening of the Orient. China and Japan for ages have been the notoriously overpopulated countries of the earth, the high birth rate, as always, accompanied by a high death rate, a high infant mortality rate and even acceptance of the widespread practice of infanticide. Famine, pestilence and flood have been the only checks to overpopulation in China, and these have been regarded even as a blessing by the yellow races. "Yang to meng ping" is a well known exclamation in China — "Many men, life cheap!"

Following my sojourn in Chir last year, the Ladies' Journal of China, the most influential women's publication there, devoted a special edition of more than one hundred pages to the problem of birth control. In this paper Tzi Sang wrote: "Since Mrs. Sanger's visit public opinion has been greatly influenced, and I understand that some educators are planning to propagate the doctrine in th interior so that our women will no longer be mere machines for breeding children. When the majority of our people know the benefits of birth control and believe that it is the remedy for plague, famine and war in China, then we can adopt the method of asking doctors to pass on their knowledge to women poor in health."

Set Lu, another writer in the same paper, points out that "if we study the actual situation in China we find that unconsciously the Chinese have attempted to practice birth control in a different way. Do we not throw away our babies?" frankly asks this writer of his compatriots. His answer is interesting: "Savages practice infanticide, but civilized people use scientific methods of prevention. Herein lies the difference between a barbarous and a civilized people. No wonder that our civilization fails to make any noticeable advance."

Both in Japan and China, as a result of my visit, and especially as the effect of the attempt upon the part of the imperial Japanese Government to suppress birth control and to shut its door in my face, the subject of birth control has aroused the deepest and most widespread interest among all classes. In both these great Oriental empires the roots of a permanent birth control movement have struck deep in popular interest, and undoubtedly will exert a great influence toward bringing down the alarmingly high birth rates to the level of those of Western civilization. The importance, the immediate necessity of an autonomous control of the birth rate by the races of the Orient is by no one more emphatically stated than by that eloquent and picturesque writer and traveler, J.O.P. Bland.

Since the first birth control clinic established in this country was raided by the New York police in Brownsville, some years ago, and its founders sentenced to jail as petty miscreants, the whole current of opinion has advanced, not merely in this country but throughout the world. The results of the intelligence tests, the menace of indiscriminate immigration, the fertility of the unfit and the increasing burden upon the healthful and vigorous members of American society of the delinquent and dependent classes, together with the growing danger of the abnormal fecundity of the feeble-minded, all emphasize the necessity of clear-sightedness and courageously facing the problem and the possibilities of birth control as a practical and feasible weapon against national and racial decadence.

With the invasion of the New York Legislature exponents of this challenging doctrine may well congratulate themselves that they have won another victory against their opponents. Whatever the outcome of the hearing on April 10, birth control in any event will have compelled serious attention from our legislators. If we can convince the assemblymen and State Senators that this is a matter which concerns not merely a group of "well-meaning" feminists, but is organically bound up with the biological welfare of the whole community, we shall consider that our efforts have not been entirely in vain.

April 8, 1923

NOTE GAINS IN WORK FOR BIRTH CONTROL

Doctors Here Report Country's Clinics Have Doubled in the Past Two Years.

23 CITIES HAVE 55 CENTRES

Rise of More Than 300 Such Places Abroad Viewed as Trend Toward Marriage Advice Stations.

Birth control centres in the United States have doubled in number during the past two years, the increase being about equal in the demonstration clinics and in the out-patient services connected with hospitals and public health centres, according to a report made public yesterday at the annual open meeting of the Committee on Maternal Health at its headquarters in the Academy of Medicine.

The report of Dr. Louis Stevens Bryant, executive secretary of the committee, to which Dr. George W. Kosmak, president of the New York County Medical Society, referred in presiding at the meeting, showed that fifty-five centres are now established in the country where organized birth control information and advice may be obtained. These centres are located, the report said, in twenty-three cities of twelve States.

Of the non-hospital group, or demonstration clinics, there are now twenty separate stations in thirteen cities of eight States, some of them highly organized with hospital affiliations, the report said. All of these are supported by lay groups but the actual work is done by physicians, and in four there is a majority medical control. These centres are located in Baltimore, Newark, Philadelphia, New York, Los Angeles, Oakland, San Francisco, Chicago, Detroit, Cleveland, Scranton, Wilkes-Barre and Reading.

Clinics in other countries, the report states, have been developed as part of general welfare programs, the work usually being supervised by physicians but actually done by midwives. More than 300 centres are reported in fourteen countries, including Great Britain, Germany, Austria, Norway, Sweden, Denmark, Russia, Holland, Egypt, Palestine, China, Japan and India. These centres are described in a forthcoming book by Mrs. Caroline H. Robinson, called "Seventy Birth Control Clinics."

Dr. Robert Latou Dickinson, discussing "The New Marriage Consultation Centres" here and abroad, told the gathering that the birth control clinic would inevitably become a "marriage advice" station and health centre as well. He urged that the church cooperate with social workers and physicians in "creating normal sex life." He said that Mary Ware Dennett's pamphlet "has its place as the Court of Appeals has shown."

Other speakers included Dr. Haven Emerson, Dr. Frederic E. Sondern and Dr. Ira S. Wile.

March 20, 1930

BIRTHS AND NATIONS.

When Theodore Roosevelt denounced race suicide he was not thinking primarily of race peril but of what might be called class peril. The problem was then domestic. It consisted in the refusal to propagate by those elements among the American people to whom the country must look for leadership. That has been until recently the main theme of subsequent concern over declining birth-rates. The eugenists were worried by a depletion of children among the "fit" and the insistence of the "unfit" in doing more than their share. But it may not be long before the eugenic propagandists in America and the countries of Western Europe will be imploring even their biologically inferior countrymen to increase and multiply. That fate would be preferable to the dwindling of the race or nation as a whole and the danger of submergence by inferior races. The scientists of the Robert Brookings Institute at Washington have lately been asserting that among the peoples of Western civilization the process of suicide is well under way. Anglo-Saxons, Germans, French and Scandinavians no longer reproduce themselves, yet it is precisely among these peoples that birth-control continues to win new victories.

When the 1930 census figures on population and allied subjects are published in the very near future, statisticians will be in a position to state at least approximately how far along the road to "stabilization" this country has advanced. That the United States is moving in that direction has for some time been made manifest in the speculations of the experts. Gone are those familiar evocations of a United States sheltering 300,000,000 inhabitants with comfort, or even half a billion with some crowding. Within the next thirty-five years our population will be stationary and the maximum will be fixed at the moderate amount of about 160 millions. Only it is well to remember that to the population expert a "stabilized" population is far from being the cheerful thing viewed by the amateur thinker. What could be pleasanter than a stationary population attained by a low birth-rate and a low death-rate, a population maintained with a minimum of physical and moral cost to the child-bearing and child-rearing masses?

Well, say the scientists, it isn't so simple as all that. The death-rate cannot conceivably be brought down much lower than it has gone in the most advanced countries, while there seems to be as yet no limit to the zeal with which people can be induced to keep down birth-rates. For a man and woman to reproduce themselves they must bear 3.2 children, and in the United States the average seems to be down already to 2.5 children, or thereabout. The statisticians have tests which correct the crude vital statistics and make them seem even more ominous. One such test is to ask how many mothers of the future do 100 mothers of today produce. In Western Europe for 100 mothers today there will be 93 mothers fifty years hence. Carry this process forward several half centuries and the results are self-evident, in the face of all future conceivable victories over death. And while the peoples of Western civilization are dwindling, the Eastern Slavs and the peoples of Asia will be growing, though they too will be experimenting with birth control. The swarms of the Orient may then be tempted to ask for a little elbow-room in the great open spaces of the birth-controlled West.

May 18, 1930

CATHOLICS ASSAIL BIRTH CONTROL BILL

Spokesmen Tell Senators That Proposal Is "Immoral" and "Inimical to Family Life."

GREEN'S OPPOSITION VOICED

Mrs. Sanger, in Rebuttal, Replies to "Misrepresentations," Calls Plan Check to Obscenity.

Special to The New York Times.

WASHINGTON, Feb. 14.—Birth control was denounced as immoral, unmoral, vicious and inimical to family life and the government of the United States and any use whatever of contraceptives as sinful and contrary to the teachings of the Catholic Church, by fifteen witnesses who appeared today before the Senate Judiciary subcommittee headed by Senator Frederick H. Gillett of Massachusetts in opposition to Senator Gillett's bill exempting physicians, hospitals and clinics from the provisions of the Federal laws forbidding the dissemination of contraceptive information or devices.

The bill itself was characterized as "diabolical and damnable" by Redmond F. Kernan Jr. of the International Federation of Catholic Alumni and by William F. Montavon, assistant executive secretary of the National Catholic Welfare Council as "most subversive and impractical," many of the arguments in behalf of which he said were based on "pure animalism."

Representatives Mary T. Norton of New Jersey and John W. McCormack of Massachusetts also opposed the bill.

Women's Support of Bill Denied.

"Marriage," Mrs. Norton said, "is or should be sacred, and the more sacrifice it entails the greater amount of happiness results."

She challenged the statement that thousands of women are sponsoring the bill, asserting it to be a fact that "a very small percentage of women know anything about it," and declared that thirty-three out of thirty-five leading doctors in her State were opposed to the dissemination of such information.

The American Federation of Labor was represented as opposed to the proposed legislation by John Magrady, who appeared by direction of William Green, its president, to present letters written by him in 1925 expressing his own disapproval, afterward confirmed by the executive council of the federation, of a bill to legalize the circulation of birth control information.

It was brought out, however, by Senator Bratton of New Mexico that the matter had never been brought up for decision at any federation convention and by Mrs. Margaret Sanger, in the ten minutes allowed for rebuttal at the conclusion of the hearing, that the measure referred to by Mr. Green was not the Gillett bill, which was introduced for the first time at this session, but a former bill with different provisions.

Misrepresentation Charged.

The references frequently made by several of the witnesses to the Soviet Government in Russia and to birth control as "one of its vicious teachings" were dismissed as "immaterial" by Mrs. Sanger, who reminded the committee that the birth control movement in the United States had preceded the formation of the present Russian Government.

Much of the "misrepresentation" contained in the statement before the committee today, Mrs. Sanger said, was the result of a pamphlet recently sent out by the National Catholic Welfare Conference, a copy of which she submitted and in answer to which she read a letter expressing the surprise and disagreement of the Jewish Bureau of Social Research in New York with the position taken by the conference.

Far from opening the "floodgates" for a "torrent of obscene and pornographic literature," as charged by many of the witnesses, Mrs. Sanger asserted that the bill and its proponents sought "to do away with the unauthorized information and literature now being surreptitiously circulated" by making available to those in need of it the advice of those competent to give advice concerning birth control.

The immensity of the need, she declared, is proved by the thousands of women who regardless of religion come for help to the more than fifty birth control clinics already legally in existence. Of the total number of women who visit the clinics, Mrs. Sanger said, 33 per cent are Protestants, 32 per cent are Catholics and 31 per cent of the Jewish faith.

"They come," Mrs. Sanger said, "not because they do not love children, but because they do love them, to give those children they already have a fair chance for life and health."

Among those who opposed the bill were: Charles Derry, president of Marymount College, New York; Judge Alfred H. Talley, representing the Catholic Club of New York; Charles F. Dolle of the National Council of Catholic Men and Henry W. Cattell, editor.

Holds Bill Degrading to Women.

Dr. Howard Kelly of Johns Hopkins declared the bill to be "infinitely degrading to women." He denounced what he termed the "gross immorality of a pamphlet published in Brooklyn" and written by a woman whose name he did not mention but who was understood to be Mrs. Mary Ware Dennett.

Dr. Kelly asserted that it was his experience that doctors "have been able to give such advice as was necessary to their patients and would continue to do so."

Among others who appeared in opposition to the bill were Miss Agness Regan, National Council of Catholic Women; Mrs. Rita McGoldrick, International Federation of Catholic Alumnae; Mrs. Alice Bicksler, Daughters of Isabella; Miss Mary Mattingly, Sodality Union, Washington, D. C.; the Rev. C. B. Austin, John Sumner, New York Society for the Suppression of Vice; John Ford, New York Supreme Court, representing the Clean Books League, and Ralph Burton, who is presenting the witnesses to Senators Gillett and Bratton of the subcommittee, warned them that "free love is the natural consequence of contraceptive teachings."

February 15, 1931

BIRTH CONTROL REJECTED

Massachusetts Margin Against Proposal Now Totals 200,000

Special to The New York Times.

BOSTON, Nov. 6—A proposal to make it legal for physicians to give contraceptive advice to married women whose health would be endangered by pregnancy was defeated, according to unofficial returns from 1,641 of 1,879 precincts by 896,597 to 695,832. Most of the missing precincts are in industrial communities where the vote in the referendum was heavy.

The proposal was opposed by the Roman Catholic Church through parish committees and supported by the Planned Parenthood League.

Former Mayor Frederick W. Mansfield of Boston, counsel to Archbishop Richard J. Cushing, said the result was "conclusive," but Mrs. Walter E. Campbell, president of the league, said her organization's fight would continue and "the next step will bring victory."

November 7, 1948

PILLS ARE TESTED IN BIRTH CONTROL

Two Studies Report Higher Degree of Effectiveness Than Present Methods

3D SURVEY DISAGREES

Dr. Guttmacher, Evaluating Results, Says Search for Ideal Tablet Persists

By ROBERT K. PLUMB

Two tests of oral contraceptive tablets over the last three years by 1,000 women were reported yesterday to have given a higher degree of conception control than contraceptives now used. However, a third test, using different pills, did not produce the same unequivocal results.

Although the two tests were said to indicate that the tablets were effective, they are not regarded as the ideal method of birth control.

The contraceptive is a combination of two hormones. In the tests, women took the tablets for twenty days of their monthly cycle. Menstruation was normal. Pregnancies occurred when the medication was discontinued.

The compound inhibits the anterior pituitary gland from production of the gonadotrophic hormone. This hormone stimulates the ova to ripen.

Two compounds, Enovid of G. D. Searle & Co., and Norlutin of Parke Davis & Co. were used in the study.

830 Women Tested

In the journal Science for July 10, Dr. Gregory Pincus and his associates at the Worcester Foundation for Experimental Biology in Shrewsbury, Mass., reported on the use of tablets by 830 women in Puerto Rico and Haiti over a time interval covering 8,133 menstrual cycles.

When the tablets were taken as directed, from the fifth to the twenty-fourth day of the cycle, the pregnancy rate for 100 woman-years was found to be 0.2 per cent.

Dr. Alan F. Guttmacher, chairman of the medical committee of the Planned Parenthood Federation of America, said in comment on the results:

"At this point, we regard the new tablets as the first important step in the development of a physiological method of conception control. We do not feel that the present tablets are ideal. In ten years a better conception control method will be available, however."

The reported pregnancy rate when women did not miss taking a tablet is lower than the rate in conventional contraception, Dr. Guttmacher noted.

Dr. Pincus summarized his study by saying:

"For the period studied, the data appear to us to answer the following questions in the manner indicated:

"Is the method contraceptively effective? Yes.

"Does it cause any significant abnormalities of the menstrual cycle? No.

"Does it adversely affect the reproductive tract and adnexae [adjuncts]? No.

"Does it have physiologically adverse effects generally? No.

"Does it affect the sex life of the subjects adversely? No.

"Does it impair fertility upon cessation? No."

Better Agent Sought

Dr. Guttmacher noted, however, that a tablet that had to be taken daily could not be considered an ideal contraceptive. The present cost of the tablets is about 50 cents each, he said. What is sought is a pill that can be taken once or twice a year, and a compound that will not alter the body hormone chemistry in a major way.

Meanwhile, Dr. Joseph Goldzieher of the Southwest Foundation, San Antonio, Tex., said that a third combination tablet, manufactured by the Syntex Corporation, had produced "remarkable" results in a recent test with 188 women over a total of 600 months. None became pregnant and there were no side effects, Dr. Goldzieher said yesterday by telephone.

A third and different study of five tablets in contraceptive use was reported in the April 18 issue of The Journal of the American Medical Association. Patients experienced good and bad side effects in a study directed by Dr. Edward T. Tyler of the University of California at Los Angeles School of Medicine. Dr. Tyler found a pregnancy rate of 8.6 per cent compared with about 4 per cent for other contraceptive methods, he said.

July 10, 1959

Excerpts From World Church Council's Birth Control Study

Following are excerpts from the report of the World Council of Churches' study group on "Responsible Parenthood and the Population Problem":

What considerations should guide parents in the means they employ for the responsible exercise of their procreative power? Responsible parenthood begins with responsible marriage. Biological maturity alone is not the only criterion of readiness for marriage.

Life in the Christian community ought to have prepared the young man and woman to raise their sexual relationship above the domination of mere biological impulse, and to have dominion over it. Further, in the life of grace, not only chastity before marriage but also periodic continence within it, when freely accepted by both the spouses, are virtues of positive worth attainable by Christian people.

But this is by no means the whole of the answer. The extremely high rates of abortion in many regions, Eastern and Western, with their toll of human suffering and violation of personality, testify to a tragic determination among parents to find some means, however bad, to prevent unwanted births. The Christian conscience cannot approve of abortion, involving as it does the destruction of human life, unless, of course, the termination of a pregnancy is necessary to save the life of the mother.

"Life," however, does not begin until the sperm has fertilized the ovum and conception has taken place. Knowing this, what means may Christians properly employ to prevent an individual act of intercourse from resulting in conception? Granted that the attempt may rightfully be made, there appears to be no moral distinction between the means now known and practiced, by the use whether of estimated periods of infertility, or of artificial barriers to the meeting of sperm and ovum—or, indeed, of drugs which would, if made effective and safe, inhibit or control ovulation in a calculable way.

It remains that the means employed be acceptable to both husband and wife in Christian conscience, and that, on the best evidence available, they do neither physical nor emotional harm. Here we would quote some words of a committee of the Lambeth Conference of the Bishops of the Anglican Communion of 1958:

"It must be emphasized once again that family planning ought to be the result of thoughtful and prayerful Christian decision. Where it is, Christian husbands and wives need feel no hesitation in offering their decision humbly to God and following it with a clear conscience. The means of family planning are in large measure matters of clinical and esthetic choice, subject to the requirement that that be admissible to the Christian conscience. Scientific studies can rightly help, and do, in assessing the effects and the usefulness of any particular means; and Christians have every right to use the gifts of science for proper ends."

In conclusion we may quote also Resolution 115 of the same conference, based on the report of this committee:

"The conference believes that the responsibility for deciding upon the number and frequency of children has been laid by God upon the consciences of parents everywhere: that this planning, in such ways as are mutually acceptable to husband and wife in Christian conscience, is a right and important factor in Christian family life and should be the result of positive choice before God. Such responsible parenthood, built on obedience to all the duties of marriage, requires a wise stewardship of the resources and abilities of the family as well as a thoughtful consideration of the varying population needs and problems of society and the claims of future generations."

Aid to Underdeveloped

It is to be observed that such deliberation, and such estimation of human, spiritual and social values, as has been outlined above is well nigh impossible in some of the regions where they are most urgently required. Where there is grinding poverty, a high birth rate, high death rate and high infant mortality, a fatalistic attitude to death is almost inevitable, and a high valuation of human personality is difficult to attain.

Christians in wealthier regions have a duty to ponder, and to act upon, this truth in order to help their fellows in less developed lands toward conditions in which they can enjoy the freedom to make personal decisions of this sort, and to exercise responsible parenthood for themselves. To secure this help the Christian is led by his faith to consider such matters as the need for capital investment and hence his opportunities as a citizen for political action.

The command to love thy neighbor as thyself (Levit. 19:18; Luke 10:27) is thus relevant at all points: it defines the duty of spouse to spouse; of parents to their children and of children to parents; of families to other families in society; of churches to churches, and of nations to nations.

October 7, 1959

Statement by Roman Catholic Bishops of U.S. on Birth Control

Following is the text of a statement in opposition to "artificial birth prevention" issued today by the Roman Catholic Bishops of the United States at the close of their annual meeting here:

For the past several years a campaign of propaganda has been gaining momentum to influence international, national and personal opinion in favor of birth prevention programs. The vehicle for this propaganda is the recently coined terror technique phrase "population explosion." The phrase, indeed, alerts all to the attention that must be given to population pressures, but it also provides a smoke screen behind which a moral evil may be foisted on the public and for obscuring the many factors that must be considered in this vital question.

More alarming is the present attempt of some representatives of Christian bodies who endeavor to elaborate the plan into a theological doctrine which envisages artificial birth prevention within the married state as the "will of God." Strangely, too, simply because of these efforts and with callous disregard of the thinking of hundreds of millions of Christians and others who reject the position, some international and national figures have made the statement that artificial birth prevention within the married state is gradually becoming acceptable even in the Catholic Church. This is simply not true.

The perennial teaching of the Catholic Church has distinguished artificial birth prevention, which is a frustration of the marital act, from other forms of control of birth which are morally permissible. Method alone, however, is not the only question involved. Equally important is the sincere and objective examination of the motives and intentions of the couples involved, in view of the nature of the marriage contract itself. As long as due recognition is not given to these fundamental questions, there can be no genuine understanding of the problem.

At the present time, too, there is abundant evidence of a systematic, concerted effort to convince United States public opinion, legislators and policy makers that United States national agencies, as well as international bodies, should provide with public funds and support, assistance in promoting artificial birth prevention for economically under-developed countries. The alleged purpose, as already remarked, is to prevent a hypothetical "population explosion." Experts, however, have not yet reached agreement on the exact meaning of this phrase. It is still a hypothesis that must stand the test of science. Yet, pessimistic population predictors seizing on the popular acceptance of the phrase, take little account of economic, social and cultural factors and changes. Moreover, it would seem that if the predictors of population explosion wish to avail themselves of the right to foretell population increases they must concede the right to predict production increases of food as well as of employment and educational opportunities.

The position of United States Catholics to the growing and needy population of the world is a realistic one which is grounded in the natural law (which, it should be made clear, is not the law of the jungle, as sometimes erroneously supposed) and in respect for the human person, his origin, freedom, responsibility and destiny. They believe that the goods of the earth were created by God for the use of all men and that men should not be arbitrarily tailored to fit a niggling and static image of what they are entitled to, as conceived by those who are more fortunate, greedy or lazy. The thus far hidden reservoirs of science and of the earth unquestionably will be uncovered in this era of marvels and offered to humanity by dedicated persons with faith in mankind, and not by those seeking short cuts to comfort at the expense of the heritage of their own or other peoples.

'Disastrous Approach'

United States Catholics believe that the promotion of artificial birth prevention is a morally, humanly, psychologically and politically disastrous approach to the population problem. Not only is such an approach ineffective in its own aims, but it spurns the basis of the real solution, sustained effort in a sense of human solidarity. Catholics are prepared to dedicate themselves to this effort, already so promisingly initiated in national and international circles. They will not, however, support any public assistance, either at home or abroad, to promote artificial birth prevention, abortion or sterilization whether through direct aid or by means of international organizations.

The fundamental reason for this position is the well considered objection to promoting a moral evil—an objection not founded solely on any typically or exclusively Catholic doctrine, but on the natural law and on basic ethical considerations. However, quite apart from the moral issue, there are other cogent reasons why Catholics would not wish to see any official support or even favor given such specious methods of "assistance."

Social

Man himself is the most valuable productive agent. Therefore, economic development and progress are best promoted by creating conditions favorable to his highest development. Such progress implies discipline, self-control and the disposition to postpone present satisfactions for future gains. The widespread use of contraceptives would hinder rather than promote the acquisition of these qualities needed for the social and economic changes in underdeveloped countries.

Immigration

Immigration and emigration—even within the same country—have their role to play in solving the population problem. It has been said that migration to other countries is no ultimate solution because of difficulties of absorbing populations into other economies. But it is a matter of record that migration has helped as a solution. Sixty million people migrated successfully from Europe to the Americas in the last 150 years. When the nomadic Indians roamed the uncultivated plains of North America before the coming of these immigrants, the entire country with its estimated Indian population of only 500,000 and its shortage of food, would have been regarded as "overpopulated" according to the norms of the exponents of Planned Parenthood. Yet, the same plains today are being retired into a "land bank" because they are overproductive in a land of 175,000,000. It is, therefore, apparent that to speak of a population explosion in the United States in these circumstances is the sheerest kind of nonsense.

Political and Psychological

The Soviets in their wooing of economically underdeveloped countries do not press artificial birth prevention propaganda on them as a remedy for their ills. Rather they allure them into the communist orbit by offering education, loans, technical assistance and trade, and they boast that their economic system is able to use human beings in constructive work and to meet all their needs. The Russian delegate to the relatively recent meeting of the United Nations Economic Commission on Asia and the Far East proclaimed, "The key to progress does not lie in a limitation of population through artificial reduction of the birth rate, but in the speedy defeat of the economic backwardness of these countries." The communist record of contempt for the value of human life gives the lie to this hypocritical propaganda, but to peoples aspiring to economic development and political status, the deceit is not immediately evident. Confronted on the one hand by the prospect of achieving their goals without sacrificing natural fertility and on the other by the insistance that reducing natural fertility is essential to the achievement of such goals, how could these peoples be reasonably expected to reject communism? Yet, the prophets of "population explosion" in alleging that contraception will thwart communism naively emphasize its specious attractiveness in these areas.

Food and Agriculture

United States Catholics do not wish to ignore or minimize the problem of population pressure, but they do deplore the studious ommission of adequate reference to the role of modern agriculture in food production. The "population explosion" alarmists do not place in proper focus the idea of increasing the acreage yield to meet the food demands of an increasing population. By hysterical terrorism and bland misrepresentation of data they dismiss these ideas as requiring too much time for the development of extensive education and new distribution methods and for the elimination of apathy, greed and superstition. Such arguments merely beg the question, for the implementation of their own program demands the fulfillment of the same conditions. It seems never to dawn on them that in a chronic condition where we have more people than food, the logical answer would be, not to decrease the number of people but to increase the food supply which is almost unlimited in potential.

We make these observations to direct attention to the very real problem of population pressures. Such remarks are not intended to exhaust this complex subject, nor to discourage demographers, economists, agricultural experts and political scientists in their endeavors to solve the problem. Rather our intention is to reaffirm the position of the Catholic Church that the only true solutions are those that are morally acceptable under the natural law of God. Never should we allow the unilateral "guesstimates" of special pleaders to stampede or terrorize the United States into a national or international policy inimical to human dignity. For, the adoption of the morally objectionable means advocated to forestall the so-called "population explosion" may backfire on the human race.

Signed by members of the Administrative Board, National Catholic Welfare Conference, in the name of the Bishops of the United States:

FRANCIS CARDINAL SPELLMAN, Archbishop of New York
JAMES FRANCIS CARDINAL MCINTYRE, Archbishop of Los Angeles.
JOHN CARDINAL O'HARA, C. S. C., Archbishop of Philadelphia
RICHARD CARDINAL CUSHING, Archbishop of Boston
ALOIS MUENCH, Cardinal-Designate, Bishop of Fargo, N. D.
ALBERT MEYER, Cardinal-Designate, Archbishop of Chicago
KARL J. ALTER, Archbishop of Cincinnati
WILLIAM O. BRADY, Archbishop of St. Paul
PATRICK A. O'BOYLE, Archbishop of Washington
LEO BINZ, Archbishop of Dubuque
EMMET M. WALSH, Bishop of Youngstown
JOSEPH M. GILMORE, Bishop of Helena
ALBERT R. ZUROWESTE, Bishop of Belleville
JOSEPH T. MCGUCKEN, Bishop of Sacramento
ALLEN J. BABCOCK, Bishop of Grand Rapids
LAWRENCE J. SHEHAN, Bishop of Bridgeport.

November 26, 1959

U. S. APPROVES PILL FOR BIRTH CONTROL

WASHINGTON, May 9 (AP)—For the first time the Food and Drug Administration has approved a pill as safe for contraceptive or birth control use.

"Approval was based on the question of safety," Associate Commissioner John L. Harvey said today. "We had no choice as to the morality that might be involved.

"When the data convinced our experts that the drug meets the requirements of the new drug provisions our own ideas of morality had nothing to do with the case."

The pill that has been approved is called Enovid. It is made by G. D. Searle and Co., Chicago.

Under the clearance granted by the agency it may be used only on doctor's prescription.

The drug has been on the market for several years but the previous clearance specified it was to be recommended only for treatment of female disorders.

May 10, 1960

RULING DECLINED IN BIRTH CONTROL

Supreme Court Dismisses Attack on Connecticut Law

By The Associated Press.

WASHINGTON, June 19—The Supreme Court declined today to rule on Connecticut laws that make it a crime to use birth control devices or for physicians to advise their use.

The state's ban, dating to 1879, had been attacked by Dr. C. Lee Buxton, chairman of the obstetrics department of Yale Medical School, and two of his married women patients.

Their suits contended that the Connecticut laws deprived them of constitutional freedoms essential to their lives and well being.

Associate Justice Felix Frankfurter announced the court's judgment and noted that Chief Justice Earl Warren and Justices Tom C. Clark and Charles E. Whittaker joined in his views.

Justice William J. Brennan Jr. concurred in a separate opinion. The court's vote thus was 5-4. Dissenters were Justices Hugo L. Black, John Marshall Harlan, Potter Stewart and William O. Douglas.

One of the women who appealed, listed as Mrs. Pauline Poe, 26 years old, has had three pregnancies, each of which produced a mongoloid child who died soon after birth. Her physician said if she had another child it would be a mongoloid and her physical and mental health would be seriously impaired.

Stillbirth Resulted

The other woman, listed as Mrs. Jane Doe, 25, had one pregnancy resulting in a stillbirth. Her physician said another pregnancy would endanger her life.

Justice Frankfurter's opinion said that the complaints by the Poes and the Does "do not clearly" allege that the state threatens to prosecute them for using contraceptive devices. Nor does the state threaten Dr. Buxton with prosecution for giving advice concerning such devices, he indicated.

During the more than three-quarters of a century that the Connecticut law prohibiting use of contraceptives has been on the state's books, Justice Frankfurter said, a prosecution seems never to have begun save in one case. The justice said the circumstances of that one case only proved the abstract character of what was before the Supreme Court today.

The court majority, in declining to rule and dismissing the appeal, said no one had been injured, such as by being jailed or fined, and therefore it was not necessary to decide the constitutional issue.

Long Harlan Dissent

One of the four dissenters, Justice Black, merely said he felt the constitutional question should be passed upon. The other dissenters, however, wrote at more length.

Justice Harlan, for example, used thirty-four printed pages to say why he would hold the law unconstitutional in so far as it purported to make criminal the conduct contemplated by the two married women.

"It follows that if their conduct cannot be made a crime, appellant Buxton cannot be an accomplice thereto," Justice Harlan said.

In a 14-page dissent, Justice Douglas said:

"Can there be any doubt that a bill of rights that in time of peace bars soldiers from being quartered in a home 'without the consent of the owner' should also bar the police from investigating the intimacies of the marriage relation? The idea of allowing the state that leeway is congenial only to a totalitarian regime."

Like Justices Douglas, Harlan and Black, Justice Stewart objected to dismissing the appeal without deciding the constitutional question. He stressed, however, that he was not indicating how he would vote if the constitutional issue were passed upon.

Controversy Is Noted

Justice Brennan, who concurred in Justice Frankfurter's opinion, said he saw no real and substantial controversy calling for a Supreme Court ruling.

"The true controversy in this case is over the opening of birth control clinics on a large scale; it is that which the state has prevented in the past, not the use of contraceptives by isolated and individual married couples," Justice Brennan said. "It will be time enough to decide the constitutional questions urged upon us when, if ever, that real controversy flares up again."

The Connecticut Supreme Court had upheld the laws as a valid exercise of the power of the state's Legislature. Anyway, the state court said, the Poes and Does have, in abstinence from sexual intercourse, an alternative to the use of contraceptives.

Fowler V. Harper of New Haven, argued the appeal on behalf of Dr. Buxton and his patients on March 1 and 2, 1961. Mrs. Harriet Pilpel of New Haven argued on behalf of the Planned Parenthood Federation of America, Inc. Raymond J. Cannon of Hartford, Assistant Attorney General of Connecticut, made the reply argument.

June 20, 1961

Birth Control Taboos Are Easing

Subject Now Open to Public Discussion—Dispute Remains

By HAROLD M. SCHMECK Jr.

Fifty years ago today Margaret Sanger unfolded a daring new tactic in her long fight for public recognition of birth control.

On Nov. 17, 1912, in The New York Call, she began a 13-week series of articles entitled "What Every Girl Should Know." Today, birth control and contraception have achieved public acceptance as important subjects that are legitimate for open discussion.

However, the subjects are still controversial and Mrs. Sanger's fight is far from finished.

Testifying to this is the fact that one of the most active clinics at Bellevue Hospital is not listed on the institution's bulletin boards.

The clinic's purpose is to dispense guidance and prescribe contraceptives for mothers who have a clear medical need for such services.

That it remains unlisted may be partly a gesture of conciliation to a dispute that erupted in the city in 1957 and was settled in 1958. This was the bitter controversy over whether New York City's municipal hospitals should be allowed to provide contraceptive guidance and materials for patients who desired and needed such aid.

Before 1957 they had not done so, although no law forbade the practice.

The Bellevue clinic opened in September, 1958, with one physicians, in a single room. Today it has three physicians, the equivalent of seven rooms, according to its director, and a waiting list so large that some patients have to be seen by appointment outside clinic hours.

Bellevue Clinic Has Long Waiting List of City Patients

Patients Given a Lecture

All advice, services, contraceptive materials or drugs are

free. Each patient is given a lecture on all presently accepted methods of contraception. Then, in consultation with a physician, she is allowed to choose among them. Most patients today choose the new contraceptive pills, according to the clinic's director. Rarely is the rythm method chosen.

The unit is not a birth control clinic in the broad sense of the word. Only mothers who have a clear medical need to avoid further pregnancy are accepted as patients.

Furthermore, each patient must be referred to the unit from one of the other established clinics at Bellevue. Because of this requirement, the clinic seems to have had one unplanned, but most welcome. effect, according to Dr. Hans Lehfeldt, director of the unit.

He said that there was clear evidence that all of the post-birth maternity clinics at Bellevue were being more heavily attended simply because the news had spread that contraceptive guidance was available at a clinic to which one could only be referred bv attending the other clinics.

Strict Criteria Used

In line with the directive of the Department of Hospitals in 1958, the criteria governing the clinic's practices are quite strict. In each case, two physicians must certify in writing their medical judgment that the patient needs to defer future pregnancy and should take contraceptive measures.

The patient must certify in writing that she desires the clinic's services. Each patient is advised to consult with her spiritual adviser and her family.

The medical indications cover a fairly broad range, but they must exit. Conditions considered valid reason for contraception include heart disease, high blood pressure, tuberculosis, diabetes and comparable illnesses that would constitute a hazard to the patient's life if she had another pregnancy. Another important indication is the number of children the patient already has and the span of time over which she has had them. The value of adequate spacing between pregnancies is commonly recognized in private practice.

First Study in 1955

"It is my personal feeling," Dr. Lehfeldt declared, "that our patients should have the same standards of care as private patients."

The vigor with which comparable programs are pursued seems to vary considerably among the other municipal hospitals. Not all have set up specific clinics for the purpose. In fact, a senior officer of the Department of Hospitals said that he did not believe that departmental reports identified any such units as separate clinics. They are simply considered part of each hospital's obstetrical and gynecological services, he said.

Until recent years, no reliable figures on national practices in contraception were available, according to Dr. Christopher Tietze, director of research of the National Committee on Maternal Health, which has offices in the New York Academy of Medicine Building, 103d Street and Fifth Avenue.

The first comprehensive study, based on a small nationwide sample of 2,713 white married women, was done in 1955. he said. There have been others since.

The gist of these seems to be that substantially more than three - quarters of all American married couples practice contraception at some time in their married lives.

Analyses of national preferences in contraceptive methods have tended to yield the same distribution, although all such estimates are probably only tentative.

The most widely used method seems to be the common device worn by the man and described in a recent report as "the male sheath."

It has been estimated that, at any given time, the sheath is the current contraceptive method of slightly more than one-quarter of all couples using any method.

Between 5,000,000 and 6,000,000 gross of the devices are manufactured in the United States annually and about one-fifth of them are exported.

Other Methods Explained

The next most widely used method is the diaphragm — a device worn by the woman to prevent sperm from the male from reaching the upper region of the female reproductive tract. One estimate for current use of this method at any time is slightly less than 25 per cent.

The third method in order of utilization is the rhythm method—the only method sanctioned by the Roman Catholic Church. This is estimated at 21 per cent of current use. One study places the rhythm method slightly above the diaphragm in percentage of users.

There are many other methods. Fourteen altogether were listed in an early draft of a still-unpublished survey of reproductive system research compiled at the National Institutes of Health, Bethesda, Md.

By a considerable margin the three methods mentioned above are the most widely used, although the new oral contraceptive pills have already had a remarkable effect. Two other methods have also attracted a great deal of recent interest among specialists.

Wide Practice Is Cited

One is the use, by the woman, of a spermicidal foam applied to the lower portion of the reproductive organ system. Field tests in Puerto Rico have shown highly promising results.

The other method involves insertion of a plastic ring or coil in the uterus. This has the advantage of acting for relatively long periods with no need for attention from the person using it. Basically, this is an old method held in low esteem by the medical profession because of doubts as to its safety. Preliminary research results suggest that modern variants may be much safer.

Studies have shown that any of the most-used methods—such as Sheath, diaphragm or rhythm—are effective in preventing pregnancy if intelligently and carefully used In practice, however, the oral contraceptive pills have had rates of effectiveness considerably higher than other means except abstinence.

The available evidence seems to indicate that contraception. using one method or another, is widely practiced in the United States and that it is recognized as proper medical practice by a large portion of the medical profession.

Nevertheless, birth control is one topic that still tends to make some public officials reticent and uneasy. It is also true that the laws governing it are full of incongruities and seeming paradoxes.

In Connecticut anyone who uses any kind of contraceptive is committing a crime, but sterilization — which amounts to permanent contraception — has been held legal in case of "medical necessity." About a year ago, a public figure discussing the Connecticut law, said that it "purports to regulate conduct in that most unregulatable of locations, bed."

In Maryland, according to a survey in 1960 of laws on contraception throughout the United States, it is illegal to sell contraceptive devices in slot machines except in places "where alcoholic beverages are sold for consumption on the premises."

States Statutes Vary

In Massachusetts, according to the same survey, the dispensing of contraceptives has been held illegal only if it can be proven that the purchaser did not buy them to prevent disease. And Wisconsin law prohibits a physician from counseling any unmarried woman on contraception.

Despite variously worded laws, however, most states do not actively interfere. The Planned Parenthood Federation of America, the agency most active in this field, considers that only in Connecticut and Massachusetts is there serious interference with birth control or family-planning activies.

Some states have no laws whatsoever concerning this. In several others that do have quite strictly worded statutes, birth control guidance is an integral part of state health department clinic practices.

It seems clear that a principal factor in making the subject of birth control and related matters so sensitive is a difference of belief between the Roman Catholic Church on the one hand and Protestant and Jewish points of view on the other. Although there is, a spread of opinion among individuals in all religious groups, Protestant and Jewish opinion has often been arrayed on the side of birth control during controversies while the Catholic opinion has not.

Ironically, however, it was Protestant majorities that passed restrictive laws related to birth control, even though Catholic opinion seems to be keeping them on the books.

The Catholic viewpoint has been most adamant in opposition to abortion and sterilization.

Roman Catholic View

In an educational pamphlet published in September with ecclesiastical approval, the Rev. Walter Imbiorski of the Cana Conference of Chicago, said:

"Direct sterilization is wrong because man has no direct dominion over his sexual faculties and cannot sterilize himself without going beyond the limits of his authority. Direct sterilization is contraceptive in its purpose and therefore a basic violation of the generative function."

In Catholic belief this attitude also applies to contraception by any method other than the periodic abstinence of the rhythm method. Indeed, Father Imbiorski was discussing the morality of using the oral contraceptive drugs in the above quotation on sterlization.

The Rev. John C. Knott, director of the Family Life Bureau of the National Catholic Welfare Conference in Washington, said that the church considered the primary objective of marriage to be the procreation and rearing of children. It is recognized, however, he said, that there can be valid reasons for a couple to abstain from having children or to limit intentionally the size of their family.

But, to do this by any "artificial" means is not proper because it usurps God's governing function in the union between man and wife. Father Knott contended.

More Research Needed

Father Knott said that further research on human reproduction was certainly needed. He questioned the wisdom of suppressing the much-discussed National Institutes of Health survey in this field. A revised version of the report is expected to be issued soon.

An early draft estimated total financial support for birth control and "closely related" research at about $5,700,000, of which the contribution from Government sources was put at $1,309,000 devoted solely to basic problems of mammalian reproduction. A panel of consultants was quoted as estimating the level of research needs at $12,000,000 yearly.

As persons who have studied it realize, birth and population control constitutes one area of broad significance, but there are two ways of looking at it.

One can think of 50,000,000 new human beings being added yearly to a planet that, in many places, is already crowded and hungry. One can think in more personal terms, of a mother 21 years old who already has six children, not enough to feed them nor enough strength to care for them and no assurance that she will not bear six more before she is a decade older.

Conversely, and this is often lost sight of, one can think of the couple adequately equipped to care for a family and yet unable to bear children.

That a population problem exists is doubted by few intelligent persons. However, at the same time, no one doubts that it will be solved. It always has been in the past. The concern of many thoughtful persons of all faiths, however, is to find, for once in human history some way of dealing with the problem other than leaving it to the traditional, natural safety valves of famine, pestilence and war.

November 18, 1962

Catholics and Birth Control: Growing Debate

By GEORGE BARRETT

The subject of birth control, long regarded by members of the Roman Catholic Church as a dangerously sensitive issue to discuss, is today stirring a profound ferment in the Catholic community.

Discussions among both the clergy and the laity turn often to birth control now as increasing numbers of Catholics discover that the issue, which they have looked upon as a matter of faith and morals beyond their right to question, actually falls within their province to examine.

The dialogues, stemming largely from the crises presented by soaring birth rates and by increasing difficulties encountered by parents trying to raise and educate properly more than two or three children, indicate that the so-called "Catholic attitude" on birth control actually encompasses many attitudes.

It is clear, however, that a shift in emphasis is occurring in large sections of the Catholic Church. The shift is from a traditional church position of almost total condemnation of birth control, a position that derives its moral authority from the story in Chapter 38 of the Book of Genesis in which God was said to have killed Onan for spilling his seed upon the ground in protest against marrying his brother's widow.

A recent meeting of three priests of the Catholic Church in the living room of an apartment on lower Fifth Avenue mirrored the kind of candid dialogues that more and more have been marking Catholic exchanges on the subject.

Quickly Turn to Issue

Their black jackets and collar dickies draped across the backs of their chairs, their shirts of two-tone blue and canary yellow standing out in abrupt contrast, the clerics touched on several of the reforms proposed for the church at the next session of the Ecumenical Council in Rome.

As they relaxed under a portrait of the Magdalena, Ribera's kneeling image of sacred and profane love, the young ecclesiastics turned very quickly to the issue that for many Catholics vividly represents the conflict of sacred and profane love —birth control, in its principle and in its means.

Prompt Disagreement

There was instant disagreement. One priest observed that if an engaged couple announced plans to build up a "family fund" and put off having children for a couple of years—using the church-approved rhythm system of birth control under which sexual relations may be confined to the "safe" period of a woman's cycle—he would refuse to solemnize their marriage.

A second priest looked at him in amazement. He flipped through the pages of the latest copy of Theological Studies. An article in the journal, published for Jesuit theological faculties in this country, instructs priests to stop imposing their theological opinions on parishioners on the issue of planned families.

It stresses that the husband and wife are "almost always the best judges of the reasons they may have for spacing their children or limiting their family."

He noted that the list of valid reasons had been made "quite broad," and he cited other authorities to show that Catholics were no longer under obligation even to consult their confessors whenever they thought it wise to limit the number of their children.

One high cleric, Bishop William M. Bekkers of 's Hertogenbosch, the Netherlands, recently put this quite bluntly in a television interview:

"This is a matter of conscience, which is nobody else's business,"

View Unchanged

As the second priest spoke, his colleague who had opened the discussion listened in silence. When he replied his voice was taut. He said he did not care what the latest theological analysis held—he intended to refuse marriage to such couples.

The dialogue that night, with its clash of opinions, dramatizes the kind of increasingly open expressions that were later disclosed in discussions and interviews with scores of theologians, philosophers, educators, scientists, editors and other members of the clergy and laity in Catholic centers in New York, Boston, Chicago, Buffalo, South Bend, Washington and in San Juan and other Puerto Rican communities. The talks covered all shades of Catholic opinion.

The dialogue also demonstrates that, while there has been an important shift in attitudes on birth control, great sections of the church remain opposed to liberalizing traditional church policies.

Francis Cardinal Spellman, Archbishop of New York, was unavailable for comment about the widening Catholic exchange on the subject. However, Msgr. George A. Kelly, official spokesman on family life for the New York Archdiocese, expressed concern that emphasis on limitation of children often tended to become a "computer operation," a philosophy that denies the richness and fulfillment that an "unplanned family" can provide for the individual, the family and the community.

'Fundamental Right'

"It is obvious that many husbands and wives are justified in practicing the rhythm method for medical, eugenic, economic or social reasons," he declares. "However, the right of the married couple to have as many children as they choose should not be endangered."

Quoting Pope Pius XII, Monsignor Kelly stresses that "the right of parents to have many children is a 'fundamental personal right' bestowed by God—one with which no human institution should tamper."

Monsignor Kelly also presents an argument that forms part of the basis of conservative Catholic opposition to birth control measures on a mass level in underdeveloped nations.

"While supporters of the contraception movement may have idealistic motives, powerful economic, social, religious and political factors are also involved — and the other peoples of the world know it," he said. "Latin Americans, Asians and Africans suspect that they are told that they should stop breeding because they are bringing 'inferior' peoples into the world to outnumber the 'superior' whites."

Some church conservatives contend that more permissiveness, even for the rhythm system, will tend gradually to encourage use of non-approved birth preventive methods, which in turn would tend to encourage sterilization and abortion.

Conservative Position

The basic conservative position is keyed to "Natural Law," which, according to theologians, forbids the use of birth control measures (other than the rhythm system) because they "clearly" interfere with the "natural" God-designed consequences of the marital act. Many conservatives contend that the "natural" purpose of a marriage is to produce as many children as possible.

Three years ago, in the magazine Christ to the World, which is published in Rome under clerical direction, the editors illustrated the conservative position in a footnote at the end of an article on "How to Fight Birth Control." The footnote said:

"Let us note that the obligation laid upon married couples by divine law refers primarily to the procreation of children and normally to the procreation of many children; and it is this duty that we must preach to them. . . . We must, therefore, stress the merit and grandeur, in the eyes of God, of fathers and mothers of big families."

But shifts in Catholic thinking on big families and birth control have been emerging gradually, often subtly.

It was Pope Pius XI, regarded by some Catholics as strict in

EXTENDED DOCTRINE: Pope Pius XII, who sanctioned limiting births in a family through the practice of periodic continence.

Associated Press

INNOVATOR: Pope John XXIII, whose role as tradition-breaker has given rise to speculations on shift in church's attitude.

Camera Press-Pix

PROGRESSIVE: Leo Josef Cardinal Suenens of Belgium, who said church loses members because of its birth control policy.

his condemnation of birth control, who in 1930 commented that married couples were not acting against nature when they practiced marital relations during the wife's sterile period. A liberalized extension was made by Pope Pius XII. He gave explicit sanction as long ago as 1951 for limiting births (through periodic continence) and even for having no children at all.

Views in the Parish

However, the gap that Catholics occasionally note between statements of the Pope and the prescripts of the parish father has been noticeable on birth control.

Until fairly recently, parish approbation customarily was reserved—in many parishes it still is reserved—for the big Catholic family. Mothers with plans to limit the number of their children have often faced parish censure.

"When the Catholic Mother of the Year turns out to be a woman with three children instead of eight or nine I'll believe the church word has reached down to my level," a mother in Chicago said, smiling.

But new trends in living, new discoveries in medicine and science and increased exchanges with non-Catholic groups have raised fundamental challenges to the traditional Catholic attitudes and customs. Consequently, throughout the Catholic world, increasing numbers of theologians, demographers, moral philosophers and sociologists are pursuing a close, and frequently bold, re-examination of many aspects of birth control.

One development in this expanding Catholic inquiry is the establishment of a population study center at Georgetown University, a Catholic institution in Washington. Working with non-Catholic research centers, the Georgetown group will explore the population problem, including ways to try to perfect the rhythm system. One major goal is to help development of what scientists are now calling the "kitchen test" formula by which a woman can easily and instantly pinpoint the period of four or five days each month that she is fertile.

Ironic Overtones

There is irony in this. It may well turn out that opposition of the church to artificial contraceptive devices and the consequent resolve to find a simple, sure rhythm method—perhaps involving a quick saliva, urine or skin test—will produce precisely the quick and uncomplicated birth control system that millions of non-Catholics have been seeking.

In fact, some non-Catholic researchers are quick to point out that there are esthetic, practical or medical faults in all artificial contraceptive devices. They now agree that a perfected rhythm-detection system would probably be welcomed as the "most natural" method and would require a period of sexual abstinence no longer than husbands and wives now usually follow.

The stress these days in Catholic journals and newspapers on the need for birth control techniques that will satisfy theological as well as medical requirements raises the No. 1 question now so often asked of Catholics, a question that plagues and infuriates most of them: "When will the Catholic Church change its stand on birth control?"

The question is resented by Catholics because it obscures the differences between birth control methods; it is resented because it implies that the church has discovered that it has been wrong about birth control and is now seeking a gracious retreat; finally, it is resented because the questioner generally predicts that the church will soon have to accept artificial contraception, which Catholics—virtually unanimously — believe will never happen.

Puzzled by 'Moralists'

(However, some daring comments have been made by Catholics on this sensitive aspect. Last July William J. Nagle, a Catholic writer in an article in The Commonweal, the liberal Catholic weekly, wrote that while he was not himself questioning the validity of the theologians' arguments against artificial contraceptives, he found "somewhat puzzling the head-in-the-sand posture of Catholic moralists on this question." He suggested that the bishops, theologians and philosophers "take a more careful look" at the theological arguments against contraceptives.)

The question about a "change" in the church attitude on contraception may never have to be answered. The birth control ferment has underscored a strange discovery: remarkably little is known by man about his own reproductive system. Men in Catholic science suggest that future physiological discoveries, as well as future refinements in birth preventives, may make the whole matter of "change" unrealistic and even undefinable.

The birth control issue has been stirred by many forces, but the population explosion, probably more than any other single development, has focused widening Catholic attention on the subject.

Catholic literature — and debates in Catholic chanceries and Catholic living rooms—echoes many of the population-growth statistics of the United Nations. These figures tell a staggering tale of permanent hunger for 2,000,000,000 of the world's 3,000,000,000 men, women and children and imply a nightmare of global starvation if births continue at the present rate. It was not so long ago that the entire church rejected any notion that there was a runaway population problem.

There are other factors that have plunged areas of the Catholic world into ferment over birth control.

Loss of Members Feared

For example, in the Catholic press, and in public and private dialogues, Catholics speak with candor these days of the membership "leakage" from the church. Leo Josef Cardinal Suenens, Primate of Belgium, who is a leader of the "progressive" group in Rome's Sacred College of Cardinals, has bluntly asked "whether many people, baptized as infants, do not fall away from the church because of birth control?"

Other elements have been accumulating to prod the church. For example, surveys of Western developed countries show that in many cases Catholic societies reflect approximately the same birth rates as non-Catholic societies. Other studies indicate that it is socio-economic-cultural attainment, rather than church canons, that basically determines the size of the family and the user's selection of a birth control method.

Citing France as an example of a Catholic country where birth control methods condemned by the church are widely in use, Cardinal Suenens has observed that "contraception has made a telling incursion into the country's way of life."

The Rev. Thomas J. Casey, writing in the American Catholic Sociological Review, says he has no reason to doubt the scientific validity of one study that shows "that, for Catholic couples who were married for at least 10 years and who were still fecund and thus likely to have more children, one out of two of them had practiced a method of birth limitation forbidden by the church."

Birth control has become a problem for many Catholics who stay away from church and even for many who faithfully attend mass. Parish priests report that many Catholics have had to be denied the sacraments because they insist on using artificial contraceptives. Parishioners who cannot afford to have more children, who are afraid to rely on the present rhythm system, are making choices that disturb them and disturb their pastors. They continue to go to church—but they go in guilt.

Church moralists have become dismayed by the high rates of abortions and sterilizations in some countries, including Catholic countries. Some clerics are now willing to encourage the practice of family planning as the lesser evil.

Medical discoveries, of course, have contributed to the new uncertainty of Catholics on birth control. Studies in human reproduction—and the discovery of such preventives as oral contraceptive pills—have made it more difficult for traditionalist theologians to apply the principle of "Natural Law" they have been able to invoke confidently against other contraceptive devices.

Finally, it is now a fact in a number of communities that both Catholics and non-Catholics are joining in dialogues in attempts to ward off future battles in the area of community policy. Catholic leaders are urging members of the faith to recognize the moral and civil rights of others in a pluralistic society and to cede gracefully—without surrendering their own moral convictions—to the rule of the majority.

Neither the issue itself nor its resolution in the teachings of the church has been the subject of an infallible utterance by a Pope This is the kind of papal pronouncement that is binding upon all Catholics, without question. One magazine, the Catholic Layman, attempting to stimulate its readers to freer discussion of birth control, assured them last February that "the subject matter, having never been defined as a matter of faith or morals, is well within the bounds of open, intelligent discussion."

The magazine staff may have been a little startled, but it printed an article by a Catholic woman strongly protesting the continued Catholic emphasis on big families and quietly noting, not with irreverence: "The Holy Family of Nazareth was a small family. One Child. And if it is said that because this Child was God there was no need for others, it might also be said that 14 children do not add up more nearly to composing God than do four. Or one."

A few weeks ago The Commonweal also reminded its readers that the teaching of the church on birth control and family planning had not been the subject of infallible pronouncement. The magazine criticized Catholic discussion of birth control as being still too restricted. It observed that, unless the Catholic writer on birth control "simply repeats verbatim the formulas in theological manuals, he is likely to arouse hostility, suspicion or condemnation; the immediate consequence of this pervasive atmosphere of fear is that those most qualified to do some theological probing and questioning shy away from publication altogether — or adopt a stilted, circumlocutionary way of expressing themselves."

To measure the mood of challenge emerging among progressive Catholic groups, go back to the same magazine 20 months ago. Here are some excerpts from that issue:

"The repeated calls by the Church for a major research effort into problems of population growth have all but been ignored. The American Catholic Church — which has the university facilities for such research — has been especially remiss. The related calls for greatly increased work on moral means of family planning have met with only a sporadic and scattered response.

"The far more difficult business of theological work on the morality of family planning has been an equally random affair. But there is, in this area, some important work afoot. To mention only one instance, the view held by many that large families are desirable is being re-examined in our theological journals."

Spirit of Challenge

There are many examples of this spirit of challenge.

A young priest declares:

"I just can't put off real answers to parishioners any more by pointing my finger at my collar and growling, 'There is your answer, that collar is your reason.'"

An eminent church moralist confesses in humility that he and others in his field have sometimes been "too quick on the trigger" to supply answers to questions about birth control by automatic references to medieval revelation theories.

A Catholic demographer, staring out across a great campus, muses: "We know so little about population and about the human physiology, yet we keep making hasty judgments."

A priest, a gentle man, soft in voice, cozily surrounded in his studio by his books, talks of the history of the church, of its famous challengers and fighters, and grins as he says: "What we need, sir, is a new Savonarola!"

When the questioner tries to find out why there has been an apparent upsurge in the spirit of inquiry into birth control matters, the answer is always the same, and even the words are very close:

"It's John."

"Credit John."

Or, simply and affectionately:

"John."

While the late Pope John XXIII has not been identified with any strong position on the birth control and population problem, his historic role as the most "tradition-shattering figure ever to occupy the Chair of Peter" (the description is by The Pilot, the Catholic newspaper in Boston) has inspired those in the church who are seeking reforms, including reforms in church attitudes on birth control.

Some say that Pope John cleared the way for the re-examination of the sensitive issue when he convoked the Ecumenical Council. The Council, which Pope Paul VI will continue, is expected to make far-reaching adjustments designed to enable the church to cope with the revolutionary scientific, political, social and economic changes sweeping the world.

There have been indications that efforts will be made to bar the birth control question from Council debate. However, the Rev. John Sheerin, editor of The Catholic World, has reported that the problem of over-population is scheduled to come up at the Council, and it is believed that this item cannot be long discussed without reference to the birth control issue.

A woman physician in Belgium, a Catholic mother of five, has reported that she wrote to the Vatican about her confusions over the church's official insistence that it is moral to practice birth prevention through rhythm but sinful to use artificial contraceptives. In her appeal for clarification from the forthcoming Council, she wrote that "in each case the intention is precisely the same." and commented that "God will not be deceived."

She has quoted a reply from the Palace of the Holy Office stating that "the question is under consideration and will certainly be dealt with at the Council." Many bishops were "well informed of the difficulties," according to the Vatican reply, "so much so that the decision of the Council will certainly be sought as a result."

Conservatives of the church, convinced that any basic changes or official shifts in attitudes on important issues might confuse the faithful and shake loyalties, are expected to offer resistance to many of the proposed reforms. Pope Paul VI, who has pledged to continue Pope John's reform efforts, may ironically turn out to be, initially at any rate, on the side of the conservatives on the birth control issue.

Three years ago, as Archbishop of Milan, he suggested that perhaps it would be better to speak a little more about the "blossoming" of many childen and a little less about their "limitation."

But the wish of much of the Catholic world for new and liberalized policies on birth control and a host of other issues has apparently crystallized too firmly now to be denied. This wish for reform was captured in a Vatican incident that is now celebrated among liberal Catholics. When Pope John was asked why he had convoked the Ecumenical Council, he opened the nearest window and remarked: "To let some fresh air into the church."

August 5, 1963

Tax Aid to Birth Control Is Rising Across Nation

Public Facilities Are Being Established in 33 States

By AUSTIN C. WEHRWEIN
Special to The New York Times

CHICAGO, March 27 — Tax-supported birth-control assistance in the form of advice, drugs and devices is increasing in all parts of the country.

Public facilities for giving information and materials have been set up or are in the process of being organized in cities and counties of 33 states and the District of Columbia.

[In New York City, because of a recent infusion of Federal funds and a more liberal interpretation of criteria for maternal health, birth-control services for needy families have been growing dramatically.]

A few years ago, the issue of governmental involvement in birth control was considered to be political dynamite. Today,

Senator Gruening of Alaska Seeks a Positive Approach

all levels of government — Federal, state and local — are engaged in birth-control aid.

The change is due to several factors: subtle shifts in the Roman Catholic viewpoint, the increasing role of the Federal Government and the development of oral contraceptive pills.

In his State of the Union Message, President Johnson called for "new ways to use our knowledge to help deal with the explosion in world population."

But even before this spur, the Federal Government had been rapidly expanding its role and encouraging local birth-control activities.

Yet there is no explicit Congressional authorization to do so, except in the District of Columbia, nor is there an exact accounting of how Federal money is spent on birth control.

This week Senator Ernest Gruening, Democrat of Alaska, moved to tidy up the situation. He drafted a bill "to coordinate the information available on birth-control research in all nations."

"Our approach at the Federal level should be positive, not permissive," he said, adding:

"Individuals have the right to know what information and aids are available to them upon request."

Mr. Gruening's move illustrated a feeling among some authorities that the change, which amounts to a social upheaval, is still too slow and confused. For others, it is much too fast.

In California, Dr. Leslie Corsa, chief of the State Board of Maternal and Child Health Bureau, said in a telephone interview:

"Everywhere birth control has been pushed, it has moved. But the speed is relative. The absolute speed is moderate."

In Milwaukee, Alderman Richard B. Nowakowski, an opponent of a proposed $59,980 Federal grant for five birth-control clinics, said:

"We will have 'sexmobiles' moving around the streets passing out birth-control information to whomever wants it — just like popcorn wagons."

Chicago to Start Program

Here in Chicago, whose population is 45 per cent Catholic, the Board of Health, using Federal funds, will start next month the voluntary dissemination of birth-control advice and pills to married and unmarried women who want them.

"There is no opposition because we aren't going to pass out pills on street corners, and the program is medically oriented," an official said.

A similar program was approved yesterday in New York, where the State Board of Social Welfare voted to make birth-control information available to unmarried welfare recipients if they were the heads of families.

The ruling, which was opposed by Catholic leaders, will provide help to unwed mothers and fathers as well as to unmarried persons who are responsible for other members of their households. It also makes explicit the board's policy of providing free birth-control service to all welfare clients who seek it on their own.

Only two years ago in Illinois a proposal for a similar state program was attacked by Catholics as one to promote "adultery, fornication and prostitution," and an avenue to later sterilization, legalized abortion and even mercy deaths.

In Corpus Christi, Tex., where the first birth-control program was approved under the anti-poverty program, the first month saw the establishment of four neighborhood Planned Parenthood clinics in the "poverty strip," a section embracing 52,000 of that seaport's 190,000 population.

In Detroit, which has a Catholic mayor and which is also the recipient of Federal funds (like Chicago, from the Department of Health, Education and Welfare), social workers may initiate the subject.

Said one of them:

"How can we teach survival and advance freedom of knowledge of our poor, all voters, mothers, all fathers responsible for directing their young, if they are not to be trusted with biological facts relating to their socio-economic plight?"

In the state, the four-member Michigan Welfare Commission, which includes a Catholic priest, adopted a policy last week similar to that of Detroit It is aimed at the 41,000 women receiving aid for dependent children.

Pill Called Significant

The development of oral contraception — the pill — and other simplified devices have made birth-control practice easier, especially among the poor, social workers say.

Along with this has been a liberalizing of the medical indications for birth control. This contrasts to the policy a few years ago in most tax-supported hospitals of withholding birth-control therapy unless life was endangered. Medical indications now cover the whole family environment.

According to the Information Center on Population Problems, there were 450 public birth-control clinics two years ago, and now there are 700. In 1963, a total of 11 states had tax-supported programs; now 33 states and the District of Columbia either have or will have public birth-control clinics serving 200,000 medically indigent women.

Symbolic of a turn in Catholic thinking, the Duluth (Minn.) Catholic Service Agency has just set up a family planning service for all faiths. Although it is confined to the church-approved rhythm method, the step was taken because of "exploding population around the world and the problems of individual familes here at home."

The switch is in part, but not entirely, due to the shift in the Catholic viewpoint. The effect of that change is still uneven.

At Notre Dame University, George N. Shuster, assistant to the president, wrote in the introduction of the Notre Dame Press Book on Population published this week:

"The population problem has two aspects, one of them statistical and the other moral. All demographers, whether they be Catholic or not, are agreed that mankind must henceforth limit its power to procreate."

But in Milwaukee, Dr. John Brennan, a spokesman for Catholic opposition, advocated in a telephone interview an individual and strictly local approach, commenting:

"The worst catastrophe would be a sudden drop in the birth rate. It would be bad for the automobile business and home building."

In Cleveland, the spokesman for the Catholic diocese, Msgr. Francis W. Carney, has denounced Dr. John A. Rock, the co-developer of a contraceptive pill, as "a moral rapist using his strength as a man of science to assault the faith of his fellow Catholics."

Nonetheless, in the light of past attitudes, Catholic opposition has generally shown a marked softening. In Massachusetts, where state law prohibits the sale, distribution and advertising of contraceptives, Richard Cardinal Cushing has lent support to repeal, saying contraception was a question of private morality.

The organized medical profession itself has shifted its attitude. Last December the American Medical Association's House of Delegates dropped its "neutral" stance and backed both private and public birth-control clinics, provided doctors ran them.

The chairman of the A.M.A. human reproduction committee, which implements the policy, is Dr. Raymond T. Holden a professor of obstetrics, at Georgetown University, in Washington. A Catholic, he said recently:

"The fact that we can begin to talk about this within the Church—and recognize a problem exists — was helpful to me."

When the A. M. A. changed its view last December it was said that the increasing use of birth-control pills was a major cause. This week the A. M. A. maternal and child care committee said that the use of plastic intrauterine contraceptive devices was generally recognized as "inexpensive and effective."

Doctors, the committee said, had a major responsibility in this area because of the "increasing demand by the public for a simple, inexpensive and effective method" of birth control.

In Albuquerque, N. M., which has applied for a $17,600 Federal grant for birth-control clinics, a planned education program (including movies) among the community's 69,000 Latin Americans, Indians and Negroes would stress both the intrauterine and the rhythm methods.

Smaller Families Sought

There has also been a sociological shift. The baby boom after World War II has given way at all social levels to a desire for smaller families.

"Women say they can take better care of the children they have when they know they're not going to become pregnant again this year, as they have in so many other years," said a public nurse in rural Williamson County, Tenn., where one of the state's 18 clinics is located.

There has been, too, a complicated set of coincidences related to the rapid urbanization of the country and the spread of the Negro ghettos.

In Cook County (Chicago) for example, annual aid to dependent children costs $90 million, and 90 per cent of those receiving such aid are found among 25 per cent of the Negro population.

Nationally, the illegitimacy rate has tripled since 1940, and the children's aid program, heavily burdened by unwed mothers, has grown to 4 million cases, costing $1.5 billion. In 1955 there were $639 million. In short, there is a tax saving in birth control.

In Mecklenberg County (Charlotte) N. C., which has a birth-control clinic considered a model of its kind, Wallace Kuralt, the county welfare director, has said that a pill program has saved taxpayers $250,000 in children's aid since 1960. "We are spending a dollar to save $25," he said.

What is the Federal role in this social change?

In 1959, President Dwight D. Eisenhower said that birth control was not a proper governmental function. Since then, and into the Kennedy Administration, the population expansion has been more and more a matter of governmental concern.

In the foreign field, the Agency for International Development, aware that aid to underdeveloped countries was outpaced by new babies, stands ready to give other nations almost any birth-control help they seek, other than contraceptives or equipment to make them.

Policy Found Fuzzy

The agency has just granted $44,800 to the Jamaica Family Planning Association, a private group, for two trucks and related equipment to be used in an educational effort.

Although millions in Federal money is already flowing into a variety of birth-control activities directly and indirectly, there is no plain record of the total amount, nor is there a clear high-level policy.

In fact, the program, of which Chicago is a part, was authorized last April by Dr. Arthur J. Lesser, deputy chief of the Children's Bureau, without asking the approval of Anthony J. Celebrezze, the Secretaty of Health, Education and Welfare. In an interview in Washington, Dr. Lesser said:

"The decision I made was consistent with the policy followed over the years."

He insisted that any "family planning" involvement of the department was a "clinical activity in accordance with the policy of state and local health departments."

Last June Mr. Gruening asked Mr. Celebrezze, a Catholic and a former Mayor of Cleveland, to detail the extent to which department funds were used for family planning. A Celebrezze assistant wrote this to the Senator:

"We have regarded the question of family planning as one for individual decision and would raise no question about the provision of such service by a physician to his patient within the normal scope of the doctor-patient relationship. Whether or not a state chooses to include such services as part of the scope of medical care for which the state will pay, using Federal-matched funds, is entirely a matter of state discretion."

The Senator's staff said that other efforts to get more details had failed.

This is how the Federal Government operates in the birth-control field:

The Office of Economic Opportunity has approved the use of funds for birth control in Corpus Christi, Tex.; Oakland, Calif., and the District of Columbia.

At least 10 other places have applied for this kind of help, although the agency declines to discuss them. The grant to Milwaukee has been stalled by Catholic opposition. The money is on a 90 per cent grant basis, and the agency must take responsibility for the projects, in effect. The bulk of the birth-control projects are proposed by existing Planned Parenthood organizations.

The Volunteers in Service to America (VISTA)—the domestic Peace Corps — also stands ready to help in birth control.

In either program the agency insists on wide community acceptance as a precondition for a grant.

At the Department of Health, Education and Welfare, there are three major avenues.

One is that of "special projects" under a $15 million appropriation last year for aid to maternal and child health and mental retardation.

It was from this appropriation that Dr. Lesser of the Children's Bureau approved family planning services in New York City, Chicago, Baltimore, Detroit, West Virginia, San Juan and Ponce, P. R.; Minneapolis, Philadelphia, Portland, Ore., and Augusta and Atlanta, Ga.

The grants vary from $73,723 for Minneapolis to $1,748,614 for New York, and the purposes also vary. Minneapolis, for example, will only make referrals to the local Planned Parenthood chapter.

Secondly, there is a Children's Bureau maternal and child health program that dates back to 1935 when the Social Security Act was passed. The current appropriation is $35 million, and it is primarily to enable states to improve a variety of services to mothers and children.

This money is channeled without strings to states. Although

Senator Ernest Gruening

it has rarely caused comment, Dr. Lesser said that to his knowledge for at least 20 years Virginia and North Carolina had used Federal money for birth-control clinics. Other experts believe this was true also for many years in Mississippi, Alabama, Florida, Georgia and South Carolina.

There is, however, no record in Washington because the states are free to use the funds for general health purposes without giving details to Washington.

"We can't get the cost [of birth control] any more than we can get the cost of taking a blood count," Dr. Lesser said.

Speaking for Mr. Celebrezze, Dr. Edward W. Dempsey, a special assistant for medical affairs, said in an interview:

"The purpose is to promote health, not to promote birth control. It is a decision by doctors on the scene, subject to local restraints."

The department does have a record of 25 states where local clinics provide family planning services. Dr. Lesser and Dr. Dempsey think all use the Children's Bureau money in this area to some degree.

Research Is Supported

(The Planned Parenthood Federation said that as recently as two years ago birth-control programs were operated in tax-supported institutions only in about a dozen states, most of them in the South.)

Thirdly, the Department of Health, Education and Welfare supports a far-flung research program through its National Institute of Child Health and Human Development. Its goal is high quality offspring. Its starting point is behavior patterns prior to mating, and the terminus is the baby at 8 weeks of age.

There are 280 research projects for which slightly more than $7 million has been earmarked.

In 1962, a report on this activity was suppressed for a time. Then it came to light that the Federal Government was financing more than half of the known research dealing directly or indirectly with birth control.

The official position is that the research, most of which is farmed out to universities, is concerned with the whole process of reproduction and that birth control is only a part of it.

March 28, 1965

High Court Bars Curbs on Birth Control; Finds Connecticut Law Invades Privacy

7-to-2 Ruling Establishes Marriage Privileges —Stirs Debate

By FRED P. GRAHAM
Special to The New York Times

WASHINGTON, June 7—The Supreme Court struck down the Connecticut birth-control law today in a sweeping decision that established a new constitutional "right of privacy."

In a 7-to-2 ruling the Court invalidated the 1879 law, which forbids the use of contraceptives by anyone, including married couples.

The seven justices in the majority were divided on the proper constitutional provision to use in striking down the law, but they agreed that married couples had private rights that could not be abridged in such a manner.

The majority ruling was written by Justice William O. Douglas. It touched off a controversy as the two dissenters, Justice Potter Stewart and Justice Hugo L. Black, charged that the decision revived the Court's earlier policy of striking down legislation that it considered unreasonable, even when the law did not violate a specific provision of the Constitution.

The dissenters said that in lieu of a specific constitutional prohibition against laws invading a citizen's privacy, the Court should not rely on vague concepts of "fundamental rights" or "liberty" to strike down a repugnant law.

The Court had avoided striking down the Connecticut law in two previous cases by holding that the law was not properly before it.

In 1942 it refused to rule on a doctor's claim that the law violated his rights to counsel his patients about contraceptives. The Court held he could not challenge the law on behalf of his patients, but only for himself.

In 1961 a group of women contended they could not get birth control advice needed for reasons of health. The Court said their claim presented no real controversy because the law had never been enforced against users of contraceptives, but only against birth control clinics.

In the case decided today two leaders of the Connecticut Planned Parenthood League had been fined $100 each for operating a birth control clinic in New Haven.

The Clinic Is Closed

Mrs. Estelle T. Griswold, executive director of the league, and Dr. C. Lee Buxton, a professor at the Yale Medical School and medical director of the clinic, were arrested on Nov. 10, 1961 and charged with aiding and abetting their patients to violate the law. After the arrests the clinic was closed.

In the majority opinion, Justice Douglas said the arrests of the Planned Parenthood leaders created a controversy that the Court could properly decide, one involving "the constitutional rights of married people with whom they had a professional relationship."

He said "the specific guarantees in the Bill of Rights have penumbras" that reached areas not specifically mentioned in the amendments. He cited six different amendments — the First, Third, Fourth, Fifth, Ninth, and Fourteenth — that create a "zone of privacy" violated by the law's restrictions on married couples.

A View of Marriage

Justice Douglas declared:

"We deal with a right of privacy older than the Bill of Rights—older than our political parties, older than our school system. Marriage is a coming together for better or for worse, hopefully enduring, and intimate to a degree of being sacred. The association promotes a way of life, not causes; a harmony in living, not political faiths; a bilateral loyalty, not commercial or social projects. Yet it is an association for as noble a purpose as any involved in our prior decisions."

Five justices joined in three concurring opinions holding there was a constitutional right of privacy, but disagreed upon which provision of the Constitution created it.

Justice Arthur J. Goldberg said in a concurring opinion signed by Chief Justice Earl Warren and Justice William J. Brennan that the Ninth Amendment protected "fundamental rights" not specifically mentioned in the Constitution and the Bill of Rights.

The Ninth Amendment says: "The enumeration in the Constitution, of certain rights, shall not be construed to deny or disparage others retained by the people."

Justice Goldberg said: "The Ninth Amendment shows a belief of the Constitution's authors that fundamental rights exist that are not expressly enumerated in the first eight amendments and an intent that the list of rights included there not be exhaustive."

Black's Doctrine Rejected

Justice Goldberg rejected the doctrine long advocated by Justice Black that the Fourteenth Amendment incorporated all of the Bill of Rights into the amendment's due-process clause and made them applicable to the states. This would limit the list of constitutionally protected rights of those specifically listed in the Bill of Rights, he said.

Instead, the due-process clause absorbs only "those specifics of the first eight amendments which express fundametnal personal rights." Justice Goldberg said. All other "fundamental rights" are protected by the Ninth Amendment, he said.

In a separate concurring opinion Justice John W. Harlan agreed that the Constitution's guarantees against state restrictions on personal liberty should not be limited to those parts of the Bill of Rights that have been "incorporated" into the Fourteenth Amendment by Supreme Court decisions.

He said the Fourteenth Amendment's due-process clause alone protects persons against state laws that violate "basic values 'implicit in the concept of ordered liberty.'"

Justice Byron R. White's concurring opinion agreed that the due-process clause, which prohibits states from depriving any person of "liberty" without due process of law, was clearly violated by the restrictions of the Connecticut law.

The willingness of the five concurring justices — Warren, Goldberg, Brennan, Harlan and White — to strike down a state law for violating such concepts as "ordered liberty," "liberty," and "fundamental rights," drew bristling dissents from Justices Black and Stewart.

They saw the case as a turning point toward increased judicial activism similar to the early years of this century, when the court struck down many state laws as "unreasonable" deprivations of property without due process of law.

Justice Black—who has been known as a "judicial activist" himself in recent years — recalled a list of cases in which the Court held invalid state and Federal laws regulating business and labor matters as "unreasonable."

These decisions eventually brought the court into conflict with the New Deal and precipitated President Roosevelt's "court-packing" plan. The Court abandoned the due-process approach in 1937 in the famous turnabout under which the Court took a "hands off" attitude toward economic legislation.

Privacy is a "broad, abstract and ambiguous concept" that can be expanded or shrunken by later court decisions, Justice Black declared.

He said the Ninth Amendment was not intended to give the Court a veto over state and Federal legislation.

In a separate dissent Justice Stewart said there was nothing in general in the Constitution that protected citizens against nvasion of their privacy by state laws. Although he thought the law was "silly," he felt it could be eliminated only by the Connecticut Legislature.

Since the decision was based on the violation of private rights by prohibiting use of contraceptives, constitutional lawyers were uncertain as to its effect on other birth control laws.

On May 13, the Hempstead, L.I., police arrested a former medical student, William R. Baird of 1269 G Street, Valley Stream, for dispensing birth control devices and advice. He told reporters that he would appeal his conviction under the New York law in an attempt to have it declared unconstitutional.

Thomas I. Emerson of New Haven argued for the appellants in today's case. Joseph B. Clark, assistant prosecutor, Sixth Circuit Court of Connecticut, argued for the state.

Today's long session was the final one of the 1964 term of the Court. After a summer recess the Justices will convene the 1965 term on Oct. 4.

June 8, 1965

Udall Offers Help On Family Planning

By WILLIAM M. BLAIR
Special to The New York Times

WASHINGTON, June 19 — The Department of the Interior became today the first Federal agency to offer direct birth-control advice and services, including contraceptives.

Secretary of the Interior Stewart L. Udall announced that three departmental agencies had been directed to offer guidance on family planning and birth control to American Indians on reservations, natives of the Pacific Trust Territory and Indians, Eskimos and Aleuts in Alaska.

These groups are all under the department's jurisdiction.

Mr. Udall's action reflected a policy laid down by President Johnson, who said in his State of the Union Message to Congress last Jan. 4 that he would "seek new ways to use our knowledge to help deal with the explosion of the world population and the growing scarcity in world resources."

Previous Role

The Federal Government heretofore has played no direct role in birth control although it has operated in areas indirectly connected with the problem. It has assisted research and training in demography and reproductive biology, and population studies and research have been encouraged in foreign aid programs.

The Interior Department's move, however, permits the supplying of contraceptives to interested persons, under the control of Federal physicians.

Whether the move would be a forerunner of other Federal action could not be immediately determined.

Behind the move is a belief by officials that the United States could not afford to tell other countries what they should do on a national level while little was being done on a Federal level in this country.

Up to now, officials noted, only local welfare programs fostered birth control services. These officials also commented that the Interior Department was the only Federal agency operating direct social and welfare programs with a group of people such as the American Indians.

The move was taken after discussions with the Public Health Service of the Department of Health, Education and Welfare. The Public Health Service administers health programs among American Indians on reservations. The Health Education and Welfare Department through the National Institute of Health, has been a main source of grants for research and training in reproduction biology.

Open debate on the population control issue appears near in Congress, where 10 bills have been introduced on the subject Most of them propose creation of offices in various departments of the Government to collect and distribute information on family planning at home and abroad. Some bills propose a White House conference to consider the problem.

President Johnson's State of the Union Message gave the Interior Department a cue. The question of furnishing information or services on birth control and planning had often arisen within the department.

The birth rate among reservation Indians and other groups under the department's jurisdiction runs well above the national average. Officials in the trust territory and among Indian tribes have posed the question in Washington from time to time in connection with various social services extended to the areas.

'Entirely Voluntary'

Mr. Udall specified that all services were to be "entirely voluntary" and that such services should "not be a prerequisite to receipt of the benefits of or participation in any program or activity."

In a memorandum to the Commissioner of Indian Affairs, the director of the Office of

Territories and the director of the Bureau of Commercial Fisheries, Mr. Udall said:

"In the past, on some Indian reservations and in some Indian communities in Alaska and in areas of the territories, inadequate education, welfare or medical services have deprived residents of the area of birth-control and family-planning advice and services generally available to other people in major metropolitan communities.

"In some of these areas the available natural resources will not be adequate in future years unless existing population growth rates decline.

"To the extent possible within the Department of the Interior's authority and resources, it is the policy of the department to seek new ways to use our knowledge to help deal with the explosion in world population and the growing scarcity in world resources."

Mr. Udall's directive authorized physicians employed by the Office of Territories "to offer appropriate birth-control advice and services to their patients, consistent with the patient's culture and conscience, or refer patients to appropriate persons."

"Social service workers," he directed, "are authorized to refer persons who for various personal reasons may decide that pregnancy should be avoided to appropriate public or private medical services."

The directive covered the contingency that some persons, particularly those in the Pacific trust islands, might have religious scruples against contraceptives or other artificial means of preventing pregnancy. The Roman Catholic Church does not sanction contraceptives but authorizes a rhythm method based on a woman's infertile days.

If Federal physicians approve requests for contraceptives, this will be the first time that the Government has dispensed them.

June 20, 1965

Margaret Sanger Is Dead at 82; Led Campaign for Birth Control

Special to The New York Times

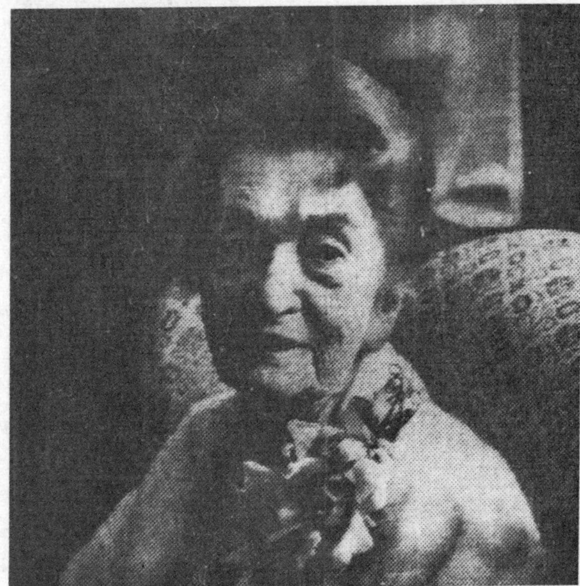

The New York Times

Mrs. Margaret Sanger as she was honored at the Waldorf-Astoria in 1961 at conference on "world population crisis."

TUCSON, Ariz., Sept. 6—Margaret Sanger, the birth control pioneer, died this afternoon of arteriosclerosis in the Valley House Convalescent Center. She would have been 83 years old on Sept. 14.

Mrs. Sanger was the widow of J. Noah H. Slee, owner of the Three-in-One Oil manufacturing concern. She is survived by two sons by her previous marriage to William Sanger, Dr. Stuart Sanger and Dr. Grant Sanger, and eight grandchildren.

A funeral service will be held at 11 a.m. on Thursday at St. Philip's-in-the-Hills Episcopal Church here. A memorial service will be conducted in Stuyvesant Square, New York City, at 11 a.m. on Wednesday, Sept., 21 Burial will be in Fishkill, N.Y.

Toward World Acceptance

As the originator of the phrase "birth control" and its best-known advocate, Margaret Sanger survived Federal indictments, a brief jail term, numerous lawsuits, hundreds of street-corner rallies and raids on her clinics to live to see much of the world accept her view that family planning is a basic human right.

The dynamic, titian-haired woman whose Irish ancestry also endowed her with unfailing charm and persuasive wit was first and foremost a feminist. She sought to create equality between the sexes by freeing women from what she saw as sexual servitude.

An active worker for the Socialist party, her friends, included radicals of all shades—John Reed, Mabel Dodge Luhan, Bill Haywood, Emma Goldman, Alexander Berkman, and Jessie Ashley.

The phrase "birth control" first appeared in 1914 in her magazine, Women Rebel, which bore the slogan "No Gods; No Masters!" on its masthead.

In her days on the barricades of the birth control movement, Mrs. Sanger presented a figure not easy to forget. Many a policeman escorting her to the station had his ears wilted by Irish invective.

Trained in the methods of public demonstrations, she also could call attention to herself and her cause in more restrained environments.

Lawrence Lader, one of Mrs. Sanger's biographers, told of meetings called by a wealthy birth control advocate to discuss the movement. When her guests were deep in discussion of the problem, she would "telephone Margaret."

"Wearing a simple black dress (the more radical the ideas the more conservative you must be in your dress) Mrs. Sanger would arrive in the doorway.

"And now here is the woman who can answer all your questions. With it was a dramatic entrance that led easily into a short talk on birth control and often won new converts."

Mrs. Sanger was the daughter of Michael Hennessy Higgins, a tombstone cutter in Corning, N.Y., who was described as "a philosopher, a rebel and an artist." Mr. Higgins specialized in chiseling angels and saints out of stone. His wife—Mrs. Sanger's tubercular mother—was Anne Purcell Higgins, who died at 48 after bearing 11 children.

Mrs. Sanger herself was afflicted with incipient tuberculosis in 1903, the year after her marriage to Mr. Sanger, an artist and architect. The Sangers moved to Saranac N.Y., in the Adirondacks, from a New York City apartment that had been a gathering place for Socialists.

"Almost without knowing it you became a 'comrade,'" Mrs. Sanger later wrote her husband of this period of their lives.

The Sanger living room had become a place where liberals, anarchists, Socialists and Wobblies (members of the Industrial Workers of the World) could meet.

"My own personal feelings drew me toward the individualist, anarchist philosophy . . . but it seemed necessary to approach the idea by way of Socialism," she later wrote.

Trained as a nurse, she was educated at Claverack College in New York. She also studied at White Plains Hospital and Manhattan Eye and Ear Hospital.

Mrs. Sanger's life work began shortly after she returned to New York in 1912. It resulted from her job as a nurse for maternity cases, principally on the Lower East Side. Many of her patients were wives of small shopkeepers, truck drivers and pushcart venders. Others were from a lower stratum of society.

"These submerged, untouched classes were beyond the scope of organized charity or religion," she wrote. "No labor union, no church, not even the Salvation Army reached them."

The young nurse saw them, weary and old at 35, resorting to self-induced abortions, which were frequently the cause of their deaths.

Mrs. Sanger nursed one mother, close to death after a self-inflicted abortion, back to health, and heard the woman plead with a doctor for protection against another pregnancy.

"Tell Jake to sleep on the roof," the physician said.

The mother died six months later during a second abortion.

Mrs. Sanger soon renounced nursing forever.

"I came to a sudden realization that my work as a nurse and my activities in social service were entirely palliative and consequently futile and useless to relieve the misery I saw all about me."

For nearly a year the ex-nurse read every scrap of material on contraception. In 1913, she went to France and Scotland to study birth control conditions, returning the following year.

Her magazine, Woman Rebel, was the spearhead of her movement. In an early issue she specified seven circumstances in which birth control should be practiced: when either spouse has a transmittable disease; when the wife suffers a temporary infection of lungs, heart or kidneys, the cure of which might be retarded in pregnancy; when a mother is physically unfit; when parents have subnormal children; if the parents are adolescents; if their income is inadequate, and during the first year of marriage.

The articles adhered to New York's Comstock law, which made it a crime to offer contraceptive information. Nevertheless, most of the issues of the Woman Rebel were banned by the New York Post Office.

In August, 1914, Mrs. Sanger was indicted on nine counts of sending birth control information through the mails and was made liable to a prison term of 45 years.

She stood virtually alone. Even progressive women, Socialists and physicians offered her no assistance. Fighters for women's suffrage seemed more concerned with the vote than with Mrs. Sanger's immediate problem.

On the eve of her trial, Mrs. Sanger fled to Europe without the court's permission. There, she met H. G. Wells and became a friend of Havelock Ellis, the author of the pioneer study "Psychology of Sex."

During her absence, Anthony Comstock, secretary of the New York Society for the Suppression of Vice, went to Mrs. Sanger's home, represented himself to Mr. Sanger as an impoverished father in search of aid and bought a birth control pamphlet from Mr. Sanger. For this sale. Mr. Sanger served a month in jail.

The indictment was quashed in 1916, shortly after she returned to this country. But Mrs. Sanger found that the indictment had aroused worldwide interest in the movement and she decided to take a step beyond the propagandizing then carried on by the National Birth Control League.

Mrs. Sanger and a sister, Mrs. Ethel Byrne, a trained nurse, opened a birth control clinic on Oct. 16, 1916, in the Brownsville section of Brooklyn. The clinic, at 46 Amboy Street, was the first birth control clinic in the United States.

Associated Press

Mrs. Margaret Sanger at a 1931 Senate hearing on bill to legalize dissemination of birth control data by physicians and clinics.

The legislative approach, Mrs. Sanger wrote, "seemed a slow and tortuous method of making clinics legal; we stood a better and quicker change by securing a favorable judicial interpretation through challenging the law directly."

Mrs. Sanger served 30 days in jail, but the case laid the groundwork for subsequent court rulings enabling physicians to give contraceptive advice "for the prevention or cure of disease."

Her sister went on an eight-day hunger strike in Brooklyn's Raymond Street Jail after her arrest.

Despite continued legal harassment, Mrs. Sanger's work was increasingly accepted. In 1937, a year after the Comstock law was reinterpreted to provide for distribution of contraceptive information, the American Medical Association adopted a report that recognized birth control as part of legitimate medical practice.

In addition, she was the author of a number of books on birth control, including "What Every Girl Should Know."

Mrs. Sanger's often picturesque struggles with the police and her differences with the Roman Catholic hierarchy furnished the birth control movement with ample publicity. On Nov. 14, 1921, when Mrs. Sanger arrived at Town Hall on West 43d Street to take part in the discussion, "Birth Control: Is It Moral?" she found the police closing the meeting.

In the angry pulling, shoving and shouting that followed, Mrs. Sanger left the platform with two policemen. A disorderly conduct charge against her was dismissed the next day. The New York Times account of the interrupted meeting stated that the police intervention was "brought about at the instance of Archbishop Patrick J. Hayes of this Roman Catholic Archdiocese."

Honors Came Later

Fifteen years later Town Hall was the scene of a ceremony in which the Town Hall Club gave Mrs. Sanger its annual Award of Honor for the most conspicuous contribution of the year to the enlargement and enrichment of life.

Three months ago her years of birth control advocacy appeared to be making an inroad in Rome. Reports from the Vatican indicated that a more liberal Roman Catholic position was possible as a result of a three-year Vatican study of the problem.

A majority of the 60 clerical and lay members of a commission originally appointed in 1963 by Pope Paul VI was reported to have accepted a position of leaving the matter of specific birth control techniques to the individual Catholic conscience.

Last month, a group of mothers, children and college students demonstrated in front of St. Patrick's Cathedral in New York to protest the Roman Catholic Church's ban on artificial methods of birth control. In contrast to police action at many rallies when Mrs. Sanger and her supporters were chased, there were no hecklers outside the cathedral. Among the mutterers and headshakers were many who accepted leaflets with smiles.

She and her adherents won a notable victory when, on Jan. 6. 1936 in the famous case of "The United States v. One Package." United States District Court Judge Grover Moscowitz decided that Dr. Hannah Stone, a physician, could legally receive a contraceptive device sent to her by a physician in Japan. Subsequent interpretations of his decision greatly broadened the scope of the circulation of birth control devices and artificial birth control information.

During one of Mrs. Sanger's visits to Europe the National Birth Control League was reorganized under the leadership of Mary Ware Dennett and Clara Stillman. Mrs. Sanger retained control of the New York State Birth Control League and later became the president of Planned Parenthood.

Mrs. Sanger's American Birth Control League, established in 1921, became the Planned Parenthood Federation of America in 1946 and led to the establishment of more than 250 Planned Parenthood Centers in 150 cities throughout the country. The movement is now worldwide, with 38 member organizations and projects in 88 countries.

Welcomed Abroad

"It was she who convinced America, and the world that control of conception is a basic human right and like other human rights must be equally available to all," said Dr. Alan F. Guttmacher, president of the Planned Parenthood World-Wide Association.

On a visit to Japan, Mrs. Sanger was received with great cordiality by members of the Japanese Government. She was the first woman to address the Japanese Diet. She was also warmly received by the late Jawarharlal Nehru of India. Her views on birth control were widely circulated throughout the Far East and in Africa.

Mrs. Sanger was heard from in firm tones when, in September, 1958, a controversy arose in New York over the refusal of Dr. Morris A. Jacobs, the city's Commissioner of Hospitals, to sanction birth control therapy in the hospitals.

Interviewed by telephone in her home in Tucson, Mrs. Sanger called the policy upheld by Dr. Jacobs "disgraceful." Mrs. Sanger was then nearing her 75th year and was still active as president of the International Planned Parenthood Federation.

Opposed Kennedy in 1960

From her Arizona home Mrs. Sanger kept up her fire of statements and letters to newspapers in behalf of birth control. Her disagreement with the Roman Catholic Church led her to say in 1960 that if Senator John F. Kennedy was elected President she would leave the United States. She opposed Mr. Kennedy because of his religion.

In an interview some weeks later Mrs. Sanger said that she had been informed that Senator and Mrs. Kennedy were both "sympathetic and understanding toward the problem of world population. I will wait out the first year of Senator Kennedy's Administration and see what happens."

During her long career many institutions honored her for her work. The degree of Doctor of Letters was conferred upon her by Smith College in 1949.

Mr. and Mrs. Sanger were divorced in 1921 after having been separated for several years.

In 1922, Mrs. Sanger was married to Mr. Slee. The industrialist, who died in 1941, contributed large sums to the birth control movement. During her marriage to Mr. Slee, she continued to use the name of Margaret Sanger.

September 7, 1966

Study Finds Birth Control Used By Most Catholic Wives 18-39

By DONALD JANSON
Special to The New York Times

SOUTH BEND, Ind., Dec. 2—A nationwide study based on interviews with 5,600 married women of all faiths indicated that a majority of Roman Catholic wives between the ages of 18 and 39 no longer conform to church doctrine on birth control.

About 25 per cent of the women in the samples were Catholic, approximately the proportion of Catholics in the population.

The survey was conducted by National Analysts, Ind., of Philadelphia. Comparable surveys for noting trends were conducted by the University of Michigan's Social Research Center in 1955 and 1960.

The results of the survey were presented tonight to the fifth annual Notre Dame Conference on Population by Prof. Charles W. Westoff of Princeton University and Prof. Norman B. Ryder of the University of Wisconsin.

The two sociologists reported that the proportion of Catholic wives complying with the church's ban on contraceptives had declined from 70 per cent in 1955 to 62 per cent in 1960 and 47 per cent last year. The 1965 study, directed by Dr. Westoff and Dr. Ryder, was sponsored by the National Institute of Child Health and Human Development.

Dr. Westoff, chairman of Princeton's department of sociology, told a dinner meeting of the conference that the proportion of married couples

Orren Jack Turner

Prof. Charles W. Westoff of Princeton, who presented results of the survey.

using contraceptives was up substantially since 1960 among Catholics and non-Catholics alike.

He said that the appearance of the birth control pill in 1960 had contributed significantly to this rise, with proportionately greater use by non-Catholics than Catholics. He said the study showed that the pill had replaced the rhythm method for avoiding conception for many Catholics and had also attracted couples of all three major faiths who had previously used other contraceptives.

Dr. Ryder, director of the University of Wisconsin's Population Research Center, said that the increased use of contraception had been accompanied by a parallel decline in fertility, with the American birth rate falling 22 per cent since 1957.

The decline has accelerated in the last two years, he said, "and the simultaneous acceleration in the adoption of oral contraception is unlikely to be merely a coincidence."

But, he said, the decline in the birth rate also reflected a reversal in the nineteen-sixties of a post-World War II trend toward bearing children at earlier ages. In recent years, he said, women are getting married a little later, waiting longer to begin having children, and adding to their families at longer intervals.

Dr. Westoff said that defiance of church doctrine by Catholic wives included a large proportion of women who report regular church attendance.

For those who go to mass every week, he said, conformity with doctrine has plummeted from 78 per cent in 1955 to 69 per cent in 1960 to 56 per cent last year, a pattern matching the rate of decline for Catholic women as a whole.

The most recent statement by Pope Paul VI on birth control was on Oct. 29. He said that he needed more time to decide on the question and, in the meantime, Catholics must abide by church rules against artificial contraception.

The sociologists said that the deliberations of church officials may partly account for the decline in conformity since 1960 because it has created expectations of a more lenient stand.

But they noted that the trend to nonconformity had begun long before the deliberations began.

The three-day conference is being held on the Notre Dame campus under the auspices of the university's new Institute for the Study of Population and Social Change.

Prof. William T. Liu, director of the institute, said in an interview that the first two of the five conferences held here were closed, unpublicized meetings. The meeting this weekend is being attended by 50 specialists in sociology, theology, law, medicine, biology and other disciplines, many of them from the Notre Dame faculty. The meetings are also open to interested students and others.

A spokesman for the university said that research in sociological subjects and the humanities had markedly increased at Notre Dame since George N. Shuster, former president of Hunter College in New York, came to Notre Dame in 1960.

Dr. Shuster is assistant to the president at Notre Dame and director of the university's Center for the Study of Man in Contemporary Society, of which the Institute for the Study of Population and Social Change is a part.

Dr. Westoff reported tonight that the birth control pill seemed to have been adopted "primarily" by couples who would otherwise have used other methods of preventing conception.

'Increasing Rate'

He said the use of the pill had "increased at an increasing rate" since 1960 till "by the time of our interviews in late 1965, 33 per cent of white women and 29 per cent of non-white women never using any method reported having used the pill."

Among those who practiced birth control, 36 per cent of the Protestants and 25 per cent of Catholics and Jews favor the pill. Its use increases as the level of education rises, the survey shows.

Dr. Westoff said that the proportion of Catholic women who sought to regulate fertility exclusively by the use of rhythm had decreased from 27 per cent in 1955 to 25 per cent last year.

December 3, 1966

A.M.A., in Reversal, Favors Liberalizing Of Abortion Laws

By DONALD JANSON
Special to The New York Times

ATLANTIC CITY, June 21—The American Medical Association took an unequivocal stand today in favor of liberalizing abortion laws.

The action by the A.M.A.'s policy-making House of Delegates is expected to speed a slowly developing trend toward the liberalization of state laws.

It marked the association's first policy change on the subject since 1871.

The 242-member House adopted the statement by a voice vote. The presiding officer, Vice Speaker Russell B. Roth, said there was "significant but inadequate opposition." The 216,000-member association is the chief spokesman for organized medicine.

In the discussion preceding the vote, a spokesman for the opposition, Dr. Joseph P. Donnelly of Jersey City, asserted that "what you are doing here is opening up vast new changes in American medicine."

Dr. Edward C. Hughes of Syracuse, a past president of the American College of Obstetrics and Gynecology, said that the change would not "open the door to misuse."

He said it was "timely" for the association to lay down guidelines for changes in state laws because change was on the horizon anyway and association guidelines would help insure that "changes will be made properly."

The new association policy condones abortion under the following conditions:

¶To safeguard the health or life of the mother.

¶To prevent the birth of a child with a physical or mental defect.

¶To terminate pregnancies resulting from rape or incest.

The policy statement follows recommendations in the model penal code of the Ameirican Law Institute. It distinguishes between therapeutic and criminal abortion by insisting that abortions be induced only in an accredited hospital by a licensed physician, in consultation with two other qualified doctors who have examined the patient and concurred in writing on the need for the operation.

"It is to be considered consistent with the principles of ethics of the American Medical Association," the statement said, "for physicians to provide medical information to State Legislatures in their consideration of new legislation regarding therapeutic abortions."

Most state laws permit abortion only to save the mother's life. The opposition of the Roman Catholic Church to abortion for any reason has been instrumental in blocking liberalization in all parts of the country.

This year, however, California, Colorado and North Carolina modified their statutes in line with the recommendations of the model penal code.

A similar bill has been passed by the Florida Senate. Legislation was introduced this year for changes or study commissions in 19 other states.

A national public opinion poll last year found that a majority approved the kind of change now advocated by the A.M.A.

"There is unmistakable evidence of restiveness in all segments of the population regarding our current therapeutic abortion practices," said the report of the association committee recommending liberalization. "It is clear that change and reform in this area is inevitable."

The report called the new policy "a reasonable and conservative approach to the problem."

The report followed an 18-month study that the committee said confirmed that the association's 96-year-old policy intended to guide doctors had been vague and "antiquated."

The policy adopted by the House of Delegates in 1871 held it "unprofessional for any physician to induce abortion or premature labor" without consultation with another physician "and then always with a view to the safety of the child."

The new policy endorses therapeutic abortion when the doctor has "documented medical evidence" that the pregnancy could threaten the life or mental or physical health of the patient or could produce a mentally or physically defective infant.

The statement was modified in floor debate to take note that "there are many physicians who on moral or religious grounds oppose therapeutic abortion under any circumstances."

In 45 states, abortion is legal only to save the life of the mother. As many as half the therapeutic abortions performed in the United States are recommended by psychiatrists to preserve the mother's mental health.

The action was taken before more than 1,000 doctors in the crowded Pennsylvania Room of Haddon Hall. Ten thousand physicians are attending the annual convention. The total registration, including guests and industrial exhibitors, is 33,000.

The House chose Dr. Dwight L. Wibur of San Francisco as the association's president-elect by acclamation. His term will begin next June. His election marked the first time the son of a former president of the association had been elevated to the presidency of the 120-year-old organization.

Dr. Wilbur, a 63-year-old internist, is the son of Ray Lyman Wilbur, who was Secretary of the Interior in the Cabinet of President Herbert Hoover and later chancellor of Stanford University.

June 22, 1967

JESUIT MAGAZINE ASKS BIRTH CURBS

Catholic Editors See Need for Contraception in a 'Sound Family Life'

By EDWARD B. FISKE

America, the Jesuit weekly, has called for the easing of the Roman Catholic Church's ban on contraception.

In an editorial in the Sept. 30 issue, the editors ally themselves with Catholic doctors who see "the compatibility—and even necessity—of some use of contraception in the life of the genuinely Catholic family."

They say that it is "obviously too early" to determine whether such views will prevail in the church, but declare: "In our judgment, they should."

The editorial also urges that the issue of birth control be considered by the Synod of Bishops, which convenes next week in Rome.

The 58-year-old magazine, which is edited by priests in New York and has a circulation of 89,300, is an official publication of Jesuits in the United States and Canada.

It normally takes a conservative to moderate position on theological issues, although its views have become increasingly liberal in the last year or so. It has, for instance, repeatedly endorsed study of the question of whether priests should be permitted to marry.

A spokesman for the editorial board, who preferred not to be identified, said yesterday that the editorial was intended to "further responsible discussion of a thorny pastoral problem that is undoubtedly on the minds of every bishop now on his way to the synod."

The editorial quotes an unidentified but "distinguished" Catholic physician as saying that, in his opinion, "contraception is essential for a sound Catholic family life."

"Without reliance on contraception in certain situations, it is not possible for most couples to achieve the values proclaimed by the church as part of the marital state," the doctor declared.

Doctrinal Clash Seen

"The church will have to change her doctrine either on contraception or on marriage. It is no longer possible for the church to maintain them both."

The editors decline to estimate how many Catholic doctors hold similar views, but they predict that there will soon be "many" who see "positive as well as negative human values in the use of contraception in certain situations."

"Since doctors are engineers, by definition, when it comes to human life and health," the editors say, "it is impossible for many of them to see the sense of the absolute 'natural law' prohibitions on particular physical techniques.

"So long as the technique is not harmful to anyone else and can be genuinely useful for the client's bodily and psychic health, how can nature forbid it?

"Contraception, as distinguished from abortion, does not kill anybody and it can provide substantial relief for couples who have serious medical reasons for temporarily or permanently avoiding a pregnancy."

The editorial also suggests that the use of contraception could assist the "achievement of authentically Christian family values," even in the absence of medical justification.

"How can couples give themselves to each other and to their children in the unselfish traditions of Christian love when another pregnancy in the family is a constant—and justified—worry?" it asks.

The editors say the physicians endorsing such views "are not challenging the teaching authority of the church." Rather, they explain, the physicians are contributing medical data to the theological discussions going on in the church.

"They fully accept the responsibility of married couples to contribute to the continuation of the race," the editorial declares. "The doctors are talking about the use of contraception to assist in having and keeping healthy, responsibly sized and truly Christian families."

The editors do not specify the kind of contraception they would favor, and do not discuss any moral distinctions between various methods.

According to Catholic teaching the only morally permissible means of limiting births are abstinence from sexual relations and the rhythm method, or abstinence during a period of the month when the wife is able to conceive.

Pope Paul VI has reserved for his personal action a decision on whether to modify the church's traditional opposition to birth control, and the subject is not on the list of topics to be discussed by the Synod of Bishops, which will advise the Pontiff on a number of major issues, such as mixed marriages.

However, the American editorial, which was titled "Contraception and the Synod of Bishops," says:

"As the bishops meet in Rome to discuss the problems of the church, there are few questions as urgent as those surrounding the use of contraception for the achievement of a truly Christian marriage."

September 23, 1967

Birth Control Pills: A Balance Sheet on Their National Impact

By JANE E. BRODY

Mrs. David G., a lithe 35-year-old brunette, began taking oral contraceptives after the birth of her third child. But now, two years later, she has given up the pill because, she says, "I became so irritable and depressed that my family couldn't live with me."

Mrs. Richard D., a young newlywed, gave it up after she developed throbbing, incapacitating headaches that had no other apparent cause.

Still another former pill user is Mrs. William F., 25. She explains: "I didn't have any problems with the pill, but I was worried about what might happen. My mother kept showing me articles about how dangerous it could be."

These women are typical of those who have become disenchanted with the pill. Nine million women are now taking oral contraceptives, making the pill the leading birth control method in the nation today. But in recent years numbers of women have stopped taking them.

The actual number of former users cannot be determined. In the last nationwide survey, made in 1965, it was found that about one-third of women who had taken the pill had stopped using it. Birth control experts believe that about one in three pill takers are still stopping after two years of use.

The survey was done by Dr. Charles Westoff of Princeton University and Dr. Norman Ryder of the University of Wisconsin under a contract with the United States Public Health Service. It indicated that about one-fifth of the former users had stopped taking the pill because they wanted to become pregnant or because they no longer needed contraception.

But 80 per cent of the women who discontinued the pill did so because they were uneasy about the method, worried by the "scare" reports, or plagued by annoying side effects.

Various reports have linked the pill to a long list of serious illnesses, among them blood clots, strokes, sight-threatening eye disease, sterility, diabetes-like upsets in sugar tolerance and even cancer.

How much validity have these reports? What has medicine learned about the side effects and diseases that have been associated with pill use? Is the woman who takes the pill risking her life for the surety and convenience of this method of contraception? If so, how great a risk is she taking?

Interviews with many physicians in the business of prescribing and studying oral contraceptives and a review of the medical literature have revealed that no definitive answers to these questions are currently available. But, there are enough indications of problems associated with pill use to keep hundreds of researchers busy pursuing the answers.

Although most obstetricians consider oral contraceptives of minimal risk to most women, opinions about their safety vary widely from doctor to doctor, depending largely upon the physician's personal experience.

Those who are far removed from prescribing oral contraceptives, such as cancer specialists and pharmacologists, tend to be more cautious and concerned than those who deal daily with women in need of effective contraception.

Other Bigger Risks

Dr. D. M. Potts, medical secretary of the International Planned Parenthood Federation, summarized general thinking among pill proponents when he pointed out that many aspects of social behavior, such as drinking and cigarette smoking, carry a much greater risk than the pill.

"From the point of view of the health of society," he says, "it would be more justifiable to have oral contraceptives in slot machines and restrict the sale of cigarettes to a medical prescription."

Statistics are lacking on the current practices of physicians in prescribing oral contraceptives. But a 1967 survey by the American College of Obstetrics and Gynecology showed that 87 per cent of the nation's obstetricians prescribed the pill more often than any other method of contraception, and that only a tiny percentage—less than 1 per cent—would not prescribe them for anyone under any circumstances.

Recent studies of the adverse effects associated with oral contraceptives seem to have made physicians more cautious about prescribing the pill. Doctors interviewed said that they were now following their pill patients more closely than at first.

Decided pill skeptics like Dr. Louis Lasagna, a noted pharmacologist from Johns Hopkins University, hold that since the pill is not completely free of risk, it should be prescribed only for those women who are unable or unwilling to use mechanical contraceptive techniques effectively.

Hazards Not Defined

In general, pill skeptics are disturbed by the fact that assurances given to women about the pill's safety are usually based on studies that, because of their design and scope, could not have clearly defined any hazards, if indeed they exist.

The most frequent difficulties surrounding the use of the pill involve the temporary but often troublesome side effects common to the first three months on the pill. Several of these effects — nausea, vomiting and breast tenderness—represent the body's adjustment to the pseudopregnancy induced by the hormones in oral contraceptives.

The various brands of the pill all consist of man-made versions of two natural female hormones, progesterone and estrogen. They work by preventing ovulation (the release of an egg from the ovaries), which normally occurs once a month except when a woman is pregnant.

The incidence of temporary side effects associated with the pill has been substantially reduced with the recent introduction of low dose oral contraceptives. Studies show that the effects bother fewer than 10 per cent of women who use brands containing only one milligram of hormones.

Obstetricians who have both private and clinical practices note wryly that the incidence of side effects seems to be considerably higher among their private patients. Dr. Hans Lehfeldt, head of the family planning clinic at Bellevue Hospital, says, "Some of our clinic patients are so highly motivated that they won't tell us their side effects because they're afraid we'll take them off the pill."

Physicians, who have been urged to notify the Food and Drug Administration of untoward effects occurring in women who are taking oral contraceptives, reported 1,034 cases of serious disorders to the agency during a three-year period that ended Dec. 31. These cases, which included 118 fatalities, involved such disorders as blood clots, cancers and hepatitis.

An F.D.A. spokesman said that the reports merely serve as an early warning system; they do not mean necessarily that the pill was in any way responsible for the ailments in question. They simply mean, the spokesman said, that the women were taking the pill when the ailment was diagnosed.

Of the serious disorders that have been linked to the pill, clotting problems are the only ones for which there is enough evidence to have convinced the majority of physicians that a real hazard exists.

Soon after oral contraceptives were introduced in this country, doctors began noticing and reporting the occasional occurrence of thrombophlebitis (clot formation and inflammation in a vein, usually in the leg), thromboembolism (in which the clot breaks loose and moves through the blood vessels) and stroke in young women who had been taking oral contraceptives.

But there was no way of knowing how often tihs occurred nor how common clotting disorders were in nonpregnant young women who were not on the pill.

Big Risk Shown

Last spring, two British research teams published findings that indicated that women who took oral contraceptives faced a nine times greater risk of being hospitalized with thrombotic disease and a seven times greater risk of dying of it.

The hospitalization study, conducted by Dr. M. P. Vessey and Richard Doll, both of the British Medical Research

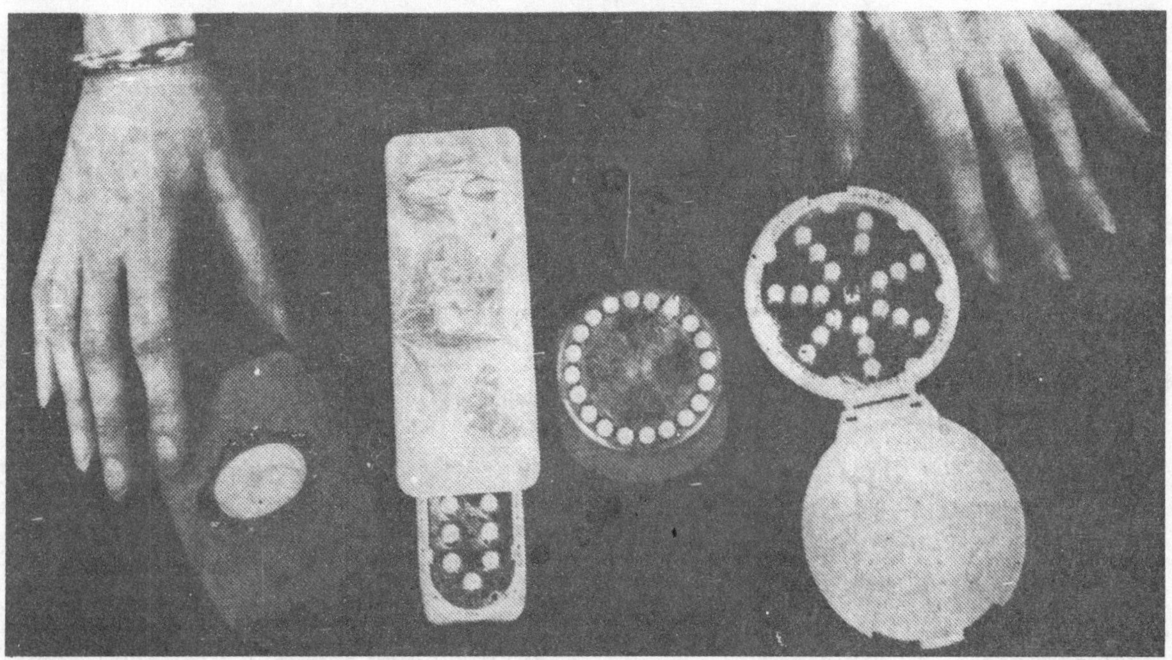

The New York Times

Contraceptive pills are supplied in various types of containers, some looking like combs and compacts and the like

Council, involved 58 women with thrombophlebitis or thromboembolism who had no condition that might have predisposed them to clotting disorders.

When the use of oral contraceptives among these women was compared with pill use among a control group of 116 women of similar age and family status who were hospitalized for other reasons, the researchers found that 45 per cent of the clot patients had been using oral contraceptives the month before they became ill, but only 9 per cent of the control group had been pill users.

In the mortality study, Dr. Vessey and Dr. W. H. W. Inman of the British Committee on Safety of Drugs investigated the use of oral contraceptives among 385 women of childbearing age who had died of clotting disorders. When compared with a control series of 998 women, the researchers found that oral contraceptives could account for an average of three deaths among 100,000 pill users each year.

Many Minimize Risk

Many doctors are inclined to minimize this risk. Dr. Potts of Planned Parenthood points out, for example, that the risk of death associated with pregnancy is about 15 times greater than that associated with the pill.

Considering the risk of pregnancy associated with other contraceptive techniques, Dr. Potts concludes that "a woman who takes oral contraceptives has more chance of being alive one year later than her sisters who choose to have a baby or use some other form of contraception."

But pill skeptics note that many women can use other contraceptives successfully and that although the pill is a virtually foolproof contraceptive if taken as directed, it is not known how many women on the pill become pregnant because they fail to follow the directions.

The British findings concerning the pill and thrombotic disease are not directly applicable to the United States because the incidence of these disorders may be different among American women.

Dr. Philip Sartwell of Johns Hopkins University is directing an extensive American study, scheduled for completion this summer, that should establish whether pill-taking American women face an increased risk of this disorder.

Meanwhile, the Food and Drug Administration has cited clotting disorders as possible side effects of oral contraceptives and has warned doctors against prescribing the pill for women with a history of such disorders. But the agency says that a cause and effect relationship has not yet been established.

Researchers are now seeking to determine which women are most likely to be prone to clotting disorders. The British study showed, for example, that women over age 35 are nearly three times more likely to suffer pill-related clotting disease than are younger women.

On the basis of British and American research, many doctors now believe that migraine headache, which is characterized by changes in the blood vessels, may be a warning sign of clotting troubles ahead. Migraine headaches nearly always occur on only one side of the head at a time and are often accompanied by nausea and visual disturbances.

Lesser Risk in Type O

An international study just published in the British journal Lancet has indicated that women with blood types A, B or AB are three times more likely to develop clotting disorders while on the pill than women with blood type O.

The authors from Sweden, Britain and the United States, say that although their findings are preliminary, they offer a further clue to physicians who are trying to determine which of their pill patients may be at high risk of developing thrombophlebitis or thromboembolism.

Another serious question related to the use of oral contraceptives is whether they may cause or promote the growth of cancer. In the last few weeks, vague reports have circulated in medical circles that pill use may lead to an increased risk of cancer-like changes in the cervix.

These reports are based on two unpublished, highly controversial studies — one by Dr. Myron Melamed of Sloan-Kettering Institute and Dr. Hilliard Dubrow, a New York gynecologist, and the other by Dr. George Wied of the University of Chicago.

Changes in Cervix

The New York study, which involved the records of 35,000 Planned Parenthood clients, reportedly found that cancer-like changes of the cervix (called carcinoma in situ) were twice as common among pill takers as among diaphragm users. The Chicago study is reported to have found a six

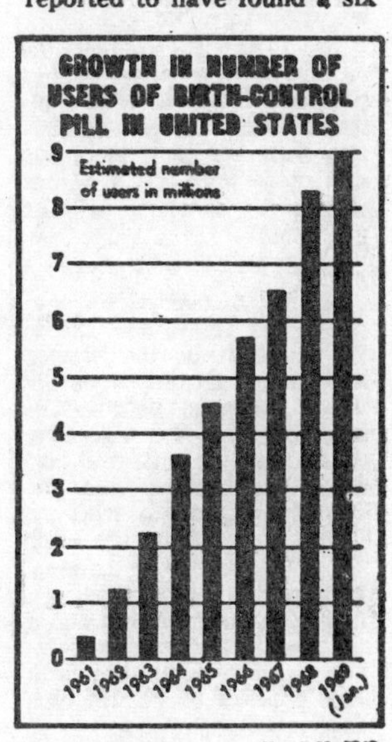

times greater risk of this disorder among women on the pill.

Two other, as yet unfinished, studies have found no evidence to date to support or refute the findings of the Melamed and Wied studies.

In a recent interview, Dr. Wied said that even with the Melamed study, "there is absolutely no evidence whatsoever that usage of the pill will per se lead to an increased incidence of cervical cancer."

Dr. Wied added that neither his nor the Melamed study took into account the fact that cervical cancer was most common among women who start having intercourse early in life and who consort with many men. He said he was now doing a study taking this fact into consideration.

Several doctors also have pointed to recent studies linking cervical cancer to a common virus, the genital herpes virus, which is known to be transmitted through sexual contact. If a virus indeed causes cervical cancer, then women who use a contraceptive like the diaphragm, which protects the cervix, would presumably be less likely to "catch" cancer.

Many physicians and virtually all clinics require their pill-taking patients to return at least once a year for a Pap smear, which is capable of detecting cervical changes up to three years before they may become cancerous.

Reports in the medical literature linking the pills to serious eye damage also have caused some concern. These reports have been based, not on controlled studies, but on a series of cases of eye abnormalities occurring in women using the pill.

Dr. Elizabeth Connell, director of the large family planning clinic at Metropolitan Hospital in Spanish Harlem, lent her own alert eye and more than 1,000 of her clients to a study of the problem.

Most Had Eye Troubles

Much to everyone's surprise, she found that about 75 per cent of the women had eye abnormalities of varying degree before they began taking the pill. Even after three years of oral contraceptive therapy, the percentage of women with eye disorders remained the same.

The Food and Drug Administration still warns physicians to be on guard for eye abnormalities in pill patients, but the concern about the problem appears to be diminishing.

Jaundice has been found to occur in a small percentage of pill takers, and the FDA advises doctors not to prescribe the pill for women who have had liver diseases or who have had jaundice during past pregnancies.

Diabetic-like disturbances in sugar metabolism have also been noted in a small percentage of pill-taking women. One authority on the subject, Dr. William Spellacy of the University of Miami Medical School, has found that the women most susceptible to increases in blood sugar while on the pill seem to have the same characteristics as women who tend to become diabetics later in life.

These characteristics include obesity, a strong family history of diabetes and abnormally high blood sugar levels during pregnancy. Affected women also tend to be older and have several children, and their babies tend to be large at birth.

Based on present knowledge, Dr. Spellacy says, "I couldn't say one way or another whether the pill can cause diabetes." He added that at this point he would only hesitate to prescribe the pills "for ladies who fit all six high-risk criteria."

Some physicians have reported that a number of women who stopped taking the pill in order to become pregnant have found themselves to be infertile for varying periods of time. These physicians suggest that the body's hormone factory responsible for producing fertile eggs may have difficulty resuming activity after being out of operation while the woman was on the pill.

Other doctors have countered that many of these women may have been infertile to begin with or became so coincidentally while they were on the pill. Some obstetricians recommend that their patients periodically go off the pill for a month or two to be sure their bodies are still functioning normally.

Other Problems

A variety of psychological problems also have been attributed to the pill. Among them are depression, irritability and decreased libido. Studies to date have shown, however, that at least as many women report an increase as report a decrease in libido while taking the pill, and many more women say they feel "better" or "happier" than say they feel "blue."

Several studies indicate that many women who do become depressed while on the pill are unhappy about having to take the pill in the first place.

Long before all the hazards of oral contraceptives are clearly defined, chances are that the pill in its present form will be passé. Several variations are currently under study that eliminate estrogen, the pill component suspected of being its main troublemaker.

Thousands of women around the world are already experimentally using one of two new nonestrogen types: a hormone injection designed to give contraceptive effects lasting one, three or six months, and a minidose oral pill that, like the present pill, is taken daily.

Some Drawbacks

Both these methods are regarded as having drawbacks: although they minimize the anxieties surrounding continuous estrogen intake, they both tend to cause irregular bleeding to an undesirable extent.

Another nonestrogen approach, still in the laboratory, involves implanting a contraceptive chemical under the skin within a time-release capsule. It is hoped that this approach will eliminate the bleeding problem by keeping constant the rate at which the body is dosed with the chemical.

Work on the "morning-after" pill, taken only after intercourse during a woman's fertile period, has been hampered by the fact that the chemical used is an estrogen that can, among other things, upset the menstrual cycle and cause nausea.

The outlook for innovations in male fertility control at present seems rather bleak.

Meanwhile, Metropolitan Hospital's Dr. Connell, who admits with some embarrassment that she is the mother of six, says:

"The pill is what we've got to work with. No one with a clinic population like ours is going to quit using the pill unless something really terrible happens."

"But," she adds, "we'll keep alert for any trouble and go ahead with our evaluations and observations. At the moment, aside from the social aspects, the odds of medical trouble with pregnancy are infinitely worse than any of the current methods of contraception."

March 23, 1969

NIXON PROPOSES BROADER U.S. AID IN BIRTH CONTROL

Urges Creation of Panel to Study the Implications of Rising Population

PRESENTS GRIM REVIEW

Message to Congress Says No One Should Be Denied Family Planning Help

By WALTER RUGABER
Special to The New York Times

WASHINGTON, July 18 — President Nixon proposed today a substantial expansion of the Government's birth control programs and the establishment of a commission to study the implications of continued population growth in the United States.

In the first message on population problems ever sent by a President to Congress, Mr. Nixon presented a grim review of national and worldwide growth projections and the problems involved.

On birth control, the President's message advocated more Federal support for family planning assistance rather than any fundamental change in the type of program the Government already underwrites.

Mr. Nixon said that nearly five million poor women of child-bearing age who wanted to limit the size of their families did not presently have adequate access to birth control information.

A Five-Year Goal

"It is my view," the President wrote in his 3,500 word message, "that no American woman should be denied access to family planning assistance because of her economic condition." He continued:

United Press International

COMMENTS ON NIXON'S MESSAGE: Daniel Patrick Moynihan, Assistant to the President for Urban Affairs, at White House news conference. Chart is an illustration for Mr. Nixon's message to Congress on growth in population.

"I believe, therefore, that we should establish as a national goal the provision of adequate family planning services within the next five years to all those who want them but cannot afford them."

The message contained an assurance that the birth control programs would not be "allowed to infringe upon the religious convictions or personal wishes and freedom of any individual."

The Roman Catholic church's opposition to artificial means of contraception once inhibited Federal efforts to restrain population growth. But Government involvement has become less controversial nowadays.

Several years ago, the government began to make grants to various agencies to finance the distribution of birth control advice and devices to low-income women who wanted them.

No religious questions are asked. A woman may obtain the sort of birth control assistance she wants, whether it involves an artificial means or information on the rhythm method of abstention during times of fertility.

Administration officials said that under the existing programs about 800,000 poor women had been able to obtain assistance but that about 5.4 million needed it.

$30-Million Annual Cost

Robert H. Finch, Secretary of Health, Education and Welfare, said at a White House news conference that according to "very conservative" estimates there were 450,000 unwanted births to low-income women in 1966.

Also the Secretary said, estimates have suggested that about 450,000 families now considered poor would not be so classified by the Government if they had three children instead of four.

Officials said the Administration's drive to reach all low-income women by the end of the five-year program would be accomplished with an annual increase in appropriations of $30-million so that the increase in yearly cost would be at least $150-million.

The President also asked the Secretary of Health, Education and Welfare and the director of the Office of Economic Opportunity to coordinate "all our domestic family planning programs." State and local government and private agencies should be involved, he said, because Federal programs "must be matched by a sizable increase in effort at other levels.

The 24-member commission that Mr. Nixon asked Congress to establish would project growth to the year 2,000, predict the resources required to meet the increase, and predict the effects of Federal, state, and local governments.

The panel, which the President called the Commission on Population Growth and the American Future, would operate for two years with an interim report required after the first year.

Mr. Nixon warned that world population might double by the end of this century, and he said the United Nations and other international bodies should take leadership in meeting the problem.

In the United States, he said, expected population increases would fill a new city of 250,000 people every month from now to the end of the century. This would raise problems in housing, employment, education, natural resources and other areas, he said.

Daniel Patrick Moynihan, Assistant to the President for Urban Affairs, said the message was the first on population growth and described the problem as the most serious issue facing the world except general disarmament.

July 19, 1969

STUDY FINDS WOMEN ACCEPT BIRTH CURBS

ANN ARBOR, Mich., Aug. 4 (UPI) — American women, regardless of their religious, racial or economic backgrounds, appear to be approaching total acceptance of birth control, according to a study by a group of scientists, medical men and experts on population.

Three University of Michigan faculty members edited the study — "Fertility and Family Planning" — published by the University of Michigan Press.

"The norm of fertility control has become universal in contemporary America," the book says.

According to the book, a change in behavior and attitude, especially among Roman Catholic and nonwhite persons took place between 1960 and 1965.

In general, the book says, American women appear to be approaching a total acceptance of some form of birth control, regardless of religious preference or devoutness; race; education; income; their husband's occupation, or the area in which they live.

The book also contends that a trend toward family planning appears to be spreading around the world.

August 4, 1969

Scientists Tell Nixon Adviser Voluntary Birth Control Is 'Insanity'

By GLADWIN HILL

Special to The New York Times

ASPEN, Colo., Sept. 21—A close adviser of President Nixon was told by scientists this weekend that the official Federal notion of limiting population by voluntary birth control was "insanity," and birth control would have to be made compulsory to avert the chaos of threatened global overpopulation.

John Erlichman, counsel to the President, was moderator of one of the principal panels at a two-day meeting of a new conservation organization, the John Muir Institute, at the Aspen Meadows conference center here.

The world's present population of three billion is expected to double within the next 35 years, and in underdeveloped nations the doubling will come sooner.

In general, the increase will not be accompanied by a consonant increase in nations' economic resources, which will mean generally lower standards of living. Many demographers and economists foresee this as precipitating, starting in the mid-1970's, mass starvation and malnutrition on a scale the world has never known.

One possible consequence, it was suggested at the conference, is that the United States, in "a frenzy of altruism" in an effort to alleviate the disaster, would futilely exhaust its natural resources, from redwood trees to food crops.

'Pregnant Pause'

To mitigate the long-term population "debacle," one conference suggestion was that the United States set an example for the world by marking the nation's bicentennial in 1976 with "a pregnant pause"—as complete a suspension of reproduction as could be organized.

Those skeptical of "voluntary" birth control in the United States—an idea enunciated by President Nixon in July — included Dr. Garrett Hardin, professor of biology at the University of California at Santa Barbara and a noted student of population problems, and Dr. Donald Aitken, a Stanford University astrophysicist.

Their views were tacitly seconded by other participants in the conference—a select group of 30 persons chosen for the diversity of their connections. They ranged from Dr. Theos J. Thompson, a physicist and member of the Atomic Energy Commission, to Jerry Mander, the San Francisco advertising man who styled the successful advertising campaign against the construction of more power dams on the Colorado River.

The institute was organized by David Brower, whose militancy in the cause of conservation caused him to be ousted in May from his post as executive director of the Sierra Club. The institute's principal financing is being provided by Robert O. Anderson, board chairman of the Atlantic Richfield Company, an oil corporation.

Other participants included the Right Rev. David Forbes, dean of the Grace Episcopal Cathedral in San Francisco; Allan Gussow, an artist of Congers, N. Y., and Ted Watkins, the leading figure in social and economic development activities in Watts, the predominantly Negro section of Los Angeles. There were 50 observers from related fields.

Idea Exchange

The chief aim of the conference, which will be reconvened within a year, Mr. Brower said, was to exchange ideas from widely divergent sources that the participants could take back to their respective fields, and to develop a program of books and other publications.

"We have to take children in their earliest years and start implanting some different ideas about the good life simply constituting getting married and multiplying," Dr. Hardin said. "We have to tell them what a good time the unmarrieds are having.

"But this approach has limitations. In the long run, voluntarism is insanity. The result will be continued uncontrolled population growth.

"It looks like a probability that in 10 or 20 years there will be a perfectly dreadful catastrophe in the world of people starving—50 or 100 million people in a single year.

"Our natural reaction will be 'We must save the starving Indians' and people of other developing countries. We'll plant marginal lands—dust bowls and redwood groves—to food crops. But it won't do much good. There won't be enough ships and planes to carry the produce.

"How can we save ourselves in terms of moral responsibility?" continued Dr. Hardin, a c onservation lecturer who frequently extends his themes, for effect, into the realm of hyperbole.

"I suggest that our big chance is to develop the idea of trust-for-posterity—to fence off certain resources as 'posterity trust areas,' and tell the world that we're preserving them not out of selfishness, but for our children and grandchildren, and the Indian grandchildren.

Seek 'Zero Birth Rate'

"Meanwhile, to establish our own good faith in the eyes of other peoples, I suggest that we celebrate 1976 as a 'year of reproductive pause' to come as close as possible to a zero birth rate."

Dr. Aitken, a consultant on the Apollo project, expressed parallel views.

"I admire Mr. Nixon's courage in making the first Presidential talks on population limitation," he said. "But he negated it all at the end by promising that the Government-al effort wouldn't interfere with religious convictions, personal convictions, etc.

"I'd like to see Mr. Nixon stand up a few years from now and say: 'Nothing has happened. Population must be controlled. We must set an example. So the Government has to step in and tamper with religion and personal convictions — and maybe even impose penalties for every child a family has beyond two."

Mr. Erlichman, who, speaking only for himself, had previously remarked that he thought conservationists should give more weight to the political viability of their proposals, commented on the compulsory birth control suggestions: "The mind boggles at the enforcement problems."

Mr. Watkins, the only Negro in the group, is chairman of the Watts Labor Community Action Committee, which is backed by 14 labor unions and has organized business and transportation enterprises and many youth activities.

After listening to several hours of generalizations by other conference participants, he asked:

"What are you going to sacrifice to do the kind of conserving we want to do? Which teacher is going to give up his nice two-story home? What doctor, what architect, is going to sacrifice some of his practice to help this cause along? What advertising man is going out and campaign to raise funds without a 25 or 30 per cent fee?

"Who of you in this room is ready to make a sacrifice

to do what you say you are going to do?"

There were no responses.

Dr. Forbes, the clergyman, said: "Sociologically, we've got problems, brothers, with the church members. The church represents primarily the Establishment, no matter how you cut it. The maximum interest is in the status quo. Sociologically, the church is a dubious ally for conservation."

The Muir Institute is one of two new conservation organizations announced by Mr. Brower last Tuesday. It will concentrate on exchanges of ideas and publications.

The other organization is Friends of the Earth, which is planned as a broad-membership nonpartisan political action group, pressing for conservation legislation and campaigning for or against candidates at all levels.

John Muir was a pioneer 19th-century California naturalist and founder of the Sierra Club, a leading conservation organization.

September 22, 1969

F.D.A. RESTRICTING WARNING ON PILL

A Draft Revision Indicates Original Is Toned Down

WASHINGTON, March 23 (AP)—The Food and Drug Administration is toning down its announced package warning for 8.5 million users of oral contraceptives after pressure from physicians, drug manufacturers and high Government officials.

An F.D.A. spokesman and sources in the Department of Health, Education and Welfare confirmed today that the 600-word leaflet announced earlier this month was being extensively reworded.

The original leaflet referred to such serious possible reactions to the pill as blood clots, mental depression, swelling, skin rash, jaundice, high blood pressure, and elevation of blood sugar levels similar to that seen in diabetes.

One draft revision runs less than 100 words, mentions only a single specific danger from oral contraceptive use, and deletes detailed suggestions on when women using the pill should see a physician.

"Any similarity between this draft and what the F.D.A. proposed is purely coincidental," said one knowledgeable Senate source.

Dr. Charles C. Edwards, F.D.A. commissioner, read to a Senate monopoly subcommittee on March 4 the leaflet's specific wording, which he said, "We are going to publish in The Federal Register so that all interested parties will have an opportunity to comment on it."

Warning on Packages

The warning would be contained in all packages of oral contraceptives for the education of users.

It is not unusual for an agency to revise a proposed regulation after publication and after receipt of comments. But it is unusual, informed sources said, for the regulation to be drastically reworded before publication and before formal comment is received.

When asked about the revision, Dr. Edwards said today that the drafting process still was under way and the agency would require some kind of a warning leaflet—a first for prescription drugs.

He did not disavow the authenticity of one draft revision obtained by a reporter. Other F.D.A. officials said the draft had been ordered lengthened.

One member of the Senate subcommittee, Senator Thomas J. McIntyre, Democrat of New Hampshire, said he was deeply disturbed on hearing that the F.D.A. had watered down the warning label.

"It is my understanding that since the story broke in the press, F.D.A. is again rewriting the label statement to put some of the original information back in," Senator McIntyre said. "I hope that this is true, and I shall look forward to reviewing this statement when it is published."

Sources in the office of the Assistant Secretary for Health, Education and Welfare said revision of the leaflet was necessary for "legal and professional acceptance."

Dr. Edwards ruffled bureaucratic feathers when he told the Senate subcommittee about the leaflet and its specific warning without first informing his superior, Dr. Roger O. Egeberg, Assistant Secretary of Health Education and Welfare.

The American Medical Association complained to Dr. Egeberg and the H.E.W. Secretary, Robert H. Finch, that the leaflet would interfere with the doctor-patient relationship and possibly could lead to malpractice suits.

The drug industry objected, contending that the leaflet overemphasized dangers and minimized benefits from oral contraceptives.

The revised draft leaflet has this to say about the pill's dangers:

"As with all effective drugs, they may cause side effects in some cases and should not be taken at all by some. Rare instances of blood clotting are the most important known complications of the oral contraceptives."

The original wording was much sharper on clots. It said:

"There is a definite association between blood clotting disorders and the use of contraceptives. The risk of this complication is six times higher for users than for nonusers."

The original warning offered signpost symptoms requiring immediate medical attention. It also said:

"Your doctor has taken your medical history and has given you a careful physical examination."

The revised draft said the contraceptives "should be taken only under the supervision of a physician," and users should have "periodic examinations at intervals set by your doctors."

March 24, 1970

FINAL APPROVAL OF ABORTION BILL VOTED IN ALBANY

4-YEAR DRIVE IS ENDED

31-to-26 Tally Unchanged From Senate's March 18 Roll-Call—Some Weep

By BILL KOVACH
Special to The New York Times

ALBANY, April 10—The State Senate, after more than two hours of quiet but emotional debate, voted 31 to 26 today to accept an Assembly bill that strikes the state's 140-year-old abortion law from the books.

Cardinal Cooke issued an appeal on behalf of the Roman Catholic bishops of the state for Governor Rockefeller to veto the bill, but the Governor said in New York that he would sign the bill tomorrow morning.

Today's vote successfully ended a bitter and tenacious campaign begun in 1966 by a Manhattan Democrat Assemblyman, Albert H. Blumenthal, to reform the law passed in 1830 that permits an abortion only to save a woman's life.

The new law makes an abortions a matter between a woman and her doctor up to the 24th week of pregnancy. After the 24th week, the new law would allow an abortion only when necessary to save the woman's life. However, abortions generally are performed during the first 12 weeks of pregnancy.

Started in Colorado

Today's vote added New York to a growing list of states caught up in a national wave of abortion reform, beginning with a 1967 Colorado reform law, and is considered a key to possible reform in other states.

Emotions continued to run high in the Senate debate today, but they did not reach the depth and scope of the eight-hour session on March 18 when the Senate passed an even more liberal version of the reform bill—one without the 24-week time limit added in the Assembly. The vote today was identical to that of March 18.

Senate Majority Leader Earl W. Brydges, a Niagara Falls Republican whose opposition to reform in past years prevented consideration of such a bill, openly wept as the bill passed.

Mr. Brydges, whose craggy features and gritty voice generally reflect complete control, rose to end debate on the bill by reading from what he described as "The Dairy of an Unborn Child."

He began to read of a child on the day of conception—when—"it is already determined even that I will love flowers." His voice broke and television lights reflected from the tears on his cheeks.

"I'm sorry, Mr. President," he stammered, "I try to keep myself under control...I cannot read it all, sir, but I want to read the final entry in this diary, dated Dec. 28 and it says, 'Today', my parents killed me.'" He dropped to his seat, trembling.

Debate Lacks Conviction

Except for two of the 13 other speeches, debate lacked any of the conviction that words would sway votes.

Fighting to the end, Senator James H. Donovan, Oneida County Republican, pointed an accusing finger at his colleagues and said:

"Your hands will reach into the womb with the doctor and you are going to kill, K-I-L-L, when you pass this law. I urge you in God's name not to do this . . .Instead, kill this bill and you will please the people of New York. What's more, you will please God."

Senator Thomas Laverne, Rochester Republican, who like Mr. Donovan is a Roman Catholic and has been under pressure from his church not to vote for the bill, responded angrily to the religious tone of Mr. Donovan's argument.

"How dare anyone say because I believe this way everyone else should believe this way," Mr. Laverne said. "I have been told I am obviously not a good Catholic . . .Even that I am a phony . . .But many do not support the church on this issue, 60 per cent of the Catholics in my district don't agree with the church on this issue."

"I don't think," he concluded, "I have the right to force my morality on anyone else."

The new law, which will take effect July 1, has raised a number of hopes and fears, all of which have been expressed during the three major debates during this session.

Primarily, supporters hope the law will end the illegal abortion business that has resulted in the death or mutilation of the women involved. These same sponsors, however, warn against what they call "probably unrealizable" hopes that the new law will cause a major reduction in welfare case loads—especially in aid to dependent children.

One reason cited for this is that medical societies and hospitals in those states—as in New York—generally oppose broadly liberal laws and devise regulations that make abortions difficult to obtain even under reformed laws.

Doctors to Make Rules

The New York State Medical Society has announced that it will devise rules designed to control abortions under the new law, in part to head of the possibility that the state will attract many women from less liberal states and lead to "abortion mills."

Hospitals also are expected to discourage abortion practices, primarily because of limited and overcrowded facilities.

Assemblymen have already moved to further restrict the new law by amendments they hope to pass next week. The amendments would limit abortions to "licensed hospitals and clinics" and provide that no doctor or hospital can be cited for malpractice for refusing to perform an abortion.

The malpractice amendment is designed to calm fears of some Catholic doctors and hospitals that they might be forced under the new law to perform abortions or face lawsuits.

Supports of abortion reform, including women's lobbies and minority group coalitions, are expected to begin campaigns now that the new law is passed to offsset any attempt by medical organizations to restrict the law with their own regulations.

One lobbyist said today that the campaign would probably take the form of "a person-to-person education and pressure program aimed at individual doctors rather than a struggle with the medical associations."

April 11, 1970

ABORTION RULES RELAXED BY A.M.A.

Social Reasons Accepted

By RICHARD D. LYONS

Special to The New York Times

CHICAGO, June 25 — The American Medical Association voted for the first time in its 123-year history today to allow doctors to perform abortions for social and economic reasons, as well as medical.

After a bitter controversy at the association's annual convention, the A.M.A.'s House of Delegates voted 103 to 73 to consider the performing of abortions ethical if the following conditions are met:

¶That the doctor be properly licensed to practice medicine.

¶That the operation be performed in a hospital accredited by various public health organizations.

¶That two other physicians be called in for consultation.

Today's stand, which was regarded as a surprising turnabout by many physicians here, is not quite so liberal as the newly enacted abortion laws in New York, Hawaii, and Alaska. The New York law, for example, does not require the last two conditions.

But the new position has far fewer legal qualifications than laws in the 47 other states and it is bound to affect abortion reform campaigns in them.

The Judicial Council of the A.M.A., as a matter of information, told the organization today that the legal jurisdiction of the locality in which the physician practiced superseded the ethic of the medical group.

After the vote, Dr. Gino Papola of Upper Darby, Pa., the president of the 6,000-member National Federation of Catholic Physicians Guild, said he intended to resign from the A.M.A. and he urged the nation's other 35,000 Catholic doctors to do the same.

"In effect, the A.M.A. has made it ethical for doctors to become paid executioners," Dr. Papola said in a telephone interview. "I certainly don't want to be a doctor in the A.M.A. under these circumstances."

However, the resolution adopted by the House of Delegates, which sets policy for the group, specifically states that a doctor cannot be compelled to perform an abortion if it "violated his good medical judgment" or is "violative of personally held moral principles."

Today's action is not expected to affect Roman Catholic hospitals, which contain nearly one-third of the nation's general hospital beds, since the resolution also states that hospitals do not have to perform abortions if their directors do not want them to. Few abortions, if any, are performed in Catholic institutions

For 120 years the A.M.A. considered abortions unethical, stating in 1871, for example, "that it to be the duty of every physician in the United States to resort to every honorable and legal means in his power to rid society of this practice."

Over the years, however, some respected physicians would perform abortions if they believed that the pregnancy was a threat to the health of the mother.

Three years ago the House of Delegates voted to consider the performing of an abortion ethical if there were a threat to the mother's physical or mental health, a threat that the child might be born deformed, or if conception had taken place under criminal conditions such as rape or incest.

A dozen states and the District of Columbia subsequently altered their abortion laws. This fall the Supreme Court is to take under consideration the issue of whether a law that restricts abortion is a violation of a woman's constitutional rights.

The A.M.A.'s shift on abortion was prompted by a report issued last month by the association's 15-man Board of Trustees that "recommends that the House of Delegates establish a policy on abortion that would permit the decision to interrupt pregnancy to be made by the woman and her physician."

The trustees said they were worried that the new state laws might force doctors practicing in those states that have liberalized their abortion laws into what might be construed as an unethical position.

A special A.M.A. committee on Monday heard 52 witnesses testify on the Board of Trustees' recommendation with many Catholic physicians urging that it not be adopted. The Catholic policy on abortion is that the practice is immoral except when medical treatment, such as radiation for cancer, might kill the fetus.

Dr. Wesley W. Hall of Reno was voted president-elect of the A.M.A. Dr. Hall, a member of the Board of Trustees, will succeed Dr. Walter C. Bornmeier when his term expires at the 1971 convention.

Dr. H. Thomas McGuire of New Castle, Del., was elected vice president.

June 26, 1970

Abortion Laws Gaining Favor As New Statutes Spur Debate

By JANE E. BRODY

A dramatic liberalization of public attitudes and practices regarding abortions appears to be sweeping the country, even in a number of states that still have restrictive abortion laws.

The change in the way Americans view abortions can be seen in the tremendous increase in legal abortions in this country, the growing participation of clergymen as prime movers in abortion reform and referral and the increasingly liberal interpretation of existing state laws by the medical profession.

Earlier this month, in the first instance in which a liberal abortion law was put to a public referendum, 55.5 per cent of voters in the State of Washington favored an eased law that leaves the decision to have an abortion up to the woman and her physician.

As abortion laws and attitudes relax, more and more doctors and hospitals are doing abortions. Dr. Christopher Tietze of the Population Council estimates that as many as 200,000 legal abortions will be performed in the United States this year, compared with about 18,000 just two years ago.

The new view of abortions reflects the combined action of many social forces, among them a growing concern with overpopulation, increasing demands for women's rights and roles outside the home, rising welfare rolls and illegitimacy rates, growing numbers of child abuse and child neglect cases and a general easing of sexual proscriptions.

Perhaps the most important liberalizing force has been the recent relaxation of restrictive abortion laws in 16 states and the publicity that surround these legal changes.

As one observer of the abortion scene remarked recently, "People tend to equate illegality with immorality; when abortion is no longer illegal, the stigma of immorality tends to fall away."

Reports from around the country this month revealed that fewer and fewer people tend to regard abortion as starting with a red letter "A." In some cases, in fact, the traditional hard-line opposition to abortion appears to be declining among Roman Catholics, laymen and clergy alike.

"A liberal abortion law shows a mature attitude of society," said Mrs. Myrtle Carr, a Portland, Ore., mother of one. "I used to feel that it was morally wrong to have an abortion—sinful, but I have read more on it, thought more about it."

Mrs. Q. Kenneth Bogaard, a middle-aged mother of two grown sons in Cedar Rapids, Iowa, remarked: "My attitude has changed over the last three years because of increasing published material presenting new information and the other side of the argument. I have misgivings about making abortions too easy for unwed mothers but I prefer this to the clandestine 'coat hanger' operation in back rooms by unskilled, unscrupulous operators."

Opponents Shift Views

Even among people who disapprove of abortions, many are broadening their views. As a West Coast father of two said, "Morally, I've thought abortion is wrong and I still do, but there are too many people for the bread that is available."

In Madison, Wis., several women made comments similar to this housewife: "I wouldn't have one myself, but if someone else wants to, why shouldn't they be able to?"

Although the Roman Catholic Church remains firmly opposed to abortions, the comments of the Rev. Carl Lezak, associate pastor of St. Sebastian's Roman Catholic Church in Chicago, were typical of a small but growing number of Catholic clergymen:

"I'm not taking any public position on the morality of abortion. I'm saying we ought to get out of legislating public morality in private matters. I'm certain there has been a great swing among Catholics toward favoring abortion reform."

One of those Catholics is Mrs. Arnold Geiger, a 26-year-old mother from Anchorage, Alaska. She said she had opposed abortions "as a matter of religious philosophy," but that recently her view has changed.

"I find there's more to a baby than having it—like supporting it, caring for it," she remarked. "I don't think adoption agencies are solving the problem of unwanted children. There's still too many kids around that aren't wanted."

Exceptions Are Asked

In Pittsburgh, where several Catholic physicians were reported doing abortions, Dr. Rose Middleman, medical coordinator of the Planned Parenthood center, said, "Quite often patients will say 'I'm Catholic but I feel I have to have this abortion,' or 'I'm Catholic but I don't agree with my church on abortion.'"

In the meantime, non-Catholic clergymen throughout the country are becoming increasingly active in the movement toward liberal abortion laws. There are now 28 Clergy Consultation Services on Abortion in 22 states, compared with just 11 eight months ago.

November 29, 1970

PRESIDENT SIGNS BIRTH CURB BILL

Programs Are Expanded—Nixon Kills Measure on More Family Doctors

By The Associated Press

WASHINGTON, Dec. 26—President Nixon has signed into law a $382-million, three-year expansion of the family planning service and creation of a Federal office to coordinate ways to control population growth, the White House announced today.

The White House also announced that Mr. Nixon had vetoed a bill that would have set up a three-year, $225-million program to train family doctors. Efforts were under way to learn if Congress could override the veto.

The bill signed by the President authorizes funds to be distributed to public and nonprofit private organizations to advise persons on means of controlling birth and issuing contraceptives.

Law Called 'Landmark'

But it bars the use of any of the funds where abortion is used as a method of birth control.

The White House announcement noted that, under the new law, acceptance of the family planning services and birth control information must be voluntary. Also, it said, the program must not be a prerequisite for eligibility for other services by the agencies that receive the grants.

Mr. Nixon said in a statement, "It is noteworthy that this landmark legislation has had strong bipartisan support. I am confident that by working together—at Federal, state and local levels—we can achieve the goal of providing adequate family planning services within the next five years to all those who want them but cannot afford them."

Funds to implement the authorizing measure must be provided by separate legislation.

Mr. Nixon noted that he proposed to Congress on July 18, 1969, creation of a Commission on Population Growth and the American Future, which Congress approved. The commission, he said, is now functioning and its interim report will be due next spring with a final report the following spring.

"The bill before me today, 'the Family Planning Services and Population Research Act of 1970,' completes the legislation I requested in my message on population," Mr. Nixon said.

The Secretary of Health, Education and Welfare will allocate the grants on the basis of local need and capacity to make effective use of the Federal assistance. The Secretary may also make grants to the state health authorities on a formula basis to aid them in establishing, maintaining, coordinating and evaluating family planning services.

Will Form New Office

The Office of Population Affairs created in the department is to be headed by a deputy assistant secretary.

The legislation is a compromise between Senate and House versions. The Senate had passed a bill providing for expenditures of $967-million over a five-year period while the House had voted to spend $267-million over three years.

A White House spokesman said that Mr. Nixon's action on the family doctor's bill was a pocket veto. He said Congress was "adjourned" at the end of the 10-day period in which the President had to act on the measure, so his only means of vetoing it was not to sign it.

Congress went home for the Christmas holidays last Tuesday evening and returns Monday.

Senator Ralph W. Yarborough, Democrat of Texas, chief sponsor of the legislation, said that he had Congress staff members studying the action to "see whether Congress will have a right to override the veto under the manner in which it was vetoed."

Mr. Yarborough said a decision "depends on records locked up until Monday morning." He called the veto "a sad blow not only to those working in the health care field, but to all Americans."

The President normally signs a bill within 10 days, excluding Sundays, of the time it is sent to him, or he vetoes it by sending it back to Congress with his objections. If he takes neither action, the bill becomes law without his signature.

But if Congress, by its adjournment, prevents him from returning a bill to which he objects, he can kill it by merely refusing to sign it.

The President himself was at his retreat at Camp David, Md. He flew up from Washington by helicopter late Christmas afternoon with Mrs. Nixon, their son-in-law and daughter, Mr. and Mrs. David Eisenhower.

Mr. Yarborough noted that earlier this year Mr. Nixon vetoed two other health-connected bills, appropriations included in an omnibus health-education-welfare measure and a $1.25-billion hospital construction bill. Congress later agreed to a scaled-down appropriations bill and overrode the veto of the construction measure.

Mr. Nixon, in a statement dated Thursday, said he was not signing the family doctor bill because "the authority provided in this bill is unnecessary and represents the wrong approach to the solution of the nation's health problems."

Finds Action Delayed

The President said that the Administration would propose next year "a broad pattern of reforms to deal with the nation's health problems and needs on a systematic and comprehensive basis."

He said that the vetoed measure "simply continues the traditional approach of adding more programs to the almost unmanageable current structure of Federal Government health efforts."

Mr. Yarborough said, "It's a safe bet that what the President proposes will be less than what the Congress has done this year. His new, delayed proposals will effectively postpone the vast, imperative health needs of the nation for another year."

The vetoed bill would have trained family doctors in medical schools and teaching hospitals, but Mr. Nixon said that the Government "already has at least four programs on the books that provide funds which can be used to promote the training of family medicine practitioners."

Mr. Yarborough said that the nation lacked 50,000 physicians, with the greatest need in the field of family medicine.

Mr. Nixon's veto was his ninth since taking office and the third by pocket veto, the White House said.

December 27, 1970

Popularity of Big Families Put At a Record Low in Gallup Poll

The percentage of Americans who favor large families has declined dramatically since 1967, according to the Gallup Poll, and is now at the lowest point in the 35 years that the polling organization has conducted regular surveys on the subject.

In the latest survey, conducted in January, only about one adult in four (23 per cent) said the ideal number of children in a family is four or more. The percentage was 40 per cent in the fall of 1967, the last time the subject was dealt with in a survey.

Three basic reasons emerge from the survey to explain the decline in interest in large families since 1967:

1. The cost of living, particularly the cost of education.
2. Concern over crowded conditions and overpopulation.
3. Uncertainty of the future.

To obtain the results reported today, personal interviews were conducted Jan. 9-10 with a total of 1,502 adults in more than 300 scientifically selected localities across the nation. This question was asked, as in all previous surveys: What do you think is the ideal number of children for a family to have?

The previous low point in the percentage of adults favoring four or more children was recorded in the Depression year of 1936: 34 per cent. The high point over the 35-year period (49 per cent) was recorded in 1945, reflecting the high birth rate of the war years. Following is the trend since 1936:

Percentage Saying 4 or More Is Ideal Number of Children

Year	Per cent
1936	34%
1941	41
1945	49
1947	47
1953	41
1957	38
1960	45
1963	42
1966	35
1967	40
1971	23

The following table shows the change in views between the two latest surveys by key population groups:

Percentage Saying 4 or More Is Ideal Number of Children

	1971	1967
National	23%	40%
Men	19	34
Women	26	45
21-29 years old	15	34
30-49 years	24	40
50 and over	27	42
Protestants	22	37
Roman Catholics	28	50
College	14	34
High School	22	40
Grade School	33	44

February 21, 1971

Nixon Abortion Statement

Special to The New York Times

SAN CLEMENTE, Calif., April 3—Following is the statement by President Nixon on Abortion:

Historically, laws regulating abortion in the United States have been the province of states, not the Federal Government. That remains the situation today, as one state after another takes up this question, debates it and decides it. That is where the decisions should be made.

Partly, for that reason, I have directed that the policy on abortions at American military bases in the United States be made to correspond with the laws of the states where those bases are located. If the laws in a particular state restrict abortions, the rule at the military base hospitals are to correspond to that law.

The effect of this directive is to reverse service regulations issued last summer, which had liberalized the rules on abortions at military hospitals. The new ruling supersedes this—and has been put into effect by the Secretary of Defense.

But while this matter is being debated in state capitals, and weighed by various courts, the country has a right to know my personal views.

From personal and religious beliefs I consider abortion an unacceptable form of population control. Further, unrestricted abortion policies, or abortion on demand, I cannot square with my personal belief in the sanctity of human life—including the life of the yet unborn. For, surely, the unborn have rights also, recognized in law, recognized even in principles expounded by the United Nations.

Ours is a nation with a Judeo-Christian heritage. It is also a nation with serious social problems—problems of malnutrition, of broken homes, of poverty and of delinquency. But none of these problems justifies such a solution.

A good and generous people will not opt, in my view, for this kind of alternative to its social dilemmas. Rather, it will open its hearts and homes to the unwanted children of its own, as it has done for the unwanted millions of other lands.

April 4, 1971

High Court Upholds D.C. Abortion Law

By FRED P. GRAHAM
Special to The New York Times

WASHINGTON, April 21—In its first decision on the constitutionality of anti-abortion laws, the Supreme Court upheld the District of Columbia's abortion statute today by a 5-to-2 vote.

The opinion by Justice Hugo L. Black held that the district's law, which is typical of anti-abortion statutes in a number of states, is not unconstitutionally vague.

However, Justice Black declined to rule on the further question of whether all anti-abortion laws violated women's constitutional right of privacy, by denying them the right to decide whether or not to continue an unwanted pregnancy.

This issue is posed by seven appeals now pending before the Court. In some of them, state laws were upheld and in others the laws were overturned, raising the likelihood that the Supreme Court will quickly agree to hear one or more of the cases to settle the issue.

In the case decided today, Dr. Milan Vuitch was indicted under the district law that outlaws all abortions except those performed by physicians when the abortions are "necessary for the preservation of the mother's life or health."

The law was declared unconstitutional and the Vuitch indictment was thrown out by Federal District Judge Gerhard A. Gesell, son of Dr. Arnold Gesell, the noted pediatrician.

Judge Gesell found that the law was so vague that a physician would not know if he was committing a crime when he performed an abortion, because a jury might later disagree with his opinion that the mother's health required it. He said that the doctors' problem was particularly acute because the burden was on them to prove that the abortion was justified.

The Justice Department appealed to the Supreme Court, charging that Dr. Vuitch operated an "abortion mill" and performed abortions for any woman who desired one, without considering the woman's health.

Justice Black's opinion, although reversing Judge Gesell, interpreted the district law to give physicians here considerable latitude to perform legal abortions. He declared that in future abortion prosecutions, the Government must bear the burden of proving that the mother's health was not endangered.

Moreover, in considering a woman's health, doctors may consider "psychological as well as physical well-being," even if the woman has no previous history of mental defects.

This interpretation was taken to be so permissive by Preterm, an abortion clinic that opened here after the Gesell decision, that its officials announced this afternoon that the clinic would continue to perform abortions.

Chief Justice Warren E. Burger and Justices Harry A. Blackmun, John M. Harlan and Byron R. White joined the majority opinion. Justice Potter Stewart dissented, saying that if a licensed physician performed an abortion the law should accept that the patient's health required it. In another dissent, Justice William O. Douglas agreed with Judge Gesell that the law was unconstitutionally vague.

Justices William J. Brennan Jr. and Thurgood Marshall expressed no view because they felt that the Supreme Court lacked jurisdiction to hear the case upon direct appeal from a district court, without a ruling from the United States Court of Appeals for the District of Columbia.

Samuel Huntington of the Solicitor General's Office argued for the Government. Joseph L. Nellis of Washington and Norman Drosen of New York argued for Dr. Vuitch.

In a 5-to-4 ruling today, the Court interpreted the refugee provisions of the immigration laws to permit the Government to deny permanent entry to persons who have fled Communist countries, if they settled temporarily in another country on the way.

The ruling was supported by Justices Black, Burger, Blackmun, Harlan and White. Justices Stewart, Douglas, Brennan and Marshal dissented.

The Court also upheld, 6 to 3, a Selective Service regulation that blocks a draftee from making a conscientious objector application after he has been told to report for induction. The majority opinion by Justice Stewart noted that men could apply for C.O. discharges, after induction. Justices Brennan, Marshall and Douglas dissented.

April 22, 1971

Notes on People

Dick Gregory, the comedian, says he has the black man's answer to genocide: big families. "I'm one black cat who's going to have all the kids he wants," he wrote in the current issue of Ebony magazine. "White folks can have their birth control. Personally, I've never trusted anything white folks tried to give us with the word 'control' of it. For years they told us where to sit, where to eat and where to live. Now they want to dictate our bedroom habits. First the white man tells me to sit in the back of the bus. Now it looks like he wants me to sleep under the bed." Mr. Gregory is practicing what he preaches. He and his wife, Lillian, have eight children.

ALBIN KREBS.

October 12, 1971

Survey Finds 50% Back Liberalization Of Abortion Policy

By JACK ROSENTHAL
Special to The New York Times

WASHINGTON, Oct. 27—General concern over population growth has become so intense, a new Federal study shows, that half the public now favors liberalization of restrictions on abortion.

That finding, the authorities say, represents a dramatic change in public attitudes. As recently as 1968, survey data showed that 85 per cent of the public opposed more liberal abortion policies.

Results of the new study were made available today by the Commission on Population Growth and the American Future, for which the study was made.

The survey, involving interviews with a national sample of 1,700 adults, was conducted by the Opinion Research Corporation. One question concerned the circumstances under which abortion should be permitted.

Among all persons, 50 per cent said the decision should be one left up to persons involved and their doctor. Forty-one per cent said abortion was permissible only in certain circumstances. Only 6 per cent said it should not be allowed under any circumstances. The remaining 3 per cent had no opinion.

Almost identical results were obtained in answer to a second question: "Do you think abortions should be permitted where the parents already have all the children they want?" Forty-nine per cent said yes, 42 per cent said no, and 9 per cent had no opinion.

Wide public attention to population growth was reflected in a series of findings, including the following:

¶Almost 80 per cent of those surveyed favored voluntary sterilization. This represented a significant increase over the 64 per cent approval found in a 1966 survey.

¶More than half think Government should try to slow population growth and to promote the development of smaller cities for better population distribution.

¶An equally large number believe people should voluntarily limit the size of their families even if they can afford more children.

¶This belief is strong enough that about 56 per cent — a surprising total to experts — said they would consider adoption if they decided to have more than two children. Of those, half said they would approve of adopting a child of a different race.

John D. Rockefeller 3d, the population commission's chairman, said today, "While we had expected to see considerable public interest in population growth problems, we were quite surprised at the extent of this interest."

The commission, proposed by President Nixon, was established by Congress in March, 1970. It is expected to begin issuing a series of public reports next spring.

Officials also were struck by the specific abortion findings. "Frankly, I'm surprised," said

Charles F. Westoff, executive director of the commission, "at the extent of apparent support for easing of legal restrictions surrounding abortion."

Earlier surveys have showed that in 1965, 91 per cent disapproved of liberalized abortion policies. By 1968, this dropped to 85 per cent, and by 1969 to 79 per cent.

While the new survey showed 50 per cent in favor of liberalized abortion policies, there were variations among subgroups. Percentages in favor of leaving the decision solely up to the couple and their doctor were as follows:

Under age 30, 58 per cent; over age 30, 45 per cent.

White, 51 per cent; black, 33 per cent.

Men, 53 per cent; women, 45 per cent.

Protestant, 48 per cent; Roman Catholic, 39 per cent; Jewish, 91 per cent.

In accord with the commission's responsibility, the new survey covered issues of population distribution as well as growth. One finding was that residents of rural areas are far happier with the kind of area they live in than are big-city residents.

When asked if they prefer their present area to others, 39 per cent of those in large metropolitan areas said yes. For residents of medium-size metropolitan areas, the figure was 55 per cent. For those outside metropolitan areas, the figure was 88 per cent.

Another finding showed that blacks are highly impatient with the pace of integration of suburbs. Among whites, 18 per cent said it was proceeding too slowly, with the rest divided between "too fast" and "just right." But among blacks, 56 per cent said "too slowly."

October 28, 1971

Population Report Excerpts

Special to The New York Times

Washington, March 16— Following are excerpts from the second report of the Federal Commission on Population Growth and the American Future, made today to the President, Congress and the public:

HUMAN REPRODUCTION

Contemporary American couples are planning to have an average of between two and three children. Given the fact of youthful marriage, far-from-perfect means of fertility control, and varying motivation, many of these couples will have children before they want them and a significant fraction will ultimately exceed the number they want.

Recent research has disclosed a substantial incidence of such unplanned pregnancies and unwanted births in the United States. According to estimates developed in the 1970 National Fertility Study conducted by the Office of Population Research at Princeton University, 44 percent of all births to currently married women during the five years between 1966 and 1970 were unplanned; 15 percent were reported by the parents as having never been wanted.

In theory, this incidence of unwanted births implies that 2.65 million births occurring in that five-year period would never have occurred had the complete availability of perfect fertility control permitted couples to realize their preferences. And these estimates are all conservative.

Unwanted fertility is highest among those whose levels of education and income are lowest. For example, in 1970, women with no high school education reported that 31 per cent of their births in the preceding five years were unwanted at the time they were conceived; the figure for women college graduates was 7 per cent. Mainly because of differences in education and income—and a general exclusion from the socio-economic mainstream—unwanted fertility weighs most heavily on certain minority groups in our population.

For example, if blacks could have the number of children they want and no more, their fertility and that of the majority white population would be very similar.

Not all unwanted births become unwanted children. Many, perhaps most, are eventually accepted and loved indistinguishably from earlier births that were deliberately planned. But many are not; and the costs to them, to their siblings and parents, and to society at large are considerable, though not easy to measure.

We conclude that there are many "costs" associated with unwanted fertility, not only financial, but health, social, psychological and demographic costs as well.

The commission believes that all Americans, regardless of age, marital status or income should be enabled to avoid unwanted births. Major efforts should be made to enlarge and improve the opportunity for individuals to control their own fertility, aiming toward the development of a basic ethical principle that only wanted children are brought into the world.

ABORTION

The Law

Currently, in over two-thirds of the states, abortion is a crime except to preserve the life of the mother; 12 states have changed their abortion statutes consistent with the American Law Institute Model Penal Code provision on abortion which prohibits abortion except in cases where the mother's life or her mental or physical health is in danger, or to prevent the birth of defective offspring, or in cases of rape or incest.

In 1970, abortion laws in Alaska, Hawaii and New York were liberalized by law and in the State of Washington by popular referendum. Currently, abortion is being reviewed in the courts in over half of the states.

At its 1972 meeting, the House of Delegates of the American Bar Association approved a Uniform Abortion Act recommended by the Commissioners on Uniform State Laws stating that abortion may be performed by a duly licensed physician upon request.

The Moral Question

In the development of western culture, the tendency has been toward a greater protection of life. At the same time, there is a deep commitment in our moral tradition to individual freedom and social justice.

The commission believes that the various prohibitions against abortion throughout the United States stand as obstacles to the exercise of individual freedom: the freedom of women to make difficult moral choices based on their personal values, the freedom of women to control their own fertility, and finally, freedom from the burdens of unwanted childbearing.

Restrictive statutes also violate social justice, for when abortion is prohibited, women resort to illegal abortions to prevent unwanted births.

Medically safe abortions have always been available to the wealthy, to those who could afford the high costs of physicians and trips abroad; but the poor woman has been forced to risk her life and health with folk remedies and disreputable practitioners.

Public Health

Abortion is not new; it has been an alternative to unwanted birth for large numbers of American women (estimates ranged from 200,000 to 1,200,000 illegal abortions per year in the United States).

The commission regards the issue of illegal abortion with great concern and supports measures to bring this medical procedure from the backrooms to the hospitals and clinics of this country. It is becoming increasingly clear that, where abortion is available on request, one result is a reduction in the number of illegal abortions.

A reduction in the number of illegal abortions has an important impact on maternal mortality. Maternal mortality ratios (including the 12 deaths out of 278,122 abortions performed under legal auspices) in New York City dropped by two-thirds the year after abortion became available on request.

For 1971, New York City experienced the lowest ratio of maternal deaths ever recorded. Judging from the experience in other countries, there is reason to suspect that the maternal death ratio will continue to decline.

What is the effect of abortion on illegitimacy? The best information comes from New York, where out-of-wedlock births have been on the rise since they were first recorded in 1954.

Statistics for the first eight months of 1971 indicate that, for the first time, the rate is declining. Moreover, the New York City programs for unmarried pregnant girls have reported a sharp decline in the number of applicants this year.

In summary, we are impressed that the availability of abortion on request causes a reduction in the number of illegal abortions, maternal and infant deaths and out-of-wedlock births, thereby greatly improving the health of women and children.

RECOMMENDATIONS

The majority of the commission believes that women should be free to determine their own fertility, that the matter of abortion should be left to the conscience of the individual concerned, in consultation with her physician, and that states should be encouraged to enact affirmative statutes creating a clear and positive framework for the practice of abortion on request.

Therefore, with the admonition that abortion not be considered a primary means of fertility control, the commission recommends that present state laws restricting abortion be liberalized along the lines of the New York State statute, such abortions to be performed on request by duly licensed physicians under conditions of medical safety.

In carrying out this policy, the commission recommends:

That Federal, state, and local governments make funds available to support abortion services in states with liberalized statutes.

That abortion be specifically included in comprehensive health insurance benefits, both public and private.

Services for Teenagers

As a society, we have been reluctant to acknowledge that there is a considerable amount of sexual activity among unmarried young people. The national study [a public opinion survey made for the commission] which disclosed that 27 per cent of unmarried girls 15 to 19 years old had had sexual relations further revealed that girls have a considerable acquaintance with contraceptive methods; over 95 per cent of all girls 15 to 19, for example, know about the pill.

Contraceptive practice, however, contrasts sharply with this picture. Although many young women who have had intercourse have used a contraceptive at some time, this age group is characterized by a great deal of "chance taking." The majority of these young women have either never used or, at best, have sometimes used birth control methods.

We deplore the various consequences of teen-age pregnancy, including the recent report from New York that teen-agers account for about one-quarter of the abortions performed under their new statute during its first year.

Adolescent pregnancy offers a generally bleak picture of serious physical, psychological and social implications for the teen-ager and the child. Once a teen-ager becomes pregnant, her chances of enjoying a rewarding, satisfying life are diminished. Pregnancy is the number one cause of school drop-out among females in the United States.

The psychological effects of adolescent pregnancy are indicated by a recent study that estimated that teen-age mothers have a suicide attempt rate 10 times that of the general population.

The commission is not addressing the moral questions involved in teen-age sexual behavior. However, we are concerned with the complex issue of teen-age pregnancy. Therefore, the commission believes that young people must be given access to contraceptive information and services.

Toward the goal of reducing unwanted pregnancies and childbearing among the young, the commission recommends that birth control information and services be made available to teen-agers in appropriate facilities sensitive to their needs and concerns.

SEPARATE STATEMENTS

By Marilyn Brandt Chandler

The commission report does stress that abortion should not be a substitute for birth control but has not intimated that liberal abortion takes the responsibility away from sexual activity. Impulsive, irresponsible sexual involvement can be rationalized without fear of pregnancy if abortion is open, legal, and free.

By Paul B. Cornley, M.D.

The Law: The argumentative posture of these paragraphs [of the commission report] is exclusively that of the pro-abortionists, namely, that abortion legislation has been no more than a health measure postulated on the welfare of the mother only. This section of the report does not even make an attempt to provide a legal accounting for the unborn developing child.

The Moral Question: This section of the report proposes that only one moral principle be the controlling factor in the abortion situation: the woman's freedom to reproduce. Such moralistic monism, simplistic as it is, at bottom fails to consider the freedom of the unborn child to live.

By Rep. John N. Erlenborn

Since this is a "population" commission and not a "birth control" commission, what compelling consideration leads the commission to make this very controversial [abortion] recommendation when it has little or no population or demographic consequence?

March 17, 1972

PRESIDENT BARS BIRTH CURB PLANS

Rejects Panel's Proposals on Eased Abortion Laws and Aid for Teen-Agers

By ROBERT B. SEMPLE Jr.
Special to The New York Times

WASHINGTON, May 5 — President Nixon rejected today two recommendations from his own Commission on Population Growth.

The commission, in reports published in March, recommended that all states greatly liberalize abortion laws and permit a doctor to perform an abortion at a patient's request.

The commission also encouraged states to make contraceptive devices and other family planning services widely available to teen-agers.

In a written statement issued today after he formally received the commission's final, three-volume report, Mr. Nixon said that he still regarded abortion as "an unacceptable means of population control" and that he did not support what he called "unrestricted abortion policies."

As for the widespread distribution of contraceptives to minors, Mr. Nixon said, "Such measures would do nothing to preserve and strengthen close family relations." He did not elaborate.

The President said that he would place his trust in the American people themselves. He said he felt confident that they would make "sound judgments that are conducive both to the public interest and to personal family goals." Moreover, he said, he retained a firm belief "in the right of married couples to make these judgments by themselves."

Mr. Nixon's reaffirmation of the "right" of married couples to determine family size carried, at least to some observers here, a faintly ironic ring—for it was precisely this same right on which the commission based its contention that abortion rules should be liberalized. Its report said, in part:

"The commission believes that the various prohibitions against abortion throughout the United States stand as obstacles to the exercise of individual freedom: the freedom of women to make difficult moral choices based on their own personal values, the freedom of women to control their own fertility, and finally, freedom from the burden of unwanted childbearing."

Despite these disagreements, the President said he thought the commission's findings and conclusions would be "of great value in assisting governments at all levels of public policy." He did not, however, say which provisions he had found to be valuable, and it was not immediately clear how his Administration intended to proceed on the commission's suggestions.

No Comment on Growth Halt

Nor did Mr. Nixon comment on the commission's basic proposal that the United States should slow — and gradually stop—the growth of its population, or on another suggestion that continuing migration out of rural areas be diverted away from larger cities into economically healthier smaller cities.

The first suggestion runs counter to the notion that population growth is essential to economic growth; the second has many adherents within the Administration.

The President's opposition to the commission's proposals on abortion and the distribution of contraceptive devices was not unexpected. On April 3, 1971, he revised liberalized abortion rules in military hospitals, stating then, for the first time, that he regarded abortion as an "unacceptable" means of population control.

Fully aware of the President's views, the commission carefully explained that it was recommending new abortion laws not as a means of controlling population but as a means of enlarging individual freedom. But this did not satisfy many Roman Catholic leaders, some conservatives, and, as it turned out, Mr. Nixon.

The chairman of the 24-member commission, whose full title is the Commission on Population Growth and the American Future, is John D. Rockefeller 3d, who presented the report to Mr. Nixon. The report was the result of two years' work.

May 6, 1972

Antiabortion Forces Demonstrate a Growing Influence in State Legislatures Across the Country

Special to The New York Times

WASHINGTON, June 27 — Forces fighting the trend toward more liberal abortion laws, which some states began implementing about five years ago, are demonstrating a growing influence on state legislatures across the country.

In some states, including California, Florida, Colorado and Hawaii, antiabortion activity is aimed at rolling back liberalized laws already on the books. In New York State, the Legislature's repeal of the state's two-year-old abortion law—allowing abortion on demand until the 24th week of pregnancy—was vetoed last month by Governor Rockefeller, who contended that the repeal was "unjustified."

In other states, including Connecticut, Iowa, Illinois, Michigan, Massachusetts and Pennsylvania, the goal is to prevent liberal abortion bills from being passed.

A check in the capitals of these states indicates that, in both cases, pressure from a number of organized efforts—particularly a confederation of local committees called Right to Life—are being felt and acknowledged by state officials.

Too Far Afield

Complaints have been heard in Sacramento, Calif., for example, that the antiabortion forces are going too far afield, to the extent of opposing any type of birth control legislation. One member of a committee considering a bill to stimulate distribution of birth control information said, "It sounds like a good bill but why have I gotten 3,000 letters against it?"

The National Right to Life Committee just ended its third annual convention in Philadelphia with a unanimous resolution in "support of President Nixon's public opposition to permissive abortion laws.' Michael Taylor, the group's executive secretary, said in an interview that groups were being set up to lobby with members of the Democratic party's Platform Committee to forestall "any possible attempt by liberals" to draft a proabortion plank in the party's 1972 platform.

The organization, which Mr. Taylor said had a chapter in "nearly every state," started around 1967, but "really got going in 1969 when the proabortionists started their push for abortion-on-demand."

Earlier this month, Mrs. Sargeant Shriver addressed the national convention of Birthright-U.S.A. in Atlantic City. Founded in 1968, Birthright operates urban counseling centers where pregnant women are encouraged to shun abortion and have their babies.

A National Campaign

Disputing that there is such a thing as an "unwanted baby," Mrs. Shriver proposed a national campaign, to be called One Million for Life, for a million couples who want to adopt an infant to register with Birthright.

For every woman who is considering having an abortion, Mrs. Shriver told the delegates, "there is at least one family and probably many more who would be eager to adopt a baby and give it the chance to develop a life of grace and physical and emotional perfection."

Most of the antiabortion groups are "grass roots" organizations, as described by an attorney representing them in one state, and were formed in reaction to the move toward more liberal policies on abortion. Legislators interviewed in the survey who had helped to loosen the laws in several states remarked that, if the organizations had existed at the time, with the strength they now demonstrate, the measure probably would not have passed.

Membership tends to be heavily Roman Catholic along with some conservative elements of Protestants and Jews. In California, for example, "Catholics are the strongest single force," reported a spokesman for Assemblyman Robert H. Burke, a Republican who has introduced a number of bills aimed at tightening California's broadened rules. "But we are bending over backward to keep the religion angle out of it," he said. "We don't want one religious conviction against another."

Generally, the active membership of the individual groups is not large, but observers on both sides of the controversy say they are able to muster participation by many thousands in a crisis campaign.

Visits and Demonstrations

The members apply tactics that range from the traditional mass-mailings and personal visits to legislators to demonstrations and counterdemonstrations at state capitols.

Lobbying in the New York Assembly this spring became so intense that, on one day, the Speaker was provoked into barring all lobbyists from the chamber. In New York, the major antiabortion forces are the Roman Catholic Church and more than 50 Right to Life groups, whose leaders say they have a following of 200,000 people.

"When it comes down to the wire," according to Robert M. Brake, a former Florida legislator and now treasurer of the Miami-area Right to Life Committee, "the Catholic archbishop generally has a letter read in the churches urging parishioners to call for defeat of the bill."

Political activity aimed at state legislators can be highly intense, with some groups circulating legislators' voting records throughout their districts. State Senator Hugh Fowler, a proabortion Republican in Colorado, expressed a common theme — that many legislators who would like to vote for easier abortions "have been terrorized" out of doing so.

"We get inundated with mail and direct verbal threats of retaliation at the polls," said Illinois Representative Bruce Douglas, a Democrat of Chicago. A bill he introduced that would have allowed abortions on demand within the first 12 weeks of pregnancy was killed in committee last year, and he has no plans to try again this year.

Illinois Representative Leland H. Rayson, a Democrat who has sponsored abortion bills since 1967, has been the target of a special campaign—to make an example of him, he believes, to prevent other legislators from voting for abortion reform.

A group called Illinois Citizens Concerned for Life flooded his district with literature bearing a picture captioned, "These are the remains of an aborted baby in a hospital bucket awaiting disposal," and exhorting voters to "prevent this needless killing . . . work for the defeat of Leland Rayson."

Mr. Rayson believes the tactic lost him enough votes in the primary to get him the bottom ballot position in the November election. In any case, other liberals in the Legislature said privately that they had given up on the abortion issue in the foreseeable future. "It's a hopeless cause here," said one, who did not want his name used.

In Michigan, where a liberal reform proposition has qualified for listing on the November general election ballot, a leader in favor of reform in the State House of Representatives attributed the political power of antiabortion forces to local organizations' ability.

"There isn't a week goes by that I don't hear from some of them on this issue," Representative Richard J. Allen said in an interview.

"They've got the passionate voters who will swing on a single issue," he continued. "You can favor financial support for nonpublic schools and everything else, but you're done if you cross over their line on abortion."

Mr. Allen said the groups had a major role in the 1970 defeat of N. Lorraine Beebe, then Michigan's only woman

Senator and a leading figure in the abortion reform movement.

"I had a therapeutic abortion 20 years ago," she once recalled in an emotional speech during a Senate debate. Mrs. Beebe was defeated by 4,700 votes, out of 75,000 cast, by 22-year-old David Plawecki, who became the youngest State Senator in the country.

The major antiabortion force in Connecticut is the Roman Catholic Church, which campaigned in a special session of the General Assembly last month and succeeded in putting a new antiabortion law on the state books soon after a United States District Court declared the state's 112-year-old abortion law unconstitutional.

The new law, which was passed with vigorous prompting from Connecticut's Republican Governor, Thomas J. Meskill, provides an even tougher penalty for performing or advising an abortion than did the 19th-century law—a maximum sentence of five years, rather than two.

To prevent another court case, the new Connecticut law includes a preamble stating that "it is the intent of the Legislature to protect and preserve human life from the moment of conception."

In a similar move a few days ago, the Massachusetts Legislature voted initial approval to a proposed constitutional amendment that would grant every child, from the moment of conception, "the rights of all citizens." State Representative David S. Liederman argued that the amendment was "dangerous" because voting districts would have to be changed because fetuses would have to be counted as citizens.

The Pennsylvania House voted last week in favor of a bill to outlaw abortions except in cases where there was "reasonable medical certainty" that the woman would die without the operation. The measure is awaiting further action in the State Senate.

Representative Martin P. Mullen, chairman of the Appropriations Committee in the Pennsylvania House, has become known as "St. Martin the First" for his diligence in furthering the legislative interests of the Catholic Church. Last year, he threatened to hold the state budget in his committee until the State Public Welfare Department stopped subsidizing abortions of women on relief. But the department stood firm, and Mr. Mullen relented.

June 28, 1972

High Court Rules Abortions Legal the First 3 Months

State Bans Ruled Out Until Last 10 Weeks

National Guidelines Set by 7-to-2 Vote

By WARREN WEAVER Jr.

Special to The New York Times

WASHINGTON, Jan. 22 — The Supreme Court overruled today all state laws that prohibit or restrict a woman's right to obtain an abortion during her first three months of pregnancy. The vote was 7 to 2.

In a historic resolution of a fiercely controversial issue, the Court drafted a new set of national guidelines that will result in broadly liberalized anti-abortion laws in 46 states but will not abolish restrictions altogether.

Establishing an unusually detailed timetable for the relative legal rights of pregnant women and the states that would control their acts, the majority specified the following:

¶For the first three months of pregnancy the decision to have an abortion lies with the woman and her doctor, and the state's interest in her welfare is not "compelling" enough to warrant any interference.

¶For the next six months of pregnancy a state may "regulate the abortion procedure in ways that are reasonably related to maternal health," such as licensing and regulating the persons and facilities involved.

¶For the last 10 weeks of pregnancy, the period during which the fetus is judged to be capable of surviving if born, any state may prohibit abortions, if it wishes, except where they may be necessary to preserve the life or health of the mother.

Today's action will not affect existing laws in New York, Alaska, Hawaii and Washington, where abortions are now legally available in the early months of pregnancy. But it will require rewriting of statutes in every other state.

The basic Texas case decided by the Court today will invalidate strict anti-abortion laws in 31 states; a second decision involving Georgia will require considerable rewriting of more liberal statutes in 15 others.

Justice Harry A. Blackmun wrote the majority opinion in which Chief Justice Warren E. Burger and Justices William O. Douglas, William J. Brennan Jr., Potter Stewart, Thurgood Marshall and Lewis F. Powell Jr. joined.

Dissenting were Justices Byron R. White and William H. Rehnquist.

Justice White, calling the decision "an exercise of raw judicial power," wrote that "the Court apparently values the convenience of the pregnant mother more than the continued existence and development of the life or potential life which she carries."

The Court's decision was at odds with the expressed views of President Nixon. Last May, in a letter to Cardinal Cooke, he opposed "liberalized abortion policies" and spoke out for "the right to life of literally hundreds of thousands of unborn children."

But three of the four Justices Mr. Nixon has appointed to the Supreme Court voted with the majority, with only Mr. Rehnquist dissenting.

The majority rejected the idea that a fetus becomes a "person" upon conception and is thus entitled to the due process and equal protection guarantees of the Constitution. This view was pressed by opponents of liberalized abortion, including the Roman Catholic Church.

Justice Blackmun concluded that "the word 'person,' as used in the 14th Amendment, does not include the unborn," although states may acquire, "at some point in time" of pregnancy, an interest in the "potential human life" that the fetus represents, to permit regulation.

It is that interest, the Court said, that permits states to prohibit abortion during the last 10 weeks of pregnancy, after the fetus has developed the capacity to survive.

In both cases decided today, the plaintiffs had based their protest on an assertion that state laws limiting the availability of abortion had circumscribed rights and freedoms guaranteed them by the Constitution: due process of law, equal protection of the laws, freedom of action and a particular privacy involving a personal and family matter.

In its decision on the challenge to the Georgia abortion law, the high court majority struck down several requirements that a woman seeking to terminate her pregnancy in that state would have to meet.

Decision for Doctors

Among them were a flat prohibition on abortions for out-of-state residents and requirements that hospitals be accredited by a private agency, that applicants be screened by a hospital committee and that two independent doctors certify the potential danger to the applicant's health.

The Georgia law permitted abortions when a doctor found in "his best clinical judgment" that continued pregnancy would threaten the woman's life or health, that the fetus would be likely to be born defective or that the pregnancy was the result of rape.

The same Supreme Court majority, with Justice Blackmun writing the opinion again, emphasized that this medical judgment should cover all relevant factors—"physical, emotional, psychological familial and the woman's age."

In some of the 15 states with laws similar to Georgia's, doctors have tended to take a relatively narrow view of what constituted a woman's health in deciding whether an abortion was legally justified.

The Texas law that the Court invalidated entirely was typical of the criminal statutes passed in the last half of the 19th century prohibiting all abortions except those to save a mother's life. The Georgia law, approved in 1972 and altered by the Court today, was patterned after the model penal code of the American Law Institute.

In the Texas case, Justice Blackmun wrote that the con-

United Press International

Justice Harry A. Blackmun

stitutional right of privacy, developed by the Court in a long series of decisions, was "broad enough to encompass a woman's decision whether or not to terminate her pregnancy."

He rejected, however, the argument of women's rights groups that this right was absolute "and she is entitled to terminate her pregnancy at whatever time, in whatever way and for whatever reason she alone chooses."

"With this we do not agree," the Justice declared.

"A state may properly assert important interests in safeguarding health in maintaining medical standards and in protecting potential life," Mr. Blackmun observed. "At some point in pregnancy, these respective interests become sufficiently compelling to sustain regulation of the factors that govern the abortion decision."

The majority concluded that this "compelling" state interest arose at the end of the first three months of pregnancy because of the "now established medical fact" that until then, fewer women die from abortions than from normal childbirth.

During this three-month period, the Court said, a doctor can recommend an abortion to his patient "without regulation by the state" and the resulting operations can be conducted "free of interference by the state."

The "compelling state interest" in the fetus does not arise, however, until the time of "viability," Justice Blackmun wrote, when it has "the capability of meaningful life outside the mother's womb." This occurs about 10 weeks before delivery.

In reading an abbreviated version of his two opinions to the Court this morning, Justice Blackmun noted that most state legislatures were in session now and would thus be able to rewrite their states' abortion laws to conform to the Court's decision.

Both of today's cases wound up with anonymous parties winning victories over state officials. In the Texas case, "Jane Roe," an unmarried pregnant woman who was allowed to bring the case without further identity, was the only plaintiff after the Supreme Court disqualified a doctor and a childless couple who said that the wife's health would be endangered by pregnancy.

In the Georgia case, the surviving plaintiff was "Mary Doe," who, when she brought the action. was a 22-year-old married woman 11 weeks pregnant with her fourth child.

January 23, 1973

Abortions, Legal for Year, Performed for Thousands

Supreme Court Decision Has Removed Much of Social Stigma and Brought Them Into Medical Mainstream

A 30-year-old divorcee who was eight weeks pregnant entered the brightly colored offices of Women's Health Services, an abortion clinic in downtown Pittsburgh, and within three hours had had an abortion, rested in the clinic's recovery room, paid the $150 fee and gone home.

A year ago the procedure would have been illegal in Pennsylvania and in almost every other state, but today, almost a year after the Supreme Court ruled that abortions are legal, similar scenes are being played out in clinics and hospitals in virtually every part of the country.

The sweeping change that has resulted from the Court decision has removed much of the social stigma associated with the operation and has taken abortions out of the backrooms of the illegal abortionist and brought them into the mainstream of modern medical care.

While there are few official figures on the number of legal abortions performed since the Court decision, interviews conducted by The New York Times in a dozen major cities disclose that tens of thousands of abortions are being performed in cities where a year ago it was impossible to obtain the operation.

Used False Names

"Before the decision, women would come begging for abortions," said Marilyn Cringer, a counselor for Arkansas Woman's Rights, an abortion referral agency. "Many used false names, and most were extraordinarily concerned over our confidentiality."

"Now, when women call, they feel that an abortion is their right," she added. "We don't have to assuage their guilt. Women just want the facts—where they can go for the best and least expensive abortion."

The Times survey also indicates that in some states roadblocks, such as restrictive state laws and high prices, still exist for women seeking the operation. However, in most cases, legal abortion facilities can be found in a neighboring state, only a few hours' drive away.

The Supreme Court ruled last Jan. 22 that all state laws that prohibit or restrict a woman's right to obtain an abortion during the first three months of pregnancy are unconstitutional. The Court also ruled that abortions after the first three months are also legal but are subject to limited state regulations.

For All But 4 States

The decision, in effect, overruled laws in all but four states — Alaska, Hawaii, New York and Washington, which already had liberalized laws. Since the decision, there has been a decline in the number of abortions performed in these states.

New York City, where the operation has been legal under a liberalized law since 1970, recently released a report that showed that more than a half million abortions had been performed since the law was enacted. In the year from July 1, 1971, to June 30, 1972, before the Supreme Court ruling, 228,094 abortions were performed in the city. In the following year, when the decision was handed down, the number of abortions declined by 15 per cent to 196,224.

22 Clinics in Detroit

According to the city's Health Services Administration, the decline resulted in part from a decrease in the number of out-of-state residents who sought abortions in New York.

Atlanta, which until January was subject to Georgia's stringent anti-abortion law, now has seven abortion clinics, some of which are performing 100 cases a week. Almost all of the city's hospitals, except for the Roman Catholic ones, are also performing them.

Detroit, which serves as an abortion center for much of the Middle West, has 22 abortion clinics and referral agencies listed in the telephone directory. The average cost for a first trimester abortion at the clinics is $150, while the hospitals charge an average of

$350. Second trimester cases can run as high as $1,400 at the hospitals.

Not Challenged

Until the Massachusetts anti-abortion law was struck down by the Supreme Court, most women from the state seeking abortions would come to New York. This year, the Massachusetts Department of Public Health estimates that 40,000 women will get abortions in Massachusetts. Most of these abortions will be performed during the first three months of pregnancy, the agency says.

In some states, however, the situation has not changed despite the Court decision. Arkansas, for example, enforces a state law specifying that abortions may be performed only if the pregnancy "threatens the life or health" of a woman. A pro-abortion group in Little Rock refers its clients to clinics in Dallas or Kansas City, Mo.

To date, the Arkansas law has not been challenged in court, but an attorney general's ruling has declared it unconstitutional.

"It's just easier for a person to go out of state than it is to go through the legal hassles involved in a court case," an abortion counselor in Little Rock explained.

Half Do Not Comply

In Virginia, the 1973 session of the state legislature refused to make the Virginia law conform with the Supreme Court ruling. Instead, the General Assembly passed a resolution requesting the Court to reconsider its decision.

"The General Assembly's action had a chilling effect on doctors and hospitals around the state," said Mrs. Shalom DuBow, director of the Virginia Civil Liberties Union. "In Virginia, there is still the attitude that abortion is immoral. The General Assembly reinforced that."

After the Court ruling was issued, Virginia's attorney general, Andrew P. Miller, issued an advisory opinion that the state's medical profession should be guided by the Supreme Court ruling rather than by the state's restrictive law.

As a result of the conflicting rulings by the state legislature and the attorney general, about 50 per cent of Virginia hospitals still do not comply with the Court ruling.

Mrs. DuBow said the state's Civil Liberties Union was seeking a test case to attack the state law.

In almost all of the states in which such suits have been filed and ruled upon, the courts have ordered compliance with the Supreme Court ruling.

Hasn't Heard of One

In Pennsylvania, a Federal judge ordered the state Department of Social Welfare to pay abortion costs for those on public assistance. And in Florida, a judge ruled unconstitutional a provision of the state law that required the consent of the patient's parent or spouse before an abortion could be performed.

Another apparent effect of the ruling has been to put the illegal abortionists out of business. In Dayton, Ohio, which has a clinic that performs 200 abortions a month, law enforcement officials could not remember the last time an illegal abortionist was apprehended.

In Tacoma, Wash., where a liberal law was approved in 1970, a state health official said she had not heard of an illegal abortion in several years.

"They probably would be less expensive legally," she said.

National organizations that have taken major stands on the abortion law have redirected their efforts in the year since the Court decision.

The National Association for Repeal of Abortion Laws, known as N.A.R.A.L., has preserved its acronym but has changed its name because the laws have already been repealed. The organization, which was in the forefront of the fight to legalize abortion, is now called the National Abortion Rights Action League. It now concentrates on preserving and enforcing the new laws.

The National Right to Life Committee, which for many years supported the status quo, is now seeking to change the law. The group plans to push for a constitutional amendment, in Congress and in the state legislatures, to guarantee the rights of a fetus, thereby nullifying the Supreme Court decision.

December 31, 1973

Population Growth of U.S. Approaching the Zero Level

Population growth in the United States is now below 1 per cent a year and approaching zero, according to a United Nations report.

The Economic and Social Council, reporting on the social situation in North America, put United States population growth at an average of nine-tenths of 1 per cent for the first four years of the seventies. The average in the previous decade was 1.3 per cent a year, according to United Press International.

The report said that with the replacement level of the population at 2.2 children per wife, surveys had found that young American wives expected an average of 2.3 children. Immigration had also slowed.

The United States, it said, appeared "to be approaching a natural rate of increase close to zero."

November 29, 1974

Funding Sterilization and Abortion for the Poor

By Sheila M. Rothman

A Department of Health, Education and Welfare proposal, now under study, to fund 90 per cent of the costs of sterilization for the poor but only to match state funds for abortion for the poor, is but the latest example of an ongoing disregard for individual freedom of choice.

By such an action, the poor would be deprived of the opportunity to select equally between sterilization and abortion. Worse yet, H.E.W. is encouraging the states to make sterilization the predominant mode of contraception among the poor. And given the history of coercion that characterizes sterilization programs, this proposal should be disallowed.

When the Federal Government first entered the field of family planning, in 1970, it pledged to provide a wide variety of contraceptive services to the poor while respecting individual conscience and rights of choice. But a gap between rhetoric and reality quickly emerged.

Although the Family Planning Act did not mention sterilization as a contraceptive service, the new clinics were soon sterilizing 100,000 to 150,000 women each year. The department justified this initiative by insisting that voluntary consent was always obtained first.

Unfortunately, family planners' zeal to sterilize the poor often outran their regard for genuine voluntary consent. Convinced that lowering the birth rate among the poor was an apt solution to a host of social problems, from increasing welfare costs to the strain on environmental resources, they paid too little attention to fundamental rights of autonomy.

In 1973 and 1974, a few headline cases captured attention. Two black teen-age girls in Alabama were sterilized without their consent or that of their parents; a South Carolina woman about to deliver her fourth child was threatened with a cutoff of medical and welfare services unless she "agreed" to sterilization. But abuses are not limited to a few Southern states, and are not the fault of a handful of overenthusiastic doctors. Rather, family-planning officials in many states freely prescribed Depo-Provera as a contraceptive drug even though the Food and Drug Administration had prohibited such use of it because permanent sterilization was one of its adverse side-effects. The patients who received this drug, not aware of this danger, could not give informed consent.

Moreover, national surveys of medical practices have discovered that women in nonprivate hospital wards and black women are sterilized far more frequently, and at younger ages, and after having had fewer children, than women in private wards or white women. One may well wonder how their informed consent was obtained.

The coalition of forces ready to impose sterilization on the poor is overwhelming. It is the professionals, the doctors, social workers, and community-action workers who in the name of doing good and delivering services have often deprived the poor of their rights.

The slogan of "reproductive freedom" has come to mean the right to have fewer children, not the right to have more children. Perhaps some of the poor do wish to undergo sterilization, although probably just as many of them, as research has made clear, find having children one remaining source of gratification in otherwise grim lives.

Perhaps a reduction of the birth rate among the poor would reduce the environmental crisis (but one doubts it). Perhaps smaller families would elevate the standard of living among the poor (but this reasoning is a variant on the theme of blaming the poor for their poverty). Neverthless, in a society committed to the integrity of the individual other solutions to these problems must be found.

Hence, when H.E.W. proposes to fund sterilization but not abortion it selects the worst possible option.

Abortion, at least, has none of the finality of sterilization; the woman can later decide to have another child.

If the original mandate of the Family Planning Act is to stand, all types of contraceptive techniques must be available to the poor. Ninety per cent funding for sterilization offers a seductive incentive to clinics and hospitals to promote this service that they are already overcommitted to. Better to fund 90 per cent of both programs or to fund neither, than to resolve, as H.E.W. has done, to fund that program which is most irreversible and most susceptible to abuse.

Sheila M. Rothman, research associate at the Center for Policy Research, is author of a forthcoming book about American social policy toward women, children and the family.

February 22, 1975

Contraception Study Slows as Costly Testing Curbs Industry's Prospects of Profits

By JANE E. BRODY

The development of new and safer methods of contraception for American couples is being seriously hampered by a combination of factors that has removed the drug industry's main incentive for developing new products: the prospect of a profitable return on research investment.

As a result, many researchers in the field say, it is highly unlikely that any major new contraceptives that overcome the main difficulties associated with current methods will be placed on the American market within the next decade and perhaps not before 1990.

"There are a number of interesting new items in the pipeline that will produce small increases in safety and acceptability of existing methods, but there is very little innovative research being done in contraception either in or out of industry," said Dr. Gordon Duncan, associate director of Battelle Memorial Institute's Population Study Center who recently completed a survey of drug industry involvement in contraceptive research.

"There is also very little fundamental biological research being done that would support truly innovative developments," Dr. Duncan added.

Interviews with research leaders within the drug industry and outside it indicate that this situation is largely the result of inherent conflicts among science, Government and public and commercial interests. Some of the conflicts invoke a fundamental challenge to the tradition of profit as the moving force behind scientific developments, particularly in medicine.

Conflicts Are Intense

Given the intensity of these conflicts in the United States today, Dr. Allan C. Barnes, vice president for biomedical affairs of the Rockefeller Foundation, has concluded, "It is entirely possible that if the ideal contraceptive were developed today, it would never be introduced in the United States. It would be taken to someplace like India, where there's a large and eager market."

While similar conflicts exist for all new drug development, for varying reasons the impact is being felt most intensely in the contraceptive area.

Those interviewed, some of whom asked not to be identified for fear that the association of their names with their statements would reveal company secrets, said that the factors discouraging development of new birth control methods by private industry include the following:

¶Increasingly stringent, lengthy and expensive premarket tests required by the Federal Government.

¶A growing number of lawsuits related to the adverse health effects of existing contraceptives.

¶A general social climate that demands absolute safety from agents that can never be totally without risk.

Faced with a 17-year patent limitation and the need for up to 15 years of research, development and testing before a new contraceptive agent can be approved for marketing, drug companies have only a few years after introducing a new agent in which to realize a return on their investment.

It is true that there is a potential for tremendous profits in the contraceptive business, but there is also more economic risk than is usually associated with drug development. Contraceptive agents are more vulnerable to Government rejection, with their demise often occurring when they are at or near marketing stage after a decade or more of study and heavy research expenditures.

Tougher Safety Standards

Since birth control agents are used by millions of essentially healthy persons for prolonged periods of time, far more rigid safety standards are set for them than for ordinary drugs. Several initially promising agents have had to be withdrawn after long-term tests on animals suggested a potential unacceptable hazard.

When the first oral contraceptive was approved for sale in the United States in 1960, there were relatively few standards to go by to judge the adequacy of premarket tests.

As unanticipated side-effects began to show up, the Federal Food and Drug Administration increased its premarket and postmarket testing requirements—some say too much, others say not enough.

Current testing procedures, which in part require extended

tests of all chemical contraceptives on beagle dogs that are highly susceptible to breast tumors, forced the withdrawal of several promising agents, including chlormadinone acetate, the first progestogen-only mini-pill that 'avoided the serious hazards associated with estrogen.

At the time it was withdrawn, chlormadinone acetate had already been tested in thousands of women for several years. The approval of two already marketed oral contraceptives was withdrawn at the same time because they contained the same chemical.

More recently, at the urging of Congressmen and consumer groups, approval for a three-month injectable contraceptive, Depo-Provera, was suspended indefinitely after it was linked to a possible increased risk of cervical cancer in women (although the validity of the key study is still in dispute) and breast tumors in beagles.

Since there are already a number of highly effective—albeit, not entirely safe—contraceptives on the market, the F.D.A. now takes a much harder look at the possible adverse effects of new agents. As a result, in weighing benefits against risks, the benefits of new agents are less likely to come out ahead than they were for the original oral contraceptives, which represented a revolution in birth control technology.

Several Companies Quit

Thus, in the last year or two, several major companies that had been heavily involved in contraceptive research and development in the nineteen-sixties have left the field entirely, deciding that it would be more profitable to spend their research dollars in other areas. Other companies have adopted more limited horizons when it comes to contraceptive research.

The survey that Dr. Duncan conducted for the Ford Foundation indicates that the drug industry as a whole is planning to spend nearly as much on contraceptive research and development in the remaining half of the decade as it did in the early nineteen-seventies—about $15-million a year. But with inflation, that money will not go as far.

And an analysis of how this money is being spent shows that only a small percentage is going toward the development of radically new and improved contraceptive methods.

Instead, the great bulk of research money is being devoted to modifications of already existing birth control methods—changes that might make these methods more convenient or associated with fewer annoying side-effects but that will not remove the more serious limitations and health concerns associated with them.

The diminishing involvement of private industry in new contraceptive development is in part being countered by several organizations in the public sector that have established research programs to develop promising new leads in the contraceptive field.

The main groups involved are the World Health Organization, the National Institutes of Health and the International Committee for Contraceptive Research, an international group of scientists organized by The Population Council and funded by foundation grants.

Outlay of $15-Million

Together they are spending up to $15-million a year on contraceptive development, about the same as the entire American drug industry. The groups, which coordinate their efforts to avoid duplication, all have essentially the same goal—to develop to marketing stage approaches to contraception that will be more acceptable to people, especially to people in developing countries.

According to Dr. Sheldon Segal, medical director of The Population Council and organizer of the international group, "The decisions as to what kinds of contraceptives to develop that are made by industry in the privacy of board rooms are not necessarily compatible with what people need.

"Since industry's goal is to make money, they are concerned with how good a product will be—its patentability, profit potential, the magnitude of the market, the product liability."

The research groups are exploring a wide variety of promising new contraceptives, many of them agents that had been lying undeveloped on some drug company shelf. Included are oral contraceptives for men, biodegradable capsules containing contraceptive hormones, medicated intrauterine and vaginal devices, a once-a-week pill, contraceptive "vaccines" and long-acting injections.

To make a major impact on the contraceptive field in the United States, birth control experts say, a new method should ideally have the following attributes: It should be simple to use, have only local action on the reproductive system, require infrequent administration at a time separate from the sex act, and relatively free of long-term hazards to health as well as annoying side-effects that discourage use.

Once-a-Month Pill

Such methods might include a once-a-month pill that would eliminate a fertilized egg should one be present and a male contraceptive that acts locally, does not require daily administration and does not interfere with sexual desire or performance.

"When it comes to really new methods that overcome basic objections to current methods, the prospects are atrocious," said Dr. Carl Djerassi, professor of chemistry at Stanford University and a former director of research at Syntex, until recently a leader in contraceptive research.

In 1970, Dr. Djerassi wrote in the journal Science that unless "important incentives for continued active participation by the pharmaceutical industry [are developed], birth control in 1984 will not differ significantly from that of today."

Now, Dr. Djerassi said, he has "turned out to be 120 per cent right," Five years ago, he estimated that it would take 10 to 15 years of research at a cost of between $10- and $30-million to develop a totally new contraceptive; today, he said, with additional testing requirements and a 50 per cent inflation factor, the cost is probably much higher.

None of those interviewed in or outside of industry doubted the advisability of stringent premarket testing requirements for contraceptives. As Dr. Earl Gerard, manager of fertility research at The Upjohn Company, commented, "When you're talking about contraception, it's a nondisease you're treating and the safety of the treatment becomes paramount."

But serious questions were raised by some about the tendency to consider only the risk side of the coin when evaluating the effects of contraceptives.

As Dr. Barnes of the Rockefeller Foundation remarked, "A mood for absolute safety is sweeping the country as part of the whole consumerism movement. We've all begun to assume benefit and concentrate only on risks.

"This is very damaging to women and to research, leading to extended delays in approval of new methods, costly animal tests of questionable validity for human beings, Senate hearings and harassment from consumer groups."

March 5, 1975

World's Backward Are Told to Curb Births; Educator Says Truman Aid Needs This Step

WASHINGTON, March 5 (UP)—The United States must teach the world's backward peoples to delay marriage and reduce their birth rates if President Truman's Point Four program to improve underdeveloped areas is to succeed, the Foreign Policy Association said today.

A report prepared by J. B. Condliffe, director of the University of California's Teaching Institute, said the question of population increase was a major factor in economic development.

Therefore, he said, President Truman's plan to develop backward countries would not pay off until the peoples of Africa and Asia followed the population pattern of Europe, which has a declining birth rate.

"The only way in which to make sure that productivity outstrips the survival rate," Mr. Condliffe said, "is to use educational processes to reinforce the desire for improved living standards."

This could be brought about, he said, by teaching "postponement of marriage, limitation of the birth rate within marriage and the provision of educational opportunities for children."

He said these proposals ran counter to the "traditional folkways," and therefore progress would be slow.

But, he said, "economic development, if it is to succeed, must be a slow process of remaking the social organization and aspirations of communities that for centuries have followed a pattern of behavior inherited from time immemorial."

March 6, 1950

KENNEDY OPPOSES ADVOCACY BY U. S. OF BIRTH CONTROL

Says He Was Against 'Advice' to Other Nations Before Catholic Bishops Spoke

CALLS IT OBJECTIONABLE

Would Decide in Country's Best Interest if He Were President, Senator Says

By JAMES RESTON
Special to The New York Times.

WASHINGTON, Nov. 27—Senator John F. Kennedy, Democrat of Massachusetts, commented today on a statement by the Roman Catholic Bishops of the United States, who recently opposed the use of public funds to promote artificial birth control at home and abroad.

In a telephone interview, Senator Kennedy, a Roman Catholic who is seeking the Presidency, made these points:

¶ Long before last Wednesday's statement by members of the Administrative board of the National Catholic Welfare Conference, in the name of the Bishops, he had felt it would be a "mistake" for the United States Government to advocate birth control in other countries.

¶ This was a decision for the countries concerned to make for themselves. United States intervention would undoubtedly be regarded as "objectionable."

¶ However, the Senator said, if he were President and the question came before him in the form of legislation, or a recommendation from within the Executive Branch of Government, he would decide it in accordance with his oath to do whatever was best in the interests of the United States.

The statement by the bishops said there was "abundant evidence" of a systematic, concerted effort to convince public opinion, legislators, and policy makers in this country that United States national agencies and international organizations should provide public funds for promoting artificial birth prevention.

It expressed confidence in future scientific discoveries, rather than in birth-control policies, to meet the needs of the expanding world population. It stated that Catholics were prepared to "dedicate themselves" to this scientific effort to increase the production of food and other human needs, but it added:

"They [the Catholics] will not, however, support any public assistance, whether at home or abroad, to promote artificial birth prevention, abortion or sterilization, whether through direct aid or by means of international organizations."

The Right Rev. James A. Pike, Protestant Episcopal Bishop of San Francisco, said Wednesday that the policy favored by the Roman Catholic Bishops would "condemn rapidly increasing millions of people in less fortunate parts of the world to starvation, bondage, misery and dispair."

He asked whether the Catholic statement was "binding on Roman Catholic candidates for public office."

Reached at his home in Massachusetts this afternoon, Senator Kennedy said that it might have been fairer for Dean Pike to raise the political question with all Presidential candidates instead of merely those who were Roman Catholics.

Nevertheless, he said that he would be bound by his oath of office in any judgment he was called to make concerning public policy on birth-control questions.

Senator Kennedy did not deal with the moral and ecclesiastical questions involved. He will undoubtedly deal with this in a formal statement later. For the time being, he concentrated on the wisdom of any public United States policy that advocated birth control in the new, young developing countries of Asia and Africa.

Wary of Giving Advice

"We have to be very careful about how we give advice on this subject," he said. "The United States Government does not advocate any policy concerning birth control here in the United States. Nor have we ever advocated such a policy in Western Europe.

"Accordingly, I think it would be the greatest psychological mistake for us to appear to advocate limitation of the black, or brown, or yellow peoples whose population is increasing no faster than in the United States."

This question comes up often in official discussions about giving economic aid to other countries. For example, when a nation applies for aid, the United States Government studies the economic situation in the country concerned to see whether conditions there are such as to justify the conclusion that the United States funds or aid given will achieve their purpose.

Washington does not say to the recipient country: You must do this or that to put your internal house in order. But it often does say that while the country concerned can do what it likes, the United States Government must be satisfied, before putting out public funds, that the funds are going to have a chance to be effective.

A population increasing faster than aid can help it, therefore, has often been a factor in foreign aid negotiations. There is no evidence, however, that Washington has ever insisted on a birth-control policy in say, Japan or India, before agreeing to allocate funds to those countries.

World Population Zooming

According to official United States documents, the population of the world is increasing at the rate of about 50,000,000 a year. These documents concede that, because of inadequate census data in many countries, the figures are subject to a wide margin of error. However, the estimates of demographers regarded by officials here as reliable put the population of the earth in 1950 at 2,497,000,000 and at 2,790,000,000 in 1957—an increase of 293,000,000.

Population experts point out that the increase in the less developed areas of Africa, the Middle East and Latin America is not primarily caused by an increase in the birth rate, but by declines in the death rate.

Birth rates have remained at the high levels associated with these areas, but the introduction of modern medicine and public health methods has produced astounding declines in death rates.

Thus the net increase is now believed to be much higher than ever in history. The estimates here note that world population doubled during the two centuries between 1650 and 1850 and then more than doubled once more in the single century between 1850 and 1950. The present estimates are that, at the current rate of increase of 1.7 per cent a year, the population of the world will double in forty-one years.

Senator Kennedy emphasized, today, as the Roman Catholic bishops had done earlier in the week, that it was misleading merely to concentrate on the net increase in world population.

"The question I think we all have to address ourselves to," he said, "is whether the available resources of the world are increasing as fast as the population. That is the over-all question. My belief is that they are, though their management may not be."

The Unitarian Fellowship for

Social Justice issued a statement today saying that it would support "all efforts by the United States, in foreign aid or through the United Nations, to help birth control state programs in India, Japan, Puerto Rico, and all other countries where the population explosion is outstripping improved methods in food production."

Statement Called 'Unfair'

The statement criticized the Catholic bishops for lumping together in a single sentence "birth control, abortion and sterilization." This, the fellowship asserted, is "grossly unfair."

The questions put to Senator Kennedy, answered by him, and later corrected by him when typed, were as follows:

Q.—The bishops of the United States have said that United States Catholics "will not support any public assistance, either at home or abroad, to promote artificial birth prevention, abortion, or sterilization, whether through direct aid or by means of international organizations." What is your position on this?

A.—I think it would be a mistake for the United States Government to attempt to advocate the limitation of the population of under-developed countries. This problem involves important social and economic questions which must be solved by the people of those countries themselves. For the United States to intervene on this basis would involve a kind of mean paternalism, which I think they would find most objectionable.

Q.—Is your position on this influenced in any way by the pronouncement of the sixteen Roman Catholic bishops in Washington last Wednesday?

A.—My judgment on this has been held for many years, and it continues.

Poses 'Over-all' Question

Q.—You mean your present views are not the result of this statement by the bishops?

A.—No. The question I think we all have to address ourselves to is whether the available resources of the world are increasing as fast as the population. That is the over-all question. My belief is that they are, though their management may not be.

Nevertheless, we have to be very careful about how we give advice on this subject. The United States Government does not advocate any policy concerning birth control here in the United States. Nor have we ever advocated such a policy in Western Europe. Accordingly, I think it would be the greatest psychological mistake for us to appear to advocate the limitation of the black or brown or yellow peoples whose population is increasing no faster than in the United States. They must reach decisions on these matters based on their own experience and judgment.

Q.—What would be your position as President if the Indian Government, for example, decided on birth control as a matter of national policy? If they did so decide that it was in their interest to suggest limiting births in their national territory, would this in any way trouble you if you were President in giving aid to a country that followed such a policy?

A.—As I said before, I believe this is a matter to be determined by the country itself. I would not think it was wise for the United States to refuse to grant assistance to a country which is pursuing a policy it feels to be in its own best interest. To do so would be a kind of intervention in their national life, which I would think was unwise.

Q.—What if the Congress passed a law stating or recommending that countries receiving foreign aid should not allow their population to exceed their capacity to make the foreign aid funds effective?

A.—I would base my determination as to whether I should approve such a law on my personal judgment as President as to what would be in the interest of the United States. If it became a law of the land, I would uphold it as the law of the land.

Q.—What would you do if your Secretary of State and the head of the International Cooperation Administration recommended executive action suggesting birth control as a means of making foreign aid funds effective in another country?

A.—Well, again I would make a judgment on that matter as to what I considered to be in the best interest of the United States.

November 28, 1959

U. S. SURVEY FINDS POPULATION PERIL IN NEEDY NATIONS

Symington Favors the Giving of Birth-Control Help to Fight Poverty Abroad

OTHERS DIVULGE VIEWS

I.C.A. Says 'Not One Penny' of Aid Funds Was Used on Contraception Data

By E. W. KENWORTHY
Special to The New York Times.

WASHINGTON, Nov. 28—Most under-developed nations are fighting a nip-and-tuck battle to keep their economies abreast of their expanding populations.

This was the principal conclusion of a State Department intelligence report, prepared last July and made available today, on the problems created by the "unprecedented" population growth in the less-developed areas.

"In Latin America," the report stated, "the per capita product is now rising more slowly than during the early postwar years. And in most of Africa and Asia there appears to have been no really profound improvement in levels of living despite the fact that intensive programs of economic development have been in operation in some countries for more than a decade."

Bishops Take Firm Stand

The State Department document became available today amid growing indications that the population problem and proposals for dealing with it might become an issue in the United States Presidential campaign next year.

Last Wednesday the Roman Catholic Bishops of the United States set themselves firmly against the use of American foreign-aid funds to promote artificial birth control in less-developed countries.

In an interview yesterday with The New York Times, Senator John F. Kennedy of Massachusetts, a Catholic who is seeking the Democratic Presidential nomination, said he thought it would be a "mistake" for the United States to advocate birth control in other countries.

Favors Information

Today, another Democratic Senator who is regarded as a Presidential aspirant, Stuart Symington of Missouri, said that he favored the dissemination abroad by this country of information on planned parenthood.

Several other Democratic Presidential possibilities also gave their views on the issue.

The International Cooperation Administration described the discussion as academic today because "not one penny of foreign-aid funds ever has been used for dissemination of birth-control information and there are no plans to do so."

The State Department study pointed out that while the world's population was now increasing at a rate of 1.7 per cent a year, the growth rate in many less-developed countries was 3 to 3.5 per cent.

If the present trend continues, the world population, now estimated at 2,890,000,000, will be doubled in forty-one years. If the rate of growth increases to 2 per cent, the population will double in thirty-five years.

The State Department study emphasizes that the phenomenal growth in less-developed countries is not due to an increase in the birth rate but to a decline in the death rate accompanying the introduction of modern drugs and public health services. In nearly all these countries, especially in their rural areas, the birth rate continues at its former high level without much change, the report stated.

"If birth rates remain at high levels," the report pointed out, "economic expansion must eventually be achieved or death rates will be forced up again. In the long run, a country can have low death rates with all that they imply in the way of economic and social well being only if a reasonable balance is maintained between population growth and available resources."

The report said that "it can be theoretically demonstrated that, given sufficient development and utilization of the world's resources, the earth can adequately support a much larger population than any that can be expected by the year 2000."

However, the report noted, the real problem is how the less-developed areas are "to make the jump to this state of adequacy from the present situation in which most of their people are living at bare subsistence levels."

The report stated that the situation in the under-developed countries was quite different from that in the industrialized nations of North America and Western Europe when they first began to benefit from modern medicine and improved public health.

By 1900, the report noted, as a result of economic improvement, the pattern of small families was well on the way to being established in the leading industrialized nations. This made up in some measure for the decline in the mortality rate with improved medical services and a higher standard of living.

"Not only are the less-developed countries experiencing declines in mortality that are much more rapid than they ever were in the advanced industrial nations," the report went on, "they are also experiencing them at a much earlier stage of development before there has been any real substantial improvement in levels of living or fundamental changes in economic and social structure."

As an indication of how modern medicine had promoted population growth, the report cited the experience of Ceylon as a result of spraying with DDT to control malaria.

From 1946 to 1947, the death rate declined 30 per cent; the expectation of life at birth rose from 44 to almost 53 years for males, and from 42 to 51 years for females.

The accelerating population, the report said, could aggravate the problem of capital shortage in less-developed areas.

"The faster the population grows, the larger the share of each year's income which must be invested in increasing the stock of productive equipment merely to maintain the existing level of equipment per worker," it was said.

November 29, 1959

President Bars U. S. Help For Birth Control Abroad

Asserts Issue Is Religious and Should Not Enter Realm of Politics

By JOHN D. MORRIS
Special to The New York Times.

WASHINGTON, Dec. 2—President Eisenhower forcefully ruled out today the use of foreign aid funds for the promotion of birth control in under-developed countries.

He said the United States would maintain a hands-off policy "as long as I am here."

"That's not our business," he asserted.

Going a step further, the President held that birth control was a religious question.

"I cannot imagine anything more emphatically a subject that is not a proper political or governmental activity or function or responsibility," he said.

[In San Francisco, the Right Rev. James A. Pike, Protestant Episcopal Bishop of California, said the President's stand had ignored the recommendations of several governmental committees.]

The question was raised at the President's news conference in the context of continuing controversy aroused by a statement Nov. 25 by the Roman Catholic Bishops of the United States.

The Bishops declared that Catholics would not support "any public assistance, whether at home or abroad, to promote artificial birth prevention, abortion or sterilization, whether through direct aid or by means of international organizations."

The prelates' statement was prompted partly by recommendations last July by the President's Committee to Study the United States Military Assistance Program.

The committee, headed by William H. Draper Jr., suggested that the United States help other countries, on request, "in the formulation of their plans designed to deal with the problem of rapid population growth."

The committee also proposed United States support in the United Nations and as a part of its own mutual security program of studies that would be useful to such countries in formulating programs to meet "the serious challenges posed by rapidly expanding populations."

Comments on Report

President Eisenhower stated his position today when asked for his reaction to the Draper committee's report. It had been generally interpreted, he was told, as a recommendation that that the United States distribute birth control information on request.

The President expressed admiration and respect for the Catholic Church but added that the birth control issue "has nothing to do with governmental contact with other governments."

The United States, he went on, does not intend to interfere in the internal affairs of any government.

Population problems of other countries, he maintained, are entirely their business. He said they would unquestionably go to professional groups, and not to another government, for any help they felt was needed.

The Catholic bishops' statement, and reaction to it, has plunged the population-control issue into the 1960 Presidential campaign. It is an especially keen one because one of the leading Presidential contenders, Senator John F. Kennedy, Democrat of Massachusetts, is a Catholic. He and several others have now stated their position.

Senator Kennedy said Friday that he had long felt it would be a "mistake" for the United States Government to advocate birth control in other countries. However, he added, if the question should come before him as President he would decide it in accordance with his oath to do whatever was best in the interests of the United States.

The views of some of the other potential Presidential candidates, as stated publicly in recent days, include these:

Adlai E. Stevenson — the United States should not "impose" birth control programs on other countries but should not hesitate to consider requests for aid in such programs "where population growth is inimical to economic well-being."

Governor Rockefeller — the United States "would want to cooperate" with the people of a country seeking technical assistance in such a field "if it was in the interest of the other country."

Senator Hubert H. Humphrey, Democrat of Minnesota—the United States should not "deny information and assistance if such nations determine it is essential to their national welfare."

Senator Stewart Symington, Democrat of Missouri—"I approve the Government's furnishing of planned parenthood information abroad where it believes the action is to the interest of our country."

Mr. Stevenson is a Unitarian, Governor Rockefeller a Baptist, Senator Humphrey a Congregationalist and Senator Symington an Episcopalian.

Vice President Richard M. Nixon and Senator Lyndon B. Johnson, Democrat of Texas, have not taken a public stand on the issue.

The International Cooperation Administration announced Sunday that "not one penny of foreign-aid funds ever has been used for dissemination of birth-control information and there are no plans to do so."

Pike Critical of President

SAN FRANCISCO, Dec. 2 (AP)—The Right Rev. James A. Pike, Protestant Episcopal Bishop of California, commented today that President Eisenhower's statement had ignored recommendations of his own and other governmental committees.

The Bishop said in a statement that the President "has chosen to refuse to allow this nation of abundance to meet a primary need of countries who want aid toward population control to help avert increasing starvation and misery."

The Bishop noted that the President had mentioned the position of the Roman Catholic Church but not "the positive teaching to the contrary of other religious bodies."

Bishop Pike is chairman of the Episcopal Clergymen's Advisory Committee for the Planned Parenthood Federation of America.

Statement Given

Following is the text of Bishop Pike's statement:

The President has chosen to refuse, during the remainder of his Administration to allow this nation of abundance to meet a primary need of countries which want aid towards population control to help avert increasing starvation and misery—and this in the face of the recommendations of the President's own committee ("The Draper Report"), the report to the Senate Foreign Relations Committee by the Stanford Research Institute, the State Department's intelligence report prepared in July and just made public, and the clear indication from the head of India's United Nations delegation and its Commissioner-General for Economic Affairs that their country needs and wants such help. We can only be grateful that this is a democratic country in which Congressional leaders and candidates for public office are free to declare themselves in favor of our assuming our Christian responsibilities to these less fortunate peoples.

According to reports of the

press conference, the President, in discussing the religious aspect of this issue, mentioned only the position of the Roman Catholic hierarchy on the subject. I am sure that there are other leaders who, while respecting the right of this particular church to take this special position, will take into account the positive teaching to the contrary of other religious bodies. I trust public interest in the expressed attitudes on this issue of all candidates to succeed Mr. Eisenhower as President will continue.

Catholics Pleased

MILWAUKEE, Wis., Dec. 2 (UPI)—The chancery office of the Milwaukee Archdioceses, representing 567,000 Roman Catholics issued the following statement today:

"The reaction on the part of the President was not unexpected inasmuch as the recent bishops' statement on the subject of birth control was based on solid reason. While the approach of the bishops' statement was from the moral viewpoint, it did have international repercussions and the decision not to interfere in the private life of nations is well received."

December 3, 1959

U. S. DISDAINS A ROLE IN POPULATION CURBS

The United States will not impose population control on any nation receiving foreign aid, the deputy United States Representative to the United Nations said last night.

Ambassador T. P. Plimpton explained, however, that the Kennedy Administration would encourage attention to the population problem by governments, international organizations and private groups to develop apropriate solutions for countries faced with mushrooming population growth.

Addressing 8850 persons at the annual dinner of the Planned Parenthood Federation of America in the Plaza Hotel, Mr. Plimpton stressed that without "proper balance between production and reproduction," efforts at economic progress in underdeveloped countries might fail.

The Lasker Award in Planned Parenthood was presented to John D. Rockefelled 3d, chairman of the Rockefeller Foundation and the Population Council, for leadership in calling attention to the need for governmental action to cope with the growth of world population.

Another speaker, Dr. Donald J. Bogue, University of Chicago sociologist, said American cities were faced with a population explosion as acute as any in Asia and Africa. Fertility rates among low-income and minority groups in the nation's cities are only a few points below the highest rates recorded in India and other overpopulated countries, he said.

October 25, 1961

Kennedy Would Give Out Data on Population Curbs

By ROBERT C. TOTH

Special to The New York Times

WASHINGTON, April 24 —President Kennedy expressed support today for any United States effort to provide information on population control to any nations requesting it.

He told his news conference that the Government "certainly could support" increased research in fertility and human reproduction, and programs to make the results "more available to the world so that everyone can make their own judgment."

Federal funds are currently being spent by the National Institutes of Health on such research, he said. These were "important studies" that "should be continued," he added.

His comments came against the background of a report last week by the National Academy of Sciences that called for the United States to "participate in fostering" international birth control studies.

The United States, in a statement last December before the United Nations, said it would not advocate any birth control measures but would help other countries, on request, to find sources of information and assistance in dealing with their population problems.

While campaigning for the Presidency in 1960, Mr. Kennedy promised to deal with such issues as birth control "in accordance with what my conscience tells me to be the national interest, and without regard to outside religious pressures or dictates."

The President is a member of the Roman Catholic Church, the largest religious organization to oppose artificial methods of contraception.

Another development in the controversy came with the publication last week of a book by Prof. John Rock of Harvard University. Dr. Rock, himself a Catholic, said birth control techniques acceptable to both Catholics and non-Catholics could be found.

He suggested that the Government appropriate money for research into contraceptive techniques, including the rhythm method, and expressed hope that an oral contraceptive pill would be acceptable to the Catholic church.

Richard Cardinal Cushing of Boston, who is Dr. Rock's Bishop and presumably President Kennedy's as well, said there was "much that is good" in Dr. Rock's book, "The Time Has Come." Some of the scientist's conclusions, however, were "not in agreement with Catholic teaching," Cardinal Cushing said in a statement.

Meanwhile, it was reported that any foreign requests for help in population problems would be handled through the Agency for International Development and its professional science advisory groups.

Contracts are usually let by the agency to private groups and universities for studies or assistance to requesting nations.

The agency can consult with the National Institutes of Health, but the research-oriented charter of the N. I. H. would seem to preclude technical assistance.

Last year, the United States spent about $6,000,000 on various studies related to birth and population control. This was virtually all the research on the subject that was conducted in the world. Of this, the Federal Government supplied $4,098,000 for fundamental studies in fertility and reproduction.

More than usual multiple births have occurred among women who took a fertility-aiding drug called Clomiphene before they became pregnant, it was reported here yesterday.

Across the nation, a few hundred women have taken the drug because they were unable to conceive. Of these, 80 have now given birth and the number of multiple births among the group is high.

The finding is inexplicable. No compound that can cause multiple birth is known. Nor is the exact mechanism through which multiple birth is caused known, although it is assumed that the drug stimulates the ovaries to form more than one egg.

A brief report on the subject was given here yesterday at the clinical meeting of the American College of Obstetricians and Gynecologists by Dr. Abraham Rakoff, Professor of Obstetric andGynecologic Endocrinology at Jefferson Medical College in Philadelphia.

April 25, 1963

U.S. Gives Policy For Birth Control Under Foreign Aid

WASHINGTON, March 4 (AP)—The United States is prepared to help foreign birth control programs with information, educational material, training and auxiliary equipment, but will not supply any contraceptives.

A circular outlining aid policy in birth control has been sent to United States missions around the world in a follow-up to President Johnson's Jan. 4 statement concerning the problem of rapidly expanding populations in less - developed countries.

Mr. Johnson said in his State of the Union Message.

"I will seek new ways to use our knowledge to help deal with the explosion of world population and the growing scarcity of world resources."

The Agency for International Development, which administers foreign aid, said that it did not advocate family planning policies for developing nations and that the United States opposed any effort to dictate birth control programs for another country.

It said the agency did not advocate any particular method of family planning. The United States believes every family should have complete freedom of choice of what methods to use, if any, it said.

A birth control program is not a condition for receiving United States aid, it said, and help on family planning will be provided only by specific request.

March 5, 1965

U.S. Offering Birth Control Help To the Underdeveloped Nations

By JOHN FINNEY

Special to The New York Times

WASHINGTON, June 21 — Cautiously and as unobtrusively as possible, the Administration is going ahead in helping underdeveloped nations curb their growing populations.

Formal and informal requests for American assistance in developing and implementing birth control programs have been received from India, Pakistan and Turkey. The expectation is that the requests will be approved in the next few months by the Agency for International Development.

Approval of the requests will mark a significant step in the Government's evolving policy toward a more positive position on population control.

This policy will come under what is expected to be sympathetic Congressional examination tomorrow when a Senate Government Operations subcommittee opens hearings on Government population control programs.

The hearings will mark the first time that a legislative committee has dared to look publicly into the politically sensitive question of the Government's role in birth control.

The subcommittee is headed by Senator Ernest Gruening, Democrat of Alaska, an outspoken advocate of population control ever since his graduation from Harvard Medical School in 1912. To provide a springboard for public hearings on the issue, he has introduced legislation proposing that an assistant secretary for population be established in the State Department and in the Health, Education and Welfare Department.

Until recently it has been the policy of the Agency for International Development to refer all foreign requests for information and assistance in birth control to private agencies. The most the agency was willing to do was provide funds for demographic studies of population growth and sociological studies of attitudes about family planning.

This policy began to come under critical review within the agency about a year ago, as it was realized that in most of the underdeveloped countries economic development could not hope to keep pace with population growth brought about by high birth rates and declining death rates.

Within an agency that was already unpopular on Capitol Hill, however, there was a reluctance to add to its difficulties by embarking upon a program a birth-control assistance to foreign countries.

The door to a more active program was opened in January when President Johnson declared in his State of the Union Message that "I will seek new ways to use our knowledge to help deal with the explosion of the world population and the growing scarcity of world resources."

In an "aerogramme" on March 4 to all its missions, the Agency for International Development laid down a policy with the following provisions:

¶It was prepared to entertain requests, approved by foreign governments, for technical assistance in family planning. Where appropriate, the requests will continue to be referred to private agencies.

¶Whatever family planning program is proposed should provide freedom of choice to the individual on what type of birth control, if any, is to be used.

¶The agency was not prepared to entertain requests for contraceptive devices or the equipment to manufacture them. But their cost was viewed as too small to present a stumbling block to an effective program.

¶The agency was, however, prepared to provide other assistance, such as administrators, doctors and nurses to help establish a program; "commodity aid," such as vehicles and education equipment, and training opportunities in this country. It also was prepared to make available local "counterpart" funds held by the United States to help finance family planning programs.

Turkey Seeks Vehicles

It was under this policy that requests were received recently from Turkey, Pakistan and India.

Turkey which only recently repealed a ban on contraceptives, is asking for several hundred jeeps to carry family planning groups into rural areas.

India has asked for technical and financial assistance, but it is not clear yet specifically what it needs.

Pakistan, which has a better defined program, has requested administrative assistance as well as counterpart funds to help pay doctors and midwives.

There is a possibility that a request for aid will be received soon from Honduras.

One of the potential problems in implementing the new policy, the agency has discovered, is a shortage, even in this country, of medical personnel and technicians trained in carrying out birth-control programs.

As a result the agency has given contracts to the University of California, Notre Dame, Johns Hopkins University and the University of North Carolina to develop training programs in population control for foreign and American students. Training will be made available to foreign students starting this fall.

In the coming fiscal year, which begins July 1, the agency expects to spend more than $3 million in carrying out the new policy.

June 22, 1965

Letter by Eisenhower on Birth Control

Special to The New York Times

WASHINGTON, June 22—Following is the text of a letter on population explosion from former President Dwight D. Eisenhower to Senator Ernest Gruening, Democrat of Alaska, who is chairman of the Senate Government Operations subcommittee on foreign aid expenditures:

Dear Senator Gruening:

I am complimented by your invitation for me to comment on the many problems arising out of the extraordinary and rapid increase in the world's population. I am taking advantage of your suggestion that should it be more convenient to me to submit a written statement than to appear before you in person, this would be satisfactory to your committee.

As a first comment I must say that I am delighted that your committee is concerning itself with this subject, one that I consider constitutes one of the most, if not the most, of the critical problems facing mankind today.

While it is true that there remain areas of the world in which there are still unexploited resources for food production and of irreplaceable subsurface minerals, it is still quite clear that in spite of great technical progress in production of the necessaries of life, we are scarcely keeping up, in over-all production and distribution, with the requirements of burgeoning and underfed populations. Moreover, since the earth is finite in area and physical resources, it is clear that unless something is done to bring an essential equilibrium between human requirements and available supply, there is going to be in some regions not only a series of riotous explosions but a lowering of standards of all peoples, including our own.

Viewpoint Has Changed

Ten years ago, although aware of some of these growing dangers abroad, I did not then believe it to be the function of the Federal Government to interfere in the social structures of other nations by using, except through private institutions, American resources to assist them in a partial stabilization of their numbers. I expressed this view publicly but soon abandoned it.

After watching and studying results of some of the aid programs of the early fifties, I became convinced that without parallel programs looking to population stabilization all that we could do, at the very best, would be to maintain rather than improve standards in those who need our help.

We now know that the problem is not only one for foreign nations to study and to act accordingly, but it has also serious portents for us.

I realize that in important segments of our people and of other nations this question is regarded as a moral one and therefore scarcely a fit subject for Federal legislation. With their feelings I can and do sympathize. But I cannot help believe that the prevention of human degradation and starvation is likewise a moral—as well as a material—obligation resting upon every enlightened Government.

If we now ignore the plight of those unborn generations which, because of our unreadiness to take corrective action in controlling population growth, will be denied any expectations beyond abject poverty and suffering, then history will rightly condemn us.

Two Issues Underlined

I have two specific suggestions respecting S. 1676. First, I doubt the wisdom of authorizing two new "assistant secretaries" and the establishment of new bureaucratic groupings, but if this is the only way to handle the administrative activities so created I could not seriously object.

Second, I must refer to reported instances, by no means exceptional, of the repetitive production of children by unwed mothers, apparently lured by the resulting increase in income from welfare funds.

To err is human and certainly none of us would want to deny needed support for anyone who because of some emotional pressure gave birth to an illegitimate child. But, when this is repeated to the point of habit, society will find itself in the curious position of spending money with one hand to slow up population growth among responsible families and with the other providing financial incentive for increased production by the ignorant, feeble-minded or lazy. Corrective action will require careful study, for even if research should uncover no effective measures other than legal sterilization, a final resort to this method unquestionably would shock great segments of our citizenry.

I would not endanger the passage of your bill by any mention of this subject, but I submit that we have a situation here that unless corrected could become far more serious than it is today.

Along with former President Truman I am cochairman of the Honorary Sponsors Committee, Planned Parenthood — World Population. I accepted this position in order to demonstrate my recognition of the urgency of the entire problem and the alarming consequences that are certain to follow its neglect.

Being sure that other witnesses, far more competent than I in specialized and professional fields, will discuss this matter in detail before your committee, I content myself merely by saying that I devoutly hope that necessary measures will be enacted into law to authorize the Federal Government, as well as appropriate private and semipublic organizations, so to cooperate among themselves that the necessary human and material resources can be promptly mobilized and employed to cope effectively with the great need of slowing down and finally stabilizing the growth in the world's population.

June 23, 1965

U.S. Aid Plan Offers Pill To Countries Asking It

Food Shortage Feared

By FELIX BELAIR Jr.
Special to The New York Times

WASHINGTON, April 5 — The Agency for International Development, in a major policy shift, plans to finance the manufacture and distribution of contraceptive pills for developing countries that have voluntary family planning programs.

William S. Gaud, agency administrator, explained the agency's position today to the House Foreign Affairs Committee. He said, however, that "family planning is a matter of great delicacy, and we do not feel it is appropriate to make the existence of a family planning program a condition of assistance."

He continued:

"But family planning is also a matter of great urgency, and we will provide aid to those countries which have voluntary family planning programs which allow for individual freedom of choice."

Mr. Gaud was the opening witness before the committee considering President Johnson's foreign aid request for $3.1-billion in the fiscal year beginning July 1. He said that population control measures were an essential part of the campaign against hunger.

"For no matter how successful the world is in increasing agricultural productivity," he said, "the time is sure to come when there will not be enough food if present population trends continue."

His agency is spending about $10-million this year for education, research and clinical and other equipment in support of family planning promotion in less developed countries. It has not thus far provided any contraceptive devices.

In the next fiscal year, the $10-million figure will be doubled at least, Mr. Gaud told newsmen after the committee hearing. He said this was because pills to prevent pregnancies cost considerably more than conventional methods of birth control, which even the poorer countries promoting them could pay for from their own resources.

Although there have been no requests from any countries for oral contraceptives, Mr. Gaud said, experience in India and some other areas indicated that the "coil" or "loop" device was not so effective as had been expected and that pills may be the answer. He said the agency had "received some feelers from the Population Council."

Another reason given by Mr. Gaud to newsmen for the expected policy change was that "the pressure we're getting from Congress has changed and more seem to think that we're going too slow."

To the House panel, he said: "Progress has been too slow. Many Governments lack a full appreciation of the enormous impact of fast growing populations on the life of their people, not only on their food supply but in their entire development effort.

"As a result, many countries have not yet faced up to the need to deal with the problem, or have not pushed forward vigorously with well planned programs. In these countries the basic obstacle to progress in family planning is not so much a lack of capital as a lack of awareness."

He went on:

"We at AID plan to do more than we have in the past to awaken other Governments to a full realization of the true nature of the population problem. And as more and more countries adopt sound programs, they will find us ready to provide the assistance they need to carry out their programs.

"I consider that we have no higher priority than to do everything we can today to see that tomorrow the world will continue to be able to feed itself and that the balance between food and mouths will be maintained."

April 6, 1967

India to Get Contraceptives Under New U.S. Aid Plan

By BENJAMIN WELLES

Special to The New York Times

WASHINGTON, Sept. 14—The United States announced plans today to give India $1.3-million to buy contraceptives.

It was the first time this country had ever included funds for that purpose in a foreign aid program.

William S. Gaud, administrator of the Agency for International Development, said that India would purchase the contraceptives in the United States and distribute them through her own commercial channels.

Of the $1.3-million total, Mr Gaud said, $800,000 will go to supply 100 million contraceptives for males as the beginning of what he termed a "large continuing program of commercial distribution of condoms throughout India."

The remaining $500,000, Mr. Gaud said, will go to provide birth control pills for 100,000 Indian women participating in a test over a period of a year and a half.

Officials at the aid agency said that this would be the first time the United States Government had ever shipped condoms overseas, except for those issued to servicemen during World War II and the Korean conflict.

Explains New Policy

Other aid officals said later that plans were under way to furnish contraceptives to other countries that have requested them, including the Philippines, Jamaica, Morocco, Tunisia and certain Latin-American nations that have asked not to be identified until pending negotiations are complete.

Mr. Gaud, addressing the General Federation of Women's Clubs in the State Department's International Conference Room, made the following points about the significance of the new policy:

¶The expenditure will be the largest ever extended by one country to another for the purchase of contraceptives.

¶It will be the first substantial United States commodities assistance for India's family planning program.

¶The program also will support India's plans to make effective contraceptives available throughout the country for the first time.

India, with a population of 523 million to 550 million, contains one-third of the people of the less developed free world. At present growth rates (2.5 per cent to 2.7 per cent yearly) India can be expected to double her present population to more than one billion within 25 years.

Faces Vast Problems

Given the soaring birth rate, lagging food production and periodic droughts, it was noted here, India must either begin intensive population control measures at once or face mounting internal problems that can be alleviated only partially by outside help.

India's population problem is so "immense" and the variety of attitudes toward birth control so vast, Mr. Gaud said, that the Indian government has decided on a vast array of acceptable family planning techniques—"a whole cafeteria," as he put it.

Under the plan to provide contraceptives for men, Mr. Gaud said, a single "brand name" contraceptive will be packaged and distributed under auspices of the Hindustan Latex Corporation, an affiliate of the Indian Government.

Hindustan Latex will contract with a half-dozen or more of India's largest concerns to promote and distribute the contraceptive as a "sideline."

Companies Listed

These concerns, which have sales networks reaching down to small rural and urban shopkeepers, include Lipton Tea, Brooke Bond Tea, Union Carbide, Imperial Tobacco, Tata Oil and Hindustan Lever, Mr. Gaud said. He described them as "already recruited and enthusiastic."

An Indian Government subsidy will reduce the prohibitively high price of condoms in India — 13 cents — to approximately 2 cents for a pack of three, Mr. Gaud said. If the market grows large enough, he said, it should permit unsubsidized production and sale within this price range.

Mr. Gaud announced a second program in population control. The United States, he said, will soon increase its subsidy to the International Planned Parenthood Federation by $2.5-million.

Of the total, he said, $1-million will be used for the purchase of United States commodities — including contraceptives — and the rest for training programs in India, Pakistan and Turkey as well as in Latin America and East Asia.

Dr. R. T. Ravenholt, director of the aid agency's population service, said that the introduction two years ago of intrauterine devices or loops in India had not lived up to its initial expectations.

Because of internal bleeding or discomfort as well as a lack of clinical facilities, he said, about half of the two million loops inserted in the course of the program had been removed.

September 15, 1967

'Food for Peace' Extended

WASHINGTON, July 29 (UPI) —President Johnson signed today a two-year extension of the food for peace program. The act provides $6.2-billion in food aid for 1969 and 1970. It makes family planning one of the guidelines the President must consider in deciding whether a nation seeking United States food aid is making a "self-help" effort to improve its food-population balance.

July 30, 1968

FAMILY PLANNING IS CALLED FUTILE

Demographer Urges New Ways to Curb Population

By ROBERT REINHOLD

Special to The New York Times

BERKELEY, Calif. — "I call it collective gold displacement," Kingsley Davis, the population expert, said with a sneer. "The Federal Government is spending millions of dollars under the illusion it is getting population control. All it is getting is bad advice."

Professor Davis, director of International Population and Urban Research at the University of California at Berkeley, reflects a growing conviction among demographers that "family planning" programs are a hopelessly futile means of controlling population explosion.

"The Government says all you need is 100 per cent effective birth control devices—this is nonsense," says the 61-year-old father of three. "You cannot just duck out and think by some technological gimmick you are going to solve the problem — the basic motivation to have children is very strong in society."

Unless this motivation is undermined by making large families undesirable or impossible, he believes, the availability of more and better contraceptives will do little to stem population growth.

Points to Motivations

To support this view, he cites evidence developed at Berkeley that fertility control has not been effective in lowering overall population growth in any country. Even in countries where stability has been achieved, such as Japan and Taiwan, the success is attributed not to distribution of contraceptive devices, but to motivations such as crowded living space that create demand for the devices.

Professor Davis does not suggest direct controls, such as compulsory sterilization or abortion. Rather, he poses two indirect approaches to population control policy through "selective restructuring of the family in relation to the rest of society."

First, he would have governments postpone the age of marriage, thus reducing the childbearing years, while maintaining current proscriptions against illegitimate birth. Second, he would impose conditions designed to motivate couples to keep their families small.

For example, he suggests, government could stop taxing single persons more heavily than married ones, end tax exemptions for children, pay the cost of abortions, levy a "child tax," and give women equality in educational and job opportunities so that they would develop interests competing with family interest.

In Eastern Europe

Measures such as these, the population expert says, have stemmed population growth in the Communist countries of Eastern Europe, where married women generally must work and where housing and consumer goods are scarce and abortions are free.

"So, if you want to control population, there's your answer," he says. "How do you do it here? The social organization is the problem. That's why you are not going to get it."

In the meantime, he sees the world moving ostrich-like and inexorably toward disaster.

"We may have fewer people in the world all right," he says with more than a tinge of sarcasm. "Nigeria is trying to help out Africa's problem."

As for the argument that large populations are needed to maintain national strength, Professor Davis cites Israel.

"From the point of view of population control," he says, "we owe a great debt to Israel because she has shown that manpower is of very little importance militarily, that modern wars are pushing buttons and paper work — 100 million people is perfectly adequate to defend any territory."

Not Certain Groups

He is contemptuous of birth control projects that concentrate on poor minorities.

"The population problem does not lie in some group of blacks having more children than they want," the professor argues. "It lies in the great broad classes having more than they want. You cannot brush it off on some particular group. It lays itself open to the claim of genocide. How'd you feel if someone said you were having too many babies — it would get your back up."

What would he do if he were President Nixon?

"I would devote a lot more attention to goals," he explains. "What kind of population do we want in the United States? Until we get that straightened out, we cannot talk about means.

"I happen to think this country would be better off with half the population. With our present technology and the population of the 1930's the country would be a paradise. As it is, it's getting to be like hell—too many places getting like New York City."

October 5, 1969

A STERILITY DRUG IN FOOD IS HINTED

Biologist Stresses Need to Curb Population Growth

By GLADWIN HILL

Special to The New York Times

SAN FRANCISCO, Nov. 24 —A possibility that the Government might have to put sterility drugs in reservoirs and in food shipped to foreign countries to limit human multiplication was envisioned today by a leading crusader on the population problem.

The crusader, Dr. Paul Ehrlich of Stanford University, was among a number of commentators who called attention to the "population crisis" as the United States Commission for Unesco opened its 13th national conference here today.

Unesco is the United Nations Educational, Scientific and Cultural Organization. The 100-member commission, appointed by the Secretary of State, included representatives of Government, outside organizations and the public. Some 500 conservationists and others are attending the two-day meeting at the St. Francis Hotel, devoted this year to environmental problems.

President Nixon's chief science adviser, Dr. Lee DuBridge, brought up the population question in his keynote speech last night, calling the reduction of the earth's population growth rate to zero "the first great challenge of our time."

Godfrey a Speaker

His comments went beyond recent statements of President Nixon, who in a message to Congress stressed the provision of birth control information to underprivileged women.

But the Federal Government's willingness to come to grips with population limitation was questioned by another speaker, Arthur Godfrey, radio-television star and a conservation campaigner.

"Dr. DuBridge rightly said that population control should be the prime task of every government," he said. "But is there anyone here — anyone — who thinks that this Administration, or the netx or the next, will act with the kind of force that's necessary?"

Dr. Ehrlich, who is a biologist, said:

"Our first move must be to convince all those we can that the planet Earth must be viewed as a spaceship of limited carrying capacity."

"I think that 150 million people (50 million fewer than there are now) would be an optimum number to live comfortably in the United States.

'Alternative to Armageddon'

"Some biologists feel that compulsory family regulation will be necessary to retard population growth. It is a dismal prospect—except when viewed as an alternative to Armageddon."

He urged establishing a Federal Population Commission "with a large budget for propaganda," changing tax laws to discourage reproduction and instituting mandatory birth control instruction in public schools.

He also urged "changing the pattern of Federal support of biomedical research so that the majority of it goes into the broad areas of population regulation, environment sciences, behavior sciences and related areas rather than into short-sighted programs on death control."

If such steps are unavailing, he continued, the nation might resort to "the addition of a temporary sterilant to staple food, or to the water supply," with limited distribution of antidote chemicals, perhaps by lottery.

Although it might seem that such a program could be started by doctoring foods sent to underdeveloped countries, he said, "the solution does not lie in that direction" because "other people already are suspicious of our motives."

Economic Pressure Urged

Rather, he suggested, the United States should stop economic aid to countries that do not try to limit their populations.

Dr. Barry Commoner of St. Louis, Washington University ecologist, in an ensuing discussion period differed with Dr. Ehrlich.

He said that he thought the urge to multiply was rooted in the sense of insecurity, and that the better way to reduce reproduction was by "increasing the well-being of peoples."

He also opposed chemical strategems on the ground that "every technological trick like that we've tried has caused disaster."

Recapitulating the environmental problems stemming from population, Dr. DuBridge said: "Do we need more people on the earth? We all know the answer to that is no. Do we have to have more people? Also no.

"Can we reverse the urges of a billion years of evolving life? We can. We know techniques for reducing fertility. We are not fully utilizing them."

Citing a widespread attitude, he said: "'We have the right to have as many children as we can afford,' we say. Do we, today? No.

"Can we not invent a way to reduce our population growth rate to zero? Every human institution — school, university, church, family, government and international agencies such as Unesco—should set this as its prime task."

November 25, 1969

Sin of Head Counts

"The demographic mind, which is humanitarian, believes that the poor, helpless, despised and rejected should not have been allowed to be."

By L. BRENT BOZELL

WARRENTON, Va.—Is demography a mortal sin? I say it is, although a distinction must be made which may let off some of its practitioners with the sort of venial blemish that can be cleaned up in purgatory. I mean it is possible for a man to be more or less innocently fascinated with his charts and statistics on birth and death rates and migration trends, even with (predictably wrong) projections of population explosions and deplosions. But this kind of demographer is an odd bird; he is outnumbered by far by colleagues who wish the fascinating statistics to be transposed into a judgment about the rightness or wrongness of making new people. This generality of demographers, I am afraid, will have to burn.

Demography, like every other sin, is a state of mind; and it is one of the achievements of the modern world to have put this state in reach of almost everybody. See if you have acquired it.

The demographic mind looks upon the human race as a crop—for which, alas, supply and demand are seldom equal. In Europe for instance, in the first half of this century, there were not nearly enough people to fill the armies that were designed to consume them. And today, in parts of Asia and Latin America, there are far too many people wishing to consume the goods the world is presently organized to provide. The lesson is that the economics of human production are inefficient; they are not susceptible to regulation by the free market of mating. What is needed is a beneficent intervention that will assure mankind the desired equilibrium.

The task is greatly complicated, however, by the recent discovery that the human crop is but one among many crops, and that all the world's crops are deserving of equal husbandry. The demographic mind need not deny a personal preference for a present specimen of the human crop—an old school chum, for example—over a given shrimp or bluebonnet or bucket of oil. But looking to future production, it will counsel an even-handed justice for all crops in the interests of a wholesome ecological balance.

The demographic mind is also increasingly sensitive to the several varieties of the human crop. There are young and old humans, rich and poor, white and black, Anglo-Saxon and others. Some of these varieties, obviously, present special problems to society which must be taken into account in the interests of a manageable social balance.

There is a boy in Bombay, a little fellow. His stomach is swollen. A single rag hangs about his loins. His face is drawn, well beyond his eight or nine years. He wanders, apparently aimlessly, through squalid streets. There is a greater supply of him than there is demand. He disturbs the ecological balance. He is socially inconvenient. The demographic mind eyes him and observes it would be better had his father been sterilized, or his mother aborted him—or, better still, had he never been conceived. He disagrees.

Consider more closely the boy in Bombay. Mr. McNamara and his banks, Mr. Rockefeller and his commissions, Time, Newsweek, National Review, New Republic, N.B.C., C.B.S., A.B.C., the United States Government, the Indian Government, the United Nations, the Planned Parenthood Federation, the Ford Foundation, the Hugh Moore Fund, the A.M.A., all the hired graph-plotters and figure-adders—the demographers—deplore him. What is more, they have the means—they are gods—to prevent more of him.

Do they? Well, at least they can prevent more like him. Can they? This boy is not capable of duplication. The life, the personhood he cherishes (if no one else does) is a once-given gift; there will never be another like it. (For better or for worse, there will never be another life like Mr. McNamara's.) What the demographic mind can do is prevent a life, block a gift, whose nature is known only to the giver, whose enjoyment and destiny are designed specifically for the given. What it can do is prevent the unfolding of a mystery.

Consider still more closely the boy in Bombay. He stands for all the world's poor, its helpless, its despised, its rejected. The demographic mind, which is humanitarian, believes that the poor, helpless, despised and rejected should not have been allowed to be. But the boy prefers to be. He was not wanted by Mr. McNamara and Mr. Rockefeller. But he was wanted by his maker, and probably by his parents, and now he wants himself. The boy might have had more of the world's things if the world were older than the one Mr. McNamara and Mr. Rockefeller have helped organize. But the boy does not understand that the remedy is to have denied him the one possession he has.

Consider Bombay. The demographic mind considers it hopelessly congested. Hopelessly, that is, unless the stream of life is dried up. The boy considers a different source of hope. At an earlier time Abram and his nephew Lot saw their herds and flocks so increase "that the land would not support them dwelling together." So "Abram said to Lot, Let there be no strife between you and me, nor between my herdsmen and your herdsmen; for we are kinsmen. Does not the whole land lie before you? Withdraw from me. If you go to the left, I will go to the right; or if you take the right, then I will go to the left. Then Lot looked about and saw that the whole region of the Jordan toward Segor was well-watered—this was before the Lord destroyed Sodom and Gomorra—like the Lord's garden."

L. Brent Bozell is editor of Triumph, a Catholic magazine.

Peasants know perfectly well where babies come from

Misconceptions

By Paul R. Ehrlich and Anne H. Ehrlich

An imaginary scene:

Whack-a, whack-a, whack-a—the rhythmic beat of the helicopter's rotor startles the languid cattle wandering on the parched Indian plain. Shankar Ram looks up from the shade of the doorway of his mud hut to see the machine growing rapidly as it bears down on the small village of Patala. His eight hungry children scramble past him, and his emaciated wife joins him as they all stare at this visitation from another world. Being illiterate, he cannot read the label on the side of the helicopter—"Christian Family Planning League of Texas."

Suddenly the air is filled with tiny packets fluttering to the ground. His son Krishna scampers up and hands him a small foil container. He tears it open and takes out six balloonlike objects and a folded piece of paper. Why, he wonders, would balloons be delivered from the sky? As his children assemble a small mountain of the packets, Ram unfolds the paper. In shock he turns, moves away from his wife. The diagrams! They remind him of the things a traveler once told him about Khajuraho. Then slowly he realizes the diagrams are not intended to titillate, but are rather a set of instructions. It is all clear. If he uses these "balloons," his wife will have no more babies. If everyone in his village uses them, there will be more land and food for all. If everyone in India uses them, it no longer will have problems of overpopulation. Joy fills his heart and brings tears of thanksgiving to his eyes. As he looks around the cluster of huts, he sees that his neighbors have also understood the message—there are tears in their eyes also. He offers a small prayer of thanks for the unknown people who have become his saviors.

Mrs. Dee Jay Sturdley wipes a tear from the corner of her eye and breaks out of her reverie as she turns her air-conditioned Cadillac into the driveway and pulls into her marked slot in front of the modern, two-story, air-conditioned building on the parched Dallas plain. As she steps through the door labeled "C.F.P.L.T.—Christian Family Planning League of Texas"—the vision of the imaginary peasants lingers in the back of her mind. Her determination grows—today she'll get the board to agree to a crash fund-raising program. She can't stand the thought of any more TV shows on starving people. They make her most uncomfortable.

Mrs. Sturdley has an advanced case of the "condoms from helicopters delusion"—a psychological condition that is rampant among well-meaning upper-middle and upper class Americans. Like all thinking people, she realizes that overpopulation is a desperate problem for underdeveloped countries and that birth control is the only possible humane solution to the problem. But she and many others think that the populations of these countries are growing so rapidly because people there don't have the know-how or the equipment to keep from having more babies than they want. Indeed, some think that many of the world's impoverished and primitive peoples hardly know where babies come from.

Being action-oriented, Mrs. Sturdley thinks that we Americans ought to do something to help those poor ignorant peasants. And what could be more logical than to bring a fleet of helicopters to sweep over half-a-million villages, showering a latex manna from heaven? What indeed, especially since Mrs. Sturdley's view of the problem is not different in kind from that of high officials of the United States Agency for International Development? Give them the knowledge and the equipment, and Indian couples will start "stopping at two" instead of, on the average, having five or more children.

Although Mrs. Sturdley and the C.F.P.L.T. are imaginary, they symbolize the dominant attitude of many concerned Americans toward the world population problem. Unfortunately, these attitudes are subject to serious question. To begin with, the idea that some people (especially Australian aborigines) don't understand how babies are made is an antique chestnut once put forth by some anthropologists who didn't know how to ask people about their sex lives. It is a common conceit of our culture to consider "primitive" people to be unsophisticated (even though, for instance, the dumbest aborigine keeps track of many more complex kinship relationships than the smartest Texan). Anyway, if some stranger wandered up to us and asked if we knew where babies came from, we'd tell him from under

Paul R. Ehrlich is professor and Anne H. Ehrlich is research associate in the Department of Biological Sciences at Stanford University. He is co-author, with Dennis Pirages, of "Ark II," a book that deals with social dimensions of the environment issue.

cabbage leaves. Wouldn't you? Some anthropologists given such an answer by, say, an Eskimo or Masai have been fools enough to take him seriously.

Nor is there real reason to believe that overpopulated countries are overpopulated because the people lack the know-how to have fewer children. Many cultures, when examined closely, seem to have social mechanisms that regulate population size if there is a perceived need for such regulation. In the Middle Ages, primogeniture (inheritance by the eldest son only) helped reduce population pressure in Europe. Farmland was not divided into ever smaller and less economically viable parcels. Excess sons went off on Crusades to kill heathens for Christ and often ended up getting killed themselves, or, more often, dying of disease. Some Amazonian Indians use war in a similar fashion; Eskimos used to "expose" excess female babies and old folks; the English in the last century institutionalized infanticide under the euphemism "baby farming," and Italians denied access to contraception recently had the highest known rate of illegal abortion.

When socioeconomic changes occur that make fewer children seem desirable, birth rates always start to come down *before* family planners and birth control devices arrive on the scene. It happened in almost all of today's industrialized countries in the last century; it happened in Taiwan and South Korea recently. People just aren't all that ignorant and unenterprising—and scientists are beginning to realize it. Today, for instance, natural-products chemists are scouring the world for "folk contraceptives," many of which are now suspected of being fairly effective and having possible commercial value. Access to modern contraceptives may make family planning easier, but it is not clear how much that access, in itself, will help to lower birth rates.

The question of how many children people "really want" is more complex. Much of the problem is defining "really want" and then developing techniques to make an accurate appraisal of that "want." People's desires tend to change with many things, including how many children they already have, changes in their social and economic status, attitudes of their friends and acquaintances, and so on. An "unwanted" pregnancy often turns into a "wanted" child. People are loath to admit that they have been careless if they have a child by accident, or they may be unwilling to confide that they want more children but can't afford them. Answers to questions or

For Americans concerned about the world's population problem, the best approach is to set a good example at home.

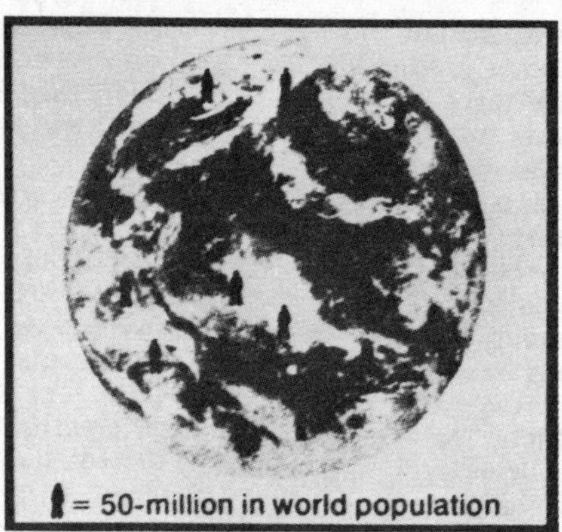

1800.

1900. ***Today.*** ***2000.***

Courtesy I.L.O.

questionnaires are often tailored by the respondents to fit what they think the questioners want to hear. This is especially common when the interviewer is perceived as a social superior—a common occurrence when social scientists conduct surveys in underdeveloped countries or ghettos.

Such considerations make it tough enough to evaluate the percentage of American children that are in some sense "unwanted"; they make it virtually impossible to determine even in a general way what proportion of children in underdeveloped countries would not be born if people had full control over their fertility. Some very competent demographers, like Charles Westoff of Princeton, think a high proportion of babies in underdeveloped countries are unwanted; others, like Kingsley Davis and Judith Blake of Berkeley, think relatively few are. It would be nice if Westoff were right, but the evidence suggests that Davis and Blake are. A prime piece of evidence is the example of India's family planning program. It started over 20 years ago, when India's birth rate was around 40 per 1,000, and shifted into high gear around 1965, when the birth rate was still around 40, but the death rate had dropped several points. In terms of governmental commitment, longevity and effectiveness in reaching a large proportion of the population (despite logistic problems virtually unmatched in any other country), India's program has been a "success." Two percent of the national budget was spent on family planning during the last five-year plan period (1966-71)—a far greater portion than was allocated by any other country. In fiscal 1972, the national budget for family planning was $101-million, and there were over 100,000 people working in the program. Until 1971, there were also substantial contributions from developed countries, including the U.S., and some assistance is still provided by the United Nations.

Statistics on the accomplishments of India's program are—superficially at least—impressive. Since 1965, 14-million people have been sterilized, nearly five-million I.U.D.'s have been inserted, over 320-million condoms have been distributed, and millions of pills and other forms of contraceptives have also been provided. It is believed that at least 13 per cent of married couples of reproductive age have been reached by the program. Yet, despite all this effort, India's birth rate is still around 40 to 42 per 1,000 (according to the U.N.; India claims 37, but its census data are extremely suspect), and the population is fast approaching 600 million. What has gone wrong?

A further examination of family planning statistics provides a clue: The average candidate for sterilization or contraceptives has *at least four* living children and has borne five or six babies. The same is true in nearly all underdeveloped countries for which figures are available. Like peasants in most countries, rural Indians (80 per cent of the population is rural) depend for security in old age on their sons. Given India's relatively high infant and child mortality rates, a couple must bear at least six children in order to ensure survival of one son to adulthood. Small wonder they view family planners' propaganda to "stop at two" as slightly insane! They aren't going to use contraceptives to reduce their family sizes because they *want* large families.

Still, the United States Agency for International Development by 1973 was providing technical assistance in demography and providing contraceptive materials (including 1.5 million gross of condoms, over 50 million cycles of the pill and three million I.U.D.'s between 1968 and 1973) to over 60 underdeveloped countries in programs that reflected the attitudes depicted above. Is there that much harm in doing so? There can be if such approaches divert funds from projects that might be more effective. And there is if they fool people into thinking a problem is being solved when it isn't—this has already happened as inflated rhetorical claims for the "green revolution" in agriculture have not been borne out in fact. When such things happen, they can only bolster existing suspicions about all the activities of overdeveloped countries that purport to help poorer lands. Many Vietnamese and other third world people will tell you that if you have Americans (or Frenchmen, or Russians, or Japanese) for friends, you don't need enemies.

Furthermore, there are other pernicious fallacies in the "what we as Americans can do about the world population problem" game. Let's start with a fallacy that the authors helped to create—the idea that we might successfully pressure governments of developing countries into launching effective population control programs. In the first edition of our book "The Population Bomb," it was suggested that the United States try to use its food aid as a lever to get recalcitrant governments moving on population control programs. The logic then (as today) was impeccable. If you deluded people into thinking that either the U.S. could (or would) supply food in perpetuity for any number of people, you were doing evil. Sooner or later, population growth would completely outstrip the capacity of the United States or any other nation to supply food. For every 1,000 people saved today, perhaps 10,000 would die when the crunch came. Simply sending food to hungry nations with population explosions is analogous to a physician prescribing aspirin as the treatment for a patient with operable cancer—in deferring something unpleasant, disaster is entrained. Yes, send food—but insist that population control measures be instituted. But despite the logic, no one in the U.S. Government paid the slightest heed to that suggestion (or to related proposals by William and Paul Paddock in their 1968 book, "Famine—1975!"), and the point is now moot, since we have no more surplus food.

A more prominent fallacy today is the "industrialize the underdeveloped countries — reduce their infant mortality rates, and their birth rates will drop" approach to population control. The thinking of this school is based on the notion that what worked in the past for today's overdeveloped countries will naturally work in the future for today's underdeveloped countries. In the United States and Western Europe, industrialization was accompanied by a decline of death rates, followed several decades later by a drop in birth rates — a so-called demographic transition. Why not try to cause a similar transition in underdeveloped countries by promoting Western-style economic development?

This theory fails for two reasons. First, because of economic and resources considerations, the underdeveloped countries can't be industrialized in the pattern of the overdeveloped countries and, if they could be, the environmental systems of the world would collapse as a result. Second, industrialization would take decades, and further decades would have to pass before a demographic transition could lower birth rates to anything like the level of replacement reproduction. And once replacement reproduction was reached, it would take an additional half-

Population control won't be achieved without cultural change; until it occurs, there is little we can do to help.

century or more for the population to stop growing — to reach zero population growth. (There is a common confusion about the relationship between reaching replacement fertility, which means each generation is just replacing itself, and zero population growth. Because several generations are alive at one time, and because growing populations have disproportionately large numbers of young people, replacement level reproduction must be maintained for about 50 to 70 years before a population will stop growing.)

Those who look to a demographic transition to solve the population problem therefore must overlook the economic realities of industrialization, the constraints imposed upon development by resource availability and environmental fragility, or—assuming these limits could be overcome—the long time necessary for such a transition to take effect. If you figure that the transition will take 100 years or so (optimistically assuming 35 years to industrialize, 15 more to reach replacement reproduction and 50 more to reach zero population growth) then you also have to count on the world's population exceeding the level of 12 billion in that time. Yet only fools believe the planet can support that many. A "solution" that involves enormous increases in death rates, with hundreds of millions of people dying prematurely, will overtake us long before then. Indeed, few knowledgeable people think the population will even reach eight billion, twice its present size, before collapse occurs.

Programs to reduce infant and child mortality alone are sometimes also promoted as the road to population control. The basic idea is that by exporting Western medical expertise, the survival of more children can be assured. Then parents in many societies will see that large families are no longer required to guarantee the survival of at least one son to support them in their old age. It sounds like a fine program for situations where lack of social security is a major reason for large families, until you realize the time lags involved—optimistically perhaps a decade for the program to be implemented and a generation or so (say 35 years) for people to perceive the change. All through that period, population growth would be accelerated by further lowering of the death rate. And then, of course, there is the minimum 50-year gap between reaching replacement reproduction and reaching zero population growth. "Population control by reducing infant mortality" is another scenario that won't stand the test of arithmetic.

Does this mean there is nothing Americans can do to help hold back the world population flood? Should we not ship pills and condoms to the underdeveloped countries; should we not help them industrialize; should we not send them medical aid to lower their infant mortality rates? We probably should not, except under very special circumstances, but we probably will anyway. Who could morally deny aid to dying children, even if that aid promotes the death of many more children in the future? The only hope seems to be that these countries themselves will change the kinds of aid they request.

The underdeveloped countries must break away from the ridiculous patterns of development that the overdeveloped countries followed and come up with their own goals and plans—ones that are appropriate to their cultures and realistic in terms of their resources and the need to maintain environmental quality. They must carefully control outside agencies, especially multinational corporations, that attempt to impose dangerous or unnecessary programs on them. These revised development plans should incorporate measures designed to reduce birth rates as rapidly as possible in ways that recognize the special characteristics of each country. Rather than trying to emulate the U.S. and other overdeveloped countries, they might look to China, whose population policies are fully integrated with the health program and efforts to "develop." Unfortunately, China has also pursued a course of massive industrialization, but in recent years, her goals have become relatively realistic. When realistic development plans are formulated, underdeveloped countries may ask for American aid, and hopefully we will be wise and compassionate enough to supply it.

In a few countries, development and population control may involve limited industrialization. If their plans make sense and they want help, we should give it to them. In most countries, the best population control program may involve such approaches as the institution of social-security systems and the expansion of maternal and child health programs, combined with intensive promotion of birth control. If these plans seem justifiable, the United States might help bankroll them. (A social-security program showed promise at a pilot level in India). But it is clear that simply providing contraceptives without profound changes in the social system will have little effect. Other useful programs might include efforts to raise the status and educational level of women and a reversal of migration from farm to city. If underdeveloped countries want technical help, we could supply it. American helicopters might yet end up flying birth control devices around. But the point is that such aid should not be granted until the motivation has been provided by cultural change. Then and only then can aid in providing family planning services prove helpful. And the responsibility for planning and execution must remain with each country itself.

It is questionable whether the underdeveloped countries can or will institute such programs in a way that can outrun the arithmetic of growth —many of their leaders are as infatuated with industrialization as most of ours (after all, a lot of them were trained in the London School of Economics)—but their choice is to change or die. In the meantime, what can Mrs. Sturdley and other concerned Americans actually do to help solve the world population problem? The very best thing they can do is to forget about clumsily conceived overseas programs and concentrate on setting a good example here at home. That might seem a limited goal, but since the U.S. has for years stood as such a model of development for underdeveloped countries to emulate, it could make an important difference.

The fact is that even at its current rapidly declining level, population growth in the U.S. is the most serious in the world, because of our enormously wasteful economy. We put the greatest per capita drain on irreplaceable resources. We launch the heaviest per capita assault on the global environmental systems on which civilization depends utterly for its existence. We have, it is true, recently dipped slightly below the replacement level of reproduction, but because of the lag time after achievement of low fertility, about 50 million Americans will be added to our population before we reach a state of zero population growth if the low fertility continues. In terms of damage to the planet, those 50 million are the equivalent of about 2 billion people added to the populations of the underdeveloped countries.

So if Mrs. Sturdley truly wants to do something about the world population problem, she will have to make some sacrifices. She could have her tubes tied before she has her second child. She could disconnect the air-conditioning in her Cadillac, drive it at no more than 55 miles per hour until it falls apart, and then replace it with a subcompact. She could urge C.F.P.L.T. to institute a crash program designed to keep the birth rate in the United States well below the replacement level— and to make sure it is designed to hit the superconsumers more than the poor.

Mrs. Sturdley could pressure her oil millionaire husband to buy a few Senators and Congressmen and have them join forces with the few people already in the Government who understand the population problem in an effort to buttress the trend to fewer births with an explicit policy. They could urge Congress or the President to announce that not only is America overpopulated, it is too greedy for resources and too destructive of the environment. "Two at the most" could be declared the national childbearing goal, and the weight of Government propaganda could be thrown into achieving that goal.

In addition to setting a direct example on the population control front, the United States could also take action on the consumption-pollution "multipliers" that add so much to the impact of American population growth. Numerous steps could be instituted to reduce wasteful consumption and minimize environmental deterioration—tough, meaningful steps like bans on big cars, on most air-conditioning and on most illuminated outdoor advertising. Adequate insulation could be required on all buildings. In short, the Government could adopt a tough population policy and move the economy into a period of "de-development"; it could admit that we have gone too far down the road of growthmania. Perhaps if we did that, some underdeveloped countries would move more rapidly to change their development goals—after all, who would want to emulate self-admitted mistakes?

Such an approach, of course, would not be as easy or as comfortable as authorizing funds for programs of technical aid or supply, and for that reason, it is not likely to occur. But it might be a lot more meaningful, in the shrinking time that is left, than condoms from helicopters, and it would certainly be more honest. ■

June 16, 1974

CHAPTER 4

The Richest Land On Earth

The face of poverty in South Carolina.

Courtesy The New York Times.

It Isn't True That Nobody Starves In America

By ROBERT SHERRILL

HEYWOOD BROUN, watching a breadline in 1932, is said to have remarked with cynical sympathy, "Poor people wouldn't be such a bother if they didn't starve so publicly." Since the end of the Depression, and especially in recent years with the development of more sophisticated welfare programs, poor people have been much more discreet about their starving.

Occasionally, the public peace of mind is elbowed by a news story indicating that something may not be quite right—a Mississippi family is reported to have eaten a cat; some Kentucky coal miners are seen eating only potato peelings for lunch; in Washington, D. C., pensioners scramble for discarded lettuce and cabbage leaves behind one of the largest markets. But most poor people are not observed in their ingenuities, and, in any event, the Government lists only 1,279 deaths from "malnutrition" and 197 deaths from "hunger, thirst, and exposure" in 1965, the last year for which there are statistics.

This, coupled with the natural optimism of Americans, has pushed into public faith an almost religious tenet—a second miracle of the loaves and fishes—called Nobody Starves in America, with the alternate title, No Adult Is Completely Broke For Long.

As with most economic dogmas, both are false, yet the foundation heaves a bit when either is challenged. And this may account for the present unease and unhappiness among some high Washington officials as they observe the Senate Anti-Poverty Subcommittee going around the country holding meetings and reviving the political topic of hunger as it has not been revived since the nineteen-thirties. (When, on Senator George Murphy's motion, the subcommittee unanimously asked President Johnson to send emergency food to Mississippi to stop wide starvation, even the Office of Economic Opportunity jumped in to belittle the subcommittee's findings.) With all the powerful antagonisms the tour is arousing, its revival mood would probably not achieve much, except that one of the evangelists on the subcommittee happens to be Senator Robert F. Kennedy, whose disciples fill many a grotto and thrive on opposition.

THE problem that a majority on this subcommittee—Joseph Clark of Pennsylvania, both Kennedy brothers, Jacob Javits of New York, *et al.*—is attempting to attack is illustrated perfectly in the two charity food programs administered by the U. S. Department of Agriculture.

The older program deals in surplus commodities. The men who put it through Congress never posed as humanitarians—the basic purpose of the commodities program is to support and stabilize farm prices, not support and stabilize needy people. It distributes free food from a larder stocked with whatever the Government's price support program has piled up, and the major items include flour, cornmeal, rice, grits and dry beans.

None of this is expected to supply more than three-fourths of minimum diet requirements. The only meat, when there is any, is a canned variety which the department states in its literature is not expected to provide a family with more than one-seventh of its needs. Each member of the family gets about $5.50 worth of food a month, but the food never includes eggs, citrus fruits, green or yellow vegetables, potatoes, sugars or sweets.

A diet of nothing but "commodities" is guaranteed to produce physical lethargy, mental depression and frequent onslaughts of disease. But, after all, this is called a supplemental program, and the optimistic Agriculture Department assumes that there is other food in the house to be supplemented. As for the quality of the commodities, that is debated. I attended a welfare rights conference at which the delegate from New York City said the commodities are "not fit for pigs." This came as something of a surprise to the delegate from Mississippi, who pointed out that in those relatively few parts of the South which have permitted this Federal program to operate, thousands of Negroes live on nothing else.

The other Federal anti-hunger program run by the Agriculture Department is f[illegible] stamps.

Enaction of this program was the first thing President Kennedy did in the White House. Today 41 states participate to varying degrees; all major cities are in it except New York and Boston, and New York may join if pending Congressional legislation increases its funds.

Theoretically, it is a gorgeous program, constructed around the notion that everybody spends something for food each month, but poor people just don't spend enough. Solution: Allow the poor people to pay the Department of Agriculture what they would ordinarily spend for food, and in return give them bonus stamps which are just as good as money for buying any U. S.-produced food in the stores. A scale had to be worked out arbitrarily to decide what people "ordinarily" spend, but the department had no trouble settling on a scale starting at $2 a head, with a maximum payment of $12 a month for the largest family with the lowest income. In exchange for the $12, the family would get $70 worth of tickets.

The assumption is that *any* adult breadwinner can manage to raise $2 for each member of his family once a month. For Congressman Jamie Whitten of Mississippi, chairman of the House Subcommittee for Agriculture Appropriations, this is more than an assumption; it is a certainty. Whitten is a powerful man in agriculture. Secretary of Agriculture Orville Freeman sometimes says, "I have two bosses. One is President Johnson. The other is Jamie Whitten." So when Freeman wants to clear something important, he takes it to Whitten.

Recently he went to Whitten for a private consultation on the idea of lowering the food stamp prices, maybe to 50 cents for people with no income. After all, there was a lot of rumbling in Mississippi. There were rumors, even, that some Negroes were so desperate they were contemplating breaking into Government warehouses. Well, what did Whitten think about it? "Nonsense," said Whitten. "There's nobody in Mississippi who can't raise $2 a month. If there is, just bring me a list of them and we'll take care of them." Freeman left the proposal at that.

If he ever gets around to making up the list—which should be about the longest noncensus list in history—Miss Marian Wright, Jackson attorney for the N.A.A.C.P., will be glad

---

ROBERT SHERRILL is the Washington correspondent for The Nation and author of "The Accidental President."

to give him her file of several hundred sworn paupers. Gene Roberts, head of The New York Times bureau in Atlanta, can probably add plenty of names. He recently wrote of one Locket Mayze, 59, who said "he could not remember when he last had a dollar in his pocket or when—with the exception of a hog's head given him by a friend—his wife and eight children had eaten anything other than surplus farm commodities." A couple of weeks ago Jim Hyatt told, in The Wall Street Journal, of meeting Richard Bogen, 62-year-old Negro farmhand, in an Arkansas plantation store, where he sat "with cap in hand and tears filling his eyes" because "'Right now I've got just 2 pennies in my pocket.'" These people may be invisible to politicians, but any reporter who covers the South is constantly running into the Mayzes and the Bogens.

"Government administrators seem not to understand," Negro leader A. Philip Randolph told the National Advisory Commission on Rural Poverty, "that the poorest people simply don't have money." The South is thick with Negroes who live in a primitive world of barter. They work or they don't work, but when they do work it is for past debts or to establish future credit. No money changes hands. They wear cast-off clothes, they eat charity food. They buy nothing. The sharecroppers wound up the season last October either in debt to their landlords or coming out of the cotton year with, say, $50—which promptly went to pay debts in town. Their pockets have been empty for six or seven months, at least. To them, $2 a head—or even 50 cents a head—for the stamp program might as well be $2,000 a head. They simply can't raise it. If they could raise it, it would only be by borrowing from their landlords, who charge up to 50 per cent interest.

The best proof of the nonexistence of money in some areas lies in the Agriculture Department's own file cabinets, where records show that in eight Mississippi counties that changed over from commodities to food stamps (the department won't permit both programs to operate in the same county because, with its usual optimism, it assumes a family getting cheap food doesn't need additional free food) the list of participants fell off by 21,000—which can be presumed to be the number who did not have the money to stay in.

Although these two programs at present are social booby traps, with relatively minor adjustments they could be perfected and with even fewer changes could be spread. Agriculture officials concede that in the South there are 17.5 million people in poverty (nearly half the nation's total) but only two million are receiving Federal food.

Of the 283 poorest counties in 15 Southern and border states, 93 counties—the home of three million people considered poor by O.E.O. standards—have no form of food distribution whatever. In the other 190 counties live 7,100,367 poor people, but only 1,029,331 get food aid. There are several reasons the other six million may have been excluded: maybe they can't afford to pay for the stamps; maybe the commodities distribution center is too far from their home; maybe local welfare workers have not bothered to tell them about the programs or welfare officials have refused to qualify them for help. In some states it isn't easy to qualify. Department of Agriculture officials acknowledge, for example, that if a four-person family in South Carolina earns more than $1,400 a year it cannot qualify for the stamp program (the only aid available), although the O.E.O. rates nonfarm families of four as poor if they don't earn more than $2,250 a year.

Hard times aren't limited to the back country. Of the 310,000 persons living in Mobile County, Alabama, 99,000 are judged poor by Federal standards. None has access to either commodities or food stamps. Of the 67,000 poor in Pulaski County (Little Rock), Arkansas, only 3,483 get Federal food. In Harris County, Texas, location of the South's largest city, Houston, there are a quarter of a million poor people but only 20,000 get food aid, and only the commodities.

Unquestionably it is easier, however, to exist in the urban clumps. The odd job is easier to come by. Proximity helps—it is more convenient to send the children to a neighbor's table, or to borrow a dollar from a relative whose welfare check hasn't been held up. It is easier to wangle an Aid to Dependent Children check in urban counties because hunger is unsightly and the cities are more sensitive to esthetics these days.

The family living in the shanty on the "back 40" of the old plantation is out of sight, out of the county officials' minds, and therefore usually out of luck. In this respect, the forces squeezing the blacks out of the rural South and into the Northern cities may be nutritionally beneficial. The squeezing forces are fourfold: there's a cotton cutback in some areas; mechanization of many jobs is almost total; weed-killing chemicals are eliminating the need for a human being on the end of a hoe; and the $1-an-hour minimum wage that went into effect this year is re-hardening many a planter's heart. The same people who were considered "good ol' darkies" a few years ago are now considered deadwood, hardly worth keeping alive.

NOWHERE are the faults and the promises of the Government's food distribution program seen better than in Mississippi, which has one of the most complete programs in America. Every county in the state participates in some form of Federal assistance, which is rare not merely by Southern standards but by national standards. Nowhere else in the Bible Belt are poor folks given anything like a comparable amount of assistance.

One-fourth of all Mississippians (about 470,000) are eating federally paid-for food, more even than New York's charity food population (440,000). The food comes via Washington, but at least Mississippi lets it in. By comparison, South Carolina won't let

TIMES CHANGE—Now that farming has become almost totally mechanized (right, a cotton-picking machine), field hands are, as one planter put it, "as useless as a mule."

the commodities program into the state at all and permits the stamp program to operate in only 10 of 46 counties; in only three of the 20 poorest counties are the stamps sold, and on such a tight basis that only 10,900 of the 715,000 poor in these counties are assisted. Virginia has food programs for only 1.9 per cent of its impoverished people; Texas covers only 5.6 per cent; Louisiana, 7.9 per cent. In the Deep South no state but Mississippi allows more than 10.9 per cent of its poor people to participate in food programs—and Mississippi offers them to 42.3 per cent.

Yet Mississippi is a laboratory of hunger and of Federal fumbling. On the Delta—that northwestern bulge of the state that arches along the river from Memphis to Vicksburg—one can stand on a steaming summer day and be persuaded that God created the world simply to give Adam a cotton allotment. There is big money here. Delta plantation owners will take out of the soil more than a quarter of a billion dollars this year, most of it in tax-supported crops. In the same area, because of newly mechanized farming techniques, Government officials estimate there will be between 60,000 and 100,000 unemployed hands by this summer. And, since Mississippi has no general state or local welfare programs, these people must depend on Federal largesse.

Choose any shanty; only the number of bodies inside will vary. Here is a mother and six children, residents of Washington County, against the river. Four of the children are asleep on the floor. They sleep most of the day as well as all night. Their lips and legs are covered with scabs and open sores. The youngest has a distended stomach and from it the umbilical knot sticks out like a valve from an inner-tube. Some days they eat nothing. Most days they have one meal, of cornmeal. Washington County quit the commodities program in March and went on food stamps. Left-over commodities are all this family has. Now, it is after 2 P.M. and they have eaten nothing, but the mother says she will cook "a little something" later on. She points to a bag on the floor by the stove; a couple of inches of meal are left of what has lasted them two weeks. When she runs out of cornmeal, she will borrow something from a neighbor. Yes, she nods, the neighbors are in bad shape, too. But she will get something.

This must be an extreme case, so drive on, northeast into the Delta's proudest county, Sunflower, home of Senator James O. ("Our Jim") Eastland, who operates a 5,800-acre plantation near Ruleville, which is also the home of Sunflower County's next best-known politician, Mrs. Fannie Lou Hamer, a leader of the Mississippi Freedom Democratic party. Mrs. Hamer used to be a sharecropper, but, like many thousands of others, she was chased off the land. Being well imbedded in the 32-million in this country officially designated as impoverished, Mrs. Hamer speaks empirically: "The main problem about bein' poor is that it only leaves you the choice between not eatin' at all and eatin' so bad you wonder if that is a improvement."

Although reared on a farm and now middle-aged, she has eaten turkey only twice in her life, once a couple of years ago when comedian Dick Gregory shipped a batch of the birds to Mississippi Negroes and the other time when she bought a turkey on the installment plan and paid for it at the rate of 70 cents a week. When the conversation turns to food, Mrs. Hamer will always mention those two turkeys, because otherwise she has nothing to talk about except the customary meat that gets on her table—meat that is thinly attached to hog neckbones (she broke off a front tooth discovering just how thinly attached). She is a big woman, built out in rings of starch—rice and grits and more grits and flour—held together by bean proteins. Perhaps once a year she eats fruit, but only if a friend who has moved to the relatively luxurious welfare rolls of the North sends it. She cannot afford it herself.

Even the little towns of Mississippi, places like Indianola, county seat of Sunflower, have their slums and they are full of farm hands who no longer have a farm to work on and have come into town to do their starving. I met a boy in Indianola who had had nothing to eat that day but a plate of butterbeans; the day before it had been bread and butterbeans; the day before that, again just butterbeans. Sometimes, he said, it was bread alone. One-course diets are commonplace. Kenneth Dean, executive director of the Mississippi Council on Human Relations, who has moved among these people for many months, describes a typical hardship case:

"Breakfast will be grits, molasses and biscuit. For lunch, the adults will eat nothing, and the children who are at home will be given a piece of bread and a drink of Kool-Aid or water. The evening meal usually consists of boiled beans and cornbread." In the worst cases, which are not uncommon, "there is usually no table on which to eat, and what little food there is is eaten by hand out of a bowl or from a newspaper on the floor."

WITH hunger so abundant and easy to find, it might be anticipated that the Department of Agriculture would react to it in a dramatic fashion. But this has not been the case. Seventeen months ago, Congressman Joseph Resnick, Democrat of New York, made a tour of Mississippi and came back to Washington writing letters to all the appropriate Administration leaders about the "desperation point of . . . starving Negroes." Nothing happened.

A month later 35 Negroes invaded the abandoned Greenville, Miss., Air Force Base, and before a phalanx of troops was flown in to evict them they distributed leaflets explaining: "We are here because we are hungry and cold and we have no jobs or land." It made the front pages as a protest story, but their appeal for food somehow went astray. Last summer the Department of Agriculture's own Civil Rights Advisory Council held hearings in Jackson, Miss., and made confidential recommendations to Secretary Freeman that he act upon their "deep sense of urgency" that something must be done swiftly "before suffering, hopelessness and frustration make an evolutionary approach extremely difficult and infinitely more expensive, if not—for an interim — impossible." About the same time, across the Mississippi River, Arkansas State Welfare Director A. J. Moss was writing letters to Freeman, warning that thousands of families would soon be unemployed on the Arkansas Delta and that the food situation was critical. Neither warning disquieted the adamant Agriculture Department calm.

Then, in April, the Clark-Kennedy troupe hit Mississippi, accompanied by TV cameramen, journalistic jongleurs and the usual ballyhoo machinery. It made a difference. At this point Freeman began to move cautiously. He dispatched two of his aides—Howard Davis and William Seabron—to Mississippi for a confidential report. Davis and Seabron found, of course, what everyone else had been reporting for more than a year: many Mississippians are limp with malnutrition, many cannot afford to buy the food stamps, and some landlords are profiteering off the programs. Among the cases of suffering they cited a man in Winstonville, father of six, who got into the food stamp program only because "a New York A.B.C. newsman on assignment in Mississippi gave him $12 twice to buy food stamps. He does not know what he will do when his present commodities and stamp supplies are gone."

Another case: Mrs. Effie Mae Jackson of Billy May Plantation, mother of five, "has a problem of having the date to buy stamps come prior to receipt of her check from welfare. To meet this she borrows from her landlord the $22 each month, and when her check comes he charges her 50 cents on the dollar, which means she has to pay $33 for the stamps each month." This, plus her $10-a-month rent, means that she must pay $43 for food and rent out of the $55 she gets from welfare.

For some reason, the story Davis and Seabron brought back penetrated where others had failed. Freeman wrote Senator Clark that he was "deeply concerned about their findings" and that he might change the rules to make persons with no income pay only a fourth as much as at present. He said this before talking with Congressman Whitten. After the latest Whitten conversation, Freeman told Jack Conway, head of the Industrial Union Department of the A.F.L.-C.I.O. and unofficial boss of Walter Reuther's Citizens Crusade Against Poverty, that he isn't going to try to cut the stamps' cost "until the department budget gets out of Whitten's committee."

AND that is where reform of the program stands today. It hasn't started.

Civil rights leaders damn Freeman for not opening his ears until two winters had passed since he was first alerted to the predicament of the foodless Southern Negro. But Freeman is not his own man in this dispute. In many respects he is the prisoner of the Southerners who command the agriculture committees and the

Though poor people are "much more discreet about their starving" than they used to be, hunger is a hotter political issue today than at any time since the '30's.

FACT-FINDER—Robert Kennedy tours the Mississippi Delta for the Senate Anti-Poverty Subcommittee. U.S. food programs reach only 2 million of the 17.5 million poor in the South.

agriculture appropriations subcommittees in both houses of Congress. As human-support programs, neither the free commodities nor the food stamps are popular with these groups. A bill is now being pushed by some House Southerners that would kill the food stamp program by making it prohibitively costly for many states, particularly those states in Dixie with the highest concentrations of Negroes. Many farm-oriented legislators have a hoary suspicion that any give-away program promotes shiftlessness among the menials.

Nowhere is this attitude better seen than in Alabama, where the distribution of Federal rood is made inversely to need, and also inversely to the concentration of Negroes. The 30 richest counties, in the top half of the state, participate in the free-food program; the 37 poorest counties in the bottom do not. Although not notorious for pampering Negroes, the Alabama administration nevertheless encourages the acceptance of Federal surplus foods by the counties because it is a sure-fire way of "beating" Washington. For a very small expense—about one or two cents a day per recipient—the counties receive a cornucopia of food. Montgomery County, for example, would pay about $15,000 a year as the cost of distributing almost $1,000,000 in commodities to its people.

But Montgomery County won't enter the program. Neither will other counties where most of the state's Negroes live. Tallapoosa County, home of the State Welfare Commissioner, refuses to pay the $10,000 required to distribute $700,000 worth of surplus foods. The Negro leaders of Hale County have been trying for two years to get county officials to bring in a food program. First the officials said it was too expensive, but when Washington offered to bear the total cost, they still refused. Agriculture officials refuse to fight this kind of local obstinacy. Secretary Freeman promised a commodities program for Hale last August, but he hasn't delivered it yet.

Could the Federal Government just send the food in anyway, without local approval, and have Federal workers distribute it or let the poor people distribute it themselves? Yes; for 30 years the Secretary of Agriculture has had power to distribute food where emergencies exist. And, when pressed hard enough, he will. When Negroes in Dallas County, already warmed up by the Selma civil rights activities in 1965, began demonstrating loudly because they wanted food, Federal officials told Dallas County leaders the food was coming in, and if they wouldn't distribute it, civil rights leaders would. Dallas County surrendered and took the goods, but the scope of the victory is disputed. Some say it only hardened the will of surrounding counties to resist.

THIS kind of tugging and heaving reveals the great weakness of the food programs: commercial interests of the South use them for reprisal and coercion. They are the political and social weapons of a region. Free Federal food was valued by the Delta planters for many years because, by allowing their hired hands to live off it through the winter, it became a kind of subsidy for the farmers. (Free commodities were never given to Delta Negroes after spring plowing time, because a little hunger was expected to make them eager to earn $3 a day in the fields.)

But now that farming has become almost totally mechanized, field hands are, as one planter put it, "as useless as a mule." They and their shotgun shanties only clutter the landscape, chafing the consciences and the pocketbooks of the region. Get rid of them. And what better way than to shift to a food program they cannot afford? Half of the Delta counties have already dropped the commodities and put in food stamps. "What does that mean?" asked Amzie Moore, a Negro leader from Cleveland, Miss. "That means starve or go to Chicago. Well, we're not going to Chicago. We don't want the stamps unless it's a free stamp program."

The angry Negroes have some support. That faint thunder in the distance may develop into a real challenge. The U.S. Commission on Civil Rights has circulated a memo implying that Freeman has ignored his obvious powers to bring relief. The commission urges free food stamps for the penniless and both programs operating simultaneously in the poorest counties. The leaders of Reuther's Citizens Crusade want to strip Freeman of his role in distributing food and turn the whole job over to the Department of Health, Education and Welfare—which was in fact Senator John Kennedy's proposal in 1959. The Crusade is putting out some pretty snappish statements about the preeminence of nutrition over profits. And now Senator Javits has asked the Senate Executive Reorganization Subcommittee to consider the "strip Freeman" proposal.

If impoverished Southerners are judged strictly as an economic factor, more food to keep them alive can be viewed skeptically as merely a temporary solution to the problem of making them profitable. But for them temporariness has always been a relative matter, and they would probably just as soon be fed even on that basis—for, as one high Citizens Crusade official pointed out: "We've been keeping them alive on a temporary basis for 300 years." Something more permanent, he felt, is not wholly impossible and is "limited only by the amount of money that American capitalism, with its Dixiecrat-dominated agriculture committees in Congress, is willing to spend to create a 20th-century civilization in the South." The vagueness of the statement is important; here is a man who for a lifetime has been professionally concerned with labor and housing conditions of the Southern poor, and yet he has no specific plans to improve them, and the specific planners have not come much farther.

Many say that the salvation of the hungry Negro lies in modification of the agricultural South with industry. It is an old dream. Since the days of Gov. Hugh White's "Balance Agriculture With Industry" program a generation ago, Mississippi has been trying to bring in the smokestacks, and the same has been true for the South as a whole since the days of Henry Grady. Yet the skies over the South's vast boondocks are just about as blue and unsmudged as ever. Others, including such practical groups as the Southern Regional Council, are pushing for farm cooperatives to give the landed Negro independence from a repressive social structure. But this, too, though spottily successful, is something that has been tried off and on for years without more than denting the general poverty of the black farmer.

These efforts and failures are quite beside the point to the Negro who faces another one-meal, beans-only day. Very much to the point is the knowledge that his life can be changed, and immediately, by the simplest of Agriculture Department fiats.

IF change does come, it will probably take some powerful motivating emotion to achieve it. But there is hope for that, too. When Robert Kennedy returned from his safari into Mississippi's shanty jungles, he told of seeing people who eat one meal every two days, but he described the results only as "extreme hunger." For politicians, "starvation" is a smut word. They don't like to come right out and say it exists in this country—so it becomes "hunger" or "malnutrition"—and even less do they like to see that which the taboo word describes; it embarrasses them. Testifying before a Senate group about swollen bellies and running sores and all the cottonpatch grotesqueries he had seen, Kennedy several times became so embarrassed he laughed. The last best hope of "extremely hungry" folks is that that discomfort will spread. ■

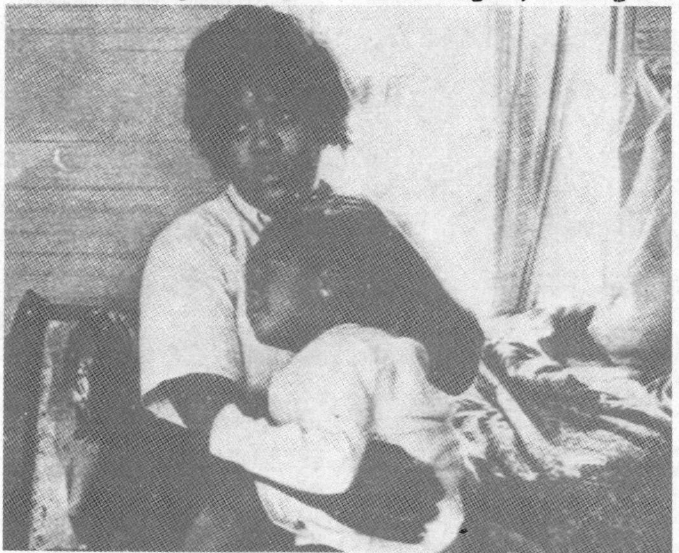

FOOD AID PROGRAM REVAMPED BY U.S.

Cost of Stamps Cut in Half in Mississippi in First Step of National Plan

Special to The New York Times

GREENVILLE, Miss., June 26—The Federal Government has drastically revamped its food aid program in Mississippi in an effort to reach more poor people.

The changes, which will be extended eventually throughout the South and the rest of the country, were in response to demands of civil rights groups and to the finding, by a team of doctors, of hunger approaching starvation among hundreds of Negro children.

The changes are being made in the face of rising criticism of the Administration on grounds that it has not overcome the hunger problem in the South. At the same time, powerful Congressional forces, mainly Southerners, have balked at Administration efforts to increase aid in the South.

Secretary of Agriculture Orville L. Freeman initiated the new program, which was worked out with state and Federal officials. It includes the following:

¶A reduction of more than one half in the cost of food stamps, effective Saturday.

¶A reduction in the required minimum purchase by families from $2 a person a month to 50 cents a person. For $12 a family of six has been getting tickets for the purchase of $70 of food at prevailing prices at local stores.

¶An attempt, through state and local officials, to get county boards of supervisors to underwrite the cost of minimum purchases of stamps for families that have no income.

¶An increase of trained Federal workers to handle the increased efforts and to recruit, hire and train new "program aides," including Negroes, to reach more of the poor people.

¶Establishment of five new Federal commodity marketing and service offices in Mississippi by Sept. 1, raising the total to 10. The offices are operated by the Agricultural Department to distribute the food stamps.

No immediate estimate of the cost of the program was made.

The new "program aides" will be trained to work with the poor on nutrition, food buying and preparation of food. These aides will be solicited from civil rights groups and from employment agencies.

Welfare Plan Conversion

Findings of hunger among Negro children were made by a team of doctors who returned from Mississippi earlier this month and informed Congress of the situation. The team was sponsored by the Field Foundation of New York, which focuses on child welfare and interracial relations.

The revised program became known as Secretary Freeman flew here on a tour of rural development projects designed to overcome rural poverty and to bolster rural economies.

Mr. Freeman was scheduled to meet with civil rights leaders to explain the changes he plans to start by Aug. 1.

Mr. Freeman's action will also include a longer conversion period for the changeover from the direct distribution of Federal food by state and local welfare agencies to the food stamp program.

This will provide a transition period to make certain that some recipients will not be cut off from direct state aid before they are able to make use of the Federal food stamps.

Mr. Freeman has been sharply criticized for not using his powers to make food stamps quickly available to all the poor, particularly those without income. He sought recently to cut the price of food stamps but was rebuffed by powerful Southern Congressional forces, who have sought to abolish the food stamp program.

Mr. Freeman consulted with Southern Congressmen on the Agriculture and Appropriations committees that deal with the budget and program of the Department of Agriculture, because he does not want to antagonize them unnecessarily. Despite their disapproval, however, he used his administrative authority to carry out the change in the food stamp program.

Many Southerners remain opposed to cutting the price of the food stamps on the ground that this would assist hard-core unemployed persons and discourage them from seeking employment.

The conversion from direct distribution of welfare food to the food stamp plan has been a thorny problem and has left hundreds of families without aid, adding to the criticism of Mr. Freeman.

For example, figures from the Department of Agriculture show that in April, 1966, 208,000 persons in 28 counties in Mississippi were getting direct food aid. As a result of the change from direct distribution to the food stamp plan, the number being aided dropped to 128,000 in April of this year.

In Washington County (Greenville) 20,218 were getting direct food aid a year ago, but last April the number under the food stamp plan totaled 10,160.

One of the most delicate areas facing Federal and state officials is that of inducing the county boards of supervisors to pay the cost of stamps for those unable to buy them.

State officials, including Miss Francis Gandy, state welfare commissioner, were understood to have asked Federal officials to let the local people work on this problem. State officials will ask the Legislature at its next session in January to budget funds to provide stamps for the poor without money.

An assistant to Mr. Freeman recently briefed Governor Paul B. Johnson Jr. on the proposed Federal actions.

June 27, 1967

$220-Million to Aid the Hungry Is Returned to Treasury Unused

By JOSEPH A. LOFTUS
Special to The New York Times

WASHINGTON, April 23—The Agriculture Department said today that it had money and food for hungry people but that bureaucratic conflicts with county officials often blocked the distribution machinery.

As a result, the department is returning $220-million in unused funds to the Treasury this year.

The department's statement today was an official reaction to publication of a report, "Hunger, U.S.A.," by a private organization called the Citizens Board of Inquiry on Hunger and Malnutrition in the United States.

The report said that 10 million was probably a conservative estimate of the number of persons suffering from a shortage of food and that the shortage was acute in 256 counties.

There are two food distribution methods, a spokesman explained—the food stamp plan, which operates through local retail stores, and direct distribution of commodities through local welfare machinery.

Stamp Money Committed

If a county official said today that he wanted only the food stamp plan, his county would not get any surplus food because all the available Federal money for food stamps has been committed. The department would not attempt to impose direct distribution of commodities on such a county.

If county officials said that they wanted no Federal food aid whatever, the department then would set up its own machinery for distributing commodities to the poor, but that takes a long time. It is undertaking that procedure in one county, Elmore in Alabama, and is considering such action is six to 18 other counties in several states.

On the other hand, the spokesman conceded that the department had recommended a rise of only $20-million in the food stamp authorization for the coming fiscal year. That would mean, if the dapartment got the authorization and the cash to go with it, that food stamp money would amount to $245-million instead of $225-million, which is the amount now carried in the budget for the fiscal year 1969.

In the current fiscal year, the food stamp money amounts to $185-million plus $2.5-million transferred from the Office of Economic Opportunity.

Secretary of Agriculture Orville L. Freeman, in a prepared comment on the "Hunger" report, said that many of the report's findings "parallel findings of Department of Agriculture studies and my own personal observations on field trips to hunger areas."

"The feelings of board

members at the disgraceful paradox of hunger amidst plenty are my feelings, also," he said.

Gains Since 1961 Cited

Mr. Freeman's only quarrel with the report was that it did not record the progress made since 1961.

He said that when he became Secretary of Agriculture, only 1,200 counties—out of 3,091 in the country—had a food program. It consisted of the distribution of five surplus commodities worth about $2.20 a person a month. Only 3.5 million persons were reached.

Today, he said, 2,200 counties have food programs, and 5.8 million persons are being fed.

The Secretary added: "Those still on direct distribution now receive 16 different foods worth four times the amount they received in 1961. Food stamp recipients multiply their food dollars by $15-million a month, $180-million a year, in additional food purchasing power. They have a much more nutritious diet than is possible with direct distribution."

April 24, 1968

House Unit Doubts Report of Starvation in U.S.

By JOSEPH A. LOFTUS
Special to The New York Times

WASHINGTON, June 16—The House Agriculture Committee reported today it had not been able to find a single case of starvation in the United States.

There are many cases of malnutrition, its report said, but these were attributed to local custom and ignorance.

The sources of the committee's information were county health officers who responded to a letter of inquiry signed by the committee chairman, Representative W. R. Poage, Democrat of Texas.

The incentive for Mr. Poage's letter was a publication, "Hunger—U.S.A.," based on a private study by a group calling itself the Citizens Board of Inquiry into Hunger and Malnutrition in the United States. Its report cited 256 "emergency hunger counties." The board was supported by church, union and civil rights groups and individuals.

Mr. Poage wrote to the health officer of each county on April 27 and went to press with replies from 181.

"Do you have any personal knowledge of any actual starvation in your county?" he asked. "Second, do you have any personal knowledge of any serious hunger in your county occasioned by inability of the individual to either buy food or receive public assistance?"

"Our committee," Mr. Poage wrote to the health officers, "is greatly concerned with any possible lack of ability of our people to obtain an adequate supply of food." He also made this point:

"From my limited knowledge of nutrition I would assume that it was true that many Americans suffer from an improper diet, but the problem there is one of education and of personal decisions. It differs greatly from the inability of citizens to secure either through gainful employment or public relief the needed nutrients."

Many of the replies were written in kind. J. P. Chism, health administrator of Hale County, Ala., wrote:

"All our employes are of the opinion that there are those in the county who do not receive proper nutrition, but none knew of any starvation. Further, it was the unanimous feeling of each member of our staff that any malnutrition which may exist in this county is due to problems of education and personal decisions plus questionable ability to rationalize rather than any inability to buy food or receive public assistance."

Macon County Replies

Macon County, Ala., was represented in the replies by Dr. Ruth Berree, who said:

"The public health nurses and I do see some children who do not have adequate diets. Often it is because the parents do not know where to get free commodities and cannot read the directions for preparing powdered milk and other foods they are not acquainted with."

Dr. O. R. Hunt, director of the Suwannee County Health Department in Florida, wrote:

"Voltaire once said: 'A man has the right to kill himself anyway he wishes.' Americans who continue to smoke, drink, and eat poor diets despite widespread knowledge of the consequences of such are apparently practicing that right. No one need go hungry in Suwannee County. An adequate diet is available, but we cannot make them eat it."

The summary in the committee document issued today said:

"While some criticism may be raised to the effect that these responses came from officials who are 'part of the Establishment' and therefore might not be expected to fully disclose conditions over which they had a responsibility, the question may be voiced as to where can be found citizens of greater responsibility who can speak more knowledgeably as to the conditions into which we are looking."

Staff reports issued on Friday by the United States Commission on Civil Rights, based largely on public hearings in Montgomery, Ala., three weeks ago, reported that the average payment for aid to dependent children in that state in March was $15 per person.

In testimony on that point, Dr. Ruben King, Commissioner of the Alabama State Department of Pensions and Security, said:

"Fifteen dollars is not enough. There are many children in this state, both black and white, who go to bed hungry at night."

Some witnesses testified they could not participate in a food stamp plan because they did not have the money to buy the stamps or for the transportation ($1 in some cases) to go for the stamps.

Participants are expected to pay for stamps the amount they would ordinarily pay for food. The stamps, however, carry bonus values.

Counties without food stamp plans—a choice made by county officials in most cases—often have a surplus commodity distribution plan. The Agriculture Department, which furnishes the commodities, concedes that these are no more than supplementary foods and do not constitute a balanced diet.

June 17, 1968

SENATE UNIT TOLD OF HUNGER IN U.S.

'Alarming' Rate of Disease Also Disclosed in Survey of 12,000, Mostly Poor

By HOMER BIGART
Special to The New York Times

WASHINGTON, Jan. 22—The phenomenon of chronic hunger and malnutrition in a land fat with agricultural surpluses was officially verified for the first time today in a Government medical survey.

Preliminary findings after complete physical examination of 12,000 Americans selected at random in low-income areas of Texas, Louisiana, New York and Kentucky showed an "alarming prevalence" of diseases commonly associated with undernourishment.

They also disclosed the presence of exotic diseases that were thought to exist only among the ill-fed peoples of backward countries, and a return of endemic goiter, a disease thought virtually eradicated in the United States 30 years ago.

A Senate committee listened in silence as Dr. Arnold E. Schaefer of the Public Health Service reported that the nutritional level of the people examined was as low as the level found in similar surveys in Central America.

The survey made no attempt to go into the reasons why people were hungry.

When Senator Jacob K. Javits, Republican of New York, asked Dr. Schaefer if he could relate the problems of malnutrition to low-income levels, Dr. Schaefer replied, "Honestly, we cannot at this point."

But Dr. Schaefer suggested during his testimony that ignorance of diet was a major factor. Other observers have noted as causes a good deal of functional illiteracy, especially in the rural South, the dearth of county welfare officers and nurses, and the difficulty of getting an improvised and apathetic population to respond to the rigid rules of local officials administering the food programs.

The first sampling of the National Nutrition Survey, a study of the eating habits of the poor that will eventually cover 10 states, disclosed seven cases of extreme malnutrition diagnosed as marasmus, primarily a caloric deficiency, and kwashiorkor, a severe protein and multiple nutrient deficiency.

These seven were starving, Dr. Schaefer told the Senate Select Committee on Nutrition and Human Needs.

"We did not expect to find such cases in the United States," he said. "In many of the developing areas where we have worked—Africa, Latin America and Asia—these severe cases of malnutrition only rarely are found. They either are hospitalized or have died."

One victim of marasmus, an emaciated baby with staring eyes and matchstick arms and legs, was shown on film. Dr. Schaefer called attention to the lack of muscle tissue on the arms and the protruding shoulder blades, a condition known as winged scapula.

Eighteen cases of rickets were found, Dr. Schaefer reported. Like goiter, rickets was thought to have been wiped out in the nineteen-thirties. Rickets is a children's disease caused by a vitamin D deficiency and marked by soft, deformed bones.

Diseases Make Comeback

Rickets and goiter have staged a comeback because of changes in the processing of food, Dr. Schaefer said. When milk was fortified with vitamin D in a public health nutrition program during the Depression years, rickets virtually vanished.

This program has lagged, Dr. Schaefer said. Although fortified milk is required for American food programs overseas, he added, only recently has the Government ordered vitamin D milk for its charity food programs at home. Not all milk in United States stores has vitamin D added.

Goiter is considered endemic when 5 per cent of the population has enlarged thyroid glands. The nutrition survey found that 5 per cent of the people examined had enlarged thyroid glands associated with low iodine intake.

The eradication of goiter was achieved in the nineteen-thirties by the introduction of iodized salt, Dr. Schaefer recalled.

"One does not eradicate goiter one generation and then forget about the problem," he said.

Texas is in a "goiter belt" that stretches from the Great Lakes down through the heart of the nation, where water and land are lacking in iodine, he said. Yet 40 per cent of the local markets in Texas do not stock iodized salt, though it costs no more, Dr. Schaefer said.

Chickens and swine in the goiter belt are carefully fed an iodized salt mineral mix, Dr. Schaefer said, yet humans are neglectful of their own diet. People have forgotten they need the iodine, he explained.

Most of the 12,000 persons examined were in Texas (4,500) and Louisiana (3,000,). The survey in New York has reached about 700 so far.

Dr. Ogden C. Johnson, head of the Food Science Research Unit of the National Institutes of Health, said those 700 were from rural areas and small towns upstate, and tended to be older than the people examined in the other states.

No Extreme Cases

No extreme cases of malnutrition have been uncovered among the 250 New York State residents whose records have been processed, Dr. Johnson said. The survey will reach New York City in mid-February and continue until June or July, with 200 slum families to be sampled.

Senator George S. McGovern, Democrat of South Dakota and chairman of the committee, wanted to know why Mississippi had not been among the first states surveyed. Widespread hunger, particularly in the Delta counties, was reported by Senator Robert F. Kennedy and other Senators after a tour of Mississippi a year ago.

Dr. Schaefer did not reply directly but indicated to reporters after the session that Representative Jamie L. Whitten, Democrat of Mississippi and chairman of the House Agriculture Appropriations Subcommittee, had opposed the survey in his state. Dr. Schaefer confirmed that agents from the Federal Bureau of Investigation attached to the House Agriculture Committee had questioned him on the reasons for the survey.

No opposition was encountered in the other states, according to Dr. Schaefer. State health departments were responsible for conducting the examinations under methods laid down by the United States Public Health Service. The survey will provide the first comprehensive scientific study of nutrition in America.

The survey was ordered by an act of Congress in late 1967. The assignment was to make a comprehensive survey of the incidence and location of serious hunger and malnutrition and health problems in the United States. The survey will draft recommendations. It began a year ago and its duration may depend on Congressional funding.

States were selected on the basis of "broad geographic representations, rural and urban populations, and the diversity of economic, ethnic and socio-cultural patterns within the United States," among other criteria.

Under questioning from Senator Edward M. Kennedy, Democrat of Massachusetts, who wanted an estimate on starvation in the country, Dr. Schaefer said he could not guess the extent of chronic hunger. But he said that 16 per cent to 17 per cent of the persons examined were "real risks" and needed medical attention.

Children up to 6 years old constituted 19 per cent of the total group examined, and children 10 to 16 constituted 25 per cent.

Dr. Schaefer reported a startling incidence of growth retardation.

"The length of most children at birth is similar in both poorly nourished and well-nourished populations," he said. "In the sample we have studied thus far, the children between 1 and 3 years of age fall below the average height reported for children in the U.S.A."

An analysis of the first 120 X-rays of these children indicated that about 3.5 per cent of the children were physically stunted, he said.

One-third of the children under 6 were anemic, Dr. Schaefer reported. Nearly one-third had a vitamin A deficiency at "unacceptable levels," below the level at which night blindness appears. Advanced stages may lead to permanent blindness, Dr. Schaefer said.

He had found no such cases, he said, but 13 per cent of the population studied were in a "high risk" category.

"We do not know how long these people have had these low levels or whether their vitamin intake is now being increased or decreased," he said. "We can't afford the risk that any of these people will develop the severe deficiency."

Mental Retardation

Severe dental problems assailed the group. Eighteen per cent of all subjects 10 years of age and over reported that it was difficult and painful to bite or chew food. Ninety-six per cent had an average of 10 teeth either decayed, filled or missing. Only 15 of each 1,000 decayed teeth had been filled.

Asked by Senator Kennedy whether mental retardation had been observed, Dr. Schaefer said there was sufficient medical evidence to suggest that stunted bone growth was accompanied by retardation of brain growth in small children.

Dr. Schaefer, a long-time public health officer who has conducted nutrition surveys for the Government in 33 developing countries, said the report indicated that malnutrition was just as bad in the United States as in the Central-American countries of Guatemala, Costa Rica, Panama, Honduras, Nicaragua and El Salvador that were recently surveyed.

The samplings covered persons with incomes ranging from $180 a year to $40,000 a year, although 80 per cent had incomes of less than $5,000.

Negroes made up 55 per cent of the sample, and 25 per cent were Spanish-Americans.

Dr. William J. McGanity of the University of Texas medical branch testified that the findings did not indicate that any one ethnic group was primarily affected by malnutrition.

The survey has been completed in Texas, is nearly completed in Louisiana, and is in progress in New York and Kentucky. A similar study is under way under Navajo Indians of Arizona. Six more states—Californa, Massachusetts, Washington, West Virginia, Michigan and South Carolina — will be surveyed later.

"Serious malnutrition is inexcusable in a country as rich as the United States," Senator McGovern commented. "I was shocked by what the survey has shown."

The report showed that 8 per cent of the families surveyed in Texas participated in the Federal food programs. Of 254 counties in Texas, 114 have either the food stamp or the direct food distribution plan.

January 23, 1969

Hunger in America: Stark Deprivation Haunts a Land of Plenty

By HOMER BIGART
Special to The New York Times

BLUFFTON, S. C.—Hunger is a noun that means, among other things, a compelling desire for food, a nagging emptiness of stomach and gut. Persons old enough to remember the Great Depression may recall going hungry, but today it is a sensation generally reserved for those mired in poverty.

Chronic hunger seems so remote in this bounteous land that reports of extreme malnutrition among Negroes in the rural South, among migrant farm workers, among Mexican-Americans and reservation Indians have been set down as exaggerations and lies, the observers frequently assailed as charlatans or do-gooders who would sap the initiative of the hungry poor by expanding "giveaway" Federal food programs or even conspiring for adoption of a guaranteed minimum wage.

Here in Beaufort County, Donald E. Gatch, an intense youthful-looking country doctor, has been shunned by the white community for insisting that hunger is a daily fact of life among the black families of this mossy tidewater.

He began losing his white patients two years ago after he charged publicly that he had seen children dying of starvation, **that most black children of his area were infested with worms, and that families were living in hovels worse than the pigsties of his native Nebraska.**

The Beaufort Gazette accused him of "running his mouth." Every other doctor in the county signed a statement deploring his "unsubstantiated allegations," contending that the "rare cases of infant malnutrition" that came to their attention were invariably due to

The New York Times Feb. 17, 1969

"parental inexperience, indifference or gross neglect." And the County Health Officer, Dr. H. Parker Jones, said he had "never seen a case of starvation or extreme malnutrition."

Ostracized by the staff of Beaufort County Memorial Hospital, annoyed by threatening telephone calls, boycotted by white patients, Dr. Gatch closed his Beaufort office, sold his home and moved with his British-born wife and two young sons back to Bluffton (pop. 356), where he had started his practice 10 years ago.

One chilly, overcast day at the tag end of January Dr. Gatch consented to take a visitor on a tour of Negro shanties near Bluffton.

Like a Missionary Outpost

The doctor, who sometimes appears disconsolate and withdrawn, peered glumly at the scene through horn-rimmed spectacles that kept sliding down his nose. From the clay road the weathered shanties, woodsmoke curling from the chimneys, looked quite charming. But Dr. Gatch, in his low, tired voice, spoke only of the overcrowding, the filth and the smell of poverty within.

The Gatches had taken over a group of summer cottages on the bank of a tidal creek, living in one, using another for

Photographs for The New York Times by EDWARD HAUSNER

A shack near Bluffton, S. C. Disease, caused by poor living conditions, is companion to hunger in depressed areas.

Listless, a boy recovering from rickets sits in the sun

frequent guests (nutritionists and sociologists from all over are coming to see him) and hoping to convert a third into a clinic. (The doctor maintains a large, well-equipped office in the center of the village.)

The Gatch compound, shaded by live oaks decked in Spanish moss, had the quiet, mournful isolation of a missionary outpost in central Africa. The African connection was further strengthened when Dr. Gatch remarked that he had treated several children for kwashiorkor, a disease generally thought to exist only in underdeveloped countries.

Kwashiorkor is a Ghanaian word meaning literally "the disease that takes the child after it leaves the mother's breast." It is a disease of extreme protein deficiency, a starvation often brought on by a mother's inability to breast-feed an infant.

Down a dirt road Dr. Gatch paused at the decaying stoop of a family named Kinnard. Silent children with skinny legs sat listlessly on floors and beds. Fifteen people lived in the shack, Dr. Gatch said, and there was no privy.

Comfortable While Still

He went directly to a young woman who was holding a crying, seven-month-old baby girl. He had examined the baby before, he said, and had detected symptoms of both kwashiorkor and scurvy. He remarked how the baby's hair had thinned, how the hairline had receded about an inch, and how the hair color had changed from black to dirty gray. These were the stigmata of kwashiorkor, he said.

He took the infant girl from the mother's arms and placed her on a sofa. The baby kept her matchstick legs drawn up and raised her arms until the tiny hands were bent close to her head. Then she stopped crying.

"As long as the baby is completely still, she's comfortable," Dr. Gatch said, "but pick her up and she'll start crying again."

He noted the extreme dryness of the skin, the absence of subcutaneous tissue. He said the baby's diet was so deficient in iron that her hemoglobin count was "half of what it should be."

The baby's mother had been out of work since December. Dr. Gatch said the infant was now getting some baby formula food. It would probably live, he said, but he feared it had suffered irreversible damage through growth retardation of bones and brain cells.

As he left, Dr. Gatch noticed a 3-year-old girl sitting on the stoop, staring vacantly at the brown fields. Her legs and face were bloated by edematose swellings, the result probably of Vitamin A deficiency, the physician said, and the same deficiency was impairing her vision.

"There's just no excuse for rickets in this country," complained Dr. Gatch as he drove to another shack, hunting this time a whole family that he said was rachitic, a mother and five children.

Rickets is a disease of infancy and childhood resulting from a deficiency of vitamin D and characterized by soft, deformed bones. The rachitic family was not at home, but Dr. Gatch found them on the stoop of a neighboring house.

All Have Misshapen Legs

The victims had gotten some relief and were now on a proper diet, Dr. Gatch said. All had misshapen legs. The mother, who seemed stout and cheerful, was very bow-legged; her children were either bowlegged or knock-kneed. Dr. Gatch commented that the legs of the three older children seemed to have straightened somewhat.

Living room in a shanty. Many farm hands live under lower-than marginal conditions.

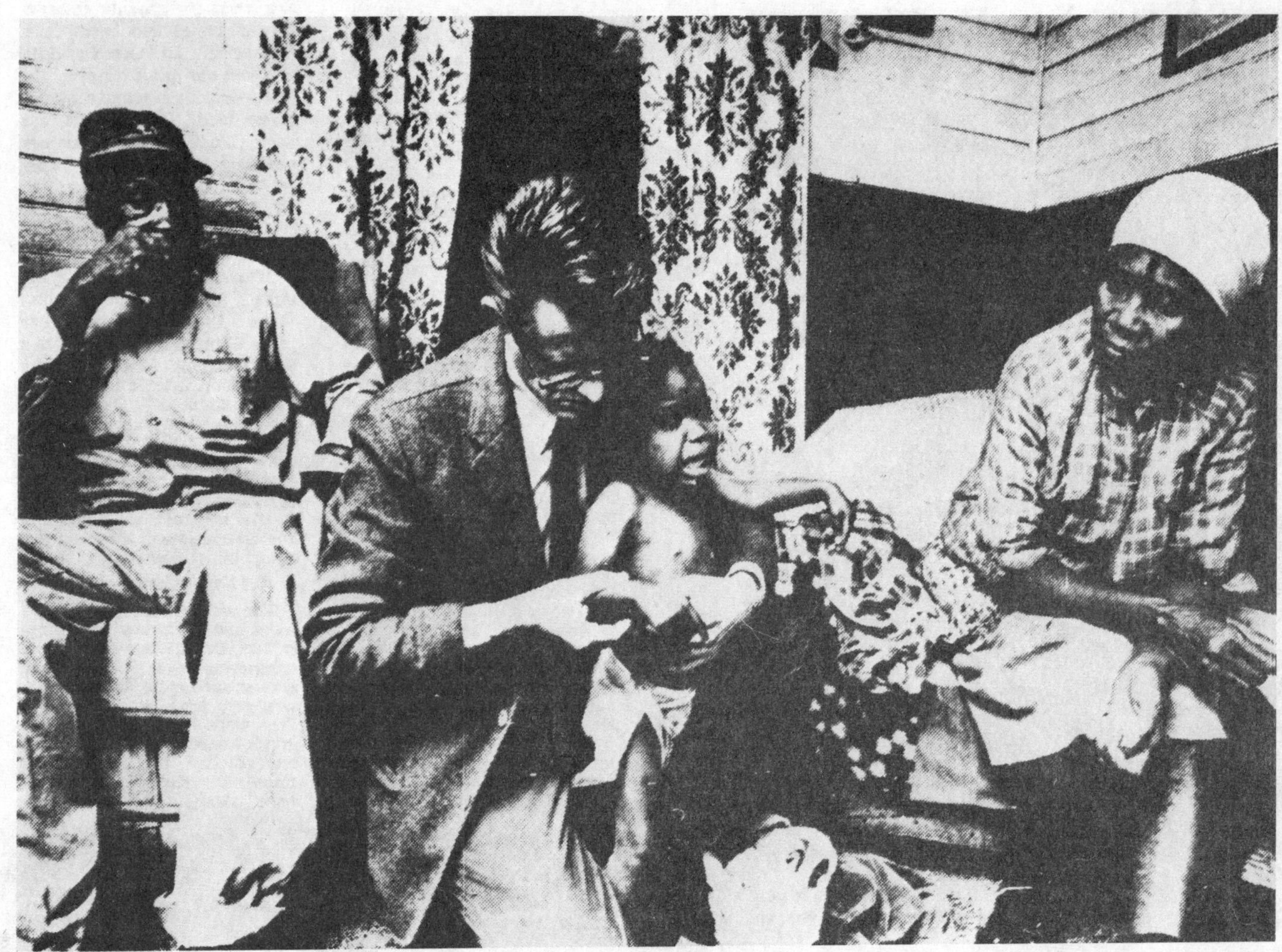

The New York Times (by Edward Hausner)

Dr. Donald E. Gatch at a home in Pritchardville, S. C. The child suffers from rickets, caused by Vitamin D deficiency, and scurvy, lack of Vitamin C.

but the twisted spindly legs of the two youngest remained badly deformed.

Milk is the main source of vitamin D, Dr. Gatch noted, and the family might never have been blighted with rickets if fortified milk had been available to them.

But the Government's food donation programs for the domestic poor did not provide fortified dry milk until the end of 1968. Dr. Gatch might have been angrier had he known that since 1965, at the insistence of the United States Public Health Service, the Department of Agriculture had been shipping dry milk enriched by vitamins A and D to American aid programs overseas.

The three-year gap during which fortified milk was sent overseas while being denied to the poor at home came to light last month in testimony before the Senate Select Committee on Nutrition and Human Needs.

Dr. Gatch stopped at an abandoned country store. Inside, two bedridden old ladies had found terminal shelter. One of them, crippled by rheumatoid arthritis, had been rescued from a mouldering shack where the bedding stank of urine and feces. The other was afflicted by Wernicke Syndrome, which Dr. Gatch said was characterized by loss of memory and confabulation (filling in a memory gap by falsifications that the patient accepts as correct).

Diet of Rice and Grits

Dr. Gatch said he believed Wernicke Syndrome could have been induced by lack of thiamine, which is essential for growth, normal function of the nervous system and normal metabolism. Thiamine is found in liver, lean meat, eggs, whole grain or enriched cereal and cereal products. The old ladies, Dr. Gatch suspected, had been eating little more than rice and grits.

Now they were on Medicare and presumably getting a better diet. The old store was spotlessly clean, neater than most nursing homes.

Dr. Gatch was asked if he had encountered pellagra, one of the more dreaded of the dietary dificiency diseases. This disease, caused mainly by a deficiency of niacin, but also of thiamine, riboflavin, folic acid and other essential nutrients, is marked in its late stages by the classical four D's: dermatitis, diarrhea, dementia and death.

Dr. Gatch said it was not even rare. He produced an old man of about 70 who, he said, had pellagrin symptoms, including hyperpigmentation of elbows and knees. There the flesh had thickened and roughened until it felt like sandpaper.

How many pellagra victims had he seen?

"I would guess 150 to 200 cases," Dr. Gatch replied.

Deaths by starvation, deaths by any of the diseases of malnutrition, were never counted, he said. Too many death certificates simply read "natural causes," Dr. Gatch said, and he intended to campaign for postmortems in those cases.

Over the years Dr. Gatch became convinced that there was close correlation between malnutrition and intestinal parasites. Most of the undernourished children he examined were wormy. Many Negro shacks, he observed, had no privies; people relieved themselves in the fields and woods. Children treated for worms quickly became reinfested by stepping on feces that contained the eggs of parasites.

"If you have 100 or 200 of these foot-long roundworms in your belly they're going to take a lot of food," he said. "They migrate to the stomach and actually get the food before the child does."

Some notion of the extent of infestation in the Negro children of Beaufort County. was given a few days later. A study of 178 Negro preschool children showed that nearly three of every four had intestinal parasites, either ascaris (roundworm) or trichuris (whipworm), or both.

"Fantastic," said Dr. James P. Carter, nutritionist of the Vanderbilt University School of Medicine, who participated in the survey. "Parasitism in Beaufort County ranks with some Central American countries and with Egypt."

In Nashville, Dr. Carter said the nutritional status of the 178 children was "in most cases inadequate and in all instances minimal." He said that by minimal he meant that the children had a low margin of safety, particularly from pneumonia and diarrhea.

The survey, financed by the Field Foundation, was conducted by researchers from the University of South Carolina, the Meharry Medical College, in Nashville, and Vanderbilt University.

The results were considered so shocking that some even suggested that the data be withheld from general publication. Many white Southerners feel that poverty conditions among the rural blacks have been exploited by civil rights zealots.

Dr. E. John Lease, nutritionist of the University of South Carolina, was among those who feared that the report, if given wide publicity, would anger the white establishment and perhaps wreck the chances of cooperation on remedial projects.

Dr. Lease wrote to his collaborators suggesting that the distribution of data be restricted and that "none of the work coming from the University of South Carolina should be published or mentioned on radio or television as the results of the university or any of its staff members."

Later, Dr. Lease apparently had a change of heart, for the material was released to the press in Columbia, S. C.

There were other indications that the establishment now wanted the situation exposed. On Jan. 31, to the astonishment and gratification of Dr. Gatch, Senator Ernest F. Hollings, the former Governor, turned up in Bluffton and made the hunger tour.

Federal Delays Charged

The Senator saw a near-starving baby, a reputed pellagrin, a rachitic child and another child said to be recovering from scurvy. Deeply impressed, Senator Hollings said he would demand an end to "Federal roadblocks and red tape," which, he said were frustrating local efforts to help the poor.

The local State Senator, James M. Waddell, also blamed the "Feds." He charged that the Office of Economic Opportunity had refused to fund a project that included privies for the poor.

"We can send a man to the moon," he cried on the floor of the South Carolina Senate, "but we can't build an outhouse."

Senator Hollings plans to testify next week before the Senate Select Committee on Nutrition and Human Needs.

The committee, headed by Senator George S. McGovern, Democrat of South Dakota, and dominated by liberals, had been planning field trips to suspected areas of hunger in a dozen states.

However, last week the Senate Rules Committee, dominated by conservatives, slashed the select committee's $250,000 budget request by $100,000. Senator Jacob K. Javits of New York, minority leader of the select committee, said he intended to carry the fight for the full appropriation to the Senate floor. But if the cut remains, the committee will have to curtail its travel plans, visiting perhaps only five or six states.

It means that the committee members will not see Beaufort County.

They still plan to visit the camps of migrant farm workers, such as those in Immokalee, Fla., where life seems even more degrading than in the shacks of Beaufort County.

February 16, 1969

Hunger in America: Mississippi Delta

Poorly Fed Despite Federal Aid

By HOMER BIGART

Special to The New York Times

YAZOO CITY, Miss.—"They aren't starving, really, but they are undernourished as hell."

Dr. Aaron Shirley, a Jackson pediatrician and civil rights leader, made this diagnosis during a recent visit to Negro homes in the Delta.

The degree of hunger among Delta Negroes has been a political issue ever since April, 1967, when Senator Robert F. Kennedy of New York and Senator Joseph S. Clark of Pennsylvania toured the Delta and reported that many people were "slowly starving."

Indignant denials came from the white establishment. The general response was "we treat our niggers fine," Dr. Shirley recalled. Gov. Paul B. Johnson Jr. reportedly described as "fat and shiny" every Magnolia State Negro that met his eye.

The issue flared up anew after a team of doctors headed by Dr. Raymond M. Wheeler of Charlotte, N. C., reported to the Southern Regional Council a widespread and "desperate" need for food and medical care.

The Federal food programs were not only inadequate, they said, but were run by local authorities with flagrant political or racial bias. The doctors' indictment was harsh: "It is unbelievable to us that a nation as rich as ours, with all its technological and scientific resources, has to permit thousands and thousands of children to go hungry, go sick, and die grim and premature deaths."

Though many people may think first of Mississippi when the subject of hunger comes up, the state actually has a good record of participation in Federal food programs.

Each of its 82 counties is enrolled in either food stamp or direct commodity distribution programs, a better record than New York's, where six counties (Sullivan, Rockland, Putnam, Chenango, Ontario and Otsego) do not participate and have no plans for joining the programs.

Nor are the Delta counties the hungriest in the land. Stomachs of reservation Indians are probably emptier more often than stomachs of Delta blacks.

No one knows how many Americans are chronically hungry. The best educated guess comes from Dr. Thomas E. Bryant, assistant direc-

tor of the Office of Economic Opportunity for Health Affairs.

According to Dr. Bryant, there are 12 to 15 million "hard-core poor." The "hard-core" are defined as those families with an annual income of less than $2,000, based on a family of four. Since the Department of Agriculture estimates that a family of four must spend $1,284 for an adequate diet, Dr. Bryant concludes that a family earning less than $2,000 would find it impossible to buy enough food to meet minimum nutrition standards after meeting other essential human needs.

At present, the food programs of the Department of Agriculture reach about 6,333,000 persons, many of whom are better off than the "hard-core poor." So, by some official estimates, there are at least six to nine million Americans for whom hunger may be almost a daily fact of life.

Newspapers Cover Walls

It was cold and rainy the day Dr. Shirley led a visitor into a back-street shack where a Negro couple and several children were huddling at a fireplace. Most of the windows were plugged with cardboard, which rattled dismally against the wind and rain; old newspapers covered the walls.

Eight children were counted in the room and Dr. Shirley, poking carefully into a pile of ragged, musty quilts, found two more infants asleep in the bed. He said the woman had given birth to triplets four months before; one died at birth, and one of the survivors had nearly expired of diarrhea and was just back from a Jackson hospital. The infant was almost certain to get diarrhea very soon again under these living conditions, the doctor said.

The family was unable to get on the welfare rolls because the husband was considered able-bodied. He earned $100 last month, but now, in midwinter, there was no farm work available. The family had nearly used up its food stamps, all that was left was sweet potatoes, condensed milk and grits, the mother said.

Dr. Shirley examined the babies, calling attention to the lack of subcutaneous tissue on their tiny arms and legs. "They need protein, calories and iron," he said.

"Too many people sleeping in that bed," the woman muttered from the fireplace.

"If I can run across a baby bed, I'll get it to you," Dr. Shirley promised.

In another shack, where daylight could be seen through a corner rat hole, a mother with seven children, living on Social Security payments of $95.40 a month, described her budget. She had to make a cash contribution of $38 to obtain $96 in food stamps and "I run out of food in the third week." Her rent, she said, was $16 a month, plus $5 or $6 for gas, plus $8 for lights and $3 for water. That left about $25 for all other essentials — clothes, soap and supplemental food to get eight people through the rest of the month.

Occasional housework for white families paid $3.50 to $5 a day, she said, then she had to hire a baby sitter. Baby sitters charge 50 cents a head, and with four children under six years that would come to $2, leaving $1.50 to $3 for the day's work.

"If you could get a job would you work?" Dr. Shirley asked.

"I sure would," said the mother emphatically. "I never want to be on welfare, period."

"That's the tale you always hear in town: 'They don't want to work,' " Dr. Shirley said.

Negroes who get sick in Yazoo City are sent to the Afro-American Hospital, a county-supported institution that cannot afford a pathologist nor even a laboratory technician. There, Dr. Cyril A. Walwyn, the director, contended that hunger in the Delta was not decreasing, as most whites insisted; he had seen too many pot-bellied, worm-infested youngsters.

"I feel they are slowly starving," he said. Dr. Walwyn was one of the six doctors who wrote the Delta hunger report.

"I have a quarrel with the welfare people," he continued. "They just don't care. Often they show a patronizing attitude toward the poor. If I am not as suppliant and cringing as they think I should be, they won't give me help."

Driving back to Jackson, Dr. Shirley said: "Black people have changed. A lot of the old fear is gone. But people are still dying unnecessarily of disease, and poor nutrition has contributed to their dying."

Chances Are Diminished

"A baby's chances of recovering from pneumonia or severe diarrhea are diminished considerably if he's undernourished. So this kid will die, and it's listed on the death certificate as diarrhea. Now, this kid didn't starve to death. But if he'd been in fairly good nutritive status he wouldn't have died.

Dr. Shirley said he had seen people eat almost anything they could chew, including tar from telephone poles — "They say it's good for the gums" — and even clay. Pregnant women, especially, would pop a piece of earth in their mouths, explaining they "had a taste for it."

"And they might get some essential minerals out of it," he said.

Describing the plight of thousands of Delta families displaced by the mechanization of the cotton plantations, Dr. Shirley said he sometimes wondered if Negroes were not better off in slavery days.

"In open slavery times human life was of some value," he mused. "If master paid $100 for a man he'd see that his property was well taken care of, just like a prize bull. But now the black people are no longer on the plantations. There is no feeling of responsibility toward them, no need to help them."

Dr. Shirley, as head of Mississippi Action For Progress, a Head Start program, recently received $106,000 from the Office of Economic Opportunity to provide free food stamps for the desperately poor of three counties — LeFlore, Scott and Claiborne — where the situation was called "critical."

But he accused the state welfare department of trying to frustrate the effort by refusing to accept checks in payment for the stamps, even though the checks were backed by special cash deposits in the county banks. Meanwhile he had helped some families out of emergencies by giving them cash.

The main complaint about the Federal food programs in the Delta was that they simply were not reaching the most desperately poor.

Mystery Finally Solved

Even though the minimum cash investment for food stamps by the poorest families — those with an income of less than $20 a month — had been reduced from $2 to 50 cents, there were still hundreds of families that couldn't raise 50 cents.

It had taken former Secretary of Agriculture Orville L. Freeman several years to solve the mystery of why the number of participants in food programs always dropped sharply whenever a county switched from free distribution of Federal surplus commodities to food stamps. Finally, some of his aides went to Mississippi and brought back the startling news: "There are families existing with no discernible income."

Today, families in the food stamp program complain that the amount of monthly food they obtain usually is exhausted after the third week. A board of inquiry headed by Dr. Leslie W. Dunbar, executive director of the Field Foundation, and Dr. Benjamin E. Mays, president emeritus of Morehouse College, and sponsored by the Citizens' Crusade Against Poverty, an organization with the backing of the United Auto Workers, reported a year ago that the money value of the stamps fell "consistently and deliberately below the amount necessary to secure a minimally adequate diet."

This indictment was substantiated last month when a preliminary report of the National Nutrition Survey, the first scientific attempt by the Federal Government to measure malnutrition in the United States, called the food programs inadequate.

In Greenville, Mrs. Frances Young said she had to feed herself and nine children on $118 worth of food a month purchased by stamps for which she paid $33. Her monthly income was $55 from Aid to Dependent Children, plus $50 sent by her eldest daughter in Detroit. Total, $105.

Rent took $25 a month, she said, and bills were overdue for gas, electricity and water. She had doctor bills totaling $233.

"I can't feed this family," said Mrs. Young despairingly. "We have pinto beans and bread. That's all for supper."

"And this here's what I'm sweeping with," she said, wrathfully snatching up a stringy broom worn down to a final clutch of straws.

But at least the Youngs were better off than some aged and lonely Negroes that remained in rural cabins after their youngsters had gone North to find work. The only nursing home for Negroes in the area burned down on Jan. 18, killing seven of the aged and destitute, including an old woman who had been restrained by chicken wire because she was senile.

The whole town was shocked, but no one, white or black, could find it in his heart to blame Carrie Weaver and her husband Wash, who ran the firetrap. After all, the victims had no other place to live.

Wash Weaver told of finding

old Ann House, who must have been 80, he said, lying helplessly in her cabin, wasted down to 100 pounds because no one had brought food.

"She must have been layin' on the floor for days," Wash Weaver said. "I had to cut her clothes off with a knife."

Mrs. House was one of the fire victims.

Down in Isaquena County, one of the poorest counties in the Delta, Mrs. Unita Blackwell, a leader of the Freedom Democratic Party, said a few more commodities had become available under the direct distribution program but that people still weren't getting a balanced diet from the free surplus foods. The Agriculture Department offers each county a choice between a free but very limited commodities distribution and the stamp program; no county can have both.

Mrs. Blackwell was worried about the children.

"Grown folks have been hungry a long, long time," she said, "but the kids just got here and we don't want them mixed up with blood disorders. If you can't get enough food, your brain won't work."

There are two developments in the Delta that promise better times.

A distinguished biracial group of Mississippians, including Dr. Temple Ainsworth, former president of the State Medical Association, and the Right Rev. John Allin, Protestant Episcopal Bishop of Mississippi; Dr. Robert E. Carter, dean of the Mississippi School of Medicine, and Dr. Albert B. Britton, a leading Negro doctor in Jackson, have proposed Federal funding for a crash program to lower the infant, maternal and child mortality rates in five Delta counties.

Delta counties have a history of the highest infant mortality rate among Negroes in the country — 72.7 per 1,000 live births in 1965. The maternal death rate among Negroes was 25.1 in the same year.

The biracial committee proposes as a "short-term objective" a 20 per cent cut in the excessively high infant, maternal and child mortality rates in the five counties — Sharkey, Isaquena, Holmes, Humphreys and Washington — in the first year. Health services in the counties would be strengthened, scores of midwives and health aides trained and sanitation improved. The committee asked the Federal Department of Health, Education and Welfare for $3,405,000.

Some Negro leaders, including Dr. Shirley, have criticized the project, saying it would be dominated by whites. The committee is composed of five whites and four Negroes.

The other development is the further expansion of the Tufts Delta Health Project, sponsored by Tufts University, in Bolivar County.

Convinced of the "enormous futility" of trying to tackle health problems without changing other aspects of Delta life, such as housing, employment and education, Jack Geiger, director of the project, and other leaders, are now helping Negroes operate a farm co-operative, rebuild houses and plan Negro enterprises.

With guidance from the Government of Israel — Zev Barash, representative of Histadruth in New York City, has sent several Delta Negroes to Israel to study farm cooperatives there — the project has formed the Northern Bolivar Farm Co-operative, which last year grew over a million pounds of produce on rented land. Starting with 120 acres, the cooperative hopes to expand to 500 acres this year.

Cannery for 'Soul Food'

There are tentative plans for a $400,000 cannery that would process "soul food" for the ethnic market, such as collards, gumboes and mustard greens.

Meanwhile, Dr. Roy Brown, associate professor of pediatrics and preventive medicine at Tufts, and Dr. Florence Halpern, a psychologist from New York, are surveying the medical and social backgrounds of 400 Negro children up to age three.

Dr. Brown and Dr. Halpern are convinced that Negro children brought up in the Delta already suffer brain retardation because of crushing poverty before they are old enough — three — to enter the Head Start programs.

"One of the things that pulls them down is the lack of verbal stimulation at home," Dr. Brown said. "Perhaps we should bring them into Head Start programs at three months, instead of three years."

February 18, 1969

Hunger in America: Mexicans And Indians Its Stoical Victims

By HOMER BIGART
Special to The New York Times

SAN ANTONIO, Tex. — Tacked on the wall of the Inner City Apostolate were four new slips from hungry Mexican-American families asking for food.

The Rev. Ralph H. Ruiz, who runs the mission for the Roman Catholic Archdiocese of San Antonio, glanced at the slips and exclaimed angrily: "The whole welfare system in Texas stinks."

The mission is on the fringe of Alazan-Apache Courts, the city's oldest public housing project, where some 6,000 Mexican-Americans live in wretched poverty and frequent hunger. Of all the nation's ethnic groups — white, black, brown or red — the "Mexicanos" are suspected by nutritionists of being most vulnerable to hunger.

For although there are nearly five million of them scattered through the Southwest, the Mexican-Americans have generally been undemonstrative about their misery, complaining so seldom of empty stomachs that the "Anglos" (the non-Mexican whites) give them scant attention. "Brown Power" has not yet taken to the streets of San Antonio.

Hungrier even than the Mexican-Americans, but less obtrusive because they are smaller in number and confined mainly to isolated wastelands, are the reservation Indians. Of the more than 300,000 Indians living on reservations, the largest tribe by far is the Navajo of northeastern Arizona. Altogether, 115,000 Navajos exist on an arid plateau bigger than the whole state of West Virginia.

The Last Frontier

The western half of this remote region, the state's last frontier, was not opened up by roads until about 13 years ago. Even today there are Navajos who live 50 miles from the nearest improved road. Last year 20 infants were brought in dead at medical stations, according to Dr. George E. Bock, the United States Public Health Service medical director, and 18 of those deaths were attributable to delay in reaching medical aid.

At Tuba City, administrative center for the western half of the reservation, Dr. Jean Van Duzen, chief of pediatrics at the Indian Hospital, reported 27 cases of marasmus (calory starvation) and 17 cases of kwashiorkor (extreme protein deficiency) among Navajo children in the last five years. The high incidence of those two rarely found diseases would be considered fantastic anywhere else in the nation. Dr. Van Duzen said that 15 of the 44 victims died.

Among Mexican-Americans in the slums of San Antonio the ravages of hunger may be less spectacular but more degrading. Father Ruiz said Mexican-Americans found the welfare apparatus unbearably cold and inhuman.

Father Ruiz's irritation with Texas welfare was mainly prompted, he explained, by a recent lowering of the ceiling on monthly welfare payments from $135, for a family of four or more, to $123.

"Texas is the only state, I believe, that requires legislation every time it wants to raise the level of welfare. A referendum to increase the payments was defeated last year. The cut was made because the increasing relief load threatened to exhaust the welfare appropriation. And now there is talk of another cut."

Food Stamps Run Short

He took a visitor on a tour of Alazan-Apache Courts, a

The New York Times Feb. 19, 1969

Cross-hatched area defines Navajo reservation, which surrounds Hopi Indian land.

sprawling expanse of low, concrete block buildings with small apartments. In one home, sparsely furnished but very clean, Mrs. Joanne Gutierrez told how she and her four children existed on a $123-a-month welfare check.

"I buy no clothes for myself," she said. "I wear castoffs from my mother and sister-in-law.

Each month she paid $54 to get food stamps that bought her $94 worth of commodities. She echoed a familiar complaint about the food stamp program—instead of providing enough food to last a month, the supply ran out in about two weeks. Fortunately two of the children were getting free lunches in school, she said.

The rent was $23 a month, plus $1.20 for extra utilities and 50 cents for "pest control." The baby's diapers required "decent soap," and there were pencils and crayons to be bought for the three daughters of school age. There were only two beds; the three girls, Mrs. Gutierrez explained, "slept crosswise" on one.

In worse plight was a Mrs. Espinosa, found with 10 children in another tiny flat. She, too, was getting the maximum $123 monthly welfare payment, out of which she had to invest $58 to get $128 worth of food stamps, and pay $39 rent. That left only $26 for all other expenses. The family subsisted mainly on tortillas and beans. Three of the children had no shoes.

Nothing infuriates a Mexican-American more than to have some Anglo suggest to him that all his troubles would vanish if he would only stop eating beans and tortillas and get on a "balanced diet."

"If you have one dollar," explained Father Ruiz patiently, "and you can buy either one pound of meat or 10 pounds of pinto beans, what are you going to buy? You are going to fill the stomachs of your kids with beans. And they call this ignorance!

"I'd like to meet the home economist who says you can take care of 10 kids on $123 a month! It would take a genius to survive on that amount of money."

He said he had been asked to appear on a television show called "Buen Apetito," an educational program intended to get Mexicans off starch. He had told the producers that the idea was preposterous: the poor simply did not have the means to buy the "balanced" foods.

Downtown, Albert A. Pena Jr., a Mexican-American member of the Bexar (San Antonio) County Commission, said he believed there were "100,000 hungry people" in Bexar (pronounced Bear) which has a population of about 800,000 (48 per cent Mexican-American, 40 per cent Anglo, 12 per cent Negro).

They are hungry, he said, because San Antonio is a "a cheap-labor town—about one-third of the wage earners earn less than the accepted poverty level of $3,000 a year."

Cites Mexican Pride

Yet Anglos, he said, cling to the myth best expressed last year by a state welfare official: "You can give a Mexican mother a bushel of money and she'll still feed her children beans and tortillas."

"This is a base canard and he knows it," Commissioner Pena said.

Many Mexican-Americans are too proud to admit they cannot feed their children properly, Father Ruiz explained, and are bruised by the coldness of welfare personnel. So "cells" have been set up in the housing project to detect and report families in trouble. Rummage sales and bingo parties are held to assist the unfortunate.

Texas was the first state to complete a nutrition study of its low-income population for a national survey by the United States Public Health Service.

The findings confirmed the presence of serious malnutrition among the Mexican-American, Anglo-American and Negro poor.

In the lower Rio Grande Valley, the investigators discovered an infant suffering from marasmus and another afflicted with what Dr. William M. McGanity, one of the directors of the survey, called "pre-kwashiorkor."

The findings of malnutrition and of evidence of growth retardation among children gave some substance to an earlier report by Dr. Francis J. Peirce of the eating habits of low-income families in San Antonio.

Dr. Peirce, who is an associate professor at the Worden School of Social Service of Our Lady of the Lake College, directed a staff of students and faculty in interviews with 967 adults and 561 children, most of them Mexican-Americans.

The findings were somber. Of the children studied, 272, or nearly half, were judged as having an inadequate diet. A total of 650, or 67 per cent of the adults, had inadequate food intake in the 24 hours preceding the interview.

Some critics challenged the validity of Dr. Peirce's survey. Dr. Peirce said he had "great conviction" that it was reliable.

He was pleased that the preliminary report of the National Nutrition Survey tended to support his bleak picture of diet inadequacy. But he said he was disturbed by a tendency to "explain away" the exposed malnutrition as the product of "ignorance."

"Let's face it," he said. "People are hungry because they are poor."

On the windswept Navajo reservation, Indians are suffering the traumas of converting from a pastoral living to a cash economy. Traditionally, the Navajos have been sheep and goat herders. But the land is arid ("it takes 10 lousy acres to graze one sheep," Dr. Van Duzen explained) and the population has grown so rapidly that most Indians can no longer live on goats and sheep.

Associated Press

A Navajo Indian family in their hogan, the traditional circular hut made of cedar logs and mud, during a blizzard. Doctors found that many Navajo children were permanently stunted by hunger, and that in classrooms their attention spans were abnormally limited.

Efforts to bring industry have had minimal success, providing a few hundred jobs, mostly for women. For most of the population poverty seems to have deepened. The average Navajo sees about $400 in cash a year, including welfare payments. Dr. Van Duzen said there were many families with no visible income who were kept alive by charity from their clan.

"I'm not saying Navajos are dropping dead of starvation," she said, "but there is hunger—and it shouldn't happen in the United States."

In the children's ward, Dr. Van Duzen observed Navajo infants who she feared had suffered irreversible brain damage from undernourishment. The babies were gaining weight, but some still showed growth retardation. Dr. Van Duzen noted a three-month-old-baby described as "marasmic," whose flesh hung loose, like an old man's skin, on pathetically thin arms and legs.

She said she was convinced that many were permanently stunted by hunger.

"Some say these are small little kids that won't grow because they are Navajos," she said. "I say these are small little kids that won't grow because they haven't got food."

At Many Farms, Dr. Robert Roessel, Jr., president of Navajo Community College, the reservation's first junior college, called malnutrition one of the most acute obstacles for Indian children in classrooms.

Attention Limited

"They look weak and gaunt to begin with," he said. "Their attention span is abnormally limited."

He charged that some public school superintendents prided themselves on virtually eliminating free lunches for Indian children. They did this, he said, on the mistaken notion that they were "teaching the Navajos responsibility and helping the children adjust to the world in which they live." But they were driving away Indian children unable to pay $1.50 a week for lunches, he said.

The community college is the first reservation school with an all-Indian school board. Six board members have never been to school and the seventh has only a second-grade education. Yet Dr. Roessel said the involvement of Indian parents in the operation of the school had eliminated so many tensions and hostilities that the students were already showing marked improvement in achievement rates.

Impoverished Navajos, he said, received free food under the commodities distribution program. But the commodities available were "woefully inadequate" and "didn't begin to meet the need."

At Window Rock, capital of the Navajo nation, Dr. Bock, the health service director, spoke of some of the difficulties of administering health over the vast reservation with a small, overworked staff.

30-Mile Walk With Baby

He told of a woman who had walked 30 miles from her hogan, the traditional circular hut made of cedar logs and mud, to the nearest traveled road, carrying a sick baby.

He had been urging the training of at least 110 Navajos as local health aides who would teach certain basic health practices and principles to the Indians of their localities. Funds for the project had finally been allocated, he said, but only for the training of 35 to 40 Indians.

Dr. Bock mentioned one promising development—the provision, since Christmas, of supplementary rations for infants and pregnant or lactating mothers who obviously were malnourished. Doctors were authorized to fill out prescriptions for food, he explained, just as though they were issuing prescriptions for medicine.

And the Office of Economic Opportunity has provided $42,000 for the purchase of a special baby formula fortified with Vitamins A, C and D, niacin, riboflavin, thiamin, calcium, phosphorous and iron to be given to premature babies.

Unfortunately a year's supply of the formula costs $308, so only about 130 infants, or just about half of the 250 to 300 premature babies born each year on the Navajo reservation, will be taken care of.

February 19, 1969

Hunger in America: Appalachia Ill-Fed Despite a National Effort

By HOMER BIGART
Special to The New York Times

PRESTONSBURG, Ky. — The hollows of Appalachia and their hidden nests of tarpaper shacks are breeding another generation stunted by hunger and programed for a lifetime of poverty.

Eight years have passed since President Kennedy focused the nation's attention on the hardships of thousands of unemployed miners and marginal farmers and their families existing in these mountains. Vast sums of Federal money have been poured into the area. There has been a reduction in human misery. The miners no longer riot. But unemployment is heavy and poverty remains endemic.

When Senator Robert F. Kennedy visited this area a year ago, he found a county (Wolfe) where some 5,000 of the 6,500 residents lived below the poverty line—an income of $3,000 a year for a family of four—and where half the total amount of food consumed was acquired through the Federal food stamp program. Today the reliance on Federal help has not diminished.

Here in eastern Kentucky as in the rural South, in the migrant farm labor camps of Florida, in the Mexican-American slums of San Antonio and in the Indian reservations of the Southwest a visitor hears this constant complaint: the Federal food programs, whether food stamps or direct distribution of surplus commodities, do not provide enough sustenance each month to stave off hunger.

The monthly allotment of food for a family usually runs out in the third week. People complain that the food stamps cost too much, although there is general agreement that the stamp program, in principle, is better than free distribution of commodities that often fail to meet nutritional requirements.

Persons eligible for stamps pay in "an amount equivalent to their mormal expenditure for food," according to the plan, and then exchange the stamps, which are worth more than their pay-in value by varying amounts, for any food of their choice at groceries.

But the plan is unrealistic, Marian Wright Edelman, civil rights lawyer and counsel to last year's Poor People's Campaign, explained in the capital, because despite some lowering of the buy-in scale, the assumption remains that people with little or no income need less to eat than people with more income. Families with no income—and there are many of them, she said — can hardly have a "normal expenditure for food."

Robert B. Choate, a transplanted Boston Brahmin who became a leading advocate in Washington for the hungry poor after a decade of philanthropic involvement with poverty programs in the Southwest, raised additional criticisms.

He noted that in Appalachia, fair distribution of food to the needy was impeded more by political and economic considerations than by racial bias. Here, as well as in much of the rest of rural America, most of the abject poor are not only white but Anglo-Saxon and Protestant as well. Of an estimated total of 12 million rural poor in the nation, he said, only three million were black.

Role of County Politics

Mr. Choate said that welfare in Eastern Kentucky was often dominated by the county political machines, and a man's eligibility for food was conferred as a political favor.

He was not impressed by the Department of Agriculture's contention that all but 472 counties and independent cities in the United States were participating (or about to participate) in either the food stamp or the commodities program.

"Many counties," he charged, "have less than 10 per cent of their poor involved in the programs." (The latest Department of Agriculture figures—for November, 1968 — show 3,672,000 enrolled for commodities and 2,661,000 for food stamps, a total participation of 6,333,000. The department estimates that 8 to 10 million Americans are eligible.)

Recalling a trip through Eastern Kentucky last May, Mr. Choate said that fundamentalist preachers, who always thrive in areas of poverty, seemd to "condone" conditions

The New York Times Feb. 20, 1969

of hunger, ignoring the mental and physical retardation that accompanies the phenomenon and dooms another generation to a life of deprivation.

A liberal Republican, Mr. Choate has been quietly urging friends in the Nixon Administration to drastically revise the handling of the food programs. He believes there may be as many as five million "chronically hungry" Americans and five to ten million more undernourished because of poverty-induced diets.

He would reduce the price of food stamps and expand the volume and variety of the free commodity distribution program to insure that every stomach got at least a minimum balanced intake. And while reluctant to join others who demand that the food programs be transferred from the Department of Agriculture to the Department of Health, Education and Welfare, Mr. Choate conceded that the Agricultural Committees of Congress, dominated by conservatives and inclined to look upon the food programs as mechanisms for getting rid of surpluses and shoring up farm prices, showed little empathy for the poor.

Back in the hollows, meanwhile, the Appalachian Volunteers, an antipoverty organization, reported finding many mountaineers still ignorant of their rights to receive welfare payments and participate in the food programs. Rejected by the county officials in a first bid for welfare, the hungry parents would often return dejectedly to cabins swarming with children without first demanding a hearing.

During a tour of Floyd County hollows, when shanties perched precariously above the sulphur-polluted creeks, Hank Zingg, an Appalachian Volunteer, showed a visitor some families that had been refused relief because the father, an idle miner, was considered able-bodied.

William Strode—Black Star

Ignorant of their rights to receive welfare payments and to participate in Federal food programs, many mountaineers in Appalachia live, dejectedly, in stark poverty.

$3 Rarely Available

In one cabin, Russell Johnson, 41, father of seven small children, produced a letter from a doctor saying that Mr. Johnson had silicosis, a disease of the lungs common among miners, induced by the inhalation of coal dust, and that "any type of exertion causes shortness of breath and smothering."

But Mr. Johnson said he had been turned down by the welfare board because he was not considered "totally and permanently disabled."

His family's only income, he said, was the few dollars his wife earned keeping house for her grandfather. The family had to pay $3 a month to obtain food stamps worth $82, and because it rarely had $3 available at one time the amount had to be provided by the food emergency fund of the Office of Economic Opportunity. Even so, the food seldom lasted into the third week, Mr. Johnson said.

"The rest of the month it's nothing but bread and gravy," he said.

And some families had to start watering the gravy during the fourth week.

"They're all puny but I never had no sickness out of 'em," declared Mrs. Milford Newsome, surveying some of her nine pallid children in a cabin beside a mine spur on the Ligon Branch. She was comparatively well-off, getting a total of $309 a month from welfare and Social Security. But she had to pay out $94 a month to obtain $144 in stamps, she said, and the rent was $15 a month plus light bills and the books for the seven children who were going to school.

She said the children received "free worm medicine" 18 months ago, thanks to a state demonstration anti-worm project, and she was getting free "blood pills" for anemia through Medicaid.

Up another hollow, two old women, one crippled by arthritis, the other ill with diabetes, said they had to drop out of the food stamp program because they could not afford to pay $5 for transportation into Prestonsburg.

Emergency Food Fund

Last year Congress approved an emergency food and medical fund to be used by the O.E.O. for families who were too destitute to pay even 50 cents for food stamps or who had run out of stamps and were on the verge of starvation.

But the fund was inadequate.

At Whitesburg, Ky., Mrs. Irene Whittaker, coordinator of O.E.O.'s emergency program for Letcher, Leslie, Knott and Perry Counties, said that only about $3,500 a month was available for emergency food supplements for the four counties, plus $800 for medicine for diseases of malnutrition.

This monthly allocation was quickly exhausted, Mrs. Whittaker said, pointing out that one-third of the 95,000 residents of the four counties belonged to families with incomes of less than $1,500 a year.

She could not say whether hunger was becoming more acute, but disclosed that during January, in Letcher County alone, 40 new families reported incomes of less than $29 for the month, thus becoming eligible for the minimum (50 cents) pay-in for food stamps.

Mrs. Whittaker said she was troubled by the people she could not help. Some local observers said that her compassion was more the rule than the exception among the dispensers of welfare, that very few were callous although many were often made to appear insensitive because of the inadequacies and red tape of the programs.

Sometimes, even in the deep South, state and local officials are angels, they said. One who came to mind was William H. Burson, the 39-year-old State Welfare Director of Georgia.

Mr. Burson, a war correspondent with United Press International in Korea and a former aide to Senator Herman E. Talmadge, startled conservatives in the administration of Gov. Lester G. Maddox by vigorously attempting to install Federal food aid programs in every Georgian county often over the opposition of county leaders.

In a telephone interview from Atlanta, Mr. Burson said that every county except Troup, a relatively high income area, was now on commodities or stamps. "Some of the other counties had denied any hunger existed," he said. "Others said, 'If you feed 'em they won't work.'"

Particularly troublesome was Glascock County. There, Mr. Burson recalled, Sheriff James English ran two welfare representatives out of the county, declaring that a food program would "just mean a lot of niggers lined up."

Eventually the Federal Department of Agriculture had to come in, and set up a program, paying the administrative costs that the county had refused to pay, Mr. Burson said. But he had heard Glascock was reconsidering, and might cooperate on food stamps.

Elsewhere in the nation, local resistance to food programs seems to be softening. Nutritionists and social workers are discovering they can talk about the existence of hunger without being accused of giving aid and comfort to the Communists. They were helped by the publication in January of a preliminary report on a sampling of the United States Health Service's national nutrition survey, the first scientific attempt to measure malnutrition in America.

The report revealed an "alarming prevalence" of diseases associated with undernourished groups and was based on examinations of 12,000 persons selected at random in low-income areas of Texas, Louisiana, Kentucky and New York (but mostly in Texas and Louisiana).

Dr. Charles Upton Lowe, chairman of the Committee on Nutrition of the American Academy of Pediatrics and a member of a group that will interpret the ongoing survey, commented:

"This unambiguous and objective data documents scientifically that substantial malnutrition exists in the United States.

"We cannot tolerate malnutrition in this country."

Dr. Lowe is convinced that proper nutrition is the key to normal development of infants. He feels that the quality and quantity of nutrition given during the first two, three or four years of life may have the effect of "programing" the child for all the years of his life.

This country could wipe out malnutrition with an added expenditure of a billion dollars, Dr. Lowe said. He saw an "overlay of puritanism" in the opposition to adequate food programs, an opposition reflected, he thought, in the notion that "it's bad to give anything away."

"Poverty is much more than a lack of cash," he said. "It is a way of life, all pervading, crushing, immobilizing, and destructive. It is self-perpetuating and infectious, spreading through regions like an infectious illness. And it is cruel, enervating, and dehumanizing."

February 20, 1969

SENATE RESCINDS HUNGER STUDY CUT

$100,000 Restored for U.S. Inquiry—Hollings Tells of Poverty in South Carolina

By WARREN WEAVER Jr.
Special to The New York Times

WASHINGTON, Feb. 18 — The Senate struck down today the $100,000 cut that its Rules Committee had made in the budget of Senator George S. McGovern's committee investigating hunger and malnutrition in the United States.

After three hours of speeches, nearly all of them favoring a full $250,000 authorization for the inquiry, the 40 per cent cut was restored by a relatively anonymous voice vote. No more than a half-dozen Senators could be heard calling "No."

The action reflected both growing national concern over hunger as a social and political issue and the receding influence of the Southern and farm blocs in the Senate. Members of these groups have been critical of the initial efforts of the McGovern committee.

A few hours earlier, at a hearing of the committee, Senator Ernest F. Hollings of South Carolina became one of the first political leaders from the deep South to acknowledge openly both the existence of widespread hunger among his constituents and his own share of the responsibility for it.

Senator Hollings, who has been touring some of the poorest urban and rural areas in his home state, said that, as Governor, he had supported "the public policy of covering up the problem of hunger" in the interest of attracting new industry and creating jobs.

"I know the need for jobs, but what I am talking about here to this committee is downright hunger," he said. "The people I saw couldn't possibly work."

The Senator also conceded that "as a public official, I am late to the problem." But he insisted that his conversion should not be interpreted as raising either a racial or a political issue. South Carolina's

Gary Ludwick for The New York Times

AS SENATOR TOURED POVERTY AREAS: Senator Ernest F. Hollings, left, South Carolina Democrat, during his visit to a rural slum in his state. Yesterday he told the Senate that while he was Governor he stressed appeals to new industry and minimized the problems of the poor. Supporting a successful move to strike down cut in funds for study of problems, he called them urgent and nonracial. He spoke at hearing of committee that regained funds.

hunger is both white and Negro, he said.

"Many is the time that my friends have pointed a finger and said, 'Look at that dumb Negro,'" Mr. Hollings declared. "The charge too often is accurate—he is dumb. But not because of the color of his skin. He is dumb because we denied him food. Dumb in infancy, he has been blighted for life."

Only two Senators took the floor against the $100,000 restoration today. Both of them approached the issue obliquely. One of them, Senator Carl T. Curtis, Republican of Nebraska, said he thought the McGovern committee was the wrong vehicle for such a big project.

"A charge has been made against America around the world," Senator Curtis said of the hunger reports. "We can't get the answer this way."

The other, Senator Spessard L. Holland, Democrat of Florida, questioned principally the prospect that the McGovern committee might get involved in some agricultural programs outside what he saw as its jurisdiction.

Holland Critical of Article

Mr. Holland was also critical of an article on poverty and hunger in Collier County, Fla., that appeared in The New York Times on Monday. He said the reporter, Homer Bigart, would have given "a very different description" if he had visited "an established migratory labor camp" instead of shacks and hovels.

Senator Allen J. Ellender, Democrat of Louisiana, proposed giving the McGovern committee $165,000 — more than the Rules Committee's $150,000 but far less than the eventual $250,000. His proposal was defeated by a voice vote.

When the debate opened, the Senators had agreed to a vote on the record on the money question. Later, however, to cloak the identity of opponents of the higher authorization and mollify the rejected Rules Committee, the leaders decided to shift to a voice vote.

In leading the debate, Senator McGovern said that his group, known officially as the Senate Select Committee on Nutrition and Human Needs, would be forced into an intolerable slowdown if the "drastic cuts" imposed by the Rules Committee were supported by the Senate.

A surprise supporter of the higher authorization was Senator Harry F. Byrd Jr., Democrat of Virginia, normally like his father an unremitting advocate of government economy. He said he thought the problem was too serious to cut the committee's budget.

Controversy Avoided

In his testimony before the committee during the morning, Senator Hollings declined to be drawn into a controversy with his Republican colleague from South Carolina, Senator Strom Thurmond, who has tended to deny past reports of hunger in his home state.

"The worst thing that could happen would be to get into an argument, to see if Hollings was right and Thurmond was wrong," Senator Hollings said.

When Senator McGovern, Democrat of South Dakota, praised him for a "powerful and compelling and dramatic statement," Mr. Hollings replied that there was no political profit for him in the stand and "the quickest way to kill me off is to ask me to come to Washington and make a dramatic statement like this."

Senator Hollings has never been as conservative as many of his Southern colleagues. He served as a John F. Kennedy aide in that area.

First elected to an abbreviated term in the Senate by a narrow margin in 1966, he appeared less moderate than his inclinations until he won a full six-year term last fall.

Nutrition Education Plan

Special to The New York Times

ALBANY, Feb. 18—New York State announced today a program under which Cornell University home economists would join with social workers and Federal farm agents "to teach poor people how to get more nutrition from their food dollar."

The federally funded educational program will be aimed first at those persons already receiving Federal food and food stamps.

February 19, 1969

Senators on Hunger Tour See Squalor in Florida

Group Headed by McGovern Is Met by Angry Governor, Who Was Not Notified

By MARJORIE HUNTER
Special to The New York Times

IMMOKALEE, Fla., March 10—A special Senate committee investigating hunger in America found migrant squalor and a furious Florida Governor waiting for them here today.

Angered by the committee's failure to notify him of a hunger tour in his state, Gov. Claude Kirk flew here from the state capital about noon.

Four Senators—two Democrats and two Republicans—had just spent nearly five hours trooping through squalid labor camps, peeping into nearly empty refrigerators and ducking under clotheslines outside dilapidated shacks that in some places house families of 10 or more.

The sign at the city limits proclaimed "Welcome to Immokalee, New World of Opportunity."

"Simply shocking," Senator George S. McGovern, Democrat of South Dakota, said later of what he had seen. Senator Jacob K. Javits, Republican of New York, termed it "distressing." Senator Marlow W. Cook, Republican of Kentucky, said: "You see and you wonder."

Governor Kirk left no doubt that he too was distressed and shocked—that the committee had failed to tell him it was coming to his state.

"I wish my office had been asked so I could have supplied you with information about my previous trips here," the Governor said coldly, as the committee opened afternoon hearings in a crowded school auditorium.

It was the first of a series of field trips in which the McGovern committee plans to investigate hunger and malnutrition across the continent.

By singling out Florida as a starting place, they angered not only Governor Kirk, a Republican, but also Democratic county officials here in Collier County, a farming area sometimes described as the watermelon capital of the world.

For years, county officials have thwarted all attempts to bring in Federally aided food programs, such as surplus commodities and food stamps for the poor.

They have argued that such aid would be too costly, that migrant farm laborers might be tempted to settle down here instead of moving North and that the poor might refuse to pick crops if they received free food.

"We want to get to the bottom of this," Senator McGovern said. "If the county won't cooperate, maybe we'll have to set up a wholly Federally supported food feeding program."

But there is dissension even within the ranks of his own committee.

Senator Allen J. Ellender, a peppery, 78-year-old Louisiana Democrat, protested today that the committee was touring only the worst areas.

"Why?" he asked. "That's what I want to know, why? This isn't typical of Florida. I've been here many times and I know."

While conceding that "con-

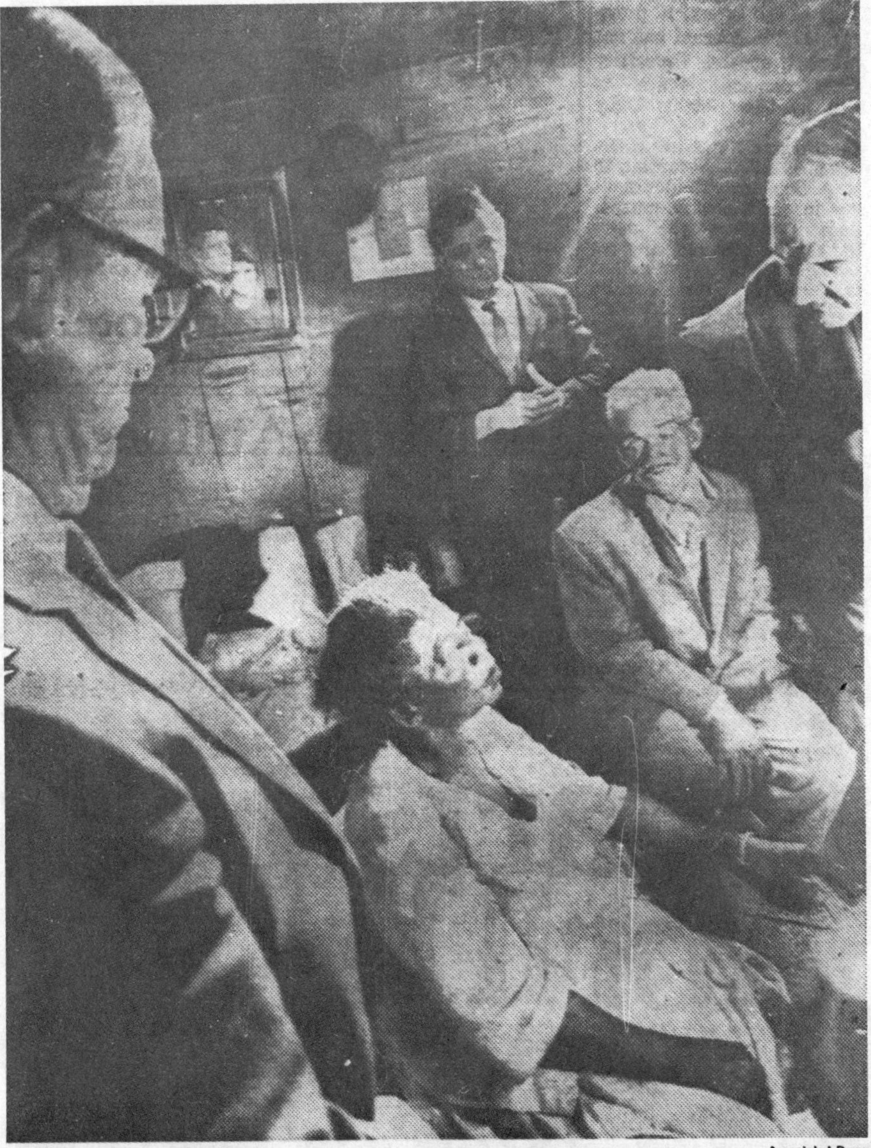

Associated Press

INSPECTING A MIGRANT LABOR CAMP: Senator George S. McGovern, right, Democrat of South Dakota, questioning Mr. and Mrs. George Adderson in their home at a camp in Immokalee, Fla. At left is Senator Allen J. Ellender, Democrat of Louisiana, a member of Senator McGovern's committee, which is investigating hunger in the United States.

ditions certainly aren't good here," Senator Ellender gestured toward a clump of shacks and said, "The people we talked to here today seemed to be happy. I haven't seen anyone who isn't contented."

He and others had just left a rotting shack where an elderly Negro man and his one-legged wife live with a 6-year-old granddaughter.

"All I need is a new leg," Mrs. Mary Adderson told them. She said that she had plenty to eat, "peas and beans and sometimes a piece of fatback."

The Addersons have an income of $136 a month, from Social Security and Old Age Assistance.

One 19-year-old migrant worker, an unwed mother of four children, was wearing a sweatshirt emblazoned with "Flower Power" as she opened the door to the touring Senators.

A few weeks earlier she had told antipoverty investigators that she had trouble feeding her family. Today, she said that they "eat well."

Refrigerators at most of the shacks visited today contained little more than fatback, sodden corn bread and plates of cold string beans.

But at one shack, Collier County Commissioner Les Whitaker took Senator McGovern in tow and said, "Come look in this refrigerator." It was jammed with milk and fruit juices and packages of meats and butter and other staples.

A staff investigator for the committee said that just two days before he had found only fatback and cold beans in that refrigerator.

"It's passing strange," Senator McGovern said.

March 11, 1969

NIXON PROPOSES $1-BILLION DRIVE TO FIGHT HUNGER

Would Broaden Food Stamp Plan to Provide Adequate Diet to Poor Families

NO BUDGET RISE NEEDED

A 'Reprograming' of Funds Is Sought for Outset of Effort in Early 1970

By WALTER RUGABER
Special to The New York Times

WASHINGTON, May 6 — President Nixon, under intense Congressional and public pressure for an expanded effort to fight hunger, proposed a Government food program today that would eventually cost more than $1-billion a year.

But the President suggested, in a message to Congress late today, that his broad-based program could not be fully implemented until sometime in the second half of the 1970 fiscal year, which begins July 1.

If started sometime after Jan. 1, 1970—the White House was vague on the precise date—the effort would require $270-million at first. That sum would be obtained without increasing Federal expenditures, Mr. Nixon said.

Thus, by what was described as "reprograming" the budget so as not to disturb the large surplus the President has demanded, Mr. Nixon continued to cling to his anti-inflationary priority.

Cuts Not Pinpointed

Officials who explained details of the expanded drive professed ignorance about what programs the Administration would cut to find the $270-million.

Daniel Patrick Moynihan, assistant to the President for urban affairs, said only that the sum would not be taken from any "poverty-related program" and not "solely" from the Agriculture Department.

There was a report that the Defense Department might be

a source for the money. The Administration was criticized for taking, in its recent 1970 budget cuts, $3 from domestic programs for every $1 it took from the military.

In his enthusiastic message, Mr. Nixon said:

"The moment is at hand to put an end to hunger in America itself for all time. It is a moment to act with vigor; it is a moment to be recalled with pride."

Most of the extra effort outlined in the President's message, which Mr. Nixon said would double Federal food outlays from $1.5-billion to $2.5-billion annually, involved the food stamp program.

Poor families who qualify are now entitled to buy stamps that are worth more than their face value in buying groceries. The cost and the redeemable value depend on family size and income.

Mr. Nixon proposed that each family taking part in the program should get enough stamps to provide what the Department of Agriculture considers a nutritionally complete diet. This is not now the case.

Under the present arrangement, for example, a family of four with an income of $20 a month or less can purchase for $2 stamps redeemable for $60. The Agriculture Department says a complete diet would cost about $100.

Under a second proposal, Mr. Nixon would offer the stamps free to "those in the very lowest income brackets." These were later described as persons who received less than $30 a month.

A number of Senators, including such politically diverse figures as George S. McGovern of South Dakota and Herman E. Talmadge of Georgia, have suggested higher cutoff points.

Free stamps for the very poor are prohibited under present law. Clifford M. Hardin, the Secretary of Agriculture, has provided them on an emergency basis in two South Carolina counties.

A breakdown of the cost of giving stamps to those with incomes of $30 a month or less was not provided by the President in his message. None of the other separate changes carried individual price tags.

30% of Income for Food

A third proposal advanced today would insure that none of the poor spent more than 30 per cent of their income to buy stamps.

At present, some of the most extremely impoverished families are forced to budget more than 60 per cent of their funds in order to participate in the stamp program. Partial purchases of stamps are not permitted.

In two other proposals, Mr. Nixon promised to blend the stamp program with a revised welfare system he expects to propose later and to provide both stamps and surplus commodities in the same county.

Under the present system, the county must choose either the stamps or the direct distribution of food packages—not both. There were two main reasons for the new proposal.

First, the Government is convinced that the stamp program is much more efficient. It would like eventually to reduce direct distribution considerably, and a county could shift more readily if it could get both programs at once for a while.

Need for Surplus Food

The Administration also believes that some areas, including big cities such as New York, may always need a little surplus food. The possibility of providing both programs, the President said today, would help meet "extraordinary or emergency situations."

In addition to broadening the food stamp effort, the President proposed issuing vouchers for infant formulas and other "highly nutritious special foods" to prevent "serious malnutrition during pregnancy and infancy."

In a series of other moves, the President:

¶Said the Administration would consider setting up a new agency, the Food and Nutrition Service, "whose exclusive concern will be the administration of the Federal food programs." These are now operated with many unrelated programs.

¶Announced that he would call a White House Conference on Food and Nutrition, with executives from food processing and food distribution companies and trade unions taking part. They would work on ways to improve the private market and the Government programs, Mr. Nixon said.

¶Asked for efforts in such areas as research, medical training and health and sanitation by the Department of Health, Education and Welfare and the Office of Economic Opportunity.

May 7, 1969

HIGH COST PLACED ON ENDING HUNGER

$4-Billion Estimate Issued by Senate Committee

By MARJORIE HUNTER

Special to The New York Times

WASHINGTON, Aug. 7 — A Senate committee concluded today that it would cost $4-billion a year adequately to feed the nation's estimated 25 million hungry and malnourished.

"We have a long, long way to go before we succeed in eliminating hunger in America," Senator George S. McGovern of South Dakota said in releasing findings of his Select Committee on Nutrition and Human Needs.

The cost of closing what the committee called the "hunger gap" was far in excess of any figure previously mentioned.

The Federal investment in food assistance to the poor was $671.9-million in the fiscal year just ended. The Administration has budgeted $1.3-billion for the current fiscal year.

While concentrating on food needs, the committee said that the gap between actual income of the nation's estimated 25 million poor and the minimum they need to meet all basic necessities is at least $10-billion a year.

While not actually endorsing a $10-billion program of income subsidies for the poor, the committee indicated it felt some sort of welfare reform or family income maintenance plan was necessary.

However, the committee said that even if this $10-billion "poverty gap" was filled, supplementary funds would be needed to provide the poor and near poor with nutritionally adequate diets.

The committee findings were based on six months of investigation into the extent of hunger and malnutrition in this country. The committee heard more than 200 witnesses and visited five states.

Pending legislation in Congress falls far short of the sums the committee said is needed.

President Nixon asked Congress this year to increase funds for the Federal food stamp program from the current $300-million a year to $610-million.

The Senate voted unanimously a few weeks ago to authorize $750-million for food stamps — a program under which the poor purchase stamps at below face value, redeemable for food in grocery stores.

The Federal Government also has other food assistance programs, including distribution of free commodities and free or low-cost school lunches.

Senator McGovern and 30 other Senators are sponsoring a bill calling for a $1.5-billion annual increase in food stamps for the needy. The bill has not emerged from the Senate Agriculture Committee.

Just yesterday, Senator Jacob K. Javits, Republican of New York, introduced a bill calling for $1.3-billion for food stamps and $415-million for other food assistance to the poor.

The Javits bill calls for expanded nutrition education programs; establishment of food store cooperative in city slums and rural poverty areas; and incentives for private industry to develop and promote fortified foods.

The bill would also permit distribution of free commodities in the same areas where food stamps are issued, and it calls for broad involvement of volunteer groups in alerting the poor to available food assistance.

August 8, 1969

Emergency Hunger Aid Given First Priority by Food Parley

By JACK ROSENTHAL
Special to The New York Times

WASHINGTON, Dec. 3—Immediate emergency action against hunger won priority tonight over a proposal for a guaranteed income for the poor at the White House Conference on Food, Nutrition and Health.

A drafting committee of conference leaders completed a controversial five-point statement of national hunger and health priorities to be presented to the closing session of the conference tomorrow and then presumably to President Nixon.

Sources reported that the statement reversed an earlier decision and put emergency hunger relief at the top of the priority list. This first priority asked that the President "free funds to feed all hungry Americans this winter."

Previously, a call for a guaranteed annual income of $5,500 for a family of four had been proposed as the conference's most urgent priority.

Income Proposal Second

In the final statement that proposal, still endorsed as the proper permanent solution to hunger, was listed second. It was linked with a strong consumer-oriented statement.

This called for effective regulation of food processing, packaging and labeling. It criticized pricing, packaing and promotion practices for what was termed adding needlessly to the cost of food. This has been damaging to every consumer, the statement said, "and disastrous to the poor."

The other priorities in order, were:

¶Interim reform and expansion of what were called present inadequate food benefit programs, including food stamps and commodities.

¶A free school food program available to all children.

¶Reorganization of the operation of food benefit programs, especally shifting them from the Departmen of Agriculture to the Department of Health, Education and Welfare.

The final statement of priorities represented a victory for Dr. Jean Mayer, director of the conference and a special consultant to the President. It was a loss for groups that had been pressing for the conference to focus primarily on the guaranteed income proposal.

Two minority groups issued strong calls for urgent food programs as the "absolute first priority." A third group, which had generated a measure of support for focusing solely on a guaranteed annual income of $5,500, broadened its position to include emergency food action.

One of the minority groups, La Raza, a coalition of Spanish speaking people, threatened to remain in Washington until President Nixon acted immediately against hunger

The Rev. Ralph Ruiz, who headed the group of 120 members of La Raza at a news conferenc, criticized Mr. Nixon's speech to the conference yesterday because he said it failed to propose emergency action.

"Poor people can't eat paper," he said. "Poor people can't eat promises."

The National Welfare Rights Organization, which has been the principal proponent of a $5,500 guaranteed income, even to the exclusion of other issues, today adopted an expanded position.

At a morning caucus, the 30 menbers of the organization at the conference decided on a parallel demand—that President Nixon order the distribution of food stamps at no cost to everyone in need. Such stamps are now sold to the poor at varying discounts, depending on income.

In a speech to an informal conference session tonight, the Rev. Ralph David Abernathy, head of the Southern Christian Leadership Conference, emphasized hunger relief as the "first priority." He also endorsed the $5,500 minimum income proposal as a long-range objective.

December 4, 1969

Books of The Times

Seven Million Hungry Children

By JOHN LEONARD

LET THEM EAT PROMISES. The Politics of Hunger in America. By Nick Kotz. Introduction by Senator George S. McGovern. 272 pages. Prentice-Hall. $6.95.

THIS savage, eloquent, fact-filled book seems a sort of Unhappy Birthday card to Martin Luther King. Dr. King proposed the 1968 Poor People's March on Washington less than a week before his assassination, and "Let Them Eat Promises" is partly a body count of that abortive engagement. It's as though our national conscience were a cement block, and Nick Kotz resolved with a sledge hammer to drive spike after spike of reproach into it until it crumbles or is shaped into something not quite so ugly. No more sophistry, he insists: "The poorest Americans who have been buried in the Deep South, the Indian reservations, the barrios of the Southwest, and the big city ghetto did not fail to make it in America because they lacked ambition or ability. The plantation system, the migrant system, the mining system, the Indian welfare system all created long odds against a man's breaking out of a cycle of abject, dependent peonage."

Nick Kotz

We have officially admitted that some 16 million Americans go hungry. Richard Nixon is perturbed about it: "Something very like the honor of American democracy is at issue," he said. Yet while they hunger we persist in quibbling: Which Federal agency should feed them, and how; does "hunger" mean "starvation"; is malnutrition a consequence of ignorance or lack of income?

An Appalling Picture

Mr. Kotz, a Pulitzer Prize-winning Washington correspondent for The Des Moines Register, paints an appalling picture of political persiflage, bureaucratic ineptitude and moral obtuseness. His is investigative reportage of the highest order, telling us what we need to know about a Congressional seniority system that elevates and perpetuates satraps like Jamie Whitten; Orville Freeman's floundering at the Department of Agriculture; the indifference of Lyndon Johnson to anything but Vietnam and inflation; the ethical callousness of the food industry; the anxiety of the white Southern Establishment to drive blacks off the land and up north before blacks vote the Establishment out of office, and the arrangement by which liberals buy a little food for the hungry by voting for farm subsidies.

What about malnutrition? Mr. Kotz demonstrates that (1) it retards the development of mind and body; and (2) the poor, according to an Agriculture Department study, "actually make *better* use of their nutritional dollars" than do the rest of us.

What about the food industry? He informs us that food technologists have developed inexpensive synthetic or fortified food products—e.g., the corn, soy and dried milk concentrate called CSM—containing all those proteins and vitamins missing from a poor man's diet. While such products are available to underdeveloped countries, they aren't available to Harlem or Appalachia or Mississippi, because then they would be competing with established commercial staples. Meanwhile, the industry takes iodine out of salt, iron out of bread, vitamins A and D out of milk, and compensates by putting more fat into frankfurters.

What about national priorities? Despite Mr. Nixon's perturbation, ABM and SST went sailing through budgetary review, and all the other problems had to scramble for any loose change: "Education was pitted against welfare, which competed with mass transit, which vied with air pollution, which competed with food programs." We have notes Mr. Kotz, a Gross National Product of $900-billion. We pay farmers $3-billion a year not to plant food. Each family has 1.2 cars and 1.3 TV sets. There are eight million pleasure boats in the Great Society . . . and seven million children don't have enough to eat; we feed them pieties.

No Aspect Is Overlooked

There isn't an aspect of this "dismal story" that Mr. Kotz neglects: the food stamp and commodities programs; the "cost benefit ratio" of feeding a child versus what we will eventually have to pay in welfare, hospitalization and other expenses for neglecting him originally; the inadequacy of the hot lunch program for school children; the names of the lobbyists involved and synopses of their rationalizations; the absence of over-all economic planning; the wretched coverage Resurrection City received from the mass media; the penitence of Ernest Hollings.

His conclusions are compelling. Some kind of income maintenance or guaranteed annual wage is inevitable, he argues, but while we argue about it, the food stamp and commodity distribution programs should be reformed "to supply adequate nutrition at minimum cost to all poor families." We must expand the school lunch program, require enrichment of food staples, encourage the development of synthetic and fortified products, and transfer jurisdiction over Federal food aid projects from the Department of Agriculture to the Department of Health, Education and Welfare.

Finally, Mr. Kotz touches on a dimension of "the politics of hunger" that should excite whichever ethical faculties in us remain unatrophied: statistical morality. He quotes a doctor: "If the infant mortality rate [in the United States] was on a par with modern European countries, 50,000 children would not die unnecessarily in this nation each year." In other words, if Norway can do it, we should be able to. And if we don't, are we not, as a nation, collectively guilty of the murder of 50,000 children? It is only one question in this excellent book of questions and answers, but what a frightening one it is.

January 15, 1970

Why Can't We Just Give Them Food?

By ROBERT SHERRILL

WASHINGTON.

"WHEN they know there's a need," Mrs. Richard Nixon said not long ago, "people step right in and help." If by "people" she means all or even most politicians and bureaucrats, why, bless her heart, that is a remark of unusual innocence.

There is still, for example, the matter of hunger in the United States. Every literate American must know about it by now: not hunger of a scope that can be controlled by baskets of food from church circles, which perhaps is the kind of need the First Lady had in mind, but hunger that is so widespread and perpetual—affecting the health and welfare of at least 20 million people—that it almost seems to demand its own loyalty and flag and folklore.

For three years, ever since the spring of 1967 when the late Senator Robert Kennedy and former Senator Joseph Clark led a troop of investigators through the backbush areas of the South and discovered it, hunger has been a favorite political topic. Of course, millions of Americans had already discovered hunger by experiencing it in varying degrees on a day-by-day basis, but since such information seeps down slowly to the political recluses of Washington, the 1967 tour was of great importance: two United States Senators had actually seen hunger and had officially taken note of it.

Others pounced on the discovery and expanded it. Since 1968 Senators George McGovern, chairman, and Jacob Javits, ranking Republican, have been running an exciting bipartisan bit of hunger muckraking through the *ad hoc* Select Committee on Nutrition and Human Needs (in titles, the word hunger is carefully avoided). The committee has cranked out more than 5,000 pages crammed with grim data, including some of the findings of the National Nutrition Survey, authorized by Congress in its first outburst of concern in 1967, showing that children on poverty diets sometimes lag by more than two years in physical development and are much more likely to suffer mental retardation.

Orville Freeman, voicing a benevolence he had not shown during his eight years as Secretary of Agriculture, left that office insisting the Government has a duty to feed any hungry American, whether or not he can pay for the food; and Freeman's successor, Clifford Hardin, came into office saying the same thing. The business-minded U. S. Department of Agriculture (U.S.D.A.) even unbent enough to find room for a new bureaucratic wing for the needy consumer, the Food and Nutrition Service, and hired a former biscuit-company executive to head it up. And then a few months ago Washington was the scene of that ultimate political parry to the thrust of necessity—a White House Conference. On hunger.

THERE has also been an impressive outpouring of nonpolitical attention. This magazine gave hunger its first comprehensive write-up ("It Isn't True That Nobody Starves in America," June 4, 1967), which was followed by countless newspaper stories, 58 magazine articles of sufficient status to be indexed in Readers' Guide, the powerful C.B.S. documentary, "Hunger in America," and

ROBERT SHERRILL is Washington correspondent of The Nation.

at least one book, Nick Kotz's first-rate retrospective, "Let Them Eat Promises: The Politics of Hunger," published this year. Prentice-Hall says it has already sold about 20,000 copies, which isn't bad for such a disagreeable subject.

So there has been, obviously, no shortage of studies, hearings, journalistic regrets and official concern. And what has come of it all?

By one measure, a great deal has come of it. Considering the vulnerability of the Johnson Administration to charges of indifference, Nixon was strangely reluctant to pick up the issue during his 1968 campaign and he did not make reference in a major speech to wiping out malnutrition until less than a month before the vote. Two months after being sworn in, Nixon's commitment to the problem was still in doubt; at his first strategy session on hunger with Secretary Hardin—Kotz reports in his book, using White House minutes—Nixon told Hardin, "You can say that this Administration will have the first complete, far-reaching attack on the problem of hunger in history. Use all the rhetoric, so long as it doesn't cost any money." But Nixon's performance has been better than that sounds.

The machinery he inherited consisted of the two standard programs: food commodities and food stamps, neither of which has ever been used as it could have been, or used with much bureaucratic grace. Since the nineteen-thirties, when the Government began shoring up farm prices by buying surplus production, food commodities have been handed out to welfare-level families. Benevolence plays a very small part. The 24 staple items — beans, cheese, cornmeal, flour, etc.—are given away simply because that is cheaper than storing them. Ideally the program provides a monthly 38 pounds of food worth $15.69 retail to every

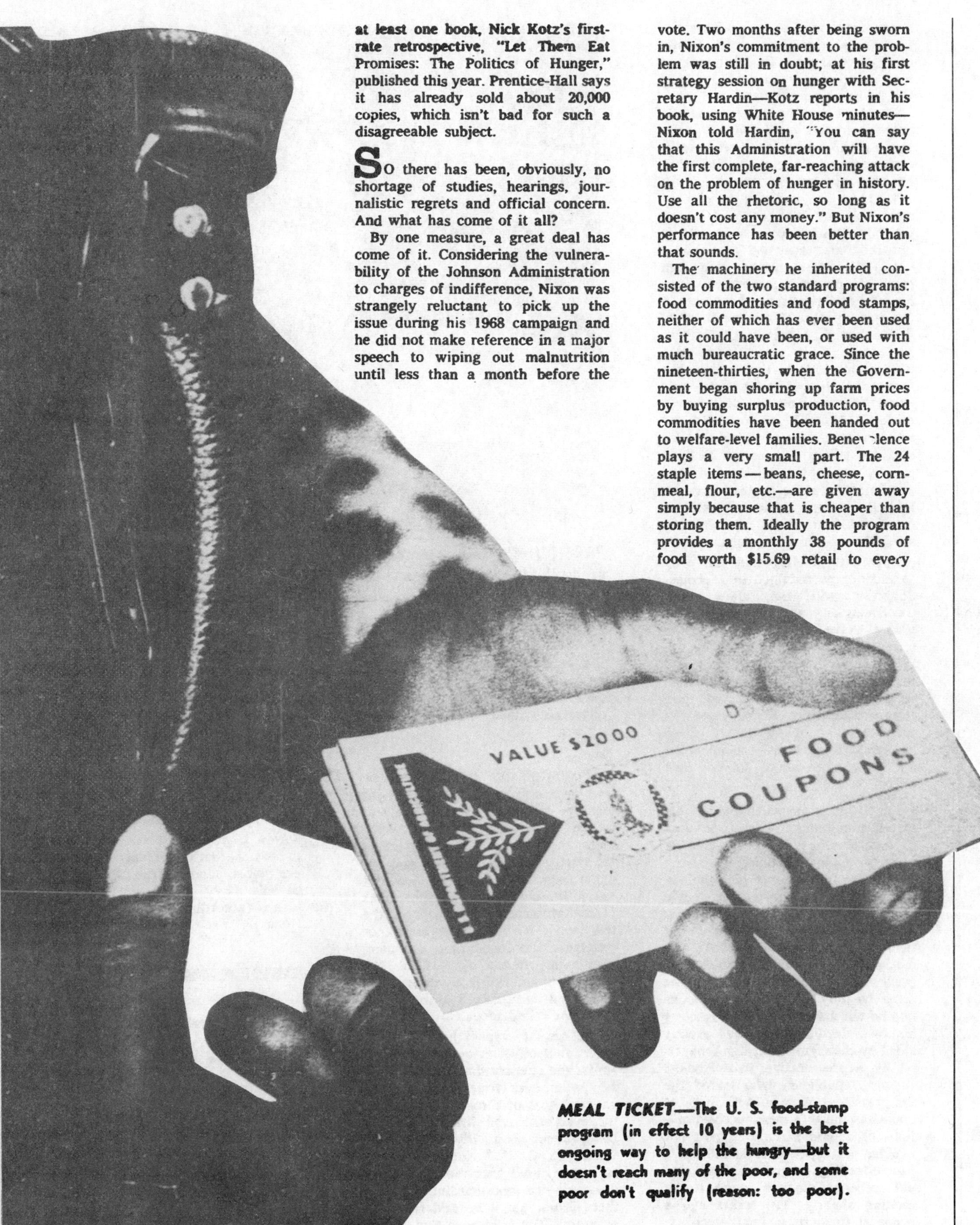

***MEAL TICKET*—The U. S. food-stamp program (in effect 10 years) is the best ongoing way to help the hungry—but it doesn't reach many of the poor, and some poor don't qualify (reason: too poor).**

eligible person, but in practice virtually no participating county distributes every commodity, and quite a few counties give only 14 or 15 of the 24 items on the list.

The food-stamp program, which is only about 10 years old, is vastly the superior way to feed people. Commodities will keep a person alive, but they are boring; stamps, on the other hand, are traded at the grocery store for any kind of food money can buy. The stamps cost something, but they are redeemed at a bonus value. Whether a needy person can get in the program depends on where he lives and how much he earns. In the state of New York, the U.S.D.A. won't permit a family of four to participate if it earns more than $350 a month. With that income, the family would pay $80 for stamps that could be redeemed for $106 worth of food. A family of four with *no* income would—presumably after stealing it—pay $2 and get $106 in stamps. This is considerable improvement over the program prior to last December, when a penniless family of four would have had to steal $3 in order to participate.

Apparently feeling that the poor should not be indulged in a choice, Congress will not allow both the commodity and food-stamp programs to be offered in the same place. In fact, unless goaded by the White House, Congress has been reluctant to make much use of either program. Eisenhower ignored food stamps completely; Kennedy got the program going; it was kicked up to an insignificant level—around $200-million yearly—before Johnson left office.

But Nixon, notwithstanding his stated preference for rhetoric over expenditures, is energetically pushing both programs, doubling the stamp budget the first year of his Administration and now trying to double that budget again. When he took office, more than 600 counties offered neither free commodities nor the food-stamp program; he promised that every county would have one or the other by July 1, 1970, and it looks like he will have no problem meeting his own deadline. (He was greatly aided by the shame campaign conducted by Representative Paul Findley, Illinois Republican, who larded the Congressional Record with lists of counties whose farmers received millions of dollars in crop support but avoided participation in the U.S.D.A.'s people-feeding programs.) Even that old iceberg Congress seems to be melting slightly. Two years ago a proposal to increase family-food assistance by $50-million was overwhelmed in a stiff debate; now proposed increases of more than a billion dollars are talked of in a matter-of-fact way.

FREE LUNCH in Brooklyn's P.S. 84. "Nixon has promised that every needy child in the country will be getting a free lunch by next Thanksgiving. It is an awesome objective, with a quarter-million still unfed in New York City, 82,000 in Los Angeles, 154,000 in Chicago—and on around the country for a total of several million to go."

CONSIDERING this progress, it may seem cranky to look now at the negative side. But the negative side is too enormous to ignore, being large enough also to make one of the McGovern committee's last reports seem fairly accurate when it says: "In relation to the dimensions of the problems, the impact of the two major Federal food-assistance programs, the food-stamp and commodity-distribution programs, has been minimal." Nor is anything likely to happen immediately to make that judgment sound foolish.

The newest crop of benign statistics cannot offset evidence turned up across the country that we are about as far as ever from achieving the national goal of three squares a day for everyone. And little enough is being done about it. In Winston-Salem, N. C., for example, where reporters found that "some children dine on rice and sardine grease," there is not yet a Federal free-food program. The Chicago Sun-Times found that some of the elderly citizens of that city, receiving only $26.18 for food from the Cook County Department of Public Aid each month, were literally starving to death; of the county's more than five-million residents, only 133,012 are in the food-stamp program because of what The Sun-Times calls "the bureaucratic tangle."

New Hampshire, whose wage scale is near the bottom among Northeastern states, supplies free commodities to only 12,000 of its residents; this means (according to a University of

“The cash-assistance plan for the poor would not take effect before July, 1971—or 1,270 meals away.”

Photographs by HARRY BENSON

A CHILD GROWS IN BROOKLYN; **or, free lunch time again at P.S. 84. The food industry seems to have as much to say about the school-lunch program as the Government. In fact, two Presidents have had their plans for the program vetoed by the milk lobby.**

New Hampshire study) that only 10 per cent of the people on "poor" diets are being reached. In one sampling of 141 old people eligible to get surplus foods, only 15 were in the program. The vast majority of townships in Massachusetts have no school-lunch program; although in the last three years Massachusetts has more than doubled the number of people to whom it gives commodities — 32,900 then, 75,500 now — it remains an island of the most acute indifference to what its needy people eat. Fewer than 500 people in the whole state receive food stamps.

New York City, which is now trying to move to the food-stamp program, has one of the nation's worst records in the distribution of free commodities; only about half of the 24 available commodities are offered to its poor, and in only half the quantity per person given elsewhere. New York's commodity-distribution centers are notorious for running out of foods before the month is up.

In a historic breakthrough, the U.S.D.A. is operating a free food-stamp program. Orville Freeman refused to budge on this matter, claiming that he had no legal right to give away stamps, even to people with no income. Hardin also takes the position that free stamps are illegal, but he's giving away a few anyway, on an experimental basis. He isn't bending the law—when a Secretary of Agriculture bends the law in favor of the poor instead of the plantation owner or the agribusinessman, the U.S.D.A. will indeed have entered a new era —but Hardin is at least making some use of an emergency fund to offset extreme hardships created by the law.

But the U.S.D.A.'s free food-stamp program means about as much to the nation's poor as NASA's moon trips mean to the average traveler. By count of the Office of Economic Opportunity (which is always conservative in such tallies) there are at least 1.3 million Americans who have *no* income, not a penny. The experts who estimate these things believe that in the crannies of the slums and behind the hedgerows of rural America, another six million or so exist on less than $300 a year.

Yet the U.S.D.A.'s free stamps are distributed in only two counties—Beaufort and Jasper, both in South Carolina—where one can qualify by earning less than $1 a day. Narrow as that opening may seem, the new regulations have doubled the participation in the food program in Beaufort and increased it by more than 50 per cent in Jasper, which proves that the broke folks are indeed out there in the back country and it only takes knowledge of free stamps—many never get the word—to bring them out.

Assistant Agriculture Secretary Richard Lyng claims that a nationwide free-stamp program, if limited to people earning $1 a day or less, would cost only $6-million annually. That may seem an unreasonably low guess, considering the O.E.O.'s head count; but to the Congressional farm committees, which have to approve such matters, it seems unreasonably high. Nixon has asked Congress for a national free-stamp program. The Senate Agriculture Committee turned him down, but the provision was restored to the food bill on the Senate floor; now that the fight has moved to the House, once again free stamps are in peril. The House Ag Committee is against them, and so, for that matter, are such strange opponents as Representative Leonor Sullivan of Missouri, who, because of her early work on behalf of the program, likes to have people call her the "Mother of Food Stamps," but who, in fact, has been one of the most adamant opponents of making stamps available to the 1.3 million identified people who can't pay a penny for them. Her reasoning: "That's charity, and we don't want to make the stamps charity."

CONGRESSIONAL unwillingness to establish a free-stamp program means that when counties and cities shift from commodities to stamps, they often automatically shut out many residents who cannot afford to pay even the minimum. In Mississippi, for example, where 12 counties shifted programs, participation in commodity handouts dropped by 95,000 during the last three years while participation in the food-stamp programs increased by only about 2,500. Are the other 92,500 cupboards bare? No official body has bothered to check.

Although it has made no effort to cushion the fall-off in participation, Congress cannot pretend ignorance of what is happening. The 40 per cent drop in Mississippi assistance is no **sharper than the drop wherever the shift in programs has been made; 1.1 million who once received commodities are not now receiving food stamps. Congress has made no provisions for these people, who must think the Federal food programs have started working backward.**

Why do difficulties like these keep coming up, forcing the Government to retreat in one sector when it advances in another? There are so many surplus crops, including food, lying around that it costs the Government nearly a quarter billion dollars a year just to store the stuff. Why is Congress so stingy with it? Why not shovel it out with wasteful abandon, if that is necessary to see everyone is fed? And, inasmuch as the Budget Bureau has said a full

application of the food-stamp program could be handled at a reasonable expense, why are we, three years after the Great Hunger Discovery, still moving toward stamps so hesitantly?

A lot of nice people, including Mrs. Nixon, would probably like to know the answer to that. There are several answers, not one, and among them are these:

Political Calvinism. The legislative halls and bureaus of Government are occupied at every level by men who believe that anyone who is hungry and seeks help must be a bum. Back in the days when John Gardner was trying to do something with Health, Education and Welfare, he ordered a survey run to find out if there are a great many loafers on welfare, as some critics charged. The finding was that of the 7.3 million persons then on welfare, only 50,000 were able-bodied, able-brained men. Otherwise there were 2.1 million persons over 65; nearly a million younger mothers; 3.5 million dependent children; 700,000 blind or unemployably handicapped; and 100,000 men who for one reason or another were judged to be hopelessly untrainable. Some of the 50,000 able-bodied men doubtless had good excuses for freeloading, but even if they didn't, they made up less than 1 per cent of the total. There is no reason to suppose things have changed much since Gardner's day, so one could justifiably conclude that assistance programs have little appeal to anyone who can stay off them.

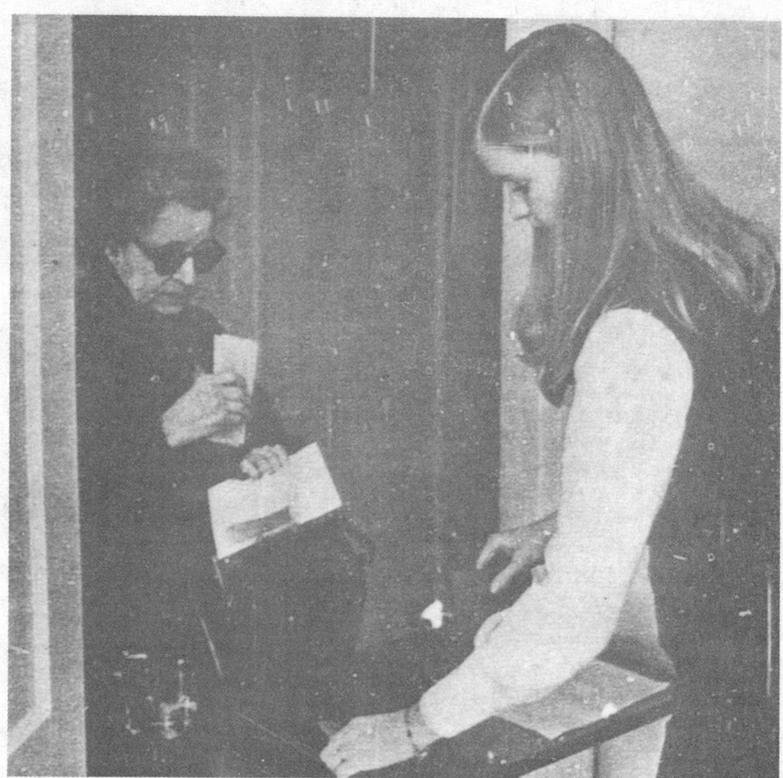

STAMP-COLLECTING—In Beaufort County, S. C. One reason that the country which virtually invented 20th-century efficiency hasn't applied it to its antihunger drive is that "Congressional jousting over food legislation often takes on the character of a territorial struggle between rival dukes."

STILL, the belief persists among most politicians that if a person is hungry it must be because he is sinful and shiftless. This is the predominant philosophy in both Congressional farm committees, but it is found most acutely in the House Agriculture Committee, which reflects the religio-political creed of its chairman, W. R. Poage of Texas, who owns two farms and whose home state leads the nation both in the amount of Federal subsidies received by its farmers and in the number of counties which refuse to feed the needy.

One day during the food-stamp hearings last October, a fascinating exchange took place between Chairman Poage and Stephen Kurzman, a Washington attorney who is special counsel to the Urban Coalition Action Council. It went, in part, like this:

Poage: "People do not work for nothing. To go back even further than 2,000 years, go back somewhere in the dim past and the Book that most all of us accept, it says somewhere, 'By the sweat of thy brow shalt thou eat bread.'

"Now I think that is true. I think it is true when old Adam was kicked out, and I think it is still true. 'By the sweat of thy brow' means work, as I understand it. Now, I have not any objection to helping the individual who needs help, and I do not want you to go away from here and say that Bob Poage said that he would not help some poor widow and her kids. He never said anything of the kind. But he has said that he was not going to help some deadbeat who is sitting down at the pool hall waiting for his wife and kids to go out and see what the neighbors bring in."

Kurzman: "I do not think that the average $6.75 a month that recipients of food stamps are now getting out of the general treasury constitute an overwhelming incentive to spend your life in a pool hall."

Poage: "The point I am making is I have not understood why you and others who have appeared before this committee, who have a legitimate and proper concern for the needy, are also so concerned in maintaining a bunch of drones.

"You know what happens in the beehive. They kill those drones. That is what happens in most primitive societies. Maybe we have just gotten too far away from the situation of primitive man."

That last paragraph was stricken from the record and does not appear in the official transcript of the hearing, presumably because Representative Poage felt that some people might interpret it to mean he favors killing the people on Federal food programs. He doesn't really go that far.

Poage has written one provision into his committee's version of the food bill that would prohibit giving stamps to a family if any of its members between the ages of 18 and 65 refused to take a job at either the Federal or state minimum wages. Two things are obviously wrong with the provision. In the first place, it would force people into peonage. The Federal minimum wage doesn't cover clerks in small retail stores, for example; if a woman took such a job in Kentucky, she would, however, be covered by the state minimum wage which would guarantee her an income of—$26 a week, or $1,356 a year. And Kentucky is quite protective compared with a dozen other states, mostly in the Southeast, which have no minimum wage at all.

The most critical defect in the Poage provision was pointed out by Representative Thomas Foley of Washington. "I don't want to feed bums," Foley argued, "but neither do I think we should visit the sins of the parents upon the children." To which Poage responded in his rasping, jeremianic voice: "You didn't make that law, Mr. Foley. That law came from a higher authority. That law has lasted throughout history. You aren't going to change that law."

THOUGH Foley—who is No. 7 down on the Democratic side, the highest-ranking member not from Dixie or a border state—spends much of his time combating this philosophy from within, he is quick to defend the backers of the Poage creed against charges of quackery or opportunism:

"The problem with the committee is that it is a residue of the Puritan ethic attitude: that if you do something to provide assistance to Americans who don't otherwise have the resources, this is going to strike a blow against initiative. What it essentially comes out to is viewing food as a spur for people to work. This is the most conservative committee in the House in terms of traditional attitude toward welfare. In working on the farm bill [the food legislation is Title II of the farm bill; Title I takes care of the juicy crop subsidies] the committee began to do things that the House itself had already rejected, like putting in a provision that anybody on strike couldn't get food stamps.

"The majority of the committee agree so strongly that the social-welfare climate is wrong and devastating of national strength, they believe it so sincerely that they are willing to act unpolitically with respect to their immediate constituent interests. If politics were their motive, they would come out with the best damn food bill ever conceived to get the city guys to back their farm subsidy. They aren't stupid. They must know the kind of bill that's going to come out of committee now is going to make the city people mad.

"But they did it anyway. Right in the middle of the General Electric strike, despite the fact that organized labor could have a veto power over the farm bill, they came out with the antistriker provision. If that is judged within the context of politics, you have to admit that people jumping out of planes without parachutes have better sense than that. It isn't politics. They are ideologically hung-up. This is their sincere view of the world, of how right and truth and justice fall into place."

Jurisdictional Jealousies. Congressional jousting over food legislation often takes on the character of a territorial struggle between rival dukes. Any legislation relating to food that bypasses the agriculture committees is interpreted by most of their members as an attempt not only to destroy their jurisdiction but probably also to destroy the nation.

When McGovern induced the Senate to substitute his more generous food bill for one passed out of the farm committee, he was denounced as a Frankenstein. Those Senators who had supported McGovern's bill, said Georgia's Herman Talmadge, had "established a monster."

One of the monstrous provisions of the McGovern bill would permit food stamps to be used to buy items for personal hygiene and household sanitation. A few weeks earlier, when the food-stamp bill was being debated in executive session in the Senate farm committee, McGovern tried to stick in this provision. Since it is commonplace for critics of welfare programs to condemn recipients as dirty as well as shiftless, McGovern thought the old bulls of the committee would like the idea of letting poor people buy soap, toothpaste and brooms with their stamps.

It didn't turn out that way. Senator Spessard Holland, Florida's ancient, thought it was horrible even to contemplate. One observer at these executive wrangles reported, "When McGovern tried to bring up this section and discuss it calmly, Holland started complaining that he didn't want to let food stamps be used to buy sanitary napkins. He kept repeating it—he didn't think the Senate had any business buying poor women sanitary napkins."

EVEN illogical arguments are enough to spike most legislation in the Senate Ag committee if the arguments are offered by one of the three patriarchs: Chairman Allen Ellender, 79, Holland, 77, or George Aiken, 77. Most of the other members of the committee are very eager to please these three who see eye to eye. Though Aiken is from Vermont, he has always felt close to the Southern viewpoint on farm matters. When he came to the Senate 30 years ago he was sponsored for a seat on the Senate Agriculture Committee by South Carolina's Cotton Ed Smith (that was in the days when the farm committee had some status and Senators actually sought

TO MARKET **with food stamps. A South Carolina woman buys her stamps at the Beaufort County office and then shops in the supermarket next door. The stamps may be used to buy any food, but not (and this is a hot Congress issue now) anything else.**

to get on it; freshmen had a hard time making it without a powerful sponsor).

A couple of years earlier Cotton Ed and Aiken, who was then Governor of Vermont, had shared a speaking engagement at the famous "Amen Corner" in Pittsburgh and they discovered that they had just about the same thing to say on every topic brought up. So when Aiken arrived in the Senate, the colorful South Carolinian took him under his wing.

Aiken never let him down. Now the ranking Republican, Aiken works closely with his colleagues to protect the big cotton and wheat subsidies, and, of course, to do what he can along the way for Vermont's dairy industry. For them and him, the system has worked well, and he resents all seeming attempts to reduce the farm committee's authority over anything relating to food. He did not forgive McGovern for slipping through the soap-toothpaste-and broom-clause on the Senate floor. So, when authorization for extension and expansion of McGovern's hunger committee came up for a vote this year, Aiken told his colleagues it looked to him like somebody was seeking "ways and means of completely changing our Government over and setting up a complete Federal welfare state," and he added darkly, though he did stop short of mentioning names, that it reminded him of the fact that "there is an organization around the country that certainly thinks the U.S. Government is set up all wrong and has to be made over." And finally he alluded to McGovern's ultimate treachery, ambition for higher office. "Thank God," cried Aiken, "thank God I do not want to be President of the United States."

When this kind of debate gets to churning around in the Senate chambers, the original topic, hungry people, is often forgotten.

Rusty Bureaucratic Machines. Edward J. Hekman, the former biscuit-company executive who now is administrator of the U.S.D.A.'s Food and Nutrition Service, says he has been "impressed by the dedication" of the people who handle the food programs on the local level. "It is," he says, "the same sort of dedication that I find among our Federal staff." Well, *that* may be true, but that isn't saying much. Whatever his competence, Hekman himself seems enthusiastic about getting the food out where it is needed. But the Federal bureaucracy with which he must work is made up of the same people who have accomplished little under previous Administrations. They have consistently permitted local officials to get by with racial discrimination, and they have made no serious effort even to learn what is going on at the local level.

This is true not only in the family-assistance programs but in the school-lunch programs as well. The guidelines put out by the Government base eligibility for free lunches on family incomes and the size of families. But as William Smith, director of the Senate Select Committee on Nutrition, points out, "As a matter of practice all over the country, the permission to get in the program is arbitrarily up to the school principals and they have in many, many instances been extremely unjust in their decisions. Nobody at the U.S.D.A. monitors the program full time. The U.S.D.A. allows the school principals to run the program just about any way they want to. Anybody who has ever studied the school-lunch program knows this is going on all over the country."

One Georgia school, for example, has an application form for free lunches which states: "Parents with TV sets, telephones, automobiles, etc., should not request free lunches unless dire circumstances have suddenly overtaken them." The form also asks these two questions, both illegal by Federal standards and yet both approved by Federal administrators: "Would you be willing to let your children do a small amount of work, such as picking up paper, as part payment for the lunches they receive? Are you willing for a committee from the P.T.A. to visit your home to investigate this application for free lunches?"

The letter of the free-lunch program law is meant to protect needy students from being singled out in this way, but Washington's enforcement of the law is so lax that in some schools children getting free lunches must line up separately, eat at a different time or use lunch tickets of a different color—and the schools of New York have been among those caught breaking the law in these ways.

LAST summer 200 high-school and college students, backed by the American Friends Service Committee, spent two months talking to local officials in 35 counties in 15 states to find out what their attitudes were toward running food programs for the poor. Rarely did they find an official who thought it might be a good idea to learn how many sub-poverty-level families lived in his county, hunt them up and tell them about available food programs. Often, of course, the reasoning was impeccably pious. A school official in New Jersey, for example, said free lunches were not publicized in his county "because it might embarrass the children."

Representative Carl Perkins pushed an extra $45-million through Congress in 1968 as emergency school-lunch funds for needy pupils; late last year Rodney Leonard, former administrator of the U.S.D.A.'s Consumer and Marketing Services, investigated the use of these emergency funds and found that "most states apparently are using these funds to hold down the prices of regular school lunches —in effect, benefiting the middle-class youngsters and diluting a special effort to provide an adequate diet for the poor." Perkins thought the money would feed an extra 1,000,000 children. Only 400,000 more were fed; Leonard found that more than half the money was diverted where it wasn't supposed to go, with eight states misusing *all* of their extra money (New York was more restrained than that; it diverted only 45 per cent of the money).

Leonard also turned up a shining example of the economic pressures that shape food programs. In March, 1969, the U.S.D.A. requested a $10-million increase for a program started the previous year which allows children to be fed meals outside of school. A month later, however, the U.S.D.A. told Congress to forget that request and instead to pump more money into the milk programs at summer camps, child-care centers and schools that do not have food-service programs.

Leonard's interpretation: "This shifting of fiscal gears has all the hallmarks of paring a budget to fit both the dictates of the Bureau of the Budget and the dairy interests. It helps to understand priorities when a program to provide a complete meal for children is slashed in favor of one which provides only milk."

EXCEPT for the American Farm Bureau Federation, which takes the quaint position of opposing Federal help for anyone, including farmers, the milk producers are the only strictly farm lobby opposing food for the needy. Partly because only 7 per cent of the $125,000,000 special milk program for schools is spent on poor children, both Presidents Johnson and Nixon have tried to transfer this money over to the lunch program instead; but so powerful is the milk lobby that it has not only easily blocked that move, it overwhelmingly defeated efforts in Congress to spend the milk money *first* on needy children. The lobby won't open the door to reform even a crack.

The U.S.D.A.'s traditional priorities are identical with those of the Appropriations Committee of both houses: money is to be spent where the agriculture market needs it. Leonard, who sat in the center of this decision-making from 1967 to 1969, says that "while the Appropriations Committees tell the Administration to go slow on the school-breakfast and other child-nutrition programs, there is no similar record of caution on funds to purchase meat when cattle prices fall or to buy frozen orange concentrate when a surplus in the citrus crop exists." In 1964, he recalls, only $43-million was spent on beef for school lunches, but the next year the purchases jumped to $173-million, and then in 1966 fell back to $49-million; the explanation being a slump in cattle prices in 1965, which called for the schoolchildren to "eat their way through excessive supplies of hamburgers and beef roasts."

Progress has been made. The U.S.D.A. can point to places like Baltimore, where a year ago only 5,000 youngsters were getting free lunches; today, because of U.S.D.A. funds used to reach children in schools without cafeterias, 30,000 are getting free lunches.

Nixon has promised that every needy child in the country will be getting a free lunch by next Thanksgiving. It is an awesome objective, with a quarter million still unfed in New York City, an estimated 82,000 needy youngsters unfed in Los Angeles, 154,000 left out in Chicago—and on around the country for a total of several million to go. So lackadaisical has the U.S.D.A. been up to this point that it can't really be sure how many needy children are waiting. It claims there are 6.7-million of school age who can't afford lunch. Other expert observers, however, contend that the total may be higher than 8 million.

It makes a difference who's right. The McGovern committee, which accepts the higher figure, says that the Nixon budget for feeding schoolchildren next year will fall short by at least 30 per cent.

And waiting down at the state and local levels to deal with the situation in their own way are such officials as the head of the Ohio Department of Education's lunch program who suggested that the best way to cut down on hunger is to cut down on children, and who urged the McGovern committee to "explore the possibilities of legalizing sterilization for retarded parents and others," the others including "welfare mothers who continue to have large families . . . and *other* mentally incompetents."

"At a bare minimum, it would take between $5-billion and $7-billion to close the hunger gap."

Even easier to find at the local level are such cheerful fellows as county judge Don Weaver Davis of McKinney, Tex., who says they don't need any Federal food programs where he lives because "there's nobody hungry in Collin County. If they were, I'd give them money for food out of my own pocket." Sixty thousand people live in Collin County. Last year $7,007 was distributed in emergency food funds. If 10 per cent of the residents are needy, which is less than the national average, it means they got about $1.16 per hungry person last year. Goodwill can begin in a flood at the White House, but by the time it leaks out through the cracks in the U.S.D.A., and in the state and local bureaucracy, there's often nothing left.

Do-Gooding Schisms. The White House Conference on hunger was not called anything as basically descriptive as that, naturally; it was called the Conference on Food, Nutrition and Health. About 4,000 persons showed up, including 100 or so authentic poor folks shipped in at the expense of the Government. Everybody immediately cliqued up and fell into fighting postures. One group wanted to concentrate on the lousy Government feeding programs; another group wanted to kick the discussion up to a more scientific level at which riboflavin and thiamine would be the topics of the day; and a third group wanted to forget about

food programs or nutritional additives and concentrate instead on straight cash handouts from Government.

Supposedly running the show, and gamely trying to do so, was Dr. Jean Mayer, the noted nutritionist from Harvard, who was under tremendous pressure from the Administration, from the food industry and from old-guard academic nutritionists to make it a predictably middle-class conference with the primary objective of showing President Nixon's concern. Just before the conference opened, several food industrialists who planned to take part reportedly drew Mayer aside and told him not to let the poor speak. As it turned out, not only did the poor speak, they spoke even louder than Mayer, who was heard to say such nasty things about parts of the food industry (about snack chips of various sorts: "Fried worms would be better. At least you'd get some protein.") that Donald Kendall of Pepsico, Inc., makers not only of soft drinks but of potato chips and corn snacks, quit the conference and went home mad.

By the end of the conference, Mayer, it is said, was without portfolio at the White House. Doubly without portfolio was his assistant, Robert Choate, a former adviser on food matters for H.E.W., who was such an irritant that some people around the White House discussed firing him almost daily.

Choate's sin was that he wanted to make the conference zero-in on hunger, and he was not above snitching on intra-White House activities. "I saw draft No. 3 of the President's speech that he planned to deliver to the conference," said Choate. "He had very little in it on welfare, lots of gutsy stuff on hunger. But the speech he gave on Dec. 2 was virtually all [White House urban adviser Patrick] Moynihan's family cash-assistance plan."

Presidential aide Raymond Price Jr. thinks the conference emphasis on cash assistance was a mistake. "When people across the country heard that that was what we talked about," he recalls sorrowfully, "I think they just turned off. Especially when they heard one group of poor people at the conference was insisting on a cash assistance of up to $12,000 for large families."

Risky Alternatives. If the Nixon Administration gets every cent it asks for in the food budget for 1971, it will—by the admission of its own experts—still have less than half what is needed to feed the malnourished in this country. For more than a year, $2.9-billion has been commonly quoted as the minimum budgetary need for closing the hunger gap. This figure had its origin in the Bureau of the Budget. But since October the White House has had an updated report from the Bureau—unpublicized—which shows that at a bare minimum it would take between $5-billion and $7-billion to close the gap; the estimate is based on a six-team study done by the U.S.D.A., O.E.O. and H.E.W.

But as one of these investigators explained, the Administration would never seek as much as $5-billion because it wants eventually to phase out the "food-stamp, funny-money and commodity programs" and swing to the proposed cash assistance. (To begin with, however, the program would be a combination: a family of four with no income would receive $1,600 in cash, from which it could spend $408 for $1,272 in food stamps.)

TO Richard P. Nathan, assistant director of the Budget Bureau, it all seems translucently obvious. "Not long ago," he says, "I went on a trip to study welfare programs and when I returned my 5-year-old daughter asked me where I had been. I said I had gone to see someone about how to help poor people. She replied, 'That's easy, Daddy, just give them money.' "

The White House is full of just-give-them-money optimism. Says Presidential aide Price, "You must always understand that in the President's mind there is an unbreakable linkage between the family-cash-assistance program and the food program. Our best estimates are that if we get the family cash assistance that he proposes and the food increase that he proposes, we would wipe out in one fell swoop 60 per cent of what most economists consider the poverty gap in America. It took 10 years for the economy and public-assistance programs to work down that gap from $14-billion in 1959 to $10-billion in 1963. The President's two programs combined would chop another $6-billion out of that gap."

So far the White House's airy cheerfulness on this subject has been justified. After months of hesitation, Ways and Means Chairman Wilbur Mills finally sent along with his endorsement a family-cash-assistance bill which Democratic liberals and Nixon loyalists will join in giving a hospitable welcome on the House floor. No companion legislation has yet begun to move seriously through the Senate, but there it will probably receive as much criticism from those who believe it to be too stingy (Senator Fred Harris of Oklahoma, for example, wants $3,600 for a family of four within three years) as from those who consider it too generous. So, although it would not take effect before July 1971—which is about 1,270 meals away— something in the way of cash-assistance legislation appears to have a chance of passing this year.

But not everyone in Congress joins in that optimistic forecast. Among the pessimists, or realists, are some who criticize the cash-assistance movement for sopping off energies that could be better spent this year in pushing for a more comprehensive feeding program.

Says Senator Ernest Hollings, one of the most enthusiastic champions of bigger food programs, "It is like Bossy, the cow, kicking over the pail of milk. When we are getting the program started, Mr. Moynihan starts across the street and kicks it over. Congress will argue for the next 10 years before it ever adopts such a program [as cash assistance]. And during that 10 years of debate we still will not have a program that would solve the poor's plight."

Then Hollings adds: "We provide $11-billion for pollution control. We could not have passed a bill to provide even $1-billion for that a few years ago. But now we get an $11-billion program because everybody can see or smell the need for that."

Hollings has touched on the major obstacle that still confronts the hungry. Assistant Agriculture Secretary Lyng makes the same point: "I can drive from my office to my apartment in Northwest Washington and never lay my eyes on a starving person." Perhaps not even a malnourished one, although a panel headed by Dr. Leroy A. Jackson, chief of the D.C. Health Department's maternal health division, reported a few weeks ago that one-third of the capital's residents are underfed. Other doctors have told Congress that malnutrition afflicts more than 70 per cent of the infants in the capital's slums. Close as this is to the men who are dealing with the problem, the intervening few blocks changes it all into statistics, and the pollution of hunger remains not only odorless and tasteless but, to official Washington, largely invisible. ■

Administration Making Significant Gains in Antihunger Drive

By JACK ROSENTHAL
Special to The New York Times

WASHINGTON, Feb. 4—The Nixon Administration's antihunger program has produced significant, often dramatic gains, reports on the program from 10 areas around the country disclosed today. Bt the job is only half done, many of the poor people and experts interviewed said, and they now fear a leveling off of Federal efforts.

"Half a loaf is better than none," said one expert. "But it's still half a loaf."

On the eve of the second White House conference on nutrition, both critics and beneficiaries cite gains in the number of needy people receiving food stamps, subsidized school lunches and other Federal food assistance.

In New York City, for example, the number of people benefited has jumped four times since the Nixon Administration took office. It has doubled just since September.

But at the same time, large numbers of needy people still are not reached, reports from the 10 areas indicated. The 750,000 people now receiving foodstamps in New York City are estimated to be only 38 per cent of those eligible.

Depressed Conditions

In such places as Seattle and Detroit, depressed economic conditions, appear, even in the face of sharply increased Federal food assistance, to have swollen the number of the needy. And, despite Presidential assertions of "an impressive record indeed," a number of antihunger groups insisted today in a joint press release here that only half the needy children were being fed.

The Administration's budget for antihunger programs, meanwhile, is leveling off, says Robert B. Choate, a leading Washington authority on hunger. The Administration deserves recognition for what it has done, he said today, "but the new budget figures seem to be more of an epitaph than a progress report."

The Administration, under continuing pressure from Congressional liberals, for the third year in a row has asked Congress for sizable increases in antihunger programs.

The new White House conference is a follow-up to the broad, contentious conference of 3,000 consumers, industry representatives and poor people that was held in Washington for three days in December, 1969.

By contrast, the one-day meeting tomorrow will be limited to about 200 participants, few if any of them poor, and will be held in distant colonial Williamsburg, Va.

The participants, in their evaluation of progress since the 1969 conference, will hear reports of significant gains from Administration spokesmen.

Many of these gains are confirmed strikingly by the check, which covered 10 disparate areas from Maine to Arizona.

In every area checked, there has been substantial improvement in Federal assistance. In Pennsylvania, for example, the number of free or reduced-price lunches for needy children has jumped from 25,000 a month in January, 1969, to almost 2.8 million a month.

In South Carolina, the number of recipients of food stamps has gone from 118,000 to almost 270,000 in the same period. In Maine, the number receiving either stamps or surplus food has inreased in a year from 68,000 to 91,000.

In a food stamp line in Collier County, Fla., a mother of 10 said recently: "We never had nothing to eat at all, hardly, until we got stamps. We don't have as much as we like, but it's more than we ever had before in our lives."

Nationally, Administration statistics show that the food stamp program has risen from 3.6 million recipients to 9.3 million in the last year. Spending has increased in three years from $248-million in 1969 to a projected $2-billion starting next July.

The number of needy children receiving free or subsidized school lunches, the Administration says, has doubled in two years, and such lunches should now be available to all eligible children.

Severe Problems Remain

Despite such increases, hunger and malnutrition remain severe problems in several of the areas surveyed.

The number of food stamp recipients in West Virginia has increased almost 50 per cent in two years Yet authorities believe that more than a fifth of the state's families still exist on poor diets.

Margaret Leishman, a nutritionist who works with welfare families in rural Lincoln County, W. Va., says they don't have hunger pangs, but she adds:

"If they didn't have beans, they would all die. That's why you see so many fat people among the poor. But it's not healthy fat."

In Arizona, the authorities estimate that only half of the needy schoolchildren are receiving subsidized school lunches. And, as is true with an estimated 18,000 inter-city schools around the country, those schools with the most needy students often cannot participate.

"They lack cafeteria facilities and can't afford to buy them," says Frances Shenberger, the state's school food services director.

In South Carolina "things are improving," says Paul Matthias, director of the State Human Relations Council, "but too slowly." The number of children in the lunch program has jumped 40,000 in two years, to 182,000. But Mr. Matthias estimates that more than 70,000 other needy children are not served.

Reaching the hard-core poor is only part of the problem, the check discloses. In a number of communities there have been rapid increases among the "newly needy."

In Seattle, unemployment has climbed from almost zero to 15 per cent in 30 months, and the unemployed ironically describe themselves as "inflation fighters."

In the same period, says Mayor Wes Uhlman, the number of food stamp recipients has grown from "next to nothing to 80,000."

Some Obstacles

In feeding the hard-core needy as opposed to the newly needy, says Robert Hatch, Indiana director of the National Welfare Rights Organization, "we've slipped backwards, but we don't know how much."

The obstacles to broader participation are by no means limited to Federal spending levels. In many areas, particularly where surplus food continues to be used rather than stamps some people are too proud to participate. Others do not know how to enroll. Still others are deterred by often complex regulations.

"There are times when they just don't have the $41 needed to purchase the stamps—and two weeks later they will have to come up with another $41," says Arthur Schiff, director of the food stamp program in New York City. "Six consecutive misses and they are dropped from the program. It takes a long time to reapply."

But in several other areas, the Administration is credited with heroic triumphs over red tape. A Detroit official says the subsidized lunch program "is the least cumbersome Federal application I've ever worked with." In South Carolina, remote areas will now get food stamps by mail and from mobile offices.

February 5, 1971

Hunger:

Half a Bowl, Say Critics, Is Not Good Enough

WASHINGTON — Four years ago the affluent society began to discover, incredulously, widespread hunger amidst its plenty. Senators Joseph Clark and Robert Kennedy bore personal — and angry — witness to this fact after a trip through the hovels of the Mississippi Delta. Soon there arose a national demand for Federal action.

The Government's response, grudging at first, has accelerated. But a central question has persisted: Is it enough?

Three public panels have recently reviewed Federal programs to help the hungry, and all have rendered similar answers. In the words of Mrs. Patricia Young, a leading national churchwoman from Scranton, Pa.: "Half-way to the moon would not be considered success and neither should feeding half our hungry citizens."

President Nixon won considerable credit from all three studies — a White House panel, a citizens' board and the Senate Nutrition Committee — for increasing Federal anti-hunger spending dramatically. President Johnson's last budget provided $900-million to finance food programs for six million hungry people. This year's Nixon budget provides $2.8-billion to help 13 million people. An additional $500-million proposed for fiscal 1972 would enlarge the total number helped to nearly 16 million.

But, as witnesses before the review panels pointed out, there are 24 million people living below the Federal poverty standard. At least eight million, therefore, would still go hungry at the end of fiscal 1972.

And so the witnesses asked, what has happened to the spirit of urgency, to President Nixon's "national commitment to put an end to hunger and malnutrition due to poverty"?

That was one of two pledges made by the President in December, 1969, at his massive White House Conference on Food, Nutrition and Health. The other was to hold a conference a year later. It was this follow-up conference Feb. 5 that triggered the current wave of attention to the hunger issue.

The location, however, seemed more calculated to keep the lid on. "It was a candlelit closet in which to hide hunger," one participant said of the follow-up conference, held 150 miles from Washington in colonial Williamsburg for some 80 select participants. Many were sorrowed by the isolation, and at the end of the one-day session more than 20 joined in a rump meeting.

The tenor of the formal and the rump sessions was severe: While the Administration deserves credit for what it has done, it must be more forthright

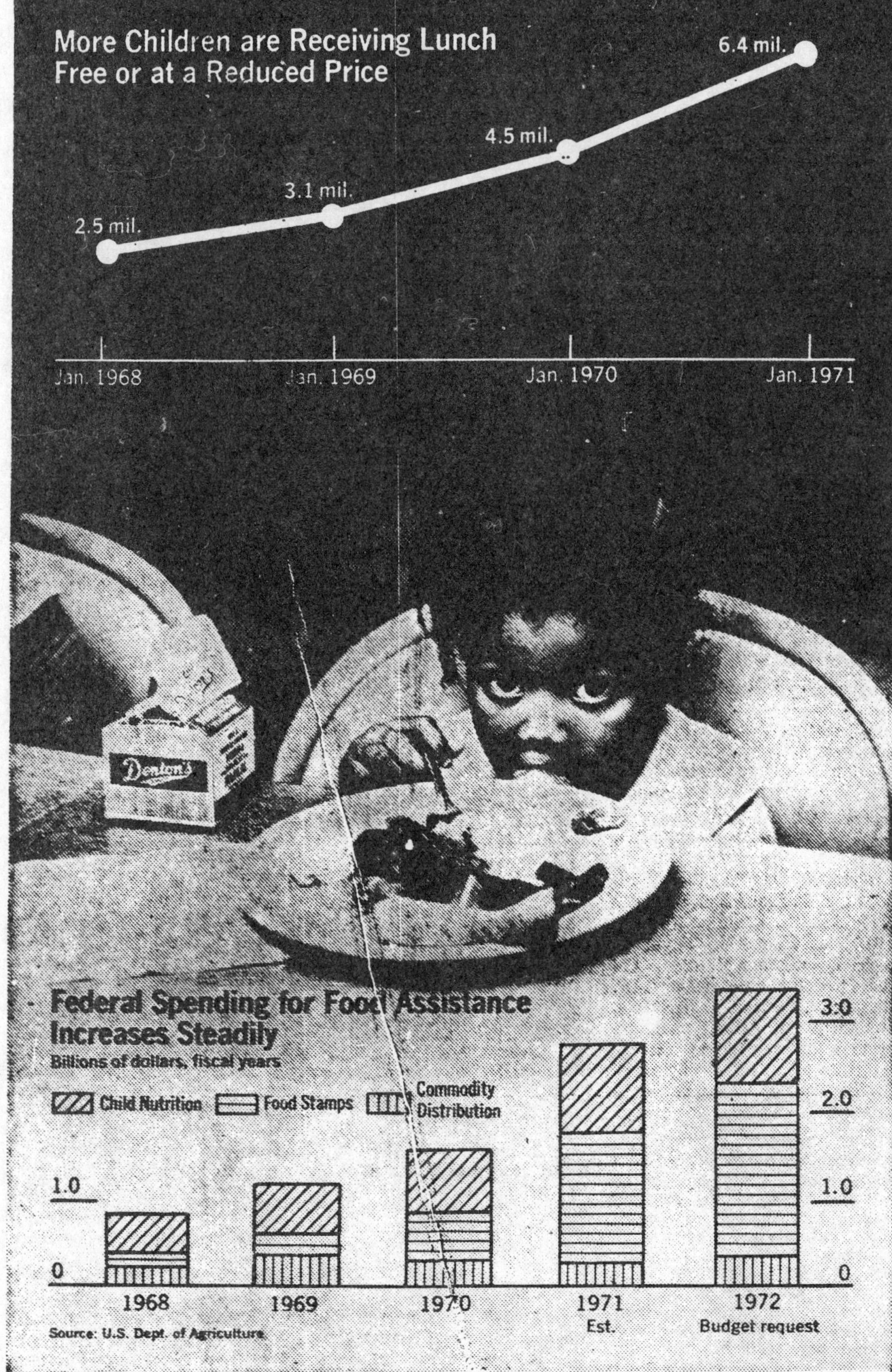

James McKnight

National programs to feed the hungry are increasing, as the charts show, but millions still go hungry. Critics ask: What happened to the spirit of urgency?

— and less frugal — in recognizing how much remains to be done.

These unexpectedly stern noises took some of the edge off the second review of the original White House conference. This was a meeting of the Citizens Board of Inquiry into Hunger, a broadly based body which helped generate the original attention to the issue. It met in Washington Feb. 15.

Where the Williamsburg conferees emphasized the need for more Federal funds, witnesses before the citizens board repeatedly assailed the callousness of state and local food program administrators.

The third round of review came before George McGovern's Senate Nutrition Committee, the leading liberal forum for stronger action against hunger. Hearings to review the program concluded last week with Administration witnesses describing their record as one of "dramatic achievement."

What the committee found most dramatic, however, was the largely technical testimony of Dr. H. Peter Chase, a Colorado pediatrician and student of malnutrition among migrant workers' children.

There were bored whispers in the gallery as he talked about low serum vitamin A, hyperketatosis, and hypertrophic tongue papillae. But then the slide projector flickered and the gallery fell abruptly silent.

For on the wall had come a color picture of a bloated baby, with matchstick arms and legs, named Jesus. "He had marasmus [calorie deficiency] as bad as anything ever seen in Africa," Dr. Chase continued calmly. "He had scurvy, rickets, pneumonia and no detectable Vitamin C in his blood. He was still at his birth weight after four and a half months."

It was an extreme case, Dr. Chase acknowledged. But malnutrition serious enough to stunt growth and jeopardize mental development is widespread among migrant children.

The hunger emergency sensed by the country four years ago, said Senator McGovern soberly, is far from over.

—JACK ROSENTHAL

March 7, 1971

ANEMIA IS FOUND COMMON IN POOR

One-fourth in Survey Have It —Study Is Largest in U.S.

By RICHARD D. LYONS

Special to The New York Times

WASHINGTON, April 29—The Federal Government released results today of a nutritional survey, the largest ever made in the United States, that found anemia and serious vitamin deficiencies in large numbers of the poor.

Of the persons surveyed who were living below the poverty level, one-fourth were found to be anemic to the degree that they needed medical attention.

The $5-million survey conducted by the Department of Health, Education and Welfare also found, in the sampling of 83,000 persons in 10 states, that there were serious deficiencies in vitamins A, B-2 and C.

Caution Advised

While Appalachian and Southern states recorded many of the worst results, the poor who were surveyed in New York City were found to have more serious nutritional deficiencies in some categories than residents of those states.

The introduction to the "Ten-State Nutrition Survey in the United States, 1968-1970, Preliminary Report to the Congress," noted that "one should be cautious in drawing conclusions [because] there is not a precise relationship between these evidences of malnutrition and occurrence of clinical abnormalities."

The release of the report prompted two Democratic Senators to assert that the problem was even worse than the statistics showed.

Senator Ernest F. Hollings of South Carolina, author of the book "The Case Against Hunger," which was published six months ago, complained that the issuance of the report with its interpretations was "an outrage."

"They are continuing to obscure the facts about serious malnutrition in the United States," he said. "They have given a msleading interpretation to these figures and have made the problem appear less than it really is."

Had Urged Release

Seven weeks ago Senator Hollings introduced a Senate resolution urging the Department of Health, Education and Welfare to release the results of the survey, which he then said had been completed a year ago. At that time he complained that the report was being suppressed.

Senator George S. McGovern of South Dakota said that the survey was "long overdue" and complained that he had not been able to read it and offer criticism before publication.

During a hearing of his Select Senate Committee on Hunger and Human Needs, Mr. McGovern said the release of the report was "typical of the shabby treatment of Dr. Schaefer."

The reference was to Dr. Arnold E. Schaefer, the director of the survey, who resigned two months ago from H.E.W. because, according to departmental sources, he felt the report had been downgraded. Dr. Schaefer, who is now with the World Health Organization in Washington, was reported by his office today to be traveling in Europe and unavailable for comment.

Muzzling Was Alleged

Representative Thomas S. Foley, Democrat of Washington, two years ago accused Nixon Administration aides of attempting to "muzzle" Dr. Schaefer when he failed to appear before the House Agriculture Committee to discuss the findings of the study.

At that time, H.E.W. officials denied the charge, but they acknowledged that Dr. Schaefer had been advised not to testify because he had not received departmental clearance to appear before the committee.

Dr. Schaefer's name appears nowhere in the report.

Most of the report's 64 pages contain statistical tables of the data obtained. The survey was conducted in New York, Texas, Louisiana, Kentucky, Michigan, West Virginia, California, Washington, South Carolina and Massachusetts.

Data is presented for race, age, income, education, participation in Federal food programs, heights and weights of children, and the four biochemical tests made: levels of hemoglobin (a component of blood that measures anemia), and vitamins A, C and B-2. The latter also in known as riboflavin.

The hemoglobin level of 25 per cent of 10,629 persons living below the poverty level were found to be either deficient or low. The "deficient or low" category was defined by Dr. Mary McCann, a physician and nutritional expert who worked on the survey, as being a level at which "some kind of medical treatment was indicated."

Twelve per cent of persons living above the poverty level — $3,350 a year for urban families of four—were found to have deficient or low hemoglobin levels.

The number of poor having deficient and low hemoglobin levels ranged from 11 per cent in Massachusetts to 38.9 per cent in Louisiana. The New York City figure was 19.9.

Eight per cent of persons below the poverty level were found to be either low or deficient in vitamin A, which is essential to bone growth and vision. This compares with 7 per cent of persons above the poverty level.

More than 7 per cent of 6,693 poverty-level persons tested for their vitamin C levels scored in the deficient or low range. As to vitamin B-2, 17 per cent of the poor were found to be in the low category, twice the rate of those above the poverty line.

April 30, 1971

FOOD STAMP PLAN BROADLY REVISED

Will Add 1.7 Million Persons —A Move to Bar 275,000 on Welfare Is Dropped

By WILLIAM M. BLAIR

Special to The New York Times

WASHINGTON, July 22—The Nixon Administration backed down today on a controversial proposal that would have cut an estimated 275,000 welfare recipients from the Federal food stamp program.

The Department of Agriculture proposed last April that anyone on welfare in counties and cities participating in the program be ruled ineligible for food stamps. But under bipartisan pressure from members of Congress, the department retained the current provision that households in which all members get public assistance will remain eligible for stamps even if those households exceed new uniform national income standards.

The new and liberalized regulations announced today were described as "sweeping" by Assistant Secretary of Agriculture Richard E. Lyng at a news conference. The revised rules, he said, will add 1.7 million persons to the stamp program. Further, the rules will enable "the poorest of the poor"—an estimated 900,000—to get free stamps for the first time.

Hippies to Lose Stamps

At the same time, revised eligibility requirements will eliminate 65,000 persons from the program and reduce stamp benefits for about two million persons at the upper end of the eligibility scale.

The regulations will also deny food stamps to hippie-type communes and to some college students and other unrelated groups living in the same households. This provision was retained in accordance with the new food stamp law.

Mr. Lyng said that he expected migrant farm workers would benefit from the new regulations.

"More migrants will be eligible simply because of the fact that they are families and can be certified wherever they move," he said. The Department of Health, Education and Welfare had protested to the Agriculture Department that the definition of households would hurt migrants because many live in communal situations.

The revised regulations also retained a hotly debated provision to require all able-bodied adults to register for and accept jobs in return for food stamps. This provision was amended, however, to exempt persons whose health or safety would be jeopardized by work.

Mr. Lyng said that the new program should be in full operation by Jan. 1. He estimated that the $2-billion program would cover 12.5 million persons by the end of the current fiscal year, June 30, 1972. This would be an increase of two million persons over the number now covered.

"Dropouts and eliminations will be more than offset by increases," he said.

He declined to speculate on what would happen if Congress adopted President Nixon's welfare reform proposals, including a family assistance plan. He said that 164 counties had applied for food stamps before the introduction in Congress of the President's plan, but that budget limitations were holding up action on the applications.

Food stamps are sold at rates based on household monthly income. Bonus stamps are given to raise buying power in the grocery store.

Under the previous proposals, the department would have cut off all families with incomes higher than uniform national income eligibility standards, including welfare recipients in states where some persons draw benefits above the standards.

For families in the upper levels of the revised regulations, however, cash benefits will be lower than at present. For example, a family of four now pays $82 in cash for $106 worth of food stamps, thus getting a bonus of $24. Under the new regulations, a family of four at the top of the eligibility scale will pay $99 for $108 worth of stamps, receiving a bonus of only $9 in stamps.

Major benefits will go to families at the lower end of the eligibility standards. A family of four with income of less than $30 a month now pays $2 a month for $106 worth of food stamps. This family will pay nothing for $108 in stamps under the new rules.

July 23, 1971

The Cat Lady's Trying to Survive, Like Everyone Else

By SHANE STEVENS

The old woman with the bandaged legs and flat feet always carries a bunch of bags around. At night she picks up stray cats and sells them to an animal laboratory for fifty cents each. Everybody around here knows the cat lady. We don't like what she's doing but we don't say anything. She's just trying to survive, like everyone else.

The block is crowded. East Ninth Street in what we call the Far East. Down a few houses from me is a mother with five children, one of whom is brain-damaged. When the boy was three, he developed lead poisoning from eating peeling wall paint. The mother remembers he had eaten nothing that day because she had no money and no food in the house. She's not aware that he must have been eating the paint for some time.

Around the corner is a ten-year-old boy who loses whole patches of skin because of a chronic vitamin deficiency. Doctors say it is irreversible.

We have lost the war on poverty. It has ended, this war, not with a bang but with a whimper. The whimpering will go on.

You can hear it, should you want to hear it, in the walls of my tenement on the Lower East Side. The Spanish-speaking couple upstairs, old and infirm, sitting at the window all day, waiting to die far from home. The overweight white woman next door, unable to work, measuring her life in pennies for cheap starches to stay alive. The young black mother with her infant daughter downstairs, husband gone, existing hand-to-mouth on emergency relief.

Or the 47-year-old man up the street who feeds himself and his wife and three children on one dollar a day. Or the innumerable families who live on bread and powdered milk for breakfast, free lunch for the children at school, when there is school, and beans for supper. Or the countless others, mostly old, who eat only one meal a day and have no supper, and so have given up worrying about the rats coming at night because there is nothing for them to eat.

Malnutrition is a major contributory factor in the high infant mortality rate in this country. (We rank thirteenth in infant mortality rate — *thirteenth* — in

David Attie

this richest of all nations.) Malnutrition causes irreversible brain damage to millions of our youngsters. Malnutrition brings on rickets, goiter and the dread kwashiorkor.

Several years ago a doctors' study group (for the Southern Regional Council) reported that the children it saw "were hungry—weak, in pain, sick. They are suffering from hunger and disease, and directly or indirectly they are dying from them—which is exactly what starvation means." More recently a Citizens' Board of Inquiry into Hunger and Malnutrition documented the fact that each year thousands of infants die from lack of food. And another group reported to the Senate Select Committee on Nutrition and Health that malnutrition was so prevalent that it "constitutes a danger to the nation."

It is estimated that ten million Americans are slowly dying from chronic hunger and malnutrition. Another ten million are running growl hungry all the time. At least thirty million are classified poor (the Government-defined poverty level is $3,335 for a family of four). Here in New York almost a million people are getting some kind of welfare assistance. How much assistance? Two years ago the State Legislature cut payments to 66 cents per person per day. Sixty-six cents per person for food—and such luxuries as clothing, household supplies and transportation. Still, even that's better than states such as Texas and Mississippi that give each person about ten cents a day.

It is surely easier to go to work than to starve slowly. Unfortunately, in New York City 97 per cent of those on welfare are mothers, children, the aged and the handicapped, most of whom are eminently unemployable. The story is about the same throughout the country. Perhaps the real tragedy is that the starvation is gradual—and therefore not dramatic. Fact is, it's hardly even noticeable because it occurs in pockets of poverty called slums.

The people in America's slums are eating stale bread that crumbles in your mouth when you chew it. They're eating tomcat stew when they can get the fatback and whatever else can be found to throw in. They're eating sugar and water on a piece of bread, making believe it's a whole meal. They're eating gummy candy bars that drown the teeth but if you eat one slow it can last all day. They're eating grits and gravy for breakfast. They're eating fried flour when there's nothing else. They're eating nothing when there's nothing.

I have been through most of the big towns and many of the smaller cities of this affluent society of ours. I have seen the hungry people. They are easy to see, except for the fact that they are invisible. They're the ones you pass on the street, your eyes straight ahead. They're the ones you dump into shacks on the other side of town or herd into slums. They're the ones you curse for wasting your tax money.

There are millions of them.

There will be no hunger revolution in America. Their bodies are too weak to fight. There will be no hunger marches on Washington. Their spirits are too apathetic to move. And there will be no hunger strikes because to go on strike you first got to have something to strike against. The poor have nothing.

Shane Stevens, novelist, is author of "Way Uptown in Another World."

10% IS IMPOUNDED IN FOOD STAMP AID

Withholding of $202-Million by Administration Brings Capitol Hill Criticism

By JACK ROSENTHAL
Special to The New York Times

WASHINGTON, Jan. 11—Confidential budgetary documents obtained today disclose that the Nixon Administration has impounded $202-million in funds for the campaign against hunger.

The impoundment totals almost 10 per cent of the $2.2-billion in spending appropriated by Congress for the food-stamp program, the major Federal effort for food assistance.

The disclosure stirred some sharp criticism today on Capitol Hill. It is expected to provoke more next week, when Congress reconvenes.

Imminent cuts in the food-stamp program in New York and other industrial states have already prompted rising Congressional and state opposition.

Senator Clifford P. Case, Republican of New Jersey, said that he would seek prompt Congressional action. It appeared likely that he would be joined by Senator George McGovern, Democratic Presidential candidate from South Dakota, who is chairman of the Senate Nutrition Committee.

Administration officials differed today over who ordered the $202-million impoundment. But there was no challenge to the fact of the action.

The Administration's budget request for food stamps for the current fiscal year was $2-billion. Congress, seeking enlargement of the program, last summer added $200-million.

The documents obtained today, however, showed that "adjusted" allowable spending had been cut back to $2-billion, despite the Congressional appropriation.

Sources at the Department of Agriculture, which administers the food stamp program, said that the $202-million impoundment had resulted from decisions made by White House budget officials.

The Office of Management and Budget denied, "without equivocation," that it had ordered the funds held back. The funds are not being spent, an official said, because the Agriculture Department has found they have not been needed.

"I suppose the real answer," a high Government official said, "is that it is neither an Agriculture nor an O.M.B. [Office of Management and Budget] but an Administration decision."

Disclosure of the impoundment, together with rising national opposition to the food stamp cuts, appeared to be prompting an internal reassessment of the cuts.

A week ago, Richard E. Lyng, Assistant Secretary of Agriculture, said, "We're not contemplating any change." Today, asked if his position had changed, he said, "No comment."

The Nixon Administration has expanded the food stamp program dramatically in three years. Since it took office, participation has increased from 3.2 million to 10.5 million people.

The underlying question in a time of budget stringency, officials have said, is "How much is enough?"

Senator Case took a different view today in his statement to the press:

"Since last June, the Department of Agriculture has argued that a prime reason for the food stamp cutback was that it did not have sufficient funds, even though the final legislation signed into law by the President included a $200-million increase."

He continued: "But the department never publicly said that the $200-million had been impounded."

Executive branch impoundment of Congressionally appropriated funds has been a major issue recently. A bill now pending would require the Administration to release about $3-billion in such funds before it can spend new money for foreign aid.

This legislation apparently would not affect the Agriculture Department funds, however, since it is limited to fiscal 1971. The Agriculture Department impounding applies to fiscal 1972, which ends next June 30.

The cuts in the food stamp program result from Agriculture Department regulations implementing the 1971 Food Stamp Act. These are generally effective Feb. 1.

Shift in Recipients

The regulations would bring an estimated 1.7 million additional persons in the South and West into the program. The additional costs are to be offset by reducing or eliminating benefits for an estimated 2.1 million recipients, largely from Northeastern states.

These cuts were protested by 28 Senators in a joint letter to the Agriculture Department on Dec. 19. This letter has not yet been answered, Kenneth Schlossberg, director of the Senate Nutrition Committee, said, today.

"There's no question now that there will be further protest to the Administration," he said.

January 12, 1972

2.1 MILLION TO GET FULL RESTORATION OF FOOD STAMP AID

Administration Reverses Its Policy on Planned Cuts—500,000 Affected Here

By JACK ROSENTHAL
Special to The New York Times

WASHINGTON, Jan. 16—In a major policy turnaround, the Nixon Administration ordered the restoration today of full food stamp benefits to 2.1 million needy poor persons in New York and other industrial states.

The action reverses cuts that would have begun Feb. 1 in most of these states. About 500,000 people would have been affected in New York City alone.

The reversal was announced by Earl L. Butz, the Secretary of Agriculture. It came after extensive Senate and state pressure, notably from leading Republican Governors.

The Administration had resisted these pressures for weeks. But once the turnaround was announced, the Government machinery went to work immediately.

Specialists Called In

If revised regulations can be issued quickly, the food stamp cuts now will never go into effect. Hence, Agriculture Department specialists were called in for Sunday work to begin the complex task of revising the regulations and detailed benefit tables.

Food stamps are certificates sold to the poor at discount prices for use in buying food. A typical participant now pays $4.50 for stamps worth $10 in food.

The program, which is the Federal Government's major antihunger effort, already reaches 11 million needy people and is expected to reach 13 million by March.

Congress has appropriated $2.2-billion for the program in the current fiscal year, ending June 30. It was disclosed last week, however, that the Administration planned to withhold about $200-million of this total.

The disclosure intensified criticism of the announced cuts in the program. Secretary Butz made it clear today that this withheld money would be used to offset the now-eliminated cuts.

The annual cost of the new policy announced today is estimated at $300-million. The cost for the remainder of the current fiscal year is estimated at more than $100-million.

Prior to today's announcement, about 75,000 persons would have been eliminated from the program and 2 million would have seen their benefits reduced.

Thus, a family of four in New York City with a monthly in-

United Press International
Earl L. Butz

come of $360 would have been eligible only for a $9 monthly bonus—paying $99 for stamps worth $108. The family's present bonus is $24.

Mr. Butz said in his statement today, however, that he had ordered new regulations insuring that "the benefits available to each household are as high or higher than they were under the old regulations."

Thus, the same New York City family of four will continue to receive a $24 bonus—paying $84 for stamps worth $108.

Praised by McGovern

Mr. Butz's announcement was immediately hailed by Senator George McGovern of South Dakota, a candidate for the Democratic Presidential nomination and chairman of the Select Committee on Nutrition and Human Needs.

"This decision is not a victory for the Congress nor for the Department of Agriculture," Senator McGovern said. "It is a victory only for the hungry poor."

Mr. McGovern and other Senators had criticized the cuts as an ironic result of a national uniform eligibility standard that was intended to broaden the program, which Congress passed last year.

Pursuant to this legislation, the Agriculture Department limited participation in the food stamp program to persons with a family income of less than $360 a month.

The cutoff point meant that 1.7 million people would be added to the program for the first time. Most of them are residents of Southern and Western states, which had previously set much lower income levels as the cutoff points for participation in the program. But at the same time, the $360 limit is lower than the cutoff point set in industrial states such as New York, where living costs are higher.

Thus, 2.1 million people in those states would have had their benefits eliminated or reduced. The principal effect may have been even greater. Officials have expressed fears that bonus levels as low as $9 would have discouraged needy people from entering the food stamp program in the first place.

The Agriculture Department defended the regulations by saying it only made sense, given limited funds, to give priority to "the poorest of the poor."

But the department was extensively criticized for serving some poor people at the expense of others, particularly when it was learned that the Administration was withholding $200-million in appropriated funds.

The criticism reached its highest point nine days ago, when representatives of 15 Governors and New York City met in Hartford and issued a strong appeal for abandonment of the cuts. They also called the new administrative requirements an "intolerable burden."

Secretary Butz did not alter these requirements, which are mandated by law, in his policy statement today. But he did promise technical assistance to the states to minimize any difficulty in implementing the newly revised regulations.

January 17, 1972

Panel Finds Half of Poor Still Hungry

By JACK ROSENTHAL
Special to The New York Times

WASHINGTON, Oct. 26—Despite massive gains during the Nixon Administration, half the nation's poor are still going hungry, according to the findings of a leading citizens' organization on malnutrition.

The answer to this "hunger gap," according to the Citizens' Board of Inquiry into Hunger and Malnutrition, is to give cash to the poor and to abandon what the board calls callous and costly bureaucratic alternatives.

The board is a panel of doctors, lawyers, university and foundation officials and other persons whose efforts in 1967 and 1968 were instrumental in turning national attention to hunger as a widespread reality.

Its new findings and recommendations are made in a detailed report, "Hunger U.S.A. Revisited," which is to be published shortly.

Nixon Given Credit

The board gives credit to the Nixon Administration, which, it says, "far more than was true of its predecessor, has had a willingness to move forward."

Since 1967, the report said, Federal antihunger spending has risen from $687-million to $4.3-billion and the number of people served by the food stamp program has risen from 1.8-million to 11.8-million.

Despite these gains, a study by the board found that 43 per cent of the nation's 26 million poor people still received no Federal help. In addition, 12 per cent, the study found, receive substantially less than recommended dietary allowances.

Achieving even these levels has required "the most bitter and exhausting kind of bureaucratic in-fighting" against the Department of Agriculture, the board said.

The department is so cost-conscious, the study found, that last June the department returned $418-million in unspent food assistance funds to the Treasury—more than 10 per cent of the total budgeted for all feeding programs.

The report said that the poor have been left with a system that is so studded with regulation that they can use food stamps to buy ice cream at a carry-out stand but are forbidden to use them to buy fried chicken.

The report said that the system, moreover, was a "jigsaw puzzle" of food programs—32 in the area of child nutrition alone.

The country, according to the report, is not indifferent to its poor but has so far asked the wrong question: "How can we feed the poor?"

"The question," the report said, "ought to have been—from the beginning—not how 'we' can feed 'them' but how they can feed themselves." Instead of an administrative "jungle of mechanisms," the nation should turn to cash assistance, the board concluded.

Tinkering with this complex system, the board said, "has not worked, is not working, and never will work."

Cost Question Left Open

The board did not explicitly deal with the cost of a cash-assistance alternative, but it appeared prepared to endorse a guaranteed income for families suffering hunger and malnutrition that equals the federally defined poverty level. This is now about $4,000 for an urban family of four.

This is significantly higher than the guarantee of $2,400 that would have been provided by the Administration's welfare reform plan, which died in the Senate early this month.

The board of inquiry's cash-aid solution would also involve substantially larger Federal subsidies for the school lunch program. The board would have the Federal Government support free school lunches for all children, not merely, as now, for needy children.

According to an analysis made for the board by John Kramer, director of the National Council on Hunger, there are major "hunger gaps" in most current Federal programs.

The largest occurs in the food stamp program, under which needy persons can buy coupons worth more than their face value when exchanged for food. This is now the major family feeding program.

Mr. Kramer reported that 11.8 million persons were now participating in the program, plus three million others who receive food parcels rather than stamps. That leaves some 11 million of the nation's 26 million poor people outside the reach of Federal programs.

In the school lunch program, the gap was considerably narrower. Of about 10 million needy children, some 8.4 million are now being served. But the board found that children in 18,000 schools without kitchen equipment remained unable to participate.

The Administration has opposed making sizable sums available to provide such equipment, the board said.

The board gives substantial credit for the antihunger gains to Congressional vigilance and pressure, notably by Senator George McGovern and his Senate nutrition subcommittee.

October 27, 1972

NATION IS TERMED BADLY NOURISHED

Hearing Is Told Nutritional Ignorance Costs Billions

By JACK ROSENTHAL
Special to The New York Times

WASHINGTON, Dec. 5 — Americans have turned into a nation of nutritional illiterates who know so little about what to eat that the annual cost of malnutrition among rich and poor alike may be $30-billion, several experts told a Senate committee today.

One of them, Dr. Jean Mayer, a Harvard professor who is an adviser to the President, said the answer was for the public and private sectors together to spend at least $100-million a year on public nutrition education.

Such an amount, he said at a hearing of the Senate Committee of Nutrition and Human Needs, would be only a tenth of one per cent of total food expenditures. And it would be less than is now spent on food advertising, which, he said, "too often represents a massive threat to nutrition education."

He and other witnesses outlined a catalog of social costs now exacted by public ignorance of nutrition that included the following:

¶There is extensive malnutrition in America today. Only some of it is attributable to poverty. Even among those who can afford to eat properly, there is unhealthy overuse of fats, sugar and alcohol, and overconfidence in "health" foods.

¶The public engages in what Dr. Mayer called widespread, "foolish" over-reliance on "the ridiculous propaganda" of faddish diet book authors. People have no clear idea that weight is a function of how many calories go in from food and how many go out from exercise.

¶Advertising has "glorified, out of proportion to their nutritional contribution," some processed foods, said Robert Choate, a noted critic of "empty calorie" products and their merchandising.

¶Children, particularly, have been converted, through television ads, into in-the-home hucksters of junk food. "Few men sitting on this hill," Mr. Choate testified, "understand the nagging capacity of a child who views 5,000 food commercials a year—the figure for even a moderate TV-watching child."

Schweiker in the Chair

The characterization of the United States as a nation of nutritional illiterates came from Senator Richard S. Schweiker, Republican of Pennsylvania, who chaired the hearing in the absence of Senator George McGovern, Democrat of South Dakota.

The hearing, the first in a series, marked a new direction for the committee. In the last four years it has repeatedly sought to goad the executive branch into more effective action against hunger on behalf of the poor.

All the witnesses at today's hearing strongly recommended an effort toward national nutritional education, for persons at all levels.

"We estimate the annual cost to our country from hunger and . . . personal mismanagement of food to the detriment of one's health is approximately $30-billion," said Dr. George M. Briggs and Helen D. Ullrich, two California nutrition experts.

They exhorted the food industry to live up to "the responsibility to produce nutritious fods."

"The development of fabricated foods containing nothing but calories is irresponsible," they said.

And, like Dr. George Christakis of the Mount Sinai School of Medicine in New York, they called for nutrition education in schools and for doctors, dentists, and other health professionals.

Children once had first-hand exposure to food and to nutrition, Mr. Choate said in his testimony, at least until World War II, he continued.

"Whether it was shelling peas, scrubbing potatoes, rolling pie crust or cleaning fish, the child of that generation picked up food knowledge by helping in the kitchen."

But with new food technology, he went on, "fun foods and convenience foods became the rallying cry of food merchandising . . . nutrition losses in the ever more sophisticated manufacturing processes were ignored."

Mr. Choate won wide attention two years ago with his criticism of the nutritional content of dry breakfast cereals.

His concern over nutrition ignorance was paralleled by Dr. Briggs: "Mother is no longer the major source of knowledge for food selection. The sources now are the label, the ad, the menu, the grocery store or the school."

"People are eating even less than in 1900," he said, but exercise has decreased so much faster "that the resulting excess of food is there for all to see" around people's middles.

December 6, 1972

12 MILLION FOUND INADEQUATELY FED

Senate Study Notes Recent Rise in Food Prices

By RICHARD D. LYONS
Special to The New York Times

WASHINGTON, May 6—Despite the steady abatement of hunger as a problem since it drew significant national attention five years ago, more than 12 million Americans are still malnourished, according to a Senate study made public today.

While the study found a steady drop in the number of malnourished Americans since 1968, when the figure was 18 million, it said that recent rises in food costs may have reversed the trend. Then it added:

"A critical deterioration of the nutritional value of Federal food assistance has happened recently as a direct result of unprecedented food-price rises in the past few months."

The report, "Hunger—1973," was prepared by the staff of the Senate Select Committee on Nutrition and Human Needs under the chairmanship of Senator George McGovern, Democrat of South Dakota.

Many More Fed

Since Federal efforts to feed the poor started in the late nineteen-sixties, the number of people receiving aid has risen from five million to 15 million at a cost of $4-billion a year for food stamps, school breakfast and lunch programs, day care and surplus food for families in institutions. A food program for the elderly has yet to start.

Noting that from 25 million to 30 million people are eligible for food assistance, the report added, "The fact that only 15 million of the poor participate in any food assistance program, and that none of the programs assure nutritional adequacy for those being served, indicates that the hunger gap is far from closed either for the country or the individuals concerned."

Some Federal food programs have been unable to buy meat, fruit and dairy products in the last two months because of high prices, the report said, adding that if food costs continued to increase, "the poor on commodity distribution may soon find themselves having nothing at all."

Comparison Made With '68

The study was undertaken to determine the effect of Federal food programs since a 1968 report, "Hunger, U.S.A.," was instrumental in turning national attention to the problem. The initial report was issued by a citizens' board of inquiry that was composed of doctors, lawyers and officials of universities and foundations.

Both the 1968 report and the one issued today were intended to prompt greater Federal efforts to continue or increase programs aimed at feeding larger numbers of hungry Americans.

The Senate committee's survey, on a county-by-county basis, identified 263 current "hunger counties," as against 280 in 1968. Neither study found any of these counties in New York, New Jersey or Connecticut. Most were in Southern or Border States.

The report noted, however, "One of the most striking changes in food assistance in the past five years is the overall improvement in program participation in the South. Generally speaking, the Southern states, which included the poorest and hungriest of our nation's poor in 1968, now are feeding a significant percentage of their poor." Exceptions to this trend were noted in Arkansas, North Carolina and Virginia.

Two Areas Praised

The report continued, "The states which do the best job of feeding their poor are the New England states and the states of the Far West. In California, for example, 30 of the 56 counties provide food assistance to over 60 per cent of the poor in those counties. On the other hand, the states in the Midwest are less successful in terms of the percentage of poor who participate in the food programs."

The report concluded that food assistance programs enacted by Congress in the nineteen-sixties may have become outdated because of differing conditions today, such as the rapid rises in food prices.

It also said that recipients of food stamps living in high-cost urban areas, especially in the Northeast or Middle West, "cannot even afford to buy the nationally averaged foods on which the plan is based."

"For a family of four," the report said, "the food stamp program offers less than $1 per person per day. For larger families, the benefits are substantially smaller. And although food costs continue to spiral upward, Department of Agriculture increases in food-stamp benefits lag behind.

"The poor who must depend on the donated foods program get far less. At its theoretical best, the commodity program provides only 53 cents per person per day in food value. In actual practice, the average value of the foods distributed is only about $7 per month, or 23 cents per person per day."

But, the report said, "each of the 3.3 million recipients of donated foods shows up on the charts that proclaim the food gap is closed. Those who must depend on the irregularly delivered, monotonous, poorly packaged lard, pinto beans and peanut butter that the program provides would probably not come to the same conclusion."

May 7, 1973

Hunger's Lifelong Effects

The "proven reserves" of a nation's human resources are babies. Yet, when some babies and their mothers are hungry and malnourished, part of the resource is being wasted, and that, according to a recent staff report from the Senate's Select Committee on Nutrition and Human Needs, is what is happening in the United States.

The discussion is both humanitarian and pragmatic. A hungry baby is heart-breaking when there is no food to give him. But to leave him hungry for months or years may be to mar him for life.

The reason is that the period of fetal development and the first year-and-a-half after birth are crucial for the physiological growth of human beings. Human brain cells multiply most rapidly in the fifth and sixth months of pregnancy, and progressively slower after birth. By the time he is 18 months old, a baby has all the neurons, or brain nerve cells, he will ever have. If a baby has been starved of protein, the building block of body tissues, during the critical period immediately before and after birth, there may be no way of undoing the damage to his brain.

Even without postulating such severe physiological damage, current statistics demonstrate that malnutrition is the common denominator of a series of major health problems. They also show that disease and social deprivation are concomitants of destructive effects on mind and personality, and that malnutrition and poverty are inextricably linked. The Senate committee report, for example, estimated that 75 to 85 per cent of the approximately 150,000 reported mentally defective and retarded children born in the United States each year are born in poverty. In 1970, according to the United States Census Bureau, the number of families at poverty level ($4,900 or under) with retarded children under 18 was 3,490,419.

Just how many of the reported cases of defective and retarded children are direct results of poor nourishment of the growing child, and how many the result of social deprivation, is not known. But in one important sense, it makes little difference. As Dr. Charles U. Lowe, chairman of the Committee on Nutrition of the American Academy of Pediatrics, put it a few years ago: "There is no evidence that feeding people makes them smart. But it is indisputable that hunger makes them dull."

Among the findings of recent scientific studies on infant and maternal nutrition are:

- Mothers who are poorly nourished during pregnancy are likely to give birth to low-birth-weight, or premature, babies. Researchers have also found evidence that suggests that a mother who was herself poorly nourished as a child may not be able to provide the nourishment the baby in her womb needs. And if such a mother is not properly fed while she is pregnant, her baby's potential handicap is even greater.
- Low-birth-weight babies are more likely than other babies to die at birth or during the first year of their lives. The American Academy of Pediatrics Committee on Nutrition has estimated that 70 per cent of the at least 50,000 infant deaths reported in the United States are deaths of low-birth-weight babies.
- The survivors who have been poorly nourished before birth are more likely to suffer from physical and behavioral problems. If they are themselves deprived of a proper diet, their problems are accentuated. According to the American Academy on Pediatrics Committee, a significant number have demonstrable intellectual or behavioral deficits by the time they reach school age. Growth retardation and susceptibility to infectious diseases are also considered by some experts to be malnutrition based.

Through Malnutrition, Wasting Human Resources—Babies

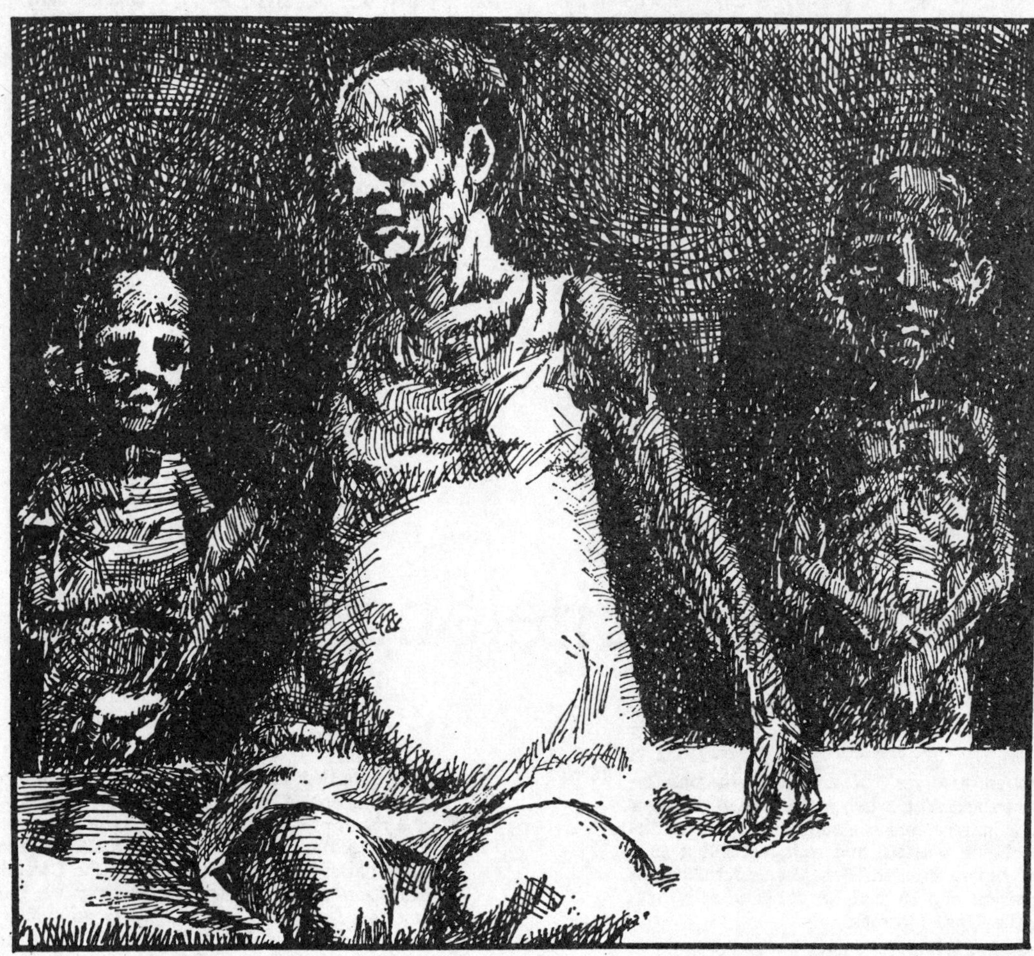

Lloyd Stevens

How severe does malnutrition have to be to cause irreversible damage? Research in rats, for example, has proven that severe malnutrition during pregnancy means that mothers produce young whose brains not only have fewer nerve cells than normal, but also are smaller than normal. Studies of gravely malnourished human babies who have died during infancy have shown the same thing.

Disagreement on Effects

In scientific terms, there are three degrees of malnutrition: severe, moderate, and mild. Experts have argued about the extent to which the findings in severely malnourished animal and human populations, such as Chile or Biafra, can be applied to the moderate and mild degrees of malnutrition generally found in the United States, where the material standard of living is the highest in the world. Statistical comparisons of infant mortality and mother and infant malnutrition rates don't give the answer because few countries' (including the United States') records are complete, and most countries maintain their records in different ways.

Scientists also disagree about how permanent the effects of moderate and mild malnutrition might be. Conceivably, the damage might not be entirely irreversible.

But few argue with the fact that whatever the degree of malnutrition, it wastes lives, or at least portions of them, and in a tragic and expensive fashion. And almost all agree that in the United States, malnutrition is not only almost totally preventable, but prevention is cheaper than coping with its aftereffects. A supplemental feeding program funded through the United States Department of Agriculture that provides families with checks for use in retail food stores started operation April 19, in Newark, N. J. It is expected to serve about 7,000 people and cost $1.6-million a year. Total Federal funding for similar programs is $35-million for the current fiscal year. Four years ago, New York State alone spent nearly $126-million on the 26,459 mentally retarded children and adults in the 14 public institutions for their care.

While scientists continue to work on the exact degree to which the three classes of malnutrition affect mental retardation, nutritionists, and the Senate select committee's report, argue that there is no need for the Government to wait for the conclusive answer to justify providing mothers and babies with good food.

U.S. NEEDY FOUND POORER, HUNGRIER THAN 4 YEARS AGO

Senate Unit Also Hears Rise in World Food Output Is of Little Benefit Abroad

REPORT OF 100 EXPERTS

Prospect for Improvement Called Grim Without Big Changes on Broad Front

By WILLIAM ROBBINS
Special to The New York Times

WASHINGTON, June 19 — The needy in this country are hungrier and poorer than they were four years ago, despite great increases in spending on food programs, and rising world agricultural output has brought little benefit to the hungry abroad, a wide range of experts told the Senate today.

Furthermore, the outlook for improvement is grim without massive changes in production and distribution systems, population patterns, income levels and aid programs, the experts told the Senate Select Committee on Nutrition and Human Needs.

These were among the conclusions of a four-month study by about 100 specialists from universities, business and the professions, who had been commissioned by the committee to explore world food and nutrition problems.

The committee was divided into two panels to conduct hearings on the experts' reports in two large conference rooms crowded with listeners. The hearings will continue through Friday.

'Plowshares for Peace'

In opening one of the hearings, Senator George McGovern, Democrat of South Dakota, who is chairman of the committee, proposed a "great American initiative" that he called "plowshares for peace."

"I believe this conference should be an opportunity for a new, bolder initiative," Senator McGovern said. "If food for peace was the great American international agricultural initiative of the nineteen-sixties, then I believe that another kind of program — one that might be called plowshares for peace — might be the great American initiative for the nineteen-seventies and beyond."

His proposal, especially, was a program that would help developing countries become more productive and incorporate some of the recommendations from the study group.

In the United States, inflation has exacted a heavy toll on the poor and the aged, the head of one panel of the experts reported.

"Over the past three to four years, our nation's needy have become hungrier and poorer," said Ronald Pollack, director of the Food Research and Action Center of New York, who headed a 26-member study panel on "nutrition and special groups."

Mr. Pollack noted that Federal spending on food programs had increased three-fold between the fiscal year 1970 and the fiscal year 1974. But he said:

"I would be pleased to tell you that we have made substantial progress in the effort to eradicate hunger. However, to do so would be untruthful. For the sad and tragic truth is that, over the past several years, we have moved backwards in our struggle to end hunger, poverty and malnutrition."

Mr. Pollack's testimony was based on a 185-page report by his group, which illustrated the slide of the needy into deeper poverty.

Between March, 1973, and last March, the study showed, the retail cost of the Agriculture Department's Economy Food Plan—that on which food stamp allocations are based—increased 21 per cent, while the retail cost of the department's Liberal Food Plan — designed for higher-income families — increased 16.9 per cent.

'Spending Down'

One reason, the report showed, is that the low-income family spends a larger proportion of its income for food. Another is that higher-income families have been "spending down," that is, buying cheaper types of food, an option that is not available to the poor.

"There simply were no cheaper food items to which they could 'spend down,'" Mr. Pollack said.

And because of the increased pressures on the cheaper types of food, their costs have increased disproportionately. He cited these examples:

While pork sausages increased in price by 68.8 per cent between December, 1970, and last March, rib roasts increased 43.3 per cent, hamburgers increased 60.3 per cent, porterhouse steaks increased 38.2 per cent, and while dried beans increased 256 per cent, canned tomatoes increased 20.5 per cent.

The report brought the effects to life on the basis of an interview among a small sample of low-income families around the country. It cited families that had switched to buying dog food for protein, and others with little or no food in their homes and little or no money to buy any, such as the following:

"Several Indian families were found surviving on chocolate bars and stale coffee.

"In Walton County, north Georgia, we visited a family who had been illegally denied food stamps. There was nothing to eat in the house but Wonder Bread and hog jowls.

One reason for the backward slide of poor families, the report showed, was that food costs have risen faster than food stamp allowances and other forms of food assistance and faster than welfare payments.

Improvements Urged

But in the absence of improved incomes or an income-maintenance system, it recommended a number of improvements in food programs.

The report said the aid provided needs to be increased to supply adequate nutritional balance, but — noting that only 35.7 per cent of the 37 million people eligible now receive food stamps — administration of aid programs needs to be improved and greater efforts made to reach those eligible but unaware of the help available.

In another report, on the international food situation, the Senate committee was told that "population growth has literally 'eaten up' almost all of the rather considerable expansion of food production achieved in the developing countries between 1962 and 1972."

The report was presented by D. Gale Johnson of the University of Chicago, co-chairman of a separate panel along with Peter G. Peterson, who is head of Lenman Brothers, Inc., investment bankers, and a former Secretary of Commerce.

Per capita incomes have increased in the developing countries, Mr. Johnson said, but they have been unevenly distributed, and the greater affluence of some has taken food away from poorer people.

Another report recommended increased emphasis on programs to curb population growth as well as the setting aside of world food reserves for emergency needs of developing countries.

Meals for the Elderly

WASHINGTON, June 19 (AP) —The Senate passed by a vote of 90 to 0 today a bill authorizing $600-million to extend the program of providing meals for the elderly in the next three years. Sponsors said the program is providing 188,000 meals daily to low-income old persons at 4,714 meal sites.

June 20, 1974

FOOD STAMP FUND FREED BY JUDGE

$280-Million in '73 Surplus Is Ordered Released

Special to The New York Times

MINNEAPOLIS, Oct. 13 — A Federal district judge has ordered the Department of Agriculture to spend nearly $280-million of 1973 funds on the food stamp program instead of returning the money to the United States Treasury.

In a summary judgment Friterday, Judge Miles Lord ruled that the department and Agriculture Secretary Earl L. Butz had violated the law when they refused to spend the money Congress had appropriated for food stamps.

Judge Lord held that Dr. Butz and the department had failed to implement the Food Stamp Act's "outreach" requirement for the development of a program to inform low-income families of their rights to food relief.

Ronald Pollack, director of the Food Research and Action Center of New York, called the ruling "the most important anti-hunger decision that's come down."

Many Held Ignored

According to Mr. Pollack, some 37 million people are eligible for food stamps in the United States but only 14 million are receiving them.

"One of the most important reasons for these people not getting the stamps is that they are not aware they are eligible," he said. "We can now go into every state, force an implemented outreach and get those people into the program."

Mr. Pollack's organization, a legal advocacy program for the poor, brought the suit together with the Minneapolis Legal Aid Society on behalf of the National Welfare Rights Organization and three plaintiffs residing in Minnesota.

For the 1973 fiscal year, ending June 30, 1973, $2.5-billion was allocated by Congress for the food stamp program. At the end of the year, $278-million remained unspent.

The suit charged that the surplus had accumulated because the food stamp program had been inadequately administered by Dr. Butz.

Judge Lord, in his ruling, said: "The Court finds that the budget surplus at issue here would have been spent if the defendants had complied with Congressional directives regarding outreach allowance.

"For example, had there been only a 13 per cent increase in food stamp participation during fiscal year 1973, an increase the Court considers minimal if effective action had been required throughout the fiscal year, the entire appropriation would have been spent and this lawsuit would never have been brought.

"The data presented to the Court indicates that food stamp participation in fiscal 1973 was essentially static and that the needs of millions of persons remained unmet. The defendants have not challenged the accuracy of that data nor the method of analysis followed by the plaintiffs."

Fewer Found Aided

Although there was an increase of 690,000 persons in the program from April, 1972, to June, 1973, this was offset by a decrease of 893,000 in the commodities distribution program during the same period.

"Taking these two Federal food programs together," said Judge Lord, "there were fewer people receiving Federal food aid in June, 1973, than in April, 1972."

The Food Stamp Act approved by President Nixon in January, 1971, included a provision requiring outreach plans by the states to be approved and enforced by Mr. Butz.

Judge Lord said that many states had delayed more than two years the submission of outreach plans and that most of the plans "evidence a lack of analysis of the state's needs, a lack of thought in devising a plan to meet those needs and a lack of commitment to utilize resources that would satisfy those needs."

"Congress intended outreach action; but inaction at both the state and the Federal level was what actually took place," said Judge Lord. "[Butz's] response to the Congressional directive, when viewed in its totality, is fairly described as a total failure on his part to do what Congress clearly intended him to do."

The judge directed Dr. Butz and his staff to reassess the existing outreach plans and the implementation of those plans by the states to see if they are consistent with the Food Stamp Act requirements. Dr. Butz is to subbmit a report of his findings within 60 days to Judge Lord.

Since 1973, Congress has passed a law requiring that surplus food stamp funds be retained in the program at the end of the fiscal year.

In the past week, however, suits have been filed in 17 states—including Minnesota—against state officials for failure to implement outreach programs.

Mr. Pollack said that Judge Lord's decision would have "a substantial impact" on the 17 new suits. "Now we can just mop up," he said.

October 14, 1974

Food Stamps Draw Miami Beach Outcry

By B. DRUMMOND AYRES Jr.
Special to The New York Times

MIAMI BEACH, March 4— In a striking demonstration of the puzzling nature of the current recession, the poor gathered here today in a steamy community center to bemoan the inadequacies of food stamps while record numbers of the rich frolicked in the cool azure pools at Gold Coast resorts.

"My tongue is hanging out for a dollar for some food," cried Mrs. Goldie Fisher, a frail, 78-year-old woman who was one of several dozen persons to testify in the community center during a special hearing of the Select Senate Committee on Nutrition and Human Needs.

Just down the street, the well-to-do stood in grocery stores, picking through the colorful bins of fresh Florida fruit.

Farther on, the pastel facades of $100,000 condominiums and $100-a-day beach hotels soared from the golden sand toward the warm tropical sun.

A Good Season

Miami Beach is having one of the best tourist seasons in its 50-year history. No one is quite sure why.

Mrs. Fisher is having one of the worst years of her long life, along with 18 million other Americans who must depend on food stamps for subsistence. Today, she and some of her friends tried to explain why to Senator George McGovern, the South Dakota Democrat who is chairman of the special Congressional committee.

They said the $4-billion food stamp program, administered by the Department of Agriculture, is bogged down in red tape, that it is inadequate in these times of high inflation and, worst of all, that it is demeaning.

Procedure Criticized

Earl L. Butz, the Secretary of Agriculture, was the target of a nunber of emotional outbursts that brought cheers from the several hundred persons who came to the hearing, one of a series being held by the Senate committee.

Hy Sachs was one who denounced Dr. Butz. Then, discussing the detailed eight-page form that food stamp applicants must fill out, Mr. Sachs added:

"I'm not asking for charity, only justice. I was made to feel like . . . like . . . well, I won't use the word because ladies are present. I was made to feel like dirt.

"I've worked. I've paid my taxes. I've fought for my country. It's ridiculous."

After a visit at dawn today to a food stamp distribution center in Miami, Senator McGovern also called the registration procedure "ridiculous."

Applicant after applicant—some had been in line since shortly after midnight—told him that the form was too

Associated Press

Senator George McGovern listening to a housewife yesterday at a food stamp distribution center in Miami. He called registration procedures "ridiculous" after finding some applicants had waited on line since shortly after midnight.

complicated, that too many receipts for such items as rent and medical bills were required, and that too many clerks seemed to regard applicants as second-class citizens.

"I waited in line three hours," said Al Langston, "and then when I got ready to buy some stamps they told me they wouldn't take a check, something they'd never warned me about."

Based on Income

Mr. Langston, an unemployed warehouseman, pays $58 in cash each month for stamps that will purchase $122 worth of food. Stamp allotments are based on family income, whether from work or welfare sources.

Senator McGovern said that Secretary Butz was "violating" the food stamp law by not clearing up the the confusion.

"What we need is a form on which a person simply declares a need for stamps, a form that can be picked up at any post office or bank," the Senator said. He added:

"If Mr. Butz is so worried about fraud, let him spot-check the way the tax people do. They have very short forms for low-income people and they have very little fraud, I might note."

Max Serchuk, the president of a senior citizens group, told Mr. McGovern that many persons in the Miami area were going to soup kitchens in search of food.

"I've seen some hot-meal recipients taking leftover food out of the trash can as they turned in their plates," he said.

Naomi Benson, a social worker specializing in nutritional needs, said:

"People will come in [to nongovernment facilities] for hot meals because they are treated with dignity. But they say they won't stand in line for food stamps."

Joseph Cander, a blind recipient of food stamps, said he had been forced by hunger to apply for aid despite his pride.

"It's humiliating," he asserted. "I didn't want to go through that. Oh, the humiliation. I have to come down every four weeks and be recertified. Why?" He added:

"I'd like to see that Mr. Butz investigated. Why did he send all of that grain to Russia and here we are with all these people over here with malnutrition?"

March 5, 1975

EUROPE'S FOOD CRISIS HAS POLITICAL ASPECTS

Humanitarian Reasons Held Coupled With Intent to Halt Radicalism

By MALLORY BROWNE

By Wireless to THE NEW YORK TIMES.

LONDON, April 27—Viewed from London, the present grave food crisis has two connected yet completely different aspects. One is immediate and humanitarian. It is the problem of tiding certain countries of Europe and Asia over the acute hunger period of the next ninety days.

The second is less urgent and more political. It is the question of whether Europe can be helped by food and other forms of economic assistance to choose the way of Western democracy or whether under the pressure of hunger, despair and propaganda, many peoples of the European continent will throw in their lot with Russian communism.

The urgent need for helping to feed the hungry millions of Europe and Asia is fully appreciated in Britain. In London as in Washington it is realized that President Truman summed up this aspect of the world food crisis exactly when he said, "The time for talk is past."

The British Government has acted. It has reduced the standard British two-pound loaf of bread to one and three-quarter pounds, with no reduction in price, to save wheat. It has cut beer supplies by more than 15 per cent to save barley. And it has agreed to divert 200,000 tons of grain from its own stocks during April and May "as an immediate contribution to the urgent problems facing India and South Africa, certain colonial territories, the UNRRA countries and the British zone in Germany.

Willing Sacrifice

Despite the fact that they are and have been for six years rationed right down to the drab dull edge of undernourishment, the people of Britain have taken these fresh cuts without murmuring.

The long-term political implications of the food crisis, on the contrary, are not plain to the general public in Britain. But they are obvious to the Government in Whitehall which is seriously concerned and far from optimistic over the outlook.

For the problem is uncomfortably complex. The underlying issue is fairly clear so long as it is kept carefully in perspective: it is essentially that during the coming months many nations of Europe and Asia must decide on their post-war political course. Germany, Greece, Italy, France, India, among other countries, are all entering or approaching a period during which crucial decisions will be taken affecting their political future for years to come. In greater or less degree these decisions will decide whether the peoples concerned will follow the path of democracy as the Western nations and the United States and Britain understand it, or whether they will feel themselves driven under the lash of hunger to some totalitarian extreme.

Broadly and somewhat oversimplified, that is the picture. But it will not stay in perspective. When you come down to cases it gets fuzzy and out of focus and all sorts of complications creep in.

Importer and Exporter

For instance, the United States and Britain plainly have a common interest in acting jointly to prevent the countries of western Europe, the Mediterranean and the Pacific from going Communist whether from hunger or a combination of that and other causes. But to obtain a common policy in practice is not easy.

The trouble is that Britain is an importer of food, particularly cereals, while the United States, on the contrary, is a producer and exporter. This difference, combined with the fact that the British find it hard to understand the American habit of feeding large quantities of grain to livestock, has led to some tension and even bitterness in the councils of the Joint Food Board. Furthermore, while Britain and the United States—or rather the British and American Governments—are equally aware of the importance of a common, or at least a parallel food policy, aimed at supporting the democratic elements in Europe, they have differences of opinion as to just how it ought to be done.

For example, Britain takes the attitude that nothing is more important than to relieve the famine threat in India. The United States, on the other hand, is inclined to feel that India is Britain's burden so far as food is concerned and wants priority in food relief given to UNRRA countries such as Italy, Czechoslovakia, Poland, etc.

Another instance: the British Government feels that in central Europe the most urgent task is to bring the people of the British zone in Germany up above the low calory level—less than 1,000—to which they have fallen.

The American authorities, on the other hand, view the Austria area where there is direct need for food relief as of greater importance. But both agree that it is in Germany—or rather generally along the fringe of the "iron curtain" which separates the Soviet belt of "friendly Governments" from those still retaining some contact with the west—that the political aspect of the food crisis is most important.

For the plain fact is that it has not proved possible to keep politics out of food.

Food in Politics

Not long ago the Communist Daily Worker in London said that food is "an international political weapon." Moscow brandished this weapon openly when it agreed to send wheat to France on the eve of the coming elections, while re-

"AND THE HARVEST?"

Hutton in The Philadelphia Inquirer

WHAT THE NATIONS EAT AND WHAT THEY NEED

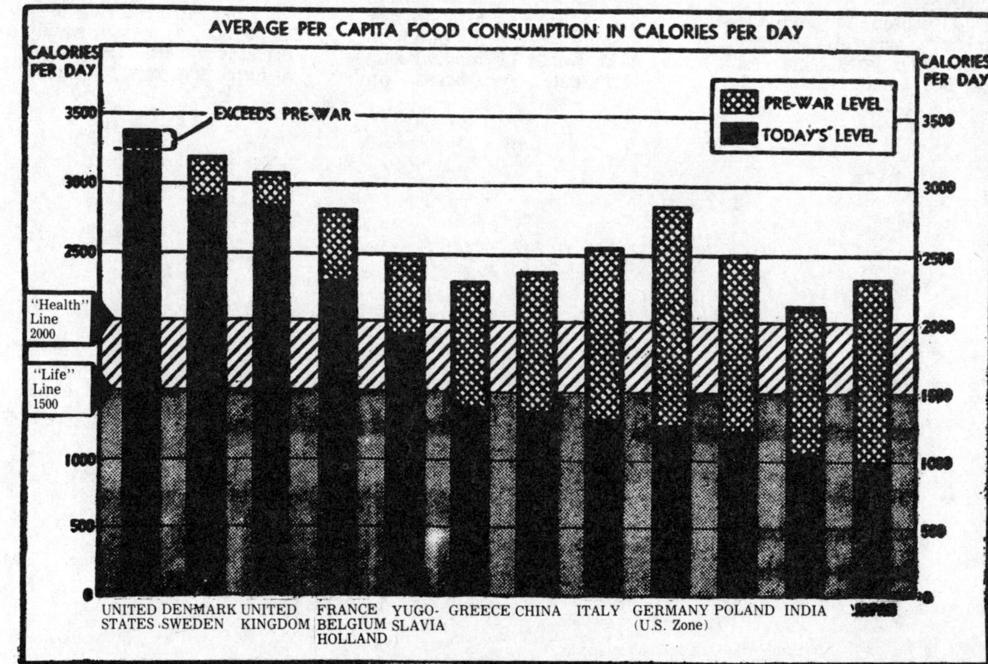

The chart is based on information from the OFAR, the UNRRA and various relief organizations.

fusing to take part in the emergency conference in London. With the exception of Poland, not a single nation in the Russian orbit agreed to attend this meeting. Yet the Soviets have left Czechoslovakia, Yugoslavia and Poland to be helped by the UNRRA, though all three are behind her "iron curtain."

In Germany, on the contrary, such slender evidence as is available indicates that the Russians are taking good care to feed the Germans in their zone so as to help the Communist party in Germany. Actually the eastern portion of Germany inside the Russian zone grows ample wheat and most other foods, while the British zone in the west is mainly industrial.

One fact that is beginning to be appreciated in London is that, politically speaking, it is no use feeding the Germans unless they know it. In other words, while the Russians in their zone have a propaganda machine which makes the most of the little it does for the Germans and turns it to the use of its pet, the German Communist party, in the British zone, until lately, Germans were not even being told in the press and on the radio that a large portion of their food ration was supplied by Britain, or rather by the Allies. This is now being remedied.

The Case of Greece

It remains to be seen just how much the food factor really weighs in this political struggle not only in Germany but in other countries of Europe and Asia. In Greece, for instance, there were so many conflicting elements in the situation that it is impossible to say exactly or even approximately how big a part hunger played in the results of the Greek elections and how much the effect of hunger was offset by the assistance of UNRRA in providing food and clothes.

Taking the longer view, however, it is generally believed that neither hunger nor food gifts will decide any one particular election; in the end the economic state of a people, including its standard of living, will influence its political course, perhaps decisively.

And so the struggle, half humanitarian, half political, and not without some mixture of commercial motives as well, goes on. Britain and the United States are doing if not their best at least a great deal to help the hungry peoples of other countries and at the same time to encourage them to follow the ways of the west rather than the communism of Moscow.

The outlook as seen from London is not bright though neither could it be called black. Britain's Labor Government, believing in Social democracy for Britons, clings to a belief in it for Europe as well. Less doctrinaire observers are less optimistic. All agree that the prospects in Europe will not be bright until the specter of hunger has been banished, and it looks at present as if that task alone may be a long and hard one.

April 28, 1946

CABINET REJECTS WORLD FOOD PLAN

Truman Aides Oppose Board to Control Prices—British May Back This View

By JOHN H. CRIDER
Special to THE NEW YORK TIMES.

WASHINGTON, Aug. 8—The proposals for a World Food Board, published yesterday by the Food and Agricultural Organization, already have been unanimously rejected by the Cabinet of President Truman. There is also reason to believe that the United Kingdom may support the United States' position at the international conference at Copenhagen on Sept. 2, which will consider the proposed board.

The plan for an international body to control prices of international food commodities by "buffer stock operations" is referred to by agricultural experts as "the Orr Plan" because Sir John Boyd Orr, Director General of FAO, is regarded as its principal author.

It also is described as an internationalization of the "ever-normal granary" plan instituted in the United States by Henry A. Wallace, as Secretary of Agriculture, in the 1930's.

Because of the alluring possibilities which the Orr plan would hold for countries whose economies depend on exports of agricultural commodities, and, as well, for those countries short on food which would benefit from the relief aspects of the plan, the United States is not expected to have an easy time sidetracking the Orr proposals. The possible help of Great Britain would not avert difficulty, it was said.

In any event, the plan is expected to provoke a fight which will be the highlight of the Copenhagen conference. It will gain in popularity in some quarters, it is felt, because some will be able to argue that the scheme provides a substitute, at least in part, for the expiring United Nations Relief and Rehabilitation Administration.

Norris E. Dodd, Under-Secretary of Agriculture, the United States delegate to the Copenhagen conference, has been instructed to propose that the conference name a committee to study and report back by Dec. 31 on an "alternative" plan to that of Sir John.

The Orr report proposes that the conference name a committee to report back by Dec. 31 on means to implement that specific plan.

Opposition to the plan for a World Food Board plan originated in the Inter-Agency Committee of the American Government which makes policy recommendations on international economic policies. The committee proposed that the American delegate be instructed to ask for appointment of a conference committee to report back on "alternative" plans, which meant it opposed the Orr proposals.

Cabinet Reported in Unity

The Cabinet was reported to have accepted the committee's recommendations unanimously with the result that Mr. Dodd was so instructed.

When some surprise was expressed that Secretary Wallace joined in the Cabinet's action, or at least did not count himself against it, informed officials said that Mr. Wallace took his position of non-opposition to the Cabinet's stand after informing his colleagues that he felt something of this general nature would ultimately have to be adopted.

The ever-normal granary idea, following the story of Joseph in the Old Testament, provides for storing up supplies in time of excess production so that they may be used in time of shortages. One economic effect is supposed to be the support of prices.

Sir John, a British food authority, former representative of the Scottish Universities in Parliament, and author of the study called "Food, Health, and Income," has applied this general idea to the critical problem of food commodities in the world market.

Technically classed as part of "a buffer stock" operation, the proposed World Food Board would fix a minimum and maximum permissible price range for each of the controlled commodities, buying them when they fell below the minimum, and selling them when they rose above the maximum.

The Orr proposal is said to differ from the conventional "buffer stock" operation in that it adds an additional operation under which the board would dispose of "surplus agricultural products on special terms to countries where the need for them is most urgent." This is the relief aspect of the plan.

What most amazed American experts, it was stated, was the sidetracking in the plan of the financial issue. The plan would, on its face, involve very large expenditures making the proposed board, in the view of some critics, the most potentially expensive of any international organization heretofore proposed.

There is a suspicion among some experts, of course, that the United States would be required to pay any such bill, or at least the greater part of it. William L. Clayton, Under-Secretary of State for Economic Affairs, recently stated, apropos of UNRRA, that "the gravy train is going round for the last time."

Just as apprehensive as United States officials, but not in so good a position to stem the tide, are said to be officials of the World Bank, who read with some concern the following paragraph of the Orr report.

"The means whereby the credits are made available is a question for the consideration of financial experts, to whom this aspect of the policy must be referred. This would clearly be a matter suitable for the consideration of the International (World) Bank for Reconstruction and Development."

Officials of the world financial institution had never regarded their organization as intended to finance the dietary relief of undernourished populations, officials said. Sir John, however, connected his plan with at least the official title of the world financial institution by saying in his report that "development can proceed rapidly only on a basis of improved education and health services." That was regarded as his interpretation of the word "development" in the "International Bank for Reconstruction and Development."

Probably as important a criticism of the plan from the United States viewpoint as the financial one is what is classed in official quarters as a direct conflict with the commodity proposals contained in the "charter" of trade principles promulgated by the State Department. These have been subscribed to "in principle" by the United Kingdom.

The basic idea of these commodity proposals, which will be moved for adoption at the World Trade Conference next summer, is to use international commodity controls only as interim devices until the causes of surpluses and maldistribution of food can be removed.

The British, major world purchasers of food commodities, are said to oppose the idea of an international board controlling the prices of such a large part of their essential imports.

August 9, 1946

WORLD FOOD BOARD ENDORSED BY FAO

Orr Plan for Stabilizing Prices of Basic Foods Also Backed as Conference Ends

DIRECTOR STRESSES SPEED

Presses Projects as Means of Dispelling Fear of War—Hungary Is Admitted

By **WALTER H. WAGGONER**

Special to THE NEW YORK TIMES.

COPENHAGEN, Denmark, Sept. 13—Sir John Boyd Orr, Director General of the United Nations Food and Agriculture Organization, appealed today to the world to speed action on a humanitarian food plan to dispel the fear of war, which he said was already "casting its shadow on mankind."

Sir John addressed the closing general session of the second FAO meeting after the conference, with virtually no debate, had formally accepted his proposals for a world food board and an international price stabilization program for basic foodstuffs.

The conference adopted a resolution approving the objectives of raising the world's health standards by improving the production and distribution of foods at prices "fair to producers and consumers alike" and added that it considered international machinery necessary to achieve these objectives.

The session did not formally adjourn but only recessed to convene quickly when a sixteen-member commission has drafted in detail a world food program along the recommended lines. Thus the so-called Orr plan became a United Nations project, the first step in a concrete program for ending world hunger that was conceived in the Hot Springs conference of May, 1943. The Quebec meeting last October was a preparation for this program.

Says Fear Grips World

In a brief message Sir John reminded the forty-seven FAO member nations that "things are not going well in international affairs." He said that fear of another war was gripping the world but that there would be no war if the nations cooperated on a world food plan "based on human needs."

He warned that nations must be prepared to take risks and act on an even broader program than was put forward at the emergency food conference in Washington in May.

AMERICAN FOOD FOR A HUNGRY CZECHOSLOVAK FAMILY

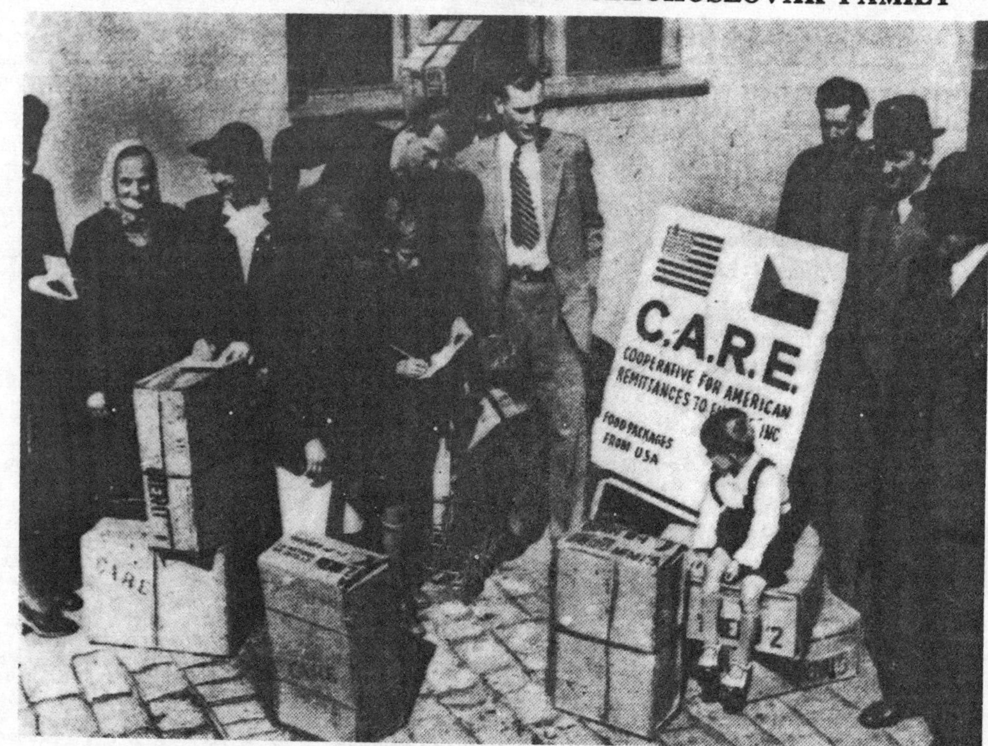

The first "Care" package to be distributed in Prague is turned over to a mother of four. Containing twenty-nine pounds of food, it was one of a large order sent by students of Hunter College here.

There is need for quick action, he said.

Alluding to the absence of the Soviet Union and Argentina from membership, Sir John expressed a hope that more members would be admitted at the next conference.

Hungary was elected to the organization today, joining Italy, Switzerland, Portugal and Ireland, which became members earlier in the conference.

The only opposition to acceptance of a world food board and international price stabilization program put forward today came first from the Union of South Africa, whose delegate said he had been instructed by his Government to approve only "examination" of the project. He explained that he believed that the final resolution, put forward by France and seconded by Australia, carried him beyond this instruction. He said he would have to dissent.

The Canadian and Indian representatives then said that if the South African interpretation was correct they, too, would be unable to support the resolution. Henrik de Kauffman of Denmark, chairman, said he felt that the session needed a review of the resolution, and called on Herbert Broadley of the United Kingdom delegation.

Conflict Is Doubted

Mr. Broadley said he could see no conflict between the French version of the proposal and that discussed in committee. He concluded that it meant that the conference approved the objectives of the world food plan and the price stabilization program, and not necessarily the details of the plan to be prepared by the special commission.

He added that, beyond that, he believed the resolution merely recognized the need for international machinery to achieve the goals desired by the conference.

The text of the resolution:

The conference

Approves the report of its commission of proposals for a world food board,

Accepts the general objectives of the proposals, namely,

Developing and organizing the production, distribution and utilization of the basic foods to provide diets on a health standard for the peoples of all countries,

Stabilizing agricultural prices at levels fair to the producers and consumers alike,

And, considering that international machinery is necessary to achieve these objectives, resolves to establish the preparatory commission suggested in the report of its commission to consider further the proposals and submit recommendations regarding the necessary machinery.

WORLD FOOD PLANS CALLED A U. S. PERIL

Commodity Group Assails FAO, Wallace and La Guardia as Aiding Collectivization Plan

WASHINGTON, Oct. 13 (AP)—Warning that "our whole American system" was in danger, the National Association of Commodity Exchanges and Allied Trades declared tonight that officials sought to subject the country's food distribution to "a world-wide totalitarian system."

The criticism was issued on the eve of a meeting of the International Emergency Food Council here tomorrow. The council of twenty-five nations will review steps to improve the world's food supplies amid reports that the outlook has become darker in recent weeks.

The council is among the international groups which the Exchange Association listed as "involved in the plan" for "regimentation of our agriculture on a worldwide scale."

The association released a letter to Chairman John W. Flannagan Jr. of the House Agriculture Committee urging his group to study what it called "this grave threat" aimed at "collectivization of agriculture on the Soviet model."

In addition to assailing the Council, the letter said that the agency "principally involved" was the United Nations Food and Agricultural Organization.

It declared statements dealing with world food planning had been made by Henry A. Wallace, when he was Secretary of Commerce; F. H. La Guardia, UNRRA director general, and Howard R. Tolley, an official of FAO, which, if spoken "with authority," represented "imminent peril" to American institutions.

In announcing the International Emergency Food Council meeting, D. A. Fitzgerald, its secretary-general, said early forecasts of good crops throughout the world had been hampered by recent reports of the bad harvest weather in Northern Europe.

"The Council is not concerned one way or the other with commodity exchanges," Mr. Fitzgerald said when informed of the criticism of the Association of Commodity Exchanges.

October 14, 1946

U. S. SOFTENS VIEW ON RELIEF SET-UP

Stevenson in U. N. Opposes International Food Body but Does Not Bar Group Aid

Special to THE NEW YORK TIMES.

LAKE SUCCESS, N. Y., Nov. 14—The United States took the position today that it was opposed categorically to the formation of any international organization to take over the problems of the United Nations Relief and Rehabilitation Administration when it goes out of existence.

Adlai Stevenson said at the same time that, in line with this country's determination to continue to help in giving relief, the United States favored "direct and informal" consultations between surplus and deficit countries, with the object of effecting prompt and efficient action.

"Help will be available when it is needed and where it is needed," Mr. Stevenson declared, as he summed up the United States position in a brief and conciliatory statement. This was the high point of a day of speeches in the General Assembly's Economic and Financial Committee as ten nations presented their views on the solution of the world food crisis.

Stevenson's Tone Mild

As he addressed the delegates of the fifty-one member nations, Mr. Stevenson took a mild tone compared with that used in Washington on Tuesday by Dean Acheson, Acting Secretary of State. Mr. Acheson had bluntly stated that Administration opposition to UNRRA Director General Fiorello H. La Guardia's plan for a $400,000,000 emergency food fund was likely.

Today, observers and delegates expressed the view that Mr. Stevenson's more moderate stand opened the way for a possible compromise between the previously stated United States position and that of Mr. La Guardia. This referred particularly to the manner in which consultation between those nations with food to export, and those desirous of importing it, would be carried out.

Mr. Acheson had talked in terms of bilateral discussions between the United States and the individual needy governments. Mr. Stevenson expressed the view that international cooperation should take the simple form of "direct and informal consultation between governments in concerting their efforts."

Mr. La Guardia, present at the meeting to answer any questions that the delegates might address to him, voiced a conviction that a compromise could be worked out between his views and those of Mr. Stevenson.

One such possible basis of compromise was submitted by the Brazilian delegate, Joao Carlos Muniz, in the form of a proposal for an international pool of voluntary contributions to meet the residual needs of countries not satisfactorily benefited by bilateral agreements.

At the same time, through the creation of a committee of representatives of specialized agencies, such as UNRRA, the International Emergency Food Council, surveys and information could be gathered with a view to providing food exporting and food importing countries essential information. The committee would then administer the contribution pool and eliminate disparities between needs and available or anticipated supplies wherever possible.

Norway Is for UNRRA

Aake Ordning of Norway led a list of speakers, who for numerous reasons called for the continuation of UNRRA's functions in one form or another. Declaring that international cooperation should not be a one-man show, Mr. Ordning observed that if every citizen member of the United Nations were to give one day's pay to a fund for unity and peace, the proceeds would total between $750,000,000 and $800,000,000. If only the members of the World Federation of Trade Unions contributed to such a fund, he said, the result would exceed $300,000,000.

Possibly alluding to the recent Yugoslav incident, Mr. Ordning offered one reason that the United States has resisted entering further international agreements for furnishing relief.

"They feel that when you ask a man to help people who not only scold him, but even shoot at him, you really ask a little too much," he said. "Good-will that is shown genuinely and repeatedly deserves a response. Cooperation must be mutual."

Ole B. Kraft of Denmark, endorsing world cooperation in the field of relief, observed that if the United Nations failed in such a practical field as relief, little measure of success could be looked for in other fields. Jan Masaryk of Czechoslovakia and Alexandre Argyropoulos of Greece added their endorsements of Mr. La Guardia's plan.

Mr. Stevenson, pointing to the leading part that the United States had played in the planning and discussions that led up to the formation of UNRRA, declared that it was clear from the outset "that the United States, because we were not bombed, because we were not occupied, and because of our great resources, would have to bear and should bear a large share of the burden during the period immediately following the war."

Discussing the needs for 1947, Mr. Stevenson declared that the countries still needing help would be few and the amount of assistance required would be relatively small.

"This situation requires very different treatment from that which faced us in the immediate post-war emergency," he said. "It is the view of the United States Government that there is no necessity under these circumstances for a new international organization to meet this residual problem. It is not a complicated one and we feel it can best and most efficiently be met by simple and direct means."

November 15, 1946

YUGOSLAV DENOUNCES AIM

Protests Bilateral Aid—Assembly Acts to End UNRRA

Ljubo Leontitch of Yugoslavia, at the session of the United Nations General Assembly at Flushing Meadow last night, denounced the relief resolution approved by the Economic and Financial Committee as the very negation of the principle of international cooperation.

A few minutes later, however, the resolution, which sounded the death knell to the United Nations Relief and Rehabilitation Administration and its method of handling the problem of relief by international concerted action, was adopted unopposed by the Assembly.

As a recipient of nearly $400,000,000 worth of supplies under the UNRRA, Yugoslavia is considered one of the nations that may suffer under the handling of relief by bilateral arrangements.

Mr. Leontitch pointed out that these arrangements would in no way be between equal parties, but between the expression of will on one hand and obedience to necessity on the other.

"Obedience precludes freedom of will," he said. "The United Nations cannot approve of such an action, and still less themselves take part in it."

Adlai E. Stevenson of the United States, who had proposed the original resolution jointly with delegates from the United Kingdom and Brazil, had urged unanimous adoption of the resolution.

"In the considered judgment of my Government, it will be effective—it will serve our common purpose—and relief will be available when needed and where needed," he said.

Through the action of the Assembly, the handling of 1947 relief will be through bilateral arrangements between governments after informal consultation. The only semblance of international action on the problem that remains calls for the setting up of a technical committee to assess needs.

December 12, 1946

FAO Food Plan Backs U. S. On Voluntary Cooperation

By WALTER H. WAGGONER
Special to THE NEW YORK TIMES.

WASHINGTON, Jan. 24—The Preparatory Commission of the United Nations Food and Agriculture Organization proposed today a world food program explicitly placing the responsibility for future international action upon voluntary cooperation by individual nations.

The final report of a three-month session here, at which seventeen nations sought to provide detailed proposals to curb world-wide hunger, was released at a closing general meeting. The outcome clearly represents a victory for the United States, most observers believe.

The United States delegation has opposed from the outset of the meeting on Oct. 28 the formation of a new international body with executive powers or the establishment of the World Food Board proposed by Sir John Boyd Orr, Director-General of the FAO.

Instead of an autonomous and executive World Food Board, with authority over international surpluses and price stabilization plans, the FAO commission has proposed a World Food Council, primarily of an advisory nature. The recommended agency would be a limb of the present FAO, and a "policy link" between that organization and member Governments. An official summary statement outlines the functions of the proposed council as follows:

"Review commodity situations and initiate studies by representatives of interested governments, to examine needs for new commodity agreements or other intergovernmental action, review operating and proposed commodity agreements from the viewpoint of food and agriculture, and aid the FAO Director-General in preparing the agenda and material for the annual program review."

The council would consist of eighteen member governments of the FAO. Several of the other specialized international agencies would be invited to send representatives to meetings. It is emphasized in the report that the United Nations Economic and Social Council should make every possible effort to achieve the cooperation of other agencies with the Council's program.

Led by the State Department, whose choice for a mechanism directing international commodity agreements is the forthcoming International Trade Organization, the United States delegation to the FAO commission has maintained from the start that distribution of food between nations can best be handled on an individual commodity basis through multilateral and inter-governmental pacts.

As a consequence, the report of the FAO group set forth today outlines of recommended programs of several commodities moving in world trade. These included wheat, cotton, sugar, cocoa, rice, livestock products, wool, tea, fish fats and oils, timber and even some non-perishable fruits and vegetables.

The projected agreements would be put into effect much as the program for wheat is directed by the International Wheat Council. In addition, cooperating nations would be asked to maintain special reserves derived from surplus production, so that importing and needy countries might get supplies in times of serious shortages or famines.

Other reserves might be accumulated for price stabilization. When prices rose above a certain predetermined level, supplies would be sold from the reserve. As prices dropped below an established minimum, quantities of the commodity would be diverted into the reserves from surplus production.

Under this plan, needy countries would be expected to limit their distribution of supplies from other nations' reserves to persons actually in need of food.

Emphasizing the need for international cooperation in assuring the success of the proposed program, Lord Bruce, commission chairman, expressed regret that the Soviet Union had not participated in the formulation of the program. He said that he "earnestly" trusted that the Soviet Government would cooperate in putting it into effect.

January 25, 1947

AID BILL IS SIGNED BY TRUMAN AS REPLY TO FOES OF LIBERTY

MARSHALL PRAISES STEP

Hails 'Courage and Wisdom' of Congress—Goods Reported Already on Way to Europe

By HAROLD B. HINTON
Special to THE NEW YORK TIMES.

WASHINGTON, April 3—President Truman signed today the Foreign Assistance Act of 1948, which made the long debated European Recovery Program an actuality. "This measure," he said, "is America's answer to the challenge facing the free world."

The Chief Executive affixed his signature shortly after his return to the capital aboard the Presidential yacht, Williamsburg, from a visit to Williamsburg, Va. A number of the chief architects of the measure witnessed the signing.

It took the European Recovery Program ten months to develop from the bare suggestion known as the Marshall Plan to the detailed legislative project signed today. It originator, George C. Marshall, the Secretary of State, was attending the Inter-American Conference at Bogota, but the following statement was issued on his behalf at the White House:

"The decision of the United States Government as confirmed by the Foreign Assistance Act of 1948 is, I think, an historic step in the foreign policy of this country. The leaders in the Congress and the membership generally have faced a great crisis with courage and wisdom, and with legislative skill, richly deserving of the approval and the determined support of the people."

Witness President's Signature

Mr. Truman, in his own statement, pointed to the efficacy of a Democratic system of free debate under which a bipartisan foreign policy could effectively be enacted into law. Senator Arthur H. Vandenburg, Republican, of Michigan, President Pro Tempore of the Senate and chairman of its Foreign Relations Committee, who is generally credited with guiding the measure to successful passage, witnessed the signature in the president's office.

Others there who had had a hand in forwarding the progress of the legislation included Secretary of the Interior Julius A. Krug, who headed a committee to study whether the nation's resources would stand the strain of a program of this magnitude; Secretary of the Treasury John W. Snyder; Attorney General Tom C. Clark; Postmaster General Jesse M. Donaldson; Secretary of Agriculture Clinton P. Anderson; Under Secretary of State Robert A. Lovett; Senator Tom Connally, Democrat, of Texas; Speaker Joseph W. Martin Jr., and representatives Charles A. Eaton, Republican of New Jersey, chairman of the House Foreign Affairs Committee, and Sol Bloom, Democrat, of New York, its ranking minority member.

Dozen Pens Are Used

The President used a dozen pens to complete his signature to the bill, giving one to each of the witnesses as a souvenir of the occasion.

The measure, which Mr. Truman called "perhaps the greatest venture in constructive statesmanship that any nation has undertaken," authorizes the expenditure in the next twelve months of $6,098,000,000 to provide economic assistance to the sixteen nations of Western Europe along with Western Germany, as well as economic and military aid to China, Greece and Turkey.

It provided for an advance by the Reconstruction Finance Corporation of $1,000,000,000 for European aid and another $100,000,000 for China to finance procurement and shipment until Congress is able to pass the necessary appropriations. The State Department will coordinate all the relief activities for the first thirty days, or until President Truman appoints the Economic Cooperation Administrator provided by the law.

Mr. Lovett, who called the enactment "a terrific accomplishment—a magnificent exhibit of what this government can do in handling a really monumental job," said that some supplies for the program were already moving.

Other officials indicated that Italy, France, Austria, Greece and The Netherlands, where the need is considered urgent, would be among the first to receive shipments.

THE PRESIDENT SIGNING THE FOREIGN AID BILL

Mr. Truman making the ERP measure a law in ceremony at the White House. Looking on (left to right) are Senator Arthur H. Vandenberg, Secretary of the Treasury John W. Snyder, Representative Charles A. Eaton, Senator Tom Connally, Secretary of Interior Julius A. Krug, House Speaker Joseph W. Martin Jr., Representative Sol Bloom and, partly hidden, Secretary of Agriculture Clinton Anderson.

The New York Times (by Tames)

Mr. Lovett said that requests from recipient countries must undergo a continual screening. Many of the desired items are in short supply, he pointed out, and substitutions may have to be made. Because of the petroleum shortage, it had been believed that coal could be substituted, but the coal strike has lessened this possibility.

Truman Requests Largely Met

The authorized program with some exceptions, particularly on the administrative set-up, is what President Truman requested in his message to Congress of last Dec. 19. It received final passage a day after the deadline of April 1 which he set at that time.

A major change in the measure was the addition of $463,000,000 for China, of which $125,000,000 may be spent on military equipment. It also authorized $275,000,000 for military equipment for Greece and Turkey beyond the $400,000,000 granted last year.

Foreign developments, including the Communist coup in Czechoslovakia and the electoral maneuvers the Communists are making in Italy, greatly helped the passage of the bill. Another factor was the acceptance by the Administration of practical advice offered by Senator Vandenberg in regard to minor changes which would lessen opposition among the Congressional majority.

The European Recovery Program had its genesis in a suggestion advanced by Secretary Marshall during a speech at Harvard University on June 5, 1947. He recommended that the European nations get together to see what they could do among themselves to speed economic rehabilitation and to calculate the deficiency. He intimated that the United States would consider to what extent it could make up this deficiency, in the interest of re-establishing peace and security in the world.

The suggestion, informal though it was, met widespread favor in Europe at once. A meeting of the Foreign Ministers of Great Britain, France and the Soviet Union was convoked in Paris within three weeks, but on July 2 Foreign Minister Vyacheslav M. Molotov announced that his Government could not see any merit in the plan and walked out. The Soviet satellite states then imitated its abstention.

Effect of ERP on U. S. Studied

However, representatives of sixteen nations met in Paris on Aug. 30. Under-Secretary of State William L. Clayton went to Paris and offered advice to the conferees. By Sept. 22 they had cast up their accounts and estimated their mutual efforts would fail by a deficit of $19,000,000,000 to assure recovery in the next four years.

While the Paris meeting was still in session a Congressional committee under Representative Christian A. Herter, Republican, of Massachusetts, was traveling around Western Europe securing data by which to evaluate the requests for aid. At home, President Truman called for three reports.

The Council of Economic Advisers was asked to predict the impact of such a program on the economy of the United States. A committee under Secretary Krug was set to work on an inventory of the national natural resources. Another under Secretary of Commerce W. Averell Harriman was directed to consider the industrial and financial strains such a program would impose.

The Soviet satellite states united, on Oct. 5, in what came to be known as the Cominform, in Belgrade and pledged undying opposition to the so-called Marshall Plan.

Congressional committees gathered in Washington early in November to hold hearings on the project. Lewis W. Douglas, Ambassador to Great Britain was brought back to Washington to act as a consultant for Congress on behalf of the Administration.

As the situation in Europe grew more acute, President Truman called a session of Congress to meet on Nov. 17. On Dec. 15, it passed an interim aid bill of $590,000,000 to tide over the neediest countries until April 1.

In another message on Dec. 19, just before the session adjourned, President Truman asked for $17,000,000,000 to be made available for European aid over the next four years. When Congress assembled in January, Senator Vandenberg persuaded the administration to scale down the request to $6,800,000,000 for a period of fifteen months.

April 4, 1948

U. N. SEES GREAT HOPE IN POINT FOUR PLANS

Much Good, It Is Believed, Can Be Done With Support of the U. S.

By THOMAS J. HAMILTON

Special to THE NEW YORK TIMES.

LAKE SUCCESS, Oct. 15 — The effort to raise living standards in the underdeveloped areas of the world is being made in two places.

One is in Washington, where legislation to carry out President Truman's Point Four program—the world "fair deal"—is now before Congress. Although no final action will be taken on the bills at this session, the legislation is expected to have a high priority when Congress reassembles in January.

The second is at Lake Success, where a program for the underdeveloped areas is an outstanding topic of the current session of the United Nations General Assembly. With surprising unanimity the Assembly's Economic and Financial Committee adopted this week proposals of the U. N. Economic and Social Council which call for technical assistance to underdeveloped countries.

Point Four got its name when President Truman listed it in his inaugural address as the fourth element in American foreign policy. The President expressed the need for such a program in these words:

"More than half the people of the world are living in conditions approaching misery. Their food is inadequate. They are victims of disease. Their economic life is primitive and stagnant. Their poverty is a handicap and a threat, both to them and to more prosperous areas."

"Technical and Financial"

The need of these people, Mr. Truman said, was for technical and financial assistance which would help them improve their own living conditions. Such a need would have existed even without the staggering cost of the recent war. The Soviet Union's endorsement of the Point Four program in the U. N.—of course, without acknowledging the fact that it had been sponsored by the United States—is an indication of how much the undeveloped countries need the assistance of engineers, foresters, experts on education, government finance and technology in general.

How can this aid be given? There are several examples of programs already in existence with objectives similar to Point Four's. One is carried on by the Institute of Inter-American Affairs, a State Department agency, and the Interdepartmental Advisory Committee on Technological Assistance, which is now spending $5,000,000 a year. The institute, whose activities are confined to Latin America, has been sending out experts in health, agriculture and education for the past decade. The interdepartmental committee, which began work after the war, has a more general program, including the training of experts in American technical institutions.

ON 'POINT FOUR'

Herblock in The Washington Post

"Want to knock off some Communist allies?"

The United Nations and affiliated international organizations have been trying to do much the same thing, but with much less money—the United Nations has only $288,000 for the current year. An admirable Food and Agricultural Organization study of Greece, and a recent United Nations survey of Haiti, are outstanding examples of its work.

Rockefeller an Example

A third example is found in the activities of Nelson A. Rockefeller, whose International Basic Economy Corporation is going ahead with its own Point Four program without waiting for encouragement from the United States Government or the United Nations.

Operating with only about $22,500,000, part supplied by Mr. Rockefeller and his brothers, the remainder locally, the corporation is successfully using American personnel and techniques to supply milk, fish, farm products and truck transportation to communities in Brazil and Venezuela.

The corporation enlists the help of local capital, limits its earnings to a reasonable figure, and pledges itself to sell out to local enterprises within ten years if they want to take over. Non-profit development work also is being carried out in Brazil and Venezuela by Mr. Rockefeller's American International Association for Social and Economic Development.

As for the why of a new American program, there are many down-to-earth reasons favoring it. The victories of the Chinese Communists have shown what might happen in other underdeveloped areas, and it is obviously in the interests of the United States to take corrective measures while there is still time.

From the economic point of view, sponsors of the program point out that American exports, which have reached unprecedented heights since the war because of the exhaustion of other countries, must be kept at those heights if our present level of prosperity is to be maintained.

Bought in America

The program ultimately would involve the purchase of large quantities of industrial and farm machinery, a large part of which would be bought in the United States.

Since the war the United States has voted $22 billion from the Federal Treasury to aid other countries. Most of this was in outright gifts, and the remainder was in loans, few of which will ever be repaid. Point Four, its sponsors say, offers Americans a chance to get something tangible for their money in the form of factories, railroads and other solid assets.

Just what would Point Four involve for the United States? President Truman has asked Congress for several bills which add up to a rounded Point Four proposal. First of all, he has requested appropriatio of $35,000,000 for a first year of the program. That amount would be in addition to $10,000,000 now being spent annually by the United States for technical aid.

The President intends the $35,000,000 for use by two hands—the United States Government and the United Nations. Perhaps $13,000,000 or $14,000,000 would be contributed to the program of the United Nations and its agencies, and the remainder would be used to expand the work now being carried on by the United States agencies.

These areas have been listed by Mr. Truman as eligible for help under the United States program: Africa, the Near and Far East, and certain regions of Central and South America. The Soviet Union and countries under Soviet control would be excluded from the United States program, but they would be free to take part in the U. N. program—in fact the United States hopes they will.

The $35,000,000 is sufficient only for the preparatory studies. As far as the billions that will be necessary to carry out the projects are concerned, the United States Export-Import Bank will be the only United States Government agency involved. The bulk of the money is to come from the World Bank, the countries where the projects are carried out and, above all, American private investors.

In addition, the Truman Administration is supporting a bill to encourage American investors to put up the money for the projects by giving them guarantees that (1) their property would not be expropriated; (2) they would be reimbursed for losses resulting from war; (3) they would be allowed to transfer their earnings into dollars despite currency controls in countries where they operate.

United Nations Plan

As for the United Nations, its budget for the coming year—to which all members of the United Nations contribute, the United States' share being about 40 per cent—includes a $676,000 program to continue the present activities. Secretary General Trygve Lie has proposed $35,000,000 for the first year to expand this program. However, the exact amount will depend on how much the various countries, in particular the United States, will offer to contribute when an international conference is held next spring to work out a detailed program. The chances are that the first year the United Nations program will cost about $20,000,000, with the United States contributing something less than 70 per cent.

United States support of the program, whatever its size, is indispensable. Unless Congress appropriates the money asked by Mr. Truman, both the United States and the United Nations programs will remain of very limited scope.

Looking further ahead, it is obvious that unless American investors can be persuaded to put up the money, most of the projects will remain in the blueprint stage. The American investing public, after having lost heavily on a number of Latin American bond issues during the depression, has been ex-

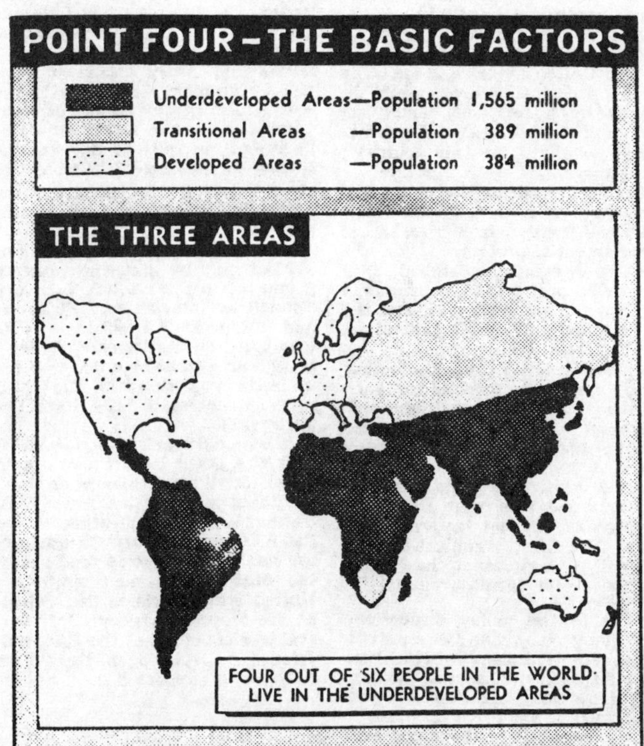

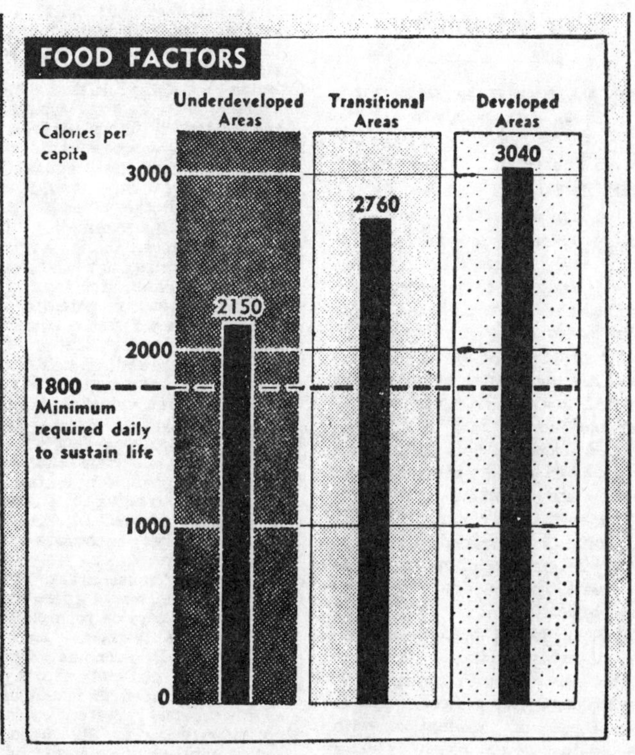

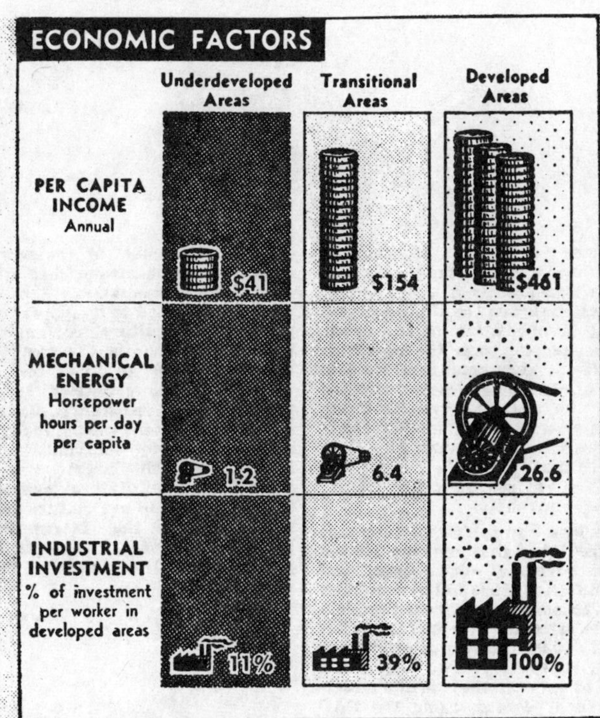

tremely slow since then to risk its money abroad.

An American Government guarantee of such investments would of course be a big help. With it, provided the Point Four program reveals genuinely profitable opportunities, the United States may be able to emulate the feat of Victorian and Edwardian England, which used its export surplus to pile up $22 billion in overseas investments. The importance of these investments is demonstrated by the fact that their depletion during two World Wars is mainly responsible for Britain's present economic difficulties.

U.S. TO FIGHT F.A.O. ON FARM SURPLUSES

Washington Dislike for Global Commodity Clearing House Likely to Defeat Move

By WALTER H. WAGGONER
Special to THE NEW YORK TIMES.

WASHINGTON, Nov. 2—The United States will oppose, and in effect defeat, the proposal by the United Nations Food and Agriculture Organization for an "international commodity clearing house" designed to transfer farm surpluses to shortage areas, it became known today.

The project will be voted on at the FAO conference opening here Nov. 21 to consider again ways to increase food output in underdeveloped areas while preventing surpluses from piling up in high-production and exporting countries.

The world-wide commodity clearing house is the second major recommendation made by the FAO for reaching this dual objective, and opposition by the United States will have the effect of stopping it in its tracks.

This Government's position on the $5,000,000,000 project is now in the process of formulation, with discussions going on in several quarters, but strong objections have already been marshaled for presentation to the conference later this month. Although these objections have not yet been formally stated, the following points are raised by policy-making officials:

1. The clearing house is designed to "maintain the flow of trade during periods of disequilibrium," such as now exists, by negotiating sales of food surpluses in "inconvertible" or "soft" currencies that could not otherwise be made. But it is believed possible here that this arrangement would prolong rather than shorten the present imbalance and period of "inconvertibility."
2. The country whose surplus commodities might be handled by the clearing house would lose control over the ultimate destination of the commodity. The United States, it is argued, might make surplus wheat available to Poland, for example, without knowing whether it would be traded for a currency usable for buying arms. The question is raised: Would Congress finance the disposal of surpluses without evidence of better controls?
3. There is a growing fear among trade policy officials that the world agency would be a step toward state trading and away from the "normal" or private trade relations encouraged by this Government.
4. The clearing house, according to its opponents, would operate on the basis of a price formula determined by so-called "normal conditions." It is considered possible that artificial shortages could be induced and unnecessary surpluses created by one nation refusing to buy the output of another. This would have the effect, it is argued, of bringing pressure on the exporter to lower the sights on "normal" conditions determined by the formula, to which the importer would readily agree.

But behind all these arguments, which are put forward principally by the economists and argued on economic grounds, is the conviction of United States trade policy representatives that this country will support bilateral commodity agreements rather than the collective arrangements planned by the FAO.

Such a bilateral agreement, for example, is now being negotiated by the United States and India, in which American wheat would be traded by a form of barter for Indian mica and other critical materials required for this country's stockpile.

Bilateral trade is the policy put forward chiefly by the State Department today. It expresses the Department's preference for the free-trade principals embodied in the Reciprocal Trade Agreements Act, on the domestic side, and the International Trade Organization, on the world level.

Agriculturalists, on the other hand, are more inclined to such planning programs as that proposed by the FAO. United States farmers have benefitted for many years from the same sort of planned agriculture and marketing arrangements that the FAO now seeks on an international basis. The farm organizations, as a result, strongly favor the "clearing house" for farm surpluses.

Even in the policy discussions now going on in this Government, however—discussions in which the State Department assumes the burden of opposing the FAO plan—a basic issue is yet to be resolved. It is the contention of the supporters of the "clearing house" that the disposal of United States farm surpluses is as much a domestic as a foreign policy problem.

On this assumption, they express surprise that policies dealing with such crucial matters as farm surpluses and farm prices should be handled exclusively by Executive decision, rather than by consultation or in cooperation with Congress.

The center of the discussions today is, in addition to the State and Agriculture Departments themselves, the Inter-Agency Committee on the FAO. This organization, a collection of both those departments and others concerned with the Government's relations to the world food agency, is led, at least nominally, by the Agriculture Department. In spite of this, the influence of the State Department is strong, and its decisions on this particular question are expected to prevail.

The "clearing house" is also under scrutiny by a special working group of the National Advisory Council on International Financial and Monetary Problems. This group, led by the Treasury Department, can also be expected to come up with objections to the FAO proposal not unlike the State Department's.

It became clear in January, 1947, that the State Department would dominate all conversations on United States participation in the FAO. On that occasion, a meeting here of the FAO Preparatory Commission for setting up a world food board, the State Department wrote the United States decision that rejected the proposed agency. Only several weeks before, at the FAO conference in Copenhagen, the United States had supported it.

November 3, 1949

NEW SURPLUS PLAN APPROVED IN F.A.O.

Calls for Group to Channel Commodities to Areas of Need —Endorsed by Brannan

Special to THE NEW YORK TIMES

WASHINGTON, Dec. 5—A working party plan substituting a fourteen-nation committee on commodity problems for the international commodity clearing house plan was accepted today by a commission of the Food and Agriculture Organization of the United Nations.

This action will have to be endorsed by a plenary session of the sixty-three-nation FAO conference before it becomes final. FAO was increased late today from sixty-two to sixty-three nations by the admission of Sweden.

Secretary of Agriculture Charles F. Brannan, United States delegate, put the full approbation of this Government behind the commodity committee plan during today's discussions. He called it the "workable heart of the clearing house proposal" that would make it possible for genuine surpluses to be channeled into areas of need outside normal trade channels. Only "the corporate superstructure" of the clearing house plan was rejected by the delegates here, he said. The part rejected was the creation of a finance agency to purchase surpluses at reduced prices or in soft currency.

Mr. Brannan said that one of the basic reasons the United States joined in opposition to the clearing house plan was the objection of soft-currency countries. He said most of them had clearly indicated that "the fiscal operations under the international commodity clearing house would jeopardize their own efforts" to regain a trade balance and restore the convertibility of their currencies.

Mr. Brannan said at a press conference later that current United States surpluses—dried eggs, butter and dried skim milk—would do little to raise world nutrition levels. He estimated, for instance, that the 67,000,000 pounds of dried eggs would supply only two and a half eggs to each of the world's undernourished persons, using the FAO estimate that half of the world's population is undernourished.

Secretary Brannan said that this country intended to do more stockpiling of agricultural commodities than it had done in the past; and that the real solution for the underdeveloped countries lay in the technical assistance plan, to which this country was ready to make a constant contribution. He also said that this country had not changed its multilateral approach to world trade in agriculture "as is evidenced by the International Wheat Agreement, the sugar discussions, and the reciprocal trade agreements."

December 6, 1949

POINT FOUR TO URGE CAPITALIST FARMS

Dr. Bennett Says He Will Seek Reforms Abroad as Incentive to Tenants to Raise Output

WASHINGTON, Jan. 7 (UP)—Dr. Henry G. Bennett, newly appointed head of the Point Four program, said today that he would urge backward countries to carry out a capitalistic-type land reform.

He said this would help increase food production and at the same time combat the appeal of widely publicized Communist land reform.

Secretary of Agriculture Charles F. Brannan already has preached this theme abroad and at home, indicating that the Administration has set out to use it as a strong anti-Moscow propaganda weapon.

Dr. Bennett outlined his plans in an interview. It was believed to be the first he had given since he left his post as president of Oklahoma Agricultural and Mechanical College to head the Point Four program.

Under this program, the United States is sending agents into thirty-six countries to teach underdeveloped peoples the latest methods of public health, education and agriculture.

"Our biggest problem is to produce more food," Dr. Bennett said. "One way to do that is for us to teach these peoples how to get more per acre through better planting, better seeds or better livestock strains.

"Another way is to get people to work harder. They have to have incentive."

Plan to Help Tenants

As a result, he said, Point Four representatives will quietly urge local governments abroad to try to give the farm workers a better chance. This policy will be aimed particularly at helping tenant farmers or the lowest-class farm workers who often are exploited in areas that have only two classes—the very rich and the very poor.

"The American farmer will work from dawn to dusk." Dr. Bennett said. "He is encouraged to do so because he gets a lot of the profit.

"The more a man gets for himself from his own production, the more incentive he has. If a tenant farmer, for instance, has to give up three-fourths of his production as rent, he won't work as hard as if he had to give up only one-fourth.

"That is the philosophy that will guide our suggestions to local authorities."

Dr. Bennett saw food production as the key to the Point Four program and peace. Must of the world's unrest could be avoided, he said, if people had the food that they are capable of producing.

He said the world's population was increasing 55,000 a day, but that food production could keep step if all the free world would use the agricultural methods the United States has developed.

"A county agent from North Carolina, for instance, has been working for three years on a private basis in India," he related. "He instructed farmers on a 100-square-mile area north of Calcutta and in the three years increased wheat production 67 per cent and potato production 200 per cent. The only expense was his salary."

Dr. Bennett hopes to repeat this feat ir. other parts of India and other Point Four countries.

Communists in such countries as China have been loud advocates of land reform. This has involved confiscation of large estates owned by the rich, and division of the land among farm workers.

But many Americans feel that this is only a temporary expedient because communism basically favors large collective farms run by the state.

January 8, 1951

U. S. to Press Land Reform For 3 Continents in U. N.

By MICHAEL L. HOFFMAN
Special to The New York Times.

GENEVA, Aug. 1—The United States will make land reform in Asia, Africa and Latin America a main plank in its platform for world economic development. At the appropriate time, the United States delegation will introduce a comprehensive resolution to the Economic and Social Council of the United Nations, now in session here, setting forth its views of the role of land reform in economic development and the battle against poverty. United States sources here say that this action will mark an important stage in the evolution of United States foreign policy.

Espousal of land reform, which is by no means simply a matter of dividing big farms into little ones, is one example of what the United States Government has learned from its recent experience in meeting new problems of being a dominant world power. It is an effort to meet criticism that United States influence in Asia and Africa particularly is always negative and backward-looking or else confined to giving away money that very often is badly used.

In seeking to use the United Nations to further changes in ownership and the method of exploitation of land, the United States, among other things, will be seeking to supplement the United Nations general activities in aiding underdeveloped countries. The United States believes that there has been too much talk in the United Nations about what Washington should do for underdeveloped countries and too little about what underdeveloped countries could do for themselves.

As groundwork for the attack on land tenure and land use problems, there now exists for the first time a comprehensive survey of land reform experiments that have been made in many parts of the world. Prepared largely by the United Nations Food and Agriculture Organization, this report also evaluates the different kinds of problems covered in the broad term "reform." The document has not yet been circulated to members of the Economic and Social Council, but has been given to members of the council of the F. A. O.

Among other conclusions, this report finds that "unsatisfactory forms of the agrarian structure and in particular systems of land tenure tend to impede economic development in underdeveloped countries in a number of ways."

This new United States interest in land reform will not be popular with most governments of underdeveloped countries, although some, like India and Mexico appear to be trying to improve land ownership systems. The United States is aware of this, but believes the interests of the United States necessitate taking positions that will appeal to peoples of those countries. It is the people not the present governments who are in danger of being sold the Communist Utopia.

Fundamental to the whole United States approach is the belief that the security of the United States is not assured so long as the yield of land to the person engaged in agriculture is on a scale of twenty-five in the United States and Canada to five in South America, two in Asia and one in Africa—differences in basic productivity too enormous to be consistent with anything but tension, distrust and hostility between those regions and the Atlantic community which needs all the support it can get from the rest of the world.

August 2, 1951

President Starts Program to Sell Federal Farm Surpluses Abroad

By JOSEPH A. LOFTUS
Special to The New York Times.

DENVER, Sept. 9—President Eisenhower set in motion today a three-year program to sell $700,000,000 in surplus farm products abroad.

A 1954 law provides for the sale of the commodities for local currencies. Another $300,000,000 worth may be given to friendly peoples in the event of national disaster.

The President declared that the policy of this Government would be to sell the surplus products at competitive prices abroad without demoralizing world markets and alienating friendly nations.

How to do that is a challenging administrative problem that remains to be solved. The expressed ideal is to seek increased consumption in areas where there is demonstrable underconsumption and where practical opportunities for increased consumption exist, or can be developed in a constructive manner.

A policy statement approved by President Eisenhower said that although this country had no intention of pursuing a reckless selling policy abroad, it could not accept the role of limiting its sales in world markets until other countries had disposed of their production.

"The adjustment of world supply to world demand," the statement added, "will require adjustments of production in other countries as well as the United States."

The statement was drafted by an interdepartmental committee under the chairmanship of Clarence Francis, board chairman of the General Foods Corporation, who is a special consultant to the President.

The achievements of the surplus sales program could bear directly on the income of United States farmers next year. The program is tied intimately with the success or failure of the Administration's flexible price support policy.

With a flexible policy, the Government theoretically can encourage or discourage the production of particular commodities as the supply and demand situation warrants.

The Government has in storage great quantities of wheat, corn, butter, cheese, cottonseed oil, dry edible beans and dried milk. The butter, for example, totals 460,000,000 pounds; cheddar cheese, 425,000,000 pounds; cottonseed oil, refined, 788,000,000 pounds, and corn, 51,000,000 bushels.

'Reckless Selling' Opposed

The magnitude of United States holdings "is such as to be capable of demoralizing world commodity markets should a policy of reckless selling abroad be pursued," the policy statement said, adding:

"This potential greatly alarms other countries despite the fact that past behavior of the United States has shown no intention of pursuing a harmful policy.

"The capacity of certain areas of the world to produce food and fiber in excess of current market takings presents a basis and a hope for improving living standards around the world—provided ways can be found for improving marketing and distribution systems and enlarging the purchasing power of consumers.

"This represents a challenge to the nations of the world to develop sound means for utilizing their productive capacity in the improvement of living standards."

The statement stressed that the liquidation of United States surpluses would be "orderly and gradual."

The Government will try to assure conditions of comme'ce that wi" permit the private trader to function effectively, the statement added.

President Eisenhower issued an executive order making the Secretary of Agriculture primarily responsible for sales. A number of other Federal agencies will participate to coordinate their work, and the President established an interagency advisory committee with Mr. Francis as chairman.

Uses for Money Outlined

The executive order provides that the local currency proceeds of overseas sales shall be released by the Budget Bureau for the following uses, as authorized by the law:

¶The development of new markets for United States agricultural commodities.

¶The acquisition of strategic and critical materials.

¶The procurement of military equipment, materials and facilities.

¶The purchase of goods or services for other friendly countries.

¶The promotion of balanced economic development and trade among nations.

¶The payment of United States obligations abroad.

¶The promotion of multilateral trade and economic developments.

The money also could be used for international educational exchange activities.

September 10, 1954

EISENHOWER URGES 'FOOD FOR PEACE' AS A FARM POLICY

In Message He Asks Allies to Use Surplus in Drive for World Harmony

PARITY REVISION SOUGHT

President Wants Supports Linked to Prices—Benson Bids Congress Act

By FELIX BELAIR Jr.
Special to The New York Times.

WASHINGTON, Jan. 29—President Eisenhower asked Congress today to scrap the Government's costly system of rewarding farmers for planting less. He urged that the United States and its allies join in harnessing their surplus food production for the cause of universal peace.

The President, in his message, gave only a broad hint of what he had in mind for a "food for peace" drive. Other sources have disclosed a plan for an international conference of food and agriculture ministers and experts of allied countries here this summer or early fall to dramatize food as an instrument for building a durable peace.

"Food can be a powerful instrument for all the free world in building a durable peace," the President said.

'All Practical Means'

"I am setting steps in motion to explore anew with other surplus-producing nations all practical means of utilizing the various agricultural surpluses of each in the interest of reinforcing peace and the well-being of friendly peoples throughout the world—in short, using food for peace."

The food-for-peace plan is much further advanced than the President's message indicated. Cabinet meeting at the White House have discussed plans for the conference.

One possible approach contemplates the storing of foodstuffs and other agricultural products at strategic points throughout the world. These depots would make food available for relief and welfare in countries struck by famine or other disasters and provide a source of supply in defense emergency.

The Parity Formula

Most of the President's message was devoted to his argument for abandoning farm price supports tied to a "parity" formula based on prices and costs prevailing in the period 1910-14. The formula is designed to give farmers the same purchasing power they enjoyed in that favorable period.

Instead of the parity concept that has been the basis of farm legislation in the last twenty-five years, the President urged that the Secretary of Agriculture be given discretion to fix price supports between 75 and 90 per cent of average market prices during an immediately preceding period. The average of the three years preceding was suggested.

The present attempt to control production by acreage allotments and marketing quotas would be abandoned under the President's major recommendation and farmers permitted to produce as they saw fit. Presumably, supply and demand factors reflected in current prices would act as a sufficient brake on overproduction.

Both in the President's message and an accompanying memorandum by Secretary of Agriculture Ezra Taft Benson, price supports related to past average market prices and without control on production were given the benefit of the argument. But neither insisted that Congress adopt this course.

Responsibility of Congress

An alternative course was presented to permit the continued use of the parity concept in fixing price supports but at lower levels and with production controls so strengthened as to impose what Mr. Benson called "drastic regimentation."

The effect as well as the design of the President's method was to place responsibility for whatever happens to farm legislation at this session on the Democratic majority in the Senate and House of Representatives. Secretary Benson said he certainly hoped for this effect, since "that's certainly where the responsibility belongs."

The Agriculture Secretary gave his views at a news conference after the President's message was read in the Senate and House. He said that if Congress adopted the course preferred by the Administration, the Government's loss on price-support activities could be cut in half.

The President branded the present system of supports and controls as "intolerable." He said the controls did not control while most of the money spent in price supports went "to a relatively few large producers."

The President summed up the results of the present system as compelling higher prices to consumers, vanished foreign markets and staggering surpluses in the hand of the Federal Government, which had to pay $1,000,000,000 a year for carrying charges.

Secretary Benson's memorandum proposed changes as soon as possible in legislative directives on wheat, tobacco and peanuts. Following a vote of corn-hog farmers last year, Congress adopted the past average market price standard for 65-90 per cent price supports. Cotton farmers have indicated that they favor the same shift.

The Secretary recommended the indefinite extension of the surplus disposal law authorizing sales abroad for local currency.

In Congress, Democrats from farm states denounced the President's message and the alternatives it presented in a reaction that indicated small chance of its adoption.

Senator Allen J. Ellender of Louisiana, chairman of the Senate Agriculture Committee, said the proposal "doesn't stand a ghost of a chance." He complained that it would make the Secretary of Agriculture "more or less a czar."

Representatve Harold D. Cooley of North Carolina, chairman of the House farm group, said the President had sent Congress an anti-farmer message.

Senator Hubert H. Humphrey, Democrat of Minnesota, called the message "a tragic failure of executive responsibility."

Senator Everett M. Dirksen, the minority leader, suggested that the message "makes sense" since the Federal Government could not continue indefinitely piling up surplus commodities that would cost $10,500,000,000 by next year.

January 30, 1959

Humphrey, at Refugee Meeting, Asks Use of Food as Policy Tool

Senator Hubert E. Humphrey called upon the United States yesterday to use its "God-given abundance of food" to further its foreign policy.

"If the United States and our allies cannot figure out what to do with our surplus * * * without wrecking world economy * * * then we are incapable of defending ourselves," he said.

The Minnesota Democrat spoke at a luncheon marking the start of World Refugee Year in the United States and celebrating the sixteenth anniversary of the American Council of Voluntary Agencies for Foreign Service.

The luncheon, sponsored by the council, was held at the Plaza Hotel. More than 600 persons attended.

World Refugee Year was established in a United Nations General Assembly resolution that called upon all governments to assist the millions of refugees in Europe, Asia, North Africa and the Middle East.

Senator Humphrey said he had introduced an amendment to the Mutual Security Bill authorizing the use of $10,000,000 this year to fulfill some of the needs of refugees.

He also said he would fight for "permanent authorization for the President to admit refugees without the dubious status of parolees" and called for the end of the national-origin quota system.

July 2, 1959

PRESIDENT APPLAUDS SURPLUS SHIPMENTS

NEWPORT, R. I., July 23 (AP)—President Eisenhower reported today that almost 6,500 shiploads of American farm surplus products were sent abroad under his Food-for-Peace program in the years from 1954 through 1959.

About half the shipments were sold for foreign currency; some were donated and some bartered.

The President said he was gratified by the achievement in "the world-wide war against want and hunger."

"There is no form of overseas assistance which this country is better able to provide than the supplying of American farm products and agricultural science," he said.

He said the accomplishment could be further improved with emphasis on continued efforts to guard against hazards of the program—such as upsetting national economies of other countries that export farm products.

President Eisenhower issued his statement at the summer White House after receiving an interim report on the program from Don Paarlberg, the Food-for-Peace coordinator.

Mr. Paarlberg, a White House economic adviser and a former aide to Agriculture Secretary Ezra Taft Benson, was appointed to the post last spring to coordinate various farm product export programs.

July 24, 1960

FEW GAINS FOUND IN FOOD-FOR-PEACE

Program Given to McGovern Largely Consists of Aid Under 1954 Surplus Act

Special to The New York Times.

WASHINGTON, Dec. 15—The so-called Food-for-Peace program assigned today to Representative George McGovern has never attained the noble grandeur suggested by its name.

As an idea, it has thrived for the last fifteen years. As an appealing slogan, it has been widely advertised by the Eisenhower Administration and seized upon by both this year's Presidential candidates.

As a program, it consists largely of surplus food distribution under the aridly titled Agricultural Trade Development and Assistance Act of 1954.

This provides for surplus food grants abroad under certain emergency conditions and for surplus sales to foreign countries for local currencies if such sales are not competitive with world traders.

Under President Eisenhower, the program has been directed by Secretary of Agriculture Ezra Taft Benson, but the idea has advanced little beyond the distribution program provided by the 1954 act.

Food Glut Produced

The idea was simple. The North American granary produces a food glut while millions about the earth live at starvation's edge. Why not work off the American surpluses by feeding the world's hungry, and coincidentally, profit from the goodwill and added stability abroad that accompanies the easing of hunger?

The idea was propounded shortly after World War II by Sir John Boyd-Orr, former head of the United Nations Food and Agricultural Organization, who advocated a system of "food banks" abroad.

The problem in translating the ideal into a successful program has been finding a method for getting the surplus to people who need it without driving established traders out of their traditional markets and thus depressing the world agricultural economy.

Various complicated proprosals have been made and Mr. Benson has been criticized on the ground that he took an inert approach to the problem.

The Democrats now get their chance to act, though there is only a vague idea of how Mr. Kennedy proposes to reorganize for the effort. Finding the solution will be Mr. McGovern's problem.

Mr. McGovern is a Democrat by conversion in an area long addicted to Republican leadership. He has long believed that surplus food is not, as some have suggested, a burden to this country.

The first Democratic Representative from South Dakota in two decades, Mr. McGovern believes that stored food commodities are good insurance against drought and other emergencies and can play a major role in this country's dealings with less fortunate nations.

"We should thank God that we have have a good abundance and use the oversupply among the under-privileged at home and abroad," he has said.

Mr. McGovern, 38 years old, waged a strong but unsuccessful race for Karl Mundt's Senate seat this fall. He is credited with a large part in efforts to rebuild the Democratic party in South Dakota.

Yet he was originally a Republican. Mr. McGovern, the son of a Methodist minister, said he became a Democrat while studying American history.

"It convinced me that the Democratic party was more on the side of the average person," he said.

Mr. McGovern received a Ph.D. in history from Northwestern University and taught political science at Dakota Wesleyan. He became interested in politics and made statements that the long Republican rule in the state was unhealthy.

In 1953 Mr. McGovern became executive secretary of the Democratic party at a time when the Democrats held no state-wide office and held only two of the state's 110 seats in the Legislature.

For three years he worked on building the party; in 1956 he ran for Congress and won; two years later he beat off a challenge by a formidable Republican opponent, former Gov. Joe Foss.

In congress Mr. McGovern was known as a liberal. He supported high supports for farm commodities, Federal aid to small-business men and farmers, medical aid for the aged and Federal aid at all levels of education.

During World War II, Mr. McGovern served as a B-24 bomber pilot and won the Distinguished Flying Cross. He is married and the father of three daughters and two sons.

December 16, 1960

U. S. BARS SENDING OF FOOD TO CHINA

President Indicates Peiping Political Use of Supplies Rules Against Aid Now

By FELIX BELAIR Jr.
Special to The New York Times.

WASHINGTON, Jan. 25 — The United States said today that it had no present intention of using its surplus food stocks for relief of starvation in Communist China.

Without entirely foreclosing the possibility of such shipments and stating that this Government would "consider" any request for food from the Peiping Government, President Kennedy appeared more interested in discouraging the idea than in holding out hope for it.

The American people do not want anybody to starve anywhere in the world, the President said at his news conference. If there was a real need for the food and it was requested by the Communist Chinese Government, his Administration certainly would consider the request.

In the same context, however, the President recalled that the Peiping Government had quite recently been shipping quantities of its own food supplies to Africa and Cuba for propaganda purposes. He indicated some misgivings that any food sent to mainland China by the United States would go for relief of people in the drought-stricken areas.

Humphrey Also Dubious

These same misgivings were shared by Senator Hubert Humphrey, Democrat of Minnesota, in suggesting that some surplus United States food stocks held by the Commodity Credit Corporation might usefully be sent to Communist China to alleviate actual starvation.

In an interview broadcast recently by the Voice of America, Senator Humphrey suggested that relief food shipments might be an effective way of letting the people of mainland China know that the American people continued to be their friends and were not enemies as pictured by their Communist Government.

A member of the President's food-for-peace task force, Senator Humphrey said there was evidence that famine conditions were becoming widespread on the China mainland, but he insisted that in no event should surplus American food be turned over to the Peiping Government, which might use it for its propaganda ends.

It was the Senator's suggestion that the food might be turned over to the International Red Cross or other voluntary agency for distribution directly to the Chinese people. His main purpose, Mr. Humphrey said, was that the United States should make known its willingness to send the food to the Chinese people.

In his response to a question, President Kennedy said the Peiping Government may not really need the food [Question 24, Page 10]. The President mentioned that Peiping's food shipments to Africa and Cuba were a matter of recent history.

"I'm not anxious to offer food if it's regarded merely as a propaganda effort by the United States," Mr. Kennedy went on. "If there is a desire for food or need for food, the United States would be glad to consider that need, regardless of the source.

"If people's lives are involved —if there is a desire for food— the United States will consider it carefully. I do say in this case, however, there are these examples of food being exported during this present time, or in recent history, and secondly, there has been a rather belligerent attitude expressed toward us in recent days by the Chinese Communists and there is no indication, direct or indirect, private, or public, that they would respond favorably to any action by the United States."

Australia Selling Wheat

Dispatch of The Times, London.

CANBERRA, Australia, Jan. 25—More than twenty ships are loading in Australian ports with wheat and flour for Communist China, officials here said today. Further large purchases are said to be imminent.

Australia, like the United States, does not recognize Communist China.

January 26, 1961

U.S. to Offer Surplus Seed To Aid Latin Land Reform

By FELIX BELAIR Jr.
Special to The New York Times.

WASHINGTON, Feb. 9—Feed grains and other surplus foods will be offered as inducements to South American countries initiating land reforms as part of a program to improve living conditions.

This was described today by George McGovern, director of the President's Food-for-Peace program, as the primary aim of a six-member team that will visit ten South American capitals next week.

The mission, headed by James Symington, Mr. McGovern's deputy, will include officials of the State and Agriculture Departments and the International Cooperation Administration.

As Mr. McGovern described the plan, feed grain could be sold for local currencies at bargain prices to various governments. The feed would be given to new farmers to feed poultry and livestock until the farmers could supply their own needs.

How much of the grain and other surplus supplies might be sold, lent or given away through the new land program approach would be conjectural, Mr. McGovern said, until it was learned how far the recipient governments might be willing to go in providing new farmsteads. Existing tracts would have to be split up for the purpose.

Funds to Be Sought

Congress has authorized a $500,000,000 aid program for Latin America. It will be asked by the Kennedy Administration to appropriate the money at the current session as a start on Operation Pan America, to which the United States pledged its support in signing the Act of Bogota.

Land reform and more equitable taxation systems have been prescribed as the minimum conditions on which the Government will insist before beginning the hemisphere economic cooperation plan.

While the six-member team is visiting the ten capital cities, Mr. McGovern and Arthur M. Schlesinger Jr. will spend three

Associated Press

OFFERS SURPLUS FOOD: George McGovern, director of Food-for-Peace program.

days in Argentina, Brazil and possibly Uruguay, conferring with government officials there.

Mr. McGovern said his major purpose on the trip would be to assure the chief exporters and importers of foods in Latin America that no interruption of commercial channels was intended in carrying out the Food-for-Peace program.

He said Mr. Schlesinger would accompany him as a personal representative of the President. Mr. Schlesinger said he would give "White House support to the mission."

At a news conference Mr. McGovern challenged contentions of some farm leaders that the Food-for-Peace program might aggravate and perpetuate the farm surplus problem rather than relieve it.

That might be the result of an "indiscriminate" distribution of surplus stocks in overseas market, he said. But he explained that "we expect to relate our overseas distribution to what we are trying to do at home."

The Food-for-Peace director said the Administration planned to ask Congress soon for a supplemental appropriation of $2,000,000,000 to finance surplus food disposal during the fiscal year ending June 30. This was necessary because the five-year grain-disposal arrangement with India had virtually depleted Commodity Credit Corporation funds, he said.

February 10, 1961

FREEMAN URGES FOOD DIPLOMACY

Bids U. S. Use Superiority in Agriculture 'to Shape Future of the World'

By IRVING SPIEGEL

Special to The New York Times.

PITTSBURGH, March 23—Secretary of Agriculture Orville L. Freeman emphasized tonight that the United States must use its agricultural superiority over the Soviet Union as a diplomatic weapon "to shape the future of the world."

He asserted that in the rivalry between the West and the Communist world "agriculture is one area in which we have clear, demonstrated, incontestable superiority."

The United States, he said, must view its abundance in perspective—as part of a massive social, economic, health and welfare drive toward an age of plenty for all the world's people.

He cautioned that the United States "must stop thinking of abundance in terms 'surplus disposal'—as something to be got rid of and kept from happening again."

"Abundance is a dynamic instrument of health, progress and peace," he declared.

Mr. Freeman spoke to more than 1,000 delegates at the dinner session closing the five-day biennial convention here of the National Council of Jewish Women.

Food Is Called Power

In stressing that "many of the world's people live in a nutritional twilight zone" Mr. Freeman warned that "one way or another, with us or without us," people in newly developing nations "intend to raise their standard of living." He said that they had "awakened to the hope that their long unsatisfied basic needs can be met."

"Food, therefore," he said, "has become a weapon of diplomacy. Food is persuasive. Food is power."

Contrasting the United States and Soviet agricultural strength, he termed as "remarkable" that only 8.7 per cent of the American people now lived on farms. In the Soviet Union, the corresponding figure is about 50 per cent. He said that only one person in twelve in the United States was engaged in agriculture in contrast to one of every three in the Soviet Union.

The 8.7 per cent of the United States population "provides enough food and fiber not only to meet the needs of every man, woman and child, but in addition vast quantities for export," Mr. Freeman said.

Opposes Relief Only

Noting that "most of our national food-sharing efforts in the past have been relief operations," he asserted that the United States must do more.

"We must help the world's agriculture to provide a minimum adequate diet—a healthful diet—a balanced diet," he declared.

Mr. Freeman called for the development of the food-for-peace program "not as an emergency year-to-year operation but as a long-term task."

Mrs. Charles Hymes of Minneapolis was re-elected president of the sixty-eight-year-old educational service organization.

Among other officers elected were Mrs. Lawrence G. Anathan and Mrs. Bernard Heineman of New York as honorary vice presidents.

Re-elected as national vice presidents were Mrs. Ronald Brown of Cleveland; Mrs. Stanley C. Myers of Coral Gables, Fla.; Mrs. Edward F. Stern of Seattle; Mrs. Leonard Weiner of Detroit and Mrs. Joseph Willen of New York.

March 24, 1961

PRESIDENT HAILS FOOD FOR PEACE

His Views on Its Policy Role Differ From Freeman's

By FELIX BELAIR Jr.

Special to The New York Times.

WASHINGTON, June 28—President Kennedy and his Secretary of Agriculture expressed differing views today on whether the Food for Peace program is an instrument of the nation's over-all foreign policy.

Secretary Orville L. Freeman said the Administration's basic farm program and the policy of using surplus farm products to feed the hungry overseas had to be carefully integrated "to meet the demands of our foreign policy."

President Kennedy told the same audience that the Food for Peace program "is not an element of the cold war—not an arm of the foreign policy of the United States." He said of the expanded scheme of giving away or selling farm surpluses for local currencies at bargain prices:

"It is an opportunity which we have because of the generosity of nature and because of the energies of our own people to play, in a critical time in the life of the world, an important role in easing and helping the lives of millions of people who are in less fortunate circumstances."

Address New Group

Both men addressed the first national conference of the American Food for Peace Council, which was set up recently under White House auspices. Both were challenged before the end of the first day's sessions by Senator Allen J. Ellender, Democrat of Louisiana, chairman of the Senate Agriculture Committee.

Senator Ellender demanded that surplus-food donations be placed on a repayable dollar-loan basis and substituted for part of the President's foreign-aid program. He also warned against Secretary Freeman's idea of paying farmers to produce greater surpluses to give away to under-developed areas.

"It is my feeling," said Senator Ellender, "that our agricultural abundance can be used to supplant in a large measure some of the dollar aid we now provide."

An opposite view was expressed by Representative Harold D. Cooley, chairman of the House Agriculture Committee. The North Carolina Democrat said "We have to step up the tempo of the program."

June 29, 1961

House Votes Omnibus Farm Bill But Adds Curb on Sales Abroad

Special to The New York Times.

WASHINGTON, July 27—The House of Representatives passed the omnibus farm bill today in virtually the same form approved by the Senate last night. Passage was by voice vote.

The House and Senate versions of the bill will now go to a conference where minor differences must be resolved.

The heart of the bill seeks to reduce crops of wheat, corn, barley and grain sorghum in 1962 to cut costs of storing and handling surpluses.

During today's voting, the House shouted through an amendment stating that it was the intent of Congress that subsidized surplus crops be exported only to friendly countries.

It was uncertain what effect this provision might have on programs such as surplus sales to Poland if it survived the conference.

The amendment was offered by Representative Delbert L. Latta, Republican of Ohio. It was an expression of Congressional resentment toward a Department of Commerce order permitting surplus sales to Communist states.

A Republican attempt to knock out the one-year extension of the emergency feed-grains program requested by the President was beaten by a standing vote of 123 to 76, without a roll-call. A similar Republican move in the Senate was beaten yesterday.

The feed-grains program—covering corn, grain sorghums and barley—requires growers to cut acreage by 20 per cent to qualify for price support payments. It also provides for compensating Federal payments in reimbursal for the production cuts.

The program was begun in the spring for this year's crop. The new bill will extend it to cover the 1962 crop.

The new wheat program, applying only to the 1962 crops, will operate on a similar principle. Growers must cut acreage by 10 per cent. To compensate, the Government will increase the support price from $1.79 to about $2 a bushel and pay growers 40 per cent of the value of the potential yield of the land taken out of production.

Wheat growers may voluntarily take an additional 30 per cent of their acreage out of production and get payments worth half the potential yield's price.

Other elements of the bill broaden the authority for the Food For Peace Plan, extend the wool price support program for three years and extend authorization to operate marketing order programs to a variety of commodities previously uncovered.

The House bill authorizes new marketing-order programs for turkeys, peanut products and naval stores as well as apples grown in New York, New Jersey, Michigan, Indiana, Maryland, California and New England. The Senate version authorizes new programs for cherries and cranberries for canning and freezing, for lambs, turkeys, apples produced in Michigan, New York and New England, and chicken and turkey hatching eggs.

Although its passage was urged by the President, the bill represents one of his major legislative setbacks of the year. The major feature of his farm proposal—centralizing power to devise new subsidy programs and productions controls in the Secretary of Agriculture—was defeated in committee voting.

There was no attempt to restore it on the floor of either house.

July 28, 1961

FOOD IS REPLACING U. S. AID DOLLARS

Officials Are Told to Use Surplus in Needy Nations

By FELIX BELAIR Jr.

Special to The New York Times.

WASHINGTON, Nov. 11 — Government surplus food stocks will be used instead of foreign aid dollars as far as possible in the Administration's program of helping under-developed areas of the world toward economic self-reliance.

Instruction going out from the State Department to all ambassadors require that whenever possible the surplus food be used to pay wages of workers on development projects, for national school lunch programs and in the form of feed grains to help tide over resettlement farmers until their first crop of pigs, poultry and other livestock.

The instructions were in the form of a memorandum prepared by James W. Symington, deputy director of the Office of Food for Peace. It was sent to all ambassadors and heads of operating missions by Under Secretary of State Chester Bowles.

Recalling that social and economic progress must go hand in hand to attain the goals of the International Development Program, the memorandum said that large sums would have to be spent on school construction and other educational improvements.

Proper Feeding Cited

They would be wasted unless students and teachers, for that matter, were properly fed, the document suggested. It added:

"In many areas of the world education lags even if there are a few schools, because the children are too hungry or poorly fed either to walk to school or to pay attention to their lessons on arrval.

"Often the school day is cut short for just such reasons. The United States provides a supplemental school lunch from surplus stocks for over 15,000,000 children. Other developed nations have such programs. But they are novel experiments in the under-developed nations.

"The dedicated efforts of the voluntary agencies hardly ripple the surface of the deep need for food and nutrition of the children of school and preschool age in such countries. It is a national responsibility but one which most such nations cannot assume for some time to come without outside aid."

The memorandum specifically directed all ambassadors and mission chiefs to explore the nutritional needs of children of such ages in the countries to which they are accredited. It acknowledged that lack of port facilities, inland transport or distribution facilities had heretofore been an obstacle to further national school lunch programs under the foreign aid program.

High Priority Listed

But the document sent out by Mr. Bowles suggested that "questions of equipment and technical assistance, will not be allowed to terminate the analysis [of nutritional needs] but will be considered as a high-ranking priority for aid funds."

It was stated at the outset in the Symington thesis that the nation's $4,000,000,000 investment in the progress and security of the under-developed southern half of the world had little chance of success unless its people were reasonably well nourished.

"Two-thirds of the world's people suffer from hunger and malnutrition," the memorandum said. "The crisis conditions which we hear about and to which we generally respond are those created by droughts, floods, earthquakes, and other spectacular phenomena.

"Yet a world-wide continuum of suffering exists in crisis proportions—only sub rosa. It is identified only in solemn but obscure governmental reports and nutritional studies. These countries have now entered a period characterized as the 'revolution of rising expectations,' and the United States has been called upon to help them.

"As we prepare to extend such help, we should not forget that the first and foremost 'expectation' of hungry people is for food. As we focus on the developmental needs of nations asking for our assistance, we should bear in mind:

"1. That the aid we provide should reach down to the neediest people and lift them a little, so the gap between them and the wealthier elements of their society tends not to increase but to decrease.

"2. That the amount of available aid dollars is limited."

Integrating Abundance

It was suggested that these two points argued "the value of seeking every appropriate way to integrate such abundance into our over-all aid effort." This was called especially true "in the light of the fact that the United States holds over 3,000,000,000 bushels of wheat and corn products, together with millions of pounds of dried milk and vegetable fats and oils as well as other agricultural commodities."

The value of these surplus food stocks, while carried on the books of the Department of Agriculture at $5,300,000,000, actually cost the Commodity Credit Corporation $9,000,000,000. The book value of the surplus food is based on world market prices, whereas the C. C. C. acquired the stocks at United States support price level. The C. C. C. is the Government's price support agency.

"One of the chief objections raised against Food for Peace is that it is a substitute for dollar "aid," the memorandum said. "Properly implemented, it should be just that. Food aid can stretch dollar aid and free dollars for a variety of other priorities."

It was part of the Bowles-Symington memorandum that objections of local producers and agricultural countries who sell to the country involved had the "greatest relevance" when aimed at this country's Food for Peace efforts. It acknowledged that "these purchases could conceivably displace sales of food either domestically produced or imported commercially."

Local Objections Raised

The success of the Food for Peace plan since its inception as a surplus disposal program—some $10,000,000,000 in such farm products having been exported—only added to the apprehensions of countries like Argentina, which relies on farm exports for about 90 per cent of its foreign exchange earnings.

But with this acknowledgment the memorandum went on to press the positive side of the Food for Peace effort.

In Tunisia alone, it said, 300,000 men have been working on some 6,000 development projects involving as few as ten and as many as 3,000 workers—all of them accepting American surplus food for a third of their wages and the remainder in Tunisian currency. This method is being used in eleven other countries and negotiations are in progress with twenty other nations.

In the drought-stricken Puna area of Peru 30,000 children are getting free school lunches made possible by surplus United States foods in agreement with that Government.

By encouraging the cooperative movement, especially in Latin America, a start has been made toward a new idea of feed grain loans by recipient governments to farm cooperatives. The loans would be repaid in the form of poultry, eggs or livestock and used for government school lunch programs or their equivalent.

The diplomatic chiefs and other heads of missions were warned not to mistake high calorie counts with proper nutrition and that "the protein level is determinative here and this is all too often substandard."

Indicative of the magnitude of the program contemplated or in being, it was pointed out that the Office of Food for Peace had already earmarked funds sufficient for the purchase this year of 500,000,000 pounds of dry skim milk for distribution abroad by voluntary agencies "which could use much more."

Finally, the memorandum reminded all ambassadors and operating mission chiefs that they should "not only make recommendation concerning the suitability of aid requests by the countries to which they are accredited, but should in the first instance make evaluations as to the most crucial needs of these countries in order to be better able to assess the sincerity and the feasibility of aid requests."

November 12, 1961

U.S. AGENCIES SPLIT ON FOOD FOR PEACE

Aid Officials Want to Use More of Surplus Abroad—Farm Authorities Wary

By FELIX BELAIR Jr.

Special to The New York Times.

WASHINGTON, Jan 10—A basic difference within the Administration over what to do about the farm surplus was disclosed today in a report to President Kennedy.

George S. McGovern, director of the Food for Peace program, said that the State Department and the Agency for International Development had become keenly aware of the importance of food in foreign aid programs.

They have learned, he said, that surplus food can be used instead of dollars in foreign aid and are planning to use more of it in development programs abroad.

"They are now actually indicating a desire to use more food abroad in foreign assistance than the U. S. Department of Agriculture believes it can justify on a concessional basis," Mr. McGovern said in his first annual report.

The concessional basis referred to involve bargain "sales" of surplus farm products for local currencies in which there is no cash return to the Treasury. It also covers various methods of giving away the commodities by using them instead of money to pay wages of workers on irrigation, sanitation and other development projects in the foreign aid program.

After resisting such practices for months, State Department and A. I. D. officials found such enthusiasm fo food wages overseas that they are demanding more and more surplus supplies.

Mr McGovern told the President that the "positive view" this changed attitude represented "has given rural America an appreciable stake in American foreign policy."

"It can make farm families the new internationalists of America and give them a greater stake in foreign assistance," he said.

But Mr. McGovern said there was still room for enlightenment among Federal loan agencies and foreign aid planners "on the possibilities of using food to supplement dollar aid."

"No United States official should give final clearance to a foreign loan until he is convinced that the possibility of using food as a substitute or supplement for aid dollars has been fully evaluated," he said.

Agriculture officials assert that Mr. McGovern's approach would cost much more than they want added to the expense of farm abundance, which now costs the nation about $6,000,000,000 a year.

They say that it is all very well to make the nation's farm surpluses "an instrument of American foreign policy." But they are beginning to ask why the cost of buying and storing such surpluses should not be included in the State Department budget.

The surplus farm commodities that are the muscle of Mr. McGovern's Food for Peace program are paid for out of Congressional appropriations to the Commodity Credit Corporation. The corporation takes them from the farmers at guaranteed support prices fixed by the Secretary of Agriculture.

There is real concern among agriculture officials that, unless a way is found to curtail mounting spending on farm programs, public reaction will trigger some arbitrary cutbacks by Congress regardless of the effect on farm income.

This concern was reflected today in an appeal by Secretary of Agriculture Orville L. Freeman to a national conference of farm leaders to help him solve the "crisis of abundance."

January 11, 1962

U.S. Aid and Health

Food for Peace Program Reduces Vast Supplies and Helps the World's Hungry

By HOWARD R. RUSK, M. D.

One of the brightest spots in American foreign aid is our Food for Peace program.

This is the name given to activities carried on primarily under Public Law 480, enacted in 1954 during the Eisenhower Administration.

One purpose of the program is to reduce vast supplies of agricultural products that accumulated through Government purchases to support prices.

These agricultural products are then shipped to other countries under provisions including complicated international sales agreements, financing of American students abroad under Fulbright Fellowships, payment for United States embassy and consul expenses, direct donations and multimillion-dollar loans to support medical and rehabilitation research.

$1.6 Billion Last Year

Last month President Johnson reported to the Congress that $1.6 billion worth of commodities were shipped overseas during 1963.

It is significant that while this new record for the distribution of surplus products was being set, commercial exports of agricultural commodities reached a high of $4 billion.

Currently an average of five 10,000-ton ships leave American ports every day carrying Food for Peace cargoes for the hungry of the world.

One of the most dramatic of the many activities of the Food for Peace program is the Alliance for Progress child-feeding program known as Operation Ninos, or Operation Children.

Under Agency for International Development auspices, 10 million children in Latin America are receiving school lunches under programs administered by host governments frequently in cooperation with United States voluntary agencies.

School Attendance Rises

Feedings range in method from the simplest mixing of powdered dry milk in the child's own cup to full-scale school lunches. Since the program started there has been increased school attendance, better scholastic achievement and a drastic reduction in absenteeism.

School lunches, for example, have helped double attendance in Peru's rural schools.

Third graders in Santiago, Chile, showed an average weight increase of eight pounds in the first four months of the program.

By the end of this year 350,000 children, more than one-half of the primary grade students in El Salvador, will participate in the national school-lunch program. Many of these children will be assured of a wholesome meal on a daily basis for the first time in their lives.

The children who are able to pay a nominal fee of around 20 cents a month do so. The El Salvador Government supplies internal transportation for the food and personnel to supervise its distribution.

Catholic Relief Service, National Catholic Welfare Conference, helps administer the program.

In other countries such voluntary agencies as CARE and Church World Service are the on-site coordinators.

Clubs, schools and organizations in the United States who wish to participate can do so. For example, $60 will provide all the necessary kitchen equipment to enable a school in Ecuador to serve hot lunches. Ten dollars will provide a desk and bench for two children in Guatemala.

In country after country there has been a shift from family-relief feeding programs to food-for-work and other "bootstrap" community development programs.

Annually 700,000 workers are earning food for an estimated four million persons in their families in part-payment for their labor on projects ranging from school construction to land reclamation.

In another aspect of the program, national currencies accumulated through the sale of food are in turn loaned for the developmental activities.

In Brazil, for example, $20 million in cruzeiros has been loaned to eight states in the impoverished northeast area for school construction and the training of teachers.

In Tunisia a loan of $5,581,000 in dinars will supplement their funds to assist the Tunisian Government in a massive effort to reclaim arid lands.

The program includes help for the needy and disaster relief.

Last year a total of 2.5 million refugees were helped in Burundi, Nepal and Tanganyika, and in the Palestinian refugee camps nearly 10 million persons in 14 countries were assisted through disaster relief.

Food for Peace is the perfect example of enlightened self-interest. It successfully combines our political, economic and humanitarian motives.

May 17, 1964

Extension Is Voted On Food for Peace

By FELIX BELAIR Jr.
Special to The New York Times

WASHINGTON, Sept. 3 — The House voted a three-year extension of the Food for Peace program today and an authorization of $6.4 billion to finance its operation.

The vote on final passage was 349 to 6.

Earlier, by 182 to 175, the House declared "any nation or area dominated or controlled by a Communist government or by the world Communist movement" ineligible to purchase surplus food commodities from the United States at bargain prices under the program.

This language, amounting to the strictest anti-Communist legislative sanction to date, was incorporated in the bill on a Republican-sponsored motion in which 143 Republicans and 39 Democrats joined.

The restriction was opposed by 162 Democrats and 13 Republicans. It was introduced by Representative Paul Findley, Republican of Illinois.

A similar restriction has been included in foreign aid legislation during the last year, but with provision that the President could waive it if this was in the interest of the United States. The idea behind the waiver provisio has been to encourage greater independence from Moscow on the part of countries like Yugoslavia and Poland.

Such policy restrictions on the executive branch have heretofore specifically excluded the Food for Peace program.

The restriction that was adopted today would leave the President free to make gifts of food from United States surplus stocks to any country, Communist or otherwise, in the event of famine or natural disaster.

The over-all House action on the measure was generally considered a major victory for the Administration. It began with a voice vote reversing a position taken by the House yesterday.

The result of the reversal was to continue Presidential discretion to authorize use of local currencies acquired from surplus food sales for common defense and development purposes in the recipient countries.

Representative John J. Rooney, Democrat of Brooklyn, who argued effectively yesterday for withdrawing the 10-year-old Presidential authority in favor of Congressional appropriation of all local currencies for specific projects, led today's démarche.

Mr. Rooney told the House he had been convinced overnight that unless the Presidential power over use of local currencies were continued, the war effort in South Vietnam would suffer. He said he had learned that about 90 per cent of local currencies controlled by the United States in that country went back directly into the war effort.

Administration forces won a second and, in the realm of foreign policy, more important triumph in narrowly defeating another Republican-sponsored proposal, which would have prohibited any new surplus-food sales to the United Arab Republic.

The ban, proposed by Representative Oliver P. Bolton, Republican of Ohio, was rejected 117 to 113 after emotional debate. Recriminations continued long after the verdict was in.

Substitute Adopted

The 117-to-113 vote approved a substitute by Representative James Roosevelt, Democrat of California. Only last night Mr. Roosevelt had signed a joint letter to all House members urging their support of the Bolton proposal and his successful effort against it today prompted charges of Administration "arm-twisting" from Bolton supporters.

The Californian's substitute provides, instead of a flat ban on surplus food sales to the United Arab Republic, that "no funds under this act shall be spent in any country unless the President finds such country is not (a) an aggressor in the military sense against any country having diplomatic relations with the United States or, (b) using funds from any source from the United States for purposes inimicable to the foreign policies of the United States."

The purpose of the Bolton proposal had been to curb President Gamal Abdel Nasser's aggressive posture toward Israel and some Arab states. During the debate it was charged that surplus food shipments were making it possible for the Nasser regime to divert its agricultural economy from food to cotton, which it was shipping to the Soviet Union in payment for modern military weapons.

In a statement explaining his turnabout, Mr. Roosevelt said the Bolton proposal "undoubtedly would not have survived the conference [with the Senate] and we would end up with nothing."

"My substitute proposal makes it mandatory on the President—and for the first time—that before any surplus food goes to any country—not just Egypt—he must find and declare that the recipient is not an aggressor and that it is not following a course opposed to the policies of the United States."

The Senate has voted a two-year extension of the Food for Peace program. A Senate-House conference will be required to reach a compromise on the two measures.

Associated Press

Representative John J. Rooney, Democrat of Brooklyn, who changed his stand on the Food for Peace measure.

September 4, 1964

HUNGER IMPERILS U.S. AID PROGRAM

Report to Johnson Calls for a Shift in Emphasis

By FELIX BELAIR Jr.
Special to The New York Times

WASHINGTON, July 17 — Widespread hunger and malnutrition in underdeveloped countries are undermining United States efforts to promote their economic growth and contributing to political instability in such areas, according to an interagency task force report for President Johnson.

Now undergoing a final revision after six months of investigation and discussion, the report recommends dramatic changes in the policy and direction of the foreign assistance and Food for Peace programs and, ultimately, in the domestic farm program.

Some of its proposals have been put in effect. Others are in process of policy formulation.

The Agency for International Development has devoted $3 million to vitamin A and D fortification of all food for peace shipments of non-fat dry milk beginning Aug. 1.

The same agency is considering a $10 million expenditure for vitamin and mineral fortification of wheat flour and corn meal milled here and in recipient countries under Food for Peace donation programs and for processing and packaging so-called "formulated" foods for child feeding.

Priority Assigned

In addition, the foreign aid chief, David E. Bell, has ordered all chiefs of mission in underdeveloped countries to give top priority to the problems of food supply, malnutrition and population increase in preparing country development plans.

Mr. Bell said that while development plans of some countries need not address themselves to all three priority problems, he would nevertheless require a statement of the reasons for omitting them in mission presentations.

At the same time, the agency has placed malnutrition ahead of all other health problems its country teams are trying to solve—including the provision of sanitary water systems, long at the top of the list — and malaria eradication.

Among the chief findings of the task force report were the following:

¶The high prevalance of hunger and malnutrition in the world is a leading contributor to human misery, apathy, disease, economic stagnation, and political instability.

¶The problems associated with malnutrition cannot be separated from the basic problems related to social and economic development such as agricultural production, industrial production and population growth.

¶About 50 per cent of preschool-age children in the developing countries are suffering from malnutrition, and there is evidence that this condition produces a retardation of mental and physical development of 10 to 25 per cent.

¶Overcoming the vitamin and protein deficiencies of young children in most less-developed countries would do more to reduce disease and eventually raise productivity than any other health measure that could be taken.

The significance of these findings is that the United States has been investing at least $2 billion a year through foreign economic aid in the economic growth of under-developed countries of the non-Communist world. Part of the military aid program is applied to the same purpose.

As matters now stand in the stymied Senate-House negotiations on the aid authorization bill, some $2.5 billion of the $3.6 billion total would go for economic loans and grants to promote economic growth in developing countries.

Look to Tomorrow

But as the task force report stresses at one point, the children of today will be the working adults of tomorrow — the leaders, the factory workers, the teachers and the farmers in these countries.

It says that economic and social growth of a seriously undernourished country will be impaired, if it must rely on adults who have been weakened by malnutrition in their childhood.

The report defines malnutrition as a lack of the vitamins, proteins and minerals needed for normal growth.

It estimated that about 70 per cent of children in less-developed countries were either undernourished or malnourished.

About 50 per cent of children in the preschool age group, up to 6 years, and 30 per cent of the group from 7 to 14 were described as "seriously undernourished."

The report called for official recognition through legislation of the new role that the Food for Peace program has been called upon to fill since its origin in 1954 as a scheme for disposal of agricultural surpluses.

It also outlined plans already taking shape in the Food for Peace office for revamping its operating practices.

But the important thing was to redraft the policy declaration of Public Law 480, authorizing the program, in a way that would reflect the use of American agricultural abundance in helping to alleviate hunger and malnutrition and their underlying causes.

If the surplus disposal tag could be removed, a relatively small additional investment would place the program in an entirely different political context in the eyes of recipient countries, the report suggested.

Primarily, the move would encourage increased host country participation and support of the things needed to diminish present malnutrition.

One of the principal conclusions of the report in this context was that the problem of hunger and malnutrition as well as the widening gap between increasing populations and food supply was one that the developing countries had ultimately to solve for themselves.

The United States and other donor countries and their food industries particularly could help in the short run. But the only lasting solution was for the developing countries to produce more food and fewer children.

July 18, 1965

U.S. ACTS TO RAISE WORLD NUTRITION

Plans Projects, in 8 Lands, Geared to Needs of Young

By FELIX BELAIR Jr.
Special to The New York Times

WASHINGTON, July 31 — A bold new program designed to reduce and eventually eradicate serious malnutrition among preschool children of underdeveloped countries was quietly set in motion this week by the Agency for International Development.

Orders went out to A.I.D. mission chiefs in 14 countries to sound out host governments on their willingness, with local private enterprise, to join the United States Government and food industry as well as private investors in an effort to break the biggest single bottleneck to economic development.

Depending on the responses from the 14 countries, it is planned to start experimental programs in some eight of them.

The immediate objective would be to increase indigenous food production by more intensive cultivation through fertilizers, bringing new lands into cultivation, and providing farmers with greater incentive to produce by land redistribution and pricing policies.

Countries finally selected for the pilot programs would be expected promptly to encourage local processors to market commercially a grain-based "complete," or formulated, food that utilizes locally available proteins and is enriched and fortified with vitamin, mineral and amino-acid additives.

Countries Listed

The 14 nations from which mission chiefs were ordered to report were chosen because of the availability of facilities for the production and distribution of formulated foods especially suitable for children.

These countries are Brazil, Chile, Colombia, El Salvador, Guatemala, Peru, India, Pakistan, Turkey, Korea, the Philippines, Thailand, Morocco and Uganda.

The experimental programs would look to an expansion of the facilities as well as the development of distribution systems. Where needed vitamin-mineral additives were not available locally, or were beyond the capacity of the Government to finance, they would be supplied by A.I.D. loans or grants.

In addition to providing the wheat flour, cornmeal and vegetable oil through continued Food for Peace shipments of United States farm surpluses, the United States would provide metering machines for accurately measuring the enrichment and fortifying process.

About 25 per cent of the grain donated through Food for Peace is milled in the recipient countries. Unlike commodities shipped from this country, the locally milled grain has not been locally enriched. This would be required under the experimental programs.

In addition, recipient governments would be urged to fix and enforce standards for enrichment of flour and other commodities and to sponsor and support local research on the development and marketing of low-cost protein foods.

Host governments would also be asked to assume progressively larger responsibility for the storage, processing and distribution costs of donated Food for Peace shipments with the ultimate goal of complete assumption of responsibility for child feeding programs.

Food for Peace operations in recipient underdeveloped countries are already in the process of shifting from the "doling out" system of family and child feeding through religious and other voluntary relief organizations.

Gradually the emphasis is being shifted from charity to the principle of "food for work." The voluntary agencies will continue to play an important role but distribution is being tied more and more to development projects approved by the A.I.D. with recipients required to shift from "relief" to "earning their keep."

In his message to mission chiefs, the foreign aid administrator, David E. Bell, said it was now a settled policy of the agency that "correcting serious protein deficiencies of preschool children would make a greater contribution to development than any other health measures — malaria eradication, sanitation and water supply not excluded." He added:

"It is also clear that Food for Peace donations alone cannot solve this problem; and that coordinated efforts by our agriculture, health, industry and community development programs will be required if progress is to be made."

'Mix of Methods'

Regarding the hoped for results of the experimental programs, Mr. Bell said that "we would hope that after a year or two we would be able to come to some conclusions on the best mix of methods for reaching target groups."

"At the same time," he said, "attention should be given to, and work initiated on, the longer-run and more basic aspects of the situation requiring research on such things as increased production of protein-rich food stuffs, nutritional habits, cultural factors, taboos, food processing, storage and distribution."

To illustrate, Mr. Bell pointed out that ground nuts were not exploited for human nutrition in a number of countries that grow them for oil or for export. As for local taboos, it was recalled, for example, that in some underdeveloped areas it was axiomatic that meat could not be digested by children while in others milk was for babies only.

As an example of the way in which the experimental programs would operate to bolster or expand child food industries, Mr. Bell included in his message to mission chiefs the following:

"The type of assistance required will vary but might include exchange or purchase of specific amounts of the final products for use in welfare-type feeding programs. Such arrangements should be structured to do away with the 'doling out' type of operations. "plans should proceed for the role" of private industry in these projects to be increased progressively, as the private sector can achieve results not attainable through government efforts.

"The United States could, for example, contract with a local processing firm to mix the locally produced protein and vitamin elements with the Food for Peace grain donations and commercial products, thus combining the feeding operation with a market promotion function for the private firm.

"New private enterprise, including United States firms, and United States firms in coventure with existing or new local firms, can be encouraged. Local currency funds jointly controlled by the United States and recipient governments, investment feasibility surveys, investment guarantees and other A.I.D. tools could also be used to bolster the child food industry in host countries.

"Loans could be made to existing firms for the extention of their facilities for production, market development or other activities. These loans should take into consideration the cost of production, advertising, surveys for acceptability and education."

The experimental programs are intended to carry out findings of an executive branch study group on nutritional needs of developing countries.

Conclusion of Study

Mr. Bell attached to his directive to mission chiefs these principal conclusions:

"1. That the high prevalence of hunger and malnutrition in the world is a leading contributor to human misery, apathy, disease, economic stagnation and political instability.

"2. That the problems associated with hunger and malnutrition cannot be separated from the basic problems related to social and economic development such as agricultural production, industrial production and population growth.

"3. That an estimated 50 per cent of the preschool-age children in the developing countries are suffering from malnutrition, and that there is evidence that this condition produces a non-reversible retardation of mental and physical development of 10 to 25 per cent.

"4. That overcoming the protein and vitamin deficiencies of young children in most less-developed countries would do more to reduce disease and eventually raise productivity than any other health measure that could be taken."

August 1, 1965

U.S. PUTS OFF INDIA ON LONG-TERM AID

Wants New Delhi to Better Its Own Farm Output

By JOHN W. FINNEY

Special to The New York Times

WASHINGTON, Nov. 2 —The United States is preparing to provide India with another monthly allotment of surplus wheat. But it is holding back on a long-term food commitment until India takes steps to improve her agricultural production.

Within the next few days, the Johnson Administration is expected to agree to an additional shipment of 500,000 tons of wheat to India under the Food for Peace Program. This would be enough to meet Indian food needs through December.

Since last June, when a one-year food agreement expired, the Administration has been providing surplus food to India only on a monthly basis. This policy has become a source of considerable irritation to India, which has been pressing for a renewal of long-term American commitments.

Misunderstandings Cited

Some misunderstanding apparently has developed between the two Governments about the purpose of this policy.

Among some diplomats, there is a suspicion that the United States, by placing India on what is interpreted as a monthly "dole," is attempting to use the Food for Peace Program for the political purpose of forcing Indian agreement with Pakistan on the Kashmir issue.

Administration officials, who are aware of these Indian suspicions, are now emphasizing to Indian diplomats that the food is not being used as a political club to force Indian concessions on Kashmir. As evidence, they point to the fact that the suspension of long-term food commitments actually predated the outbreak of the Indian - Pakistani conflict in September and October.

Within the Johnson Administration, there is concern that India may have been using the extensive surplus food shipments from the United States as a crutch and neglecting the steps she should be taking to increase domestic food production.

Administration officials feel that India has been devoting a disproportionate amount of her resources to industrial development in the last 10 years.

In the new five-year program now being drafted by India, therefore, Administration officials hope that there will be a greater investment in the agriculttural segment, particularly for increasing fertilizer production, extending irrigation and improving seed stocks.

In recent years, India has been the major recipient of surplus food from the United States. Since 1960, she has received 20 million tons of American wheat and 1.35 million tons of rice.

At present, about one American wheat farmer in five is growing wheat indirectly for India.

November 3, 1965

New Turn Ahead in Farm Policy

Special to The New York Times

WASHINGTON, Nov. 13 —In his famous Johns Hopkins speech earlier this year, when he offered "unconditional discussions" to settle the war in Vietnam, President Johnson also outlined a program of economic development in the Southeast Asia region, including the short-term shipment of surplus American rice to meet immediate food needs.

What he did not know was that there was no surplus rice. Later the Administration had to stretch existing law to its limits to procure and ship the rice on a give-away basis.

The incident is a revealing example of a profound change that is developing in the United States farm and food surplus situation. With the exception of wheat, the U.S. is running out of food surpluses, and even the excess wheat supply is rapidly dwindling.

Food has been an element of American foreign policy for ten years since Congress, in despair at mounting surpluses, passed a law in 1954 allowing their "sale" for foreign currencies to poor countries that could not pay dollars. Some of the food has been sent on an outright donation basis. Food will continue to be an element in foreign policy, but the techniques will probably have to change.

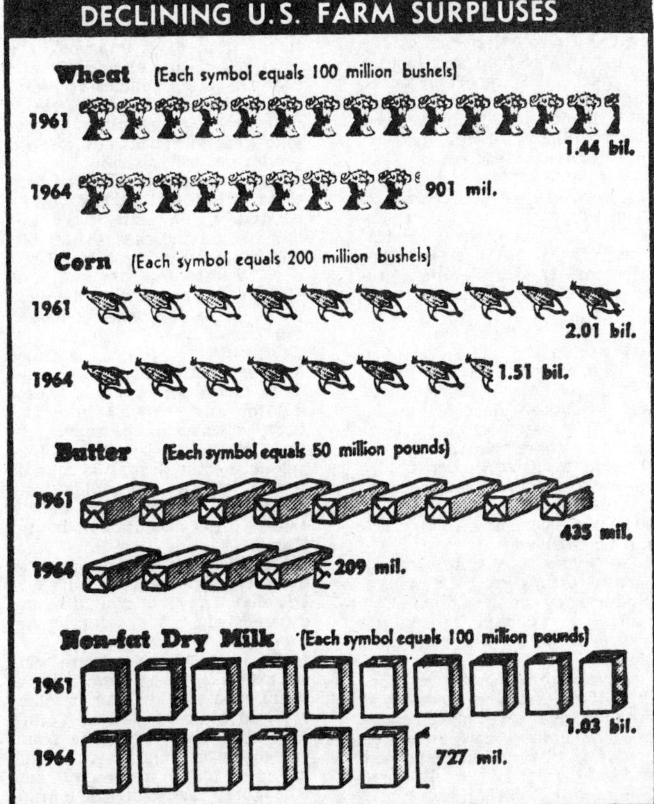

United States farm surpluses, on the decline since 1961, have fallen off sharply and may affect Administration policy on food shipments to underdeveloped nations. A percentage of the surplus (key commodities of which are shown in chart) is carried over from one year to the next as a necessary reserve food supply for the country.

Four Reasons

The reduction of the carry-over of excess food has come about for four main reasons.

First, there is a gradually rising domestic consumption, augmented by the new "food stamp" and other programs of food distribution to the poor and to schoolchildren.

Second, as living standards rise in Europe and Japan, there is a rising demand for some key American crops, such as corn for livestock feed. Agricultural exports paid for in cash reached a record last year, quite apart from food give-aways. Part of the reason is that Government support prices have been sharply cut, with farmers' income kept up by cash subsidies, thus making U.S. crops competitive.

Third, acreage controls at home check the growth in output, even if they do not actually cut it back.

And finally, there are the food give-aways abroad, which is what sales for foreign currencies amount to. This is so because most of the foreign currencies are then loaned back to the recipient country.

None of this implies any impending shortage, either for home consumption or for shipment abroad. U.S. output of most crops can be expanded any time we want, and production of other items such as dairy products can be increased with a relatively small time lag.

At the same time as the U.S. food surpluses are dwindling, however, the public and the Government have become increasingly aware of the problem of world hunger, if not starvation. This is the now familiar problem of population growth outrunning food supply.

Although the threat of malnutrition has been known about for years, it was not until quite recently that large numbers of poor countries began to think of themselves as seriously deficient in food supply and to need imports on a give-away basis from abroad. Last year the U.S. sent food—under the old surplus disposal concept—to 31 less developed countries.

In any event, the new situation at home, combined with the expiration next year of the present "Food for Peace" law, is leading the Government toward three conclusions.

First, food give-aways will have to be based less and less on what the U.S. happens to have on hand in Government stocks arising from the domestic price support program. Instead, the food will have to be bought to an increasing extent in the open market, with the advance intention of giving it away.

Second, this being so, food give-aways should be planned more rationally—based on what given countries and age groups in the population can best use.

But third, because the U.S. will never be able to feed the whole world if population continues to explode, there must be a firm condition on U.S. give-aways. This is an insistence on a major effort at agricultural development in the poor countries themselves.

None of this will lead to any radical early change in the food that actually is placed aboard ship and sent abroad. Wheat, which has made up two-thirds of food give-aways, will continue to constitute a major part of the program—both because it is badly needed in such countries as India and because without give-aways abroad, U.S. surpluses would quickly start piling up again. At present almost one out of every five bushels of American wheat produced each year winds up in Indian stomachs.

But if there will be no overnight change, the food program seems bound to be modified, with effects on domestic farmers as well as the hungry abroad.

For example, there could well be heavier concentration on oils, such as soybean oil, even though they may not be in surplus at home, because they are an important part of the diet in nations that lack fats.

Further Sales

There will be as much attention as ever on cash exports, in light of the U.S. balance of payments problem. There may yet even be another big sale of wheat for cash to the Soviet Union, if shipping restrictions and labor problems can be solved—a sale, incidentally, that would bring the existing wheat surplus down to a level close to the amount needed for an ordinary reserve.

But in the future American food give-aways abroad will be more and more a conscious policy, probably paid for by the taxpayers as aid rather than farm price supports. The debate next year in Congress seems sure to make Americans think more deeply about the issue of "feeding the world" than ever before.

E. L. D. Jr

November 14, 1965

U.S. Urged to Spur Farm Output To Alleviate World Food Crisis

By FELIX BELAIR Jr.
Special to The New York Times

WASHINGTON, Dec. 4 — A dramatic reversal of national agricultural policy is urged in a report by a select panel of businessmen, educators, economists, nutritionists and Federal officials.

The panel recommends that farmers produce more, instead of less, to help meet the world food crisis.

The report, now quitely making the rounds of top Government levels, proposes a direct

linking up of the productive capacity of American agriculture—"the most efficient farm system in the world"—to the nation's foreign policy objectives, including economic aid to underdeveloped countries.

Several months in preparation, the report calls for the return to cultivation of all or part of 50 million idle acres capable of productng 40 million tons of grain that farmers now are being induced not to plant.

The report looks to a gradual phasing out of the present complicated system of price supports and other subsidies and to eventual reliance on the market place for producer rewards.

Existing price support programs would be retained during an indefinite transition period to keep a floor under farm income.

But the $1.7 billion annual cost of the Food for Peace program, which disposes of "surplus" commodities abroad for local currencies, would be assigned to the foreign policy budget instead of the domestic farm policy budget as at present, along with any additional costs.

The report attempts to define the elements of a United States food policy in relation to world food needs. It had its inception in a week-long seminar last July at the Center for Research and Education at Estes Park, Colo.

Financed by Foundation

Co-chairmen of these sessions were Prof. Roger Revelle, director of the Harvard Center for Population Studies, and Richard W. Reuter, special assistant to the President and director of the office of Food for Peace, which was recently transferred to the State Department.

Thirty other representatives of various disciplines took part in the study, which was financed by the Rockefeller Foundation.

In terms of food and mouths to feed, the report reached these over-all conclusions:

"1. Under any circumstances, the population of the developing countries is destined to increase very rapidly for at least the next 10 to 15 years. To meet this rapid increase in population, efforts in food production both in the Western countries and the developing countries, must be dramatically increased.

"2. The reproductive potential will rise so high by 1980 that a continuing rate of reproduction at present levels would presage worldwide disaster.

"3. It is essential that means be found to reduce the rate of population growth drastically in two-thirds of the world. Unless this is done, there is scant possibility that the food crisis can be resolved.

"4. A massive and intensive parallel campaign, both in food production and in population control, is essential to the future peace and welfare of mankind."

Such arrangements, it said, should require increased food production by recipient countries, including more intensive use of fertilizers and pesticides and the introduction of new lands into cultivation.

The report urged a tougher approach by this Government in negotiating agreements, through the Food for Peace program, to ship food abroad at bargain prices.

Negotiators for the United States should insist on greater use of fertilizer whether locally manufactured or imported, the report said, and should demand that the price policies of recipient underdeveloped countries be revised where necessary to provide greater incentives to food producers and distributors.

The report cited United Nations estimates that the world's population, now about 3.5 billion, would increase to 4.6 billion by 1980 and to some 6 billion by the year 2000. About 85 per cent of this increase would be in the underdeveloped countries.

Projecting present average food production into the immediate future and without allowing for any increase in nutritional standards, the report estimated the food deficit of developing countries at 30 million tons in 1970 and 48 million tons in 1980. The estimated deficit takes into account mainland China.

The panel made no finding as to the amount by which nutritional standards should be increased in the developing countries.

But it said that if there was no increase, there would be a significant rise in the number of children, now put at 3 million, who die every year from protein-calorie malnutrition and in "the many more millions who are retarded in the physiological development by this condition."

"These malnourished, retarded survivors are major deterrents to the future social and economic development of their countries," the report said. "They will be the retarded young adults of 1985."

The study made the point, in stressing the need for increased local food production and for population control, that even if the more advanced nations had supplies available "the world's shipping and distribution facilities are inadequate for the large food transfers that would be needed."

"U. S. 'surplus' today more and more exists in its capacity to produce than in accumulated stocks," the panel said. To harness the capacity of the American farm plant to the nation's foreign policy objectives, it argued, would only give official recognition to the facts as they are.

"As far as the future is concerned," it said, "surplus disposal is not the real problem; rather it is a distraction from the real problem — how can American agriculture aid in meeting the needs of the less developed countries?"

"Certainly American agriculture can help meet this challenge," the panel declared. "It can do it primarily by planning production, not on the basis of what is easy to produce, but on the basis of what the world needs."

December 5, 1965

Farm Aide Bars Loosening Controls

By FELIX BELAIR
Special to The New York Times

WASHINGTON, Dec. 9 — The Administration responded today to mounting demands for programs to permit the cultivation of more acres to meet the world food crisis.

Under Secretary of Agriculture John A. Schnittker said in a statement that his department was well aware of the food situation abroad as well as at home but that he saw no reason to reverse the Administration's farm policy by relaxing controls designed to hold down production.

The statement was issued as a procession of speakers at an organization meeting of the Committee on the World Food Crisis endorsed an expansion of the United States farm plant by bringing back into cultivation some 55 million acres that farmers were being paid to withhold from production.

"There are vast needs for American grains abroad, particularly in India," Mr. Schnittker said. "But there are limitations on the quantity we are able to supply. The major limitation is the ability of many needy countries, and this includes India, to handle, process and distribute supplies."

Postponement Sought

Concerned that the meeting of the new organization might result in snowballing demands for an expansionist policy in domestic farm programs and in a top-heavy agricultural budget, the Administration sought to have the session postponed or abandoned. The suggestion through Secretary of Agriculture Orville L. Freeman, however, came too late.

In a major address this morning to an audience that filled the ballroom of the Washington Hilton Hotel, Representative Harold D. Cooley, chairman of the House Agriculture Committee, called for "an about face" in domestic farm policy.

The objective of this major policy switch, the North Carolina Democrat said, will be to "loosen the cords that now bind our agriculture, and then set up on a vastly expanded attack on starvation around the world — in programs aimed ultimately at developing the potentials for food sufficiency in those areas where hunger now is rampant."

Representative Cooley said that besides the 55 million farm acres not being used, the cropland adjustment program passed during the recent Congressional session would result in the retirement of an additional 40 million acres in the next 10 years.

Senator George McGovern, former director of the Food for Peace program, told an afternoon panel discussion of legislative objectives that hearings on his bill to ease crop controls would be held early next month by the Senate Foreign Relations Committee.

The McGovern bill would permit farmers to produce for indicated world needs and reward them with a fair price in an assured market at home and abroad if they followed guidelines provided by the Secretary of Agriculture.

Estimates of the cost of the South Carolina Democrat's plan run as high as $3.5 billion annually, or about the same as the current outlay for the price support program. An additional $1.7 billion is going to the Food for Peace program in which the Commodity Credit Corporation acquires title to the surpluses of farmers participating in crop control programs.

The new organization said it would seek a farm program of unfettered production to meet foreign as well as domestic needs. It said United States agricultural productive capacity could help promote the nation's foreign policy objectives.

Gov. William H. Avery of Kansas told the organization, however, that any expanded farm output would have to be accompanied by a price structure that rewarded the farmer for his increased efforts and investments.

Louis H. Bean, agricultural economist and assistant to several Secretaries of Agriculture, cautioned against imposing on developing countries this country's "wasteful" emphasis on livestock production for meat proteins. He reminded the conference that livestock returned only a third of the vegetable protein they consumed in the form of meat for human consumption.

Representative Paul H. Todd Jr., Democrat of Michigan, said no amount of increased food production, by itself, could close the gap between increasing population and food supplies. Any such effort would fail, he said, "unless strong programs of family planning are initiated and assiduously followed."

Before adjourning, the committee named Herschel D. Newsom, master of the National Grange, as its chairman. James J. O'Connor, president of the American Freedom from Hunger Foundation, was appointed vice chairman; Robert Koch, president of the National Limestone Institute, executive director, and Dr. Flemmie P. Kittrell of Howard University's home economics department, secretary.

December 10, 1965

SHUMAN OPPOSES FOOD AID PROGRAM

Scores Johnson Proposal as Breeder of Socialism

Special to The New York Times

WASHINGTON, Feb. 28 — The nation's largest farm organization urged Congress today to reject President Johnson's $3.3-billion-a-year Food for Freedom program as a breeder of unwanted surpluses and "Socialist farm planning."

In a statement to the House Agriculture Committee, Charles B. Shuman, president of the American Farm Bureau Federation, sounded the first dissenting note in the chorus of approval from Administration and academic witnesses during two weeks of hearings on the plan.

The farm leader demanded the gradual abandonment of acreage allotments, marketing quotas and other restrictions on producers. He called for ultimate reliance on the "market price system' of rewarding efficient farmers instead of the present system of government price supports, direct payments and commodity loans to those curtailing output.

Instead of telling farmers what they must do to be eligible for various Federal subsidies, Mr. Shuman proposed that they be informed of prospective domestic and foreign demand and then let the laws of supply and demand establish the price of the product in a free market. He favored retention of commodity loans temporarily.

A Willingness Test

While favoring food aid to poorer countries through loans during the present and prospective emergency period, Mr. Shuman demanded that only those governments receive such aid that agreed to adopt "the American success formula" of the private incentive system.

The farm leader proposed as a test of the willingness of recipient government to liberalize their agricultural policies the abandonment of ceilings on farm prices wherever they prevailed. He said the $25-billion of food aid shipped abroad in the past decade had been used largely "to prop up sagging Socialist systems around the world" instead of "showing the direct correlation between Socialism and increasing hunger."

"Foreign aid to India has failed as a program," he said. "It has only prolonged the life of the Socialist government of that country and is responsible, more than anything else, for the present hunger there. The incentive system of free market prices could enable India to feed itself in ten years."

Spokesmen for two smaller farm organizations—the National Farmers Union and the Midcontinent Farmers Association—urged approval of the Administration's program of food aid combined with self-help conditions on such credit sales. They also urged continued price protection for farmers.

March 1, 1966

WORLD FOOD DRIVE IS URGED FOR POOR

Presidential Panel Suggests a Multibillion-Dollar Effort to Avert Mass Starvation

By FELIX BELAIR Jr.

Special to The New York Times

WASHINGTON, June 17—A Presidential study group proposed today that the United States and other advanced non-Communist nations join in a multibillion-dollar economic development program for poor developing countries to avert impending mass starvation and its threat to world peace.

To double food production and curb population growth in the next 20 years within a framework of increased economic activity in the underdeveloped two-thirds of the world, the blue ribbon panel proposed a mobilization of capital and technical resources on a scale never attempted in time of peace.

Without fixing any ceiling on the combined capital outlay to do the job, the study estimated that to realize a 4 per cent annual increase in food supply and demand in the developing countries would require an annual investment of $12-billion more than the 1965 "input" level of about $45-billion.

The United States' contribution toward this additional investment requirement would be about $7-billion, assuming a continuation of its 58 per cent share in the total economic development contribution by non-Communist nations in recent years. Private capital investment would reduce the amount of Federal funds required, but this would indicate an economic foreign aid request to Congress of about $6-billion a year.

These estimates were given at a news briefing on a three-volume report setting forth conclusions from a year-long investigation by more than 100 experts and consultants enlisted by the President's Science Advisory Committee from the universities, industry, foundations and Federal agencies.

The only indication of the Administration's intentions concerning the long list of recommendations by the panel had to be read between the lines of President Johnson's foreword in the first volume of the report.

'Must Join With Others'

The President wrote:

"The world food problem is one of the foremost challenges of mankind today," the President wrote. The dimensions of the challenge will define the dimension of our response and the means for that response.

"We must join with others in a massive effort to help the less fortunate of the earth to help themselves. I am making this report public because of its significance for the American people and people all over the world."

Dr. Ivan L. Bennett Jr., deputy director of the White House Office of Science and Technology, told the briefing session that it had not been possible to brief members of the Senate and House prior to publication. He said it was hoped that this could be done later.

There was no indication that the far-reaching proposals would be brought to bear on the President's pending economic aid request for $2.5-billion in the fiscal year beginning July 1. However, some of them, such as a drastic overhaul of the administrative organization for development aid and the asserted need for a national commitment to such development for the rest of this century, are certain to figure in the floor debates on the request.

Two related concepts ran through the report. One was that the increased food production needed to meet the calorie-protein requirements of developing countries must take place almost entirely within these countries. The other was that the food-population imbalance cannot be solved by successful programs of family planning alone.

It was emphasized, however, that this did not mean that population control measures were defective or in any way secondary in importance to increasing food production.

'Sobering and Alarming'

The panel pictured economic development prospects in the poor and hungry nations as "both sobering and alarming."

"By the year 2000, if present rates of growth continue, there will be more than four times as many people in the developing countries as are in the developed nations," said the report.

"To avoid a threat to the peace of the world as well as to our own national security," it said, "we cannot afford to be too little and too late with our development assistance. It is to be hoped that some measure of their ambitions can be realized by peaceful means."

The report made no attempt to minimize the task involved in trying to make the poor countries reasonably self-sufficient in food. It mentioned "the necessity of capital investments of almost staggering proportions."

But the panel said that since the main hope for increasing total food production in the poor countries was through increased yield per unit of land, there could be no substitute for this higher investment in improved seed, fertilizers, pesticides machinery and water for irrigation.

Education and Training

Even more difficult would be the vast educational and training programs required to create, distribute and properly use modern crop production input and the transportation to distribute, process and market the output of farms, the panel concluded.

Stressing the need for the earliest possible beginning of the economic and agricultural development effort, the report observed that "even under the most favorable circumstances, the interval between the inauguration of such programs and their realization in the form of increased production of crops will be at least 5 to 10 years."

"It is by no means certain that this task [modernization of traditional farming] can be accomplished to the extent or at the rate needed to meet food requirements during the next two decades, even with a 'warlike' mobilization of the developed countries," the panel concluded.

A maximum effort would be required from all nations, developing and developed alike, said the report, "if the pangs of hunger are to be alleviated, if the irreparable damages of infant and childhood malnutrition are to be prevented, and if the growing threat of mass starvation is to be turned aside."

The panel experts saw the United States faced with two choices in trying to spur lagging economic development in hungry countries. One was to continue providing capital assistance and private investment to poor countries willing to make the self-help effort to achieve self-sustaining growth.

They said this course might bring about some improvement in the status quo but would not meet the food problem "because, for all its economic resources, the United States cannot possibly accompish the immense task of alleviating the world food problem alone."

"The other alternative is for the United States to take the lead in mounting a global effort in concert with other developed nations and with international organizations that will bring to bear the technical skills and capital resources needed to reverse the downward trend of the developing countries and to restore the chance of their people for a better life.

"We are unanimous in the belief that the United States must assume leadership of the free world and all its international institutions in a coordinated, long-range development strategy for raising the economic level of the poor nations, thereby meeting the hunger, increasing the volume of world trade and economic activity and contributing to the achievement of the goal of ultimate importance, a lasting peace."

June 18, 1967

Time to Rethink World Farm Policy

By ROBERT KLEIMAN

The long-predicted exhaustion of American food surpluses, now increasingly a fact, is beginning to have significant repercussions on United States foreign policy as well as on the American farmer and consumer.

The belief that a world food crisis is still two decades off is proving a miscalculation. The notion that idle American farmland could meet growing domestic and foreign food needs until 1984 has misjudged the critical difference between surplus food in storage and surplus land. Surplus food can be shipped on short notice. Surplus land requires many months—plus complex economic and governmental decisions—to produce a crop.

Facing a New War

The decisions, it is now evident, have not been made in time. The generals on the economic front have made the classic mistake of their military counterparts—fighting the last war too long. The shift from a long war against surpluses to a new war against world hunger is under way, but it comes late.

Wheat acreage now is being enlarged 32 per cent, but the crop will not come in until next spring. Meanwhile, wheat stocks have declined below the level needed for domestic American reserves. Much the same is true for feed grains, cheese, butter and dried milk, a crucial high-protein item in aid programs. Not only are surpluses gone but supplies in some items are beginning to resemble shortage conditions—a factor in the rising bread and milk prices in New York and elsewhere.

Senator George McGovern of South Dakota has revealed, with State Department confirmation, that American wheat shipments under foreign-aid programs are being cut back 25 per cent this year. The current commitment to ship nine to ten million tons of grain to India—newly made, to stave off impending famine—is being reappraised, as are future programs there. The pledge can be met only at the price of far larger cutbacks than 25 per cent in wheat shipments to other countries or by a further rundown of reserves.

Until the new crop comes in, "we will just have to sweat it out," A.I.D. Administrator William S. Gaud said last week. Delicate choices will have to be made that undoubtedly will bring charges—similar to those already being made by Egypt's President Nasser — that Washington is playing politics with food. Recipient countries with critical monetary problems are being notified that payment for grain will have to be made in dollars rather than local currency.

Need for Monetary Approach

This particular tightening of conditions under the new "Food for Freedom" program may be justified by the need to put food aid on the same cost basis as industrial assistance. Certainly it is vital to stimulate food production and population control in the developing countries rather than over-rapid investment in industry.

But the dollar mechanism has been chosen because of the aggravation of the American payments deficit as a result of the stepped-up war in Vietnam. This device disregards the rising debt burden that is braking the development of the Southern Hemisphere. And it raises again serious questions of whether the United States should restrict output and refuse to sell food to the Communist world. The Communist countries are paying billions of dollars to other suppliers for record grain imports, which are substantially larger this year than total wheat consumption in the United States.

It is evident that contradictions abound—and are increasing—in the American policies now evolving. President Johnson last month, in a little-noticed move, summoned the full National Security Council for the first time in memory to address itself to problems of this kind. And, as Times correspondent William M. Blair has reported, Vice President Humphrey gave a sharp private warning to the advanced countries of the West during the recent Washington meeting of the O.E.C.D. Development Assistance Committee. He put them on notice that they can no longer increase commercial food sales at the expense of American markets, shirk their burden of agricultural aid to the underdeveloped world and expect the United States to feed the poor countries.

This warning—addressed primarily to food-exporting countries such as France, Canada, Australia, Holland, Denmark and Argentina—was not misplaced. But the prime responsibility is that of the free world's leader and chief producer, the United States, which clearly has been lacking in foresight.

Reluctance to Reappraise

The West's agricultural problem, whether one of surpluses or world shortages, has long been beyond the American capability to manage alone. Yet there has been a prolonged reluctance in Washington to respond imaginatively to proposals from France and the Common Market Commission for an international grains agreement covering subsidies, production controls, prices and exports.

In the Kennedy Round in Geneva, the chief American emphasis still is on holding down prices, "protectionism" and production in Europe, although American farm sales to Europe have risen substantially in recent years. Both in Geneva and in American domestic and food aid programs, the moment has clearly come for a thorough reappraisal of policies. For world population is growing faster than food output. Hunger in the poor nations, long ignored by the rich, is increasing. And the world is getting a first preview right now of the food crisis that was supposed to be two decades off.

ROBERT KLEIMAN is a member of the editorial board of The Times.

August 15, 1966

Letters to the Editor of The Times

Freeman Defends Policy on Agriculture

To the Editor:

Robert Kleiman's editorial page column of Aug. 15 "Time to Rethink Farm Policy" presents a faulty impression of the food situation in this country and the world. It fails particularly to recognize that while we have been successful in eliminating burdensome and price-depressing surpluses, we still have large reserves on hand to meet our needs. These reserves are meant to be used as needed, and replenished—not locked up for all time.

On July 1, the start of the new crop year, we had 536 million bushels of wheat on hand. This is almost exactly the amount we had determined upon as the signal to expand production and thus increase our reserves against possible larger demands at home and abroad.

Having arrived at that point, we have increased wheat acreage for next year by one-third. But even the 400 million bushels we expect to have on hand next June 30 would get us through another bad year in 1967-68 if it came to that. Or some of it could be used this fiscal year if conditions warrant it.

The same is true for feed grains. An expected supply of 47 million tons on Oct. 1 is our signal that 1967 will be the year in which to plant more corn, sorghum and barley, after six years of planting less.

Grain to India

Regarding food assistance, it simply is not true that the Government is reappraising our commitment of early this year to send nine or ten million tons of grain to India. Most of that amount has been shipped, and more is on the way. The timely action of this nation in assessing the danger and in sending unprecedented quantities on short notice has actually prevented famine in India this year.

We have made it clear that our grain will be carefully programmed. The total program laid out for the year ahead looks adequate, barring serious droughts abroad. It is in fact comparable to last year's program, if we adjust for the fact that India required an extra three to four million tons of grain last year which we do not expect to be repeated this year.

It has been our policy for five years to seek a supply-demand balance in food and fiber to avoid both surpluses and shortages. We have increased soybean acreages in each of the past several years, but a record 1966 crop still will not be large enough to provide a comfortable reserve. We reduced cotton this year by 28 per cent because of excessive stocks. These illustrations demonstrate that we now have flexibility in our farm programs and we are prepared to use it.

Population Growth

Mr. Kleiman is correct, of course, in suggesting that we must wage war on hunger rather than on surpluses. But that is a shift that has already been made in the Food for Freedom bill now before the Congress. The United States cannot win a worldwide war on hunger, however, simply by producing more for shipment overseas. Our food-producing capability, which loomed so large a decade ago, is not so imposing in a world that is adding 65 million people a year, most of them in the food-short developing countries.

It is absolutely essential that developing countries give agricultural development the attention it requires. The only hope for permanent victory in the war on hunger is greatly accelerated food production in the hungry nations. Our policies and the pending legislation are geared to this need.

Finally, it is distressing to find The New York Times attributing constructive proposals for an international grains arrangement to France and the Common Market Commission after three years in which the European Economic Community has been unable or unwilling to participate seriously in grain talks or the other agricultural negotiations in Geneva. You suggest that the United States, which together with Canada and Australia has taken the initiative in the Geneva grain talks since 1963, ought to respond "imaginatively" to the E.E.C.

Indeed it is the proposals of the United States and other exporters—not the Common Market—which outline a possible grains arrangement that includes a major international program of food aid to needy countries, access to importer markets, rules for commercial trade, and prices related to world supply and demand. E.E.C. proposals, in contrast, would do no more than allow the Community to increase her self-sufficiency in food. The E.E.C. would only provide food aid when they happened to produce a surplus, still leaving to the United States the burden of feeding the poor nations and adjusting world supply to demand. ORVILLE L. FREEMAN

Washington, Aug. 23, 1966

September 1, 1966

Food Aid Policy

With Senate passage of the revised Food for Peace bill, both houses of Congress now have approved a radically new concept for American aid in feeding a hungry world.

Instead of giving away surpluses, the new program calls for planned production of food for foreign aid. Instead of trying to hold down production at home and abroad, the emphasis now is on stimulating farm yield in the developing nations and increasing American output, to the extent necessary, to close the gap. All this because food needs are rising everywhere—most rapidly in the poor countries—just as American surpluses have finally disappeared.

"We are beginning the most complex farm policy period in our history," Under Secretary of Agriculture John Schnittker said last week. "Decisions by United States farmers and program administrators must be geared to domestic and export markets and to food aid as far as thirty months ahead."

The new Food for Peace bill is intended to provide new financing and other mechanisms for this task. It will do so far more effectively if the Senate-House conference acts wisely now to excise the restrictive amendments each house inserted. For the future, the critical question is whether Washington's "program administrators" will make the right decisions and make them sufficiently well in advance. The shortages now developing—which have lifted farm prices 9 per cent in a year and 2 per cent in the midst of the current harvest—indicate that such foresight has been inadequate in the past.

Despite the strong defense of Administration food policy Secretary Freeman makes in a letter on this page today, the recent increases in wheat acreage will not augment supplies until next spring. It will take even longer to ease the tightness in food grains, soybeans, cheese, butter and dry milk, an important high-protein item in aid programs.

To help meanwhile, American reserves can be drawn down, for they are large, as Mr. Freeman says. Unfortunately, they are not large enough — or it would not be necessary to inform American embassies abroad that wheat aid this year will be cut back 25 per cent.

"We had far better risk having too much food in our warehouses than too little," President Kennedy's Food for Peace Administrator told the Senate last week. It is wise counsel for a program that, in effect, substitutes production planning for the ever-normal granary the United States has hitherto maintained for the world.

September 1, 1966

PRESIDENT SIGNS FOOD PEACE PLAN BUT SCORES CURBS

Asserts Congress Limited His Flexibility in Dealing With Communist Nations

$5-BILLION AUTHORIZED

Johnson Disturbed by Ban on Countries Selling to North Vietnam and Cuba

By ROBERT B. SEMPLE Jr.
Special to The New York Times

SAN ANTONIO, Tex., Nov. 12—President Johnson signed today a $5-billion, two-year expansion of the Food for Peace program despite strong complaints that certain provisions of the bill would "create major difficulties for our foreign policy."

The act, which authorizes slightly more than $2.5-billion in each of calendar years 1967 and 1968, includes two provisions added by Congress regarding the shipment by third countries of materials to North Vietnam and Cuba.

The first bans all food shipments under Public Law 480—the original Food for Peace law passed in 1954—to any country selling or transporting any goods, strategic or otherwise, to North Vietnam.

The second imposes a similar ban on countries making shipments to Cuba, but gives the President authority to waive the ban when the transactions involve certain specified nonmilitary goods—medical supplies, nonstrategic raw materials for agriculture and nonstrategic agricultural or food commodities.

Troubled by Curbs

In a statement issued by the White House here, the President said he was "particularly troubled" by these provisions, despite the fact that the second gave "some latitude for Presidential discretion."

He said he was not objecting to the substance of the provisions.

"The position of this Administration is quite clear as to Free World trade and shipping to both North Vietnam and Cuba," he declared. "We oppose it. We have conducted and will continue a very active effort against this trade. No Free World countries now furnish arms or strategic items to either area."

However, the Administration, particularly the State Department, has argued that the inclusion of such directives in the bill would severely restrict the President's ability to use the Food for Peace program as a bargaining tool with nonaligned nations and as a device to woo Communist nations.

"I believe we should have the flexibility to use food aid to further the full range of our important national objectives," the President said. "Restrictions on its use deprive us of this flexibility. They inhibit us in meeting objectives to which four Administrations have dedicated themselves."

Reconsideration Asked

Accordingly, he said he hoped that the next Congress would "reconsider these provisions of the bill, passed in the closing days of the session, which create major difficulties for our foreign policy."

The bill amends and enlarges the existing Food for Peace program, which was scheduled to expire Dec. 31. It made three major changes in the old program, all of which Mr. Johnson endorsed.

The first shifts the emphasis of the program from disposal of American surplus food to planned production for export. The President noted that surpluses had dwindled but that recent agricultural legislation would return to production half of the nation's 60-million-acre cropland reserve by removing acreage and other limitations.

The second requires recipient countries to improve their own agricultural production as a condition for receiving American food. The President has long urged such a move and applauded it vigorously today.

"Even the food producing capability of United States farmers—unmatched in history—cannot suffice indefinitely in a world that must feed a million new human beings each week," he said. "The only long-term solution is self-help."

Nine Areas Cited

The bill directs the President, before entering into a sales agreement, to consider the extent to which the recipient country is undertaking self-help measures in nine areas of agricultural development. They range from production of needed food rather than nonfood crops to the development of fertilizer, farm equipment and other farm-related industries to the training of farmers in agricultural techniques.

A third major change encourages recipient nations to undertake population control programs by requiring the President, before making agreements, to "take into account" a nation's efforts to meet the problems of "population growth."

"Rapid population growth is putting relentless pressure on food supplies," Mr. Johnson said. "For six consecutive years world food consumption has exceeded production."

He noted that "sound population programs, encouraged in this measure, freely and voluntarily undertaken, are vital to meeting the food crisis, and to the broader efforts of the developing nations to attain higher standards of living for their people."

November 13, 1966

INDIANS TO LIMIT TRADE WITH REDS

Sales Restrictions to Hanoi and Havana Approved to Assure U.S. Grain Flow

By J. ANTHONY LUKAS
Special to The New York Times

NEW DELHI, Jan. 22—Prime Minister Indira Gandhi said today that India had accepted new restrictions on trade with North Vietnam and Cuba in order to get badly needed American grain.

However, the Prime Minister said this did not compromise the country's honor because India had not been trading with North Vietnam and because her trade with Cuba was limited to the selling of jute goods, to which the United States did not object.

Mrs. Gandhi assured a large crowd at an election meeting in Nagpur that if any conditions were imposed that violated India's self-respect, she would reject them.

"We would rather starve than sell our national honor," she declared.

The Prime Minister was replying to recent charges by leftist leaders and the left-wing press that India had accepted "humiliating conditions" to get American grain.

They were speaking of restrictions in the American Food for Peace act that went into effect Jan. 1. The restrictions prevent the United States from supplying food to countries that trade in any fashion with North Vietnam or that sell anything but medicine or nonstrategic food and agricultural commodities to Cuba.

V. K. Krishna Menon, a former leader of the governing Congress party's left wing who is running for Parliament as an independent, said at a Bombay election meeting yesterday that if India had agreed to such restrictions she had abandoned self-respect and independence.

Contending that Mrs. Gandhi's Government had given in to one Western pressure after another, Mr. Menon said, "This rot must stop."

'Spineless Pusillanimity'

The Patriot, a pro-Communist daily newspaper, called the Government's reported decision "spineless pusillanimity." It charged that Mrs. Gandhi was now openly accepting "dictation by the State Department."

These and other charges suggest that the left is hoping to make the new restrictions a major issue in the closing weeks of the campaign for the general elections from Feb. 17 to 25.

Mrs. Gandhi's remarks in Nagpur were clearly designed to cut the ground from under her critics by an open discussion of the matter.

However, some observers believe she may unwittingly have added fuel to the controversy

United Press International

Mrs. Indira Gandhi

by further dramatizing the decision.

She said India had had to decide "whether to accept food with political strings attached or to say, 'No, we don't want your food'."

She said the strings were attached when "the Americans told us that we must stop our trade with Cuba and North Vietnam if we wanted food from them."

"Our position was that we had already stopped trade with North Vietnam since 1962, though for different reasons," she said. "Our fear then was that anything we exported to North Vietnam might find its way to China."

"As regards Cuba," she continued, "we told them that we had been exporting jute to Cuba for a long time. Then they said, 'All right, but don't send them any arms.' This we were not doing anyway."

Mrs. Gandhi said that when these conditions were set the Government considered the matter and even consulted with the chief ministers of several Indian states.

Finally, she said, the Government decided that "the conditions put by the United States did not affect our position or honor in any way. So we decided to take the much-needed food."

Another Drought Ahead

India is in particularly bad need of American grain this year because she is facing her second consecutive drought and the threat of serious famine in Bihar and Uttar states. Indian officials estimated that they will need at least 11 million tons of grain over the next year, most of which they would like from the United States.

American officials here expressed some surprise at Mrs. Gandhi's formulation. They said the matter had not been a serious issue between the United States and India because it was known that India was not violating the restrictions in the new law.

They said the clause that permitted exemption of countries selling only medicines or nonstrategic agricultural commodities to Cuba had been written into the law specifically to meet India's case.

This waiver can be made only if the President feels that a food agreement with such a country would be in "the national interest of the United States." However, officials said they were sure it would be waived in India's case.

Most Trade in Jute

From April, 1965, to February, 1966, India sold $3.866-million worth of commodities to Cuba. Of these, $3.856-million worth was in jute sacking, which is defined as a nonstrategic agricultural commodity.

Officials said the remaining $10,000 worth was in medicines, also included in the waiver provision.

American officials said that since India so clearly did not run afoul of the law there had been no need for negotiations on the matter.

They said it had not come up for serious discussion at the meeting that Eugene V. Rostow, Under Secretary of State for Political Affairs, held with Indian officials here last week.

Mr. Rostow was here as part of an eight-nation tour he is undertaking for President Johnson to seek a broader, international approach to India's food crisis. He is trying to organize a new food consortium in which all the advanced nations would contribute to meet India's needs.

Officials said the consideration that Mrs. Gandhi described in her speech evidently occurred several months ago, after the new Food for Peace legislation was enacted.

One official said: "If they [the Indians] took any decision on the matter, they took it by themselves and did not communicate it to us. Nor did we ask them for any decision."

January 23, 1967

JOHNSON REVAMPS FOOD AID PROGRAM

Places Control in the Hands of 2 New Committees

By FELIX BELAIR Jr.
Special to The New York Times

WASHINGTON, March 15—President Johnson has signed an executive order designed to end the bureaucratic struggle for control of the $7.4-billion Food for Freedom Program.

The order places over-all direction of the program in a War on Hunger Policy Committee. The Secretary of State will be chairman. Other members include the Secretary of Agriculture, the Director of the Budget and the administrator of the Agency for International Development.

The order provides for an additional executive committee to be headed by the assistant administrator of the Agency for International Development, Herbert J. Waters, who is chief of the agency's War on Hunger Office.

This second group would have immediate control of the program, for which Congress last year appropriated $3.7-million a year.

If the reorganization operates as intended, it will provide positive leadership and direction to the Food for Freedom Program for the first time since October, 1965.

Office Downgraded

President Johnson at that time downgraded the office of Food for Peace from an adjunct of the White House to a small advisory office in the State Department.

The office ceased to function in any capacity when Richard W. Reuter resigned in dismay as a special assistant to the Secretary of State.

The President's order defining jurisdictions and the chain of command in the campaign against hunger came as the Senate gave routine approval to a resolution supporting Mr. Johnson's request for authority to send 3 million more tons of food grains to India and for $190-million more to pay for it.

The voice vote approving the measure came after an explanation of the proposal by Senator Jack Miller, Republican of Iowa. The House approved the resolution last week. The Senate Agriculture Committee added its endorsement yesterday.

President Johnson had ample authority under existing law to allocate the extra 3 million tons for India. A total of 3.6 million tons was committed for shipment earlier this year. But the President requested the resolution as a means of establishing the concept of matching contributions by other donor countries.

The resolution authorizes the allocation of "up to 3 million tons" of food grains to India, provided this amount is matched by other contributions of food. capital, fertilizer or farm equipment by other countries, including the Soviet Union.

The President's executive order defined the purpose of the War on Hunger Policy Committee as reviewing and coordinating policies for the new Food for Peace Act as well as those involving capital and technical assistance, research related to food production and distribution, voluntary population control programs in developing countries and agricultural self-help activities in such areas.

The executive committee would be established at the discretion of the top policy group. It would have an advisory role, but it could undertake any assignments approved by the policy committee. Actually, plans were well advanced for the executive group to become the operating arm of the Secretary of State

A third group to be known as the Interagency Staff Committee on Food for Freedom is also provided for in the President's order. Its members would be representatives of the Departments of State, Agriculture, the Treasury, Commerce and Defense; the Bureau of the Budget and the Agency for International Development.

The chairman of this group would be the representative of the Agriculture Department. It would develop and review proposed programs under the new law and coordinate functions delegated or assigned by the new order.

"ALWAYS SMOLDERING"

Little in The Nashville Tennessean

March 17, 1967

ADVISERS OPPOSED U.S. WHEAT SLASH

Presidential Panel Asserted a Cut Was 'Unthinkable'

By FELIX BELAIR Jr.
Special to The New York Times

WASHINGTON, July 2—The day before the Johnson Administration decided to cut back this year's wheat acreage by 13 per cent a Presidential advisory committee told Mr. Johnson that it was "unthinkable that this country would consider a reduction in our own food production."

The committee's conclusion was based on a report the week before by a White House study group on the world food situation. It was explained in a letter to the President by James A. Perkins, president of Cornell University who was writing as chairman of the General Advisory Committee on Foreign Assistance Programs. The letter said:

"We cannot believe that this country should so flatly turn its back on starvation."

The decision to cut back wheat acreage by 13 per cent was announced by Secretary of Agriculture Orville L. Freeman on June 23 while President Johnson was meeting with Premier Aleksei N. Kosygin of the Soviet Union.

Letter Delayed on Way

The Perkins letter was forwarded to the White House the day before the Freeman announcement but informed officials report that it did not get to the President's attention until later.

Coming on the heels of the White House study group report citing the "alarming" status of agricultural production in developing countries, the Freeman announcement had a stunning impact in both the executive and legislative branches on supporters of a vigorous drive against hunger.

What everybody knows and nobody says out loud is that something had to be done to shore up sagging wheat prices before next year when disgruntled farmers will help elect a President of the United States, a new House of Representatives and a third of the Senate.

This explains why Congressional spokesmen from wheat states have had nothing to say about the cutback that none of them likes. As one of them put it during the last week:

"You can't argue against any plan to bring about better prices and incomes for farmers."

World Consideration Asked

The Perkins letter to the President was widely discussed by policy officials following the wheat acreage cut.

Apparently on the assumption that its advice would be adopted, the Perkins advisory group urged that the White House study group's report be brought officially to the attention of the Organization for Economic Cooperation and Development as well as the legislative and executive branches of this Government at the earliest opportunity.

The Organization for Economic Cooperation and Development is composed of government representatives of most industrialized nations of the non-Communist world. Its headquarters in Paris provides a forum for discussion for trade, aid and related international economic and monetary policies of member nations.

It was to this organization that President Johnson addressed his proposal earlier this year that the United States contribution of three million tons of food grains to India this year be matched by other advanced countries either in kind or by other appropriate means such as fertilizer, farm equipment or capital grants.

Before the Freeman announcement, arguments for and against the cut had already split the Administration down the middle, with the State and Agriculture Departments on opposite sides.

The Agency for International Development, with State Department backing, argued for enough additional wheat acreage to produce a wheat crop of 100 million bushels over this year's record total of 1.5 billion bushels. This would have provided a reserve of some 600 million bushels, given normal weather conditions and better than average yields.

But in the end the Budget Bureau sided with the Department of Agriculture in setting the wheat acreage allotment at 59.3 million acres against the current year's allotment of 68 million, or a reduction of 13 per cent.

Doubled Output Urged

The general advisory committee headed by Dr. Perkins includes 15 members representative of business and industry, banking, education, agriculture, organized labor and the foundations. Its most recent meeting on June 21 was devoted to the report on the world food situation by 100 scientists and economists under direction of the White House Office of Science and Technology.

Based on a year's study of the food population problem the study group report found that "mass starvation" was inevitable unless the United States acted now to help double food production in the next 20 years in advanced, non-Communist nations.

Secretary Freeman's announcement suggested that the decision had taken account of a lower food requirement than in recent years under the Food for Peace program authorizing sales to developing countries. He mentioned specifically the ineligibility of Yugoslavia for food aid because of its trade and aid to North Vietnam and of Algeria because of its expropriation of American private property without proper compensation.

It was learned that a week before the decision Mr. Freeman advised the Catholic Relief Agency that the department would be unable to renew its contract for 2.3 million bushels of wheat and large quantities of nonfat dry milk at less than world market prices.

The Perkins letter to President Johnson was actually a mild version of the consensus developed during the all-day meeting of the general advisory group. A morning session was devoted to a briefing on the 800-page study group report by Dr. Ivan L. Bennett Jr., deputy director of the White House Office of Science and Technology.

In the aftermath of the wheat acreage decision Secretary Freeman has been accused privately by some officials of "gambling" that both weather and yields per acre will be above average in recent years. The Secretary acknowledged that the expectation of a 1.5 billion bushel crop assumed "normal" weather between next fall planting and the following July 1 and the highest yields ever.

July 3, 1967

The Muffled War on Hunger

The President's Science Advisory Committee has called on the United States as a matter of "highest priority" to lead a vastly expanded and redirected international effort to solve the world food problem or face consequences of "alarming" proportions.

The committee recently released a three-volume report, based on a year's study by more than 100 scientists, which spells out in compelling detail both the magnitude of the problem and the nature and scope of the programs that must be undertaken if the world is to avoid mass starvation and resultant widespread civil strife.

Unfortunately, although President Johnson gave the study his personal endorsement in an introductory note, there is as yet no indication that the Johnson Administration or Congress is prepared to meet the rising challenge of a world food crisis. For example:

The report calls for a substantial increase in United States foreign assistance, both for agriculture and for general economic development, but the Administration continues to make only a half-hearted case for another "bare bones" aid budget that is under heavy fire in both houses.

The report deplores "the steadily diminishing role that true technical assistance has played in foreign aid," but there are no signs of a move to strengthen the modest technical assistance component of the new aid budget.

Meanwhile, the war on hunger that the President proclaimed with such fervor last year is being prosecuted with considerably less conviction than Mr. Johnson's rhetoric conveyed.

Seven months ago the director of the Food for Peace program resigned in dismay over his lack of authority and the bureaucratic wrangling between the State Department and the Department of Agriculture.

The program is being administered on an *ad hoc* basis by interdepartmental committees. It is reported that because of the absence of clearcut authority, many important decisions are being set aside.

One decision that has been made was announced not long ago by the Secretary of Agriculture. It was to cut back the wheat acreage for next year's crop by 13 per cent.

The cutback announcement came only one day after the President's General Advisory Committee on Foreign Assistance Programs had written that it was "unthinkable that this country would consider a reduction in our own food production." In a letter to the President, James A. Perkins, president of Cornell University and chairman of the advisory panel, wrote:

"We cannot believe that this country should so flatly turn its back on starvation."

This is indeed a strange way to demonstrate America's readiness to lead a worldwide crusade against hunger.

July 9, 1967

U.S. INDUSTRY SET TO FEED THE POOR

Growing Market Emerges in Underdeveloped Lands

By JAMES J. NAGLE

Efforts to feed the undernourished people of the world now and in the future bode well for numerous segments of American industry as well as farmers.

Needed are fertilizers, drugs, agricultural equipment, a coordinated plan for raising the economic levels of the developing countries through increasing crop yields and the development of new types of food.

As pointed out by Professors Nevin S. Scrimshaw and Samuel A. Goldblith of the Massachusetts Institute of Technology, not only do many people have too little food but what they do have contains little or no proteins. Dr. Scrimshaw is head and Dr. Goldblith is executive officer of M.I.T.'s Department of Nutrition and Food Science. Both are active in various organizations — both national and international — engaged in finding solutions to the world food problem.

Among the objectives of these groups are the promotion of increased quantity and quality of conventional plant and animal protein sources suitable for direct human consumption; improvement in the efficiency and scope of both marine and freshwater fisheries operations, and the prevention of unnecessary losses of foods in field, storage, transport and the home.

They also seek an increase in the direct food use of oilseeds and oil-seed protein concentrates by humans; promotion of the production and use of fish-protein concentrates; an increase in the production and use of synthetic amino acids to improve the quality of protein in cereals and other vegetables and the development of other synthetic nutrients and, finally, the promotion of the development of single-cell protein for both animal feeding and direct consumption by humans.

The oil industry already is working on the production of a single-cell protein from crude oil, and some other companies are recovering algae from waters surrounding their plants. As one cynical observer pointed out, however, these moves are not purely altruistic since the oil companies usually are in underdeveloped countries and the production of protein also helps produce their oil products. The companies recovering algae get credit for aiding the fight on water pollution.

According to Alfred Champagnat, research director of the Société Française des Pétroles, the micro-organisms that emerge as protein feed mainly on the wax in the paraffinic oil. With the wax removed, the oil is more fluid and is suitable for diesel engines and domestic heating. Because they are grown in tanks, the proteins require no soil, sunlight or even assistance from human labor and because they belong to the plant kingdom they are not outlawed by religious or traditional taboos anywhere in the world.

Dr. Champagnat already has produced in a pilot plant in France, imitations of standard human foods ranging from meats such as beef, pork and chicken to cookies and sauces.

Professor Scrimshaw pointed out that American companies were accomplishing almost the same results with oil seeds. Three companies, Ralton-Purina, General Foods and General Mills have produced sample foodkits containing chunks of ham, beef, scallops, bacon chips and chicken — all made from oil seed meal.

The latter development is important because about eight million metric tons of fermented or cooked soybean products are consumed each year in the Far East. Another three million tons of peanuts, coconuts and other oil seeds are consumed in various parts of the world, but almost none of the remaining 90 million tons of oil seeds produced is fed to humans. That goes for export, is fed to animals or is used as an inefficient fertilizer, Dr. Scrimshaw said. Most developing countries, he added, have enough oil seed meal to meet the protein needs of their children if the meal was properly processed.

Samuel A. Goldblith

Nevin S. Scrimshaw

Dr. Scrimshaw and Dr. Goldblith emphasize that whatever the United States Government does in connection with alleviating the world food problem, it should be done through business and on a business-like basis.

Among the American companies already deeply involved in the problem, according to the First Hanover Corporation, are the Potash Company of America, Olin Mathieson, Kerr-McGee, American Cyanamid, International Minerals and Chemicals, Continental Oil, Cities Service, and the Homco division of Houston Oil Field Materials — all of which are providing fertilizers.

The drug industry is active in producing herbicides, fungicides and food preservatives, new products for the controlled breeding of animals, new feed additives, antibiotics, synthetic amino acids, vitamins and veterinary medicines. Considerable research in these fields is being made.

Drug companies particularly active in this field include Merck, Eli Lilly and Charles Pfizer, according to First Hanover,

Among the American companies providing better tools and implements in the battle against undernourishment are John Deere, Allis-Chalmers, Massey-Ferguson, and the Homco division of Houston Oil Field Materials, the report said.

In addition to the three general fields of improved fertilizers, drugs and equipment, there are other problems, such as administration and the development of new types of food, in which American companies are active.

They apparently recognize that the job of feeding the world does not have to be wholly an altruistic one.

August 13, 1967

U.S. IS EXPANDING FOOD AID ABROAD AS SPUR TO PRICES

Authorizes Negotiations in Eight Countries for Sales Under Freedom Program

By FELIX BELAIR Jr.
Special to The New York Times

WASHINGTON, Oct. 24—A rapid expansion of the Food for Freedom program in underdeveloped countries has been authorized by the Administration under pressure of sagging farm prices in the United States and sharp cuts in foreign aid funds.

Negotiations are actively under way with eight countries looking to concessional sales of wheat, feed grains and edible oil for local currency, as well as repayable dollar credit. In addition, restrictions on donated food to combat malnutrition, particularly among children, have been quietly removed.

The Agency for International Development has cabled its missions in less developed countries that supplies are now ample for donation programs linked to self-help efforts in agricultural development. Two conditions for eligibility are that the donated food should be used to increase local farm production and should not displace commercial sales.

Notice Revoked

The message on donation food had the effect of revoking a notice to missions in August, 1966, that 25 per cent less wheat and feed grains would be available as food aid—whether on a concessional sales basis or for donations programs—and that their requests should be tailored accordingly.

Food aid shipments dwindled to a trickle in the last half of 1966. Requests for donation food, which many underdeveloped countries use instead of money to pay workers on agricultural projects, all but stopped. To reverse this psychology of scarcity, the agency cable said in part:

"There is ample food available to meet program requirements which were curtailed last fiscal year because of limited supplies of some commodities. Our task now is to utilize more effectively Title II [donation] authority to help developing countries gain ground in the food and population race and speed up social and economic progress.

Nutrition Programs

"Increased availability of Public Law 480 commodities, particularly wheat and wheat products, coarse grains and vegetable oils, offer opportunities to help offset the economic and political effects of reduced levels of other forms of assistance."

As originally enacted in 1959, Public Law 480 authorized concessional sales or donation abroad of surplus agricultural products. The requirement that commodities be in "surplus" was eliminated by Congress last year in extending the law two more years. The extended law also authorized the Secretary of Agriculture to buy in the open market to meet foreign requirements.

The A.I.D. message to missions went on to say:

"The President has a personal interest in seeing that our food resources are used to improve nutrition and child feeding and he has been assured by the Secretary of Agriculture and the A.I.D. administrator that special attention will be given to using our food resources for this purpose.

"We believe there are additional opportunities for imaginative use of donation commodities for the expansion or establishment of meaningful programs to combat malnutrition, particularly in infants and preschool age children, to provide school children with nutritious meals, and to promote community development and other self-activities, with special emphasis on increasing agricultural production."

The message added that all such self-help activities could be carried out under the auspices of voluntary agencies such as CARE, World Church Service and Catholic Relief Service as well as under government-to-government programs.

Although unwilling to identify the countries with which negotiations are under way for concessional food sales, agriculture officials are frankly hopeful that revival of food aid shipments will have a buoyant effect on farm prices in this country.

On the threshold of the Presidential election year there has been widespread discontent among farmers of the Corn Belt and the Plains States over current price levels. Wheat that brought $1.71 a bushel on the farm a year ago was at $1.39 last Sept. 15, and corn that brought $1.35 a bushel a year ago was worth $1.12 a bushel a month ago.

Farmers generally are blaming the Administration for the persistent low level of prices beyond the period of surplus supplies of wheat and feed grains.

Secretary of Agriculture Orville L. Freeman had publicly "shared" their frustration, explaining that while there was no wheat surplus in the United States today," bumper crops around the world were "prompting irregular and discouraging short-term market action."

Because all wheat-producing countries have better than average crops in prospect, some grain-trade experts are skeptical about an Agriculture Department forecast of wheat exports of 750 million bushels this year.

A year ago, Mr. Freeman asked wheat farmers to increase their planted acres by 32 per cent. They responded with a 26 per cent increase, and a crop officially estimated at 1.55 billion bushels resulted. Producers are angry because their response has been rewarded with materially lower prices.

To make matters worse, Congress appears in no mood to act on food reserve legislation at this time so that the addition to the wheat carryover from this year's indicated harvest cannot be expected to be lessened by that possibility.

October 25, 1967

Flip-Flop on Food Aid

The Administration has performed another flip-flop on food aid this week in a context that suggests there may be as much political expediency as enlightened policy in execution of the President's proclaimed War on Hunger.

Citing an increasing threat of world famine, Mr. Johnson asked and received last year new legislation designed to step up American food production to help meet world needs through an expanded Food for Freedom program. The new act replaced a 1954 law under which United States food aid depended on the availability of surpluses that by last year had virtually vanished.

No sooner had the new legislation gone into effect, however, than the Administration began to cut back on food aid because of tight supplies and rising prices. Statements by agriculture officials belittled fears of a growing world food shortage and suggested a new policy of stringency in food aid from the United States.

This policy, which many regarded as a retreat from the War on Hunger, was abruptly reversed within the last few days when the Administration announced plans for a rapid expansion of food assistance. It would be gratifying to think that this expansion represented a renewed determination to fulfill the commitment the President made last year. But there is evidence to suggest that the new enthusiasm for shipping food abroad to the needy is prompted by urgent political pressures from the Farm Belt, where bumper crops have brought sharply declining prices. It looks suspiciously like a return to the old expediency of dumping surpluses through food aid.

This dismal view is reinforced by the Administration's announcement that it is cutting corn and other feed grain acreage, as it has already cut wheat acreage. Such actions may boost prices and cheer farmers, but they are not in keeping with the President's promise of an all-out War on Hunger.

The erratic performance of Food for Freedom cannot be blamed entirely on the Administration, however. Because it is impossible to predict with any assurance what world food production and needs will be from one year to the next, President Johnson requested, as part of the Food for Freedom bill, authority to establish a food reserve. Congress has not yet granted that authority. If it were granted, the United States would be in a better position to meet its responsibilities to its own farmers while responding consistently to the needs of the hungry abroad.

October 28, 1967

AID HELD LAGGING TO NEEDY NATIONS AT CRITICAL POINT

Pearson Commission Study Calls for Sharp Increase in Richer Countries' Help

REPORT TO WORLD BANK

Global Survey Notes Heavy Distrust of Foreign Relief, Especially in America

By EDWIN L. DALE Jr.
Special to The New York Times

WASHINGTON, Oct. 1—The first international study of aid to the poor countries by an independent commission of eight distinguished citizens from as many countries, concluded today that the aid effort was "flagging" at the very time that the drive for economic development was beginning to produce results.

The Commission on International Development, headed by Lester B. Pearson, former Prime Minister of Canada, presented its 230-page report, with appendices, to the World Bank and to the bank's governors, assembled here for the annual meeting.

All the member governments of the World Bank will receive the report. President Nixon has instructed his special commission studying the future of foreign aid to take it into account. The commission is headed by Rudolph A. Peterson president of the Bank of America.

Dilon Takes U.S. Role

The United States member of the Commission was Douglas Dillon, former Secretary of the Treasury. The other members were Sir Edward Boyle from Britain, Roberto Campos from Brazil, Wilfried Guth from West Germany, Arthur Lewis from Jamaica, Robert Marjolin from France and Saburo Okita from Japan.

The report began by conceding that "the climate surrounding foreign aid programs is heavy with disillusion and distrust," particularly in the United States, but said that in actual fact, "economic growth in many of the developing countries has proceeded at faster rates than the industrial countries ever enjoyed at a similar state in their own history."

Widening Gap Cited

Saying that "the widening gap between the developed and developing countries has become a central issue of our time," the report asserted that "it is the progress that has been made and the lessons that have been learned that would make any weakening at this time of the commitment to international development so foolish and so tragic."

In a personal address to the bank's governors Mr. Pearson said, "I know that the road to nowhere is paved with good reports—and some not so good. I hope that ours may deserve a better fate. But that will be up to Governments. They dispose of what commissions propose."

The Commission advocated a large increase in Government aid (as distinct from private investment), to seven-tenths of one per cent of the gross national product of the industrial countries by 1975, compared with just under four-tenths in 1968. For the United States, this would mean an aid program of more than $8-billion, with probably less than at present in the form of surplus food already paid for by the taxpayers under the farm program.

The Commission also made numerous other recommendations, ranging from techniques of aid to population, from trade policy to private investment.

Rise in Aid Urged

It urged that 20 per cent of aid by 1975 be channeled through the World Bank and other international institutions, compared with 10 per cent now.

And it proposed a new form of political relationship between donor and receiver to avoid some of the problems of the past.

In probably its most eloquent section, the report sought to answer the question of "why aid?" It noted that the answer "goes to the very root of the weakening of the will to continue, let alone strengthen, development cooperation," and is affected by the present fact that "even the richest countries are saddled with heavy social and economic problems within their own borders."

The report gave several answers. The simplest, it said, was moral—"that it is only right for those who have to share with those who have not." It added:

"Concern with the needs of other and poorer nations is the expression of a new and fundamental aspect of the modern age—the awareness that we live in a village world, that we belong to a world community.

The New York Times (by Mike Lien)

REPORTS ON INTERNATIONAL AID: Lester B. Pearson, head of an eight-nation commission on economic aid, addressing governors of the World Bank in Washington.

'Social Imperative'

"It is this which makes the desire to help into more than a moral impulse felt by an individual; makes it into a political and social imperative for governments, which now accept at least a degree of accountability in their relations with each other."

The report readily conceded that economic development did not guarantee political stability and that "aid for development does not usually buy dependable friends." But it said: "Who can now ask where his country will be in a few decades without asking where the world will be?"

Shortly before Mr. Pearson spoke today, the feelings of the 80 poorer members of the World Bank about the current situaton were summarized by Edward Seaga, Finance Minister of Jamaica.

"At the same time that official capital flows from rich to poor nations (last year) were less than $7-billion per annum," he said, "the world was actively spending $150-billion per annum for arms and the means of destruction . . . in the first six years of this decade, per capita income in the wealthy countries grew more than $200 per annum. Compare this with the growth over this period among the poorer nations — $7 per annum."

Correlation Traced

The Pearson report conceded that there is a "weak" correlation in the past between the countries that grew fastest and those that received the most aid. One reason, it said, was that much aid was allocated for military or political reasons, rather than for development.

"Nonetheless," said the report, "it is clear that aid, increasingly focused on the imperatives of long-term development, has helped to make possible a good record of development in the past two decades."

Mr. Pearson told the meeting that 41 countries had achieved 2 per cent growth a year in per capita income since 1955, "roughly what the developed countries of Western Europe and North America achieved in the century starting in 1850."

And yet, said the report, "official development assistance increased rapidly between 1956 and 1961, increased very slowly through 1967, and began to decline in 1968." Private investment flows, which have risen, "represents a compensation for only a limited number of countries, the report said."

"The stagnation of official development assistance," said the report, "is perhaps the principal element in the increasing dissatisfaction and sensitiveness of the less developed countries, fully matching the aid weariness of some of the donors."

Among the more innovative proposals in the report was that the aid-giving countries use part of their large and rising inflow of interest and principal on past loans to "subsidize interest rates on some World Bank lending."

Trade Liberalization Plan

Another suggestion involved a staged plan of trade liberalization by the rich countries, to give the less developed countries a gradually rising share of the market from some agricultural products and a growing range of manufactured products.

The report emphasized the diversity of the poor countries and of their problems. This was one example:

"India has 17 states, the largest with more people than any European country; Gabon has fewer people than a single borough in London."

On the population issue, the report strongly refuted the "widespread belief that in small or sparsely settled countries, rapid population growth is in the national interest and raises no problem, as there is much empty land" — a belief widespread in Latin America.

The report set as a specific goal "to slow the growth of population" and said: "We believe that the right to knowledge and means of family planning should be available to all, and that no child should be born unwanted." Aid-giving countries, it added, "cannot be indifferent to whether population problems receive the attention they require."

The basic goal set by the report was real economic growth averaging 6 per cent a year for the poor countries in the next decade and "self-sustaining" growth by the end of the century. It said the majority of the developing countries can "clearly" attain the goal.

Aid as Part of GNP

The following is a list of official development aid as a percentage of the gross national product (1968) of major countries:

France	0.72	United States	0.38
Australia	0.57	Canada	0.28
Netherlands	0.54	Sweden	0.28
Britain	0.42	Japan	0.25
West Germany	0.42	Italy	0.23
Belgium	0.42		

Sources: Organization for Economic Cooperation and Development and the Development Assistance Committee.

October 2, 1969

Congressmen Told of $693-Million Arms Sales Under Food for Peace Program

By JOHN W. FINNEY
Special to The New York Times

WASHINGTON, Jan. 4 — The General Accounting Office told a Congressional subcommittee today that the Food for Peace program had permitted foreign countries to purchase nearly $700-million in military equipment in the last five years.

Senator William Proxmire, chairman of a joint economic subcommittee, said that the use of Food for Peace funds to purchase weapons smacked of an "Orwellian operation," an example in "double-think" in which "Food for Peace has been converted into Food for War."

But Controller General Elmer B. Staats, the head of the General Accounting Office, pointed out to the Senator that there was nothing illegal in using foreign currencies obtained for Food for Peace shipments for military purposes. In fact, he said, such use was specifically authorized under a provision of the Food for Peace Law—known as Public Law 480 — passed by Congress in 1954.

Under the Food for Peace program, foreign countries deposit local currency with the United States in payment for food. With the approval of the United States, the foreign countries can then use this currency for domestic purposes, and one purpose specifically authorized under the law is the purchase of military equipment needed for defense, including internal security.

A study by the General Accounting Office presented to the subcommittee by Mr. Staats showed that from the 1965 fiscal year through the 1970 fiscal year, which ended last June 30, a total of $693-million of the local currency obtained through the Food for Peace program had been used to buy military equipment.

Mr. Staats was the first witness as the subcommittee headed by Senator Proxmire, Democrat of Wisconsin, opened hearings into the extent of United States military assistance through grants, sales and such indirect methods as the Food for Peace program. One of Senator Proxmire's stated purposes is to demonstrate that vast amounts are being spent on military assistance without the full knowledge of Congress.

As what he termed a shocking case in point, Senator Proxmire cited the Food for Peace program. "The issue is not whether we should do those things," he said, "the issue is whether Congress has full knowledge they are being done."

Differing Jurisdiction

Mr. Staats suggested that part of the problem could be traced to the structure of Congress. The Agricultural Committees, he noted, have jurisdiction over the Food for Peace programs, but these committees have no direct knowledge of other military-grant programs, which are handled by the committees dealing with foreign policy and the armed services.

But he added that the G.A.O.

Associated Press

Controller General Elmer B. Staats, head of General Accounting Office, explaining use of Food for Peace funds at hearing.

study showed that the problem extended to the executive branch. The military aid program, he said, involves so many agencies in the executive branch and committees in Congress that it is doubtful that any one has the "full story" on how much the United States is spending on military aid.

The study estimated that total military assistance came to about $5-billion in the last fiscal year. But Mr. Staats suggested that not even the Defense Department knew the precise total.

For example, he said, the Defense Department told the G.A.O. that it did not know how much surplus military equipment had been turned over to South Vietnam and Thailand. And, he said, the State Department, which grants licenses for foreign military sales, did not know how much was actually sold by United States corporations.

Senator J. W. Fulbright, chairman of the Senate Foreign Relations Committee, estimated that total military assistance would reach $7-billion in the current fiscal year. "Those who believe that military assistance consists largely of the military component of our foreign aid program, amounting to something in the neighborhood of $375- to $400-million for the current fiscal year, are only dimly perceiving the tip of this particular iceberg," he told the subcommittee.

January 5, 1971

FOOD AID, ABUSED, IS CUT IN VIETNAM

U.S. Program Drops a City and 9 Provinces—Some Items Sold for Pigs

By RALPH BLUMENTHAL
Special to The New York Times

SAIGON, South Vietnam, Jan. 7—The United States aid mission in South Vietnam has quietly suspended a significant part of the Food for Peace program after Federal investigators uncovered widespread abuses, including the sale of war victims' food aid as pig feed.

The mission eliminated one city and nine of South Vietnam's 44 provinces from the program last month for violations of the regulation that the food has to be consumed by the recipient and not sold.

In addition, the mission canceled all imports of bulgur wheat, corn meal and rolled oats—three of the seven commodities imported under the Food for Peace program—and will allow imports only by institutions where the food would go to a common kitchen and not to individuals. This will mainly affect those who live at home rather than in camps.

The other commodities for war victims—widows and their dependents, refugees, disabled veterans and schoolchildren—are wheat flour, corn soya milk, vegetable oil and nonfat dry milk. Aid officials said that bulgur wheat and corn soya milk were high-nutrient foods that were meant to be mixed with local foods to make them palatable.

But, a worker with South Vietnam's refugees said, "The people just don't eat the bulgur wheat, and the corn soya milk upsets their stomachs." He continued:

"The only people I've ever seen use it are Cambodian refugees. The people found it makes excellent pig feed. The only way to control it is for someone to go home with them and watch them eat it."

The distaste for the two foods has led to the most widespread abuse in the Food for Peace program: Recipients sell products they disdain to eat to merchants who then sell the commodities to farmers, usually for pig feed.

Decision in a Letter

The decision to suspend part of the program was communicated in a letter on Dec. 14 from H. E. Kosters, associate director for commercial and capital assistance for United States aid in Saigon, to the South Vietnamese Minister of Social Welfare, Tran Nguon Phieu. He is also chairman of the central Food for Peace coordinating committee.

Dr. Cao Xuan An, an official at the Ministry of Social Welfare, described the suspension today as "a unilateral action" by the Agency for International Development and said "We are not very clear which kind of irregularity is being referred to."

Dr. An said that on Tuesday the minister would lead a meeting of South Vietnamese and United States officials to try to win restoration of the program.

However, American officials, who reported the suspensions today in response to inquiries, indicated that the South Vietnamese would have to carry out substantial reforms before the program would be restored.

Two Ships Diverted

The United States was so serious about the suspensions, the officials said, that two ships under way with wheat, corn meal and oats had been diverted to the Philippines.

The suspensions are expected to remove $5-million from the program of $19,569,987 for the 1971 fiscal year, which ends June 30.

The cuts are also expected to result in a drop of 737,000 recipients in the 2,856,704 war victims the program was aimed at this fiscal year.

Under Title II of Public Law 480, the Food for Peace program makes high-nutrient foods from the United States available to other countries, usually under long-term loans repayable in local currency. The foods must be consumed personally by the recipient. In South Vietnam, the foods are distributed by seven religious and social charities in conjunction with the Government and under the final supervision of American pacification and aid officials.

Title I of the program empowers the United States to sell consumer items to South Vietnamese importers and to use the piasters earned to pay American overhead expenses and to buy items for the South Vietnamese. The fact that this money has been used to buy military equipment generated controversy at a Congressional hearing in Washington on Monday.

Although United States refugee workers in the provinces have long known of abuses of the program and often reported on them, and a few provinces have been temporarily suspended from time to time, the strong United States action came only after investigators from Washington had witnessed instances of corruption here at first hand.

According to aid officials, investigators from the State Department's Office of the Inspector General for Foreign Assistance and the Agency for International Development's Auditor General's Office visited centers of the Food for Peace program in November and December.

"On one occasion," an aid official recalled, "an investigator watched food being handed to war victims—who carried it to a truck to be sold and driven away."

On another occasion, a field worker reported, an investigator watched a similar illegal sale in Tayninh—one of the suspended provinces—and another time flour supplied by the United States was discovered in a Vietcong cache in Binhtuy Province, less than 100 miles from Saigon.

Such events did not surprise the aid workers in those provinces, some of them recalled today. "It happens all the time," said one from the region surrounding Saigon, "only this time the people from Saigon and Washington finally saw it."

At a meeting of United States refugee advisers from the provinces that was held in Saigon on Dec. 11 and Dec. 12, one aide reported that he helped refugees sell the commodities to supplement their small incomes. This help was not unusual, officials said later.

Some Applaud Decision

It was at this meeting that aid officials announced to the advisers that the program would be cut. Many advisers applauded the decision but some were angry that they had not been consulted on the decision affecting their provinces.

Besides the city of Camranh, the nine affected provinces are: Darlac, Khanhhoa, Tayninh, Binhtuy, Chuongthien, Vinhlong, Anxuyen, Vinhbinh and Chaudoc.

The conclusions of the investigators, who left South Vietnam just before Christmas, have been presented in secret reports, which are unavailable for inspection.

However, an official who saw the report of the Inspector

The New York Times Jan. 8, 1971

Nine provinces (shown in black) and Camranh were affected by U.S. order.

General's Office said that auditors had estimated that between 10 and 75 per cent of the Food for Peace commodities in South Vietnam were illegally sold. The auditors were said to have been unable to come up with a more precise percentage or to say which commodities had been most involved in the corruption.

The program has been in effect here for 12 years.

Another abuse of the program, officials said, was the theft of commodities before they reach the war victims.

30 Per Cent Off the Top

Although officials disclosed no figures from the investigators' reports, an adviser in Binhduong Province, 25 miles from Saigon, recently reported that by the time Vietnamese officials in his province had taken their cuts, 30 per cent of the commodities were gone before they reached the intended recipients.

In explanation of the abuses, aid officials recently prepared a telegram for transmission to Washington. One part read: "Without going into detail, it should be understood that many times when a [Vietnamese] social service chief in the Ministry of Social Welfare attempts to prevent the sale of commodities, he finds the buyers, who are wives" of national police or army officers, 'capable of exerting considerable counterpressure, often far in excess of his ability to resist."

January 8, 1971

'Agent Blue' in Vietnam

A Deadly Chemical Has Been Destroying Crops for Years

By ARTHUR H. WESTING

The United States has been destroying growing crops in South Vietnam since at least November 1961 as part of its "resource denial" program. This is accomplished largely by the aerial application of an aqueous solution of sodium dimethyl arsenate, "Agent Blue"; applied at the rate of 9.3 pounds of active ingredients per acre. This is a highly persistent (and potentially hazardous) chemical not domestically registered for use on or near crops.

Based on available Department of Defense data, some 6,397,000 pounds of active ingredients were expended between the beginning of 1962 and the end of 1969. Figures for 1970 are not available, although the program continues. Annual acreage treated, according to the Defense Department is:

Year	Acres
1962	1,000
1963	250
1964	10,000
1965	66,000
1966	104,000
1967	221,000
1968	170,000
1969	115,000
Total	**688,000**

The 688,000 acres sprayed during eight years for which data are available represent 9 per cent of South Vietnam's 7.6 million acres of agricultural lands. Actually, most crop destruction occurs in the Central Highlands so that the percentage of destruction is regionally much higher. These regions have been traditionally food poor; their population consists largely of primitive hill tribes (Montagnards). Spraying is usually carried out near harvest time, destroying the standing crop and rendering the land useless until at least the next growing season.

Additionally, foods are purposely destroyed by various other ground techniques. Foods are also destroyed incidentally in the large-scale forest destruction program in which, according to the Pentagon, some 5,517,000 acres or 13 per cent of South Vietnam, have been aerially sprayed through the end of 1969. No data are available to me on how much food has been destroyed in these ways.

Some estimates can be made for the amount of food destruction via herbicides aerially applied for that purpose. A conservative yield estimate for upland rice fields (the major target) is 500 pounds of milled rice per acre per year. (Crops other than rice are also destroyed but we can assume for our purposes that their food yield is equivalent to that of upland rice.) One Vietnamese apparently can live on 1.1 pounds of milled rice per day, or 400 pounds per year. Using the above listed acreages, one arrives at the following figures of destruction:

Year	Pounds of Rice Destroyed	Annual Diets Denied
1962	500,000	1,250
1963	120,000	300
1964	5,000,000	12,500
1965	33,000,000	82,500
1966	52,000,000	130,000
1967	110,500,000	276,250
1968	85,000,000	212,500
1969	57,500,000	143,750
Total	**344,000,000**	**860,000**

The main avowed purpose of the food destruction program is to deny food to the enemy soldier. Since the Vietcong number only about 260,000 out of 17.5 million (or 1.5 per cent) but control perhaps 80 per cent or 90 per cent of the rural economy of South Vietnam, enormous amounts of food must be destroyed in order to create a hardship for the Vietcong. In fact, classified studies performed for and by the U. S. in 1967 and 1968 revealed that food destruction has had no significant impact on the enemy soldier. Civilians, in contrast, did and do suffer. Estimates in these studies varied between 10 and 100 for how many civilians have to be denied food in order to deny it to one guerrilla. In other words, of the 860,000 total annual diets destroyed during 1962-1969, between 774,000 and 851,000 were destined for civilian stomachs. Moreover, it is not unreasonable to assume that the brunt of this civilian burden is borne by infants, aged, fetuses, pregnant and lactating women, and sick.

By way of more specific example I single out Quangngai Province, a particularly war torn northern province of South Vietnam. During a visit there this past August I learned that 15 crop-destruction missions had been approved for 1970, totalling 182,000 acres. (An additional 13 forest-destruction missions were scheduled for 1970, totalling another 107,000 acres.) A study done for the Department of Defense in 1969 states that 215,000 acres in the province (out of a total of 1,418,000 acres) were then being used agriculturally. Thus approximately 85 per cent of the crop lands of Quangngai were scheduled for aerial destruction in 1970, presumably virtually all not under physical United States control. I must add that I have no knowledge of how many acres were actually sprayed in Quangngai Province in 1970 (or in previous years), only the number officially approved for that year.

Our nation's food-destruction program in South Vietnam, although not secret, has received only scant attention. It is clear that the acceptability of food destruction as a means of warfare requires an immediate and searching re-evaluation by the Congress, the Pentagon, and ultimately, the White House.

Arthur H. Westing, chairman of the biology department at Windham College in Putney, Vermont, has made two trips to Indochina.

July 12, 1971

U.S. Cuts Its Contribution To World Food Program

UNITED NATIONS, N. Y., Jan. 31—The United States has cut its contribution to the World Food Program from 50 per cent of the program to 40 per cent, explaining it wanted other governments to share more fully in the international undertaking.

The United States, as a pledging conference today, announced it would give up to $136-million toward a target goal of $340-million for the years 1973 and 1974. A total of 45 countries pledged $266-million during the conference.

The United States and Canada have been the financial mainstay of the program.

February 1, 1972

U.S. Relief Aid to Laos Reported to Be Diverted

By TAD SZULC

Special to The New York Times

WASHINGTON, April 22 — The General Accounting Office has reported that United States refugee relief programs in Laos are being used in part to support paramilitary forces there. These forces, it was said, include Meo tribesmen who serve in the clandestine army operated by the Central Intelligence Agency.

In reporting that the refugee programs are being used as a cover by the C.I.A., the General Accounting Office was expanding on a report last month that the civilian health program was being used for the same purpose.

The new report, prepared for Senator Edward M. Kennedy's Senate Subcommittee on Refugees, declared that funds from the Agency for International Development and the Agriculture Department's Food for Peace program had been diverted to feed and otherwise assist "paramilitary forces and their dependents." It said that of 306,000 Laotians on refugee relief rolls, entirely administered by the Agency for International Development, 125,000 were paramilitary personnel and their families.

Senator Kennedy, Democrat of Massachusetts and chairman of the subcommittee, released today what his office termed a "heavily sanitized" summary of the report by the General Accounting Office, which is the Congressional investigative agency. However, sections of the report itself, including the numbers of paramilitary Laotians on refugee rolls and financial aid details, were obtained separately by The New York Times.

The accounting office's report said that as of June 30, 1971 the refugee programs supported 20,000 "paramilitary personnel" and 105,000 of their dependents. Most were said to be Meo tribesmen in the northern Xiengkhouang Province serving in the C.I.A.'s clandestine army under Gen. Vang Pao.

Additional Spending Reported

Agency for International Development refugee programs in Laos during the current fiscal year are estimated to cost $16.2-million, and the cost of food donated by the Agriculture Department is $1.4-million. The accounting office's new report said that the C.I.A. and Defense Department were spending $52.2-million more under the guise of aid to refugees.

One section of the report said that the total United States commitment this year on all forms of refugee aid in Laos was $69.8-million.

The General Accounting Office report last month, also prepared for Senator Kennedy, said that the Central Intelligence Agency had been using the Agency for International Development public-health programs as a "cover" for some of its military activities in Laos. The Agency for International Development's administrator, Dr. John Hannah, publicly acknowledged last year that the C.I.A. had used his organization as a "cover" but said that this practice was being halted.

However, the new accounting office report not only charged that the refugee program was a partial cover for the C.I.A. but also for the first time connected the Agriculture Department with the paramilitary operation.

Termed Violation of Law

The report said that the department was providing in the 1972 fiscal year, which ends June 30, commodities worth $1.4-million, a part of which goes to the clandestine army's tribesmen, as well as unspecified funds to transport the food from the United States to Thailand and then on to Laos.

Senator Kennedy, commenting on the report, said that the diversion of Food for Peace commodities to the paramilitary units violated the spirit of Public Law 480, under which this program is administered.

The accounting agency's report said: "Refugee relief in Laos is administered under the terms of a project agreement between the United States Government and the Royal Laotian Government. This agreement provides that basic necessities of life such as food, clothing, medicine, feeds and tools be furnished to persons uprooted by the war and temporarily unable to care for themselves."

The food is supplied under a provision of Public Law 480, providing for "donations" in order "to meet famine or other urgent or extraordinary relief requirements."

But the accounting office said that in Laos refugees had been classified for assistance purposes as "fully dependent, partially dependent, in need of no food assistance but requiring other types of support, and paramilitary forces and their dependents."

Senator Kennedy said in a statement accompanying the summary of the report that the decision to involve the Agency for International Development "as a cover for support of Lao military," including direct military-logistical support, "was made at a high level of the U. S. Government."

He said, "Tens of thousands of Laos refugees are still being pushed around and dying needlessly for our strategic reasons—under the cover of humanitarian programs administered by the Agency for International Development."

April 23, 1972

U.S. and India Taking Up Blocked-Rupees Problem

By BERNARD WEINRAUB

Special to The New York Times

NEW DELHI, June 17—The United States is seeking to remove a key barrier to good relations with India by trying to settle the complex and politically emotional "rupee problem," in which millions of rupees meant to pay back food loans of the nineteen-sixties are piling up in an American bank account here.

The problem has deeply involved the United States Treasury, the State Department and the United States Ambassador to India, Daniel P. Moynihan. The ambassador is scheduled to leave for Washington early Tuesday for final White House approval of the United States' position in dealing with India over the tangled and mutually embarrassing source of friction.

The rupee problem involves the agreements from 1956 until 1971 under which the United States sup ied India with tons of food to ward off famine. The surplus food was sold at cheap, concessional rates to India, and she was to pay back the loan over 40 years.

The assistance turned into an unexpected and bizarre problem because the money was to be repaid in Indian rupees and placed in an American account for use here. As mass hunger threatened India in the nineteen-sixties and food assistance increased abruptly, the United States rupee account began growing into a mountain of money, at least on the ledger sheets of the Reserve Bank of India. Even without imports over the past year, the accumulations are spiraling because of interest — at least $100-million a year.

Though estimates vary sharply, officials say that in 40 years, the total of American-owned rupees will finally reach the equivalent of $7-billion to $8-billion. The figure alarms the Indian Government and deeply distrubs the United States since it represents a permanent American asset here that, if paid and spent, would jolt the Indian economy and place the United States in the position of owning 20 per cent of the local money supply.

"We could never spend this amount of money," said Mr. Moynihan in an interview. "Twice as much is now coming in as going out. There's no possible escape from indebtedness for India. It could go on into the 22d century."

"This is the big test of whether or not the United Stat?s and India can work out a good, healthy, normal relationship," Mr. Moynihan said. "This problem is a psychological barier that's poisonous to the relationship of equality between the United States and India. It harms our relationship in terms of trade. It's simply not in the interests of either country to have this rupee problem, this legacy of the past."

$840-Million in Banks

The current American holdings in rupees amount to the equivalent of $840-million. Only a portion of the money is used, to pay United States Embassy expenses and those of various projects totaling some $50-million a year. The rupees themselves are "blocked," cannot be transferred out of the country, and are placed each year on the United States ledger in the Indian bank.

Beyond the debt itself, the issue has powerful political overtones. India views the rupees as a source of American manipulation and leverage, as a "fantastic anachronism" under which a foreign government is allowed to create money and aggravate inflation.

"The rupees are like a monster, uncontrollable and growing," said a senior Indian official, who asked to remain unidentified. The account, he said, was "used for years to establish and pay for an American presence that was twice as big as any other country. It was used to build up a big American establishment that was resented. It was used to waste money, to lavish it because the rupees are to be spent."

"Psychologically, I'm not anti-American — and I don't think many Indans are — but this accumulating rupee fund represents permanent bondage, a source of unending debt," the Indian official went on.

Some Indian officials, including L. K. Jha, the former Ambassador to the United States, say that the "simple solution" is that "the money has got to be buried and put out of circulation." The Indians and some Americans agree that food aid essentially should involve free donations or straight commercial sales. They point out that Canada has given tons of food free to India without loan commitments and they say that the United States should simply erase the debt.

'Some Point in Between'

Mr. Moynihan cannot see the United States doing that. "There's an intermediate point between zero and infinity," he said. "The present arrangement could, of course, run into infinity. We won't accept zero. Negotiations will reach some point in between."

Americans outside Mr. Moynihan's office say that the rupee funds have been somewhat misused, for plane fares and junkets for State Department officials and other Government officers. Mr. Moynihan himself has made the settlement of "the rupee problem" a major goal of his mission here.

Essentially, the main reasons that the United States cannot spend the money on family planning, farming and relief projects here is that it would distort and upset the planned Indian economy, lead to rapid inflation and a sharp increase of American involvement and personnel, and place the United States on a virtually permanent basis, in an aggressively paternalistic role.

June 18, 1973

U.S. Shortages Peril World Food-Aid Plan

By KATHLEEN TELTSCH

Special to The New York Times

UNITED NATIONS, N. Y., Aug. 18 — In Colombia's poorest rural areas, a school-lunch program faces shutdown. Elderly patients ina hospital in Haiti will have to go without an extra daily hot meal, and in India, the promising development of a new food for babies is threatened.

These operations and hundreds more will be abandoned or drastically cut back in coming weeks because private United States relief agencies will no longer have the commodities to continue helping 80 million to 100 million needy people in 100 countries around the world.

The agencies have been informed in the last week by Washington officials that the Department of Agriculture will not be able to purchase commodities for the Food for Peace program during August and possibly not in September.

Moreover, the agencies were told the commodity situation was so unsettled that it was uncertain when they could again expect to get supplies of wheat, flour, vegetable oil and other foodstuffs on which they have based their free distribution of relief overseas for almost 20 years.

Calamitous Effect Seen

The effect will be calamitous, according to administrators of the voluntary agencies, as they are called.

"I have not seen a situation like this in my 28 years in overseas assistance," said Fred W. Devine of CARE — the Cooperative for American Relief Everywhere. "It's going to be disastrous."

CARE and Catholic Relief Services operate the two most extensive programs supplying supplementary foods to the poor. The Catholic agency cares for 10 million of the "poorest ot the poor," said Bishop Edward E. Swanstrom, executive director. The relief activities in more than 50 countries will have to be terminated by the end of the year, he said, unless the Agriculture Department resumes buying and distributing commodities.

The voluntary agencies get their relief goods for distribution without cost under United States Public Law 480, which is the basis for the Food for Peace program. The same legislation provides for assistance to such operations as the United Nations Children's Fund, the Aid Program for Palestinian Refugees and the World Food Program. So far they have not been advised officially of pending cutbacks.

Agencies Come Last

Under the law the Administration must first satisfy domestic requirements including aid for poor Americans, must meet foreign sales commitments and provide a carry-over of supplies before taking care of the agencies, which are at the bottom of the list.

When the law was enacted in 1954 there were surplus supplies of dairy products and free distribution to the needy — a humanitarian way of disposing of the surpluses. Later, with bumper crops of wheat on hand, grains were added.

But all of the commodities traditionally used for relief have been in short supply in recent years. The Soviet Union's purchase last year of one-quarter of the United States wheat crop sent the market price soaring, but in trade circles spokesmen maintain that the crisis in grain was brought on by a combination of circumstances, including droughts, poor harvests and floods in many of the wheat-producing areas as well as the big Soviet purchases.

Because officials of the voluntary agencies have been anxiously watching the commodity market, they anticipated difficulties even before they were invited to a recent meeting with Daniel E. Shaughnessy, associate coordinator of the Food for Peace office of the Agency for International Development.

Sandwiches for Lunch

At the meeting at the headquarters of CARE the message was as plain as the luncheon fare of hero sandwiches and coffee in containers.

Mr. Shaughnessy said that the Agriculture Department had made no purchases in July or August and probably only small quantities of commodities would be procured in September. He said that the department was not going into the grain market to make further purchases until it completely reviewed the commodity situation and assessed the needs for domestic use and foreign sales in light of a revised crop estimate. This estimate showed lower production of wheat and other grains than had been forecast earlier.

Some of the agencies countered with an appeal saying they did not want foods to be diverted from American consumers but asked that 1 per cent be held back from allocations for sales abroad and be earmarked for Food for Peace.

An extensive review of the commodities situation now is under way in Washington and the decision will be made "at the highest level," according to spokesmen at the Agriculture and State Departments.

Shipments 'Will Be Nil'

Meanwhile, Church World Service has sent its representatives in the field a terse announcement that shipments for October through December "will be nil."

The American-Jewish Joint Distribution Committee intends cutting back on some of its services so as to be able to buy bread for such operations as the soup kitchens run in Morocco.

CARE Will Juggle

CARE will juggle what's left of its dwindling supplies as long as it can, but unless the Agriculture Department provides new commodities by September, there will be a breakdown in the pipeline of supplies in 20 countries, according to Frank Goffio, CARE's executive director.

All of the agencies' directors stress that a delay of even three months in shipments risks the collapse of distribution services that have been developed over many years.

"We have tried to get people to learn to help themselves by using food as a tool," explained Anthony Foddai of Catholic Relief Services.

"We have asked countries to buy vehicles to distribute food, we've taught them about general nutrition," he said. "When dry milk supplies became unavailable a few years back, we persuaded them to learn to use alternative foodstuffs. They did learn. Now we have to go back and say we have nothing for you."

Mr. Foddai apologized for sounding emotional. "I am an adopted American," said the Italian-born administrator. "To me this work, done by voluntary agencies is peculiarly American. It is a beautiful thing, this people-to-people help. I cannot believe the Government will let this happen."

August 19, 1973

Farmers Fear New Federal Crop Policy May Lead to Scarcities

By WILLIAM ROBBINS

Special to The New York Times

WASHINGTON, Nov. 13—The big combine clattered to a stop at the edge of a soybean field and Kenneth Cheers climbed down from its glass-walled cab to greet a waiting visitor. A friendly smile creased the dust smudges of the young Iowa farmer's face as he remarked:

"It's kinda hard to stop when you're taking in beans at the rate of $1,200 an hour."

Mr. Cheers is one of an army of farmers sweeping the rolling hills and plains of the Midwest with their tank-sized harvesting machines. And most of them are smiling, because their crops are the biggest ever, and the prices are good.

The smiles start to sag, however, when they try to look beyond this year's harvests. Like many economists, in and out of the Government, they are concerned about a new direction in farm policy that now militates against any sizable accumulations of Federal grain reserves in years of plenty to guard against scarcity in bad years.

Those economists fear that the Government is gambling with food supplies, risking possible shortages and high prices here and the specter of increased hunger and death in some parts of the world.

Concern Is General

A sampling of farmer opinion in one community in the heart of the Midwestern grain country, around Creston, Iowa, found those interviewed all concerned that a policy against Government accumulation of grain reserves could lead to wide fluctuations—to cycles of boom and bust, surplus and scarcity, and sharp swings in farm and consumer prices.

The issue, which increasingly preoccupies experts and food agencies around the world, has divided Secretary of Agriculture Earl L. Butz and some of his top advisers.

Dr. Butz opposes Government holdings of grain stockpiles. His chief economist, Don Paarlberg, takes "a kind of different" view from the Secretary's, as do other top economic advisers interviewed, although Dr. Paarlberg is the only one who was willing to bring the conflict into the open.

The change in policy is largely one of degree. Under United States agricultural law, the Government accumulates grain stocks when farmers forfeit their grain rather than repay price-support loans. In the past, when the farmers were allowed loans that were generally very close to market prices, large accumulations occurred in periods of market declines.

Such accumulations are considered unlikely under the new law, enacted this year. When the law was under consideration in Congress, **Secretary Butz successfully resisted demands to increase loan rates enough to reflect rising costs.**

The old loan rate for wheat, for example, was $1.25 a bushel, which until mid-1972 was generally close to the market price. The new loan rate is $1.37 a bushel, which is less than one-third of current market prices.

The issue of grain reserves was the principal concern found in interviews over the last several weeks with farmers and Government and private economists, conducted as part of an unsuccessful search for a coherent concept of a national food policy.

The importance of the question has been underscored because grain is the basic element in the world's diets. Grain supplies directly help to determine

the adequacy of bread, pastries and cereals, and they also indirectly govern supplies and costs of meats, which are the biggest items in family food budgets in the United States and other developed nations.

Grain has moved to the forefront of food economists' concerns because of a reversal that has occurred over the last two years in the world supply situation. In early 1973, the United States had large stockpiles of wheat and corn, farm prices had dropped, and the Government was urging growers to cut back their production.

Peruvian Phenomenon

That situation changed radically amid developments dominated by massive grain sales to the Soviet Union. Those sales resulted from a severe winter accompanied by a light snow cover for winter wheat and subsequent drought. A drought in Australia and crop failures elsewhere reduced supplies at the same time that a mysterious phenomenon was occurring off the coast of Peru.

The Peruvian anchovy catch has normally been one of the world's major sources of protein for livestock feed. The other is the American soybean crop. But last year the cold Humboldt Current, in which the anchovies thrive, moved away from the Peruvian coast, as it does once about every seven years, and that nation's fishing fleet was coming up with empty nets.

The diminishing world supplies drove food prices inexorably upward in the United States, but two devaluations of the dollar within a 14-month period made prices of American crops more attractive abroad and spurred export demand.

By the end of the summer of 1973, the Government had virtually no stockpile of grain and the total "carryover"—supplies still held on farms and in grain company warehouses—were the lowest in decades. Forecasts indicate that the carryover will be still smaller by the end of the 1973-74 crop year.

Economists note that those developments have merely unmasked a changing condition of world supply and demand, and some, such as Lester R. Brown of the Overseas Development Council, a private nonprofit research institution, see critical pressures on limited world land resources.

Mr. Brown sums up the situation this way: Increasing population coupled with growing affluence here and abroad, has narrowed the margin between supply and demand to a critically thin ribbon.

He cites the fact of increasing meat consumption. In the United States, for example, beef consumption per capita has more than doubled since World War II.

More Land for Meat

He noted that it takes about seven pounds of grain protein to produce one pound of protein in meat—and thus more land to support meat-eaters than people who depend more on direct consumption of grain. It takes nearly a ton of grain, for example, to support the average meat-eating American in comparison with the 400 pounds of grain, consumed directly, to support the average citizen of less developed countries.

And in a world that has less than one acre of arable land per person, it takes about two acres to support the average American in the style to which he has become accustomed.

Some economists believe that the current squeeze on supplies will eventually be relieved by rising production, but those interviewed generally agreed with Philip H. Trezise, a former Assistant Secretary of State for Economic Affairs, now with the Brookings Institution, who observed: "If one major producing nation should have a crop failure right now, we'd be in real trouble."

Mr. Trezise made the remark shortly after attending an international conference at Brookings, which was attended by economists from Europe, Japan and North America. The group called for a world agreement for cooperation in maintenance of grain reserves.

The disappearance of Government grain stockpiles has been welcomed by Secretary Butz, who is firmly opposed to Federal maintenance of reserves and determined to leave that role to grain companies and farmers.

Committee Appearance

"Farmers and the private trade should keep the supply in their hands," Dr. Butz told the House Agriculture Committee at a hearing last March 20. "They should retain the marketing decision and market at the best prices for them. They should earn the profits for carrying the crop from periods of lower prices to periods of higher prices."

Recently Dr. Butz expressed satisfaction to a reporter that "we've gotten the Government out of the grain business."

As he explained it, the Secretary's view is that once foreign customers are convinced that they cannot depend on stored surpluses in the United States, they will keep their own emergency stockpiles, and thus the United States will be spared heavy storage costs.

"We've been the residual suppliers," Dr. Butz told an interviewer. "The Japanese have depended on us; international [cotton] spinners have depended on us. Now we have changed that. The Japanese, for example, are buying further ahead."

Asked what might have happened in 1972, the year of widespread crop failures, without a United States carryover of grain stocks, Dr. Butz said the answer would have been rationing of supplies.

"After all, you ration things with prices," he said, adding that, for example, higher prices caused by short supplies might have led the Russians to reduce their livestock herds rather than buy United States grain.

As for the Government-maintained reserves, he said: "I think the Government should not do this. It won't work. A year ago we had substantial reserves completely under Government control. Then when prices went up consumer pressures forced us to release them, and the result was chaos."

In a speech today at the biennial governing conference of the United Nations Food and Agriculture Organization, Dr. Butz expressed continued United States willingness to contribute food aid to distressed nations as well as to consider problems of food security in cooperation with other countries.

No Evidence in Text

But there was no evidence, in text of his speech released in Washington, of any relenting in his opposition to a "centrally controlled inventory system."

Disagreement with the Secretary ranged from mild to

The New York Times/Gary Guisinger

A combine harvesting a wheat crop in Colorado. Farmers are concerned about new policy on Federal grain reserves.

harsh. Other economists interviewed, including high economic aides in the Agriculture Department, contended that reserves of food supplies were too vital under present world conditions to leave decisions on maintenance to the business sense of the grain industry or the marketing judgement of farmers.

The Agriculture Department's chief economist, Dr. Paarlberg, observed: "My view is kind of different from the Secretary's. I think it is risky [not to keep Government reserves]." Dr. Paarlberg cited the danger of crop failure and resulting "gyrations in prices that can occur."

"For some people in the world, it's a matter of life or death," said Mr. Brown, at the Overseas Development Council.

At a round-table discussion among economists held at Brookings recently, none believed that private grain companies would foot the bill for long-term storage of substantial reserves.

In Creston, Iowa, Charles Ehm, a banker-farmer who deals daily with other producer, remarked to a visitor:

"The farmers around here are doing great now, but they are worried. You've got to have some reserves. You know the private interests are not going to do it. What if we have a blight again; what do you do with your livestock?"

One Man's Answer

Nearby, Joseph Weisshaar, a substantial hog producer, offered this answer: "I'll tell you what we'd do. We'd just have to go out of the hog business. So would a lot of others. You know what would happen to meat prices then."

A neighbor, Eugene McCann, supplied this further observation: "You'd see consumer prices go right through the roof. That's what we have for a national food policy."

Questions about a national food policy brought this answer from one of the Agriculture Department's top economists:

"We've had a farm policy that indirectly produced a food policy, but I don't think the Department of Agriculture has really had a food policy.

Both Dr. Butz and Dr. Paarlberg disagreed, in virtually the same words.

"We have a food policy, and it's one of plenty," said Dr. Butz. "We're going for all-out production."

November 14, 1973

Butz Hints U.S. Weighed Food Embargo on Arabs

By PAUL HOFMANN

Special to The New York Times

ROME, Nov. 13—Secretary of Agriculture Earl L. Butz indicated today that the United States had been contemplating an end to food exports to Arab countries in retaliation for their oil embargo, but would probably refrain from such a measure.

Mr. Butz, in a news conference at the headquarters of the United Nations Food and Agriculture Organization, said that in view of the Arab oil embargo "there is a feeling that the United States should stop food shipments to that area." he added: "We have not done so yet."

Mr. Butz was asked whether he was saying that a ban on United States food exports to Arab nations was being considered.

"I don't wish to comment on that," he replied.

In an interview, the Secretary said that the volume of food to Arab nations—mostly grains—was small and that the Soviet Union could easily make up for embargoed United States food shipments. Soviet grain crops this year are reported to be excellent.

In his news conference and in an earlier address to the conference of the Food and Agriculture Organization, Mr. Butz gave qualified support to proposals for international stockpiling of farming products to insure a minimum of food security for the world.

"Our feeling is that we need international machinery to identify needs and establish general guidelines for individual nations," the Secretary said. "We feel that continual management of such reserves should be left to individual nations, whether they be sellers or buyers."

Mr. Butz said that some quarters in the organization, which is a specialized United Nations agency, were advocating management of food reserves by an international body. "We do not subscribe to this," the secretary said.

He was refering to recommendations by Addeke H. Boerma, director general of the 130-member agency, who has urged action to provide national stocks of grains on a basis broad enough to tide countries over periods of crop failures and natural disasters.

Underdeveloped countries that must buy food are pressing for a system of international reserves that would guarantee them adequate supplies at low prices.

Mr. Butz contended that "the problem is not so much international control but encouraging production." The Secretary said that it was a matter of controversy whether this could be achieved by state controls or free markets.

Praises U. S. System

In his address to the conference, the agency's governing body, Mr. Butz said: "It is a simple fact that farmers in the United States produce in response to price and outlook for demand. We, and they, have not discovered a better alternative to assure the capitalization, managament and dedication necessary to encourage higher production."

The Secretary said that the world food situation had improved considerably since the beginning of this year's harvest, and he warned against "scare estimates."

Mr. Butz said that the United States had kept its markets open and supplies available to all buyers. "We do believe, however," he cautioned, "that importing countries and private interests should not assume that the United States Government can and will maintain commercial reserves adequate for all customers under all conditions."

He said that there was no reason that grain producing countries should carry commercial reserves for all the world's potential buying customers. He added: "There is certainly no reason why one or two countries, the United States and Canada for example, should perform the lion's share of this role."

November 14, 1973

West Africa: Neither Rain Nor Fast Relief

By Jeffrey L. Hodes

After five disastrous years of declining rainfall that culminated in drought, desolation and death, the tragedy of the sun-scorched region of former French West Africa has come to public attention. It is a tragedy that could have been avoided.

The region is losing its struggle against the environment to maintain self-sufficiency. Its fragile ecological balance is being devastated by the encroaching Sahara Desert at the rate of thirty miles per year; the livestock, on which the economy is based, are dead or dying, and unknown thousands of people have died of starvation or diseases resulting from malnutrition.

About 25 million people live in the drought area, which covers six of the world's poorest and perhaps least-known countries—Chad, Mali, Mauritania, Niger, Senegal and Upper Volta. Together they cover an area in a semiarid zone south of the Sahara the size of the continental United States.

Large-scale death was averted in 1973. But the crisis demonstrated that there was no international mechanism for effectively responding to natural disasters when simple humanitarian considerations were more immediate than those of political advantage.

Indeed, the international response to the region's needs offers a distressing example of the low premium placed on life in black Africa, the slowness of the United Nations in mobilizing itself to respond to a natural disaster, and Washington's stinginess when there is no immediate political gain in giving sustenance to the "humanitarian" aspects of United States foreign policy. Uncertainty now remains whether the international community will find the political will to deal with the region's long-range rehabilitation problems.

Unlike a flood or earthquake, drought does not immediately capture the attention. Much of the public awareness about the West African crisis dissipated last fall when newspapers reported that the crisis had passed its peak with the monsoons' arrival. Nothing could be further from the truth. In October the summer rains ceased. What rain fell was late and totally inadequate to overcome the drought's effect on crops and cattle. Despite desperate attempts to spare the crops, they withered, necessitating a continued emergency relief operation in 1974.

How extensive was the threat to human life? Statistics are hard to come by in such a desperately poor region. Last month there were reports that the drought took 50,000 lives in nearby Ethiopia. The countries of West Africa said that six million people faced starvation last summer, but some aid experts said that the figure was inflated. Shortly afterward, the League of Red Cross Societies estimated that perhaps 10 million nomads and farmers could starve in the near future.

As the drought came to public attention, there were charges in Washington that the affected countries had not heeded disaster warnings and had been slow in reacting. When the governments recognized the gravity of the situation, they did seek outside help. Diplomats representing the affected countries in Washington have said that the United States was approached for aid as early as September, 1972. They were displeased by the reception given to their requests and then by the size of aid shipments that first started arriving in early 1973.

However, the Africans' major appeal was to France, since they are former French colonies, and the European Economic Community, which is tied economically to West Africa through the Yaounde Convention, a commercial treaty.

The United Nations assumed responsibility for coordinating the global response to the drought. But its Food and Agriculture Organization did not treat the disaster as an emergency until it was well-advanced, and it failed to marshal international support at an early stage.

The F.A.O. was a poor choice to coordinate the emergency relief because it had had little experience in dealing

In Gall, Niger/Chester Higgins

with emergency operations. Headquartered in Rome and primarily a technical agency, it does not have the managerial expertise necessary for such an operation.

The organization had been working in West Africa since the brief rainfalls in the late nineteen-sixties. Yet when its own early-warning system reported "an acute emergency" in September, 1972, nothing significant was done to mobilize the international community until February, 1973. And a major appeal was not made until May!

By the time of the appeal, the United Nations agency's mishandling of relief operations had so alienated the major donors, especially the United States and France, that for all practical purposes, the appeal was an embarrassing failure. The agency asked for $15 million in a month; only $2.6 million was pledged.

Lacking confidence in the F.A.O., the major donors chose to give their aid bilaterally—France via the Common Market, and the United States through the Agency for International Development.

That agency, which usually supplies 70 per cent of the world's food assistance under the Food for Peace program, provided only about 42 per cent of the emergency food contribution. By midsummer, the most severe period of the famine, the United States had contributed only 156,000 metric tons of grain, and by October, 100,000 more metric tons had been delivered, out of a total 625,000 donated by the international community.

In addition, over $38.5 million was given in cash and services by the world community, of which the United States share was $4.6 million.

Could the United States have done more? Last year, Washington gave black Africa $307.5 million in aid, of which West Africa received $11.9 million, mostly in food. The emergency drought-relief funds came from a separate source, an Agency for International Development contingency fund that covers catastrophes. But in fiscal 1973 only half of the fund was spent on disaster relief. Among its grants were $10 million for livestock research in the Bahamas.

Under political pressure in the last quarter of the fiscal year, the Agency for International Development shifted $2 million from $10 million in funds that had been set aside for Nicaraguan relief and found another $2.6 million in reserves for West Africa.

In Congress, the black legislator Charles C. Diggs Jr. argued that if the United States committed $318 million to fight famine in Bangladesh, no less could be done to assist 26 million black Africans.

Last month, Mr. Diggs, working with Senators Edward M. Kennedy and Hubert H. Humphrey, won his point. The new foreign aid bill contains $25 million for continued emergency relief and a $50-million supplemental grant for a medium-term recovery program.

Jeffrey L. Hodes is director of the student and young adult division of the United Nations Association of the United States of America. This article was researched by four college students: Terry Garcia of American University, Leslie Friedman of Mount Holyoke, Thelma Price of Antioch and Paul Schaeffer of Washington, D. C.

January 9, 1974

On U.S. Assistance to Parched West Africa

By Maurice J. Williams

WASHINGTON—The continuing drought in the sub-Sahara region of Africa and the hardships it is bringing to the people who live there is one of the great tragedies of our time. It is, as it should be, of concern to Americans and, because of its magnitude and duration, there has been considerable comment on what the Government is doing to help, and how well we are performing our job.

The drought that has afflicted the Sahel, as the sub-Sahara region of West Africa is called, is no sudden catastrophe. It has been years in the building. United States officials in the affected countries—Senegal, Mauritania, Mali, Niger, Chad and Upper Volta—warned in the summer of 1972 that the poor rains for the fourth straight year could bring famine to this region of nomadic herdsmen and subsistence farmers.

The ecological balance of the area has been changing. The desert has been encroaching on grazing areas and farms, and the drought has accelerated the process. Trees have died. Lakes and rivers have dried up. Cattle weakened by successive years of drought have been unable to survive. Reserves of grain, including seed stocks, have vanished, and there has been a large migration of people in search of water and food.

The United States had been conducting a wide range of development programs in the Sahel region amounting to about $30 million annually to help with some of the essential needs. Nevertheless, the situation deteriorated seriously when the 1972 harvest fell far short of the need.

By November, 1972, the United States had already committed a substantial increase in food shipments to the area. By the time the six affected governments formally called for worldwide help in March, 1973, the first United States pledge of over $21 million in 156,000 metric tons of food was beginning to arrive. The United States Agency for International Development also provided $3.5 million in contingency funds to speed the delivery of this food to the rural areas in greatest need.

Other donors quickly joined in these relief efforts to provide food, medicines and other assistance—the total international effort in 1973 was over $120 million. A major limitation on effective relief in 1973 was not the over-all level of relief aid but the capacity of West African ports and transport to move food inland to the drought-afflicted areas. This capacity

Roland Topor

was augmented by airlifting food in planes from Belgium, the United Kingdom, West Germany, Canada and the United States, among other countries. The drought deeply affected some two million nomads, many of whom were left destitute, as well as millions of others who became dependent on relief food. Widespread starvation was averted, but without the international relief effort millions would have died of starvation.

The summer rains in 1973 initially were believed to have been adequate for improved cereal crops and, hence, able to give the people of the Sahel a breathing spell to turn their attention to recovery and longer-term development needs. But the critical late-summer rains again failed. So in 1974 the Sahel—in particular Mali, Mauritania, Niger and Chad—again faces a potentially disastrous situation.

The United States and its partners in the international relief effort are already acting to assure that food, transport, medicines and other essential supplies are available to meet needs. The Food and Agriculture Organization of the United Nations estimates that over 550,000 tons of food grains will be needed this year before the October harvest. The United States has already committed 250,000 tons of food to meet this need, most of which will arrive this spring.

Food commitments from other donors and the United States should more than meet the F.A.O. target of minimum essential need.

Since the first warnings, the United States has provided more than $129-million in emergency drought relief food and other assistance—over 35 per cent of the over-all $340 million furnished by all donor countries and agencies. Food commitments have totaled 506,000 metric tons—more than twice the amount provided by any other single donor and about 46 per cent of all food shipments.

Solutions to restoration of the land must be found in new development approaches and the innovative application of what we have learned from experience elsewhere in the world.

A start has been made. Congress has authorized and appropriated $25-million in special relief funds for the Sahel and another $50 million has been appropriated and is being actively considered by the authorization committees. From the $25 million that is now available, the Agency for International Development has already committed $20 million for programs to rehabilitate and develop livestock herds, start vegetable and other garden projects, provide proteins and vitamins, make available health facilities and medical teams, dig wells and construct small reservoirs.

Maurice J. Williams, Deputy Administrator of the Agency for International Development, is President Nixon's special coordinator for emergency assistance to sub-Sahara Africa.

100,000 Deaths in Africa Linked to Drought Neglect

By DAVID BINDER

Special to The New York Times

WASHINGTON, March 4—A newly published study of relief efforts by the United States Government and international agencies for the victims of last year's drought in West Africa has charged that gross neglect and outright failures contributed to the deaths of more than 100,000 people.

The study was prepared for the Carnegie Endowment for International Peace by Roger Morris, a former aide to Secretary of State Kissinger, and his assistant, Hal Sheets.

The 66-page study asserted that officials of the United States Agency for International Development and other relief organizations had known that a long-term drought was developing in the sub-Saharan region of West Africa for the last five years. Yet no contingency plans were drawn, the authors say.

The region covers six countries—Senegal, Mauritania, Mali, Upper Volta, Niger and Chad—with a population estimated at 22 million. The drought directly affected about two million people, primarily nomadic herdsmen.

Mr. Morris and Mr. Sheets hold that "a pattern of neglect and inertia" by the United States aid agency and the United Nations Food and Agriculture Organization caused emergency food and medical supplies to reach the nomads too late.

The study, released last night, drew a four-page response from the Agency for International Development, acknowledging that there had been no emergency plan for the region. It also acknowledged that the United States relief effort in West Africa, totaling $129-million, or 35 per cent of the international contribution, was not "a model operation."

But the agency rejected charges of neglect or inertia, as well as the report's allegation that "an administrative and bureaucratic disaster was added to the natural calamity."

The Carnegie Endowment, which sponsored the report, was established by the steel magnate Andrew Carnegie in 1910 with a bequest of $10-million. It operates on a budget of a little more than $2-million a year and has a staff of about 60 in Washington, New York and Geneva. Funds are used for study, projects and publications dealing with questions of war and peace.

The study on African drought relief is entitled "Disaster in the Desert" and is based on extensive interviews with American officials and on previously unpublished documents.

It makes its strongest charges on the basis of the discovery of a United States Public Health Service survey dated September, 1973. That survey said that thousands of inadequately fed nomadic children faced imminent death from measles, for which vaccine was lacking.

The Carnegie Endowment

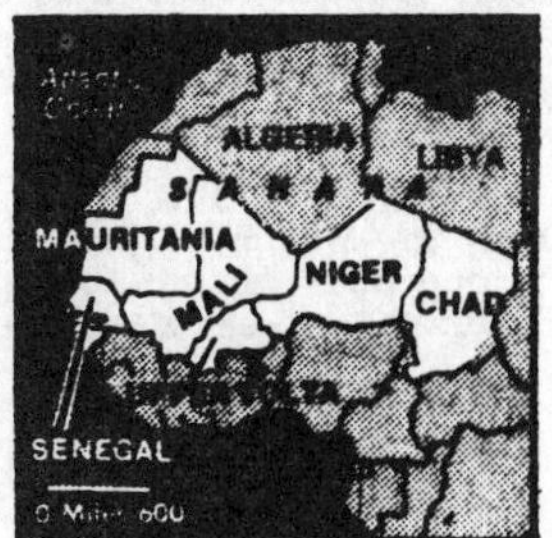

The New York Times/March 5, 1974

study asserts that the health findings, prepared by field teams of the Center for Disease Control in Atlanta, had made clear the acute malnutrition and rampant measles epidemics many months before relief supplies were sent.

Yet the teams' reports remained in the files of the American and international agencies until it was too late to save many children, Mr. Morris and Mr. Sheets charged.

They added that emergency food shipments often consisted of sorghum, which they said was fit for cattle feed but not for starving children who needed milk.

March 5, 1974

INDIANS ASK U.S. TO RESTORE AID

Request Emphasizes Anxiety Over Economic Travails—U.S. Was Major Donor

By BERNARD WEINRAUB

Special to The New York Times

NEW DELHI, April 4—India has quietly asked the United States to resume aid, a move that underlines the anxiety here about food shortages and the faltering economy.

Within the last month, Indian officials in New Delhi and in Washington have informed Americans that India wants to receive aid again and would begin discussions soon on the scope of specific projects.

Major American aid to India broke off in December, 1971, when the Nixon Administration was leaning to Pakistan during the war in East Pakistan. Total American aid to India since 1950 had totaled nearly $10-billion, the largest amount of assistance given to any country.

U.S. Made Offer

Last summer, Daniel P. Moynihan, the American Ambassador, presented a private memorandum to Indian officials saying that Washington was willing to resume assistance. But only in recent weeks has the Indian Government, facing severe economic strains and food shortages, quietly decided to ask for renewed assistance. No figures have been set.

Mr. Moynihan, now in Washington, is said to be working on the details. Some sources here say that the aid would focus on agriculture and health as well as some technical assistance, under which the Indians would specifically select both the projects and the Americans working on them.

In some ways, Americans here are almost as nervous about aid as the Indians. Americans insist that the aid bureaucracy of the nineteen sixties, and the flood of technical assistance and projects, will not be revived and that the new program will be mutted and carefully selected.

Indians Criticized Aid

Although American aid in the fifties and sixties thwarted famine, spurred the "green revolution" in rice production and resulted in the eradication of malaria—800,000 Indians died of the disease 20 years ago—Indians have said that the assistance crippled initiative and was a source of humiliation. To the anger of Americans, the Indians also maintain that aid was largely a vehicle of dominance and that "goodwill" was a secondary motive.

Indicative of India's sensitivity about aid, it took the Government months to decide to approach the United States. India's decision was in large part a result of threatening food and fertilizer shortages, the oil-price increase and a stumbling economy.

The World Bank has estimated that India will need $12-billion in international aid over the next five years and has said that oil-producing nations must be tapped for help. India's planners had hoped for self-sufficiency by 1979, but this hope was shattered even before the Middle East war last October.

$75-Million Set Aside

One puzzling element about American aid to India is that for the fiscal year 1974, which ends June 30, $75-million was set aside by the United States Agency for International Development to provide economic assistance. Currently, officials here are unsure whether the money is still being held or has been spent elsewhere.

In the last two years, the only American aid here has been a program under which American food worth $50-million is distributed annually to children and pregnant women by three groups, CARE, the Catholic Relief Organization and Church World Services-Lutheran World Relief.

The $10-billion in American aid provided since 1950 is broken down as follows: About 40 per cent in development loans, 55 per cent in concessional wheat sales and grants and 5 per cent in grants for technical assistance.

April 5, 1974

Civil Defense Biscuits Feed Drought Victims

Special to The New York Times

UNITED NATIONS, N. Y., June 20—Million of pounds of nutritious biscuits being distributed these days to drought victims in Niger and Chad are one of the tangible benefits of improved Soviet-American relations.

The biscuits were made 12 years ago at the height of the cold war, sealed in survival packs and stored by the Federal Government at specified sites around New York where they would be available in a nuclear attack.

The Government since decided to offer the supplies free to a relief organization and CARE quickly accepted. Despite their age the supplies were in excellent condition, according to Fred Devine, deputy executive director of CARE. The agency shipped them to Africa to starving drought victims.

"They really became survival biscuits," he said.

June 21, 1974

Tackling the World Food Problem

By George McGovern

WASHINGTON — We have a new President and it is a time for new beginnings. It is an opportunity to grapple with the great problems that confront our nation and the world.

In his inaugural speech, President Ford identified inflation as the nation's most urgent problem.

Every American farmer and consumer knows all too well that the cost of producing and marketing food has been skyrocketing. Furthermore, this food problem is one that is not confined within our borders; it is a problem affecting every human on earth.

High food-production costs and consumer prices in the United States inevitably signal food shortages, hunger and even starvation in other, less affluent parts of the globe.

We all remember the food price panic just a year ago. Among its causes were a worldwide crop reduction arising from the changing weather, discovery that critical fertilizers were in short supply and finding that surplus food had practically disappeared after the large grain sale to the Soviet Union.

The most dramatic visible evidence of the crisis is the tragic situation in West Africa, where millions are already severely undernourished and hundreds of thousands have died, and in South Asia, where floods and drought have created a critical food shortage.

We had hoped that this feeling of crisis and panic would ease this year as our own and other nations' bumper crops came in. In this country alone, we have put fifty million acres back into wheat and corn production in the last two years. Earlier this year, crop prospects looked excellent as farmers sowed in record numbers.

Now, however, hope is turning to fear again. As some weather experts had predicted, the American farm belt is experiencing its worst drought since the nineteen-thirties.

Predictions of feed grain crops have already dropped from an original 6.7-billion bushels to 4.9 billion or less. If yields in other major grain-producing nations such as Argentina, Canada and the Soviet Union are also down, the world is in serious trouble.

At the very least, these developments mean continued high food prices. But high food prices do not help the farmer because of his own high production costs, particularly the cost of fertilizer, fuel and machinery, which are wiping out potential profits, and in the cattle industry wiping out producers altogether.

For all of these reasons, the United States and the world community need to develop a new set of national and international policies that promote maximum food production at the lowest possible cost to provide ample nutrition for mankind.

Secretary of State Kissinger, last year in his maiden speech to the United Nations, proposed a world food conference to be held in Rome this November. This conference represents an opportunity to make major progress.

I have proposed outlines of a program for our Government to take to Rome. Called "Plowshares for Peace," the proposal consists of the following components:

First is the need for agricultural research. Without the kind of basic research already being carried on by men such as Norman Borlaug, the American Nobel laureate and father of the so-called Green Revolution, millions more of the world's population would be starving today. We also need to intensify our research into weather prediction and weather control to anticipate or prevent periodic drought and floods.

Second, equally important, is the assurance of adequate supplies of those key elements without which crops cannot grow—land, water, fuel and fertilizer. The United States and the world need a large new investment in fertilizer factories over the next two decades to enable food production to keep pace with population growth.

Third, we need to increase technological assistance in the harvesting, storing, processing and distributing of crops to assure maximum use and minimum waste—assistance that American farmers' cooperative associations and American industry are uniquely qualified to render.

Fourth, there must be established a minimum emergency food reserve on a worldwide basis, isolated from commercial marketing, to be used solely for famine relief.

Richard M. Nixon and Secretary Kissinger raised the world food issue at the Moscow summit meeting. As a result, the Soviet Union is seriously considering officially joining the United Nations Food and Agriculture Organization—a major step forward in the possible development of a world food program.

I hope that President Ford will continue this initiative by making the Rome conference an opportunity to deal in a fundamental way with the food and inflation problems.

There is a natural community of interest on these two great problems. The United States and the other grain-exporting nations have the technology and food to carry out a "Plowshares for Peace" program. The Arab world has the oil and investment capital to finance vitally needed fertilizer capacity and to help support food-research and famine-relief programs. The less-developed countries, which need this agricultural assistance desperately, have many of the scarce raw materials that make possible the advanced technology of the United States, Western Europe and Japan.

This is the potential negotiating environment of the conference. But a major leadership effort is required of the United States to take full advantage of that environment.

George McGovern, Democrat, is senior Senator from South Dakota.

August 19, 1974

FARM EXPERTS SEE A U.S. OPPORTUNITY TO LESSEN HUNGER

But Assert a Reversal in Policy Is Needed to Spur Expansion to Aid World

ECONOMIC FACTOR CITED

Research Seeks New Ways of Increasing Food Output Without Federal Aid

By WILLIAM ROBBINS

Special to The New York Times

WASHINGTON, Aug. 24—The United States has substantial reserves of agricultural resources that could help feed the world's hungry if there were sufficient economic incentives and significant changes in traditional Federal farm policy, a number of leading agricultural experts agree.

Exploitation of anything approaching the nation's full potential, however, would require enormous investments in land, resources and technology. These, in turn, would have to be stimulated by Government action and a change of Federal farm policy, which has never involved an active role in stimulating farm expansion. Virtually no one foresees such a reversal.

In fact, Secretary of Agriculture Earl L. Butz continued yesterday to sound an optimistic note about the nation's and the world's capacity to produce an abundance of food.

Despite a "shrill outcry from professional doomsdayers," Dr. Butz said in a speech in Indianapolis, the world is "a long way from running out of food."

Recent indications of imminent food shortages in India and other world areas, however, have forced many other agricultural experts in Government and the private sector to take a new look at agricultural procedures in the United States.

50 Per Cent Increase

Estimates of increases in food production that could be achieved with reasonable effort and without Government intervention in the next 10 years range up to 50 per cent of the present output. Such estimates assume the use of additional land, continuing advances in technology and a favorable economic climate, including attractive prices for farmers.

"Of all the factors involved, the major one is economic—the price has to be right," according to Marion Clawson, acting president of Resources for the Future, Inc., a private research organization.

"It's not only present prices, but how well farmers feel those prices will hold up. Many are unwilling to make the investment to bring new land into production, not knowing. They are showing commendable caution," Mr. Clawson commented.

Dr. Sylvan H. Wittwer of Michigan State University, one of the nation's leading agricultural scientists, sees research as the key to expansion and feels that the Government has been too conservative in its support of scientific work.

"The resource base changes with time and technology," he said recently, summing up in a wide-ranging interview his view of an attainable future of abundance.

And even in the face of a drought that dashed this year's hopes for crop production great enough to meet all demand, the Department of Agriculture's chief economist, Don Paarlberg, expresses his view with rhetoric equal to his soaring optimism.

"These are exciting times," he said. "Ours is the first generation that could hope to wipe the specter of Malthus from this globe."

1985 Estimates

While expressing concern over the precarious balance between food production and world needs, Dr. Paarlberg estimated that by 1985, this country could be producing 9.1 billion bushels of corn a year, up from this year's drought-reduced crop of about 5 billion and earlier estimates of record production above 6 billion.

He said the soybean crop could go to 2.3 billion bushels in 1985, up about a billion, and wheat to 2.3 billion bushels, up from this year's record of 1.8 billion.

Dr. Paarlberg's projections were based on the work of a long-range planning unit in the Department's Economic Research Service. About eight economists in the group draw on help and advice from other economists and scientists in divisions throughout the department.

Their products are projections, or "scenarios," based on varied assumptions of future economic conditions and influences. Normally they project what is likely to happen rather than what can be caused by Government programs.

Those projections filter up through administrators to the department's policy makers, such as Dr. Paarlberg and his chief, Secretary of Agriculture Butz. At that level, government activism is an alien philosophy.

"We want to keep the Government out of agriculture," Dr. Butz says. His view is reflected among other department officials.

"There may come a time when we will need Government action," said J. Dawson Ahalt, Dr. Paarlberg's deputy. "But we think farmers should get their signal from prices, and they will react best to that kind of signal."

Population Curbs Advocated

Like many others in the department, Dr. Ahalt feels that governmental influence would be better directed to population controls rather than to pressures for all-out expansion of productive capacity.

The long-range planners' most recent projection, on which Dr. Paarlberg's estimates were based, looks at resources that could be brought into use by 1985.

The projection starts with the land, about 325 million acres of which are being cultivated this year. More than 250 million additional acres of the nation's land not under cultivation are suited for crop production.

Most of that is now in competing uses, such as forests and pastures, but about 25 million acres could reasonably be expected as additions to the present farmland, the planners say. Part of that would come from land clearing and drainage operations in the Southeast and Delta regions, part from expanded dry-land cropping in the West and part from continuing irrigation projects.

The long-range planning group also took into consideration a projection of continued trends in technological progress, such as improved grain hybrids and fertilizers, but with no reliance on any major scientific breakthrough.

It also projected some further spread of improved farming practices and productivity, noting that the leading 10 per cent of today's farmers already get 50 per cent more production per acre than the national average.

"We're not saying that is what will happen," said Dr. Leroy Quance, who heads the planning group, called Economic Projections and Analytical Systems. "But the results were encouraging when he summed up what we can do."

Grandiose Irrigation Plan

Much more could be done, many agricultural experts say, with stepped-up Government investment in irrigation and research.

One of the most grandiose schemes advanced is a vast engineering proposal, known generally as the Parsons plan, that would take excess water from great rivers of the northwestern corner of North America, impound it in a Rocky Mountain trench reservoir, pump it from there into another reservoir in central Idaho and then let it flow by gravity through the Western states and down to Mexico.

The author of the plan, the Ralph M. Parsons Company, a big engineering organization, estimated that the project's water could be used to irrigate 40 million acres in the United States and said that as a by-product it would generate 70 million more kilowatts of power than would be needed for its own pumps.

Although the plan has been talked about since its conception in the early nineteen-sixties, few agricultural experts foresee a time when it would be undertaken.

"The engineering is possible, but it would be enormously costly," Mr. Clawson commented. "It would take 20 years to complete and the political problems are enormous."

The Parsons company estimated the cost of the project at $100-billion in 1964 dollars.

Based on less ambitious projects, economists in the Department of the Interior's Bureau of Reclamation have projected expansion of irrigated land by about 3 million acres through 1980, 6 million by 1990 and 8.8 million by 2000.

Inclusive Projections

The projections include land fully irrigated and that supplied with supplemental water and both authorized and merely potential work.

"The easy private development has already been done," Aldon D. Nielson, chief of the bureau's economics and statistics branch, said during a discussion with several aides in his office. "You can hardly find a simple dam site anymore."

Dick L. Porter of the bureau's division of planning observed: "When you talk about big ideas, you're talking about something like the Canadian scheme. Water is a more limiting factor than land."

Mr. Nielson responded: "It will probably take a crisis to get anything like that going.

And then you will be 10 years too late."

Many scientists believe that research can augment United States potential far beyond that projected by the Agriculture Department's long-range planning group.

In a study for the National Science Foundation on research needs, Dr. Wittwer of Michigan State called for a "national program for increasing the research investment," citing the potential payoffs already indicated by the work of some scientists.

Dr. Wittwer, who is assistant dean of Michigan State's Agricultural College and director of the Michigan Agricultural Experiment Station, is also chairman of the board of agriculture and renewable resources of the National Academy of Sciences National Research Council.

Among possible breakthroughs that he cited in the study and explained in an interview were some that could greatly increase the productivity of plants.

One area is that of photosynthesis, the growth process generated by sunlight on plant leaves. Experiments to alter plant structures and expose more leaves to the sun promise greater and faster growth and productivity, he said.

The rate of photosynthesis has also been increased experimentally, he noted, by enriching the atmosphere around plants with more carbon dioxide than is naturally present. But, he said, "Little work has been done to bring the results of research into the field."

Related studies that show great promise, he said, are in the area of nitrogen fixation, a process by which bacteria associated with certain plants—the legumes, such as peas and beans—convert atmospheric nitrogen for soil enrichment.

Nitrogen fixation has been increased as much as 500 per cent by carbon dioxide enrichment of the atmosphere around plants, he said.

In addition, Dr. Wittwer cited efforts to develop strains of nitrogen-fixing bacteria that might be associated with other plants besides legumes. The result, he noted, would improve growth rates of many plants and relieve pressures on increasingly scarce fertilizer resources.

Oregon State Experiments

One scientist working in this area, Harold Evans of Oregon State University, said in a telephone interview that he had found strains of bacteria with low-level nitrogen fixation on wheat, fescue and corn. He said he was also working with strains of bacteria found on wild grasses of South America.

"The problem is to develop more productive strains," Dr. Evans said. "Our hope is in mutations and manipulation of genes in plants and bacteria to achieve the goal."

"It's a gamble," he continued, "but the stakes are high. In order to feed all the humans on this earth we're going to need all the nitrogen fixation we can get, and all the chemical fertilizers, too."

Other agricultural scientists, meanwhile, are at work on experiments seeking to make livestock more productive. Among the projects are some to increase fertility.

One person involved in the work, R. A. Bellows of the United States Range Livestock Experimental Station at Miles City, Mont., is trying to produce multiple births in beef cattle. His goal is a 200 per cent annual reproduction rate in breeding herbs.

The payoff would be obvious. The more fertile the breeding cows the fewer would be needed, the less grain would be required and the less land area they would use.

Dr. Bellows has had some success. Using hormone treatments, he has been able to induce four sets of twin calves and one set of triplets in a herd of 30 cows.

In a telephone interview, he said that he believes his work will emerge in commercial applications by the nineteen-eighties. With greater funding, increased staff and more test animals, he said, it could be much sooner.

Agricultural specialists generally agree that all the nation's available land and all the fruits of research will be needed to meet domestic and foreign demand for United States food output in the not too distant future. And many also agree with Kenneth R. Farrell, Deputy Administrator of the economic research service, who observed recently:

"Long-range projections of current rates of population growth simply run off the chart and beyond the range of agricultural solutions that are either possessed or conceivable."

August 25, 1974

Toward Easing Hunger

To the Editor:

Regarding the Aug. 25 news story "Farm Experts See Potential in U. S. for Easing Hunger," the philosophy of Secretary of Agriculture Butz and his colleagues "to keep the Government out of agriculture" and let farmers "get their signals from prices" hardly seems likely to ease world hunger.

First of all, U. S. food prices have never been higher, which should normally encourage agricultural production. However, the farmer's costs are so high that even with inflated prices he is struggling to break even. Second, how are U. S. prices ever going to inspire U. S. farmers to produce food for starving millions who have no money? Third, not that U. S. efforts to produce more food should be restrained, it is a delusion that U. S. surplus food production can successfully contend with the expanding hunger problem of the world.

In a few major commodities we may produce a 10 to 15 per cent surplus beyond our own needs (200,000,000 people), but the projected world need is to feed several more billion people. A further point, as aptly described in The Times Magazine article of a few weeks ago, having food produced and available for starving people is only the beginning; problems in getting it to them are staggering. Indeed, a most worthwhile ultimate goal is to teach these people how to produce their own food.

The most profound part of the report, placed at the very end, was the comment by K. R. Farrell of the U.S.D.A. to the effect that projections of population growth simply outstrip agricultural solutions to the problem. This statement coupled with the philosophy of Secretary Butz do not add up to any "potential in the U. S. for easing hunger." At the very least shouldn't our Government be actively stimulating U. S. food production and agricultural research directed toward increased food production?

STUART PATTON
University Park, Pa., Aug. 26, 1974

September 1, 1974

SENATE UNIT CALLS FOOD AID POLITICAL

Vietnam Reduction Is Held Offset by Assistance to Egypt and Chile

By WILLIAM ROBBINS

Special to The New York Times

WASHINGTON, Sept. 9 — A staff report for the Senate Select Committee on Nutrition today criticized the United States for using a large portion of its food aid for political purposes and called on the United States to take the lead at the upcoming World Food Conference in efforts to alleviate human suffering.

"A review of the U.S. food effort shows not only that it was shrinking but that in the struggle over short supplies, political concerns have taken high priority," the report said.

It noted that Congress, finding heavy use of food aid for military purposes in South Vietnam, had acted to end the practice, but said that "the use of food for strategic diplomatic purposes has not been reduced significantly." The report added that the Vietnam cutoff had beeu offset in part by the recent commitment, under special terms, of 100,000 tons of grain for Egypt and a $34-million increase in aid for Chile.

The report, summing up testimony by panels of experts on world food problems at three days of hearings last June, also calls for American cooperation in an international system of grain reserves as well as increased aid in improving production of food in poorer countries.

In a preface, Senator George McGovern, Democrat of South Dakota and the chairman of the committee, criticized what he called "the unyielding official position of the Department of Agriculture." He said he would introduce a resolution in the Senate requiring United States Representatives at the food conference, scheduled to be held Nov. 5 to 16 in Rome, "worthy of the moral and economic position of our nation."

The conference, proposed by Secertary of State Kissinger and sponsored by the United Nations, will bring together representatives of about 130 countries.

A spokesman for the Department of Agriculture said that its officials would withhold comment on the Senate committee report until they had had a chance to study it. However, he cited the text of an address by Secretary of Agriculture Earl L. Butz, prepared for a Sept. 4 meeting at the State Department, on plans for the conference.

In his text Mr. Butz, who will head the United States delegation in Rome, said that this country would make a "firm commitment" on food aid and was prepared to discuss "an appropriate over-all reserve target level."

Mr. Butz—who departed from his text when he spoke—reminded representatives of nongovermental organizations attending the meeting that $1-billion had been budgeted for food aid this fiscal year, an amount that is expected to buy less than the $800-million spent by the United States for the purpose in the fiscal year ended June 30.

He also indicated that he would continue to insist that each participating country in an international system be free to determine how it would maintain its share of grain reserves. In the United States, he said, he would insist that the function of holding reserves be left in private hands.

Experts at the June hearings had called for a system of reserves to be built up by the Government in good years to guard against scarcity in years of poor production. Senator McGovern reiterated that view today, saying:

"In reality, a reserve in private hands is no reserve at all. It is indeed precisely the same market mechanism that has produced the situation we face today."

September 10, 1974

The Food Weapon

To the Editor:

In his United Nations speech on Sept. 18, President Ford said, "It has not been our policy to use food as a political weapon." Yet the U.S. apparently stopped large-scale food assistance to Chile after the election of Salvador Allende to the Presidency and then resumed it soon after a repressive military dictatorship took with sickening brutality and in the name of "peace with honor"), the fact remains—and plainer than ever as *this* all-but-mortal wound is reopened—that without such resistance on the part of its youth our nation would still be fighting, in Burma or Bangladesh by now.

I fail to see, or feel, how any one of these three actions has the effect of "binding up [our] nation's wounds." In fact, with our soaring crime, these young Americans should remain in their deserved exile until their homeland can restore its original sanity—and reclaim that once very *common* decency, out of which they were manifestly bred.

Clearly, in our as yet-unsettled "evil upheaval" of the past thirteen years, the old scum persists in masquerading as our fresh cream.

MARY MENZIES

Goleta, Calif., Sept. 20, 1974

September 29, 1974

U. S. Food Aid Expected

WASHINGTON, Oct. 10 — India, overcoming her reluctance to make a direct request, has called on the United States for food assistance to ease a threat of widespread famine, and officials here say the response is sure to be affirmative.

Clayton Yeutter, Assistant Secretary of Agriculture for International Trade Relations, confirmed reports that India had made a direct appeal for shipments under the long-term low-interest arrangements available through the United States foreign food assistance program.

Secretary of State Kissinger, who is due to visit New Delhi later this month after his current Middle Eastern tour, was said to be determined before he left Washington not to go to India empty-handed or with only token aid.

But, according to several United States Government sources, the amount of aid that will be provided will be determined by budgetary, foreign policy and other considerations.

These sources noted that food-program planners were operating under guidelines that include a series of specific priorities. Foreign policy and strategic considerations in Indochina and the Middle East were said to be placed highest in that series, ahead of humanitarian uses of this country's food-assistance program.

Those priorities were laid out last month at a meeting of an interagency food group headed by an official of the Office of Management and Budget, according to sources familiar with the results of that session.

Aides to Secretary Kissinger acknowledge that foreign-policy objectives continue to have top priority in allocation of food assistance, but they note that the Secretary also continues to insist on expanding the purely humanitarian uses of the program to help countries where hunger is greatest.

Secretary of Agriculture Earl L. Butz said Tuesday that such needs were among considerations in this week's decision to impose limited controls over commercial exports.

"We simply have to have the supplies to meet our humanitarian obligations," he told the Senate permanent subcommittee on investigations.

Although the exact amount of food shipments for India has not been determined for this fiscal year, diplomatic and Government sources say that the most probable level is 500,000 tons.

Food assistance is provided under Public Law 480, the so-called Food for Peace Program.

October 11, 1974

U.S. Ending 'Food for Peace' Despite Rising Hunger Abroad

By H. J. MAIDENBERG

When World War II ended, Washington embarked on an unusual and far-reaching program to feed millions of hungry people overseas, most of whom paid little or nothing for the basic foodstuffs they received.

Now, with even greater numbers in desperate need of food, Washington is quietly winding down its so-called "Food for Peace" programs.

One such program has already ended. There were no shipments of powdered milk, upon which millions of children depended, during the fiscal year that ended last June 30.

Lester R. Brown, a food expert at the Overseas Development Council, observed in Washington recently that in 1972 some 90 million of the world's poorest people depended on food received from these programs. He added:

"An estimated 20 million nutritionally vulnerable people have been cut off from these programs in the past year."

In addition, many more millions are now confronted with costly food bills they cannot afford. Shamsher Singh, chief of the commodity division of the World Bank, declared the other day:

"The poor countries have had their energy bill raised by $10-billion the past year. Their minimum imported food bill equals that unobtainable sum. Obviously, their situation is untenable even in the short term."

It was also obvious to the many commodity specialists interviewed in recent weeks that producers of basic foodstuffs are attempting to use their surpluses to pay for their vastly increased energy bills. That is one reason, the experts pointed out, that prices of such key foodstuffs as grain, soybeans and sugar have recently risen almost as much as petroleum.

Another reason is that the current tonnages of surplus foods, while they equal those in the years immediately after World War II, must now feed far greater numbers of people born in the last generation.

Economic Weapon

Actually, the use of food surpluses as an economic weapon was a child of the cold war that followed World War II. During the war the United States sent huge amounts of food to its allies regardless of political ideology. But after the war Washington expanded its food shipments to relieve hunger in ravaged parts of Asia and Europe not only for humanitarian reasons but also to prevent those regions from leaning toward Communism.

According to Government officials involved in that effort, food played a vital role in the Marshall Plan, the United Nations Relief and Rehabilitation Administration and other programs that sprouted in the late nineteen-forties.

Meanwhile, the huge handouts of foodstuffs provided a vital support for American agriculture, which had been geared for massive production during the war.

Washington's aid programs were also stimulated by scientific advances that stunningly raised corn's yield per acre, for example, from 30 bushels to more than 90 bushels in the postwar years.

So great was the productive power of the United States farmer that, by the end of the Korean War in 1953, this nation faced a flood of surplus food each year. So did Argentina, Canada, Australia, New Zealand, South Africa and other countries that had geared up to help feed the world during World War II.

To cope with domestic crop surpluses and increasing foreign competition, Washington strengthened its tariff barriers to imported food and, in 1954, swept up many relief programs into the Agricultural Trade Development and Assistance Act (Public Law 480), known as the "Food for Peace" program.

Attractive Terms

Under Title I of the program, foodstuffs were shipped to America's political allies under extremely attractive terms. The recipient country usually paid in local currency or over a period of up to 40 years at very low interest rates.

Washington aid officials point out that the large sums amassed by their food loans were often used in the recipient countries for improving health, communications and education systems, all of which also eventually increased the demand for food.

American surplus food was also given away outright under Title II of P.L. 480, which accounted for roughly half the $1-billion to $1.5-billion a year involved in the over-all plan.

But the cost was often canceled by Washington's ability to unload tremendous tonnages of surplus foodstuffs, which it had to carry at taxpayer cost. These surpluses accumulated because farmers often didn't redeem their crops after they had pawned them under the various subsidy programs offered by the Government since the Depression.

The American merchant marine also benefited by carrying the bulk of the food surpluses at a time when foreign-flag carriers were driving the nation's shipping companies out of business with lower freight charges.

Washington also earned the friendship of millions of hungry people abroad who received the precious food either at no cost or at subsidized low prices

Until the Soviet Union's massive grain purchases in the United States and elsewhere in 1972-73 and the surge in petroleum prices late last year, the private traders and exporters of basic foodstuffs depended largely on a crop failure somewhere, a minor war or some natural disaster to bring them business.

The bulk of this nation's surpluses were finally erased by Moscow's purchase of 10 million metric tons of grain and soybeans here and 11 million tons elsewere in 1972 because of a poor Soviet crop.

The Chinese, Too

Equally important, President Nixon opened the American food market to China for the first time in 24 years at a time when Japan and other developed nations were becoming increasingly dependent on North America for their key agricultural products.

For the millions of poor who depended on American food giveaways, the events of 1972-73 mean more than an economic disaster—their very lives are at stake. Indeed, their exposure to starvation today is far greater than it was in the post-World War II period, when the aid programs began.

First, there are about 900 million more people on this planet now than in the late nineteen-forties. Science has not been able to duplicate its earlier crop miracles because of shortages of pure water, cheap fertilizers and other chemicals made from crude oil

Wheat from the United States being prepared for division in the village of Rajasthan in India in 1966.

as well as the normal vicissitudes of weather.

The last quarter century also has seen vast movements of people from rural areas, where they could provide their own basic food, to urban centers. It was th availability of relatively cheap food that permitted this mass migration.

The decades of surpluses also permitted the wealthier countries to indulge in their taste for animal protein. For example, meat consumption in the United States and the Soviet Union doubled between 1960 and 1972.

While it takes a pound of grain to make a pound of bread, it takes two pounds of grain to produce a pound of chicken, four pounds of grain to make a pound of pork and eight pounds of grain to produce a pound of beef.

In this country beef consumption exceeded pork consumption for the first time in 1954; the average American ate 56 pounds of beef that year. Now with the United States population much bigger and beef prices much higher, the per capita consumption of beef is 109 pounds a year.

Commodity experts point out that most of the grain and soybeans grown in the United States are consumed by animals, and so is an ever-increasing amount elsewhere in the world.

Another factor that the experts stress is that there will be 72 million more humans for the world to feed one year from today. They will require 30 million tons of grain. That is 40 per cent of America's present grain exports—or the combined sales of Canada, Australia, Argentina and South Africa last year.

Meantime, the poorer nations that require food aid now face another problem. During the years of American aid, many of these countries either neglected their own agricultural potential or used it to produce cash crops for export.

One obvious need, the experts insist, is some worldwide control on population growth. Another need is to invest heavily in unused land in the less developed countries to make them productive.

Much of this land is now owned either by the state or by private persons who are unwilling or economically unable to develop it for crops or as pasture for animals.

As the commodity experts see it, piecemeal land reform measures are not the answer because small holdings preclude efficient production. In this country, where only 2 per cent of the farm and ranch acreage is owned by large corporations, 25 per cent of the units produce 80 per cent of the nation's agricultural output.

The pressures on the poorer countries have placed a heavy burden on global aid agencies such as the International Bank for Reconstruction and Development (better known as the World Bank) and the younger regional lenders, the Inter-American Development Bank and the Asian Development Bank.

Loans Set Record

The World Bank, by far the largest of the three major lenders, will make loans totaling a record $4.5-billion this year, of which $800-million is expected to involve agricultural projects. The rest of the loans are earmarked for industrially related or socially oriented programs.

Another needed measure in the poorer countries, commodity specialists insist, is incentives for rural people to stay on the farm.

Several Chicago grain exporters observed recently that China has apparently taken the lead in this sector. They commented recently that only 11 per cent of China's land mass is arable but that 80 per cent of that country's population works there, often double-cropping arable acreage.

Undoubtedly, the political fabric that cloaks the problems of the hungry countries will be high on the list of tropics when the United Nations Food and Agriculture Organization meets in Rome next week to discuss the world's food needs.

However the less developed nations may approach the food shortage and high price of food, one thing is certain to American commodity experts: They can no longer count on Washington for cheap surplus foodstuffs—or cash.

October 29, 1974

Excerpts From Kissinger's Speech at World Food Parley in Rome

ROME, Nov. 5 (AP)—Following are excerpts from Secretary of State Kissinger's speech today at the opening of the World Food Conference:

We must begin here with the challenge of food. No social system, ideology or principle of justice can tolerate a world in which the spiritual and physical potential of hundreds of millions is stunted from elemental hunger or inadequate nutrition. National pride or regional suspicions lose any moral and practical justification if they prevent us from overcoming this scourge.

A generation ago many farmers were self-sufficient; today fuel, fertilizer, capital and technology are essential for their economic survival. A generation ago many nations were self-sufficient. Today a few food exporters provide the margin between life and death for many millions.

World population is projected to double by the end of the century. It is clear that we must meet the food need that this entails. But it is equally clear that population cannot continue indefinitely to double every generation. At some point we will inevitably exceed the earth's capacity to sustain human life.

Help Is Needed

The responsibility for financing food imports cannot, however, rest with the food exporters alone. Over the next few years in particular, the financing needs of the food-deficit developing countries will simply be too large for either their own limited resources or the traditional food aid donors.

The oil exporters have a special responsibility in this regard. Many of them have income far in excess of that needed to balance their international payments or to finance their economic development. The continuing massive transfer of wealth and the resulting impetus to world-wide inflation have shattered the ability of the developing countries to purchase food, fertilizer and other goods. And the economic crisis has severely reduced the imports of the industrialized countries from the developing nations.

Therefore, ways must be found to move more of the surplus oil revenue into long-term lending or grants to the poorer countries. The United States proposes that the development committee, created at the recent session of the governors of the International Bank and Monetary Fund, be charged with the urgent study of whether existing sources of financing are sufficient to meet the expected import requirements of developing countries.

If these sources are not sufficient, new means must be found to supplement them. This must become one of the priority objectives of the countries and institutions that have the major influence in the international monetary system.

Serious Health Problems

Supplies alone do not guarantee man's nutritional requirements. Even in developed countries, with ample supplies, serious health problems are caused by the wrong kinds and amounts of food. In developing countries, the problem is magnified. Not only inadequate distribution but also the rising cost of food dooms the poorest and the most vulnerable groups —children and mothers—to inferior quality as well as insufficient quantity of food. Even with massive gains in food production, the world could still be haunted by the specter of inadequate nutrition.

First, we must understand the problem better. We know a good deal about the state of global production. But our knowledge of the state of global nutrition is abysmal. Therefore, the United States proposes that a global nutrition surveillance system be established by the World Health Organization, the Food and Agriculture Organization and the United Nations International Children's Emergency Fund. Particular attention should be devoted to the special needs of mothers and young children and to respond quickly to local emergencies affecting these particular vulnerable groups. Nutrition surveying is a field with which the

United States has considerable experience; we are ready to share our knowledge and techniques.

Second, we need new methods for combatting malnutrition. The United States invites the W.H.O., F.A.O. and UNICEF to arrange for an internationally coordinated program in applied nutritional research. Such a program should set priorities, identify the best centers for research, and generate the necessary funding. The United States is willing to contribute $5-million to initiate such a program.

Third, we need to act on problems which are already clear. The United States proposes an immediate campaign against two of the most prevalent and blighting effects of malnutrition: Vitamin-A blindness and iron-deficiency anemia. The former is responsible for well over half of the millions of cases of blindness in less developed countries; the current food shortages will predictably increase this number. Iron-deficiency anemia is responsible for low productivity in many parts of the world.

The events of the past few years have brought home the grave vulnerability of mankind to food emergencies caused by crop failures, floods, wars and other disasters. The world has come to depend on a few exporting countries, and particularly the United States, to maintain the necessary reserves. But reserves no longer exist, despite the fact that the United States has removed virtually all of its restrictions on production and our farmers have made an all-out effort to maximize output. A worldwide reserve of as much as 60 million tons of food above present carry-over levels may be needed to assure adequate food security.

It is neither prudent nor practical for one or even a few countries to be the world's sole holder of reserves. Nations with a history of radical fluctuations in import requirements have an obligation, both to their own people and to the world community, to participate in a system which shares that responsibility more widely. And exporting countries can no longer afford to be caught by surprise. They must have advance information to plan production and exports.

F.A.O. Chief Praised

We commend F.A.O. Director General Boerma for his initiative in the area of reserves. The United States shares his view that a cooperative multilateral system is essential for greater equity and efficiency. We therefore propose that this conference organize a reserves-coordinating group to negotiate a detailed agreement on an international system of nationally held grain reserves at the earliest possible time. It should include all the major exporters as well as those whose import needs are likely to be greatest. This group's work should be carried out in close cooperation with other international efforts to improve the world trading system.

An international reserve system should include the following elements:

¶ Exchange of information on levels of reserves and working reserves.

¶ Guidelines on the management of national reserves, defining the conditions for adding to reserves and for releasing from them.

¶ Preference for cooperating countries in the distribution of reserves.

¶ Procedures for adjustment of targets and settlement of disputes and measures for dealing with noncompliance.

The challenge before this conference is to translate needs into programs and programs into results. We have no time to lose.

A 5-Point Platform

I have set forth a five-point platform for joint action:

1. To concert the efforts of the major surplus countries to help meet the global demand.
2. To expand the capacity of chronic food-deficit developing nations for growth and greater self-sufficiency.
3. To transfer resources and food to meet the gaps which remain.
4. To improve the quality of food to insure adequate nutrition.
5. To safeguard men and nations from sudden emergencies and the vagaries of weather.

I have outlined the contributions that the United States is prepared to make in national or multinational programs to achieve each of these goals. And I have proposed three new international groups to strengthen national efforts, coordinate them and give them global focus:

¶ The Exporters Planning Group.

¶ The Food Production and Investment Coordinating Group.

¶ The Reserves Coordinating Group.

A number of suggestions have been made for a central body to fuse our efforts and provide leadership. The United States is open-minded about such an institution. We strongly believe, however, that whatever the mechanisms, a unified, concerted and comprehensive approach is an absolute requirement. The American delegation headed by our distinguished Secretary of Agriculture Earl Butz is prepared to begin urgent discussions to implement our proposals. We welcome the suggestions of other nations gathered here. We will work hard and we will work cooperatively.

November 6, 1974

World Food Parley Looking to U.S. For Half of Emergency Aid

By WILLIAM ROBBINS
Special to The New York Times

ROME, Nov. 11—Half of the additional food supplies needed to stave off widespread famine will have to be found in the United States, an official of the World Food Conference secretariat said today.

"It has to come from the United States—nobody else has it," the official said, speaking on the basis of surveys made in preparation for the conference.

The United States delegation planned to meet privately tomorrow with other grain producers to try to determine where the needed food might be found.

By the time of that meeting, the Americans expect to have a reply from President Ford on their request for permission to announced that the United States will provide a million tons more of food assistance than was provided last year, an American official said.

The conference secretariat and the United Nations Food and Agriculture organization have determined that 8 million to 10 million tons of additional food aid will be needed this year.

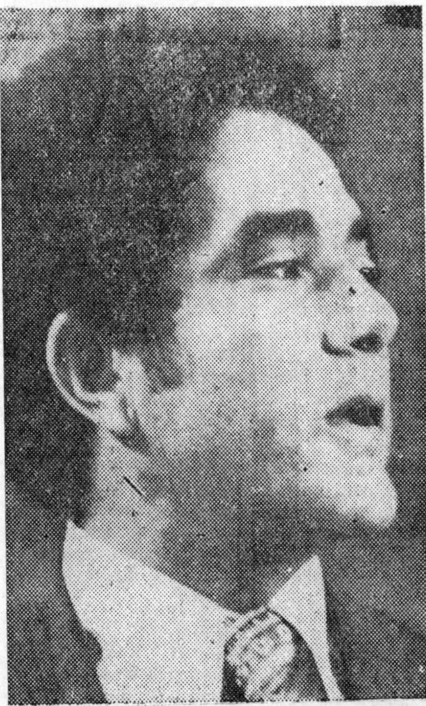

United Press International

Muhammad Ali al-Tabu, left, Libyan Agriculture Minister, and Salem Ibrahim al-Manai, the assistant Under Secretary of Agriculture in Kuwait, at the World Food Conference yesterday in Rome. Mr. Tabu said Libya would allocate part of her oil income for foreign agricultural projects if big powers halted "limitless spending on arms."

Four to five million tons will have to come from the United States, the secretariat aide said. He said that about a million tons more might come from Canada. Any additional grain would have to come from the European Economic Community, Australia or Argentina.

The identification of possible aid sources was one of a number of developments today, including the following:

¶Five countries — Bangladesh, India, Pakistan, Sri Lanka and Indonesia, planned to call tomorrow for food grants totaling 10 million tons to meet the present emergency and for additional tonnage to be made available on long-term credit.

¶Some oil-exporting countries, led by Algeria, Iran and Venezuela, prepared a resolution calling for creation of an agency to channel agricultural aid to the poorer countries. The agency would include representatives of donor countries, oil producers and aid recipients.

¶Senator Dick Clark, Democrat of Iowa, said he would introduce legislation in Congress to carry out the intent of an American resolution offered Friday calling for restraints on nonagricultural uses of fertilizer.

¶President Luis Echeverría Alvarez of Mexico, the first head of state to address the conference, reiterated a Mexican proposal for a world food and agricultural research bank and, at a news conference, said his country had begun discussions with Venezuela on creation of a separate fund for Latin America if the conference failed to act.

The secretariat's attempt to identify possible sources of emergency grain dealt only with availability, not with financing arrangements. Besides seeking funds from the traditional donor nations, the secretariat and the Food and Agriculture Organization are expected to turn to the oil countries.

The four to five million tons of grain reportedly needed from the United States does not take into account the one million tons of American aid yet to be announced.

Contract Review Urged

Much of any additional aid would be expected to come from the 28 million tons of wheat that the United States has for export. All but seven million tons of that has been committed to foreign buyers, United States officials have said.

But the Secretariat aide said it was believed that the United States, through its continuing review of sales contracts, might find some that were not true commitments and some involving tonnage that might be deferred until after next June, when new wheat harvests start coming in.

It is thought that other countries, similarly committed, might find additional grain available through the same process.

The imminent threat of famine is increasingly overtaking the emphasis on long-term solutions that were given priority in the original planning of the World Food Conference.

Long-Term Fund Planned

Among the resolutions drafted to deal with the long-term questions is a proposal for a ood aid fund equal to the immediate relief sought by the five needy countries.

For that fund of 10 million tons a year, the secretariat has also identified possible sources of supplies. Again the United States would be the major supplier, followed by Western Europe, Canada and Australia.

The United States would probably have to supply 5 million to 5.5 million tons. Canada has already pledged a million tons a year for the next three years, and Australia said she would give 550,000 to 600,000 tons a year. The European Economic Community is considered a possible source for 2 to 2.5 million tons.

These supplies fall short of the 10 million tons sought, but it is thought that the rest could be obtained from smaller producers, primarily Argentina.

In his address, President Echeverría laid much of the blame both for the food crisis and for inflation on the more affluent countries.

Famine 'Manufactured'

"The rise in prices, the confrontation of markets, and the crisis of raw materials cannot be attributed to the third world," he said. "In the final analysis, this situation has been determined and brought about by the inability of the great industrial nations to submit their production model to a system of international solidarity and shared development and interdependence based on equity and justice."

Of the food crisis, President Echeverria said:

"The famine that today is paralyzing the activities of entire nations has been manufactured with the same detachment as that employed in the construction of the atomic bomb.

"The progressive transformation of cereals and grains into meat that makes overconsumption of meat in certain affluent areas of the world possible destroys the possibility of a sufficient amount of protein in other parts of the world."

His charge was similar to a growing demand being heard during the conference for more restraint in developed nations on meat consumption.

November 12, 1974

U.S. COMMITMENT TO MORE FOOD AID REJECTED BY FORD

Butz Tells Rome Parley Step Would Hit Market—White House Denies Turndown

GAINS IN OTHER AREAS

Conference Advances Plans for Future Supplies and Long-Term Assistance

By WILLIAM ROBBINS
Special to The New York Times

ROME, Nov. 15—President Ford refused today to permit the American delegation at the World Food Conference to commit the United States to a million-ton increase in emergency food aid to nations threatened with famine.

The decision, announced by the Secretary of Agriculture, Earl L. Butz, at a news conference, overshadowed other developments on a day in which substantial progress was reported on plans for more food for the future. They included the shaping of resolutions on an international grain reserve and long-term internationally financed aid.

In explaining President Ford's decision, Dr. Butz said the increase "would have a bullish effect on the market." He cited budget constraints, tight supplies and the possible impact on American consumer prices, already sharply inflated.

Fear of Falling Short

Another reason, given privately, is that the Administration is unwilling to commit itself for fear that if prices do rise, budgeted funds would buy less grain than the commitment would call for. Decisions on food aid have been made on a quarterly basis to maintain flexibility even though shipments have been at a rate that would produce a 1.5-million-ton increase, Administration sources say.

Commodity experts here question the idea of an impact on grain markets. "The traders have already discounted it," a source close to the Administration said of the purchasing. "They know as well as anybody that the Government is already doing it."

[The White House press secretary said that it would not be proper to assert that President Ford had "turned down" the delegation's request. It said the United States would honor Secretary of State Kissinger's commitment of increased contributions in the current fiscal year.]

Last Friday the American delegation requested President Ford to give it permission to announce that the United States would increase its aid for humanitarian purposes from one million to two million tons.

The request followed a meeting at which major grain-producing nations were presented with a report estimating that South Asia and the sub-Sahara region of Africa face a grain shortage of seven to 11 million tons in the next year.

Dr. Butz, at his news conference, charged that three Democratic Senators attending the conference, acting "for partisan political gain," had placed the United States in a defensive position by pressing Mr. Ford to announce an increase in humanitarian aid. Of the Senators who led the initiative the only one whose name he mentioned was Hubert H. Humphrey of Minnesota. The others were Dick Clark of Iowa and George McGovern of South Dakota.

Referring to their public statements, Dr. Butz asserted: "These things have placed the United States in a position of seeming reluctant to go along with food aid. Nothing could be further from the truth."

Though the Secretary acknowledged signing the cablegram requesting permission to announce an increase, he said he was only passing along the Senators' position which they had pressin private meetings and then in public statements. However, a copy of the message obtained by The New York Times makes it seem that the proposal was the sense of the American delegation.

"Suggest minimum one-million-ton increase current fiscal year 1975," the cable said. It expressed the belief that such an increase was feasible both in terms of budget considerations and "in terms of the supply situation."

"Belief here is that shipment of 4.3 million tons will likely develop anyway," it said, "and announcement here would be extremely constructive at this time in view of Canadian and Australian announcements:"

American shipments last year totaled 3.3-million tons. The Canadians have pledged a million tons a year over the next three years and Austrialia has pledged a fixed proportion of gross national product.

History of U.S. Food Aid

In announcing the American position, Dr. Butz detailed the history of the United States food aid to developing countries and noted that it had given 46 per cent of such assistance worldwide since 1962. He also said that more wheat and rice were scheduled for food aid this year than last, with lower shipments of livestock feed. Now, he said, "you need food for people rather than for animals."

"We are indeed shipping more food to the critical areas of the world," he added, citing commitments already made to Bangladesh this year totaling 250,000 tons.

In a recent interview Dr. Butz said that the United States would probably increase shipments this fiscal year as much as the cablegram proposed.

With the American statement the focus of the 12-day conference, which ends tomorrow, shifted from the issue of immediate relief for countries threatened with famine, which had overwhelmed attention, to the long-term problems that the United States delegation has insisted are its primary concern.

Further Talks Scheduled

"The immediate problem of world hunger is not going to be solved by this conference," Secretary Butz, who is the delegation chairman, had said. "Somehow we have to find a way to solve this critical problem. But it has to be found where the supplies are—in the United States, Canada, Argentina, Australia and the European Economic Community."

He and his principal aides have been conferring privately with ministers from the other major grain producers on steps to solve the immediate problem, among other subjects.

His assessment appeared to many to be confirmed Wednesday when a meeting of major producers and importers with A. H. Boerma, Director General of the United Nations Food and Agriculture Organization, failed to identify sources for the 7 million to 11 million tons of grain that the F.A.O. estimates are needed by five most seriously threatened countries—Bangladesh, India, Pakistan, Sri Lanka and Tanzania.

Another such meeting is scheduled here Nov. 29. An Administration source said the United States questioned the F.A.O. estimate and expected to tell Mr. Boerma that the five-million-ton-need estimated by the United States will be no problem if financing can be obtained.

Others here have not been willing to accept the United States position on conference priorities. Sayed A. Marei, secretary general of the conference, said this week that pledges for immediate relief would be a measure of its success, and, breaking a diplomatic silence, called on the United States to pledge an increase.

Senator Clark, at a news conference with Mr. McGovern and Mr. Humphrey, expressed the urgency felt by many delegates and observers: "It would be unfortunate to say we are concerned about future generations but not interested here in the half-billion that may die now."

An Optimistic Outook

However, Sartaj Aziz, deputy secretary general of the conference, took an optimistic view, saying: "If the position is unchanged it doesn't mean it gets worse. This may not be the last word because the meeting scheduled for Nov. 29 is due to take up this question." He also said he could see that there might be "all kinds of domestic reasons" for the American stand.

Other reactions were mixed. The Pakistani Agriculture Minister, Khuda Buksh Bucha, said: "I hope it won't have a negative effect on the conference. Perhaps this is internal politics. I think that the American decision to contribute with other donor countries toward a 10-million-ton-a-year goal in food aid is a major achievement of this conference. The United States will be a major contributor."

Joseph Mungai, Agriculture Minister of Tanzania, said: "It is a disappointing outcome in that quite a number of countries were banking on these food supplies."

Some progress in committees working on plans for food for the future were detailed by Richard E. Bell, a Deputy Assistant Secretary of Agriculture, who accompanied Dr. Butz at the news conference. Work is "essentially completed," he said, on an early-warning system to provide information that could help avert serious crises or deal with them expeditiously, on the international grain-reserve plan and on the 10-million-ton-a-year food aid plan.

Details to Come Later

All such plans are embodied in resolutions, with details to be worked out by negotiating groups.

Mr. Bell said he was encouraged by a statement made in committee sessions that Moscow would be willing to consider an information system.

While noting that the 10-million-ton goal was a substantial increase over present levels, he said it was "feasible provided there are new donors."

In another committee, a proposal by Arab countries for an agricultural development fund has been put in the form of a resolution calling for voluntary participation. The United States usually prefers bilateral aid rather than submerge its help in multilateral funds.

Plea Not 'Turned Down'

Special to The New York Times

WASHINGTON, Nov. 15—The White House press secretary, Ron Nessen, said today that it would not be proper to say that President Ford had "turned down" the request by the United States delegation to increase American food aid by a million tons.

At a White House briefing he said that the United States would honor the commitment by Secretary of State Kissinger, who pledged increased food contributions in the current fiscal year despite adverse weather.

Mr. Nessen, who said that the United States could not be more specific about the amount of assistance until more information was obtained about crop levels, explained that the Administration feared it would compound inflationary problems if it committed itself to a figure.

To avoid adding to inflationary pressures, Mr. Nessen said, commitments will be made on a quarterly basis and will depend on the most up-to-date crop reports.

The United States will do everything it can to insure larger contributions in the future, he added.

Senator Clark, an Iowan, issued a statement saying that the White House decision "means that we as a nation are unwilling to put forward any meaningful additional assistance to meet the immediate problem of world famine."

"The White House is wrong in defending its refusal to approve the proposal on grounds that the purchase of an additional one million tons would drive prices higher and cause inflation," he added. "In fact, the President just approved a sale of grain to the Soviet Union which was more than twice as large, and it caused no increase in prices."

Meanwhile, at a news conference Secretary of State Kissinger said that he expected that before the year was over the United States would increase not only the dollar amount but also the quantity of food aid it would provide to hungry nations.

He expressed regret that the question of emergency food assistance had come up during a conference that the United States had proposed to deal with long-range solutions to food-supply problems.

November 16, 1974

Butz Tells Rome Conference Food Is a 'Tool in Kit of American Diplomacy'

By CLYDE H. FARNSWORTH
Special to The New York Times

ROME, Nov. 16—Agriculture Secretary Earl L. Butz said repeatedly at the World Food Conference that food is a "tool in the kit of American diplomacy," underscoring the belief of the Ford administration, like that of earlier ones, that the top priority in food aid should be to further foreign policy objectives. Food was in fact used as a weapon in the Vietnam war.

Some Democratic Senators who brought reformist ideas to the Rome forum as advisers to the American delegation think the priority should be to fulfill humanitarian needs.

The Senators got the delegation to cable Mr. Ford asking permission to announce here that the United States would increase by one million tons its emergency food aid to nations threatened with famine. The President refused.

A proposal submitted to the conference by the American delegation, after considerable infighting, represents something of a compromise between the two philosophies. The proposal requests donor Governments to:

"Reaffirm a commitment to continually review their food assistance programs toward assuring that the neediest countries are receiving adequate priority in the allocation of available food supplies."

Those close to the Democratic Senators — George McGovern of South Dakota, Hubert H. Humphrey of Minnesota and Dick Clark of Iowa—see in the wording of the draft resolution a subtle shift in the official American position.

According to sources close to the proceedings, a meeting of Administration officials last month, convened to reassess the priorities, had still placed humanitarian objectives second to foreign policy.

The battle to force a full-scale reversal in priorities was seen in American political clashes at the Rome conference, which ended today, and is expected to continue when Administration food officials and the Senators get back to Washington.

Legislation setting up the so-called American Food for Peace program goes back to the mid-ninteen-fifties, under Public Law 480. At that time the United States had a lot of surplus grain, which was costing millions of dollars to store. In some cases, such as the scandal surrounding Billie Sol Estes, a Texas financial operator, grain storage led to profiteering.

There were four objectives in Public Law 480: to dispose of surpluses, develop markets, advance foreign policy and meet humanitarian needs. Now that the surpluses have disappeared, the first two objectives no longer apply. In recent years much of the Food for Peace has gone to Southeast Asia under Title I of the legislation.

November 17, 1974

America: Abused and Fed Up

By Anthony Harrigan

NASHVILLE—The World Food Conference in Rome, like many other United Nations gatherings, turned into a hate-America session. Delegates from Communist and so-called nonaligned nations charged that "imperialists" were responsible for the food shortages in the Southern Hemisphere. They demanded that Americans eat less and give away more.

It is amazing that those nations that want the United States to feed them also are determined to abuse the American people and attribute to them the worst of motives.

In any case, however, the American people aren't about to accept reduced diets or support new, massive giveaways of food to third-world nations. Indeed, none of the advanced nations of the Northern Hemisphere are likely to introduce austerity measures in order to provide the food sought by India and other food-deficient countries.

For an entire generation, Americans have been shipping food to India and elsewhere. They have lavished billions of dollars on food giveaways without receiving any thanks in return. By and large, the American people are very tired of all types of foreign aid.

Today, the United States faces severe economic difficulty at home. The nation can't afford to be as generous as it was in the past. The United States needs to expand food production in order to lower food prices for the American people.

Where possible, the United States needs to sell food overseas in order to redress the balance of payments which worsens each month because of the outflow of dollars for foreign oil.

Each country will have to solve its food problems. To be sure, the problems facing some countries are horrendous. But, in many cases, the suffering nations have brought on their troubles. India experimented with socialism and weakened its private sector, including its farmers. It has wasted money on creating a nuclear capability.

Beyond that, many of the countries now short of food are incompetent nations. To use a fashionable word, they aren't "viable" countries. They lack the leadership, resources, educational élites and the capitalist economic structures necessary for effective production of food and long-term national existence.

The United States cannot save all the inadequate nations of the world from their inadequacies or follies. The United States is not under any moral obligation to feed the entire world. In any case, that would be an impossible task. The responsibility of America's leadership is to America's people.

Indeed we are in a period when our Government must stress economic nationalism. We need to maximize all our advantages, including sale of our food. Dependent nations must look to their own resources and attempt to curb their extravagant population growth.

Our Government, for its part, should be more candid in stating the concerns of the American people. It should not urge establishment of international food reserves, as though food were an international resource. It should discourage talk of world food redistribution, for our people won't support such measures.

The food crisis will worsen in many nations that can't carry out their basic responsibility for feeding their people. Unfortunately, the American people will be subjected to emotion-laden appeals and to threats of third-world retaliation if the United States doesn't come across with more food giveaways.

The United States must not cease all charity but it will have to become very firm in dealing with the appeals and threats.

Anthony Harrigan is executive vice president of the United States Industrial Council, a nationwide association of conservative businessmen. This is a press release offered by the council as a newspaper column.

December 2, 1974

Ford Signs Aid Bill but Attacks Cuts in Funds to Help Indochina

By JAMES P. STERBA
Special to The New York Times

VAIL, Colo., Dec. 30—President Ford today signed the $2.7-billion foreign military and economic aid bill, but complained that Congressional cuts in aid for Indochina threatened to undermine efforts to negotiate an end to the fighting in Cambodia and to retard efforts to bring economic stability to South Vietnam.

The President said he would meet with Congressional leaders, "at the earliest possible time" to "discuss this critical issue."

"The economic and military assistance levels for Cambodia, particularly, are clearly inadequate to meet minimum basic needs," he said in a statement issued to newsmen. "Our support is vital to help effect an early end to the fighting and a negotiated settlement."

The act authorizes a total of $625-million in military and economic aid for Israel. Of that, $300-million was earmarked for the credit sale of military equipment, of which $100-million will be "forgiven"—that is, Israel will not have to pay it back.

Congress imposed a ceiling of $449.9-million on economic aid to South Vietnam in the 1975 fiscal year and imposed certain restrictions on its use. The Administration had requested $750-million, with no restrictions. Congress also imposed a limit of 4,000 United States Government employes in South Vietnam and told the Administration to reduce that number to 3,000 within a year.

The authorization act also imposes a limit of $377-million on total military and economic aid to Cambodia. It limits military assistance to $200-million. President Ford had requested $500-million for Cambodia, with $390-million earmarked for military aid.

President Ford said he regretted that Congress had cut off a modest program of $15-million to $20-million yearly in military aid to Chile. The act authorized $25-million exclusively for economic aid to Chile during fiscal 1975.

"Although I share the concern of the Congress for the protection of human rights and look forward to continuing consultations with the Chilean Government on this matter, I do not regard this measure as an effective means for promoting that interest," the President said.

Mr. Ford also objected to the Feb. 5, 1975, cut-off date for military aid to Turkey imposed by Congress.

"The threat of cut-off of aid, even if unfulfilled, cannot fail to have a damaging effect on our relations with one of our staunch NATO allies whose geographic position is of great strategic importance," Mr. Ford said. "This, in turn, could have a detrimental effect on our efforts to help achieve a negotiated solution to the Cyprus problem."

The act provides for an authorization of $500-million for food and nutritional aid around the world. That is $46-million less than was requested. Congress, however, added $20-million to the amount requested by the President for population control and health aid, earmarking $150-million specifically for efforts aimed at curbing world population growth.

On food aid, Congress directed that no more than 30 per cent of the concessional food program—that is, commodities sold on long-term, low interest loan agreements—should go to countries such as South Vietnam, without serious food shortages. The bulk of this food, Congress said, should go to countries beset by famine.

December 31, 1974

Press and Politicians

By Anthony Lewis

BOSTON, Jan. 22—In the wake of Watergate the American press has acquired the image of a tiger—a remorseless antagonist of official deceit, probing for the truth. In this vision, journalists are no longer co-opted by officials or overcome by awe of them; if anything, the poor officials are intimidated by the powerful press.

There is some danger that the press itself may be starting to believe that myth. But myth it is.

For a realistic example of the relationship between journalists and political figures consider the first program in the new public television series of Bill Moyers' Journal: an interview with Secretary Kissinger.

Mr. Moyers got into the question of American food aid. He said: "A lot of the food that we're giving right now is going for political—into political areas, strategic areas, rather than humanitarian. . . ."

Mr. Kissinger said that in considering proposed increases in food aid, "we have opted, after all the discussions, for the highest proposal," totaling nearly $1.5 billion. Then there was this exchange:

Kissinger: "I also don't agree with you that we're giving most of our food aid for strategic purposes."

Moyers: "I didn't say most. I didn't mean to say most. I meant a substantial amount."

Kissinger: "We're giving some in countries in which political relationships are of importance to us. . . . But the vast majority—the considerable majority of our food aid goes for humanitarian purposes. . . ."

The ordinary viewer would naturally assume that Mr. Kissinger and the Administration have chosen to give the "vast" or at least "considerable majority" of U. S. aid to feed the starving rather than to keep governments we support in office. What are the facts?

The most important U. S. food program is one of concessional sales—sales on much less than commercial terms—under Title I of Public Law 480. In the most recent fiscal year, ended last June 30, the budget for this program was $748 million.

Thirty-two countries in the world are officially classified by the United Nations as "most seriously affected" by food shortages and poverty. Of these, six were in the 1974 Title I program: Guinea, the Sudan, Sri Lanka, Pakistan, Bangladesh and Cambodia.

Of the $748 million, these six most desperately needy countries were allotted $275 million. The overwhelming proportion of that, $194 million, went to Cambodia, which is both hungry and a military-political client of the United States. Even counting Title I aid to Cambodia as wholly "humanitarian," these countries got only 37 per cent of the money.

The other 63 per cent, $473 million, went to thirteen countries *not* on the needy list, such as Thailand, Israel, Jordan, Iran. By far the largest amount went to South Vietnam: $305 million.

For the current fiscal year, ending next June 30, the Administration has considered three options. Their total costs for food under Title I would be $582 million, $886 million or slightly over $1 billion. In addition, the three options include between $312 and $394 million in a separate humanitarian program of food gifts under Title II.

Under the lowest option, just over half of the Title I money would go to the most needy countries, the largest amount to Cambodia: $139 million. This is a shift toward the needy from the previous year, but it was not a shift desired by Mr. Kissinger. It was forced on him by Congress, which was so outraged by his political use of food aid that it said no more than 30 per cent could henceforth go to countries outside the needy list.

When Mr. Kissinger said on television that the highest option had been chosen, that decision had not in fact been made. He was then trying to work out a deal with Congressmen who want to give more aid to the most desperate countries. He would do that, he said, if Congress would allow him to include South Vietnam in the list of the needy—and then, under the 30 per cent ceiling, give more to other political clients.

Thus, under the Kissinger third option, India would get more Title I aid (up from $53 to $131 million), as would Bangladesh ($56 to $149 million) and Pakistan ($18 to $53 million). But so would South Korea (up from $30 to $124 million), Chile ($33 to $65 million), Indonesia (zero to $43 million) and Egypt ($53 to $88 million). Of the Title I total, the neediest countries would get slightly less than half.

The figures are complicated, but their import is not. Henry Kissinger is determined to make up for Congressional cuts in general aid to such countries as South Korea by sending them food that they could afford to buy commercially. His reason for doing so is political, but on the Moyers' program he got away with the pose of a humanitarian.

Bill Moyers is a man of integrity and experience who deserves his reputation as a serious journalist. That he was overborne by Mr. Kissinger shows how many advantages the official skilled in manipulation still has over the press.

January 23, 1975

U.S. TO INCREASE FOREIGN FOOD AID

Administration Raising to $1.6-Billion Grant for Current Fiscal Year

By WILLIAM ROBBINS

Special to The New York Times

WASHINGTON, Feb. 3—The Ford Administration announced today an increase of more than $600-million in foreign food aid for the fiscal year ending June 30 over the total provided the previous year.

The announcement, made by Secretary of Agriculture Earl L. Butz, said that $1.6-billion in foreign food aid would be provided by the United States this year. A total of $981-million had been projected earlier. The $1.6-billion figure is more than $600-million higher than the $963-million outlay in the fiscal year that ended last June 30.

Agriculture officials said the money now budgeted would provide about 5.5 million tons of food compared with 3.3 million tons the year before.

The Administration has latitude on spending in the food-aid program under Public Law 480. It is authorized to draw funds from the Commodity Credit Corporation for the purpose, although at some future date such funds must be replaced by a Congressional appropriation.

The Butz announcement ended a long period of speculation and conflict within the Government over the extent of efforts to help meet world food needs.

"This confirms once again the U.S. intention to share fully in the supplying of needy nations even during a period of decreased supplies in the United States," Dr. Butz said.

Both the funding of $1.6-billion and the amount of food it will provide correspond roughly with the highest of three budget options top advisers proposed to President Ford nearly two months ago.

The figure cited includes costs of ocean transportation, which department experts estimated at about $150-million.

Point of Contention

The question of an increase in food aid has been a point of

contention in the Government as well as between Administration officials and nongovernment groups since before the World Food Conference in Rome last November.

At the conference, a controversy arose between Administration representatives and several Senators accompanying the United States delegation who pressed for an announcement that this country would increase food aid by at least a million tons.

Today's announcement indicated a 2-million-ton increase but did not make clear how much of the increase would go to the hungriest nations.

Senator Dick Clark, Democrat of Iowa, one of the leaders of the Senatorial group in Rome, said today he was "delighted" that the Administration had "finally gone along with the increase."

The use of United States food to further political and strategic goals, as opposed to aid for purely humanitarian reasons, has also been a subject of controversy.

Congress recently imposed a restriction against use of more than 30 per cent of food aid for countries other than those that have been designated by the United Nations as most seriously affected by food shortages.

Conflicts over that restriction and efforts to reach a compromise on its interpretation are given privately by Government officials as one reason for the lng delay in a budget announcement. Those conflicts still have not been resolved, officials said today.

There has also been uncertainty about supplies of food and the possible effects increased aid could have on world markets.

February 4, 1975

Books of The Times

Granary Row

By LAWRENCE M. BENSKY

FAMINE—1975! America's Decision: Who Will Survive? By William and Paul Paddock. 276 pages. Little, Brown. $6.50.

SOMETIMES it is useful to read a book not from the beginning but from the point where its announced thesis is explained. The Paddock brothers, an agronomist and a former Foreign Service officer, don't really deal with "America's Decision: Who Will Survive?" until the last of their book's three parts, when they advocate a "triage" technique for supplying food to the world's hungry nations in 1975. Triage is the term used by military doctors for assigning priority of treatment to battlefield wounded. "Call triage cold-blooded," the authors say, "but it is derived from the hard experience of medical humaneness during a crisis."

As we apply it with the Paddocks, we learn that Haiti ("the people are sunk in ignorance and indifference"), Egypt (Nasser is in "open, active support of anti-American regimes throughout the area"), and India (whose leadership is not evil, "it is just childish") aren't worth saving and can't be saved. Tunisia (because of the "intelligent supervision of the Tunisian leadership") and Pakistan (a surprising choice politically, but explicable because "if adequate fertilizer is available . . . Pakistan can be exporting wheat by 1970") should be helped. And such countries as Gambia and Libya, it is reasoned, won't need food if only they can hold down their expectations, which are "spiraling upward like an unchecked hot air balloon."

Echoes of a Modest Proposal

Triage, as you may have gathered, sounds like a Swiftian Modest Proposal for Solving Mankind's Needs; thus the virtue in first reading the last third of "Famine—1975!" is that one can thereby come to terms more easily with the problems presented earlier in the book. If those problems seem serious to you, you'll know they cannot be as bad as what the authors have coming later.

The Paddocks' major contribution is a well-supported analysis of the world's agricultural situation and the failure of most smaller nations to encourage efficient food production. Even here, one is made aware of the authors' bias: Though they boast of extensive work and travel all over the world, they use United States publications and officials as sources almost exclusively—only 10 of 387 footnotes cite foreign publications.

Their arguments, then, become impossible. We can't feed everyone on that great famine day, say the Paddocks, because our self-interest dictates, first of all, that we "help maintain the economic viability and relative prosperity of the United States during the Time of Famine." Furthermore, just giving away all that lovely wheat might alienate American public opinion, which will "demand that this food be distributed in a manner which will give them their 'money's worth.'" We're surely not going to get *that* unless we sternly insist that those we help help themselves. And if, occasionally, we have to step on some toes for political reasons, such as in Cuba, where "the economy was highly prosperous at the time Castro came to power" (the "economy," "government" and "people" are seemingly unrelated entities in this book) why that's our right, we've got all the wheat in Iowa.

Hungry people mean "civil tensions, riots, and military take-overs." That's why we'd better sharpen up our triage right now, and the authors provide a handy checklist of 111 countries to ponder when we're not trading wheat futures or polishing our machine guns. More useful than such a list would have been some discussion of America's effort to institute a cooperative method of agricultural aid with the Common Market, an initiative of the Johnson Administration that was blocked by Germany. Or some discussion of the monstrous disproportion between America's military aid and its economic aid—one month's expenditures on the Vietnam war would more than pay for providing every woman in the world with contraceptives for a year. And, as Senator Edward Kennedy recently pointed out, the aid budget proposed for South Vietnam this year is greater than for all Latin-American nations combined.

Not the Lordly Presence

Though the United States, and the other "have" nations, could never use agricultural surpluses to deal with a global famine of the proportions described in "Famine—1975!" there is some evidence that this country's wheat potential is much greater than the Paddocks think it is. And there is, beyond anything else, the certainty that if we come to that point of famine predicted by the Paddocks, Washington will not be the lordly presence that the Paddocks esteem, judging the "dreams and wishful thinking . . . misconceptions and faulty theories of progress" of the rest of the world. By that time, the pestilence and turmoil they dismiss as inconsequential when compared to the orderly "servicing of debts" and transactions in "funny money" (U.S.-controlled foreign currency) might well have transformed international relations to a different kind of debate.

May 26, 1967

TRIAGE

Who shall be fed? Who shall starve?

On the battlefield, the triage decision is made on the basis of which sufferer wi gain decisive benefit. Our food allocation these days seems to be based on how much it benefits us—by helping our balance of payments or balance of power.

By Wade Greene

During the trench-warfare slaughters of World War I, a system for separating the wounded into three groups was practiced in Allied medical tents. The groups consisted of those likely to die no matter what was done for them, those who would probably recover even if untreated, and those who could survive only if cared for immediately. With supplies and manpower limited, the third group alone received attention. Such a practice was called triage—from the French verb *trier*, to sort. While it is still little discussed, triage has become a standard wartime procedure for making the most efficient use of scarce medical resources.

With severe food shortages in many parts of the world today, some people are advocating the unsentimental, morally uncomfortable practice of the medical tent for dealing with nations that are victims of the battle against starvation. The triage analogy is the basis of a scenario as bleak, as unthinkable, as any of those thoughts about life-after-holocaust that issued from the Hudson Institute in the nineteen-fifties:

Instead of floundering in nuclear ruin, the world is swept by famine as the populations of many regions outstrip their agricultural capacities. Only one nation, the United States, has a sizable surplus of food. And, with godlike finality, we dispense it, after systematically deciding which people are salvageable and should be fed, which will survive without help, and which are hopeless and should be left to the ravages of famine.

Unthinkable, perhaps, but no longer unthought. The idea has haunted recent discussions of mounting global food shortages. Some observers detected it in the halls of the recent World Food Conference in Rome. It has cropped up in graduate seminars and Congressional committees. ("Will you and I as American citizens some day have to participate in the choice of 'Food Triage'?" wondered a House agriculture subcommittee in a recent report.) And triage-type thinking was recently expressed by no less respectable a figure than the president of the American Academy of Sciences.

The current attention to the idea represents, in effect, a delayed reaction. Food triage was first proposed in 1967 in a book entitled "Famine—1975!" The authors, William and Paul Paddock, one an agronomist and the other a

Wade Greene, a frequent contributor to this Magazine, writes on social issues.

retired career officer of the Foreign Service, prescribed triage as a mode of U.S. food allocation in a coming time of widespread famine. With experts now estimating that as many as 10 million people may starve to death this year and that as many as half a billion are hovering on the brink of starvation, "Famine—1975!" may prove to have been precisely prescient. Whether its prescription for dealing with famine was equally inspired is another matter.

"Triage is not a system to cut off aid. It is not a system to reduce help," William Paddock said emphatically the other day when I talked by phone to him at his home on the Bahamian island of Eleuthera. "It's a system to make it more effective."

That may be, but the focus of attention has fallen on the morally disturbing notion that some countries should be cut off from food aid for the benefit of the rest. Which countries? The book describes them: "Nations in which the population growth trend has already passed the agricultural potential. This, combined with inadequate leadership and other divisive factors, makes catastrophic disasters inevitable. . . . To send food to them is to throw sand in the ocean." The book looks at a number of examples, invites the reader to do some triage reckoning himself, aided by three check boxes following each example, and gives the authors' own judgments at the end of the grim game. The biggest loser is India. ". . . Today's trends show it will be beyond the resources of the United States to keep famine out of India during the nineteen-seventies. Indian agriculture is too antiquated. Its present government is too inefficient to inaugurate long-range agricultural development programs. Its population tidal wave is too overwhelming, more than 11,800,000 are added each year to the current half-billion population."

If triage struck a responsive chord in some circles, it was not, predictably enough, well received in others. As the authors note in the book itself, some who read the manuscript before publication reacted with "complete horror." As for critical reaction after publication, "we were thoroughly clobbered," recalled William Paddock.

But for the most part, the book and the triage idea went relatively unnoticed outside of special-interest circles. The book had been written during a severe drought in India where famine was staved off only by the shipment of millions of tons of American grain. But the weather improved as the book appeared, and soon after the Green Revolution was proclaimed. Miracle rice and

Lifeboat ethic": A scene from a 1957 movie, "Abandon Ship," based on an 1841 incident in which some survivors of a shipwreck were forced from their overloaded lifeboat so that the rest might live. Today, in a world of starving millions and scarce food supplies, the lifeboat analogy is frequently cited by proponents of triage.

wonder wheats seemed to promise nearly limitless expansion of the world's food production. The Paddocks' dire projection and even direr prescription tended to be dismissed as crop yields did in fact increase and the threat of famine faded for a while.

At about the same time, however, anxiety over the unprecedented expansion of world populations began to inspire other proposals challenging traditional humanitarian values, including Western respect for individual freedom, even the sanctity of life itself. Paul Ehrlich's "The Population Bomb" appeared (in 1968) a year after the Paddocks' book and approvingly referred to "triage" while also declaring that "many apparently brutal and heartless decisions" will have to be made in order to bring birth rates down. That same year, the hardest and most relentlessly reasoned thoughts about population appeared in the respected professional publication Science. The article was entitled "The Tragedy of the Commons," and its author—whose name among populationists has since become almost synonymous with thinking the unthinkable—was a University of California ecologist-biologist, Garrett Hardin.

I had lunch with Dr. Hardin the other day after watching him testify before a House subcommittee. He had calmly advised the lawmakers that we would be doing a favor to starving countries as well as ourselves if we refused to send them any more food. He seemed good-natured and was surprisingly humorous, however. "I'm supposed to be gloomy," he said at one point when we were talking about another member of what some in the New York- and Princeton-based population establishment call the "California camp." "But he's much gloomier than I am." Dr. Hardin wore a vasectomy pin in his lapel, a golden replica of the male symbol in biology with a chunk out of the circle. When I asked him about it, he said he had had himself vasectomized 20 years ago, after having had four children. "Just like in India," he said, an ironic allusion to the contention that many Indian men who have vasectomies in exchange for incentive payments or food bonuses already have as many children as they want.

Dr. Hardin's writing is deadly earnest by comparison to the person at lunch, both in its style and in its message. "The Tragedy of the Commons" proposed compulsory birth control on the grounds that those who do not practice birth control will otherwise outbreed those who do to the detriment of an overpopulated society as a whole—just as a commons, a pasturing area open to all, will tend to be overgrazed because it is in each user's interest to put as many cattle on it as he can. "The only way we can preserve and nurture other and more precious freedoms is by relinquishing the freedom to breed, and that very soon," Dr. Hardin concluded. He drew broader social and moral implications, too, borrowing some thoughts from a recent book on "situation ethics." "The morality of an act," he wrote, "is a function of the state of the system at the time it is performed." In other words, freedom to have as many children as one wanted was properly valued in a sparsely populated planet but should be limited in an increasingly crowded one. Other values are changing as well in our heavily peopled world, he suggested.

The relativity of right and wrong was at the same time beginning to be argued by Jay Forrester, the management professor at the Massachusetts Institute of Technology, who invented the memory device central to the operation of digital computers and whose disciples subsequently put together computerized projections of doom under the auspices of the Club of Rome. In turning his attention from corporations to social systems (which he has described as "multiple-loop, nonlinear feedback mechanisms"), Dr. Forrester looked first at the city of Boston, later at the world. And he came to the conclusion that we no longer intuitively understand the outcome of some societal actions, not because of population growth per se, but because of the increasing complexity of social systems. So what in the short run may seem to be an unqualified good may lead in the long run to undesirable—bad—results. Is the good then good?

Dr. Forrester espoused his gospel of moral complexity in 1971 in a speech before an unlikely audience, the Division of Overseas Ministries of the National Council of Churches. He advised the church group to reconsider traditional international humanitarianism in the light of what he regarded as the long-range inhumanities of some supposedly humane acts. "Consider a country that is overpopulated," he said. "Its standard of living is low, food is insufficient, health is poor, and misery abounds. . . . The country is operating in the overextended mode where all adversities are resolved by a rise in the death rate. The process is part of a natural mechanism for limiting further growth in population. But suppose that humanitarian impulses lead to massive relief efforts from the outside for each natural disaster. What is the long-term result? The people who are saved raise the population still higher. . . . Relief leads to more people in crisis, to still-greater need for relief, and, eventually, to a situation that even relief cannot handle." . . . "The church should begin to examine the limits and consequences of humanitarianism," the technologist advised the theists.

A doctoral student of Dr. Forrester, Dale Runge, later expanded this theme in an unpublished but widely-read paper, "The Ethics of Humanitarian Food Relief," in which, with the aid of computerized projections, he came to the conclusion that such relief is "not ethical" because by itself it creates more misery over the long run than it alleviates.

As this course of thinking developed in recent years, so did its relevancy. The climate, generally favorable for decades in the world's main agricultural areas, reverted to its haphazard ravages, drastically reducing crop yields in several parts of the world. Energy costs soared, and because of the Green Revolution's heavy dependence on energy (for pumping water and for petroleum-based fertilizer), the cost of food also soared—out of reach for millions in impoverished areas. Increasing cries for food relief have added an immediacy to proposals that we should not answer all, or perhaps any, such appeals. Other economic factors added an extra dimension to these proposals. Until recently, the U.S. found it quite painless to give or sell food cheaply to countries that needed it. We produced far more than we could use and were paying $1-million a day just to store excess grain. But U.S. grain reserves are gone now, mostly to Russia. Meantime, quadrupled oil prices have made us increasingly dependent on international food sales to maintain our balance of payments; these sales have grown from $8-billion to $21-billion annually in the last three years and now head the U.S. export list.

Doubts about our humanitarian impulses have been generally phrased in terms of whether these impulses were good for the "beneficiaries" or for the world as a whole; some doubters now feel it is appropriate also to ask whether they are good for us. Garrett Hardin, for one. His "Tragedy of the Commons" has been anthologized in no less than 48 different collections, and he revived and extended the commons theme last fall, reasoning that our generosity not only does no long-range good for others but imperils us in the process.

In articles in Psychology Today and BioScience magazines, he argues for an adjusted ethics of survival dominated by unsqueamish self-interest: lifeboat ethics, he calls it, in an analogy that has already begun to rival triage. The rich nations of the world, he writes, are adrift in lifeboats. "In the ocean outside each lifeboat swim the poor of the world, who would like to get in, or at least to share some of the wealth. What should the lifeboat passengers do?" We could try to take everyone aboard, but we would sink the lifeboat if we did, he says. "The boat swamps, everyone drowns. Complete justice, complete catastrophe." Because he thinks we have already exceeded the carrying capacity of our land in some ways, Dr. Hardin suggests that it would be prudent not to take anyone aboard. "For the foreseeable future," he concludes, "our survival demands that we govern our actions by the ethics of a lifeboat, harsh though they may be."

Harsh indeed in light of Americans' ingrained image of themselves as international benefactors and rescuers. The lifeboat ethic was denounced as an "obscene doctrine" in a guest editorial in November's Science by Roger Revelle, head of Harvard's Center for Population Studies. Dr. Hardin says that mail from his Psychology Today article has been running about 95 per cent against his doctrine, accusing him of "being a scoundrel."

Cutting off aid to starving

nations was proposed recently from another more surprising source — Philip Handler, president of the National Academy of Sciences. But he adds a significant proviso that offers little moral comfort. We should not give food aid, he said, if we aren't *willing* to do enough to effect long-range solutions. Dr. Handler contended, in a speech in late September, that if we are going truly to help hungry countries, food aid has to be accompanied by further assistance aimed at setting those we help on the road to both agricultural self-sufficiency and lower population growth rates, which tend to fall as standards of living rise. Anything short of that, says Dr. Handler, with a clear echo of Forrester and Runge, is "probably intrinsically counterproductive," and only leads to later misery "on a larger scale."

"Cruel as it may sound," Dr. Handler said, "if the developed and affluent nations do not intend the colossal, all-out effort commensurate with this task"—and he indicated his doubts that they do—"then it may be wiser to 'let nature take its course.'" Asked later whether he was saying that a policy of triage should be considered, Dr. Handler replied: "That's what I was saying, gently."

Such are the major contours of the recent challenges to America's humanitarian instincts—or at least what we like to think are our instincts—toward the starving, suffering millions in the rest of the world. How persuasive are the analogies and the arguments?

In recent weeks I talked to most of the principal advocates involved, some of their supporters and some of their dissenters. These are gloomy times, of course, and the burden of proof in many situations rests almost wholly on those prophets who claim things are not bad and are not getting worse. Still, I found experts who have considered—and dismissed—the triage and lifeboat reasonings because they feel the world can and will surmount disparities between food supplies and population. People like the Paddocks, however, seem more convinced of their pessimistic premises than ever. "Everything is so much worse than when we wrote that book," said William Paddock. "You have a couple of hundred million more people to worry about, you've got the energy crisis, you've got inflation. . . . Another thing is that we have less land under production today than we did in 1967 due to losing land from salting and advancing deserts."

The facts are not all on one side or the other. To some extent, one's opinion about them and about the harsh measures being proposed depends on an *a priori* sense either that material progress and a little bit of luck are part of man's boundless destiny or, as many ecologists and philosophers and Forrester's computers contend, that nature sets firm limits, which we are approaching, on how much an ever-larger population can extract from a finite planet.

The major, recurrent argument I encountered against the triage concept was that, even if there are such limits, we are not close enough to them to justify triage — not while much of the world enjoys an overabundance of its fruits. This viewpoint was not limited to the U. S. It extended to other countries that produce or consume disproportionate amounts of food and energy — wealthy, food-surplus countries like Canada and Australia, the newly-rich oil-producing countries and Western Europe and Japan. Nonetheless, it was the U. S., according to this argument, with its unmatched capacity for food production and widely disproportionate consumption of global resources, which figuratively has the most fat to trim before it can justify dictating the starvation of others. It has been noted, for example, that if Americans cut their meat-consumption by only one-tenth, the saving in grain used for cattle feed would totally eliminate the estimated grain shortage of countries now verging on starvation.

"As long as the wealthy societies are consuming at the rate we are, I think there's an awful lot that can be done short of triage," says Roger Shimm, president of Union Theological Seminary and one of many religious leaders who are considering anew the dimensions of the age-old scriptural injunction to feed the hungry. And as long as cutting back on consumption is a possibility, he added, "I would find it extremely hard to say that I would deliberately consign people to starvation by any act, positive or negative."

But how much of a possibility is this, in terms of the will if not the way? The question arose at a recent three-day meeting near Baltimore, sponsored by the Aspen Institute, at which experts from government, private groups and the academy who have been concerned with food, population and ethics gathered to consider the world food situation. In one vigorous exchange, the protagonists were Jay Forrester, to whom many of the questions were directed, and Peter Henriot, a Jesuit, who works with the Center for Concern in Washington. Their disagreement grew out of a discussion of Dr. Hardin's lifeboat analogy. Dr. Forrester asked whether it would be moral to rescue the drowning poor if it meant swamping the boat. To which Peter Henriot replied that the moral thing to do would be first to make the boat more efficient—get rid of the excess baggage. That's just so much preaching, Dr. Forrester answered.

In any case, could the United States adopt a deliberate, explicit policy by which it determined which countries were to be helped and which left to the inexorable course of nature—a governmental version of the Paddocks' triage check list? I asked Representative John Dingell, before whose House subcommittee Garrett Hardin testified. "In terms of U. S. politics," Representative Dingell said, "we can't do it either morally or politically." But many policies aren't arrived at "clearly and explicitly . . . they sort of grow and evolve. And whether we make a conscious decision of the kind that Hardin has discussed in his papers, the hard fact of the matter is that nature is probably going to make those judgements for us. . . . Triage is going to come upon us whether we like it or not."

Some others say it already has, that we have begun practicing triage without declaring it. "There has always been a degree of triage in the world," said Dr. Forrester in the course of a recent scientific conference at the Franklin Institute in Philadelphia.

John Steinhart, professor of geology and geophysics at the University of Wisconsin, was more specific and less philosophic as he discussed the subject at Representative Dingell's hearings. "I guess I would argue," he said, "that we are already practicing triage, whether we call it by that name or not. The decision, for instance, that the President not respond to Secretary Butz's or Senator Humphrey's request for additional food for India, but, instead, supply some additional food to Syria means a triage decision. That decides that some Indians will die and some Syrians will live. It is as simple as that."

Both Dr. Forrester and Dr. Steinhart were using the term loosely, however. In the battlefield analogy, the triage decision is made on the basis of which sufferer will gain some decisive benefit. Our food allocation these days seems to be based almost entirely on how it benefits us—the donors rather than the recipients—either by helping our balance of payments through export sales or our balance of power, by keeping strategically important countries friendly. In fact, in recent years, most of our food aid, in the form of low-interest, long-term loans for food purchases, has gone to countries like South Vietnam, South Korea, Pakistan, Indonesia, Egypt, Syria and Israel. While this has had the effect of reducing "humanitarian" shipments to much needier countries, the effect seems to have been incidental rather than a result of the harsh logic of triage. That Washington policy - makers may be moving toward a harder look at humanitarian food relief in its own right, however, was evidenced by a National Security Council representative's recent remark that "to give food aid to countries just because people are starving is a pretty weak reason."

Perhaps the ultimate obstacle to triage, or the lifeboat ethic, is a moral self-image with which Americans cannot tamper without severe, perhaps devastating, consequences. "I have certain moral feelings about letting some poor bastard starve," concedes Representative Dingell. Somewhat more elegantly, Ronald Jager, a professor of philosophy at Yale University, who took part in the Aspen Institute meeting, asks: "What happens to us, to our whole conception of what a moral life is, if we force ourselves to turn callously away? What happens when a nation does that, when a nation has to tell itself, when its leaders have to tell its people: this is what we must do, the moral thing to do is let Bangladesh disappear in anguish? . . . What you create is an internal situation which I think is just disintegrative."

I asked Garrett Hardin about this. "I'm not sure I can exactly answer you," he said, "but I've got a sort of reply. We have gotten ourselves into a difficult position in the last 25 years. . . . The success of the Marshall Plan in Europe was one of the great motivations for embarking on AID [Agency for International Development]. Now this was the first time that the nation ever embarked on such a project as trying to save the whole world. People have been starving to death for centuries—and even in large numbers. There's nothing new about that. But now, because of the feeling that has been built up over the last 25 years—that we somehow can, we have an obligation to, save the world—we're in a difficult position. That, coupled with television so that the person who is dying 8,000 miles away can be brought into our living room. . . But quite apart from whether it's desirable or not, I think the realities are that we simply don't have the ability to take care of the rest of the world and we better adjust to that. I think we have a very hard psychological adjustment to make. My only point is that we don't have to go up against the sentiment of the ages, it's only the sentiment of the last 25 years."

Several people I talked to, however, said that they were not prepared to adjust to some realities. Richard Neuhaus, author of the book, "In Defense of People," and a Lutheran minister, said, "A world that would choose Garrett Hardin's options is a world in which I for one would not care to survive."

When I pressed Dr. Hardin on this point, he admitted that the question of whether we could live with ourselves by the values he is espousing was probably the strongest challenge to his case. "But I firmly believe that we can," he said. "I'm doing it. I don't think it's easy. But—it's like gravity. We may not like the law of gravity either. But once you know it's true, you don't sit down and cry about it. That's the way the world is."

Philosophers have been arguing the fundamental ethical question posed by triage at least since Plato: the weighing of "good" ends against "bad" means. This problem has cropped up in very concrete form throughout history, also. It has been solved notoriously in some cases—in Nazi atrocities, for example. Other solutions have been less easy to condemn, however, including a legally famous application of Dr. Hardin's lifeboat ethics, the case of *United States v. Holmes*. Holmes was a sailor on a passenger ship that was wrecked on an iceberg in 1841. He and a number of passengers found themselves in a dangerously overloaded lifeboat, so Holmes directed that several passengers be thrown overboard. He and the rest were eventually rescued. Holmes was tried for manslaughter, convicted and then pardoned by President Tyler.

The ultimate course of the law in not punishing Holmes seems just in this case, and it may appear to offer some support to the ethics of food triage and of Dr. Hardin's lifeboat analogy. But, in the view of several people I talked to, the difference between a literal situation involving individuals and the analogous one involving nations may make precisely the difference between right and wrong.

In the Holmes case, the likelihood of everyone's dying unless a few were sacrificed was presumably immediate and total. But even with computer projections, the future is far from being absolutely predictable in the complex realm of food and population. Who can be sure that tens or hundreds of millions of people will eventually starve to death if we are not willing to write off a lesser number now—sure enough, that is, to make the decision to do so?

Another distinction generally acknowledged at the Aspen Institute meeting is that life and death terms don't apply to nations as they do to individuals. Gerald Barney of the Rockefeller Brothers Fund raised the point that nations don't die, they don't disappear. And not helping them does not eliminate them as a problem; it may even create a larger problem of prolonged social upheaval and violence.

Dr. Forrester, who had shown considerable interest in the triage concept when he came to the Baltimore meeting, seemed to have become disillusioned with it during the discussions, for when I talked with him afterwards, he was saying some of the same things Mr. Barney had said. He was far from abandoning his underlying moral arguments over whether help is really helpful, however. "There's an implication going along with the word [triage]," he said, "that there are those who, if you help them, will survive and some who, if you don't help them, won't. And neither of these is true. It seems to me that those we help are not going to be better off than those we don't help. In many ways the problems we see around us today are related to past attempts to help that haven't succeeded."

Part of the gloom of the times is the pervasiveness of at least one aspect of Dr. Forrester's viewpoint — the feeling that many social programs aren't working, at least not the way we want them to. But even he is said to have left the Aspen Institute meeting expressing the hope that his computers might still come up with ways of helping that really do help.

Meantime, there appears to be a great deal of soul-searching in and out of Government to try to determine just what we can and should do to stem the tide of hunger and famine, something more than muddling from crisis to crisis. Some people are quite happy to use the specter of triage as a moral prod.

Some, too, while deploring such a viewpoint, feel that the population explosion in some parts of the world may have pushed the search for answers beyond the framework of traditional liberal values. Several people I talked to mentioned China. Though I am sure these people view China's repressive society as intolerable, they still look at China's improving living standards and rapidly declining birth rate and find repression an acceptable alternative to the degradation and death of millions.

Many of the same people felt, however, that a great deal more to alleviate hunger could be done by the world's wealthy nations within their traditional humanitarian standards. Whether Americans, among others, have the will to do so is another matter. I encountered considerable doubt about that. Yet the feeling, frequently expressed, was that if we turn our backs on the world's starving because we have not summoned the will to provide effective help regardless of its cost, it will be at a bitter loss in self-esteem, no matter how sophisticated our ethical justifications. In such an event, as sociologist Daniel Patrick Moynihan has put it, "We are going to have to face up to the fact that we're a different people than we thought we were." ■

January 5, 1975

Suggested Reading

The World in Crisis

Borgstrom, George, *The Hungry Planet: The Modern World at the Edge of Famine.* rev.ed. New York: Macmillan, 1972. Pb*

Give Us this Day ...: A Report on the World Food Crisis by the Staff of the New York Times. New York: Arno Press, 1975.

Laffin, John. *The Hunger to Come.* New York: Abelard-Schulman, 1972.

Simon, Paul and Arthur Simon. *The Politics of World Hunger.* New York: Harper Magazine Press, 1973.

Food

Brown, Lester. *Seeds of Change: The Green Revolution & Development in the 1970's.* New York: Praeger, 1970. Pb.

Clark, Colin. *Starvation or Plenty?* New York: Taplinger Publishing Company, 1970.

Freeman, Orville L. *World Without Hunger.* New York: Praeger, 1968.

Hambidge, Gove. *The Story of FAO.* New York: Van Nostrand, 1955.

Idyll, C. P. *Sea Against Hunger.* New York: Crowell, 1970.

Johnson, Glenn L. and C. Leroy Quance, eds. *The Overproduction Trap in U.S. Agriculture: A Study of Resource Allocation from World War I to the Late 1960's.* Baltimore: Johns Hopkins University Press, 1972.

Johnson, Stanley. *The Green Revolution.* New York: Harper & Row, 1972. Pb.

McGovern, George S., ed. *Agricultural Thought in the Twentieth Century.* New York: Bobbs-Merrill Company, 1967. Pb.

Prentice, Ezra P. *Hunger and History.* New York: Harper & Brothers, 1939.

Population

Borgstrom, George. *Too Many: The Biological Limitations of Our Earth.* New York: Macmillan, 1969. Pb.

Cepede, M. et al. *Population & Food.* New York: Sheed & Ward, 1964.

Ehrlich, Paul R. *The Population Bomb,* new rev. ed. New York: Ballantine, 1971. Pb.

Hauser, Philip M., ed. *The Population Dilemma.* 2d ed. Englewood Cliffs, N.J.: Prentice-Hall, 1970. Pb.

Lowry, J. H. *World Population & Food Supply.* New York: Crane, Russak & Company, 1970. Pb.

Malthus, Thomas R. *An Essay on the Principle of Population.* Anthony Flew, ed. Baltimore: Penguin Books, 1971. Pb.

The Richest Land on Earth

Citizen's Board of Inquiry. *Hunger, U.S.A.* Boston: Beacon Press, 1968. Pb.

Kotz, Nick. *Let Them Eat Promises: The Politics of Hunger in America.* Englewood Cliffs, N.J.; Prentice-Hall, 1969. Pb.

McGovern, George S. *War Against Want: America's Food for Peace Program.* New York: Walker, 1964.

Paddock, William and Paul Paddock. *Famine Nineteen Seventy-Five!: America's Decision, Who Will Survive.* Boston: Little, Brown, 1968. Pb.

Segal, Judith A. *Food for the Hungry: The Reluctant Society.* Baltimore: Johns Hopkins University Press, 1970. Pb.

Stanley, Robert G. *Food for Peace: Hope & Reality of U.S. Food Aid.* New York: Gordon & Breach, 1972.

Toma, Peter A. *The Politics of Food for Peace.* Tucson, Ariz.: University of Arizona Press, 1967.

Index